WATERLOO PUBLIC LIBRARY
3 3420 00671 598 2

W9-BLR-589

Waterloo
Public
Library

DEC - 2003

ENCYCLOPEDIA OF 20TH-CENTURY ARCHITECTURE

Board of Advisors

ENCYCLOPEDIA OF 20TH-CENTURY ARCHITECTURE

Volume 1
A–F

R. Stephen Sennott, Editor

Fitzroy Dearborn
New York London

Editorial Staff
Sponsoring Editor: Marie-Claire Antoine
Development Editor: Lynn M. Somers-Davis
Editorial Assistant: Mary Funchion
Production Editor: Jeanne Shu

Published in 2004 by
Fitzroy Dearborn
An imprint of the Taylor & Francis Group
29 West 35th Street
New York, NY 10001

Published in Great Britain by
Fitzroy Dearborn
An imprint of the Taylor & Francis Group
11 New Fetter Lane
London EC4P 4EE

10 9 8 7 6 5 4 3 2 1

Library of Congress Cataloging-in-Publication Data

Encyclopedia of 20th-century architecture / R. Stephen Sennott, editor.
p. cm.
Includes bibliographical references and index.
ISBN 1-57958-243-5 (set : alk. paper) — ISBN 1-57958-433-0 (vol. 1 : alk. paper) — ISBN 1-57958-434-9 (vol. 2 : alk. paper) — ISBN 1-57958-435-7 (vol. 3 : alk. paper)
1. Architecture, Modern—20th century—Encyclopedias. I. Title: Encyclopedia of twentieth-century architecture. II. Sennott, Stephen.
NA680.E495 2004
724'.6'03—dc22

2003015674

ISBN 1-57958-243-5 (Set)

Printed in the United States on acid-free paper.

Contents

Acknowledgments

Resembling a large-scale comprehensive building design, an encyclopedia necessitates the collaborative efforts of countless individuals and may take considerable time to complete. It seems long ago that Fitzroy Dearborn Publishers invited me to edit a two-volume encyclopedia about 20th-century architecture. In 1998, I was teaching the history of architecture in a landmark 1890s Richardsonian Romanesque building at Lake Forest College, a small liberal arts college north of Chicago. Immersed in interdisciplinary studies, I was working alongside many architectural historians at the end of the century to endorse what Spiro Kostof termed "a broader, more embracing view of the built environment." To that end, I was soon conferring with editors to propose various organizational and thematic strategies for a comprehensive reference work. Recognizing that architecture and its debates had occupied broad popular interest, the Fitzroy editors held a keen belief that well-educated general readers, scholars, teachers, and professionals alike would benefit from an encyclopedia that explained far more about 20th-century architecture than the conventional group of famous buildings and architects. Following the careful selection of a diverse and highly qualified board of advisors, editors and specialists vigorously discussed lists of proposed topics sufficient in number and importance to justify a third volume. I wish to thank editors, advisors, and many contributors for their valuable insights and recommendations. At Lake Forest College, I wish to thank Professor Ann Roberts and Art Department colleagues for a productive teaching and research environment, as well as friends from numerous departments for their keen support as this project was launched. Thank you to the students enrolled in "Global Architecture and Urbanism," where we pursued the topics of this encyclopedia, considering why contributors flocked to the ranch house or fled from modernism.

On the completion of final edits to the Introduction of the *Encyclopedia of 20th-Century Architecture* in the spring of 2003, I continue to teach the history of architecture, but now in a national historic landmark, S. R. Crown Hall, designed by Ludwig Mies van der Rohe to hold the College of Architecture on the Illinois Institute of Technology campus. Begun in a massive building of load-bearing stone walls, the encyclopedia has been finished in this light-filled structure of steel, glass, and concrete. In the very last editorial stages, I benefited by virtue of being surrounded by inspired teachers and architects and an international student body whose engagement with the built environment taught me the genuine meaning of global. I wish to thank Dean Donna Robertson and the entire faculty for the opportunity to work in a space to which Mies referred as "a home for ideas and adventure."

The *Encyclopedia of 20th-Century Architecture*'s chief aim is to capture the significance of a century of global architectural practice and production. Seeking to be far-reaching and inclusive, the encyclopedia has been shaped in its contents to emphasize the diversity and complexity of 20th-century architecture. The difficult and lengthy selection process provoked useful debate; it has been my intention to preserve this diversity of perspective in the published volumes. For their consistent support and reliable participation, I would like to thank the following persons who graciously and diligently served as the board of advisors on this project.

Their widely regarded expertise, varied perspectives, and most generous efforts provided the *Encyclopedia of 20th-Century Architecture* with a widespread and critical range of entries and themes. They include Diana Agrest (Agrest and Gandelsonas Architects, New York City), Nezar AlSayyad (University of California, Berkeley), Eve Blau (Harvard University, Cambridge, Massachusetts), Robert Bruegmann (University of Illinois at Chicago), William Brumfield (Tulane University, New Orleans, Louisiana), Jeffrey Cody (Chinese University of Hong Kong), Nnamdi Elleh (University of Cincinnati, Ohio), Stephen Fox (Rice University, Houston, Texas), Kenneth Frampton (Columbia University, New York City), Diane Ghirardo (University of Southern California, Los Angeles), Michael Graves (Michael Graves and Associates, Princeton, New Jersey), Renata Holod (University of Pennsylvania, Philadelphia, Pennsylvania), Steven Izenour (deceased, Venturi, Scott Brown, and Associates, Philadelphia, Pennsylvania), Richard Longstreth (George Washington University, Washington, D.C.), Christian F. Otto (Cornell University, Ithaca, New York), Michèle Picard (Montreal, Quebec), Franz Schulze (Lake Forest College, Lake Forest, Illinois), Denise Scott Brown (Venturi, Scott Brown, and Associates, Philadelphia), Helen Searing (Smith College, Northhampton, Massachusetts), Joseph Siry (Wesleyan University, Middletown, Connecticut), Martha Thorne (curator, Department of Architecture, The Art Institute of Chicago), and Dell Upton (University of California, Berkeley). Their spirited advice resolved numerous questions about contents and organization, they recruited qualified and articulate contributors from around the world, and several advisors asked to write important entries.

In addition, I would like to thank the many individuals who assisted in the early portion of research and editing while the project was under the auspices of Fitzroy Dearborn Publishers in Chicago. Under the wise and enthusiastic guidance of editor Paul Schellinger, commissioning editors Chris Hudson and Lorraine Murray were enormously helpful in administering the database, communicating with authors, and directing the editing cycle. Copyeditor Bruce Owens compiled hundreds of references. From the start, the Fitzroy Dearborn staff truly gave the project its consistency, scope, and form. In addition, I wish to give special thanks to Emily Urban, a Richter Scholar and publishing intern from Lake Forest College, who wrote dozens of capsule biographies as well as proofread manuscripts under the guidance of Fitzroy editors.

The published table of contents, as predicted, varies from the very first list sent out to hundreds of contributors. At a time when the 20th century seems somewhat distant, a five-year editorial process has inevitably called for adjustments, to the benefit of the project. With all parts in place, and following numerous editorial stages, I am profoundly grateful to each contributor for their commitment, generosity, critical thinking, and imagination as they met and surpassed the challenges posed by this ambitious project. Authors have given their entries remarkable depth and scope, ensuring that this *Encyclopedia of 20th-Century Architecture* has met its charge to be international, interdisciplinary, and inclusive. On behalf of the editors and contributors, I trust that the project—for its inclusions and exclusions—will stimulate innovative approaches and provoke constructive debate.

Finally, and with deep appreciation for their collective precision and grace under unrelenting pressure to publish, I wish to offer my thanks to the Routledge team of professionals who brought this project to its outstanding conclusion. From unpacking boxes in New York to editing hundreds of manuscripts, the Routledge editors tirelessly made their experience and wisdom available at a crucial moment of conversion from one publisher to another. Years of writing and editing would have perished without the Routledge editors. These include the Sponsoring Editor Marie-Claire Antoine, Development Editor Lynn M. Somers-Davis, Senior Production Editor Jeanne Shu, Editorial Assistant Mary Funchion, Development Director Kate Aker, and Publishing Director Sylvia Miller. Their enthusiasm for this project and commitment to seeing it through, despite the difficulties of transition, is truly appreciated. In closing, I wish to offer praise and heartfelt gratitude to my three lifelong muses and amusers, Ann Jordahl, Brianna Sennott, and Hille Sennott, for their inspiration and constant delight in our shared world of words and images. Carry on.

R. Stephen Sennott

Introduction

In its broad coverage of architecture produced between 1900 and 2000, the *Encyclopedia of 20th-Century Architecture* provides a three-volume, English-language reference work for scholars, professionals, students, and the general public seeking a basic understanding of interdependent topics that define the production of architecture in the developed cities, countries, and regions of the world. Seeking the breadth and diversity of any encyclopedic endeavor, the project extends its coverage beyond the conventional study of prominent architects and their buildings to address important related facets of 20th-century architectural production that motivate architects and their clients and give form and meaning to their buildings.

Arranged in alphabetical order, the entries fall into three broad areas: persons, places, and architecture topics. Persons include architects and firms, critics, and historians; places include countries and regions, cities, specific buildings and sites, and unbuilt projects; architecture topics include materials and building technology, building types, stylistic and theoretical terms, schools and movements, architectural practice and the profession, and planning. Ranging in length from 1,000 to 4,000 words, each article is written for the well-informed general reader and signed by an established scholar or professional with expertise in the subject. In addition, each architecture topic and places entry includes a selected bibliography; each person's entry includes a capsule biography, a list of selected works, and a selected bibliography. The bibliographies consist of standard works and recent scholarship to enable the student or scholar to expand his or her research.

This project set out in 1998 in Chicago with the editorial staff of Fitzroy Dearborn Publishers to shape a broad and inclusive reference work designed to provide description and analysis of 20th-century architects, buildings, and places from a global perspective. In its review of an enormously inventive century of ambitious architectural production, the editorial team quickly recognized that the most useful reference work would include far more than buildings and architects alone. The *Encyclopedia of 20th-Century Architecture* therefore aims to explain the range of technological, professional, and historical factors that the architectural process entails, from drawings to the completed building. The far-reaching influence of important architects, sustainability and new materials, new digital technologies, and global proliferation of large-scale building types, for example, has altered the scope of modern architectural practice. Moreover, 20th-century architecture profoundly engaged many new constituencies, including the general public. In its efforts to provide a broader audience with a more inclusive understanding of architectural practice, the project seeks to frame a vast scope of selected topics that have defined and directed 20th-century architecture and its consumption worldwide.

The practice of architecture has become enormously complex, as modern airports and skyscrapers make clear. Wherever constructed, a single building requires the design team to understand traditional and innovative materials, new construction technologies, building types, historic precedent, and related planning needs. Readers of the *Encyclopedia of 20th-Century Architecture* will benefit from an understanding of these interconnections. It is the editorial team's belief that one strength of this project is the selective inclusion of a diverse range of architecture subjects rarely examined together with important buildings and their architects. To facilitate these connections, the book provides readers with extensive internal cross-references in the majority of entries and a comprehensive, analytical index.

International coverage required a variety of critical perspectives from a diverse group of scholarly and professional experts. From the start, the task of defining the scope and content of this project reiterated the complexity of architectural production in the last hundred years. Consulting for several months with a distinguished international advisory board of scholars and architects, architectural historian and volume editor R. Stephen Sennott has organized a far-reaching investigation of architecture from all regions of the world. The final selection of topics found in these three volumes is the result of a long and careful evaluation of a much longer list of proposed topics.

To the benefit of this project, the advisory board's contributions were both contradictory and consistent in their careful explanations of what should be included or excluded from these pages. This debate served to balance the book's perspective and content. In short, the principal criteria for inclusion were, first, that the individual or topic had had a lasting or formative effect on architecture or, second, that the individual or topic reinforced the international scope of the encyclopedia. One strength of this reference work is its deliberate effort to accommodate these differences and contradictions by including a diverse range of advisors and a balanced variety of expert writers able to recognize the global character of architectural practice in the 20th century. In concert with the advisory board's recommendations, the book profiles this century's vast chronicle of architectural achievements within and well beyond the confines of mid-century modernism. Even so, and with apologies to readers who note the absence of a subject they hold as significant, it has obviously not been possible to include every architect, building, or topic of architectural significance. Indeed, following this challenging editorial process, and in light of compelling scholarship of the last 15 years, it is the editorial team's collective hope that this project will encourage further study of the global, interconnected character of architecture and its production. The encyclopedia will provide an effective starting point for researchers and readers for years ahead.

Whatever the risks of this ambitious reference work, an international team of 300 writers—architectural historians, architects, engineers, preservationists, urban historians, critics, and independent scholars—has presented a wide-ranging and critical assessment of buildings, architects, cities, and related architecture topics to provide professionals and general readers alike with an integrated view of architectural production around the world. Scholars and practitioners from related design and building professions have written more than 700 entries that collectively provide readers with a distinct approach to 20th-century architecture's materials, theory, design, and practice. Such a broad and sweeping study invites complexities and risks; to leave some of these as unresolved defines some aspects of modern and contemporary architectural practice. This diversity of authorship and critical viewpoints makes this a requisite source for general readers and the architectural profession alike as they seek basic information about 20th-century architecture. Given its expansive sweep, the *Encyclopedia of 20th-Century Architecture* is directed at a diverse readership and provides a wide variety of information on a great number of subjects.

Architectural Topics (179 entries)

From broad and inclusive entries to shorter entries, topics have been selected because of their generally acknowledged importance in directing architectural form, fulfilling programmatic needs, directing style and change, and otherwise affecting the practice of architecture during the 20th century. Entries describe the topic and evaluate its effect on buildings, architects, or places around the world.

Materials and Building Technology (35 entries)

Entries on traditional or innovative materials describe the origins, needs, and purposes of an important building material as it evolved during the 20th century (e.g., Aluminum, Reinforced Concrete, and Truss Systems). For example, concrete has a long history; however, its dramatic new capacities have generated new construction methods as well as innovative architectural form. The 20th century witnessed the invention of many new building technologies and systems, making significant contributions to architectural function. For example, air conditioning has allowed large-scale buildings to be built with new standards for comfort in extreme climatic conditions.

Building Types (53 entries)

Building types vary in their associations with form, function, or program. Many types resulted from new needs that served new methods of transportation or evolving social, industrial, recreational, or economic needs. Entries describe the building types' forms and uses, with focus on how established building types changed during the 20th century (such as Church, House, School, Skyscraper). For example, the skyscraper has been exported from American cities to rapidly developing cities in Asia, and the resulting designs have transformed the scale and appearance of these corporate emblems.

Stylistic and Theoretical Terms (34 entries)

Entries vary among stylistic categories and theoretical ideas that have guided architects, their clients, and recent writers and critics. Brief essays on stylistic terms characterize the features that define the style (e.g., Craftsman Style, Prairie School) while contextualizing their subject within broad regional or global applications. Longer essays on theoretical terms (e.g., Art Deco, Modernism, and Postmodernism) seek to synthesize the generally accepted meaning of these terms for the general reader, identifying key writers, architects, and representative buildings as examples.

Schools and Movements (12 entries)

Frequently, like-minded architects and supportive critics or historians have banded together to form groups, schools, and movements (both organized and loosely collective) to promote their design ideals, or retrospectively, historians have designated members of a movement on the basis of formal and historical analyses. These types of entries (e.g., Constructivism, De Stijl, Memphis Group) identify significant leaders and explain the goals or intentions of these groups, where and for how long each school or movement has been influential or successful, and their contributions to subsequent generations.

Architectural Practice and the Profession (20 entries)

In its attention to 20th-century architectural practice and education, this section includes topics that examine some of the important changes in the profession and its administration. Similarly, entries address how architects and their buildings are evaluated and awarded (e.g., Architectural Drawing, Education of Architects/Schools, Environmental Issues, Pritzker Architecture Prize).

Planning (24 entries)

The 20th century is marked by the evolution of the planning profession in response to new and large-scale transportation and infrastructure needs. Architects and planners have often collaborated to bring about new kinds of urban, suburban, and rural development. Examples of these entries include Campus Planning, Garden City Movement, New Urbanism, and Plan of Chicago.

Persons (292 entries)

Individuals have been chosen because they have contributed significantly to the history of 20th-century architecture. Regardless of where they practice in the world, individuals have typically been recognized as founders or leaders in their own time or documented as highly influential practitioners for subsequent generations. Typically, they have been recognized professionally by well-known awards, prizes, or other honors. These entries consist of a signed critical essay, a capsule biography, a list of important buildings (in the case of architect entries), and a bibliography of useful sources.

Architects and Firms (267 entries)

Architects and firms have been chosen because of their important contributions throughout the world or within the boundaries of the country or regions where they practice. In addition to the world's well-known architects and firms, the editor and advisory board sought to include a diverse group of architects not frequently included in standard reference works. Their work has often been recognized by their peers and juries for the superior quality of their architectural designs at a regional, national, or international level.

Critics and Historians (25 entries)

In these entries, influential critics and historians represent ways in which primary writings and assorted publications have significantly affected 20th-century architecture and its reception within professional circles and the public realm.

Places (277 entries)

Given the rapid changes that define this century's political and geographical boundaries, the advisory board chose to blend regional and national surveys with the project's deliberate focus on major and progressive cities around the world that can be evaluated for their architectural significance. These essays will inevitably privilege the most well-known places (including countries and major cities), but they also will provide a far more diverse selection than currently is available in architecture reference works.

With the 2002 acquisition of this project from Fitzroy Dearborn Publishers by the Taylor and Francis Group, an inspiring and experienced editorial team at Routledge Reference brought this *Encyclopedia of 20th-Century Architecture* to fruition. In the course of editing and producing this book, they have researched and assembled over 500 photographs and illustrations that trace the developments in architecture around the globe and across the 20th century. In addition, each of the three volumes has an eight-page insert of color photographs. The result is an encyclopedia that provides not only depth and breadth of scholarship but also beautifully illustrates the many facets of 20th-century architecture.

The few existing reference works related to architecture include dictionaries of individual architects or individual countries and a range of encyclopedia topics; however, the *Encyclopedia of 20th-Century Architecture* is distinguished by its global scope and purposeful integration of architects and buildings with a selected set of highly important architectural topics. It is the hope of the practicing architects and engineers, architectural historians, preservationists, and other experts, who have together created this multilayered examination of 20th-century architecture, that this reference work will be an indispensable addition to any art, architecture, or history library.

Entry List

D

E

H

I

N

O

S

Thematic List of Entries

Architects and Firms

Aalto, Alvar (Finland)
Abraham, Raimund (Austria and United States)
Adler, David (United States)
Agrest, Diana, and Mario Gandelsonas (United States)
Alvarez, Mario Roberto (Argentina)
Ambasz, Emilio (Argentina and United States)
Ando, Tadao (Japan)
Ardalan, Nader (Iran)
Arquitectonica (United States)
Arup, Ove (England)
Ashbee, C.R. (England)
Asplund, Erik Gunnar (Sweden)
Aulenti, Gae (Italy)
Baker, Herbert (England)
Barnes, Edward Larrabee (United States)
Barragán, Luis (Mexico)
Bawa, Geoffrey (Sri Lanka)
Behrens, Peter (Germany)
Berlage, Hendrik Petrus (The Netherlands)
Birkerts, Gunnar (United States)
Blomstedt, Aulis (Finland)
Bò Bardi, Lina (Brazil)
Bofill, Ricardo (Spain)
Böhm, Gottfried (Germany)
Botta, Mario (Switzerland)
Breuer, Marcel (United States)
Bunshaft, Gordon (United States)
Bureaux d'Etudes Henri Chomette (France and West Africa)
Burle Marx, Roberto (Brazil)
Burnham, Daniel H. (United States)
Calatrava, Santiago (Spain)
Candela, Félix (Spain)
Carrère, John Mervin, and Thomas Hastings (United States)
Chadirji, Rifat (Iraq)
Chareau, Pierre (France)
Coderch y de Sentmenat, José Antonio (Spain)
Connell, Amyas, Colin Lucas, and Basil Ward (England)
Coop Himmelb(l)au (Austria)
Corbusier, Le (Jeanneret, Charles Édouard) (France)
Correa, Charles Mark (India)
Costa, Lúcio (Brazil)
Cram, Ralph Adams (United States)
Cret, Paul Philippe (United States)
Czech, Hermann (Austria)
De Carlo, Giancarlo (Italy)
De Klerk, Michel (Netherlands)
Dieste, Eladio (Uruguay)
Diener and Diener (Switzerland)
Doshi, Balkrishna (India)
Duany and Plater-Zyberk (United States)
Dudok, Willem Marinus (Netherlands)
Duiker, Johannes (Netherlands)
Eames, Charles and Ray (United States)
Eisenman, Peter (United States)
Eldem, Sedad Hakkí (Turkey)
Ellwood, Craig (United States)
Erskine, Ralph (England)
Eyck, Aldo van (Netherlands)
Eyre, Wilson Jr. (United States)
Fathy, Hassan (Egypt)
Fehn, Sverre (Norway)
Ferriss, Hugh (United States)
Fisker, Kay (Denmark)
Foster, Norman (England)
Frank, Josef (Austria)
Frey, Albert (United States)
Fuller, Richard Buckminster (United States)
Gabr, A. Labib (Africa)
Garnier, Tony (France)
Gaudí, Antoni (Spain)
Gehry, Frank (United States)
Gilbert, Cass (United States)
Gill, Irving (United States)
Ginzburg, Moisei (Russia)
Goff, Bruce (United States)
Goldberg, Bertrand (United States)
Golosov, Ilya (Russia)

González de Léon, Teodoro, and Abraham Zabludovsky (Mexico)
Goodhue, Bertram Grosvenor (United States)
Goody, Joan (United States)
Graham, Anderson, Probst, and White (United States)
Graves, Michael (United States)
Gray, Eileen (Ireland and France)
Greene, Henry M. and Charles S. (United States)
Gregotti, Vittorio (Italy)
Griffin, Walter Burley, and Marion Mahony Griffin (United States)
Grimshaw, Nicholas, and Partners (England)
Gropius, Walter (Germany)
Gruen, Victor David (United States)
Gullichsen, Kristian (Finland)
Gwathmey, Charles, and Robert Siegel (United States)
Hadid, Zaha (Iraq)
Häring, Hugo (Germany)
Harrison, Wallace K., and Max Abramovitz (United States)
Hasegawa Itsuko (Japan)
Heikkinen and Komonen (Finland)
Hejduk, John (United States)
Hertzberger, Herman (Netherlands)
Herzog, Jacques, and Pierre de Meuron (Switzerland)
Hilberseimer, Ludwig (United States and Germany)
Hodgetts and Fung (United States)
Hoffmann, Josef (Austria)
Holabird, William, and John Wellborn Root (United States)
Holabird, William, and Martin Roche (United States)
Holl, Steven (United States)
Hollein, Hans (Austria)
Hood, Raymond (United States)
Hopkins, Michael and Patty (England)
Horta, Victor (Belgium)
Howe, George, and William Lescaze (United States)
Islam, Muzharul (Bangladesh)
Isozaki, Arata (Japan)
Ito, Toyo (Japan)
Jacobsen, Arne (Denmark)
Jahn, Helmut (United States)
Jiricna, Eva (England)
Johnson, Philip (United States)
Kada, Klaus (Austria)
Kahn, Albert (United States)
Kahn, Louis (United States)
Kalach, Alberto (Mexico)
Kohn Pederson Fox (United States)
Koolhaas, Rem (Netherlands)
Kurokawa, Kisho (Japan)
Lapidus, Morris (United States)
Larsen, Henning (Denmark)
Lasdun, Denys (England)
Legorreta, Ricardo (Mexico)
Leonidov, Ivan Ilich (Russia)
Levi, Rino (Brazil)
Lewerentz, Sigurd (Sweden)
Liang Sicheng (China)
Libera, Adalberto (Italy)
Libeskind, Daniel (United States)
Lin, Maya (United States)
Loos, Adolf (Austria)
Lu Yanzhi (China)
Lubetkin and Tecton (England)
Lutyens, Edwin (England)
Mackintosh, Charles Rennie (Scotland)
Maillart, Robert (Switzerland)
Maki, Fumihiko (Japan)
Mallet-Stevens, Robert (France)
Manteola, Sánchez Gómez, Santos, Solsona, Viñoly (Argentina)
Markelius, Sven (Sweden)
May, Ernst (Germany)
Maybeck, Bernard R. (United States)
McKim, Mead and White (United States)
Medgyaszay, István (Hungary)
Meier, Richard (United States)
Melnikov, Konstantin (Russia)
Memphis (Group) (Italy)
Mendelsohn, Erich (Germany and United States)
Meyer, Hannes (Germany)
Mies van der Rohe, Ludwig (Germany)
Miralles, Enric, and Carme Pinós (Spain)
Molnár, Farkas (Hungary)
Moneo, Rafael (Spain)
Moore, Charles (United States)
Moral, Enrique del (Mexico)
Moretti, Luigi (Italy)
Morgan, Julia (United States)
Morphosis (United States)
Muthesius, Hermann (Germany)
Navarro Baldeweg, Juan (Spain)
Nervi, Pier Luigi (Italy)
Neutra, Richard (Austria)
Niemeyer, Oscar (Brazil)
Nitzschke, Oscar (France)
Norten, Enrique (Mexico)
Nouvel, Jean (France)
O'Gorman, Juan (Mexico)
Olbrich, Joseph Maria (Austria)
Otto, Frei (Germany)
Oud, J.J.P. (Netherlands)
Pallasmaa, Juhani (Finland)
Patkau, Patricia and John (Canada)
Paul, Bruno (Germany)
Pei, I.M. (United States)
Pelli, Cesar (Argentina and United States)
Perkins and Will (United States)
Perrault, Dominique (France)
Perret, Auguste (France)
Perriand, Charlotte (France)
Piano, Renzo (Italy)
Pietilä, Reima and Raili (Finland)
Platt, Charles Adams (United States)
Plečnik, Jože (Yugoslavia)
Poelzig, Hans (Germany)
Polshek, James Stewart (United States)
Ponti, Gio (Italy)
Pope, John Russell (United States)
Portman, John C. (United States)
Predock, Antoine (United States)
Puig i Cadalfalch, Josep (Catalan)
Purcell, William Gray, and George Grant Elmslie (United States)
Raymond, Eleanor (United States)

Revell, Viljo (Canada)
Rewal, Raj (India)
Rietveld, Gerrit (Netherlands)
Roche, Kevin, and John Dinkeloo (United States)
Rogers, Richard (England)
Romañach, Mario (Cuba)
Rossi, Aldo (Italy)
Rudolph, Paul (United States)
Saarinen, Eero (Finland)
Saarinen, Eliel (Finland)
Safdie, Moshe (Canada and Israel)
Salmona, Rogelio (Colombia)
Sant'Elia, Antonio (Italy)
Santos, Adèle Naudé (South Africa)
Scarpa, Carlo (Italy)
Scharoun, Hans (Germany)
Schindler, Rudolph M. (Austria and United States)
Scott Brown, Denise (United States)
Seidler, Harry (Australia)
Sejima, Kazuyo (Japan)
Sert, Josep Lluís (United States)
Shaw, Howard Van Doren (United States)
Shekhtel, Fedor (Russia)
Shinohara, Kazuo (Japan)
Síren, Heikki and Kaija (Finland)
Siza Vieira, Álvaro J.M. (Portugal)
Skidmore, Owings and Merrill (United States)
Smith, Chloethiel Woodard (United States)
Smithson, Peter and Alison (England)
Soleri, Paolo (United States)
Sota, Alejandro de la (Spain)
Souto de Moura, Eduardo (Portugal)
Stern, Robert A.M. (United States)
Stickley, Gustav (United States)
Stirling, James (Scotland and England)
Stone, Edward Durell (United States)
Studio Per (Spain)
Sullivan, Louis (United States)
Tange, Kenzo (Japan)
Taniguchi, Yoshio (Japan)
Taut, Bruno (Germany)
Távora, Fernando (Portugal)
Taylor, Robert R. (United States)
Team X (Netherlands)
Terragni, Giuseppe (Italy)
Tessenow, Heinrich (Germany)
Testa, Clorindo (Argentina)
The Architects Collaborative (TAC) (United States)
Torre, Susanna (United States)
Tschumi, Bernard (France)
Ungers, Oswald Mathias (Germany)
Utzon, Jørn (Denmark)
van Doesburg, Theo (Netherlands)
Velde, Henri van de (Belgium)
Venturi, Robert (United States)
Vesnin, Alexander, Leonid, and Viktor (Russia)
Villanueva, Carlos Raul (Venezuela)
Voysey, Charles F.A. (England)
Wagner, Otto (Austria)
Wissa Wassef, Rames (Africa)
Williams, Amancio (Argentina)
Williams, E. Owen (England)
Williams, Paul Revere (United States)
Williams, Tod, and Billie Tsien (United States)
Wilson, Colin St. John (England)
Wright, Frank Lloyd (United States)
Wu Liangyong (China)
Wurster, William (United States)
Yamasaki, Minoru (United States)
Zumthor, Peter (Switzerland)

Architectural Practice and the Profession

Adaptive Re-Use
Aga Khan Award
American Institute of Architects
Architectural Drawing
Architectural Photography
Athens Charter (1943)
Competitions
Computers and Architecture
Congrès Internationaux d'Architecture Moderne (CIAM, 1927–)
Education and Schools
Energy-Efficient Design
Environmental Issues
Historic Preservation
Historiography
Institute for Architecture and Urban Studies
Institutes and Associations
Pritzker Architecture Prize
Royal Institute of British Architects
Sustainability/Sustainable Architects
Tribune Tower International Competition (1922), Chicago

Building Types

Agricultural Buildings
Airport and Aviation Building
American Foursquare
Amusement Park
Apartment Building
Bungalow
Bus Terminal
Church
City Hall
Corporate Office Park, Estate, and Campus
Country Club
Department Store
Embassy
Exhibition Building
Factory
Fallout Shelter
Gas Station
Grain Elevator
Hospital
Hotel
House
Library
Maidan
Memorial
Mobile Home

Mosque
Motel
Movie Theater
Museum
Office Building
Parking Garage
Plaza
Power Plant
Prison
Public Housing
Railroad Station
Ranch House
Research Center
Resort Hotel
Restaurant
Roadside Architecture
Row House
School
Shopping Center
Skyscraper
Stadium
Subway
Synagogue
Tensile Structures
Tent
Visitor Center
Warehouse

Buildings and Sites

Abteiberg Municipal Museum, Mönchengladbach, Germany
Abuja, Federal Capital Complex of Nigeria
AEG Turbine Factory, Berlin
Alliance Franco-Sénégalaise, Kaolack, Senegal
Aluminaire House, Long Island, New York
Arcosanti, Arizona
AT&T Building, New York
Baiyoke Tower, Bangkok
Bank of China Tower, Hong Kong
Bank of London and South America, Buenos Aires
Bauhaus, Dessau
Benneton Factory, Italy
Berlin Philharmonic Concert Hall
Berlin Wall, Berlin
Best Products Showroom, Houston
Boots Factory, Nottingham, England
Boston City Hall
British Library, London
Carson Pirie Scott Store, Chicago
Casa Malaparte, Capri
Casa Milá, Barcelona
Celebration, Florida
Center for Integrated Systems, Stanford University
Century of Progress Exposition, Chicago (1933)
Channel 4 Headquarters, London
Chapel of Notre-Dame-du-Haut, Ronchamp, France
Chrysler Building, New York
Church of St. Francis of Assisi, Brazil
Church on the Water, Hokkaido, Japan
Ciudad Universitaria Campus and Stadium, Mexico City
Ciudad Universitaria, Caracas
Concert Hall, Hälsingborg, Sweden
Cranbrook, Michigan
Cultural Centre Jean-Marie Tjibaro-Nouméa, New Caledonia
Disney Theme Parks
Dulles International Airport, Chantilly, Virginia
Eigen Haard Housing Estate, Amsterdam
Einstein Tower, Potsdam, Germany
Empire State Building, New York
Entrepreneurship Development Institute, Ahmedabad, India
Exhibition Hall, Turin
Expo 1958, Brussels
Expo 1967, Montreal
Expo 1992, Seville
Exposition Universelle, Paris (1900)
Fagus Werk, Alfeld, Germany
Fallingwater, Bear Run, Pennsylvania
Farnsworth House, Plano, Illinois
Federal Capital Complex, Brasília
Fiat Works, Turin
Flatiron Building, New York
Gateway Arch, St. Louis, Missouri
German Pavilion, Barcelona (1929)
Getty Center, Los Angeles
Glacier Museum, Fjærland Fjord, Norway
Glasgow School of Art, Glasgow
Glass House, New Canaan, Connecticut
Grand Central Terminal, New York
Grande Arche de la Défense, Paris
Great Mosque of Niono, Mali
Gropius House, Lincoln, Massachusetts
Grundtvig Church, Copenhagen
Guggenheim Museum, Bilbao, Spain
Guggenheim Museum, New York
Gürel Family Summer Residence, Çanakkale, Turkey
Habitat 1967, Montreal
Haj Terminal, Jeddah Airport
Hassan II Mosque, Casablanca
Helsinki Railway Station, Finland
High Museum of Art, Atlanta, Georgia
Highpoint I Apartment Block, London
Hilversum Town Hall, Netherlands
Holocaust Memorial Museum, Washington, DC
Hong Kong International Airport, Hong Kong
HongKong and Shanghai Bank, Shanghai
Illinois Institute of Technology, Chicago
Imperial Hotel, Tokyo
Indian Institute of Management, Ahmedabad
International Exhibition of Decorative Arts, Paris (1925)
International Style Exhibition, New York (1932)
Jewish Museum, Berlin
Johnson Wax Building, Racine, Wisconsin
Kansai International Airport Terminal, Osaka
Karl Marx Hof, Vienna
Kimbell Art Museum, Fort Worth, Texas
Larkin Administration Building, Buffalo, New York
Lever House, New York
Lincoln Center, New York
Lincoln Memorial, Washington, DC
L'Innovation Department Store, Brussels
Lisbon World Exposition (1998)

Cities

London, England
Los Angeles, California
Melbourne, Australia
Mexico City, Mexico
Miami, Florida
Montreal, (Quebec), Canada
Moscow, Russia
New Delhi, India
New York, New York
Paris, France
Philadelphia, Pennsylvania
Prague, Czech Republic
Rio de Janeiro, Brazil
Riyadh, Saudi Arabia
Rome, Italy
Rotterdam, Netherlands
Santiago, Chile
São Paolo, Brazil
St. Petersburg, Russia
Stockholm, Sweden
Stuttgart, Germany
Sydney, Australia
Tokyo, Japan
Toronto, Ontario, Canada
Vancouver, BC, Canada
Washington, DC, United States

Countries and Regions

Africa: Northern Africa
Africa: Southern and Central Africa
Argentina
Australia
Austria
Belgium
Brazil
Canada
Chile
China
Cuba
Czech Republic/Czechoslovakia
Denmark
Finland
Germany
Greece
Hungary
India
Iran
Israel
Mexico
Netherlands
New Zealand
Norway
Romania
Russia and Soviet Union
Saudi Arabia
Southeast Asia
Spain
Sweden
Switzerland
Turkey
United Kingdom
United States
Yugoslavia

Critics and Historians

Banham, Reyner (England)
Benevolo, Leonardo (Italy)
Choisy, Auguste (France)
Cohen, Jean-Louis (France)
Collins, Peter (England)
Colquhoun, Alan (England)
Frampton, Kenneth (United States)
Giedion, Sigfried (Switzerland)
Guadet, Julien (France)
Hamlin, Talbot Faulkner (United States)
Hegemann, Werner (Germany)
Hitchcock, Henry-Russell Jr. (United States)
Huxtable, Ada Louise (United States)
Jacobs, Jane (United States)
Lynch, Kevin (United States)
Mumford, Lewis (United States)
Norberg-Schulze, Christian (Norway)
Pevsner, Nikolaus (England)
Portoghesi, Paolo (Italy)
Rasmussen, Steen Eiler (Denmark)
Rowe, Colin (United States)
Scully, Vincent Jr. (United States)
Tafuri, Manfredo (Italy)
Von Moos, Stanislaus (Switzerland)
Zevi, Bruno (Italy)

Influential Projects (unbuilt)

Broadacre City (1934–35)
Cité Industrielle, Une (1901–04)
Città Nuova (1914)
Contemporary City for Three Million Inhabitants
Dom-ino Houses (1914–15)
Glass Skyscraper (1920–21)
Monument to the Third International (1920)
Palace of the Soviets Competition (1931)
Ville Radieuse (c. 1930)
Voisin Plan for Paris

Materials and Building Technology

Acoustics
Aluminum
Brick
Catalan (Guastavino) Vaults
Climate
Concrete
Concrete-Shell Structure
Curtain-Wall System
Demolition
Earthen Building
Elevator
Engineered Lumber
Escalator

Planning

Schools and Movements

Stylistic and Theoretical Terms

AALTO, ALVAR 1898–1976

Architect, Finland

Hugo Alvar Henrik Aalto, whose architecture is often described as organic and close to nature, is regarded as one of the most significant architects of the 20th century. The majority of historians and critics emphasize three aspects in Aalto's architecture that set it apart from any other architect's work and explain his importance: his concern for the human qualities of the environment, his love of nature, and his Finnish heritage.

It seems that Aalto's architecture is a socially refined reflection of Le Corbusier's work, a masterly connection of avant-garde culture with traditional values. Despite being well integrated into the art world, apparently Aalto did not hesitate to include in his designs unfashionable issues that were dismissed by other architects of his time: individuality in mass housing, social equality in theaters, and his foible for details, such as extreme, carefully planned light systems in public buildings. From this angle, Aalto turns out to be a pure dissident of the avant-garde, emphasizing the complexity of architecture by leaving aesthetic values behind him.

Even before adopting the language of modernist architecture, the young Aalto was determined to be as avant-garde as possible, which in Scandinavia in the early 1920s meant a sophisticated and mannerist neoclassicism. His early work shows the influence of anonymous irregular Italian architecture and neoclassical formality as developed by 19th-century architects such as Carl Ludwig Engel, and these strategies were to remain important throughout his career. His most interesting buildings from this time are the Jyväskylä Workers' Club (1925), the church (1929) in Muurame, and the Seinäjoki Civil Guard Building (1926) and the Defense Corps Building (1929) in Jyväskylä. Aalto organized the facade of the Workers' Club like the Palazzo Ducale in Venice by setting a heavy, closed volume on airy Doric columns on the ground floor. The almost symmetrical facade is challenged by a Palladian-style window that is shifted to one side, marking the location of a theater on the first floor. The church in Muurame, which also recalls an Italian motif, namely, Alberti's Sant Andrea at Mantua, is on the outside very much into the neoclassical tradition, whereas its interior emphasis on light anticipates later church designs, such as the churches in Imatra and Wolfsburg.

In 1924 Aalto traveled to Vienna and Italy with his wife and partner Aino Marsio, where he made several sketches that had a great effect on their later work. However, Aalto did not ignore the development in continental Europe, either, and his conversion to international functionalism can be traced back to the autumn of 1927, when he and Erik Bryggman jointly designed a modernist proposal for the Kauppiaitten Osakeyhtiö office building competition. Le Corbusier's reputation among Scandinavian architects had been widely disseminated by a 1926 article in the Swedish magazine *Byggmästaren* by Uno Åhren, and Aalto's first functionalist buildings, the Standardized Apartment Building in Turku (1928) and, more important, the Turun Sanomat office building (1929), demonstrated all of Le Corbusier's five points.

The beginning of international recognition was marked in 1929, when Aalto was invited to join the newly founded CIAM (Congrès Internationaux d'Architecture Moderne) and he attended the second congress of CIAM in Frankfurt on the theme of "Housing for the Existenzminimum." Other masterpieces of functionalism were created by Aalto in the following years, including the Paimio Tuberculosis Sanatorium (1933) and the Viipuri Library (1935). During this time, Aalto started designing bent-plywood furniture, which he later developed into standard types. From 1942 Aino Aalto directed the Artek Company, which had been set up in 1935 for the manufacture of this furniture. These experiments also affected the architectural designs: in the mid-1930s, Aalto introduced the famous curved, suspended wooden ceiling as an acoustical device for the lecture room of the Viipuri Library. Although the functioning of this element is very questionable, curved walls and ceilings became typical of his later work.

In the 1930s, surprisingly enough, Aalto, who had until this point been known as the most modern of Finnish architects, began returning to the vernacular tradition. With the Finnish Pavilions to the World Exhibitions in Paris (1937) and New York (1939), he infused functionalism with his own organic alternative and radically parted ways with mainstream International Style. The critics appreciated this move, for they saw Aalto's primitivism in connection with his origin in the exotic and unspoiled Finland.

Most important for Aalto's architectural reputation was Sigfried Giedion's analysis in the second edition of *Space, Time and*

Architecture (1949). Giedion's interpretation of Aalto's work as Finnish, organic, and irrational helped Aalto to achieve worldwide fame after World War II. The integration of building and nature emerged as a central theme in Aalto's work; this is exemplified in his designs for the Sunila pulp mill (1937) and the Sunila housing for employees (1939). In the engineering staff housing, the first fan-plan motif appears, which became a crucial element in his designs. Characteristic of this period is his interest in natural materials, such as wood, brick, and grass roofs, as he demonstrated in one of his masterpieces, the Villa Mairea (1939) in Noormarkku. The villa is often praised for its harmonious relationship with nature and reference to old Finnish farmsteads. However, Finnish critics did not originally recognize Aalto's buildings as particularly Finnish but, rather, as Le Corbusiersian with Japanese touches. Gustaf Strengell noted that the interiors of the Viipuri Library exhibited strikingly Japanese characteristics in their use of light wood in its natural state. The Villa Mairea was originally a collage of Le Corbusian modernism with Japanese tearooms, African columns, Cubist paintings, and continental Heimatstil until it slowly became a paradigm of "Finnish" or "natural" architecture in the modern architectural discourse.

After the war Aalto was again commissioned by the Massachusetts Institute of Technology to build a student dormitory, where brick was a typical material for the other campus facades. The Baker Dormitory (1949) was Aalto's first experiment with brick, and throughout the 1950s his oeuvre was dominated by the use of red brick. Later, he used the brick as a metaphor for standardization, claiming that the cell was the module of nature, and the brick would occupy an analogous position in architecture. His most important works of this period include the Expressionist House of Culture (1958) and the National Pensions Institute office building (1957), both in Helsinki. The House of Culture consists of a curvilinear theater and a rectangular office block, a typical Aalto arrangement of organic versus orthogonal shapes, where the public space is articulated in a free form and more private functions are placed in rectangular shapes. As in most of his designs, all elements including the apparently free form follow a hidden geometric grid, with the center being a fountain in the courtyard, where a giant hand presents a tiny model of the building. Inside the theater, he experimented again with the acoustic ceiling but also drew on references to the facade of Le Corbusier's Villa Savoye. The Säynätsalo Town Hall (1952), another brick building, is a small version of the piazza theme that Aalto elaborated further in the town center of Seinäjoki (1956–69). After the death of Aino in 1949, Aalto married the architect Elissa Mäkiniemi, for whom he built the Muuratsalo Summer House (1953), or experimental

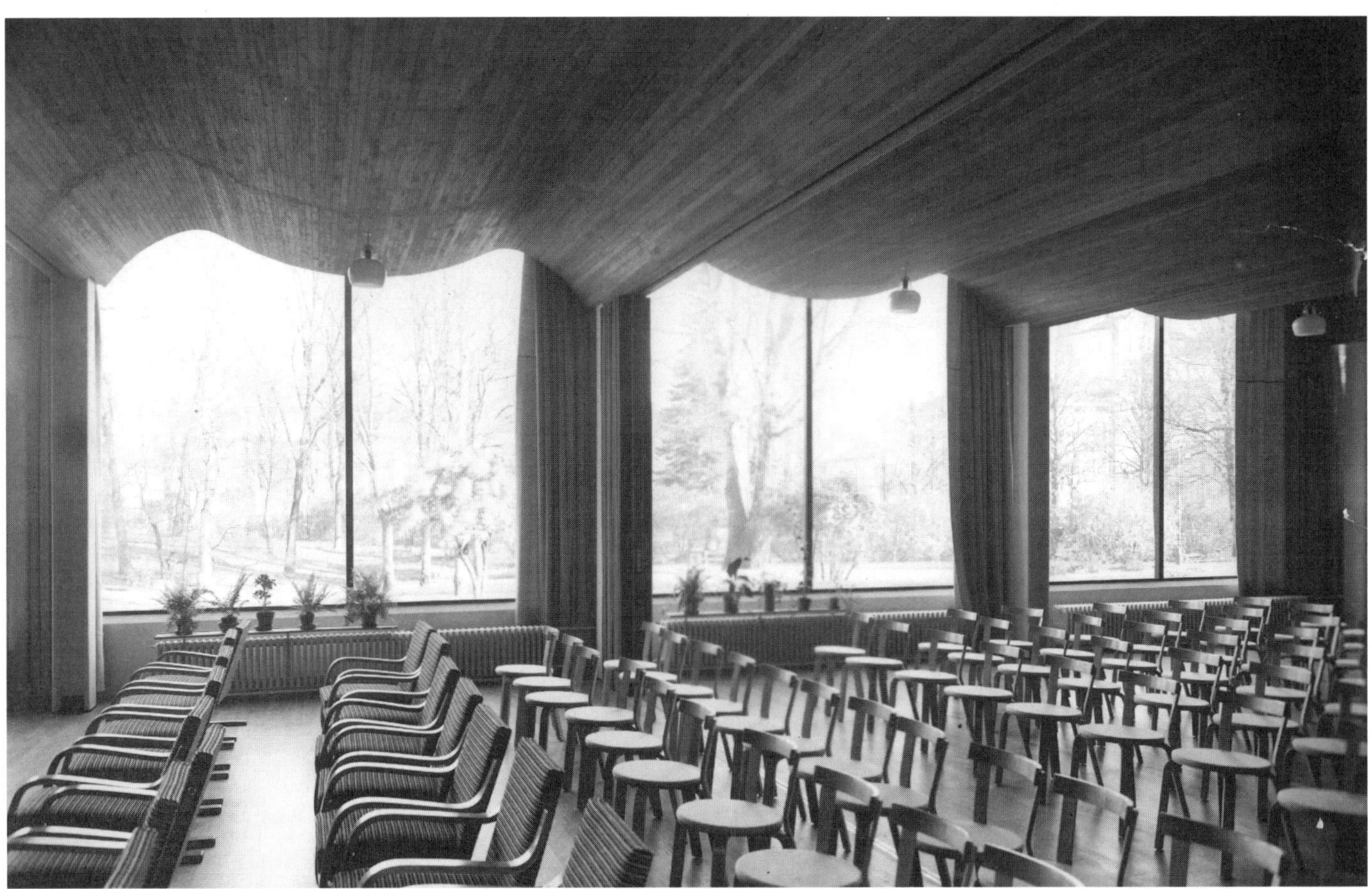

Viipuri Library Lecture Hall, Vyborg, Russia, designed by Alvar Aalto (1927)
Photo © G. Welin 1935/Alvar Aalto Archives

House of Culture, Helsinki, designed by Alvar Aalto (1952–58)
Photo © H. Havas/Alvar Aalto Archives

house with an inner courtyard. The exterior walls are painted white, whereas the inner walls show brick patterns of various De Stijl compositions.

Although Aalto's brick buildings from the late 1940s and 1950s won international critical acclaim, for his commissions in Germany—the Hansaviertel House (1957) in Berlin, the Neue Vahr Apartment building (1962), and the parish centers in Detmerode (1968) and Wolfsburg (1962)—he chose international white modernism while at the same time continuing to use brick in the Otaniemi (1974) and Jyväskylä (1971) universities. This choice may seem surprising, given that brick had a strong regional connotation in Hanseatic cities, whereas in Finland the dominant building material was wood. Hence, Aalto's use of brick in Finland cannot be understood as primitive or regional, and he himself connected brick rather with Central Europe, whereas Finnish architects of around 1900 tended to view it as Russian. Aalto did not want to simply reproduce tradition, and so he worked in both Finland and Germany explicitly against tradition and concentrated more on the symbolic self-identity of the community than on local traditions or building techniques.

The German project Neue Vahr, a slender skyscraper in a suburb of Bremen and the most daring use of the fan plan, is odd in another way. Although in 1934 he had proposed high-rise housing for Munkkiniemi, Helsinki, Aalto was generally known as an outspoken critic of tall buildings. He argued that high-rise apartments were, both socially and architecturally, a considerably more dangerous form of building than single-family houses or low-rise apartments, and therefore they needed a more stringent architectural standard and greater artistry and social responsibility. Despite these reservations, in June 1958 he was appointed to build the 22-story tower Neue Vahr and later the Schönbühl high-rise block of flats (1968) in Lucerne, Switzerland. However, his solutions were praised as outstanding examples of modern housing, and both the Hansaviertel House and the Neue Vahr supported his reputation as a humanist architect among his modernists colleagues.

In 1959 he received the commission for the Enso-Gutzeit headquarters on a prestigous site next to the harbor of Helsinki. In this work he referred partly to the notion of an Italian *palazzo* while at the same time responding to Engel's neoclassical harbor front. With its location right next to the Russian Orthodox Uspensky Cathedral, the strange composition of the House of Culture is repeated: a rectangular modernist office building adjacent to a curved public brick building. Aalto's public buildings of this time are in the tradition of Bruno Taut's Stadtkrone: they are meant to support the identification of the individual with the community and—appropriate for monuments—are usually cladded with marble tiles. The striped marble facade of the Cultural Center (1962) in Wolfsburg is reminiscent of Siena, whereas the white Finlandia hall (1971) looks more like a snowy hill. Both the Finlandia and the Essen Opera House (competition 1959, completed 1988) are very much in the Expressionist tradition and seem to celebrate the social event of visiting a theater rather than responding to the functional needs of an opera.

Aalto's image in crticism does not really reflect his sensitivity to region, nature, or the human being in an abstract sense but rather in the context of critical debates on the lack of regional, natural, and human qualities in international modernism. Thus, in Göran Schildt's characterization of Aalto as the secret opponent within the Modern movement, the word "within" should be emphasized. Aalto did not undermine the cultural field of modernism but exercised his critique internally. Many of his 1950s buildings, for example, addressed the placelessness of modern architecture, which critics had complained about. His Rautatalo office building (Helsinki, 1955) in particular was singled out by critics as a successful example of contextualism because the brick corner pilasters could be read as minimal markers that indicated respect for the built context, the adjacent brick facade of the bank by Eliel Saarinen, without giving up the modern agenda.

DÖRTE KUHLMANN

See also **Contextualism; Corbusier, Le (Jeanneret, Charles-Édouard) (France); Finland; Helsinki, Finland; International Style; Paimio Sanatorium, near Turku, Finland; Villa Mairea, Noormarkku, Finland; Villa Savoye, Poissy, France**

Biography

Born 3 February 1898, Kuortane, Finland; graduated in 1916 from Jyväskylä Classical Lyceum; earned diploma of architecture at the Institute of Technology, Helsinki, 1921. Married Aino

Marsio (1892–1949) in 1924; established private architectural office in Jyväskylä (from 1924 in collaboration with Aino Aalto), 1923–27. Private architectural office in Turku (1927–33); private architectural office in Helsinki (1933–76). Appointed visiting professor, Massachussetts Institute of Technology (MIT) 1940; returned to Finland 1941; returned to United States, Professor, MIT (1946–48); Chairman of the Association of Finnish Architects SAFA (Honorary Member 1943–58); married architect Elissa Mäkiniemi, 1952; Member of the Finnish Academy, 1955 (Emeritus Member since 1968); President of the Finnish Academy, 1963–68; died 11 May 1976 in Helsinki.

Selected Works

Jyväskylä Workers' Club, Jyväskylä, Finland, 1925
Seinäjoki Civil Guard Building, Jyväskylä, Finland, 1926
Standardized Apartment Building, Turku, Finland, 1928
Defense Corps Building, Jyväskylä, Finland, 1929
Muurame Church, Muurame, Finland, 1929
Turun Sanomat office building, Turku, Finland, 1929
Paimio Tuberculosis Sanatorium, Paimio, Finland, 1933
Viipuri Library, Viipuri, Russia, 1935
Finnish Pavilion, World Exhibition in Paris, 1937
Finnish Pavilion, World Exhibition in New York, 1939
Sunila Pulp Mill, Kotka, Finland, 1937
Sunila Housing, Kotka, Finland, 1939
Villa Mairea, Noormarkku, Finland, 1939
Baker Dormitory, Massachusetts Institute of Technology, Cambridge, 1949
Säynätsalo Town Hall, Säynätsalo, Finland, 1952
Muuratsalo Summer (Experimental) House, Muuratsalo, Finland, 1953
Rautatalo Office Building, Helsinki, Finland, 1955
National Pensions Institute office building, Helsinki, Finland, 1957
Hansaviertel House, Berlin, Germany, 1957
Expressionist House of Culture, Helsinki, Finland, 1958
Neue Vahr Apartment building, Bremen, Germany, 1962
Heilig Geist Parish Center, Wolfsburg, Germany, 1962
Enso-Gutzeit Headquarters, Helsinki, Finland, 1962
Schönbühl Apartments, Lucerne, Switzerland, 1968

Further Reading

Fleig, Karl (editor), *Alvar Aalto, Oeuvre Completes I-III*, Zurich: Artemis, 1963–78
Giedion, Sigfried, *Space, Time and Architecture: The Growth of a New Tradition*, Cambridge, Massachusetts: Harvard University Press, 1941, 2nd revised edition, 1949
Jormakka, Kari, "House of Culture," *Datutop 20* (1999)
Kuhlmann, Dörte (editor), *Mensch & Natur, Alvar Aalto in Deutschland* (Human & Nature, Alvar Aalto in Germany), Weimar: Bauhaus Universität, 1999
Porphyrios, Demetri, *Sources of Modern Eclecticism: Studies on Alvar Aalto*, London: Academy Editions, 1982
Quantrill, Malcolm, *Alvar Aalto. A Critical Study*, New York: Schocken Books, 1989
Reed, Peter (editor), *Alvar Aalto. Between Humanism and Materialism* (exhib. cat.), New York: Museum of Modern Art, 1998
Schildt, Göran, *Alvar Aalto. The Complete Catalogue of Architecture, Design and Art*, translated by Timothy Binham, New York: Rizzoli, 1994
Weston, Richard, *Alvar Aalto*, London: Phaidon Press, 1995

ABRAHAM, RAIMUND 1933–

Architect, Austria and United States

The Austrian-born architect Raimund Abraham has played an influential role in architectural discourse and education over the last four decades. His challenging oeuvre of unbuilt work, consisting almost entirely of seductive architectural renderings, delineates a complex architectural position revolving around subversion, metaphor, and a fascination with archetypal forms. His recently completed high-rise in Manhattan for the Austrian Cultural Institute is the most recognizable of a portfolio of built work that has brought together many of the philosophical themes that have preoccupied this enigmatic architect over a prolonged period.

Raimund Abraham was born in Lienz, Austria, in 1933 and was educated at the Technical University in Graz, graduating in 1958. In the early sixties Abraham followed in the footsteps of avant-garde groups such as Archigram, the Metabolists, and fellow Austrians Coop Himmelb(l)au in offering proposals for technology-driven Utopias providing modular living environments capable of embodying the future requirements of civilization. In these early projects, Abraham imagined cellular capsules that would be inserted into vast organic communities comprising monolithic megastructures and colossal bridges. These early idealistic visions demonstrated Abraham's mastery of drawing and collage that would suffuse his later work.

In 1964 Abraham moved to the United States to further a career in architectural education, taking up a position as assistant professor at the Rhode Island School of Design. Since 1971 Abraham has been involved in education at a range of major international universities, holding professorships at the Cooper Union, the Pratt Institute, and the graduate schools of Yale and Harvard. In 30 years of academic life, he has also held visiting professorships at the University of California, Los Angeles; the Architectural Association; and various other North American and European universities.

Abraham's attitude to education, and his architectural practice, is subversive, and his position is often critical of the architectural establishment and its compliance with the principles of modern architecture. Abraham sees in modern architectural discourse a rupture with history that has prevented architects from understanding completely the elemental process of architecture. For Abraham, the 20th-century preoccupation with fashion and style has prevented a thorough understanding of the principles of building and the clarity of thought that they demand. Abraham urges a return to the a priori principles of construction concerned with the nature of materials, site, and program. Abraham posits architectural drawing as an equivalent means of expression, where the paper becomes a site for the poetry of architecture. The intellectual act of building surpasses the ultimate physical product. For Abraham, built architecture is often endemic to the forces of compromise.

Throughout the 1970s, Abraham galvanized his theoretical position by undertaking an extensive series of unbuilt houses concerned primarily with Heidegger's notion of dwelling. Abraham maintains that "collision" is the "ontological basis of architecture," offering as an example the horizon as the most basic junction between the earth and the sky. Abraham defines the process of architecture as either digging into the earth, or reaching for the sky—all building is intrinsically related to these primordial elements. These elements become central to many of Abraham's designs of the period, such as House for the Sun and House with Two Horizons. The abstract house designs sought to strip architecture down to its most essential state, arranging architectonic elements within a formal language of rectilinear forms often embedded within the topology of a generic natural site. Presented largely in rendered axonometric projection, the designs crystallized complex theoretical principles into simple spatial meditations, as is evidenced by titles such as House without Rooms, House with Three Walls, and House for Euclid.

In the 1980s Abraham's attention turned toward monuments, concentrating on historic European centers such as Venice, Berlin, and Paris. Abraham's unbuilt projects from this period interweave themes of juxtaposition and subversion to arrive at a new monumentality capable of questioning the historical significance of architectural form. The instability inherent in Abraham's immersion within the historical landscape is most evident in his projects for the city of Venice, the Les Halles Redevelopment in Paris, and the competition entry for the New Acropolis Museum in Athens (for which he was short-listed).

One of the most poignant projects from this period is the Monument to a Fallen Building, completed in 1980. The project commemorates the collapse of the Berlin Congress Hall in the same year, proposing a prism-like vault in which traces of the former structure are symbolically revealed. Similar themes are inherent in his 1981 project for a Monument to the Absence of the Painting *Guernica*, which mourns the loss of Picasso's masterpiece from its provincial base to another larger museum in Spain. Abraham also addresses the issue of ownership in his project of 1982 for a monumental church that would straddle the Berlin Wall, bringing a transcendental spirituality to the contested space of the wall. All of Abraham's projects from this period deeply question the foundations of architecture and languish after a lost or forgotten meaning in architectural discourse.

As well as his portfolio of unbuilt work, Abraham has also contributed important buildings both in America and in his homeland of Austria. These include individual houses, low-cost housing, and several commercial buildings. The completed buildings demonstrate a fascination similar to his unbuilt work, using archetypal forms, layering, and concision to question conventional architectural form.

In 1988 Abraham was runner-up to Daniel Libeskind in the competition for the extension to the Jewish Museum in Berlin. Two years later, he successfully won the commission to build the New Austrian Cultural Institute in Manhattan (other nominees included Hans Hollein and Coop Himmelb(l)au). The recently completed 20-story tower rises in the shape of a dramatic wedge from a narrow and heavily constrained site obscured almost entirely by neighboring buildings. The front facade is layered with a sloping curtain of cascading planes of glass punctuated by solid elements. Celebrating the link between earth and sky, the powerful form of the tower and the heavy plinth of the podium reinforces Abraham's intention to return architecture to its most basic and primeval elements.

Abraham's challenging and often confronting work occupies an important place within architectural discourse, fostering principles of resistance and legislating against mediocrity. His attempts to return architecture to its philosophical origins in both built and unbuilt projects are intrinsic of a position that attempts to blend the disparate forces of philosophy, poetry, and architecture.

Michael Chapman

See also **Archigram; Coop Himmelb(l)au (Austria); Metabolists**

Selected Works

New Austrian Cultural Institute in Manhattan, New York City, United States, 2002

Further Reading

The 1996 monograph on Raimund Abraham, edited by Brigitte Groihofer, is by far the most thorough collection of his work to date. The work brings together various essays by other authors as well as some of the architect's own writings. It contains an extensive bibliography and color images of many of his drawings.

Groihofer, Brigitte (editor), *Raimund Abraham: [Un]Built*, Vienna: Springer-Verlag, 1996

ABSTRACTION

The 20th century is indelibly marked by the new vision realized by modern art. This vision is no doubt a response to the success of material science, but it is also a cultural phenomenon, an invention that helps us adjust to the new and often daunting horizons that science and technology have opened up. Architecture has benefited as much from that new artistic vision as it has from directly adopting new technology, and the invention of abstract art is one of the important strands of this development.

Abstract art is a product of modern times. It can be seen to follow from the loss of conviction sustained by the ancient view of art as imitation, or mimesis, that is, representing the visible world and placing humanity into a visible narrative. To say that photography supplanted representational art would be to oversimplify the story, but it certainly played a part, and throughout the 19th century one can trace the steps by which another standard gradually took the place of the time-honored one. In British Romantic painter J.M.W. Turner's tumultuous landscapes and in the Impressionist Claude Monet's freely composed water lilies, we see a progression in which more and more weight is given to the artist's feelings in front of the motif, or the subject. It is through personal selection that the artist abstracts the aspects that he or she desires to emphasize and out of them constructs the composition, no longer bound by verisimilitude. Abstract art thus has two principle components: abstraction and expression.

It was perhaps the fin-de-siècle French painter Paul Cézanne who brought the movement to its point of precipitation since it was largely he who substituted the actual vertical plane of the canvas for the virtual horizontal plane of Renaissance perspective. His painting of a curve in the road creates a feeling about the road disappearing from view, not through perspective but by the multiple relations invented in a flat composition (*Turn in the Road*, 1882, Boston Museum of Fine Arts, Massachusetts). Equally, it was Vincent van Gogh who painted with swirling pigment what he felt rather than what he saw. By 1907 the promptings of popular science were suggesting that physical reality must be quite different from appearance, the search was on for the "fourth dimension," and the time was ripe for the invention of Cubism. Analytical Cubism allowed the artist to give a metaphysically complex visual account of the subject, and

Synthetic Cubism introduced fragmented material from the world (newsprint, textiles, paper, string) into the picture plane, or the artist's composition. During World War I, abstraction progressed toward the sublime purism of Piet Mondrian's gridded, neoplasticist compositions and the ineffable weightless rectangles of Kasimir Malevich, who opened a perspective with Russian Suprematism that reaches through to the end of the century in the language of abstract planes used by architects such as Peter Eisenman, Richard Meier, Rem Koolhaas, and Zaha Hadid.

Architecture in the 20th century made its first steps in the shadow of the Arts and Crafts tradition, with Charles Rennie Mackintosh, Josef Hoffmann, and Michel de Klerk, among others. Architecture was as much in need of liberation as the plastic arts, but it was at the same time in need of a new authority to replace ancient authority, something more compelling than the intuition of the artist. One answer was found in the authority of science. For architects, the innovative language of abstraction was not so much a gateway to freer personal expression as an escape from the conventions of traditional construction. It was no longer necessary to affix the Antique orders to facades or to follow academic rules of ordonnance and symmetry in drawing plans. Abstract forms opposed no difficulties of a formal kind to the idea of a plan freely following the program and so freed architecture to create its own myth, that of functionalism. To the subjective intuition of the artist, functionalism opposed a firm objective law similar to the laws of nature.

There was a short time, hardly more than a year, when architecture came close to sharing with art a complete autonomy of form. The year was 1923–24, when De Stijl leader Theo van Doesburg collaborated with the architect Cornelius van Eesteren in designs for villas. In projects such as *Space-Time Construction No. 3* of 1923, his use of axomometric projection obscures for a moment the difference between an art composition created on the flat plane of the canvas for contemplation and the three-dimensional equivalent constructed in real life for use. When van Doesburg designed the interior for the dance hall L'Aubette in Strasbourg, using dramatic rectangles set diagonally on the walls and ceiling, he could not compensate for the ordinariness of banal adjuncts, such as balcony rails and fixed seating, which seem to remove the viewer completely from the world of contemplation proper to fine art. An even more poignant case is that of the Schröder House in Utrecht, where Gerrit Rietveld's exterior, like his famous chair, can certainly be contemplated as a kind of artwork, while the interior is mediated by the dynamic use of movable screens for privacy, reducing the object of contemplation to a practical convenience.

The paradox was fed by the polemical ideology of such protagonists of the Modern movement in architecture as J.J.P. Oud and Le Corbusier, who led the way in identifying architecture with engineering, thereby conceptualizing it as a subject that develops through research and discovery, in which the interest will always be in the novel and not in the already known. According to the credo of International Style, decisions in architectural design should result from rational analysis of the functions, replacing the traditional practice of starting from precedent, which was suffused by convention and custom.

For some, the architect could not claim to shape his building from his inner perceptions; it had to be shaped from something more socially relevant. Functionality provided a rule apart from the purely subjective, and it was a rule that had little precedent in the visual arts. The impact of abstraction within architecture was to create a new duty toward the social function of the building and toward the physical material of construction. Empirical needs would guide form, and form would be free to follow function in the ecstatic exercise of liberation. Within architecture, then, abstraction and functionalism appeared to share a common destiny.

In fine art, Mondrian remained the most extreme purist, and there is no question that he identified avoidance of figuration as an expression of spirituality. In the heroic 1920s and 1930s, artists such as Pablo Picasso and Henri Matisse preferred to distort appearances rather than abandon them. In the case of Fernand Leger, his Communist sympathies kept him firmly focused on the essence of the worker, and between *Le Mécanicien* (1918) and *Abstract Composition* (1919), there is only a difference of degree; the figure remains. This enables us to say something clear about abstraction, namely, that it is not exclusive. It is clearly possible to employ abstraction in due measure without abandoning figuration.

The nascence of abstract art seemed to suggest a solution for architecture by redefining nature itself as a kind of artist. This was the argument advanced in an influential book by D'Arcy Thompson, *On Growth and Form* (1917). Thompson conceived of nature as the supreme designer, producing functional structures that were also intrinsically beautiful. Not only do the skeletons of dinosaurs follow engineering principles, but the patterns of growth in hard-shell mollusks observe strict mathematical rules, as the strictly logarithmic series preserves a constant proportion. Nature thus seems to be the penultimate designer, and the products of nature are "naturally" beautiful. As art approached nature in following natural law, it could appropriate nature's beauty. In the book *Circle*, edited by Leslie Martin, Ben Nicholson, and Naum Gabo (1937), it is clear that abstract form had taken on an aura of objectivity at odds with the reality of its subjective origins.

It is not until De Stijl in the Netherlands and the Abstract Expressionists of the New York School in the 1950s that one finds another impulse to abandon figuration, above all with the mural-scale abstract canvases of Jackson Pollock, Robert Motherwell, and Mark Rothko. In postwar painting the expressive gesture generated the source of meaning, and the authenticity of that gesture became the guarantee of artistic truth. However, this immediacy was difficult to achieve within architecture, with its reliance on physical reality. The urge toward purity that the viewer found in Mondrian and later in Rothko is marked with renunciation, and renunciation is truly difficult to reconcile with functionalism. In art, all arguments are ad hominem, and what one person can do is always exceptional. The idea that abstract art approached a deeper level of reality than figurative art proved difficult to sustain as a general principle, and to this extent it seemed that the hopes of objective validity pinned on bringing abstraction into architecture have proved illusory.

During the crystallization of Modernism in the 1930s, it was simply not possible to eliminate appearances; as long as buildings had to have openings such as doors and windows, as long as they could be entered and used, they clearly served as utilities. Use created meaning, at the most basic level, because doors not only permit entry but also denote entry. The struggle for purity turned into a struggle to eliminate ornament, and this was accentuated by the belief that only through standardization could the building's economy be fully realized. To match transparency in art, we have austerity in architecture, epitomized by the German architect Mies van der Rohe. Standardization was considered the key to realizing the full benefits of mass production. With standardization went repetition, and the monotony of the curtain wall in identical glass panels reduced the possibility of expressive form. It was enough that buildings were massive and impressive, tailored to the demands of modern business, and expression was demonstrated in seeing which city had the tallest building.

From the pluralism of Postmodernism, it became evident that standardization was not as effective in economic terms as marketing. The appearance of a steel-frame building could be changed at will in order to present a spectacular image; the facade became a surface of signification, and irony, humor, and eclectic style were manipulated in such a transformation. Strict economy of construction held less expressive importance. With the end of the 20th century, it became possible to see that the authenticity attributed to abstract forms was balanced by the freedom they conferred upon expression. This was manifest in the 1960s and 1970s within fine art but not within architecture. Today, in the work of Frank Gehry, Peter Eisenman, Daniel Libeskind, and Zaha Hadid, there is no longer any concealment of the expressive gesture.

Except in extreme cases, such as aircraft design, forms are primarily derived not from a scientific analysis of the functional requirements but from the creative feelings of the designer. The architect can have feelings about the function as well as everything else, but he or she is now permitted to sublimate these into a more general concept of the purpose and meaning of a building. So, for example, Libeskind's Holocaust Museum in Berlin is conceived from a universal set of emotions including suffering and persecution, and the jagged forms of the windows are an expression of this emotive tenor and not a response to the practical uses of daylight. In the Solomon R. Guggenheim Museum in Bilbao, Spain, Gehry's abstract, dynamic forms derive from the capacity of the computer to control the fabrication of complex components and allow him to generate an architectural composition as powerful as anything displayed inside the functional building that it also is. In this way, the architect has acquired the technical means that will allow him or her to "build" gesture with all the immediacy of the painter. Abstraction emerges as an acknowledged means of expression.

ROBERT MAXWELL

See also **Arts and Crafts Movement; Le Corbusier, Le (Jeanneret, Charles-Édouard) (France); Cubism; Curtain Wall System; de Klerk, Michel (Netherlands); De Stijl; Eisenman, Peter (United States); Gehry, Frank (United States); Guggenheim Museum, Bilbao, Spain; Guggenheim Museum, New York; Hoffmann, Josef (Austria); International Style; Koolhaas, Rem (Netherlands); Mackintosh, Charles Rennie (Scotland); Meier, Richard (United States); Oud, J.J.P. (Netherlands); Postmodernism; Rietveld, Gerrit (Netherlands); van Doesburg, Theo (Netherlands).**

Further Reading

Frampton, Kenneth, *Modern Architecture: A Critical History*, New York: Oxford University Press, 1980

Henderson, Linda D., *The Fourth Dimension and Non-Euclidean Geometry in Modern Art*, Princeton, New Jersey: Princeton University Press, 1983

Jaffé, Hans Ludwig C., *De Stijl, 1917–1931: The Dutch Contribution to Modern Art*, Amsterdam: Meulenhoff, 1956

Jencks, Charles, *Late Modern Architecture and Other Essays*, New York: Rizzoli, 1980

Jencks, Charles, *The New Moderns: From Late to Neo-Modernism*, New York: Rizzoli International, 1990

Martin, J.L., Ben Nicholson, and Naum Gabo (editors), *Circle: International Survey of Constructive Art*, London: Faber, 1937

Rowland, Kurt F., *A History of the Modern Movement: Art, Architecture, Design*, New York: Van Nostrand Reinhold, 1973

Thompson, D'Arcy Wentworth, *On Growth and Form*, Cambridge: University Press, 1917; abridged edition, edited by John Tyler Bonner, Cambridge: Cambridge University Press, 1961

ABTEIBERG MUNICIPAL MUSEUM, MÖNCHENGLADBACH, GERMANY

Designed by Hans Hollein; completed 1982

Since the 1990s, it has not been uncommon for architects and their clients to break with the two previously prevailing alternatives—temple or warehouse—for art museums, but such a typological rupture had been dramatically anticipated two decades earlier. by Hans Hollein in the Museum Abteiberg, a unique building tailored to an unusual site and a distinctive collection. The Pritzker Prize laureate of 1985, who was born in Vienna in 1934 and is an artist, teacher, and creator of furniture, interiors, and exhibitions, has at Mönchengladbach assembled a virtual primer of museum design, one that has brought a heretofore unknown visceral excitement to the vocation of museum going. In contrast to later attempts in this genre, however, Hollein's achievement has contributed to an intensified appreciation of the museum's contents rather than making a personal statement at their expense.

Although Hollein has learned from the institutional buildings of Louis I. Kahn and Alvar Aalto, he listens to his own music, which—to pursue the metaphor—includes concerti from the 18th, symphonies from the 19th, and popular songs from the 20th centuries. His eclecticism served him well in this complex commission, made more difficult by the need for the museum to serve urban as well as aesthetic ends. Hollein has linked Mönchengladbach's town center on the heights with the medieval Ettal Abbey (today the city hall) on the slopes below, assembling a multi-tiered museum from a series of discrete elements of different sizes and shapes that provide a series of delightfully varied indoor and outdoor rooms. Distributing the individual volumes in space rather than containing them within a monolithic whole allowed him to maintain the picturesque scale of the town; at the subterranean level, the disparate sections are united.

Although designing a museum is always challenging, it is perhaps less onerous when, in contrast to those encyclopedic institutions that are in continual flux, its holdings consist of a focused group of works. Kahn found such a golden opportunity in the Kimbell Museum, and Hollein has exploited the similar possibilities here, where he worked closely with the director, Jonathan Cladders, in formulating the program. They believe that today the museum itself represents a *Gesamtkunstwerk* (total work of art), "a huge scenario into which the individual work is fitted . . . not the autonomy of the work at any price but the deliberately staged correspondence between space and work of

Abteiburg Museum, Mönchengladbach, Germany, designed by Hans Hollein (1972–82)
© Donald Corner and Jenny Young/GreatBuildings.com

art" (Klotz, 1985, p. 19). This especially applies to contemporary art, which frequently is deliberately produced for a museum setting. The plan that Hollein and Cladders evolved is without precedent for this building type. None of the customary tropes, whether conventional or modern—vaulted galleries arranged symmetrically, the universal space, the proverbial white cube—are present. Instead, the combination of small, contained cabinets and larger rooms perfectly accommodates a collection that, although including some historical pieces, is mainly focused on the post–World War II period and, although international, is richly endowed with work by American artists of such competing movements as Minimalism, Post-Painterly Abstraction, and Pop. Many works are in the form of installations without customary boundaries or frames and do not necessarily require natural light.

From the town, one enters the museum precinct via an elevated walkway that leads to a stone-faced platform whereon is set a tower containing administrative offices; a library; workshops and storage; a cubic, top-lighted undivided volume for temporary displays; the shedroofed, zinc-clad "clover-leaf" pavilion for the permanent collection; and the entrance temple. The platform also covers museum spaces excavated into the hill, and from it, one can descend gradually to curving terraces, furnished with sculpture, that border the gardens of the former abbey; beneath a portion of the terraces are additional exhibition areas.

Hollein has rejected the prescribed routes encountered in traditional museums for mysterious, polymorphous paths that compel the viewer to wander on her own and discover unexpected places, then to turn back on them or chance on new chambers. Because chronology is not the issue it would be for a historically based collection, the ad hoc character is stimulating rather than frustrating. Upstairs and downstairs, under- and above-ground, the variously configured galleries illuminated by diverse means—daylight through windows and skylights and artificial light via incandescent, neon, and fluorescent fixtures—permit individual works to be perceived in the setting most sympathetic to their makers' intentions. The most organized part of the display areas comprises what Hollein calls the "clover-leaf"—a group of seven "kissing squares," to use Kahn's formulation, that are traversed at the corners. Set under saw-toothed skylights, these rooms are ideal for big pieces by such artists as Andy Warhol, Frank Stella, Carl Andre, and Roy Lichtenstein. There are also curved rooms, some with undulating walls that are positively Baroque in character; double-height spaces and circular steps add further drama. Hollein's rejection of the convention of amorphous flexible areas, dominant since the 1940s, in favor of a rich variety of specific and distinctive spaces, would in the 1990s become a popular solution for art museums—yet another example of the way the Museum Abteiberg adumbrates many later schemes for this type of institution.

Also prescient is Hollein's interjection of playfulness and irony into the reverence that typically pervades museum design. Although marble clads some of the surfaces, it is combined with less elevated masonry materials like brick and sandstone. Reflective as well as transparent glass appears; zinc is placed beside chromium and steel. One side of the temple-like pavilion that forms the main entrance sports graffiti in red paint, matching the color of some of the railings. Exterior light fixtures have an industrial character in contrast to the lush surrounding landscape and the textured brick walls and paths. The visitor, constantly encountering the unpredictable, is sensitized to the daring originality of the art displayed.

It is instructive to compare Museum Abteiberg with another German museum from the same period that similarly had a profound effect on subsequent museum design—James Stirling's Neue Staatsgalerie (1977–84) at Stuttgart. Both are set on irregular terrain and require urbanistic interventions, but Stirling's solution revives and updates the 19th-century museum paradigm, whereas Hollein has jettisoned all previous solutions. Both make reference to industrial as well as classical buildings and use the technique of compositional collage, yet their differences illuminate the manifold possibilities inherent in the museum program.

HELEN SEARING

See also **Aalto, Alvar (Finland); Hollein, Hans (Austria); Kahn, Louis (United States); Kimbell Art Museum, Fort Worth, Texas; Neue Staatsgalerie, Stuttgart; Stirling, James (England)**

Further Reading

Allégret, Laurence, *Musées* (Tome 2), Paris: Editions du Moniteur, 1992

Cladders, Johannes, "Museum Abteiberg Mönchengladbach," *Architektur und Wettbewerbe* (March 1980)

Davis, Douglas, *The Museum Transformed*, New York: Abbeville, 1990

Frampton, Kenneth, "Meditations on an Aircraft Carrier: Hollein's Mönchengladbach," *A+U* (E8502) (1985), pp. 142–144

Gössel, Peter, and Gabriele Leuthäuser, *Architecture in the Twentieth Century*, Cologne: Taschen, 1991

Klotz, Heinrich, and Waltraud Krase, *New Museum Buildings in the Federal Republic of Germany*, Frankfurt: Ernst Klett Verlage, 1985

Krämer, Steffen, *Die postmoderne Architekturlandschaft: Museumsprojekte von James Stirling und Hans Hollein*, Hildesheim, New York: Georg Ulms, 1998

Montaner, Josep, and Jorid Oliveras, *The Museums of the Last Generation*, Stuttgart/Zurich: Karl Kramer Verlag, 1987

Pettana, Gianni, *Hans Hollein: Works 1960–1988*, Milan and New York: Idea Books, 1988

ABUJA, FEDERAL CAPITAL COMPLEX OF NIGERIA

Designed by Kenzo Tange; completed 1981

In 1976 the Nigerian state authorities believed that a new federal capital city would facilitate the creation of a "federal character" and thus resolve the problem of nepotism and relieve ethnic tensions among the 250 cultural groups that constitute the Nigerian nation. Abuja and its architecture, it was believed, would also remove the colonial identity that the erstwhile capital city of Lagos was thought to bestow on the Nigerian people.

As a result, the role of Lagos as the federal capital of Nigeria has been in question from 1960, when Nigeria became independent, to 9 August 1975, when General Murutala Mohammed set up an eight-member Committee on the Location of the Federal Capital of Nigeria. The task of the committee was to review the multiple roles of Lagos as the federal capital of Nigeria, the capital of the state of Lagos, and the economic capital of the country.

The committee concluded that a new federal capital would improve Nigeria's national security, enhance Nigerian interior development, encourage the decentralization of economic infrastructures from Lagos, and enhance the development of an indigenous Nigerian building culture and industry. Finally, the new capital would emphasize Nigeria's emergence from the civil war of 1967–70 as a more united, stable, and confident country. Nigerian lawmakers who shared the opinions of the committee justified the idea of developing a new federal capital by suggesting that there existed a fundamental need for a place where all Nigerians could come together on an equal basis to help foster national unity. Moreover, advocates of a new federal capital city raised the problems of overcrowding and lack of land for future expansion at Lagos as well as the existence of severe social inequality in the colonial cities of Nigeria. As a result, Abuja was conceived as a place that symbolized Nigeria's autonomy from British colonization, urban segregation, and a federal character that all Nigerians could share in regardless of ethnic heritage. According to the committee and the International Planning Association (IPA), the new capitol would provide "a balanced development focus for the nation" (see *The Master Plan for Abuja*, 1979). They chose Japanese modernist Kenzo Tange, a protégé of Le Corbusier, as the principal architect for the city plan.

The federal government of Nigeria produced a schedule for implementing the committee's recommendations on 4 February 1976. Decree No. 6 established for Nigeria a Federal Capital Territory—an African version of the District of Columbia—a neutral ground where a Nigerian federal character would be developed for the good of all Nigerians. The government took an 8,000-square-kilometer parcel (more than twice the size of the state of Lagos) out of three minority states. Abuja is located on the Gwagwa Plains in the middle of Nigeria; its high elevation and numerous hills contribute to a year-round pleasant climate, one of the major attractions that influenced the committee to select the site.

Abuja was conceived as a city for three million people to be developed in 20 years, and its master plan symbolized the themes of democracy and Nigerian unity. Construction began at Abuja in 1981 under the leadership of President Shehu Shagari (who was later deposed), who was anxious to move from Lagos to the new Federal Capital Territory.

The Nigerian authorities of state insisted that Aso Hill must be the most prominent element within the Federal Capital Territory. Aso Hill is a huge granite outcrop (1,300 feet high) that dominates the landscape of Abuja and its vicinity visually and physically, giving the city a natural east–west axis. Moreover, creating the image of a democratic landscape that emblemizes

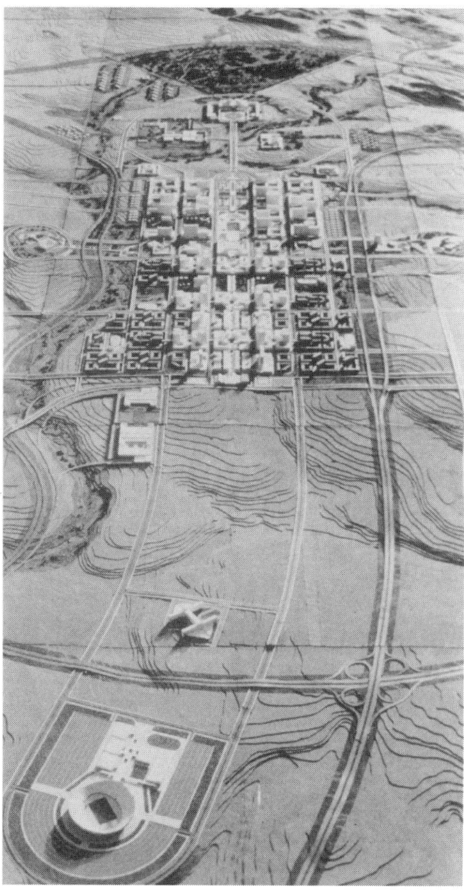

Abuja, Federal Capital Territory of Nigeria
Urban design model of Abuja, Nigeria, designed by Kenzo Tange
© Nnamdi Elleh

the Constitution of the Federal Republic of Nigeria (patterned after the United States' checks-and-balances system of government) was also an integral part of the Abuja urban design scheme. As a result, a democratic shrine called the Three Arms Zone was created at the foot of Aso Hill, making it the focal point of the city and the locus of power of the federal government of Nigeria. Abuja's Three Arms Zone is one kilometer in diameter, and the buildings of the National Assembly, the Presidential Palace, and the Supreme Court are located within it. From Aso Hill in the east end of the city, one moves through the ceremonial Abuja National Mall, which is also patterned after that of Washington, D.C. However, the axial view of the mall is flanked by high-rise federal office buildings on both sides, terminating first at the quintuple towers of the Nigerian National Petroleum Corporation and finally at the National Stadium in the west of the city.

Although the Abuja master plan also aspires to position the city as a major pan-African commercial, financial, and political center, it is dominated by a rhetoric of Nigerian unity, national identity, and democracy. As a result, it is characterized by unresolved tensions between its nationalist themes, the intentions of the emergent Nigerian intelligentsia who inherited political power from Britain, and the intentions of the architect. First, Tange's fundamental concept for Abuja's master plan resembles the plan for Tokyo. One could argue that Tange's plan to incorporate the Japanese modernism of Tokyo represented an attempt to meet the needs of Nigerian national identity; but concerns remained as to whether the architect's uniform design for the monumental federal buildings reflected the interests of the emergent Nigerian elite who inherited political power from Britain, or whether the new structure contributed to the erasure of certain ethnically based social boundaries. The insistence of the federal government of Nigeria that Aso Hill be the most prominent object in the Federal Capital Territory suggests that it was adopting an ancient "pagan" ritual site (Aso Hill) as a means of reinventing a Nigerian "federal character," something quite different from the version of modernity that Tange envisioned. Advocates of the Aso Hill complex envisioned it as a sign of stability, nationality, and cultural myth making in the vibrant, new capital city.

Military dictators interpreted Abuja's master plan as a document that required the isolation of the Three Arms Zone (as a shrine to power) from the rest of the city to make it inaccessible for public gathering. The river that runs down the foot of Aso Hill forms a moat between the central part of the city and the Zone. This moat can be crossed only by bridge, and the bridge is designed to be easily barricaded in time of civil disturbances. Hence, marching to the shrine of power, as is the case in most democratic societies, has been neutralized by the manner in which the master plan was interpreted and implemented. Any march in the city will stop at the national mall in the central district. This outcome was not by accident but by the careful intentions of the military dictators who built Abuja and who deliberately chose to ignore existing traditional urban examples in Nigeria. The ideology that privileges a landscape that can forge national unity in Nigeria will face several practical challenges with the national assembly and the civilian president, who took over power on 29 May 1999 after 15 years of continuous military dictatorship.

NNAMDI ELLEH

See also **Africa: Northern Africa; Corbusier, Le (Jeanneret, Charles-Édouard) (France); Tange, Kenzo (Japan)**

Further Reading

Afigbo, A.E., *Federal Character: Its Meaning and History*, Owerri, Nigeria: RADA, 1986

Ajayi, J.F., *The Problems of National Integration in Nigeria: A Historical Perspective*, Ibadan, Nigeria: Nigerian Institute of Social and Economic Research, 1984

Elleh, Nnamdi, *African Architecture: Evolution and Transformation*, New York: McGraw Hill, 1997

The Master Plan for Abuja, the New Federal Capital of Nigeria, Lagos, Nigeria: The Federal Capital Development Authority, Federal Republic of Nigeria, 1979

Report of the Committee on the Location of the Federal Capital of Nigeria, Lagos, Nigeria: s.n., 1975

Vale, Lawrence, *Architecture, Power, and National Identity*, New Haven, Connecticut: Yale University Press, 1992

ACOUSTICS

As Charles Garnier prepared the design for the Paris Opera House in 1861, the lack of acoustical design information and the contradictory nature of the information that he found forced him to leave the acoustic quality to chance and hope for the best. With few exceptions, this was the condition of architectural acoustics at the beginning of the 20th century. In 1900, with the pioneering work of Wallace Clement Sabine, the dark mysteries of "good acoustics" began to be illuminated. In his efforts to remedy the poor acoustics in the Fogg Art Museum Lecture Hall (1895–1973) at Harvard University, Sabine began experiments that revealed the relationship among the architectural materials of a space, the physical volume of the space, and the time that sound would persist in the space after a source was stopped (the reverberation time). Predicting the reverberation time of a room provided the first scientific foundation for reliable acoustic design in architecture. This method is still regularly used as a benchmark to design a range of listening environments, from concert halls to school classrooms.

The first application of this new acoustical knowledge occurred during the design of the Boston Symphony Hall (1906) by McKim, Mead and White. Original plans for the hall called for an enlarged version of the Leipzig Neues Gewandhaus (1884), a classical Greek Revival theater. The increased size would have been acoustically inappropriate, as it doubled the room volume, leading to excessive reverberation. Sabine worked with the architects to develop a scheme with a smaller room volume in the traditional "shoe box" concert hall shape. The Boston Symphony Hall remains one of the best in the world. Adler and Sullivan's Auditorium Building (1889) in Chicago was praised for its architectural and engineering achievements as well as for the theater's superb acoustics. As the profession of acoustical consulting emerged in the design of listening spaces, the firm of Bolt, Beranek and Newman made a significant impact on the development of architectural acoustics in the 20th century. Their work with architects Harrison and Abramovitz on Avery Fisher Hall (1962) in New York City represented a legitimate attempt to incorporate new scientific principles of acoustical design rather than merely copying previous halls that were known to be good. Although it presented several failures, one key acoustic point gleaned from a study of European halls for Avery Fisher Hall was that the room should hold 1,400 to 1,800 seats. Yielding to economic pressures, the architect increased seating to almost 3,000.

A more successful implementation of modern acoustical theories is the Berlin Philharmonie (1963). Architect Hans Scharoun's vision of a hall in the round blurs the traditional distinction between performer and audience. The approach posed quite an acoustical challenge, given the directionality of many orchestral instruments; it required an extremely unconventional acoustical design. The resulting "vineyard terrace" seating arrangement resolved many potential acoustical difficulties while creating a spatial vitality that resonates outward to form the profile of the building. This collaboration between Scharoun and the acoustic consultant Lothar Cremer engendered a truly inspired architectural design.

Possibly inspired by the failure of Avery Fisher Hall and the desire to understand what went wrong, concert halls, as the crucible for applying sonic theories, gave rise to an acoustical renaissance in the latter part of the 20th century. Acoustically designed spaces need high-quality direct sound, strong sound reflections from the ceiling and side wall surfaces soon after the direct sound, a highly diffuse and controlled reverberance, and heavy solid sound reflecting materials. Formerly thought to be mutually exclusive, these sonic properties exist together in the latest halls of the 20th century through an integration of both historic precedent and new understandings of room acoustics and listening. An extraordinary example of this union is the 1,840-seat Concert Hall in the Cultural Congress Center (1999) in Lucerne, Switzerland, by architect Jean Nouvel and acoustic consultant Russell Johnson.

New techniques for improved acoustic environments are applied in many building types, including school classrooms, music practice rooms, church sanctuaries, movie theaters, transportation hubs, and industrial facilities. Simultaneously, with more and more exposure to digital-quality sound, clients have become keenly aware of their sonic environment and expect high levels of performance. Speech intelligibility in classrooms has been related to learning, with efforts to reduce excessive background noise from mechanical equipment. The issue has become the focus of a U.S. federal government assessment and proposal for a nationwide acoustical standard for schools. Additionally, careful selection of materials, their quantities, and their locations in classrooms are important to enhance speech intelligibility. Music practice spaces require adequate room volume with both sound-absorbent and sound-diffusing materials to control loudness and reduce the risk of noise-induced hearing loss to musicians and teachers. Religious liturgy relies more heavily on intimate spoken sermons, cathedral-like choir singing, and high-powered amplified music in many denominations. These trends, coupled with a prevailing increase in sanctuary size and the desire for more congregational interaction, have demanded sophisticated sound reinforcement systems and carefully configured room acoustic design strategies to strike a balance among divergent sonic criteria. Digital surround sound, the new standard in movie theater entertainment, incorporates the environmental acoustic character as part of the movie sound track, which should not be colored by the theater space. This requires very low reverberance, low background noise levels from mechanical equipment, and exceptional sound isolation from adjacent theaters. Unintelligible announcements, the bane of transportation hubs, have been the focus of many recent acoustical studies, affirming the need to consider room geometry, size, and material selection as they play as great a role as the actual announcement system itself in the success of these spaces.

Many meaningful advances in acoustic knowledge were made in the 20th century. The application and integration of this information within architectural design leaves much room for advancement. Alvar Aalto's famous acoustical ray tracing diagrams for the lecture room of the Viipuri Public Library (1933–35) in Viipuri, Finland, represent acoustical thinking in the earliest phases of design. Developing sophisticated methods to assimilate newer acoustical knowledge as part of the architectural design process is the work at hand in the 21st century.

MARTIN A. GOLD

See also **Aalto, Alvar (Finland); Adler, David (United States); Church; Concert Hall; Harrison, Wallace K., and Max Abramovitz (United States); Library; McKim, Mead and White (United States); Nouvel, Jean (France)**

Further Reading

Barron, Michael, *Auditorium Acoustics and Architectural Design*, London and New York: Spon, 1993

Beranek, Leo, "Acoustical Consultation: Brief History before 1960," in *Wallace Clement Sabine Centennial Symposium, Proceedings*, New York: Acoustical Society of America, 1994
Cavanaugh, William J., and Joseph A. Wilkes (editors), *Architectural Acoustics: Principles and Practice*, New York: Wiley, 1999
Egan, M. David, *Architectural Acoustics*, New York: McGraw-Hill, 1988
Fitch, James Marston, and William Bobenhausen, *American Building: The Environmental Forces That Shape It*, New York: Oxford University Press, 1999
Harris, Cyril M. (editor), *Handbook of Noise Control*, New York: McGraw-Hill, 1957; 3rd revised edition, as *Handbook of Acoustical Measurements and Noise Control*, New York: McGraw-Hill, 1991
Mehta, Madan, James Johnson, and Jorge Rocafort, *Architectural Acoustics: Principles and Design*, Upper Saddle River, New Jersey: Prentice Hall, 1999

ADAPTIVE RE-USE

Buildings often outlive their function; however, their inherent durability often gives the building another life. There is a long tradition of buildings being adapted to suit new functions. Roman basilicas were converted to serve as worship spaces for the nascent Christian church. In medieval times, Roman fortifications were resurrected to form part of the fabric of the mercantile cities. It was not until the advent of ready demolition and the mechanization of the building process during the Industrial Revolution that the practice of adapting old buildings to new uses became less the norm.

Following World War II, the pace of change in urban form, precipitated by technological advances and social upheavals, quickened. As buildings became obsolete and shifting land values directed economic development away from central cities, particularly in North America, large-scale demolition became commonplace. In some cases, well-built warehouses and industrial structures stood on land that had become more valuable for other commercial and office uses, further accelerating demolition. Housing that stood in the pathway of proposed highways was also torn down. Urban renewal stopped short of its promise, and vacant buildings quickly became vacant land. To combat these failures, preservation strategies were developed that employed the existing built environment to suit new uses.

There are four distinct building types in which adaptive re-use of older structures can be seen. Public buildings, which includes large transportation facilities like train stations and civic buildings built in the 19th and 20th centuries being converted to new public and private uses. Industrial buildings, with their large clear structural spans and, typically, large expanses of windows or skylight, lend themselves particularly well to housing an enormous variety of new use groups. Private buildings, like large houses, can serve multiple functions because of the inherent flexibility of the prototype. Finally, commercial buildings, the structures that are so emblematic of the advances in architectural technology in the 20th century, are being recycled with different uses, presenting unique preservation problems, as architects must address issues related to preserving buildings that employed contemporary technology.

The U. S. government owns many magnificent historic structures and has taken the lead in finding new uses for its stock of buildings, serving as an example for private sector development. In Washington, D.C., the Pension Building, an imposing brick edifice, was constructed shortly after the Civil War to provide office space for agencies distributing pensions to war veterans and their families. Its primary distinctive feature is a large, central skylit atrium space that allows the ring of offices access to natural light. The building stood dormant for many years until a major restoration project started in 1984 enabled the National Building Museum to occupy the lower floors of the building, with the bulk of the building retained for government offices. The soaring splendor of the building's interior serves as an excellent advertisement of its function as a museum for the built environment.

Also in Washington, D.C., is the Old Post Office Building, another atrium building. Completed in 1899, the neo-Romanesque building was almost demolished in the early 1970s. Fortunately, as a result of the dedicated efforts of local preservationists and the daunting cost of demolishing such a huge structure, the building was renovated in 1978. The three lower levels of the building, including the atrium, were converted to restaurants and retail, with the perimeter of the building on the upper level retained as office space.

One of the most well-known re-uses of a dormant train station is Gae Aulenti's remaking of the *Gare d'Orsay* in Paris as the national museum of art and civilization. Originally opened for train traffic in 1900, both the building's short platform lengths and changes in travel patterns lead to the abandonment of the station shortly after World War II. Reopened as a museum in 1986, the renovation makes use of the original attached hotel within the head house as exhibition space. Built within the volume of the train shed are smaller structures that house more intimate display space for sculpture. Despite the somewhat awkward intrusion of these galleries within the shed, the sense of the original great volume of the space is still preserved.

In the United States, the nation's private railroad system developed a legacy of magnificent structures throughout the country. When train traffic declined following World War II, these buildings, centrally located in the downtowns of virtually every American city, sometimes were virtually abandoned or, worse, torn down in the case of McKim, Mead and White's Pennsylvania Station in New York. Union Station in St. Louis (Theodore C. Link), built in 1894 and renovated and modified in the early 1980s, is a good example of an important building restored to a new life. The barrel-vaulted Grand Hall functions in much the same way as it was originally intended, now serving as a hotel lobby and entrance to a multiuse complex that includes a parking garage and a restaurant and retail center within the former train shed. The shed, the largest of its type ever built, is organized into "neighborhoods" to make the integration of the building's multiple functions more coherent. When Union Station was renovated, the ornate and eclectic spaces within the head house were restored and glass was inserted into the vaulted train shed, flooding the interior with natural light.

In Philadelphia, a large commuter train station built for the Reading Railroad in 1893 became redundant in 1984 when a subterranean tunnel was constructed below it, linking the area's railways to a regional network. The beautiful steel and glass-vaulted shed and Renaissance revival terra-cotta facade were empty for several years as several different alternatives were studied for a possible re-use. Critical to the success of the project was the maintenance of the historic food market below the train shed. The Pennsylvania Convention Center, built in 1992 (Thompson, Ventulett, Stainback and Association), incorporates the Reading Terminal into the new construction, maintaining both this vital piece of urban architecture and the market's social importance in the city fabric. The head house serves as the ceremonial entrance for the convention center as well as a hotel. The train shed links the entrance from the principal street to the new large convention center that spans over two adjacent blocks.

The first International Style skyscraper, the PSFS Building (George Howe and William Lescaze), also in Philadelphia, was constructed in 1932 and served for many years as the headquarters for a local bank and office building. The building had retail on the ground floor with a cool modern banking hall on the second floor. After the bank went out of business in the early 1990s, the building stayed dormant for many years. Despite the high esteem held for the building locally, its relatively small floor plate did not attract the interest of businesses seeking space where the need for a large floor negated the desire to have ready access for natural light. Fortunately for the building, developers converted it to a hotel that uses the original banking hall as a multipurpose room. The former retail space now serves as a ground floor lobby and restaurant. The renovation is truly successful and the building retains its landmark neon sign, first lit to advertise the bank during the depths of the Depression.

Private buildings that have been adaptively re-used range in size and character from urban townhouses to urban palaces and castles set alone in the countryside. Museums are the most common new use for these buildings, often commemorating the house and holdings of the original occupant, as in the Hearst Castle in San Simeon, California, and the Biltmore House in Asheville, North Carolina. Alternatively, the urban mansions are often converted to art museums, making use of the variety of spaces, both small and grand. Institutions like the Cooper-Hewitt Museum in the former Carnegie mansion and the Frick Museum, both in New York City, serve as excellent display space for sculpture and paintings of all manners of style and size. In European countries like France, Spain, and Portugal, châteaus and castles have been converted into hotels. The Spanish government, in particular, has made the conversions of these castles into *paradores* for the latter half of the 20th century a matter of restoration policy.

Industrial buildings offer the most flexible typology for conversion. Mills and old factory structures are typically solidly built and often offer large expanses of natural light. Industrial buildings are generally anonymous buildings that, in the early part of the 20th century, were executed, if not by architects, then by highly competent vernacular builders. The prototype was a relatively recent phenomenon, and the pace of construction of these buildings accelerated during the time of great urban industrialization that coincided with a particularly eclectic period in architecture. Consequently, these buildings hold important social and physical significance in the urban context. The solid structures of these buildings may have contributed to their long-term survival; in some cases, the cost of demolition made their destruction not as viable an option, allowing time for alternative uses to be found.

Housing has been a popular choice to occupy these spaces. In the United States, the vanguard of the movement to convert former industrial properties to housing was the SoHo neighborhood in New York City. What started as flexible and inexpensive space serving as artist studios became coveted by those looking for expansive living quarters in neighborhoods that the artists had helped to become fashionable. Outside of New York, one of the better-known early preservation and conversion projects is Lowell Mills in Lowell, Massachusetts, a mixed-use complex that helped to revitalize a portion of that moribund town.

These mill buildings are now also adapted to house the industries of the information age, the economic successor to the industrial revolution. Offices for computer technology firms, professional offices, and material and product showrooms in early 20th-century industrial loft buildings are such a commonplace sight in urban centers that it is often forgotten that those buildings were not originally constructed to house those functions. One particularly striking conversion is the Templeton Factory in Glasgow, Scotland, a former carpet mill built in a colorful and stylized Venetian Gothic style in 1898. The building complex was considered for demolition following its abandonment in 1978 as the result of changes in manufacturing technology. Preservation as a museum was rejected. In the early 1980s, a scheme was devised to convert the building into a hybrid research and business incubator center run by a local government development agency.

Winston Churchill's aphorism—"We shape our buildings; thereafter they shape us"—rings true. Preservationists seeking to link the past with the future take exception to this rule as we continue to shape our buildings, adapting them to new functions. Adaptive re-use as a tool used by architects, like the larger preservation movement, is a 20th-century phenomenon. The preservation of older buildings by giving them new uses also serves as part of an overall strategy for urban designers, city planners, and the consortium of public and private forces that view this approach as a tool of economic development. The supply of older and significant buildings is a source of sound urban ecological regeneration. As preservation practice evolves, the emphasis is shifting away from strict restoration to an attitude that frees the building from its former use.

SCOTT KALNER

See also **Aulenti, Gae (Italy); Howe, George, and William Lescaze (United States); McKim, Mead, and White (United States); Pennsylvania Station, New York**

Further Reading

Burchell, Robert W., *Adaptive Reuse Handbook: Procedures to Inventory, Control, Manage, and Reemploy Surplus Municipal Properties*, New Brunswick, New Jersey: CUPR Press, 1981

Cantacuzino, Sherban, *Re/Architecture*, New York: Abbeville Press Publishers, 1989

Collins, Richard, A. Bruce Dotson, and Elizabeth B. Masters, *America's Downtowns: Growth, Politics & Preservation*, Washington, D.C.: Preservation Press, 1991

Diamonstein, Barbara, *Buildings Reborn: New Uses, Old Places*, New York: Harper & Row, 1978

Fitch, James Marston, *Historic Preservation: Curatorial Management of the Built World*, New York: McGraw-Hill Publishers, 1982

Greer, Nora Richter, *Architecture Transformed, New Life for Old Buildings*, Gloucester, Massachusetts: Rockport Publishers, Inc., 1998

Lee, Antoinette (editor), *Past Meets Future: Saving America's Historic Environments*, Washington, D.C.: Preservation Press, 1992

Lee, Vinny, and Ray Main, *Recycled Spaces: Converting Buildings into Homes*, San Francisco: Soma Publishing, 2000
Moore, Arthur Cotton, *The Powers of Preservation: New Life for Urban Historic Places*, New York: McGraw Hill Publishing Company, 1998
Partners for Livable Communities (editor), *The Livable City: Revitalizing Urban Communities*, New York: McGraw Hill Professional Publishing Company, 2000
Powell, Kenneth, *Architecture Reborn: Converting Old Buildings for New Uses*, New York: Rizzoli International Publications, 1999
Stratton, Michael (editor), *Industrial Buildings: Conservation and Regeneration*, London: E & FN Spon, 2000
Tyler, Norman, *Historic Preservation: An Introduction to Its History, Principles and Practice*, New York: W.W. Norton and Company, 1999

ADLER, DAVID 1882–1949

Architect, United States

David Adler, a proponent of Paris's École des Beaux-Arts and its classical teachings of symmetry, balance, and superb proportions and an all-inclusive plan whereby a building relates to its surroundings, was one of America's most important great-house architects. Born to Isaac David, a prosperous second-generation wholesale clothier, and his wife, Theresa Hyman, in Milwaukee, Wisconsin, Adler was educated at the Lawrenceville School and Princeton University. After graduating from Princeton in 1904, Adler moved to Europe, where he traveled extensively and studied architecture at the Polytechnikum (1904–06) in Munich and at the École des Beaux-Arts (1908–11), whose curriculum included lessons in structural and technical applications. However, because Adler was interested exclusively in design, he returned to the United States without mastering these key assignments, bringing with him a collection of 500 picture postcards that documented the important architecture and gardens he had seen and to which he referred throughout his 38-year career.

Before venturing out on his own, Adler apprenticed in Chicago in the office of Howard Van Doren Shaw, a devotee of the Arts and Crafts movement. Shaw (1869–1926) was among the most prolific country house architects on Chicago's North Shore, particularly in Lake Forest, where Adler also forged his eminent reputation.

Henry C. Dangler, Adler's closest friend from the École and the person who introduced Adler to Katherine Keith, whom he married in 1916, also worked in Shaw's office. Adler and Dangler did not stay long with Shaw; they decided to form their own partnership. Dangler left first, and Adler remained with Shaw only until he completed the design of his first house (1911), which was for uncle and benefactor Charles A. Stonehill, in the North Shore community of Glencoe. Stonehill had paid for his nephew's living expenses while he was studying in Europe.

The Stonehill house, a Louis XIII–style building inspired by the Château de Balleroy in Normandy, set the tone for what became a recognizable trait of Adler's exemplary oeuvre. Symmetry guided the house's entrance facade of pink brick, limestone trim, and offsetting tall windows and steeply pitched roof. Perched on a high bluff overlooking Lake Michigan, Adler's first charge was one of the most outstanding country houses in Chicago. Unfortunately, the house, with its classically detailed interiors furnished in Mediterranean pieces, was razed during the early 1960s.

Among the most important houses executed by the Adler–Dangler partnership was its first country house (1912), for Ralph H. Poole, in Lake Bluff, Illinois. With this commission, Adler brought the Loire valley to the Illinois prairie, designing a Louis XV–style château that perpetuated, with its symmetrical facade of low horizontal lines rising to a slate mansard roof, classical French architecture. Inside the house, a checker-floored entrance hall led to the principal rooms: living porch, library, living room, music room, and dining room, all arranged enfilade across the entire length of the house, another indication that Adler understood French design.

Henry Dangler's death in 1917 left both a personal and a professional void in Adler's life, for he had lost not only his partner but also his best friend. Adler was not certified to practice architecture in Illinois; he obtained a New York license in 1917. Although Adler was the designer, the signature on his plans had always been Dangler's. Therefore, Adler was compelled to sit for the Illinois exam, and as presaged by his incomplete studies at the École, he failed. Adler had already built 17 houses, in French, Georgian, and Mediterranean styles, but he was forced to find another architect who could replace Dangler professionally. The solution came in another former associate from Shaw's office, Robert Work. Their association, marking the second phase of Adler's career, was strictly one of convenience.

While associated with Work, Adler applied the styles of his early houses but also added to his eclectic oeuvre early American, South African Dutch colonial, and a modernist design inspired by Viennese architect Josef Hoffmann (1870–1956). Of these three styles, it was the house in early American (1926) for William McCormick Blair in Lake Bluff that deviated from Adler's usual approach to design. The irregular massing of colonial architecture, whereby a house grows larger over time, dictated the asymmetrical design for the Blairs. Although the house was built all at once, Adler's adaptation flawlessly suggested an organic progression of growth from the principal block, shingled and gambrel roofed, to the appended wings.

Adler's largest undertaking was also completed during the mid-1920s. Castle Hill, the imposing English manor house (1925) for Richard T. Crane Jr., in Ipswich, Massachusetts, with its pedimented entrance pavilion, balustraded hip roof, and crowning cupola, followed closely the architecture of 17th-century England, particularly the work of Sir Christopher Wren (1632–1723) and the Wren-like Belton House (1689). Adler's ability lay not only in his proficient design but also in his choice of small Holland brick with a soft pink patina that softened the imposing scale of the house, rising at the foot of a 160-foot-wide aisle of grass that undulated toward the Atlantic Ocean.

Adler built 16 houses during the second phase of his career, including a Louis XVI–style townhouse (1921) for Joseph and Annie Ryerson in Chicago. The Ryerson townhouse, a classically elegant building—with its symmetrical limestone facade, crowning mansard roof, and period detailing—was Adler's only townhouse design in the French style (Adler built eight townhouses during his career).

By 1929, because Adler had practiced as a principal architect for ten years, he became eligible for Illinois's oral examination, which he passed, therefore ending his 12-year association with Robert Work. Unfortunately, Adler's professional achievement

House-on-Hill (Celia Tobin Clark House), Hillsborough, California, designed by David Adler (1930)
Ezra Stoller © Esto

was marred by personal tragedy. In May 1930 Katherine (1893–1930), his wife of 14 years, was killed in an automobile accident while she and Adler were motoring on a rain-slick road in Normandy. Adler sustained only minor physical injuries, but he was extremely distraught.

Regardless of this setback, the late 1920s through the mid-1930s resulted in the culmination of Adler's career, starting with his masterpiece: the Cotswold-influenced house of Celia Tobin Clark in Hillsborough, California, called House-on-Hill (1930). Here, Adler created a house that, despite its underlying grandeur and nearly 400 acres of property, was inconspicuous and unpretentious. For example, because Adler nestled House-on-Hill into the hillside of its vast property, from the entrance forecourt it appeared to be only one-and-a-half stories. The house's full magnitude became apparent only at the back, from the south terrace, where Adler's most outstanding elevation—an Elizabethan half-timbered facade of oak and intricately patterned brick nogging—rose majestically, as if it grew from the landscape.

Inside the Clark house, a beamed and oak-paneled reception gallery, floored in a harlequin-patterned black-and-white marble tile, opened into the house's principal stair hall. Here, a monumental and skillfully carved staircase gave the first indication of the opulence of House-on-Hill. Because the reception gallery was on the second floor, the staircase, with its substantial balustrade, led downstairs to an impressive procession of rooms: library, music room, and dining room. Warmth and comfort pervaded the library, whose antique pine paneling, Grinling Gibbon's overmantel, and pegged parquetry were imported from Europe. In the commodious and imposing music room, classically detailed spruce walls served as foundation for a high plaster ceiling with its patterns of rosettes, garlands, and musical instruments, while in the dining room, panels of hand-painted 18th-century Chinese wallpaper were framed by exquisite woodwork in sugar pine.

Another outstanding design from this period was the Pennsylvania Dutch–style Georgian for Helen Shedd Reed (1931), unquestionably Adler's finest house on the North Shore. The Reed house, consisting of a center block balanced by a pair of wings, was sited beyond a grass forecourt with a small pool and surrounding U-shaped gravel drive and exemplified the symmetry, balance, and elegance of Adler's work. The house's shimmering dark gray mica stone also added to its magnificence.

The interior of the Reed house was the most important collaboration between Adler and his sister, interior decorator Frances Elkins (1888–1953). Adler and Elkins were extremely close, and during his tenure in Paris, she traveled with him,

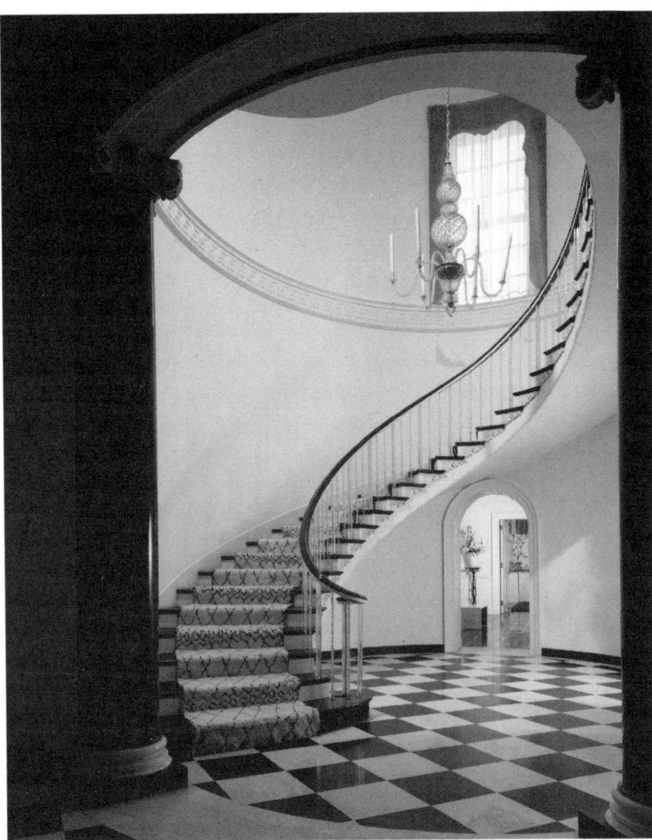

Freestanding staircase, Mrs. Kersey Coates Reed House, by David Adler (1931)
Ezra Stoller © Esto

meeting several avant-garde artisans, including Jean-Michel Frank (1895–1941), the French interior decorator, and furniture designer, and Alberto Giacometti (1902–85), the sculptor who designed furniture for Frank. Nowhere is Elkins's relationship with these designers more apparent than in the Reed house, where Adler's skilled architecture guided the most notable interiors of her career. Elkins lived in California, and although she worked independently of her brother, they collaborated on at least 16 commissions, undoubtedly her best work, from 1919 until 1949, when Adler died unexpectedly of a heart attack.

The Reed house's interiors blended the traditional and the avant-garde, starting in the entrance hall, where a slick black-and-white marble floor led to the ladies' powder room, the gentlemen's cloakroom, and the gallery. In the gallery, stately black Belgian marble columns framed the crowning element of the interior: a dramatic, freestanding staircase of ebony and wrought-glass spindles. The gallery led to each of the principal rooms: living room, library, and dining room, all aligned overlooking Lake Michigan.

Adler gave each of these rooms his usual dose of exquisite and brilliantly executed detailing. In the living room and dining room, a dentiled cornice, as well as mantels and door casings, all intricately carved, complemented Elkins's selection of English antiques and accoutrements, including the dining room's hand-painted Chinese wallpaper. In the library, although the most avant-garde room in the house, walls of tan Hermès goatskin and leather-upholstered furnishings by Frank were adroitly tempered by Adler's traditional foundation: antique French parquetry, a finely carved fireplace mantel, and doors and casings, resulting in the perfectly balanced eclecticism for which he was renowned.

Any discussion of the Reed commission would be remiss without mentioning the tennis house that Adler designed several years before the main house. Located at the foot of the formal gardens, across the street from the main house, the Georgian building, with its central lounge, his-and-hers changing rooms, and second-floor bedrooms, was ingeniously sited at the edge of a ravine, allowing Adler to reduce the apparent scale of the mammoth building by positioning the court ten feet below ground level. The end result: a sunken indoor court where natural light flooded the space through a pitched glass roof, creating, along with interior ivy-covered walls, the illusion of an outdoor setting.

The mid-1930s signaled the end to Adler's career as an architect of the great house. Adler's declining health from a riding accident in 1935, as well as altered economic conditions in the United States, prompted him to adapt to designing smaller, less grand houses and to spend more time executing apartment interiors and the alterations and additions that had always been a part of his demanding schedule.

Adler's last house (he built 45 houses, 18 of which were located outside of the Chicago area), in Pebble Beach, California, was designed for Paul and Ruth Winslow (1948). Built low to the ground, one storied, and sided in flush boards painted white, the Winslow house consisted of a central living room balanced by two symmetrical wings: the dining room and service wing and the master bedroom wing. Despite the house's modest size, Adler's last house was one that exemplified his ability to create grandeur and elegance, albeit on a much smaller scale.

STEPHEN SALNY

See also **Arts and Crafts Movement; Shaw, Howard Van Doren (United States); Historicism**

Selected Works

Charles A. Stonehill House, Chicago, Illinois, 1911
Ralph H. Poole House, Lake Bluff, Illinois (with Henry Dangler), 1912
Castle Hill, Ipswich, Massachusetts, 1925
William McCormick Blair House, Lake Bluff, Illinois (with Robert Work), 1926
House-on-Hill (Celia Tobin Clark House), Hillsborough, California, 1930
Helen Shedd Reed House, Lake Forest, Illinois (with Frances Elkins), 1931

Further Reading

Hampton, Mark, *Legendary Decorators of the Twentieth Century*, New York: Doubleday, 1992
Pratt, Richard, *David Adler*, New York: M. Evans and Company, 1970
Salny, Stephen M., *The Country Houses of David Adler*, New York: W.W. Norton, 2001

AEG TURBINE FACTORY

Designed by Peter Behrens and Karl Bernhard; completed 1910
Berlin, Germany

Largely misunderstood by the historians of the Modern movement who celebrated it as the first major work of frank industrial architecture endowed with exceptional "functional directness," the AEG Turbine Factory—designed by Peter Behrens and Karl Bernhard and completed 1910—remains the most admired and most influential of Behrens's works.

Designed between 1908 and 1909 for the Allgemeine Elektricitäts Gesesells (AEG)—a German electrical concern founded by Emil Rathenau in 1883—the factory was placed strategically at the southern edge of the factory complex along Huttenstrasse and Berlichingenstrasse, facing Berlin and the world as a show front of the prosperous industrial magnate. Complying with such expectations and following his own ideological stance, Behrens built a magnificent iron and glass hybrid of two eminently classical temple traditions—the Greek and the Egyptian—meant to glorify industrial might.

In accepting the challenge of designing his first industrial building, Behrens's concern was not to recast all of architecture in terms of industry and the machine, as was most often the case with the next generation of modern architects. Rather, "his concern was . . . with elevating so dominant a societal force as the factory to the level of established cultural standard" (see Anderson, 1977).

As an adept of the Austrian art historian and critic Alois Riegel's theory of *Kunstwollen* (literally, "artistic will" or the evolutionary force of style) and of Georg Wilhelm Friedrich Hegel's aesthetic historicism, exemplified in the concept of the Zeitgeist, Behrens applied in the design of the Turbine Factory the principles that he had evolved as the leader of the Darmstadt artists' colony after 1901. In direct opposition to Gottfried Semper's "materialism," central to Behrens's approach was belief in the force of the artist, and art, to transform brute everyday life into a dignified existence. Akin to the carbon transformed under extreme conditions into a praised diamond, everyday life—and in this case raw industry, the factory, and the machine—could be transformed under the artist's *Kunstwollen* into an entity of high culture. Such an ideological position, applied to industry, spread into a number of aesthetic and symbolic themes clearly reflected in the Turbine Factory. Far from depending on primary concerns for material, technical, and functional purposes, the factory was, in Behrens's mind, the result of a specific concretization of selected industrial features, filtered through the artist's transcendental will to form. The result was a vast crystal symbolizing the victory of art over the banality of life in an emerging machine society. If the industrial fact at hand could not be ignored, it was not the role of the artist to succumb to it helplessly, either. It is largely because of this position that Behrens's first industrial building was unprecedented in industrial architecture and design.

In aesthetic terms, the central conflict that Behrens faced in the design of the Turbine Factory was the tectonic character of the ferro-vitreous wide span offered by his engineer, Karl Bernhard, as the necessary solution for mastering the vastness of the structure and Behrens's adherence to the concept of *Stereotomie* since his 1905 pavilions at the Oldenburg Northwest German Art Exhibition. The challenge was, therefore, to find a solution that would be flexible enough to accommodate the dictates of a particular technology—including the use of given industrial materials—while preserving architecture as the eminent symbol of established cultural values of a modern capitalist state. The culmination of this synthetic process was expressed in the factory's triumphal templelike facade with its crystalline central window of staggering dimensions that only advanced technology could have brought about.

With his limited knowledge of any kind of building technology, Behrens had to rely on the support of an engineer for such a vast and technically complex building. The shifting priorities between ideology and technology in the conception of the building necessarily resulted in a series of ambiguities and concealments that Behrens provoked rather than avoided in a strained collaboration with Bernhard.

The structural makeup of the factory consists of an asymmetrical three-hinged arch reinforced by a transversal tie-rod. The longer half of the arch springs vertically up to the second hinge and then breaks in three facets before reaching the third hinge at the apex of the arch. In properly structural terms, there was no reason for breaking the second arm into segments. The decision was a willful intervention in the engineer's work by Behrens the artist. Historically, a variety of reasons have been advanced as an explanation for such a move. Whereas Kenneth Frampton, for example, refers to a rather improbable desire to create the shape of a farmer's barn with its typical polygonal gable, Reyner Banham offers a technological explanation: the need for clearance for the huge internal traveling crane—even though the section shows that the tying rods forced the crane to run much lower.

The chiseled gable was, in fact, the result of two specific exigencies of Behrens's *Kunstwollen*: the urge for enforced *Stereotomie* and the evocation of *Zeichen* (sign), the crystalline symbol of life as art. Indeed, the comparison between Behrens's earlier representation of the priestess of Darmstadt carrying the redemptive crystal high above her head, as well as the majestic front of the temple–factory, reinforces the idea of a crystal-shaped gable springing high above the ground in delicate balance over the equally crystalline abstracted robe of a priestess.

Furthermore, using the given technology for more ambitious aims, Behrens concealed the fact that the actual structural system of the factory was made up of a series of hinged arches by capping the building with a voluminous cornice cutting the arch at the top of its vertical member. In so doing, Behrens created the visual impression of a trabeated system in which the vertical members of the arches represented so many columns of a classical temple. By the same token, the somewhat inwardly inclined glazed surfaces between the structural members of the side elevation, along with the blown-up roofline and the massive concrete nonbearing "corner stones" wrapping around a streamlined trapezoidal silhouette, created a convincing case of a perfectly "stereotomic" volume inflated with space. Thus undermining the iron framing, Behrens prevented the construction from dematerializing into a dispersed tectonic grid—as would have been the case with the Dutert-Contamin Gallerie des Machines—and clearly subverted any engineering directness. The formulation of a symbolic structure, however, did not preclude Behrens from addressing forcefully the nature and purpose of the building.

AEG Turbine Factory, Berlin, designed by Peter Behrens with Karl Bernhard (1910)
© Alan Windsor

Still remaining in the realm of powerful symbolism, Behrens allowed the function of the building to express itself allegorically not only through the exclusive use of industrial materials on a large scale but also by evoking forcefully the dominant societal role of the machine in the most memorable details of the building, such as the giant base hinges of the arches set on high concrete pedestals. As has been noted, what makes the significance and the importance of the AEG Turbine Factory, aside from actual achievement, "is that Behrens understood that the established cultural standards must be transformed in the process of assimilating modern industry."

Danilo Udovicki-Selb

See also **Banham, Reyner (United States); Behrens, Peter (Germany); Darmstadt, Germany; Frampton, Kenneth (United States); Modernism**

Further Reading

Anderson, Stanford, "Modern Architecture and Industry: Peter Behrens and the Cultural Politics of Historical Determinism," *Oppositions* 11 (Winter 1977)

Anderson, Stanford, "Modern Architecture and Industry: Peter Behrens, the AEG, and Industrial Design," *Oppositions* 21 (Summer 1980)

Buddensieg, Tilmann, with Henning Rogge, *Industriekultur: Peter Behrens und die AEG, 1907–1914*, Berlin: Mann, 1979; as *Industriekultur: Peter Behrens and the AEG, 1907–1914*, translated by Iain Boyd Whyte, Cambridge, Massachusetts: MIT Press, 1984

Buderath, Bernhard, with Tilmann Buddensieg (editors), *Peter Behrens, umbautes Licht: Das Verwaltungsgebäude der Hoechst AG*, Frankfurt: Prestel, 1990

Le Corbusier, *Étude sur le mouvement d'art décoratif en Allemagne*, La Chaux-de-Fonds, Switzerland: Haefeli, 1912; reprint, New York: Da Capo Press, 1968

Dohrn, W., "Das Vorbild der AEG," *März* 3 (3 September 1909)

Giedion, Sigfried, *Space, Time, and Architecture: The Growth of a New Tradition*, Cambridge, Massachusetts: Harvard University Press, and London: Oxford University Press, 1941; 5th edition, revised and enlarged, Cambridge, Massachusetts: Harvard University Press, 1967

Kadatz, Hans-Joachim, *Peter Behrens: Architekt, Maler, Grafiker und Formgestalter, 1868–1940*, Leipzig: Seemann, 1977

Kalkschmidt, E., "Deutsches Kunstgewerbe und der Weltmarkt," *Dekorative Kunst* 19 (July 1911)

Pevsner, Nikolaus, *Pioneers of the Modern Movement from William Morris to Walter Gropius*, London: Faber, 1936; revised edition, as *Pioneers of Modern Design: From William Morris to Walter Gropius*, London: Penguin, 1975

AFRICA: NORTHERN AFRICA

Compared with the rest of the continent, the countries of North Africa form an immediately recognizable region and appear as a more cohesive bloc than do their neighbors south of the Sahara Desert. They derive their apparent cohesion from a common language (Arabic), a common religion (Islam), and a shared cultural identity as heirs of the Ottoman Empire. Like their sub-Saharan neighbors, all shared the historical experience of European colonialism and of the struggle for independence. Unlike their sub-Saharan neighbors, however, pan-Arabism has been a more powerful force than African unity.

On closer examination, all the countries of North Africa have developed their own distinctive cultural identity and historic perception of themselves and their role in the world. Egypt, with its overpowering legacy of its Pharaonic past and its small but influential Coptic Christian minority, has always perceived itself as distinctively different from the Maghreb (the countries to the west) and more naturally internationalist in outlook. Morocco, which was the only country in North Africa that did not suffer the experience of Ottoman rule, prided itself on the purity of its national culture and the dignity of its sultanate.

At the beginning of the 20th century, the Ottoman Empire was collapsing all around the Mediterranean: Its final death throes came after it allied itself with the German and Austro-Hungarian Empires at the beginning of World War I. Egypt had effectively become a protectorate of Britain in 1882, to the intense annoyance of France, which had enjoyed most-favored-nation status in Egypt since Napoleon's short-lived expedition to Egypt in 1799–1801. Algeria (or at least the coastal strip) became a French colony in 1830, to which the mountainous hinterland and the desert interior were added in 1848, and by 1900 it was effectively part of metropolitan France. Tunisia, as a consequence of the dey of Tunis's indebtedness to French bankers, was annexed by France in 1881. The Sudan, over which vast territory British troops had campaigned sporadically for 20 years, was absorbed into the British Empire in 1899 as an Anglo-Egyptian condominium. Libya was invaded by Italy and incorporated into the infant Italian Empire in 1912; in the same year, Morocco became a protectorate of France by treaty, proudly safeguarding its cultural independence as the brightest jewel in the French imperial crown.

The European colonial experience was, with the exception of Algeria, short-lived and, again with the exception of Algeria, relatively bloodless. Egypt gained its independence in 1922 under the Albanian dynasty, whose founder, Mohammed Ali, had seized power from the Ottomans and imposed himself as khedive on the long-suffering Egyptian people in 1805, shortly after Napoleon's expedition to Egypt. Effective independence was not really secured until the revolution under General Neguib and until Colonel Nasser overthrew King Farouk and seized power in 1952. With the exception of Algeria, all other North African states gained their independence in the 1950s: Algeria, after a long, bloody civil war between the European settlers (10 percent of the population) and the indigenous Africans, finally followed suit in 1962. (A couple of insignificant Spanish enclaves on the Mediterranean coast of Morocco still owe allegiance to Europe.)

For the first half of the 20th century, the architectural and urban development of North Africa was European directed and European driven. At the beginning of the century, European imperialism was at its apogee, and between 1900 and the outbreak of World War I in 1914, with a few significant exceptions, colonial governments, architects, and developers aimed to re-create Europe in Africa. By 1900 regionalism and vernacular revivalism had become respectable, even fashionable, architectural styles in Europe in a period when eclecticism reigned.

Physical manifestations of imperialistic rule, such as the Union Jack–inspired town plan of the new capital of the Sudan (Khartoum) and the Hausmannesque boulevards imposed on the organic city plan of Algiers were characteristic of this period but by no means were universal. Equally popular were the garden suburb, garden city developments that were fashionable in Europe: the Garden Suburb along the Nile in Cairo, the more ambitious New Town of Heliopolis on the desert fringe of the same city, and the Parc d'Hydra and the hilly suburbs of El Biar in Algiers were laid out in European lines for a mainly European settler population.

Arabisance (Arabism) and the Hispano-Mauresque Revival were eagerly adopted by French architects in Algeria, as the Saracenic, Coptic, and even Pharaonic styles were adopted by the polyglot architects practicing in Egypt.

Representative buildings of the pre–World War I period, when European imperialism reigned supreme, were the Post Office (1890–1900, Algiers) by Tondoir and Voinot, the Galerie Algerienne (1902, Algiers) by Voinot, and the Prefecture (1904, Algiers) and the Hotel St. Georges (1910; now the Hotel El Djezair, Algiers), all in a highly decorative and stylized part Ottoman, part Hispano–Mauresque style inspired by the wealth of handsome 18th-century Ottoman buildings in the city. Also representative, in Cairo, are the eclectically classicist Egyptian Museum (1900), the vernacular revivalist Coptic Museum (1910), and the Beaux-Artian, symmetrically planned buildings of the Cairo University (founded as Fuad University in 1908); in Khartoum, the neo-Byzantine Anglican All Saints' Cathedral (1909–12) by Robert Weir Schulz and the late Ottoman-style Gordon Memorial College (*c.* 1905; now the University of Khartoum) by Fabricius Bey and Gorringe are representative.

Lieutenant Gorringe was a British army officer serving with the Royal Engineers; Fabricius Bey was architect to the khedive in Cairo and of southern European (probably Maltese) origin. Under the autocratic rule of Lord Cromer, British consul-general in Egypt from 1883 to 1907, whose job title concealed the virtually absolute power he wielded, Cairo and Alexandria were boom cities, and architects and engineers flocked to Egypt from all over Europe. The indigenous Egyptian elite—the educated middle classes who had enjoyed a privileged position in society under the Francophile rule of Khedive Ismail before the British invasion of Egypt in 1882—were increasingly sidelined under Cromer's administration and agitated for a national university and for a school of fine arts under Egyptian control. The foundation of the École des Beaux-Arts in 1906 and of Fuad University in 1908 were the results of their efforts. By 1920 both institutions (now the University of Helwan at Zamalek and Cairo University, respectively) had schools of architecture. Not until the 1920s, therefore, were indigenous Egyptians able to study architecture in their own country. The few Egyptian architects who were in practice in the early decades of the century had studied abroad at the École des Beaux-Arts in Paris or at Constantinople. A similar situation prevailed throughout North Af-

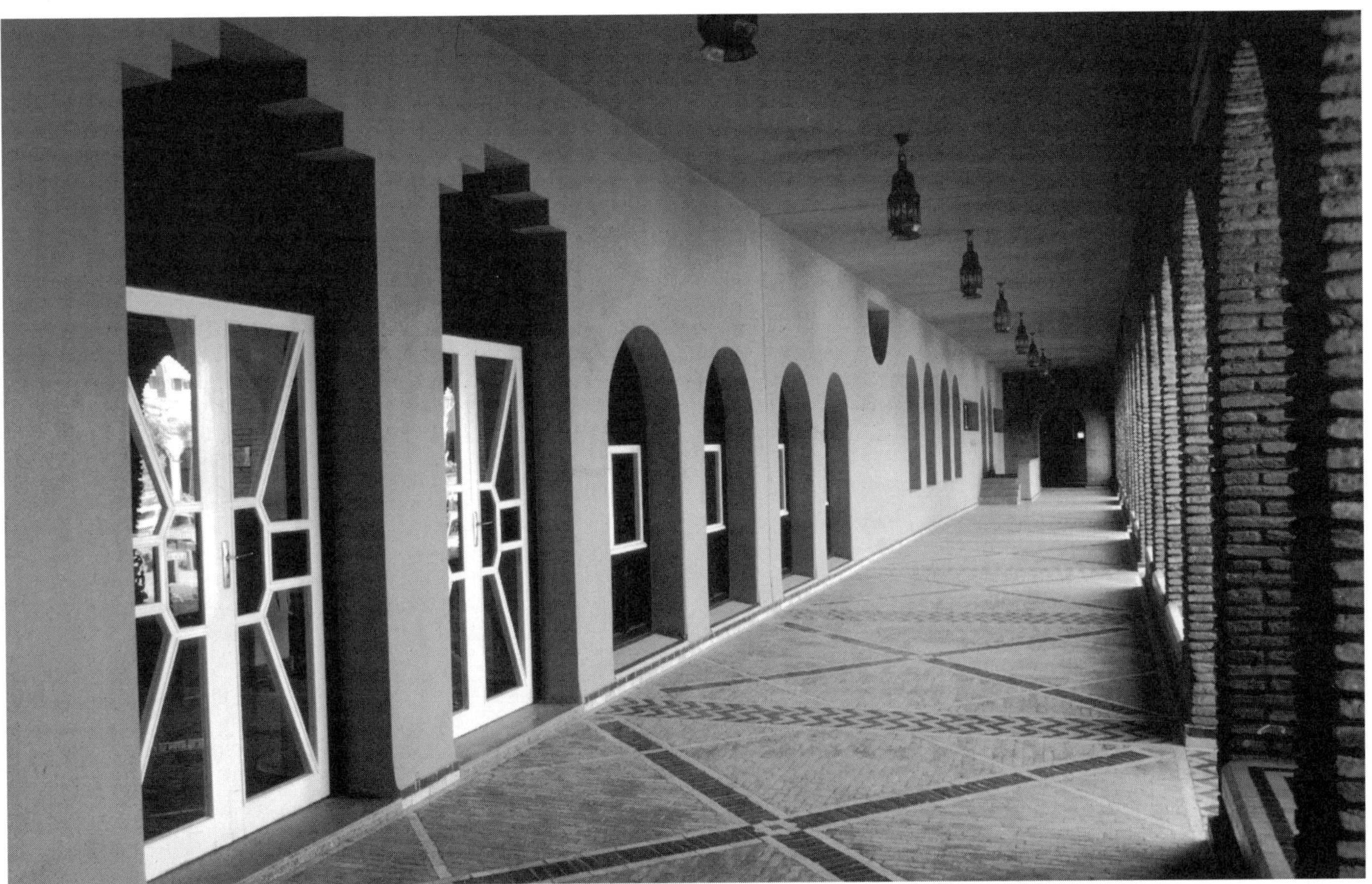

Regional Military Hospital (1982), Marrakesh, designed by Charles Boccaro
Photo by Christian Lignon © Aga Khan Trust for Culture

rica: not until the École Polytechnique d'Architecture et Urbanisme (EPAU) was founded in Algiers after World War II were there any schools of architecture in North Africa outside Egypt. Inevitably, it was well into the second half of the century before indigenous African architects were able to make a major contribution to the physical development of their homelands.

If the period before World War I was the high point of European imperialism, the period between the world wars was the decline of empire; however, the architectural and urban development of North Africa was still almost entirely European driven. Morocco, under its first French resident-general, Hubert Lyautey (1912–25), pursued a clear-sighted policy of state intervention in urban development (as did Libya) after Benito Mussolini seized power in Italy in 1922 and sought to revive the splendors of Rome's imperial past in Africa.

Marshal Lyautey sought conscientiously to conserve what remained of the Moroccan architectural heritage—Hispano–Mauresque, Arab, and Berber. He stated, "While in other parts of North Africa we only found social debris, here . . . we have found a constituted empire, and with it a beautiful and great civilization. . . . A remarkable Morocco can be created, that will remain Moroccan and Islamic" (quoted in Betts, 1978). However, he was not averse to contemporary architectural developments: Auguste and Gustave Perret designed and built the Dock Installations and Warehouses (1915) in Casablanca, but the cities of Casablanca and Rabat were replanned on grandiloquent lines and had public buildings that were both neoclassical and embellished with Hispano–Mauresque decoration, as in the Law Courts (1915) in Casablanca by J. Marrast and the Post Office (*c.*1920) in Rabat by J. Laforgue.

The Italian administration showed no such sensitivity in Libya, except toward the imperial Roman sites. Tripoli was replanned as the colonial capital, and the new town was created on provincial Italian lines, designed by the architects A. Novello and O. Cabiatti; in building during the 1920s and 1930s, it was a prototype of Giovanni Pellegrini's *Manifesto dell' architettura coloniale* (1936).

No such high-mindedness drove the architectural development of the other North African countries. Where appropriate, *arabisance* prevailed, as in the Waqf Ministry Building (1925) by Mahmould Fahmy Pasha and the Bank Misr (1927) by A. Laseiac in Cairo; in general, however, North Africa followed European precedents: a pared-down Neoclassicism in the 1920s with some commercial Art Deco in the downtown streets of major cities, a tentative adoption of modernism, and the International Style in the 1930s. Algeria generally set the pace: the Palais du Gouvernement General (1930; now the Palace of Government) designed by M.J. Guiauchain with A. and G. Perret, the

Maison des Etudiants (1933) by C. Montaland, and the Town Hall (1935) by L. Claro, all in Algiers, are no less advanced than are their contemporaries in Europe. In addition, Algiers was the subject of Le Corbusier's most sustained urban-planning initiatives. Between 1933 and 1942, he published no fewer than three major plans for the city; formal concepts first proposed for Algiers were eventually realized elsewhere (such as the Ministry of Education building in Rio de Janeiro and the UNESCO headquarters in Paris).

The struggle for independence and the consolidation of power after achieving it preoccupied the governments of all North African countries during the first decade and a half after the end of World War II (part of which was fought over North African terrain), and the series of Arab–Israeli wars, culminating in the disastrous war of 1973 and the devastation of the Suez Canal Zone, deprived the region of the economic security and political stability that is a prerequisite for sound and sustained physical development. In contrast, the final quarter of the century saw massive investment in building and a transformation of the built environment throughout the region (with the exception of Sudan, where a civil war has been waging for 20 years).

The provision of adequate housing for the mass of the people has been a major priority of all governments in the region since independence. The rehousing of immigrant squatters on the outskirts of all major cities, the protection of the limited areas of fertile agricultural land from population invasion, the reconstruction of the devastated Suez Canal cities, and the creation of new towns to accommodate the overflow of population from the major cities have become major areas of architectural activity. Hassan Fathy was one of the first North African architects to engage seriously with the problems of popular housing: his modest book *Architecture for the Poor*, which describes his attempt to create a humane environment in the resettlement village of New Gourna on the west bank of the Nile at Thebes in Upper Egypt, has been acclaimed worldwide and has transformed architects' perceptions of their social responsibility as housing providers. Hassan Fathy was also one of the pioneers, along with his contemporary Ramses Wissa Wassef, in the revival of traditional materials, constructional systems, and craft skills. The bulk of his practice, however, was the design of individual houses and villas for private clients. Abdel Wahid El Wakil is an accomplished younger Egyptian architect designing in a similar manner.

Inevitably, however, given the enormous shortfall in housing provision, the emphasis in most state-funded social housing schemes has been on quantity rather than quality, and four-, five-, or six-story walk-up blocks of apartments have become the norm. Some architects have handled such assignments well (for example, Elie Azagury's apartment blocks in Rabat and Casablanca [1960s] or Candilis, Josic, Woods and Pons's residential estate Sidi-bel-Abbes in Oran, Algeria [1950s]), but the scale of most state housing schemes necessitates the formation of large international multidisciplinary teams of architects and engineers, as in the huge new cities in the desert hinterland of Cairo established by the Egyptian Ministry of Reconstruction, New Communities, and Land Reclamation in the 1980s: Sadat City, 10th Ramadan City, and 6th October City.

Also in the state sector, major building programs for education and health care have sought to remedy the neglect of these areas by the colonial authorities and to demonstrate governments' commitment to the provision of education and health care for all. Provincial universities and regional hospitals are perceived as flagships of government policy, and architects of international reputation are commissioned for major projects (such as James Cubitt and Partners for the University of Garyounis, Benghazi, Libya; Oscar Niemeyer for the University of Constantine, Algeria; and Charles Boccara for the 1982 Regional Hospital, Marrakesh, Morocco).

Tourism has generated large downtown hotels and holiday resorts. Good examples of the latter include work by architects A. Faraoui and P. de Mazieres in Morocco, Fernand Pouillon in Algeria, and Serge Santelli in Tunisia. In addition, the demands of tourism undoubtedly generated several major historic and archaeological conservation projects, the most spectacular being the UNESCO-sponsored re-erection of the temple of Rameses II at Abu Simbel on an elevated site overlooking Lake Nasser in Upper Egypt.

A major factor that was instrumental in the evident raising of standards of architectural service and of the quality of architectural design in the last 20 years of the century was the institution of the Aga Khan Award for Architecture (AKAA). Conservation of the environment, community involvement in the design decision-making process, and the appropriateness as well as the quality of the executed design are among the criteria for selecting buildings for an award. The patronage of the Aga Khan through this award scheme has both publicized and promoted, as models for other architects to emulate, several excellent buildings and conservation schemes in North Africa, among them the Arts Center at Harrania near Giza in Egypt by Wissa Wassef, the revitalization of the Hafsia quarter of the Medina in Tunis, and the Dar Lamane Housing Community in Casablanca, Morocco.

Finally, two outstanding buildings that have become icons of their countries' commitment to excellence in architecture and the arts are the new Cairo Opera House and Cultural Center (1987–92) on Gezira Island by the Japanese consortium Nikkei Sekkai Planners Architects and Engineers and the Great Mosque (1986–93) in Casablanca, commissioned by King Hassan II from the French architect Marcel Pinseau. By way of postscript, with about 20 schools of architecture in the region at the turn of the millennium, the 21st century can expect a much higher proportion of buildings in North Africa to be designed by indigenous architects than was true in the 20th century.

ANTHONY D.C. HYLAND

See also **Aga Khan Award (1977–); Art Deco; Cairo, Egypt; Le Corbusier, Le (Jeanneret, Charles-Édouard) (France); Egyptian Revival; Fathy, Hassan (Egypt); Hassan II Mosque, Casablanca; International Style; Niemeyer, Oscar (Brazil); Public Housing; Ramses Wissa Wassef Arts Centre, Giza, Egypt; Wassef, Wissa (Egypt)**

Further Reading

Abel, Colin, "Work of El-Wakil," *Architectural Review* 180 (1986)

Abu-Lughod, Janet L., *Cairo: 1001 Years of the City Victorious*, Princeton, New Jersey: Princeton University Press, 1971

Abu-Lughod, Janet L., *Rabat: Urban Apartheid in Morocco*, Princeton, New Jersey: Princeton University Press, 1980

Béguin, François, with Gildas Bandez, Denis Lesage, and Lucien Godin, *Arabisances: Décor architectural et tracé urbain en Afrique du Nord, 1830–1950*, Paris: Dunod, 1983

Betts, Raymond F., *Tricouleur: The French Overseas Empire*, London and New York: Gordon and Cremonesi, 1978
Danby, Miles, *Moorish Style*, London: Phaidon, 1995
Elleh, Nnamdi, *African Architecture: Evolution and Transformation*, New York: McGraw Hill, 1997
Fathy, Hassan, *Gourna: A Tale of Two Villages*, Cairo: Ministry of Culture, 1969; as *Architecture for the Poor: An Experiment in Rural Egypt*, Chicago: University of Chicago Press, 1973
Holod, Renata, and Darl Rastorfer (editors), *Architecture and Community: Building in the Islamic World Today*, Millerton, New York: Aperture, 1983
Huet, Bernard, "The Modernity in a Tradition: The Arab Muslim Culture of North Africa," *Mimar* 10 (1983)
Kultermann, Udo, *New Directions in African Architecture*, translated by John Maass, London: Studio Vista, and New York: Braziller, 1969
Kultermann, Udo, "Contemporary Arab Architecture: The Architects of Egypt," *Mimar* 4 (1982)
Kultermann, Udo, "Contemporary Arab Architecture: The Architects of Algeria, Tunisia, and Libya," *Mimar* 9 (1983)
Linstrum, Derek, "The Architecture of the Colonial and Post-Colonial Periods outside Europe: Africa," and "The Architecture of the Twentieth Century: Africa," in *Sir Banister Fletcher's A History of Architecture*, 20th edition, edited by Dan Cruickshank with Andrew-Saint Peter Blundell Jones, Kenneth Frampton, and Fleur Richard, Oxford and Boston: Architectural Press, 1996
Reading the Contemporary African City: Architectural Transformation in the Islamic World, Singapore: Concept Media, 1983
Richards, James Maude, Ismail Serageldin, and Darl Rastorfer, *Hassan Fathy*, Singapore: Concept Media, and London: Architectural Press, 1985
Taylor, Brian Brace, "Demythologizing Colonial Architecture," *Mimar* 13 (1984)

AFRICA: SOUTHERN AND CENTRAL AFRICA

Architectural expression of the southern subcontinent and eastern seaboard of Africa in the 20th century resonates with broader international concerns. In the first half of the century, before decolonization, the regional styling was a direct reflection of that of the European colonial powers—an embodiment of empire and what architecturally might appropriately reflect statehood and civic order. After World War II, postcolonial Africa engaged the international architectural debate.

At the turn of the 20th century, the so-called scramble for Africa by the European nations had created the geography of the continent, the larger portion of which bore the pink mapping that demarcated the British Empire. The southeast and southwest seaboards were flanked by Portuguese East and West Africa (since 1974, Mozambique and Angola, respectively), which were at that time administered as provinces and not nations, and German South West (to the south) and East Africa (to the north), now Namibia (1992) and Tanzania (since 1964; in 1961, Tanganyika), respectively. On the *highveld* (flat grasslands above the escarpment) lay two independent Boer republics. While being the political domain of farmer-pioneers of European extraction of some 200 years before, their numbers swelled a wave of immigration of the gold rush to the Zuid-Afrikaansche Republiek (South African Republic) of the 1880s.

The subcontinent, as it entered the 20th century, was heir to the aspirations of one man, Cecil John Rhodes (1853–1902), with his stated ambition to have the area from the Cape to Cairo as a dominion of the British Empire. Architecture, through his architect-protégé Herbert Baker (1862–1946), was to embody the expression of this ambition. Baker can take credit for coining a style, Cape Dutch Revival, a derivative of the domestic baroque of white-walled and curvilinear gabled homesteads of the Dutch farmers who had settled the Cape peninsula and beyond. This was probably fired by the Queen Anne style then fashionable in Britain, although the appreciation for vernacular and traditional architecture fostered by the Arts and Crafts movement also played its part. His first example of this revival, the "restoration" of Grootte Schuur (1896; since 1994, the state president's guest house) for his patron, Rhodes, has been shown to be a fantastical reinvention of a once-sedate Georgian barn conversion. His homes for the wealthy "Randbarons" on Parktown Ridge of Johannesburg follow in the Arts and Crafts tradition, as, for example, the house known as Northwards.

A colonial war (Anglo-Boer War, 1899–1902) heralded the new century. The British had to maintain long lines of supply and communication, and so industrialization came into its own. Kit wood-and-iron utility buildings, popular in the diamond rush to Kimberley and the gold rush to the Witwatersrand in the latter half of the 19th century, came back into their own for military use. The crowning achievement of prefabrication was the supply of parts of buildings as fortification—loopholes, ladders, and hatches—in steel. These were built into blockhouses, the rest constructed from any immediately available material. Thousands were erected, and many survive.

At that time, the independent Boer (farmer-trekkers of Dutch descent) republics had their own architectural patrimony, a European eclecticism rooted in the Beaux Arts. The Department of Public Works was newly established in 1887 by President Paul Kruger (1825–1904). The Dutch contingent of architect immigrants, with Sytze Wierda (1839–1911) as head, brought with them current European practice. The best examples are the Raadsaal (Legislature, 1892) and Palace of Justice (1900). This same styling manifested in the then German colonies of German South West Africa and German East Africa, best represented by the "Tintenpalast" ("Ink Palace," Administrative Building, 1913, Windhoek, Namibia). In the northern countries of Europe, Schinkel's influence was still strong—the tradition of brick buildings for public commissions in particular. This was reflected in the schools, magistrate's courts, and other utility buildings of the period, as in the Johannesburg Post Office (1897). The colonial tradition of the Germans persists in Dar Es Salaam and, while contributing to the architectural character of the city, was one of the motivating factors for moving the capital inland to Dodoma. The term "Wilhelmine," deriving from both Wilhelm II (1859–1942), German emperor and ninth king of Prussia, and Wilhelmina (1880–1962), queen of the Netherlands, is used for the stylistic influences of northern European architects in German colonial Africa. It is the equivalent of Victorian style in that both show eclecticism and revivalist styling (particularly neo-Romanesque and neo-Gothic) but differ in their sources and treatment of style elements, particularly domes and decorative trimmings. The style found its most ebullient expression in his turn-of-the-19th-century Ostrich Feather Palaces, designed by

Johannes Egbertus Vixseboxse (1863–1943), in Oudshoorn (South Africa).

In the Union of South Africa (1910), which formed from the colonies of Cape and Natal and the defeated Boer republics of the Orange Free State (Orange River Colony, 1902–10) and the South African Republic (Transvaal Colony, 1902–10), Baker and his office, as official architect to the Church of England (Anglican Church) and favored architect of the Department of Public Works, received numerous commissions, with the Union Buildings (1912) in Pretoria being his crowning achievement.

A vast array of state and private commissions by the young coterie of architects was brought into the Department of Public Works by the British administration. They belong to the so-called Baker School, a collective term coined by Pearce (first head of school of the University of the Witwatersrand, Johannesburg—himself a Baker boy) to cover the works of the young architects who worked either in Baker's office or in the employ in the Department of Public Works in the colonies of the Free State and Transvaal (1902–10). With its attention to craftsmanship in detail, traditional use of material to suit circumstances, and free borrowing of styles, it dominated architectural thought for decades after Baker's departure. Included in the school are the works produced in his own office and of his own imagination in the years 1902–13, when he was resident in South Africa; commissions carried out by his successors in the firm in the period 1913–20 at the dissolution of the partnership; work done by previous members of the partnership after 1920 or former assistants who established independent practices on leaving; and then contemporary architects inspired by his work but having little or no direct association in practice. This styling of the Edwardian period in the other British colonies, with a mix of Arts and Crafts revivalism and neoclassicism, particularly in its state and civic expression, was meant to aggrandize the sense of empire and, hence, is known as the Empire style. Lutyens's (1869–1944) New Delhi Secretariat complex, to which he had been jointly appointed with Baker, epitomized this style in India. Lutyens too has his legacy in South Africa: the Johannesburg Civic Art Gallery (1915).

Opportunities for these architects expanded to the northern colonies of Southern and Northern Rhodesia (since 1964, Zambia, and since 1980, Zimbabwe, respectively), Bechuanaland (1885; since 1966, Botswana), and beyond to Nyasaland (1891; since 1964, Malawi) and the East African Protectorate (now Kenya).

A reaction to British imperialism was to be found in the person of Gerhard Moerdyk (1890–1958). Born on African soil and educated at the Architectural Association in London, he looked to northern European precedent, particularly the Ro-

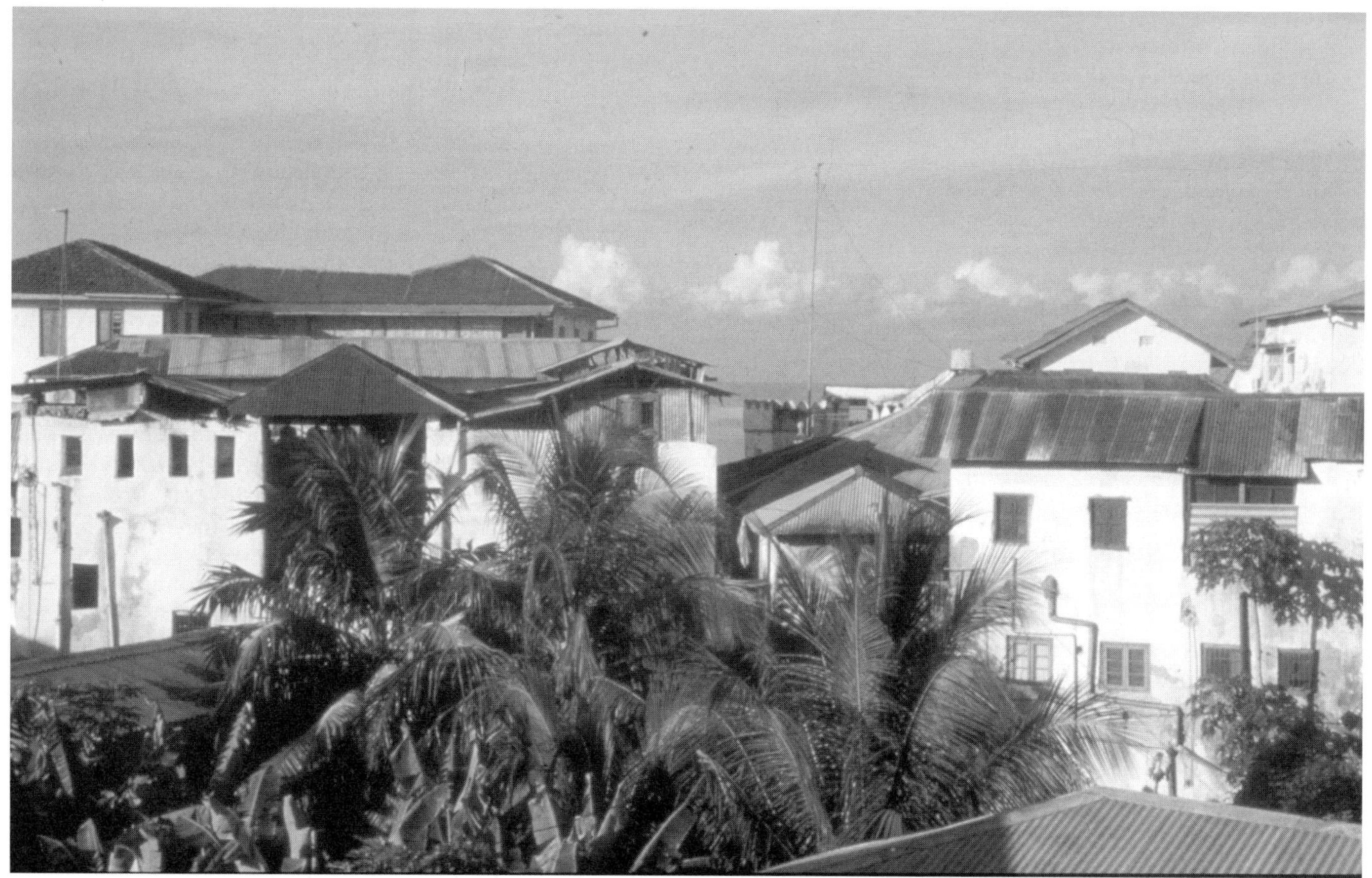

Old Stone Town, Zanzibar, Pwani Region, Tanzania
Photo by Francesco Siravo © Historic Cities Support Programme/Aga Khan Trust for Culture

mantic Nationalism (the term derives from Kidder Smith as applied to certain early 20th-century trends in Sweden) of the Baltic peninsula. The brooding and somber Voortrekker Monument (1949) remains his personal triumph, although he matched the number of Baker's Anglo-Saxon ecclesiastic architecture with more than 80 Afrikaans Protestant churches, built from Windhoek, South West Africa (now Namibia), to Salisbury (now Harare, Zimbabwe). His joint appointment to the Johannesburg Station (1932) with Gordon Leith gave opportunity for demonstrating the use of local materials and decorative motifs and artworks (their school colleague Henk Pierneef was commissioned for these) on a public scale. These Romantic Nationalists show diverse stylistic influences, but central to their endeavor is an expression of the use of local material and decorative devices. There is usually an underlying classicism and thus sometimes the use of classical elements, although often in modern guise.

Until the 1920s, architects of the southern African subcontinent were obliged to study abroad. The first local architectural graduates were from the Witwatersrand School (established in 1923) and made their mark internationally. The students brought the Modern movement to the subcontinent with their publication *zero hour* (1933; the sans-serif uncapitalized lettering a deliberate choice, showing solidarity with the Bauhaus). In their seminal publication, Ludwig Mies van der Rohe and Le Corbusier were heralded as role models. Le Corbusier was sent an issue and responded with an approving letter, published in the *South African Architectural Record* (vol. 20, no. 11 [1936], 381–83) and used to preface his *Oeuvre Complète*. In this he coined the term "the Transvaal Group," a name that has stuck. South Africa was thus at the cutting edge of the Modern movement in the post-Depression years. Monuments to the period are the residential blocks built in the developing higher-density suburbs of Johannesburg and Pretoria.

In the years directly following World War II, Expressionist modernism became popular on the subcontinent, fired by the "Brazil Builds" exhibition (1943) and the subsequent publication of the same name. Graduates from the architectural schools of the Witwatersrand and Pretoria (established 1943) had a particular affinity for the style, and the *highveld* became a "Little Brazil," a style term used by Chipkin (1993) and derived from Pevsner's (1953) observation that Johannesburg was "a little Brazil within the Commonwealth." The appellation has expanded to all southern African architecture of the 1950s and 1960s that reflects Brazilian influence. The idiom is most flamboyant in the then-Portuguese colonies of Angola and Mozambique, particularly in Lorenço Marques (now Maputo), with Pancho Guedes (1925–) being its distinguished exponent. Graduates from the Witwatersrand and Pretoria Schools (the latter established 1943) had a particular affinity for the style, and the *highveld* became a "Little Brazil," typified by buildings that were overtly styled against sun penetration—exaggerated louvers, *brises-soleil*, and egg-crate sun guards, with the first such building being Helmut Stauch's Meat Board Building (1952).

A movement with nationalist roots but without an overt political agenda was the emergence of a regionalist school, and Norman Eaton (1902–66) was its recognized founder and master. He frequently traveled to East Africa, sketching and photographing, bringing these motifs to his buildings as sculptured elements and patterning in brickwork and paving; his Bank of Netherlands buildings (Pretoria, 1953, and Durban, 1966) are his finest testimonies. This style, termed Pretoria Regionalism, epitomized by Eaton, is a variant of the Modern movement where the tenets of modernism are tempered by considerations of local material, techniques, traditions, and climate. Graduates of the Pretoria School moved away from the aesthetic of large expanses of window and clipped eaves toward an architectural expression of deeply recessed or screened windows and wide eaves, verandas, and pergolas. Materials of choice were stock bricks, gum poles, stone, and roughcast exposed concrete. Traditional elements such as downpipes and shutters were employed, although they were reinterpreted in modern idiom.

World War II brought with it the demise of the European colonial empires. Postcolonial Africa needed new symbols of independence. Nairobi, Kenya, as the capital of one of the first independent southern African British colonies, engaged in a program of high-rise building. High-rises were not new to the subcontinent. Johannesburg (South Africa) had always been at the forefront of the tallest modern structures on the continent, the most innovative being the Standard Bank tower, the most ambitious the Carlton Complex. Today, it is the Reserve Bank (1990, Pretoria), in neo-Miesian style, that holds the honor.

In the 1970s, New Brutalism, a term associated with Peter and Allison Smithson of England, found its way across the continent through the offices of the Transvaal Institute of Architects and the Witwatersrand School, who invited the Smithsons to visit South Africa. Similar influences were through the frequent visits of Fry and Drew and Paul Rudolph from the United States. The aesthetic was an uncompromising ruthlessness, intellectual clarity, and honest presentation of structure and materials. The University of South Africa (Pretoria) best epitomizes this period and is possibly the largest single commission in the world that can be ascribed to only one architect—namely, Brian Sandrock.

Louis Kahn was also highly influential and established a committed following among local students who had gone to Philadelphia to do postgraduate studies under him. Roelof Uytenbogaardt (1933–98) is possibly the most esteemed local protégé, and his Steinkopf Community Centre (1985) is probably the best architectural example, although his contribution as teacher of urban design at the University of Cape Town remains his enduring legacy. Unfortunately, his honest opposition to the apartheid state denied him any commissions of substance.

In the late 1960s there arose an international interest in traditional African construction and styling provoked by the Museum of Modern Art exhibition "Architecture without Architects" (1964). A concern for alternative low-tech architecture gained further impetus with the oil crisis of the 1970s. Hasan Fathy (1900–89) was teaching mud construction up north, where both tradition and vernacular were explored as precedent; his critical sensitivity catalyzed a reevaluation of the architectural heritage of the subcontinent. There is now a concern for conserving traditionally African cities, monuments, and settlements (such as Zanzibar, Mozambique Island, and Great Zimbabwe). Restoration in the 1990s of Stone City, an Arabic heritage of Zanzibar, with assistance by the Aga Khan Foundation, is a case in point. A rise and growth of Islam has witnessed a revival in the tradition of mosque buildings, with Mohammed Mayet being a practitioner particularly skilled in interpreting the type. The largest such building to date is the Kerk Street Mosque (started 1994, under construction) in Johannesburg.

Attempts to translate an understanding of the architecture of Africa into a body of theory have been termed "Afrocentricity" (Hughes, 1994), an understanding directed at African-American practitioners that has searched find a theory of Afrocentric architecture through a process of using observed empirical data based on three principal areas of the built environment: historic precedent (including ancient civilizations and monuments), cultural elements (including customs, ceremonies, and living patterns as well as representational aspects of artifacts), and elements of the environment (including climate) and ecology (including geologic conditions and physical features).

African sensibilities in architecture find their best expression in buildings as ensembles rather than as individual set pieces. Liberated states needed new capitals, and it is here that the expression of African spaces is made. Dodoma, as the newly conceived capital for Tanzania, is a people's forum, a space for the meeting of governance and populace. Lilongwe, the designated new capital of Malawi that was meant to replace Blantyre, has ambitious intentions of pedestrianized boulevards and vehicular routes but languishes as it derives from the personal ambitions for aggrandizement of the president. An interesting new capital is Mafikeng, provincial capital of North West Province, South Africa, conceived as the "capital," Mmbatho, of "the independent homeland" of Boputhutswana. This had been done as part of the apartheid ideology of Bantustans (the suffix "-stan" being a cynical attempt at exploiting Balkanization through association with the separation of India and Pakistan at independence, which had the support of the international community). It was meant to supplant nearby afiking, which had served as the out-of-country administrative center for the Bechaunaland protectorate until the protectorate became the independent state of Botswana and relocated its capital to Gaborone. In the Legislative Administration Building (1982), Britz and Scholes explore the traditional *kagotla*, or place of gathering, built in monumental brickwork and expressed in Kahnian style and scale. Yet there is a pervasive sense of an African place in the spaces.

At present, some practitioners on the African continent meet the ongoing challenge of designing affordable, appropriate, and sustainable architecture. The Eastgate Building (1996, Pearce Partnership) in Harare serves as an example, as does the Appropriate Technology Centre (1999, Stauch Vorster, MOM) in Gabarone, Botswana. There are, outside the mainstream of commercialism, architects who engage with communities as clients and attempt to express their clients' concerns and financial circumstances in built form; for example, Liebenberg Masojada (Kwadengezi Cemetery reception area, 1995, Kwa-Zulu Natal, South Africa), Design Workshop (Warwick Avenue Bridge Market, 1999, Durban, South Africa), and CS Studio (Uthago Lotyebiselwano [Learning Centre], Nyanga East, South Africa).

Under the auspices of the Commonwealth Association of Architects, those schools of architecture established in the emergent independent African states once under British rule partake in academic exchange and scrutiny of their teaching programs by accreditation boards. More and more architectural graduates are emerging from these institutions, and as time passes, their contribution should become more apparent.

ROGER C. FISHER

See also **Aga Khan Award; Baker, Herbert (England and South Africa); Lutyens, Edwin (England)**

Further Reading

There is not much by way of contemporary writing on the architecture of the southern subcontinent of Africa. Various tourist guides give access to some of the buildings as part of the tourist itinerary but often lack pertinent architectural information. Recent publications relating directly to architecture are listed below.

Beck, Haig (editor), *Southern Africa–Natal Cape Province Transvaal Boputhatswana Lesotho Zambia Swaziland Zimbabwe*, London: International Architect, 1985

Chipkin, Clive, *Johannesburg Style: Architecture & Society 1880s–1960s*, Cape Town: David Philip, 1993

Elleh, Nnamdi, *African Architecture: Evolution and Transformation*, New York: McGraw-Hill, 1997

Fisher, Roger, Schalk le Roux, and Estelle Mareé (editors), *Architecture of the Transvaal*, Pretoria: UNISA, 1998

Judin, Hilton, and Ivan Vladislavic (editors), *Blank—: Architecture, Apartheid and After*, Rotterdam: Netherlands Institute of Architects, 1998

Muwanga, Christina, *South Africa: A Guide to Recent Architecture*, London: Elipsis, 1998

Prinsloo, Ivor (editor), *Architecture 2000: A Review of South African Architecture*, Cape Town: Picasso Headline

AGA KHAN AWARD 1977–

The Aga Khan Award for Architecture was established in 1977 by His Highness the Aga Khan, the 49th hereditary Imam of the Shia Ismaili Muslims, to enhance the understanding of Islamic culture and its architecture. The program, administered by the Aga Khan Trust for Culture, recognizes and awards architectural excellence, with special concern for contemporary design, social housing, community development, restoration, conservation, and environmentalism. One of the principles of the Aga Khan Foundation has been to encourage sustainability whereby recipients of the Aga Khan's largesse would themselves be able to reinvest in the future of their own communities. The Aga Khan's influence is widespread and includes the establishment in the United States of the Aga Khan Program for Islamic Architecture (1979), jointly run by the Massachusetts Institute for Technology and Harvard University, and the creation of the Aga Khan Award for Architecture.

In 1976 the Aga Khan announced that he would establish an architectural award as a means of fostering the growth of a modern and vibrant Islamic architecture within the context of rich and valuable traditions. In spanning political and geographical boundaries, a major objective of the award was to create an overarching sense of unity for the Muslim world, in spite of distinctive and sometimes disparate cultures. "Excellence in architecture" was attributed not only to examples of finely designed architecture, but also to community projects, such as housing for the poor and civil engineering works, clearly demonstrating the future direction of the Aga Khan Award for Architecture.

In 1988, the Aga Khan reorganized his network of philanthropic institutions. The Aga Khan Award for Architecture was transferred from the Aga Khan Foundation to the newly established Aga Khan Trust for Culture, also responsible for the Historic Cities Support Programme and the Education and Culture Programme. The goals of these cultural agencies were aligned with the Aga Khan's original list of challenges for the Islamic world—pursuit of excellence in architecture and related disciplines, conservation and re-use of historic buildings and spaces, and education for architects and urban planners. A fourth objective of the Trust for Culture was to encourage the interchange of ideas to enhance awareness of the relationship between historic and contemporary Muslim cultures and their built environments.

On occasion, the Aga Khan has bestowed a special Chairman's Award to recognize outstanding achievement in Muslim architecture. In 1980 the first was presented to Egypt's Hassan Fathy, architect, artist, and poet, particularly acknowledging his encouragement of vernacular building systems and his work improving the built environment of impoverished peoples. Others have followed and include Rifat Chadirji of Iraq and Geoffrey Bawa of Sri Lanka.

Recipients of the Aga Khan Award for Architecture have now totalled 80, and they have been as diverse as the cultures they represent. One of the most prevalent themes throughout the history of the award has been the social responsibility of architecture. This was reflected in the 1980 award to the Kampung Improvement Programme in Jakarta, the Grameen Bank Housing Programme in Bangladesh (1989 award), and the multiphased Hafsia Quarter project in Tunis (1983 and 1995 awards). Such humanitarian considerations were also evident in awards given for educational and medical facilities, such as the Medical Centre in Mopti, Mali (1980 award) and the Lepers Hospital, Maharashtra Province, India (1998 award). Another major award theme was heritage preservation, as evidenced by the awards for restoration of Jerusalem's Al-Aqsa Mosque (1986 award), conservation of Old Sana'a in Yemen (1995 award), and restoration of Bukhara Old City, Uzbekistan (1995 award). Juries concerned with self-sustainability often appreciated projects demonstrating the viability of vernacular construction techniques and traditional building forms or the use of locally available materials. This priority is evident in the Yaama Mosque in Tahoua, Niger (1986 award) and the Stone Building System employed in Dar'a Province, Syria (1992 award).

Despite the fact that the Aga Khan Awards for Architecture have so far been principally bestowed on projects in North Africa, the Middle East, and Asia (the only central European recipient was the Institut du Monde Arabe in Paris), the international architectural community has steadily developed an interest in the awards. Because cultural, religious, and economic conditions in most Muslim countries differ so much from Western societies, a lack of sympathy for the priorities of the award program persists, although the expanding cadre of skilled Islamic architects and planners is helping to alleviate this.

This awards program has significantly inspired the architectural representation of Islamic culture during the past 25 years. At a time when many of these cultures were threatened by Western influence, by economic failure, and by political violence, the Aga Khan's initiative reminded everyone of the quality of this cultural heritage. At the same time, the award's broad scope, with its emphasis on alleviating living conditions of the poor, on sustainability, and on the environment, has encouraged innovative solutions to rapidly worsening societal problems. Although this award does not fit the mold of Western architectural perceptions, its initial priorities were clearly established and are constantly evolving to meet the needs of many cultural communities. Emphasizing not only contemporary architecture, but also historic architectural traditions threatened by reconstruction and development, the Aga Khan Award for Architecture has helped to create a means of expressing Islamic ideals in a modern context. The award promotes a sense of pride in Muslim culture, and the vast number of submissions has facilitated documentation of over 6,000 works of modern Islamic architecture, providing inspiration for future generations.

RHODA BELLAMY

See also **Alliance Franco-Sénégalaise, Kaolack, Senegal; Bawa, Geoffrey (Sri Lanka); Chadirji, Rifat (Iraq); Entrepreneurship Development Institute, Ahmedabad, India; Fathy, Hassan (Egypt); Great Mosque of Niono, Mali; Gürel Family Summer Residence, Çanakkale, Turkey; Haj Terminal, Jeddah Airport; Ministry of Foreign Affairs, Riyadh, Mosque; Mosque of the Grand National Assembly, Ankara, Turkey; National Assembly Building, Sher-e-Bangla Nagar, Dhaka; Social Security Complex, Istanbul; Sustainability/Sustainable Architecture; Vidhan Bhavan (State Assembly), Bhopal; Yaama Mosque, Tahoua, Niger**

Further Reading

A monograph has been published for each cycle of the Aga Khan Award for Architecture that reviews the successful entries, describing the jury and the selection process. These volumes also include essays discussing contemporary issues pertaining to Islamic architecture.

Daftary, Farhad, *A Short History of the Ismailis: Traditions of a Muslim Community*, Princeton, New Jersey: Markus Wiener Publishers, 1998 and 2001

Davidson, Cynthia C. (editor), *Legacies for the Future: Contemporary Architecture in Islamic Societies*, London: Thames and Hudson Ltd. and The Aga Khan Award for Architecture, 1998

Davidson, Cynthia C., and Ismaïl Serageldin (editors), *Architecture Beyond Architecture*, London: The Aga Khan Award for Architecture and Academy Editions, 1995

Ivy, Robert, "An Interview with the Aga Khan," *Architectural Record* (February 2002)

Michell, George (editor), *Architecture of the Islamic World: Its History and Social Meaning*, London: Thames and Hudson Ltd., 1995

Özhan, Suha, "Legacies of the Future" in *Legacies for the Future: Contemporary Architecture in Islamic Societies*, edited by Cynthia Davidson, London: Thames and Hudson Ltd. and The Aga Khan Award for Architecture, 1998

Robson, David (editor) with Kenneth Frampton and Charles Correa, *Modernity and Community: Architecture in the Islamic World*, London: Thames and Hudson Ltd. and The Aga Khan Award for Architecture, 2001

Steele, James (editor), *Architecture for a Changing World*, London: The Aga Khan Award for Architecture and Academy Editions, 1992

AGREST, DIANA, AND MARIO GANDELSONAS

Architects, United States

Agrest and Gandelsonas, Architects, is an internationally recognized firm that was established by its principals, Diana Agrest and Mario Gandelsonas, in New York in 1980. With a focus on architecture, urban design, and interior design in relation to the city, the firm has been an integral part of New York's architecture community. Celebrated for their work in developing an understanding and practice of architecture through linguistics and semiotics, Agrest and Gandelsonas have been instrumental in advancing the course of contemporary architecture in the wake of late modernism. Establishing a self-named critical practice in which writing, drawing, and building would have equal weight, they have played a key role in the architecture community's reevaluation of design as part of a larger cultural context.

Natives of Buenos Aires, both Agrest and Gandelsonas were educated at the University of Buenos Aires School of Architecture and studied linguistics with the French semiotician and philosopher Roland Barthes in Paris. Arriving in New York in the late 1970s, they became Fellows of the Institute of Architecture and Urban Studies, where they played key roles in establishing the institute as both educational venue and publisher of periodicals such as *Skyline* and *Oppositions*. Agrest is adjunct professor of architecture at The Cooper Union for the Advancement of Science and AA in New York and has taught at Princeton, Yale, and Columbia universities in addition to lecturing throughout the world. Gandelsonas is the 1913 Professor of Architecture at Princeton and has taught at Yale, Harvard, the University of Illinois, and the University of Southern California. He has also lectured widely throughout the world. Authors and coauthors of a number of books on architecture, urbanism, and architectural theory, Agrest and Gandelsonas are also responsible for a series of seminal essays and articles that have fixed their place in the history of architecture. Agrest is the author of *Architecture from Without: Theoretical Framings for a Critical Practice* (1991), a collection of essays on the relationship between architecture and larger cultural phenomena, as well as editor of another collection of essays, *The Sex of Architecture* (1996), whereas Gandelsonas has published two books documenting his unique approach to the formal analysis of the American city: *The UrbanText* (1991) and *X-Urbanism* (1999). Jointly, Agrest and Gandelsonas produced their own monongraph, *Agrest and Gandelsonas: Works* (1995).

Moving away from the rational, purist, and autonomous architecture that characterized so much of modernism, Agrest and Gandelsonas have looked outside and around the actual discipline of architecture to inform their approach to working within the field. Drawing on such diverse sources as history, semiotics, language, psychology, and film, they have taken their architecture beyond exercises in formal manipulation to reflect culture and society at large. Their point of reference has been that of a broad sociocultural spectrum rather than strict formalism. Agrest's insightful essay, "Design versus Non-Design," originally published in *Communication* (1979), is a poignant refutation of

Melrose Community Center, view from south garden, Bronx, New York, designed by Agrest and Gandelsonas Architects (2000)
© David Sunberg/Esto

an unthinking formulaic attitude toward design and a call to acknowledge the merits of that which is less self-consciously designed. Gandelsonas's often-quoted "On Reading Architecture" (1972) asked the design world to pause and recognize the textual capacity of architectural design as a language in and of itself.

An intensely felt and highly unique perception of the city has formed the basis of this firm's work, whether it has been for competitions, buildings, or interiors. Reading the city as a text, the architects have continuously analyzed, both verbally and visually, the forms, programs, signs, and symbols of the urban condition. Taking the American city as their primary subject, they have identified on a number of levels the systems and hierarchy of the structure of the city while deriving meaning from their forms and compositions. Continuously reassessing the relationships between fabric and monument, street and plan, and nature and artifice, the duo keeps the analysis fresh and ready for further interrogation. Gandelsonas's striking analytic diagrams of the American city, which have become a trademark of his investigation into urban morphology, have brought plan, street, building fabric, monument, and nature into a concert of form that is at once artistically appealing and scientifically legible.

A clearly defined idea or concept is central to every project that the firm of Agrest and Gandelsonas develops. Intertwining theory with practice, they treat research, analysis, and writing as part of their practice and practice as part of their theory. They perceive architecture as possessing three distinct phases—writing (text), drawing (graphic), and place (building)—and embrace each for what it brings to furthering the role of architecture within the culture at large.

While giving careful consideration to historic and contextual parameters, they explore material and technical possibilities for giving shape and meaning to the projects they design, whether it is for a building, an interior, or an object.

A trio of apartment buildings in Buenos Aires (1977) that explored issues of scale, typology, and material while responding to historical and contextual conditions within both classical and modern idioms established the identity of Agrest and Gandelsonas in the built environment. A series of much published and exhibited proposals for reshaping the American city have acted as a barometer of their intellectual investigations at the level of urban design and have ultimately led to practical applications. Their Vision Plan for Des Moines, Iowa (1992), rejects the notion of the master plan and instead embraces the fluid permutations and idiosyncrasies that sociopolitical and economic factors can lend to urban design. Their South Bronx Community Center (2000) presents a footprint that is contextual and object like at once. Although a linear blocklike element refers both to the tower-in-the-park type of housing project in which it is set as well as a generic block of fabric, its prominent oval form acts as both marker in the city and reference to the idea of object endemic to the midcentury modernism of the housing project it is built within. Designs for houses, both built and unbuilt, have provided exercises for the architects in the manipulation of typology, scale, and compositional sequence. The Villa Amore (1990) in Southampton, New York, reinterprets the Shingle-style house as a grouping of "found objects" in a modern idiom. The urban interiors of this pair of designers have been directly responsive to the city while acting as testing grounds for the design of objects that blur the distinction between furniture and architecture. The design of an apartment on Central Park West (1988) was a veritable laboratory for the testing of material and form as catalyst between furniture and architecture.

Architects, writers, and educators with an indomitable spirit for exploration and the shedding of light on the multiple perceptions of architecture, Agrest and Gandelsonas have had a profound influence on generations of students, critics, architects, and the general public. They continue to read and research the city as both foundation and testing ground for their work while slowly but surely enhancing the urban landscape with the fruit of that investigation.

CHRISTIAN ZAPATKA

Selected Works

Building 1, Buenos Aires, Argentina, 1977
Building 2, Buenos Aires, Argentina, 1977
Building 3, Buenos Aires, Argentina, 1977
Upper East Side Townhouse, Manhattan, 1985
Framings, Bill Robinson Showroom, New York, 1985
Interior on Park Avenue, New York, New York, 1986
Interior on Central Park West, New York, New York, 1987–88
House on Sag Pond, Southampton, New York, 1989–90
Vision Plan, Des Moines, Iowa, 1990–92
Des Moines International Airport, Des Moines, Iowa, 1992
A Town Plan for 10,000, Shanghai, People's Republic of China, 1996
Vision Plan, Red Bank, New Jersey, 1992–97
Pool House, Sagaponack, New York, 1998–99
Las Casas, Jose Ignacio, Uruguay, 1997–02
Melrose Community Center, South Bronx, New York, 2001
Breukelen Community Center, Brooklyn, New York, 2002–05 (expected completion date)

Selected Publications

By Diana Agrest and Mario Gandelsonas:
"Critical Remarks on Semiology and Architecture," *Semiotica* 9, no. 3 (1973)
"Semiology and Architecture: Ideological Consumption or Theoretical Work?" *Oppositions* 1 (1973)
"Semiotics and the Limits of Architecture," in *A Perfusion of Signs*, edited by Thomas A. Sebeok, 1977
"Architecture as Cultural Practice," *Architecture and Urbanism* 114 (March 1980)
"On Practice," *Architecture and Urbanism* 114 (March 1980)
Agrest and Gandelsonas: Works, 1995

By Diana Agrest:
"The Sky's the Limit," *Architecture and Urbanism* 60 (December 1975)
"Architectural Anagrams: The Symbolic Performance of Skyscrapers," *Oppositions* 11 (Winter 1977)
"Towards a Theory of Production of Sense in the Built Environment (1968–72)," in *On Streets*, edited by Stanford Anderson, 1978
"The Architecture of the City" (interview with Aldo Rossi), *Skyline* (September 1979)
"Design versus Non-Design," *Communication* 27 (1979)
"The City as the Place of Representation," *Design Quarterly* 113–114 (City Segments) (January 1980)
"Notes on Film and Architecture," *Skyline* (September 1981)
A Romance with the City: The Work of Irwin S. Chanin, edited and principal essay by Agrest, 1982
"Architecture of Mirror/Mirror of Architecture," *Oppositions* 26 (1984)

"Architecture from Without: Body, Logic and Sex," *Assemblage* 7 (1987)
Architecture from Without: Theoretical Framings for a Critical Practice, 1991
The Sex of Architecture, edited by Agrest with Patricia Conway and Leslie Kanes Weisman, 1996

By Mario Gandelsonas:
"On Reading Architecture," *Progressive Architecture* (March 1972)
"Linguistics, Poetics and Architectural Theory," *Semiotexte* 1, no. 2 (Fall 1974)
"Semiotics and Architecture," *Architecture and Urbanism* 64 (April 1976)
"Theoretical Landscapes," *Lotus International* 11 (1976)
"On Reading Eisenstein, Reading Piranesi," *Oppositions* 11 (1978)
"From Structure to Subject," *Oppositions* 17 (1979)
"From Structure to Subject: The Foundation of an Architectural Language," in *House X*, edited by Peter Eisenman, 1982

AGRICULTURAL BUILDINGS

The critic Robert Venturi has referred to gas stations and other vernacular structures located along commercial strips as "decorated sheds." His use of the name of a utilitarian, work-oriented structure suggests that sheds, barns, and other such structures are most importantly utilitarian; nevertheless, they also possess meaning that is based on a definable structural program. Buildings used in American agriculture possess clear structural forms, but their emphasis as work buildings also allows them to function as a material artifact of changes in the social and economic context of labor on the American farm.

The agricultural landscape is a composite of many structures designed around the natural cycles of planting, harvest, and maintenance that define farm labor. Such component structures might include those designed for a specific animal (such as chicken houses), specific storage (milk houses or springhouses), limited processes (smokehouses, summer kitchens, sugarhouses, evaporators), grain and fodder storage (granaries, corncribs, silos), and even fencing. Most important, however, such structures are sublimated in the overall layout to the central barn. The American plantation serves as an example that did not use the central barn and instead relied on sprawling compounds of smaller buildings around one central home (the big house); most American agriculture, however, operates on a central plan defined by the barn.

The American barn is one of the nation's most ubiquitous architectural signifiers. In addition to its obvious utilitarian function, to many observers the barn is a symbol of the rugged individualism that Thomas Jefferson and others connected to the American yeoman farmer. The barn and the farm that it supports became one of the most flexible mechanisms for American expansion. A closer analysis of specific barn styles and types reveals overall diversity while suggesting continuity between region, ethnic groups, and general agricultural function.

Prior to 1900, barns were primarily wood, although sometimes constructed from brick or stone. Most barns function as a mixed-use facility, prioritizing storage, shelter, and ventilation. Many barn styles integrated stables and other areas to shelter animals. Often, silos or areas in which to store feed were then also integrated into the site. Crib barns, for instance, contained storage facilities within the structure; more often, tall, cylindrical silos would be incorporated into the overall plan in order to free up the interior space for storing machinery. Thus the program of the American barn prioritizes functionality.

Barns, like many of the site's supporting structures, followed the most general design patterns. Plank framing supported expansive walls, which were then normally covered in planking. Traditional Anglo-American joining (based on carving joints to make them interlock), of course, served as the ancestor of the better-known balloon frame, which replaced such joints with nails. Standardized parts, simplified joints, and two-story studs and bearers link the balloon-frame form to traditional carpentry. In such a design, studding was placed at a minimum. As tools and mechanization changed by 1900, balloon framing became a standard form, and even as materials changed in the 20th century, the balloon frame remained the norm. Although many farmers or agricultural corporations have opted for manufactured buildings sided in fiberglass or aluminum panels, the structural support remains extremely similar to the original balloon frame. Flooring, however, has added structural support by incorporating a solid cement founding where formerly dirt or planks served the facility.

Prefabrication, as an architectural pattern, grew out of increased technology. By the turn of the century, the timber-rich Pacific Northwest, upper Midwest, and Southeast were the headquarters of corporations that sold prefabricated, mail-order farm buildings and commercial structures. During World War II, the Seabees, a portion of the U.S. Navy, created prefabricated, all-purpose buildings that could be manufactured in the United States and shipped anywhere. The Quonset hut was made from preformed wooden ribs sheathed with corrugated sheet steel and fitted with pressed-wood interior linings. After use in the war, more than 170,000 of these structures would return to the United States for use in agriculture and industry. Prefabrication had even more application in the utilitarian world of agricultural structures than in the suburban countryside, where it would be applied by William Levitt (1947) and others.

As agriculture expanded westward, infrastructural links became major components in connecting the agricultural hinterland to railroad corridors. Following the completion of the transcontinental railroad in 1869, the entire American West would be linked by technology as "hinterland" to Chicago and other developing shipping centers. The program of the rural, agrarian landscape remains dominated by this economic relationship. Most prolific, grain elevators serve as tremendous storage facilities at railroad termini. Industrial architecture of the early 1900s was widely influenced by European modernism and particularly Walter Gropius, including these massive compounds for grain storage and transshipment of steel or concrete tubes (from one to hundreds). Located in towns and shipping ports, these facilities became fully automated with electricity in the 20th century.

Technology has allowed the contemporary agricultural landscape to sprawl over land often hostile to farming. Hydraulic management allows vast tracts of the American West, particularly the Great Plains and California's Central Valley, to produce enough goods to feed the entire world. Located west of the isohyetal line of 20 inches, such locations lack the necessary rainfall for agriculture. Building on hydraulic concepts developed by natives of the Southwest and of Utah Mormons, federal subsidies initiated by the 1902 Reclamation Act have helped to finance infrastructure that spreads the limited water resources of the West among the arid regions. Additionally, many farmers in the Great Plains have drilled into aquifers, including the Ogallala, and then planted circular fields irrigated by center-pivot watering systems. The extension of agriculture into such regions is a technological wonder of American society; however, it also makes farmers precariously dependent on the management of a limited resource.

Patterns in agricultural buildings have not all solely followed a program of utility. As large agricultural corporations have taken over lands of the midwestern and western United States, preservationists throughout the nation have sought to preserve the image of the independent yeoman farmer. Most often, this effort has seen organizations such as the National Farmland Trust raising funds to preserve older farmsteads that are threatened by suburban or urban expansion. Another social change to the farm structure relates to Venturi's idea of the decorated shed. For many years, the largest shed, the barn, was viewed as a billboard-in-the-making. Tobacco companies often painted an entire side of the barn with advertisements for Mail Pouch or Red Man. As part of the antismoking furor of the late 1990s, these billboards were banned and removed. The barn has consistently belied its status as purely a utilitarian structure to inspire and exhibit social ideas and ideals.

BRIAN BLACK

Further Reading

Banham, Reyner, *A Concrete Atlantis: U.S. Industrial Building and European Modern Architecture, 1900–1925*, Cambridge, Massachusetts: MIT Press, 1986

Cronon, William, *Nature's Metropolis: Chicago and the Great West*, New York: Norton, 1991

Jackson, Donald C., *Building the Ultimate Dam: John S. Eastwood and the Control of Water in the West*, Lawrence: University Press of Kansas, 1995

McMurry, Sally, *Families and Farmhouses in Nineteenth-Century America: Vernacular Design and Social Change*, New York: Oxford University Press, 1988

Noble, Allen G., and Richard K. Cleek, *The Old Barn Book: A Field Guide to North American Barns and Other Farm Structures*, New Brunswick, New Jersey: Rutgers University Press, 1995

Worster, Donald, *Rivers of Empire: Water, Aridity, and the Growth of the American West*, New York: Pantheon, 1985; Oxford: Oxford University Press, 1992

AHMEDABAD, INDIA

Described by 16th-century European travelers as "the handsomest town in Hindustan, perhaps in the world," in the 17th century as a "city comparable in size and wealth to London" and as "the Manchester of the East" for its thriving textile industry, Ahmedabad eventually hosted an architectural treasure trove in the 20th century. This metropolis in western India, with a population of more than 2.8 million, is home to four key buildings designed by Le Corbusier (1887–1965), the well-crafted Indian Institute of Management Campus (1962–73) by American architect Louis I. Kahn (1901–74), and outstanding projects by leading Indian architects Charles Correa (1930), Balkrishna Doshi (1927), and Achyut Kanvinde (1916).

Named after its founder, Ahmed Shah, Ahmedabad was established in 1411 on the site of Ashawal, an earlier trading settlement that was abandoned in the 11th century. Occupying the east bank of the Sabarmai River, the original city of Ahmedabad, popularly known as the Old City, continues to serve as a distinct commercial and residential core of the present-day metropolis. With the building of the Ellis Bridge in 1870 (a wooden structure replaced by steel in 1882) and subsequent construction of a series of reinforced-concrete bridges capable of withstanding monsoon floods, the city started to expand across to the west bank. New bridges opened the less crowded west, or right, bank of the river. The empty west bank was more attractive for development compared with the crowded east side. This remains so today, even as the city is now spread equally on both sides of the river. The expansion of the west bank in the 20th century encouraged a wide range of new architecture. It would be a mistake, however, to overlook the Old City, because the living architectural heritage from the last five centuries can be found alongside 20th-century buildings. Noteworthy modern projects in the Old City include the Premabhai Hall (1972) and the Central Bank of India Head Office (1966) by Doshi, the Reserve Bank Headquarters (1969) by Hasmukh Patel (1933), the Roman Catholic Church of Gaekwad-ni-Haveli (1979) by Leo Pereira (1943), and the Geodesic Domed Calico Shop (1962) by Gautam (1917–95) and Gira Sarabhai (1923).

Foundations of 20th-century architecture of Ahmedabad are primarily Western in origin, beginning in the early 19th century, when the British took control of the city from the Maratha kings. They established a military cantonment to the northeast of the Old City in 1830. The railway was introduced in the 1860s with the first textile mill. In the 1870s, new gates were opened in the city wall, and large portions of it were pulled down after World War I. Early expansion of modern Ahmedabad occurred on the side of the Old City and in the direction of the cantonment. Suburban Shahibagh still holds a number of well-designed homes of the rich mercantile class, including the Retreat (1936) designed by Surendranath Kar (1892–1970), and Le Corbusier's ground-hugging, vaulted structure of the Sarabhai House (1951).

The completion of the Ellis Bridge was followed by increased development on the west side of the river. Not too far from the bridgehead emerged the educational complex of Gujarat College (*c.*1890), an eclectic Public Works Department project with Gothic, Tudor, and local touches, where the George V Hall (1910) was renamed Mahatma Gandhi Hall after India's independence. Other important buildings include the Town Hall (1940), designed by an influential British architect, Claude Batley (1879–1956); the Bombay-based partnership of Gregson, Batley, and King is inspired by Indian traditions and Western classical orders. The Town Hall, the Relief Cinema (1940), and the Electricity House (*c.*1940) do not bear the typical stylistic imprint of these architects; rather, the Art Deco and the International Style architecture seem to have inspired all three buildings.

The Postindependence Era

Ashram Road, the main traffic artery connecting all bridgeheads along the west bank of the Sabarmati River, begins near the Subhas Bridge to the north and ends near Sardar Bridge to the south. A host of important civic structures are located along this road, including Charles Correa's Gandhi Smarak Sangrahalaya (1963), located less than 100 yards from the Hriday Kunj (heart grove) in the Sabarmati Ashram, where Gandhi resided from 1917 to 1930. Built around 20-foot-square modules only 7 feet high with hutlike structures that are interconnected and with courtyards, this modest and inspiring edifice holds letters, photographs, and other documents of Gandhi. Kanvinde's Darpana Dance Academy (1968) fits beautifully with nature and its surroundings. To the south of the Gandhi Bridge lies the well-known Mill Owners's Association Building by Le Corbusier. The southernmost crossing of the river at Sardar Bridge is the cultural prescient of Ahmedabad; Le Corbusier's recently refurbished museum, or the Sanakar Kendra (1954–57), the reinforced-concrete folded plate structure of Tagore Memorial Theater (1962) by Doshi, and the rambling National Institute of Design Campus (1961) by Gautam and Gira Sarabahi are all located here.

The westward growth of suburban Ahmedabad continued rapidly in the postindependence period. A number of well-designed private residences can be found in these neighborhoods, including the Shodhan Villa (1951–54) by Le Corbusier, which, according to his *Oeuvre complète*, "recalls the ingenuity of the Villa Savoye . . . in a tropical Indian setting."

A number of educational and research institutions beyond these suburbs represent significant contemporary architecture of Ahmedabad, including the Gujarat University main buildings (1947) by Atmaram Gajjar (1901–61); a fine range of projects by architect Doshi, including the Institute of Indology (1957–62), science buildings (1959–62) for Gujarat University, the School of Architecture (1966–68), the Gandhi Labor Institute (1980–84), and the Hussain-Doshi Gufa (1992–94), a mosaic-covered cavelike exhibition structure; the Ahmedabad Textile Industries Research Association Facility (1950–52) and the Physical Research Laboratory (1954) by Kanvinde; and the Newman Hall (1970) and the Indian Space Research Organization (1975), two beautiful brick complexes, by Hasmukh Patel. The Nehru Center for Environmental Education (1988–90) by Neelkanth Chhaya (1951) and the Entrepreneur Development Institute (1985–87) by Bimal Patel (1960) represent projects by young Indian architects. Louis Kahn's brooding brick complex of the Indian Institute of Management has served as an inspiration to many of these projects.

Although the recent urban growth of Ahmedabad has not been very coherent and is continuing in a rather uncontrolled fashion, a few housing projects provide attractive and affordable places to live. For example, the Ahmedabad Study Action Group's Housing Rehabilitation Project (1973–75) provides housing for about 2,500 flood-affected families in the southern suburb of Vasna. It combines a series of housing clusters around a sequence of open spaces, well suited for community activities. In his Life Insurance Corporation Project (1973–76), Doshi employed a stackable urban row house model that allows users to expand their units. Architect Kamal Mangaldas's (1938) narrow-front row house project for Sanjay Park (1985) and the duplex-type Gulmohur Luxury Housing (1986) support a sense of community and self-sufficiency by organizing rows of housing around a cluster of amenities. However, such projects are few and far between. Nevertheless, these enlightened housing and architectural projects distinguish Ahmedabad from other rapidly expanding Indian cities.

VIKRAM BHATT

See also **Art Deco; Corbusier, Le (Jeanneret, Charles-Édouard) (France); Correa, Charles Mark (India); Doshi, Balkrishna (India); Indian Institute of Management, Ahmedabad; International Style; Kahn, Louis (United States); Villa Savoye, Poissy, France**

Further Reading

Ashraf, Kazi Khaleed, and James Belluardo (editors), *An Architecture of Independence: The Making of Modern South Asia: Charles Correa, Balkrishna Doshi, Muzharul Islam, Achyut Kanvinde*, New York: Architectural League of New York, 1998

Bhatia, Gautam, "Indian Archetypes," *Architectural Review* 197, no. 1179 (May 1995)

Bhatt, Vikram, and Peter Scriver, *After the Masters*, Ahmedabad: Mapin, 1990

Caine, William Sproston, *Picturesque India: A Handbook for European Travellers*, London and New York: Routledge, 1890; reprint, Delhi: Neeraj, 1982

Charles Correa, Singapore: Concept Media, 1984; revised edition, by Hasan-Uddin Khan, Singapore: Concept Media, and New York: Aperture, 1987

Chhaya, Neelkanth, "Centre for Environmental Education, Ahmedabad," *Architecture + Design* 7, no. 3 (May–June 1990)

Corbusier, Le *Oeuvre complète, 1952–1953*, New York: G. Wittenborn, 1957

Cruickshank, Dan, "I Like a Brick," *Architects' Journal* 195, no. 9 (March 1992)

Curtis, William J.R., *Le Corbusier: Ideas and Forms*, New York: Rizzoli, and Oxford: Phaidon, 1986

Curtis, William J.R., *Balkrishna Doshi: An Architecture for India*, Ahmedabad: Mapin, and New York: Rizzoli, 1988

Desai, Madhavi, and Miki Desai, "Ahmedabad: The City as Palimpsest," *Architecture + Design* 8, no. 3 (1991)

Gillion, Kenneth L., *Ahmedabad: A Study in Indian Urban History*, Berkeley: University of California Press, 1968

Gujarat State Gazetteers, 19 vols., Ahmedabad: Directorate of Government Printing, Stationery, and Publications, Gujarat State, 1961–84; see especially vol. 18, *Ahmadabad*, 1984

A Handbook for Travellers in India, Burma, and Ceylon, London: John Murray, 1892; 21st edition, as *A Handbook for Travellers in India, Pakistan, Burma, and Ceylon*, edited by L.F. Rushbrook Williams, 1968

India: A Travel Survival Kit, South Yarra, Victoria: Lonely Planet, 1981; 6th edition, as *India: A Lonely Planet Travel Survival Kit*, by Hugh Finlay et al., Hawthorn, Victoria, and London: Lonely Planet, 1996

Lang, Jon T., Madhavi Desai, and Miki Desai, *Architecture and Independence: The Search for Identity, India 1880 to 1980*, Delhi, Oxford, and New York: Oxford University Press, 1997

Mehta, Meera, and Dinesh Mehta, *Metropolitan Housing Market: A Study of Ahmedabad*, New Delhi, London, and Newburry Park, California: Sage, 1989

Mellin, Robert, "Sites and Services: Case Study, Ahmedabad," *Open House International* no. 1 (1984)

Michell, George, and Philip Davies, *The Penguin Guide to the Monuments of India*, 2 vols., London and New York: Viking, 1989

Michell, George, and Snehal Shah (editors), *Ahmadabad*, Bombay: Marg, 1988

Pandya, Yatin, "Balkrishna V. Doshi: Hussain-Doshi Gufa, Ahmedabad, India," *GA Document* 40 (July1994)

Steele, James, *Rethinking Modernism for the Developing World: The Complete Architecture of Balkrishna Doshi*, New York: Whitney Library of Design, 1998; as *The Complete Architecture of Balkrishna Doshi: Rethinking Modernism for the Developing World*, London: Thames and Hudson, 1998

Wadhva, Kiran, *Role of Private Sector in Urban Housing: Case Study of Ahmedabad*, New Delhi: Human Settlement Management Institute, and Rotterdam: Institute for Housing Studies, 1989

Wisloscki, Peter, "Ahmedabad Authority: The Gijerat High Court Complex," *World Architecture* 58 (July–August 1997)

AIRPORT AND AVIATION BUILDING

Airports were a novel development without precedent. Although similar to railway stations, aircraft had quite different architectural requirements to passenger trains. This did not deter designers in the early 20th century from using the styling of train stations and train interiors in their designs for the new airport terminals and aircraft cabin interiors. Much as the great railway stations encapsulated the engineering achievements of the 19th century, airport terminals were to become highly visible indicators of technological advancement for nations and global cities in the 20th century.

The symbolism of airport terminals was present almost from the outset, but it has undergone significant alteration over time, from the oversized modern designs of the 1930s; to expressive structures such as Eero Saarinen's eaglelike TWA Terminal, Idlewild, New York (1962); to the futurist high-tech terminals of the 1980s and 1990s. In the mid-1960s, Paul Andréau's centralized Terminal 1 at Charles de Gaulle International Airport, Roisy-en-France (1974), demonstrates how air terminals had evolved into large complex megastructures that were purely systems to deal with enormous numbers of travelers. The air terminal type embodied an inevitable romanticism about flight and movement in contrast with the reality of scale and flexibility in an environment subject to rapid unrelenting change.

Aircraft have changed enormously since that first flight at Kitty Hawk, North Carolina, in 1903. The changes in commercial aircraft design over the 34 years that separate the Douglas DC-3 (1935) from the Boeing 747–100 (1969) have been staggering; airports raced to keep up with the new aircraft and airline needs. The much increased seating capacities, safety, reliability, speed and range of aircraft lowered costs and increased the popularity of air travel, which encouraged ever greater numbers to fly; in turn, airport terminals around the globe were confronted by new pressures to expand facilities. The one constant factor in airport terminal design was change—swift, unrelenting, and unpredictable. Airport terminal design is a contest between the rival claims of centralization and dispersal, between providing minimum passenger walking distances on the landside and dispersal on the airside to take advantage of the maneuverability of airplanes.

The challenge of mass air travel in the 1990s led to the building of extremely large terminals to handle upward of 35 million passengers per year in an unprecedented expansion of airports around the world that culminated in a stunning new architectural synthesis. This new generation of terminals were hugely complex, giant high-tech steel sheds that responded to the demands of extreme efficiency and a renewed emphasis on architectural expression. Indeed, it is hardly an original observation to say that much as train stations were the great popular monuments to 19th century industrialism, in the 20th century, these extraordinary airport terminals similarly express the pinnacle of 20th century achievement in architecture and construction.

The new terminals are almost cities unto themselves, albeit rampant metropolitan fragments, populated by hoards of transient nomads. The introduction of lightweight tent and tensile forms in Saarinen's elegant terminal at Dulles International Airport, Washington, D.C. (1962), and later in the new Haj Terminal, Jeddah, Saudi Arabia (1978), and at Denver, Colorado (1995), and Kuala Lumpur, Malaysia (1998), international terminals reinforced this incipient nomadic connection.

Whether the strategy of building ever-larger terminals proves effective and they are the forerunners of even larger terminals in the future, or whether other factors—air traffic density, weariness of the traveling public—intervene to limit size, time alone will tell. The great size and cost of the new terminals may yet prove to be their undoing. Of all the new building types to emerge in the 20th century, and notwithstanding the skyscraper, these new terminals speak more vividly and eloquently than any other mass movement by peoples across the globe. Starkly contrasting with the tragic events of the 20th century, the horizontal steel-and-glass terminal is a cathedral whose standardized open space, immersed in light, encapsulates mankind's dream of freedom.

The earliest airline routes—both national and international—began across Europe in spring 1919. The first generation of airfields was primitive, little more than grassy fields—unobstructed flat surfaces used for recreational purposes at the weekend or for military training and parades. The Dugny-Le Bourget (Paris) and Croydon (London) airports, which opened in 1920, signaled the arrival of second-generation airports having purpose-built terminals, the beginning of the concept of the modern air terminal complex. The second-generation terminal, unlike the earlier primitive landing fields, comprised a multifunctional building that was normally separated from the hangars and workshops but that usually incorporated the control tower. Except for this control tower, the building had a low profile to avoid obstructing flight passes, and the roofs were designed on the airfield side as flat platforms for use by the public at air shows.

Terminals often resembled grandstands with tiered viewing terraces for the public to watch air shows. More monumental than necessary, in Europe, architectural overstatement was usually a product of local ambition or national pride. The air terminal and modern architecture thus emerged concurrently. Terminal architecture was frequently uncompromisingly modern, with examples such as the Schipol International Terminal (1928) by Dirk Roosenberg serving as models. Schipol had an L-shaped layout, with a tall control tower as a central feature and roof terraces for visitor viewing. The importance of the tower was typical: At Lyon's V-shaped terminal by Antonin Chomel and Pierre Veriere (1930), the control tower is on the corner and advances toward the field, and at Birmingham (1939), by Graham Dawbarn and Nigel Norman, the tower sprouts sheltering wings on either side.

Gatwick terminal (1936), designed by Hoar Marlow and Lovett, was circular, with the control tower mounted on top in the center. It had rail-mounted telescopic passageways connected to the gates of the beehive to protect passengers from the weather

Stansted Airport exterior, Essex, England, designed by Norman Foster and Partners (1981–91)
© Ken Kirkwood. Courtesy Foster and Partners

and from propellers. Gatwick was the first airport with a railway connection, and it initiated the satellite concept for airport terminals. Significantly, Gatwick's canvas passageways connecting to aircraft are precursors of modern telescopic passenger-loading bridges or jetties.

The postwar terminals coincided with the engineering and machine aesthetic of modern architecture as expressed succinctly by Le Corbusier in *Vers une architecture* (1923), in which he dedicated an entire chapter to airport architecture. Aircraft fascinated other architects as well. Erich Mendelson sketched a hangar with workshops for airships and airplanes in 1914, and Peter Behrens designed an airplane factory at Henningsdorf near Berlin (1915) for AEG. In the 1926 film *Metropolis*, a rooftop airport was included on top of a tower, and in 1932 Andre Lurcat suggested building airports in the River Seine, Paris. Manmade islands to service transatlantic airplanes were proposed, an idea that, 70 years on, was realized in the futuristic artificial island airports of Kansai (1994, Osaka Bay) and Chek Lap Kok (1997, Hong Kong).

In the United States air services were started by the Post Office, which developed and operated an airmail service from 1918 to 1925. After the passage of the contract Air Mail Act of 1925, many private entrepreneurs and companies entered commercial aviation. The history of American air transport policy contrasts with that of Europe, where the responsibility for forming airlines, building navigation aids, and constructing airports nearly always rested in the hands of each country's central government. In America airport designers generally simulated ideas from the architects and engineers of railway terminals, combining the best of railroad station design with important airport elements that became common features in later decades. On occasion, a regional style was chosen for terminals, such as in San Francisco (1937) and Albuquerque (1939).

After 1927 increases in flight movements and passenger capacities and the weight of commercial aircraft placed new demands on concepts for the buildings and for the entire airfield and caused the third generation of airport construction. Expensive take-off and landing strips with paved surfaces, standard at all airports in the United States since 1928, now became mandatory in Europe. Usually, four or more strips were planned to respond to varying wind directions. The airport at Bromma near Stockholm became the first to be so equipped. Doubts now arose about the common practice of building on the periphery, and in 1929, the French proposed the idea of a wedge-shaped building zone projecting forward from the edge of the airport into the center of the airfield, leaving more than 80 percent of the edge undeveloped.

The introduction of flying boats in the 1930s led to the construction of amphibian airports on coasts, such as the International Air Terminal and Dinner Key Seaplane Base at Miami (1934) and Marine Air Terminal, LaGuardia Airport (1939), where one could transfer to a land airplane. The 1930s saw some striking terminal buildings erected, such as Ramsgate Municipal Airport (1937) by David Pleydell-Bouverie in Great Britain.

Resulting from the tremendous advances in aviation made during World War II and the introduction of new types of commercial aircraft carrying 80 to 100 passengers, existing arrival and departure halls were rendered inadequate. Airport construction and modernization was delayed in the immediate postwar period and only got going properly in Europe in the 1950s. The frontal system or transporter configuration of terminal design dominated: Aircraft stood out on aprons, separate from the terminals, and passengers had to walk out across the tarmac to the planes. The Zurich International Airport (1953) by Alfred and Heinrich Oeschger is typical of this fourth generation of airports. Other examples are Heathrow (1956, London) and Orly (1961, Paris), which had a terminal located at the center with two fingers on either side, stretching 2,300 feet from end to end.

Finger- and star-shaped terminals arrived in the 1950s in the United States and soon afterward in Europe. The terminal at London's Gatwick Airport in 1958, a rectangular building with a single finger, was the first example of a fifth-generation airport, with two more added in 1964; Rome, Milan, Copenhagen, London, and Amsterdam soon adopted the system. Toronto airport (1961) in North America and Geneva's Cointrin airport (1968) and the Cologne-Bonn airport (1970) in Europe are leading examples of satellite terminal design.

The basic assumption inherent in fifth-generation airports—minimum distances between landside and airside—came under great pressure in the 1970s when international terrorism surfaced. Since then, airports have been subject to strict safety regulations.

The main feature of the next, sixth, generation of airports, dealt with the terrorist threat by applying the bottleneck principle, with the arrival and departure halls once again centrally located (often on separate floors), in combination with a strict division between the "secure" area and the "open" area. As a consequence, well-designed terminals assure a discreet transition from public area to a zone of differentiated security, thereby avoiding any feeling of restricted freedom.

The 1990s brought a climax in terminal design with the creation of some 40 major new terminals around the globe, replacing older obsolete facilities for cities as far apart as Osaka, Hong Kong, Bilbao, London, Paris, Inchon, Barcelona, Seville, and Shanghai. Although they are very varied architecturally, they share many common features; namely, great size, openness, lightweight construction, high-tech detail of structure and services, and a new lyrical freedom. The new high-tech megaterminals frequently combine extensive areas of retail, hotel and conference facilities, bars, and movie theaters. At a minimum, the 1990s terminals are the products of a 40-year evolution and, hence, bring together many existing trends in a striking new synthesis. Constructional ingenuity and bravado, large, curved, roofs, the application and celebration of advanced technology—all this and more has been applied obsessively to every facet of terminal performance. Although the dominant high-tech expression was not confined to air terminal design, there is an immediate appropriateness about its use. Sir Norman Foster and Partners, Sir Richard Rogers, and Renzo Piano, as well as a host of other designers and followers, were inspired by 19th-century English industrial buildings, and more critically, by Sir Joseph Paxton's 1851 Crystal Palace.

Foster and Partner's Stansted Airport in Essex, England (1991), is such an example. Stansted is a single-level building that incorporated an evenly spaced grid of columns that is clearly and intentionally reminiscent of Mies van der Rohe's steel-and-glass pavilion concept. Its plan was for an elegant and directionless neutral terminal with a detached satellite in a flat English landscape, a step farther on from his previous Sainsbury Center for the Visual Arts at Norwich (1978), which resembles an aircraft hangar.

The new airport at Kansai, which was designed by Renzo Piano Building Workshop and that opened in 1994, displays with great authority the characteristic features of contemporary airport architecture such as scale (it has a 1.7-km-long departure lounge), planning complexity, engineering prowess, and technological splendor. Kansai was the first airport of its size (it was designed to handle 25 million passengers a year) to be developed entirely on a man-made island. The architect anticipated later terminal designs by exploiting open, curvaceous roofs that are ecologically sound and by using natural light to mark the passenger routes through the terminal. It is a multinodal transportation center as much as an airport.

Hong Kong's new Chek Lap Kok (1997) terminal, also by Foster and Partners, planned for 35 million passengers per year and extended the architectural language of Stansted. The roof has a 36-meter structural grid and appears from above as a cutout silhouette of a plane. On three main levels between two parallel runways, Chek Lap Kok also has train and expressway links to Hong Kong.

The 1990s generation of megaterminals, although they make the most of available technological resources, push beyond mere technological expression: They seek to become more "natural" and less artificial as they acquire an outdoors–indoors character, making the most of natural light and ventilation. This trend may be the result of technology fatigue, the onset of boredom with technology in isolation, and an acknowledgment that people require a deeper, more meaningful, relationship with natural things for harmony and balance. It is not surprising to find terminal designers using words such as "calm and visual clarity" to express their aims.

PHILIP DREW

See also **Dulles International Airport, Chantilly, Virginia; Foster, Norman (England); Haj Terminal, Jeddah Airport; Hong Kong International Airport, Hong Kong; Kansai International Airport Terminal, Osaka; O'Hare Airport, Chicago; TWA Airport Terminal, New York**

Further Reading

The literature on airport design and architecture is extensive and far ranging, which makes it difficult to approach. Much of it is of a highly technical nature, on planning and engineering and transportation, environmental impact, and sound problems. For information on design standards, refer to De Chiara (1990) and Edwards (1991). Technical standards are continually being revised and updated, so it is important to confirm the applicability of information. In 1937 the Royal Institute of British Architects (RIBA), London, held an exhibition on airport design and published an accompanying catalog, as did the Art Institute of Chicago (see Zukowsky, 1996). For a good introduction to the extensive literature, see Binney (1999), who provides information alphabetically on 46 new terminal projects. On airports before 1940, the Council of Europe–sponsored Raphael program *Europe de l'air* monograph on Tempelhof, Speke, and Le Bourget (2000) is most useful, complemented by Zukowsky for the American account.

Aeroport de Paris: Aerogare D 'Orly, L Agence, Paris: Havas, 1961
Airport Architecture of the Thirties: Berlin: Tempelhof; Liverpool: Speke; Paris: Le Bourget, Paris: Editions du patrimone, 2000
Airports and Airways (exhib. cat.), London: Royal Institute of British Architects, 1937
Ashford, N.J., and P. Wright, *Airport Engineering*, New York: Wiley, 1991
Binney, Marcus, *Airport Builders*, Chichester: Academy Editions and John Wiley, 1999
Blow, Christopher J., *The Airport Passenger Terminal*, New York: Wiley-Interscience, 1985
Bode, Stephen, and Jeremy Millar (editors), *Airport—Most Important of the Century*, London: Photographers Gallery, 1997
Ceerver, Ascensio, *The Architecture of Stations and Terminals*, Arco for Hearst Books, 1997
De Chiara, Joseph, and John Callender, *Time-Saver Standards of Building Types*, 3rd edition, New York: McGraw-Hill, 1990
Doganis, R., *The Airport Business*, London: Rutledge, 1992
Edwards, Brian, *The Modern Terminal: New Approaches to Airport Architecture*, London: E and FN Spon, Rutledge, 1991
Horonjeff, Robert M., and F.X. McKelevey, *Planning and Design of Airports*, 3rd edition, New York: McGraw-Hill, 1983
Jahn, Helmut, *Airports*, edited by Werner Blaser, Boston: Birkhauser, 1991
Powell, Kenneth, *Stansted: Norman Foster and the Architecture of Flight*, London: Fourth Estate, 1992
Whitelaw, J. (editor), *Airports of the 21st Century*, London: Thomas Telford Publications, 1995
Wickens, A.H., and L.R. Yates (editors), *Passenger Transport after 2000 AD*, London: Chapman & Hall, 1995
Wilkes, Joseph A., *Encyclopedia of Architecture, Design, Engineering & Construction*, Vol. 1, AIA, New York: Wiley, 1988
Wilkinson, Chris, *Supersheds: The Architecture of Long-span Large Volume Buildings*, Oxford: Butterworth Architecture, 1991
Zukowsky, John (editor), *Building for Air Travel*, Munich and New York: The Art Institute of Chicago and Prestel-Verlag, 1996

ALLIANCE FRANCO-SÉNÉGALAISE

Designed by Patrick Dujarric; completed in 1994
Kaolack, Senegal

With his project for a new French cultural center in rural Senegal, architect-anthropologist Patrick Dujarric gave a new twist to an indigenous architectural style. The Alliance Franco-Sénégalaise that he completed in 1994 in Kaolack, links a vernacular tradition to a new decorative program. Kaolack is a rural city, with a population of approximately 150,000, that lies 160 kilometers southeast of Dakar in west-central Senegal on the right bank of the Saloum River. French cultural centers in West Africa ostensibly act to promote and disseminate French culture and language, but they are also important venues for showing African art forms, from films to paintings. With its reinvention of local architectural traditions, the Alliance Franco-Sénégalaise makes clear that this building does not simply house an institution affiliated with the French government but is also a local community center.

Senegal is a former French colony, and Dujarric is a longtime resident. He completed this project in 1994, the client being the Mission de Coopération et d'Action Culturelle. Unlike French cultural centers in Dakar and Saint-Louis du Sénégal that are housed in Colonial-style buildings, Dujarric's work is both French and Senegalese.

The plan for the center is loosely modeled on an African village or compound. (Although the project borrows eclectically from several West African artistic traditions, the ethnic groups most prominent in this region are Sereer, Wolof, and Djola.) The complex comprises three main blocks that are separated by courtyards and that themselves have open-air courts. The main block houses the administrative and public exhibition areas. It also contains the center's office, an exhibition hall, a library, and audiovisual and pressrooms. Two courtyards puncture this main block, bringing air and light to the interior spaces.

A smaller block contains four classrooms. Three small courts separate the classrooms and can be used as additional lecture space. The third element is an open-air theater that can be used for many purposes, such as showing French newscasts, screening films, and presenting live performances.

Anyone visiting the center is immediately awestruck by its profuse decoration. The decoration is sometimes geometric, as many of the walls, piers, and columns are painted with stripes. It is sometimes figural, showing people and animals in scenes derived from local graphic traditions. Although the graphic forms are traditional, many of them are traditional to nonarchitectural art forms, such as pottery and textiles. In a move that is unusual today, patterns cover almost all visible surfaces. Dujarric decorated everything: floors, walls, ceilings, and columns. Such an exuberant profusion of decoration is associated with Gothic, Byzantine, and Islamic religious architecture but is rare in modern secular buildings.

Reviewers of the project (many of whom were French) have frequently claimed that Dujarric's Kaolack structure was an architectural embodiment of French literary Poststructuralism. The building itself, because of its elaborate decorative program, was a "text" that had to be read and interpreted by viewers. According to many critics, the postmodern decoration and graphics act as an interactive text, inviting visitors to create their own textual and visual meanings. For a building that houses and exhibits a variety of media, the structure itself has become a form of media. Architecture is thus integrated into the larger realm of popular art and graphics.

In addition to the local iconographic programs that it draws on, the Alliance building incorporated another traditional artistic practice: the use of perforated *claustra* walls. *Claustra* walls are a feature of Tukulor houses and mosques, and their open-air grillwork treats light as a raw material that can be transformed into patterns. When light patterns move across already decorated planes, surfaces come alive, and painted figures dance, thus imbuing graphic representations with video-like qualities.

This project was one of the recipients of the 1995 Aga Khan Awards for Architecture. Previous rounds of the Aga Khan Awards, in 1983 and 1986, had recognized few modern buildings, and traditional buildings dominated the winners. This left the awards program open to criticism (from such notable Aga

Alliance Franco-Sénégalaise, Kaolack, Senegal, designed by Patrick Dujarric (1994)
© Aga Khan Trust for Culture

Khan jurors as Mehmet Doruk Pamir and Hans Hollein) that it was reactionary, anti-modern, anti-Western, and anti-technology. The Alliance Franco-Sénégalaise puts much of that criticism to rest, for it is a project that grows out of local traditions yet houses modern functions and uses new materials.

The materials of this low-budget project include terrazzo floors in which stones from the Thiès region provide local color. Cement block can no longer be considered a modern or foreign material, for much of the architecture around the Kaolack region is made from it. Dujarric ingeniously created columns by pouring concrete into PVC pipes that were then richly painted with horizontal stripes. The project is economical not only with its materials but with its energy costs as well. It is not air-conditioned but relies on crosswinds, ceiling fans, and shaded areas to keep the place cool and well ventilated.

The largely favorable reviews that Dujarric has received for this building suggest a need to see new kinds of architecture that grow out of African traditions. Successful or not, this building does affirm that Africa is not importing modernity from the West but, rather, is creating its own.

MARK HINCHMAN

See also **Aga Khan Award (1977–); Hollein, Hans (Austria)**

Further Reading

"1995 Aga Khan Awards for Architecture," *Architect and Builder* (May 1996)

"Aga Khan Awards," *Architectural Review* 198 (November 1995)

"Alliance Franco-Sénégalaise, Kaolack, Senegal," *Metropolis* (September 1997)

Chaslin, François, "Palmares Aga Khan 1995," *L'architecture d'aujourd'hui* 303 (February 1996)

ALUMINAIRE HOUSE

Designed by Albert Frey; completed 1931
Long Island, New York

Designed by Albert Frey and Lawrence Kocher and completed 1931, the Aluminaire House represents one of the earliest examples of European-inspired Modern architecture in the eastern United States. The Aluminaire was one of only six American buildings chosen by Henry-Russell Hitchcock and Phillip Johnson in 1932 for the New York Museum of Modern Art's International Style exhibition and book, and of those six, it was the only private residence other than Richard Neutra's Lovell House (1927–29). Like the Lovell House, the Aluminaire represented a merger of advanced building technology and advanced architectural expression, and as such, it exemplified many of Le Corbusier's five points of architecture. This was mainly the result of the contributions of Albert Frey, a Swiss-born designer who worked in Le Corbusier's studio before imigrating to the United States in 1930. Co-designer Lawrence Kocher, a Beaux-Arts–trained architect from California, was managing editor of *Archi-*

tectural Record at the time of his partnership with Frey, and it was through the journal's contacts that the firm received the Aluminaire commission.

Designed for the 1931 Allied Arts and Building Products Exhibition in New York, the Aluminaire House was intended as an attention-getting display to draw in the public. Eventually, more than 100,000 visitors toured the full-scale model of what the architects described as "a House for Contemporary Life," filled with light and air ("alumin" + "aire"). To be occupied by a couple living near a city, the house contained a covered porch, entrance hall, boiler room, and garage on the ground floor; a kitchen, living and dining rooms, bedroom, bathroom, and exercise room on the second floor; and a skylit library, toilet, and terrace on the third floor. As a model dwelling, the Aluminaire was intended as a prototype for prefabricated housing that, if produced in adequate quantities (10,000 units), would have been relatively low cost ($3,200). As a three-story block with *pilotis*, ribbon windows, a roof garden, and freely composed facades, the Aluminaire House had much in common with a building that Frey knew firsthand: Le Corbusier's detached single-family house (1927) in the Weissenhofsiedlung (the exhibition of domestic modern architecture initiated by the German Werkbund in Stuttgart). If the Aluminaire lacked the spatial complexity typical of a Corbusian *plan libre*, it nonetheless featured a combination living and dining area that stretched the full width of the house, with a double-height ceiling above the living space. This gave the house a feeling of openness despite its small size, a perception augmented by folding screens and translucent partitions that transformed individual rooms into flexible, multiuse spaces.

Aluminaire House, Syosset, New York, designed by Albert Frey (1931)
© RIBA Library Photographs Collection

Using lightweight skeletal construction, the house was erected in the exhibition hall in less than ten days. All building materials, many of which were experimental, were donated by national manufacturers eager to associate themselves with modern architecture. Of these materials, aluminum and steel were prominent in the structure and fittings. Six five-inch aluminum pipe columns set in concrete supported the entire weight of the building, with many columns left exposed. Fastened to the columns was a framework of channel girders and steel beams supporting steel floor decking and steel stairs. Steel-framed windows were used throughout the house, as were steel-faced, chrome-trimmed doors, including the overhead doors of the drive-through garage. The non–load-bearing, exterior walls were only three inches thick, consisting of a steel frame, wood nailers, and insulation board. They were sheathed in three-foot panels of corrugated aluminum fastened with aluminum screws and washers. Practically, the panels' vertical corrugations added rigidity, and the polished surface deflected the sun's rays, but they also gave the Aluminaire a desirable metallic sheen and a gloss of the modern.

A similar effect was evident inside in the nontraditional details and finishes. Fabrikoid covered the walls in the living spaces, and black Vitrolite clad those in the bathroom. Neon tubes running above the windows lit the interior with dial controls, allowing the occupant to adjust the level and color of illumination. The house also featured built-in metal, glass, and rubber fixtures designed by Kocher and Frey to save space and minimize maintenance. Beds were suspended from metal cables. A combination china cupboard and retractable dining table had legs on wheels to allow easy extension. A suite of air-filled rubber chairs could be deflated for easy storage; although never fabricated, these designs anticipated the inflatable furniture of the 1960s.

Public response to the Aluminaire House was generally positive, as evident in the extensive coverage the house received in the general and architectural press in the early 1930s. Local journalists were impressed with its ease and rapidity of construction, dubbing it the "zipper" and "magic" house and heralding it as a portend of future dwellings. In *The Modern House* (1934), British architect F.R.S. Yorke praised the weather-resistant qualities of its laminate wall structure and noted that its design was well adapted to standardization.

After its display at the Allied Arts exhibition, the Aluminaire House was dismantled in only six hours and transported to Syosset, Long Island, to the estate of architect Wallace K. Harrison, who had purchased it for $1,000. In the spring of 1931, it was reerected as Harrison's weekend retreat, but it was structurally compromised because of construction delays. Harrison altered the house during the next decade, adding two one-story additions, enclosing the roof deck, and relocating it to a hillside site that transformed the first floor into a basement. The Aluminaire gradually deteriorated in the ensuing four decades, and in 1986, after the Harrison estate was sold, it was threatened with demolition. Although the Harrison estate was listed on the National Register of Historic Places, the Aluminaire House itself did not have the individual local listing needed to ensure its protection. Largely through the efforts of Joseph Rosa, an architect researching a book on Albert Frey, the architecture community in New York City rallied to save the Aluminaire House, deeming it too significant a landmark of American modernism not to be preserved. In 1987 the house was moved to the Central Islip campus of the New York Institute of Technology, where, under the auspices of the School of Architecture, the Aluminaire is gradually being reconstructed and restored to its original condition.

GABRIELLE ESPERDY

See also **Corbusier, Le (Jeanneret Charles-Édouard) (France); Hitchcock, Henry-Russell (United States); International Style; Johnson, Philip (United States); Lovell Health House, Los Angeles; Neutra, Richard (Austria); Weissenhofsiedlung, Deutscher Werkbund (Stuttgart, 1927)**

Further Reading

"Aluminaire: A House for Contemporary Life," *Shelter* (May 1932)

Jandl, H. Ward, *Yesterday's Houses of Tomorrow: Innovative American Homes, 1850 to 1950*, Washington, D.C.: Preservation Press, 1991

Rosa, Joseph, "A. Lawrence Kocher, Albert Frey, The Aluminaire House, 1930–31," *Assemblage* 11 (April 1990)

Rosa, Joseph, *Albert Frey, Architect*, New York: Rizzoli, 1990

Yorke, F.R.S., *The Modern House*, London: Architectural Press, 1934; 8th edition, 1957

ALUMINUM

Aluminum is such a ubiquitous material in 20th-century architecture that it is hard to appreciate how relatively late it came on to the scene. Aluminum had considerable advantages, including its light weight, its malleability, its corrosion resistance, and its alloyability for special properties. For the first third of the 20th century, however, it had to compete with similarly reliable materials, especially steel. Nevertheless, aluminum was seen as a thoroughly modern material without historical associations, making it indispensable to the Modern movement. This did not preclude some designers from using the material for historicist styles, but its functional role in architecture kept pace with architectural design and building technology.

The particular strengths of aluminum were proven during World War II in a wide range of applications. However, after the war, the primary producers put aluminum into large-scale market development to advocate for its use in all sectors, architecture being no exception. In fact, by 1965 an estimated 905,000 tons of aluminum were used in building construction in the United States, more than in any other field of application. Aluminum's most significant and specific contributions to 20th-century architecture have been in windows, storefronts, and curtain walling. Aluminum has also been widely employed in decorative features and hardware, windows and doors, and siding for a range of structures.

Although aluminum had been known for much of the 19th century, one of its first architectural uses was for the capping of the Washington Monument (Robert Mills, 1884). Aluminum was introduced commercially after 1886, when American Charles Hall and Frenchman Paul Héroult independently and almost simultaneously discovered that alumina, or aluminum oxide, would dissolve in fused cryolite, which could then be decomposed electrolytically to become a crude molten metal. A low-cost technique, the Hall-Héroult process remains as the major method used for the commercial production of aluminum.

Another early application of aluminum in architecture came in 1891, when Burnham and Root used the material for the interior fittings of the Monadnock Building (1889–91) in Chicago. In 1897 Raffaele Ingami used unalloyed aluminum sheets with aluminum rivets to surface the cupola of the Church of San Gioacchino (1897) in Rome. In the same year in Montreal, the Canada Life Building (Brown and Vallance, 1897) was finished with a decorative aluminum cornice. In all these cases, the metal was used as a practical substitute and did not contribute significantly to the design.

The Austrian Otto Wagner developed the use of aluminum as a deliberate and specific architectural feature in his Post Office Savings Bank (1904–06) in Vienna. He used aluminum bolts to hold the exterior marble panels, and he used aluminum for interior cladding and details, such as the grilles and vents. Although it would be some 30 years before the material came into the mainstream of architecture, Wagner's designs represented a breakthrough and began to establish aluminum as a modern material, one that could be associated with the ideals of modern architecture, including technology and theories of modernism.

Despite these early precedents, aluminum's large-scale application as a constructive and decorative architectural material was developed most significantly during the 1930s. Even in Pittsburgh, the aluminum capital of the United States, the tower of the Smithfield United Church (Henry Hornbostel, 1926) used aluminum, but still only as a substitute for other metals and in a design that was strangely traditional and imitative.

Modernist architects began to value aluminum as a building material with vast potential. With the development of steel-framed skyscrapers and curtain walls, architects used aluminum for glazing bars and spandrels. Aluminum could save space, reduce weight, and shorten building time. Aluminum's strength-to-weight ratio meant that thinner and lighter sections could be used for spandrels and windows, thus significantly increasing rentable floor area. In addition, these elements could be prefabricated and hoisted into position on-site, thus saving considerable time and money over conventional materials. These factors were directly related to considerations of industrial building and mass production of component parts. Many skyscrapers were fitted with aluminum spandrels in the 1930s, including the panels of the Empire State Building (Shreve, Lamb and Harmon, 1930). The Daily Express Building (1931) on London's Fleet Street by Ellis and Clarke combined glazing bars with glass panels. Another noteworthy use of aluminum was in the fabrication of storefronts and window frames. During the 1930s, the American Kawneer Company developed extrusion technology that was particularly appropriate for fabricating metal windows and storefronts. The combination of reduced maintenance, technical efficiency, and ease of assembly encouraged the use of prefabricated aluminum components.

These applications to commercial buildings were paralleled by experiments in housing and space frame architecture. In 1931 the Aluminaire House was erected by Lawrence Kocher and Albert Frey as a demonstration building within the Allied Arts and Building Products Exhibition in New York City. The house was built using aluminum-pipe columns and panels fixed on the

Alloy girders support the framework of the Dome of Discovery, for the 1951 Festival of Britain. (Photograph taken July 1950.)

interior frame with screws and washers. The Aluminum Company of America subsidized the aluminum parts, probably with the intention of developing another area of aluminum application. In the late 1920s, Buckminster Fuller intended his 4D house to be fabricated from aluminum alloys, which at that time were yet to be developed. By the early 1930s, new heat-treated alloys were available, yet Fuller's experimental ideas were not accepted by the American Institute of Architects (AIA), where prefabrication in domestic building was disfavored. These early attempts at prefabrication did nonetheless set a precedent for later postwar architects who produced a range of prefabricated buildings that employed aluminum in many different applications.

This potential for prefabrication and portability was developed after World War II. For example, the British aircraft industry produced 86,000 prefabricated bungalows using aluminum as the main material immediately after 1945, and in America after 1940 the National Homes Corporation designed and manufactured prefabricated houses using aluminum cladding and roofing. The prefabrication ideal was also used in England for schools and portable buildings. During the 1950s, a British firm developed the supply of prefabricated, pressed, aluminum-framed huts for use in rural areas of Africa.

After World War II the aluminum companies began promoting their material for use in construction and architecture. In 1947 the R.S. Reynolds Company, a specialist aluminum supplier, set up a Memorial Award, which was offered by the AIA for architects who "made the most significant contribution to the use of aluminum aesthetically or structurally, in the building field." Notable examples of award winners include I.M. Pei's 88 Pine St., New York (1974), Philip Johnson's Pennzoil Place (1978), Foster and Partner Hong Kong Shanghai Bank Headquarters (1986), and Helmut Jahn's United Airlines Terminal, Chicago (1988). In France, the work of Jean Prouvé (who had already developed an interest in aluminum prior to 1940) was greatly enhanced when, in 1949, the French trade association L'aluminium Français purchased an interest in his workshop. He used aluminum curtain walls for the Féderation Nationale du Bâtiment building in Paris and continued to develop aluminum components for commercial, residential, and overseas commissions.

The demand for "space frames" grew with a demand for exhibition halls, aircraft hangars, warehouses, and storage facilities. One of the most elegant solutions for space frames was the dome. The Festival of Britain's Dome of Discovery (1951) was fabricated mainly from extruded triangular lattice aluminum framework and, at a span of 110 meters, was the largest aluminum structure at the time. By the later 1950s, the American Kaiser Aluminum Corporation was developing a prefabricated dome system that use shaped panels to create domed space frames. Structures, with a diameter of 145 feet and able to hold up to 2,000 people, could be erected in a matter of hours. A gold-anodized Kaiser dome was erected in Moscow in 1959 for a U.S. cultural and industrial exhibition.

Although these structural uses of aluminum were impressive, the most successful postwar application was undoubtedly the further development of the curtain wall. The aluminum-clad 30-story Alcoa Building (1950) in Pittsburgh by Harrison and Abramovitz was the lightest permanent office building of its size in the world at one time and required approximately less than half the constructional material of a similar building that used structural steel in the framework. In Chicago, where skyscraper curtain walls of the post–World War II era consisted of stainless steel, rusting steel, and glass, Naess & Murphy's Prudential Building (1955) was significant not only for its temporary status as the city's tallest building but also for its limestone and aluminum facade.

Modern Japanese architects have also embraced the material. Arata Isozaki's Prefectural Museum of Modern Art (1971–74) in Gunma and the Museum of Contemporary Art (1981–86) in Los Angeles make extensive use of aluminum panels. The use of aluminum as a component in the structure of buildings continued in the 1970s, especially as an element of High-Tech style. The works of Norman Foster, including the Sainsbury Centre for the Visual Arts (1977) at the University of East Anglia and his Hong Kong and Shanghai Bank (1985); parts of the Lloyds Building (1979–87) in London by Richard Rogers; and the outer frameworks of I.M. Pei's Bank of China (1990) in Hong Kong exemplify this trend.

Aluminum is now a standard and unexceptional material for buildings. It has been specified for cladding, roofing, and interior applications of all kinds, including partitions, ceilings, ducting and trunking, grilles, and hardware fittings, including gates grills, balcony rails, lamp casings, and ornamental and practical fittings of all kinds.

CLIVE EDWARDS

See also **Aluminaire House, Long Island, New York; Empire State Building, New York; Foster, Norman (Great Britain); Fuller, Richard Buckminster (United States); Isozaki, Arata (Japan); Prefabrication**

Further Reading

Aluminum Company of America, *Aluminum in Architecture*, Pittsburgh: Alcoa, 1932

Aluminium Development Association, A symposium on aluminium in building. (Proceedings) Convened by the Aluminium Development Association and held at the Royal Institute of British Architects, London: July 9–10, 1959

Dorre, E., et al., *Alumina: Processing, Properties, and Applications*, Berlin and New York: Springer Verlag, 1984

Dwight, J., *Aluminium Design and Construction*, London: Publisher E. F. and N. Spon, and New York: Routledge, 1999

Hornbostel, C., *Construction Materials: Types, Uses, and Applications*, New York: John Wiley, 1991

Lane, J., *Aluminium in Building*, Aldershot, England: Ashgate, 1992

Northern Aluminium Company, *Aluminium in Building*, London: The Company, c. 1952

Peter, J., and P. Weidlinger (editors), *Aluminum in Modern Architecture*, 2 vols., Louisville, Kentucky: Reynolds Metals Company, 1956

Simpson, Tracy, *Aluminum Extrusions in Architecture*, Oakland, California: Kaiser Aluminum and Chemical Sales, 1968

Van Horn, Kent R., *Aluminum*, 2 vols., Metals Park, Ohio: American Society for Metals, 1967

ALVAREZ, MARIO ROBERTO 1913–

Architect, Argentina

Mario Roberto Alvarez is considered one of the most prominent and prolific representatives of the rationalist approach to architecture in Argentina. Born in Buenos Aires on 14 November, 1913, he graduated with a degree in architecture from the University of Buenos Aires in 1937. He worked first at the Ministry of Public Works and later become a municipal architect for Avellaneda City. Alvarez opened his architectural office in 1947, when the modernist ideas were firmly established in Latin America. Ever since, his practice has been characterized by the variety, quantity, and solid professionalism of his work.

His most refined and important contribution is The Municipal Theater General San Martin, designed in association with Macedonio Oscar Ruiz (1960) and located on Corrientes Avenue, the area of spectacles and theaters. The facade has a curtain wall that announces adherence to a functional and rational approach, articulated with a marquee that makes a subtle reference to the history of the area. The lobby is one of the best examples of high modernism in Latin America. This space, which echoes some of the developments in Brazilian modernism at that time, combines tilted columns supporting the suspended volume of one of the auditoriums. It also incorporates a flying staircase and a large mural, as well as modernist furniture and rich materials.

The entire complex, with four auditoriums dedicated to experimental theater, contemporary dance, and chamber music, incorporated the best stage equipment and technology available at the time. The interior spaces of the auditoriums are characterized by a calm artistic sensibility that relies on the combination of very few materials while using elongated, sweeping lines and lighting. The complex was later extended and connected to the San Martin Cultural Center (1970), also designed by Alvarez. The cultural center is located in a very dense urban area, and the entrance incorporates a dry plaza that opens up the space of the old Spanish colonial grid.

The studio also expanded some of the finest cultural institutions of the country, among them the prestigious Colón Theater (1968) and the Cervantes National Theater (1969), both in Buenos Aires.

By the 1970s, the firm Alvarez and Associates had acquired a reputation for incorporating modern technology in its rational approach to design problems. This approach was further explored with the SOMISA building (1975), a technological challenge, as it was the first building in the world completely welded together.

Alvarez was always very conscious of the effect of a building in the environment. This is exemplified by the Galeria Jardin (1983), a commercial center located on Florida Street at the core of the city center. The complex has an underground garage, with three levels of shops and offices, and also includes two towers with offices and apartments. The basic parti revolves around the idea of opening an internal street, which was unified by two submerged patios opened up to the sky and to natural light. The complex is linked visually and functionally by stairs and balconies, thus enriching the urban fabric with this refuge in the core of the block.

Among several towers designed by Alvarez, one of the most remarkable is the IBM building (1983). The IBM headquarters is located in the Catalinas Norte area, the gateway to the metropolis from the estuary of the river. The tower is in the middle of a hub of relevant buildings from the turn of the century, including corporate headquarters, monuments, and parks.

The solution is a highly sculptural yet simple type that follows the tripartite model of a base, a middle, and a top, which exemplifies Alvarez classical affinities. However, Alvarez incorporates subtle reflections on the theme. The building aesthetic is characterized by the distinction between the circulation of the areas served. The tower is related to the site by an elongated, pure platform forming a base. The prism of the tower is linked to the platform by the elevator shafts' smaller volume, generating the impression that the tower is floating. The fenestration recedes and the horizontal bands of concrete slabs composing each floor give the building its dynamic simplicity. A clean and powerful entablature ends the composition.

The conscious expression of the structure, care for the programmatic requirements, and the ascetic elegance of the interiors characterize most of the multistory flats, health centers, and office buildings designed by Alvarez's studio. One of the most significant landmarks in the Buenos Aires skyline is Le Parc tower. Forty-six stories high, it is one of the tallest towers in South America (1995). Instead of the typical Miesian rectangular prism used in many of his other projects, Alvarez approaches this structure differently. The floor plan is expressed in volume through balconies and circulation. The highly articulated yet restrained facade is the result of interior variations needed to provide sun and views. The expressive richness of this tower comes from the joints in the exposed concrete and from the marks left by the shuttering bolts securing the formwork.

Instead of radical transformation, Alvarez's philosophy has been to explore a limited set of forms as variations of a theme: to do more with less. His work was immune to the sweeping changes and explorations of the 1970s and to the notions of fragmentation, historical allusion, or the search for complexity and richness of meaning. Alvarez's production remained involved in solutions that advanced an uncompromising classicist attitude. His work belongs to a generation that absorbed most of Ludwig Mies van der Rohe's contributions and adopted them to a country with a developing economy.

After more than 50 years of professional work, innumerable awards, and many competitions won, Alvarez's studio remains committed to a stable, gradual evolution instead of revolutionary changes in architecture. His extensive work is an accrued reflection on some of the tenets of high modernism. As with many other rationalist architects, his practice is an ascetic and rigorous search that aspires to order and continuity.

JOSE BERNARDI

See also **Argentina; Buenos Aires, Argentina; Mies van der Rohe, Ludwig (Germany)**

Biography

Born in Buenos Aires on 14 November 1913. Graduated with a degree in architecture in 1937, and opened his architectural office in 1947. Honorary member of the AIA since 1976, his office is one of the most prestigious in Latin America.

Further Reading

Alvarez, Mario Roberto, *Arq. Mario Roberto Alvarez y Asociados: obras 1937–1993*, [Argentina]: M.R. Alvarez, c. 1993

AMBASZ, EMILIO 1943–

Architect, Argentina and United States

Emilio Ambasz is an Argentinia-born architect and designer whose international design and architectural projects have made him a significant contributor to the history of contextualized modernism in 20th-century architecture.

After completing military obligations, Ambasz applied to universities in the United States and (with the recommendation of Williams) entered Princeton University under a Palmer Fellowship to the School of Architecture as a freshman in 1963, placed in the junior-year design studio his first semester, and switched to the first-year graduate program his second semester. He completed his studies as a graduate student, receiving his professional degree (a Master of Fine Arts) in two years, having been waived from the undergraduate curriculum, and joined the faculty in 1966. Appointed as a lecturer, Ambasz was promoted to assistant professor during 1966–69. In 1968 Princeton awarded him the Philip Freneau (Class of 1771, Poet of the Revolution) Preceptorship, established in 1949 as a bicentennial endowment to provide three years of research funds in recognition of scholarship. In addition, he served as a visiting professor at the Hochschule für Gestaltung in Ulm, Germany.

Ambasz drafted the charter for the Institute for Architecture and Urban Studies (IAUS) in New York while on the faculty at Princeton and served as its deputy director, dividing his time initially after joining the Architecture and Design Department of the Museum of Modern Art of New York in mid-1969, where he served as its curator of design from 1970 to 1976. His philosophical manifesto for design as the basis of interdisciplinary discourse was articulated in "Institutions for a Post-Technological Society: The Universitas Project" (1971), a working paper produced under the joint auspices of both the Institute for Architecture and Urban Studies and the Museum of Modern Art, from which several of his published writings were subsequently drawn. Derived in part from the thought of Argentine philosopher Tomas Maldonado, Ambasz's work postulated the complementary nature of science and design, where the former deals with the given (to reveal order) and the latter seeks to alter the future (to create order).

The Museum of Modern Art's design collection reflects Ambasz's vision of dialectic between American high technology and the value-added qualities of European design. In addition, he initiated several milestone exhibitions on architecture and industrial design. "Italy: The New Domestic Landscape" (1972) was not only a comprehensive investigation of the 1960s effect of

Lucile Halsell Conservatory, Main Courtyard (1987), San Antonio, Texas, designed by Emilio Ambasz

Italian product design but also an intellectual challenge to design "boundaries." It included the designed conversion of the objects' shipping containers into exterior display kiosks that populated the Museum of Modern Art's Garden Court, effectively extending the exhibition beyond its programmed domain. His exhibit "The Architecture of Luis Barragán" (1974) reintroduced a minimalist modernism at a time when the historicist revivalism of postmodernism was emerging yet emphasized the Mexican architect's lyrical and symbolic underpinnings. In "The Taxi Project" (1976), Ambasz developed a "performance specification" for urban taxis and, in a manner similar to his "Italy" show, called on industry to respond with prototypes anticipating the "smart cars" of the late 1990s.

In 1976 Ambasz represented the United States in the Venice Biennale, the first of many subsequent international exhibitions of his work. This coincided with the formal opening of his firm, Emilio Ambasz & Associates, and the first of a series of design awards in the program of the journal *Progressive Architecture*, awarded to his design for the Grand Rapids (Michigan) Art Museum. This building combined adaptive re-use of an existing Beaux Arts building, contextual urban revitalization, and reformation of the building with the intervention of an abstract transparent inclined planar roof, filling the interior of its C shape and creating a major interior public space. At the same time, this building served as a symbolic sign for the museum and an allegorical reference by means of a water cascade over this roof surface.

Ambasz has characterized himself as an inventor. His design work has essentially straddled the boundaries of a "critical" discourse, at all levels of its definition. This embraces the tradition of Le Corbusier's notion of normative standards and architectural projects as prototypes of larger issues as well as Amancio Williams's belief that architecture is a creative act, postulating alternative models to the present condition. In a method that combines the rational and the lyrical, and quoting Walter Gropius, "Develop a technique, then give way to intuition," Ambasz asserts that he does not design with words; instead, he is a maker of images.

Ambasz's images, moreover, might best be characterized as a fundamental purism characterized by a process of extreme reduction in which the object aspect of the architecture disappears, or at least nearly vanishes, through integration with the landscape. As a basic leitmotif of his work, this idea represents more than merely a philosophical giving back of the land that the building occupies. It is a strategic gesture to address the crisis of the object in mid-1980s design, to do away with the edifice.

It becomes the frame from within which to harness the site, as in much of the visual arts of the preceding decades.

Among Ambasz's works are the Fukuoka Prefectural International Hall (Fukuoka, Japan), a Janus-like building addressing its urban streetfront and embracing an existing park at its rear, which literally ascends the 16-story building, a theme extended in his Phoenix Museum of History (Arizona) and the Myca Cultural and Athletic Center (Shin-Sanda, Japan). Landscape-in-building include the Union Station (Kansas City) and the Nichi Obihiro Department Store (Hokkaido, Japan), where interior spaces become great winter gardens, as if the landscape had developed internally. Building-in-landscape are the Schlumbeger Research Laboratory complex (Austin, Texas), the House for Leo Castelli (East Hampton, New York), the Lucille Halsell Conservatory (San Antonio, Texas), Thermal Gardens (Sirmione, Italy), the Baron Edmond de Rothschild Memorial Museum (Ramat Hanadiv, Israel), and the Barbie Doll Museum (Pasadena, California); in all cases, these are fundamentally underground earth-sheltered structures as well as "marked sites" in which man-made structures emerge from a seemingly continuous landscape.

Projects that emphasize an aformal strategy of change and indeterminacy include the Center for Applied Computer Research (Mexico City, Mexico), the New Orleans Museum of Art (Louisiana), and at an urban scale, the Master Plan for the 1992 Universal Exposition (Seville, Spain), which incorporate floating structures in a parklike setting or themes of evolution grounded in a rigorous armature whose fabric is intended to incorporate variety or actually devolve, such as with the Cooperative of Mexican-American Grape Growers (California) or "Pro Memoria" Gardens (Ludenshausen, Germany).

Ambasz's career includes design in graphics, installations, and products for which he holds a number of patents. His industrial design has involved formulating the process from concept through manufacture: design, detail, patent, tools, and product. Often, there is a mechanical invention fundamental to the concept: the "Vertebra" furniture series (included in the design collections of both the Museum of Modern Art and the Metropolitan Museum of Art) involved a dynamic reconfiguration to adjust to position, further extended in the "Vertair" series, which developed a patented upholstery system that expands and contracts. Ambasz has a wide range of products, from toothbrushes to mechanical pens, including the development of diesel engines as chief design consultant to Cummins Engine since 1980.

In 1989 he was featured in an exhibition, "Emilio Ambasz: Architecture," at the Museum of Modern Art (which traveled through 1995) and subsequently a one-man show, "Emilio Ambasz: Architecture, Exhibition, Industrial and Graphic Design," which was designed by Shigeru Ban and traveled from 1989 to 1991. Although his work continues to be published, particularly internationally, his products and graphics are recognized by awards (several have also been accessioned to the Design Collection of the Museum of Modern Art).

A citizen of Monaco with several international residences and offices in New York and Bologna, Italy, Ambasz continues his production despite the demands of practice. In his publications, no projects are dated, and it is never clear whether they were built. In a sense, this is the essence of Ambasz: to leave behind a Chinese puzzle that appears as one thing but that contains complex interlockings to be revealed and discovered by others.

PETER C. PAPADEMETRIOU

Biography

Born in Resistencia, Argentina, June 1943. Received master's degree in architecture from Princeton University, New Jersey. Curator of design, Museum of Modern Art, New York 1969–76. Taught at Princeton University, Carnegie Institute of Technology, Pittsburgh, and Hochschule für Gestaltung, Ulm, Germany. Exhibition, *Italy: The New Domestic Landscape*, the Museum of Modern Art, New York 1972.

AMERICAN FOURSQUARE

"American foursquare" refers to a house type that is little recognized in traditional architectural history sources yet is visible in virtually any urban neighborhood developed during the period 1900–40. Despite its lack of official approval, this hardy survivor was far and away the dwelling of choice for generations of people with modest means constructing or purchasing homes. The design was eminently practical: it was spacious, it was passably attractive, and it was cheap.

Variously called "Builder's Houses," "American Basic," "Square Houses," "Box Houses," "double-deckers," "double cubes," "American Farm Houses" (something of a misnomer, since the vast majority of these homes were built in cities and suburbs), or, because of their sheer numbers across the land, "National Houses," the houses themselves remain clearly boxlike in their design.

The foursquare design is often not truly square. In its rectilinear proportions, low-hipped roof, square plan, and simple facades, the foursquare resembles early prairie houses of the Midwest made popular by the Prairie School architects. As American cities grew, land values soared. Urban blocks were jammed with narrow lots, usually rectangles with the short side abutting the street. Thus, the foursquare could often be somewhat narrower in front and back and have longer sides to accommodate the site. As cities expanded, urban—and finally suburban—growth allowed greater flexibility in building. The foursquare house, once removed from the strictures of cramped, rectangular lots, usually grew in size and, in the process, frequently became more ornamented. As a rule, box houses located closer to traditional "downtowns" tend to be smaller and less ornate than those found in outlying neighborhoods and suburbs.

The essentially cubelike shape is the initial indicator of the type. The American foursquare is an efficient, self-contained box. No matter how many bays, wings, porches, or other appendages the house might offer, the basic shape of the building should be apparent. In addition, broad, overhanging eaves follow the upper perimeter of the building, providing shade for the second story and the bedrooms therein and a settled look for the house as a whole. The rooflines growing from these extended eaves are usually pyramidal. Unlike more expensive homes, chimneys are seldom of any great aesthetic importance and are often made of concrete or brick. A large front dormer, usually hipped like the roof, serves as a trademark and helps provide light and air to the attic sections.

Windows are simple in both arrangement and presentation, usually standard, mass-produced, double-hung models that can

American Foursquare house, Lynchburg, Virginia, architect unknown (1919)
© William H. Young

be opened for maximum ventilation. As a rule, the lower half is a sheet of plain glass; the upper portion usually consists of smaller panes grouped in one frame and divided by thin muntins. In some of the more unadorned box houses, even the upper half of the window is a single glass pane, further reducing costs. Because these homes were designed more for utility than for architectural or stylistic purity, the windows are often irregularly spaced, thereby serving the interior of the house in the all-important admission of light and air in the most efficient way.

Virtually every foursquare has a porch across its front. Decorative style for this appendage varies, from a simple raised floor with an equally simple roof over it to elaborate classical columns and railings that support an ornamented roof complete with garlands, friezes, and fancy shingles.

A major selling point of the box house was its interior arrangement. Because these homes are normally two-story structures, the first floor contains a spacious living room, a formal dining area, a den, and an airy, well-equipped kitchen with pantry. The second floor commonly consists of four large bedrooms, each with its own closet. Finishing off this emphasis on livable space is an attic that offers either storage or the potential of still more rooms. A full basement—or "cellar," as they were usually called at the time, a dank, dark hole beneath the dwelling with a bare earth floor and no living amenities whatsoever—typically houses the furnace and accompanying coal bin and little else.

As this immensely popular residential style gained momentum with buyers, it moved from its initial simplicity to ever-more applied decoration. Plain clapboard or stucco walls evolved into brick or shingle facades, and vestigial turrets, towers, and bays sprouted out of the basic cube. The hipped roof might feature a widow's walk at its apex, or a balustrade might appear above the broad overhanging eaves.

Catalogs of simple plans—usually done by draftsmen, not architects—flooded the market, offering, in essence, a mass-produced house to anyone. Sears and Roebuck, Montgomery Ward, Aladdin, Gordon Van Tine, and a host of other merchandisers had long offered dwellings in kit form, and their box-style houses promptly became some of their most popular models.

Following World War II, the style was completely eclipsed by innumerable tract subdivisions that seemingly sprang up everywhere. The box house never achieved a comeback, but in its brief 40-year history it has left its mark nonetheless. How many thousands and thousands of box houses were built will never be known, but their legacy endures in myriad ways. In many eastern American cities, the foursquare house—in sheer numbers of extant structures—remains the dominant residential design.

Historians have at times attempted to link the origins of the box house to Federal-style townhouses and to aspects of Italianate design and have even suggested that the foursquare is really a reborn Georgian mansion, one more suited to the tastes and means of the middle class. Although each of these theories contains an element of truth, each also tends to overlook the pragmatism of the basic box house. The foursquare house, as found in most of the nation's cities, stands as the triumph of vernacular design on a massive scale.

The foursquare house might find little space in the annals of American residential design, but it has had a lasting impact on perceptions of what constitutes adequate housing. In the early 20th century, middle-class Americans wanted more spacious homes and larger lots. The box-type house satisfied both desires: substantially larger than most other dwellings then available, the foursquare in turn required more land. More than has been realized, the foursquare helped define both urban and suburban housing needs throughout the country.

William H. Young

See also **Prairie School**

Further Reading

Definitive studies of the American foursquare await writing. Aside from brief mention in larger works, the style has received little scholarly or popular attention. The following books acknowledge the style and its popularity among homebuyers. Little attention, however, is paid to the architectural qualities of foursquare design.

Baker, John Milnes, *American House Styles*, New York: Norton, 1994

Gowans, Alan, *Styles and Types of North American Architecture: Social Function and Cultural Expression*, New York: Icon Editions, 1991

McAlester, Virginia, and A. Lee McAlester, *A Field Guide to American Houses*, New York: Knopf, 1984

Schweitzer, Robert, and Michael W.R. Davis, *America's Favorite Homes: Mail-Order Catalogues as a Guide to Popular Early 20th-Century Houses*, Detroit, Michigan: Wayne State University Press, 1990

AMERICAN INSTITUTE OF ARCHITECTS

The American Institute of Architects (AIA) is an organization that sought, in its infancy, to bring a degree of professionalism and recognition to certified architects in the United States. When the organization was established in 1857, few people understood the role an architect plays in the design of new buildings, and engineers and construction workers often assumed the design role in building projects of the late 19th and early 20th centuries. The role of the AIA continues today in coordinating a degree of both professional and ethical conduct among members, offering recognition for well-designed projects, and working to continue the development of architects in the United States.

In the middle of the 19th century, architects were few in number, and most of those were unskilled. With westward expansion, towns bloomed into cities in a haphazard fashion, and a new "Stick style" of architecture took hold throughout the United States. Where the flat-roofed brownstone residential row houses of New York or the Greek Revival along the Atlantic coast had been popular, builders' patterns now emphasized an asymmetrical plan, lively outline, and the use of thin wooden framing. This Stick style represented the skilled carpenter—a populist view of architecture. Professional architects, located mainly in the larger eastern cities, organized a defense against the informality of plebeian style.

A new architecture, oriented to future change, was taking shape in the United States. It grew rapidly and found wide acceptance. "In the new world, there was less resistance imposed by an earlier culture or social order. Industrial and engineering progress were equated with national development. The enthusiasm for major engineering works was whetted by continental expansion, especially in the field of transportation. In building it was furthered by the lack of a hard and fast professional line between architecture and engineering," wrote Frederick Gutheim in *One Hundred Years of Architecture in America*.

The blurred lines of architecture and engineering led to the establishment of the American Institution of Architects in 1836, founded by a talented artist and architect, William Strickland. He and five other skilled designers met in New York to organize the institution. Although the group never became active, it is seen as the forerunner of the AIA. Thomas Walter, an original member of the 1836 group, helped found the AIA in New York City in 1857 along with Alexander Davis, also an original member of the 1836 group, and 12 other architects. Richard Morris Hunt, the first American to study at the École des Beaux-Arts in Paris, was one of the spirited 12 architects at the first AIA meeting in 1857.

According to historian Spiro Kostof, Hunt and other founders of the AIA "pitted the cultured, disciplined procedures of the architect against the free-wheeling creativity of builders whose do-it-yourself philosophy they considered a threat to their status."

Although the École encouraged creativity, a strict academic curriculum emphasized design principles and professional acclimation. Promoting training, accreditation, and overall professionalism, Hunt sought to bring the formal training of the École to the United States, where training was less organized or codified. The first school of architecture, housed at the Massachusetts Institute of Technology in 1865, was modeled on the École. By 1868, the first architectural journal began publication in Philadelphia.

As the AIA took hold, bringing professional standards to certified and licensed architects, they met engineers on an intellectual battlefield. With engineers, they fought over the science—the "how," or the mechanics—of building design. Where engineers sought to limit creative expression, architects sought an increasing scope of control in architectural design.

This battle came to a head after the U.S. Civil War when the country worked at rebuilding. In Washington, D.C., the rebuilding occurred not only through physical buildings but also through the image that the country hoped to project to countries abroad. Modeling the official architectural styles of Paris and London, the federal government of the United States led the way in boastful public architecture. Thomas Walter designed the dome for the U.S. Capitol building in which he simulated the overwrought classicism of Second Empire Paris, and this new monumentalism fit the federal presence.

National headquarters building for the American Institute of Architects, designed by T.A.C. (The Architects Collaborative) (1973)

As technology advanced, architects were faced with the subsequent challenges of mechanization within architectural building and design, for example heating, air-conditioning, lighting, and power systems. Moreover, according to Gutheim, industrialization of the building industry (factory-produced windows, spandrels, roofing, flooring, equipment, and other elements designed by others) as well as increasingly stringent tests of comparative economy, operating performance, or standards set by hospital administrators, military engineers, educators, and other specialists complicated matters.

In the early part of the 20th century, architects were concerned with a range of public and institutional buildings—banks, libraries, schools, business offices, and hospitals; increasingly, however, the importance of these designs extended beyond the limits of the building and its construction. School buildings were seen as community institutions as well as educational centers. Libraries came to reflect amenable, open plans devoted to free access to learning. The informality of family life led to increasing influence on nonpublic buildings, such as residences.

"Architects are also dealing with clients who are frequently inexperienced, often confused, and unprepared to recognize the time and cost required by good building," states Gutheim. This is where the AIA aids its members in professional development and services to promote the field of architecture in the United States. In keeping with this spirit, the AIA has instituted an AIM (Aligning the Institute for the Millennium) program. In a call for a culture of innovation, AIM is redefining the mission of the AIA and developing "Seven Core Values" to identify what architects and the industry can expect of the AIA in the future, including architectural education, knowledge delivery, and advancement.

LISA A. WROBLE

Further Reading

Gutheim, Frederick, *One Hundred Years of Architecture in America, 1857–1957: Celebrating the Centennial of the American Institute of Architects* (exhib. cat.), New York: Reinhold, 1957

Kostof, Spiro, *A History of Architecture: Settings and Rituals*, New York: Oxford University Press, 1985

Wilson, Richard Guy, *The AIA Gold Medal*, New York: McGraw-Hill, 1984

AMSTERDAM, NETHERLANDS

Although not the seat of government, Amsterdam, in the province of North Holland, is the acknowledged capital (*hoofdstad*) of the Netherlands and, until World War II, was its architectural leader. Its local professional groups—Architectura et Amicitia, De 8, and Groep 32—were successively at the forefront of innovation, and despite the subsequent evaporation of regional hierarchies, the city has retained its prominence. Its inclusive and diversified buildings, especially those from the first third of the century as well as from its final decade, are endowed with a specifically local flavor, even when responding to more global design trends. Amsterdam's watery foundations (many of the buildings rest on wooden pilings) and extensive network of canals and islands, no less than its distribution into distinctive quarters, ensure its unique character. Although 20th-century structures are interspersed among the picturesque remnants of the older city, the majority of these buildings were planted in an encircling girdle that extends dramatically but deliberately from the historic core. In Amsterdam, chronology and geography coalesce: for the most part, one can recognize the era of construction from the location.

After the Golden Age of the 17th century, the cosmopolitan and prosperous harbor city became a somnolent town with a declining population until belated industrialization and the construction of international canals and railways commenced in the late 19th century and Amsterdam awoke to an expansive future, with concomitant woes (a desperate housing shortage, ruthless demolition, tactless road building, and the filling in of canals and open space) and wonders (prosperity generating provocative new construction). Thanks to the National Housing Act (Woningwet) of 1901, which required Dutch municipalities to provide extension plans and building codes (which in Amsterdam included aesthetic prescriptions), the city's development proceeded responsibly. Initially, the main augmentations were southward, but eventually rings of buildings surrounded it in all directions. In the 1920s, Amsterdam was called the "Mecca of housing"; its social democratic administration insisted that dwellings answer artistic demands, serve the community, and embody the cultural aspirations of the working and lower-middle classes. Housing has continued to be the dominant building type.

Although at the turn of the century eclecticism ruled in Amsterdam as elsewhere, two contrasting yet complementary buildings signaled a fresh start. One was the vast Bourse (1897–1903) by H.P. Berlage, its sources in medieval architecture and the theories of Gottfried Semper and E.E. Viollet-le-Duc transformed by Berlage's personal quest for a universal language suitable for all programs and viewers; the other was the American Hotel (1898–1902) by Willem Kromhout (1864–1940), a more playful design incorporating Byzantine and Arabic motifs as well as Romanesque. Both are unusually monumental for the time and place, with corner towers that anchor and announce their presence in the cityscape. Each is constructed from Amsterdam's traditional material: unplastered brick (glowing red in a large "cloister" format for the Bourse, pale yellow and slender for the hotel) with stone trim kept within the sleek plane of the masonry walls. The elevations and plans obey a proportional system intended to harmonize the parts with the whole, characteristic of Amsterdam practice. Gifted applied artists executed the details and contributed to the interiors, which are representative of Nieuwe Kunst, the geometric and restrained Dutch version of Art Nouveau. A third building, the imposing polytonal masonry headquarters (1919–26) for the Dutch Trading Company (Nederlandsche Handelsmaatschappij, today ABN-Amro Bank), extended this aesthetic into the 1920s. The concrete-frame construction, rare at the time, was articulated by projecting vertical piers that unite five stories, an American formula seen previously only in the Scheepvaarthuis (1912–16; see Amsterdam School). Its theosophically inclined designer, K.P.C. de Bazel (1869–1923), one of the first Dutch architects to employ proportional systems, further interpreted his contemporaries' goals in a personal manner in his housing projects for the municipality and the philanthropic organization De Arbeiderswoning.

Berlage was the author of the first modern extension, Amsterdam Zuid (South); in 1915, he exchanged his picturesque plan of 1905 for a more formal and practical layout to accommodate large-scale housing. The formula behind his acclaimed design, executed mainly between 1917 and 1927, was "in layout monumental, in detail picturesque" (Berlage quoted in Fraenkel, 1976, 46), meaning individualized and intimately scaled; discrete neighborhoods were composed of turbine plazas, winding streets, and perimeter blocks, often enclosing communal gardens, with the typical Amsterdam arrangement of floor-through dwellings ranged to either side of entries and stairs, creating a vertical punctuation in the long facades. These smaller urban units were woven into a larger tapestry of avenues leading, in Berlage's original vision, to major public structures. The latter were replaced by four-story multiple dwellings, but since these were designed mainly by the Amsterdam School, the grandeur, exuberance, and luxury associated with institutional buildings invigorate the housing and the accompanying schools, shops, communal bathhouses, branch libraries, bridges, electrical transformers, and so on that form an integral part of Amsterdam Zuid. A stylistic and typological anomaly in Plaz Zuid is the Wrightian Olympic Stadium (1926–28) by Jan Wils (1891–1972), who was briefly a member of De Stijl.

Other important districts created in the period during and immediately after World War I under the guidance of the dynamic director of housing Ary Keppler include the Spaarndammerbuurt north of the railroad tracks, best known for Michel de Klerk's dwellings for the workers' housing society, Eigen Haard (1915–20), but with interesting ensembles for other such organizations established by union members with government support, most notably Zwanenhof (1915–20) by H.J.M. Walenkamp (1871–1933). On reclaimed land north of the IJ estuary (Amsterdam Noord), a series of garden suburbs with more conventional two-story row housing offered an alternative to the denser matrix of Amsterdam Zuid. A significant municipal experiment of 1921 was Betondorp in Watergraafsmeer, annexed by Amsterdam in that same year, where a number of different systems employing concrete for rapid and cheap construction were tested. Some 1,000 dwellings were added to the housing stock; some of the experiments provided useful precedents, while others proved but temporary expedients. Architects included those of Amsterdam School persuasion, such as Dirk Greiner (1891–1964) and Jan Gratama (1877–1947), and budding functionalists, such as the Haarlem-based J.B. van Loghem (1881–1940).

Amsterdam's belt of new extensions, with buildings firmly defining streets and squares, was scornfully decried as the "stone city" by a younger generation touched by the ideas of Le Corbusier, the Bauhaus, and CIAM (Congrès Internationaux d'Architecture Moderne). In 1927 these polemicists founded De 8 and issued a manifesto denouncing the putatively antiutilitarian and defiantly aesthetic schemes then dominant and demanding the introduction of Zakelijkheid (Nieuwe Bouwen in the Netherlands). The most distinguished examples of this tendency in Amsterdam comprise the school and cinema by Johannes Duiker; the glazed Apollohal (Apollolaan, 1933–35) by A. Boeken (1891–1951), a founder of Groep 32; the steel-framed, unplastered brick atelier dwellings with artists' studios combining single- and double-height spaces (Zomerdijkstraat, 1934) by P. Zanstra (1905–), K.L. Sijmons, and J.H.L. Giesen; and the strikingly transparent "Drive-In Dwellings" with garages below (Anthonie van Dijkstraat, 1936–37) by Mart Stam, Lotte Stam-Beese (1903–), W. van Tijen (1894–1974), and H.A. Maaskant (1907–77). Buildings that also display modern materials and functionalist concepts but that, while devoid of Amsterdam School decorative flourishes, have a distinctly local rather than international character include the brick "Wolkenkrabber" (Amsterdam's first "Skyscraper"; Victorieplein, 1930), its glazed stair separating the two apartments on each floor designed by an apostate from the Amsterdam School, J.F. Staal (1879–1940), and the curvaceous white National Insurance Bank (Apollolaan, 1937–39) by Dirk Roosenburg (1887–1962).

De 8 had published proposals to replace perimeter blocks with Germanic open-row housing and four-story tiers of dwellings with high, horizontally layered flats accessed by galleries or corridors and served by a single stair or elevator. When Cornelis van Eesteren designed the AUP (Algemene Uitbreidungsplan [General Extension Plan]) of 1934, he likewise envisaged tall slabs standing free in parklike settings and, according to CIAM prescriptions, segregated the city according to use: dwelling, working, recreation, and transport. Although World War II prevented complete realization, his scheme guided development until the late 1980s: Bos en Lommer (1937 and later, by De 8 members Ben Merkelbach [1901–61] and Ch. Karsten [1904–79]) and Frankendael (1947–51, by Merkelbach and Karsten and Merkelbach and P. Elling [1897–1962] with Mart Stam) are examples of such worthy but architecturally undistinguished solutions.

In the postwar period, only on occasion did modernists escape tired formulas. The curtain wall appeared first in 1959 in the unusually elegant Geillustreerde Pers (Illustrated Press) headquarters by Merkelbach and Stam. Reconstruction focused on social housing, and the strict economic guidelines enforced by a government bureaucracy led to monotony and mediocrity. The culmination of CIAM thinking was the enormous southeastern housing estate Bijlmermeer (1962–73), designed by the Municipal Housing Service. This dispiriting honeycomb of concrete high-rises was linked to the center by the Metro, a remarkable feat of engineering of the 1970s that unfortunately did far more damage to Amsterdam's fabric than the Nazi occupation. The precepts that produced Bijlmermeer were finally repudiated in the scheme by OMA (Office for Metropolitan Architecture, led by Rem Koolhaas) for the Ijplein in Amsterdam Noord (1980–82). Like Berlage's Amsterdam Zuid, variety was naturally achieved by employing different firms to execute the plan, which consists of tall blocks in the western sector and low-rise buildings in the east, producing a successful mix of housing types conforming to OMA's neomodernist stance.

By the 1960s, editors of the journal *Forum* urged reform. Aldo van Eyck (1918–99) criticized the sociologically driven soulless modernism that had blighted his country, called for "labyrinthine clarity" (ordered and logical complexity), proposed theories that drew inspiration from the African Dogon and the Casbah, emphasized the importance of intimacy and the thresholds between public and private space, and envisaged the city as a large house and the house as a small city, thus challenging Amsterdam's inert and self-contained enclaves. After designing many ingenious playgrounds throughout the city, he realized his ideals in the acclaimed but flawed Burgerweeshuis (City Orphanage, 1960, no longer used as such), a miniature townscape of domed units of concrete and brick scaled to its small inhabitants. A subsequent movement, Structuralism, was formed by sympathizers such as Herman Hertzberger (1932–), whose Le Corbusian Studentenhuis (Student Dormitory, 1959–66), which combines social and dining facilities with living quarters and a common terrace (a street in the sky), exemplifies this approach; within the compound, a matrix of large and small rooms offers points where social encounters, often accidental, can enrich daily life.

Since the mid-1980s, there has been an explosion of exciting new architecture in Amsterdam, comparable in magnitude and inventiveness to the period between 1915 and 1934. Postmodernism is alien to Amsterdam, although the neo-Expressionist, ecologically prescient "sand castle" that houses the NMB (today ING) bank (1979–87) by A. (Ton) Alberts (1927–1999) and M. van Huut might be categorized as such, in that Alberts has revived the anthroposophical organicism of the early 20th century. Instead, an exuberant, triumphantly contemporary and quintessentially Dutch architecture has reappeared. Housing projects are again a cause for celebration, no longer constrained by politically correct but architecturally lifeless requirements. Redeveloped sites such as Kattenburg and Wittenburg (post office and flats by A.W. van Herk and S.E. de Kleijn, 1984) and KNSM-, Java-, and Borneo-Eilanden (the harbor's decline left the islands free for other uses) display housing less indebted to modernist dogma and more to vernacular and Amsterdam School sources, although Nieuwe Bouwen is not forgotten (towers and slabs by Wiel Arets [1955–], J. Coenen [1949–], and Sjoerd Soeters [1947–], among others, 1988–96). Clusters of colorful and individualistic apartment blocks by firms such as Atelier Pro (who inclusively invited six foreign firms to provide facades for their housing development on the site of a former Army Barracks on the Alexanderkade, 1988–92) and Mecanoo (housing estate Haagseweg, 1988–92) reinvigorate the city and reinforce the identity of particular places. There has been a return to four- or five-story buildings organized according to the traditional Amsterdam entry system (Nova Zemblastraat by Girod and Groeneveld, 1977), each with its own distinctive details and massing, vigorously plastic with dramatic projections in plan and elevation. Wood and aluminum, as well as steel and stucco, often brightly painted, have joined brick, tile, and concrete as popular materials. Equally significant is the reconfiguration of older buildings—warehouses, arsenals, grain silos, customs houses, churches, and canal residences—for new purposes, again mostly residential; effectively active here is J. van Stigt (1934–). Amsterdam thus completed the century as it began: simultaneously socially responsible and architecturally on the cutting edge.

HELEN SEARING

See also **Amsterdam School; Art Nouveau (Jugendstil); Berlage, Hendrik Petrus (Netherlands); De Stijl; van Eyck, Aldo (Netherlands); Hertzberger, Herman (Netherlands)**

Further Reading

The bibliography in the Dutch language is huge but is specialized in terms of building types, time periods, and issues of urbanism and preservation; several items take the form of annotated guide books in Dutch and English. There is also a plethora of publications issued by the municipality, especially the Departments of Urban Planning (Stedebouw) and of Housing (Volkshuisvesting). Since 1986 ARCAM (Amsterdam Center for Architecture) has regularly commissioned a series of pocketbooks in English on various topics concerning the buildings of the city.

Amsterdam: Planning and Development, Amsterdam: Amsterdam Physical Planning Department, 1983

Bock, Manfred, Jet Collee, and Hester Coucke, *H.P. Berlage in Amsterdam*, edited by Martin Kloos, Amsterdam: Architectura and Natura, 1992

Forgeur, Brigitte, *Living in Amsterdam*, London: Thames and Hudson, 1992

Fraenkel, Francis Frederik, *Het Plan Amsterdam-Zuid van H. P. Berlage*, Alphen aan den Rijn, The Netherlands: Canaletto, 1976 (with English summary)

Gemeentelijke Dienst Volkshuisvesting, *Amsterdam/wonen, 1900–1975*, Amsterdam: Bureau Voorlichting Gemeente Amsterdam, 1975

Groenendijk, Paul, and Piet Vollaard, *Gids voor moderne architectuur in Nederland; Guide to Modern Architecture in the Netherlands* (bilingual English and Dutch edition), Rotterdam: Uitgeverij 010, 1986; 4th edition, 1992

Haagsma, Ids, and Hilde de Haan, Anna de Haas, H. J. Schoo, *Amsterdamse Gebouwen, 1880–1980*, Utrecht: Spectrum, 1981

Het Nieuwe Bouwen, Amsterdam, 1920–1960 (exhib. cat.), Delft: Delft University Press, and Amsterdam: Stedilijk Museum, 1983

Huisman, Jaap, Michel Clans, Jan Derwig, and Ger van der Vlugt, *100 jaar bouwkunst in Amsterdam*, Amsterdam: Architectura en Natura, 1999

Kemme, Guus (editor), *Amsterdam Architecture: A Guide*, Amsterdam: Thoth, 1987; 4th edition, 1996

Kloos, Maarten (editor), *Amsterdam Architecture, 1991–93*, Amsterdam: Architectura en Natura, 1994

Kloos, Maarten (editor), *Amsterdam's High-Rise: Considerations, Problems, and Realizations*, Amsterdam: Architectura en Natura, 1995

Kloos, Maarten (editor), *Amsterdam Architecture, 1994–96*, Amsterdam: Architectura en Natura, 1997

Kloos, Maarten, and Marhes Buurman (editors), *Amsterdam Architecture 1997–1999*, Amsterdam: Architectura en Natura, 2000

Koster, Egbert, *Oostelijk Havengebied Amsterdam; Eastern Docklands*, Amsterdam: Architectura en Natura, 1995

Paulen, Françoise (editor), *Sociale woningbouw Amsterdam atlas; The Amsterdam Social Housing Atlas* (bilingual Dutch-English edition), Amsterdam: Amstaerdamse Feratie van Woningcorporaties, 1992

Roy van Zuydewijn, H.J.F. de, *Amsterdamse bouwkunst, 1815–1940*, Amsterdam: De Bussy, 1969

Searing, Helen, "Architecture and the Public Works in Metropolitan Amsterdam," *Modulus* 17 (1984)

Searing, Helen, "Betondorp: Amsterdam's Concrete Garden Suburb," *Assemblage* 3 (July 1987)

Stieber, Nancy, *Housing Design and Society in Amsterdam: Reconfiguring Urban Order and Identity, 1900–1920*, Chicago: University of Chicago Press, 1998

AMSTERDAM SCHOOL

The Amsterdam School was comprised of Dutch architects active between 1910 and 1930 whose work was associated with Expressionism and promulgated by the publication *Wendingen*. During World War I and for a decade thereafter, the striking and controversial work of the Amsterdam School transformed entire portions of its eponymous city and influenced architecture throughout the Netherlands. Although almost every building type was addressed, the major monuments are government-funded ensembles of workers' dwellings arranged in perimeter blocks that brought a new scale to Dutch cities. Paradoxically, although its members sought unique solutions for each commission, a readily identifiable group style emerged, and collaborations were frequent. Characterized by a luxurious fantasy and individualistic details, the work came under fire in the later 1920s from proponents of the functionalist *Nieuwe Bouwen*; subsequently, the Amsterdam School was written out of the literature. But in the 1970s, reevaluation commenced; many of the buildings have been restored and once again are a magnet for architects and urbanists.

The cradle of the Amsterdam School was the atelier of Eduard Cuypers (1859–1927). Working there at various times during the first decade were its future leader, Michel de Klerk (1884–1923) and such important representatives as Johann Melchior van der Mey (1878–1949) and Pieter Lodewjik Kramer (1881–1961). Other future acolytes in that office who absorbed Cuypers's credo that architecture was first and foremost an art that must transcend, while serving the pragmatic realities of program and resources, included G.F. LaCroix (1877–1923), Nicolaas Landsdorp (1885–1968), B.T. Boeyinga (1886–1969), Jan Boterenbrood (1886–1932), J.M. Luthmann (1890–1973), and Dick Greiner (1891–1964).

Cuyper's peculiar synthesis of Austrian and German Jugendstil (Art Nouveau), British Arts and Crafts, Belgian Art Nouveau, 17th-century Dutch architecture, and Indonesian art appears in more abstract guise in all of their work. Better known architects of Cuypers's generation such as Willem Kromhout (1864–1940) and K.P.C. de Bazel (1869–1923) also were admired exemplars but with the doyen of Dutch architecture, H.P. Berlage (1856–1934), they had a more complicated relationship. In his one published statement of 1916, de Klerk criticized Berlage's work for its excessive sobriety and lack of representational character in both materials and function. Yet they followed his use of geometric systems to proportion plans and elevations, and in the late teens and early 1920s, Berlage worked with members of the Amsterdam School and responded to their delight in piquant invention; his housing around the Mercatorplein (1925–27) indicates a mutual regard.

Although the Amsterdam School, unlike its rival, De Stijl, embraced no specific theoretical program, its members were united not only by stylistic practice and the conviction that architecture was first and foremost an inclusive art that should be aesthetically accessible to people of all classes, but also by training (many were autodidacts or studied in courses outside the main professional school at Delft). To understand the movement's rapid and widespread—if short-lived—influence, it is necessary to review several peculiarly Dutch institutions through which its "members" exercised power. The club Architectura et Amicitia (A et A), founded in 1855, during the teens and twenties was led by those sympathetic to the artistic ideals of the Amsterdam School, whose work was privileged in its publications, especially *Wendingen* (literally, "Turnings," but in the sense of departures or deviations), which under the partisan editorship of Hendricus Theodorus Wijdeveld (1885–1987) appeared monthly from 1918 to 1928. The club also held competitions and exhibitions that disseminated designs conforming to the group's aesthetic position; it was in a review of the display mounted by A et A in 1916 that the name *Amsterdamse School* first appeared in print.

Amsterdam's municipal organizations also played a role. The Department of Public Works was staffed by its adherents, as testified by the street furniture, bridges, public baths, schools, and offices for city agencies that were designed and executed between 1917 and 1930. The Social Democrats responsible for housing policy in Amsterdam were admirers, for they believed that the work of the Amsterdam School dignified the neighborhoods of the working- and lower-middle-class families for whom they were responsible. The Commission of Aesthetic Advice (*Schoonheidscommissie*), which passed judgment on exterior design, also was dominated by its advocates, much to the chagrin of architects of other stylistic persuasions, who often had to change their designs to conform to Amsterdam School conceptions.

Multicolored brick and tile, quintessentially Dutch materials, were employed for structure and cladding but used in unprecedented ways, in combination with concrete, stone, and powerful new mortars, to create unique configurations that pulsate with vitality. The dynamism of the modern metropolis inspired many of the formal strategies employed by the Amsterdam School, yet vernacular, historical, and even naturalistic references, as well as motifs from German and Scandinavian architecture and Frank Lloyd Wright, leavened the imagery. This was a narrative architecture that used massing and ornament iconographically, to contextualize each commission. Accusations of irrationalism and facadism were exaggerated; when commissions allowed, interior spaces were as ingenious as exterior envelopes and in each case expressed the realities of the program. After 1925 socioeconomic events curtailed the extravagant conceits of the Amsterdam School and led to a more repetitious and less imaginative vocabulary, but during its reign in the Netherlands it was responsible for such remarkable buildings as the Scheepvaarthuis, 1912–16 (by Van der Meij, Kramer, and de Klerk), and the housing estates Eigen Haard, 1914–18 (de Klerk) and De Dageraad, 1919–21 (de Klerk and Kramer), all in Amsterdam, plus the villas compromising Park Meerwijk, 1917, in Bergen (Kramer, La Croix, plus J.F Staal [1879–1940] and Margaret Staal-Kropholler [1891–1966], the Netherlands' first female architect), the Bijenkorf Department Store in The Hague, 1925–26, by Kramer, and the post office in Utrecht 1917–24, by Joseph Crouwel (1885–1962).

HELEN SEARING

See also **Amsterdam, Netherlands; Berlage, Hendrik Petrus (Netherlands); de Klerk, Michel (Netherlands); De Stijl; Expressionism; Netherlands**

Further Reading

Baeten, Jean Paul, *De onbekende Amsterdamse School – The Unknown Amsterdam School*, Rotterdam: NAi Publishers, 1994

Bock, Manfred (editor), *Michel de Klerk: Architect and Artist of the Amsterdam School*, Rotterdam: NAi, 1977

Casciato, Maristella, *The Amsterdam School*, Rotterdam: 010, 1996

Fanelli, Giovanni, and Ezio Godoli, *Wendingen 1918–1931: Documenti dell'arte olandese del Novecento*, Florence: Centro Di, 1982

Frank, Suzanne S., *Michel de Klerk (1884–1923): An Architect of the Amsterdam School*, Ann Arbor: UMI Research Press, 1984

Mattig, Eric, and Jan Derwig, *Amsterdam School*, Amsterdam: Architectura et Natura, 1991

Mieras, J.P., and Francis Yerbury, *Dutch Architecture of the Twentieth Century*, London: Ernest Benn, 1926

Destruction of Dreamland, Coney Island, Brooklyn, New York
© 1911 Charles E. Stacy, Brooklyn, NY/Library of Congress

Pehnt, Wolfgang, *Expressionist Architecture*, London: Thames and Hudson and New York: Praeger, 1973. Trans J. Underwood and Edith Kuestner. Originally in German, *Die Architektur des Expressionismus*, Stuttgart: Gerd Hatje, 1973
Searing, Helen, "Amsterdam South: Social Democracy's Elusive Housing Ideal," *VIA IV: Culture and the Social Vision*, (1980)
Searing, Helen, "Architecture and the Public Works in Metropolitan Amsterdam," *Modulus*, 17 (1984)

AMUSEMENT PARK

Amusement parks are controlled environments that entertain visitors through the simulation of space, place, and experience. It is the element of control that is initially most important in defining the building type because the amusement park presents itself as a safe, and indeed sanitized, environment wherein conventionally dangerous or arduous activities can be undertaken without fear of their consequences. The desire for control leads to the necessity of simulating or fictionalizing each and every space and event that the visitor to the park will experience. For this reason, amusement park designers often treat their buildings and settings simply as film sets, facades that are divorced from the function of their interiors and that are dismantled and changed at will. In the early years of the 20th century, this transience was exacerbated by the fact that a single designer was rarely responsible for more than one part of any park. In combination, these factors render the task of determining who has designed the park, and even its date of completion, difficult. This situation has changed in recent years, with many respected architects, including Michael Graves, Robert Stern, Antoine Predock, Frank Gehry, Robert Venturi, and Denise Scott Brown, accepting commissions for the design of amusement parks and associated facilities (hotels and training centers). Major 20th-century amusement parks include Disneyland (1955) in Anaheim, Florida; Six Flags over Texas (1961) near Fort Worth, Texas; Walt Disney World (1965) in Orlando, Florida; Universal Studios (1970–80) in Los Angeles, California; Tokyo Disneyland (1983) in Tokyo; and Fox Studios (1996–99) in Sydney.

One particular type of amusement park, the theme park, also rose to prominence in the last half of the 20th century. The theme park is characterized by a limited set of well-defined thematic boundaries. Typical theme parks include the Old West-flavored Knotts Berry Farm (1940, 1970) in Anaheim, California; the theologically focused Bible World (1975) in Orlando, Florida; the evolutionary-themed Darwin Centre (1995) in Edinburgh; and the piratical Mundomar (1996) by Estudio Nombela on Spain's Costa Blanca. Despite these differences, the terms "theme park" and "amusement park" are often used interchangeably to refer to any space that promotes enjoyment through simulation.

The origins of the amusement park are frequently traced to the 17th-century pleasure gardens of England and France. One of the most famous of these parks was Vauxhall Gardens in London, which first opened in 1661 and by 1728 contained mechanical rides, parachute jumps, and balloon ascensions. Perhaps the most popular of these early amusement parks was the Prater in Vienna, which became the site of the 1873 Vienna World's Fair and which featured both a primitive wooden Ferris wheel and one of the first large carousels. However, although amusement parks first came to prominence in Europe, it was in North America that they enjoyed their greatest success. One of the first large American amusement parks was Jones's Wood, which opened in New York in the early years of the 19th century. Jones's Wood comprised a loose collection of beer halls, music

houses, viewing platforms, dioramas, and shooting galleries. Rapid development of the surrounding areas forced Jones's Wood to close in the late 1860s just as a new era in amusement park design was beginning on nearby Coney Island.

In 1897 George Tilyou erected a walled enclosure around his Steeplechase ride on Coney Island. This act of enclosing the site and controlling entry to his rides is regarded as a defining moment in 20th-century amusement park design. Of similar significance is Tilyou's claim that if "Paris is France, Coney Island, between June and September, is the World" (McCullough, 1957, 291). With this statement, Tilyou set in motion the 20th-century amusement park obsession with spatial and cultural simulation. Tilyou believed that by constructing replicas of famous building types from different parts of the world, he could simulate the entire planet in such a way that it could be quickly, efficiently, and safely experienced by large numbers of paying customers. Such was the success of Steeplechase Park (1897) that two new Coney Island amusement parks, Luna Park (1903) and Dreamland (1904), soon followed. Luna Park simulated a trip to the moon, and Dreamland featured a number of attractions, including a partial reconstruction of Pompeii (complete with simulated eruptions on the hour) and a six-story building where customers could experience an office fire firsthand. Such was the success of this building type that by 1919 there were more than 1,500 amusement parks in North America, although the Depression saw this figure drop to barely 200 financially viable parks in the 1940s. It was not until the 1950s that Walt Disney revitalized the industry with his themed zones (Fantasyland, Adventureland, Frontierland, and Tomorrowland) and his focus on the traditional values of middle America. The success of Disneyland at Anaheim saw a string of similar Disney parks opened around the world, including EPCOT (1982) in Florida and the more controversial EuroDisney (1992) near Paris. This friction between the "real" and the "simulated" or "virtual" is evident in many recent amusement park designs. At one extreme, amusement parks are increasingly producing more complex and realistic electronic simulations. Virtual World (1981–92) in San Diego, California; Acurinto (1996) in Nagasaki; and SegaWorld (1996–98) in Sydney each feature extensive electronic, or video game, environments. In sharp contrast to this trend is the rise in amusement parks that promote ecotourism as a "real" experience. Mitsuru Man Senda's Asahikawa Shunkodai Park (1994) and his Urawa Living Museum (1995) in Urawa are examples of parks that advocate a "genuine" appreciation of the environment or history of the "real world." Ironically, in many respects each of these extremes is as artificial as the other. The only difference is that in one environment the simulation is glorified, whereas in the other it is repressed or hidden.

MICHAEL J. OSTWALD

See also **Disney Theme Parks; Gehry, Frank (United States); Graves, Michael (United States); Predock, Antoine (United States); Scott Brown, Denise (United States); Stern, Robert A.M. (United States); Venturi, Robert (United States)**

Further Reading

Asensio Cerver, Francisco, *Theme and Amusement Parks*, New York: Arco, 1997

Dunlop, Beth, *Building a Dream: The Art of Disney Architecture*, New York: Abrams, 1996

Koolhaas, Rem, *Delirious New York*, New York: Oxford University Press, and London: Thames and Hudson, 1978; 2nd edition, New York: Monacelli, 1994

Kyriazi, Gary, *The Great American Amusement Parks*, Secaucus, New Jersey: Citadel Press, 1976

Marling, Karal Ann (editor), *Designing Disney's Theme Parks: The Architecture of Reassurance*, Paris and Montreal: Flammarion, 1997

McCullough, E., *Good Old Coney Island*, New York: Charles Scribner's Sons, 1957

Sorkin, Michael (editor), *Variations on a Theme Park: The New American City and the End of Public Space*, New York: Hill and Wang, 1992

ANDO, TADAO 1941–

Architect, Japan

Tadao Ando, one of the most important contemporary Japanese architects, has pursued what he calls an architecture that moves people with its poetic and creative power. His numerous buildings yield intensely meaningful and didactic experiences. In so doing, Ando has engaged the discipline in the core philosophical questions on humanistic values, such as the end and purpose of creativity, or what architecture can contribute to improve the quality of human existence. To study his architecture is to examine how architecture can conceivably enhance the world as a humanistic discipline.

On the tangible level, Ando's works may be characterized by their primary walls, constructed out of limited materials and composed of purely geometric forms. Raw, unfinished reinforced concrete has been Ando's material of choice since his earliest years; later he added a shorter list of wooden buildings. These rather reductive methods, however, should never be taken to demonstrate a lack of intention, nor do they result in poor spatial qualities; instead, they are the consequence of Ando's willful determination to stage, though intangible they may be, rich architectural experiences. Ando's simple materials and forms engage a viewer in an appreciation of architecture, making the piece significant to that person. Ando is therefore in no respect a formalist—his interest in the tangible stems solely from his much deeper concern for their ontological relation to the intangible aspects of architecture.

Ando's decision to limit his materials and forms comes from the belief that their intrinsic natures heighten the viewer's experience of buildings, especially when they reveal their utmost state of existence. Therefore, Ando compares himself to the poet who chooses words carefully and gives them the most appropriate forms of expression. Ando is keenly interested in and highly knowledgeable about building materials. Once, in the early 1980s, Ando joined other sculptors, industrial designers, and architects in an exhibition, held in Tokyo, of objects made out of glass. Ando's entry, nothing but numerous sheets of glass laid horizontally on top of one another, brought to the viewer's attention the intrinsic nature of float glass. Produced by pouring liquid glass on a flat bed, ordinary float glass inevitably has minute irregularities on the upper-side surface. Compiling such sheets magnifies the irregularities, eventually causing them to shatter. Ando's project celebrated almost perfect sheets that withstood the challenge and quietly acknowledged the great care the manufacturer took in producing them.

It is also in building projects that Ando reveals the material's properties to the physical extreme with a high degree of care. The intention is to present the materials in their utmost essence. In fact, Ando believes that the more austere his wall, the more it speaks to mankind. Ando's specification of hard concrete mixture stirred up the Japanese building industry in 1970s, when both contractors and architects were used to the norm of much softer mixes for the sake of its easy distribution into the forms. The specification demanded Ando's attentive supervision, apt instruction, and even some on-site demonstration—he is said to have tapped the wooden panels incessantly while concrete was being poured. Once constructed, however, the walls were worthy of a critical gaze and required no finishing materials that would ordinarily hide the faults of construction.

Ando's efforts to provide an intense architectural experience rest not only with materials but also with building form and open space. As one becomes familiar with Ando's floor plans, one recognizes in them the persistent recurrence of pure geometry. However, once inside his building, a visitor is confronted with an enriched sequence of spatial experiences rather than a mere confirmation of simple forms. The ultimate goal is to draw attention to the space's architectural qualities. Ando once commented that an unexpected experience generates a stronger impression and elevates man's spirit. In such an experience, geometry is no longer an abstract factor but instead serves to generate the real human existence.

Ando's interests in the spatial sequence led him to explore the potential significance of vertical circulation. A staircase is, in the utilitarian sense, nothing but the means to traverse between different floor levels. With Ando, ascending and descending become almost a spiritual opportunity of preparation before entering a place of religion, as in the Water Temple (1991) on Awaji Island. Or, as in the Oyamazaki Villa Museum (1996) in Kyoto, ascension is an awakening experience of one's body while discovering the daylight reflected delicately on each step's rounded nose, which in turn draws attention to the cascading waterfall just outside, which shines similarly under the sun.

The simplicity and purity of form and materials also support what Ando has called the nature—in particular, light, air, and water—of his architecture. Ando once commented that architecture should not be loud but rather that it should let nature, in the guise of sunlight and wind, speak. His concrete wall captures on its surface an ever-changing pattern of light and shadow. In return, the austere surface of the wall is enlivened, made rich with character. When his concrete walls, taller than eye level, bound a space, as in the Vitra Seminar House (1993) in Weil-am-Rhein, Germany, the observer's attention is naturally drawn to the sky, both visually and spatially. When an opening is made in a wall at floor level, as in a number of residential buildings, the sight is directed specifically to the pebbled or grassed ground outside. A vertical sheet of water, as in the Forest of Tombs Museum (1992) in Kumamoto, or a serene horizontal surface of water, as in the Church on the Water (1998) in Hokkaido, could be waiting to fill the viewer's hearing or vision. In these settings, man is in an immediate confrontation with nature, with only Ando's architecture serving as a mediator.

Ando has acknowledged that the way he brings nature into architecture could require some severe living conditions. For example, in Row House Sumiyoshi (1976) in Osaka, the residents are faced with every element of weather each time they pass the courtyard on the way from one room to another. Ando's rather forceful mediation between man and nature is not always without criticism. Some critics have commented that it leads to a spatial impoverishment. On the contrary, however, Ando believes that a close confrontation with nature is crucial for the enrichment of man's life, which makes man keenly aware of the season and which nurtures within man a finer sensitivity. This insistence on austerity and severity reflects his critical stance against modern society's materialistic way of life. In this regard, Ando has taken a critical stance against the modern ways of living that may be materialistically rich and yet spiritually impoverished. He has made incessant inquiries as to what enriches an individual's life in the contemporary age. He considers it critical to discover through his architectural works what is essential to human life. Ando believes that abundance does not necessarily enrich one's life and instead thinks that an architectural space stripped of all excess and composed simply from bare necessities is true and convincing because it is appropriate and satisfying. In this understanding of the human conditions, Ando's architecture constitutes a challenge to contemporary civilization.

Just as Ando is suspicious of the materialistic view of life, he is equally doubtful about what many modern and contemporary architects have taken to be an unquestionable goal: timeliness of design. Rather, Ando's is a quest for the essence that allows architecture to endure the test of time. In the same regard, Ando is in a constant search for the kind of architectural heritages that have withstood various conditions of both time and place. Ando's attitude toward architectural heritage should, however, be distinguished from the Postmodern regionalism in which traditional forms are replicated by modern, universally available industrial materials and technology, to which Ando is not at all sympathetic. A pseudo-authentic application is for him not a pursuit of the material's intrinsic potential and therefore not essentially architectural.

Ando's desire to scrutinize the time-earned architectural heritage and to appropriate it in his projects makes his practice critically cross-cultural. On the one hand, Ando is not hesitant to draw both from his native Japanese and from other, especially Western, traditions. On the other hand, his reference to the heritage is always based on the critical and creative appropriation that often brings the heritage one step beyond its traditional boundaries. For example, it is not at all difficult to discern a Vitruvian ideal with four equilateral triangles in his temporary theater, Kara-za in Tokyo (1988). Ando chose the dodecagon because of a certain order and perfection that the human mind tends to find in the number 12. This also referred to the 12-year cycle of the Eastern calendar and the 12 months of the Western year. Then Vitruvius's recommendation is, for Ando, not restricted to the West but rather is cross-culturally human. For Ando, the dodecagon is the most appropriate form to give to the project in which theatrical events represent a construction of a temporary microcosm.

With Ando's Church of the Light (1989), a cross becomes more than a Christian symbol. Instead, a vertical and horizontal linear opening in the otherwise solid concrete wall is a void at the end of the space. It embodies the sense of time and space beyond reach, so appropriate for religious contemplation. It encourages a respect for the past, a commitment to the future, and a trust in the universal applicability and effectiveness of one's

Modern Art Museum, Fort Worth, Texas, designed by Tadao Ando (2002)
© Mary Ann Sullivan

particular religious activity, which in turn is limited by its place and time.

Ando has an extraordinary background as an architect. He did not receive any formal architectural education, nor did he apprentice in an office. As for career preparation, Ando often refers to the study tours he made on his own and the books he read, including Le Corbusier's oeuvre, during the period between 1962 and 1969, before he opened his architectural office in Osaka. This specific location was also somewhat out of ordinary, for many well-known, well-established architects are in Tokyo, by far Japan's largest center of economic activity. Because of this and because of the strong regional accent in his Japanese, Ando had often compared himself to a stray warrier, half mockingly and half proudly. His is the proof that still, in the economically driven contemporary societies, architecture can provide a spiritual and even sacred dimension of the human existence.

Although his early practice was limited primarily to residences and small commercial building in the nearby regions of his office, Ando gradually gained domestic and international acclaim and extended his practice to cultural and religious institutions. Ando has received virtually every award there is for an architect, including the Annual Prize from the Architectural Institute of Japan (1979), the Alvar Aalto Medal from the Finnish Association of Architects (1985), the Gold Medal of Architecture from the French Academy of Architecture (1989), the Arnold W. Brunner Memorial Prize from the American Academy and Institute of Arts and Letters (1991), the Carlsberg Architectural Prize of Denmark (1992), the Asahi Prize (1995), the 18th Pritzker Architecture Prize (1995), the eighth Premium Imperiale (1996), and the Royal Gold Medal from the Royal Institute of British Architects (1997). His vigorous influence is manifest in the range of exhibitions of his work, including the Museum of Modern Art, New York (1991); the Centre Georges Pompidou, Paris (1993); the Royal Institute of British Architects, London (1993); the Basilica Palladiana, Vicenza (1995); the Sixth Venice Biennale (1996); the National Museum of Contemporary Art, Seoul (1998); and the Royal Academy of Arts, London (1998). His winning competition entries include the Modern Art Museum of Fort Worth, Texas (1997); the Hyogo Prefectural Museum of Modern Art (1997); and the Manchester City Centre Piccadilly Gardens Regeneration (1999).

RUMIKO HANDA

See also **Church on the Water, Hokkaido, Japan; Modernism; Postmodernism**

Biography

Born in Osaka, Japan, 13 September 1941. Self-taught in architecture, traveled in the United States, Europe, and Africa 1962–

69. Married Yumiko Kato 1970. Founder and director, Tadao Ando Architect and Associates, Osaka from 1969. Visiting professor, Yale University, New Haven, Connecticut 1987; visiting professor, Columbia University, New York 1988; visiting professor, Harvard University, Cambridge, Massachusetts 1990; visiting professor, University of Tokyo 1997. Honorary Fellow, American Institute of Architects 1991. Alvar Aalto Medal, Finnish Association of Architects, 1985; Gold Medal, French Academy of Architecture 1989; Carlsberg Architectural Prize of Denmark 1992; Pritzker Prize 1995; Royal Gold Medal, Royal Institute of British Architect 1997.

Selected Works

Row House Sumiyoshi, Osaka, 1976
Water Temple, on Awaji Island, 1991
Forest of Tombs Museum, Kumamoto, 1992
Vitra Seminar House, Weil-am-Rhein, Germany, 1993
Oyamazaki Villa Museum, Kyoto, 1996
Hyogo Prefectural Museum of Modern Art (first prize, competition), 1997
Church on the Water, Hokkaido, 1998
Manchester City Centre Piccadilly Gardens Regeneration (first prize, competition), 1999
Modern Art Museum of Fort Worth (first prize, competition), Texas, 2002

Further Reading

Ando, Tadao, and Richard Pare, *The Colours of Light*, London: Phaidon, 1996
Ando, Tadao, George T. Kunihiro, and Peter Eisenman, *Tadao Ando: The Yale Studio and Current Works*, New York: Rizzoli, 1989
Dal Co, Francesco (editor), *Tadao Ando: Complete Works*, London: Phaidon, 1995
Documenti di architettura Tadao Ando, Milan: Electa, 1994
Futagawa, Yukio (editor), *Tadao Ando*, Tokyo: A.D.A. Edita, 1987
Futagawa, Yukio (editor), *Tadao Ando: Details*, Tokyo: A.D.A. Edita, 1991
Futagawa, Yukio (editor), *Tadao Ando: Vol. 2, 1988–1993*, Tokyo: A.D.A. Edita, 1993
Futagawa, Yukio (editor), *Tadao Ando: Details 2*, Tokyo: A.D.A. Edita, 1997
Jodidio, Philip, *Tadao Ando*, Cologne and New York: Taschen, 1997
Kawamukai, Masato, Tadao Ando, and Mirko Zardini, *Tadao Ando*, London: Academy Editions, and New York: St. Martin's Press, 1990

APARTMENT BUILDING

Population growth and the increasing density of cities created a housing crisis in the 20th century. The apartment building emerged as a solution for housing large numbers of people in small areas. Although a preexisting type, during the 20th century the development of the apartment building dramatically reshaped the built environment of cities and their surrounding suburbs. Apartment buildings developed in locations convenient to transportation networks and services that encouraged dense residential land use. The increase in apartment living subsequently inspired continued international dissemination of the modern apartment building type.

An apartment building contains multiple dwelling units of one or more rooms. Other basic aspects of the 20th-century apartment building's program are a bathroom and kitchen for each unit and the provision of heating, ventilation, air conditioning, and other systems. As with other commercial building types, efficient use of space is integral to good apartment building design. Public areas of the apartment building are normally minimal, with a small lobby and laundry room or, in more luxurious examples, a roof deck, recreation room, or swimming pool. All apartment buildings share the basic function of providing shelter for numerous household groups, but the features and appointments of a building can vary greatly, depending on the socioeconomic level of the intended residents. Apartment buildings need to balance efficiency with comfort; this requirement is challenging, especially when building for low-income tenants.

In the early 20th century, most architecturally notable apartment buildings were intended for upper-class tenants. Living in a full-service apartment building could provide a luxurious home at much smaller cost than maintaining a single-family house. Rising land values in many cities made sole ownership prohibitively expensive even for the relatively well off. Use of Classical Revival and Italian Renaissance Revival decorative modes was prevalent, as evidenced by the lavish examples built in cities such as New York, Chicago, Los Angeles, London, Paris, and Vienna. The dominance of historical styles in apartment building design indicated the fashionable design mode for most commercial and domestic structures during the early part of the century.

For low- and middle-income tenants, apartment building design was characterized by tension between aesthetics and economic viability. Tenement house design frequently sacrificed aesthetic and sanitary concerns to create a profitable investment. By the 1920s, apartment buildings were integral to the international debate over housing and social reform. European avant-garde architects used the apartment building type to explore the potential of modernism and prefabricated structural systems for providing affordable worker housing. Government sponsorship of housing projects provided important opportunities for architectural experimentation not available in the commercial real estate market of the United States despite housing reform efforts. The housing policy of the Weimar Republic generated pioneering modern apartment buildings for German cities, such as Breslau, Hamburg, Celle, Berlin, and Frankfurt. Another example is J.J.P. Oud's Kiefhoek housing (1925), an International Style garden apartment complex built in Rotterdam. Both the garden apartment and the high-rise form of the apartment building were explored by architects throughout the mid-20th century. A key high-rise example in London is Highpoint I (1933–35), designed by Berthold Lubetkin and Tecton.

These two primary apartment building forms—the mainly urban high-rise and the suburban garden apartment—became internationally prevalent by the 1930s. High-rise apartment buildings, alone and later in planned groups, capitalized on an economy of scale. They distributed the rising cost of elevators, ventilation, and other systems-related apparatus by using modern building materials to create taller structures with more living units. Garden apartments were suitable for lower-density development on the urban periphery, where land was less expensive. Groups of two- or three-story buildings arranged on landscaped sites contained units that shared an entrance stairwell. The garden apartment form did not require formal public areas or expensive elevators but was not as efficient in land use or building materials as a more compact high-rise apartment building.

A housing estate being completed in Southwark, London, in 1959 (architect unknown)

In the post–World War II period, the housing crisis became more acute owing to years of postponed building and wartime destruction. European governments again sponsored the construction of major apartment housing projects. In the United States, the new Federal Housing Administration and later the Department of Housing and Urban Development began to fulfill a role similar to that of their European counterparts, although more limited in scope. International Style modernism, particularly the slab-form high-rise developed by Le Corbusier, dominated these construction efforts.

The key postwar example is Le Corbusier's Unité d'Habitation (1947–53) at Marseilles, France. Unite d'Habitation is a 12-story horizontal slab raised on heavy tapered *pilotis*. A roof deck and an interior commercial "street" seek to create a unified community, but this quality of self-containment also separates the building from its neighborhood context. Other large apartment buildings based on this model experience mixed results when applied in other contexts. Noteworthy examples of apartment buildings done in a postwar modernist vocabulary include ATBAT housing (1951–56, Shadrach Woods and J. Bodiansky) in Morocco and Peabody Terraces (1964, José Luis Sert) in Cambridge, Massachusetts.

During the postwar period, large-scale developments, including multiple high-rise apartment buildings, site planning, and amenities such as shopping and recreational facilities, became more prevalent. In the United States, federal urban-renewal funding cleared sizable portions of blighted urban neighborhoods to be replaced by large public housing projects. These projects reflected the modernist vision of social reform through environmental determinism. Commercial interests built more luxurious and well-maintained versions of these high-rises for middle-class and wealthier tenants. These projects could be successful when integrated into existing community services, but they failed miserably when they isolated poor residents from economically stable parts of the urban landscape.

Apartment buildings have been a source of controversy over zoning and land use in the United States. As a multi-dwelling structure, the apartment building threatens the American ideal of the single-family house. However, economic reality, even in the United States and the prosperous nations of Europe, is that apartments fulfill an important need. The apartment building has transformed the urban and suburban landscape of the 20th-century city and by extension the lived experience of many residents.

LISA DAVIDSON

See also **Corbusier, Le (Jeanneret, Charles-Éduoard) (France); Eigen Haard Housing Estate, Amsterdam; Oud, J.J.P. (Netherlands); Public Housing; Unite d'Habitation, Marseilles/Cité Radieuse**

Further Reading

The most current architectural histories of the apartment building type focus on specific cities. Sociological literature provides additional information on housing issues connected with the apartment building.

Abel, Joseph Henry, "The Apartment House," in *Forms and Functions of Twentieth-Century Architecture*, by Talbot Hamlin, volume 3, New York: Columbia University Press, 1952

Cerver, Francisco Asensio, *The Architecture of Multiresidential Buildings*, New York: Arco, 1997

Cromley, Elizabeth Collins, *Alone Together: A History of New York's Early Apartments*, Ithaca, New York: Cornell University Press, 1990

Goode, James M., *Best Addresses: A Century of Washington's Distinguished Apartment Houses*, Washington, D.C.: Smithsonian Institution Press, 1988

Paul, Samuel, *Apartments: Their Design and Development*, New York: Reinhold, 1967

ARCHIGRAM

Architecture firm, England

Archigram is both a group of British architects and their architectural periodical, which gave the group its name. Between 1960 and 1972, Archigram published nine issues of the periodical, staged exhibitions and conferences, and devised a number of influential architectural projects. Founded by Peter Cook (1936–), the group consisted of Cook, David Greene (1937–), Mike Webb (1937–), Warren Chalk (1927–88), Dennis Crompton (1935–), and Ron Herron (1930–94). Their avant-garde architecture rejected heroic modernism in favor of expendable, variable, and often mobile combinations of component units plugged into superstructures. Although Archigram gained worldwide recognition, their utopian project owed much to the intense architectural debate fermented by the massive rebuilding projects of postwar Britain. The group drew on eclectic sources, including R. Buckminster Fuller, the Independent Group, Reyner Banham, comic books, science fiction, consumer imagery, and contemporary technology, such as the *Telstar* satellite, the U.S. National Aeronautics and Space Administration's mobile launch towers, and the more modest Airstream trailer.

In late 1960, Cook, Greene, and Webb began meeting in an effort to perpetuate the vibrant intellectual climate that they had experienced at architecture school. Their publication both augmented their activities, providing a forum for ideas as well as a publication venue for student work, and gave the group its name. *Archigram* not only suggested the immediacy of a telegram or an aerogram (i.e. "archi[tecture]-gram") and the urgency of their ideas but also described the broadsheet format of the fledgling publication. The first issue, published in 1961, featured both Greene's poetry and a collage composed of provocative statements that wound around and through images of architectural projects, a metaphor for the group's desire to break down traditional barriers between form and statement. The document proclaimed their response to postwar British architecture: "we have chosen to by pass the decaying Bauhaus image/which is an insult to functionalism" in favor of organic forms that "flow," signaling their enduring interest in the inventive use of architecture to foster communication.

By 1963 the group had coalesced. That year they produced both *Archigram 3* and the *Living City* exhibition, staged at the Institute of Contemporary Arts (London). *Archigram 3* celebrated expendability, claiming that the change in "user-habits" occasioned by expendable items such as food packaging should prompt a comparable change in "user-habitats," an argument for "throwaway architecture" that would mirror the consumerist lifestyle of the late 20th century. Inspired by William H. Whyte and Jane Jacobs, *Living City* examined the urban matrix of which architecture was but one component. The group claimed that "when it is raining in Oxford Street, the architecture is no more important than the rain, in fact the weather has probably more to do with the pulsation of the living city at a moment in time" (*Living Arts* 2 [June 1963]). The installation comprised seven "Gloops," spaces that defined constituent elements of the living city, such as Communications, Crowd, and Movement. This "city stimulator," a Postmodern pastiche inspired by the Independent Group's *This Is Tomorrow* exhibition, installed at the Whitechapel Art Gallery (London) in 1956, urged the spectator toward an awareness of the vitality and the value of city life. Both *Archigram 3* and *Living City* consolidated the group's conviction that modernist architecture mistakenly prioritized heroic permanent structures over the user's changing needs, thereby failing to respond to contemporary developments, such as technology, the consumer economy, and modern communications.

With *Archigram 4* (1964), the group embarked on a series of celebrated projects that revolved around the notion of individual capsules that clipped onto or plugged into a structural framework. These capsules were mobile, expendable, and responsive to human desires, thereby embodying Archigram's central concerns. Cook's Entertainments Tower (1963), an entertainment center proposed for the Montreal Exposition (1967), consisted of a concrete tower on which hung facilities (such as an auditorium) that could be removed or replaced after the exposition. Similarly, his Plug-In City, a series of ideas developed between 1962 and 1966, proposed expendable capsules plugged into the network structure by means of integrated cranes. In 1964 Herron proposed Walking City, mobile megastructures that walked across both sea and land on robotic, spiderlike legs. Subsequent projects deployed these ideas on a smaller and perhaps more attainable scale. Webb proposed the Cushicle (1966–67), a personalized enclosure that enabled a human to carry a complete environment in a backpack that inflated when needed, and the Suitaloon (1968), a space suit that inflated to serve as a minimal house. These projects enabled the consumer to construct a personalized environment, free of the strictures of modernist architecture.

Archigram 4 not only initiated a series of celebrated projects but also brought the group worldwide attention. Pages were widely reproduced in magazines, providing the model for other anti-architecture groups, such as the Italian Archizoom group, and group members were invited to lecture worldwide. In 1966 they organized the International Dialogues on Experimental Architecture (IDEA), an exhibition and conference in Folkestone, Kent, England, which attracted notable speakers. In 1967 the *Weekend Telegraph* commissioned Archigram to design a house for the year 1990 and received a structure that could be adjusted to accommodate various daily activities, which was exhibited at Harrods in London. Archigram was invited to exhibit at both the 1968 Milan Triennale and Expo '70 in Osaka, Japan. In

1970 the group was invited by the Ministre d'Etat of Monaco to participate in a limited competition for a seaside entertainment center in Monte Carlo. True to the group's anti-heroic stance, their winning project was an underground structure that preserved the view of the sea. Because of the difficult economic climate of the 1970s, the Monte Carlo project was never built.

Archigram's significant collective activities ended in 1972, although its members remained active as designers, teachers, and archivists of their own history. Archigram remained influential: a sequence of exhibitions and publications has celebrated their work, and their anti-architecture stance figures in any history of 20th-century architecture. Their legacy proves difficult to quantify not only because the members contributed to a diffuse international discourse about architecture but also because their projects seem to presage innumerable contemporary trends, including both high-tech and sustainable approaches to design. More concrete influence can be seen in the work of Richard Rogers, Norman Foster, and Renzo Piano and Richard Rogers's Pompidou Centre (1976) in Paris. Archigram's medium has proven as powerful as its message. Its members' combination of intricate draftsmanship and collaged elements—including comic books, advertising imagery, and Day-Glo colors—produced a vivid visual record that typifies the decade of pop art, Marshall McLuhan, the Beatles' *Yellow Submarine*, and Rowan and Martin's *Laugh-In*. Similarly, both their anti-authoritarian stance and their focus on the individual reflect the social concerns of the 1960s. Nostalgia for the decade, as well as the continuing aptness of Archigram's inventive architecture, continues to spur interest in the group, as evidenced by the 1998–99 retrospective exhibition *Archigram: Experimental Architecture, 1961–1974*.

KRISTIN FEDDERS

See also **Banham, Reyner (United States); Bauhaus; Corbusier, Le (Jeanneret, Charles-Édouard) (France); Foster, Norman (Great Britain); Piano, Renzo (Italy); Pompidou Center, Paris; Rogers, Richard (Great Britain)**

Further Reading

Although *Archigram* was published in limited editions and circulated primarily through the international architectural community, both the group and its members have written extensively for mainstream publications. Moreover, since 1972, Archigram has produced three volumes that reprint pages and projects from *Archigram*, as well as additional projects, commentary, and bibliography.

Cook, Peter, et al. (editors), *Archigram*, London: Studio Vista, 1972; New York: Praeger, 1973; revised edition, New York: Princeton Architectural Press, 1999

Crompton, Dennis, et al., *A Guide to Archigram, 1961–74; Ein Archigram-Program, 1961–74* (bilingual English-German edition), London: Academy Editions, and Berlin: Ernst, 1994

Crompton, Dennis (editor), *Concerning Archigram*, London: Archigram Archives, 1998

ARCHITECTURAL DRAWING

In the 20th century and throughout the history of the discipline, drawing has been the dominant means of architectural communication and is considered to be the "language" of architecture. Through drawings, an architect can record new ideas, concepts, and even visionary projects in addition to projects intended for construction. To facilitate this communication, a number of drawing conventions have evolved.

Orthographic Projections

The most commonly used projective drawing in 20th-century architectural practice is the orthographic projection. The primary orthographic projections are plan, section, and elevation views in which the observer's line of sight is perpendicular to both the drawing plane and the surfaces of the building viewed and in which the drawing surface is parallel to the principal surfaces of the building. The floor plan and building section are both sections, or cuts. The floor plan, a sectional view looking down after a horizontal plane, cut through the building with the top section removed, typically shows the location of major vertical elements and all door and window openings. Building sections are transverse or cross sections or longitudinal. A transverse section is created by cutting at right angles to the long axis, and conversely, a longitudinal section is an orthographic projection made by cutting at right angles to the shorter axis. Elevations are drawings of the exterior of a building and are labeled north, south, east, or west for the direction from which you see it (which is also the direction it faces). As no single orthographic projection can communicate all aspects of a three-dimensional object, the drawings must be considered as a series of related views. The advantage of an orthographic projection is that the faces of an object parallel to the drawing surface are represented without distortion or foreshortening, retaining their true size to scale, their shape, and their proportion.

Pictorial Projections

This type of drawing shows the three dimensions of a building simultaneously. They are generally divided into parallel and perspective drawings. The most common parallel drawings are oblique and isometric. Oblique projections can be further subdivided into plan and elevation oblique projections. The plan oblique, or axonometric, is the most popular of the parallel (or paraline) drawings. A scale drawing of the plan is tilted at either a 45-degree angle giving equal views of two perpendicular planes or a 30/60-degree angle giving emphasis to one plane over the other. All lines parallel to the three main axes are drawn to scale.

Perspective drawings employ various techniques for representing three-dimensional objects on a two-dimensional surface in a more realistic manner than paraline drawings. All points of the object are projected to a picture plane by straight lines converging at an arbitrary fixed point. In a one-point perspective, a principal face of the object is parallel to the picture plane. Vertical lines remain vertical, horizontal lines remain horizontal, and lines perpendicular to the picture plane converge on a vanishing point. In two-point perspective, vertical lines remain vertical and both sets of horizontal lines converge on their own vanishing points.

At different points in the 20th century, preferences for various drawing types and rendering techniques have been inextricably linked with artistic movements. The birth of the Modern Movement early in the century and the influence of Cubism resulted in the rejection of architectural perspective drawing in favor of the more analytical and objective axonometric plan projections, which were considered more appropriate for an architecture cubic in nature and devoid of ornamentation. In fact, several movements in the first half of the century were known primarily through the production and circulation of architectural drawings and not as a result of built works. The break with tradition that characterized Modernism was also evident in the graphic representation of the movement.

One of the early 20th-century movements that was expressed primarily through drawings was Futurism. The theoretical focus of Futurism, the Italian architectural movement founded in 1909 by Filippo Tommaso Marinetti (1876–1944), was made manifest through graphic representations of industrial buildings, skyscrapers, and utopian visions of the city of the future. These images glorified technology, machines, speed, dynamism, and movement. The fact that drawings of futuristic cities by architects such as Antonio Sant'Elia (1888–1916) do not include plans underscores the notion that they were never intended for construction.

Architects of the De Stijl movement (1917–28) relied heavily on the use of axonometric projections to illustrate the development of spaces. The antihistorical movement advocated a clarity of expression through the use of straight lines, decomposed cubes, pure planes, right angles, and primary colors. These qualities were effectively represented in the orthographic projections, which were repeatedly published and exhibited.

Similarly, Russian avant-garde architecture of the revolutionary era (1917–34) is known principally through drawings of work that, in many cases, was neither structurally viable nor ever intended for construction. The new relationship between architecture and the plastic arts that was central to De Stijl was also prevalent in the Russian architectural drawings. The formal language of the architecture followed explorations in the fine arts. Visionary drawings by Iakov Chernikov (1889–1951) celebrated technology and demonstrated the possibilities of constructivist design to contemporary and subsequent generations of architects.

The Expressionist movement, affected by unstable conditions in Germany after the First World War, is characterized by drawings that emphasize force and massiveness. Buildings were conceived in terms of volume, and drawings by Erich Mendelsohn (1887–1953) and others were devoid of the detail found in earlier architectural representation.

In 1975 an exhibition at the Museum of Modern Art in New York of drawings from the archives of the École des Beaux-Arts exposed a new generation of architects and designers to the meticulous watercolor renderings that had been supplanted earlier in the century by axonometric projections. The contemporary Postmodern once again used historical forms as a source of design inspiration and the movement was characterized by a resurgence in the Beaux- Arts style of rendering and the architectural drawing, as *objet d'art*, became important in its own right removed from the context of built work.

With the advent of Deconstruction late in the 20th century, the language of technology was concerned with breaking, splintering, diagonal overlapping, and superimposition of elements, and again, as in previous periods, these formal aspects of the architecture were reflected in the drawings of architects such as Bernard Tschumi (1944–).

Undoubtedly, the method of graphic representation that will have the greatest influence on the future generation of architects is that involving the use of the computer. Computer-aided design, three-dimensional modeling, and programs allowing a client to "walk through" a space that does not yet exist in reality are revolutionizing the way in which architects conceive of and represent space. Computers have transformed the design process into one of continuous and nearly limitless experimentation.

LINDA HART

Further Reading

Ching, Francis, *Architectural Drawing*, New York: Van Nostrand Reinhold, 1985

Fraser, Iain, and Rod Henmi, *Envisioning Architecture: An Analysis of Drawing*, New York: Van Nostrand Reinhold, 1994

Gebhard, David, and Deborah Nevins, *100 Years of American Architectural Drawing*, New York: Whitney Library of Design, 1977

Nevins, Deborah, and Robert Stern, *The Architect's Eye: American Architectural Drawings from 1799–1978*, New York: Pantheon Press, 1979

Powell, Helen, and David Leatherbarrow (editors), *Masterpieces of Architectural Drawing*, New York: Abbeville Press, 1982

Robbins, Edward, *Why Architects Draw*, Cambridge, Massachusetts: MIT Press, 1997

Stamp, Gavin, *The Great Perspectivists, RIBA Drawing Series*, London: Trefoil Books, 1982

ARCHITECTURAL PHOTOGRAPHY

At the turn of the 20th century, architectural photography was just emerging as a subfield of photography and ever since has affected the practice of architecture and its representation. Governments and organizations made accurate photographic records of historic buildings, whereas architects found the photograph to be the perfect medium for sharing their exotic travels with colleagues. Today architectural photography is its own industry, an inseparable part of the architectural profession and the primary vehicle through which the public receives information about the built world.

The century began with a type of architectural photography very different from the precision-obsessed documentary style of the 1870s and 1880s. These new photographs gave viewers much less detail about the architecture, instead preferring to elicit an emotive response about the atmosphere of a place. The work of the "Photo-Secession," a group led by Alfred Stieglitz (1864–1946), characterizes this approach.

As a result of this expanding definition of photography, new equipment, such as lighter, faster lenses and smaller, handheld cameras, started to appear. Travel photographs by Le Corbusier illustrate the spontaneous aesthetic of easier-to-use equipment. Similarly, the snapshots by architect Erich Mendelsohn and others, compiled in a publication titled *Amerika* (1925, rev. 1928), were taken from nontraditional angles, featured people, and considered a wide range of vernacular subjects in an attempt to describe the architect's physical and conceptual impressions of the United States.

It was in the late 1930s that the history of architectural photography made a dramatic shift. Until this time, although many photographers excelled at making images of architecture, no one had yet dedicated their entire career to this task. Like Margaret Bourke-White (1904–71), whose powerful 1936 photograph titled "Fort Peck Dam, Montana" appeared on the first cover of *Life* magazine, some photographers worked as journalists for a variety of publications. Others, such as Berenice Abbott (1898–1991), who spent years photographing New York for the Federal Art Project, eventually moved on to other subjects. Toward the end of the decade, however, there appeared professional architectural photographers whose only business was to make photographs of buildings, primarily for use in publications and by architects as marketing tools.

Magazines and journals produced internationally in major cities were quick to include architectural photographs with their articles. These mass-produced images circulated widely in magazines such as *Architectural Record* and *Architectural Review*, to name only two, and kept clients and the profession informed of new trends, emerging architects, award-winning designs, and buildings that were important at local, regional, national, and international levels. With the emergence of architectural history as an academic discipline in the 19th and 20th centuries, the important history texts illustrated the canonic works of architecture with photographs that in some cases would become iconic representations of famous buildings.

It is not coincidental that the International Style gained popularity and influence at the same time that a few talented photographers started to specialize in architectural images. Among the many factors that contributed to this, two are particularly noteworthy. The first is that, generally speaking, the representation of modern architecture was inherently well suited to the formal language of modernism. Photography seemed well suited to showing either layered planes or the subtle lights and darks of curved surfaces. Because color had not yet become the standard, black-and-white photography's emphasis on tone and depth worked well with modern architecture's use of translucent materials and interest in space. Moreover, photography's ability to isolate a single viewpoint provided endless possibilities for abstract compositions. Some historians argue that the widespread acceptance of black-and-white photography in the early days of the International Style encouraged and perpetuated the movement's monochromatic aesthetic. Photography surely served to distribute the movement's imagery and ideals to an international audience.

A second factor appearing simultaneously with modernism and professional architectural photography was the rising status of commercialism in society. Editors and advertisers hungered for images of modern life, giving rise, particularly after World War II, to an immense market for architectural photographs that could be serviced only by a new group of specialized photographers. In the United States, this was particularly true of photographs of the "American dream home," which were in high demand and resembled fashion photographs in style and attitude. The potential for images to become marketing tools for architecture as a whole was recognized by Walter Gropius, Frank Lloyd Wright, and others, who immediately used architectural photography to promote their ideas.

Several figures of the architectural photography community emerged in the late 1930s and early 1940s, including Ezra Stoller (1915–) and Julius Shulman (1910). The first well-known architectural photography firm, Hedrich-Blessing, also came about during this period. Begun in Chicago by Ken Hedrich (1908–72), Hedrich-Blessing has been known for dramatic composition, a high level of craftsmanship, and an understanding of architects' need for marketable images.

The introduction of color photography in the 1960s and 1970s presented challenges and opportunities that earlier photographers had not encountered. In addition to an image's formal composition and the craftsmanship of the final product, photographers now had to consider the color of every element that fell within the photograph's boundaries. This was made more complicated by the nature of color film, which is slower than black-and-white film and sensitive to differences between daylight, incandescent, and other types of light. Despite the technical difficulties, color photography became very popular among architects and publications because it provided a new, important layer of information. Two photographs by Richard Bryant (1947–) illustrate how color photography has been used effectively. In his 1983 photograph of the Camden Town TV-am Building, the slower film speed records an object emitting light passing across the bottom-left corner of the frame as a zigzag line of light that becomes the photograph's only suggestion of life or movement. More recent photographers, such as Norman McGrath (1931–), Tim Street-Porter (1939–), Timothy Hursley (1955–), Cervin Robinson (1928–), and Yukio Futagawa (1932–), have spent much of their careers in the age of color photography.

Today, architectural photography, particularly in color, has also become the dominant mode of architectural representation in publications. This is because it is perceived as more accurate and immediate than sketches or renderings. However, with the increasing number of photographers and the rising importance of the photograph to the business of architecture, the inability of photography to represent reality has become a significant issue. Most agree that architecture is unique among the arts because it uses the passage of time and all the audience's senses in combination to create an unreproducible, three-dimensional experience. Photography, on the other hand, isolates a single moment and view in two dimensions, often giving the viewer an inaccurate idea of how a building looks or what it is like inside. Still, photographers have been able to create many well-known and highly published photographs by making educated decisions about distortions and working closely with architects and publishers to create photographs by understanding the medium's limitations and creatively using its distortions to communicate ideas about buildings.

SARAH M. DRELLER

Further Reading

Given photography's importance to the architectural profession, surprisingly little has been written on its history. The only survey of the entire history of architectural photography is Robinson and Herschman, now slightly outdated. Several photographers have published books on their careers, including Stoller and Shulman, whereas Busch offers short profiles and a series of photographs for Stoller, Shulman, and ten other important architectural photographers. Perspectives on architectural photography and modernism can be found in Benson and Naegele. For basic information on the history of photography in general, the two standard texts are Newhall and Rosenblum.

Benson, Robert, "The Image and The Reality," *Inland Architect*, 35, no. 2 (March/April 1991)

Busch, Akiko, *The Photography of Architecture: Twelve Views*, New York and Wokingham, Berkshire: Van Nostrand Reinhold, 1987
Museum of Modern Art, *Photography, 1839–1937*, with introduction by Beaumont Newhall, New York: Museum of Modern Art, 1937; as *The History of Photography: From 1839 to the Present*, by Newhall, New York: The Museum of Modern Art, 1937; revised and enlarged edition, London: Secker and Warburg, 1972; 5th edition, 1994
Naegele, Daniel (editor), *History of Photography*, 22, no. 2 (Summer 1998)
Robinson, Cervin, and Joel Herschman, *Architecture Transformed: A History of the Photography of Buildings from 1839 to the Present*, New York: Architectural League of New York, 1986
Rosenblum, Naomi, *A World History of Photography*, New York: Abbeville Press, 1984; revised edition, New York, 1989; 3rd edition, New York, 1997
Saunders, William S., *Modern Architecture: Photographs by Ezra Stoller*, New York: Abrams, 1990
Shulman, Julius, *Architecture and Its Photography*, edited by Peter Gössel, Cologne, Germany, New York, and London: Taschen, 1998

ARCOSANTI, ARIZONA

Arcosanti, found in the desert of Arizona, is a prototype urban development by the visionary architect and planner Paolo Soleri. The site is an experimental "urban laboratory" where Soleri applies his ideas concerning architecture, ecology, and urban planning. Born on 21 June 1919 in Turin, Italy, Soleri, shortly after completing Ph.D. studies in architecture at the Turin Politecnico in 1946, joined Frank Lloyd Wright at Taliesin in Spring Green, Wisconsin, and at Taliesin West in Scottsdale, Arizona, with a fellowship for 16 months. He immigrated to the United States in 1955 and by 1970 had completed designs for some 30 "arcologies."

Soleri uses the term "arcology" for alternative urban habitats (architecture and ecology). Arcologies are high-density structures that will be capable of containing close to six million inhabitants. Arcosanti is the 13th of these arcologies, and it was the most feasible to build. It is a laboratory for a community that conserves energy, land, and raw materials and is composed of studios, apartments, a swimming pool, a restaurant, cultural facilities, a casting workshop, a community farm, a sewage pond, and greenhouses.

Soleri, beginning construction at Arcosanti in 1970, has increased the initial projection of 1,500 inhabitants to 5,000. It is built on the south slope of a canyon on an 860-acre site at Cordes Junction. Arcosanti lies approximately 65 miles north of Scottsdale, where in 1956 Soleri had begun constructing Cosanti, a nonprofit educational foundation.

Cosanti was built on five acres of land, and it is where Soleri began his experiments in concrete-casting techniques that were later to be applied at a larger scale at Arcosanti. Experiments have also been carried out on surface decorations and moldings at Arcosanti as well as the construction of large vaults and solar apses. Silt from streambeds on the site was used to create forms for sections of vaults, cast-in-place vaulting, and the precast wall panels. Silt is used as a parting agent and can be easily carved to produce ribs where needed. Coloring matter then is applied over the silt and adheres to the concrete along with some of the silt to create various shades of color and texture. Linoleum sheets are used for large areas when silt carving is inefficient. They are cut to predetermined shapes and used to create indentations and transfer color to the concrete. The use of ordinary wood formwork is used for the pouring of foundations, columns, beams, and slabs. There are a few floor slabs where silt is used on top of the formwork to create curved, ribbed undersides.

Soleri has designed advanced solar systems in building structures with assistance from the University of Arizona. At Cosanti, Soleri also began creating his ceramic wind-bells. This effort eventually led to the creation of a foundry and workshop on its site for casting metal bells. The Soleri bells soon became the main income source for Cosanti and, later, Arcosanti.

There are more than 50,000 annual visitors to Arcosanti who may participate in workshops and conferences or tour the grounds. The main builders of Arcosanti have been mainly volunteers, summer student apprentices, and a few employed workers.

The urban planning at Arcosanti takes its stand against suburban sprawl, which Soleri sees as an extremely destructive force. As an alternative to spread-out cities and suburban sprawl, Arcosanti is based on a miniaturization of elements into large urban structures. To Soleri, energy problems are largely the result of suburban sprawl and the use of the automobile. It is avoiding the use of automobiles and creating a series of ministructures, not megastructures, that Soleri believes will help create a better prototype for urban dwelling.

It is Soleri's notion that cities are vital but that contemporary cities tend to isolate people from one another and to have transportation systems that are cumbersome and polluting. Cities also tend to segregate people on the basis of age, race, ethnicity, occupation, and wealth as well as to create problems such as natural resource depletion, food scarcity, and a depletion of the quality of life. Arcosanti is designed to include the positive attributes of an urban environment, such as human interaction, and availability of consumer goods and services along with integrating these urban qualities in an interaction with the surrounding desert. When completed, Arcosanti will be 25 stories high. With a footprint that covers 15 acres of the 860-acre site, it will represent one of the highest population densities ever known.

The architectural historian Hanno-Walter Kruft claims in *A History of Architectural Theory: From Vitruvius to the Present* (1994) that Arcosanti explores an alternative to the functionalist and technologist concerns within architecture occurring in the United States at the time of its inception. According to Kruft, Arcosanti is a "transtechnological" utopian city in which Soleri believes that by improving social conditions, humankind's genetic structure would also be improved (p. 439). Like many modernists, Soleri believes in the morality of architecture: better living conditions produce better humans. However, following the philosopher Teilhard de Chardin, Soleri extends this to include humankind's genetic composition as being effected by better living conditions. The architectural historian Charles Jencks, in *Architecture Today* (1982), stated that in the early 1970s, Soleri's Arcosanti presented a "highly saturated super-urbanism" that differed from many counter-cultural movements of the time that emphasized a movement away from the urban environment (p. 284). Jencks also described Soleri as a late modernist having similarity with Luis Barragan and John Hejduk in his emphasis on pure sculptural form (p. 178).

Soleri insists that Arcosanti is not a megastructure. However, it is a structure after the architectural tradition of Archigram

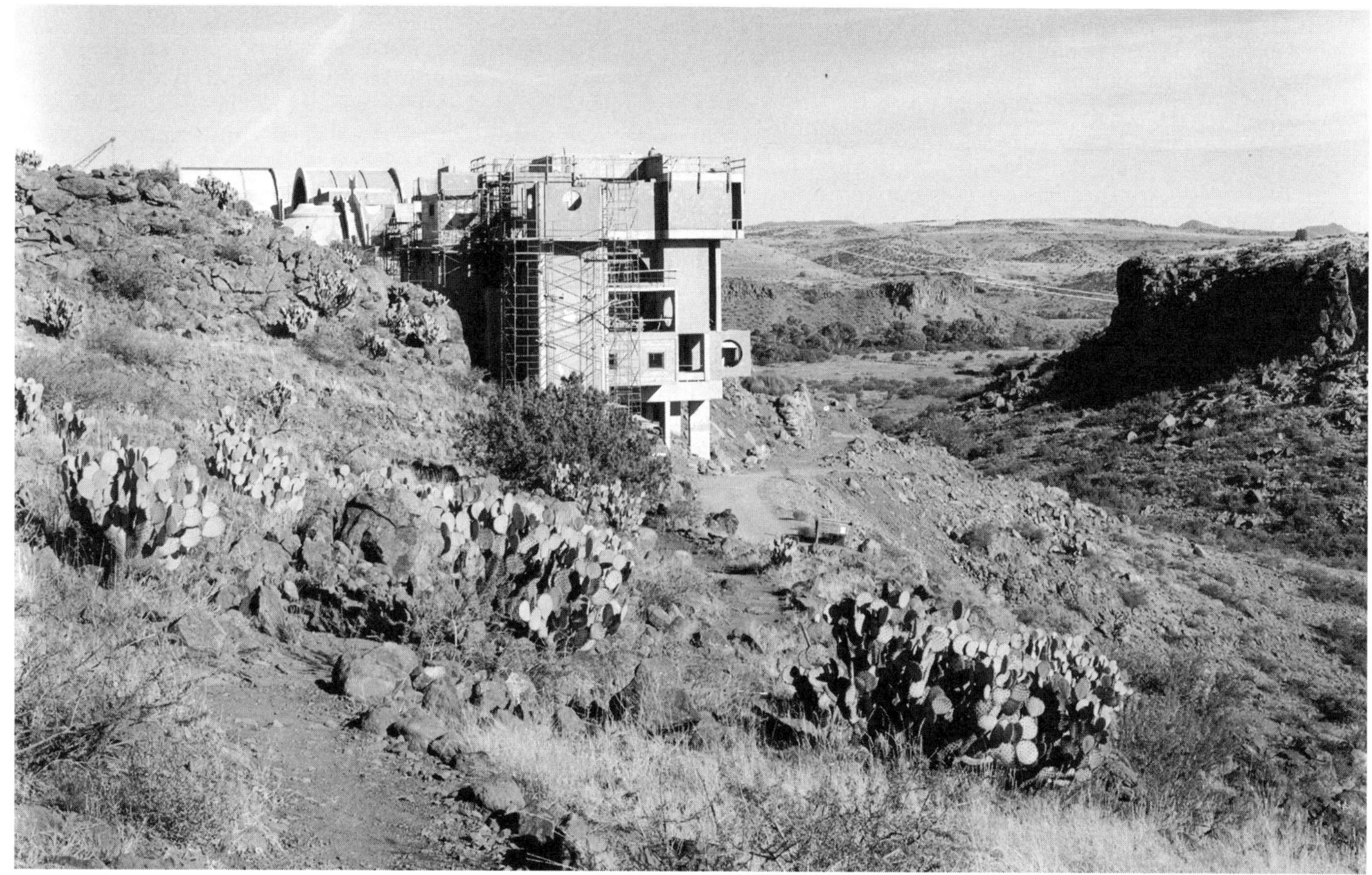

Crafts III Building at Arcosanti, Cordes Junction, Arizona (1977)
© G.E. Kidder Smith/CORBIS

and Buckminster Fuller. Soleri is similar to Fuller, who discussed the environment and ecological issues beyond conventional ideas of architecture. However, unlike Fuller's tendency to emphasize self-sufficiency and applied technology, Soleri's ideas on technology are based on analogies and the belief that a person is never self-sufficient.

Arcosanti today has approximately 100 occupants who still aid Soleri in its continuation. Its slow growth has been largely caused by lack of funding, but it remains an experimental city and an alternative to suburban sprawl in the United States.

REBECCA DALVESCO

Further Reading

Arcidi, Philip, "Paolo Soleri's Arcology: Updating the Prognosis-Interview," *Progressive Architecture* (March 1991)

Bazan Giordano, Michele "Il Mondo de Soleri = The World of Soleri," *Arca* (April 1990)

Cook, Jeffrey "Architettura e biosfera = Architecture and Biosphere-(Interview)," *Arca* (September 1999)

Dixon, J.M., "Arcosanti, Arizona: Job Site for Utopia," *Progressive Architecture* (April 1973)

Gavinelli, Corrado, "Arcosanti 2000 di Paolo Soleri," *Arca* (December 1993)

Jencks, Charles, *Architecture Today*, London: Academy Editions, 1988

Jensen, Robert, "Arcosanti as a Practical Place," *Arts & Architecture* (Winter 1983)

Kostof, Spiro, "Soleri's Arcology: A New Design for the City," *Art in America* (March–April 1971)

Moholy-Nagy, Sybil, "Arcology of Paolo Soleri," *Architectural Forum* (May 1970)

Plagen, Peter, "Journal: A Visit to Soleri's El Dorado," *Art in America* (May–June 1979)

Sharp, Dennis, "Paolo Soleri," *Building* (November 1972)

Shipsky, James, "Diary of an Arcosanti Experience: What It's Like to Be a Soleri 'Workshopper'," *AIA Journal* (May 1982)

Skolimowski, Henryk, "Paolo Soleri: The Philosophy of Urban Life," *Architectural Association Quarterly (London)* (Winter 1971)

Spinelli, Luigi, "Soleri e l'Arizona = Soleri's Arizona," *Domus* (February 1999)

Stanishev, Georgi, "Soleri's Laboratory-Interview," *World Architecture* (January 1993)

Zevi, Luca, "La Ricerca di Paolo Soleri = Paolo Soleri's Research," *Architettura: Cronache e Storia* (December 1990)

ARDALAN, NADER 1939–

Architect, Iran and United States

On his return to his native Iran from the United States in 1964, Nader Ardalan influenced contemporary architecture in the country through his modernist designs and his concern with Islamic and regional expressions. These concerns have remained with him throughout his career and are reflected clearly in his work. Ardalan has been influential not only in his native country but also in the Middle East as an architect, urban planner, and theoretician.

Ardalan is a designer influenced by the internationalist agendas of the 1960s, although his interests are wide ranging. He was also among those who formulated the "Habitat Bill of Rights" presented to the United Nations Habitat Conference in Vancouver in 1971, where issues of inequity between East and West and those related to culture were considered. His architectural and planning work reflects particular attention to cultural and ecological considerations. In Iran, this was made evident through his understanding of the traditions and forms of the vernacular and of Iranian (Shiite) Islam, although manifested in a totally contemporary idiom.

His best-known work in Iran is the Center for Management Studies (1972, Tehran), now the University of Imam Sadegh in Tehran, which consists of vaulted buildings arranged formally around courtyards. The geometric forms and axial arrangements and the reinterpretation of the Persian "paradise garden" are revealed in the low concrete structures that sit comfortably in a landscape of gardens and fruit orchards. His Tehran Center for the Celebration of Music (1978) continues this exploration, with an effective use of water and natural light. Other innovative works in the country include the Behshar Home Offices (1974), now used as the Ministry of Industry, and Bu Ali Sina University (1978, with Georges Candilis) in Hamadan. He planned several new towns, such as Nuran (1978) near Isfahan, which was designed with the paradise garden as its central spine and having two symbolic heads or ends signifying the imaginative or spiritual and the thinking or material.

Ardalan coauthored a book with Lela Bakhtiar, *The Sense of Unity: The Sufi Tradition in Architecture*, that in the last quarter of the 20th century has influenced many architects and scholars interested in contemporary "Islamic architecture." In this book, the authors explore both the spiritual and the geometric aspects of Islamic architecture, presenting the metaphysical doctrines and symbolism within natural, geometric, and harmonic orders. Subsequently, Ardalan wrote a number of articles that built on these themes, and his preoccupation with what he calls "transcendent design" continued. The Sea Palace Paradise Garden (1994–97), a residence on the Persian Gulf coast of Abu Dhabi, uses the *hasht bihisht*, or octagonal "eight paradise," concept and a mandala plan set in long axial gardens and courtyards.

Ardalan moved to the United States two years before the Islamic Revolution of 1979, first continuing his practice in

Al-Sharq Waterfront, view of piazza, Kuwait City, designed by Nader Ardalan (1998)
Photo courtesy Nader Ardalan © Aga Khan Award for Architecture

Boston and then working there for Jung-Brannen International. His international work included the Preservation Plan (1984) for the Old City of Jerusalem and the Ankara Sheraton Hotel (1984). In the United States, his work became more concerned with corporate image making and new technologies, a departure from his earlier concerns. His prize-winning competition entry for the Citizens Plaza Office (1989), a triangular-shaped building with a tall entry atrium, is set against the background of a historic area in Providence, Rhode Island. This manifestation of the atrium as an organizing and monumental element is used subsequently in other projects, as in the 23-story, 54,000-square-meter ADMA-OPCO and ADGAS Office Building (1994–96) in Abu Dhabi. By and large, in his later work the spiritual dimension of architecture has given way to more formal and economic factors in his corporate and commercial buildings.

Perhaps Ardalan was never truly satisfied working in the United States, for when the opportunity arose to move to Kuwait to work on major projects there, he did so. In 1994 he joined the Kuwait Engineers Office as its principal designer. His subsequent work all over the Middle East has focused on the theme of modernity and the integration of tradition interpreted through historic Islamic architecture and the desert vernacular of the region. This has led to a contemporary historicism, a kind of synthesis, akin to Postmodernism found in the West. A good example of this is the buildings along a 2.4-kilometer-long waterside development in Kuwait City. The project consists of a seafront esplanade with low-rise buildings and a large retail complex, the Al Sharq *souk*, completed in 1998. The complex with its plazas overlooks the sea and marina on one side and the city on the other and is conceived as a connector to the urban fabric. The design itself uses traditional elements, such as wind towers, shaded arcades, and *mashribiya* (wood screens), although much of the building is mechanically air conditioned and consists of large shopping-mall types of spaces that have been imported from contemporary commercial practices, including the idea of anchor stores on either end of the so-called *souk*. It is also noteworthy that at the ground-floor level, in "places one can touch," the materials used evoke tradition—ceramic tiles, stone bases, and pilasters—whereas the upper levels are finished in gypsum-reinforced concrete. The large interior spaces are finished in marble and other rich materials. Overall, the effect is a cross between a modern shopping mall and a traditional *khan* (the covered bazaar).

The struggle to reconcile his notions about culture and spirit with those of having to work in a competitive marketplace places Ardalan in a curious position. His current architectural projects carry within them the imagery of the past; this is also prevalent among many architects practicing in the region. This sense of fusion is embodied in his current work, but what distinguishes Ardalan's work is his consistent fine sense of design and place making.

HASAN-UDDIN KHAN

See also **Iran**

Biography

Born in Tehran, Iran, 9 March 1939. Attended the Carnegie Institute of Technology, Pittsburgh, Pennsylvania 1956–61; bachelor of arts degree 1961; studied at the Harvard University Graduate School of Design, Cambridge, Massachusetts; master's degree in architecture 1962. Married (1) Laleh Bakhtiar (divorced 1976); married (2) Shahla Ganji 1977: 4 children. Worked for several firms in the United States including Skidmore, Owings and Merrill, San Francisco, California 1962–64; head of the architecture and engineering section, the National Iranian Oil Company, Masjid-i-Sulaiman, Iran 1964–66; design partner, Abdul Aziz Farman-Farmaian and Associates, Tehran 1966–72. Founder and managing director, the Mandala Collaborative, Tehran 1972–79; president, Mandala International, Boston, Massachusetts 1977–91; principal and senior vice president, Jung/Brannen International Limited, Boston from 1983. Visiting critic in architecture, University of Tehran 1969–73; visiting critic in architecture, Yale University, New Haven, Connecticut 1977; visiting critic in architecture, Harvard University Graduate School of Design 1977–78; visiting critic in architecture, Massachusetts Institute of Technology, Cambridge 1979–80; visiting critic in urban design, Harvard University Graduate School of Design 1977–78 and 1981–83. Member, steering committee, Aga Khan Awards for Architecture 1976–80; member, Designing for Islamic Cultures Workshop, Harvard University and Massachusetts Institute of Technology 1980; jury member, King Fahd Award in Architecture 1987; member, long-range planning committee, Senate of Massachusetts 1989; member, advisory board, WGBH Educational Foundation, Boston 1990–93; chairman Harvard University Graduate School of Design, New England Alumni 1990–93; jury member, State Landmark of Kuwait Competition 1993.

Selected Works

For Skidmore, Owings and Merrill:
Engineering Sciences Building, University of California at Berkeley, 1964

For the National Iranian Oil Companies (NIOC):
Dr. Eghbal Elementary School, Masjid-i-Sulaiman, Iran, 1964
Staff Housing, NIOC, Kharg Island, Iran, 1966

For Farman-Farmaian & Associates:
Asian Games Sports Center, Tehran, 1972
Iran Center for Management Studies, Tehran, 1972
Behshar Home Offices, Tehran, 1974

As the Mandala Collaborative:
Bank of Iran and Holland, Tehran (with Georges Candilis), 1977
Bu Ali Sina University Master Plan and University Sports Center, Hamadan, Iran, 1978
Development Plan and Housing, Nuran Satellite Town, Isfahan, Iran, 1978
Tehran Center for the Celebration of Music, Tehran, 1978
"Jerusalem Consciousness," Old City Promotion Plan, Jerusalem, 1984

With Jung/Brannen Associates:
Hartford Insurance Building, San Francisco, 1984
Ankara Sheraton Hotel and Retail Center, 1984
Treatment Facilities Plan, Boston, 1989
One Citizens Plaza, Providence, 1989
The Sultan Center, Kuwait, 1994
Abu Dhabi Marine Operating Company (ADMA-OPCO) and ADGAS Headquarters, Abu Dhabi, 1996

With Kuwait Engineers Office:
Al Bustan Center and Shopping Galleria, Kuwait, 1994
Sea Palace Paradise Garden, Abu Dhabi, 1997

Al Sharq Souk and Waterfront Project, Kuwait (with Sasaki Associates), 1998
Grand Hotel Redevelopment Master Plan, Abu Dhabi (project completion targeted for 2001)
Shaqab Equestrian Club, Doha, Qatar, 1999

Selected Publication

The Sense of Unity: The Sufi Tradition in Persian Architecture (with Laleh Bakhtiar), 1973

Further Reading

Ardalan, Nader, "On Mosque Architecture," in *Architecture and Community: Building in the Islamic World, Today*, edited by Renata Holod and Darl Rastorfer, Millerton, New York: Aperture, 1983
Ardalan, Nader, "Innovation and Tradition: New Design's Relevance to Cultural Heritage," *Arts and the Islamic World*, 23 (1997)
Ardalan, Nader, "The Paradise Garden Paradigm," in *Consciousness and Reality*, Tokyo: Iwanami Shoten, 1998
Badshah, Akhtar, "The Fusion of Nature and Culture in Design," *Mimar*, 40 (September 1991)
Eshraq, M., "Contemporary Iranian Architects," *Art and Architecture* (June/November 1973)
Kassarjian, J.B., and N. Ardalan, "The Iran Center for Management Studies, Tehran," in *Higher-Education Facilities*, Cambridge, Massachusetts: Aga Khan Program for Islamic Architecture, 1982
"Kuwait City Waterfront Souk by Nader Ardalan (KEO)," *The Architectural Review Middle East* (Spring 1999)
Pontoizeau, Yvette, "Architectures iraniennes," *L'architecture d'aujourd'hui* (February 1978)

ARGENTINA

In the late 19th century, a powerful group of politicians and intellectuals known as "The Generation of the Eighties" incorporated Argentina into a world economy dominated by the British Empire. The early decades of the 20th century witnessed the transformation of the social and economic foundations of the country. Administrative and educational reforms were implemented during the modernization process. Immigration and the movement of the rural population to the city generated the rapid growth of metropolitan areas. Concurrently, an ideological break with the Spanish colonial past generated a cultural identification with the ideas of the French Enlightenment. As a result of a widespread cultural debate between what was understood as civilization and progress versus barbarism and savages, the larger cities of the country, particularly Buenos Aires, were transformed by boulevards, parks, avenues, and building following the Beaux-Arts tradition.

In Argentina, modernization was implemented by conservative political powers. The ruling class was confronted with the dilemma of how to incorporate new ideas and how to deal with an unprecedented situation of quick institutional change and demographic diversity and growth. This situation generated a reaction in some sectors of society for the need to preserve the Hispanic past. Consequently, in the first two decades of the 20th century, parallel to an architectural production dominated by French-educated architects such as Alejandro Christophersen, the first attempts to generate a national style were developed.

Martin Noel adopted a neo-Colonial style in his own residence, today the Museum Fernandez Blanco of Iberoamerican Art (1924). The neo-Colonial style also produced the Cervantes Theater (1922) by Aranda and Repetto and the Bank of Boston (1924) by Paul Bell Chambers and Louis Newbery Thomas with a facade inspired by the Spanish renaissance. The search for authentic cultural roots and a national style was the first attempt to examine architectural patrimony and to systematically preserve local culture.

The first part of the 20th century was also characterized by other reactions against Beaux-Arts and academic canons. Art Nouveau appeared through varied manifestations including Catalan modernism in Rosario by Francisco Roca Simó and in Buenos Aires by Julián Garcia Nuñez with the notable Spanish Hospital (1906). Other architects who embraced Italian influences include Mario Palanti, Francisco Gianotti, and Virgilio Colombo.

The 1925 International Exhibition of Decorative Arts in Paris signaled a shift in taste identified with new materials and architectural types, such as cinemas, bars, banks, and hotels. In Buenos Aires, Alejandro Virasoro's House of Theater (1927), Santander Bank (1929), and the Equitativa del Plata office building (1929) are key examples of this tendency. Also important is the Opera Cinema (1936) by Alberto Bourdon.

The transition between Art Deco and Argentinian rationalism is exemplified in Rosario, with La Comercial de Rosario (1939), a building for offices, a theater, and apartments by De Lorenzi, Otaola, and Rocca, and the Company of Industry and Commerce Headquarters (1939) by Arman and Todeschini.

When the military regime of Uriburu took power in 1930, conservative and authoritarian tendencies desired to build a national identity strong enough to overcome the diverse mosaic of traditions brought by immigration. Parallel to these efforts, the transformation of urban culture and new minimum standards of living marked the transition from the dominance of academic and historicist styles to rational architecture. Rationalism hence in the 1930s acquired a progressive connotation and increasingly became a formal modernist alternative adopted even by architects with a traditional academic education.

Exemplary works in this period in Buenos Aires include the Comega Building (1932) by Enrique Douillet and Alfredo Joselevich, the Safico (1934) by Walter Moll, and the Kavanah building (1936) by Sanchez, Lagos, and de la Torre. Broadly considered a masterpiece of the period, the Kavanah's refined Art Deco interiors were influenced by Chicago's skyscrapers but remained attentive to local characteristics, adaptation to the site, and innovative technology. Another modernist landmark is the Cinema Rex (1937) by Alberto Prebish.

In Córdoba, representative of the period is the Sudamerica Building (1938) by Jaime Roca and Vilar, Sarmiento School (1940) by Juárez Cáceres, and the Allende House (1936) by Roca.

Argentina also manifests some of the earliest critiques of modernist stylization. The Austral Group, in its manifesto *Will and Action* (1939), declared that "present architecture is in a critical moment and lacking the spirit of the initiators." The group denounced the use of academicism and so-called narrow-minded functionalism. The Austral Group was composed of Bonet, Ferrari Hardoy, Kurchan, Le Pera, Ungar, and Zalba. Representative of the manifesto's position are the ateliers and housing for artists (1939) in Buenos Aires by Bonet, Lopez Chas, and Vera

Ramos, characterized by the use of Mediterranean vaults, rich materials, and tectonic variations.

In the 1940s, Peron initiated a plan of industrial production for Argentina. World War II promoted the industrial development of the country, and architecture became oriented toward social welfare. Public work was directed to the areas of education, housing, and health. It was only after World War II that International Style modernism gained dominance. Between 1942 and 1944, the Austral Group published three influential issues of the magazine *Tecné*, pursuing a modernism connected to landscape, climate, and regional construction materials. An important work of this decade was the Apartment (1942) in Virrey Del Pino, Belgrano, by Kurchan and Ferrari Hardoy, in which the architects incorporated a growing tree into the facade.

At the same time, Amancio Williams, with a rigorous and purist aesthetic, created two masterpieces: the House Over the Brook (1945) in Mar del Plata and studies for a Suspended Office Building Project (1946). In the late 1940s, the influential organic group Metron, composed of Tedeschi, Sacriste, Vivanco, Caminos, and Borgato, was created in Tucumán. Critical of the International Style for its negation of the past and regional architecture, Metron's ideas were promulgated by Eduardo Sacriste's site- and landscape-based works, including Barrio Jardin Elementary School (1947) and the Gómez Omil House (1951).

The most representative work of this period is the project, in 1953, for the General San Martin Theater (1960) in Buenos Aires by Mario Roberto Alvarez and Ruiz.

In the 1950s and early 1960s, institutional works were inspired by Le Corbusier's Unité d'Habitation apartment complex in Marseilles (1952). Le Corbusier's curtain wall, free plan, *pilotis*, and sculptural terraces are the dominant features of the Encotel Post Office and Auditorium (1955) in Buenos Aires by Jose Spencer and the Municipal Building (1954) in Córdoba by the group SEPRA: Sánchez Elía, Peralta Ramos, and Agostino. The Civic Center of La Pampa (1956) by Testa, Davinovic, Gaido, and Rossi shows the influence of Le Corbusier's Parliament building in Chandigarh, India.

As an alternative to the International Style, the Church of Our Lady of Fátima (1957) in Martinez (state of Buenos Aires) by Caveri and Ellis reinterpreted regional typologies and materials.

One of the most important studios of the 1960s and 1970s is Mario Roberto Alvarez and Associates. Representatives of the professionalism of the group are the Cultural Center Buenos Aires City (1970) and SOMISA (1975), the headquarters for the steel company owned by the state. Two seminal pieces of the 1960s are the project for the National Library (project, 1961; construction, 1972–92) by Clorindo Testa and the sculptural Bank of London (1966) by Testa, Sánchez Elía, Peralta Ramos, and Agostini. This bank is considered a masterpiece of Brutalist architecture.

Since the 1960s, the application of new technology and processes of construction characterized proposals such as the Hospital (1963) in Oran, Salta, by Llauró-Urgell and Associates. This hospital creates a microclimate within a basic module, allowing for expansion and, eventually, change of functions.

The 1970s were characterized by a series of relevant competitions, including the project for the Auditorium of Buenos Aires City (1972), a complex of organic fragments, by Baudizzone, Erbin, Lestard, Varas, Díaz. Moreover, the Civic Center (1971) for San Juan by Antonini, Schon, Zemborain and Associates explored flexibility and modules. In addition, several competitions for skyscrapers were held in Catalinas Norte in Buenos Aires. The most interesting response is the Conurban building (1973) by Kocourek SRL. The facade of the building is adapted to the climate and the orientations. The building for ATC (Argentinean Color TV) by Manteola, Sánchez Gómez, Santos, Solsona, and Viñoly is considered the most relevant example of the late 1970s for its integration with the context and the resolution of complex functional requirements.

In the wake of the military government years, the 1980s were characterized by diverse tendencies, ranging from the search for a rediscovery of Latin American connections to the revalorization of the urban heritage to architecture as aesthetic experience only. However, the enriching possibilities opened by a Postmodern condition also brought frivolity and superficiality. José Ignacio Díaz contributed since the 1970s to transform and enrich the urban character of Córdoba, the second-largest city in the country. Using the characteristic brick construction material of the city, Diaz designed and built more than 120 residential buildings. In the public sector, Miguel Roca's proposal for Córdoba's center and neighborhoods produced cultural centers and pedestrian malls and recuperated the river.

The 1990s continued the multiplicity of architectural tendencies. The playfulness and acceptance of many influences of this period are shown by the hybrid architecture of Testa, particularly in his complex at the Recoleta Cultural Center (1994). The intention to insert new architecture without disrupting the urban was demonstrated in Córdoba by the Nuevocentro Shopping (1990) by Gramática, Guerrero, Morini, Pisani, Rampulla, and Urtubey. This group also designed the new Justice Palace of Córdoba (1998).

The 1990s was also characterized by a new care for tectonics and finesse in details, as in the work of the Studio Benadon, Berdichevsky, and Cherny, particularly in the Organon Argentina offices (1997) in Bajo Belgrano and the CAPSA, Capex, offices (1997) in Vicente Lopez.

Popular architecture, environmental issues, hybridization, identity, regionalism, and rehabilitation, all involving both practical and poetic considerations, have been the dominant elements of Argentinean architecture in the last 20 years. In a country where economic and cultural dependence is still debated, the late decades have been marked by an architecture more responsive to ecological and social concerns and the search for the appropriate use of technology with local resources. The tension between these local concerns and its universal vocation makes the architecture of the 20th century in Argentina one of the most vital and interesting in the world.

JOSE BERNARDI

See also **Alvarez, Mario Roberto (Argentina); Ambasz, Emilio (Argentina, United States); Buenos Aires, Argentina; Manteola, Sánchez Gómez, Santos, Solsona, Viñoly (Argentina); Pelli, Cesar (Argentina); Testa, Clorindo (Argentina); Williams, Amancio (Argentina)**

Further Reading

There is no available historical survey of architecture in Argentina available in English. Neither are there comprehensive studies of architectural tendencies and movements within the larger context of society. Partial chapters or critical essays on architectural issues in Argentina written by the most important historians and critics of the country can be found scattered in recent books dealing with Latin America or in magazines devoted to particular architects or works. The most relevant critics of the country are Marina Waisman, Ramón Gutierrez, Jorge Glusberg, and Jorge Francisco Liernur. They represent distinct yet very influential points of view. Some of the books mentioned here reflect the renewed interest in regionalist architecture and the dialogue among major protagonists of architecture in Latin America in general and Argentina in particular.

A&V 48 (July–August 1994) (special issue titled "America Latina")
Argentina—Arquitetture 1880–2004, edited by Daniela Pastore, Gangemi Editore, 1998
Braun, Clara, and Julio Cacciatore (coordinación), *Arquitectos europeos y Buenos Aires [European Architects and Buenos Aires], 1860–1940*, Buenos Aires, Argentina: Fundación TIAU, 1996
Bullrich, Francisco, *Arquitectura Argentina Contemporánea, Panorama de la arquitectura Argentenia 1950–1963* [Contemporary Argentinean Architecture: A Survey of Architecture from 1950 to 1963 in Argentina], Buenos Aires: Ediciones Nueva Visión, 1963
Bullrich, Francisco, *Arquitectura Latinoamericana, 1930–1970* [Latin American Architecture, 1930–1970], Buenos Aires: Editorial Sudamericana, 1969
Design Book Review 32/33 (Spring/Summer 1994) (special issue titled "Other Americas," edited by John Loomis)
Fernández Cox, Cristián, et al., *Modernidad y Postmodernidad en América Latina* [Modernity and Postmodernity in Latin America], Bogotá, Colombia: ESCALA, 1991
Glusberg, Jorge, *Miguel Angel Roca/texts by Jorge Glusberg & Oriol Bohigas*, (English and Spanish in parallel texts), London: Academy Editions, 1981
Glusberg, Jorge, *Breve Historia de la Arquitectura Argentina* [Brief History of Architecture in Argentina], Buenos Aires: Editoral Claridad, 1991
Gutiérrez Z., Ramón, *Arquitectura y Urbanismo en Iberoamerica* [Architecture and Urbanism in Ibero America], Madrid: Ediciones Cátedra, 1983
Hitchcock, Henry-Russell, *Latin American Architecture since 1945*, New York: Museum of Modern Art, 1955
Instituto Argentino de Investigaciones en Historia de la Arquitectura y el Urbanismo, *Arquitectura Latinoamericana, Pensamiento y Propuesta* [Latin American Architecture: Thinking and Proposals], Buenos Aires: Ediciones Summa, 1991
Liernur, Jorge Francisco, *America Latina, Architettura: gli ultimi vent'anni* [Latin American Architecture: The Last Twenty Years], Milan: Electa, 1990
Liernur, Jorge Francisco (proyecto y dirección general), *Diccionario histórico de arquitectura, habitat, y urbanismo en la Argentina* [Historical Dictionary of Architecture: Habitat and Urbanism in Argentina], Buenos Aires: Sociedad Central de Arquitectos, 1992
Liernut, Jorge Francisco, *Twentieth Century Architecture in Argentina: The Construction of Modernity*, Buenos Aires: Fondo Nacional de las Artes, 2001
Pinilla Acevedo, Mauricio (coordinador), *Togo Díaz: el arquitecto y su ciudad* [Togo Díaz: The Architect and His City], Bogotá, Colombia: Escala, 1993
Roca, Miguel Angel (editor), *The Architecture of Latin America*, London: Academy Editions, 1995
Taylor, Brian Brace, *Miguel Angel Roca*, London: Mimar Publications, 1992
Waisman, Marina, and César Naselli, *10 Arquitectos latinoamericanos* [Ten Latin American Architects], Seville: Consejería de Obras Públicas y Transportes, 1989
ZODIAC 8 (September 1992–February 1993) (Guido Canella, editor)

ARQUITECTONICA

Architecture firm, United States

Arquitectonica began as a Miami firm created in 1976 by a group of young architects under the leadership of Hervin A.R. Romney and Bernado Fort-Brescia. Andrés Duany and Elizabeth Plater-Zyberk joined the pair a few months later, with Laurinda Spear arriving the following year. By 1984 Plater-Zyberk and Duany and Romney had left to establish their own firms. Arquitectonica's current principles include Sergio Bakas and Jenifer Briley, who joined the firm in the early 1980s.

Under the leadership of Spear and Fort-Brescia, Arquitectonica expanded to design buildings in several countries, particularly in Fort-Brescia's birthplace of Lima, Peru, and in the Pacific Rim nations of Asia. Although it has some small residential designs to its credit, Arquitectonica has become known for large-scale projects: apartment towers, hotels and convention centers, sports facilities, government institutions, shopping malls, and financial office complexes.

Arquitectonica's design approach has been described as Latin modern, tropical modern, new modernism, Postmodern surrealism, Mediterranean, or Caribbean and as manifesting influences of Russian Constructivism, Deconstructivism, and Art Deco. One of Laurinda Spears's early designs that attracted widespread attention was The Spear House (1978), also known as the Pink House, the firm's first completed work. Located on the Biscayne Bay waterfront in suburban Miami Shores, this building uses glass block, concrete, and stucco, rendered in five different shades of pink, with angular geometric forms highlighted in white, to boldly proclaim its allegiance to its tropical setting. The long, narrow plan stretches along the street with a high wall of opaque glass, assuring privacy. In contrast, the elevation overlooking the Bay is a busy collage of windows, balconies, and recesses based on multiples of a square. This motif is repeated, both front and rear, in a landscaped grid of square patio stones.

The first large-scale designs by Arquitectonica included a quartet of Miami apartment buildings: the Babylon (1979), followed by the Atlantis Condominiums (1982), the Palace (1982), and the Imperial (1984). The Atlantis Condominiums, in particular, captured international interest with their deconstructivist forms. This long and narrow high-rise, with its single curved end, was designed to be seen from a moving vehicle. The street elevation was a glazed curtain wall, whereas a large-scale, brilliant royal blue grid defined the opposite facade. The element that attracted most attention for the firm was the building's sky court: a four-story-high opening punched clean through the center of the building. By audaciously playing with a building's fundamental sense of enclosure, the Atlantis building was a success and was followed by numerous commissions within the Miami region.

Some of Arquitectonica's entertainment and retail projects, such as the All-Star Sports and Music Resorts (1994) at Lake Buena Vista, Florida, play with popular imagery and imagination. Designed for Disney World's visitors, Arquitectonica used brilliantly colored and oversized sports paraphernalia, such as basketballs and hoops, baseball bats, sports pennants, and megaphones, to decorate these resort motels and ancillary facilities. Eschewing subtlety in favor of the blatantly obvious, such motifs assault both the senses and the imagination, yet manage to

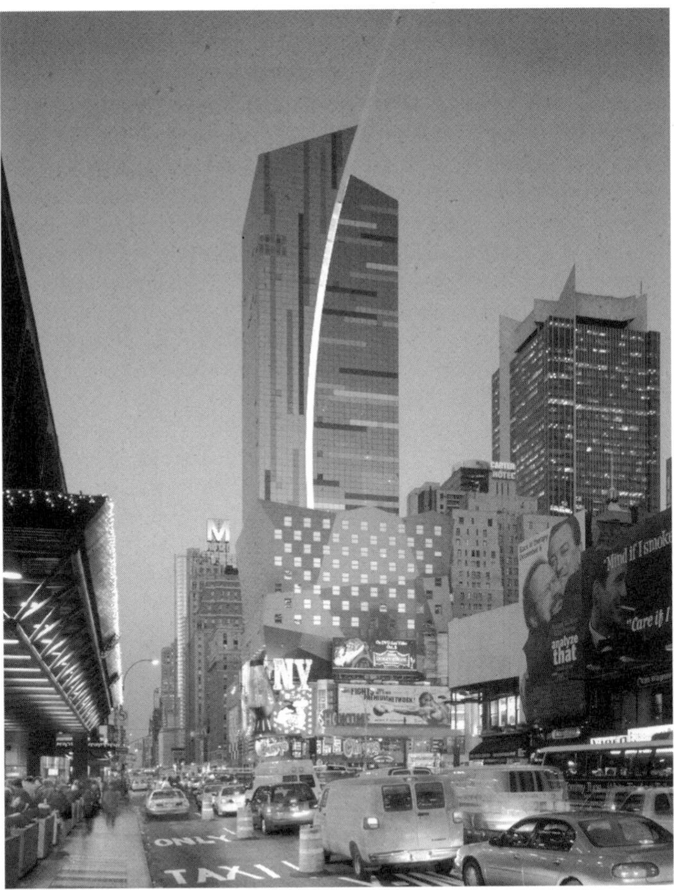

Westin Times Square Hotel, New York City, designed by Arquitectonica (2002)
Photo © Norman McGrath

complement and enhance the visitor experience of Disney's fantasy world.

The Banque de Luxembourg's headquarters (1994) respects the character of its owners and its urban context. Situated on a site at the end of a homogenous range of traditional European financial institutions, the Banque's interlocked solid and transparent volumes allude to both stability and progressiveness. The core section of the Banque is a dark black parallelogram, enclosed on three sides by a stolid and rational cantilevered facade of locally available Chassagne stone. The contrasting volume, a dark green, curved glass tower, slices abruptly into its stone counterpart at the point where the Royal Boulevard curves around the site. To keep within the footprint of the relatively small and angular site and to conform with the profile of the existing streetscape, several office and parking levels were constructed below grade. To the rear of the main building is a formal garden linking it with a reception area in a house constructed to mimic others along the street.

Although the massive United States Embassy (1996) in Lima was designed according to the stringent security and safety requirements required for American government facilities in foreign countries, Arquitectonica's designers enlivened a conventional building type with multicolored brick, metal, and tinted glass, laid in complex geometric patterns. The exposed portion of the entrance facade contains few windows, but behind a high courtyard wall of Inca-style stone panels welded to steel plates, and at the rear of the Embassy, an irregular arrangement of windows and squares of gold-plated metal, interspersed with elongated strips of tinted glass, help to create an intricate geometric collage, intended to be reminiscent of a pre-Colombian textile. On this elevation, a grandly scaled ceremonial entrance of alternating stone and metal frames steps out to the face of the building.

Arquitectonica's first major commission in New York, the Westin Times Square Hotel (2002), is but one component in a massive and, at times, controversial redevelopment project called E-Walk. Even though the actual project site on 42nd Street is removed from the Square itself, the lower levels of the hotel and entertainment complex emulate the big and brassy commercial ambience of Times Square. The 47-story hotel is visually split in two by a recessed convex chasm containing lighting systems that project a broad swath of light skyward. One side of the structure is clad in blue glass panels, and the opposite is covered with gold-tinted glass. Because the tower's base is supported above the lower entertainment complex, innovative seismic insulators were designed to enable the tower to sway with the wind, whereas the lower building remains stationary.

RHODA BELLAMY

See also **Deconstructivism; Duany and Plater-Zyberk (United States); Lapidus, Morris (United States); Miami (FL), United States; Supermodernism**

Selected Works

Spear House, Biscayne Bay, Miami, 1978
Babylon Apartment House, Miami, 1979
Atlantis Condominiums, Miami, 1982
Palace Apartment House, Miami, 1982
Imperial Apartment House, Miami, 1984
All-Star Sports and Music Resorts, Lake Buena Vista, Florida, 1994
Banque de Luxembourg headquarters, 1994
United States Embassy, Lima, Peru, 1996
Philips Arena, Atlanta, Georgia, 1996
Westin Times Square Hotel, New York City, 2002

Further Reading

Dunlop, Beth, *Architectonica*, Washington D.C.: American Institute of Architects, 1991

Dunlop, Beth, and Roberto Schezen (photographer), *Miami: Trends and Traditions*, New York: The Monacelli Press Inc., 1996

Leon, Luis Aguilar, "El nuevo rostro urbano," *El Nuevo Herald* (January 2000)

Stein, Karen D., "A Fortress with No Apologies," *Architectural Record* (October 1996)

Stein, Karen D., "Gaining Currency," *Architectural Record* (January 1995)

Vonier, Françoise, and Thomas Vonier, "Auditorium de Dijon, Dijon, France," *Architectural Record* (May 1999)

Zevon, Susan, "Florida House for a Family of Eight," *House Beautiful* (July 1998)

ART DECO

The term *Art Deco* is a now firmly established designation for an aesthetic of the late 1920s and 1930s that in its own day was called *art moderne*. In architecture, the style took various forms, each of which has prompted historians to devise different identifying terminology. In the 1960s, the more ornamental phase of popular modernism was dubbed Art Deco, echoing the name of the 1925 Parisian *Exposition des Arts Decoratifs et Industriels Modernes*, where the style's formal design motifs, patterns, and decorative predilections were first observed. Recognizing in Deco a character both modern and abstract but a style that nevertheless avoided the white, volumetric, and planar reductivism of the emerging 1920s "Bauhaus Modern," some historians referred to the style as "modernistic," that is, pseudomodern or approaching modern. These and other design terms and stylistic labels have been applied to the several dimensions of Art Deco architecture after the mid-1920s.

Inspired by the aerodynamic forms and kinetic lines emerging from the drafting boards of industrial designers, a "Streamline Moderne" architectural style (dubbed "nautical moderne" when marine imagery was most explicit) evolved as one of the quintessential styles of the 1930s. In architecture, it borrowed from the streamlining evidenced in the forms of new transportation machines—planes, trains, ships, and automobiles—and streamlining was most frequently applied to buildings that served these transportation machines: air terminal buildings, bus terminals, marinas, and especially such roadside buildings as diners, gas stations, and car dealerships. Recognizing that streamlining's paring down of moderne forms to the ultimate teardrop was paralleled by a general economy of line and form and that this restraint was considered appropriate in a period of economic depression, writers employed the term Depression modern to describe elements of selected examples of the later Deco-era aesthetic. Finally, when 1930s government architects looked to a restrained classicism to communicate an image of authority and order, a Deco-era "modern classic" derivation presented itself in county courthouses, New Deal–era post offices, and other government architecture.

The Art Deco period in architecture, therefore, was polyglot and multifarious, an age in which Progressivism and modernity were embedded in different forms in which the more conservative Deco stylists, often traditional Beaux-Arts–trained designers, might express their ornamental predispositions in more abstract modern terms. Likewise, classicists might mollify earlier Edwardian enthusiasm for the baroque in favor of a new monumentalism that was simpler, plain surfaced, and grand without being grandiloquent. Finally, the more avant-garde modernists offered a populist, ornamental, and colorful *l'art decoratif* of recognized, albeit abstracted, motifs.

The Art Deco era was fundamentally a 20th-century machine age. In Deco reliefs and architectural ornament, a knife-edged profile transformed human, animal, and plant forms into low-relief sculptural representations treated as faceted machine-cut patterns of light and shadow. Similarly, a Streamline Moderne building's curved corners, neon signage, marquees, and "drive-through" features, as found in diners, bus terminals, and gas stations alike, merely borrowed forms from the period's machine, especially from transportation and industrial designs. Architecture was characterized by a transmogrification of aerodynamic shapes and surfaces from streamlined fenders, curved car bodies, and zephyrlike lines of speed that, by the 1930s, shaped and accented Chrysler Air Flows, Hupmobiles, Cords, and other contemporary sedans and coupes of the day. Comparable architectural elements emerged from designs first shaping airplane fuselages and wing sections, from the aerodynamic shrouds enveloping the Pennsylvania S-1 locomotive or bull-nosed Studebakers of Raymond Loewy, or from the hydrodynamic hull of a Norman Bel Geddes futuristic ocean liner. Moreover, during the Deco era, technology (in the form of steel-frame construction, reinforced concrete, and plate glass) provided the means to build skyscrapers higher than ever before, making the Chrysler Building (1930), the Empire State Building (1930–31), Rockefeller Center (1931–40), and indeed, the entire skyline of New York icons of the age.

The period was also quintessentially an era of popular modernism. Cosmetic Deco and moderne facades brought a face-lift to Main Street America by an applied architectonic skin of colorful, glazed terra-cotta, Vitrolite, ceramic or gloss metallic panels, glass brick, neon, and other Deco-era materials. At the same moment that European modernists such as Le Corbusier, Walter Gropius, and Ludwig Mies van der Rohe were defining an avant-garde modern style based on lack of or minimal color, no ornament, and an emphasis of volume over mass, popular ornamentalists in America rejected the utilitarian for the visual, the intellectual for the sensual, the rational for the expressive, and the sociological for the purely decorative. Art Deco was jazzy, bright, sexy, loud, and visually appealing. If Bauhaus modernism and the International Style appeared to limit its focus to functionalism at the exclusion of emotionalism or expressionism, Art Deco found its appeal in the very color and excitement that polychromatic stylized facades, neon lighting, and zigzag profiles communicated.

Recognizing Deco's increasing presence on Main Street, in Kress and F.W. Woolworth five-and-dimes, in arty neighborhood theaters with their sunburst splashed facades, and in chic department stores and other commercial emporia, historians have characterized the Art Deco style as transcending social class, as egalitarian and democratic, and as the modern aesthetic of the people. Even today, a revived Art Deco is in evidence at populist marketplaces as the preferred style of perfumeries and at the cosmetic displays of department stores. This neo-Deco, both chic and cheap, parallels the rebirth in the 1980s of the Streamline Moderne in roadside architecture as evidenced in nostalgic diners and drive-through hamburger chains.

Landmarks of Art Deco architecture, therefore, are less often palaces of royalty, cathedrals, or monumental institutional buildings and more often commercial, Main Street, and roadside structures—indeed, department stores were nicknamed "people's palaces," and skyscrapers of the period were called modernistic cathedrals of commerce. Among the most noteworthy were Timothy Pflueger's Paramount Theater (1929) in Oakland, California; G. Albert Lansberg's Warner Brothers' Western (Wiltern) Theater (1930) in Los Angeles; B. Marcus Priteca's Pantages Theater (1929) in Hollywood; and Donald Deskey's Radio City Music Hall (1931) in New York. Only occasionally was the style

Barbizon Apartment Hotel, Ocean Drive, Art Deco district, Miami Beach
© Historic American Buildings Survey/Library of Congress

of cathedrals of commerce applied to genuinely religious edifices: First Church of Christ, Scientist, in Perth, Western Australia, designed by Ochiltree and Hargreave, is a notable late Deco church of 1939, although perhaps the best-known religious building of the idiom is the 1929 Boston Avenue Methodist Episcopal Church in Tulsa, Oklahoma, by Ada M. Robinson and Bruce Goff.

The true cathedral of commerce on Main Street, however, was the department store, which ranged from such landmarks as Bullock's Wiltshire store (Los Angeles, 1928) by John and Donald Parkinson to scores of F.W. Woolworths, Kress five-and-dimes, and small boutiques in small towns nationwide. However, the vertical giants of commerce were the skyscrapers. These were sometimes actually dressed in a Gothic Deco, as at Atlanta's City Hall (1930) by G. Lloyd Preacher. Generally, however, the Deco skyscraper rose skyward to form towering commercial ziggurats and office buildings in New York whose prominence advertised sponsoring companies. McGraw-Hill (1931, Raymond Hood), Barclay-Vesey Telephone (1923–26, Ralph T. Walker), Chrysler (1930, William Van Alen), and RCA Victor (1931, Cross and Cross) were the ultimate Deco exemplars of capitalist architecture.

Indeed, the extensive construction of taller urban office buildings and apartment towers during the Deco era has prompted some historians to label Art Deco the "skyscraper style." Distinctive zigzag setbacks brought Deco skyscrapers a jazz-aged syncopated profile, a feature that was initially required by the 1916 zoning ordinance in New York but soon developed as a style. Beyond the New York landmarks cited previously, Manhattan's Deco masterpieces included the Waldorf Astoria Hotel (1930, Schultze and Weaver), the Chanin Building (1927–29, Sloan and Robertson), the Panhellenic Tower (1929, John Mead Howells), and the Film Center Building (1928–29, Ely Jacques Kahn). The 450 Sutter Building (1928, Timothy Pflueger) in San Francisco and the W.W. Orr Building (1930, Pringle and Smith) in Atlanta are two medical office buildings whose relief panels and ornament reflect the popular modern style, the former's decoration employing Mayan elements, the latter a Deco-esque serpent and staff of Asclepius. Among the ornamentalists enriching Deco buildings were muralists and sculptors. Among the most representative period murals were those executed between 1934 and 1943 for 1,100 local post offices under the sponsorship of the U.S. Treasury Department's Section of Painting and Sculpture (later known as the Section of Fine Arts). Most notable among Deco sculptors was Lee Lawry, whose relief carvings and sculpture may be seen at the Nebraska State Capitol (1919–32, Bertram G. Goodhue), the Louisiana State Capitol (1930–32, Weiss, Dreyfous, and Seiferth), and Bok Tower (Mountain Lake Singing Tower, 1929, Milton B. Medary) as well as at Rockefeller Center.

In southern Florida, Miami Beach preserves an entire historic district of Art Deco hotels, apartment buildings, and other period landmarks by architects Henry Hohauser, L. Murray Dixon, Anton Skislewicz, and others. Notable works include Hohauser's Hotel Park Central (1937) and Hotel Cardozo (1939), Dixon's Marlin Hotel (1939) and Ritz Plaza (1940), and Skislewicz's Breakwater Hotel (1939) and Plymouth Hotel (1940). These works synthesize modern and Art Deco elements into a unique blend of 1930s ornament, streamlining, and ribbon windows accented in these oceanside structures with local decorative references and regional themes, including waves, palm trees, fountains, flamingos, fish, sails, portholes, ship bows, and rising bubbles. Since the 1980s, revitalization of the beachfront Deco color palette on refurbished facades and in rehabilitated hotel lobbies in a Postmodern vein has created a "tropical Deco" style that has transformed an originally predominantly white architecture into a wash of pastels, rainbow figure-ground profiles, and neon-enhanced pizzazz. In Los Angeles, Sunset Towers (1929, Leland A. Bryant) is comparable in form to Miami Beach's smaller-scale residential blocks, and further echoes of this domestic Deco found its way into private residences.

The only large collection of like Art Deco structures to rival Miami Beach is the town of Napier, New Zealand, substantially destroyed by an earthquake and rebuilt within a short period of the 1930s. Both a Mediterranean or Spanish Mission style and a Deco-informed international modern informed nearby Hastings, New Zealand, but the rebuilding of the commercial district of Napier provides an unusual concentration of period architecture in a city well off the beaten track. Moreover, a remarkable body of Art Deco architecture survives in major Australian cities including theater architecture by William Leighton (Windsor, 1937, in Nedlands and Perth) and Samuel Rosenthal

(Beacon, 1937, South Fremantle) as well as Deco office buildings in Sydney (City Mutual Building, 1934–36, Emil Sodersten) and Melbourne (ACA Building, *c.*1936, attributed to Hennessy and Hennessy). A strong presence of streamlining and flat-roofed, ribbon-windowed modernism informed this region's international Deco, with Australian architects achieving designs of additional interest when ornamental accents included kookaburra birds and other native references. Australia's quintessential Art Deco landmark, however, is a monumental Deco classic: C. Bruce Dellit's powerful Anzac Memorial in Hyde Park, Sydney, dating from 1934. Embodying the monumental form, decorative detail, and spirit of the best formal, public side of the Art Deco style, the Anzac Memorial, like smaller monuments of the period nationwide, is an emotionally charged memorial to the Australian and New Zealand fallen from the world wars.

Such a restrained yet monumental modern classic was foreshadowed in the World War I memorials by British architect Sir Edwin Lutyens, including his Whitehall Cenotaph (1919–22) in London and reflected in the work of Paul Cret (Folger's Shakespeare Library, 1929–31, Washington, D.C., and National Naval Medical Center, 1939–41, Bethesda, Maryland). The Palais de Chaillot (1937) by Carlu, Boileau, and Azéma is Paris's best example. In the United States during the same period, the modern classic phase of Art Deco architecture is represented by Goodhue's Los Angeles City Hall (1922), San Francisco's Veterans Hospital (1934, designed by the U.S. Treasury Department's supervising architect), and Atlanta's Federal Post Office Annex (1931–33, A. Ten Eyck Brown).

The modern classic and Depression modern character finds its way into Holabird and Roche's Chicago Board of Trade Building (1929–30) and the same architects' Chicago Daily News Building (1929). However, it is given its most evocative representation in Hugh Ferriss's renderings of dramatic urban towers, as published in his *Metropolis* of 1929, whose images appeared immediately brought to fruition in Buffalo's City Hall (1929–31) by George J. Dietel and John J. Wade. Indeed, Ferriss's influence is seen as late as the 1990s, as evidenced by Rabun Hatch and Associates' GLG Grand (1992) in Atlanta.

The 1939 New York World's Fair closed the late moderne era with clear evidence that the decade had been dominated by streamlining. At the fair, the General Motors Highways and Horizons Exhibit, including the Futurama, presented the World of Tomorrow as envisioned by Norman Bel Geddes, a world of and for the automobile encouraging the free-flowing movement of goods and people across the continent. In 1932 Bel Geddes had published his industrial designs (particularly planes, trains, and cars) in *Horizons*. The streamlined phase of Art Deco focused the attention of designers on roadside architecture. W.W. Arrasmith of Louisville, Kentucky, designed bus depots for Greyhound, including those for Evansville, Indiana (1938), Washington, D.C. (1939), and Atlanta (1940), the latter now hidden under a hideous "modernization" two decades ago. George D. Brown's Atlantic Greyhound Bus Terminal in Columbia, South Carolina, shows the influence of Arrasmith's streamlining that informed such structures nationally. Similarly, Texaco commissioned Walter Dorwin Teague to design standardized service stations, and variations on five models were sited at prime corner building sites nationwide.

In private and public realms alike, electronics, transportation, radio communication, and other scientific and technological advances were viewed as signs of the progress of the age, and images of these modern marvels adorned murals and ceiling paintings and shaped neon outlines in signage and advertising. Representations of the machine informed industrial photography, motion picture and theater sets, and the sharp-edged profiles of Charles Sheeler landscapes and Ferdinand Leger figures. In architecture, the Deco-era design impulses, in Streamline Moderne, modern classic, or faceted Art Deco style, were a synthesis of tradition and Progressive design, nature and the machine, and the ornamental as well as the abstract. In all, Art Deco architecture was both modern and popular, and although associated with known designers and stylists, some of its most ubiquitous forms are anonymous and found along the roadside.

ROBERT M. CRAIG

See also **Bauhaus; Chrysler Building, New York City; Empire State Building, New York City; Movie Theater/Cinema; Roadside Architecture; Rockefeller Center, New York City**

Further Reading

Appelbaum, Stanley, and Richard Wurts, *The New York World's Fair, 1939–40, in 155 Photographs*, New York: Dover, 1977

Battersby, Martin, *The Decorative Thirties*, New York: Walker, and London: Studio Vista, 1971

Battersby, Martin, *The Decorative Twenties*, New York: Walker, and London: Studio Vista, 1969

Bayer, Patricia, *Art Deco Source Book*, Secaucus, New Jersey: Wellfleet Press, and Oxford: Phaidon, 1988

Breeze, Carla, *L.A. Deco*, New York: Rizzoli, 1991

Bush, Donald J., *The Streamlined Decade*, New York: Braziller, 1975

Capitman, Barbara Baer, *Deco Delights: Preserving the Beauty and Joy of Miami Beach Architecture*, New York: Dutton, 1988

Capitman, Barbara Baer, Michael D. Kinerk, and Dennis W. Wilhelm, *Rediscovering Art Deco U.S.A.*, New York: Viking Studio Books, 1994

Craig, Robert M., *Atlanta Architecture: Art Deco to Modern Classic, 1929–59*, Gretna, Louisiana: Pelican, 1995

Craig, Robert M., "Atlanta's Moderne Diner Revival: History, Nostalgia, Youth, and Car Culture," *Studies in Popular Culture*, 19, no. 2 (1996)

Crowe, Michael F., *Deco by the Bay: Art Deco Architecture in the San Francisco Bay Area*, New York: Viking Studio Books, 1995

Duncan, Alastair, *American Art Deco*, London: Thames and Hudson, and New York: Abrams, 1986

Ferriss, Hugh, *The Metropolis of Tomorrow*, New York: Washburn, 1929; reprint, Princeton, New Jersey: Princeton Architectural Press, 1986

Gebhard, David, *The National Trust Guide to Art Deco in America*, New York and Chichester, West Sussex: Wiley, 1996

Geddes, Norman Bel, *Horizons*, Boston: Little Brown, 1932; London: Lane, 1934

Greif, Martin, *Depression Modern: The Thirties Style in America*, New York: Universe Books, 1975

Gutman, Richard J.S., and Elliott Kaufman, *American Diner*, New York: Harper and Row, 1979; revised edition, as *American Diner: Then and Now*, by Gutman, New York: HarperPerennial, 1993

Hillier, Bevis, *Art Deco of the 20s and 30s*, London: Studio Vista, 1968; revised edition, New York: Schocken Books, 1985

Hillier, Bevis, *The World of Art Deco* (exhib. cat.), New York: Dutton, and London: Studio Vista, 1971

Jennings, Jan (editor), *Roadside America: The Automobile in Design and Culture*, Ames: Iowa State University Press, 1990

Meikle, Jeffrey L., *Twentieth Century Limited: Industrial Design in America, 1925–39*, Philadelphia, Pennsylvania: Temple University Press, 1979
Pulos, Arthur J., *The American Design Ethic: A History of Industrial Design to 1940*, Cambridge, Massachusetts: MIT Press, 1983
Robinson, Cervin, and Rosemarie Haag Bletter, *The Skyscraper Style: Art Deco, New York*, New York: Oxford University Press, 1975
Trétiack, Philippe, *Loewy*, Paris: Assouline, 1998; as *Raymond Loewy and Streamlined Design*, translated by Cynthia Calder, New York: Universe/Vendome, 1999
Vieyra, Daniel I., *"Fill 'er Up": An Architectural History of America's Gas Stations*, New York: Collier Books, and London: Collier Macmillan, 1979
Vlack, Don, *Art Deco Architecture in New York, 1920–40*, New York: Harper and Row, 1974
Weber, Eva, *Art Deco in America*, New York: Exeter Books, 1985; as *Art Deco in North America*, London: Bison Books, 1985
Weingartner, Fannia (editor), *Streamlining America: A Henry Ford Museum Exhibit* (exhib. cat.), Dearborn, Michigan: Henry Ford Museum and Greenfield Village, 1986
Wilson, Richard Guy, Dianne Pilgrim, and Dickran Tashjian, *The Machine Age in America, 1918–41* (exhib. cat.), New York: Brooklyn Museum, 1986
Wirz, Hans, and Richard Striner, *Washington Deco: Art Deco Design in the Nation's Capital*, Washington, D.C.: Smithsonian Institution Press, 1984

ART NOUVEAU (JUGENDSTIL)

Art Nouveau was a vibrant but short-lived phenomenon that flourished but from 1890 to 1910 and touched on all the visual arts. Fashion and furniture, pots and paintings, books and buildings, no object was too small or too large, too precious or too ordinary, to be shaped by the designer working according to the ideals—moral and social as well as aesthetic—associated with the Art Nouveau, even though these ideals were never codified in a coherent manifesto and were inflected according to the place wherein they were practiced.

Although historians may question the extent, chronologically and geographically, as well as the very validity of an Art Nouveau style, several characteristics that bind its representatives together may be credibly summarized: first, a desire to avoid the historicism so dominant during the 19th century, using as inspiration Nature in all its fertility and heterogeneity; second, an emphasis on the expressive power of form and color and an aspiration to refine and elevate the material world; third, a determination to erase the distinction between the fine and the applied arts, between the designer and the craftsperson, between art and everyday life; and fourth, a willingness to experiment with materials, transforming the character of traditional ones, like stone, stained glass, and mosaic, and inventing new uses and shapes for recently developed ones, above all cast and wrought iron. In architecture and the decorative arts, there is a heightened appreciation of the role of ornament, but ornament that was novel in its formal character and was not merely applied to, but integrated with, structure.

If there were influences from the distant past in time and space, they did not lead to the imitative revivals so typical of the 19th century. Although Japanese, Islamic, and Javanese art, medieval architecture, and rococo interiors were studied, the lessons learned were assimilated into a creative synthesis intended to respond to the dawning of the new century. More immediate sources were the critic-theorists of the Gothic Revival, notably John Ruskin (1819–1900) and E.E. Viollet-le-Duc (1814–79), and figures associated with the English Arts and Crafts and Aesthetic Movements, such as William Morris (1834–96). If their goals were at times interpreted in contradictory ways, the social and professional reforms these thinkers embraced anticipated many aspects of the positive revolution in design accomplished under Art Nouveau's aegis.

The drive to embrace the new and to break from the past is embodied in the very names that designate this *fin-de-siècle* phenomenon: *Modern Style* in France, *Jugendstil* in Germany, *Modernismo* in Spain, *Nieuwe Kunst* in the Netherlands, *stil modern* in Russia, and Art Nouveau in English-speaking lands. Its antiacademic stance is embodied in the term *Secessionstil*, used in Austria and Eastern Europe. The two Italian designations identify sources: *stilo Liberty*, suggesting both the quest for freedom and the English influence (the shop, Liberty's of London, was one of the earliest purveyors of goods that appealed to Art Nouveau sensibilities), and *stilo floreale*, implying formal genesis in the world of plants. Its detractors may have dubbed it the *Vermicelli-stijl* (Netherlands) or the Spook Style (Great Britain), but these epithets did not prevent its widespread adoption.

Art Nouveau was at once international and regional. The principles of originality, organic integrity, and symbolic employment of ornament were translated according to national traditions. Especially in Scandinavia, Scotland, Switzerland, Russia, and Eastern Europe, National Romanticism was a component of Art Nouveau, and stylized peasant and vernacular motifs as well as the memory of local medieval buildings flavored its productions. Yet another principle of differentiation is whether the language is predominately curvilinear or rectilinear. In Belgium, France, and Spain, the curvilinear branch, where symmetry and repetition were assiduously avoided and sinuous vegetal shapes informed both structure and ornament, held sway; the rectilinear, where geometry controlled the stylization of natural forms, was preponderant in the Netherlands, the Austro-Hungarian empire, Scotland, and the United States. Nevertheless, one can instantly recognize in the particular national or local permutations the visual and tactile elements associated with the Art Nouveau.

Art Nouveau architects sought the challenge of unprecedented building types, like rapid transit stations and department stores, and did not confine their commissions to domestic architecture, although private houses—Hill House, Helensborough (1902–04) by Charles Rennie Mackintosh (1868–1928); the David Gamble house in Pasadena (1908) by Greene and Greene (Charles Sumner [1868–1957] and Henry Mather [1870–1954])—and blocks of flats—Castel Beranger, Paris (1895–97) by Hector Guimard (1967–1942); Majolikahaus, Vienna (1898–99) by Otto Wagner (1841–1918)—provide some of the most noteworthy examples. Thus, the Paris Metro employed Guimard, and the Viennese Stadtbahn commissioned Wagner to create appropriate structures for this most contemporary of urban facilities. La Samaritaine, Paris (1903–05) by Frantz Jourdain (1847–1935) and Carson, Pirie, Scott, Chicago (1899–1904) by Louis Sullivan (1856–1924) testify to Art Nouveau's commercial attraction for shoppers.

Various paradoxes complicate the definition of Art Nouveau. Fantastic elements have led commentators to dub its disciples

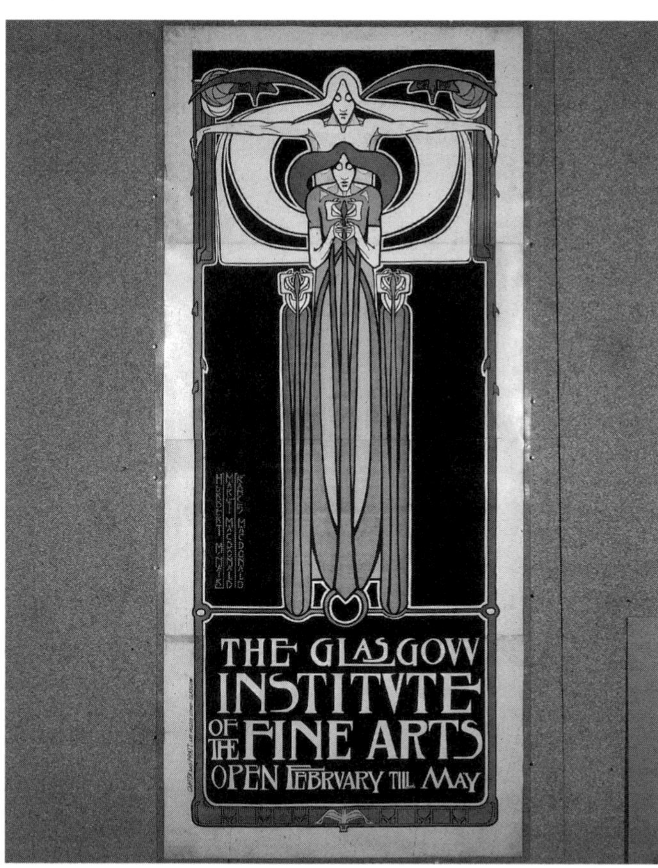

Art Nouveau lithograph poster for the opening of The Glasgow Institute of the Fine Arts, designed by Frances Macdonald (*c.* 1985) © Library of Congress

"irrational," yet many of the architects were rationalist in their sophisticated approach to technology, just as most were motivated by a wish to democratize society. Some of its acolytes were fiercely individualistic, yet others worked cooperatively in communes and workshops. Its products frequently were extravagantly luxurious and made to order for rich patrons, yet many were mass-produced, and the vocabulary, as manifested in posters, tableware, and textiles, appealed markedly to popular taste. The antagonism between the machine-made and the handcrafted that raged during the 19th century was to some extent reconciled in the Art Nouveau.

It was one of the first movements to be disseminated via specialized periodicals that enhanced its reach: *Van Nu en Straks* (Brussels-Antwerp, 1892), *The Studio* (London, 1893), *Pan* (Berlin, 1895), *Dekorative Kunst* (Munich, 1897), *Deutsche Kunst und Dekoration* (Darmstadt, 1897), *L'Art Decoratif* (Paris, 1898), and *Ver Sacrum* (Vienna, 1898) are only a few of the magazines that proselytized for Art Nouveau architecture and design.

The concept of the *Gesamtkunstwerk* (total work of art) was more potent than at any time since the 18th century. Thus, designers and artisans in many media played a crucial role, although the architect, who controlled the overall setting, was especially powerful. One of the most striking cases is the Belgian, Henri van de Velde (1863–1957), who began his career as a painter and in 1895, at his home in Uccle, established an influential decorating enterprise. He designed not only the building but everything within: furniture, table settings, wallpaper, lighting fixtures, tapestries—even his wife's clothing. Van de Velde went on to provide Samuel Bing, the entrepreneur whose Parisian shop was called "Art Nouveau," with many of his trend-setting furnishings. A member of the avant-garde Belgian organization, *Les Vingt* (Les XX), which had ties to French symbolism and the English Arts and Crafts, Van de Velde was an important link between the various groups that fed into Art Nouveau; in 1897 he moved to Germany and helped to crystallize the nascent *Jugendstil.* His career illustrates the cosmopolitan character of Art Nouveau.

One of the engines for the rapid spread of the Art Nouveau was the international exhibition. The expositions at Paris in 1900 and Turin in 1902, where almost every pavilion and its contents proclaimed Art Nouveau's ascendency, may be considered the high point of the movement. Other means of dissemination were the schools and museums of the applied arts founded during the late 19th century, educating artisans and the general public about the significance of the built environment. The Folkwang Museum in Hagen, Germany, and the Austrian Museum of Applied Arts in Vienna followed the lead of London's Victoria and Albert Museum, established in the wake of the first international (Crystal Palace) exposition, of 1851, to display decorative arts worthy of emulation.

A curiosity of the movement was the tendency for some of its adherents, including patrons, to launch workshops, firms, and even communities of like-minded souls. The *Vereinigte Werkstätten für Kunst und Handwerk* (Munich, 1897), *The Interior,* (Amsterdam, 1900), and the *Wiener Werkstätte* (Vienna, 1903) all produced decorative objects based on Art Nouveau principles. Colonies where artists could jointly pursue the ideal of the *Gesamtkunstwerk* were initiated including the *Künstlerkolonie* at Darmstadt, Germany, where Grand Duke Ernst of Hesse in 1899 invited a number of designers to live and work.

Arguably the birthplace of mature Art Nouveau is Brussels, and the figure most associated with its brilliance is Victor Horta. His Tassel House (1893) is widely accepted as the first example of Art Nouveau architecture: the sinuous curves of the organic two- and three-dimensional ornament and the artful blending of masonry and metal, tile and stained glass, were imitated throughout the continent. Horta's greatest work, the Maison de Peuple (1895–99; demolished), demonstrated the popular aspect of the style. Not only could wealthy industrialists indulge their taste for it, but their employees too recognized that it evoked their aspirations. Thus the Belgium Social Democratic Workers' Party elected the Art Nouveau as the appropriate language for its new headquarters. The striking building, emblazoned with the names of Karl Marx and other socialists, seems to grow from its hilly site, its contours undulating as if to conform to contextual dictates. The iron frame used in combination with brick and stone permits a free plan with spaces of varied heights and dimensions, perfect for accommodating the program's differing functions, revealed on the exterior through the individualized fenestration; nothing is regular or repetitive. The main door resembles a mysterious cave or mouth that draws one into its recesses, empathy being a quality exploited by many Art Nouveau architects.

Majolikahaus, Vienna, designed by Otto Wagner (1898–99)

Comparable in terms of naturalistic appearance, irregular footprint, and bold exploration of kinesthetic and emotional responses to form and space are the Casa Mila (1906–10) in Barcelona by Antonio Gaudí, and the Humbert de Romans building in Paris (1897–1901; destroyed) by Guimard. Like the Belgian, the Catalan and the Frenchman were indebted to Viollet-le-Duc, especially his projects using the new material of iron, but where Viollet was still in thrall to his Gothic sources, this later trio subsumes them into a totally novel vocabulary derived from flora and fauna. The devout Gaudí believed that "nature is God's architect" (Collins, 1960), whereas Guimard saw Nature as "a great book from which to derive inspiration," replacing the archaeological tomes of the revivalists.

The more rectilinear version of Art Nouveau retains nature as the basic source of imagery but emphasizes the geometric substructure underlying organic forms, as described with particular insight by the German theorist Gottfried Semper (1803–79), and symmetry is not rejected. Works by H.P. Berlage, Wagner, Olbrich, and Josef Hoffmann belong in this camp, as do those by designers in Britain and the United States with roots directly in the Arts and Crafts movement (e.g., C.R. Ashbee, Mackintosh, Charles Harrison Townsend, Frank Lloyd Wright, and the brothers Greene). Right angles and straight lines prevail, the stylized decorative motifs are less intuitive and more cerebral, and metal structure, although occasionally present, is subordinated to more conventional materials like wood, stone, and brick, the latter often plastered.

Most of the architects of High Art Nouveau turned away from the style by the end of the first decade of the 20th century, those from the curvilinear branch toward Expressionism, those practicing the rectilinear version toward modernism or academicism; in France and Austria, the Art Nouveau smoothly metamorphosed into Art Deco. In the second half of the 20th century, sporadic Art Nouveau revivals have occurred. Short its reign may have been, but Art Nouveau's spell endures.

HELEN SEARING

See also **Arts and Crafts Movement; Casa Milà, Barcelona; Gaudí, Antoni (Spain); Greene, Henry M. and Charles S. (United States); Hoffmann, Josef (Austria); Horta, Victor (Belgium); Mackintosh, Charles Rennie (Scotland); Metro Station, Paris; Olbrich, Josef Maria (Austria); van de Velde, Henri (Belgium); Vienna Secession; Wagner, Otto (Austria)**

Further Reading

After its decisive rejection in the first decade of the 20th century, scholarly and popular interest in Art Nouveau evaporated (although the course of Art Deco in many ways recapitulated that of Art Nouveau), thanks in part to a revival of historicism but more definitively to the triumph of international modernism, with its proscription against ornament. Then in 1959 came the groundbreaking exhibition at New York's Museum of Modern Art. Whether renewed attention was driven by the exhibition or whether the show itself was prompted by a sudden collecting frenzy for Art Nouveau objects is difficult to ascertain, but what is clear is that the Art Nouveau gradually achieved a respectability that it has not relinquished. The MoMA catalogue was important also because it included architecture, although most subsequent publications continued to emphasize the decorative arts until 1979, when Frank Russell edited a volume devoted to architecture. Since then, the vital significance of architecture to the movement as a whole has been recognized, and surveys do not fail to include buildings that fit within the canon.

Amaya, Mario, *Art Nouveau*, London: Studio Vista, 1966

Borsi, Franco, *Bruxelles 1900*, Brussels: M. Vokaer, 1974

Borsi, Franco, and Ezio Godoli, *Paris 1900*, New York: Rizzoli, 1977

Borsi, Franco, and Ezio Godoli, *Vienna 1900: Architecture and Design*, New York: Rizzoli, 1986

Brunhammer, Yvonne, *Art Nouveau Belgium, France*, Houston: Rice University, 1976

Collins, George, *Antonio Gaudí*, New York: Braziller, 1960

Cremonan, Italo, *Il Tempo dell'Art Nouveau: Modern Style, Sezession, Jugendstil, Arts and Crafts, Floreale, Liberty*, Florence: Vallechi, 1964

Greenhalgh, Paul (editor), *Art Nouveau 1890–1914*, London: Victoria and Albert Museum, 2000

Howard, Jeremy, *Art Nouveau: International and National Styles in Europe*, Manchester and New York: Manchester University Press, 1996

Lambourne, Lionel, *Utopian Craftsmen*, Salt Lake City: Peregrine Smith, 1980

Lenning, Henry, *The Art Nouveau*, The Hague: Martinus Nijhoff, 1951

Pevsner, Nikolaus, *The Sources of Modern Architecture and Design*, New York: Praeger, 1968

Pevsner, Nikolaus, *Pioneers of the Modern Movement from William Morris to Walter Gropius*, London: Faber and Faber, 1936

Pevsner, Nicolaus, and J.M. Richards (editors), *The Anti-Rationalists*, London: The Architectural Press, 1973

Rheims, Morris, *The Flowering of Art Nouveau*, translated by Patrick Evans, New York: Abrams, [1966]

Russell, Frank (editor), *Art Nouveau Architecture*, London: Academy Editions, 1979

Schmutzler, Robert, *Art Nouveau—Jugendstil*, Stuttgart: Gerd Hatje, 1962; as *Art Nouveau*, translated by Edrouard Roditi, London: Thames and Hudson, 1964

Selz, Peter, and Mildred Constantine (editors), *Art Nouveau—Art and Design at the Turn of the Century*, New York: Museum of Modern Art, 1975

Silverman, Deborah, *Art Nouveau in Fin-de-Siècle France: Politics, Psychology, Style*, Berkeley: University of California Press, 1989

Thiébaut, Philippe, and Bruno Girveau, *Art Nouveau Architecture*, London: Thames and Hudson, 2000

Tschudi-Madsen, Stephen, *Art Nouveau*, London: Thames and Hudson, 1967

Varnedoe, Kirk, *Vienna 1900: Art, Architecture & Design*, New York: Museum of Modern Art, 1986

Weisberg, Gabriel, and Elizabeth Menon, *Art Nouveau: A Research Guide for Design Reform in France, Belgium, England and the United States*, New York: Garland, 1998

ARTS AND CRAFTS MOVEMENT

Although the Arts and Crafts movement dominated England between the years 1860 and 1915, its effects were felt around the world, especially in Western Europe and the United States, well into the 1920s. Artwork associated with the Arts and Crafts movement is characterized by a handcrafted aesthetic that embodied the principles of its English founders: C.R. Ashbee, W.R. Lethaby, and William Morris, among others. The philosophy these men advocated centered on their belief that the Industrial Revolution had produced substandard goods with little artistic merit. In response to this situation, they sought to reintroduce handmade products to the arts and to elevate the craftsman to a more prominent position in the design professions. In refocusing the production of art away from machines and toward individual designers, Arts and Crafts leaders hoped to reform society by changing the way art was created, patronized, and appreciated in English society.

The Arts and Crafts movement promoted the idea of truth in architecture, meaning that a building should clearly express its structure, function, and material. An uncluttered exterior and interior, without applied decoration to obscure the structure, was considered the ideal, partly because the aesthetic was easily achieved without machines. This idea of truth and clarity in architecture contrasted sharply with the Victorian aesthetic currently in vogue in England in which elaborate and ornate decorations, usually multicolored and machine-made, dominated architectural design. Ashbee, Lethaby, and Morris believed that Victorian interiors hid truth and clarity from the viewer by obscuring the forms and shapes of a building. To this end, the simpler aesthetic of the Arts and Crafts returned truth to architecture and contrasted with the "false" art created by the machine.

The idea of a simple aesthetic had regional, national, and historic overtones. Leaders of the Arts and Crafts movement argued that the corrupted state of artistic production resulted from the negative influence of industrialization on Western, particularly English, society. Therefore, artistic production could be reformed by reviving methods of art and craft that predated the industrial era. As viewed by the Arts and Crafts founders, the period that best exemplified the preferred mode of artistic production was the age of English medieval architecture. Not only did English medieval architecture fully embody the Arts and Crafts ideal of a simple and truthful aesthetic, but buildings of the style were local and easily available for study. Most important, the forms of English medieval structures were already synonymous with the English architectural identity, and therefore reviving English medieval art and craft promoted the English national identity through architectural form. In using English medieval models, Ashbee, Lethaby, and Morris made direct connections between the past and the present and between the historic and the modern to make the Arts and Crafts aesthetic pertain directly to England.

The use of English medieval models also embodied the vision of craftsmen working for a truthful aesthetic, which Arts and Crafts leaders strenuously advocated. In general, English medieval structures had been constructed by laborers who worked with hand tools to build a collective monument from honest artistic labor. Ashbee, Lethaby, and Morris argued that because the work of these craftsmen was not mass-produced, it had not been corrupted by the machine. Therefore, English medieval models served as examples of how the individual craftsman could enhance the design of an aesthetic masterpiece by ensuring that every part of the design received individual attention and that every form was designed and created by hand. Ashbee, Lethaby, and Morris envisioned groups of craftsmen, metalworkers, stonecutters, and carpenters working together toward a finished product that combined a variety of different media. Inspired by these medieval models, Arts and Crafts leaders believed that artistic production could separate itself from the mechanized methods of the Victorian age to create a detailed and truthful expression of its time and place.

Attention to detail resulted in an idea that was fundamental to the Arts and Crafts movement: that of a total work of art. The Arts and Crafts aesthetic was not limited to any one particular medium; in fact, Ashbee, Lethaby, and Morris argued that all arts should be used to create a complete effect such that the whole became more than the sum of its parts. Every aspect of an Arts and Crafts interior or structure, whether it was art or architecture, was considered relevant to the design, and in this way the entire environment was subject to consideration by a designer or a design team. To this end, many Arts and Crafts workers began to experiment with processes that machines had performed for decades, and crafts such as fabric dyeing and printing experienced a renaissance as new methods were investigated and new objects produced.

Because the Arts and Crafts movement is a movement largely of ideas, it is difficult to single out particular designers or works, or to identify particular forms as characteristic of the Arts and Crafts style. In terms of architecture, Philip Webb's Red House, in Upton, Kent, commissioned by Morris in 1859, serves as one outstanding example of Arts and Crafts architecture in England. Taking its name from its red brick construction, the design of the Red House avoided all decoration that recalled a direct model and instead followed the functional needs of Morris and his family. Murals, wall hangings, tapestries, and wallpapers together created a homey and medieval ambience through natural motifs that included animals, birds, flowers, and trees, all of which were native to the area or to England. Designed and crafted by Morris, his wife Jane, Philip Webb, and Morris's friend Dante Gabriel Rosetti, the Red House expressed a relaxed and informal medieval atmosphere where different artistic media conveyed a total aesthetic.

Arts and Crafts architecture relied on historic local and regional influences to ensure that each house would wholly be a product of its place. Looking back to earlier examples of Scottish domestic architecture, Charles Rennie Mackintosh intended his 1903 Hill House, in Helensburgh, Dunbartonshire, Scotland, to connect with the Scottish medieval past through a re-use of medieval and local forms. Like that at the Red House, Hill House's facade is plain, with limited applied ornament. The exterior consisted of smooth stucco with low, protective eaves; deep windows and porches; and buttresses that were borrowed

Interior designs of Hill House, Helensburgh, Scotland, designed by Charles Rennie Mackintosh (*c.* 1903)

from nearby examples of the medieval country church. Inside, Hill House embodied the same idea of a total work of art in its consideration of all aspects of the space. Dark wood shaped in simple and linear forms decorated the walls, while the beams supporting the upper stories were left open to view. Handcrafted furniture and plain, white walls created a cozy effect, while the lighting filtered through wooden screens and lampshades to warm the room. Mackintosh's appreciation for the materials and his honest expression of the structure through planar forms made Hill House fully represent the goals of the Arts and Crafts movement.

The Arts and Crafts movement had greater impact on craft than on architecture, as craftsmen were encouraged to incorporate many different artistic media into a single product. Many Arts and Crafts designers worked in groups or partnerships, with each partner specializing in a different process, such as printing or metalwork. Morris's firm, Morris, Marshall, Faulkner and Company, founded by Morris in 1861, serves as an excellent example of this diversity, as the firm could produce wallpaper, furniture, murals, stained glass, carvings, metalwork, and tapestries. The inclusion of different artistic media not only added to the overall effect of the Arts and Crafts interior but also recalled the idea of a medieval system in which different artists worked together, each providing an essential and necessary component that enhanced the overall product.

The Arts and Crafts ideology and aesthetic was not limited to English and Scottish designers. The reform efforts of Ashbee, Lethaby, Morris, and Mackintosh resonated with designers of other nations, many of whom struggled with the issue of artistic national identity, the impact of the machine on society, and the economic effect of mechanized art. Each nation, however, tended to isolate and incorporate different aspects of the ideology of the Arts and Crafts movement as they related to each nation's context. In the United States, for example, Morris's ideas were complemented by the efforts of Gustav Stickley, who promoted an agenda similar to Morris's through his magazine, *The Craftsman*. For Stickley, a return to a handcrafted aesthetic not only promoted art and social reform but also educated the public and provided many with the means to earn their own living. Unlike the English Arts and Crafts leaders, Stickley was less concerned with evoking a medieval atmosphere in his designs, especially because the medieval did not have a connection to the American past. Instead, Stickley argued that the simple Arts and Crafts aesthetic could enhance the social conditions of the worker. As a result Stickley chose to harness the power of the machine in favor of the worker rather than at the worker's expense. Ultimately, Stickley's more famous designs, such as the 1903 Morris chair, were produced by his own workers using machine technology.

Outside of Stickley's magazine and furniture empire, other American designers worked to apply Arts and Crafts principles to American design. One team of designers, Charles Sumner Greene and his brother, Henry Mather Greene, experimented with native materials in the design of the 1908 David B. Gamble House in Pasadena, California. Aesthetically, the Gamble House explored craftsmanship through a new venue that merged nature with handcraft, such that the Gamble House expressed its total work of art through a strong connection between building and landscape. In contrast to the Greene Brothers' design is the work of Frank Lloyd Wright, who used machines to create a similar effect. The Robie House (1908) in Chicago is an example of Wright's efforts to use simple forms and low-hanging eaves to evoke a sense of movement between parts. Like most other Arts and Crafts designers, Wright carefully considered the appearance of the interior, using rich materials and patterns to create a sumptuous yet planar aesthetic. Although Wright's interiors relied on machines for their production, his interest in promoting a unified interior and the straightforward use of natural materials resembled ideas from the English Arts and Crafts leaders.

Like American designers, European designers placed more and less emphasis on different aspects of the Arts and Crafts ideology. In Belgium and France, the Art Nouveau movement, spearheaded by Samuel Bing, Victor Horta, and Hector Guimard, sought to strike a new balance between modernity and handcraft through an emphasis on naturalistic forms. In Barcelona, Spain, Antoni Gaudí explored regional identity through the native materials he used to create an imaginative and unique architectural style. Likewise, in Austria, the Vienna Secession movement, under the leadership of Otto Wagner, advocated an artistic break from the past and experimented with simple forms and planar volumes. All the products—art, architecture, and crafts—produced by French, Belgian, Spanish, and Viennese designers in these movements borrowed from the Arts and Crafts ideology, even if their work resulted in vastly different forms.

By 1914 the Arts and Crafts movement had faded from the architectural scene, and new ideas moved into its place, taking English, American, and Western European designers into the machine aesthetic and the International Style. Scholars recognized that the Arts and Crafts movement had important links with the Modern movement, which had first promoted the idea that architecture could reform society. Some designers, such as Walter Gropius and Frank Lloyd Wright, had direct connections with Arts and Crafts ideology and partook in the Arts and Crafts revolution of form, helping to refocus artistic production from its classical roots to its modern agenda. Without the simplicity of the Arts and Crafts movement and its emphasis on social reform, the Modern movement would have lacked a certain strength and vigor. The Arts and Crafts movement represents an important precursor to subsequent movements and the development of new forms for architectural production.

CATHERINE W. ZIPF

See also **Gaudí, Antoni (Spain); Gropius, Walter (Germany); Horta, Victor (Belgium); Mackintosh, Charles Rennie (Scotland); Robie House, Chicago; Stickley, Gustav (United States); Wagner, Otto (Austria); Wright, Frank Lloyd (United States)**

Further Reading

A good overview of the movement and the crafts it produced appears in Naylor 1989. Cumming includes a more theoretical description of the ideas involved in the production of Arts and Crafts goods. For biographical information on Morris, see Stansky. For biographical information on Stickley, see Sanders. For women's participation in the Arts and Crafts movement, see Callen.

Anscombe, Isabelle, *Arts and Crafts Style*, New York: Rizzoli, and Oxford: Phaidon, 1991

Bowman, Leslie Greene, *American Arts and Crafts: Virtue in Design*, Los Angeles: Los Angeles County Museum of Art, and Boston: Bulfinch Press/Little Brown, 1990; London: Bulfinch/Little Brown, 1992

Brooks, H. Allen, *The Prairie School: Frank Lloyd Wright and His Midwest Contemporaries*, Toronto: University of Toronto Press, 1972; New York: Norton, 1976
Callen, Anthea, *Women Artists of the Arts and Crafts Movement, 1870–1914*, New York: Pantheon, 1979; as *Angel in the Studio: Women in the Arts and Crafts Movement, 1870–1914*, London: Astragal, 1979
Clark, Robert Judson (editor), *The Arts and Crafts Movement in America, 1876–1916*, Princeton, New Jersey: Princeton University Press, 1972
Coote, Stephen, *William Morris: His Life and Work*, London: Garamond, 1990; New York: Smithmark, 1995
Cumming, Elizabeth, and Wendy Kaplan, *The Arts and Crafts Movement*, New York: Thames and Hudson, 1991
Davey, Peter, *Architecture of the Arts and Crafts Movement*, New York: Rizzoli, 1980; as *Arts and Crafts Architecture*, London: Architectural Press, 1980
Kaplan, Wendy (editor), *"The Art That Is Life": The Arts and Crafts Movement in America, 1875–1920*, Boston: Little Brown, 1987
MacCarthy, Fiona, *William Morris: A Life for Our Time*, London: Faber and Faber, 1994; New York: Knopf, 1995
Morris, William, *News from Nowhere and Other Writings*, London and New York: Penguin, 1993
Naylor, Gillian, *The Arts and Crafts Movement: A Study of Its Sources, Ideals, and Influence on Design Theory*, London: Studio Vista, and Cambridge, Massachusetts: MIT Press, 1971; new edition, London: Trefoil, 1990
Naylor, Gillian, et al., *The Encyclopedia of Arts and Crafts: The International Arts Movement, 1850–1920*, New York: Dutton, 1989
Sanders, Barry, *A Complex Fate: Gustav Stickley and the Craftsman Movement*, New York: Wiley, 1996
Stansky, Peter, *Redesigning the World: William Morris, the 1880s, and the Arts and Crafts*, Princeton, New Jersey: Princeton University Press, 1985
Stickley, Gustav, *Craftsman Homes*, New York: Craftsmen, 1909; reprint, New York: Dover, 1979
Trapp, Kenneth R. (editor), *The Arts and Crafts Movement in California: Living the Good Life*, New York: Abbeville Press, 1993

ARUP, OVE 1895–1988

Architectural engineer, England

Ove Arup was arguably one of the greatest engineers of the 20th century. Born in 1895 in Newcastle upon Tyne in England to Scandinavian parents, he first studied philosophy and graduated from the University of Copenhagen in 1916. Six years later, he received a second degree in engineering. This wide-ranging interest and curiosity was to influence both his own work and that of others with whom he consulted. Throughout his life—his practice Ove Arup and Partners grew to include more than 50 offices in 40 countries with a staff of almost 4,000—he retained a speculative yet rigorously questioning approach to design.

Having qualified as a civil engineer and with a special interest in reinforced concrete, Arup joined the Danish company Christiani and Nielsen in 1922, a company that designed and built civil engineering structures. He worked in Hamburg before moving to their London office, where he became chief designer in 1925.

With this experience not only in the design but also in the construction of structures, Arup became increasingly interested in developing a holistic approach to design. His particular skill in the use of a new material, reinforced concrete, created opportunities for him to work with other designers who were committed to the ideals of the Modern movement. Collaborating with Tecton (a group of young architects in London) and with Berthold Lubetkin in particular, Arup was to play an influential role in the design of a several iconic buildings of the period. The first was the Gorilla House (1933) at the London Zoo, followed by the Penguin Pool (1934). Both explored the fluid forms made possible by using reinforced concrete. He went on to work with Lubetkin on the design of Highpoint One. This residential building in London was also built in reinforced concrete but explored the potential of the material to create an eight-story tower.

The construction of Highpoint coincided with Arup's move in 1934 to join J.L. Kier and Company, the contractors who built the scheme. This project was especially significant because it allowed Arup and Lubetkin to work on a design that required the complete integration of architecture, structure, and building method. As a result, Arup became increasingly enthusiastic about collaboration between the professions in building design, an enthusiasm that motivated his own practice.

Established in 1946, the practice was formerly called Ove Arup and Partners, Consulting Engineers, in 1949, flourishing

Finsbury Avenue Offices, London, designed by Ove Arup and Associates (1984)

in the postwar period with the reconstruction of cities and the design of numerous new buildings and improved infrastructure. Arup was sought out by an increasing number of architects, especially those who were interested in innovative forms of engineering, integrative design, and the use of new materials. His work at this time included the Brynmawr Rubber Factory (1952, Gwent) in Wales, designed with Architects Co-Partnership; Michael Scott's Bus Station and Offices (1952) in Dublin; and the Hunstanton School (1954, London), designed by Alison and Peter Smithson. After the young Danish architect Jørn Utzon won the competition to design the Sydney Opera House in Australia in 1957, he asked Arup to collaborate on the design. Arup played a central role in the translation of the architect's early sketches into an outstanding building defined by the famous series of elegant vaulted roofs. After the building opened to acclaim in 1973, the material research and design studies established Arup's reputation as an engineer of great creativity and international standing.

Arup designed a number of significant civil engineering projects, including the Kingsgate Footbridge (1963) over the River Wear in Durham, England. He brought together structural and civil engineers, environmental engineers, building economists, and architects in a parallel partnership, Arup Associates, to design buildings and engineering structures. Ove Arup and Partners grew as a multidisciplinary consultancy and became one of the largest engineering design practices in the world. This collaborative, interprofessional way of working enhanced talent and made the practice a center for design innovation and research. After the Sydney Opera House, Arup and his colleagues worked with the German engineer Frei Otto on the development of lightweight structures, studies that were to result in projects such as the Garden Pavilion (1975) in Mannheim. Collaboration with Richard Rogers and Renzo Piano on their competition entry for the Centre Pompidou in Paris was awarded first prize in 1971. In 1979 a further collaboration with Richard Rogers and another with Norman Foster resulted in successful designs for limited competitions for new headquarters buildings for Lloyds of London (1979–85) and the Hong Kong and Shanghai Bank (completed in 1986) in Hong Kong. Arup also continued to work with Renzo Piano on numerous projects, including the Menil Gallery (1984) and Kansai International Airport (1988–94).

Arup advocated a way of working that not only brought together many of the disciplines to generate ideas at the beginning of the design process but that also created multidisciplinary teams that directed projects through to completion. Many other significant engineers emerged from the practice, including Jack Zunz, Ted Happold, Tom Barker, Peter Rice, Jane Wernick, Chris Wise, and Cecil Balmond.

Arup received the Royal Gold Medal for Architecture in 1966 and in 1971 was knighted by the queen of England for his services to architecture and engineering. His inspiration created a practice that has been central to the development of outstanding architecture and structural design worldwide. He remained actively involved in practice until his death in 1988.

BRIAN CARTER

See also **Kansai International Airport Terminal, Osaka; Lubetkin and Tecton (Great Britain); Piano, Renzo (Italy); Rogers, Richard (Great Britain); Smithson, Peter and Alison (Great Britain); Sydney Opera House**

Biography

Born in Newcastle upon Tyne, England, to Danish parents, 16 April 1895. Studied philosophy and mathematics, University of Copenhagen, Denmark; bachelor of arts 1916; studied civil engineering, Royal Technical College, Copenhagen 1916–22; bachelor of science 1922. Married Ruth Sorenson 1925: 3 children. Designer 1922–25, chief designer 1925–34, Christiani and Nielsen, Hamburg, Germany; chief designer, J.L. Kier and Company, London 1934–38. Director, Arup Designers Ltd., London and Arup and Arup Ltd. with cousin 1938–46; consultant engineer to the Air Ministry, London 1938–45; private practice as engineering consultant, London 1946–49; senior partner, Ove Arup and Partners, London from 1949; senior partner, Arup Associates, London from 1963. Visiting lecturer, Harvard University, Cambridge, Massachusetts 1955; Alfred Bossom Lecturer, Royal Society of Arts, London 1970. Founding member, MARS (Modern Architecture Research Group), London 1933; fellow, Institute of Structural Engineers 1940; fellow, Institute of Civil Engineers 1951; chairman, Society of Danish Civil Engineers in Great Britain and Ireland 1955–59; fellow, American Concrete Institute 1975. Commander, Order of the British Empire 1953; Gold Medal, Royal Institute of British Architects 1966; Knight Bachelor 1971; Chevalier 1965, Commander 1975, Order of the Dannebrog, Denmark; Aga Khan Award for Architecture 1980. Died in London, England, 2 February 1988.

Selected Works

Gorilla House, London Zoo, 1933
Penguin Pool, London Zoo, 1934
Highpoint I Apartment Building, Highgate, London, 1936
Brynmawr Rubber Company Factory, Gwent, Wales (with Architects Co-Partnership), 1952
Bus Station, Dublin, 1952
Hunstanton School, London, 1954
Kingsgate Footbridge, Durham, England, 1963
Sydney Opera House (first prize, 1957 competition; with Jørn Utzon), 1973
Garden Pavilion, Mannheim, Germany (with Frei Otto), 1975
Centre Georges Pompidou (first prize, 1971 competition; with Renzo Piano and Richard Rogers), Paris, 1977
Finsbury Avenue Offices, London, 1984
Menil Gallery, Houston (with Piano), 1984
Lloyds of London Headquarters (first prize, 1978 competition; with Rogers), London, 1985
Hong Kong and Shanghai Bank (first prize, 1980 competition; with Norman Foster), Hong Kong, 1986
Kansai International Airport, Osaka (with Piano), 1994

Selected Publications

Design, Cost, Construction, and Relative Safety of Trench, Surface, Bombproof, and Other Air Raid Shelters, 1939
London's Shelter Problem, 1940
Safe Housing in Wartime, 1941
Ove Arup and Partners 1946–1986, 1986

Further Reading

Arup, Ove, *Ove Arup*, London: Institution of Civil Engineers, 1995
Dunster, David (editor), *Arups on Engineering*, London: Ernst and Sohn, 1996
Rice, Peter, *An Engineer Imagines*, London: Artemis, 1994; 2nd edition, London: Ellipsis, 1996
Silver, Nathan, *The Making of Beaubourg: A Building Biography of the Centre Pompidou, Paris*, Cambridge, Massachusetts: MIT Press, 1994
Sommer, Degenhard, Herbert Stöcher, and Lutz Weisser, *Ove Arup and Partners: Engineering the Built Environment: Philosophpy, Projects, Experience*, Basel and Boston: Birkhäuser Verlag, 1994

ASHBEE, C.R. 1863–1942

Architect, England

C.R. Ashbee was one of the best-known figures of the British Arts and Crafts movement. He was born on 17 May 1863 in Spring Grove, Isleworth, on the western fringe of London. Ashbee attended Wellington College from 1877 to 1882 and graduated from King's College, Cambridge, in 1886. At King's College, Ashbee became exposed to the thoughts of Ruskin, which were to influence his lifelong commitment to the Arts and Crafts. Among Ashbee's noteworthy accomplishments were the founding of the Guild of Handicraft; a series of houses on Cheyne Walk, London; the development of the Survey of London; and his role as civic adviser to the city of Jerusalem during renovations to the old city.

Following King's College, Ashbee joined the architectural firm of Bodley and Garner, the leading English church architects of their day. For the next two years, Ashbee lived at Toynbee Hall, meeting William Morris for the first time on 4 January 1886. Ashbee drew on his experiences at Toynbee Hall in founding his own School and Guild of Handicraft, inaugurated on 23 January 1888. The School and Guild grew in part from Ashbee's reading class on Ruskin in the winter of 1896–97 and a later class on drawing and decoration (both at Toynbee Hall). Ashbee rented for two years the top floor of a warehouse on Commercial Street, which served as a combined workshop and schoolroom. The primary goal of the School and Guild, observed Ashbee, was "the application of Art to Industry" (Burrough, 1969, p. 85). The School lasted only until 1895, but the Guild (which produced furniture, silver and metalwork, jewelry, and later, books) was Ashbee's constant focus until it began to decline in 1905. Shortly after its inauguration, the Guild's work was favorably received at the first exhibition of the Fine Arts and Crafts Exhibition Society in September 1888. After William Morris's death in 1896, the Guild purchased and operated his Kelmscott Press. For most of his career, Ashbee maintained an architectural office as well as the Guild of Handicraft. His first architectural office opened in September 1890 at 15 Lincoln's End Fields, London. Soon the volume of work required a larger space, and the firm moved to Essex House on Mile End Road in 1891.

A major undertaking of Ashbee's career was the large-scale movement of the Guild of Handicraft, its workers, and their families to Chipping Campden in the Gloucestershire countryside in 1902. Inspired by Ruskin's 1882 explanation of his St. George's Guild, focusing on the value of rural life, work, and community, Ashbee and his Guild renovated buildings in the small rural town for their purposes. Chief among the renovated buildings was the old Silk Mill (1902, woodshed and engine house; 1909, pottery kilns), which became the center of the Chipping Campden site. By 1905, however, the Guild was in decline. Its distance from London made marketing its wares more difficult, and competitors, such as Liberty, began to produce comparatively inexpensive copies of its silver work. The dismal economic times and remote location of the Guild made letting workers go an impractical solution to these problems. Instead, the Guild began to liquidate its assets in 1907. Despite the Guild's eventual demise, it served as a model for other socially conscious projects, such as Jane Addams's Hull House in Chicago.

In addition to his work with the Guild, Ashbee designed, built, and renovated many houses, including several on Cheyne Walk, London, where his work is perhaps best known. He combined the ambiance of old London, brickwork, and an asymmetrical arrangement of elements to produce simple and functional houses appropriate for their riverside setting. In 1893 Ashbee began work on the first house—The Ancient Magpie and Stump at 37 Cheyne Walk—which became his mother's house and was Ashbee's first executed design. He then bought land that he

38 Cheyne Walk, London, designed by C.R. Ashbee (1898–99)
© Philippa Lewis, Edifice/CORBIS

was interested in developing, designed houses for the land, and showed the homes to friends, colleagues, and real estate agents to attract a clientele. Ashbee created drawings for 21 sites, often designing multiple schemes simultaneously. Other homes in the area with which Ashbee was involved as architect or renovator were 24 Cheyne Row (1895) and the following structures on Cheyne Walk: 72–73 (1896–97), 118–119 (1897–98), 74 (1897–98), 38–39 (1898–99), and 75 (1901–02). Of these houses, only 38–39 survives.

Ashbee also made significant contributions to architecture and the study of its history through two additional projects. In 1894 he began work on the Survey of London, one of his most enduring legacies to English architectural history. The aim of this ambitious project was to record all historic buildings in London. Today, the Survey of London is a continuing and scholarly record. Following the Guild's demise, Ashbee was appointed civic adviser to the city of Jerusalem to survey the old city and to begin the restoration process. Ashbee worked on the restoration of Jerusalem between 1919 and 1922, when he resigned and retired to Godden Green, Kent.

In addition to his architectural and crafts pursuits, Ashbee traveled and lectured extensively in the United States in 1896 and 1900–01 (the East and Midwest) and in 1908–09 (California), visiting some 14 states on his coast-to-coast tour. Some time in late November or early December 1900, Ashbee met Frank Lloyd Wright, with whom he was to keep up a lifelong correspondence and friendship. During his 1909 visit to California, Ashbee met Charles Sumner Greene and was impressed by the architectural and furniture work of the firm, which was just completing work on the Blacker and Gamble Houses in Pasadena, California.

Ashbee died on 23 May 1942. His multidimensional life had been dedicated to his belief that "the things which made for good craftsmanship were in the end neither technical nor aesthetic, but moral and social" (Crawford, 1985, p. 213).

CYNTHIA DUQUETTE SMITH

See also **Arts and Crafts Movement; Greene, Henry M. and Charles S. (United States); Wright, Frank Lloyd (United States)**

Further Reading

The most comprehensive and authoritative examination of Ashbee's life and work is provided by Crawford (1985). MacCarthy (1981) focuses on the social aspects of Ashbee's family and Guild life and the movement of the Guild to the Cotswolds. Burrough's (1969) two-part article in *Connoisseur*, offers a thorough overview of the Guild's history and handicrafts, but less focus on the architectural aspects of Ashbee's career.

Burrough, B.G., "Three Disciples of William Morris: 2 Charles Robert Ashbee, Part 1," *Connoisseur*, 171 (October 1969)

Burrough, B.G., "Three Disciples of William Morris: 2 Charles Robert Ashbee, Part 1," *Connoisseur*, 171 (December 1969)

Crawford, Alan, *C.R. Ashbee: Architect, Designer & Romantic Socialist*, New Haven, Connecticut: Yale University Press, 1985

Crawford, Alan, "Ten Letters from Frank Lloyd Wright to Charles Robert Ashbee," *Architectural History*, 13 (1970)

MacCarthy, Fiona, *The Simple Life: C.R. Ashbee in the Cotswolds*, Berkeley: University of California Press, 1981

Winter, Robert W., "American Sheaves from 'C.R.A.' and Janet Ashbee," *Society of Architectural Historians Journal*, 30 (December 1971)

ASPLUND, ERIK GUNNAR 1885–1940

Architect, Sweden

Erik Gunnar Asplund was among the most important Scandinavian architects of the first half of the 20th century. His early work evolved from National Romanticism through the sparse Nordic classicism of the World War I period and by 1930 embraced canonic modernism. At the time of his death in 1940, his work assumed a personal direction, influenced more by traditional architecture and a desire for symbolic content than by contemporaneous design tenets. Asplund had a unique ability to create a sense of place in his architecture, to manifest directly the context in which his works were situated through manipulating landscape elements as forcefully as architectural ones. His untimely death at age 55 occurred at the height of his creative powers and productivity.

Born in Stockholm, Asplund studied architecture at the Royal Institute of Technology. After traveling to Germany on an Institute Scholarship, he returned to Stockholm and helped establish, with some fellow students, the Klara School, an independent academy of design. Supplanting the more normative neoclassical training of the period, the Klara School, under the tutelage of Carl Bergsten, Ragnar Östberg, Ivar Tengbom, and Carl Westman, proposed a Romantic sensibility incorporating the influence of Scandinavian vernacular design and handicrafts. The inclusion of vernacular and traditional sources of expression had influenced Nordic architecture since the turn of the century, creating a style known as National Romanticism. The National Romantic influences of Westman and Östberg, and especially Östberg's ability to combine symmetrical facade composition with informal plan organization, informed Asplund's early work: examples include the villa project for Ivar Asplund (1911), the Karlshamn School competition entry (1912), and the Villa Ruth (1914). These works are characterized by a vernacular imagery created through using traditional board and batten siding, tile-covered gable-roof forms, and carefully placed and proportioned window openings.

Asplund, while continuing to use vernacular imagery, began to use classical motifs in his work, as witnessed in the first-place competition entry for the Woodland Cemetery (1915, Stockholm; in collaboration with Sigurd Lewerentz) and his Woodland Chapel (1919, Stockholm), which blends Romanticism and Classicism. The simple, steeply pitched chapel roof recalls Swedish vernacular buildings, whereas the austere Doric portico, domed interior space, and white-rendered stucco walls reference classicism. The Villa Snellman (1918), located in Djursholm, a Stockholm suburb, continues Asplund's dialogue between classicism and Romanticism, as does the Lister County Courthouse (1921, Sölvesborg). In the Courthouse, however, the detail qualities of the building become somewhat idiosyncratic, even exaggerated, in execution. Three competition entries for urban projects entered during the period 1917–22—the Göta Square (1917) and the Gustaf Adolf Square (1918), both in Göteborg, and the Royal Chancellery (1922) in Stockholm—indicate that

Woodland Chapel, Stockholm, Sweden, designed by Erik Gunnar Asplund (1919)

Asplund's sensitivity in designing buildings within the historical context of the city is equal to that within the natural landscape.

Paralleling the development of classicism in Scandinavia during the 1920s, the classical-Romantic duality of Asplund's earlier work gave way to a more explicit expression of classical principles. The work of this period represents a serious attempt at innovation within the context of classicism rather than a nascent eclecticism. Two buildings in Stockholm, the Skandia Cinema (1923) and the Public Library (1928), demonstrated his leadership position in this pan-Nordic movement. Whereas the Skandia Cinema projects a certain playful and idiosyncratic use of classical elements, motifs, and images, the Public Library has a simplicity and austerity reminiscent of the neoclassical architecture of the French Enlightenment. Although the initial design for the library was explicitly classical, with coffered dome, columnar entry porticos, and *palazzo*-like facade treatment, the built work, while maintaining the organizational *parti*, was abstracted into two simple volumetric elements: cube and cylinder. Preceded by a large reflecting pool, the building sits slightly rotated in its parklike setting, further enhancing the monumentality of the austere volumes. The cylinder houses a great rotunda, which contains the tiered, open-stack lending hall. It is a monumental clerestoried space that recalls the work of the French 18th-century architect Etienne-Louis Boullée. Exterior and interior surfaces are rendered in stucco, with finely proportioned openings and excellently crafted and integrated sculptural detail that provide the building with a subtle power.

The Stockholm Public Library marks the end of Nordic classicism, for "functionalism," as modernism was termed in Scandinavia, had appeared in Sweden. Asplund's 1930 Stockholm Exhibition celebrated the emergence of functionalism in Sweden and represented a fundamental change in sensibility for the architect. The design for the Exhibition complex underwent three phases, the last occurring after Asplund traveled to the Continent to visit extant examples of the new "modern" architecture. The Stockholm Exhibition not only epitomized the mechanistic aesthetics of modernism but also served as a propaganda instrument for illustrating its social programs. However, unlike many modernist compositions that were isolated objects sitting in green, parklike settings, Asplund's complex assumed a more dense, urban configuration. The light, machinelike pavilions were tied together by such traditional urban elements as squares, concourses, cul-de-sacs, and garden courtyards. Here, space was as important as form. The tall, constructivist-inspired advertising mast was a light, steel structure that held signs and flags and provided a festive and energetic quality to the Exhibition.

Although Asplund's Bredenberg Department Store (1935, Stockholm) was a functionalist work, the State Bacteriological

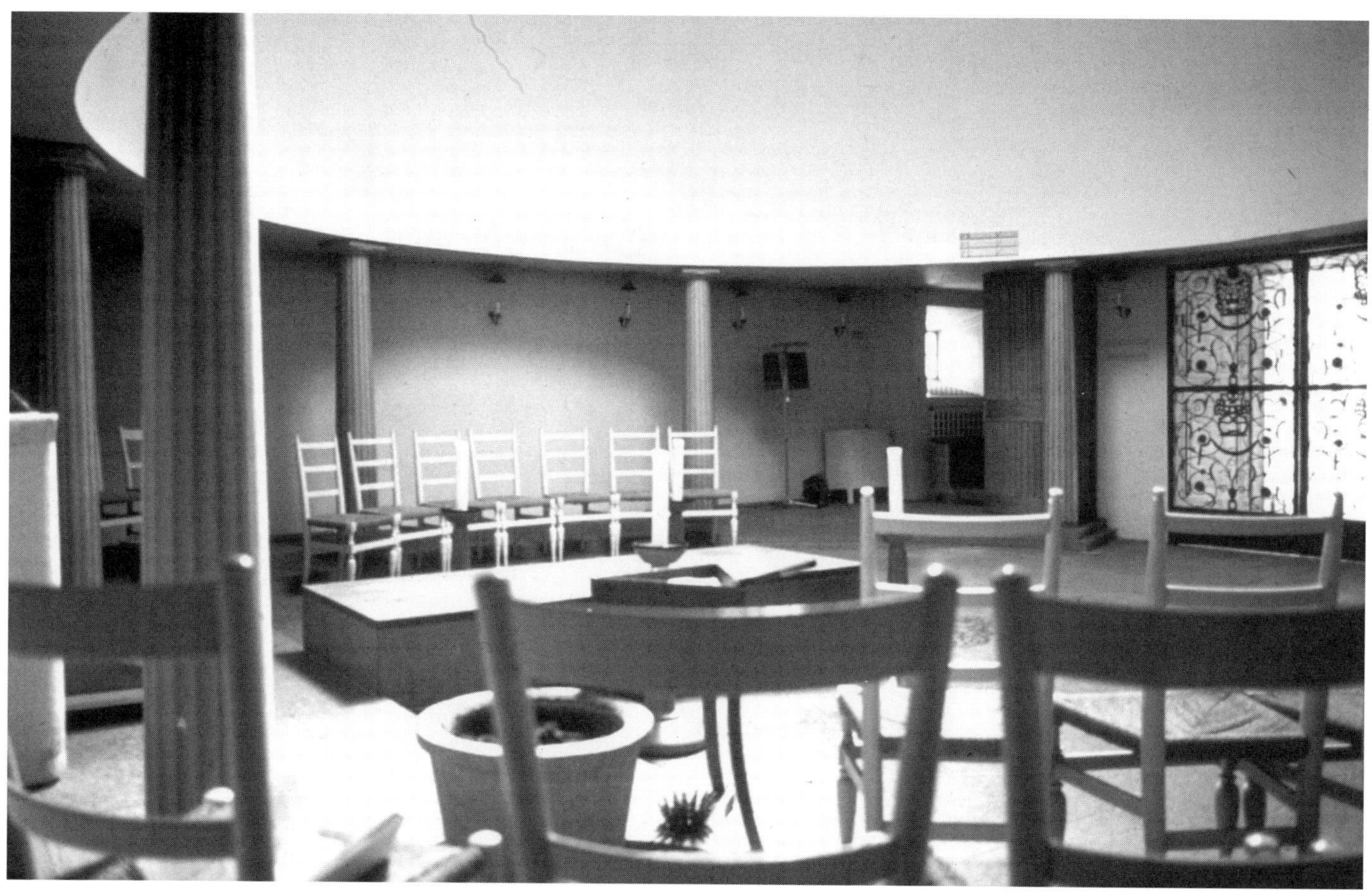

Woodland Chapel, Stockholm, Sweden, interior, designed by Eric Gunnar Asplund (1919)

Laboratories (1937, Stockholm) signaled a move away from the canons of modernism. In his last two major commissions, the Göteborg Law Courts Annex (won in competition in 1913, redesigned in 1925, and completed in 1936) and the Woodland Crematorium (1940), Asplund's reaction to functionalism solidified. The addition to the Law Courts, which were designed by Nicodemus Tessin in 1672, was initially conceived of as a direct extension of the original facade. In the final design, Asplund attempted the difficult proposition of developing a facade that would create a contrasting yet harmonizing tension between the old and the new. The result extends the rhythm of the original facade with a modern vocabulary while containing classical inferences. The central interior atrium, composed of a delicate concrete framework and staircases and superbly detailed wood paneling, has a timeless quality that transcends stylistic preferences.

Asplund's final major work, the Woodland Crematorium, is a composition dominated by the manipulation of the naturalistic qualities of the landscape, making the buildings seem secondary on approach. Yet the positioning of the primary architectural elements of loggia, wall, and cross actively gathers the surrounding landscape into a dynamic, emotional experience. The complex contains references to traditional, classical, and modern architecture: the planar quality of the buildings stems from modernism and the loggia and *impluvium* from classical sources, whereas the material usage and landscape design root the building to its Nordic context. The integration that Asplund achieved in the complex through the synthesis of modern with classical and vernacular precedents makes the Woodland Crematorium, in the final analysis, one of the truly compelling buildings of the 20th century.

William C. Miller

See also **Classicism; Stockholm Public Library; Stockholm, Sweden**

Biography

Born in Stockholm, Sweden, 22 September 1885. Studied architecture at the Royal Institute of Technology, Stockholm 1905–09; attended the Klara Academy of Architecture under Carl Bergsten, Ivar Tengbom, Carl Westman, and Ragnar Östberg 1910–11; studied the architecture of Italy and Greece 1913–14. Married (1) Gerda Sellman (divorced); married (2) Ingrid Katarina Kling 1934. Worked for I.G. Clason, Stockholm 1910–11; private practice, Stockholm 1911–40; editor, *Arkitektur* magazine, Stockholm 1917–20. Founded the Klara Academy with six others, including Sigurd Lewerentz and Osvald Almquist 1910;

assistant lecturer, Royal Institute of Technology, Stockholm 1912–13; special instructor in ornamental art, Royal Institute of Technology, Stockholm 1917–18; professor of architecture, Royal Institute of Technology, Stockholm 1931–40. Died in Stockholm, Sweden, 20 October 1940.

Selected Works

Villa Project for Ivar Asplund, Sweden, 1911
Villa Ruth, Kuusankoski, Finland, 1914
Woodland Cemetery (with Sigurd Lewerentz; first place, competition), Stockholm, 1915
Göta Square (competition project), Göteborg, Sweden, 1917
Gustaf Adolf Square (competition project), Göteborg, Sweden, 1918
Karlshaam Secondary School, Sweden, 1918
Villa Snellman, Djursholm, Sweden, 1918
Woodland Chapel, Stockholm, 1919
Lister County Courthouse, Sölvesborg, Sweden, 1921
Royal Chancellery (competition entry), Stockholm, 1922
Skandia Cinema, Stockholm, 1923
Public Library, Stockholm, 1928
Stockholm Exhibition, 1930
Bredenburg Department Store, Stockholm, 1935
Göteborg Law Courts Annex (won in competition 1913; redesigned 1925), 1936
State Bacteriological Labs, Stockholm, 1937
Woodland Crematorium, Stockholm, 1940

Selected Publication

Acceptera (with W. Gahn, S. Markelius, G. Paulsson, E. Sundahl, and U. Ahrén), 1931

Further Reading

Interest in Asplund's work has increased over the last quarter-century, as architects look to designers who were able to synthesize, during the late 1930s, a number of competing architectural traditions in a compelling and personal manner. This, coupled with Asplund's understanding of the interactive relationship between built elements and the landscape and the creation of appropriate urban spaces, forms, and additions, has stimulated more in-depth analysis of his work. This interest is witnessed by the number of publications that have appeared on his work since 1980.

Alison, Filippo, *Erik Gunnar Asplund: Mobili e Ogetti*, Milan: Electa, 1985
Caldenby, Claes, and Olof Hultin (editors), *Asplund*, Stockholm: Arkitektur Förlag, 1985; New York: Rizzoli, 1986
Constant, Caroline, *The Woodland Cemetery: Toward a Spiritual Landscape*, Stockholm: Byggförlaget, 1994
Cruickshank, Dan (editor), *Erik Gunnar Asplund*, London: Architect's Journal, 1988
de Maré, Erik, *Gunnar Asplund: A Great Modern Architect*, London: Art and Technics, 1955
Engfors, Christina, *E.G. Asplund: Arkitekt, vän och kollega*, Stockholm: Arkitektur Förlag, 1990; as *E.G. Asplund: Architect, Friend, and Colleague*, Stockholm: Arkitektur Förlag, 1990
Hasegawa, A., *Erik Gunnar Asplund*, Tokyo: Space Design, 1982
Holmdahl, Gustaf, Sven Ivar Lind, and Kjell Ödeen (editors), *Gunnar Asplund, arkitekt, 1885–1940: Ritningar, skisser, och fotografier*, Stockholm: Tidskriften Byggmästaren, 1943; as *Gunnar Asplund, Architect, 1885–1940: Plans, Sketches, and Photographs*, Stockholm: Tidskriften Byggmästaren, 1950; 2nd edition, Stockholm: Byggförlaget, 1981
Lindvall, Jöran (editor), *Asplund: 1885–1940*, Stockholm: Arkitekturmuseet and Arkitektur Förlag, 1985
St. John Wilson, Colin (editor), *Gunnar Asplund, 1885–1940: The Dilemma of Classicism*, London: Architectural Association, 1988
Wrede, Stuart, *The Architecture of Erik Gunnar Asplund*, Cambridge, Massachusetts: MIT Press, 1980
Zevi, Bruno, *Erik Gunnar Asplund*, Milan: Il Balcone, 1948

AT&T BUILDING

Designed by Philip Johnson; completed 1984
New York, New York

As arguably the first Postmodern building designed on a monumental, commercial scale, the AT&T Building (completed in 1984 by Philip Johnson) generated sufficient popular interest to be front-page news in the *New York Times* on 31 March 1978 and the cover story in *Time* on 8 January 1979, which portrayed the architect Philip Johnson cradling a model of the proposed design. In legitimizing Postmodern style and ideas, it reversed almost three decades of modern principles espoused by Mies van der Rohe that Johnson himself had practiced with the master in the Seagram Building (1958). Gone are the open plaza (the externalization of universal space); the understated, monochromatic, almost mute metal-and-glass curtain wall; and the nonconformist, neo-Baroque setback from the avenue. Instead, Johnson's building presses directly against the site line along the entire block of Madison Avenue between East 55th and East 56th Streets and introduces a newer type of urban amenity: a glass-canopied atrium with retail establishments. Several similarities to the Seagram Building remain, however, in the deeply recessed ground-story lobbies, overall floor plans, and steel construction. In fact, the plan is typical of postwar high-rise office buildings, comprising a sizable service core of elevators, emergency stairwells, and rest rooms, with resultant narrow office spaces.

Discussions for the design began in the mid-1970s with AT&T, ironically one of the world's largest corporations before its divestiture only shortly after the erection of the building. At a cost of $200 million, the 648-foot-high, 37-story building dedicated ten of its stories to its eponymous corporation, with the remaining rented as general office floors.

Its two central Postmodern features are the selection of a masonry enclosure, a light pink granite, and the addition of a crowning broken pediment. The latter feature fueled the nickname the "Chippendale" skyscraper, presumably because of its association with Thomas Chippendale's highboy chest-on-chests rather than with its actual but much rarer architectural source in 18th-century Georgian entrances. Because of the density of the location, the pedestrian experiences the building at two scales: from the street, the ground-level arcades, and from a considerable distance, the signature broken pediment.

Originally, the ground level of the tower comprised open arcades around the small entrance lobby and service core. The unenclosed public space beneath the tower, compared to an Egyptian hypostyle hall by one historian, was intended to mitigate the intensive use of the site and to repay the absence of setbacks in the tower. At the rear of the site, a glass-canopied galleria in the spirit of Milan's Galleria Vittorio Emanuele (1867) contains a three-story row of shops. A quarter of a barrel vault, the canopy is supported by quarter-round arches, not un-

Top of the AT&T Building showing Chippendale detail, designed by Phillip Johnson and John Burgee (1984)
© Mary Ann Sullivan

like the Romanesque tunnel-vaulted nave of St.-Sernin (1100) in Toulouse, France. Concentric diamond and chevron patterns animate the granite floors. In 1994 Gwathmey Siegel and Associates, in an effort to respond to criticism of insufficiently sheltered public spaces, enclosed both the public arcades beneath the tower and the galleria, which was extended into one bay on either side of the elevator core. By creating deep shadows, Gwathmey Siegel's bay windows for storefronts retain the feeling of depth in the arcade openings.

The most tactile experience occurs at the street level, where the flame-finished pale pink Stony Creek granite cladding meets the ground. Above substantial square column bases rise piers with reentrant corners, and quarter pyramids mark this articulation. Johnson has claimed that the entrance composition, with its central arch flanked by narrower trabeated openings, recalled Filippo Brunelleschi's Pazzi Chapel (1429) at Santa Croce, Florence, although critics did not hold both in equal esteem. Following the rhythm of openings established at the ground level, uninterrupted vertical bays contain granite mullions between piers, anchored underneath to steel tubes and originally intended to be round sectioned. Cost containment prevented the materialization of this feature, and in combination with the insufficient suppression of windows into the wall, AT&T's resultant thinness has been a frequent source of criticism, which compared the building unfavorably with Louis Sullivan's Wainwright Building (1891) in St. Louis, Missouri, admired for the expressive qualities of its brick masonry and molded terra-cotta. More successful, however, are the upper-level executive floors, where deeper suppression of the glazing and round-sectioned mullions were realized. Also lamented were the bare expanses of granite between the entrance arcade and the office floors as well as between the upper-level executive office floors and the sloping edges of the pediment, the subtle cornice of which, however, was praised.

At the main entrance, a suppressed glazed entrance arch, with an oculus above, echoes the narrow 116-foot central arch. Lavish detailing of the material includes a diamond pattern, or *opus reticulatum*, in the apron around the openings and fully three-dimensional articulated moldings around the arch and in corners. Capped with a gilded cross vault that springs from corner brackets, the compact but well-proportioned 65-foot-tall lobby has a black-and-white marble floor pattern recalling Durbar Hall (1931) at the Viceroy's House in New Delhi, India, designed by Sir Edwin Lutyens. Lined with granite walls as well, the lobby precedes a barrel-vaulted elevator hall; columns with abstracted Byzantine capitals demarcate the two spaces. Among the renovations supervised by Gwathmey Siegel and Associates, black glass replaced the diamond-patterned granite in the blind lobby arches. Bronze elevator doors, set in a blind arcade, repeat the arched forms. The regilded sculpture *Genius of Electricity* (1916), by Evelyn Beatrice Longman, known popularly as *Golden Boy*, from the top of the earlier headquarters, was replaced, after the Sony Corporation purchased the building, by an untitled non-objective Joel Shapiro (1941–) sculpture.

Called the "sky lobby," the main reception area sits one level above ground behind the entrance oculus. Its veined Breccia Strazzema marble forms a central aedicule enclosed by half-round arches springing from linteled openings. Gwathmey Siegel and Associates softened surfaces with wood panels, black glass, and murals. In the middle section of the building, there are 27 standard office floors, with ten-foot heights, and the executive offices occupy the 33rd and 34th floors. In them, Johnson specified molded wood panels and a double grand staircase connecting the two levels. Ventilation is diffused between vinyl-clad metal acoustical ceiling panels, and task lighting illuminates each workstation.

Considered flamboyant and arbitrary by some, frivolous and stylistically promiscuous by others, the building design generated ample criticism. Its historical references, reduced to two dimensions, were said to lack symbolic weight. Still, in its superficial use of the grammar of architecture, the AT&T Building expresses a perhaps unconscious camp quality, and as an object of the resentment of Postmodernism for its esoteric references and ad hoc assembly of historical images, AT&T represents at the same time the overthrow of orthodox modernism.

PAUL GLASSMAN

See also **Gwathmey, Charles, and Robert Siegel (United States); Mies van der Rohe, Ludwig (Germany); Postmodernism; Sullivan, Louis (United States)**

Further Reading

Periodical literature published when the building was completed provides the strongest analyses and most insightful critical responses.

Banham, Reyner, "AT&T Offices, New York: The Post–Déco Skyscraper," *Architectural Review*, 176 (August 1984)

Canty, Donald, "AT&T: The Tower, the Skyline, and the Street," *Architecture*, 74 (February 1985)

Curtis, William J.R., "Modern Transformation of Classicism," *Architectural Review*, 176 (August 1984)

Doubilet, Susan, "Not Enough Said: AT&T Headquarters, New York, N.Y.," *Progressive Architecture*, 65 (February 1984)

Frampton, Kenneth (editor), *Philip Johnson, Processes: The Glass House, 1949, and the AT&T Corporate Headquarters, 1978* (exhib. cat.), New York: Institute for Architecture and Urban Studies, 1978

Goldberger, Paul, "A Monument to Post-Modernism," *New York Times* (31 March 1978)

Hughes, Robert, "Doing Their Own Thing," *Time* (8 January 1979)

Huxtable, Ada Louise, "Johnson's Latest—Clever Tricks or True Art?" *New York Times* (16 April 1978)

"John Burgee Architects with Philip Johnson: AT&T Headquarters, New York, New York ground breaking: January 1979; completion: 1984," *GA Document*, 12 (January 1985)

Knight, Carleton, "Significant Clients: Ma Bell Builds Big," *Architecture: The AIA Journal*, 72 (July 1983)

Philip Johnson/John Burgee: Architecture 1979–1985, New York: Rizzoli, 1985; revised edition, 1989

Schulze, Franz, *Philip Johnson: Life and Work*, New York: Knopf, 1994

ATHENS CHARTER (1943)

The "Athens Charter" was the name given by Le Corbusier to his version of the results of the fourth congress (1933) of the Congrès Internationaux d'Architecture Moderne (CIAM). This congress was organized on the theme of the "Functional City," a concept developed in part by the Dutch town planner Cornelis van Eesteren, who became president of CIAM in 1930. In contrast to what he called the "cardboard architecture" of classical urbanism, van Eesteren and other CIAM members advocated an approach to city planning based on the most rational siting of functional elements, such as workplaces and transportation centers. This idea was linked to the belief that city planning should be based on the creation of separate zones for each of the "four functions" of dwelling, work, recreation, and transportation. At the fourth congress, held on a cruise ship traveling from Marseilles to Athens and back in July–August 1933, CIAM members from Eastern and Western Europe analyzed the same-scale plans of 33 existing cities prepared by CIAM members according to guidelines developed by the Dutch CIAM group. At the end of the congress, the CIAM members present had planned to draw conclusions from these analyses and to issue resolutions about how cities should be reorganized according to CIAM principles. Disagreements over whether CIAM should call for the expropriation of existing property for such a reorganization and over Le Corbusier and others' promotion of high-rise housing delayed the issuing of these resolutions. In the fall of 1933, the congress instead published what it termed preliminary *Constatations* (Observations) in French and *Festellungen* (Findings) in German.

In both the French and the German versions, which were not completely consistent with each other, the text emphasized that cities are part of an economic, social, and political system. Under "Dwelling," CIAM found that population densities were typically too high in historic centers and that open spaces were lacking. It demanded that housing districts should occupy the best sites and that a minimum amount of solar exposure should be required in all dwellings. For hygienic reasons, CIAM asserted that buildings should not be built along transportation routes and that modern techniques should be used to construct high apartment buildings widely spaced apart to free the soil for large green parks. Under "Leisure," CIAM found that existing open areas were generally insufficient for recreation or not well situated to benefit the inhabitants of dense central areas. It called for the demolition of these central areas so that they could be turned into green spaces, with schools and other collective facilities sited in them. Under "Work," CIAM found that the relationship between dwelling and places of work was not rational, as it usually required long commutes. It determined that travel distances should be reduced to a minimum and called for the separation of industrial quarters from housing, buffered by a neutral zone of green areas and sports fields.

Under "Transportation," CIAM found that most cities had street patterns that had become unsuitable for modern means of transportation, such as streetcars and automobiles. It proposed that rigorous statistical methods be used to establish rational street widths, classified according to the speed of different modes of transport. Under "Historic Districts of the City," CIAM stated that historic monuments should be respected when they "are a pure expression of previous cultures and are of general interest" and when their conservation did not mean that their inhabitants had to live in unhealthy conditions.

In the *Constatations*, CIAM concluded that the chaotic conditions of present cities do not correspond to the "primordial biological and psychological necessities of the population." It declared that the city should be organized according to the four functions and that city plans should conform with these biological and psychological needs. CIAM also emphasized that urbanism was "a three-dimensional science" and that the "element of height" could be used to solve traffic problems and efficiently create green spaces for leisure.

Le Corbusier's *La charte d'Athènes*, published in Paris in 1943, is an expanded version of the *Constatations* that was published in various European journals in 1933 and later. Le Corbusier began to call the results of the fourth congress "La charte d'Athènes" in his "Pavillon des Temps Nouveaux" at the 1937 Paris Exposition. In 1941, while serving on an urbanism commission of the Nazi-controlled Vichy government, he began to prepare a new publication of the *Constatations*. By November 1941, as Vichy officials grew increasingly hostile to him, he decided to publish the Athens Charter anonymously. He also established a new French CIAM group, ASCORAL (Assemblée de Constructeurs pour une Rénovation Architecturale), which began to issue a series of publications on urbanism in anticipation of postwar reconstruction. One of these publications, authored by "CIAM-France" (later Le Corbusier), was *La charte d'Athènes*.

Although the book was based on the *Constatations* issued after the fourth congress, the immediate inspiration for it had been Le Corbusier's involvement with the reconstruction committee in Vichy, where it was intended to provide a basis for legislation governing postwar reconstruction. By publishing it with its 1941 introduction by Jean Giraudoux, the book linked Le Corbusier and ASCORAL to the pre-Vichy era and paved the way for its acceptance by the government after liberation. Although the text maintains the same sectional headings (the four functions and the "Historic Districts of the City") as the original 1933 *Constatations*, much new material was added, and existing points were significantly modified. For example, the first point on the city in the original text is expanded into an eight-point section called "The City and Its Region" in the Athens Charter, and what had been simply termed "Summing Up" is retitled the more directive "Points of Doctrine." Without Le Corbusier and his associates' urban plans, which are the text's absent illustrations, the Athens Charter is less clear than the terse 1933 CIAM *Constatations*, and it often reads as a series of platitudes. Nevertheless, it was widely referred to in postwar Europe as the key text of the urbanism of the Modern movement. Later, it became the focus of much of the Postmodernist reaction against this brand of urbanism.

Eric Mumford

See also **Corbusier, Le (Jeanneret, Charles-Édouard) (France)**

Further Reading

CIAM, "Constatations du IVe Congrès," *TECHNIKA CHRONIKA-Les Annales Techniques 44–46* (November 1933); as "Statements of the Athens Congress, 1933," in *Het nieuwe bouwen Internationaal/International: CIAM, Volkshuisvesting, Stedebouw; Het nieuwe bouwen Internationaal: CIAM, Housing, Town Planning*, by Auke van der Woud, Delft, Netherlands: Delft University Press, 1983

CIAM-France, *La charte d'Athènes*, Paris: Plon, 1943; as *The Athens Charter*, by Le Corbusier, translated by Anthony Eardley, New York: Grossman, 1973

Goldfinger, Ernö, "A Meeting of the Minds," *Architects' Journal*, 14 (December 1983)

Moholy-Nagy, Laszlo, *Film Diary [of the] Architect[s'] Congress* (videorecording), New York: Windsor Video, 1986

Mumford, Eric, *The CIAM Discourse on Urbanism, 1928–1960*, Cambridge, Massachusetts: MIT Press, 2000

Sert, José Luis, *Can Our Cities Survive?: An ABC of Urban Problems, Their Analyses, Their Solutions, Based on the Proposals Formulated by the CIAM*, Cambridge, Massachusetts: Harvard University Press, and London: Milford and Oxford University Press, 1942

AULENTI, GAE 1927–

Architect, Italy

Gae Aulenti is one of Italy's best-known architects and one of the leading female architects in the world. She has made her reputation in a versatile career that has combined architecture with designs for theater, furniture, museums, exhibitions, showrooms, gardens, and city-planning projects. In this way, she is very much a product of Milan in the 1950s, 1960s, and 1970s, when many architects, such as Vittorio Gregotti, combined architecture with design.

Aulenti graduated from the Faculty of Architecture at the Milan Polytechnic University in 1954. From 1955 to 1965, she was an editor in charge of layout at *Casabella* magazine in Milan, directed by Ernesto Rogers, her mentor. She was a member of a group of disciples of Rogers that included Vittorio Gregotti and Aldo Rossi, both of whom also were editors at *Casabella*. Her career as an architect began with a series of designs for showrooms: Olivetti (1967) in Paris; Olivetti (1968) in Buenos Aires; Knoll International (1970) in New York; and Fiat (1970) in Brussels, Zurich, and Turin. She also designed offices, such as Max Mara (1965) in Milan. She designed a traveling exhibition (1970) for Olivetti and participated in the exhibition, "Italy: The New Domestic Landscape," at the Museum of Modern Art in New York (1972). In the 1960s, her interior designs are kaleidoscopic explosions of forms into space, though later they become calm and restrained, with curvilinear, surreal, and suggestive forms. The early showrooms are experiments in the breaking up of space without interfering with its functional use.

During the 1980s, Aulenti's attention turned toward the design of museums and exhibition spaces. Her best-known project is the design of the Musée d'Orsay (1980–86) in Paris, made in collaboration with a team of French architects and the lighting designer Piero Castiglioni. This beautiful museum combines the iron structure and stucco decoration of a railway station into a modern architectural composition. Aulenti also worked on exhibition spaces for the National Museum of Modern Art at the Georges Pompidou Center in Paris (1982–85), the National Museum of Catalan Art in Barcelona (1987–95), and the Palazzo Grassi in Venice (1985–93). She designed "The Italian Metamorphosis 1943–68" exhibit at the Guggenheim Museum in New York (1994). The museum and exhibition designs always take into account, according to Aulenti, how the art is viewed by the visitor from different perspectives and combinations. Her exhibitions develop contrasts between open and closed spaces as well as between the autonomy and integration of spaces.

Throughout the 1980s and 1990s, Aulenti designed a series of stage sets for theatrical productions. These include sets for

Museé d'Orsay, Paris, France, designed by Gae Aulenti (1986)

Rossini's *La Donna del Lago* (1981–89), Rimski-Korsakov's *Zar Saltan* at the Teatro alla Scala in Milan (1988), Strauss's *Electra* in Milan (1994), and Shakespeare's *King Lear* at the Teatro Argentina in Rome (1995). Aulenti's stage sets contain beautiful dreamlike imagery that juxtaposes color and evocative forms that transgress the rules of perspectival construction. Aulenti sees the theater as a space of continuous transformation, where a relation between time and space is enacted.

During the 1990s, Aulenti received several commissions for residences and public buildings. The residences include a villa (1990) at Saint-Tropez, where four autonomous cubic structures are arranged on a square plan and connected in various ways, opening between interior and exterior. The public commissions include the entranceway to a train station in Florence, a college in Biella, and the Italian Pavilion at Expo '92 in Seville. At the Italian Pavilion, Aulenti emulates Mies van der Rohe in the aesthetic refinement and use of materials. Aulenti's architecture always combines the application of an aesthetic order and the synthetic analysis of space. The designs take into account how space is experienced and how spaces and masses are combined. She experiments with relations among materials, distances, measurements, and equilibriums: primarily concerning how the body is experienced in the space.

In Italy, Aulenti's work has been the subject of important critical essays by Ernesto Rogers, Vittorio Gregotti, Aldo Rossi, Manfredo Tafuri, and Francesco Dal Co. Although she is Italy's most famous woman architect, Aulenti's work has had very little influence on architectural practice in Italy and no theoretical influence in the architecture schools, as opposed to her peers Vittorio Gregotti and Aldo Rossi.

JOHN HENDRIX

See also **Gregotti, Vittorio (Italy); Mies van der Rohe, Ludwig (Germany); Museum of Modern Art, New York; Rossi, Aldo (Italy)**

Biography

Born in Palazzolo dello Stella, Italy, 4 December 1927. Graduated from the School of Architecture, Milan Polytechnic 1954. In private practice, Milan from 1954; exhibition and industrial designer since 1954; member, editorial staff, *Casabella-Continuità*, Milan 1955–65; member, board of directors, *Lotus International*, Venice from 1974. Assistant professor of architectural composition, faculty of architecture, University of Venice 1960–62; assistant professor of the elements of architectural composition, faculty of architecture, Milan Polytechnic 1964–67; visiting lecturer, the College of Architecture, Barcelona and the Cultural Center, Stockholm 1969–75. Member, Movimenti Studi per l'Architettura, Milan 1955–61; member, from 1960, vice president, 1966, Associazione per il Disegno Industriale, Milan; honorary member, Italian National Society of Interior Designers 1967; honorary member, American Society of Interior Designers 1967; joint executive member, *Triennale*, Milan 1977–80; corresponding member, Accademia Nazionale di San Luca, Rome from 1984; honorary member, Bund Deutscher Architekten 1990; honorary fellow, American Institute of Architects. Chevalier, Legion d'Honneur 1987; Commander, Ordre des Arts et Lettres 1987.

Selected Works

Max Mara Office, Milan, 1965
Olivetti Showroom, Paris, 1967
Olivetti Showroom, Buenos Aires, 1968
Traveling Olivetti Exhibition, 1970
Knoll International Showroom, New York, 1970
Fiat Showroom, Brussels, Zurich, and Turin, 1970
National Museum of Modern Art, Exhibition Designs, Georges Pompidou Center, Paris, 1985
Musée d'Orsay, Paris, 1986
Stage sets for Rossini's *La Donna del Lago*, 1989
Marina B Store, Milan, 1989
Villa at Saint-Tropez, 1990
Italian Pavilion, Expo '92, Seville, 1992
Palazzo Grassi, Venice, Restoration, 1993
"The Italian Metamorphosis 1943–68" Exhibition, Guggenheim Museum, New York, 1994
National Museum of Catalan Art, Exhibition Designs, Barcelona, 1995
Palazzo Grassi, Venice, Exhibition Designs, 1996

Selected Publications

Un nuova scuola di base (with others), 1973
Il laboratorio di Prato (with Franco Quadri and Luca Ronconi), 1981

Further Reading

Bianchetti, Fabrizio, *Le grandi architetture contemporanee*, Faenza, Italy: C.E.L.I., 1991
Gae Aulenti (exhib. cat.), Milan: Electa, 1979
Galbiati, Augusta, Claudio Raboni, and Simonetta Rasponi, *Venti progetti per il futuro del Lingotto*, Milan: Etas, 1984
Petranzan, Margherita, *Gae Aulenti*, Milan: Rizzoli, 1996; as *Gae Aulenti*, translated by Susan Meadows, New York: Rizzoli, 1997

AUSTRALIA

The 1901 federation of sovereign states and territories that formed the Commonwealth of Australia centralized cultural developments. A new nationalism subdued regional differences. A new federal capital, Canberra was chosen, as it was equidistant between the cities of Melbourne and Sydney. These two metropolitan cities became the primary settings for major 20th-century architectural movements, although many gems have been built throughout the whole country: the modernist Education Department Building (1982, Perth, Western Australia), by Cameron Chisholm and Nicol; Student Union Building, University of Adelaide (1973, South Australia), by Dickson and Platten; St Ann's Geriatric Hospital (1979, Hobart, Tasmania), by Heffernan Nation Rees and Viney; Queensland Art Gallery (1982, Brisbane), by Robin Gibson and Partners; and the contextual "Pee Wees at the Point" restaurant in tropical Darwin (1998, Northern Territory), by Troppo Architects. The most beautifully crafted building in the nation is the Postmodern Parliament House complex in Canberra (1988, Australian Capital Territory), by the Italian-American Romaldo Giurgola (Mitchell Giurgola and Thorpe), nowadays a resident of Canberra.

The architectural forms of the vast terminal buildings for the suburban electric railway networks in Melbourne and Sydney were indicative of fin-de-siècle tension between Arts and Crafts Movement principles and a shift to rational Classicism. The ornate Flinders Street Station (1911, Melbourne), by J.W. Fawcett and H.P.C. Ashworth, was an Edwardian Baroque masterpiece and emulated not only buildings in London but also some in Otto Wagner's Vienna. The entry on a diagonal to the street intersection has a generous semicircular arched opening below a band of squat columns compressed between a heavy lintel and sill, both being familiar tectonic elements in Henry H. Richardson's and Louis Sullivan's Chicago of the 1880s. The sedate facade of the Central Railway Station in Sydney (1908), by Walter Liberty Vernon, has a heavily rusticated base in front of an austere neoclassical elevation.

Garden suburbs grew rapidly, starting early in the twentieth century. The detached house in its own garden became the norm. The middle classes abandoned their 19th-century inner-city terrace houses, renting them to industrial workers of the inner belt of factories and warehouses. Brick-walled and terracotta-roofed Federation Style bungalows that amalgamated English and American Queen Anne traits dominated the new grids of Melbourne's tree-lined streets. Typically, the Arthur Norman house (1910, Kew), by Ussher and Kemp, combined elements of Richard Norman Shaw's English Domestic Revival and the American Shingle Style and included the latter's diagonal compositions in plan and silhouette.

Exceptions in Melbourne were Robert Haddon's Art Nouveau red brick Anselm (1906, Caulfield) and Harold Desbrowe Annear's half-timbered Chadwick House (1903, Eaglemont), with inventive Arts and Crafts details and curved forms. In Sydney, W. Hardy Wilson revived an elegant Regency colonial domestic architecture, Eryldene (1913, Gordon), which has his famous Chinese garden pavilion. During the late teens and the 1920s, architects led the way with the ubiquitous California bungalow–type homes in the suburbs of both cities. The major central city buildings at this time were the reinforced concrete Capitol House office block and the adjacent Capitol Theatre (1924, Melbourne), with its crystalline plaster ceiling. This complex was designed by Walter Burley Griffin and Marion Mahony Griffin, who had settled in Australia in 1914 to achieve the realization of their 1911 competition-winning design for the city of Canberra.

After the Great Depression, the images of modernism were embraced in Australia in the mid-1930s. Initially, the styling of the outer fabric of the suburban house was affected, rather than its planning. Having visited the United States, Harry A. Norris employed an expressive Jazz Moderne for the reinforced concrete house Burnham Beeches (1933, Sassafras, Victoria). Roy Grounds, in designing Portland Lodge (1934, Frankston, Victoria), showed fascination with the linear timber houses of William W. Wurster of California. Having worked in England, Sydney Ancher, in the Prevost House (1937, Bellevue Hill, New South Wales) incorporated the open living room idea and the curved dining screen element found in Ludwig Mies van der Rohe's Tugendhat House (1930, Brno, Czechoslovakia). Ancher's younger office colleague in the post–World War II years, Glenn Murcutt, took as his exemplar the Farnsworth House (1950) by Mies and consequently created a vibrant series of climate-controlled universal-box houses (1985, Magney house, Bingy Point, New South Wales) that also reflect Alvar Aalto's involvement with materials and their potential for exquisite empathetic detailing.

In Melbourne's central business district, Marcus Barlow in the Manchester Unity office block (1932) displayed his enthusiasm for the work of Raymond Hood, for this example providing a corner marker based on the Chicago Tribune Tower (1922), with Chicago Gothic verticality in the two street elevations. Norman Seabrook in the MacPherson Robertson Girls High School (1934, South Melbourne) gave testimony to a pilgrimage often made by Australian architects to the Frank Lloyd Wright–inspired Hilversum Town Hall (1931) by Willem Marinus Dudok of the Netherlands.

Despite the privations of World War II, a large, reinforced concrete block of flats of great sculptural power, Stanhill (1950, Queens Road, Melbourne), by the Swiss-trained architect Frederick Romberg, was eventually completed. The irregular plan and block massing, reminiscent of the superstructure of an ocean liner, was composed of International Style figures in an accomplished and idiosyncratic fashion. This compares with the rationally simple indented crescent of "urban co-operative multi-home units" in reinforced concrete (1951, Potts Point Sydney) by Aaron Bolot, a former employee of the Griffins.

The estate of three family houses at Turramurra, on the outskirts of Sydney, by the Gropius- and Breuer-trained, Austrian-born Harry Seidler, reformed and consolidated International Modernism in Australia. The Rose Seidler House (1950, Wahroonga) is similar in plan to the American East Coast houses created by his teachers, and its appearance also reflected De Stijl principles. However, Seidler imaginatively overlaid aspects of Le Corbusier's 1920s imagery, specifically, of the white cube thrust up on thin *piloti*, the cube cut and sliced, and the ramp as an element of the architectural promenade. Seidler, in his own house (1967, Killara), enriched the idea of circulation, and the forms became robust and muscular in reinforced concrete.

Counter to Seidler's international rationalism, Peter Muller, a University of Pennsylvania graduate, and Bruce Rickard independently created site-sensitive houses around Sydney that were largely based on the characteristics of the Usonian houses of Frank Lloyd Wright. Muller composed Kumale (1956, Palm Beach) out of circles, and Rickard formed Mirrabooka (1964, Castle Hill) of rectangles. Hoyts Cinema Centre (1969, Bourke Street, Melbourne) was designed by Muller. Melbourne architects Chancellor and Patrick also referred to American organic sensibilities, but in their former ES&A Bank (1960, Elizabeth Street, Melbourne), the massive corner piers and vertical concrete ribs were typical of the Griffins's work, not Wright's.

Daring use of tensile steel proved to be more feasible than fanciful shell concrete conceptions for the Olympic Swimming Stadium (1956, Flinders Park Melbourne), by Kevin Borland, Peter McIntyre, John and Phyllis Murphy (1982, Borland Brown alterations), and the Sidney Myer Music Bowl (1959, Kings Domain, Melbourne), by Yuncken Freeman Brothers Griffiths and Simpson (1999, Gregory Burgess refurbishment). Inspired by expressionistic works by Eero Saarinen, Bruce Goff, and Paul Rudolph, structural experiments and formal adventures by Melbourne architects in the 1950s were discerned as a "Melbourne School" by the prolific Melbourne commentator and architect, Robin Boyd. In "The State of Australian Architecture" (1967), Boyd also identified a "Sydney School" of "nutty crunchy textures," referring to a disciplined but picturesque first-hand interpretation of English Brutalism by architects such as Ken Woolley. His own house (1962, Mosman) consisted of exposed timber-floor terrace levels stepping down a heavily vegetated natural bush site, enclosed by klinker-brick walls and terracotta Roman roof tiles.

Boyd was a staunch advocate for the Modern movement and used absolutes derived from the writings of Walter Gropius to measure and criticize his contemporaries. He grew to understand, however, that eclectic diversity was real. His *The Puzzle of Architecture* (1965) reviewed the plurality of theories and solutions in the world architectural scene. Sharing Gropius's belief that Japanese architecture of the 1960s fulfilled the dream of a universal modern architecture possessing a regional flavor, Boyd wrote *Kenzo Tange* (1962) and *New Directions in Japanese Architecture* (1968).

The Sydney Opera House commission, in an international competition judged by Eero Saarinen, was won by the Danish architect Jorn Utzon (1957). He proposed free-form layered roof shells, which proved to be structurally indeterminate. Utzon developed a reinforced concrete ribbed structural system finished in curved white ceramic tiles, each "shell" being a segment of a sphere. Political maneuvering soon deprived Utzon of design control, and he resigned in 1963. The interiors and glass walling were finished by Hall Todd & Littlemore (1973).

Australian architects have built abroad, including Sydney-trained John Andrews. His seminal Scarborough College (1965, Toronto, Canada), and Gund Hall, Graduate School of Design (1968, Harvard University, Cambridge, Massachusetts) are like rigourous zoning and circulation diagrams realized in elegantly detailed reinforced concrete and glass. Another significant geometrically abstract work was Seidler's Australian Embassy in Paris (1977), dominated by two curved-in-counterpoint blocks of office suites. Ken Woolley assembled relaxed reinforced concrete pavilion forms in a tropical garden in the Australian Embassy, Bangkok, Thailand (1985, Ancher Mortlock Woolley). Embassy architects from Melbourne have included strong architectural references to the host countries. Daryl Jackson, for the Australian Chancery complex, Riyadh (1989, Saudi Arabia), used grillwork-shaded courts and robust heavy walls. Denton Corker Marshall in Beijing (1992, Peoples Republic of China) used as a theme Chinese courtyard houses, with solid wall enclosures and large-scaled square openings. Their design for Tokyo (1991) is a sparkling assembly of metal blockforms reflecting the vitality of new Japanese architecture. Hank Koning and Julie Eizenberg from Melbourne successfully practice in Los Angeles, California.

The dichotomy of geometric–abstract versus free-style modes still haunts Australian architectural production. Giurgola, in the new parliament buildings in Canberra (1988), integrated a classical severity and repose, with an "itinerary" of "fragments" embedded in a hill. With the RMIT University Building #8 (constructed on top of a low-rise student union building by John Andrews [1982]), Edmond and Corrigan (in association with Demaine Partnership [1994]) introduced a variety of pop figures into the ground of rectangular block wall facing the major Melbourne thoroughfare of Swanston Street. Peter Corrigan studied at Yale University during the Charles Moore and Robert Venturi era, enhancing his predilection for startling shapes and juxtapositions, polychromy, and contrasting patterns. Next door is the restoration and additions for Storey Hall (1995, former Hibernian Hall, RMITU) by Ashton Raggatt McDougall, which contributes another masterpiece in the tradition of Melbourne expressionism. Pea-green and purple paint was sprayed on the multifaceted raw concrete facade, to which a network of cast-bronze computer-generated geometric figures was attached. These two buildings contributed compatibly to the wall of the streetscape.

The values of craftmanship and organicism have also survived in current work by architects in various cities. Rex Addison, in his own house (1999, Brisbane), freely interprets the regional qualities of the typical timber and corrugated-iron 19th-century tropical Queensland house. Richard Leplastrier in a house for the Australian novelist Peter Carey (1982, Bellingen, New South Wales) provided an airy elevated timber pavilion beside a native forest. Gregory Burgess lived on site with aboriginal people before designing their Brambuk Cultural Centre (1990, Halls Gap, Victoria), a birdlike undulating corrugated-iron roofscape supported on peeled tree-trunk poles in-filled with timber-clad framing. Similarly, Gregory Burgess designed the aboriginal landowners' information centre at Uluru (1998, Northern Territory), an icon for Australia at the end of the millennium.

JEFF TURNBULL

See also **Art Nouveau (Jugendstil); Canberra, Australia; Gropius, Walter (Germany); Melbourne, Australia; Plan of Canberra; Seidler, Harry (Australia); Sydney, Australia; Sydney Opera House; Tugendhat House, Brno, Czech Republic; Wright, Frank Lloyd (United States); Wurster, William (United States)**

Further Reading

Boyd, Robin, *Kenzo Tange*, New York: Braziller, 1962
Boyd, Robin, *The Puzzle of Architecture*, [Carlton, Australia]: Melbourne University Press and New York: Cambridge University Press, 1965
Boyd, Robin, "The State of Australian Architecture," *Architecture in Australia*, 56 (June 1967)
Boyd, Robin, *Australia's Home: Its Origins, Builders and Occupiers*, Melbourne: University of Melbourne Press, 1952; Penguin Books, 1968
Boyd, Robin, *New Directions in Japanese Architecture*, New York: Braziller, 1968
Johnson, Donald Leslie, *Australian Architecture 1901–1951: Sources of Modernism*, Sydney: University of Sydney Press, 1980
Taylor, Jennifer, *Australian Architecture Since 1960*, Sydney: The Law Book Company, 1986

AUSTRIA

Despite enduring the disruption of two world wars and decades of political, social, and economic turmoil, Austria has been among the most fertile centers of 20th-century architecture. From Otto Wagner at the beginning of the century to Co-op Himmelb(l)au at its end, Austrian architects have often been at the forefront of the struggle to confront the rapidly changing dictates of the modern age. Those efforts have been marked less by technical innovation than in many other countries—until recently Austria's building industries lagged behind those of most other European nations—but rather by a remarkable openness to new forms and ideas. On the one hand, modern Austrian architecture has been characterized by a strong inclination to embrace novelty, to originate and develop innovative expressions. But Austrian architects have also exhibited exceptional skill in manipulating and re-using elements from the past, engaging, in the process, in a sophisticated dialogue with history. In the works of many of the best Austrian architects, these two tendencies have been combined to yield designs of unusual power and expressiveness. Often the results have been quite distinctive: the works of figures like Adolf Loos or Gustav Peichl remain uniquely individual and parochial, even while they have drawn worldwide attention. And when Austrian architects have followed wider tendencies, their works nonetheless frequently show original adaptations to culture and place.

The origins of 20th-century Austrian architecture stem in great part from Otto Wagner. In his roles as practitioner, revolutionary, and teacher, Wagner inaugurated the headlong search for the new. His call for an architecture suited to "modern life" and "new materials and the demands of the present" proved decisive in shaping the distinctive look of the Viennese *Moderne* at the beginning of the century. Yet Wagner, like many of those who came after him, never fully abandoned the past; even his most spare works are redolent of Austria's rich building history, especially its legacy from the Renaissance and the Baroque. Early on, Wagner developed a new form language that mixed freely the curvilinear lines of the Art Nouveau (Jugendstil) with classical features, compositional strategies, and planning. By 1904, however, he had begun to pursue a more rectilinear, abstract style that brought together elements of the old and new. The resulting fusion of the classical and the modern characterized his most famous works, including the Postal Savings Bank (1904–05) and the Church am Steinhof (1902–07).

Wagner's many protégés and followers, although often tracing their own special paths, continued to investigate the possibilities of innovation and historical revivalism. Joseph Maria Olbrich, who worked in Wagner's atelier around the turn of the century, sought a new architectonic ideal in the florid lines and patterning of the Jugendstil. But Olbrich was simultaneously drawn to archaic, Asian, and Near Eastern motifs, resulting in a discernible note of exoticism in his designs, a tendency that has reappeared in the works of many later Austrian architects. Josef Hoffmann, another of the architects who was influenced by Wagner, sought to foster a new idiom from the language of rectilinear geometry: the *Quatratstil*—the square style—that Hoffmann pioneered along with the graphic artist and designer Koloman Moser, became the most widely admired—and imitated—images of early Austrian modernism. Yet Hoffmann, after his brief flirtation with a geometric purism, returned to employing elements from former times, experimenting at various times with the Biedermeier, Baroque, Rococo, folk art, and Anglo-American traditions. Many of Wagner's former students from the Academy of Fine Arts in Vienna, among them Hubert Gessner, Franz Gesser, Karl Ehn, and Rudolf Perco, adopted this same approach in the 1920s and 1930s, combining features of Wagner's modernized classicism and other historical imagery.

A parallel, but equally important strain of Viennese modernism is descended from Adolf Loos. During the early years of the 20th century, Loos formulated an alternative vision of modern architecture based on his own idiosyncratic ideas of culture and form. He rejected the Jugendstil as contrived and inappropriate, calling instead for an architecture that would reflect honestly the inherent modernity he found in contemporary urban life. This approach led Loos toward a new architecture of complexity and pluralism most brilliantly expressed in his Goldman and Salatsch store on the Michaelerplatz in Vienna (1910–11). Loos's renunciation of the notion of a universal modern style was also embraced by a number of Vienna's younger generation of modernists, most notably Oskar Strnad and Josef Frank, who in the years prior to 1914 developed their own progressive critique of the Viennese *Moderne*.

The implications of Loos's ideas extended beyond traditional concepts of style. Inspired by the linguistic and ethical writings of his friend Karl Kraus, Loos sought to establish a modern architectonic language that would articulate his notions of propriety and civility without sacrificing older conventions of material comfort. In his Goldman and Salatsch Building, Loos also began to investigate a new spatial idea, the *Raumplan*, or space-plan, a system of interlocking rooms on multiple levels. In a series of later designs, most notably the Moeller (1927–28) and Müller (1929–30) houses, he raised the *Raumplan* concept to a high art, creating some of the most extraordinary spatial assemblages of the modern era. Both of these notions—the concept of linguistic "appropriateness" and the idea of intricate spatial play—exerted a strong influence on Loos's followers and later Austrian architects, including the philosopher-builder Ludwig Wittgenstein, Josef Frank, and Hermann Czech.

World War I marked a caesura in the development of Austrian architecture. After 1918 the prosperity and stability of the prewar years gave way to a long period of economic hardship and political uncertainty that ended only after 1945. Vienna, which before the war had been the capital of an empire of 60 million inhabitants, was reduced to a provincial city in a country of barely 6 million. The centerpiece of Austrian building activity in the interwar years was a massive program launched by the Social Democratic municipal government in Vienna to combat the city's severe postwar housing shortage. In contrast to similar housing programs in Germany and the Netherlands, however, the Viennese experimented little with new construction technologies, relying instead on conventional, labor-intensive building practices as a means of ensuring employment for as many workers as possible.

With few exceptions, the Austrians of the interwar years also showed a decided aversion to the modernist purism of Le Corbusier and the Bauhaus. The vast majority of the Vienna communal housing projects were the work of the former Wagner students, and their buildings, like Karl Ehn's massive Karl-Marx-Hof (1926–30), reflected older, traditional ideas of massing and composition. Even those architects like Ernst Lichtblau and Walter Sobotka who subscribed to the general ideas of the Modern movement exhibited a notable tendency in the 1920s and early 1930s to introduce historical forms and complex patterning into their designs.

Among the few Austrians of the interwar period who conformed to tenets of the so-called International Style were Ernst Plischke, Lois Welzenbacher, and Richard Neutra. Plischke's Liesing Labor Office in Vienna (1930–32) and Welzenbacher's Turmhotel Seeber in Solbad Hall (1930–31) both brilliantly encapsulated the best features of the functionalist idiom, but neither architect was able to realize more than a handful of works. Far more successful was the young Neutra, who immigrated to the United States in the early 1920s and settled in California where he practiced for a time with Rudolph M. Schindler, another Viennese-trained modernist. Together with Frederick Kiesler, who moved to New York in the mid-1920s, the three architects would have a decisive impact on American modern design, but their work exerted little, if any, influence in their homeland.

The period between 1933 and 1938 formed the second major break in the history of 20th-century Austrian architecture. With the rise of the conservative Austrian clerical party and the later German annexation of Austria, many of the country's leading architects were forced to flee. Josef Frank moved to Sweden and Clemens Holzmeister to Turkey, but the majority of Austrian exiles—among them Felix Augenfeld, Victor Gruen, Ernst Lichtblau, and Bernard Rudofsky—sought refuge in the United States. Very few of these exiles returned to Austria after 1945, depriving the country of some of its best architectural talent.

The arduous task of rebuilding Austria after World War II fell to a small group of mostly middle-aged architects who had been trained in the 1920s and 1930s. The most significant of these figures were Holzmeister, who promoted an older, traditional, and popular approach; Oswald Haerdtl, Hoffmann's former assistant, whose buildings and interiors carried on the tradition of a distinctive Austrian modernism; and Roland Rainer, who developed a rational, decidedly antihistoricist architectural idiom. But it was a new generation, most of whom had been students of Holzmeister at the Vienna Academy of Fine Arts, including Friedrich Achleitner, Johann Gsteu, Hans Hollein, Wilhelm Holzbauer, Friedrich Kurrent, Josef Lackner, Gustav Peichl, Anton Schweighofer, and Johannes Spalt, who took the lead in shaping the direction of Austrian architecture after the late 1950s. Gsteu, Holzbauer, Peichl, and the others sought to reestablish the links with Austria's prewar modernist tradition while at the same time responding to contemporary trends abroad. The result was a more resolutely modernist and constructivist architecture, one that for the first time began to explore fully the possibilities of the newest construction methods. Also important in this development was Karl Schwanzer, whose

Museum des 20. Jahrhunderts (1959–62) and Philips Building (1962–64) were widely admired.

In the midst of this fascination with technology and tectonics, Hollein, in his Retti Candle Shop (1964–65) and subsequent works, demonstrated a renewed interest in aestheticism, one that pointed firmly in the direction of Postmodernism. Like Holzmeister before him, Hollein probed the potential of symbolism and representation, articulated not only in formal terms, but also through materials and space. Other Austrian architects of the 1960s, among them Haus-Rucker-Co (Laurids Ortner, Manfred Ortner, and Günther Zamp), Co-op Himmelb(l)au (Wolf D. Prix and Helmut Swiczinsky), and Missing Link (Adolf Krischanitz, Angela Heiterer, and Otto Kapfinger), rebelled against the avant-garde of the previous decade, seeking to substitute a new architecture—visionary, dynamic, and socially responsive—in the place of the dominant modernist monumentalism of the time.

By the 1970s, the works of both the old and the new avant-garde began to attract worldwide attention. Many of the old avant-garde—including Gsteu, Hollein, Kurrent, Lackner, Peichl, and Spalt—received academic appointments, and both groups found increasing numbers of commissions in Austria and abroad. Their position was challenged in the mid-1970s by two new movements that arose outside Vienna, the Vorarlberger Baukünstler (Vorarlberg architect-builders) and the Grazer Schule (Graz School). The former, concentrated in Bregenz near the border with Switzerland and represented by Carlo Baumschlager, Dietmar Eberle, Roland Gnaiger, and Hermann Kaufmann, stressed structural refinement and clear tectonic expression; the Graz School, led by Günther Domenig, Volker Giencke, and Klaus Kada, took an almost diametrically opposite approach, emphasizing the organic and expressive aspects of building.

The designs of the Vorarlberger Baukünstler, in spite of their use of regional, Alpine elements, followed the broader development of late modernism. The work of the Graz School, on the other hand, suggested a much more radical reinterpretation of 20th-century architecture, at once nervous, irrational, complex, and sometimes even disturbing. Forged at a moment when the faith in modernism had been broken, the architects of the Graz School and their counterparts in Vienna, including Coop Himmelb(l)au and Helmut Richter, challenged conventional notions of functionality, compositional form, and spatial enclosure. Domenig's Zentralsparkasse branch bank in the Favoriten section of Vienna (1975–79), perhaps the most significant example of the early phase of the Graz School, proffered a trembling assemblage of forms, evoking allusions to biomorphism. The more recent works of Giencke, Kada, and the others evince this same interest in visual dynamism, but add to it a greater formal and geometric complexity. Coop Himmelb(l)au's Falkenstrasse Roof Construction Project in Vienna (1983–88), among the most celebrated Austrian designs of the last two decades, introduced not only a potent construction-based aesthetic, but also a novel kind of space that is both challenging and inspiring.

Austria in the 1990s presented an unusually rich and diverse architectural scene. At one extreme were the buildings of Rob Krier, Heinz Tesar, and Hans Hollein, which sought to reintroduce historical concepts and forms into the contemporary discourse about urbanism and place. Hollein's Haas House in Vienna (1985–90), among the most controversial buildings of the era, demonstrated the long-standing Austrian attitude toward combining and blending varied elements of the past and present. Hermann Czech and Gustav Peichl, by contrast, made more specific allusions to the past, drawing in particular from the early Austrian *Moderne*. Others, like Wilhelm Holzbauer, Adolf Krischanitz, and Boris Podrecca, worked more or less within the codes of late modernism, albeit also with occasional backward glances. Younger architects, such as Florian Riegler and Roger Riewe, designers of the Graz Airport (1992–94), sought to frame a new austerity within the wrappings of technology. At the same time, Ortner & Ortner, Coop Himmelb(l)au, Völker Giencke, Klaus Kada, Helmut Richter, and their followers continued to challenge the old orthodoxies, even while their buildings had become firmly positioned within the mainstream.

CHRISTOPHER LONG

See also **Art Nouveau (Jugendstil); Co-op Himmelb(l)au (Austria); Czech, Hermann (Austria); Frank, Josef (Austria); Hoffmann, Josef (Austria); Hollein, Hans (Austria); Kada, Klaus (Austria); Karl Marx Hof, Vienna; Loos, Adolf (Austria); Neutra, Richard (Austria); Olbrich, Josef Maria (Austria); Post Office Savings Bank, Vienna; Steiner House, Vienna; Vienna, Austria; Vienna Secession; Wagner, Otto (Austria)**

Further Reading

Achleitner, Friedrich, *Neue Architektur in Österreich 1945–1970*, Vienna: Österreichische Fachzeitschriften, 1969

Achleitner, Friedrich, *Österreichische Architektur im 20. Jahrhundert: Ein Führer in vier Bänden*, 4 vols., Salzburg and Vienna: Residenz Verlag, 1980–

Achleitner, Friedrich, *Wiener Architektur: Zwischen typologischem Fatalismus und semantischem Schlamassel*, Vienna: Böhlau Verlag, 1996

Baujahre. Österreichische Architektur 1967–1991 (exh. cat.), Zentralvereinigung der Architekten Österreichs/Vienna, Cologne, and Weimar: Böhlau Verlag, 1992

Becker, Annette, Dietmar Steiner, and Wilfried Wang (editors), *Architektur im 20. Jahrhundert: Österreich: Von Otto Wagner bis Coop Himmelb(l)au* (exh. cat.), Munich and New York: Prestel Verlag, 1995

Blau, Eve, *The Architecture of Red Vienna, 1919–1934*, Cambridge, Mass., and London: MIT Press, 1999

Boeckl, Matthias, *Visionäre und Vertriebe: Österreichische Spuren in der modernen amerikanischen Architektur* (exh. cat.), Berlin: Ernst & Sohn, 1995

Co-op Himmelb(l)au, *Coop Himmelb(l)au: Architecture Is Now: Projects, (Un)Buildings, Actions, Statements, Sketches, Commentaries 1968–1983*, New York: Rizzoli, 1983

Dimster, Frank, *The New Austrian Architecture*, New York: Rizzoli, 1995

Domenig, Günther, et al., *Architektur-Investionen: Grazer "Schule" 13 Standpunkte*, Graz: Akademische Druck- und Verlagsanstalt, 1984

Feuerstein, Günter, *Visionäre Architektur Wien 1958–88*, Berlin: Ernst & Sohn, 1988

Frampton, Kenneth (editor), *A New Wave of Austrian Architecture* (exh. cat.), New York: Institute for Architecture and Urban Studies, 1980

Haiko, Peter, *Vienna 1850–1930 Architecture*, New York: Rizzoli, 1992

Kapfinger, Otto, Dietmar Steiner, and Adolph Stiller (editors), *Architecture in Austria: A Survey of the 20th Century*, Barcelona: ACTAR, and Basel: Birkhäuser, 1999

Österreichische Architektur 1945–75. Zeitentwicklungsübersicht, Utopien-Konzeptionen. Beispielhafte Objekte (exh. cat.), Vienna: Österreichische Gesellschaft für Architektur, 1976
Pelkonen, Eeva-Liisa, *Achtung Architektur! Image and Phantasm in Contemporary Austrian Architecture*, Cambridge, Massachusetts, and London: MIT Press, 1996
Sarnitz, August, *Drei Wiener Architekten: Wilhelm Holzbauer, Gustav Peichl, Roland Rainer*, Vienna: Edition Tusch, 1984
Tabor, Jan, *Architektur und Industrie: Betriebs- und Bürogebäude in Österreich 1950–90*, Vienna and Munich, 1992
Uhl, Ottokar, *Moderne Architektur in Wien, von Otto Wagner bis heute*, Vienna and Munich: Schroll, 1966
Zukowsky, John, and Ian Wardropper, *Austrian Architecture and Design: Beyond Tradition in the 1990s* (exh. cat.), Chicago: Chicago Art Institute, Berlin: Ernst & Sohn, 1991

AUTOMOBILE

At the close of the millennium, many local and national politicians admitted what many architectural critics and planners had noted for years: the landscape of post–World War II America had been planned around automobiles more than around people. Reflecting the nation's great enthusiasm for automobility, the 20th-century landscape integrated this transportation infrastructure and allowed it a defining influence. In some ways, this dominance snuck up on many Americans; yet such change is more attributable to blinded free choice than to naïveté: the 20th-century American lived under the spell of the open road.

Although the United States seized the invention, the automobile was first developed in Europe in the 1890s. French manufacturers marketed the first successful automobile in 1894. Inconvenience from a lack of roads and infrastructure as well as a dependence on transportation technologies such as trolleys precluded Americans from rapidly accepting the new "horseless carriage." The manufacturing and marketing efforts of Henry Ford and others changed this attitude by 1913, when there was one motor vehicle to every eight Americans. Mass production made sure that by the 1920s, the car had become no longer a luxury but a necessity of American middle-class life. The landscape, however, had been designed around other modes of transport, including an urban scene dependent on foot travel. Cars enabled an independence never before possible, if they were supported with the necessary service structure. Massive architectural shifts were necessary to make way for the automobile, as architects and planners reconfigured urban street forms or designed new building types to accommodate the automobile. Congested streets forced motorists to park and store their automobiles in a new building, the parking garage. Early garages included mechanical systems and elevators to carry cars into tall skyscraper-like garages. Smaller garages affiliated with hotels or commercial districts proliferated. After World War II, motorists could select garages with attendants or, more commonly by the 1970s and after, they could use self-park garages. By the 1990s, architects were designing tall garages for hundreds of cars. With retail storefronts at the pedestrian level, many urban garages were designed to blend in with neighboring buildings and styles.

Although the motorcar was the quintessential private instrument, its owners had to operate it over public spaces. Who would pay for these public thoroughfares? After a period of acclimation, Americans viewed highway building as a form of social and economic therapy. They justified public financing for such projects on the theory that roadway improvements would pay for themselves by increasing property-tax revenues along the route. At this time, asphalt, macadam, and concrete were each used on different roadways.

By the 1920s, the congested streets of urban areas pressed road building into other areas. Most urban regions soon proposed express streets without stoplights or intersections. These aesthetically conceived roadways, normally following the natural topography of the land, soon took the name "parkways." Long Island and Westchester County, New York, used parkways with bridges and tunnels to separate these express routes from local cross traffic. The Bronx River Parkway (1906), for instance, follows a river park and forest; it also is the first roadway to be declared a national historic site. In addition to pleasure driving, such roads stimulated automobile commuting.

The Federal Road Act of 1916 offered funds to states that organized highway departments, designating 200,000 miles of road as primary and thus eligible for federal funds. More important, ensuing legislation also created a Bureau of Public Roads to plan a highway network to connect all cities of 50,000 or more inhabitants. Some states adopted gasoline taxes to help finance the new roads. By 1925 the value of highway construction projects exceeded $1 billion. Expansion continued through the Great Depression, with road building becoming integral to city and town development.

Robert Moses of New York defined this new role as road builder and social planner. Through his work in the greater New York City area (1928–60), Moses created a model for a metropolis that included and even emphasized the automobile as opposed to mass transportation. This was a dramatic change in the motivation of design. Historian Clay McShane (1994) writes, "In their headlong search for modernity through mobility, American urbanites made a decision to destroy the living environments of nineteenth-century neighborhoods by converting their gathering places into traffic jams, their playgrounds into motorways, and their shopping places into elongated parking lots."

Outside of cities in the United States, major efforts were underway to knit the nation together on a larger scale. In the 1910s, motorists and commercial forces joined in the good-roads movement to establish early national highways, such as the Lincoln Highway and the Dixie Highway. Route 66, stretching southwest from Chicago through Illinois, Missouri, Kansas, Oklahoma, Texas, New Mexico, Arizona, and California, ending at Los Angeles, was to become the most celebrated interstate roadway. While the road supplied an exodus for many Dust Bowl sufferers in the 1930s, Route 66 became even more important as a symbol. "Get your kicks on Route 66" echoed through many musical moments as well as in minutes of personal longing. For Americans, "America's Main Street" opened up westward and ushered in a period of comfortable cruising in American automobiles. Probably more than any other roadway, Route 66 allowed the automobile to become a means for expressing the American tradition of independence and freedom. Planners, designers, and entrepreneurs sought methods to stimulate and take advantage of this new American passion.

Aerial view of a housing development in Levittown, New York, under construction
© Collection of New York World-Telegram and the Sun Newspaper Photograph Collection (Library of Congress, United States). Photo by Thomas Airviews, Bayside, New York

Drivers through the 1930s often slept in roadside yards, so developers soon took advantage of this opportunity by devising the roadside camp or motel. Independently owned tourist camps graduated from tents to cabins, which were often called "motor courts." After World War II, the form became a motel, in which all the rooms were tied together in one structure. Still independently owned, by 1956 there were 70,000 motels nationwide. Best Western and Holiday Inn soon used ideas of prefabrication to create chains of motels throughout the United States. Holiday Inn defined this new part of the automobile landscape by emphasizing uniformity so that travelers felt as if they were in a familiar environment no matter where they traveled.

The automobile landscape, of course, needed to effectively incorporate its essential raw material: petroleum. The gas station, which originally existed as little more than a roadside shack, mirrors the evolution of the automobile-related architecture in general. By the 1920s, filling stations had integrated garages and service facilities. These facilities were privately owned and uniquely constructed. By the mid-1930s, oil giants, such as Shell and Texaco, developed a range of prototype gas stations that would re-create the site as a showroom for tires, motor oil, or other services. The architectural style clearly derived from the International Style, with a sleek, white appearance. While carefully dressed attendants were a vital part of the experience at many service stations, George Urich introduced the United States' first self-service gas station in California in 1947. By the 1990s, this form had been further streamlined to include convenience stores and the opportunity to pay at the pump. The gas station experience would steadily become less personalized.

As automobiles became more familiar in everyday Americans' lives, planners and developers formalized refueling stations for the human drivers as well. Food stands informally provided refreshment during these early days, but soon restaurants were developed that utilized marketing strategies from the motel and petroleum industries. Diners and family restaurants sought prime locations along frequently traveled roads; however, these forms did not alter dining patterns significantly. White Castle (1921) combined the food stand with the restaurant to create a restaurant that could be put almost anywhere. Drive-in restaurants would evolve around the idea of quick service, often allowing drivers to remain in their automobile. Fast food as a concept, of course, derives specifically from Ray Kroc and the McDonald's concept that he marketed out of California (1952). Clearly the idea of providing service to automobile drivers had created an entire offshoot of the restaurant industry.

Whereas most roadside building types evolved gradually, the drive-in theater was deliberately invented. Richard M. Hollingshead Jr., of New Jersey, believed that entertainment needed to incorporate the automobile. Hollingshead patented the first drive-in in 1933, but the invention would not proliferate until the 1950s. Viewing outdoor films in one's car has become a symbol of the culture of consumption that overtook the American middle class during the postwar era. Of course, it also established the automobile as a portable, private oasis where youth could express their sexuality as well as experiment with drugs and alcohol.

Most of these developments redefined the local landscape while creating few national thoroughfares. President Dwight D. Eisenhower changed this in the 1950s. In 1920 he had led troops across the American road system in a military call for new roads. Then he had witnessed the spectacle of Hitler's Autobahn firsthand. When he became president, he worked with automobile manufacturers and others to devise a 1956 plan to connect America's future to the automobile. The interstate highway system was the most expensive public works project in human history. The public rationale for this hefty project revolved around fear of nuclear war: such roadways would assist in exiting urban centers in the event of such a calamity. The emphasis, however, was clearly economic expansion. At the cost of many older urban neighborhoods—often occupied by minority groups—the huge wave of concrete was unrolled that linked all the major cities of the nation.

With the national future clearly tied to cars, planners began perfecting ways of further integrating the automobile into American domestic life. Initially, these tactics were quite literal. In the early 20th century, many homes of wealthy Americans soon required the ability to store vehicles. Most often, these homes had carriage houses or stables that could be converted. Soon, of course, architects devised an appendage to the home and gave it the French name "garage." From this early point, housing in the United States closely followed the integration of the automobile and roads into American life.

Upper- and middle-class Americans had begun moving to suburban areas in the late 1800s. The first suburban developments, such as Llewellyn Park, New Jersey (1856), followed train lines or the corridors of other early mass transit. The automobile allowed access to vast areas between and beyond these corridors. Suddenly, the suburban hinterland around every city compounded. As early as 1940, about 13 million people lived in communities beyond the reach of public transportation. Because of these changes, suburbs could be planned for less wealthy Americans.

Modeled after the original Gustav Stickley homes or similar designs from *Ladies Home Journal* and other popular magazines, middle-class suburbs appealed to working- and middle-class Americans. The bungalow became one of the most popular designs in the nation. The construction halt of the Great Depression set the stage for more recent ideas and designs, including the ranch house. The basic features of the ranch house—its simple, informal, one-story structure; its low-pitched eaves; and its large expanse of glass that included "picture" windows—were fused in the public mind with the easygoing lifestyle identified with the Southwest and West Coast.

Planners used home styles such as these to develop one site after another with the automobile linking each one to the outside world. The world of Levittown (the first of which was constructed in 1947) involved a complete dependence on automobile travel. This shift to suburban living became a hallmark of the late 20th century, with over half the nation residing in suburbs by the 1990s. The planning system that supported this residential world, however, involved much more than roads. The services necessary to support outlying, suburban communities also needed to be integrated by planners.

Instead of the Main Street prototype, the automobile suburbs demanded a new form. Initially, planners such as Jesse Clyde Nichols devised shopping areas, such as Kansas City's Country Club District (1922), that appeared a hybrid of previous forms. In Lake Forest, Illinois, Howard Van Doren Shaw designed Market Square (1916), perhaps the first shopping center planned to address the automobile. Soon, however, the "strip" had evolved as the commercial corridor of the future. These sites quickly became part of suburban development in order to provide basic services close to home. A shopper rarely arrived without an automobile; therefore, the car needed to be part of the design program. The most obvious architectural development for speed was signage: integrated into the overall site plan would be towering neon aberrations that identified services. In addition, parking lots and drive-through windows suggest the integral role of transportation in this new commerce.

These developments culminated in the shopping mall, which quickly became a necessary portion of strip planning. By the 1970s, developers' initiatives clearly included regional economic development for a newly evolving service and retail world. Incorporating suburbs into such development plans, designs for these pseudocommunities were held together by the automobile. The marketplace for this culture quickly became the shopping mall. Strip malls, which open onto roadways and parking lots, were installed near residential areas as suburbs extended further from the city center. Developers then perfected the self-sustained, enclosed shopping mall, which became the symbol of a culture of conspicuous consumption that many Americans have criticized since its first appearance. Try as they might, developers could never re-create the culture of local communities in these new artificial environments.

Critics such as Jane Jacobs and James Kunstler identified an intrinsic bias on the American landscape in the 1970s. Kunstler writes, "Americans have been living car-centered lives for so long that the collective memory of what used to make a landscape or a townscape or even a suburb humanly rewarding has nearly been erased." The 1990s closed with the unfolding of the new politics of urban sprawl. "I've come to the conclusion," explained Vice President Al Gore on the campaign trail in 1999, "that what we really are faced with here is a systematic change from a pattern of uncontrolled sprawl toward a brand new path that makes quality of life the goal of all our urban, suburban, and farmland policies." During the 20th century, planners and designers gave Americans what they wanted: a life and landscape married to the automobile. A divorce will require an entirely revised architectural program.

BRIAN BLACK

See also **Roadside Architecture; Shaw, Howard Van Doren (United States); Shopping Center; Suburban Planning**

Further Reading

Belasco, Warren James, *Americans on the Road: From Autocamp to Motel, 1910–1945*, Cambridge, Massachusetts: MIT Press, 1979

Calthorpe, Peter, *The Next American Metropolis: Ecology, Community, and the American Dream*, New York: Princeton Architectural Press, 1993
Clark, Clifford Edward, *The American Family Home, 1800–1960*, Chapel Hill: University of North Carolina Press, 1986
Flink, James J., *The Automobile Age*, Cambridge, Massachusetts: MIT Press, 1988
Hart, John Fraser (editor), *Our Changing Cities*, Baltimore, Maryland: Johns Hopkins University Press, 1991
Jackson, Kenneth T., *Crabgrass Frontier: The Suburbanization of the United States*, New York: Oxford University Press, 1985
Jacobs, Jane, *The Death and Life of Great American Cities*, New York: Random House, 1961; London: Jonathan Cape, 1962
Kay, Jane Holtz, *Asphalt Nation: How the Automobile Took Over America and How We Can Take It Back*, New York: Crown, 1997
Kunstler, James H., *The Geography of Nowhere: The Rise and Decline of America's Man-Made Landscape*, New York: Simon and Schuster, 1993
Lewis, Tom, *Divided Highways*, New York: Viking, 1997
Liebs, Chester H., *Main Street to Miracle Mile: American Roadside Architecture*, Boston: Little Brown, 1985
McShane, Clay, *Down the Asphalt Path: The Automobile and the American City*, New York: Columbia University Press, 1994
Relph, Edward, *The Modern Urban Landscape*, Baltimore, Maryland: Johns Hopkins University Press, and London: Croom Helm, 1987
Wright, Gwendolyn, *Building the Dream: A Social History of Housing in America*, New York: Pantheon, 1981

AVANT-GARDE

Taken literally, the avant-garde refers to the front part of a marching army, the scouts that first head into unknown territory. As a metaphor, the word has been used from the 19th century onward to refer to progressive political and artistic movements that considered themselves to be ahead of their time. The avant-garde is struggling against the old, heading toward the new. It is radical and controversial, fighting against consensus and looking for disruption. The avant-garde radicalizes the basic principle of modernity: the urge toward continual change and development. According to Matei Calinescu (1987), its very radicality drives it to a conscious quest for crisis: Because the avant-garde attitude implies the bluntest rejection of such traditional ideas as those of order, intelligibility, or even success, its protagonists seek for an art that is to become an experience, deliberately conducted, of failure and crisis. The most characteristic feature of the avant-garde, therefore, might be the continuous cycling of short-lived movements that emerge and whither away in rapid succession.

As early as 1962, Renato Poggioli described the avant-garde as characterized by four moments: activism, antagonism, nihilism, and agonism. The activist moment meant adventure and dynamism, an urge to action that is not necessarily linked to any positive goal. The antagonistic character of the avant-garde refers to its combativeness; the avant-garde is always struggling against something—against tradition, against the public, or against the establishment. Activism and antagonism are often pursued in such a way that an avant-garde movement finally overtakes itself in a nihilistic quest, in an uninterrupted search for purity, ending up by dissolving into nothing. The avant-garde is indeed inclined to sacrifice itself on the altar of progress—a characteristic that Poggioli labels agonistic.

During the last decades, the term avant-garde has acquired a more precise theoretical meaning because of the work of Peter Bürger (1974). The avant-garde is clearly distinguished from modernism in that it is confined to a more limited range of ideas and movements. According to Bürger, the avant-garde in the visual arts and literature was concerned to abolish the autonomy of art as an institution. Its aim was to put an end to the existence of art as something separate from everyday life—of art, that is, as an autonomous domain that has no real impact on the social system. The avant-garde, says Bürger, aims for a new life praxis, a praxis that is based on art and that constitutes an alternative for the existing order. This alternative would no longer organize social life on the basis of economic rationality and bourgeois conventions. It would rather found itself on aesthetic sensibilities and on the creative potentialities of each individual.

Avant-gardism has been most prominent in literature and the arts, whereas its use in the context of architecture was less common. Nevertheless, there has been a tendency to identify the Modern movement as the avant-garde in architecture. The theoretical fine-tuning urged by Bürger, however, necessitates a modification of this too-simple identification. Bürger's work also brought about a growing consensus to distinguish between the historical avant-garde, chronologically situated before World War II, and the neo-avant-garde, which is a more recent phenomenon.

The issues and themes around which the Modern movement in architecture crystallized were surely related to the avant-garde logic of destruction of the old and construction of the new. The Modern movement was based on a rejection of the bourgeois culture of philistinism that used pretentious ornament and kitsch and that took the form of eclecticism (Gusevich, 1987). In its stead, the movement gave precedence to purity and authenticity. In the 1920s, these themes acquired a distinct political dimension: The new architecture became associated with the desire for a more socially balanced and egalitarian form of society in which the ideals of equal rights and emancipation would be realized. The architectural vanguard, nevertheless, did not become as uncompromising and as radical as its counterpart in art and literature. Most architects, for example, never renounced the principle of rationality, even if it stood for a bourgeois value.

Therefore, it might be more productive not to speak of the Modern movement as *the* avant-garde but, rather, to distinguish certain avant-garde moments within its discourse, for the movement was hardly a unified whole; rather, it consisted of widely differing trends and tendencies. Manfredo Tafuri and Francesco Dal Co cite tendencies such as De Stijl in Holland, Productivism and Constructivism in Russia, and the late Expressionist currents of the Arbeitsrat für Kunst and the Novembergruppe in Germany among the architectural avant-garde. These movements, they argue, were inspired by an intensive exchange between visual arts and architecture and a new social reality that was based on a new, artistic outlook on the world.

The early writings of Swiss historian and critic Sigfried Giedion testify to an aspiration to abolish architecture as a typology or segregated discipline. In *Bauen in Frankreich, Eisen, Eisenbeton* (1928; *Building in France, Building in Iron, Building in Ferroconcrete*), Giedion questions the very idea of an architecture with definitive boundaries, and his implicit suggestion is that architecture no longer has anything to do with objects. If it is to survive at all, it must become part of a broader domain in which spatial relations and concerns are of central importance. Herewith, Giedion formulates as a goal for architecture that it would break out of the limits imposed on it by tradition and by its functioning as an institution.

Although Giedion did not develop these potentially subversive considerations in any radical way in his consecutive work, they were not completely idiosyncratic, either. The thought that architecture should no longer limit itself to the design of representative buildings but rather should develop into a more comprehensive discipline that is focusing on the whole of the environment and that merges with social reality and with life itself was shared by many prominent modern architects from the 1920s. Avant-garde architects such as Walter Gropius, Hannes Meyer, and Ernst May believed that their mission had to do with the design of all aspects of life, and they aimed at a reconceptualization of the whole process of building, including construction techniques, housing typologies, and urbanism. One of the most radical interpretations of such beliefs was to be found in the work of Walter Benjamin.

Benjamin thought that the destructive gestures of the avant-garde, which aimed at purification, were necessary to free the way for a revolutionary future. The transparency and openness of the new architecture pointed for Benjamin to a revolutionary, classless society based on emancipation and flexibility. He interpreted this architecture as part of the avant-garde's attack on bourgeois culture. The new architecture schooled inhabitants and users to adapt to new social conditions that prefigured the future transparent society. Benjamin saw architecture as a discipline that was capable of stimulating people to align their attitudes with those required by the new society to come (Heynen, 1999).

The alignment between modern architecture and politically progressive tendencies was thus clearly present in the 1920s and the early 1930s, in the self-reflection of its representatives as well as in the discourse of major critics. This avant-garde position claimed a new, more open and more socially relevant mission for architecture. It was utopian and critical, believing that the new future could be reached only by starting from scratch. This position, however, did not dominate very long. When Henry-Russell Hitchcock and Philip Johnson introduced modern architecture to the United States, they presented it as the latest and most topical style, leaving aside any social or political issues (*The International Style*, 1932). Giedion himself gravitated toward a similar position with his later *Space, Time and Architecture* (1941). In presenting the space-time concept as a "secret synthesis" that was capable of building a unity across very different disciplines, Giedion no longer referred to social experiments or to the revolutionizing aims of the new architecture. Instead, he strove toward the formulation of a common denominator that could unite rather diverse trends under the banner of one "modern architecture," thus formulating a certain orthodoxy that was at odds with the continuous longing for change characteristic of the avant-garde.

This tendency toward consensus and orthodoxy in modern architecture was only reinforced in the postwar years, when modern architecture was accepted by many administrations as the most appropriate answer to the building needs of the Reconstruction era. Modern architecture thus became institutionalized as part of the establishment, and consequently, it took its leave from the avant-garde aspirations of the 1920s. It was therefore no coincidence that after World War II a gap opened up between modern architecture and the avant-garde in the arts. They soon drifted quite apart. The most vehement criticism that was leveled against modern architecture in the early postwar years came from movements such as Lettrism and International Situationism rather than from right-wing conservatives. International Situationism was based on the program for a "unitary urbanism," which consisted of a vigorous critique of current modernist urbanism. Unitary urbanism rejected the utilitarian logic of the consumer society, aiming instead for the realization of a dynamic city, a city in which freedom and play would have a central role. By operating collectively, the Situationists aimed to achieve a creative interpretation of their everyday surroundings, and they created situations that subverted the normal state of affairs. The Situationists belonged to the neo-avant-garde movements that formed an "avant-garde beyond modernism." This neo-avant-garde considered itself to be ahead of the masses in its search for the future but took its distance from the more conciliatory, consensus-oriented mainstream modernism because it was much more radical and utopian.

Within the field of architecture, there were also groups, such as Archizoom, Archigram, and Superstudio that moved beyond modernist ideas and could be called neo-avant-garde. It is less clear, however, what the meanings of the terms "avant-garde" and "neo-avant-garde" have become in the most recent decades. On the one hand, there is a clear rejection of the avant-garde logic of destruction of the old and utopian construction of the new. It is stated that this logic is based on an ideology of progress, which has since been proven to be false; that it gave rise to an elitist hermeticism that rendered its ideals completely inaccessible to a general public; and that its supposedly radical innovations and inventions nevertheless lend themselves all too well to appropriation by the culture industry. This widely spread criticism would lead one to think that the avant-garde is dead—a claim that has been made repeatedly. On the other hand, in the 1980s and the '90s, the notion of a contemporary neo-avant-garde has resurged in the work of Peter Eisenman, Bernard Tschumi, and others. It seems clear, however, that this use of the term *neo-avant-garde* is based on a perception of their position within a discursive field and that its application has nothing to do with how they, contentwise, think about architecture. The avant-garde and its significance for 20th-century architecture rests, then, with the constant obliteration of boundaries between the arts and architecture, image and text, and the meanings of old and new.

HILDE HEYNEN

Further Reading

The theoretization of what the avant-garde was all about took place mostly in fields outside architectural theory or history. Poggioli presented an early *Theory of the Avant-Garde*, focusing on the arts. Bürger published his seminal work in 1974 (it was translated in 1984). He took his clues mainly from surrealism and Dadaism in literature and in the arts. Bürger's book gave rise to an interesting debate in Germany, resulting in the publication of Lindner (1976) and of Müller (1984). Calinescu (1987) offers a very interesting and reliable source for clarifying terminological questions, but he does not focus on architecture.

Tafuri is the most important architectural historian who theoretically distinguishes between avant-garde and modernism. Although there are no full-length books in English dealing with the theme of architecture and avant-garde, there are some important collections of essays (Ockman, 1988; Somol, 1997) as well as individual articles raising interesting questions (Gusevich, 1987; Heynen, 1999). McLeod offers a feminist criticism on the neo-avant-garde of the 1980s and the 1990s (1996).

Bürger, Peter, *Theorie der Avant-Garde*, Frankfurt am Main: Suhrkamp, 1974; as *Theory of the Avant-Garde*, translated by Michael Shaw, Minneapolis: University of Minnesota Press, 1984

Calinescu, Matei, *Five Faces of Modernity: Modernism, Avant-Garde, Decadence, Kitsch, Postmodernism*, Durham: Duke University Press, 1987; revised edition of *Faces of Modernity: Avant-Garde, Decadence, Kitsch*, Bloomington: Indiana University Press, 1977

Colomina, Beatriz and Joan Ockman (editors), *Architectureproduction*, New York: Princeton Architectural Press, 1988

Giedion, Sigfried, *Bauen in Frankreich, Eisen, Eisenbeton*, Leipzig: Klinkhardt and Biermann, 1928; as *Building in France, Building in Iron, Building in Ferroconcrete*, translated by J. Duncan Berry, with an introduction by Sokratis Georgiadis, Santa Monica, California: Getty Center for the History of Art and the Humanities, 1995

Gusevich, Miriam, "Purity and Transgression: Reflection on the Architectural Avantgarde's Rejection of Kitsch," *Discourse*, 10, no. 1 (Fall–Winter 1987–88)

Heynen, Hilde, " 'What Belongs to Architecture?' Avant-garde Ideas in the Modern Movement," *The Journal of Architecture*, 4, no. 2 (1999)

Lüdke, Werner Martin, et al. (editors), *Theorie der Avantgarde: Antworten auf Peter Bürgers Bestimmung von Kunst und bürgerlicher Gesellschaft*, Frankfurt am Main: Suhrkamp, 1976

McLeod, Mary, "Everyday and 'Other' Spaces," in *Architecture and Feminism: Yale Publications on Architecture*, edited by Debra Coleman, Elizabeth Danze, and Carol Henderson, New York: Princeton Architectural Press, 1996

Müller, Michael, *Architektur und Avantgarde: ein vergessenes Projekt der Moderne?* Frankfurt am Main: Syndikat, 1984

Poggioli, Renato, *Teoria dell'arte d'avanguardia*, Bologna: Il Mulino, 1962; as *The Theory of the Avant-Garde*, translated by Gerald Fitzgerald, Cambridge, Massachusetts: Belknap Press of Harvard University Press, 1981

Somol, R.E. (editor), *Autonomy and Ideology: Positioning an Avant-Garde in America*, New York: Monacceli Press, 1997

Tafuri, Manfredo, and Francesco Dal Co, *Architettura contemporanea*, Milano: Electa, 1976; as *Modern Architecture*, 2 vols., translated by Robert Erich Wolf, New York: Electa/Rizzoli, 1986

Tafuri, Manfredo, *La sfera e il labirinto: avanguardie e architettura da Piranesi agli anni '70*, Torino: Einaudi, 1980; as *The Sphere and the Labyrinth. Avant-Gardes and Architecture from Piranesi to the 1970s*, translated by Pellegrino d'Acierno and Robert Connolly, Cambridge, Massachusetts: MIT Press, 1987

B

BAIYOKE TOWER

Designed by Plan Architects; completed 1987
Bangkok, Thailand

Distinctive for its horizontal strips of rainbow color and a gable-shaped roof, the first Baiyoke tower in Bangkok, Thailand, was famously known as the one-time tallest reinforced-concrete building in Asia. This skyscraper signified the start of Thai high-rise architectural development. Land Development, a real estate company dominated by the Baiyoke family, the project developer and landowner, proposed this 42-story building to serve as both a commercial and a residential complex. The company turned the site on Rachaprarob Road, which once had been occupied by a large-scale theater, into a garment and cloth market and a residential tower for the Pratunam district. Not only did the garment and cloth business inside the building fit in well with the neighborhood's business in general, but it also eventually became one of the most significant wholesale cloth markets in Bangkok for years to come.

Although the Baiyoke tower established the Baiyoke family among Bangkok's business society, the tower itself promoted its design firm, Plan Architect, for their use of bright color and the composition of geometric forms. The design team represented a collaboration between Plan Architect and Inter Arkitek. Sinn Phonghanyudh, Plan Architect's executive architect, was in charge of the design team, which included Theeraphon Niyom (firm owner), Krongsak Chulamorkodt (partner), Boonrit Kordilokrat, Chenkit Napawan, Sapark Aksharanugraha, and Songsak Visudharom. Their design won the 1984 competition sponsored by the Baiyoke family. The winning design proposed the most functional exploitation of the limited site as well as the remarkable concept of building the tallest building in the region.

On its completion in 1987, the building contained 55,000 square meters, including two main parts: podium and tower. The large-scale column-and-beam reinforced-concrete podium covered almost the entire site. Each floor was marked by different color, forming a vertical rainbow in downtown Bangkok. The ground, first, and second floors were devoted to the garment and cloth market. The third floor was originally designed as offices for rent but later was turned, in part, into cloth shops to serve the growing market. The fourth floor held a gigantic food center and several minitheaters. The next five floors served as a parking garage for over 500 cars, an estimation approximated to accommodate the high density of car drivers in Bangkok during the 1980s. Architects designed the roof at the top of the podium as a recreation center, including a swimming pool and health center, serving residents of the tower above. The residential floors were eventually converted to a hotel complex. Its structure, supported by the shared structure of the podium, was erected with flat-slab layers of a cross shape. Each residential floor combined eight units, each with a single shared wall. Four elevators at the tower core ran from the ground floor to the top, separating the tower's access from that of the podium. Other facilities were likewise designed separately for serving the tower's residents and the users inside the podium area. Despite the shared structure of the podium and tower parts, Baiyoke tower was designed as two very different buildings. In fact, this design reflected a common trend of multifunction complex favored among Bangkok's real estate development during the late 20th century.

Shortly following the success of the project, the Baiyoke real estate developer decided in 1988 to initiate a second project, Baiyoke II, with a similar publicized theme of establishing another record for the world's tallest reinforced-concrete building. This follow-up project, however, was interrupted a few times during Thai financial turbulence in the 1990s. The building was finally opened to the public in 1999, taking more than ten years to complete. This long wait contrasted to the three-year construction period of its fellow building, the first Baiyoke.

The Baiyoke II consisted of 172,000 square meters, more than three times the first Baiyoke's space. The project comprised 88 floors, 309 meters in total height above ground (including the tower's antenna but excluding the two underground floors). The building functioned mainly as a hotel and included a shopping plaza and a parking garage—an intrinsic element of contemporary Bangkok's architecture. The ground floor through the fourth floor served as retail shops, and the next ten floors consisted of parking space. The hotel business occupied space from the 15th floor up, with the top ten floors designed to serve as space for sky lounges, restaurants, and kitchen areas. The main observation lounge for tourists and visitors was located on the 76th floor, whereas access to the very top floors remained exclusive to hotel guests and the restaurants' clients.

Unlike the first Baiyoke's colorful theme, the Plan Architect design team conceptualized the second Baiyoke building as a massive red block rising from the ground, with a glittering gold roof that signified the golden roof of a Thai temple, an omnipresent metaphoric symbol of Thai culture. In the design proposal of Plan Architects, the design team once mentioned that the mass of colorful red sandstone represented "the image of natural sandstone rising from the earth, punched out to provide space for human's various activities. The higher it goes, the more modernized and sophisticated these various voids become."

To be modernized or not remains an unfinished argument for which there is hardly an answer, not only for both Baiyoke towers but also for contemporary Bangkok architecture in general. The issues of "modern" and "modernity" have led many Thai architects to confront problems in interpreting and defining designs to suit the terms. Along with layers of interpretation and influences from foreign architectural development, definitions vary and thus have brought up various designs. The Baiyoke towers' significant contribution to the city, with extension to the Southeast Asian region, was essential in that they challenged the general geographic condition and virtually turned Bangkok's architectural development into a new phase of high-rise architectural development.

VIMALIN RUJIVACHARAKUL

See also **Bangkok, Thailand**

Further Reading

Association of Siamese Architects, research by Vimolsidhi Horayangkura, Kobkul Indaravichitr, Santi Chantavilaswons, Veera Inpantang. *Phattanakarn Naew Kwamkid lae Rupbab kong Ngan Satapattayakarm: Adeet, Patjuban, lae Anakot* (Development of Architectural Form: The Past, Present, and Future), Bangkok: Amarintr Publishing, 1993

BAKER, HERBERT 1862–1946

Architect, England and South Africa

Herbert Baker's prolific practice produced a wide variety of work in England and abroad. His work ranged from country houses to ecclesiastical work and public buildings and most notably includes the government Houses in both South Africa and India. Indeed, Baker is credited with the creation of a South African architecture by giving expression to the dreams of his great patron, Cecil Rhodes, who wished to create a distinguished and permanent culture.

As a contemporary of Edwin Lutyens, Baker's particular distinction lay in his ability to range from Arts and Crafts in his domestic work, to a dignified monumental style, sensitively modified to accommodate technology, and different national and climatic conditions.

Baker was born in Kent, and attended the Royal Academy School, London, from 1879 until 1881, when he was apprenticed to his cousin, Arthur Baker. Between 1882 and 1887, he served as lead assistant in the office of celebrated domestic architects, George and Peto, where he claimed to have gained invaluable experience. Emphasis was placed on the importance of working drawings, sketching tours, and above all, respect for high levels of craftsmanship. It was there that he met Lutyens, who was an apprentice with the firm from 1887.

In 1892 Baker began his own practice in Cape Town, South Africa, where he met Rhodes, who commissioned the restoration of his home, Groote Schuur. It was originally completed in 1895 but destroyed by fire and rebuilt by Baker. The final design was an adaptation of the old Cape Dutch style and alerted South Africans to the supremacy of their 17th- and 18th-century buildings over recent 19th-century work. The interiors are indebted to George and Peto, in Baker's elaborate amalgamation of English Tudor and Cape Dutch and in his employment of a consistent group of craftsmen.

Baker was appointed diocesan architect for Cape Town, and was responsible for building many churches, including St. George's Cathedral (1898, Cape Town), all of which were characterized by a round-arched style that combined rough-hewn stone and white plaster. A flow of both domestic and commercial buildings followed.

Baker designed many houses in Johannesburg built in response to the short-lived mining boom. His style provided a synthesis of indigenous sources, including Mediterranean vernacular, and English Arts and Crafts, which were emulated in numerous suburbs.

In 1900 Baker retraced Rhodes's steps while on a tour of Egypt, Greece, and Italy. Rhodes's tour had inspired him to a series of classical architectural dreams that sadly were to materialize only in his memorial, which was built by Baker at Mowbray, Cape Town. Baker also designed memorials to the Shangani tribe for the Matabele War of 1897 and a monument, the *Honored Dead* (1905), at Kimberley, Cape Province, that was inspired by Rome and Agrigentum. Following Rhodes's death in 1902, Lord Milner assumed responsibility for reconstruction in the Transvaal and Orange River Colony after the Boer War.

Baker and his partner, Francis E. Masey, produced government buildings, churches, houses, and agricultural and mining settlements. Pretoria Cathedral was begun in 1905, but was only partially completed. Government House (1907, Pretoria) and Pretoria Railway Station (1909) heralded the Union Buildings style. The work was commissioned by General Botha, South Africa's first prime minister, and came as a result of the legislature remaining in Cape Town; the Pretoria Union Buildings (1912) represent Baker's most important work in South Africa, and lend expression to his belief that a nation should demonstrate pride by the creation of noble monuments. In this work, traditional European Neoclassical forms were combined with a serious concern to adapt to local materials and technology. Twin cupola towers, evoking Wren's Greenwich Hospital, were linked by a concave hemicycle to prevent them from dominating the low ground that they crowned.

Lutyens recommended that Baker share with him in the building of the new government buildings in New Delhi. Unfortunately a disagreement over the leveling of the central King's Way leading to Lutyen's Viceregal Lodge led to a long estrangement. Whereas Baker's designs were sympathetic to the Mogul tradition, those by Lutyens were rather more dispassionate and individual. In 1913 Baker returned to England and, with his subsequent partner, Francis Fleming, designed the twin-domed Secretariat Building and the circular Legislature Building.

Pretoria Railway Station, Pretoria, South Africa (1909), photographed designed by Herbert Baker

In 1917 the War Graves Commission invited Baker to make recommendations about cemeteries and monuments that were designed to give expression to inarticulated grief. Compared with Lutyens, who strove for abstract monumentality, Baker favored a more literal symbolism, reveling in the intricacies of heraldry and literary quotation. His designs included the Indian Memorial at Neuve Chapelle and the South African Memorial at Deville Wood. He produced a formidable number of buildings in England following World War I, culminating in South Africa House (1935) in London.

Following a distinguished career, Baker was knighted in 1926.

HILARY J. GRAINGER

See also **Africa: Southern and Central Africa; Arts and Crafts Movement; Lutyens, Edwin (Great Britain)**

Biography

Born in Cobham, Kent, England, 9 June 1862. Studied at the Royal Academy School of Architecture, London 1879–81; apprenticed to cousin Arthur Baker, architect 1879–82. Married Florence Edmeades 1904: 4 children. Worked for Ernest George and Harold Peto, London 1882–87. Opened office in Gravesend, Kent 1890; moved to Cape Town, South Africa and was appointed architect to Cecil Rhodes 1892; opened office in Johannesburg, South Africa 1902; formed partnership first with Willmott Sloper, then Francis Flemming; returned to London in 1913 and continued practice until 1946; worked with Edwin Lutyens in New Delhi, India 1913–31; principal architect to Imperial War Graves Commission 1918–28; architect to the Bank of England from 1921. Fellow, Royal Institute of British Architects 1900; founder and member, South African Society of Architects 1901; associate, Royal Academy 1922; member, Royal Academy 1932. Knighted 1926; Gold Medal, Royal Institute of British Architects 1927. Died in Cobham, Kent, England, 4 February 1946.

Selected Works

Groote Schuur (Cecil Rhodes House), Rondesbosch, South Africa, 1895; rebuilt after fire, 1897
St. George's Cathedral, Cape Town, 1898
Kimberley Siege Memorial, Cape Province, 1905
Pretoria Cathedral (incomplete), Pretoria, 1905
Government House, Pretoria, 1907

Cecil Rhodes Memorial, Mowbray, 1908
Railway Station, Pretoria, 1909
Union Buildings, Pretoria, 1912
Numerous war cemeteries and memorials, Belgium, France, England, 1918–28
India House, Aldwych, London, 1925
Secretariat Building, New Delhi, 1927
Legislative Assembly Building, New Delhi, 1928
South Africa House, Trafalgar Square, London, 1935

Selected Publications

Plas Mawr, Conway, North Wales (with Arthur Baker), 1888
Cecil Rhodes by His Architect, 1934
Architecture and Personalities, 1944

Further Reading

There is no published monograph on Baker. For a complete account, including notes on his assistants and partners, see Greig. Baker's autobiographical work (1944; see above) and Reilly provide an interesting contemporary context in which to locate Baker's practice. The following texts examine various aspects of his life, career, and individual commissions.

"The Government Buildings of Pretoria, New Delhi, Rhodesia and Kenya," *Royal Institute of British Architects Journal* (December 1927)
Gradidge, Roderick, *Dream Houses: The Edwardian Ideal*, London: Constable, and New York: Braziller, 1980
Gray, A. Stuart, *Edwardian Architecture: A Biographical Dictionary*, London: Duckworth, 1985; Iowa City: University of Iowa Press, 1986
Greig, Doreen E., *Herbert Baker in South Africa*, Cape Town and New York: Purnell, 1970
Irving, Robert G., *Indian Summer: Lutyens, Baker, and Imperial Delhi*, New Haven, Connecticut: Yale University Press, 1981
Le Roux, W.J. (editor), *Groote Schuur: Residence of South Africa's Prime Minister*, Pretoria: South Africa Department of Information, 1970
Reilly, C.H., *Representative British Architects of the Present Day*, London: Batsford, 1931; Freeport, New York: Books for Libraries Press, 1967
Stringer, P., "Sir Herbert Baker and His Collaboration with Sir Edwin Lutyens at New Delhi" (M.Phil. thesis), Thames Polytechnic

BANGKOK, THAILAND

With the abrupt change that accompanied the arrival of European art and architectural styles during the late 19th century, Bangkok of the 20th century emerged as an international city, emulating Western urban formation and leaving behind its former structure of canals and teak buildings along the riverside. "Venice of the East" was effaced; replacing it are layers of different modern architectural styles, in which "modern" is defined variously according to different contemporaneous Euro-American architectural currents, imported into Thailand through different means. Over the century, however, the fabrication of "the East-meets-West" architecture occasionally occurred. But by the end of the century, the mass of concrete high-rise buildings has become an unprecedented image of Bangkok's skyline.

The proliferation of Western influence on Bangkok architecture during the first half of the century was largely due to the sociopolitical reformation during the late 19th and early 20th centuries. It began in the last decades of the 19th century when King Rama V (Chulalongkorn, 1853–1910) officially introduced Western practices of both sociopolitical structure and city formation. Given the government's incentive to modernize Thailand, the imported culture was no longer perceived as foreign practice, but as fundamental composition of national modernization process, to which Western-style practices were not only imposed on, but also adapted to, the existing condition of Thai society.

By 1920 neoclassical architecture outshone other types of buildings, particularly in the heart of the present-day Bangkok's old town due to the large number of royally imported Italian artists and architects. The Grand Palace's new complex, including the Barommabhiman Palace and the Royal Innercourt division, the Dusit Palace complex, and a group of Ministries' buildings along Rajdamnern Road, were among the foremost evidences. Some of the outstanding Thai and foreign architects of the period included Prince Narissaranuwattiwongs (Vimanmek Palace and Benjamabopitr temple), Carl Dohring (Bangkhunprom Palace), and M. Tamanyo (Anantasamakom Palace).

As favor for European-derived architecture grew, foreign artists, architects, and engineers flooded into the country to design new buildings, while many young Thai scholars went aboard to study and also to experience the culture of the other hemisphere. When they returned to Thailand, many of them reset the standard of the Thai lifestyle, which in turn radically altered Thai mentality and daily life practices, and their influence could be observed even more clearly in architecture of the later period; Western influence was manifested not merely by the exterior, but more importantly through the use of space and the emulation of Western daily life practices inside the building. Consequently, the development of Thai architectural design from the 1910s through the 1930s could be called an experimental period, the moment in which Thai architects attempted to create space that not only accompanied more "modern/civilized" practices, but also suited tropical weather. Different combinations of materials and technology gave rise to various architectural styles and building forms, as can be seen in the architectural evidences of the Marukkatayawan and the Klaikangvol Palaces.

Meanwhile, in 1934, seven professional Thai architects, Pra-Sarojrattananimman, Luang-Burakarmkovit, Nart Pothiprasat, M.J. Ithithepsan Kridakorn, M.J. Votayakorn Voravan, Sivavong Kunchorn na Ayudthaya, M.J. Prasomsavat Suksavat, and Chitrasen Sanitwongs, established the first national association of architectural professionals under the name of Association of Siamese Architects (ASA). The book *Pattanakarn Tang Satapatayakarm*, one of a few comprehensive books on modern Thai architectural history, mentioned that the designs of these seven architects, exemplifying that of other contemporaneous Thai architects, were influenced largely by the concept taught during the early 20th century at the Beaux-Arts School, a place where many of them were trained. In fact, the omnipresent trend of the Beaux-Arts school during the early 20th century was known for its search for national identity within the formation of modern-style architecture; consequently, an emulating political concept was indeed gradually implanted and flourished among Thai architects during that period of time.

Vimanmek Palace, Bangkok, designed by Prince Narissaranuwattiwongs (*c.*1900)

Such political incentive in architectural design became even more solidified through the rise of different political leaders after the political situations of the 1932 revolution, which changed the national political structure from absolute monarchy to democracy, and after the rise of nationalism during World War II. The political fragments unwittingly geared Thai society toward a search for a unifying discourse, a way to express the nation's identity. The idea in designing public buildings shifted from the sole expression of the government, as had occurred in the dynastic dynamic, to the representation of collective identity—a "modern" identity of democratic Thailand. The elaborate decorative styles became outdated as they were seen to symbolize feudalism; modern architectural style of different trends in Europe were adopted as a solution for an identity search, a situation resembling that of many other countries at the same period. The use of simple geometric forms and a playful arrangement of both horizontal and vertical planes became dominant. Although many of the contemporaneous buildings were destroyed during the bombing of World War II, one could still find images of buildings built during this period, such as the shophouse along Rajdamnern Road and that of the adjacent neighborhoods including the former Chalerm-Thai theater.

Within the decades following, Bangkok grew from a small Asian capital into a medium-size international metropolitan city. International economic growth during the 1960s and 1970s resulted in a surge of the importation of newer architectural influences from abroad. The design goal in general was no longer to emulate Western modernity, but to drive Bangkok to reach "the international standard," as represented by other metropolises. Modernism, particularly that of the International Style, became popular among Thai designers and architects, outdistancing other styles. High-rise buildings with sun-shading elements and cement blocks took on a major part in changing the cityscape. New business districts emerged along Sukhumvit, Silom, Rama V, and Sathorn roads, and the preceding ones around the old town began to fade away. All these changes affected the general layout of Bangkok, as the city began to grow toward the East and the North, while its old town, and the western part, including the Thonburi district across the Chao Phraya River, were left remaining more or less with its former skyline.

Another interesting architectural movement during 1960s was the revival of traditional Thai-style architecture. Several designs of M.J. Samaichalerm and M.R. Mitrarun for royal buildings and temporary ceremonial stands reflected the preference of following traditional architectural grammar, but with an adaptation of material and construction technology. A similar attempt of Luang Visalsilpakarm could be seen in his designs of several Buddhist temples, including the elegant Wat

Amarintraram. A younger generation such as Pinyo Suwankiri evoked and grounded concerns for traditional Thai architecture in many schools of architecture in Bangkok. The design of traditional Thai architecture in general, however, was utilized quite exclusively for royal and religious ceremonies and related practices.

Despite the challenges of unstable politics and military interference, the period from the 1970s to the 1980s was the beginning of the Bangkok real estate boom, which continued into the next decade before it gradually slowed down by the mid-1990s. Given the rapid growth of the population and the increasing number of immigrants from the countryside, housing and land development predominated over other forms of real estate investment. Agricultural land around Bangkok was developed into residential areas, particularly that extending from the new business districts on the north and east sides. Newly developed and/or rehabilitated villages sprang up and were eventually integrated to become the city's new districts. Consequently, Bangkok kept growing with no fully restricting zoning control and proper transportation systems. In addition, the design for Thai suburban real estate development suggested another challenging point in modern Thai architectural development in that, to begin with, it generally reflected that Thai architectural realm encompassed the most influential trend of the era, modernism, merely through the use of materials and through the Western-replicating forms.

A slightly economic decline occurred during the end of 1970s and the beginning of 1980s when fears of Communism throughout Southeast Asia were compounded by political disturbance, along with the energy crisis. Yet the city kept growing, and the number of high-rise buildings in business districts eventually increased, following the strengthening of Thai politics and international connections. By the end of the 1980s, more than half of today's high-rise buildings in Bangkok's downtown were constructed. The headquarters of banks and financial companies lined Silom, Sathorn, and Sukhumvit Roads. The offices of Bangkok Bank on Silom Road, designed by Krisda Arunwongs, and Thai Farmer Bank on Paholyuthin Road, designed by Rangsan Torsuwan, created a stir in the Thai architectural design movement, as their designs were the very first recognizable construction of the grand-scale high-rise office buildings. The completion of an international award-wining robot-shape Asia Bank building, designed by Sumet Jumsai, enhanced the world's recognition of modern Thai architecture. The peak moment of Thai high-rise building culminated with the completion of the one-time tallest reinforced concrete building in Asia, Baiyoke Building, in 1987, designed in chief by an architectural team from Plan Architect, underscoring a virtual transformation of Bangkok's skyline.

During the late 1980s, flat slab and glass wall construction came into favor in designing Bangkok's high-rise architecture. The growth of the Thai concrete and glass-wall industries supported the movement. The general design of the trend's new high-rise buildings, such as Thai Airways Building, Sin Asia Building, and Orkarn Building, thus differentiated itself from its predecessors with the surface design's material and a more elaborate interior decoration. To architects, designing with flat slab and glass wall became, for some time, fashionably intrinsic to high-rise architecture. Yet, to the general public's perception, buildings with linear strips such as the two Headquarters of Bangkok Bank and Shell Gas Company exemplified the majority of Bangkok's architecture in the 1980s, but the cloud reflection on the mirror wall of the new Thai Airways office building on Vipavadee Road induced their imagination of the future Bangkok.

Meanwhile, another architectural trend was introduced to Bangkok through the Postmodernism influence. The neoclassical style Amarintr shopping plaza twisted the atmosphere of Erawan Square, from a postwar–World War II modern architectural environment to a reconstructed 19th-century European atmosphere. Yet, as time passed, the Postmodernist trend lost its popularity among architects, but its influence was rooted in the design of individual houses, luxurious housing development in particular.

The continuing escalation of the Thai economy during the early 1990s was a key to the construction of many grand-scale buildings. The National Queen Sirikit Convention Center, designed by Design 103 Architects firm, purposely built to serve as an international convention center, shed light on the use of high-span structure and the concern for energy conservation. The form itself exemplified other buildings in which the architects attempted to combine the form of traditional Thai architecture, the pointed roof in particular, with modern architectural elements. Yet, even though the "East-meets-West" situation has been a longtime concern of modern Thai architects, thus far it has not yet been fully developed, either in terms of form or concept. The closest was that of Dan Wongsprasat's design of Regent Hotel on Sathorn Road; the architect integrated the design for tropical weather with the simplified form of Thai Panya-roof house into the design of the hotel building and its interior courts. Similar attempts, for example, included Sumet Jumsai's design of the Dome Building at the new campus of Thammasat University and the Moblex Firm's design of the Rajmongkol Conference Center inside the Suang Luang Public Garden.

In contrast to the architects' struggle in conceptualizing and refining modern Thai architecture, traditional Thai architecture during the last half of the century is well regarded and more developed. The complex of Ruen Thai architecture at Chulalongkorn University, designed by Pinyu Suwankiri, has become a significant prototype for late-20th-century central-Thai region's architecture. Its elegant atmosphere and serene landscape was occasionally epitomized as the essential characters of traditional Thai architecture. Yet, other variations do exist, such as the sacred complex of the City Shine in the old town center and the solemn Chalerm-prakiet-King-Bhumipol building in front of the National Library.

Unlike the beginning of the decade, the economic crisis in 1997 turned Bangkok into one of the most challenging moments, particularly for that of architectural development. More than 70 real estate projects in Bangkok have been pending, some were sold to foreign owners, but many were left with their half-built structure. The city was then covered with the remains of unfinished construction projects, which yet waited to be revived in times to come. As many noticed, most interruptions over the 200 years of Bangkok's growth often turned the city itself into a newer and better phase of development.

VIMALIN RUJIVACHARAKUL

See also **Baiyoke Tower, Bangkok**

Further Reading

Association of Siamese Architects, research by Vimolsidhi Horayangkura, Kobkul Indaravichitr, Santi Chantavilaswons, Veera Inpantang, *Phattanakarn Naew Kwamkid lae Rupbab kong Ngan Satapattayakarm: Adeet, Patjuban, lae Anakot* (Development of Architectural Form: The Past, Present, and Future), Bangkok: Amarintr Publishing, 1993

Kostof, Spiro, "Architecture and the State," in *A History of Architecture*, New York: Oxford University Press, 1995

Saksri, M.R. Nangnoi, Pusdee Tiptus, M.R. Chanvut Voravan, Veera Sajjakul, Lesom Stapitanont, and Bandhit Chulasai (editors), *Onkprakop Tang Kaypap Krung Rattanakosintr* (Physical Composition of Bangkok), Bangkok: Chulalongkorn University, 1991

Silpakorn University, The Italian Embassy in Thailand, The Department of Fine Arts, *Reports from the First International Conference on Italian-Thai Studies from the Nineteenth Century to the Present*, Bangkok, 1997

Tiptus, Pusdee, and Manop Pongstat, *Ban Nai Krungtep* (Houses in Bangkok), Bangkok: Chulalongkorn University, 1982

BANHAM, REYNER 1922–88

Architectural historian and critic, England

Reyner Banham was an iconoclastic British architectural historian and design critic whose irreverent writings spanned an enormous range of topics and audiences—everything from traditional architectural history to discipline-bending academic studies, from advocacy criticism for his avant-gardist contemporaries to journalistic popular culture reviews. Trained first as an aeronautical engineer and only later as an architectural historian under Nikolaus Pevsner at the Courtauld Institute in London, Banham was fascinated by questions of technology and technological expression. Acting something like modernism's guilty conscience, he challenged mid–20th-century architecture to realize its earlier unfulfilled promises of functionalism and machine aesthetics. Simultaneously, he celebrated the actual technological achievements realized by the popular cultures of the industrialized world. He turned a sharp eye toward the potato crisp, cult films, surfboards, California air shows, and London Raves and found in them the promises and achievements of a culture living at the speed of the machine.

After leaving behind his wartime career as an aeronautical engineer and a short-lived career as a newspaper art critic, Banham enrolled in the prestigious Courtauld Institute. There, he quickly won the admiration of Pevsner and within a few short years found himself in dialogue with London's most interesting architects and artists and on the staff of the *Architectural Review*. Like many around him during the difficult postwar years, Banham developed a strange joint infatuation—on the one hand obsessed with the inaccessible splendor of U.S. consumerism and on the other admiring the late Surrealist and Abstract Expressionist strategies of formlessness and material ineloquence. The fusion of these two gave rise to the so-called Independent Group in London—a group of Pop-affiliated artists and architects that included Banham, Peter and Alison Smithson, Eduardo Paolozzi, Lawrence Alloway, Richard Hamilton, John McHale, and Nigel Henderson, among others—out of which commenced Banham's struggle to craft an "*architecture autre.*" During this period, he was the studio critic for the movement known as New Brutalism and passionately endorsed its material and technological facticity and its proto-Pop interests in American advertising.

With the publication of his doctoral dissertation *Theory and Design in the First Machine Age* in 1960, Banham gave academic rigor to his earlier enthusiasms. In a rich and convincing study, he outlined two competing tendencies within the history of the Modern movement, one compositional and traditional, the other dynamic and technological. Upending the familiar arguments, Banham claimed that the International Style, often considered to be a functionalist architecture, was in fact essentially a symbolic and aesthetic movement. In contradistinction, Banham championed the work of the early-20th-century Italian Futurists and Buckminster Fuller, whom he claimed had more fully internalized the dynamism of machine-age culture. Quoting Fuller, Banham characterized technology as "the unhaltable trend to constantly accelerating change." He concluded *Theory and Design* with a polemical challenge to the profession:

> The architect who proposes to run with technology knows now that he will be in fast company, and that, in order to keep up, he may have to emulate the futurists and discard the whole cultural load, including the professional garments by which he is recognized as an architect. (Banham, 1960)

Extrapolating from the conclusions of *Theory and Design*, Banham wrote a number of essays in the 1960s that examined the impact of "second" machine-age technologies on architecture. With an eye toward things such as television, inflatable buildings, demountable geodesic domes, mobile homes, and "architecture-less" drive-in movie theaters, Banham argued that the traditional architectural virtues of permanence and monumentality were becoming increasingly irrelevant. As he put it,

> When your house contains such a complex of piping, flues, ducts, wires, lights, inlets, outlets, ovens, sinks, refuse disposers, hi-fi reverberators, antennae, conduits, freezers, heaters—when it contains so many services that the hardware could stand up by itself without any assistance from the house, why have a house to hold it up? . . . what is the house doing except concealing your mechanical pudenda from the stares of folks on the sidewalk? (Banham, 1960)

This line of argument reached its zenith, at least in an academic sense, with the publication in 1969 of Banham's discipline-stretching study *The Architecture of the Well Tempered Environment*. Discreetly posing as a history of environmental technologies (for example, lighting, ventilation, heating, and air conditioning) and loosely extrapolated from Sigfried Giedion's canonical *Mechanization Takes Command* (1950), in actuality Banham's argument was a revisionist end run around the genealogy of modernism, an attempt to imagine (and instigate) an *autre* architectural future.

However, any description of Banham would be only half complete if it ended with his vision of the good life lived mechanically in a "polythene bag." Just as surely as Banham was a careful reader of science, he was also an enthusiastic reader of science fiction. His was a pop sensibility as comfortable with robots and Martians and bikini-clad warriors as with ventilator flows. From his earliest days with the Independent Group, Banham had celebrated the excessive technological imagery of the American postwar consumer boom. He wrote lovingly of Detroit's baroque chrome ornament, the physiognomy of the American hamburger, drag racing and custom-car culture, *Star Wars*, ice cream wagons, and even Disneyland, Coca-Cola, and the Santa Monica Pier. Given these infatuations, it was probably inevitable that Banham would find himself drawn to the United States, and after several extended study and research tours in the mid-1960s, he eventually relocated for good in 1976, first to Buffalo and then to California.

It was with the California dream of a tanned noble savage—that New World polyglot of surfboards, rock and roll, balloon frames, freeways, "gizmos," and mad scientists—that Banham discovered his long-sought synthesis between the cultures of consumerist affluence and technological potlatch. His brilliant 1971 book *Los Angeles: The Architecture of Four Ecologies* paints a celebratory picture of a city infused with the rhythms of bodies and cultures in motion. With its bronzed warriors, endless sunshine, and endless freeways (which necessitated that he learn to drive in order to "read Los Angeles in the original"), Banham had found at last an urbanism in which "mobility outweighs monumentality" and that sparkled with the fantasies of endless self-invention and renewal. For Banham, Los Angeles was "a reasonable facsimile of Eden" (Banham, 1971).

The impact of Banham's writings echoed into the second half of the 20th century. If at times his critique of the profession of architecture seemed totalizing and radically pessimistic, when he did discover architects whom he liked—figures as diverse as Archigram, Bruce Goff, the Japanese megastructuralists, or James Stirling—Banham's wide-eyed enthusiasms proved disarmingly contagious. His obsessions with hygiene, waste, and the nonvisual body undoubtedly will only continue to grow in theoretical importance. His eloquence on behalf of the American techno-vernacular had, with the exception perhaps of J.B. Jackson, no equal; and, if regrettably some of Banham's writings now seem compromised by an irreverent sensibility—long on the furry, the puerile, and the machismo—the radical character of his scholarship and the eloquence and playfulness of his pen guarantee that Banham will continue to provoke, please, and astound.

RONN DANIEL

See also **Archigram; Fuller, Richard Buckminster (United States); Pevsner, Nikolaus (Great Britain); Postmodernism; Smithson, Peter and Alison (Great Britain); Vernacular Architecture**

Biography

Born in Norwich, England, 2 March 1922. Apprentice, Bristol Aeroplane Company 1939–45; studied art history, Courtauld Institute, London 1949–52; earned a doctorate under Nikolaus Pevsner; received a research fellowship in Chicago 1964–66. Married Mary Mullet, art teacher 1946. Wrote art reviews in local journals, Norwich 1946–49; lecturer, Norwich 1946–49; stage manager, Norwich theater 1946–49; editor, *Architectural Review* 1952. Lecturer, Bartlett School of Architecture, London 1960–69; chair of architectural history, Bartlett School of Architecture 1969; professor and chair of design studies, State University of New York, Buffalo 1977–80; chair of art history, University of California, Santa Cruz 1980–87; chair of architectural history and theory, University of New York 1987. Member, Independent Group from 1952. Died in London, 18 March 1988.

Selected Publications

Theory and Design in the First Machine Age, 1960
The Architecture of the Well Tempered Environment, 1969
Los Angeles: The Architecture of Four Ecologies, 1971

Further Reading

Banham's posthumously published collection of essays *A Critic Writes* is the most comprehensive source of his writings. It includes many of his most influential essays, some biographical material, and an outstanding appended bibliography. Otherwise, a comprehensive and straightforward critical overview can be found in Whiteley. Scott is more oblique but raises many theoretically interesting questions.

Banham, Reyner, *A Critic Writes: Essays by Reyner Banham*, Berkeley: University of California Press, 1996
Frampton, Kenneth, "Book Review: A Critic Writes," *ANY*, 21 (1997)
Maxwell, Robert, "Reyner Banham: The Plentitude of Presence," in *On the Methodology of Architectural History*, edited by Demetri Porphyrios, New York: St Martin's Press, and London: Architectural Design, 1981
Scott, Felicity, "Glass Eyes and Cloth Ears," *Transition*, 49–50 (1996)
Vidler, Anthony, "Peter Reyner Banham Deceased in London," *A + U*, 214 (1988)
Whiteley, Nigel, "Banham's 'Otherness': Reyner Banham and His Quest for an *architecture autre*," *Architectural History*, 33 (1990)

BANK OF CHINA TOWER

Designed by I.M. Pei and Partners; completed 1989
Hong Kong

Notable for its place in the late-20th-century skyline of Hong Kong, the Bank of China Tower, the headquarters of the Bank in Hong Kong designed by I.M. Pei and Partners and completed in 1989, is located two blocks away from the old bank building in central Hong Kong island. Surrounded by major roads on three sides, the tower rises from a square footprint placed at the center of the small two-acre trapezoidal site. Measuring 1,209 feet to the tip of the twin masts in 70 stories, the tower was the tallest structure outside the United States at completion.

The building is acclaimed for its elegant form and structural ingenuity. The tower can be divided into two parts: the curtain-walled shaft resting on a three-story granite-clad base. The base, with a castellated top, is designed to give the building visual protection from the chaotic surrounding of major roadways. The allusion to an ancient Chinese city wall in the design of the base is unmistakable. As the site slopes up from north to south, the base absorbs the slope and provides the building with two entrances at different levels. The northern entrance has an arched opening that leads into a barrel-vaulted lobby where elevator banks are placed for access to the office tower. The southern entrance at the upper level leads into the banking hall. Located right above the base, the hall is surrounded on three sides by a floor-to-ceiling curtain wall screened with heavy vertical mullions. This screen wall, decorated with a diagonally placed squares motif used in Pei's Fragrance Hill Hotel in Beijing, helps to make the transition from the heavy base to the light curtain-walled tower. Above the information counter in the hall is a 14-story square atrium that brings daylight into the center of the hall. However, because of the narrowness of the atrium, very little light manages to filter into the hall. Around the atrium are the offices for the bank, and above these floors are speculative offices. The boardroom for the bank is located at the apex of the tower under sloped glass roofs supported by massive steel trusses.

Although the building is set back from Victoria harbor by a block, its shimmering facade never fails to attract attention from across the water, the principal vantage point of the famed Hong Kong skyline. This is due entirely to the elegant form of the building. The tower is made up of a square shaft cut by the two diagonals into four triangular segments. Each segment terminates at a different height with a large sloping roof. The effect is said by Pei to be like bundling four sticks of different heights together, symbolizing rising bamboo stalks with its auspicious connotation in Chinese culture. The form of the building is said to be the result of a long search by Pei for an appropriate form for a late-20th-century skyscraper. Dissatisfied with the conventional rectangular tower of the International Style and the neoclassical pastiche of Postmodernism, Pei attempts to seek a new form in the Bank of China Tower that is structurally honest and innovative while aesthetically genuine to its region. Because of the diagonal cut, the building contains six facades tapering toward the tip, each face covered with silver-coated reflective glass that catches light from different directions at different times of the day, resulting in a glittering appearance.

Pei's tower is similarly important for its structural inventiveness. Designed in collaboration with Leslie E. Robertson, the main structure consists of four corner composite columns of reinforced concrete that carry the building load to the ground. In addition, a central column to support the four segments of the tower is placed between the top of the building to the 25th floor, at which point the load is transferred to the corners. The five-column tower is reminiscent of ancient Chinese pagoda forms with a heavy central column and four supporting corner columns. It is at these corners that both vertical and lateral loads meet and where vertical, horizontal, and diagonal steel members meet in the encasing reinforced-concrete columns. Designed to withstand the severe typhoon winds of Hong Kong, the structural frame was conceived by Robertson as a huge three-dimensional space frame, a structural solution that is extremely efficient and less costly than a conventional structural steel frame. In order to express the structure on the facade, Pei first proposed a curtain-wall system that accentuated the structural frame, resulting in a series of crosses on the elevations. This proposal was not accepted by the client, who feared that the crosses might carry negative associations. Pei then modified the design to recess the horizontal elements of the bracing system and turn them into steel. This design, explained by Pei as a series of diamonds, seamlessly integrates the structure with aesthetics.

The meaning of the building's form has been a subject of intense speculation in Hong Kong society. The four triangular shafts of the building resulted in sharp corners. According to the principles and beliefs of *feng shui*, the ancient Chinese art of reading the house form for auspicious or bad influences, these edges are regarded as exerting malignant forces on the occupants of facing buildings. Thus, the building is said to have a negative impact on neighboring buildings. For *feng shui* masters, the corners are like sharp knife blades, and devices must be placed in surrounding buildings, including the Government House (the residence and office of the colonial Governor of Hong Kong), to ward off negative influences coming from the tower.

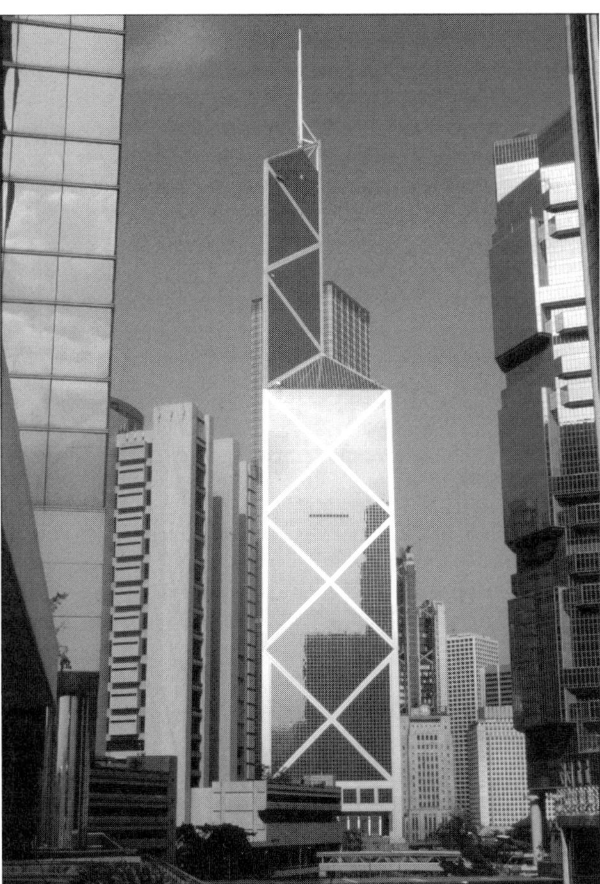

Bank of China Tower, Hong Kong, designed by I.M. Pei
© GreatBuildings.com

The taller and more elegant Bank of China Tower has always been compared to the Hong Kong and Shanghai Bank Headquarters by Norman Foster. However, what Pei has ultimately achieved in the tower, his last skyscraper, is a modernist statement of structural integrity and honesty of expression in a multifaceted sculptural form. The tower remains one of the most prominent landmarks in Hong Kong's skyline and represents an innovation in skyscraper form, a key building type in 20th-century urban architecture.

PUAY-PENG HO

See also **Feng Shui; Foster, Norman (Great Britain); Hong Kong and Shanghai Bank, Shanghai; Pei, I.M. (United States); Skyscraper**

Further Reading

The most complete architectural account of the building can be found in Jordy. Cannell and Wiseman contain narratives relating to the building from the architect's perspective. Blake and Rastorfer explain the structural design of the building.

Blake, Peter, "Scaling New Heights," *Architectural Record*, 179, no. 1 (1991)

Cannell, Michael, *I.M. Pei: Mandarin of Modernism*, New York: Carol Southern Books, 1995

Davey, Peter, "Another Prize for Pei," *The Architectural Review*, 188, no. 1121 (1990)

Gordon, Douglas E., "Curtain's Up in Hong Kong," *Architecture*, 79, no. 2 (1990)

Jordy, William H., "Bank of China Tower," *A + U*, 249, no. 6 (1991)

Rastorfer, Darl, "The Logic of Eccentricity," *Architectural Record*, 173, no. 10 (1985)

Suner, Bruno, *Pei*, Paris: Hazan, 1988

Suner, Bruno, "Banque de Chine à Hong Kong," *L'architecture d'aujourd'hui*, 270, no. 9 (1990)

Wiseman, Carter, *I.M. Pei: A Profile in American Architecture*, New York: Abrams, 1990

BANK OF LONDON AND SOUTH AMERICA, BUENOS AIRES

Designed by Clorinda Testa; completed 1966

The Bank of London and South America, located on a congested corner of Bartolomé Mitre in Buenos Aires, is one of the most significant buildings in Argentina and a landmark achievement in concrete construction. Designed by Clorindo Testa in association with SEPRA architects, the introverted building presents a robust concrete facade that belies a seductive and subdued labyrinthine interior. Set within a context of formal neoclassical architecture from the 19th century, the cleverly orchestrated design mediates between the busy and crowded Argentinian streets and the methodical operation of the bank headquarters. It compliments the urban fabric in a manner that is both charismatic and controlled.

The building was constructed at a time of tremendous economic turbulence in Argentina, resulting from political changes internally and the rampant tension across Latin America that had culminated in the Cuban revolution of 1959. The election of Arturo Frondizi as president of Argentina in 1958 had introduced sweeping reforms to the economic, political, and cultural policy of the country, designed to dispel discontent and to reform the inward-looking Argentine economy. Frondizi instigated an urgent program of westernization, targeting rapid development through increased levels of foreign investment and the growth of local industry. The new headquarters for the Bank of London and South America was the first by-product of this new economic policy. The building was to represent a rekindling of ties between Britain and Argentina that had gradually been eroded since the beginning of World War II. As a mark of sincerity toward this objective, the foundation stone for the building was laid by Prince Philip, the Duke of Edinburgh, in March 1962.

The building already on the site, the former headquarters of the bank (designed in 1867 by the architects Hunt and Schroeder), was demolished in May 1961. The first stage of construction was begun in December 1962, and the inauguration of the building took place in August 1966. The design of the building was the outcome of an invited competition undertaken by four Argentinian practices between January and May 1960. The commission was awarded to the well-established local firm SEPRA (Santiago Sanchez Elia, Fredrico Peralta Ramos, and Alfredo Agostini), who had collaborated with the local artist and architect Clorindo Testa in their design proposal. Testa, who was more than a decade younger than the other three members of the design team, had previously worked with SEPRA on numerous urban projects for the city and became instrumental in the design and realization of the finished building.

Occupying the corner of a busy intersection in the historical business district of Buenos Aires, the building responds to the demanding neoclassical context by filling the rectangular site with a chiseled, extruded block measuring 45 by 75 meters in plan. The massive structure is hewn from concrete, which, unlike steel, could be produced locally and required a less-skilled workforce. The two public facades of the building are protected by monolithic, layered concrete screens that curve outward at the top, providing a more generous pedestrian area at the base. The fluid concrete walls are punctuated by seductive rounded openings to allow light to enter. This acts as a curtain providing a mediation between the narrow street and the cavernous interior of the bank. Behind the dramatic concrete curtains, which carry the structural load of the massive roof, is another layer of glazing, which provides a climatic and acoustic barrier from the street. The two imposing skirts fold back at the corner to reveal the glazed curtain wall that marks the entrance to the building. A large, unadorned concrete blade wall folds over at the roof level in the manner of a giant eyelid, enclosing the outdoor foyer space and revealing the underside of the vaulted canopy, providing a shaded undercarriage as a refuge from the busy and confined street space beyond. The gesture at the corner addresses not only the entry but also the opposing buildings of the intersection, disappearing seamlessly into the urban context.

The building houses 1,500 employees of the bank and provides office space in excess of 10,000 meters squared. The complex yet sculptural interior layout, dominated by floating mezzanines and the powerful mass of the circulation cores, distributes the office space over six levels. Services and car parking are contained in three subterranean floors. The palette of materials consists of richly formatted reinforced concrete throughout, light timber trimmings, and a deep red painted finish.

The interior of the building is open and uncluttered by structural supports. The floating floor slabs are supported by the concrete core of the lift shafts, the separate banks of stairs, and the sculpted columns that support the exterior walls, tapering at both the base and apex. This adds a legibility to the structural system and also frees the plan of intermediate supports, allowing for a fluid and unobstructed spatiality inside the building. The fluid concrete beams on the underside of the floating intermediate levels taper back to elegantly house lighting and air-conditioning ducts.

The monumental simplicity of the building has played an important role in the context of architectural history not only in Argentina but across the world. The sculptural building can be seen as influential to avant-garde movements such as Archigram,

Metabolism, and the Brutalism of Paul Rudolph and, more recently in the curvilinear geometries of Neil Denari. In the last decade, the building, like Clorindo Testa himself, has been the subject of international critical reappraisal, elevating the profile of the building and its architect.

MICHAEL CHAPMAN

See also **Argentina; Buenos Aires, Argentina; Metabolists; Rudolph, Paul (United States); Testa, Clorindo (Argentina)**

Further Reading

Cook, Peter, "Clorinda Testa's Bank of London and South America, Buenos Aires," *Architectural Design*, 71 (September 2001)
Cuadra, Manuel, *Clorinda Testa: Architect*, Rotterdam: NAi Publishers, 2000
Glusberg, Jorge, "Banco de Londres y America del Sud, casa central," *Global Architecture*, 65 (1984)
Liernur, Jorge Francisco, "The Bank of London and South America Head Office," *AA Files*, 34 (Autumn 1997)

BARCELONA, SPAIN

Barcelona, the capital of the Spanish province of Catalonia, was an epicenter of 20th-century architectural vanguardism. The city's geographic position on the northeast face of the Iberian Peninsula—ostensibly with its back to the Castilian capital of Madrid and its face toward the Mediterranean countries of Europe and North Africa—has sustained its cosmopolitan dimensions throughout its history. From the century's onset and the separatist–regionalist concepts associated with Catalan *modernisme*, Barcelona's architectural primacy has endured two dictatorships, the suppression of its people's native language, and the dramatic social upheavals associated with industrial expansion and rapid population growth.

From the mid-19th century, Barcelona's municipal authorities sought to cope with the newly industrialized city's adolescence. The socialist Ildefonso Cerdà i Sunyer (1815–76) created a Haussmannian solution for unifying Barcelona's Old City with the independent villages of the periphery (Cerdà plan, 1859). He focused on building a new connective corridor of regularized grids—the district known as the Eixample ("extension" or "new town")—which he envisioned as the embodiment of the social panorama, where different classes could coexist harmoniously and nonhierarchically. By the early 20th century, the plan was deemed obsolete, and an international competition was announced to resolve the city's increasingly problematic geographic and demographic expansion. French Beaux-Arts architect Léon Jaussely (1875–1932) won the competition and presented the city with a less radical attempt to address the city's urbanization. This attempt was partially implemented in 1917. Barcelonese philosopher Eugeni d'Ors (1881–1954) directly observed the flowering of Catalonian culture during these years and proclaimed the new Zeitgeist "*Noucentisme*," a rebirth of ancient Rome's legacy in the region.

The dynamically autonomous spirit of Catalonian architecture proclaimed itself in a visual opponent of this heralded classicism: Barcelona's version of Spanish *modernisme*. With pronounced Art Nouveau influences combined with regionalist flair in both materials and construction techniques, Catalan *modernisme* became the province's most political aesthetic movement. Antoni y Cornet y Gaudí's (1852–1926) highly charged, colorful, and poetic combination of osteomorphic, zoomorphic, and baroque forms challenged the traditional Herreran architecture that dominated the peninsula's public commissions, thus asserting the distinctiveness of Catalonian culture as anti-Madrileño. Catalan *modernisme*'s heart was established along Barcelona's wide Passeig de Gràcia, a major artery leading from the north corner of the city's Plaça de Catalunya into, ironically enough, Cerdà's Eixample district. Here, progressive middle-class patrons, following the lead of Gaudí's Count Eusebio Güell (1847–1918), commissioned private homes from this new generation of urban architects. The personalized visions of Gaudí's Casa Batllò (1907), Lluís Domènech i Montaner's Casa Lleó Morera (1906), and Josep Puig i Cadafalch's Casa Amattler (1900) contributed expressiveness to an otherwise neoclassical urban sector, creating the district's anticontextualist *Manzana de la Discordia* (Apple of Discord).

One finds among the *modernisme* architects a romantic engagement with medieval vernacular forms and local construction materials such as brick and ceramic tile, a rhetorical vocabulary associated with cultural tradition, local topography, climate, and vegetation. A distinctively Catalonian mode of vaulting was practiced by Gaudí, Domènech, and the younger Josep Ma Jujol i Gibert (1879–1949): an elasticine fireproof vault comprised of laminated layers of ceramic tiles bonded together with reinforced concrete that could be configured into a variety of geometric or biomorphic forms and that could span considerable widths without structural reinforcement. Jujol's Church at Vistebella (1923) near Tarragona and Montserrat Sanctuary (1936) and close to Montferri, abandoned at the outbreak of Spanish civil war, employed Catalonian vaults in neo-Gothic formations, combining local brick and ceramics with iron and concrete to result in religious spaces imbued with poetic references to both God and nation.

Catalan *modernisme*'s effect on the city lessened in the 1920s, with the death of two of its major exponents: Gaudí and Domènech (d. 1923). By 1929 a new architectural language affected the city by virtue of the International Exhibition. This exhibition was dictator Miguel Primo de Rivera's (1923–30) reconstitution of an Electrical Industries Exhibition that had been conceived nearly a decade earlier. Mies van der Rohe's epoch-making German Pavilion (1929), built on the city's acropolis Montjuïc, introduced the city to the Bauhaus idiom. Farther up the hill, Poble Espanyol (1928) presented the same exhibition audience with an "ideal Spanish village," an amalgamation of the peninsula's traditional architecture and the manifestation of the Viennese Camillo Sitte's urban planning schemes. The coexistence of structural purity and folkloric vernacular would reverberate in Barcelona's architecture for much of the century.

The 1930s saw the dissolution of Rivera's dictatorship, the institution of a new state government (the Second Republic, 1931–39), and the reestablishment of a semiautonomous Catalonian government, the Generalitat (1932–39). The latter fostered an acceptance of Republican ideals and created a climate hospitable to Catalonian architects interested in using the state's ideology as the basis for urban projects. Many of these young builders were part of the Grupo de Arquitectos y Técnicos Españoles para la Arquitectura Contemporánea (GATEPAC)—

Casa Albert Lleó i Morera, Barcelona, designed by Lluís Domènech i Montaner (1905)
Photo © Mary Ann Sullivan

the Spanish wing of the Congrès Internationaux d'Architecture Moderne (CIAM) and the Comité International pour la Réalisation des Problèmes d'Architecture Contemporaine (CIRPAC)—which emerged with four distinctive regional groups: East, North, West, and South. Grup d'Artistes i Tècnics Catalans pe Progrés de l'Arquitectra Contemporània (GATCPAC), the Barcelona-based East group, was arguably the most influential of them all, establishing direct and enduring connections with its European counterparts to the extent that Le Corbusier himself assisted in creating the Macià plan (1935), a massive and radical project for reorganizing this working-class city into a communal utopia of high-density courtyard housing. GATCPAC's seven-story Casa Bloc (1936, altered) allowed the young architects to construct the distinctive type of urban dwelling associated with the Maciá plan and Le Corbusier's *à redent* housing.

Josep Lluís Sert (1902–83), later the dean of Harvard University's Graduate School of Design, inaugurated GATCPAC's rationalism both with his Muntaner Apartment Building (1931), a variation on the theme of balancing the private and the public, and most markedly with his Dispensario Central Antituberculoso (1938, by Sert, Joan Subirana, and Josep Torres i Clavé), a leading exemplar of hygienic modernism and architectural economy that made use of traditional Catalonian vaulting. Sert, who had been an assistant to Le Corbusier in Paris from 1929 to 1931, closely emulated the refined proportional relationships, sense of color, and texture that epitomized the Swiss architect's works. Sert's Spanish Pavilion at the 1937 Exposition Internationale des Artes et Techniques dans la Vie Moderne in Paris—which housed Picasso's *Guernica* and populist imagery in photomontages and other visual media—introduced the international architectural community to the group's dialectic and the Second Republic's liberalist stance. Despite GATCPAC's visionary aims of urbanistic reform and their ability to disseminate their ideals through the magazine *A.C.* (1931–37), resources were significantly limited during the period, and thus the promise of socially driven rationalism remained primarily a utopian dream and not an actuality.

Spain's civil war (1936–39) devastated the Iberian Peninsula and especially resulted in destruction in the nation's eastern provinces; in Barcelona, churches were damaged or completely destroyed and building projects effectively halted. The victorious authoritarian New Régime of General Franco (1939–75) associated the country's various avant-garde movements with left-wing political sensibilities, and subsequently, modernist movement architecture was actively discouraged. In the nation's urban centers, the new official architecture prescribed to the legacy of grandiose neoclassical academicism; in rural Spain, post–civil war architecture hearkened back to a whimsical folk vernacular. Sert and other vanguard architects exiled themselves from their homeland; those who chose to stay either sustained themselves by constructing "patriotic" buildings that followed the state's doctrines and guidelines, subsisted on the limited patronage of the private sector, or stopped building altogether.

The reclusive José Antonio Coderch y de Sentmenat (1913–84) found work designing Mediterranean villas of a regionalist and at times Expressionistic bent, such as his Ugalde House (1952; Caldetes, Barcelona), and also sought vernacular approaches to Barcelona's explosive population growth in apartment buildings, such as the Pescadores Block (1954), constructed for retired seamen in Barceloneta, a working-class port area of the city. During the 1950s and 1960s, Coderch consistently developed an architectural idiom that at its best was a subtle response to modernist "white architecture" harmonized with local expression, climate, landscape, and culture.

Sert maintained contacts with architects and patrons in Spain, especially with those in Catalonia and the Balearic Islands. His studio (1956) for the Surrealist painter Joan Miró, located on the Mediterranean island of Majorca outside Palma, united the region's whitewashed rubble surfaces and sun-shielding perforated grilles with the formal vocabulary of Le Corbusier and the hieroglyphic shapes of Miró.

Spain's isolationist tendencies dissipated during the 1950s, and interactions with democratic nations invigorated the nation's economy. Barcelona's Group R (1952–58) was founded in conjunction with the Colegio de Arquitectos de Cataluña y Baleares's municipal competition to tackle the city's constant housing problems. Josep Mª Sostres Malaquer (1915–84) was the theoretical leader of the group and an ardent admirer of Gaudí's work. His own Casa Agustí (1955) in the nearby resort town of Sitges combined a regional sensitivity to its seaside context with an understated rationalism, resulting in a structure delicately imbricated with its nearby garden and protected by a double facade from the sun's penetrating heat. Group R members Oriol Bohigas Guardiola (1939–) and Antonio Moragas Gallissà (1913–85) entered into an exchange regarding the future of Catalonian architecture and whether it should prescribe to the rationalist or neoclassical idiom. The group's formal interchanges resulted in an outlook that called for Catalonian architects to reject neoclassicism because of its associations with Francoism and instead to promote a regionalist architecture emerging from modernism, a reinterpretation of craftsmanship and materials, of generic urban structures, and of avant-garde spatial configurations. Group R espoused the belief that architecture should have a social conscience to resolve sociological problems, and the group was particularly inclined toward the rationalist architecture of the exiled Sert, the vernacular approach of Coderch, and the neorealism of the Milanese. The group's most noteworthy structure, Gustavo Gili Publishing House (1961), constructed in the interior of the Eixample for vanguard publisher Gustavo Gili by Bassó and Gili, made use of an unadorned permeable glass membrane wall raised on red *pilotis* and surmounted by a landscaped rooftop garden with pergolas.

By the late 1950s, Francoist Spain had entered a period of sizable economic expansion and unchecked urban development. Barcelona, Madrid, and Bilbao became the hubs of this growth, and their historic centers and peripheral suburbs faced the same architectural malaise that plagued many similar industrialized cities. Group R had grown significantly larger and eventually was reconstituted as the so-called Barcelona School, a less formal group of architects whose stylistic influences were markedly eclectic: *modernisme*, rationalism, Brutalism, neorealism, and Neo-Expressionism. Architects Bohigas, Josep Martorell Codina (1925–), and others came to reject modernism's utopian premises for a "poetic realist" regionalism—an architecture that emphasized traditional building practices and methods and a pragmatic knowledge of local history. The Barcelona School architects sought to redefine and reinvigorate the role of architecture in its new socioeconomic and technical context; the school thus became more politicized—more engaged with the Milanese theoretical position that architecture should be a catalyst for significant social change and that architectural practice should return to its traditional craft values. Bohigas promoted the group's ideas in a number of written works, including his influential manifesto "Cap a una arquitectura realista" (1961; "Toward a Realist Architecture"). MBM, Bohigas's partnership with Martorell and British expatriate David Mackay (1933–), focused on urban housing projects in the 1960s; their Casa del Pati Housing Block (1964) and Avenida Meridiana Flats (1965) evidenced the prominent features that have come to define the Barcelona School: tectonicity, tactile sensitivity, the so-called deep plan, communal spaces, and sun-protective patios.

Coderch developed relationships with the international community of architects called Team X, which had emerged from CIAM in 1956. He sought new humanistic solutions to urban domestic configurations in the 1960s with such projects as his Casa Uriach (1962) and Casa Luque (1963), which introduced an especially marked sensitivity to the issue of the privacy in their jagged plans, vertical window recesses, and prominent use of Venetian blinds. His nonresidential Trade Office Building (1965) revealed his admiration for Mies van der Rohe's glass skyscraper project of 1921. From his Girasol Building (1964) in Madrid and throughout the remainder of his life, Coderch also was engaged in rethinking modern urban apartment projects by creating humanistic variations on the theme, in which he sought a unified complex of distinctively autonomous apartments, a quasi-ruralization of urban life (e.g. Calle Raset, 1974; Paseo Manuel Girona, 1975).

Nearly half a century of authoritarian rule ended with General Franco's death in 1975, and change became the nation's credo. A new democratically elected government sought the partial restoration of Spain's historical autonomies and the creation of new public authorities, including the Generalitat of Catalonia. Thus, the province's distinctive culture was revitalized, its regional language was no longer outlawed, and new museums to its native sons were constructed. In 1976 Barcelona's municipal officials created a new schema for the city's rehabilitation, the General Metropolitan Plan, in 1974 the Barcelona School's *Arquitectura Bis* published its first issue, and from 1976 until 1980 Bohigas was chairman of the local school of architects. MBM continued to address Barcelona's social concerns in such projects as their more Brutalist-inspired Thau School (1975), a collaborative-based educational environment rooted in a more centralized and open plan of multiuse spaces. Ricardo Bofill's (1939–) multidisciplinary studios, Taller de Arquitectura, founded in Barcelona in 1962 and Paris in 1971, addressed urban renewal problems with a more fervent ideological underpinning. The visual manifestation of their aims, Walden 7 (1975) in Sant Just Desvern, named after B.F. Skinner's behavioralist utopia, consisted of 400 multileveled flats of various sizes in 12-story concrete towers prescribing to the Barcelona School's deep plan and sheathed in the region's terra-cotta tiles.

In 1981 the Generalitat named Bohigas the director of urbanism for the City of Barcelona and in so doing solidified the effect of the Barcelona School's new typology for urban renewal. He used the 1976 master plan as the basis for creating regulated densities and for identifying the civic areas most in need of revitalization, although he questioned the earlier plan's implementation and rejected its motorway designs. His new strategy included the establishment of a network of communal spaces—parks, plazas, and public facilities—threaded into the city's densest neighborhoods, or *barris*. Most important, Bohigas advocated a pragmatic solution—a balance between modernity and historical memory—to Barcelona's urban problems by stressing the importance of collaboration between civil servants and consultants, by selecting specific architects to resolve specific problems, and by emphasizing local design projects over total civic transformation. The first so-called *plaza dura* ("hard" square), Alberto Viaplana (1933–) and Helio Piñón's (1942–) Plaza dels Països Catalans (or Plaza de la Estación de Sants, 1983), was constructed as a flat urban area with no protective boundaries and no contextualist references to the surrounding architecture; instead, the minimalist design acknowledged the site's limitations and stark immediacy. Emblematically, Mies van der Rohe's Barcelona Pavilion was painstakingly reconstructed on Montjuïc by Ignasi de Solà-Morales, Fernando Ramos, and Cristian Cirici.

Barcelona's selection as host to the 1992 Olympic Games focused international attention on the city's renovation projects, including Santiago Calatrava's Bac de Roda Bridge (1987), Esteban Bonell and Fracesc Rius's Horta Cycle Track (1984), Araka Isozaki's Sant Jordi Palace (1991), Norman Foster's Coll serola Telecommunications Tower (1992), and Richard Meier's Museum of Contemporary Art (1995). Much of the city's waterfront was rebuilt, Montjuïc Park was remodeled, and new roads were developed around the periphery. Municipal government supported these sizable projects, and a sense of optimism pervaded among many of the city's architects, including MBM, who designed Novia Icària (Olympic Village, 1992), an attempt to reconcile the 1859 Cerdà plan with the renovation of the city's formerly industrial coastal belt. Named after a 19th-century socialist group, Novia Icària became the culmination of Bohigas's efforts to redefine the city by balancing tradition and modernity.

KELI RYLANCE

See also **Bofill, Ricardo (Spain); Calatrava, Santiago (Spain); Coderch y de Sentmenat, José Antonio (Spain); Congrès Internationaux d'Architecture Moderne (CIAM, 1927–); Gaudí, Antoni (Spain); Miralles, Enric, and Carme Pinós (Spain); Moneo, Rafael (Spain); Sert, Josep Lluís (United States)**

Further Reading

Baldellou, Miguel Ángel, and Antón Capitel, *Arquitectura española del siglo XX* (Vol. 40 of *Summa Artis*), Madrid: Espasa Calpe, 1995

Curtis, William J.R., *Modern Architecture since 1900*, 3rd edition, London: Phaidon, 1996

Flores, Carlos, and Xavier Güell, *Arquitectura de España 1929/1996*, Barcelona: Caja de Arquitectos Fundación, 1996

González, Antoni, and Raquel Lacuesta, *Barcelona Architecture Guide 1929–2000*, Barcelona: Editorial Gustavo Gili, 1999

Hughes, Robert, *Barcelona*, New York: Random House, 1992

Mackay, David, *Modern Architecture in Barcelona, 1854–1939*, New York: Rizzoli, 1989

Montaner, Josep Mª, *Después del movimiento moderno. Arquitectura de la segunda mitad del siglo XX*, Barcelona: Editorial Gustavo Gili, 1999

Rovira i Gimeno, Josep M., *La arquitectura catalana de la modernidad, 1901–1951*, Barcelona: Edicions de la Universitat Politècnica de Catalunya, 1987

Saliga, Pauline, and Martha Thorne (editors), *Building in a New Spain: Contemporary Spanish Architecture*, Chicago: The Art Institute of Chicago, 1992

Solà-Morales, Ignacio, and Antón Capitel, *Birkhäuser Architectural Guide Spain 1920–1999*, Basel: Birkhäuser Verlag, 1998

Zabalbeascoa, Anatxu, *The New Spanish Architecture*, New York: Rizzoli, 1992

BARNES, EDWARD LARRABEE 1915–

Architect, United States

The career of Edward Larrabee Barnes has encapsulated and contributed to the course of modernism across the United States. Barnes entered the architectural profession in concurrence with the arrival of Walter Gropius and Marcel Breuer into this country in 1937. He closed his office in 1994, just as a reinvention of modernism appeared to be launched. During the intervening years, Barnes crafted an array of private houses notable for their clarity in plan, volume, and landscaping. The houses exist as a series of educationl and cultural buildings, instructive for the sensitivity of their siting and responsiveness to a larger context. Barnes's body of work also includes several office buildings, noteworthy for their dedication to Louis Sullivan's theme of the tall building, artistically considered.

Barnes was born in Chicago in 1915, to parents who were successful in their chosen careers of law and writing. He attended preparatory school in the East, and received his undergraduate education at Harvard College. Following a brief teaching stint, Barnes returned to Harvard to study under Gropius and Breuer, graduating in 1942 with a master's degree in architecture.

Barnes's wartime career included a year in Washington, D.C., at the Division of Defense Housing and service as an architect with the Naval Reserve at Hunter's Point in San Francisco. At the close of the war, Barnes joined the offices of architect William W. Wurster in San Francisco, and industrial designer Henry Dreyfuss in Los Angeles. With Dreyfuss, Barnes designed a prefabricated house for Consolidated Vultee Aircraft, scheduled for mass production. In 1949 Barnes returned East with his wife, Mary, and opened an office in New York City.

Like a number of his Harvard contemporaries including Henry Cobb, Ulrich Frazen, John Johansen, Philip Johnson, and I.M. Pei, Barnes entered the profession during a time of rapid economic expansion, and increased demand for new construction at all levels, including residential, institutional, and commercial. For Barnes and the others, the national growth combined with talent, personal connections, and luck led to rapid recognition and robust practices by the mid-1950s.

Barnes's body of work, while infused with a modernist acknowledgment of the specificities of each project, exudes no dogmatic or easily definable style. His legacy is a dedication to an overall organizing idea derived from the complexities of each commission, distilled in a rationally ordered plan.

The Osborn House (1949–51) in Salisbury, Connecticut, typifies a group of early Barnes houses, with a site plan that creates a distinct precinct within an open meadow, augmented by carefully considered connections between individual rooms and the adjacent landscape. In time Barnes extended this strategy to increasingly individualized spaces, suggesting villages with individual house designs. The plan of the Cowles House (1959–63) in Wayzata, Minnesota, alludes to a farm assemblage, while sharp-peaked roofs and bold modulations of surface and void simultaneously separate the residence from the adjacent acreage.

By the late 1950s, Barnes had developed a portfolio of institutional work, with the completion of two children's summer camps for the Fresh Air Fund (Camp Bliss and Camp Anita, 1953–55, Fishkill, New York). At the Haystack Mountain School of Crafts (1958–63) in Deer Isle, Maine, Barnes combined a bold master plan—running down the site's 90-foot slope—with a typological layout and articulation of separate building elements. Although the individual buildings at Haystack are one-story volumes constructed of unfinished wood boards, their geometry and the system that orders their arrangement direct attention to both the natural site and the school as a community, making the experience of place an emotional and practical one. While Barnes described his overriding concept as the construction of "a typical Maine fishing village" (minutes of the Board of Trustees, Haystack Mountain School of Crafts, 26 July 1959), the simplicity and inevitability of such a conceit is the product of the architect's thoughtful design decisions. In 1994 Haystack Mountain School of Crafts received the American Institute of Architects (AIA) award for an exemplary American building of 25 years of age or more. It remains the masterwork of his career. Following Haystack, Barnes designed a host of buildings for educational institutions, including dormitories at St. Paul's School (1959–61 and 1969) in Concord, New Hampshire; faculty apartments and a building for the arts (1963–71) at Emma Willard School in Troy, New York; and master plans for the State University of New York at Purchase (1966–68) and Yale University (1968–78).

With the Walker Art Center (1966–71, addition in 1984) in Minneapolis, Minnesota, Barnes first tackled the program of an art museum; he arranged seven galleries and three roof terraces around a central service core. The galleries, individualized by their proportions and apertures, defer in authority to the artwork. Here, the architect emphasized movement through space over discrete destinations. At the Dallas Museum of Art (1978–83, additions in 1984 and 1993), a central passageway lends access to an array of museum functions, accommodating expansion and the distinct schedules of galleries, public spaces, and auxiliary operations. The linear arrangement reduces the scale of the overall enterprise and, as with the early houses, allows the development of independent relationships between interior galleries and exterior gardens.

Although Barnes was lauded in his commercial work, it was more for his articulation of surface than for his design plan or volume; two towers stand out for the clarity of their overall design. The New England Merchants National Bank (1963–71) in Boston, Massachusetts, addresses a sloping site and a complex of disparate civic buildings at its base, including the Old State House and the new city hall (1962–67, Kallmann McKinnell and Knowles). The articulation of the crown expresses the presence of a restaurant and an executive office suite. In between, a tight surface patterned by ribbons of window and wall convey repetitive office floors. At the IBM tower (1973–83) in New York City, a similar scheme provides for an entrance base, a clear tower shaft (here sheathed in green granite), and a differentiated top. At the entrance, Barnes carved out a triangle-shaped plaza from the first three floors, at the corner of Madison Avenue and 57th Street, over which he cantilevered the tower's remaining 40 stories. The 1973 zoning law, which allowed increases in overall square footage of commercial buildings in exchange for public amenities, made possible a greenhouse park planted with dramatic copses of bamboo on the southwestern half of the parcel.

Barnes was widely recognized for his work and received awards from the AIA for the Walker Museum of Art (Minneapolis, 1972), the Hecksher House (1977), and the private home in Dallas (1986) in addition to the AIA Firm Award in 1980. He was elected a fellow of the AIA in 1966, of the American Academy of Arts and Sciences in 1978, and of the American Academy of Arts and Letters in 1991. Harvard awarded him a 350th Anniversary Medal in 1986 and an Alumni Lifetime Achievement Award from the Graduate School of Design in 1993. In addition to teaching stints at Pratt Institute, Yale, and Harvard, Barnes served as a director of the Municipal Art Society, the American Academy in Rome, and the Museum of Modern Art, where he remains a lifetime trustee.

Although he associated with partners over the years—namely, Alistair Bevington, Percy Keck, and John M.Y. Lee—Barnes remained the signature designer of his eponymous practice during its full 45 years. In his office, he trained a number of the leading American architects of the late 20th century, including Ivan Chermayeff, Alexander Cooper, Bruce Fowle, Charles Gwathmey, Toshiko Mori, Laurie Olin, Giovanni Pasanella, Jaquelin Robertson, and Robert Siegel.

Writing in *Perspecta: The Yale Architecture Journal* early in his career, Barnes describes his design process as rooted in exploration and discovery, followed by synthesis and discipline. He demands consideration of function—both practical and psychological; site—both immediate conditions and the larger environment; structure—whose implementation requires clarity without dominance; and finally, the lasting legacy of the individual work. For all these concerns, Barnes seeks unity. He notes, "We do not solve our problems by sheer genius or sudden inspiration, but by a process of exploration and analysis" (Barnes, 1959). Throughout his career, Barnes remains true to these conditions, producing a body of work respectful of its programmatic role, expressive of its materials, structure, and volume, disciplined in its articulation, and evocative of its larger humanistic purpose.

AMY S. WEISSER

See also **Breuer, Marcel (United States); Gropius, Walter (Germany); Johnson, Philip (United States); Pei, I.M. (United States); Sullivan, Louis (United States)**

Biography

Born in Chicago, 15 April 1915. Studied at Harvard University, Cambridge, Massachusetts under Marcel Breuer and Walter Gropius; bachelor's degree 1938; master's degree in architecture 1942. Married Mary Elizabeth Coss 1944: 1 child. Lieutenant, United States Naval Reserves 1942–47. Private practice, New York from 1949; director, Municipal Art Society of New York from 1960; member, Urban Design Council of New York 1972–76; trustee, Museum of Modern Art, New York from 1975; Westchester Planning Board, New York from 1975; member, advisory council, Trust for Public Land from 1984. Architectural design critic and lecturer, Pratt Institute, Brooklyn, New York 1954–59; taught at Yale University, New Haven, Connecticut 1957–64; trustee, American Academy in Rome 1963–78; member of the visiting committee, Massachusetts Institute of Technology, Cambridge 1965–68; taught at the Graduate School of Design, Harvard University from 1978; Thomas Jefferson Professor of Architecture, University of Virginia, Charlottesville 1980. Fellow, American Institute of Architects 1966; associate 1969 and academician 1974, National Academy of Design; fellow, American Academy of Arts and Sciences 1978.

Selected Works

Osborn House and Studio, Salisbury, Connecticut, 1951
Camp Bliss, Fishkill, New York, 1955
Camp Anita, Fishkill, New York, 1955
Dormitories, St. Paul's School, Concord, New Hampshire, 1961, 1969
Haystack Mountain School of Arts and Crafts, Deer Isle, Maine, 1963
Cowles House, Wayzata, Minnesota, 1963
Master Plan and Major Buildings, State University of New York, Purchase, 1968
Music, Art, and Library Buildings and Faculty Apartments, Emma Willard School, Troy, New York, 1971

New England Merchants' National Bank Building, Boston, 1971
Walker Art Center, Minneapolis, 1972; addition, 1984
Chicago Botanical Gardens, Glencoe, Illinois, 1976
Farnum, Vanderbilt, and Durfee Halls Renovation, Yale University, Cambridge, Massachusetts, 1978
IBM World Headquarters, New York, 1983
Dallas Museum of Art, 1983; additions, 1984, 1993
Private House, Dallas, 1984

Selected Publications

"The Design Process," *Perspecta*, 5 (1959)
"Control of Graphics Essential to Good Shopping Center Design," *Architectural Record* (June 1962)
"Remarks on Continuity and Change," *Perspecta*, 9/10 (1965)

Further Reading

Barnes, Edward Larrabee, *Edward Larrabee Barnes Museum Designs*, Katonah, New York: The Katonah Gallery, 1987
Campbell, Robert, "Evaluation: A Classic That Retains Its Appeal," *Architecture*, 78 (February 1989)
Crosbie, Michael J., "8 over 80," *Progressive Architecture*, 76 (July 1995)
Edward Larrabee Barnes: Architect, New York: Rizzoli, 1994

BARRAGÁN, LUIS 1902–88

Architect, Mexico

Luis Barragán was at the forefront of a generation of Mexican architects who followed a fascination with European functionalist design; they endeavored to reconcile modernism with the indigenous architecture of Mexico, in order to express a distinct sense of place.

Barragán is best known for a small body of post–World War II buildings and landscapes that merge modern materials and minimalist cubic form, with discreet references to local culture, personal memory, figurative surrealist painting, and Mexican and Mediterranean vernacular forms. These works are marked by frequent use of brilliant saturated colors (pinks, blues, yellows, and reds are prevalent) and by a sophisticated handling of space, texture, siting, and natural light. His most significant projects involved speculative designs for residential subdivisions, and private houses for wealthy clients. Among the former are the seminal Jardines del Pedregal (1945–50), which he called his most important work; Las Arboledas (1958–59); and Los Clubes (1963–64), all in Mexico City. Among his private houses, key examples include the González Luna and Cristo houses (1928 and 1929) in Guadalajara, his private residence in Mexico City's Tacubaya district (1947), and houses for Eduardo Prieto López (1950), Antonio Galvez (1959), Folke Egerstrom (1967–68), and Francisco Gilardi (1976), all built in Mexico City as well. He also built other projects, including small chapels, such as the one for the Capuchinas Sacramentarias del Purísimo Corazón de Maria (1953–55) again in the Tacubaya district. There were also multifamily housing units, such as the apartment house he designed with José Creixell and Max Cetto for Mexico City's Plaza Melchor Ocampo (1940); public sculptures, such as the Satellite City Towers (1957), with Mathias Goeritz, for Mario Pani's Ciudad Satélite subdivision north of the City; and semipublic gardens, as those for the Hotel Pierre Marquez (1955) in Acapulco.

Barragán was born in Guadalajara to a large, wealthy, devoutly Roman Catholic family. Following long stints on his family's cattle ranch near the Jaliscan village of Mazamitla, and preparatory school in Guadalajara, he received his civil engineering degree in 1925 from Guadalajara's Escuela Libre de Ingenieros. He later completed his course in architecture there under Agustín Basave, who was a disciple of the French Beaux-Arts master Hippolyte Taine, but the school closed shortly before his degree was awarded. This formal study was followed by travel to Europe. In 1924–26, during the first of two trips, Barragán was especially impressed by visits to the Alhambra, and the Parisian *Exposition des Arts Decoratifs*, where he first encountered works by Le Corbusier (whom he met there) and French author, illustrator, and landscape gardener Ferdinand Bac. In 1930–31, he visited Bac at his home, Les Colombières, in Menton, on the French Côte d'Azur. Bac encouraged his interest in the poetic use of vernacular architecture and nostalgia. The visual impressions and contacts he gained on these voyages were to nourish Barragán's thought process and practice for many years to come.

Barragán's career can be divided neatly into three periods. The first lasted from 1927–36, and included his work in and around Guadalajara. During this time, he completed work on a city park, Parque de la Revolución (1935), with his brother Juan José, and a dozen villas and small rental houses. The houses, such as those for Efraín González Luna and Gustavo Cristo, are thick walled and cubic, with clay tile roofs, deep-set round-arched voids, and complicated spatial arrangements, and reflect a formal vocabulary indebted to Moorish and Jaliscan vernacular sources, and to Bac's illustrated books *Les Columbières* and *Les Jardines Enchantés* (both published in 1925).

In 1936 Barragán moved to Mexico City, then booming after the cessation of a long and devastating civil war. Over the next few years there, he built some 30 small houses and apartment buildings. Most of these were speculative ventures that he financed himself, and most were done in collaboration with other architects, such as Creixell and Cetto. Like much of the architecture then being built in Mexico City, Barragán's thin-walled, glass and concrete buildings, with their roof terraces and factory windows, borrowed heavily from the work of Le Corbusier. Buildings such as these, built by Barragán, Juan O'Gorman, and others, were seen by many progressive Mexicans as appropriately quick, cheap, efficient, and modern, and free of the historical and ideological baggage of earlier revival styles.

During the early 1940s, Barragán slackened his professional pace. He spent time designing a group of private gardens at his home in Tacubaya, and on property that he had acquired in the rugged lava fields south of Mexico City. This last area, known as El Pedregal, or "the rocky place," provided the inspiration and the setting for the 865-acre Jardines del Pedregal, the first major work of Barragán's third and final phase. At El Pedregal, he and his staff worked with or took inspiration from many others, including Max Cetto, sculptor Mathias Goeritz, painters Diego Rivera and Dr. Atl, financier José Alberto Bustamante, city planner Carlos Contreras, and photographer Armando Salas Portugal—and designed roads and water systems, public plazas and sculpture, demonstration houses and gardens, and launched an extensive print and broadcast advertising campaign. Roads, gardens, and modern, flat-roofed houses—some bearing subtle, formal similarity to the walled courts and high-beamed ceilings of Mexican colonial–era convents and haciendas—were fitted

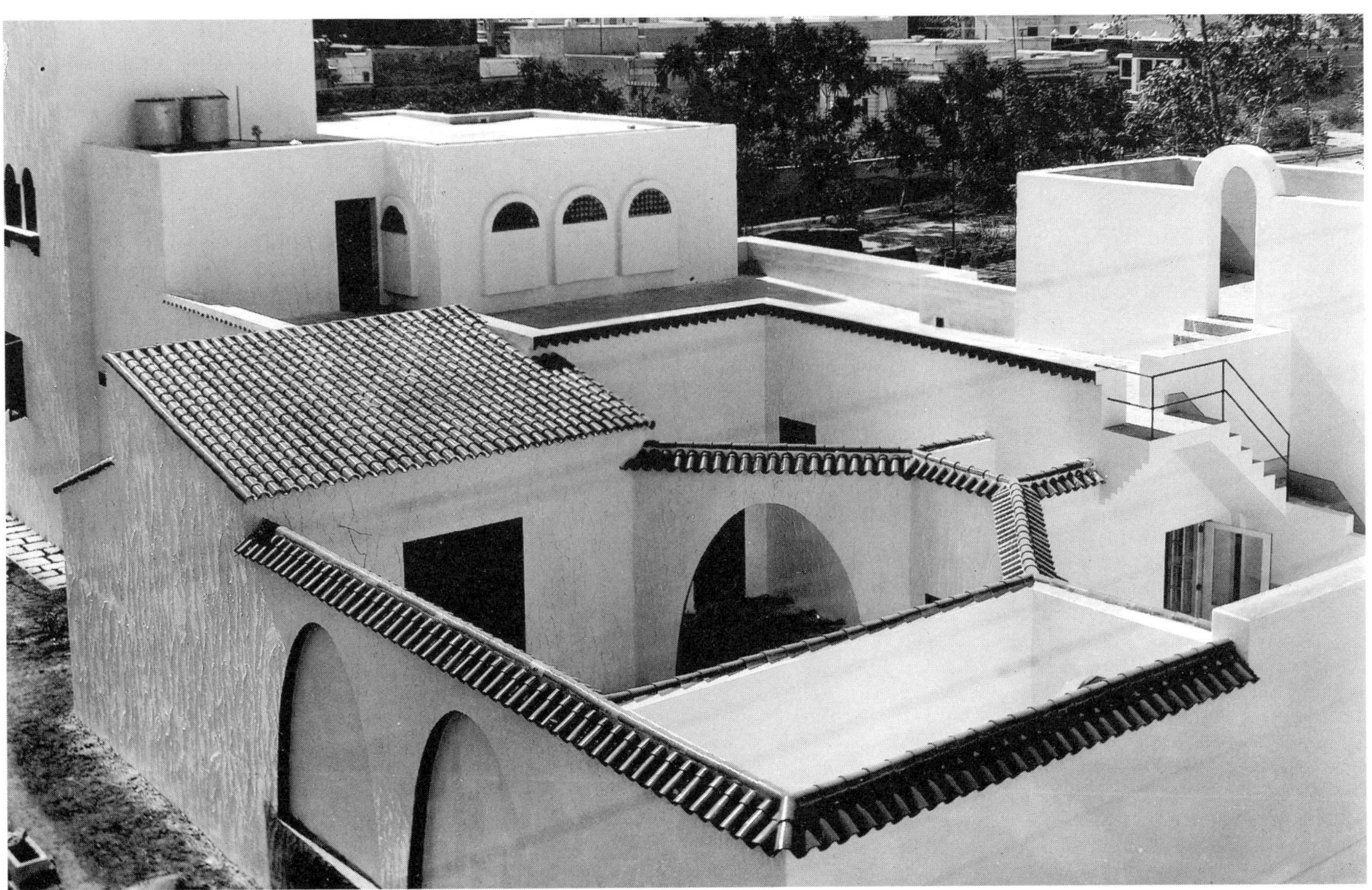

Cristo House, Guadalajara, Jalisco, designed by Luis Barragán (1929)

amidst the swirling stone eddies and distinctive native vegetation of the site. Many of Mexico's best-known modern architects, including Francisco Artigas, Enrique del Moral, and Félix Candela, built houses there. Barragán was criticized at times by his Mexican colleagues for his work's "scenography" and diversion from functional and politically progressive concerns, but during the early 1950s El Pedregal became a substantial financial and international critical success.

Barragán's subsequent projects, such as Las Arboledas and the Egerstrom and Gilardi houses, carry the themes explored in El Pedregal forward. In them, one finds more evolved versions echoing the play of light, shadow, water, and wall, its dramatic use of color and varied textures, its startling juxtapositions of the old and the new, the local and the imported, and the natural and the man-made. These designs capture scenography at its best, stage sets for unspecified yet solemn rituals, thick with silence, time, and gravitas.

Although much of Barragán's best work, including the Jardines del Pedregal, has been insensitively modified or destroyed, his influence continues to be wide ranging. Many younger Mexican architects, including Ricardo Legorreta, have treated his forms and signature colors as the basis of a distinctly Mexican modern architecture. Outside Mexico, designers as diverse as Tadao Ando and Mark Mack have attributed his work as a source of inspiration.

In 1976 the Museum of Modern Art in New York presented a retrospective exhibition of his work. This honor came as he was completing his last projects prior to suffering a long and debilitating illness and brought him renewed attention after two decades of neglect. Four years later, in 1980, he was awarded the Pritzker Prize.

KEITH L. EGGENER

See also **Ando, Tadao (Japan); Candela, Felix (Mexico); Corbusier, Le (Jeanneret, Charles-Édouard) (France); Legorreta, Ricardo (Mexico); Mexico; Mexico City, Mexico; Moral, Enrique del (Mexico); O'Gorman, Juan (Mexico)**

Biography

Born in Guadalajara, Jalisco, Mexico, 9 March 1902. Studied engineering in Guadalajara and received degree in 1925; self-taught architect; traveled in Spain and France 1924–26; attended Le Corbusier's lectures, Paris 1931–32. Practiced in Guadalajara 1927–36; worked in and near Mexico City from 1936;

concentrated on planning studies and real estate 1940–45; founder and director, with José Alberto Bustamante, Jardines del Pedregal de San Angel, SA, Mexico City 1945–52; co-founder, Las Arboledas Residential Zone Foundation, Mexico City 1957; co-founder, La Hacienda Golf Club, Mexico City 1958; partner, with Raul Ferrera, Luis Barragán y Raul Ferrera Arquitectos, Mexico City from 1976. Member, Mexican Academy of Architects; fellow, American Institute of Architects 1984; honorary member, American Academy of Arts and Letters 1984. Pritzker Prize 1980. Died in Mexico, 22 November 1988.

Selected Works

Gonzalez Luna House, Guadalajara, 1928
Cristo House, Guadalajara, 1929
Parque de la Revolución, Guadalajara (with Juan José Barragán), 1935
Apartment Building, Plaza Melchior Ocampo, Mexico City (with José Creixell), 1940
Barragán House, Tacubaya, Mexico City, 1947
Eduardo Prieto Lopez House, El Pedregal, Mexico City, 1950
Jardines del Pedregal, Mexico City, 1950
Capuchinas Sacramentarias del Purísmo Corazón de Maria, Tlalpan, Mexico City, 1955
Gardens for the Hotel Pierre Marquez, Acapulco, 1955
Satellite City Towers, Queretaro Highway, Mexico City (with Mathias Goeritz), 1957
Antonio Galvez House, Mexico City, 1959
Las Arboledas, El Pedregal, Mexico City, 1959
Los Clubes Master Plan, Public Landscaping, and Building Code, Mexico City, 1964
Folke Egerstrom House, Los Clubes, Mexico City, 1968
Francisco Gilardi House, Tacubaya, Mexico City (with Raul Ferrera and Alberto Chauvet), 1976

Selected Publications

"Gardens for Environment—Jardines del Pedregal," *Journal of the American Institute of Architects* (April 1952)
"The Construction and Enjoyment of a Garden Accustoms People to Beauty, to Its Instinctive Use, Even to Its Accomplishment," in *Via I: Ecology in Design*, 1968
"Luis Barragán," interview with Jorge Salvat, *Archetype* (Autumn 1980)

Further Reading

Ambasz, Emilio, *The Architecture of Luis Barragán*, New York: Museum of Modern Art, 1976
de Anda, Enrique (editor), *Luis Barragán: clásico del silencio*, Bogata, Colombia: Escala, 1989
Eggener, Keith, "Postwar Modernism in Mexico: Luis Barragán's Jardines del Pedregal and the International Discourse on Architecture and Place," *Journal of the Society of Architectural Historians*, 58/ 2 (1999)
González Gortazar, Fernando (editor), *La arquitectura Mexicana del siglo XX*, Mexico City: Consejo Nacional Para la Cultura y las Artes, 1994
Noelle, Louise, *Luis Barragán: búsqueda y creatividad*, Mexico City: Universidad Nacional Autonoma de Mexico, 1996
Riggen Martínez, Antonio, *Luis Barragan, 1902–1988*, Milan: Electra, 1996; as *Luis Barragán: Mexico's Modern Master, 1902–1988*, translated by Christina Bennett, New York: Monacelli Press, 1996
Rispa, Raúl (editor), *Barragán: The Complete Works*, New York: Princeton Architectural Press, and London: Thames and Hudson, 1996
San Martin, Ignacio (editor), *Luis Barragán: The Phoenix Papers*, Tempe: Arizona State University Center for Latin American Studies, 1997

BAUHAUS

Often misunderstood as a single entity with a consistent program and body of work, the Bauhaus was an educational program that occupied three successive sites in post–World War I Germany: Weimar (1919–25), Dessau (1925–32), and Berlin (1932–33). Distinguished by its changes in location, direction, and faculty, the program's turbulent history is reflected in the various articulations of the Bauhaus program that, although not wholly distinct from one another, appeared as separate phases of development.

The first Bauhaus (literally, "house of building"), located in the legendary city of German arts and letters, Weimar, was founded by the German architect Walter Gropius in April 1919, several months after the surrender of Germany and the formation of the Weimar Republic. Taking up residence in a building that formerly housed Henri van de Velde's School of Arts and Crafts, the "First Proclamation of the Weimar Bauhaus" (officially known as the Staatliches Bauhaus Weimar) declared the formation of a new school dedicated to the arts and crafts, a "new guild of craftsmen, without class distinctions which raise an arrogant barrier between craftsman and artist." Modeled on a medieval guild, Gropius's "new guild" would harbor artists and craftsmen who would "together . . . conceive and create the new building of the future, [a new building that] will embrace architecture, sculpture and painting in one unity and which will rise one day toward heaven from the hands of a million workers like the crystal symbol of a new faith." The frontispiece of the program, a woodcut designed by Lyonel Feininger, constituted an emblem of this new faith. Depicting a Gothic cathedral with three stars radiating the light of the heavens, the symbol hearkened back to another age, an age idealized in the literature and art of German Romanticism.

A director of the revolutionary group Arbeitsrat für Kunst (Work Council for Art), Gropius's early appointments to the Weimar faculty, or "Council of Masters," indicate his vision of an internationalist, pluralist program in which students and faculty alike could share their views and aspirations for artistic and social revolution. Including Gerhard Marcks, Adolf Meyer, Laszlo Moholy-Nagy, Georg Muche, Paul Klee, Oskar Schlemmer, Lyonel Feininger, Johannes Itten, Lothar Schreyer, and Wassily Kandinsky, the Bauhaus masters were supplemented by an "Honorary Council of Masters," a group whose members were drawn from countries across the whole of Europe. Ranging in age from 17 to 40, students were from the north and south of Germany and Austria, Czechoslovakia, Hungary, and the Baltic countries; two-thirds were men, and half had served in the army.

Curricular studies included mural painting, sculpture, theater, dance, and music. Reflecting the program's affiliation with medieval guilds, students developed from apprentices to journeymen in order to finally reach the title of "Master." In accordance with Gropius's vision, the early years of the Bauhaus were marked by the engagement of a variety of movements, styles, and pedagogical methods, including German Expressionism, Dada, Russian Suprematism, and Constructivism. Aptly characterized by Wolfgang Pehnt as an "expressionist art school," the Weimar Bauhaus did in fact exhibit a pronounced bias toward Romantic themes, including social unity, subjective artistic expression, vernacular Christianity, and collective artistic expression, a tendency that was modified over the course of the program's evolution. The presence of Johannes Itten, a practitioner of the Perozorastrian religious sect, further exaggerated this view. Charged with teaching the required preliminary course (*Vorkurs*), Itten espoused individual expression over collective responsibility while introducing his students to a cultlike way of living that depended on the elevation of subjective visions, the rigors of individual self-discipline, and bodily and spiritual purification. On the other hand, the empirical visualization techniques and allegorical figuration of Paul Klee (*Ways of Nature Study*; *The Thinking Eye*) and the Russian painter Wassily Kandinsky, along with the other Bauhaus masters, mediated Itten's influence.

Internal and external criticisms of the Bauhaus, a school never fully adopted by either the citizens of Weimar or the government of the state of Thuringia (where Weimar is located), were continual problems for Gropius, who spent most of his time defending the program as the controversy increased. Both as a defensive measure and as a signal of the evolving nature of the Bauhaus curriculum and aims, a new motto, "Art and Technics: A New Unity," and a new seal, Oskar Schlemmer's "Constructed Man," were adopted in 1922. Tempering Gropius's earlier proclamation of social revolution through art, the attempt to unify "art and technology" sought to counter what many Bauhäusler, students and faculty alike, perceived as the subjective and mystical excess of certain aspects of the program. Officials of Thuringia regarded the program as a waste of resources and a hotbed of foreign influence, a reading of Gropius's original intentions that was not dissuaded by the school's new motto and seal. Students, dismayed by the constant upheavals within the school and searching for an alternative to Expressionist drama, were drawn to forms of Constructivism. Sensing an opportunity to achieve an even greater impact for his own artistic ideas during the Dada-Constructivist Congress held in Weimar in 1922, Theo van Doesburg, founder of the Dutch Constructivist movement De Stijl, set up an atelier in Weimar. Students began to migrate to van Doesburg's studio, perhaps in search of an objective, delimited, and scientific (mathematical) approach to art, and this inevitably led to the import of van Doesburg's ideas and influence within the Bauhaus itself. A master of compromise bent on sustaining his educational program, Gropius approached the problem directly, hiring the Hungarian Dada-Constructivist Lazslo Moholy-Nagy, a student and associate of van Doesburg, to teach the preliminary course. This arrangement brought about a relative truce between van Doesburg and Gropius.

In further response to the criticism leveled by his peers and colleagues, Gropius sought to assuage various factions, elaborating his views with the publication of *Idee und Aufbau des Staatlichen Bauhauses Weimar* (Idea and Construction of the Weimar Bauhaus) in 1923. Although Gropius's vision of the Bauhaus program had evolved into a more comprehensive plan (including admissions policies, a program constitution, and a more carefully articulated curriculum), *Idee und Aufbau* retained several ideas from his original vision, ideas now wedded to a focus on demonstrating outcomes. The more abstract courses taught by Klee and Kandinsky were supplemented by carpentry, stained-glass, pottery, metal, weaving, stage, wall-painting, and architecture workshops. The 1923 Bauhaus exhibition—an event requested by the Thuringian Legislative Assembly—provided a report of the Bauhaus's accomplishments to date. The exhibition, spread mainly throughout the school, featured a one-family house ("Haus am Horn"), built and furnished entirely by the Bauhaus students, and included lectures, performances, and "other entertainments," such as the Bauhaus jazz band.

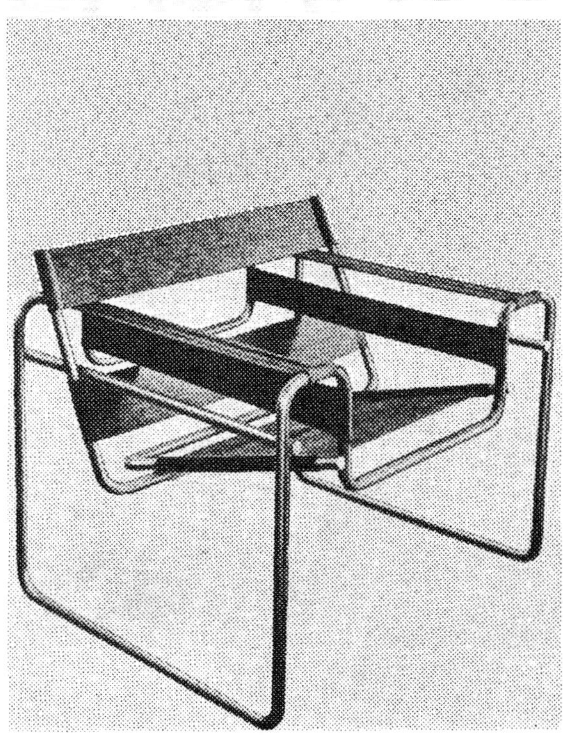

Chair by Marcel Breuer (1925); poster by Muriel Cooper
© Library of Congress, Prints and Photographs Division

A whole greater than the sum of its parts, the Weimar Bauhaus program sought to overturn the "decadence of architecture" and the "elitist and isolating effects of the academy" with an "awareness of the infinite [that can only be] given form . . . through finite means." Uniquely combining Elementarist theory, nature study, representational techniques and methods, and quasi-scientific experimentation with materials and processes, the Bauhaus curriculum sought to promote a seamless integration of "practical building, building experiments, and the engineering sciences." Seeking a revolution of art with the intention of providing a revolutionary impulse for humanistically based change, Gropius's "guiding principle" was centered on "the idea of creating a new unity through the welding together of many arts and movements: a unity having its basis in Man himself and significant only as a living organism." The prolific output of Gropius and the Bauhaus masters and students, coupled with the support of numerous critics, scientists, architects, and artists, could not forestall the antagonisms and threats of the state government (Thuringia). The decision to leave Weimar was made on 26 December 1924. Students and masters of the Bauhaus finally vacated the premises of the Bauhaus at Weimar in the first few months of 1925. By this time, 526 students had been trained at the Bauhaus, although far more took only the preliminary course.

Fortunately, the close of the Bauhaus at Weimar did not represent the end of the Bauhaus program. During the period of greatest controversy in Weimar, Gropius secured permission from the mayor of the city of Dessau, Dr. Fritz Hesse, to transfer the Bauhaus to Dessau, where it remained relatively free of state criticism for several years. Almost all the former Bauhaus masters transferred to Dessau, and five former students—including Josef Albers, Herbert Bayer, and Marcel Breuer—were appointed masters. Gropius designed a new suite of buildings to house the program, moving the program from its temporary quarters in Dessau in 1926. Sharing its premises with the Municipal Arts and Crafts School, the Dessau Bauhaus included the technically innovative school building (including a laboratory workshop, administration offices, and technical school) and a dormitory with 28 studio apartments, baths, dining hall (which acted as an auditorium and included a stage), and laundry for the students. Near the Bauhaus, Gropius designed a series of houses for the Bauhaus masters and director, all of which were supplemented by the Bauhaus workshops. The curriculum was modified as well, enlarging the architecture program and adding a department of typography and layout. The principles were also clarified, with the purpose of the Bauhaus defined as "1. The intellectual, manual and technical training of men and women of creative talent for all kinds of creative work, especially building; and 2. The execution of practical experimental work, especially building and interior decoration, as well as the development of models for industrial and manual production." A Bauhaus Corporation, chartered for the express purpose of handling the business aspects of the various Bauhaus models, was also installed.

The Dessau Bauhaus continued to thrive. In 1926 Gropius received an additional commission to design 60 housing units for a new housing community in Dessau, a commission that grew to 316 houses by 1928, all of which were partly furnished by the Bauhaus workshops. In 1926 the new generation of Bauhaus masters—Albers, Breuer, and Bayer among them—began to elaborate the practical experiments of the Bauhaus, producing furniture, typography, graphic design, photography, weaving, light fixtures, and domestic objects that have come to be known as representative of the "Bauhaus style." Parallel studies in painting and sculpture also developed, with the figurative lyricism of Klee and Schlemmer providing a foil for Kandinsky's continued experiments with analytic abstraction.

Because of the relative stability of the program, the overwhelming administrative burdens placed on him in the position of director, and a substantial increase of professional work, Gropius resigned in early 1928, recommending as his successor the head of the Department of Architecture, the Swiss architect Hannes Meyer. Because of various conflicts with municipal authorities, Meyer resigned in 1930. His replacement, the German architect Ludwig Mies van der Rohe, moved the Bauhaus to Berlin in 1932, continuing to oversee the program until it was closed by the reactionary National Socialist regime in April 1933. The closure of the Bauhaus, presaged by the program's original commitment to humanistically based change, pedagogical experimentation, innovation, and internationalism, did not in fact spell the demise of the Bauhaus. Guaranteed by the numerous graduates of the program and facilitated by its prominence as a premier program for the study of the arts and architecture, the Bauhaus program was incorporated into various design curricula throughout Europe and the United States. Bauhäusler, including Mies van der Rohe, Moholy-Nagy, Gropius, and Albers, were appointed to head schools of art and architecture, and many other members of the Bauhaus received teaching positions in universities, colleges, and schools of art. Together with their advocates, Bauhäusler revolutionized the way in which art and architecture were taught while reinforming modern American business and commerce with new ideas about modern life (domestic and corporate) and advanced methods of communication. As Mies so deftly phrased the impact of the Bauhaus, it was not a style, an institution, or even a program for study; rather, "it was an idea, and Gropius formulated this idea with great precision. . . . The fact that it was an idea, I think, is the cause of this enormous influence the Bauhaus had on every progressive school around the globe. You cannot do that with organization, you cannot do that with propaganda. Only an idea spreads so far."

ELIZABETH BURNS GAMARD

See also **Breuer, Marcel (United States) Constructivism; De Stijl; Gropius, Walter (Germany); Meyer, Hannes (Germany); Mies van der Rohe, Ludwig (Germany); van Doesburg, Theo (Netherlands)**

Further Reading

Bayer, Herbert, Walter Gropius, and Ise Gropius (editors), *Bauhaus, 1919–1928*, New York: Museum of Modern Art, 1938; London: Allen and Unwin, 1939

Droste, Magdalena, *Bauhaus, 1919–1933*, Cologne: Taschen Verlag, 1990; as *Bauhaus, 1919–1933*, translated by Karen Williams, Berlin: Taschen, 1990

Forgács, Éva, *Bauhaus*, Pècs, Hungary: Jelenkor Irodalmi és Muvészeti Kiadó, 1991; as *The Bauhaus Idea and Bauhaus Politics*, translated by John Bátki, Budapest and New York: Central European University Press, 1995

Gropius, Walter, *Scope of Total Architecture*, New York: Harper and Row, 1955; London: Allen and Unwin, 1956

Hochman, Elaine S., *Bauhaus: Crucible of Modernism*, New York: Fromm International, 1997

Kaes, Anton, Martin Jay, and Edward Dimendberg, *The Weimar Republic Sourcebook*, Berkeley: University of California Press, 1994

Kentgens-Craig, Margaret, *Bauhaus-Arkitektur: die Rezeption in Amerika, 1919–1936*, Frankfurt and New York: Lang, 1993; as *The Bauhaus in America: First Contacts, 1919–1936*, Cambridge, Massachusetts: MIT Press, 1999

Lane, Barbara Miller, *Architecture and Politics in Germany, 1918–1945*, Cambridge, Massachusetts: Harvard University Press, 1968

Whitford, Frank, *Bauhaus*, New York: Thames and Hudson, 1984

Wingler, Hans Maria, *Das Bauhaus, 1919–1933: Weimar, Dessau, Berlin*, Bramsche: Gebr. Rasch, 1962; 2nd edition, as *Das Bauhaus, 1919–1933: Weimar, Dessau, Berlin, und die Nachfolge in Chicago seit 1937*, Cologne: DuMont Schauberg, 1968; 2nd edition translated as *The Bauhaus: Weimar, Dessau, Berlin, Chicago*, translated by Wolfgang Jabs and Basil Gilbert, edited by Joseph Stein, Cambridge, Massachusetts: MIT Press, and

London: Cambridge University Press, 1969; 3rd edition, Cambridge, Massachusetts: MIT Press, 1976

BAUHAUS, DESSAU

Designed by Walter Gropius; completed 1926
Dessau, Germany

Walter Gropius (1883–1969), the founder and first director of the Bauhaus, was the architect of the Bauhaus building in Dessau, Germany, completed in 1926. This new 28,000-plus square-foot educational building, which became the symbol for the renowned avant-garde academy of design in Germany, was the second home for this architecture and design school. Gropius, whose visionary zeal created the Bauhaus School in Weimar in 1919, moved the school from Weimar to Dessau in 1925 at the invitation of Dessau's progressive mayor, Fritz Hesse. The design of the Bauhaus was begun in 1925, after he moved to Dessau, and formally opened 4–5 December 1926.

The building design exemplified Gropius's educational philosophy, "Art and Technology: A New Unity," which expressed the critical and inventive role of architects and designers within the seemingly chaotic and rapidly changing technological society of the times. This slogan, revised from "Art and Craft: A New Unity," his first 1919 Weimar Bauhaus slogan, referred to a building both designed through and fitted with up-to-date machinery that promoted the development of prototypical contemporary designs for industrial production. His design invoked debates between architects who worked within the tradition of fine arts, craft, and handicraft and those who embraced the potential for technological advances promised by modern industry. Gropius, with his partner Adolf Meyer, first explored these questions in their design of the Fagus Werk (1912, 1914) in Alfeld, Germany. Gropius's Bauhaus building extends his philosophy and synthesizes these seemingly opposing beliefs whose outcome was shared: to raise the standards of design and public taste through modern technology.

The Dessau Bauhaus building was conceived during an atmosphere of political and social turmoil in Germany. Formerly a state-supported school in Weimar, once the right-wing conservative majority in Weimar came to power, the school was denounced in 1923 as filled with avant-garde foreign Bolsheviks, and in 1925 demands leading to its closure were imminent. Gropius, who quickly searched for another home, found Dessau. Dessau, led by progressive Social Democrats, made the school a city-funded institution and provided construction funds and prime sites for the new building complex and its faculty residences (1926). Dessau's progressive roots could be traced back to Prince Leopold Friedrich Franz von Anhalt-Dessau (1740–1817), who believed that design should combine "beauty with use." Between 1765 and 1820, Prince Anhalt-Dessau, who created Europe's first English-style landscapes, redesigned Dessau and neighboring areas, including Wörlitz Park (1790 and later). Wörlitz, designed by the prince and his friend Baron Erdmannsdorff, was model for Dessau's principles of enlightened government and religious tolerance. The Bauhaus building, a landmark building for Dessau, was set in a natural parklike setting outside the city center. This permitted the design to become a counterpoint to Dessau's urban industrial fabric. Similar to Gropius's motto "Art and Technology: A New Unity," the building could be seen in light of the area's traditional promotion of visionary architects.

The mayor recognized that Dessau's design problems could become design projects for Gropius and his Bauhaus. These were typical design problems that industrial urban centers faced: the necessity for careful urban planning that directed rapid growth and carefully conceived housing that provided the resulting expanding population with housing, schools, and other institutional and civic buildings. Gropius moved his architectural practice to Dessau, leaving his partner Adolf Meyer, and began working with architects Ernst Neufert and Carl Fieger on the design and construction of the Bauhaus as well as other new projects, including the masters' houses (1926), the workers' housing estate (1928) at Törten, and the Dessau Employment Office (1929).

Architects Carl Fieger and Ernst Neufert developed the design of the Bauhaus in Dessau with Gropius. Ernst Neufert was head architect in Gropius's office, and Carl Fieger developed the initial sketches in 1925 to establish the idea of the building. Fieger had a profound effect on the design. His sketches show three parts of the building, each a distinct element of the building's program yet joined as one building by various bridging, roofing, and massing elements. Initially, the program consisted of the arts and crafts school, workshops, and administrative offices. The administration area was located between the two other areas, serving as an actual and conceptual bridge between the school and workshops and spanning a road that bisected the site. Additional areas, student housing, dining/auditorium facilities, and generous and carefully designed public spaces within the building created contiguous social gathering spaces within the institution. Spacious stairs with generous landings, well-proportioned lobbies, foyers, and hallways ("circulation areas") provided places for formal and informal gatherings.

Gropius's building was very different from those buildings designed from Renaissance or baroque principles. Unlike these historical precedents, the Bauhaus was neither symmetrical nor axial. As Gropius explained, one had to "walk right around the whole building" in order to understand the design. Otherwise, its design could be understood only from the air. His favorite photographs, which were published throughout the world, were aerial views of the building. Seen from above, Gropius's building was a series of simple cubic masses joined by planar roofs. What could not be experienced from aerial photography were the phenomenal effects of light and space captured by and within the building.

As the inventor of the "dematerialized" corner, Gropius expressed this innovation of the glass curtain wall here as well as in his Fagus factory. The metal and glass "curtain" was hung from the exterior edge of a cantilevered, unsupported (and seemingly floating) floor slab, revealing empty and open corners. This structural innovation, which permitted the corner column to disappear, allowed the workshop wing to appear as if it were wrapped in glass. A clear reference to the utopian and Expressionistic writings of German poet Paul Scheerbart, Gropius brilliantly detailed the transparent wall as curtain, taking full advantage of the technological possibilities provided by the primary structural system: a reinforced-concrete frame with cantilevered slabs (deeper than necessary due to contemporary building codes). The reinforced-concrete skeleton, with mushroom-

Bauhaus building (1926), designed by Walter Gropius, Dessau, Germany

headed columns, was in-filled with brickwork and hollow tile floors. The glass and steel curtain wall included operable steel windows (currently aluminum) whose exposed and articulated control devices created yet another sublime homage to machined technology, which remains intimately engaged to the hand and body. In many ways, this building reinforced the corporeal nature of the body as well as the building, as evidenced by the design of asphalt-tiled terrace-roofs and balconies, all part of the educational and social life of the school.

The style of this building is modern, without a doubt. However, beyond that obvious fact, others have variously described its form and style. Historians Henry-Russell Hitchcock and Philip Johnson used this building to derive their interpretations of International Style. They also claimed it to be the model for a "Bauhaus" style. Theo van Doesburg, the Dutch artist and architect, claimed it as a prime example of his De Stijl (literally, "the style"), whereas others claimed it as a part of the ambiguous *Neue Sachlickeit* (New Objectivity), implying a consistent and carefully worked out rationalism. Others see it as a modern representation of the complete or "total work of art," or *Gesamtkunstwerk*, as a collaboration of all members of the Bauhaus: the director, teachers ("masters"), and students who made furniture, fittings, hardware, and finishings in the workshops. One might argue that it has no style but rather that it addressed its own Zeitgeist (spirit of the time)—as contemporary topics and ideas.

The Dessau Bauhaus recently named one of only three modern buildings on the UNESCO world heritage list, has recently undergone a renovation that will by 2006 have fully restored the building to its pristine and original state. This honors noteworthy features that made it a model of both modern and contemporary design. Clear distinction between the building's parts and its overall layout, the large expanse of glass covering the entire street, and careful detailing remain delightful and fascinating. Gropius, who believed that architecture shapes "the patterns of life," took these "patterns" beyond simple function to create forms that shape the beauty and wonder of the activities of life. This was confirmed by Nelly Schwalacher's description of her visit, which she wrote for a German newspaper in the fall of 1927:

> I arrive in Dessau at dawn. Fog hands over the city. Our headlights occasionally penetrate the damp air. But the eye is drawn to a dazzling beam of light. A giant light cube: the new Bauhaus building. Later, with sunshine and blue sky, the building remains a focal point of lightness and brightness. Glass, glass and more glass, radiating daz-

zling white light from every wall. I have never seen such a light reflector. And the weight of the walls is neutralized by two factors, namely the high glass walls openly revealing the light steel structure of the building and the radiating whiteness. ("Das Neue Bauhaus," *Frankfurter Zeitung*, evening edition [31 October 1927]; from Droste, 1990)

However, realities derived from the design created their own problems within the building: undersized and inefficient heating, huge heat gain and heat loss from expansive, unprotected, and noninsulated glass facades; poorly maintained roofs, which led to leakage; and a lack of privacy, which, according to today's American traditions, would be unacceptable. For example, art historian Rudolf Arnheim inadvertently revealed a lack of privacy: "Looking in through the large windows, you can see people hard at work or relaxing in private" (Droste, 1990).

Gropius resigned as Bauhaus director soon after the building's completion and was followed by architects Hannes Meyer and then Ludwig Mies van der Rohe, who strengthened and focused the coursework in architecture. However, in 1932 the Bauhaus lost its municipal support and its beloved building after Dessau's Social Democrats were defeated by the National Socialist Party. Mies van der Rohe restructured the school and moved it to Berlin. The Nazis dissolved it in 1933.

The building was transformed after the Bauhaus program moved out. First, on 1 October 1932, it was dissolved as a municipal institution, and then the National Socialist majority, who described the building as a "squalid glass palace in oriental taste," pushed for its demolition. Although the building might have been saved, once the Nazis came to power, the building was raided. All documentation, drawings, furnishings, and even fittings were destroyed or stolen. During World War II, the glass curtain wall of the workshop wing was almost entirely destroyed. In 1948 it was replaced by brick walls with small square windows. The building held various institutions: a girls' finishing school, a Nazi training school, part of the Junkers military aircraft manufacturing company, a POW camp, and, after the war, a homeless shelter and the home of schools displaced by the war. In 1964 the windows were replaced by horizontal bands of glass with wide spandrels until 1974, when the East Germans included the building on their list of significant monuments and began restoration. In 1984 it became the home of the "Center of Form at the Dessau Bauhaus" and, most recently, the "Bauhaus Foundation." This organization, currently renamed the "Bauhaus Kolleg" and directed by an urban planner, addresses the "problems" and "spirit" of the present.

Few of Gropius's contemporaries and later critics agreed with the Nazis' assessment. Before World War II, the Bauhaus buildings were the epitome of modern architecture in Germany. Hundreds of visitors from Germany and abroad traveled to Dessau. Its renown extended from constant publicity through photographs, especially aerial photography, exhibits, publications, and the writings of prominent critics. In 1927 Rudolf Arnheim wrote about the clarity of structure and skillful yet honest construction. Eleven years later, Alfred H. Barr Jr., then director of the Museum of Modern Art in New York, described it as the most important structure of its decade, and in 1954 Sigfried Giedion called it the first building to employ a radically new conception of space. From the time it was completed to the present, architects and students in architecture considered the Bauhaus building in Dessau as one of the most, if not the most, influential buildings of the modern period of architecture. It remains a mecca for students, practitioners, and connoisseurs of architecture.

MARCIA F. FEUERSTEIN

See also **Bauhaus; De Stijl; Fagus Werk, Alfeld, Germany; International Style; Mies van der Rohe, Ludwig (Germany); van Doesburg, Theo (Netherlands)**

Further Reading

Most of the readings in English refer to the building in the context of the school. Few focus solely on the architectural design. Gropius's book *Bauhausbauten Dessau* is an excellent source for images and the architect's original ideas. However, it remains in German. There are many general texts about the school, its activities, masters, and background, as well as translations of documents, letters, and works from the various stages of the Bauhaus.

Droste, Magdalena, *Bauhaus, 1919–1933*, Cologne: Taschen, 1990; as *Bauhaus, 1919–1933*, translated by Karen Williams, Berlin: Taschen, 1993

Futagawa, Yukio (editor), *Walter Gropius: Bauhaus, Dessau, Germany, 1925–26: Fagus Factory, Alfeld-an-der-Leine, Germany, 1911–25 (with Adolf Meyer)*, Tokyo: A.D.A. Edita, 1994

Gropius, Walter, *Bauhausbauten Dessau*, Munich: Langen, 1930

Kentgens-Craig, Margret (editor), *Das Bauhausgebäude in Dessau, 1976–1999*, Basel and Boston: Birkhäuser, 1998; as *The Dessau Bauhaus Building, 1926–1999*, translated by Michael Robinson, Basel and Boston: Birkhäuser, 1998

Krause, R., "A History of the Development of the Plans for the Bauhaus Building in Dessau," *Architectura Zeitschrift für Geschichte der Baukunst*, 28, no. 2 (1998)

Wingler, Hans Maria, *Das Bauhaus, 1919–1933: Weimar, Dessau, Berlin*, Bramsche, Germany: Gebr. Rasch, 1962; 2nd revised edition, as *Das Bauhaus, 1919–1933: Weimar, Dessau, Berlin, und die Nachfolge in Chicago seit 1937*, Cologne: DuMont Schauberg, 1968; 2nd edition, as *The Bauhaus: Weimar, Dessau, Berlin, Chicago*, translated by Wolfgang Jabs and Basil Gilbert, edited by Joseph Stein, Cambridge, Massachusetts: MIT Press, and London: Cambridge University Press, 1969; 3rd revised edition, Cambridge, Massachusetts: MIT Press, 1976

BAWA, GEOFFREY 1919–

Architect, Sri Lanka

Geoffrey Bawa is a rare architect whose work combines an environmentally appropriate beauty with a cultural sensitivity. Bawa was educated within the modernist tradition in the West, where he was trained both as a lawyer and as an architect. An urbane, widely read, and well-traveled person, he remains rooted in the soil of his native land. His buildings are predicated on the landscape and climate—he is as much an architect of landscape as he is of buildings.

To Bawa, the pitched roof is the archetype of southern Asian architecture. It is the dominant element that governs his aesthetic, in which shape, texture, and proportion are the strongest visual factors in his buildings. The great roof, with the building's sides open to the flow of air and the view, give "presence to both function and form, to admit beauty and pleasure as well as purpose" (as told to the author, 1984). Another important feature of his work deals with movement through the building, modulated by the rooms, passages, and courtyards that frame vistas or parts of the landscape. Of equal importance is the play of light, in both the built areas and the "rooms" of the landscaping, which gives pleasure in addition to giving comfortable, functional use of the spaces. Bawa pays careful attention to detail, ranging from the expression of structure to the furnishing of rooms, regardless of the scale of the project.

Bawa has been fortunate to be in the position to choose his projects and select clients who are sympathetic to his approach. They include artists and intellectuals, private institutions, and government. The perception and organizational skills of his longtime partner, Dr. Poologasundram, an engineer, has enabled the Bawa to realize the buildings as conceived. He has worked with several others in his office for many years, and they also assist him in the development of his ideas. However, Bawa remains the principal and controls every aspect of the design.

Bawa designs using numerous freehand sketches, while simultaneously working on the site layout plan, section, elevation, and details. His partners and colleagues begin to formalize the work with schematic and working drawings. Often construction drawings and details are discussed with the craftsman and are changed. In the mode of the master architect, Bawa will alter his design on-site while the building is under construction. This technique was even used on his large Parliament Complex Colombo which was built by a Japanese company on a turnkey basis, but Bawa's on-site decisions and solutions proved better and more cost-effective than the original plan.

His personal residences best illustrate his approach to design. His country house, Lunuganga, has been a continuing project since 1950. Set in a garden of 25 acres, the house and its free-standing pavilions overlook terraces and a lake, and illustrate his concerns with site and the expression of a contemporary vernacular. He has periodically added new buildings and elements, such as a large concrete chess set and a grove of trees and benches. Each of the pavilions has its own character and fits into its natural setting. It is perhaps his masterpiece, and was once described by one of the workmen as "a sacred place." His principal residence in Colombo dates from 1969, and consists of four townhouses joined together with multiple small courtyards and a maze of rooms. It illustrates well his characteristic skill in working with small spaces to create intimacy and a sense of place.

The theme of pavilions set in a landscape typifies his architecture, as in the Ena de Silva House (Colombo, 1962) and the 12 pavilion houses (1973) built in Batujimbar, Indonesia, and designed with artist, Donald Friend. Low-cost schools such as Yahapath Endra Farm School (1966) in Hanwella extend this approach into the realm of institutional buildings. Bawa works this on an even larger scale at the University of Ruhunu (1984–86) in Matara, on the southern coast. There he not only planned the university, but also designed the Arts and Sciences faculty building as well as others. Pavilions of varying size, some of which are placed on stilts, are arranged to take advantage of the verdant site and the view to the sea.

Bawa is also known for his tourist beach hotels. Bentota Beach Hotel (Bentota, 1969) has a dramatic entry staircase that spotlights the Sinhalese batik cloths on the ceiling. The Triton Hotel (1981) in Ahungalla has open spaces and public facilities on the ground floor with bedrooms above, and all have vistas of the beach and sea. A huge, ornamental entry pool leads to an open-sided reception area, which in turn overlooks a swimming pool that appears to merge into the sea and sky. This progression of spaces and visual effects is a common theme that appears in his work. Bawa's Kandalama Hotel (1995) in Dambulla is sited on a hillside and approached from a lake. It takes full advantage of the views, and the concrete-frame structure is expressed in a modernist facade.

The Garden at Lunuganga, exterior view showing wood columns supporting overhang, Sri Lanka (1950), by Geoffrey Bawa
Photo by Helene Binet © Aga Khan Award for Architecture

This aesthetic and the use of concrete, steel, and glass mark some of his office buildings and institutional complexes. His largest single structure, the Parliamentary Complex in Kotte (1982), is set in an artificially constructed lake. Pavilions of varying size flank the ceremonial building, with its large central volume containing the government assembly chamber and ancillary spaces. The huge copper roofs are reminiscent of monastic and royal buildings of the past yet convey a contemporary image. Bawa's buildings, both public and private, cover a range of types, and although his work is often classified as "vernacular," it is executed in varying styles.

Bawa's work is contemporary yet seems to have existed in the landscape over the ages; it is a truly timeless architecture. Artist Barbara Sansoni wrote that his work "represents the distillation of centuries of shared experience, and links at the first level of achievement, its ancient architecture to that of the modern world" (Taylor 1986).

HASAN-UDDIN KHAN

Biography

Born in Colombo, Sri Lanka, 23 July 1919. Studied English literature, University of Cambridge, England; bachelor of arts 1941; studied law, Middle Temple, London; barrister-at-law 1943; attended, Architectural Association, London; degree in architecture 1956. Private practice, Colombo, from 1956; partner, Edwards Reid and Begg, Colombo 1958; collaboration with Ulrik Plesner 1958–67; adviser to the government of Fiji on the restoration of the old capital 1986. Teaching fellowship, Aga Khan Pragramme for Architecture, Massachusetts Institute of Technology, Cambridge 1986. President, Sri Lanka Institute of Architects, Colombo 1969–70; honorary fellow, American Institute of Architects 1983; member, Master Jury, 4th Aga Khan Awards for Architecture 1989. Vidya Jothi (Light of Science) 1985. Since the mid-1990s Bawa has been totally incapacitated and unable to work: his projects are being completed by his staff.

Selected Works

Almost all of Bawa's buildings are in Sri Lanka with the exception of severalin Bali, southern India, and Indian Ocean islands.

Lunuganga, the Garden House, Bentota, 1950
Carmen Gunasekera House, Colombo, 1959
Ena de Silva House, Colombo, 1962
The Architect's Office, Colombo, 1963
St. Bridget's Montessori School, Colombo, 1964
Yahapath Endera Farm School, Hanwella, 1966
Geoffrey Bawa House, Colombo, 1969
Bentota Beach Hotel, Bentota, 1969
Serendip Hotel, Bentota, 1971
Pavilions, Batujimbar, Bali, 1973
Peter White House, Mauritius, 1974
Neptune Hotel, Beruwela, 1974
Agrarian Research and Training Institute, Colombo, 1975
Mahaweli Office Building, Colombo, 1978
Triton Hotel, Ahungalla, 1981
Integral Education Center, Piliyandale, 1981
Parliament Complex, Sri Jayawardenpura, Kotte, 1982
Phase I, Science Faculty, Ruhunu University, Matara, 1984
Phase II, Arts Faculty, Library and Administration Building, Ruhunu University, 1986
Royal Oceanic Hotel, Negombo, 1986
United Nations Building, Malé, Maldives, 1992
Currumjee House, Mauritius, 1995
Kandalama Hotel, Dambulla, 1995

Selected Publication

Lunuganga (with Christoph Bon and Dominic Sansoni), Singapore: Times Editions 1990

Further Reading

Brawne, Michael, "University of Ruhunu, Matara, Sri Lanka," *Architectural Review* (November 1986)
Jayawardena, Shanti, "Bawa: A Contribution to Cultural Regeneration," *Mimar: Architecture in Development*, 19 (1986)
Laird, Simon, "Geoffrey Bawa and the Architecture of Sri Lanka," *Mackintosh School of Architecture Journal* (1984)
Lal, Ashok, "The Architecture of Geoffrey Bawa—An Intimacy of Experience and Expression," *Architecture & Design*, 11, no. 2 (March/April 1990)
Lewcock, Ronald, "Bawa—Arcadia in Sri Lanka," *RIBA Journal* (February 1986)
Nakamura, Toshio, "The Architecture of Geoffrey Bawa," *A + U*, 141 (June 1982)
Richards, Sir James, "Geoffrey Bawa," *Mimar: Architecture in Development*, 19 (1986)
Robinson, David, *Bawa: The Complete Works*, London: Thames and Hudson, 2002
Taylor, Brian Brace, *Geoffrey Bawa*, Singapore: Concept Media, and New York: Aperture, 1986; London: Butterworth Architecture, 1989; revised edition, New York: Thames and Hudson, 1995

BEHRENS, PETER 1868–1940

Architect, German

Peter Behrens was one of the most prolific architects of his generation. He created buildings ranging from embassies, monuments, bridges, churches, and giant factories to domestic houses, workers' estates, and apartment blocks. He also became the first industrial designer in the modern sense; he was responsible for mass-produced furniture, textiles, cutlery, ceramics, and glass in addition to his well-known range of electrical appliances for the AEG, or General Electric Company. His graphic work was enormously successful, and he was active in theater design, calligraphy, and typography. He was a teacher and a writer, and he had a strong influence on the development of his assistants, who were to become the most celebrated architects of the next generation. Behrens was born in St. Georg, Hamburg, and he was the son of a landowner who did not marry his mother. Both his parents died when he was young, and he was reared by a guardian from the age of 14. On leaving school in Altona in 1886, he chose to study art and attended the Gewerbeschule, Hamburg, and the Kunstschule, Karlsruhe, until 1889, before becoming first a pupil of Ferdinand Brütt in Düsseldorf and then of Hugo Kotschenreiter in Munich. Behrens went through various phases in his painting style; at first he was influenced by the realist and impressionist work of Dutch-German and Dutch artists, such as Wilhelm Leibl and Max Liebermann, before turning to studio compositions of a more symbolist approach. Behrens never sought or acquired formal qualifications as an architect. In the later 1890s, while still living in Munich, he executed a number of woodcuts in a flat, linear style and became drawn into the group that formed the Vereinigten Werkstätten für Kunst im Handwerk, designing and exhibiting ceramics, glass, jewelry, furniture, and women's clothing. His large woodcut, *Der Kuss* (1898), became one of the best-known images of Jugendstil, or German Art Nouveau.

In July 1899, as a result of his reputation as an artist and designer, he was invited to join the artists' colony at Darmstadt, which was being established under the patronage of Grand Duke Ernst Ludwig of Hessen. This colony was planned and launched with ducal, government, and industrial support to stimulate the role of applied art in the local economy and to bring prestige to the city. The seven artists brought together at Darmstadt were to be a free creative community, and to exhibit their work regularly; they were to live in houses designed by the Austrian architect Joseph Maria Olbrich, with the exception of Behrens, who designed his own.

This house, his first, was to accommodate himself, his wife, and their two young children. It was intended, like the other houses of the *Künstlerkolonie* (artists' colony), to be at once a dwelling and a permanent exhibit of the new architecture, a statement of a way of living and a model of style.

Behrens's house is basically cubic in form, with a red-tiled pyramidal roof. A gable dominates the main facade, and the plain white walls are relieved with decorative pilaster strips, quoins, and architraves in molded green-glazed bricks. Internally, the ground floor is comprised of an entrance hall with wide sliding screens that open into a music room that in turn connect to a dining room, so that virtually the whole space can be unified when desired. The studio is a principal room upstairs. Behrens designed all the interior decorations—the furniture, carpets, curtains, light fittings, cutlery, glass, china, and linen—in harmony. He and his house played a major role in the 1901 exhibition of the artists' colony, titled *Ein Dokument Deutscher Kunst* (A Document of German Art). In his first year in the colony, he wrote and published a long essay on the theater, *Feste des Lebens und der Kunst,* and designed a round, highly centralized Festival Theatre, the plans of which were published but never realized.

In 1902 Behrens's first printing type, Behrens-Schrift, was published. He was to design a number of typefaces, including a special face for the AEG that is still used today for that company's logo, and, with Anna Simons, the inscription on the portico of the Reichstag in Berlin, *Dem Deutschen Volke* (1909).

Of importance to his growing reputation was his contribution to the First International Exhibition of Modern Decorative Arts in Turin in 1902. He was responsible for the Hamburger Vorhalle, a powerfully modeled, cryptlike, top-lit hall. It may be considered the most Art Nouveau of Behrens's architectural works, and the strongest expression of his admiration for Frederich Nietzsche's philosophy. Following this, his architecture became more rectilinear and geometric, and indeed it remained so for the rest of his career.

In 1903 Behrens moved to Düsseldorf, where he had been appointed director of the School of Arts and Crafts. In that year, he traveled in England and Scotland, visiting houses by Edwin Lutyens and Charles Rennie Mackintosh. A striking demonstration of Behrens's new, coolly geometrical style was seen in the garden layout and pavilion that he designed for the Düsseldorf Gartenbau und Kunstausstellung (Garden Design and Pavilion) of 1904. In harmony with the restaurant pavilion (which Behrens furnished with Mackintosh-like ladder-backed chairs) were rectangular white latticework pergolas, creating what was described as "habitable nature, a living room in the open air" (Osborn). A lasting influence on Behrens's design procedure came from the proportional grids, based on the square and the circle evolved by the Dutch architect J.L.M. Lauweriks, who joined Behrens's staff in that year. Behrens spent the summer of that same year studying the antiquities of Rome and Pompeii.

Between 1904–06, Behrens designed a number of buildings that directly fuse the elements of simple geometry with classically derived decoration. For example, the complex of buildings for the Northwest German Art Exhibition of 1905 was symmetrically grouped on a broad rectangular space to form an ensemble

Behrens House (architect's house Künstler-Kolonie), Darmstadt, Germany, designed by Peter Behrens (1901)

of cubes, pyramids, domes, and triangles. The stark white buildings with their bold geometric surface patterns suppressed any expression of their material or constructional elements. His domed, octagonal exhibition pavilion in Dresden for the Delmenhorster Linoleumfabrik of 1906, as well as the range of linoleum patterns exhibited in it, led to Behrens's recognition as an artist who was gifted for and suited to working with modern industry.

Behrens's friendship with the patron Karl Ernst Osthaus of Hagen led to a number of commissions in the city, as well as to his famous Crematorium nearby at Delstern (1906–07). They included a lecture theater for the Folkwang Museum (1905), a shop for the firm of Josef Klein (1905–07), a large octagonal Protestant church that was never built (1906–07), and an important group of houses on an estate at Eppenhausen, for which Osthaus was the developer.

The garden suburb at Eppenhausen was divided by Osthaus into three zones, and he asked Behrens, Lauweriks, and the Belgian Henri van de Velde to prepare related groups of houses for each area. Behrens's were built between 1909 and 1912, following a dramatic new phase in his life as artistic adviser to the AEG. He moved to Berlin in 1907, and his three houses (the Cuno, Schroeder, and Goedecke houses) were detailed and supervised by Walter Gropius. Gropius was the closest to him of the team of assistants he had engaged to join his Berlin studio, to work on his now immensely expanded practice. The most impressive of the houses remains the Cuno house (1909–10). Rectangular in plan, it resembles a Palladian villa, with a nearly symmetrical disposition of the rooms on the ground floor. The living room on the garden side, centrally placed between the identically scaled dining room and the ladies' drawing room, opens through a large three-light French window onto a generous terrace. The most striking feature of the main, street facade is the curved central tower, recessed into the plane of the front walls, which rises the full height of the elevation and contains a spiral staircase. This, with its five plain narrow windows between slender piers, is flanked by a rusticated ground-floor story in local stone, above which plain, smoothly rendered wall surfaces are broken only by three square bedroom windows on either side in the upper story. The web of horizontal and vertical tensions of the design is given an asymmetrical rhythm by the stone wall of one of the balconies (which flank the house on either side), wrapping around to the front as a thick buttresslike wall. Horizontal emphasis is given by the low-pitched roof set behind a stepped-back parapet, a thin emphatic cornice, and a similar stringcourse halfway up the facade.

The most remarkable development in Behrens's career was his appointment in 1907 to the AEG. He redesigned the firm's range of arc lamps, kettles, coffee pots, fans, clocks, radiators, and motors, bringing enormous commercial success to the firm. He designed a vast range of brochures, posters, and catalogs and devised typefaces as well as the logo of the company. More important, he became responsible for the firm's industrial architecture. In 1910 the best known of his factory buildings, the Turbine Hall at Moabit, was completed. The largest steel hall in Berlin of its time, this great building is formed of 22 girder frames exposed along one side; the main facade has a huge steel-framed window under a curved segmental concrete gable; the profile is made up of six straight facets. This rests on massive-looking concrete piers, grooved horizontally, which affect the corners on either side. Its peculiar genius lies in the expressive force of steel and glass used on a large scale, without historical decorations of any kind.

Between 1908 and 1914, a range of giant factory buildings on the Humbolthain in Berlin were designed by Behrens and his team, which included Ludwig Mies van der Rohe and, for a brief period, Charles-Édouard Jeanneret (Le Corbusier) alongside Gropius. The most significant of these steel-framed buildings were the High Tension Materials Factory (1910), a powerful, expressive multistory complex with echoes of classical form in its triangular pediments and pilasterlike columns on its principal facade, and the Small Motors Factory (1910), with its vast, stoa-like range of 20-meter-high brick piers facing Voltastrasse. Also, there is the Assembly Hall (for large machines, 1912) flanking Hussitenstrasse, with its restrained grid of repeated horizontal and vertical elements framing the large rectangular windows.

A major state commission of the period was the German Embassy, St. Petersburg (1911–12), which owed inspiration to Roman *palazzi* of the 16th century and to Schinkel's Altes Museum. An astonishing number of other large projects that were completed included the head office of the Mannesmann Tube Company in Düsseldorf (1911–12), a pioneering exercise in modular planning and construction; the Continental Rubber Company Factory in Hannover (1911–12); the Frankfurt Gasworks Complex (1911–12); and the Festival Hall for the 1914 Werkbund Exhibition in Cologne.

Behrens's contract with the AEG was terminated in 1914. After the war, he published, with Heinrich de Fries, *Von sparsamen Bauen* (1918; On Economical Building), which advocated low-cost housing schemes to be built of reinforced concrete, incorporating the latest facilities and communal social services using standardized units to create varied types of accommodation with built-in storage cupboards to maximize the space.

Following a period of brick expressionism—used, for example, for the head offices of the Hoechst Dyeworks for IG Farben and the Dombauhütte (Cathedral Masons' Lodge) exhibition building in Munich (1922)—Behrens's style changed yet again. This time the change led to mainstream International Modern, a style for which his own earlier work had been formative. Other projects included blocks of flats (1924–28) for the authorities in Vienna, where he lived following his appointment as professor of the Master School for Architecture, the small house New Ways in Northampton, England (1923–25), his terrace block on the Weissenhof estate in Stuttgart (1926–27), his house for Dr. Lewin, Berlin (1929–30), and the superb villa for Clara Gans in the Taunus Mountains (1931). All of these buildings had flat roofs over plain, cubic forms with a strong horizontal emphasis. His *Ring der Frauen* pavilion for the 1931 Berlin Building Exhibition was a delightful, prototypical women's clubhouse comprising several low intersecting cylindrical elements.

During the Third Reich, despite being attacked as a Bolshevist, the elderly and sick Behrens was invited to design a new AEG headquarters (1937–39) for the North-South Axis of Berlin being planned by Albert Speer. It was never constructed.

ALAN WINDSOR

See also **AEG Turbine Factory, Berlin; Art Nouveau (Jugendstil); Corbusier, Le (Jeanneret, Charles-Édouard) (France); Gropius, Walter (Germany); Mies van der Rohe, Ludwig (Germany); Olbrich, Josef Maria (Austria); van de Velde, Henri (Belgium); Werkbund Exhibition, Cologne (1914)**

Biography

Born in Hamburg, Germany, 14 April 1868. Attended the Karlsruhe and Düsseldorf Art Schools 1886–89; studied privately in artists' studios 1887–89. Married Lili Kramer 1889. Founding member, Munich Sezession 1893; co-formed Die Seben art colony, Darmstadt, Germany 1899; designer to electrical combine AEG, Berlin 1907. Established own firm, Berlin 1907. Director, Nuremberg Master Course in Architecture, 1902; head of Düsseldorf School of Applied Arts 1903–07; director, Academy of Art, Düsseldorf, Germany 1921–22; director and professor, School of Architecture, Vienna Academy of Fine Arts, Vienna 1922–27; director, Department of Architecture, Prussian Academy of Arts, Berlin 1936–40. His pupils included Le Corbusier, Walter Gropius, and Ludwig Mies van der Rohe. Died in Berlin, 27 February 1940.

Selected Works

Behrens House, Künstler-Kolonie, Darmstadt, 1901

Hamburger Vorhalle, Exhibition of Modern Decorative Arts, Turin, 1902

Garden Design and Pavilion, Düsseldorf, 1904
Exhibition Buildings, Northwest German Art Exhibition, 1905
Lecture Hall, Folkwang Museum, Hagen, 1905
Exhibition Pavilion, Delmenhorster Linoleumfabrik, Dresden, 1906
Crematorium, Delstern, 1907
Shop for Josef Klein, Hagen, 1907
Protestant Church (unbuilt), Hagen, 1907
Schröder House, Hagen-Eppenhausen, 1909
Cuno House, Hagen-Eppenhausen, 1910
AEG Turbine Factory, Berlin (with Karl Bernhard), 1910
AEG High Tension Materials Factory, Berlin, 1910
AEG Small Motors Factory, Berlin, 1910
Goedecke House, Hagen-Eppenhausen, 1912
AEG Large Machinery Assembly Hall, Berlin, 1912
AEG Railway Equipment Factory, Berlin, 1912
German Embassy, St. Petersburg, 1912
Mannesmann Tube Company Headquarters, Düsseldorf, 1912
Continental Rubber Company Office Building, Hanover, 1912
Gas Works Complex, Frankfurt, 1912
Festhalle, Deutscher Werkbund Exhibition, Cologne, 1914
Nationale Automobil Aktien-Gesellschaft Housing and Factory, Berlin, 1917
Dombauhütte, Kunstgewerbeschule, Munich, 1922
IG Farben Dyeworks Headquarters, Hoechst, 1924
New Ways House, Northampton, 1925
Terrace House Apartments, Stuttgart, 1927
Low-income Housing Blocks, Vienna, 1929
Kurt Lewin House, Berlin, 1930
Ring der Frauen Pavilion, Berlin Building Exhibition, 1931
Clara Ganz Villa, Kronberg im Taunus, 1931
AEG Administration Building (unbuilt), Berlin, 1939

Selected Publications

Feste des Lebens und der Kunst: Eine Betrachtung des Theaters als höchsten Kultursymbols, 1900
Ein Dokument deutscher Kunst: Die Ausstellung der Künstler-Kolonie in Darmstadt 1901, 1901
"Haus Peter Behrens," Darmstadt, 1901, brochure
Behrens Schrift, 1902
Beziehungen der künstlerischen und technischen Probleme, 1917
Vom sparsmen Bauen: Ein Beitrag zur Siedlungsfrage (with Heinrich de Fries), 1918
Das Ethos un die Unlagerung der künstlerischen Probleme, 1920
Terrassen am Hause, 1927

Further Reading

A detailed and scholarly catalogue of Behrens's architecture, appliances for the AEG, and graphics appears in Buddensieg and Rogge. Furniture is catalogued in Schuster, and work for the Anker-Marke linoleum factory is listed in Asche.

Anderson, Stanford, *Peter Behrens and a New Architecture for the Twentieth Century*, Cambridge, Massachusetts: MIT Press, 2000
Asche, Kurt, *Peter Behrens und die Oldenburger Austellung 1905*, Berlin: Mann, 1992
Branchesi, Lida, "Peter Behrens" (Ph.D. dissertation), Rome, 1965
Buddensieg, Tilmann, and Henning Rogge, *Industriekultur: Peter Behrens und die AEG, 1907–1914*, Berlin: Mann, 1979; 4th edition, 1993; as *Industriekultur: Peter Behrens and the AEG, 1907–1914*, translated by Iain Boyd Whyte, Cambridge, Massachusetts: MIT Press, 1984
Buderath, Bernhard, and Tilmann Buddensieg, *Peter Behrens: umbautes Licht: das Verwaltungsgebäude der Hoechst AG*, Frankfurt: Prestel, 1990
Casabella 240 (June 1960) (special issue on Behrens)
Cremers, Paul Joseph, *Peter Behrens: Sein Werk von 1909 bis zur Gegenwart*, Essen: Baedecker, 1928
Dokumente aus Hoechster Archiv, part 4, Hoechst: Hoechst A.G., 1964
Gerber, Werner, *Nicht Gebaute Architektur. Peter Behrens und Fritz Schumacher als Kirchenplaner in Hagen. Beispiele aus den Jahren 1906–1907*, Hagen: Linepe, 1980
Hesse-Frielinghaus, Herta, *Peter Behrens und Karl Ernst Osthaus. Ein Dokumentation nach den Beständen des Osthaus-Archivs im Karl-Ernst-Osthaus Museum, Hagen*, Hagen: Karl Ernst Osthaus Museum, 1966
Hoeber, Fritz, *Peter Behrens*, Munich: Müller und Rentsch, 1913
Hoepfner, Wolfram, and Frizt Neumeyer, *Das Haus Wiegand von Peter Behrens in Berlin-Dahlem*, Mainz: Phillipp von Zabern, 1979
Kadatz, Hans-Joachim, *Peter Behrens, Architekt, Maler, Grafiker, und Formgestalter, 1868–1940*, Leipzig: Seemann, 1977
Krimmel, Bernd (editor), *Ein Dokument Deutscher Kunst. Darmstadt 1901–1976*, Darmstadt: Roether, 1976
Norberg-Schulz, Christian, *Casa Behrens: Darmstadt*, Rome: Officina Edizione, 1980; 2nd edition, 1986
Osborn, Max, *Die Düsseldorfer Ausstellung: Kunst und Künstler, Yr II*, vol. 12 (September) 1904
Pfeifer, Hans-Georg (editor), *Peter Behrens: "Wer aber will sagen, was Schönheit sei?": Grafik, Produktgestaltung, Architektur*, Düsseldorf: Beton-Verlag, 1990
Schuster, Peter-Klaus, *Peter Behrens und Nürnberg: Geschmackswandel in Deutschland* (exhib. cat.), Munich: Prestel, 1980
Windsor, Alan, *Peter Behrens, Architect and Designer 1869–1940*, London: Architectural Press, and New York: Whitney Library of Design, 1981

BEIRUT, LEBANON

The modern face of Beirut hides the city's long architectural and urban history. Recent archaeological excavations, generated by the post–civil war reconstruction, have provided further evidence that different civilizations have continuously inhabited the city since at least the Iron Age. Hardly any architectural landmarks remain from before the 19th century, with the exception of some religious buildings. Beirut remained a secondary settlement to other cities along the eastern Mediterranean coast, such as Tripoli and Damascus until 1831, when Ibrahim Pasha of Egypt, in his failed insurrection against the Ottomans, took it as a base, and attracted merchants and consuls. Since then, the city has grown from a town of 10,000 to a metropolitan district of about 1.5 million today.

The early years of growth were supported by many Ottoman modernization projects, conducted mostly through concessions to European companies. These included harbor expansion, public utilities, military facilities, and transportation networks, and most notably, the toll road to Damascus (1863). Buildings such as the Orozdi Bek Department Store (1900), the Arts and Crafts School (1914), including some of its extramural residential quarters and missionary educational facilities, display a Mediterranean architectural character that attests to the open cultural exchange at the time.

During World War I, Beirut suffered a famine, losing much of its population of 100,000. A major urban-planning endeavor was mounted by the Ottomans, that would be completed during the French mandate (1918–43) in the form of Place de l'Etoile.

The mandate created a new nation-state—Greater Lebanon—with Beirut as its capital. With the exception of urban improvements in the city center, the mandate continued the modernization-by-concession process started by the Ottomans. It was not until 1932, in the face of social tensions caused in part by the Great Depression, that an attempt at large-scale urban planning began. Two master plans were advanced: one by the Danger Brothers in 1932 and one by Michel Ecochard in 1942. The first created commercial centers for new residential areas, while the second introduced a major road network linking the port and airport with the hinterland. Neither plan was implemented.

The building of the city's new quarters and institutions was carried out by some of its established architects, including Yousif Aftimos and Mardiros Altounian. Aftimos helped develop the ornate facade architecture of the new avenues in the city center, such as the Municipality Building (1933) and Maarad Street (1930s). Altounian elevated Oriental Art Deco motifs, extending it to civic architecture for the Lebanese Parliament and the National Museum buildings. The pre–World War II period also saw the rise of a new generation of architects, such as Antoun Tabet, Farid Trad, Ilyas Murr, and Bahjat Abdulnour. Tabet's link with the studio of Auguste Perret heralded the expressive application of concrete-and-steel technology by many engineer-architects of the period, whereas the work of Murr and Trad extended the forms of late Ottoman architecture into the French mandate (1918–43) and early independence (1943–58). This extension of styles and building types attests to the continuity within the urban developmental culture across the different political epochs. Interestingly, a new vernacular architecture was developed during this period, featuring multistory residential buildings built to absorb the growing population.

Beirut's economic primacy in the region was boosted by the sudden loss of competition from the city of Haifa and the beginning of the Arab-Israeli conflict in 1948. This was supported by Lebanon's strong banking and services sectors, and by the presence of foreign business interests; it was paralleled by the strong intellectual and political life that gave Beirut the reputation of being a breeding ground for regional political and cultural movements. Architecture, however, remained cast in the professional, technical arena. Following a brief civil war in 1958, urban development was guided by a new welfare state and a new ministry of planning. Two major master plans were proposed for Beirut; one by Constantinos Doxiadis in 1957–59 and one by Michel Ecochard in 1963–64. Both master plans acknowledged the growth of the city and the need to develop physical planning at a regional, and even a national, scale. The country's new institutions and infrastructure were given a strong modern image, as exemplified by the Central Bank as designed by Swiss architects Addor et Julliard, among others. However, the buildings were distributed mostly in the suburbs including such important projects such as the Ministry of Defense (1965) and the Lebanese University (late 1960s) by Maurice Hindieh and André Wogenscky. Hence, they did nothing to improve the urban layout. Other architects of the period, such as Pierre el-Khoury, Bahije Khoury-Makdisi, Wassek Adib, Pierre Neema, George Rayes, and Assem Salam, helped to generate a professional culture that guided Lebanon's architecture more effectively than the intellectual networks and academic institutions. For example, Khoury's École Technique provided a model for institutional buildings, whereas Adib's collaborations with Polish architect Karl Schayer provided the city with a facade along the seafront. The Corniche combined a rational, structural frame with expressive ground planes and roofs. With such buildings as the Shell Building (1962) by Schayer and Adib and the more mannered work of Joseph Philippe Karam, the city acquired a new building type: a mixed-use apartment building, that would come to dominate urban as well as suburban development.

What emerged in the early 1960s as a vigorous expression of flexibility turned into a formal anonymity in the 1970s under the pressure of speculative construction. Architects, such as Pierre Neema and Michel Ecochard, sought a more institutional expressiveness, as demonstrated by Neema's Electricité du Liban (1962). Samir Khairallah and Assem Salam would consciously incorporate regional styles, with Salam actively debating with other Arab architects, such as Rifaat Chadirji (Iraq) and Jaafar Toukan (Jordan), about national and Arab identity expressed through architecture. Despite the rise of many schools of architecture, practice maintained its primacy in generating architectural attitudes. This was caused by the continuation of a technical approach to architecture and by the effectiveness of

Banque du Liban et d'Outre Mer, Beirut, Lebanon, designed by Pierre el-Khoury (1996)
Photo courtesy Pierre el-Khoury © The Aga Khan Award for Architecture

competition and open exchange that dominated the development culture.

Beirut would witness exponential growth in population, from 10,000 within the municipal district in 1920, to about 1.5 million in the metropolitan area by 1975. With about half of Lebanon's population occupying 5 percent of the land, Beirut had become a virtual city-state. This imbalance in growth and development attracted the rural population to the city, causing overcrowding in its immediate suburbs, and dire socioeconomic problems. During the same period, the city also absorbed Palestinian refugees increasing social tensions in the city. It led, along with religious and regional conflicts, to a succession of wars between 1975 and 1990, and included the invasion of the city by Israel in 1982. From 1975 to 1990, Beirut would suffer extensive damage, leaving much of the commercial center's architecture destroyed.

Since the 1990 Taef Accord, which reconciled Lebanon's warring factions, Beirut has been the focus of Lebanon's reconstruction efforts. The emphasis has been on rebuilding road networks and infrastructure services and enlarging the city's port and airport. Much of the urban planning was guided by the *Schéma Directeur* (1986), a study developed by the Mission Franco-Libanaise d'Étude et d'Aménagement, which called for decentralization of the commercial activity toward regional centers, and for a peripheral highway around the city. This study also stipulated a special project for the city center, which was the area most affected by the war. The city center was eventually developed by a private real estate holding company that was set up to execute a master plan, developed by the Arab consultant Dar al-Handasah (Shair and Partner). This plan caused controversy regarding liquidation of property into shares, destruction of old streets and buildings, and the highly speculative new development. The vague, urban design that characterized the plan was further developed by American architectural firms, including Skidmore, Owings and Merrill and Perkins and Will, but they failed to bring formal clarity to the street layout, or create continuity between the streets and buildings. New buildings in the city center have been burdened by the responsibility of recreating the lost heritage, and by an inability to project a bold urban presence. Rafael Moneo's design for the city bazaar has challenged the separation between urban design and architecture. Public institutions that had been built during the early independence period were retrofitted and enlarged. Many of them, including the Sports City, the Lebanese University, and the Presidential Palace, were clad with historicist styles, creating a link between the preservation policies of the city center and the restoration of modern buildings. The more promising architects of this period, including pre–civil war architects like Pierre el-Khoury (Ghazal Tower and Moritra Residential Building) and Jacques Ligier-Belair, as well as some of the younger architects, are experimenting with newer, more articulate building typologies for different uses.

In the late 1990s, when a constantly changing urban fabric and a rapidly disappearing architectural heritage seemed to undermine the search for continuity and invention, a postwar generation of architects was also challenged by speculative tendencies and environmental and preservation problems.

HASHIM SARKIS

Further Reading

Recent reconstruction activity in Beirut has generated extensive literature about the urban planning process as well as a renewed interest in urban and architectural history. Extensive research is currently being conducted in Beirut and in archives in Paris and Istanbul, led by a new generation of historians who are already beginning to make remarkable contributions to the understanding and reassessment of the city's architectural heritage.

Buheiry, Marwan R., *Beirut's Role in the Political Economy of the French Mandate, 1919–1939*, Oxford: Centre for Lebanese Studies, 1986

Davie, May, *Beyrouth et ses Faubourgs (1840–1940): une intégration inachevée*, Beirut: Centre d'Études et de Recherches sur le Moyen-Orient Contemporain, 1996

Debbas, Fouad, *Beyrouth: notre memoire: promenade guidée a travers la collection de cartes postales*, Beirut: Naufal, 1986; as *Beirut, Our Memory: A Guided Tour with Illustrated Postcards from the Collection of Fouad Debbas*, Beirut: Naufal, 1986

Khalaf, Samir, and Philip S. Khoury (editors), *Recovering Beirut: Urban Design and Post-War Reconstruction*, Leiden and New York: E.J. Brill, 1993

Rowe, Peter G., and Hashim Sarkis (editors), *Projecting Beirut: Episodes in the Construction and Reconstruction of a Modern City*, Munich and New York: Prestel, 1998

Saliba, Robert, *Beirut, 1920–1940: Domestic Architecture between Tradition and Modernity*, Beirut: Order of Engineers and Architects, 1998

Salibi, Kamal Suleiman, *A House of Many Mansions: The History of Lebanon Reconsidered*, London: Taurus, and Berkeley: University of California Press, 1988

BELGIUM

At the turn of the century, Belgian architecture played a vital role in the promotion of modern architecture with its Art Nouveau style, developed by the pioneers Victor Horta and Henri van de Velde. Art Nouveau was born as a reaction against the eclectic styles that had prevailed during the 19th century, such as neoclassicism, promoted by the academies, and neo-Gothic styles, taught at the St. Lucas Institutes.

Horta's design for the Tassel House (1893, Brussels) already revealed all the characteristics of this new style: a new language of elegant curvilinear forms, a dynamic manipulation of interior spaces, and a decorative use of steel and wrought iron as structural frames. This project brought him an influx of both private and public commissions in Brussels such as the Maison du Peuple (1899), the architect's own house (1898), the Aubecq House (1899), the Van Eetvelde house (1901), and the Waucquez Department Store (1906).

By 1895 Henri van de Velde, a prolific theorist and the first industrial designer, had designed his own house Bloemenwerf (1895, Uccle/Ukkel, Brussels) as a *Gesamtkunstwerk* (total work of art). Designed to the smallest details, this two-story house comprises a series of irregular polygonal rooms organized around a central hall with an upper balcony. This spatial nucleus acts as a symbolic womb from which art could be generated from within the family core to fight the ugliness that prevailed in contemporary society; the latter concept would become the basic tenet of his theoretical writings.

Reacting against the exuberant curvilinear forms of Art Nouveau, the Viennese architect Josef Hoffmann designed the Palais

Stoclet (1911, Brussels) with simple and pure cubic forms stressing their planarity and rectangularity, an implicit reference to classicism. Although it was quite rare that an international architect would be commissioned for a work in Belgium, this does illustrate the international recognition Belgian architecture received before World War I.

During the Interbellum, Belgian architecture held the function of rebuilding the country. The main task was to provide sound and hygienic houses for the working classes. Louis van der Swaelmen (1883–1929), a landscape architect and an early town planner, promoted the idea of garden cities. Under his direction, a number of architects designed some of the finest examples of collective habitations. Notorious examples are the Small Rusland Industrial District (1923, Zelzate, East Flanders) and the Kapelleveld (1926, St-Lambrechts-Woluwe, Brussels) designed with Huib Hoste (1881–1957), the Cité Moderne (1923, St.-Agatha-Berchem, Brussels) designed with Victor Bourgeois (1897–1962), and the Logis (1927, Boisfort/Bosvoorde, Brussels) developed with Jean-Jules Eggericx (1884–1963).

After his return from Germany, where during the period 1907–14 he was active in the Kunstgewerbe of Weimar, Henri van de Velde, the precursor of the Bauhaus founded by Gropius in 1919, would in 1926 become the first director of the Intsitut Supérieur des Arts Décoratifs (ISAD), also known as La Cambre. La Cambre was to become the leading educational institute where most of the modern architects were trained by the pioneers of the modern movement, such as Louis Van der Swaelmen, Huib Hoste, Victor Bourgeois, Antoine Pompe (1873–1980), and Louis Herman De Koninck (1896–1984).

In 1930 Brussels hosted the third Congrès Internationaux d'Architecture Moderne (CIAM) to discuss the problems of national housing developments and their relationship to public amenities in urban areas. To seek a solution to these architectural and urban problems was the main intent of the Charters of Athens, signed in 1933.

Individual residences remained a more graceful subject to explore the new directions modern architecture could take. In 1927 the painter Guiette invited the French architect Le Corbusier (1887–1965) to design his House and Studio as a variation of his Citronhan house. Van de Velde's built work during this period reveals a more mature modern style. Flat roofs, rounded corners, cantilevered balconies, and carefully selected material textures are some of the main characteristics of La Nouvelle Maison in Tervuren (1928, Brabant). Van de Velde's library building for the University of Ghent (1936, East Flanders) is a concrete building that forms a landmark in the city, with its vertical articulated tower and horizontal building volume that stretches a whole city block.

De Koninck and Bourgeois, two talented and influential architects, promoted the ideas of functional rationalism. Because both were professors at La Cambre, their influence on future generations of architects would be pervasive. Adapting the doctrines of Adolf Loos, De Koninck's projects, such as the Dotremont house (1932, Brussels), reveal a rational synthesis of plan, a technical virtuosity, and an acute sense for spatial composition. As meritorious as these projects are, they remained isolated instances and failed to generate a wide following as most buildings were designed without the intervention of an architect. It was only in 1939, just one year before the outbreak of World War II, that an act was voted to protect the architectural profession, which in turn led to the establishment of the Belgian Order of Architects.

After World War II, the focus once again turned to reconstruction, yet this time the pragmatism and the logic of modernism prevailed. New building programs, major public infrastructures, and sanitation were the main concerns in the larger cities such as Brussels, Ghent, Antwerp, and Liège/Luik. The National Society for Low-Cost Housing (1919), governed by politicians and technicians rather than architects, directed the building industry. CIAM members eagerly awaited commissions to put the ideas of the Athens Charter into practice. These architects proposed developing multistoried buildings; however, most of the rest of the country opted for surface building. Examples of high-rise towers for habitation are Renaat Braem's (1910–) apartment buildings in Kiel (1958, Antwerp); the group EGAU's *Plaine de Droixhe* complex in Liège/Luik (1951–70); and Willy Van Der Meeren's (1923–) social housing high-rise *Ieder Zijn Huis* in Evere (1954, Brabant).

During the 1950s, architects exposed to the progressive movements of the international scene experimented with individual housing projects. The English-born architect Peter Callebout (1916–70), who produced some of the subtlest villas during the 1950s, including his Gerard House (1949, La Plante, Namur), was inspired by Japanese architecture and influenced by Alvar Aalto. The individual residences by Jacques Dupuis (1914–84), such as his Bertrand house (1949, Uccle/Ukkel, Brussels), reveal a more organic approach. The modernism of La Cambre is exemplified by the work of Roger Bastin, such as his design for the Matagne House (1950, Namen/Namur), the architect's own house (1960, Namur/Namen, with G. van Oost), and his St. Nicholas Chapel (1961, Namur/Namen), with its elements of English Brutalism. The modern avant-garde, such as Willy Van Der Meeren—an inventive constructor with a social commitment, sporadically experimented with new formal solutions for a minimal dwelling such as the Ceca houses (1956) in Tervuren.

Early examples of modern public buildings can be found in the coastal city of Ostend. Its Post Office building (1953) designed by Gaston Eysselinck (1907–53); its Townhouse (1954) by Victor Bourgeois; and its Casino (1951) by Leon Stijnen (1899–1990) exemplify how large spatial complexes whose facades contain large portions of glass can create a monumental style.

The 1958 World Exhibition held in Brussels celebrated the victory of modernism, with traditional building being relegated to the Vieux Bruxelles (Old Brussels) area. New materials such as prestressed concrete, tension wires, glass, steel, and aluminum, and innovative structural systems such as rigid shells were exhibited to the public at large. The Philips pavilion by Le Corbusier and Xenaxis and the Marie-Thumas pavilion by L.J. Boucher (1929–), J.P. Blondel (1924–), and O. Filippone (1927–) illustrated how these new systems could be adapted to host a wide variety of functions.

During the early 1960s, project developers and architects alike exploited modernism and the International Style. Architectural practices bloomed, and an ever-spreading growth followed, during which quantity rather than quality would prevail. The different ideologies that had once distinguished the institutes of architectural education had all adopted the modern

International Style, and differences among them would become one of language (Flemish versus French) rather then differences in pedagogy.

In 1968, just ten years after Expo 58, a decisive moment marked a turning point in the Belgian architecture of the 20th century. The student revolts of May 1968 aimed to expose the devastating consequences of a consumption society in general and that of the International Style in particular. The project developers were held accountable for their ever-spreading urge to destruct the old and supplant it with the new without any consideration for social or cultural implications. The demolition of Horta's Maison du Peuple, in 1965, had gone by without any remarkable contest. As a result, two organizations for historic preservation were established that same year: the St. Lucas Archives and the Archives et Recherches de l'Architecture et de l'Urbanisme (ARAU).

Whereas initially these preservation efforts mainly pertained to buildings of previous centuries, during the 1980s attention slowly moved to include buildings from the early 20th century, such as the Interbellum Foundation (1981, Ghent) and the Livres Blancs de l'Agglomeration (1983, Brussels). The latter's main objective was not only to preserve but also to rehabilitate significant buildings to make them economically viable. Because of their efforts, for example, Horta's Wauquez Department Store (1906, Brussels) was converted with considerable success into the Belgian Center for the Strip (1988). To promote modern and contemporary architecture, other foundations were established such as the Stichting Architectuur Museum in Ghent (1983), the Singel Museum in Antwerp (1985), and the Fondation pour l'Architecture Moderne in Brussels (1986).

After the revolts of the sixties, a new generation of architects had to search for a new frame of reference, deal with the issues of how to integrate the old with the new, and reassess their role in society. New campus designs for the Université de Liege, for the Université Catholique de Louvain (UCL), and for the Free University of Brussels (VUB/ULB) offered great opportunities to put into practice some of the answers to these problems. The Sart Tilman campus in Liège created a new urban context with its modern buildings such as the Hospital (1973) by Charles Vandenhove (1927–) and its Sport complex by B. Albert (1949–). The UCL campus of Louvain-la-Neuve in Ottignies with its human scale was modeled after the old Flemish *beguinages*. The new campus for the Medical Faculties of UCL in St. Lambrechts Woluwe (1969, Brussels) offered Lucien Kroll (1929–) the opportunity to implement his methods of user participation.

Integrating modernism with classicism became the main issue during the 1970s and 1980s. Vandenhove devoted himself to create new languages of designs through the stylistic transformation of either regional vernacular or classical styles. Examples of the former are his own house in (Liège) built in 1961 and adapted in 1974; an example of the latter is the Delforge House (1983, Namur), with its reference to Palladian architecture. His assistant, Albert, designed the Villa Herzet (1985, Esneux, Liège) as a Palladian villa, transforming it to adapt it to the sloping site yet respecting its strict bilateral symmetric compostion. The plan is organized around a central hallway that stretches from the entry porch in the front to the garden in the back, where it opens into a semi-circular glass house. In Antwerp Bob van Reeth (1943–) designed the Van Roosmalen House (1988) in reference to the house Loos designed for Josephine Baker in Paris. Located along the terrace promenade of the Schelde, its design has an industrial maritime style with round windows, round corners, and roof terraces reminiscent of the deck of an elegant ocean liner.

During the 1990s, a number of Flemish architects with small practices, such as Stephane Beel (1949–), Luc Deleu (1944–), and Paul Robbrecht (1950–) and Hilde Daem (1950–) have gained some international recognition. The latter's close collaborations with artists have inspired their minimalist approach toward architecture. Noteworthy examples are their projects for the Bacob Bank (1988) in Kerksem and the Canal Houses (1997) in Ghent. The last decade of the century was also marked by the engineered architecture of one of Belgium's largest multidisciplinary firms: Philippe Samyn (1948–) and Partners. Their oeuvre counts numerous industrial projects such as the OCAS Research Center for Steel Applications (1991, Zelzate, East Flanders), the Wallonian Trade Center (1992, Marche en Famenne, Luxembourg), and the Auditorium for the Free University of Brussels (1993). Although this oeuvre can be stylistically characterized as High Tech, it does have some classical aspirations and claims to supply the framework in which life's activities can unfold.

HENDRIKA BUELINCKX

See also **Athens Charter (1943); Brussels, Belgium; Congrès Internationaux d'Architecture Moderne (CIAM, 1927–); Hoffman, Josef (Austria); Horta, Victor (Belgium); Palais Stoclet, Brussels; van de Velde, Henri (Belgium)**

Further Reading

Beekaert, Geert, *Contemporary Architecture in Belgium*, Tielt: Lannoo, 1995

Bontridder, Albert, *L'Architecture Contemporaine en Belgique. Le Dialogue de la Lumière et du Silence*, Antwerp: Hélios, 1963

De Kooning, Mil (editor), *Horta and After: 25 Masters of Modern Architecture in Belgium*, Ghent: University Press, 1999

Dubois, Marc, *Philippe Samyn: Architecture and Engineering 1990–2000*, Basel: Birkhauser, 1999

Jacobs, Steven, *Works in Architecture: Paul Robbrecht & Hide Daem*, Ghent: Ludion Press, 1998

Puttemans, Pierre, and Lucien Hervé, *Architecture Moderne en Belgique*, Brussels: Vokaer, 1974

Strauven, Francis, *L'Architecture en Belgique 1970–1980*, Louvain-la-Neuve: CRA, 1981

Van Bergeijk, Herman, and Otakar Mácel, *Birkhauser Architectural Guide: Belgium, The Netherlands, Luxembourg 20th Century*, Basel: Birkhauser, 1998

BENEVOLO, LEONARDO 1923–

Architecture historian and critic, Italy

Leonardo Benevolo is one of the most prolific writers on architecture in Italy. He was born in Orta in 1923 and graduated from the Faculty of Architecture at the University of Rome in 1946. Throughout his distinguished career as a professor of the history of architecture, he has taught in Rome, Florence, Venice, and at the University of Palermo. He has written more than 20 books on architecture over the last four decades, with a focus on urban design and the problems of the city. Although he is not as widely read as Manfredo Tafuri or Kenneth Frampton, his books serve as important texts in the study of 20th-century architecture, both in Italy and around the world.

Since the early 1960s with *Le origini dell'urbanistica moderna* (*The Origins of Modern Town Planning*), Benevolo has concerned himself with the history and transformations of the city. This book addresses the industrial city, the utopian city, and urban legislation in modern Europe. In 1968, with *L'architettura delle città nell'Italia contemporanea* (The Architecture of Cities in Contemporary Italy), Benevolo addressed the issues surrounding legislation problems in Italy, the historical environment in relation to contemporary construction, and the teaching of architecture and urban planning at the university in Italy. In the same year, his concern with the city was the main focus of *Storia dell'architettura del Rinascimento* (The Architecture of the Renaissance), with chapters on the ideal city and urban transformations in the 16th century. Here Benevolo also focused on the evolution of architectural styles, the invention of new architectures, and the architectural principles of varying periods.

In the early 1970s, Benevolo published *Le avventure della città* (The Adventures of the City), addressing the problems of the relation between the historical center of the city and the *periferia* (outskirts), and the decline and degradation of the Italian city following World War II. Many of the problems of the city are attributed to territorial organizations, which result from the interests of public administrators and private landowners, and are perpetuated by obsolete institutions and customs in Italian society. In 1960 Benevolo published his *Introduzione all'architettura* (Introduction to Architecture), in which he explained the constructive principles of architecture in relation to its historical contexts, examining a range of contexts and surveying architectural types including Greek, Hellenistic, Roman, Byzantine, Romanesque, Gothic, Renaissance, Mannerism, baroque, neoclassical, and modern.

Storia della città (*The History of the City*) is a well-illustrated, four-volume opus of the history of the city divided into antique, medieval, modern, and contemporary periods. The work is an attempt to explain the origin of the city and to tell the basic story of the development of the built environment in the history of civilization. It is intended for the average reader as well as scholars and professionals in the fields of architecture and urban planning. Written in 1960, his two-volume *Storia dell'architettura moderna* (History of Modern Architecture) has significantly impacted the architectural history of the 20th century for the last four decades. The first volume (1760–1914) examines town planning, engineering, and the emergence of the skyscraper and the avant-garde prior to World War I. The second volume (1914–66) isolates the canon of architects and buildings that characterize the Modern movement. Other books that have been translated into English are *Storia dell'architettura del Rinascimento* (*The Architecture of the Renaissance*) and *The Origins of Modern Town Planning, La casa dell'uomo* (*The House of Man*). These analyze the built environment at every level, from the room to the city, and consider the relation between the built environment and the process of design.

In the mid-1980s, Benevolo published *L'ultimo capitolo dell'architettura moderna* (The Final Chapter of Modern Architecture). The title of the book refers to the years 1970–85 and the work of individual architects, such as Kenzo Tange, James Stirling, Charles Moore, and Robert Venturi, and in Italy, Vittorio Gregotti, Renzo Piano, Paolo Portoghesi, and Aldo Rossi. Benevolo analyzes the tendencies of their work and their personalities in order to synthesize the realizations and problems of contemporary architecture. He frames his discussion of the work of this period with a discussion of the late work of the masters of modern architecture: Le Corbusier, Walter Gropius, and Mies van der Rohe.

In the early 1990s, Benevolo refocused his attention on the problems and development of the city. In *La città Italiana nel Rinascimento* (The Italian City in the Renaissance), he analyzes the transformations undergone by Italian cities during the 16th century, with a detailed examination and comparison of city plans from that period. In *La città nella storia d'Europa* (The City in the History of Europe), Benevolo addresses, in more technical terms, issues such as the detachment of the modern world from the ancient world, the idea of the city in classical culture, and the transformations of the city during the Roman Empire. He analyzes the use of perspectival construction in the Renaissance city and the adjustments made necessary by the rules of perspective. He looks at new types of cities, such as the coastal city, the international city, and the industrial city, and addresses the issues facing Europe in confrontation with the new world of the 20th century.

Benevolo is most certainly a historian dedicated to the ideas of the Modern movement and is considered among the most influential writers on architecture and urban planning and the history of the city in the 20th century, in Italy. In his preface to *History of Modern Architecture*, he writes, "The task of a history of modern architecture is to present contemporary events within the framework of their immediate precursors; it must, therefore, go far enough into past history to make a complete understanding of the present possible and to set contemporary events in adequate historical perspective."

John Hendrix

See also **Frampton, Kenneth (United States); Gregotti, Vittorio (Italy); Moore, Charles (United States); Piano, Renzo (Italy); Rossi, Aldo (Italy); Tafuri, Manfredo (Italy); Tange, Kenzo (Japan); Urban Planning; Venturi, Robert (United States)**

Biography

Born in Orta, Italy, 1923. Graduated from the Faculty of Architecture at the University of Rome in 1946. Taught in Rome, Florence, and Venice; professor of the history of architecture at the University of Palermo 2000.

Selected Publications

Introduzione all'architettura, 1960

Storia dell'architettura moderna, 2 vols., 1960; new edition, 1999; as *History of Modern Architecture*, 2 vols., translated by H.J. Landry, 1971

Le origini dell'urbanistica moderna, 1963; as *The Origins of Modern Town Planning*, translated by Judith Landry, 1967

L'architettura delle città nell'Italia contemporanea, 1968; 2nd edition, 1970

Storia dell'architettura del Rinascimento, 2 vols., 1968; 9th edition, 1993; as *The Architecture of the Renaissance*, 2 vols., translated by Judith Landry, 1978

La città Italiana nel Rinascimento, 1969; new edition, 1990
Roma da ieri a domani, 1971
Le avventure della città, 1973; 2nd edition, 1974
Storia della città, 1975; new edition, 1993; as *The History of the City*, translated by Geoffrey Culverwell, 1980
La casa dell'uomo, 1976; 5th edition, 1988
Città in discussione, Venezia e Roma, 1979
Urbanistica e crisi economica, 1979
L'ultimo capitolo dell'architettura moderna, 1985
La città nella storia d'Europa, 1993
The European City, translated by Carl Ipsen, 1993

Further Reading

Ehresmann, Donald L., *Architecture: A Bibliographic Guide to Basic Reference Works, Histories, and Handbooks*, Littleton, Colorado: Libraries Unlimited, 1984
Irace, Fulvio, "Interview with Leonardo Benevolo," *Domus*, 668 (January 1986)
Madanipour, Ali, *Design of Urban Space: An Inquiry into a Socio-Spatial Process*, Chichester, West Sussex, and New York: Wiley, 1996
Morton, P.A., "Pragmatism and Provinciality: Italian Criticism of the American Plan," *Precis*, 4 (1983)
Sutcliffe Anthony, *The History of Urban and Regional Planning: An Annotated Bibliography*, London: Mansell, 1981
Trebbi, Giorgio, "An Archaeological Park for Rome," *Parametro*, 146 (May 1986)

BENETTON FACTORY, ITALY

Designed by Alfra and Tobia Scarpa; 1967–

The Benetton Corporation was a groundbreaking manufacturer both in terms of their interest in design and the transition from manufacturer of goods to the making of a service industry toward the idea of service-oriented production industries of the late 20th century, which created a culture around a product. Their advanced, just-in-time production and continual flow of goods from manufacturing to distribution influenced the layout, design, and siting of their facilities. Spanning three decades of development, these complexes in Treviso, Northern Italy, were designed by Alfra and Tobia Scarpa, architects and industrial designers, who designed not only the factory and administration buildings, but also developed with Benetton a new approach to retail design, which was initiated with their international franchises in the 1960s.

Tobia Scarpa designed the first factory building for Benetton in 1967 in Paderno di Ponzano, Treviso, with Christiano Gasparetto and Carlo Maschietto. The complex, adjacent to an historic villa, comprises an administration building and manufacturing facility identified by the different roofscapes for the two building typologies, setting up a dialogue between the two functions, while creating a sense of the whole site.

The manufacturing facility's primary structure is a girder and parallel series of X-shaped prefabricated concrete beams. The X-shaped beams, 1.3 meters high by 1.3 meters wide with the profile exposed, have skylight glazing in the interstices, bringing light to the manufacturing floor. The beams are supported on the 84-meter-long hollow girder for the entire length of the building, forming the main axis, and by perimeter 9.2-meter-high precast panels walls with a C-shaped section. The X-shaped beams, with their sloped angles, reflect light in the interior and have the double duty of integrating the building systems of pipes and electric wiring through the hollow channel.

The long beam identifies a streetlike spine for local circulation and a wider delivery area bracketed by the production areas. The success of this layout led to its continued use for three additional facilities. Variation in the manufacturing space, through paving and spatial divisions, makes a comfortable rather than overbearing work space.

A courtyard links the manufacturing hall to the administrative offices, a custodian house, and the heating plant. Capping the offices, the architects designed pyramidal roofs with cupola skylights by assembling three triangular 3-inch-thick prefabricated concrete panels, each with a base of 3.9 or 4.5 meters, recalling the surrounding domestic landscape. Reference to the local context is also made evident in the rustic waddle and dab walls, with the sticks still visible.

In 1986 this complex was renovated and expanded to house prototype production, offices for the computer systems, a conference center, a meeting room, and the runways for fashion shows. A 600-car underground garage reduces the use of automobiles at the site and creates unobstructed views to the site. Pedestrian pathways over ramps and arched bridges above water channels create "streets" to lead to displays of Benetton prototype stores.

In 1993–95 Benetton hired the Scarpas to build a two-part manufacturing facility in Castrette di Villorba, Treviso, based on the same layouts as the earlier factories. Castrette's singularity lies in the structural system and unobstructed production space employing a high-tech industrial aesthetic and materiality. The single-story complex was built as two identical 18,000-meter-squared manufacturing buildings in seven, 25-meter modules based on the dimensions of the cotton machines. The factory layout has three distinct areas—centralized assembly, a central roadway spine, and two production areas. The just-in-time production method made the access key to the site, so the architects made the central spine a 40-meter-wide roadway, larger than the earlier factory.

To achieve the essential flexible and unobstructed manufacturing space, the architects employed a structural system developed by Bridon Ropes of Doncaster, England, normally used for bridges and here used for the first time for a factory building. A reinforced concrete pier in the center of each of the seven modules anchors pairs of 25-meter-high steel pylons from which thin steel cables extend to brace the trussed roof. The roof trusses are, in turn, supported on the exterior reinforced concrete walls. The walls are clad with insulated ribbed galvanized steel, creating a horizontal emphasis to the complex. The steel manufacturers dipped the panels in zinc coating to create a herringbone pattern resembling woven fabrics, symbolic of the activity inside. The architects recessed the building under overhanging metal eaves with a wide cantilever over the loading street. On the east and west facades the shed module profile is exposed in the framework of the seven bays. They were also concerned with maintaining the vistas and the landscape, so they lowered the building into the earth for a lower profile. In the below-ground spaces, large skylights illuminate the workers' cafeteria.

The exposed high-tech structure also conceals in its wall panel system a high-tech building technology system of robotic production and computer controls in a fiber-optic cables network and electronic systems. In the 1990s the highly automated system provided information to the administrative offices for the control of 7,500 items every eight hours as they were distributed to Benetton's 7,000 selling points in the world. Both visually and structurally, the building expresses the design, manufacturing, and distribution process of an innovative company.

NINA RAPPAPORT

See also **Factory**

Further Reading

"Scarpa: Stabilimento Benetton a Castrette," *Abitare*, no. 328 (1994)
"Scarpa: New Benetton Factory," *GA Document*, Castrette, no. 38 (1994)
"Una Presenza Forte," *Ottagono*, 28 (1993)
Zardini, Mirko, "Benetton," *Lotus International*, no. 85 (1995)

BERLAGE, HENDRIK PETRUS 1856–1934

Architect, Netherlands

Hendrik Petrus Berlage was one of the most significant European architects before World War I. Often considered the father of modern architecture in the Netherlands, Berlage greatly influenced a generation of architects that included J.J.P. Oud, Gerrit Rietveld, and Mies van der Rohe. His work is known for its transition from 19th-century historicism to new styles and theories of modern architecture. While his early designs were revivalist Dutch Renaissance, in the 1890s Berlage rejected historicism to experiment instead with stylistically innovative forms. Often considered a rationalist, Berlage was similarly noted for his restrained use of ornament and his insistence that the exterior of a building express its interior, functional design. Berlage was a pioneer in the development of 20th-century architecture, and many of his buildings are Dutch cultural landmarks.

Berlage's career falls into three periods: 1878 to 1903, his early work through the completion of the Amsterdam Exchange; 1903 to 1919, his mature period through the termination of his work for the Kröller-Müller family; and his late work from 1920 to 1934, when he turns to Cubist forms. Berlage received his formal architectural training at the Zürich Polytechnic. After extensive travels, he began working in the Amsterdam office of Theo Sanders. When Sanders retired in 1889, Berlage opened an independent office. His first major commission was the purely historicist De Algemeene office building in Amsterdam. His experiments with restrained, stylized historical forms culminated in the Amsterdam Exchange. The five successive Exchange designs (1884–98) show Berlage's transformation from historicism to modernism. Beginning as a Dutch Renaissance palace, the Exchange became an original design, reinterpreting, abstracting, and subjecting historical forms to new ideas about proportion and materials. The Exchange uses a proportional grid of triangular prisms that harmonizes and unifies the exterior. In conception, it drew on history as well, as Berlage sought to adapt a native form for 20th-century use. The first exchanges in the Low Countries had been open courtyards. Berlage kept that basic idea with glass-roofed trading halls surrounded by brick arcades.

After 1913 Berlage became "house architect" for the wealthy Kröller-Müller family and designed several innovative buildings, including the Holland House in London and St. Hubertus near Otterlo. The London building code required that Berlage cover Holland House's steel frame. He chose terra-cotta plates to fill the space and frame the windows. Inside, movable walls divided the office space. Both were innovations. St. Hubertus was an extravagant hunting lodge; its plan takes the form of stylized antlers in reference to the story of St. Hubertus and the stag. The monumental conception has been linked to Wright's designs.

After 1920 Berlage's work began to favor geometry even more vigorously. The best examples of this are the First Church of Christ, Scientist, and the Municipal Museum, both in The Hague. Both buildings are assemblages of cubic prisms in which geometry replaces historical quotations. Another late work is the Amstel Bridge, designed as part of his plan for Amsterdam South. The bridge was a joint effort between Berlage and the city engineer's office and was praised by contemporaries as a socially productive collaboration between state and artist promising cooperation for the future. It combines a decorated bridge with park space for water recreation.

Both 19th-century theorists and 20th-century innovators influenced Berlage. He drew inspiration from Gottfried Semper and Viollet-le-Duc, who admired the organic harmony and holistic creativity of great architecture of the past but who also criticized the cut-and-paste pattern-book copying that had come to dominate 19th-century architecture. Similarly, Berlage argued that the architect should shape useful spaces rather than decorate facades. In his view, a building should express its function from the interior outward rather than allow surface details to dictate room arrangement. Through lectures and essays describing his American travels, Berlage was the first major European architect to publicly declare his interest in the American innovations of Louis Sullivan and Frank Lloyd Wright. Wright's work particularly affected Berlage, confirming the path toward geometric architecture that he had already begun.

Berlage is thus an excellent example of an architect negotiating between the ancients and the moderns. He was interested in developing a newer architectural vocabulary in step with the 20th century while also retaining links to the historical past. His best-known works are modern but based in traditional forms. After 1890 he began to decorate his buildings with geometric, stylized historical motifs. Preferring simple materials to imitations and noting that "genuine plaster is better than false marble" (*Over stijl in bouw- en meubelkunst*, 1904), he liked to use materials in accordance with their natural features. Conversely, he disliked bentwood and the plaster concealment of structural elements, as the exposed iron supports in the trading rooms of the Amsterdam Exchange demonstrate. Berlage was especially fond of brick, a material traditionally associated with Dutch architecture. He retained this link to the past, but he used brick in unorthodox ways, particularly by exposing it as an interior wall element in residences, for example, the Villa Henny (1898) in The Hague. Brick gave mass, strength, and an organic pattern to architectural designs that were intrinsic to the material, not an applied ornament.

Berlage believed that the architect had a social responsibility to improve living conditions. Consequently, beginning around 1900, his interests expanded to include city planning as a means of social amelioration, resulting in expansion plans for several Dutch cities, of which only the plan for South Amsterdam (1915–17) was implemented. Social concerns affected Berlage's interior design as well, which is known for its geometric focus. He explicitly avoided the vegetative forms popular with Art Nou-

Holland House (W.H. Muller office building), London, designed by Hendrik P. Berlage (1915)

veau designers, such as Victor Horta and Henri van de Velde in Belgium, and he was a founder of the anti–Art Nouveau reform design store 't Binnenhuis (the Interior). He was interested in higher aesthetic standards for ordinary objects such as furniture, carpets, books, dishes, and wall coverings and made many designs. His work influenced De Stijl designers, although there was periodic hostility between Berlage and leading figures associated with De Stijl.

TIMOTHY PURSELL

See also **Art Nouveau (Jugendstil); De Stijl; Horta, Victor (Belgium); Mies van der Rohe, Ludwig (Germany); Oud, J.J.P. (Netherlands); Rietveld, Gerrit (Netherlands); Sullivan, Louis (United States); van de Velde, Henri (Belgium); Wright, Frank Lloyd (United States)**

Biography

Born in Amsterdam, 21 February 1856. Studied painting, Rijksakademie van Beeldende Kunsten, Amsterdam 1874–75; studied architecture under Gottfried Semper's followers at the Bauschule, Eidgenössische Polytechnikum (now Eidgenössische Technische Hochschule), Zurich 1875–78; traveled Germany 1879; traveled Italy 1880–81. Married Marie Bienfait 1887. Worked in Arnhem, Netherlands 1879; associate, later designer, office of Theodorus Sanders, Amsterdam 1881–84; partnership with Sanders 1884–89; private practice, The Hague and Amsterdam 1889–1934; after 1899, became involved primarily in urban planning; worked for Müller and Company, traders, Rotterdam 1913–19. Awarded Gold Medal, Royal Institute of British Architects 1932. Died in The Hague, 12 August 1934.

Selected Works

Office Building De Algeemene, Amsterdam, 1892
Office Building De Nederlanden van 1845, The Hague, 1895
Villa Henny, The Hague, 1898
Diamond Workers' Union Building, Amsterdam, 1900
Amsterdam Exchange, 1903
Headquarters for Wm. Müller and Co. "Holland House," London, 1915
Expansion Plan for Amsterdam South, 1917
St. Hubertus Hunting Lodge, Otterlo, 1920
Mercatorplein, Amsterdam, 1925
First Church of Christ, Scientist, The Hague, 1926
Amstel Bridge or Berlage Bridge, Amsterdam, 1932
Municipal Museum, The Hague, 1935

Selected Publications

Over stijl in bouw- en meubelkunst, 1904
Gedanken über den Stil in der Baukunst, 1905
Grundlagen und Entwicklung der Architektur, 1908
Het uitbreidingsplan van 's Gravenhage, 1909
Studies over bouwkunst, stijl en samenleving, 1910
Beschouwingen over bouwkunst en hare ontwikkeling, 1911
"Neure amerikanische Baukunst," *Schweizerische Bauzeitung*, 60, nos. 11–13 (1912)
"Art and the Community," *The Western Architect*, 18 (1912)
"Foundations and Development of Architecture," *The Western Architect*, 18 (1912)
Amerikaansche reisherinneringen, 1913
Normalisatie in woningbouw, 1918
Schoonheid in samenleving, 1919
Hendrik Petrus Berlage: Thoughts on Style, 1886–1909 (a translated anthology), 1996

Further Reading

Bazel, K.P.C. de, et al., *Dr. H.P. Berlage en zijn werk*, Rotterdam: Brusse, 1916
Berlage, Hendrik Petrus, *Dr. H.P. Berlage, bouwmeester*, Rotterdam: Brusse, 1925
Bock, Manfred, *Anfänge einer neuen Architektur: Berlages Beitrag zur architektonischen Kultur der Niederlande im ausgehenden 19. Jahrhundert*, Wiesbaden: Steiner, and The Hague: Staatsuitgeverij, 1983
Bock, Manfred, *H.P. Berlage en Amsterdam*, Amsterdam: Meulenhoff/Landshoff, 1987; as *H.P. Berlage in Amsterdam*, Amsterdam: Architectura and Natura Press, 1992
Polano, Sergio, *Hendrik Petrus Berlage: Opera completa*, Milan: Electa, 1987; as *Hendrik Petrus Berlage: Complete Works*, translated by Marie-Hélène Agüeros and Mayta Munson, London: Butterworth, and New York: Rizzoli, 1988
Reinink, Adriaan W., *Amsterdam en de Beurs van Berlage: Reacties van tijdgenoten* (with English summary), The Hague: Staatsuitgeverij, 1975
Singelenberg, Pieter, *H.P. Berlage: Idea and Style: The Quest for Modern Architecture*, Utrecht: Haentjens Dekker and Gumbert, 1972 (an important monograph)
Singelenberg, Pieter, *H.P. Berlage, bouwmeester, 1856–1934* (exhib. cat.), The Hague: Haags Gemeentemuseum, 1975

BERLIN, GERMANY

Reciprocal reasons justify historians emphasizing the modern era when studying Berlin's architectural history: the sheer amount built and the sheer amount destroyed. Unique among European capitals, Berlin exemplifies both formative dynamism and annihilative zest. Between the German unification and reunification (1871–1991), razing spoke as much as raising—and each still speaks today.

In 1800 Berlin was still a moderate, regional city. Centuries of accommodating the Hohenzollern and their baroque and neoclassical edifices (by Schülters and Schinkel, respectively) added dignity, not development. However, by 1900, Berlin emerged a continental parvenu—an empire seat whose aggregate population had multiplied 15 times (from 170,000 to 2.7 million), making it Europe's third-ranked metropolis and possibly the most densely inhabited. Heavy industry and railway centralization induced immigration, necessitating rapid, blanketing, polycentric growth. *Mietskasernen* (rental barracks) distended outward from the historical kernel on vast blocks. These massive tenements (sometimes of six stories and five communicating courtyards) housed 90 percent of Berliners. Urbanist Werner Hegemann decried this human warehousing. Uncontrolled speculation overran planning; fervid rebuilding followed demolition. Metropolitan Berlin became an amnesic place. A newly emerging citizen, the *blasé flâneur*, roamed bustling streets; sociologists (Franz Hessel and Georg Simmel) were fascinated and repelled. The only parallel to Berlin's demographic and economic dynamism was Chicago—a comparison Mark Twain made. Historical Berlin's attrition, of course, ultimately resulted from more than this recycling. The only parallel in warfare, ruination, and division was, ironically, Jerusalem—a comparison Harry Truman made.

Berlin's "tradition of no traditions" spawned the 20th century's preeminent architectural avant-garde. There was so much to build and so few precedents. While the 19th century's dawning brought Berlin Schinkel's brilliance, its ending offered no comparison. Wilhelmine architecture (1888–1918), named for Germany's last Kaiser, Wilhelm II, was an unsteady, eclectic transplant. Wallot's bombastic Reichstag (1884–94) and Kark and Raschdorff's grandiose Cathedral (1894–1905) were much criticized. Jugendstil barely touched Berlin despite Henry van de Velde's brief stay. Bland, stuccoed brick boxes defined the city. Hints toward a purposefully "reductive" architecture existed, such as Alfred Messel's Wertheim Department Store (1904). Radicalism flourished unchallenged within Berlin's aesthetic neutrality. World War I reinforced this. Although many nations were startled into modernity by mechanized war, Germany (like another subsequent architectural avant-garde center, Russia) abandoned its conservative political and social institutions through abandoning its monarchy.

Heavy industry's futurism imprinted Berlin's architecture. Berlin rode the industrial revolution's second wave, a half century after England's first push. Berlin meant not spinning mills but combustion engines, electricity, and intraurban transportation. The world's first electric trolley originated here (1881). In this utilitarian *Fabrikstadt* (factory city), functionalism was the natural order. To prosper, new building tasks—the industrial elite's manufacturing facilities, the consumer bourgeoisie's department stores and offices, and the proletariat's mass housing—needed solutions. Berlin's technological ascendancy paralleled the rise of steel, glass, and reinforced concrete. A city still becoming, not being, Berlin liberally explored these new typologies and materials.

Berlin's 20th-century architectural pageant was not just prescient but stylistically comprehensive. Berlin respected "orthodox" modernism's mode (Bauhaus rationalism/functionalism) but also cherished modernism's "other" mode (organicism/keneticism). Only 20th-century Helsinki—through Alvar Aalto—could compare in dedication to naturalistic automatism. Berlin bred strident variants of both the "orthodox" and "other" modes: *die neue Sachlichkeit* (the New Objectivity) and Expressionism. Collaborative groups offered solidarity among cacophony. Although Germany overall excelled at this (as the Deutsche Werkbund's Munich 1907 founding shows), Berlin after World War I particularly fostered associations: Walter Gropius's "Arbeitsrat für Kunst" (1918, later fused with the propagandist

"Novembergruppe"); Hugo Häring and Mies van der Rohe's antiestablishment "Der Ring" (1924); and Bruno Taut, Paul Scheerbart, and Hans Scharoun's Gläserne Kette (Glass Chain, 1919–20)—this last an utopian euphoria dedicated to crystalline mountain forms. Peter Behrens, Erich Mendelsohn, Hans Poelzig, and Ludwig Hilberseimer plied these circles. Berlin's commitment to competitions also fostered diversity (continuing into today). Paper architecture thrived. Vying visionary alternatives brought everything before the public. Architecture's exuberance paralleled Berlin's arts—the Dada montagists' nihilism, the German Expressionist painters' ferocious hues, Fritz Lang's metropolitan exposé films, and Bertolt Brecht's theater of critical verity.

Straddling World War I, two successive architectural revolutions swept Berlin. First came Behrens's reification of the industrial "idea." His AEG Turbine Factory (1908–09) created an unexpectedly monumental temple celebrating mass production. Behrens's atelier (where Gropius and Mies schooled) transformed Berlin-Moabit into the world's most technical and representational industrialized district. Berlin became symbolic: no mere metropolis but an "electropolis." The second revolution, after the war, posited and probed the aesthetic binary of *Neue Sachlichkeit* versus Expressionism—a stylistic controversy embroiling Mendelsohn, Poelzig, Mies, and others, with Gropius contributing from the Bauhaus. During the Weimar Republic, Berlin focused Europe's avant-garde architectural debate. The volumetric clarity and dryly "objective" tectonic of Mies's Concrete Office proposal (1922–23) countered against the organic complexity of Poelzig's Grosses Schauspielhaus (1919) and Mendelsohn's Einstein Tower (1920–24) in Potsdam. Yet positions fluctuated. Mendelsohn, although inspired by relativity's indeterminacy at Potsdam, celebrated constructional pragmatism in his Luckenwalde Hat Factory (1921–23). Mies's 1921 Friedrichstrasse Competition project simultaneously presented the competing aesthetics in stark, orthographic stalemate: unrelenting rationalism in section intersected by exuberant Expressionism in plan. Here, Mies fed a Glass Chain crystal through a *Sachlichkeit* slicer, saving and stacking only the repetitive segments from its middle girth. Gropius also vacillated. Expressionist balconies blurred his 1922 unbuilt Chicago Tribune Competition entry's tectonic lucidity. Gradually, Berlin architects reached better syntheses—Emil Fahrenkamp's Shellhaus office block (1930–31) or Mendelsohn's commercial Columbushaus (1931–32). The very fact that Berlin architects promoted commercial architecture to an aesthetically significant task was as important as this stylistic debate.

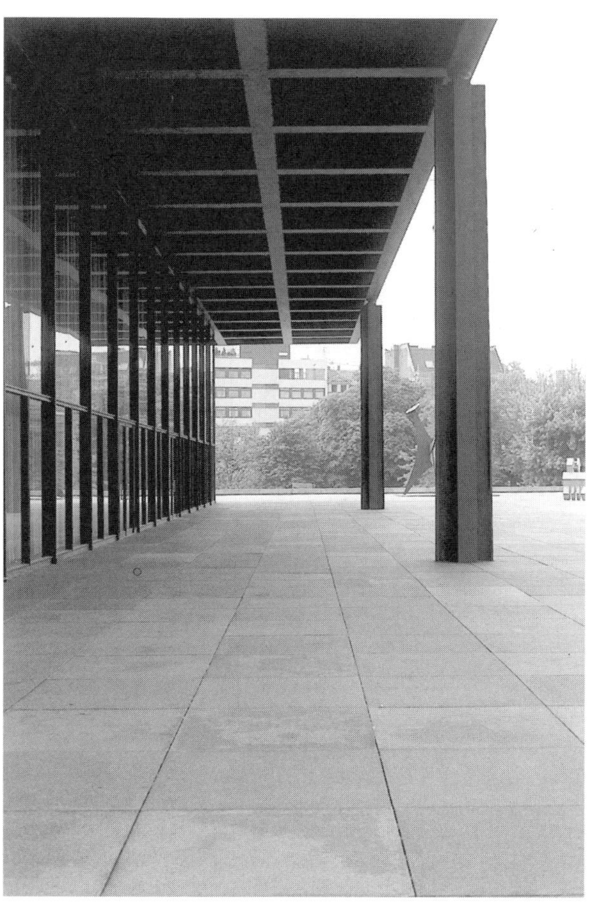

Neue Nationalgalerie, detail (New National Gallery), designed by Mies van der Rohe (1962–68)
© Randall Ott

Weimar Berlin did not ignore social issues during this aesthetic deliberation. In addition to "representing" elite industries and bourgeois commerce, Berlin sought eminence in proletariat housing. Berlin's *Mietskasernen* spawned a "back-to-the-earth" reform movement favoring decentralization. Like other German cities (such as Frankfurt under Ernst May), Berlin took inspiration from Raymond Unwin's pleas for rural tranquility. Conditions were so adverse that benevolent paternalism during late imperial Berlin generated several outlying *Siedlungen* (low-density settlements of minimum dwellings infused with light and air). Results accelerated with the Republic. Companies began paternalistically sponsoring employee housing; gradually boroughs took over, then the city. *Siedlung Lindenhof* (1919–20), an early collaboration between Martin Wagner (soon to be Berlin's Building Commissioner) and Bruno Taut (of Cologne's 1914 Werkbund Exhibition fame), had "Nuremberg" roofs and gables that mimicked "bourgeois-traditional" aesthetics. In 1920 Berlin became Greater Berlin; 93 separate polities united, creating the legal means to reconfigure what was now physically the largest city in Europe. Promulgating tax and interest relief, the Social Democrats engendered cooperatives such as GEHAG (Public Benefit Homestead, Savings, and Building Corporation). These, in aggregate, realized 135,000 units housing 500,000 people between 1924 and 1930.

Most famous was Wagner and Taut's GEHAG-sponsored *Hufeisen* (Horseshoe) *Siedlung* of garden walk-ups in outlying Britz (1925–31). Its open community green spaces and shared facilities were socially progressive. Modernist aesthetics also appeared—continuous flat roofs, horizontal lines, clean surfaces, and cantilevers. Taut felt that this appearance manifested the complex's collective goals. Similar *Siedlungen* followed, such as Wagner, Taut, and Häring's *Onkel-Toms-Hütte* (1926–32) in Zehlendorf, again GEHAG sponsored. By 1928, with the housing crisis still deteriorating citywide, this low-scaled density was questioned. Wagner speculated that only *Großsiedlungen* (taller, denser developments) could answer the need. The Bauhaus-affiliated trio of Gropius, Hilberseimer, and Marcel Breuer pro-

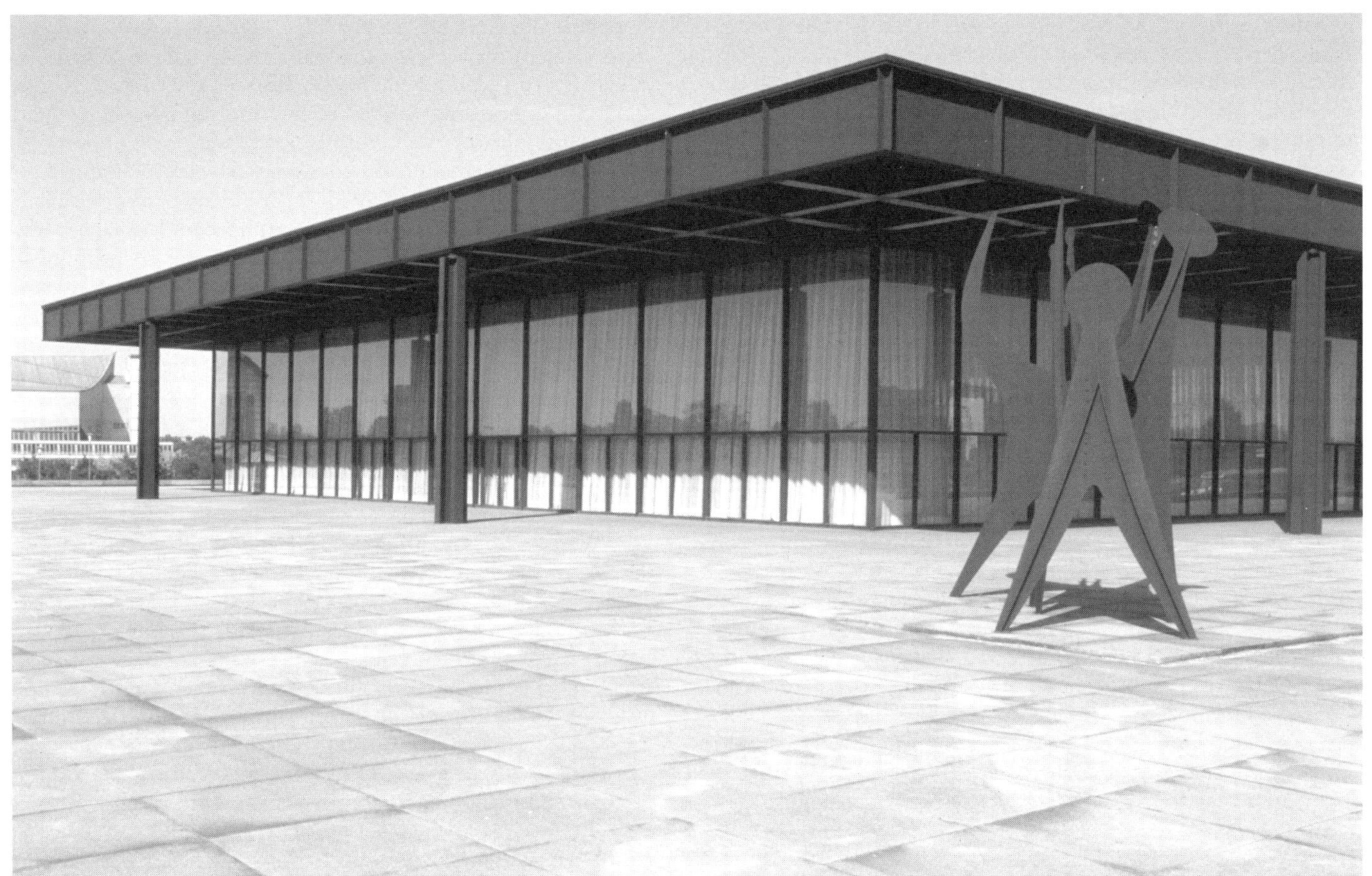

Neue Nationalgalerie, designed by Mies van der Rohe (1962–68)
© Donald Corner and Jenny Young/GreatBuildings.com

duced high-rise competition studies for Berlin reaching to 18 stories. Although no tall slabs materialized, projects of over four stories (lacking immediate access to the ground) appeared on superblocks nearer the city center, subdivided into "row form" configurations prefiguring modernism's later repetitiveness, scalelessness, and obsessiveness (regarding solar orientation). Greater density did allow further collectivist gestures, such as centralized mechanical plants.

Compared with Stuttgart's Weissenhofsiedlung (1927), these projects were technically conservative. Early talk of Fordist/Taylorist production methods was set aside. The emphasis remained on social issues and their aesthetic representation. Modernism's revolutionary "new style" was often conflated with the "new society" during Weimar, as Lane (1968) details, resulting in a highly politicized, even propagandistic, architecture. Government support reinforced this reading. The Nazis took note, deriding Weimar housing's appearance as "Bolshevist." Berlin's Communist Party, ironically, had nothing to do with these projects because it opposed any accommodation with the "corrupt" bourgeois system.

The 1930–31 worldwide economic collapse halted Berlin's social housing experiment, leaving the Nazis to beat a dead horse. Just as the "Brown" cloud approached, Berlin's 1931 Building Exhibition (titled "Dwelling of Our Time") introduced modernism to a wider audience. Berlin's historicist tradition of outstanding villas in suburban districts (Hermann Muthesius's 1907–08 half-timbered Haus Freudenberg or Behrens's 1911–12 classical Haus Wiegand) had already been updated with Hans and Wassili Luckhardt's Le Corbusian Zwei Einfamilienhäuser (1928) and Mendelsohn's Expressionist Haus Sternefeld (1924). Yet the 1931 Exhibition publicly interjected "Bolshevist" aesthetics into bourgeois—as opposed to proletariat—homes. Mies translated his German Pavilion at Barcelona into a lush exhibit house that the Nazis labeled a "horse stable."

Though grand planners, Berlin's Nazis built little. Only bits survive—such as Ernst Sagebiel's Aviation Ministry (1936–37) and Tempelhof Airport (1936–41). Hitler impacted modernism not through buildings but inadvertently through expellant "gifts" (mostly to the United States—Gropius, Mies, and ultimately Mendelsohn). Although architecture—the "Word in Stone"—was critical to Hitler's ideological program, it proved too costly after his war machine's ignition. Still, until the bitter end, Hitler crouched as amateur architect over vast models with his amanuensis, Albert Speer. How sad for the profession that the 20th-century leader most architecturally impassioned was a tasteless criminal. Hitler's architectural proclivities were vivid—a reactionary parochialism intended to resist "Bolshevist" cosmopolitanism and a perdurable monumentality in keeping with world domination. As Nazi preferences hardened, the Dessau Bauhaus was chased to Berlin (during Mies's directorate), where the Gestapo finally padlocked it. Nazi aesthetics mirrored—with opposing predilection—the Weimar Socialists' belief that architectural style symbolized specific political views. However, the Nazis added a destructive, racist edge. The Nazi-fomented *Kristallnacht* (Night of Broken Glass, 1938) saw 9 of 12 Berlin synagogues aflame, including Ehrenfried Hessel's famed Fasanenstraße Temple (1912).

Speer's New Chancellery expansion (1938–39) housed Hitler. Stretching an intimidating quarter mile, its 480-foot gallery doubled the length of Versailles' Hall of Mirrors. Hypertrophy drained Speer's classicism of all humanism (entasis, for example, disappeared). Megalomania roamed across Speer's unrealized "Germania" Berlin Plan (1937–42). This north/south avenue connected an 825-foot-diameter rotunda and 400-foot-high triumphal arch. Contemporary praise of Speer (Krier, 1985) ignores his errors. Speer blithely muffed axial transitions any Beaux-Arts journeyman could manage. Existing conditions at the Chancellery necessitated a slight axial rotation. Speer properly positioned a "Round Hall" to resolve this, then neglected to utilize it, merely crimping the bend within the *poché*. Where his Berlin Plan's axis turned, he positioned his gargantuan rotunda but again earned no profit. The existing Reichstag, which Hitler wanted incorporated into "Germania," had been built several degrees shy of due north/south. Speer merely ignored this, causing one side of his grand plaza to warp bizarrely. Speer's architectural goose-stepping could successfully accommodate only 4 of the 360 compass degrees.

In 1943 the Western Allies launched the aerial Battle of Berlin. By 1945 incendiary phosphorous had consumed 70 percent of the city's center and 1.5 million Berliners' homes. Soviet shelling came next, then tanks and capitulation. Only outlying *Mietskasernen* and *Siedlungen* escaped unscathed. "Quadrasectioning" ensued; apportionments observed Berlin's 20 districts—six falling American, four British, two French, and eight Soviet (including *Mitte*, the historical kernel containing Schinkel's battered works). From Berlin's ceremonial remnants, ideological sterilization claimed further shares. Between 1947 and 1951, the standing walls of the Hohenzollern Stadtschloss and Hitler's New Chancellery in the Soviet sector and the Gestapo's headquarters at the Prinz-Albrecht-Palais (once renovated by Schinkel) in the American were dynamited.

Devastation opened possibilities for restructuring the unplanned Moloch that Berlin had become. The Soviets, first on the scene, named Scharoun "City Architect." Though he would serve a mere year, the former Glass Chain Expressionist gained prominence in postwar Berlin. Immediately, he formed the *Planungs-Kollektiv*, which by 1946 proposed the city's dissolution into more manageable, picturesquely "organic" neighborhoods. Rubble clearance and infrastructure rigidity prevented any action. After losing his post, Scharoun pressed forward with a lyrical housing plan (1949) for the bombed-out, Soviet-controlled Friedrichshain district. However, as the Communist's massive Berlin-Treptow victory monument (1947–48) foretold, modernism had scant future in the Soviet sector. In the Soviet Union, the "Constructivist versus traditionalist" debate ended by 1934; socialist realism's pseudoclassicism triumphed. Once East Germany achieved statehood with East Berlin as capital (1949), the Stalinist aesthetic of "Progressive Tradition" was imposed. Apparatchiks attacked modernism (both Berliner modes) as formalist, cosmopolitan, and decadent. Scharoun's Friedrichshain plan was shelved. Stalinallee (1952–60) emerged instead—a mile-long avenue of housing reminiscent of Moscow's Gorky Street, with sculpted street walls of symmetrically ponderous, tripartite, pilastered facades by various architectural cooperatives (spearheaded by Hermann Henselmann, a chameleon who had conveniently renounced his own Bauhaus work).

As division's reality settled in, the West responded with showpiece housing of its own: the 1957 Interbau Hansaviertel district (a western bombed-out zone). A consciously international team of 53 architects representing 14 countries (including Aalto and Oscar Niemeyer) created a medley of loosely grouped, reinforced-concrete point blocks and slabs. Yet Hansaviertel's Progressivism rapidly seemed as superficially clichéd as Stalinallee's regressive pomposity. Conventional flats, dressed in gratuitously variegated balcony rhythms, rested on Le Corbusiersian stilts. For the same exhibition but on a distant site, Le Corbusier gave West Berlin an "authentic" knockoff of his Marseilles *Unité*. Also for the exhibition, the United States presented Berlin with Hugh Stubbins's Kongresshalle (1956–57)—a suspended hyperbolic paraboloid that became something of a technological "gift horse" when one arch collapsed in 1980. More evocative of modernism's continued viability was Egon Eiermannn's Kaiser-Wilhelm-Gedächtniskirche reconstruction (Memorial Church, 1957–63). Movingly preserving fragments of the bombing's "zero hour," when time stopped, this dark stained-glass honeycomb increasingly became the unofficial architectural symbol of West Berlin's island vigil. Western dreams of urban reunification continued with the Hauptstadt Berlin competition ignoring the city's division (1959).

In 1954 Nikita Khrushchev began attacking Stalinist architecture. Modernist slabs gradually rose in East Berlin. Yet just as the ideological combatants' aesthetics aligned, physical separation heightened. In 1961 a 102.5-mile "Wall"—Berlin's most famously infamous edifice—encircled the Western enclave as an "Antifascist Protective Barrier." The Cold War stalemate's face, it became the 20th century's most sublimely meaningful construction. As Baker (1993) notes, the Wall evolved through several "generations." First came an improvised breeze block and barbed-wire barrier. Next was a "lollipop" profile of stacked, prefabricated, asbestos-stoked concrete panels crowned with a rounded pipe denying purchase to grappling hooks. Last was a massively prefabricated L section, also round capped, with its foot pointing toward East Berlin to prevent overturning in an imagined Western attack (and also escape by digging). Formidable as these variants became, it was open space, not the Wall, that killed (122 or more times). The Wall delimited a death strip (often hundreds of meters wide, with watchtowers, lights, and dog runs), sandwiched by a second barrier of concrete or barbed wire. This strip necessitated demolition of many square miles of East Berlin's adjoining neighborhoods, including churches. To West Berlin, only the smooth backside of the L showed—the ultimate in *Neue Sachlichkeit* aesthetics, soon daubed with gorgeous graffiti. Standardization of construction components passed a critical test at the Wall. Gradually, satellite towns of grim, cratelike prefabricated housing ringed the East (the *Plattenbau* of Marzhan, Hohenschönhausen, and Hellersdorf). The West's satellites, Märkisches Viertel (1963–74) and Gropiusstadt (1962–72), bared similarity.

Absolute division exacerbated Berlin's preexisting polycentrism. Through rival "centers," both ideologies sought urban "wholeness." The East's path was governmental and bland; the West's cultural and heterogeneous. In the old kernel, the Communists' curtain-wall "Palace of the Republic" usurped the site of the Hohenzollern Stadtschloss. Schinkel's Bauakademie was razed (1961–62), making way for the Foreign Ministry's morose white slab. A symbolically assertive 365-meter Television Tower (1965–69) leapt from nearby Alexanderplatz. Vast seas of empty pavement awaited rallies. The West, lacking federal presence, responded with Kulturforum—a diffusely suburbanized zone, where Scharoun's ecstatic Philharmonie and Staatsbibliothek (1960–63, 1967–76) jostled with Mies's silent Neue Nationalgalerie (1965–68). Expressionism again confronted *Neue Sachlichkeit.* Swathes of arterial green space, as crippling to urbanism as the East's barren plazas, ran between. Nearby, Hentrich and Petschnigg's Europa Center (1965), an echo of Skidmore, Owings and Merrill's New York Lever House, capped the chic Kürfurstendamm. American design principles settled heavily on West Berlin.

Postmodernism in West Berlin invoked "critical reconstruction" as urban tonic. Promoted by Josef Paul Kleihues (1987), this "anti-Hansaviertel" methodology respected traditional street lines and block heights in healing rent urban fabric. Its manifestation was the IBA (International Building Exposition, 1984–87), celebrating Berlin's 750th anniversary. Titled "living in the city," IBA fostered midscale housing in-fill in five Berlin districts by international and German architects—Aldo Rossi, John Hejduk, Charles Moore, Peter Eisenman, Rob Krier, Oswald Mathias Ungers, and others. Nonhousing projects included James Stirling's Berlin Science Center (1984–87) and, consistent with Berlin's traditional interest in technological architecture, Gustav Peichl's Phosphate Elimination Plant (1981–85). The results, both sober and meretricious, succeeded in keeping the divided city in the architectural spotlight, even as its schizophrenic cachet aged. Critical reconstruction touched the East, too, in the historicist re-creation of the Nikolai Quarter (also celebrating the anniversary). The West snubbed this as kitsch.

The Wall and East Germany's collapse in 1989 unleashed startling development pressures. Construction cranes laced the sky, as the surreal transmogrification from ideological battleground to world corporate and financial center began. Traffic, never an issue in circumscribed West Berlin, exploded overnight. The Wall, instantaneously a commodity, was chipped to bits, its best graffiti-carrying segments sold to museums (only a few lengths remained in situ, with one inaugurated as a Wall Memorial in 1998). Public planning commenced only following German reunification and the election of a unified Berlin city council in late 1990. Berlin's close victory in the 1991 vote to move the federal seat from Bonn opened the need for a wholly reconfigured capital, a task exceeding even François Mitterrand's revitalization of Paris during the 1980s. A plethora of raucous competitions followed.

Potsdamerplatz, lying across the Wall's wound (between the East's old kernel and the West's Kulturforum), developed first, with Sony, Daimler Benz, and others grabbing turf. The city launched a competition to reassert control. The results prefigured a duality that recurred throughout the 1990s: a choice between exuberant narcissism and the "sturdy stuff" of old Prussia. A desire to celebrate Berlin's 20th-century ethos of diversity, discontinuity, and rupture clashed with a desire to return to (an imagined) 18th-century historical normalcy through critical reconstruction. Selected was Hilmer and Sattler's restatement of blocky, continuous urbanism (though this came too late to tame Helmut Jahn's gesticulating Sony complex). More conservatism would follow. Hans Stimmann, Berlin's new building commissioner, felt that Berlin was destroyed as much by postwar planners as by Allied bombs. Height limitations (22-meter facades), masonry stipulations, and requirements for housing were imposed. Stimman's ideals were attacked as a "New Teutonia."

Berlin's affinity for demolition continued into the post-Wall era. East Germany's Foreign Ministry was razed (1995), purportedly to make way for the improbable rebuilding of Schinkel's Bauakademie. A scaffold and canvas mock-up of the Stadtschloß (1993) seriously threatened the Communist "Palace of the Republic." Economic realities alone forced government re-use of a number of threatened Nazi office structures.

The 1992 Spreebogen competition for Germany's new federal zone attracted 835 entries from 44 countries (but few from Eastern architects; new Berlin began on Western terms). The site, adjoining the Reichstag, passed over the positional ghost of Speer's north/south axis. Given this "counterprecedent," an east/west axial composition was purposefully selected. This, by Axel Schultes, symbolically bridged the divided city's halves, giving attention to reestablishing the district's interrupted tissue. Schultes also won the competition for a new Federal Chancellery (1994). Both of Schultes's schemes assumed blocky forms. England's Sir Norman Foster prevailed in the Reichstag renovation competition, providing a new high-tech dome after controversy prevented his winning proposal's immense, tented canopy (1994–2000). A squat, elliptical doughnut scheme by Gruber and Kleine-Kraneburg won the Presidential Office competition (1994).

As Balfour (1995) reported, disappointment grew with each announcement. Faced with an opportunity that actually justifies the word "millennial," Berlin's almost complete reliance on "sturdy stuff" deflates imagination. A signal exception is Daniel Libeskind's Jewish Museum addition to the Berlin Museum (1993–96). Harrowed with history yet never witnessed before, this work, like Eiermann's Memorial Church, is an expression of 20th-century architecture's potential to speak of a future that mournfully roots but never enslaves itself to the past. This should be new/old Berlin—a place of reciprocal tension.

RANDALL OTT

See also **Behrens, Peter (Germany); Einstein Tower, Potsdam, Germany; Expressionism; Germany; Gropius, Walter (Germany); Mendelsohn, Erich (Germany, United States); Meyer, Hannes (Germany); Mies van der Rohe, Ludwig (Germany); Scharoun, Hans (Germany); Taut, Bruno (Germany); Wagner, Otto (Austria)**

Further Reading

Åman, Anders, *Architecture and Ideology in Eastern Europe during the Stalin Era: An Aspect of Cold War History*, Roger and Kerstin Tanner translator, Cambridge, Massachusetts: MIT Press; Architectural History Foundation, 1992

Baker, Frederick, "The Berlin Wall: Production, Preservation, and Consumption of a Twentieth-Century Monument," *Antiquity*, 67, 257 (1993)

Balfour, Alan, *Berlin: The Politics of Order, 1737–1989*, New York: Rizzoli, 1990
Balfour, Alan (editor), *World Cities: Berlin*, London: Academy Editions, 1995
Buddenseig, Tilmann (editor), *Berlin 1900–1933: Architecture and Design*, Berlin: Gebr. Mann Verlag, 1987
Buddenseig, Tilmann, Henning Rogge, et al., *Industriekulture: Peter Behrens and the AEG, 1907–1914*, Cambridge, Massachusetts: MIT Press, 1984
Helmer, Stephen D., *Hitler's Berlin: The Speer Plans for Reshaping the Central City*, Ann Arbor, Michigan: UMI Research Press, 1985
Kleihues, Josef P., and Heinrich Klotz (editors), *International Building Exposition Berlin 1987: Examples of a New Architecture*, New York: Rizzoli, 1987
Kleihues, Josef Paul, and Christina Rathgeber (editors), *Berlin-New York: Like and Unlike: Essays on Architecture and Art from 1870 to the Present*, New York: Rizzoli, 1993
Krier, Leon, *Albert Speer: Architecture, 1932–1942*, Brussels: Archives d'Architecture Moderne, Editions, 1985
Ladd, Brian, *The Ghosts of Berlin: Confronting German History in the Urban Landscape*, Chicago: University of Chicago Press, 1997
Lane, Barbara Miller, *Architecture and Politics in Germany, 1918–1945*, Cambridge, Massachusetts: Harvard University Press, 1968; reprint 1985
Taylor, Robert R., *"The Word in Stone," The Role of Architecture in the National Socialist Ideology*, Berkeley: University of California Press, 1974
Wiedenhoeft, Ronald V., *Berlin's Housing Revolution: German Reform in the 1920's*, Ann Arbor, Michigan: UMI Research Press, 1985
Wise, Michael Z., *Capital Dilemma: Germany's Search for a New Architecture of Democracy*, New York: Princeton Architectural Press, 1998

BERLIN PHILHARMONIC CONCERT HALL

Designed by Hans Scharoun; completed 1963
Berlin, Germany

In 1956 Hans Scharoun (1893–1972) won an invited competition of 12 architects to design a home for Germany's premier orchestra. Now considered to be one of Scharoun's crowning achievements, the Berlin Philharmonic Concert Hall (1963) is outstanding both for its auditorium design and for its dynamic spatial experiences. The site in Berlin originally chosen for the competition was on the Bundesallee adjacent to a 19th-century school, the Joachimsthaler. Scharoun's design used the Philharmonic building to create a public square on axis with Stüler's Matthäi Church. In 1959, however, the Berlin Senate changed the site to the Tiergarten in anticipation of the development of a new cultural center for the city of Berlin, an attempt to revitalize an area that had been devastated in the war. The basic form and concept of Scharoun's design remained the same, but he adjusted the configuration of the foyer and ancillary spaces to accommodate the new site. Scharoun completed the adaptations and overseeing of the construction in conjunction with the architect Werner Weber. Work proceeded rapidly, and within three years of the laying of the foundation stone in 1960, the auditorium opened on 15 October 1963 with a concert directed by Herbert von Karajan, a supporter of Scharoun in the early phases of the competition.

At the time of its completion, both the critics and the public lauded the auditorium design for its innovation, but they derided the exterior form, likening its sweeping roofs to a circus tent. Originally left as rough-finished concrete and painted a yellow ochre color reminiscent of many of the historic buildings in Berlin, the exterior of the auditorium was faced in the 1980s with golden anodized aluminum panels, further accentuating the central form. In a striking contrast to the dominance of the central auditorium is the three-story administrative wing, which angles away from the auditorium as a painted white rectangular mass.

Particularly significant, however, is the fact that Scharoun, who considered the creation of interior and exterior spaces of equal importance, used the foyer as a mediating space so that both site and auditorium requirements could be accommodated. The foyer reaches out into the site, drawing the visitor into the entry, where, once inside, he or she confronts a dynamic, fluid space. Angled walls break up the edges of the foyer, blurring the boundaries between one area and another. Located near the entry are amenities, such as ticket booths and coat rooms, which are split between the multiple levels. Within the foyer, dramatic stairs rise seemingly at random but are actually artfully controlled and successfully accommodate the large number of people attending the performances. Using the placement of the stairs to guide circulation, Scharoun creates a dynamic nonhierarchical yet elegant spatial experience that removes the visitor psychologically from the world outside.

Scharoun's concern for the relationship of the individual to the community carried over into his design of the Philharmonic. He assembled a group of artists and engineers whose work underscores his theories. Erich Fritz Reuter's slate mosaic floor patterns guide the visitor through the foyer toward the two main stairs, which are further highlighted by Alexander Camaro's colored-glass windows and a sloping glass skylight. Light, shadow, and subtle color activate the daytime experience of the foyer. In contrast, the evening lighting is more subdued, with pendant "dandelion" lights designed by Günther Symmank and lit handrails along the stairs.

Exceedingly aware of the cultural and political importance of the building, Scharoun designed an architectural experience that creates a community through the dissolution of traditional barriers between the listeners and the performers. Scharoun explained the generative idea for his design as "music in the centre—this, from the very beginning, has been the guiding principle which has shaped the new Philharmonic auditorium." In addition to his generative concept of the centralized performance space, Scharoun described the auditorium metaphorically as a landscape where banks of angled seating become "vineyards" sloping into the "valley" of the stage and the ceiling a "skyscape" floating above. The angled groups of seating prevent the creation of a single focal point, forcing the viewers to visually address the other listeners, thus subduing the overall symmetry of the plan. The auditorium is equipped with a 72-register organ built by Schuke with Professor Michael Schneider, facilities for television production and recording, locations throughout for small additional groups of musicians, and the ability to lower the orchestra floor in sections to accommodate a variety of performance types. None of the 2,218 seats, however, is more than 100 feet away from the stage, and only 270 seats are located

Berlin Philharmonic Concert Hall, designed by Hans Scharoun (1963)

behind the orchestra. The overall impression in the auditorium remains one of intimacy.

The acoustical design of the auditorium was one of Scharoun's primary concerns. Through his work with the engineer Lothar Cremer, they achieved reverberation times in the auditorium ranging between 2 and 2.4 seconds. A triple-shell roof system and double-wall design buffer the auditorium from outside noise, and the limestone walls surrounding the orchestra act as reflectors.

Currently, adjacent to the Philharmonic Concert Hall is the Chamber Music Hall (1978). Although the initial sketch was by Scharoun, Edgar Wisniewski completed the hall after Scharoun's death. Unfortunately, Scharoun's original ideas regarding the siting of the Philharmonic were never completed. Later, in conjunction with his design of the State Library (1967–78), Scharoun produced another site design that included the Philharmonic site. However, this was never completed either, and there remains a disjointed quality to the site.

The recent resurgence of interest in Scharoun's work in general and the Philharmonic Concert Hall in particular indicates the influence of his work beyond the labels of German Expressionist or organic architecture, an interest gained from his friend Hugo Häring. Scharoun's prioritization of spatial experiences and expressive designs has influenced many later 20th-century architects. The Berlin Philharmonic Concert Hall remains one of the most unique architectural spatial experiences, as well as one of the most successful concert halls built to date, and is a flourishing cultural addition to the city of Berlin.

KATHERINE WHEELER BORUM

See also **Acoustics; Expressionism; Scharoun, Hans (Germany)**

Further Reading

Bürkle, J. Christoph, *Hans Scharoun und die Moderne*, Frankfurt: Campus, 1986; as *Hans Scharoun*, Zurich: Artemis, 1993

Conrads, Ulrich, *Berlin Philharmonie*, Berlin: Lettner-Verlag, 1964

Frampton, Kenneth, "Genesis of the Philharmonie," *Architectural Design*, 35 (March 1965)

Futagawa, Yukio, and Hiroshi Sasaki (editors), *The Berlin Philharmonic Concert Hall, Berlin, West Germany*, Tokyo: A.D.A. Edita Tokyo, 1973; revised edition, 1976

Janofske, Eckhard, "Meaning from Contrast: Scharoun's Philharmonic in Berlin," *Daidalos*, 3 (March 1982)

Jones, Peter Blundell, *Hans Scharoun: A Monograph*, London: Gordon Frasier Gallery, 1978

Jones, Peter Blundell, "Hans Scharoun: An Introduction," *Architectural Design*, 48, no. 7 (1978)

Jones, Peter Blundell, "Organic versus Classic," *Architectural Association Quarterly*, 10, no. 10 (1978)

Jones, Peter Blundell, "From the Neoclassical Axis to Aperspective Space," *Architectural Review*, 183 (March 1988)
Jones, Peter Blundell, *Hans Scharoun*, London: Phaidon, 1995
Lanier, R.S., "Acoustics in-the-Round at the Berlin Philharmonic," *Architectural Forum*, 120 (May 1964)
Pehnt, Wolfgang, *Die Architektur des Expressionismus*, Stuttgart, Germany: Hatje, 1973; 3rd edition, Ostfildern-Ruit: Hatje, 1998; as *Expressionist Architecture*, London: Thames and Hudson, and New York: Praeger, 1973
"The Philharmonie, West Berlin," *Architectural Design*, 35 (March 1965)
Posener, Julius, "Philharmonie Concert-Hall, Berlin," *Architectural Review*, 135 (May 1964)
Segal, Walter, "Scharoun," *Architectural Review*, 153 (February 1973)

BERLIN WALL, BERLIN 1961–89

The Berlin Wall stood in Berlin, Germany, for 28 years, 2 months, and 26 days. However, it was not just any wall—it was *the* Wall: politically, a symbol of the post–World War II Cold War world order; architecturally, an example of the power of the most basic building block of architecture; and artistically, a giant 166-kilometer-long blank canvas.

After the defeat of the Third Reich in 1945, both Germany and its capital, Berlin, were partitioned into four zones, each under the administration of one of the Allies: Great Britain, France, the United States, and the USSR. The partition of Germany was done so along existing provincial boundaries. The partition of Berlin, which was located in the middle of the Soviet sector, was done so in terms of postal codes.

In 1949 the French-, British-, and American-controlled sectors were merged to form the Federal Republic of Germany (FRG), with Bonn as its capital. In that same year, the Soviet-controlled eastern quarter of Germany became the German Democratic Republic (GDR), with (East) Berlin as its capital. Although the USSR proclaimed the sovereignty of the GDR in 1954, East Germany effectively was an internally run satellite of the USSR.

Between the years 1949 and 1961, it is estimated that approximately three million people, or roughly one-sixth of the population, fled from the GDR to the West. This exodus occurred both along the 1,400-kilometer border with the FRG and from East to West Berlin. Because the refugees were from all professions and mostly under the age of 25, the GDR soon faced a social and economic crisis, especially in terms of the loss of trained and specialist personnel.

To stop this flow of refugees, armed units of the GDR began to seal off the open border between East and West Berlin in the early morning of 13 August 1961. The border between the GDR and the FRG was also sealed, and West Berlin became, in effect, an island in the middle of the GDR. The justification for these fortifications was clear in the GDR's name for them—"the anti-fascist protective barrier"—suggesting the prevention of the West from coming in, not the prevention of the East from going out.

At first the Berlin Wall was merely a hastily constructed barbed-wire fence with armed guards. During the remainder of 1961, these initial fortifications rapidly grew more sophisticated. In front of the Brandenburg Gate, soldiers constructed a seven-foot-high (2.1 meters), six-foot-deep (1.8 meters) tankproof barrier with steel posts and prefabricated concrete slabs laid flat and held with mortar. Elsewhere in Berlin, concrete slabs were laid vertically and then topped off with square concrete blocks and barbed wire.

On the eastern side of the Wall, the GDR then slowly began to construct a no-man's land. First, a second wall was built approximately one city block (100 meters) into East Berlin. This system was perfected with lookout towers, searchlights, tank traps, dog runs, trip wires, alarmed fences, and ditches in between the two walls. Then the above-ground division was doubled underground as Berlin's subway lines were severed and terminated at the border. Eventually, all roads, train lines, canals, and other transportation routes in and out of West Berlin were either severed or controlled by GDR border police.

In some areas of Berlin, the East-West border ran right down the middle of a street, thanks to the previously mentioned decision to use postal codes as the division line. In these locations, the buildings on the East were evacuated and their openings bricked up, effectively making the buildings themselves the Berlin Wall. Eventually, these buildings and also the early versions of the Wall were demolished and replaced with the superefficient "fourth generation," or 1979 version, which proved to be the most famous. It consisted of four-foot-wide (1.2 meters) prefabricated concrete L-shaped panels nearly 12 feet (3.6 meters) high, laid side-by-side in mortar and topped with a round concrete tube. Each panel weighed 2.6 tons and had to be installed with a crane.

This last version of the Berlin Wall is the one that became famous for its graffiti. Soon after the 1979 version was built, all sorts of comments, slogans, stories, constructions, figures, and grotesque fantasies began to be written, stenciled, and painted onto it. Every year, the GDR border guards would dutifully paint over these scribbles in a futile attempt to draw attention away from them, and every year the Wall would fill right back up with its multicolored messages.

The Wall soon became no longer a thorn in the side of West Berlin but rather an asset, almost a tourist attraction. Tourists from around the world no longer came to West Berlin to take in an opera or to visit a museum but rather to marvel at this three-dimensional expression of an arbitrary line on the map. The American artist Keith Haring painted a vast stretch near "Checkpoint Charlie" in 1986 and held a press conference afterward. After that point, the Wall was considered art.

The beginnings of the fall of the Berlin Wall can be traced to the 1985 election of Mikhail Gorbachev as general secretary of the Communist Party of the Soviet Union. Gorbachev's policies, which allowed the satellite nations of Eastern Europe to determine their own affairs, brought about demands in those countries for more freedom. In May 1989 the Hungarian government opened its border with Austria, thereby lifting Churchill's famous "iron curtain" and allowing GDR citizens to travel to the West via Hungary. On 9 November 1989 the GDR announced on the radio that all citizens were free to travel wherever they wanted. This decree effectively rendered the Berlin Wall useless.

Within one year, the Berlin Wall was practically destroyed by both angry East Germans and hungry souvenir hunters. Other parts were dismantled and recycled for road construction. On 3 October 1990 East and West Germany were officially unified into a single Federal Republic of Germany. In 1995 one watchtower and four stretches of the remaining Berlin Wall totaling 1.71 kilometers were placed under protection and designated as historical monuments. The Wall thus officially became history.

CHRISTOPHER WILSON

See also **Berlin, Germany; Fascist Architecture**

Further Reading

Möbius, Peter, and Helmut Trotnow, *Mauern sind nicht für ewig gebaut: zur Geschichte der Berliner Mauer* (Walls Are Not Built Forever: On the History of the Berlin Wall), Frankfurt: Propylaen, 1990

Read, Anthony, and David Fisher, *Berlin: Biography of a City*, London: Hutchinson, and New York: Norton, 1994

Schürer, Ernst, Manfred Keune, and Philip Jenkins (editors), *The Berlin Wall: Representations and Perspectives*, New York: Peter Lang, 1996

Waldenburg, Hermann, *The Berlin Wall Book*, London: Thames and Hudson, 1990

BEST PRODUCTS SHOWROOM

Designed by SITE; completed 1975
Houston, Texas

The Best Products building located in Houston, Texas, also known as the "indeterminate facade," was built in 1975 as a showroom by the architectural firm SITE for the Best Products retail chain. The building is known mainly for its idiosyncratic facade, which wraps a 65,000-square-foot, commercial-formula building with a high brick wall that appears to be in the act of collapsing. The extended cornice is given an irregular profile as though it were coming apart, and atop the entrance a massive pile of bricks tumbles through a gap, resting precariously on a thin metal canopy. The building presents a startling image when viewed within its suburban context, a strip center located between Almeda Mall Shopping Center and a residential neighborhood along the Gulf Freeway. Visitors' reactions to the building have ranged from amusement to concerns for the safety of the occupants; a common conjecture soon after the building opened was that it was damaged by a Gulf coast hurricane or an earthquake. The apocalyptic vision was, of course, apocryphal; inside the building it was business as usual.

The Houston showroom is one of several unusual designs that SITE produced for the Richmond, Virginia–based company, each of them involving an eye-catching embellishment of the facade. The commissions were in no small measure owing to the patronage of the late Sidney Lewis, then president of Best, who was an avid collector of contemporary art. Lewis was seeking ways to incorporate art into his showrooms to distinguish them from the conformity of standard shopping-strip architecture. In an earlier commission in 1972, shortly after the formation of the SITE group, the designers enlivened a Best Products showroom in Richmond, Virginia, with the Peeling Front, a facade that was molded in epoxy to create the appearance that the facing brick was peeling away from the building's backing materials. However, of all the SITE designs, the Houston showroom was the one that was most photographed and that received the most popular and critical attention.

SITE was organized in 1970 as a collaboration between Alison Skye, who was trained as an art historian; Michelle Stone, a photographer and sociologist; and James Wines, a sculptor. The confluence of their various disciplinary points of view resulted in designs that rejected conventional architectural formulas for new inspirations found in contemporary art (particularly the work of American Pop artists of the 1960s, such as Claes Oldenburg), social commentary, and popular culture.

Wines, who became the chief spokesman for the group, described SITE's work as being about "de-architecture," which he defined as a condition of reversing or removing some quality or ingredient from architecture in order to destabilize it. It was a means of defining an attitude or of changing standard reactions to the urban context, including the ubiquitous strip centers that were burgeoning along America's highways. In the Best showrooms, they attacked the most banal, contemporary building type, the commercial box, by subverting the traditional relationships between form, function, and economy. In its place they foregrounded the often ambiguous relationship between the building's contents and the external influences of a more inclusive social and cultural context. The SITE designs made the showroom buildings into memorable landmarks—no small feat among the visual complexities and commercial excesses of the suburban strip. As marketing strategies, their success could be measured in increased sales revenues for the Best Company.

Curiously, the buildings also became the focus of intense architectural commentary, perhaps because they distilled many of the interests of the Postmodernists—for example, the idea of the decorated shed advanced by architect Robert Venturi—and pushed them almost to the point of parody. Extensive critical review and coverage of the Houston showroom in both the professional and the popular press included sympathetic reviews by Gerald Allen (1977) and Bruno Zevi (1980), the latter of whose commentary was titled "The Poetics of the Unfinished." Opposite opinions were registered by architects Lebbeus Woods, who considered the building to be little more than a "one-liner" without sustaining power, and Léon Krier, who called it tragic and a setback for architecture.

The extraordinary amount of attention that was paid to the building owed partly to Wines's own polemical writings and interviews in which he described SITE's mission as a confrontation with the tenets of modern architecture, particularly the orthodoxies of formal functionalism (that is, International Style). In the Houston design, with its wholeness shattered by the appearance of chaos, the commentary went further, constructing a deliberate subversion of the glossy conformity that expressed the economic and building boom in the state of Texas. By liberating the facade and making it a plaything of the imagination, the Best Showroom signaled the arrival of wit, parody, and surreal figuration in architecture. These inversions on the standard architectural formulas were similar to the fascinations of the avant-garde artists beginning with Marcel Duchamp in the early 20th century, who worked to blur conventional categories and definitions of art.

The Best Showroom has been described as both a mock ruin and a vision of incompleteness or indeterminacy, Wines himself staunchly defending the latter interpretation. As a constructed ruin, it was never romantic or reflective, as was the case with many of the mock ruins or follies from history. Instead, it was intended to call attention to itself by creating an architectural puzzle in which the viewer is invited to fill in the missing pieces. As a cultural icon, it introduced to the strip the ambiguous sign

Best Products Showroom, Houston, Texas, designed by SITE (1976)
© G.E. Kidder Smith/CORBIS

whose meaning had little relationship either to the contents or to the usual patterns of signification that were characteristic of strip architecture. Wines used the freedom of this new formulation to pursue a fusion of art and architecture, although in this case whatever architecture there was in the design was largely devoured by the effusiveness of imagery that is, after all, decoration. Because SITE never interfered with the formula for the interior layouts of the showrooms, the projects portrayed a fundamental schism between form and content—inside and out—that was a characteristic feature of much of the work of the Postmodern architects.

Over the years, the building has settled into the landscape as an unselected period piece of popular, architectural culture from another era. Rather than defining a direction for architecture, its main accomplishment was to exhibit an ambitious and audacious, aberrant behavior. The Best Products company declared bankruptcy in 1991, closing its Houston showroom in 1992. After sitting idle for several years, the building was reoccupied as a video store and its indeterminate facade outfitted with a new, red-neon script sign advertising the new tenants.

Bruce Webb

See also **Brick; Postmodernism; Shopping Center; Venturi, Robert (United States); Vernacular Architecture; Zevi, Bruno (Italy)**

Further Reading

Balch, Barbara, and Arthur Drexler, *Buildings for Best Products*, New York: Museum of Modern Art, 1979

Bzdak, Michael J., "Indeterminate Façade, Best Products Show Room," in *The Critical Edge: Controversy in Recent American Architecture*, edited by Tod J. Marder, Cambridge, Massachusetts: MIT Press, 1985

Moore, John, "The Ruin, the Tilt, and a Gaping Hole Are Luring Customers," *Wall Street Journal* (27 February 1979)

Papademetriou, Peter, "The Joke Is Out of Site," *Progressive Architecture*, 57 (January 1967)

Site, Inc., *Best Products Co. Houston Showroom*, New York: Site, 1975

Wines, James, "De-Architecturization," *A + U*, 45 (July 1975)

BIRKERTS, GUNNAR 1925–

Architect, United States

Gunnar Birkerts is the leading American exponent of organic architecture in the generation of architects that came to maturity in the 1960s. Working in the tradition of Erich Mendelsohn, Hugo Haring, and Eero Saarinen, Birkerts received his architectural education in Stuttgart from 1945 to 1949. During his years in Germany, he was drawn to Scandinavian modernism rather than Bauhaus doctrine, which was still taught at the Technische Hochschule. In 1959 he formed a partnership with Frank Straub, and since 1962 he has been practicing independently in addition to teaching, lecturing, and writing.

Birkerts's early buildings show a rejection of the dogmas of the International Style, and a mastery of site problems that is unusual in any architect, young or old. Within their urban context, his buildings respond to other works of architecture and to dominant geographic features. Moreover, Birkerts playfully utilizes the metaphorical qualities of architecture within the design process.

The nature of his expressive design process has allowed Birkerts to adapt to some unusual clients and remarkable problems. He designed the new Federal Reserve Bank in Minneapolis under the leadership of bank president Hugh Galusha in 1973; at first glance it appears to be a monolithic Brutalist facade. Its most striking feature is a curving, catenary arch that frees up a great deal of space below ground for high-security work, and allows for office space above.

In 1984 Birkerts built the Domino's Pizza World Headquarters in Ann Arbor, a complex of buildings that included corporate headquarters, warehouses, laboratories, and public spaces. Birkerts designed the buildings as a series of long, low, broad-eaved structures that appear to shoot across the flat site as if on railroad tracks. Birkerts borrowed elements of Frank Lloyd Wright's designs (primarily the manner in which buildings relate to the natural setting) in a continuation of the organic tradition of architecture in the United States.

Birkerts' 1981 library addition to the Law School at the University of Michigan in Ann Arbor precisely melds with the existing buildings in the quad, including the neo-Gothic Legal Research building and Hutchins Hall, which are relatively recent adaptations of King's College Chapel in Cambridge, England. In order to preserve the integrity of the quadrangle, the architect's solution was to put the library addition underground. Thus, the sidewalk on the east end of the quadrangle runs along the roof of the Law Library. The building's exterior wall forms a limestone V-shaped moat along the outside of the structure, abutting a trough of glass plate windows, providing a major source of daylight. For Birkerts, light is as much a tangible material as it was to Alvar Aalto, whose aesthetic the Ann Arbor library recalls.

Birkerts's design process draws heavily upon intuition. A student of psychology, Birkerts initially relies on rough sketches that look like doodles. As a project is refined, these sketches are expanded into drawings and models that explore functioning spaces and orientation. The architect terms his process "organic synthesis" and claims that, as he responds to space needs, he

Corning Museum of Glass (renovation), Corning, New York, designed by Gunnar Birkerts (1980)

uses a free form polygonal geometry that he can adapt at will. It allows him to define space without compromising functional or aesthetic considerations.

His 1980 renovation and remodeling of the Corning Museum of Glass in Corning, New York, is a masterful synthesis of organics and plastic form that metaphorically evokes the material of glass itself. The building's exterior surface undulates like liquid glass in the furnace; this effect is carefully tempered by hard right angles that represent glass in its solid state. To create an effect of brilliant illumination and visual clarity, Birkerts designed periscope windows, with slanting mirrors to deflect direct sunlight without blocking the view.

More recently, Birkerts has begun two buildings in his native country that are still under construction (as of 2003): the Latvian National Library at Riga, and Museum of the Occupation of Latvia. The former received the 2000 Annual American Architecture Prize of the Chicago Museum of Architecture and Design. With a spectacular site near the Daugava River in the country's capital city, the Latvian National Library takes the form of a crystal mountain emerging from dark waters, and contains at its upper level, the treasures of Latvian literary history. Birkerts sees his Latvian buildings as the opportunity to create grand national symbols that express the country's layered history, character, and freedom.

LEONARD K. EATON

See also **Aalto, Alvar (Finland); Bauhaus; International Style; Saarinen, Eero (Finland); Wright, Frank Lloyd (United States); Yamasaki, Minoru (United States)**

Biography

Born in Riga, Latvia, 17 January 1925; immigrated to the United States 1949; naturalized 1954. Attended the Technische Hochschule, Stuttgart 1945–49; degree in architecture and engineering 1949. Married Sylvia Zvirbulis 1950: 3 children. Designer, office of Lawrence B. Perkins and Will, Chicago 1950–51; designer, offices of Eero Saarinen and Associates, Bloomfield Hills, Michigan 1951–54; chief designer, Minoru Yamasaki and Associates, Birmingham, Michigan 1955–59. Principal, Birkerts and Straub, Birmingham 1959–62; president, Gunnar Birkerts and Associates, Birmingham from 1962. Assistant professor, 1961, associate professor, 1963–69, professor of architecture, 1969–90, professor emeritus, from 1990, University of Michigan, Ann Arbor; architect in residence, University of Illinois, Urbana-Champaign 1982; T.S. Monaghan professor, University of Oklahoma 1990. Fellow, American Institute of Architects; fellow, Latvian Architects Association; fellow, Graham Foundation.

Selected Works

Federal Reserve Bank of Minnesota, Minneapolis, 1973
Corning Museum of Glass (renovation), Corning, New York, 1980
Allan and Alene Smith Addition, Law School, University of Michigan, Ann Arbor, 1981
Domino's Pizza World Headquarters, Ann Arbor, Michigan, 1984
American Embassy, Caracas, Venezuela, 1987
Kemper Museum of Contemporary Art and Design, Kansas City, Missouri, 1991
Geisel Library Underground Addition, University of California, San Diego (with Carrier Johnson), 1993
Church of the Servant, Kentwood, Michigan, 1994
Duke University Law School Addition, Durham, North Carolina, 1995
Latvian National Library, Riga, 1989–2000
Museum of the Occupation of Latvia, Riga, 2001–

Selected Publications

Subterranean Urban Systems, 1974
Buildings, Projects, and Thoughts 1960–1985, 1985
Process and Expression in Architectural Form, 1994

Further Reading

The most comprehensive treatment of Birkerts is Kaiser 1989, with a respectful but not overly laudatory text. The article in *World Architecture* is the most recent commentary on the Latvian National Library in Riga and contains a brief interview with the architect. A profile and extracts from an interview with Birkerts in which the author assesses the last ten years of his practice is found in Kaiser 1999. Birkerts himself has provided an excellent commentary on his projects and executed buildings in Marlin, which includes superb photographs. Birkerts has given a collection of his drawings and photographs of his work to the Bentley Historical Library at the University of Michigan.

"Gunnar Birkerts and Kevin Rochi: The Return of the Prodigal Sons to Latvia and Ireland," *World Architecture*, 80 (October 1999)
Kaiser, Kay, *The Architecture of Gunnar Birkerts*, Washington, D.C.: American Institute of Architects Press, 1989
Kaiser, Kay, "Gunnar Birkerts," *World Architecture*, 36 (1999)
Marlin, William, *Gunnar Birkerts and Associates*, edited and photographed by Yukio Futagawa, Tokyo: A.D.A. Edita, 1982

BLOMSTEDT, AULIS 1906–79

Architect, Finland

Although the international perspective of architectural developments in Finland centered on the work of Alvar Aalto in the quarter-century following World War II, Finnish architecture during this time was very much more than Aalto. This period is often viewed, again from an international perspective, as the quiet, golden age of the century, with numerous works realized in a material palette relying on brick and wood. Within Finland, while Aalto went his own way, the majority of Finnish architects continued to practice an evolved form of modernism influenced by Mies van der Rohe, among others. This work is characterized by its direct approach in the use of reinforced concrete and steel along with brick and wood, coupled with rational building planning and organizational techniques. Less romantic in conception than Aalto's work, these buildings expanded the rationalist aspect of modernism while incorporating more expressive spatial explorations with richer material vocabularies.

A major intellectual and creative force in this period—and one often not recognized internationally—was Aulis Blomstedt. Although he did not design many buildings, Blomstedt had a strong influence on Finnish architecture and is often viewed as the significant counterpoint to Aalto. More than any of his contemporaries, Blomstedt's important influence can be seen both in his work as well as in his theoretical writings and presentations. Without question, he was the foremost theoretician in Finnish architecture during the postwar period. Though his work and writings, he aimed to develop an objective theory of architecture that could be verified through practice, with simplicity, austerity, and abstraction becoming the essentials in his designs. His terraced Ketju housing complex in Tapiola (1954) and Worker's Institute Addition in Helsinki (1959) are essays indicating his rigorous process of thinking and doing, as are a series of abstract graphic and installation pieces he developed for studying proportion and dimension. In addition to practicing, Blomstedt was a professor at the Helsinki University of Technology, and his influence is seen in the works of his students, Kristian Gullichsen, Juhani Pallasmaa, Erkki Kairamo, and Kirmo Mikkola, among others, that were executed since the 1970s.

Like his contemporaries, Blomstedt received a classical education in architecture at the Helsinki Institute of Technology, and a number of his student projects are indicative of this. The work is sympathetic with the "Nordic Classicism" found throughout Scandinavia architecture during the 1920s. He made a study tour to Italy in 1927. By the time of his graduation in 1930, his work embraced the transition to functionalism that had occurred in Finland during the late 1920s: His diploma project—"A Circus for Helsinki"—bears witness to this change. The firms for which he worked immediately following graduation practiced in the classical style.

During his tenure as chief architect for the Finnish Ministry of Defense, he executed projects such as the Air Force School Hospital in Kauhava (1934) and the Aerodrome No. 6, Staff Headquarters and Barracks buildings in Imatra (1936), among others. These works demonstrate a modesty and practicality, yet are also good examples of functionalist design.

In 1942, following the Russo-Finnish War, The Finnish Association of Architects set up a reconstruction office to address the rebuilding issues facing Finland, as well as relocation problems resulting from the war (120,000 homes were destroyed or abandoned and over 400,000 citizens were resettled from territory ceded to the Soviet Union). Blomstedt worked on the development of standardized plans and prefabricated building designs with Viljo Revell, Kaj Englund, Aarne Hytönen, Yrjö Lindegren, Olli Pöyry, and Erkki Koiso-Kanttile. In this environment, Blomstedt laid the foundation for the postwar debate on aesthetic principles and social applications of modular industrial systems used for housing complexes. This work also had a powerful influence on the development of Finnish building standards immediately after the war.

Blomstedt opened his architectural practice in 1944 and was soon engaged in designing numerous housing complexes and dwellings, among other works, throughout Finland. Over his entire career, Blomstedt, like a number of his contemporaries, was an active architectural competition entrant (the architects for Finnish public buildings are selected through an open competition process). His numerous entries always combined a strong theoretical foundation with practical problem solving and planning techniques.

By the early 1950s, Finland was active in developing new towns in the forest areas near existing cities. One of the most important initial projects was Tapiola, an internationally recognized development, outside of Helsinki. In 1952 Blomstedt joined Aarne Ervi, Viljo Revell, Markus Tavio, and the town planner, Otto-I. Meurman, on the first phase of the plan for Tapiola. Several of Blomstedt's best housing projects were designed for Tapiola, including the harmonious group of three chain houses and three apartment blocks on adjacent sides of a street. With their alternating red brick and white stucco facades, the Ketju terraced row houses have two-story living quarters linked by a variable intermediate section that was designed as reserve space for future uses or needs. The apartment blocks designed for the other side of the street (but were not built) would have reinforce the streetscape, acting as a compositional foil to the row housing. Works in Tapiola include the Finnish Artists Society terraced housing (1955), the Riistapolku housing complex (1957–60), and the Helikko housing complex (1961–62), among many other types of housing projects. Much of Blomstedt's body of work resides in Tapiola.

Without question, the extension to the Helsinki Finnish Worker's Institute is Blomstedt's most important work. Adding on to Gunnar Taucher's 1927 classical work, Blomstedt derives the dimensions of his new building from the classical proportions of the original. This results in achieving a harmony between the new and the old through massing and proportions in the facades. Three times the size of the older building, the addition does not disturb the urban context of the original but is sensitively sited behind it. Blomstedt skillfully exploits the significant level change occurring between the streets that border the site. The new building is placed parallel to the existing one in a new excavated courtyard space. A rock wall clad in colored concrete slabs provides an effective boundary to the back of the court, and the new main entrance is located within the courtyard. Further, there are painterly and architectural qualities in the addition and its spaces that directly reference the Dutch De Stijl movement.

Blomstedt was also a theoretician, however, and from the 1940s onward, he focused on clarifying architecture through intellectual speculations. Modular and proportional discipline was Blomstedt's foundation, for he sought to develop a universal system derived from human measurements and dimensional harmony. The crystallization of his research was "Canon 60," a system of dimensions and proportions in which the principals of mathematical and musical harmony were applied to building. In achieving this, he was able to extend his classical training into contemporary architecture, continuing one of the oldest traditions in Western architecture—using the principles of harmonic proportions—into current practice.

Austerity and simplicity were essentials of Blomstedt's work. But his austerity and simplicity is not for the simple-minded, who would miss the subtle and poetic realizations in his work. Like that of the classical and Renaissance architects before him, Blomstedt's architecture is an architecture for both the mind and the senses.

WILLIAM C. MILLER

See also **Aalto, Alvar (Finland); Finland; Revell, Viljo (Finland)**

Biography

Born in Jyväskylä, Finland, 28 July 1906. His father Yrjö Blomstedt (1871–1912) and his brother Pauli (also known as P.E. Blomstedt, 1900–35) were also architects. His wife, Heidi Sibelius Blomstedt (1911–81), was the daughter of the renowned Finnish composer Jean Sibelius. Graduated and qualified as an architect and, while working in a variety of offices, also taught at the Central School of Applied Arts 1930. Chief architect for the Finnish Ministry of Defense 1934–37; chief editor, Finnish architectural journal, *Arkkitehti* 1941–45; co-founder of the legendary theoretical periodical, *Le Carré Bleu* 1958. Began his private practice 1944–79; Professor of Architecture at the Helsinki Technical University 1958–65; received the Finnish State Prize in Architecture 1977. Died 21 December 1979.

Selected Works

Restaurant Valhalla, Helsinki, 1947
Villa Salonen, Espoo, 1948
Block of flats, Turku, 1951
Block of flats, Helsinki, 1952
Block of flats and "chain"-houses, Tapiola, 1954
Terrace houses with studios, Tapiola, 1955
Block of flats, Tapiola, 1956–57
Atelier Aulis Blomstedt, Tapiola, 1958
Worker's Institute addition, Helsinki, 1959
Villa Pettersson, Helsinki, 1960
Block of flats, Tapiola, 1961
Terraced houses, Tapiola, 1962
Block of flats, Tapiola, 1965
Kulosaari Congregational Center, Helsinki, 1976
Warehouse, Espoo, 1976

Further Reading

Aulis Blomstedt, arkkitehti: Ajatus ja muoto Bharmonikaalisia tutkielmia (exhib. cat.), Helsinki, Museum of Finnish Architecture, 1976
Helander, Vilhelm, and Simo Rista, *Suomalainen Rakennustraide/ Modern Architecture in Finland*, Helsinki: Kirjayhtymä Oy, 1987
Norri, Marja-Riitta, Elina Standertsjöld, and Wilfred Wang, *20th Century Architecture: Finland*, Helsinki: Museum of Finnish Architecture, 2000
Pallasmaa, Juhani (editor), *Aulis Blomstedt. Architect: Thought and Form—Studies in Harmony* (exhib. cat.), Helsinki: Museum of Finnish Architecture, 1980
Pallasmaa, Juhani, "Man, Measure and Proportion: Aulis Blomstedt and the Tradition of Pythagorean harmonies," *Acanthus* (1992).
Poole, Scott, *The New Finnish Architecture*, New York: Rizzoli International, 1992
Quantrill, Malcolm, *Finnish Architecture and the Modernist Tradition*, New York: E & FN Spon, 1995
Richards, J.M., *800 Years of Finnish Architecture*, North Pomfret, Vermont: David and Charles, 1978
Salokorpi, Asko, *Modern Architecture in Finland*, New York: Frederick A. Praeger, 1970
Suhonen, Pekka, *Neue arkitektur in finnland*, Helsinki: Tammi, 1967
Suhonen, Pekka, "Aulis Blomstedt," in *Contemporary Architects*, edited by Muriel Emanuel, New York: St. Martin's Press, 1980
Tempel, Egon, *New Finnish Architecture*, New York: Frederick A. Praeger, 1968
Vanhakoski, Erkki, "Aulis Blomstedt—Works 1926–1979," *Acanthus* (1992)
Wickberg, Nils Eric, *Byggnadskonst i Finland*, Helsinki: Werner Sönderström, 1959; English edition, Helsinki: Otava, 1962

BÒ BARDI, LINA 1914–92

Architect, Brazil

Lina Bò Bardi was born in Rome, Italy, in 1914 and died in São Paolo, Brazil, in 1992. She was among the most prolific women architects of the 20th century. She was also a noted designer of furniture, jewelry, staging and installations, as well as an architectural writer and editor. Bò Bardi emerged at an early age as strong willed and unconventional and was one of a handful of women to study in the College of Architecture at Rome University in the late 1930s. Her graduation project revealed her nonconformist bent. The project was in a modern style and was at odds with the historicism of her teachers Marcello Piacentini and Gustavo Giovannoni; it was a large-scale maternity hospital for unwed mothers, and was an unusual choice of topic in the family-oriented society of prewar Italy.

On graduation, Bò Bardi left for Milan and worked for the modernist architect and designer Gio Ponti. Ponti was the director of the Triennale of Milan and of the architecture and design magazine *Domus*, both major platforms for Italian modern architecture and industrial design. At the same time, Bò Bardi, at the age of 24, opened her own one-woman architectural office, supporting herself as an illustrator for *Stile*, a woman's fashion magazine. In 1943 when Italy went to war, at the age of 25, she accepted the position of codirector of *Domus* and was also a member of the Italian resistance. After the war, in 1946, she founded the famous *A, Cultura della Vita* with Bruno Zevi, and married the art critic Pietro Bardi. Because she had been a wartime supporter of Benito Mussolini, Bò Bardi would have had a difficult professional life in Italy. Hence, the couple left for Brazil in 1947, and jointly founded the celebrated art magazine *Habitat*. Bò Bardi, then 29, again opened an architectural firm, and remained in active practice until the end of her life.

Bò Bardi's architecture is characterized by its often-daring, concrete construction engineered in pursuit of Miesian-inspired universal spaces. The Glass House (1951), which she designed for herself and Bardi just outside São Paolo, juts out from the top of a steeply inclined site and is screened by the surrounding tropical forest. It is an early example of the use of reinforced concrete and glass for a domestic building. Despite its formidable weight, it achieves an effect of airy lightness using just seven slender columns that support the structure. Her scheme for the Taba Guaianases Building, commissioned for the media conglomerate Diarios Associados in São Paolo (1951, never completed), represented yet another technical feat. The main issue in the scheme was technical: how to place a building of 1,500 apartments on top of a large theater with 1,500 seats, remaining free of columns. She collaborated on the structural engineering with the famed Italian engineer Pier Luigi Nervi. One of her most famous buildings, the Museum of São Paulo (1957–68), is a 70-meter-long glazed structure, suspended from two prestressed longitudinal concrete beams on the roof, resting on four pillars with a clear span under it. The exhibition hall thus created is an immense universal space, unencumbered by structural elements; the immense resulting space under the building (named the Belvedere because of the view it affords over São Paolo) became one of the most popular public places in the city. With its use of concrete construction and search for universal space, it recalls her uncompleted Museum on the Seashore (1951) in São Paolo. Bò Bardi's second most famous project, the Pompéia Factory (1977) in São Paolo, converted an abandoned steel-drum factory into a cultural and recreational center. She qualified this low-cost project as Arquitetura Povera, inspired by the art movement in Italy during the 1960s, called Arte Povera (literally, poor art). Located in a 19th-century industrial complex, it

São Paulo Museum of Art, designed by Lina Bò Bardi (1957–68)
© Eduardo Costa

exploits rather than rejects the gritty realism of the site. The two concrete high-rise structures that she added to the complex are reminiscent of silos, bunkers, or containers, with a series of seven prestressed-concrete walkways linking them. It contains a swimming pool, gymnasium, studios for arts and crafts, a dance hall, and a theater for 1,200 spectators, a library, a restaurant, and exhibition halls.

Bò Bardi also built or designed many small domestic buildings in a critical regionalist spirit, incorporating tropical vegetation into the concrete construction in novel ways: her Chame-Chame House (1958) in Bahia preserves a Jaca tree at the center of the design and, as in her home for Valeria P. Cirell (1958) in São Paolo, combines stones, ceramic chips, and plants in the wall slabs creating vertical garden walls. She was also involved in many renovation projects: Solar do Unhao (1963) in Bahia, the Historical Center of Bahia (1986), the House of Benin (1987) in Bahia, and Misericórdia Slope (1987) in Bahia. Moreover, she designed furniture; the most famous example is a classic of postwar furniture design, a chair called "Bardi's Bowl" (1951). Much like her early buildings, it is an exercise in structural thinking. In the form of a mobile hemispherical bowl, it rests on a light steel structure made up of a circular ring supported on four thin legs.

Bò Bardi's last project was for the conversion of the old Palace of Industries of São Paolo into the new City Hall (1992).

LIANE LEFAIVRE

See also **São Paulo, Brazil; Zevi, Bruno (Italy)**

Biography

Born in Rome, 5 December 1914. Graduated from the School of Architecture, University of Rome 1940. Married Pietro Maria Bardi 1942. Worked in the studio of Gio Ponti, Milan 1941–43; editor, *Domus* magazine, Milan 1941–43; emigrated to Brazil 1947; naturalized 1952. Assisted with the interior design of the Museu de Arte de São Paulo, Brazil 1947; director, Estúdio de Arte Palma, São Paulo, from 1947; editor, *Habitat* magazine, São Paulo 1949–53; with husband and architect Giancarlo Palanti, founded the Studio de Arte Palma, São Paulo. Organized the first industrial design course in Brazil 1948–51; professor, University of São Paulo 1954–55. Died in São Paulo, 29 March 1992.

Selected Works

Casa de Vidrio, São Paulo, Brazil, 1951
Taba Guaianases (incomplete), São Paulo, 1951

Museum on the Seashore (incomplete), São Paulo, 1951
Chame-Chame House, Bahia, Brazil, 1958
Cyrel Czerna House, São Paulo, 1958
Solar do Unhao (restoration), Museum of Popular Art, Salvador, Bahia, 1963
São Paulo Museum of Art, São Paulo, 1968
Leisure Center, SESC Fábrica Pompéia, São Paulo, 1977
Historical Center (restoration), Bahia, 1986
Benin House and Restaurant, Salvador, Bahia, 1987
Housing Development, Ladeira de Misericórdia, Salvador, Bahia, 1987
Palace of Industries (conversion), São Paulo, 1992

Selected Publications

"Terapia Intensiva, Casa do Benin," *Arquitetura e Urbanismo* (June/July 1988)
"Registro de Uma Idéia, Centro Cultural de Belem," *Arquitetura e Urbanismo* (October/November 1988)
"Lina Bò Bardi" (with others), *Projeto* (May 1991)
"Uma aula de Arquiteturas," *Projeto* (January/February 1992)

Further Reading

Bò Bardi, Lina, *Lina Bò Bardi*, edited by Marcelo Carvalho Ferraz, São Paulo: Empresa das Artes, 1993; 2nd edition, São Paulo: Instituto Lina Bò e P.M. Bardi, 1996
Bruand, Yves, *L'architecture contemporaine au Brésil*, Paris: Université de Paris IV, 1971

BOFILL, RICARDO 1939–

Architect, Spain

Ricardo Bofill is one of Europe's most prolific and provocative exponents of Postmodernism in architecture.

In 1975 French President Valéry Giscard d'Estaing described Bofill as the "world's greatest architect" for his award-winning design for Les Halles in Paris. In the following decade, a series of international exhibitions and monographs confirmed his position at the forefront of the modern classical revival. However, despite being celebrated for the manner in which he has rejuvenated the classical and baroque traditions in architecture, it is also an appreciation of geometry and the interrelation among social, spatial, and technical systems that define his work.

Bofill was born in Barcelona in 1939, and between 1955 and 1960 he studied at the Escuela Técnica Superior de Arquitectura in Barcelona and the Université de Genève in Switzerland. In 1960 he founded the multidisciplinary team *Taller de Arquitectura* (Architecture Workshop), and since that time he has worked with them in close collaboration on all his designs. Bofill and the Taller have been based in Barcelona and Sant Just Desvern in Spain since that period, but they have also opened offices in Paris, Algeria, and New York.

Bofill describes both his childhood in Catalonia and his travels with his family as being strong influences on his architectural career. It was while growing up in Barcelona that he developed a great fascination for the architecture of Antoni Gaudí (1852–1926) and for traditional Catalan craftsmanship. During his later travels throughout Western Europe and North Africa, he also cultivated an interest in the manner in which spaces shape social interaction. All of these themes suffuse his early architectural works, including the Plaza San Gregorio Apartment Building (1965) and the Nicaragua Apartment Building (1965) in Barcelona, as well as the Barrio Gaudí (1968) in Reus. All three of the buildings are constructed of simple industrial materials that are applied in traditional ways, and all feature elaborate, variegated roofscapes and richly textured and decorated facades.

Bofill's work first came to international prominence in the early 1970s, when the *Taller de Arquitectura* produced a series of brightly colored, and enigmatically titled buildings throughout Spain. All these projects, including Xanadu (1967) on the bay of Sitges, Walden-7 (1975) in Sant Just Desvern, and Kafka's Castle (1968) and Red Wall (1972), both in Alicante, display a similar theme; they share a preoccupation with the manner in which geometric systems can generate forms that are complex yet conducive to social interaction. Kafka's Castle is a resort, and is generated from a series of equations that govern the siting and distribution of cubic rooms and castellated balconies. One equation generates the number of room capsules that plug into the stair towers, and another determines the height of each spiral progression around the stair. Rather than resulting in a bland or repetitive building, the overlaying of these simple geometric rules produces a rich and evocative environment. In Walden-7, a monumental 17-story apartment complex, this same method is used to accommodate different-sized groups of people in cellular spaces. Both of these flexible-use living areas are connected by vast atriums, upper-level bridges, and roof gardens. Bofill describes these early works as being an intuitive response to issues of design and local culture that have since been termed critical regionalism. For Bofill such projects attempt to solve modern problems (mass housing) using modern materials, while retaining some essence of the region's natural complexity. However, in the years that followed, Bofill began to gradually revise this approach to design, arguing that it was becoming increasingly important to express historical and regional characteristics as well as geometric ones.

In 1975 Bofill's design for a large public park ringed by baroque colonnades won the international design competition for Les Halles in Paris. The design was already under construction when the mayor of Paris, Jacques Chirac, ordered that it be abandoned. Despite this setback, Bofill successfully developed a number of similarly monumental and historically themed projects in France, including Les Arcades du Lac (1981) and Le Viaduc (1981), both near Versailles, Les Espaces d'Abraxas (1983) at Marne-la-Vallée, Les Echelles du Baroque (1985) in Paris, and Antigone (1985) in Montpellier. Bofill describes Les Arcades du Lac and Le Viaduc as "Versailles for the people." These buildings (the latter over an artificial lake) incorporate a giant rhythmic system of precast-concrete pilasters, arched windows, and classical pediments. Below the symmetrical piazza with its classical fountains and balustrades, are cavernous parking lots. Les Espaces d'Abraxas, a development for more than 600 apartments on the outskirts of Paris, is similarly boldly derivative of French architectural history and geometry. Les Espaces d'Abraxas comprises three historic building types: a semicircular theater, an arc (a habitable arch), and the palace (a U-shaped block that frames the arc). Each of these buildings is between 10 and 15 stories high and is clad in an elegant, precast-concrete panel system. The exterior of the theater features a series of

Les Arcades du Lac (The Lake's Arches) and viaduct, St. Quentin en Yvelines, France, designed by Ricardo Bofill
© Bernard Annebicque/CORBIS SYGMA

gigantic Doric columns, each the full height of the building. The inner courtyards are lined with mirror-glass Corinthian columns, each surmounted by a triple molding (actually a series of balconies) and a cypress tree. These buildings, along with Les Echelles du Baroque and Antigone, confirmed Bofill's reputation as designer of extravagant, monumental, and theatrical buildings.

In the 1990s Bofill and the Taller continued to design buildings for clients in the United States, China, and Europe, despite society's growing rejection of the exuberance of Postmodern classicism.

By the time that Bofill's designs for the 1992 Barcelona Olympics were completed, the approach to architecture that had once earned him great praise, now drew mostly criticism. Despite this rejection, it is Bofill's appreciation of the relationship among geometry, space, and society that remains his greatest strength.

MICHAEL J. OSTWALD

See also **Gaudí, Antoni (Spain); Postmodernism**

Biography

Born in Barcelona, Spain, 5 December 1939; son of architect Emilio Bofill. Studied at the French Institute of Barcelona until 1955; attended Escuela Superior de Arquitectura, Barcelona 1955–56; studied at Geneva School of Architecture, the University of Geneva, Switzerland, 1957–60. Founded *Taller de Arquitectura*, Barcelona, 1960; opened offices in Paris, 1970, and New York 1984. Fellow, American Institute of Architects, 1985.

Selected Works

Apartment House, Calle Johannes Sebastian Bach 4, Barcelona, 1965
Schenkel Apartment Building, Calle Nicaragua 99, Barcelona, 1965
La Manzanera (Xanadu) Apartment House, Calpe, Spain, 1967
Kafka's Castle Vacation Apartments, Barcelona, 1968
Barrio Gaudí Residential Complex, Reus, Spain, 1968
La Muralla Roja Holiday Apartments, Calpe, 1972
Walden-7 Residential Complex, Sant Just Desvern, Barcelona, 1975
Le Viaduc Housing, St. Quentin en Yvelines, France, 1981
Les Arcades du Lac, St. Quentin en Yvelines, France 1981
Les Espaces d'Abraxas, Marne-la-Vallée, France, 1983
Les Echelles du Baroque Housing Development, Paris, 1985
Antigone, Montpellier, 1985
Les Temples du Lac Housing Development, St. Quentin en Yvelines, 1988
Olympic Village, Barcelona, 1992

Selected Publications

Hacia una formalización de la ciudad en el espacio, 1968
CEEX I, City in Space Experience, 1970
L'Architecture d'un homme, 1978
El Taller y la critica, 1981
Los Espacios de Abraxas-El Palacio-El Teatro-El Arco, 1981
Projets Français 1978–81: La Cité—histoire et technologie (exhib. cat.), 1981
Los Jardines del Turia (catalog), 1982
Taller de Arquitectura: City Design, Industry and Classicism, 1984
Espaces d'une vie, 1989

Further Reading

Many hundreds of books, papers, and articles have been written about Ricardo Bofill and the *Taller de Arquitectura*; however, no complete catalog of his publications, or of writings about his work has been published since 1988. James provides a fairly exhaustive list of publications prior to 1988.

Cruells, Bartomeu, *Ricardo Bofill: Works and Projects*, Barcelona: Gustavo Gili, 1995
Futagawa, Yukio (editor), *Ricardo Bofill: Taller De Arquitectura*, New York: Rizzoli, and Tokyo: A.D.A. Edita, 1985
Huart, Annabelle d' (editor), *Ricardo Bofill: Taller De Arquitectura*, Barcelona: Gustavo Gili, 1984
James, Warren A. (editor), *Ricardo Bofill: Taller De Arquitectura: Buildings and Projects, 1960–1985*, New York: Rizzoli, 1988
Jencks, Charles, "Ricardo Bofill and the Taller: Six Characters in Search of a Script," in *Taller De Arquitectura: Ricardo Bofill*, London: Architectural Association, 1981
Stern, Robert A.M., *Modern Classicism*, London: Thames and Hudson, and New York: Rizzoli, 1988

BÖHM, GOTTFRIED 1920–

Architect, Germany

Gottfried Böhm's architecture ranges from the Expressionistic to the experimental. His early sculptural concrete buildings from the 1960s and 1970s and his vast steel-and-glass secular buildings of the 1980s and 1990s find few, if any, parallels in other countries. Böhm's buildings clearly have a sculptural approach that is seen in the treatment of the outside form and woven throughout the building, manipulating interior spaces through the formation of structural elements and details.

Böhm always followed his own style and method of creating architecture. His buildings range from small-scale to large-scale projects, and his architecture embraces the simple and the complex by using diverse building materials that range from reinforced concrete and steel to glass and brick.

The son of the famous church builder Dominikus Böhm (1880–1955), Böhm gained his reputation through his early churches. In the 1960s, his architecture blended existing historic city fabrics, integrating his creation into this network of private and public zones while also interacting with its environment in form, materiality, and color.

From 1942 to 1946, Böhm studied architecture under Adolf Abel and Hans Döllgast, among others, at the Technische Hochschule (technical university) in Munich. He received his diploma in 1946 and continued his studies in sculpture under Josef Henselmann at the Akademie der Bildenden Künste (Academy of Fine Arts) in Munich. His education in both architecture and sculpture significantly influenced his work, as is clearly seen in his monumental concrete structures of the 1960s and 1970s.

In 1951 Böhm went to the United States to work for the architectural office of Brother Cajetan Baumann in New York. While there, he visited Ludwig Mies van der Rohe twice in Chicago and Walter Gropius once at Harvard University.

Although fascinated by the technical perfection of Mies's buildings, Böhm's main influence came from his father. From 1952 until 1955, he collaborated with his father on multiple church designs, a few single-family homes, a cinema, and projects (1951) for the Wallraff-Richartz Museum in Cologne. The influence of Mies on their single-family homes is evident in the Kendler House (1953) in Junkersdorf-Cologne, which clearly corresponds with Mies's row house Elmshurst III (1951). Böhm's Chapel of St. Kolumba (1950) used rendered shells attached to structural ironwork, creating a sculptural transitory appearance, as in his father's Benedictine Abbey (1922) in Vaals. These influences on his architecture were clearly evident in his early independent projects.

After the death of his father, Böhm took over the existing projects in the office, transforming the typology of his father's works, as exemplified in the Church of the Sacred Heart (1960) in Schildgen and the church project (1959) for Bernkastel-Kues. From the end of the 1950s to the end of the 1960s, Böhm's architecture developed sculpturally and departed from earlier influences. His individualized definition of architecture was characterized by extreme plasticity and dynamic forms. His was an architecture that defined masses with contrasting form and light. Böhm strayed from strict classical geometric forms to free-flowing asymmetrical compositions, which suggest crystal-shaped compositions in reinforced concrete.

The Church of St. Gertrud (1960–66) in Cologne and the Parish Church of the Resurrection of Christ and a youth center (1970) in Cologne-Melaten mark a movement toward his unique sculptural style, culminating in his two masterpieces: the Town Hall (1962–71) in Bergisch Gladbach-Bensberg and the pilgrimage church of Mary, Queen of Peace (1963–72), in Velbert-Neviges. These highly acclaimed projects drew on his father's architecture and German Expressionism of the early 20th century.

Böhm used highly advanced concrete technology to construct in the manner prophesied by Bruno Taut, Mies, Hans Poelzig, Max Taut, Hans Scharoun, and others. The town hall in Bensberg functions as a "city crown," inspired by Bruno Taut's Expressionist vision of the center of cultural–religious life in the city.

In the 1970s, the demand for churches decreased, and secular buildings formed the majority of the structures built by Böhm. The complex formwork for his concrete buildings became too expensive for public buildings. The office changed its design strategy to a more strict orthogonal typology following the ideas of system-based building, influenced by both the cluster buildings of Aldo van Eyck and Herman Hertzberger and Peter Cook's Archigram and its "Plug-in City."

In the 1970s, steel dominated in the exterior of Böhm's buildings. These new influences and materials are clearly present in the pilgrimage church of Our Lady of the Victory (1972–76) in Opfenbach-Wigratzbad, the town hall and cultural center (1970–77) in Bocholt, and the renovation and new building of Castle Saarbrücken (1977–78, 1981–89).

After his neo-Expressionist period of the 1960s and 1970s, Böhm pursued a more sumptuous strategy. His baroque-like spaces tended toward vastness in volume within mazes of axial symmetry. One design feature of the Böhm office seems to recur over and over again; namely, the basilica-based building with nave and two aisles in secular structures, as seen in the Züblin office building (1981–85) in Stuttgart and the Hotel Maritim (1989) in Cologne. In these projects, parallel office wings are arranged side to side on a central hall that has a semipublic character and that is used for hosting events, such as exhibitions and concerts.

In the later 1990s, Böhm's architecture developed away from the restraints of symmetry and axial logic. The projects become more fragmented and split into more layers as he used suspended shell-roof construction, as demonstrated in his design for the Philharmonic Hall (1997) in Luxembourg. His Peek & Cloppenburg department store (1995) in Berlin demonstrates his will of form giving, with clear origins in sculpture.

MONIKA EVELYN KÖCK

See also **Church; Expressionism; Mies van der Rohe, Ludwig (Germany); Taut, Bruno (Germany)**

Biography

Born in Offenbach, Germany, 23 January 1920 as youngest son of Dominikus and Maria Böhm. After military service from 1938 to 1942, studied at the Technische Hochschule in Munich and graduated 1946. Added a year of studying sculpture at the Akademie der Bildenden Künste in Munich. Assisted his father in his office 1947–50. Married the architect Elisabeth Haggenmüller (1948) and had with her four sons, three of them are architects: Stephan, Markus, Peter, and Paul. Worked 1950 for Rudolf Schwarz on planning the reconstruction of Cologne. Worked for six months in 1951 for Cajetan Baumann in New York. Worked 1952–55 in his father's office until the 1955 death of Dominikus Böhm, when Gottfried took over the parental office. Professor for urban planning and design at the Rheinisch-Westfälischen Technischen Hochschule in Aachen 1963–85. Member of the Akademie der Künste in Berlin-Brandenburg from 1968. Received the major prize of the Bund Deutscher Architekten 1975. Member of the Deutsche Akademie für Städtebauund Landesplanung in Berlin from 1976. Teaching appointments in Massachusetts Institute of Technology in Cambridge, Massachusetts; the University of Pennsylvania in Philadelphia; and Washington University in St. Louis. Awarded the Fritz-Schuhmacher-Prize in Hamburg 1985. Received the Pritzker Architecture Prize 1986. Was awarded with many other national and international prizes and recognitions. He practices and lives in Cologne-Marienburg.

Selected Works

Parish Church of St. Gertrud, Cologne, 1966
Bethanien Village for Children and Young People, Bergisch Gladbach-Refrath, 1968
Parish Church of the Resurrection of Christ and Youth Center, Cologne-Melaten, 1970
Town Hall, Bergisch Gladbach-Bensberg, 1971
Pilgrimage Church of Mary, Queen of Peace, Velbert-Neviges, Bergisches Land, 1972
Pilgrimage Church of Our Lady of the Victory, Opfenbach-Wigratzbad, 1976
Town Hall and Culture Center, Bocholt, 1977
Renovation and New Building of the Central Section of Castle Saarbrücken, 1978, 1989
Prager Platz Residential Development, Berlin, 1980, 1989
Office Building Züblin, Stuttgart-Vaihingen, 1985
WDR Arcades, Cologne, 1996

Selected Publications

Gottfried Böhm, Bauten und Projekte, 1950–1980. Cologne: Verlag der Buchhandlung Walther König, 1982

Further Reading

Bode, Peter, and Svetlozar Raèv, "Gottfried Böhm," *A+U*, 89 (1978)
Darius, Veronika, *Der Architekt Gottfried Böhm. Bauten der sechziger Jahre*, Düsseldorf: Beton Verlag, 1988
Pehnt, Wolfgang, "Böhm family. Dominikus, Gottfried, Elisabeth, Stephan, Peter, Paul," *A+U*, 288 (September 1994)
Pehnt, Wolfgang, *Gottfried Böhm*, Basel: Birkhäuser Verlag, 1999
Raèv, Svetlozar (editor), *Gottfried Böhm. Lectures Buildings Projects. Vorträge Bauten Projekte*, Stuttgart: Karl Krämer Verlag, 1988
Speidel, Manfred, "Gottfried Böhm," *A+U*, 240 (September 1990)
Weisner, Ulrich, *Böhm: Väter und Söhne*, Bielefeld: Kat. Kunsthalle Bielefeld, 1994

BOOTS FACTORY

Designed by Sir Owen Williams; completed 1938
Nottingham, England

The factories designed by the architect and engineer Sir Owen Williams for Boots Pure Drugs Company in Nottingham are regarded as buildings of seminal importance in the history of modern architecture in Britain.

Built between 1930 and 1938, the development consists of two large buildings designed for the manufacture of pharmaceutical products and a collection of smaller buildings including a fire station. All the buildings still exist, and the factories were refurbished in 1994.

Owen Williams was born in 1890. He qualified as an engineer in 1911 and a year later joined the Trussed Concrete and Steel Company, for which he worked as an assistant engineer prior to establishing his own practice in 1918. Three years later, he was appointed consulting engineer to the British Empire Exhibition, a commission that included the design of several large exhibition buildings together with a swimming pool and a sports stadium for 125,000 spectators at Wembley. It was a turning point in his career. The buildings, which made extensive use of reinforced concrete, were completed in record time, and, after the exhibition opened in 1924, Williams was knighted in recognition of his achievements. He subsequently became a registered architect and in 1930 was appointed to design a large new manufacturing complex for a wide range of pharmaceutical products for Boots of Nottingham.

Although Boots had originally been founded by Jesse Boots, a local chemist, it was under American ownership at the time of Williams's appointment. The United Drugs Company purchased a 300-acre site at Beeston on the outskirts of Nottingham in 1926, and their initial design brief required that the complex be contained within one huge envelope. Williams worked with the client to develop their requirements, and his first plans were for a single building planned for phased development and designed to accommodate wet and dry processes of manufacture located to either side of a central shipping dock.

The first building to be constructed, the Packed Wet Goods Factory, was completed in 1932. Planned as half of the original scheme, the vast concrete, steel, and glass complex has a footprint of 240,000 square feet. It is organized in five interrelated zones with an unloading dock to the south, a ground floor manufacturing area with upper floors for storage of raw materials, a main packaging hall connected to a four-story packed goods store, and a shipping dock to the north. Administrative offices were integrated into the scheme in a four-story block along the western edge of the complex, which was also planned to accommodate the main entrance, laboratories, and a staff canteen.

The organization of the building is dominated by an uncompromising functionalist approach and an interest in developing an overall systematic method of construction. The structure consists of reinforced-concrete flat slabs spanning in two directions and supported on square reinforced-concrete columns with flared capitals. The slabs are cantilevered at the perimeter and around light wells, and the building is clad with a glazed-curtain wall.

Like the early buildings designed by Albert Kahn for Henry Ford, the scheme for this first building was planned to feed raw materials down from the upper levels. Also like Kahn, Williams was keen to design a building that provided good working conditions, and this is perhaps most obvious in the use of natural daylight. In addition to an extensive glazed perimeter, the light wells bring daylight into the heart of the building. In the five-story packing hall, perhaps the most dramatic space in the scheme, Williams created a roofing system with 8 1/2-inch-diameter circular glass disks within a 1 3/4-inch-deep reinforced-concrete slab supported on steel trusses at 30-foot, 8-inch centers. He also used a similar system over the unloading docks and the manufacturing areas.

In 1935, after Boots Company had been bought back into British ownership, Williams was commissioned to design additional manufacturing space at Beeston. The "Drys," originally conceived as a mirror-image extension to his first building, was eventually redesigned to be independent and freestanding.

Planned for the manufacture, storage, and dispatch of powders, tablets, and other dry products, the design of this building is simpler than the earlier factory. It consists of three zones planned for incoming raw materials, manufacture, and packaging and shipping. A five-story central spine houses manufacturing processes that are top fed as in the "Wets" Building. However, the atria were omitted. Single-story spaces at either side provide for incoming raw materials to the south and for outgoing finished materials to the north.

Although built in reinforced concrete, the structural system is also different. Flat-slab construction, limited to the central spine building, is carefully integrated with the structure of the roofs over the single-story bays at either side. Nine-foot-deep Z section beams of reinforced concrete span 92 feet to the north and 215 feet to the south with extraordinary cantilevers of 30 feet and 48 feet, respectively, providing column-free unloading and loading docks. At the point where these beams meet the multistory spine, they are suspended from concrete hangers that are exposed on the elevation and that in turn are suspended from deep beams at roof level. Williams, who also sought to integrate structural and servicing systems, designed these hangers to be hollow, and they house air-extract ducts.

Perhaps it is not surprising that these buildings appear to be inspired by American practice, for the first was commissioned by an American client; designed to optimize materials and structural systems developed by engineers such as Ernest Ransome, Turner, and the Trussed Steel Concrete Company; and constructed after a series of large reinforced-concrete industrial buildings designed by Albert Kahn that had been widely publicized. However, they should also be considered in a lineage that includes the significant work of Maillart, Freysinnet, and Perret in Europe. Williams's buildings for Boots, which explore the potential of structure, rational systems, and materials at a grand scale, have been fittingly described as Joseph Paxton's Crystal Palace of the 20th century.

Brian Carter

See also **Factory; Kahn, Albert (United States)**

Further Reading

The Architects' Journal (25 November 1938)
Cottam, David, *Sir Owen Williams, 1890–1969*, London: Architectural Association, 1986
Roth, Alfred, *The New Architecture; Die neue Architektur; La nouvelle architecture* (trilingual English-German-French edition), Zurich: Girsberger, 1940; 5th edition, 1951
Whyte, Iain Boyd, "Boots Wets Factory, Beeston (Nottingham), 1927–1933," *Casabella*, 61 (December 1997–January 1998)
Williams, Owen, *Engineering News-Record* (25 May 1933)

BOSTON CITY HALL

Designed by Kallmann, McKinnell and Knowles; completed 1969
Boston, Massachusetts

The Boston City Hall is a modern architectural icon that has served and identified the citizens of Boston since 1969. It is the product of the Boston architectural firm Kallmann, McKinnell and Knowles, now Kallmann, McKinnell and Wood, and a national design competition held in 1962. The site is in the center of the historic Boston urban fabric in a plaza created by architect I.M. Pei. The trapezoidal site, comparable in scale to St. Mark's Square in Venice, provides one of the earliest modern exterior public spaces in a large American city.

Gerhard Kallmann and Michael McKinnell, along with Edward Knowles, formed their office with this project. Kallmann, the eldest member of the team, German born and English educated, provided the philosophical expressions of the theory and the design ideas. McKinnell, English born and educated, has shared Kallmann's inclusive and sensitive approach to architecture for all the years of the office's existence. Both have served as practicing architects, as educators at the Harvard Graduate School of Design, and as researchers and historians. Henry Wood joined the firm in 1965.

The Boston City Hall expresses the design quality and philosophy of the firm. It is the historical foundation of its design credits and the initial expression of its goals achieved in the built environment. It is not easy to understand the building without a context or background in architecture. At the same time, it is a building much appreciated and generally valued and approved by architects and architecture critics.

Writing in *Architecture Forum* in 1959, Gerhard Kallmann, as an educator, not yet practicing or having designed the City Hall, sought to generate a new spirit of creativity in architectural designers. Modernism as a style dominated the architectural scene, and its success was multiplied by the large amounts of construction in the postwar period that conveyed that visual image. It was a time of rigid stylistic dogma, well-established rules, and culturally defined and accepted physical forms. In the face of systems processes and deterministic products, Kallmann argued for and encouraged young architects to maintain confidence in the traditional architectural problem-solving processes and insights. As Kallmann demonstrates in the Boston City Hall, it is critical that human emotions and expressions overcome system processes that produce homogeneous and stylistically dead metropolitan environments.

In place of static modernism design approaches, Kallmann and McKinnell championed the "New Brutalism" style. The work of Le Corbusier and the refining qualities of Louis Kahn's work served as springboards for the office to create a new physical expression with a new direction affording new opportunities within the modern movement. In a lecture in 1959, Kallmann stated that this new direction "in its physical concreteness and firmness of build, strives for a confirmation of identity and existence to counter the modern fear of nothingness."

As a development of Kahn's ideas of rigor and order within the context of New Brutalism, form, symbolism, function, and technology are balanced and integrated in the Boston City Hall. Form is the classical tripartite massing of base, body, and cap. Contrast and tension in this scheme is achieved by inverting the masses. The large, ordered, and repetitive office spaces are at the top. The body, or central portion of the tower, symbolically expresses the central government process of council and mayor with clear and bold forms. The base is open and accessible, inviting and encouraging the public to enter and traverse the dramatic, interpenetrating interior arrival and circulation spaces.

The entire project is set on a brick plaza base that serves as a public gathering space and a Boston focal point. As an exterior circulation area, it encourages movement through the plaza into the building and around to Faneuil Hall, the markets, and the waterfront.

Boston City Hall, designed by Kallmann, McKinnell and Knowles (1968)
© G.E. Kidder-Smith, Courtesty of Kidder Smith Collection, Rotch Visual Collections, M.I.T.

The symbolism of the government is expressed as both authoritarian and human, inviting participation by the citizenry of Boston. There is a clear expression of the government functions within a complexity that invites interest and a desire to be included.

One element that fails in this openness and opportunity for public involvement is the long, high wall along Congress Street. It reflects the quality of monumental, institutional scale typical of the modern artifacts at the time of its design. The wall serves as a brick barrier, unsympathetic to the pedestrian path at its side.

Analysis of the architecture of the Boston City Hall reveals an uncommon balance between the need to provide form, function, and technology. The integration of environmental systems with the building structure and form is well studied and developed. In what has become for the firm an opportunity to explore and express the central concepts of their design philosophy, the structural elements serve not only to support the building loads but also to formally become elements of style that define entry, wall, space, and program.

Daylighting and electric lighting are integrated so as to reveal the total architecture and provide a cohesive fabric that underlies the total experience. The integration of the air-handling ducts within the columns and beams successfully provides the services of the system without focusing attention on the technology.

The use of exposed concrete as the building material is an issue for some of those who are accustomed to the softer textures and feel of wood and the more human scale of masonry. Concrete is a cold, hard material, lacking the scale of detail in classical masonry and stone construction. One must realize that this type of construction was new and provided the opportunity for the "Brutal" style of modern architecture to come into being. This building, through detail and complexity of form and scale, overcomes the lack of historic context and precedence. However, the grayish values remain cold and provide a counterresistance to the open, inviting appearance.

Today, although the building is recognized as an architectural icon, societal changes and the growth of the Boston City government have generated calls for renovation and even replacement. The biggest disappointment is the failure of the surrounding urban community to successfully develop the plaza boundaries and walls. The exterior space fails to provide the human qualities of scale, texture, and meaning that are so characteristic of the historic Boston urban scene. The surrounding structures have not provided the sense of place and balance of enclosure, entry, passage, and definition that is characteristic of European piazzas. The reference to the comparable size of St. Mark's Square is limited to that parameter.

Despite these qualifications, the Boston City Hall is a building of quality and historic significance. The style, program, holistic expression, and historic significance in the annals of modern architecture make it one of the truly great buildings in the United States.

JACK KREMERS

See also **Brutalism; City Hall; Corbusier, Le (Jeanneret, Charles-Édouard) (France); Kahn, Louis (United States); Pei, I.M. (United States)**

Further Reading

Huxtable, Ada Louise, "Boston's New City Hall: A Public Building of Quality," *The New York Times* (8 February 1969)

Kay, Jane Holtz, "Prizes Underscore Trend to Area Harmony," *Boston Sunday Globe* (25 May 1969)

Kennedy, Lawrence, *Planning the City upon a Hill: Boston since 1630*, Amherst: University of Massachusetts Press, 1992

Krieger, Alex (editor), *The Architecture of Kallmann, McKinnell and Wood*, New York: Rizzoli, 1998

Lyndon, Donlyn, *The City Observed: Boston: A Guide to the Architecture of the Hub*, New York: Random House, 1982

Schmertz, Mildred F., "Boston's New City Hall: A Competition-Winner Built," *Architectural Record* (February 1969)

Southworth, Michael, and Susan Southworth, *A.I.A. Guide to Boston*, Chester, Connecticut: Globe Pequot Press, 1984; 2nd edition, as *The Boston Society of Architects' A.I.A. Guide to Boston*, 1992

BOSTON, MASSACHUSETTS

Notwithstanding the influential career of Henry Hobson Richardson, the 19th century ended in Boston with the construction of one of the most important buildings in the history of American architecture: McKim, Mead and White's Boston Public Library (1895). This "People's Palace," designed in the form of an Italian Renaissance palace, monumentalizes the importance of education in a city self-consciously marking its preeminence in the various fields of learning. Using Henri Labrouste's Bibliothèque Ste.-Geneviève (1850) in Paris as his model, Charles McKim created an American paragon of Beaux-Arts design, integrating architecture, sculpture, murals, mosaics, and stained glass into an aesthetic whole.

The neoclassical architecture displayed at the Boston Public Library and the World's Columbian Exposition of 1893 in Chicago led to a renaissance of this style across the country. Boston embraced the planning principles of the "White City" with its "Boston-1915" movement, a Progressive Era crusade to remake the city by the year 1915. The most important legacy of this City Beautiful movement was the creation of the Boston Planning Board (see Kennedy, 1992) and buildings such as Shepley, Rutan and Coolidge's Harvard Medical School (1907), Guy Lowell's Museum of Fine Arts (1909), and William Welles Bosworth's Massachusetts Institute of Technology (MIT) campus (1916), called the "great white city" on the Charles River.

During the early years of skyscraper design, Boston lagged behind Chicago and New York in technological innovation. Most notably, Boston preferred not to erect numerous tall buildings. The most important historicized skyscraper in Boston from the early 20th century was the Custom House tower (1915) by Peabody and Stearns. A federal structure, the tower was not limited to Boston's height restrictions.

The first Art Deco skyscraper to appear in Boston was the United Shoe Machinery Building (1930) by Parker, Thomas and Rice. Mingled among the more recent glass box skyscrapers of Boston's financial district, one still finds a number of step-back forms, notably Cram and Ferguson's U.S. Post Office (1931). Boston architect Ralph Adams Cram was best known for his Gothic Revival ecclesiastical work in Boston and around the United States, including collegiate designs for Princeton University and West Point.

Cram's medievalism contrasts sharply with progressive architectural design, which began in earnest with the arrival of leading modernist Walter Gropius in 1937. Gropius became chairman of the Department of Architecture at Harvard University from

1938 to 1952 and reorganized the program along Bauhaus lines, transforming American architectural education in the process. The residence that Gropius built for himself (1938, with Marcel Breuer) in the suburb of Lincoln, Massachusetts, features an International Style flat roof, ribbon windows, and a factory aesthetic that was new to the New England landscape. Gropius formed The Architects' Collaborative (TAC) in 1945, an experimental group of architects responsible for the Graduate Center at Harvard (1950).

Not long after the ascendancy of Gropius at Harvard came alternatives to the International Style with Alvar Aalto's Baker House (1949) at MIT, a student dormitory featuring a serpentine plan and brick facade, and Eero Saarinen's Kresge Auditorium (1955) and Kresge Chapel (1955), also on the MIT campus. Aalto's dormitory is especially significant, as it is one of only two Aalto-designed buildings in the United States. Like those at other campuses, these buildings are examples of postwar campus expansion at Boston-area colleges and universities. The European influence on American architecture continued with Le Corbusier's only building in North America, the Carpenter Center for the Visual Arts (1963) on the Harvard campus. Constructed of reinforced concrete, the building's effect is quite sculptural with its play of voids and solids on the facade. Characteristic of Le Corbusier is the prominent ramp that extends through the center of building. Sited among Harvard's traditional brick buildings along Quincy Street, the Carpenter Center seems strikingly noncontextual at the dawn of the 21st century.

Le Corbusier's colleague, José Luis Sert, succeeded Gropius as dean of Harvard's architecture program from 1953 to 1969 and brought modern urban design principles to the city. Despite the lack of original Le Corbusier designs in Boston, his impact on the city's architecture was enormous. The prime example is the Boston City Hall (1968) by the then-unknown architectural firm of Kallman, McKinnell and Knowles, who won the national competition with a design based on Le Corbusier's Monastery of La Tourette (1955) in France. Although the American Institute of Architects voted City Hall the sixth-greatest building in American history in 1976, the fortresslike concrete structure in the Brutalist style and its vacant, windswept plaza have been a source of criticism among populists over the years.

The construction of the Boston City Hall was part of a massive urban-renewal campaign that remade the city in the 1950s and 1960s. The first target was the city's west end, a crowded immigrant neighborhood demolished in the 1950s and replaced with complexes such as Paul Rudolph's State Health, Education and Welfare Service Center (1970). The destruction of this lively streetscape has since served as a lesson for city planners, urging subsequent generations to respect Boston's unique scale and layout. Urban renewal continued in the 1960s with the "New Boston" program under Mayor John F. Collins and Boston

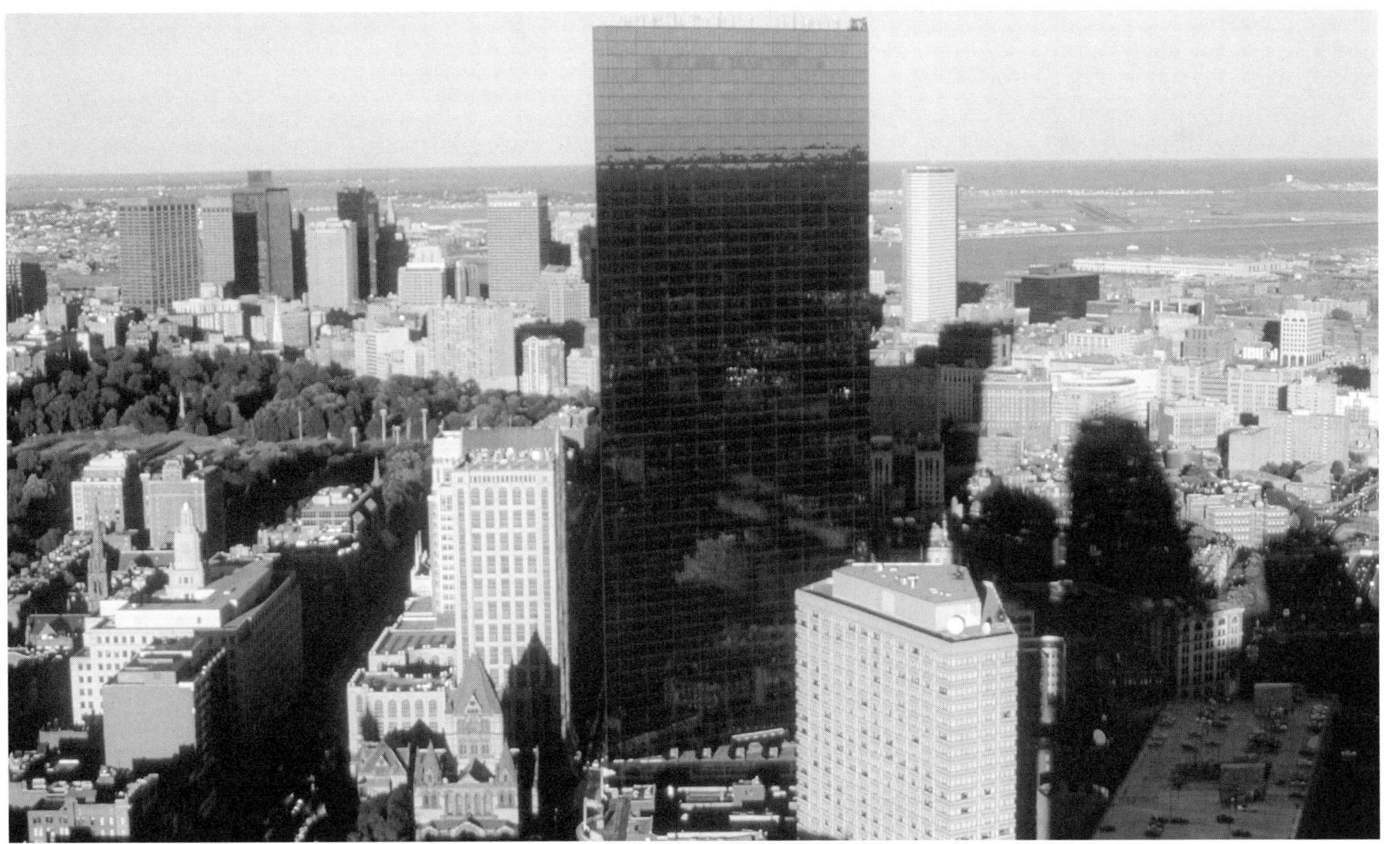

View of Hancock Tower and Copley Square buildings from one side of the skywalk at the Prudential Center. Includes Trinity Church, the Hancock Tower, and neighboring buildings. © Kevin Fleming/CORBIS

Redevelopment Authority Director Edward Logue with the demolition of Scollay Square, an area notorious for tattoo parlors and burlesque entertainment. Replacing such urban blight was the new Government Center (1960, master plan designed by I.M. Pei and Partners), a complex of modern buildings dominated by City Hall.

One outcome of postwar urban renewal in Boston was an increased interest in historic preservation. Preservation in Boston was not new; the Society for the Preservation for New England Antiquities (SPNEA), founded by William Sumner Appleton, had been purchasing and restoring colonial architecture since its establishment in 1910. Outraged by the large-scale destruction of the west end in the 1950s, preservationists rallied for saving historic structures throughout the city. Boston became a leader in this movement, and adaptive re-use became a viable alternative to demolition. A prime example is the old Boston City Hall (1865), originally designed by Arthur Gilman and Gridley J. Fox Bryant in the French Renaissance Revival style and renovated into offices and a restaurant in 1970 by Anderson, Notter Associates.

Preserving the historic character of Copley Square was the challenge faced by Henry Cobb of I.M. Pei and Associates in designing the tallest skyscraper in Boston, the John Hancock Tower (1975). Two of Boston's most important historic buildings, the Boston Public Library and Henry Hobson Richardson's Trinity Church (1877), face each other across the Square. A site to the south of the church became the location of the Hancock Tower, a 60-story reflective-glass-surface skyscraper. Cobb angled the building with the shortest facade of the trapezoidal structure facing Copley Square so that the enormous building would minimally impact Trinity Church. Although considered by many to be aesthetically successful, the building has had more than its share of structural and engineering problems, leading to the complete replacement of all its reflective-glass windows (see Robert Campbell's [1988] interview with structural engineer William Le Messurier).

The 1980s witnessed a building boom in Boston in which oversized developments sometimes caused community backlash. A case in point is the 500 Boylston Street project (1989), a Postmodern high-rise designed by John Burgee Architects with Philip Johnson. Public outcry was directed against the building's proximity to Trinity Church and its shadow-casting enormity. As a result, only half of the one-block complex was completed before Robert Stern was asked to step in and design the second tower at 222 Berkeley Street (1989), complete with Postmodernist historical references. Other important Postmodern Boston buildings include 75 State Street (1988, Graham Gund and Skidmore, Owings and Merrill), an Art Deco revival skyscraper, and Philip Johnson's International Place (1992) with its repetitive facade of Palladian windows.

History continues to play an important part in the architecture of the city, as it did with the construction of the Beaux-Arts Boston Public Library at the close of the 19th century. At the beginning of the 21st century, restoration, preservation, and historicism continue to abide in this historic American city.

KERRY DEAN CARSO

See also **Aalto, Alvar (Finland); Art Deco; Boston City Hall; City Beautiful Movement; Corbusier, Le (Jeanneret, Charles-Édouard) (France); Cram, Ralph Adams (United States); Gropius, Walter (Germany); Johnson, Philip (United States); Library; McKim, Mead and White (United States); Pei, I.M. (United States); Saarinen, Eero (Finland); Sert, Josep Lluís (United States); Skidmore, Owings and Merrill (United States); Skyscraper; The Architects Collaborative (TAC) (United States)**

Further Reading

The most comprehensive architectural history of 20th-century Boston is Douglass Shand-Tucci's *Builtin Boston.* Miller and Morgan is an excellent source for individual buildings and contains high-quality photographs. Kennedy provides a well-written history of city planning in Boston from the earliest settlement up to the late 20th century.

Campbell, Robert, "Learning from the Hancock," *Architecture*, 77 (March 1988)

Campbell, Robert, and Peter Vanderwarker, *Cityscapes of Boston: An American City through Time*, Boston: Houghton Mifflin, 1992

Curtis, William J.R., *Boston: Forty Years of Modern Architecture*, Boston: Institute of Contemporary Art, 1980

Eldredge, Joseph L., *Architecture, Boston*, Barre, Massachusetts: Barre, 1976

Goody, Joan, *New Architecture in Boston*, Cambridge, Massachusetts: MIT Press, 1965

Herdeg, Klaus, *The Decorated Diagram: Harvard Architecture and the Failure of the Bauhaus Legacy*, Cambridge, Massachusetts: MIT Press, 1983

Holleran, Michael, *Boston's "Changeful Times"; Origins of Preservation and Planning in America*, Baltimore: Johns Hopkins University Press, 1988

Kay, Jane Holtz, *Lost Boston*, Boston: Houghton Mifflin, 1980; expanded and updated edition, 1999

Kennedy, Lawrence, *Planning the City upon a Hill: Boston since 1630*, Amherst: University of Massachusetts Press, 1992

Krieger, Alex, and David Cobb (editors), *Mapping Boston*, Cambridge: MIT Press, 1999

Lindgren, James, *Preserving Historic New England: Preservation, Progressivism, and the Remaking of Memory*, New York, Oxford: University Press, 1955

Lynch, Kevin, *The Image of the City*, Cambridge, Massachusetts: MIT Press, 1960

Miller, Naomi, and Keith Morgan, *Boston Architecture, 1975–1990*, Munich: Prestel, 1990

Shand-Tucci, Douglass, *Built in Boston: City and Suburb, 1800–2000*, Amherst: University of Massachusetts Press, 1999

Southworth, Michael, and Susan Southworth, *AIA Guide to Boston*, Chester, Connecticut: Globe Pequot Press, 1984

Whitehill, Walter Muir, *Boston: A Topographical History*, Cambridge, Massachusetts: Harvard University Press, 1959; 2nd edition, 1968

BOTTA, MARIO 1943–

Architect, Switzerland

Mario Botta gained architectural fame during the early 1970s when he began designing small houses in the Ticino region of Switzerland.

Botta completed an apprenticeship with Tita Carloni and architectural studies in Milan and Venice, prior to opening his own office in 1969. The houses he designed during the early 1970s established the Ticino school and changed Swiss architecture dramatically. It is largely because of Botta's innovative work that the present generation of Swiss architects is internationally acclaimed.

During the 1970s and early 1980s, the Ticino region changed from a primarily agricultural economy, to an industrial one that emphasizes tourism. The primary cause of this change was the integration of this region into the European highway system at the beginning of the 1960s. Most of the Ticino architects built for the wealthy bourgeoisie who profited from the economic change, and Botta's first commissions came either from clients to whom he was recommended by his mentor Carloni, or from his relatives. In addition, he participated in competitions, either alone or with older colleagues, such as Luigi Snozzi, Carloni, and Aurelio Galfetti.

The Ticino school generates its designs from architectural and contextual requirements. Architecturally, the buildings exhibit their materials and construction openly. Simple forms characterize typical examples, with a focus on mass and contour line, and ornamentation derived from structure and construction technology. Contextually, these designs attempt to relate the old to the new. The old comes from architectural typology and the vernacular traditions, and the new stems from building technology. In addition, these architects intend to express a mythical topography of the Ticino region, or what is termed the natural calling of the site. This architecture attempts to continue the trends (*tendenza*) already apparent in the organization of the land, and to realize them in an architecture conceived as an act of culture, which incorporates geometry and history.

For Botta, the dignity of architecture results not from intuition, but from architecture's own rules and from history. He proposes that history is the place where architecture finds and defines its meaning. Form and meaning are determined through the relationship to historical buildings, especially the local Romanesque and baroque churches. New meanings can be derived only from these familiar themes, and it is only secondarily that meaning is created through sociocultural usage. Botta's designs aim to contrast physical, social, and cultural traditions to the transient phenomena of modern life.

Botta began in the 1960s, with designs that were inspired by the postwar work of his idols: Le Corbusier and Louis Kahn. During the 1970s, he transformed his theories into buildings that had a strong formal quality. The Bianchi House (1973) in Riva San Vitale is a mysterious, isolated tower that stands up to the surrounding mountains. It is defined by corner supports and a roof slab, and allows outside views by increasing the opening of the construction shell as it rises. The confrontational position of the house to its site emerges in the entrance bridge, which

San Francisco Museum of Modern Art, California, designed by Mario Botta (1994)
© Mary Ann Sullivan

articulates the detachment between natural and man-made, resulting in stark, bizarre forms.

Botta's buildings impress through their strong image quality, which might be interpreted as cultural resistance intent on a new order and meaning. The houses are devoid of clustered compositions or extensions. The massive exterior walls establish a sharp datum. Through such devices, the Casa Rotonda (1981) in Stabio establishes an unexpected presence within an anonymous context. The building is derived from geometric form. The seemingly impenetrable, cylindrical shape contrasts with the large cuts in its surface and suggests an opposition between fortification and openness. The Casa Rotonda questions our assumptions concerning the nature of dwellings; conventional or traditional elements are eliminated. Moreover, everything is subordinated to form. The interior is laid out symmetrically around the central slot of the stairwell and skylight, and rooms are irregular, leftover spaces resulting from inserting a rectangular grid into the house's cylinder.

In larger designs, the geometrical forms became megastructures. The Middle School (1977) in Morbio Inferiore, uses a bridge typology for the arrangement of its eight classroom clusters. The complex is an orderly architectural composition with openings, covered areas, porticoes, and passages. Modular units are repeated to generate the overall shape, and to make the organizational structure of the building easily apparent. A spatially diverse, skylit central passage creates a rich variety of spaces inside this simple form.

In the State Bank (1982) in Fribourg, Botta managed to fit his building into an existing urban situation. A protruding cylindrical volume dominates a public square, and turns the corner while the two receding wings relate to the rhythm and scale of the buildings on the flanking streets. Botta used this approach of dividing a large building into different shapes and facade articulations frequently during the 1980s.

In the late 1980s, the images of the facades became dominant in Botta's buildings; they became figures in which typical details from his earlier designs were re-used. In his Union Bank (1995) in Basel, the facade, curved toward the square, impresses as a heavy bastion. It opens into a cavity that is partly filled by a massive pier on a broad base. Although such shapes are appropriate for a bank building, they become disturbing when used for other building types. The large cubical forms used for the Housing Complex (1982) in Novazzano appear to be without scale and meaningless, because they are not finished in Botta's traditional brick veneer. The absence of this craft surface reveals the emptiness of these forms.

A disappointing aspect of Botta's architecture is that most of his buildings seem to embody the same vision. Now, his repetitive cylinders have appeared in all parts of the world for the most diverse functions, such as museums, churches, single-family homes, shopping centers, and office buildings, as well as in his furniture designs and household appliances.

Hans R. Morgenthaler

See also **Corbusier, Le (Jeanneret, Charles-Édouard) (France); Kahn, Louis (United States)**

Biography

Born in Mendrisio, Switzerland, 1 April 1943. Apprentice building draftsman, office of Carloni and Camenisch, Lugano, Switzerland 1958–61; attended the Liceo Artistico, Milan 1961–64; studied under Guiseppe Mazariol; attended the Istituto Universitario de Architettura, Venice 1964–69; received a degree in architecture 1969; studied under Carlo Scarpa. Assistant to Le Corbusier, Venice and Paris 1965. Private practice, Lugano from 1969; member, Swiss Federal Commission for the Fine Arts 1982–87. Professor, École Polytechnique Fédéral, Lausanne, Switzerland from 1983; visiting professor, Yale University, New Haven, Connecticut 1987; committee member, International Course for Architectural Planning, Andrea Palladio International Centre for Architectural Studies 1989. Member, Federation of Swiss Architects 1978; honorary fellow, Bund Deutscher Architekten 1983; honorary fellow, American Institute of Architects 1984; member, Acádemie d'Architecture, Paris 1991.

Selected Works

Bianchi House, Riva San Vitale, Switzerland, 1973
Secondary School, Morbio Inferiore, Ticino, Switzerland, 1977
Library, Capuchin Convent, Lugano, Switzerland, 1979
Casa Rotondo, Stabio, Switzerland, 1981
State Bank, Fribourg, Switzerland, 1982
Housing Complex, Novazzano, Switzerland, 1982
Ransila I Building, Lugano, Switzerland, 1985
André Malraux Maison de la Culture, Chambéry, France, 1987
Mediathéque, Villeurbanne, France, 1988
Art Gallery, Tokyo, 1990
San Francisco Museum of Modern Art, 1994
Union Bank, Basel, Switzerland, 1995

Selected Publications

"Architecture and Environment," *A + U* (June 1979)
"Swiss Transmission and Exaggerations" (interview), *Skyline*, 2/8 (1980)
"Ein Raum für Guernika," *Werk, Bauen und Wohnen*, 11 (1981)
La Casa Rotonda, 1982

Further Reading

A fairly complete and well-illustrated three-volume catalog of Botta's work has recently been published (Pizzi, 1993–98). Botta's designs usually receive ample coverage in architectural magazines, while scholarly articles are scarce.

Abrams, Janet, "Mario Botta's San Francisco Museum of Modern Art," *Lotus International*, 86 (1995)
Bedaria, Marc, "The House of Culture of Chambery: An Example of Decentralization," *Lotus International*, 43 (1984)
Botta, Mario, and Enzo Cucchi, *La cappella del Monte Tamaro: The Chapel of Monte Tamaro* (bilingual Italian-English edition), Turin: Umberto Allemandi, 1994
Carloni, Tita, "Architect of the Wall and Not of the Trilith," *Lotus International*, 86 (1983)
Dimitri, Livio, "Architecture and Morality—An Interview with Mario Botta," *Perspecta*, 20 (1983)
Frampton, Kenneth, "Mario Botta and the School of the Ticino," *Oppositions*, 14 (Fall 1978)
Musi, Pino, and Marco d'Anna, *Mario Botta: Public Buildings, 1990–1998*, edited by Luca Molinari, Milan: Skira, 1998
Nicolin, Pierluigi, *Mario Botta: Buildings and Projects, 1961–1982*, New York: Rizzoli, and London: Electra/Architectural Press, 1984
Pizzi, Emilio, *Mario Botta*, Barcelona: Gustavo Gili, 1991
Pizzi, Emilio, *Mario Botta: The Complete Works*, 3 vols., Zurich: Artemis, 1993–98

Purini, Franco, "Inner Voices: Observations on Architecture and Mario Botta," *Lotus International*, 48–49 (1986)
Zardini, Mirko, *The Architecture of Mario Botta*, New York: Rizzoli, 1985

BRASILIA, BRAZIL 1955–60

The construction of Brasilia, the much-maligned capital city of Brazil, represents an important and cathartic moment in the history of modern architecture and the International Style. As well as becoming a national emblem for the geographically disparate country, Brasilia has also become, in more recent times, a symbol for some of the perceived shortcomings of the modernist movement. Bringing together many of the European ideals that had accompanied the utopian urban plans of the postwar years, Brasilia necessitated the deployment of monumental architecture on a scale almost unprecedented in the 20th century. The emphasis on establishing a new cultural identity for the South American power was interwoven with the global architectural language of Oscar Niemeyer and the Le Corbusian-inspired planning of his mentor Lúcio Costa. The optimistic proposal was to be realized within an incredibly short construction period and in the wake of enormous political pressure.

The decision to relocate the Brazilian capital from Rio de Janeiro to Brasilia in the isolated interior of the country was set against a backdrop of domestic instability and individual ambition. In 1955 Juscelino Kubitschek had been elected president of Brazil by a slender margin and without a party majority. The decision to build a new capital was motivated by the need to consolidate the support of a marginal electorate as well as the need to project Brazil into the technological age. The geography of the country had dictated much of the political and economic structure of Brazil, concentrating most of the population and industry along the scenic Atlantic coast that housed most of Brazil's major cities. An inland capital was intended to not only symbolically relocate the seat of national power but also shift the demographic and economic focus away from the European colonial powers and toward the vast domestic hinterland. This was part of Kubitschek's nationwide industrialization process that sought to rapidly develop rural and remote regions of Brazil and bring egalitarian prosperity to the emerging country. The new capital was to be a symbol for this modernization, establishing a new national identity and offering the opportunity to reform the convoluted bureaucracy of the old capital in Rio.

The fact that Kubitschek was limited to a single five-year term in office necessitated that the epic project be realized within this period. The vast scale and enormous technical impediments to the project meant that the preliminary design of the city had to be undertaken with speed and efficiency. Brazil's most internationally renowned architect, Oscar Niemeyer, who had previously worked with Kubitschek, was appointed to direct the works and given complete control over the design and construction process. On 16 March 1957, Niemeyer announced a national competition for the master plan of the new capital and, as an important member of the jury, was instrumental in awarding the winning scheme to Lúcio Costa (his teacher and former employer). Niemeyer was to be the architect for the buildings extending a long period of successful collaboration between the two men. Construction was begun in 1957 and the new capital city was inaugurated on schedule on 21 April 1960.

Costa's plan for the city was hinged around the intersection of two monumental axes, marking Brasilia as the symbolic and geographic center of Brazil. The characteristic arrangement houses the three branches of government—legislative, executive, and judicial—along a lineal central axis that Costa calls the Plaza of the Three Powers. From here, two wings radiate in either direction, housing the ministry buildings and embassies, giving the plan a diagrammatic relationship to a modern aircraft. This cruciform plan was an important symbol aligning the new capital not only with more traditional Catholic typology but also with the pervasive imagery of modernism, progress, and flight. Unlike the congested streets of Brazil's coastal metropolises, the new capital was serviced by broad, expansive highways that celebrated automation and the technological convenience of the modern age.

Costa had followed Le Corbusier's Ville Radieuse (Radial City) (partially implemented at Chandigarh) by isolating the political and administrative centers of the new capital from the housing and recreational facilities, which radiated out from the circumference of this new monolithic center. However, it was the imposing architectural composition of Niemeyer that most clearly reiterated the formal principles of Le Corbusian modernism. The language of Niemeyer's grandiose structures betrayed a profound allegiance to Le Corbusier and, in particular, his work at Chandigarh. Niemeyer, in reverence to the Punjab capital, implemented a simple but elegant geometric language to articulate the colossal monuments of Costa's plan. The austerity of this new architectural entourage, like many modernist projects, attempted a synthesis between an idealistic social vision and pure geometric form. The attenuated scale of the buildings deployed in the capital worked with the master plan to facilitate a characteristically modernist reunification between architecture, nature, and the individual.

The Plaza of the Three Powers represents the political and architectural epicenter for the new capital. The elegant Palácio de Planalto (Highland Palace) became the new seat for Brazil's government, housed within a single structure running parallel to the plaza. Giant, curved concrete pilasters articulate the exterior of the building, allowing the roof and floors to float gracefully above the ground. Opposite the palace and separated by a broad public space is the Supreme Court, which employs a similar language of forms to the palace with the strong rhythm of sculptural pilasters that dominates the elevation. In the vast space between these two buildings, along the center of the axis, is the Museum of the City of Brasilia, characterized by a dramatic horizontal cantilever that memorializes the construction of the city. A large bust of Kubitschek faces back toward the palace, unmistakably commemorating the president responsible.

The central axis is also the site of several important cultural buildings including the National Theatre and the sculptural Metropolitan Chapel. The chapel, in particular, is an important structure subtly demarcating the roles of politics and religion within Costa's plan for a utopian urbanism. The poetic conical structure is formed by 16 bent concrete pilasters opening out at the top to form a crown. Between the concrete supports is a mosaic of colored glass (redesigned in 1970 by Marianne Peretti) transmitting a powerful spirituality to the internal space. This is heightened by the entry procedure, which takes visitors underground before depositing them dramatically in the center of the internalized crystal chamber. The National Theatre also makes use of a pyramidal form elegantly housing two theaters within a terraced subterranean crater.

The end of the Plaza of the Three Powers is punctuated by the third major administrative building—the authoritative residence of the Congress. This colossal structure dominates the surrounding landscape with two slender concrete towers on a broad horizontal plinth. The two bodies of congress (the House of Deputies and the Senate) are expressed by two enormous parabolic dishes, one inverted, that are located on either side of the two towers above the podium. The circular form of the dishes allows a seductive interior layout for the two legislative bodies, distributing, rather than focusing, power.

The playful composition of the Congress, set against the expansive public spaces of the plaza, marks the hierarchical apex of the axis forming a hinging point in the whole design. Costa's plan is reminiscent of the principles of the colonial baroque architecture (evident in many coastal cities of Brazil) that established primary and secondary functional corridors. Architecturally, Neimeyer established this hierarchy through the use of form and finish to distinguish between the sacred Plaza of the Three Powers and the secondary administrative axis that bisects it. The various ministries that make up the two curved wings of the plan are accommodated within undistinguished Cartesian office blocks, less elaborate than the parliamentary buildings in both form and execution.

Recent writers have applied a more critical eye to Brasilia and observed that Niemeyer's structures unwillingly enforced a cultural hierarchy by allocating expensive finishes and detailing to the institutional structures and neglecting the sites of work and leisure. Unlike the rough Brutalism of Chandigarh, which was uncompromising in its rough-cast concrete finish, many of the significant buildings of Brasilia are finished with luxurious yet cosmetic surfaces like marble, metal, and mirrored panels. The most pronounced contrast with this, and the subject of many contemporary critiques of the city, is embodied in the sprawling housing sectors that surround the capital and quickly became the scene of crime, poverty, and disease. As a result, Brasilia became a city of transit for politicians who generally resided in Rio de Janeiro and visited the capital only intermittently. The residents of the city, many of whom had been instrumental in its construction, were relegated to ramshackle favelas enveloping the periphery of the city. This divisive relationship between the center and the periphery seemingly enforces a rigid social stratification between the monumental majesty of the governing elite and the working-class squatters, betraying the egalitarian rhetoric that initially inspired the construction of the new capital.

Nowhere is the decadent luxury of Brasilia more evident than in the lavish presidential palace, which exists on an isolated site apart from the other institutional buildings. Known as the Alvarado Palace, the expansive residence was the first building completed at Brasilia and remains one of the most recognizable and influential of Niemeyer's buildings. It quickly became the architectural symbol of the new capital. The palace employs a similar language to the Federal Government and Supreme Court monuments, dominated by an inverted arched colonnade that sinks gracefully into a pristine reflecting pond. The palace incorporates a private chapel, signaling the seamless influence of the Catholic Church on the affairs of state. Located at the side of the imposing palace, the plan of the chapel is based on a sweeping spiral that, like the plastic forms of Le Corbusier's Ronchamp, leads the visitor from the sculptural whitewashed exterior toward a discreet and contemplative altar. The geographic and spiritual isolation of the residence, as well as its imposing scale, further elaborates the social stratification intrinsic to the program of the new Capital.

Only four years after the city's completion, Brazil was the victim of a military coup that instantaneously reversed the democratic and egalitarian principles that had initially inspired the construction of the new capital. The next 20 years within the country were characterized by a turbulent political landscape that ultimately led Niemeyer to live in exile in Europe for several years. Despite this, Niemeyer, although occasionally distancing himself from the design of the city, continued his association with the capital under the new regime, finishing the construction of several important buildings, including the Ministry of Justice. Significantly, in 1980 Niemeyer proposed a monument to commemorate the death of Juscelino Kubitschek, who had been the political and spiritual force behind the new city. The monument, whose form is reminiscent of the hammer and sickle, houses the tomb of the former president in a serene underground chamber.

However, possibly the most elegant and graceful of all of the buildings at Brasilia is the Pantheon of Liberty and Democracy, completed in 1987 in memory of Tancredo Neves. The poetic reinforced concrete sails of the pyre now enclose the southern end of the Plaza of the Three Powers, juxtaposed against the robust silhouette of the congress building at the northern end. The expressive structure subtly completes the urban composition, complementing the formal austerity of the earlier monumental structures with contemporary images of peace and harmony.

Despite failing in its intention to create a more egalitarian society through pure architectural expression, the city of Brasilia remains a powerful urban gesture, layered with symbolism of form and meaning deployed across a rich architectural tapestry. The dominant scenography, rigid geometric planning, and uniform aesthetic language effectively unite the diverse political, social, and artistic forces of the turbulent South American nation, forming a capital that is as inspirational as it is imperfect. The elegant poetry, epic scale, and often-naïfe socialism embodied in the monumental forms provide an important commentary on both the best and worst aspects of the Modern movement.

MICHAEL CHAPMAN

See also **Chandigarh, India; Corbusier, Le (Jeanneret, Charles-Édouard) (France); Costa, Lúcio (Brazil); Niemeyer, Oscar (Brazil)**

Further Reading

Botey, Joseph Ma, *Oscar Niemeyer*, Barcelona: Gustavo Gili, 1996

Evenson, Norma, *Two Brazilian Capitals: Architecture and Urbanism in Rio de Janeiro and Brasilia*, New Haven: Yale University Press, 1973

Holston, James, *The Modernist City: An Anthropological Critique of Brasilia*, Chicago: University of Chicago Press, 1989

Underwood, David, *Oscar Niemeyer and the Architecture of Brazil*, New York: Rizzoli, 1994

BRAZIL

The 20th-century architecture of Brazil became widely famous for its originality and formal freedom in contrast to more codified paradigms of modernism. Celebrated abroad as a step ahead of functionalism and rationalism, Brazilian modernism acquired international significance in the 1950s, and the effects of it can still be found in contemporary architecture. However, to grasp the full scope of Brazilian 20th-century architecture, it is necessary to understand the radical transformations in its economy and society that led to an accelerated process of urbanization. From 17 million inhabitants in 1900, 70 percent of whom were living in rural areas, Brazil closed the century with almost 170 million, with more than 60 percent living in urban areas.

Brazilians entered the 20th century under the influence of positivism and sanitary engineering as two events of 1897 indicate: the planned city of Belo Horizonte was inaugurated to replace the 18th-century Ouro Preto as the capital of the state of Minas Gerais, and Canudos, a fast-growing spontaneous settlement guided by messianic leader Antonio Conselheiro in Bahia, was destroyed by the Brazilian army. Both the plan of Belo Horizonte by engineer Aarão Reis and the Canudos war campaign reveal positivist views of sanitation and circulation in vogue at that time.

Following that direction, the 1900s would be marked in Rio by the urban reformations of Pereira Passos, with avenues being opened and slums being displaced while civic buildings in French neoclassical style took its place (for example, in Teatro Nacional, 1906). In 1927 another plan by the French urbanist Alfred Agache would be the structure for Rio's main transformations of the first half of the century. Meanwhile, São Paulo experimented an exhilarating growth brought about by the coffee-based economy that provided new developments based on garden city ideas for the emergent middle class. Around 1905 Victor Dubugras was designing railroad stations in the Art Nouveau style, initiating what would be São Paulo's cosmopolitan modernity.

Later, in the second decade of the century, a debate would arise regarding issues of local identity versus international images with the arrival of Art Deco on the one hand and the development of neo-Colonial styles on the other. The Deco tradition was manifest in many of Brazil's landmarks, such as the Cristo Redentor statue over Rio, the City Hall in Belo Horizonte, and multiple buildings and viaducts in São Paulo. On the other hand, the neo-Colonial movement, led by José Mariano Filho, would battle against the modernist avant-garde ideas during the whole of the 1920s and 1930s but would also be fundamental to give Brazilian modernism its character by valuing the forms of 18th-century baroque.

Until the 1920s, modernism had an impact only on some isolated painters and writers who were influential within architectural developments. The event that marks the starting point of Brazilian avant-garde is the Semana de Arte Moderna, a week of exhibitions, lectures, and poetry declamation organized in São Paulo in 1922. From this period, we can highlight the works of Oswald de Andrade on texts such as *Manifesto Antropófago* and the young female painters Anita Malfatti and Tarsila do Amaral. They attempted to resolve the apparently opposing forces of abstract internationalism and the representation of local identities. After the polemical introduction at the Semana, Brazilian avant-garde artists gradually turned to the issue of adapting the avant-garde to Brazilian reality and "Brazilianess." As early as 1925, articles appeared in São Paulo's newspapers by Rino Levi and Gregory Warchavchik, who were the first exponents of what contemporary historiography calls "modern architecture in Brazil" (primarily derived from European traditions) to differentiate it from "Brazilian modern architecture" (exemplified by Brazilian-derived ideas and formal vocabularies). Rino Levi (Art Palacio Movie Theater, 1936) became an exemplar of Brazilian modernism, whereas Warchavchik (House at Rua Itápolis, 1928) would play an important role as Costa's partner for a while and also as the first Latin American delegate to the CIAM (Congrès Internationaux d'Architecture Moderne).

In 1930, in what would be one of the key moments of Brazilian architecture, Lúcio Costa was named director of ENBA (National School of Beaux-Arts). As soon as he was named, Costa began a radical reformation of the art and architecture curriculum based on the Bauhaus pedagogy and Le Corbusier's ideas in architecture. The strong reaction against the changes led to Costa's replacement 11 months later, but the ideas that he installed flourished with a generation of students at that time: Oscar Niemeyer, Roberto Burle Marx, Affonso Raidy, Carlos Moreira, Milton Roberto, Luis Nunes, and Henrique Mindlin, among others. Until 1930 the ENBA still adopted the 19th-century academic approach to architectural teaching, with a strong emphasis on classical figurative drawing. This was changed in the 1930 curricular reformation, and this early generation of Brazilian modern architects took advantage of both the strong domain of classical drawing and the new architectural freedom of avant-garde techniques. After leaving the ENBA, Costa went to work for the Ministry of Education and Culture on the organization of SPHAN, the Brazilian Office for Conservation of Historic Monuments.

With the task of cataloging, protecting, and publicizing Brazilian historic and artistic heritage, the Serviço do Patrimônio Histórico e Artístico (SPHAN) was created in 1937. Costa's acumen played a major role in the articulation of Brazilian modern architecture, stitching together the past and the future into a very effective concept of architecture. Standing in defense of the 18th-century baroque, not yet valued by modern critique and diminished by the Beaux-Arts academia, Costa sought transitions and continuations rather than ruptures and breaks; he thus conceived of modern architecture as a natural continuation of the baroque style.

In 1936 Le Corbusier was invited as a supportive consultant for the team of architects commissioned to design the new building for the Brazilian Ministry of Education and Health (MES). The invitation of Le Corbusier served as a support for canceling the previous competition, as the winning design was considered by the government to be incompatible with the modern image that it was trying to establish. The MES building, one of the first high-rises of the world following Le Corbusier's five points, would catalyze a whole generation of young architects and artists, with the murals by Candido Portinari, sculptures by Bruno Giorgi, and gardens by Burle Marx, around the architecture developed by Costa, Carlos Leão, Jorge Moreira, and mainly Oscar Niemeyer, inspired by Le Corbusier.

The years before and during World War II would also witness the spread of modernist architects all around the country and the battles between modernists and traditionalists in Rio. In

Santa Efigênia Viaduct, São Paulo, Brazil (architects unknown)
© Eduardo Costa

Recife, Luis Nunes would direct the municipal building office and collaborate with structural Joaquim Cardoso (Water Tower, 1937) and Saturnino N. Brito (Anatomical Laboratory, 1940), and Burle Marx was redesigning the city's public gardens. In São Paulo, Rino Levi designed the Sedis Sapientiae building (1942), and Alvaro Vital Brasil designed the Esther Building (1937). However, Rio de Janeiro was still the country's capital, and there, in addition to the Roberto Brothers ABI (1936) and Santos Dumont Airport (1944), Atílio Correa Lima designed the Seaplane station (1940), and Niemeyer designed a nursery (Obra do Berço, 1937) and his own house (1939) at Lagoa.

Meanwhile, a vigorous debate around architecture and national identity would turn into many battles fought through competitions and commissions. The federal government maintained a twofold take on architecture all the way through the 1930s, alternating commissions between modernists and traditionalists. In 1939 a commission was done for a hotel in the city of Ouro Preto, home of the most important baroque buildings in Brazil, with SPHAN responsible for the project. Niemeyer's modernist scheme modified by Costa's advice (adding a ceramic roof like the rest of the city and wooden trellises instead of steel *brises-soleil*) was accepted and built. With the Grande Hotel de Ouro Preto (1942), a modernist design in the heart of the main historical city of Minas Gerais, the modernist group demonstrated the possibility of blending modernity with tradition.

The decade would end with the first international exposure of Brazilian modernism with the design for the Brazilian Pavilion at the 1939 New York World's Fair. The combination of Le Corbusian volumes with sensual curves caught the attention of the architectural media, and just four years later the Museum of Modern Art in New York mounted the "Brazil Builds" exhibition. The accompanying catalogue by Philip Goodwin became the first text on Brazilian modern architecture to be published in English. Goodwin's marriage of modernity and Brazilian heritage was further advanced by Costa and would be the conceptual basis for many of the most successful Brazilian buildings after the 1940s.

In 1941 Niemeyer was commissioned by the city's mayor, Jucelino Kubitschek (who would be the president who built Brasília 15 years later) to design a series of buildings around Pampulha's artificial lake, in Belo Horizonte. Niemeyer's designs of Capela da Pampulha, Casa do Baile, Casino, and Iate Clube became the model for Brazilian architectural modernism for decades. The Capela was revolutionary for breaking with the Le Corbusian paradigm, with its walls and ceiling that were not "free" (or flexible) but inseparable. Ceramic tiles *(pastilhas)* cover its parabolic vaults, and a ceramic panel *(azulejo)* decorates the rear wall. The Casino presents a free-form canopy supported by thin steel columns and the continuous glass wall on the facade. Inside the cubic main volume, the ramp dominates functionally, and the round concrete columns punctuate the rhythm of the interior space. The impact of the Pampulha buildings was considerable, initially in Brazil just after its completion in 1942 and then abroad. The international debate of the following decade would embrace Brazilian architecture in its core, with Nikolaus Pevsner labeling Pampulha as subversive work, Reyner Banham claiming it as the first national style in modern architecture, and Gino Dorfles describing Niemeyer's work as neobaroque.

The architecture of the 1950s is still considered the golden years of Brazilian modernism. Starting with Rino Levi designing the headquarters of the Brazilian Institute of Architects (1949) in São Paulo and Affonso Raidy designing the Museum of Modern Art (1952) in Rio, the 1950s would also witness innumerable fascinating buildings by Sergio Bernardes (House for Lota M. Soares and Elizabeth Bishop, 1952), Francisco Bolonha (Maternity Hospital, 1951, in Cataguases and Kindergarten, 1952, in Vitória), Alvaro Vital Brasil (Banco da Lavoura, 1951, in Belo Horizonte), and Niemeyer (Ibirapuera Pavilions, 1954), as well as the Burle Marx gardens. In a time of accelerating industrialization and urbanization, the issue of housing was at the core of the 1950s practice. The Pedregulho complex (1950) by Raidy, the Bristol apartments (1950) by Costa, and the Kubitschek complex (1953) by Niemeyer in Belo Horizonte are the most well known, but other, still little-known architects were laboring to improve housing quality and quantity in government offices, such as Carmem Portinho at the PDF (Rio's office for public building). In the 1950s, a second generation of modernist architects would emerge from the Rio–São Paulo axis including Acacio Gil Borsoi in Recife, Edgar Graeff in Porto Alegre, and Eduardo Guimarães and Sylvio de Vasconcelos in Belo Horizonte, effectively extending the achievements of modern architecture to new frontiers. However, the most important group, formed around the late 1950s, might be the later-called Escola Paulista (São Paulo School). The group, formed around João Batista Villanova Artigas, would advocate for an open architecture in terms of content while developing a unique aesthetic of exposed concrete, generous slabs, and rigorous geometry. Among many extraordinary buildings are the School of Architecture (1967) at the University of São Paulo and Morumbi Stadium (1969) by Artigas and the Brazilian Pavilion (1970) at Osaka and the Junqueira House (1976) by Paulo Mendes da Rocha, who would be of the major Brazilian architects of the late decades of the 20th century with his designs for the Museu da Escultura (Sculpture Museum, 1986) and Pinacoteca renovation (1995), both in São Paulo.

The golden years of Brazilian modernism led to the construction of Brasilia (1955–60). During the presidential term of Juscelino Kubitschek, the idea of building a new capital in the heartland was put forward, and the planning competition was won by Costa in 1956, with major buildings by Niemeyer (Congress, Cathedral, Foreign Ministry, and Presidential residence [Alvorada] and offices [Planalto], among many others). The new capital was opened on 21 April 1960. The international reaction to Brasilia is well known and ranges from the Alvorada columns being copied worldwide to a severe social criticism of the city's flaws. However, its construction would change fundamentally the panorama of Brazilian modernism after that. In the geopolitical realm, the inland capital induced a vector of penetration toward the backlands. On the symbolic level, the buildings by Niemeyer (especially the Congress with its twin towers and inverted spherical capes) would become the icons of Brazilian institutions. In terms of architecture, Brasilia marks the climax of the modernist paradigm and the beginning of its critique and revision that followed.

While Brasilia was under construction, Lina Bò Bardi (an Italian immigrant living in Brazil since 1947) was completing her Museum of Modern Art (1957) in São Paulo. In the early 1960s, Bardi worked in Salvador, where she renovated 17th-century buildings and worked with popular art exhibitions in preparation for the construction of the Museum of Art at that city. However, the military coup of 1964 aborted her plans and those of many other architects. Without ever actually leaving the architectural scene, she came back with the SESC-Pompéia (1987), a sports/cultural facility in São Paulo.

The 1970s, known in Brazil as the "economic miracle" years, experienced huge housing projects financed by the National Housing Bank in which the control was with the construction firms, marginalizing most architects to a secondary role. The military regime was also responsible for the exile of exponent architects, such as Niemeyer, Artigas, and Vasconcellos, repressing architecture schools that were a focus of cultural and political discussion on the 1960s. Although the construction industry was busy with megahousing projects, the more talented architects were revising the modernist dogmas and receiving the early Postmodern ideas from Europe and the United States. The critique of modernism carried out in Brazil during the 1970s is also associated with a demand for regional solutions, a reaction against the hegemony of the Rio and São Paulo Schools. Deep in the Amazon, Severiano Porto was experimenting with climatic and formal solutions (Architect's house, 1971; Silves hostel, 1979; Balbina's environmental center, 1984), whereas in Salvador, João Filgueiras Lima (State Administrative Center, 1973, and several Sarah hospitals since the 1970s) and Francisco Assis Reis (Chesf building, 1978) were advancing the ideas of late modernism. Also under a late-modernist approach were the buildings by Carlos E. Comas, Carlos Fayet in Porto Alegre (Centro de Abastecimento, 1972), Luis Paulo Conde in Rio (Ewerton house, 1968, and UERJ [State University] Complex, 1968), and Humberto Serpa and Marcus Vinicius Meyer in Belo Horizonte (BDMG building, 1969).

Beyond the late modernism of the 1970s, a generation of young architects in Belo Horizonte took Postmodernist ideas further away. Gravitating around *Pampulha* magazine (a direct reference to Niemeyer's buildings at that same city), founded in 1979, the "Mineiros" catalyzed the Postmodern/regionalist tendencies of the 1980s in Brazil. The Touristic Support Center building (1982; called Rainha da Sucata) by Eolo Maia and Sylvio Podestá in Belo Horizonte epitomizes their movement with its bright colors, rusted metal surfaces, and plenty of formal quotations from the surroundings. The 1980s would then have pluralism and regionalism as its axis, with an intense debate between proponents of a continuation of late-modernist ideas and the defendants of Postmodern rupture. In 1991, in a competition for the Brazilian Pavilion at the Sevilla Expo, this debate would reach its peak. The first prize (never built) was awarded for a group of Paulistas (Angelo Bucci and others); the runners-up were Eolo Maia and Joel Campolina, and a special award (Paulo Leander) was given to the Mineiros. In São Paulo, now the financial center of the new Brazilian economy, Rui Othake designed several high-rise apartment buildings while Gian F. Gasperini and Roberto Aflalo changed the face of Paulista Avenue with their design for the Citibank building.

The last decade of the 20th century also saw the rise of a very talented generation of architects in Recife galvanized by Fernando Montezuma (Camelódromo [street vendors pavilion], 1994) and in Porto Alegre with Edson Mahfuz. In Rio de Janeiro, an extensive project of urban design, public facilities, and renovation was put forward by Luis Paulo Conde, first as the Municipal Secretary of Urbanism (1992–96) and then as mayor (1996–2000). Rio Cidade (urban design of downtown areas) and Favela-bairro (improvements and infrastructure at the shanty hills) are among the successful cases of good architecture serving the public at the end of the century.

As the 20th century came to an end, Brazil showed a dynamic internal architectural scene with almost 100 schools in 20 states, despite not participating much on the international scene. That started to change in the late 1990s with the renewed interest in Brazilian modernism being exhibited and discussed worldwide, and this should project its 20th-century accomplishments well into the third millennium.

FERNANDO LARA

See also **Bò Bardi, Lina (Brazil); Brasilia, Brazil; Burle Marx, Roberto (Brazil); Church of St. Francis of Assisi, Brazil; Costa, Lúcio (Brazil); Guedes, Joaquim (Brazil); Levi, Rino (Brazil); Niemeyer, Oscar (Brazil); Pampulha Buildings, Belo Horizonte, Brazil; Rio de Janeiro, Brazil; São Paulo, Brazil**

Further Reading

Broadbent, Geoffrey, "Brazil Still Builds: Vilanova Artigas and Affonso Eduardo Reidy," *AA Files*, 37 (1998)

Bruand, Yves, *Arquitetura contemporânea no Brasil*, São Paulo: Editora Perspectiva, 1981

Lemos, Carlos Alberto Cerqueira, *Arquitetura Brasileira*, São Paulo: Melhoramentos, 1979

Mindlin, Henrique E., *Modern Architecture in Brazil*, New York: Reinhold, and London: Architectural Press, 1956

Segawa, Hugo, "The Essentials of Brazilian Modernism," *Design Book Review*, 32/33 (1994)

Segawa, Hugo, *Arquiteturas no Brasil, 1900–1990*, São Paulo: EDUSP, 1998

Underwood, David Kendrick, *Oscar Niemeyer and the Architecture of Brazil*, New York: Rizzoli, 1994

Xavier, Alberto (compiler), *Arquitetura moderna Brasileira: Depoimento de uma Geração*, São Paulo: Associação Brasileira de Ensino de Arquitetura, 1987

BREUER, MARCEL 1902–81

Architect, United States

Marcel Breuer was a master of scale. His designs ranged from the human anatomical scale of the chair to the domestic scale of his modern houses, the urban street scale of the museum, and the monumental scale of major international commissions. To observe these varied designs, Breuer's Bauhaus steel tubular chair (1928); his own houses in Lincoln, Massachusetts (1939), and New Canaan, Connecticut (1947); the Whitney Museum of American Art (1966) in New York City; and the United Nations Educational, Social and Cultural Organization (UNESCO) Headquarters (1958) in Paris will serve as excellent examples selected from his long career.

Breuer's tubular steel cantilevered chair is a primary legacy of the Bauhaus, recalled now in both its original and its ubiquitous copied forms. Breuer had come to the Bauhaus to follow Walter Gropius's belief that good design for mass production through the machine would improve living conditions for the common man. It was here, in the highly charged, creative atmosphere of prewar Germany, that Breuer first exhibited his talent, advancing from student to Bauhaus master of the furniture design workshop. The machine imagery of the Bauhaus is evident in two ways in the Breuer Bauhaus chair: first, it is a prototype for repetitive machine production, and, second, the materials of the tubular steel chair replicate the materials of another type of machine: the bicycle, a modernist icon.

Breuer further experimented with furniture, especially in bent plywood, producing his successful Isokon chair (1935) for an advanced London design firm. Isokon Furniture Company was really a rescue mission for Bauhaus refugees such as Breuer and Gropius, affording them employment and exit visas from Nazi Germany. Breuer was a very fortunate man to be helped early in his career by influential people such as Gropius and J.C. Pritchard, Isokon's founder. Pritchard supported Bauhaus refugees while they got on their feet, offering design commissions as well as stipends and living quarters in Isokon Flats, Hampstead, London. In return for Pritchard's largesse, Breuer produced some of the finest works to come out of the Isokon design line.

Gropius further aided Breuer when, after they both emigrated from Britain to the United States, Gropius brought Breuer to Harvard University to teach in the revamped design school and formed a working partnership with him as well. This led to their collaboration on an architectural compound of modern houses in rural Lincoln, Massachusetts: the Woods End Colony. Here, émigré Breuer built his first American house design for himself and began a major thread of his career in inventive forms of distinctly American domestic flavor. Domestic works of textural American wood and fieldstone, with clean lines and openness, became Breuer's first big success, as he increasingly moved away from Gropius's European white cubic architecture, eventually conceiving his signature two-wing house plan.

Breuer's Lincoln house is transitional, employing echoes of his earlier European white-box roots together with his new American tactileness, and relates both to his British Ganes Pavilion (1936) in Bristol and to Gropius's work. Breuer's American style was fully developed by the time he built his later house for himself in New Canaan, a simple statement of lightweight cantilevered construction, a wooden "crate" within rolling landscape. It is interesting to note that the cantilever form, which would organize this house and so much of Breuer's later architectural work, was first used by him in furniture design.

Breuer did not, however, confine himself to the domestic realm in which he had become so adept. Having left Harvard, teaching, and Gropius, he opened his own firm in New York City in 1946, winning important commissions for urban architecture, the most significant of which was his design for the

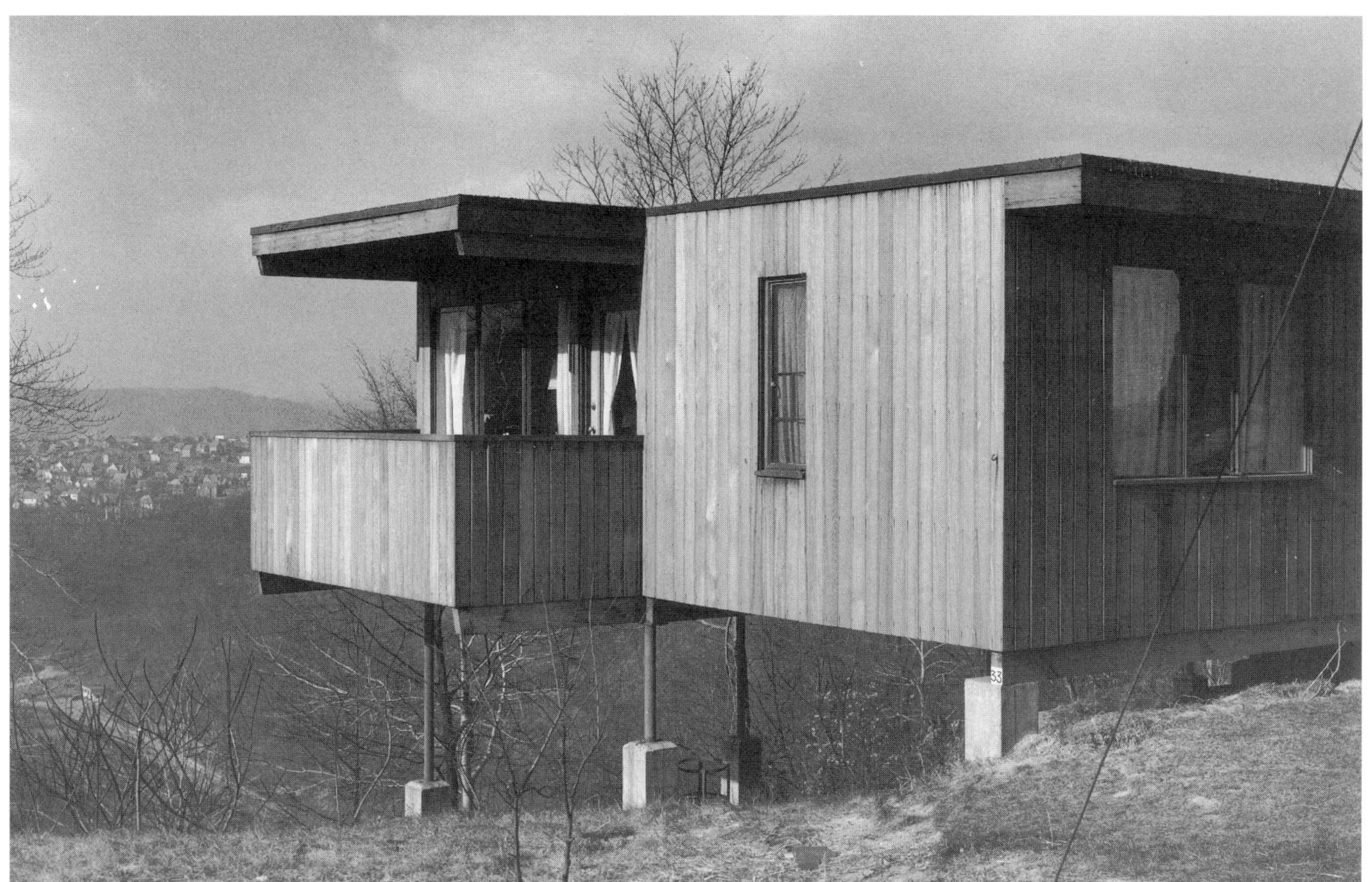

Aluminum City Terrace (Townhouse 33 out of 250), New Kensington, Pennsylvania, designed by Marcel Breuer and Walter Gropius (1941)
© Gottscho-Schleisner, Inc. photographer/Library of Congress, Prints and Photographs Division

Whitney Museum of American Art (1966) on Madison Avenue in New York City. This highly unusual design has remained controversial since its inception and was nearly effaced within a planned addition of a Postmodernist pastiche during the 1980s.

With this forceful building, Breuer broke with all expectations and sense of his former domesticity, yet he did not lose the sense of scale dictated by the urban pedestrian street. Breuer's vision of the Whitney is very brave new world, very Brutalist. It is a rare modern interpretation of the beauty of the sublime, the aesthetic of beauty heightened by awe and fear; it hangs ominously over Madison Avenue, reversing the traditional solid-void relationships of architecture, cantilevering its mass as a Breuer chair is structured. Its rock-faced hardness and aesthetic contortions speak to the hardness of the urban place and to the socially hard times of the America of its conception, the 1960s. Breuer's Whitney is a tough architecture—brutal but beautiful.

Breuer had by now moved into the international realm, which few architects reach, with such commissions as the UNESCO Headquarters in Paris, here sharing the design program with such international modern artists as Henry Moore, Alexander Calder, Jean Arp, and Pablo Picasso. For this monumental multi-use edifice, Breuer employed his sweeping Y-shaped plan in a sculptural concrete configuration. He hearkened back to his early unbuilt design for a concrete civic center (1936) for London, setting his massive tripartite building on Le Corbusian stilts. Although this work at first looks very bureaucratic, especially in its setting within the La Militaire sector of Paris, its most creative, intriguing feature—that it actually responds to the nearby landmark Eiffel Tower—is not readily apparent. In plan UNESCO's tripartite shape looks very like an Eiffel Tower laid on its side. Because this relationship, although undeniable, can be appreciated only in plan or by observation from the deck of the Eiffel Tower itself, one wonders whether the relationship was intentional or unconsciously created by Breuer in response to the Parisian site. In either case, it enriches the UNESCO design.

From the Bauhaus to New York to Paris, from the 1920s to the 1960s, Breuer created modern form. Chair to house to public monument, throughout the entire scale of the built environment, he responded to modern life. The aesthetics of Breuer have been endlessly influential in defining that place we call the modern world.

Leslie Humm Cormier

See also **Bauhaus; Bauhaus, Dessau; Brutalism; Gropius House, Lincoln, Massachusetts; Gropius, Walter (Germany)**

Biography

Born in Pécs, Hungary, 21 May 1902; emigrated to the United States 1937; naturalized 1944. Attended the Allami Föreäiskola, Pécs 1912–20; studied at the Bauhaus, Weimar, Germany 1920–24. Married (1) Martha Erps 1926; married (2) Constance Crocker 1940: 2 children. Professor, carpentry and furniture design programs, Bauhaus, Weimar 1924–28; master of the Bauhaus, Weimar 1924 and Dessau 1925–28. Independent architect and interior designer, Dessau 1925–28 and Berlin 1928–36; partnership with F.R.S. Yorke, London 1936–37; professor, Harvard University School of Design, Cambridge, Massachusetts 1937–46; collaborated with Walter Gropius, Cambridge 1937–41; private practice, Marcel Breuer and Associates, Cambridge 1941–46; moved practice to New York 1946–76; member, National Council of Architectural Registration Boards 1947; fellow, American Institute of Architects; member, National Institute of Arts and Letters; honorary member, Association of Argentine Architects 1947; honorary member, Association of Architects of Columbia 1947. Gold Medal, American Institute of Architects 1968; Gold Medal, French Academy of Architecture 1976. Died in New York, 1 July 1981.

Selected Works

Prototype Steel Furniture and Interchangeable Cabinet Units, 1924–28
Isokon Laminated Furniture (with F.R.S. Yorke), England, 1936
Gane's Exhibition Pavilion (with F.R.S. Yorke), Bristol, 1936
Civic Center of the Future (project with F.R.S. Yorke), London, 1936
Isokon Bar (with F.R.S. Yorke), London, 1937
Breuer House I, Lincoln, Massachusetts, 1939
Aluminum City Terrace housing complex, New Kensington, Pennsylvania (with Walter Gropius), 1941
Breuer House II, New Canaan, Connecticut, 1947
Institute for Advanced Study of Housing, Princeton University (with R.F. Gatje), New Jersey, 1957
UNESCO Headquarters (with Pier Luigi Nervi and Bernard Zehrfuss), Paris, 1958
IBM Research Center (with R.F. Gatje), Le Gaude, Var, France, 1961
Whitney Museum of American Art (with H. Smith), New York, 1966

Selected Publications

Sun and Shadow: The Philosophy of an Architect, edited by Peter Blake, 1955
Marcel Breuer, Buildings and Projects, 1921–62, 1962

Further Reading

Blake, Peter, *Marcel Breuer: Architect and Designer*, New York: Museum of Modern Art, 1949
Gatje, Robert F., *Marcel Breuer: A Memoir*, New York: Monacelli Press, 2000
Jordy, William H., "The Domestication of Modern," in *The Impact of European Modernism in the Mid–Twentieth Century*, by Jordy, Garden City, New York: Doubleday, 1972
Wilk, Christopher, *Marcel Breuer: Furniture and Interiors*, New York: Museum of Modern Art, 1981
Wingler, Hans Maria, *Das Bauhaus, 1919–1933: Weimar, Dessau, Berlin*, Bramsche: Gebr. Rasch, 1962; 2nd revised edition, as *Das Bauhaus, 1919–1933: Weimar, Dessau, Berlin, und die Nachfolge in Chicago seit 1937*, Cologne: DuMont Schauberg, 1968; 2nd edition translated as *The Bauhaus: Weimar, Dessau, Berlin, Chicago*, translated by Wolfgang Jabs and Basil Gilbert, edited by Joseph Stein, Cambridge, Massachusetts: MIT Press, and London: Cambridge Press, 1969; 3rd revised edition, Cambridge, Massachusetts: MIT Press, 1976

BRICK

"A common, ordinary brick," says Woody Harrelson, playing an architect in the movie *Indecent Proposal* (1993), "wants to be something more than it is." Harrelson proceeds to turn this proposition into a metaphor for the human condition, something never envisioned by the real architect who served as an inspiration for the movie's monologue. It was Louis I. Kahn (1903–74) who first posed a question in the early 1970s that has since attained legendary status within architectural circles: "What do you want, brick?" The answer, according to Kahn, is that brick wants to be an arch and not merely an in-fill or cladding material with no structural role.

In fact, a key to understanding brick as a modern architectural material lies precisely in its dual potential to be both structure and cladding. For the greater part of the history of architecture, brick walls assumed both roles, simultaneously supporting floors and roof while at the same time providing enclosure. It is only since the late 19th century that it has become possible to separate those roles by creating an independent framework of steel or reinforced concrete (structure) to which exterior brick may be attached (cladding). In this case, the brick no longer supports the floors and roof, although its appearance as cladding might well obscure this fundamental distinction.

From the Kahnian viewpoint, brick as mere cladding was inherently suspect. However, other modernists were equally distrustful of brick as load-bearing structure, as this seemed to negate the idea of the "free plan," the independence of structural framework from means of enclosure, and the opportunities for large glass areas. In fact, an influential faction of early 20th-century modern architects and theorists eschewed the use of brick in any form, associating it with the 19th-century cultural forces that they were attempting to overcome. They lobbied instead for the 20th century's revolutionary new materials of construction: glass, steel, and reinforced concrete. Where construction with brick walls was still found expedient within this context, a coat of plaster could transform the deviant surface into something acceptably plain and neutral. As a *symbol* of traditional culture and pre-industrial technology, brick was an easy target. However, brick's traditional role as load-bearing structure was also legitimately challenged by the need for greater heights and larger spans in the new commercial and industrial structures of the 19th and 20th centuries and by the ascendancy of heterogeneous, layered exterior wall systems that could accommodate air and vapor barriers, thermal insulation, and an air space (cavity) to block the migration of water through exterior walls.

Nevertheless, brick was never rejected absolutely and was, on the contrary, often found capable of embodying precisely the abstract formal values that helped define the new modernist aesthetic. Even load-bearing brick buildings remained influential well into the 20th century, acting as a kind of conservative moral datum of "honest" construction (what the brick really "wanted to be") opposed to some, but not all, modern tendencies. Architects continued to use brick with enthusiasm and, like Frank Lloyd Wright (1867–1959), boasted that in their hands the ordinary brick became "worth its weight in gold." Other practitioners, however, were less confident about the appropriateness of brick in modern construction; for them, brick represented a kind of compromise—accepted with various degrees of ambivalence—between the new culture, technology, and aesthetics of the 20th century and those that preceded it. At the same time, brick itself was subject to technological change, evidenced not only in the increased systemization of its manufacture, begun in the late 12th century and culminating in the 19th century's relentless mechanization of all aspects of the brick-making process, but in the application of Frederick Taylor's theory of scientific management to bricklaying in the first decades of the 20th century.

Brick was widely used throughout the 20th century, accommodated within virtually all styles. The chronological survey that follows is therefore necessarily incomplete and somewhat arbitrary. That being said, several key developments can be highlighted, starting with the period before World War I. Already, a number of trends can be discerned in the late 19th century that continued to be played out well into the 20th. The first can be illustrated by Daniel Burnham's design for the Monadnock Building in Chicago (1889) and H.P. Berlage's Amsterdam Stock Exchange (1903), both of which pointed the way toward a reinterpretation of brick informed by the modernist bias toward simple, relatively unornamented surfaces, even when used in load-bearing wall construction. A second, more complex tendency can be seen in the brick facade of Louis Sullivan's Wainwright Building in St. Louis (1890), which, while functioning as nonstructural cladding, was meant to express symbolically the "idea" of the steel framework behind it. What resulted, though, was a certain ambiguity—some would call it deceit—in which the actual construction of the building was severed from its outward form.

Eigen Haard Housing complex, designed by Michel de Klerk, Building #3, corner

A third trend derives from 19th-century brick-walled factory buildings characterized by flat brick surfaces, functional massing, and the use—at least internally—of heavy timber or cast-iron structural elements. In Hans Poelzig's chemical plant at Luban (1911), the asymmetric massing and unornamented surfaces were distinctly modern; in contrast, the small, rectangular and arched window openings that punctuated the brick walls evoked a premodern sensibility. On the other hand, the Fagus Werk factory in Alfeld-an-der-Leine (1911) and the model factory, Werkbund exhibition, Cologne (1914), by Walter Gropius and Adolf Meyer—both brick-clad buildings—contained elements of classical axiality in their massing while their innovative glass curtain walls, when photographed from the proper perspective, gave the buildings a dynamic modern appearance. An additional variation on this theme can be seen in Poelzig's Upper Silesia Tower in Posen (1911), where brick cladding is clearly expressed as nonstructural "in-fill" within an actual structural frame exposed on the building's surface. However, this remained a minority position, in part because the exposure of an actual skeletal framework, especially of steel, invites problems with corrosion, differential thermal movement, water and air infiltration, and the continuity of thermal insulation. Instead, it is Sullivan's attitude valuing formal expression above "truth in construction" that informs most brick architecture in the early 20th century. For example, many of Wright's early projects, including the Larkin Building in Buffalo (1904), the Robie House in Chicago (1909), and the Imperial Hotel in Tokyo (1916), although nominally load-bearing brick structures, were filled with hidden steel and concrete elements that allowed his formal vision to be actualized.

Finally, a fourth trend combining the textural possibilities of brick-bonding patterns with an interest in free-form massing and Romantic silhouette finds an analogue in certain so-called Expressionist projects from the early 20th century: examples include Michael de Klerk's Eigen Haard and Piet Kramer's De Dageraad housing estates in Amsterdam (1917 and 1923, respectively), in which otherwise straightforward brick facades are enlivened with curvilinear brick elements and decorative treatments.

Between the two world wars, brick was employed by a younger generation of European modernists experimenting with new spatial concepts informed by notions of Cartesian orthogonality and populated by interpenetrating planes and abstract cubic masses. In particular, the early work of Mies van der Rohe, starting with his brick villa project of 1923 and including his houses for Wolf (1925), Lange (1927), and Esters (1927), as well as his monument to Karl Liebknecht and Rosa Luxemburg (1926), attempted to reconcile these new formal attitudes with traditional brick-bearing wall construction. However, more commonly, where load-bearing brick was present, it was covered up with a smooth plaster finish, as in Erich Mendelsohn's Einstein Tower in Potsdam (1921), Gerrit Rietveld's Schroder House in Utrecht (1924), and J.J.P. Oud's Kiefhook Housing

Estate in Rotterdam (1930). In the United States, architects seemed less interested in the ideological struggle between an evolving modernist aesthetic and the use of traditional materials: brick was used as a primary cladding material in Raymond Hood's American Radiator (American Standard) Building (1923) and, combined with stainless steel, in William Van Alen's sumptuous Chrysler Building (1930).

After World War II, the use of brick, in both load-bearing walls and exterior cladding, was revitalized by a new interest in raw materials of construction that could be expressed in an aggressively straightforward manner. Of several such projects by Le Corbusier in France and India, the most influential was his pair of houses, the Maisons Jaoul at Neuilly-sur-Seine (1955), consisting of brick load-bearing walls supporting concrete-covered—but brick-faced—Catalan vaults. This so-called Brutalist aesthetic, in which brick was juxtaposed against deliberately exposed steel or concrete structural members, reappeared in buildings such as the Langham House Development at Ham Common, London, by James Stirling and James Gowan (1958) and in several projects by Louis Kahn, including the Phillips Exeter Academy Library in Exeter, New Hampshire (1972), and the Indian Institute of Management at Ahmedabad, India (1974). It is only with these projects by Kahn that the traditional load-bearing brick arch was finally permitted to enter the vocabulary of 20th-century architecture.

However, having been once let in, load-bearing brick, whether as wall, pier, or arch, has had little further impact on 20th-century architecture. Instead, it is primarily as nonstructural cladding that brick has made its presence felt, even within the Brutalist oeuvre. Mies's academic buildings at the Illinois Institute of Technology (IIT), designed at the end of World War II, used brick *and* steel as cladding over the actual steel framework: the brick appears ambiguously as both in-fill within, and foundation for, an elegantly detailed—but nonstructural—grid of painted steel. Yet the fact that the brick (and steel) could be seen on both the inside and the outside gave the construction a perverse kind of integrity, and it served as a role model for numerous other buildings, including the self-consciously Brutalist Hunstanton School in Norfolk, England, designed by Alison and Peter Smithson in 1949.

During this time, brick cladding became an accepted part of the modernist oeuvre, representing a compromise in which the historically resonant surface qualities of brick were fully integrated within the modernist vocabulary of unadorned orthogonal planes and cubic mass, of articulated solid and void. Kahn's influential Richards Medical Research Building at the University of Pennsylvania (1961), with its expansive, windowless brick surfaces, spawned numerous derivative works, including Ulrich Franzen's Agronomy Laboratory at Cornell University (1968) and Davis and Brody's Waterside Housing in New York City (1975). Earlier, Alvar Aalto, in his Baker House Dormitory at the Massachusetts Institute of Technology (1949) and Säynätsalo Town Hall in Finland (1952), made of the brick surface an even more explicit medium for the play of sensuality, imperfection, and historic reference.

Yet this compromise proved unstable. In the latter part of the 20th century, references to tradition involving brick, however stylized or ironic, became less constrained by the modernist formal aesthetic and more overtly rooted in historical precedent. A key moment in the development of this Postmodernism was the Guild House in Philadelphia (1963) by Robert Venturi. His axially positioned brick arch—nominally a load-bearing form but here purposefully articulated as nonstructural cladding—acted like a *sign* pointing to an intellectual attitude about history rather than as an attempt at some kind of reconciliation. James Wines and his group, SITE, produced a series of architectural projects beginning in the early 1970s that used various characteristics of brick walls as a starting point for an ironic integration of sculpture and architecture. This attitude, as in Venturi's Guild House, addressed brick forms not only as construction systems—SITE's use of "peeling," "notched," and "crumbling" brick walls was directed more at brick as cladding and at the recent banal history of big-box retail design—but also as the class-stratified culture supported by such projects. That issues of class became intertwined with the use of brick is illustrated as well by the so-called red-brick novelists in postwar Britain, associated with the "red-brick" universities (not the older and elite "stone" universities of Oxford and Cambridge), and the coincident phenomenon of Brutalist buildings in which the deployment of brick was meant to invoke a kind of working-class solidarity.

In a similar vein, American corporate Postmodern office skyscrapers of the 1980s were generally clad with thin stone veneer rather than brick. Nevertheless, brick continued to be widely used in Postmodern residences, schools, and related occupancies; a building that typifies the genre is the condominium project on 70th Street, New York, by Kohn Pedersen Fox (1987), in which a smooth, unadorned brick surface appears to support stylized stone moldings and pediments that step back much like the New York skyscrapers of the 1920s and 1930s. In Europe a far different Postmodernism emerged, favoring a synthesis of classical and Platonic geometric elements within which the Kahnian essence of brick—its weight, compressive strength, and solidity—were valued and exploited. Aldo Rossi's Burial Chapel in Giussano (1987) and Mario Botta's design for a private house in Vacallo (1989) serve as examples of this tendency.

Whether embraced, hidden, disowned, contrasted with more modern materials, or coopted within a new aesthetic, brick has played an active role within the cultures of both modern and Postmodern architecture. In contrast, so-called deconstructivist architecture in the final decades of the 20th century has virtually ignored brick, reverting to the radical modernist dogma in which abstract geometric surface and mass, the play of solid and void, the iconography of machine and grid, and the "new" materials of glass, steel, and concrete (or its nonstructural analogue, stucco) are once more combined, albeit in a self-consciously distorted and fragmented way. Characteristically, where deconstructivist brick appears most famously—in Peter Eisenman's Wexner Center for the Visual Arts (1990) in Columbus, Ohio—it is as a fragmented and stylized archaeological reconstruction of an armory denoting the site's past history rather than as "the building" itself.

During the course of the 20th century, as traditional load-bearing forms of construction encountered new structural and environmental systems, as well as new functional and spatial needs, and as traditional architectural paradigms encountered new forms of aesthetic expression, the answers to the question posed rhetorically by Kahn—"What do you want, brick?"—have shifted accordingly. That brick has continued to be commonly employed as cladding in the face of competition from more modern and technologically sophisticated materials is evidence enough that its nonstructural qualities—reasonable cost, flexibility, durability, impact resistance, and visual appearance—continue to be valued.

JONATHAN OCHSHORN

See also **Berlage, Hendrik Petrus (Netherlands); Brutalism; Burnham, Daniel H. (United States); De Klerk, Michel (Netherlands); Deconstructivism; Eisenman, Peter (United States); Fagus Werk, Alfeld, Germany; Gropius, Walter (Germany); Illinois Institute of Technology, Chicago; Imperial Hotel, Tokyo; Indian Institute of Management, Ahmadabad; Kahn, Louis (United States); Kohn Pederson Fox (United States); Larkin Building, Buffalo, New York; Mendelsohn, Erich (Germany, United States); Oud, J.J.P. (Netherlands); Poelzig, Hans (Germany); Rietveld, Gerrit (Netherlands); Robie House, Chicago; Smithson, Peter and Alison (Great Britain); Sullivan, Louis (United States); Venturi, Robert (United States); Wright, Frank Lloyd (United States)**

Further Reading

The history of brick in 20th-century architecture can be pieced together from readings in general architectural histories and in the accounts of individual architects, but sections or chapters dealing specifically with brick are unusual. Notable exceptions include Giedion and Patterson. For a good general reference work dealing with the production, properties, and historical use of brick, see the work by Plumridge and Meulenkamp. Building construction textbooks also contain information on bricks; an excellent chapter that includes a short history of brick masonry can be found in Allen. The Brick Industry Association publishes numerous books and technical articles on brick construction that can be ordered from 11290 Commerce Park Drive, Reston, VA 22091. Alternatively, refer to their web site listed below, especially their link to "technical notes."

Allen, Edward, *Fundamentals of Building Construction*, New York: Wiley, 1985; 3rd edition, 1999

Brick Industry Association <www.bia.org/>

Giedion, Sigfried, *Space, Time, and Architecture: The Growth of a New Tradition*, Cambridge, Massachusetts: Harvard University Press, and London: Oxford University Press, 1941; 5th edition, revised and enlarged, Cambridge, Massachusetts: Harvard University Press, 1967

Patterson, Terry L., *Frank Lloyd Wright and the Meaning of Materials*, New York: Van Nostrand Reinhold, 1994

Plumridge, Andrew, and Wim Meulenkamp, *Brickwork: Architecture and Design*, New York: Abrams, 1993

BRITISH LIBRARY, LONDON

Designed by Colin St. John Wilson; completed 1998
London, England

The British Library is arguably the most significant and controversial 20th-century public building in London, equal in importance to Sir Williams Chambers's Somerset House in the 18th century and Charles Barry and A.W.N. Pugin's Houses of Parliament in the 19th century, and the largest public building commissioned in the 20th century. In terms of its centrality as an institution, urbanistic visibility and impact, cost (£511 million, contrasted with £400 million for Norman Foster's Stansted Airport Outside London, and £35.5 million for the Sainsbury Wing of the National Gallery, London, 1990), size, length of gestation and realization, programmatic complexity, and architectural uniqueness, the British Library has no contemporary rivals. Its designer, the erudite Colin St. John Wilson (who earned a knighthood on its completion) enjoys a professional history nonpareil in modern Britain, comparable only to those 19th-century Beaux-Arts laureates who devoted entire careers to executing one or two major official buildings, or to his noble forebear, Sir John Soane, who labored over the Bank of England from 1788 to 1831 (although, unlike that vanished monument, destroyed in 1922, the British Library is likely to endure for several centuries).

Until 1998 the name of the British Library was synonymous with the British Museum, where it had resided since 1785; first in Montague House and after 1826 in Robert Smirke's colonnaded Greek Revival stronghold. From 1857 scholars perused books in the beloved round reading room surrounded by book stacks constructed by Sidney Smirke in the open courtyard of the museum under a ferro-vitreous dome. Exponential growth of the collection and readership led, in 1951, to a proposal for expansion. In 1962 Sir Leslie Martin (1908–2000) and his younger colleague, Colin Wilson (who by 1964 was solely in charge) were commissioned to design a new wing, adjacent to the existing museum building, which would be part of a mixed development of commercial, residential, and institutional uses.

Over the next 12 years, two different schemes were thoroughly worked out by Wilson for the Bloomsbury site, but the developing Preservationist movement demanded a different location. Furthermore, the merger in 1972 of the British Museum library with the National Science library necessitated a larger site. In 1973 the government acquired nine acres next to St. Pancras Station, for a completely independent structure. Over the next 25 years, Wilson and his partners, including his wife, library expert M.J. Long (1939–), grappled with shifting governments, altered requirements, surly bureaucrats, inflation, tight budgets, fickle architectural fashion, transformations in information technology, and fallible contractors, to bring to fruition a great library that, in the words of its architect, "embodies and protects the freedom and diversity of the human spirit in a way that borders on the sacred."

The relocation of the British Library was advantageous for many reasons. Not only did it allow for a more capacious building that would not be crammed onto an inadequate site (integral to the design was the notion of expansion; only the first phase of a three-phase program has been erected), but it represented a move to a part of London that, while more mercantile and industrial than Bloomsbury, has a great future as an international gateway, as it will provide a second terminus for cross-channel transit and is the hub of several rail and underground lines. Fortunate too is its proximity to St. Pancras Chambers (1878), now undergoing extensive restoration. Sir George Gilbert, Scott's Gothic Revival station and hotel, completed in 1878 (also fiercely criticized in its time), is a more sympathetic neighbor than the solemn stone museum, given Wilson's preference for the English Free style of the mid- and late 19th century over the neoclassical movement that preceded it. Both ensembles are multipurpose and contain very large spaces as well as more intimate rooms; both draw passersby toward them by inflecting away from the street; both have dramatic contrasts of vertical and horizontal volumes (a slender clock tower on the library gestures to the bustling silhouette of St. Pancras); and both are

British Library, London, designed by Colin St. John Wilson (1998)

polychromatic (the pinkish-red brick used in the British Library comes from the same Leicestershire source as that chosen by Scott), and in each case details are painted in contrasting hues. Further, the majestic train sheds behind the station, by engineers Ordish and Barlow, anticipate the tremendous spans encountered in the library.

The library serves a diverse assortment of functions and audiences: it is an urban stage, a forum, an art gallery, and a repository of knowledge. The generous plaza provides an inviting oasis within a dense quarter of the city and caters to the casual passerby as well as the bibliophile through impressive sculptures, generous seating, and an outdoor coffee shop; it also gives access to a conference center with auditorium, which can be entered independently when the main building is closed. Within the library, the public is immediately welcomed; the information desk and cloakrooms on the ground and lower levels and the cafeteria restaurants on the second and third floors are readily visible and accessible. To the left are the bookshop and a two-story exhibition area, properly protected from daylight, where rare manuscripts and educational materials are on display. On the fourth floor, the Friends' room leads to an ample landscaped terrace that overlooks the urban scene to the northeast. Although the sections show a complicated matrix of interlocking spaces, clear circulation patterns enable visitors to swiftly reach different destinations.

The reading rooms are flooded with inspirational, carefully controlled natural light, as is the main reception hall, which soars through the full height of the building and is the hinge between the humanities wing on the northwest and the science wing to the east. Those seeking information on technical subjects, where journals, ephemera, and electronic media are the rule, frequent the five reading rooms devoted to science. Tables are arranged around the perimeter and daylight enters through side windows; here, the reference materials are immediately available to readers, as that is the way most such researchers operate. The two humanities reading rooms, endowed with clerestories and skylights that bounce natural light off curved reflector walls, vary in proportion as well, allowing different temperaments to choose their preferred niches, open or intimate, central or peripheral. There are smaller enclosures for maps, manuscripts, and rare books and music. The books are stored in environmentally monitored levels below ground (additional volumes are stored off-site); the automated catalog and mechanized delivery make retrieval swift and efficient.

Wilson's own scholarly habits have sensitized him to the comfort of the researchers. The variety in the size, shape, and illumination of the spaces counters potential reader fatigue and contributes a sense of serenity and well-being that embraces both patrons and staff. Custom-designed furniture of wood and leather and carefully placed, beautifully detailed lamps and fittings provide a zone of concentration within the grander reaches of the reading rooms.

Wilson's credo that architectural form must derive from thoughtful attention to program and that it must be humane and inclusive means that the British Library presents no monolithic image to be captured in a single photograph. Rather, the building can be appreciated only over time by a moving and involved observer/user. This is not to say that Wilson overlooks the beauty inherent in the striking form or in materials that appeal to touch and hearing as well as sight. Besides the typical concrete, brick, and glass, the palette includes Purbeck stone, travertine, bronze, brass, leather, terra-cotta, glazed tile, luscious carpeting, American oak, African teak, and steel painted red and green; as one moves from public to private areas, the materials become softer and more sensual. The aesthetic heart of the building, a literal tour de force, is the six-story glass and bronze box that houses the King's Library, George III's collection of rare books, donated to the nation by George IV. The tower appears to arise from the watery depths beneath London, thanks to the surrounding softly lighted and reflective "moat" of polished stone. A close friend of many British artists, Wilson made certain that relevant art was included from the start, such as the tapestry by R.B. Kitaj, the colossal sculptural transcription of William Blake's Newton by Eduardo Paolozzi, the bronze-cast typographic entrance gates by David Kindersley, and the numerous busts, including, since 1999, one of the architect himself, by Celia Scott.

Committed to "the other tradition" of modern architecture, Wilson pays subtle homage in his masterwork to revered predecessors, especially Alvar Aalto and Hans Scharoun, and there are discreet references to Frank Lloyd Wright, Sigurd Lewerentz, Le Corbusier, Louis Kahn, James Stirling, H.P. Berlage, and Gunnar Asplund. However, this is no Postmodern pastiche; rather, Wilson has assimilated the lessons of those masters to forge an unmistakably personal synthesis that serves London urbanistically, aesthetically, and programmatically in its own unique way, thoughtfully designed with its users' comfort and convenience in mind no less than producing an atmosphere conducive to scholarship, contemplation, and general learning combined with sensual pleasure and intellectual enjoyment.

HELEN SEARING

See also **Foster, Norman (Great Britain); Library; Sainsbury Wing, National Gallery, London**

Further Reading

Caygill, Marjorie, and Christopher Date, *Building the British Museum*, London: British Museum Press, 1999

Frampton, Kenneth, R.B. Kitaj, and Martin Richardson, *Colin St. John Wilson*, London: Royal Institute of British Architects, 1997

Harris, Philip Rowland, *The Reading Room*, London: British Library, 1979; corrected edition, 1986

Jones, Peter Blundell, "Speaking Volumes," *The Architectural Review* (June 1998)

Wilson, Colin St. John, *The Design and Construction of the British Library*, London: British Library, 1998

Wilson, Colin St. John, *The Other Tradition of Modern Architecture*, London: Academy Editions, 1995

BROADACRE CITY 1930–35

Project (unbuilt) by Frank Lloyd Wright

Following his innovative Prairie houses of the previous decades, Broadacre City permitted Frank Lloyd Wright to pursue the subject of a new American urbanism. The opportunity for this remarkable plan was provided initially by an invitation to present the 1930 Kahn Lectures at Princeton University. After a decade of personal trials and professional inactivity and with the economic depression increasingly pressing, Wright knew that these lectures could provide an opportunity for regeneration. In those sections devoted to the city, he presented no specific layout or architectural parts. Instead, he negatively exposed the physical and social state of present cities; they were ugly, congested, dirty, badly administered, and an economic disaster. Wright's solutions were, however, mired in emotion mixed by awkwardly unclear language. Yet the vision of Broadacre City was described in all but name. His comments match those in his autobiography, written at the same time and for the same reason.

For the autobiography, Wright wrote a concluding section about Broadacre, but the publisher rejected it. Wright then had it produced as a pamphlet titled *The Disappearing City*. The first half contained philosophical reasons for change and an accounting of present ills, organized under five headings: economic (drawn from the analytical and curative ideas of Henry George); suppression of human individuality; urban concentrations and the inhuman vertical city; the failure to embrace modern resources (for example, telecommunications, mechanical systems, and new building materials); and chaotic automobile traffic.

The last half of *Disappearing City* offered some rather inexact proposals for rectification, all to be activated by adhering to George's social and economic observations and promotion of the individual as the dominant factor in opposition to collectivism and the dominating authorities of government and church. If causes and effects were properly understood and cures attended, a fresh morality and new urban and rural space would follow, joined by a new aesthetic, Broadacre City.

An article in *American Architect* briefly outlined some of Wright's thoughts from *Disappearing City*. Illustrated with a fuzzy aerial view sketched in charcoal (not by Wright), it showed roads, major highways, and a few isolated buildings on a rather desolate landscape. The text indicated some determinants for Broadacre, including "plane-stations" and the use of highways for "take off." Wright did not mention how his city might be physically laid out, but one detail to reappear was that "farm units and factories that produce [?] are within a ten mile radius . . . of each market and within walking distance of home and the workers." That radius fit the location of "plane-stations" every 20 miles.

The *New York Times Magazine* published an article in 1932 about Le Corbusier's architectonic Ville Radieuse. Many readers were aware of Wright's antagonism toward what he saw as the growing hegemonic influence of Europe's socialistic modernism. Wright followed the Le Corbusier piece with an article titled "Broadacre City: An Architect's Vision," in which he again attacked centrally clustered skyscrapers (places of both work and home, he reminded) as foolish and unnatural and said that villages harmoniously close to the land were preferred: "Ruralism as distinguished from *Urbanisme*."

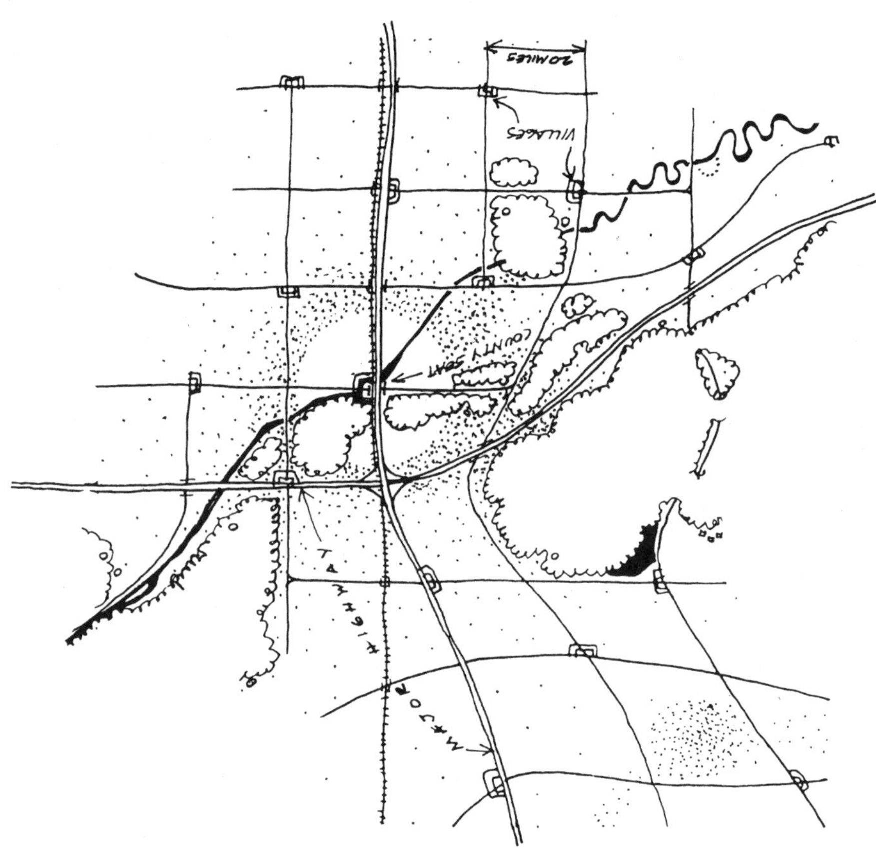

Broadacre City (1930–35)
Map of a possible regional layout incorporating Broadacre villages to an imprecise ca. 20 mile grid. Not to scale.
As extrapolated from F. L. Wright, *When Democracy Builds*, 2nd edition, Chicago: University of Chicago Press, 1945.

Broadacre City remained a verbal, nontectonic concept until November 1934, when Tom Maloney in New York City arranged to exhibit a model of a possible city. Wright prepared a plan in late 1934 intended to accommodate about 4,000 people, and this plan was published the following year. This served as the basis of plans prepared in 1945 and 1958. It was a suggestive layout for an imaginary site, perhaps typical, realizing that each actual city/village would respond to its unique physical environment. A 12-foot-square model, large display panels with illustrations and text, and a number of models of possible buildings were mounted at Rockefeller Center in April–May 1935 and then at Madison, Wisconsin; in Pittsburgh; and at the Corcoran Gallery in Washington, D.C.

The organizational device of a cruciform derived from a square gave the plan an obvious coherence. Defined by roads and functional zones, the cruciform was used as spatial geometry. The smallest element was a rectangular acre, but the design itself was organized by a square composed of 40 (8 by 5) acres, such as that for the circular stadium, or two squares at area 2 or four squares at area 4.

Housing was the heart of Broadacre—"Minimum of one acre to the family"—and constituted the large central square with schools at the center. Therefore, tall buildings (including apartments) were not clustered but rather were dispersed on the periphery. Other major areas included arts, recreational facilities, and county administration located at A; markets, other recreations, and little farms at B; orchards and "small" industry at C; and housing and higher education (and a cemetery) at D. In the cruciform's corners were nonfarm ("luxurious") housing at *e* and "games" and other administration at *f*. Juxtaposed to regional rail lines and a raised four-lane highway (with storage underneath) were distribution activities related to commerce, manufacturing, and industry, at g, C, and *h*, respectively.

Generally, the Broadacre concept was one of self-sustaining communities surrounded by nature preserves and rural agriculture, each linked regionally by transport systems. Predecessors included Arturo Soria y Mata's Linear City (1882 and later), Ebenezer Howard's Garden City (1898 and later), and William Drummond's Neighborhood Unit (1913). More in line with American sensibilities was Frederick Law Olmsted's plan (1868 and later, with Calvert Vaux) for Riverside, Illinois, a place known and admired by Wright, as were Olmsted's views about the city (it need not be synonymous with "an unhealthy density of population"), about house and home ("the advantages of 'civilization' were perhaps best realized in suburban neighborhoods"), and on Nature ideally typified by landscape and private gardens.

Although Wright had been influenced by writers, nonconformists, and philosophers ranging from Ralph Waldo Emerson to Thorsten Veblen, the practical Henry Ford was the immediate influence on Wright's ideas for Broadacre. The two men agreed that such innovations as the automobile, the airplane, and the radio were potent indicators of freedom, capable of freeing up time from work and creating a new kind of social space. To

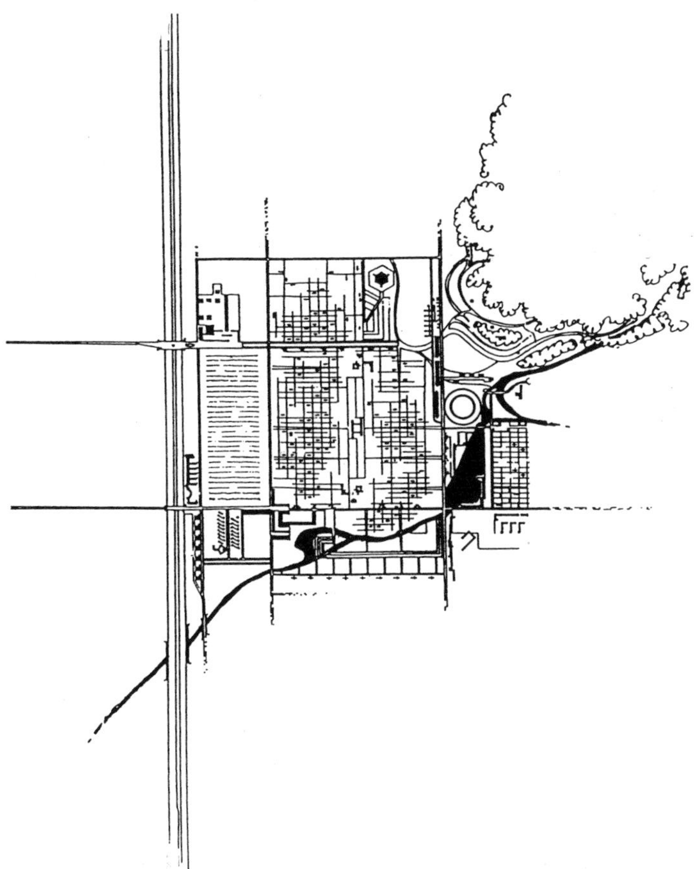

Broadacre City (1930–35)
A Broadacre City layout as a possible county seat beside a highway. The large central square is for suburban housing with educational facilities at the center. Not to scale. As extrapolated from. F.L. Wright, *When Democracy Builds*, (2nd ed.), University of Chicago Press, 1945.

Wright, Ford epitomized a properly administered capitalism, American pragmatism, gumption, verve, and a means to social change.

In 1918 Ford had said, "I am a farmer. . . . I want to see every acre of the earth's surface covered with little farms with happy, contented people living on them," and close to little markets. In 1919 he had said, "Plainly . . . the ultimate solution will be the abolition of the City. . . . We shall solve the City problem by leaving the City." Recognized as a pragmatist, Ford always put theory into practice and weighed the results. He proposed that regional car and tractor parts "manufacturing" plants be "within easy reach of farming districts," a series of village industries. One energetically pursued plan was the construction of a large scheme at Muscle Shoals on the Tennessee River, but that private enterprise was rejected by the federal government. In 1932 President Roosevelt announced a tax-supported program for the multipurpose development of the Tennessee Valley. It was similar to Ford's proposal, only more comprehensive and considerably larger. Ford's idea of village industries was reiterated in May 1932, also in the *New York Times Magazine*; it followed Wright's article on Broadacre.

Wright was clear about Ford's influence, noting that Muscle Shoals would have decentralized industry and given "every man a few acres of ground." When Wright introduced Broadacre City in 1932 in *American Architect*, he titled it "Today . . . Tomorrow." Ford's book *Today and Tomorrow* (1926) described the integration of industry and agriculture. It reads as a primer for Wright's ideas on modern villages, the work ethic, unionism, effectiveness and productivity, and much more, but not economics. Wright did not favor the plutocratic impulse of American capitalism.

Inspired by Ford, Walter V. Davidson offered a practical application, commissioning Wright in late 1931 to design prefabricated sheet-metal farm buildings composed of a house separated by an airlock from a composite farm facility to be called a "Little Farms Unit." Davidson also asked for the design of "Wayside Markets" where the produce of little farms—and from elsewhere—would be available at roadside. Made possible by inexpensive cars, the idea pre-dates the modern shopping center. A service, social, and administrative center was to be a "Little-Farms" village, laid out by Wright to contain many normal city functions. Nothing came of these commissions, but they preceded or paralleled Wright's comments later in 1932 and predicted aspects of the 1934–35 plan and related text.

The Broadacre City concept was meant to reinforce, by reinterpretation, the Jeffersonian tradition of a rural society sustained by Emersonian virtues and to encourage returning to a democratically endowed village life in modern geometric form and functional character. Broadacre was to be scattered about the landscape, integrated "along the horizontal lines" of highway and rail, with people free of capital gains tax but owning "utilities and government" and a right to "fair means of subsistence" from "their own ground," laboratory, or "common offices." However, as historian George Collins correctly observed, in the 1930s "the world was not electrified by Wright's agrarianism."

Broadacre City is not a theory. It does not contain a body of ideas or a set of terms that can be rationally measured—a treatise, yes, but not a utopia, nor was it conceived as such. Lyman Sargent's reasonable specification (in *British and American Utopian Literature, 1516–1985*, 1988) is that a utopia must describe "fairly completely an imaginary society," a nowhere. Therefore, Broadacre is not included in his compendium. As the last radical reaction to the horrors (as Wright saw the situation) imposed on cities in the 19th century by a rapacious process of centralization, Broadacre City is a provocative decentralist proposition that—if faintly—still teases urbanists.

DONALD LESLIE JOHNSON

See also **Corbusier, Le (Jeanneret, Charles-Édouard) (France); Ville Radieuse (c. 1930), Le Corbosier; Wright, Frank Lloyd (United States)**

Further Reading

Wright's arguments in the 1930s are best expressed in several of his essays (1931; March and May 1932; April and July 1935) and in his *The Disappearing City*. Brownell was committed to small town participatory democracy, and he and Wright collaborated on—but thankfully Brownell wrote—the section on Broadacre City in the work they coauthored. The most valuable evaluations are Collins, Grabow, Ciucci, Alofsin, Johnson (1990), Johnson (2000), and Zellner. Sergeant relates Broadacres to Wright's residential commissions, 1932–59.

Alexander, Stephen, "Frank Lloyd Wright's Utopia," *New Masses*, 15 (June 1935)

Alofsin, Anthony A., "Broadacre City: The Reception of a Modernist Vision, 1932–1988," *Center*, 5 (1989)

Brownell, Baker, and Frank Lloyd Wright, *Architecture and Modern Life*, New York and London: Harper, 1937

Ciucci, Giorgio, "The City in Agrarian Ideology and Frank Lloyd Wright: Origins and Development of Broadacres," in *The American City from the Civil War to the New Deal*, by Giorgio Ciucci et al., translated by Barbara Luigia La Penta, Cambridge, Massachusetts: MIT Press, 1979; London: Granada, 1980

Collins, George R., "Broadacre City: Wright's Utopia Reconsidered," in *Four Great Makers of Modern Architecture: Gropius, Le Corbusier, Mies van der Rohe, Wright*, New York: Columbia University Press, 1963

De Long, David G. (editor), *Frank Lloyd Wright and the Living City*, Weil am Rhein, Germany: Vitra Design, and Milan: Skira, 1998

Fishman, Robert, *Urban Utopias in the Twentieth Century: Ebenezer Howard, Frank Lloyd Wright, and Le Corbusier*, New York: Basic Books, 1977

Ford, Henry, *Today and Tomorrow*, Garden City, New York: Garden City Publishing, 1926; reprint, Cambridge, Massachusetts: Productivity Press, 1988

Grabow, Stephen, "Frank Lloyd Wright and the American City—The Broadacres Debate," *Journal of the American Institute of Planners*, 43 (April 1977)

Herbert, Gilbert, "The Organic Analogy in Town Planning," *Journal of the American Planning Association*, 49 (August 1983)

Hubbard, Preston J., *Origins of the TVA: The Muscle Shoals Controversy, 1920–1932*, Nashville, Tennessee: Vanderbilt University Press, 1961

Johnson, Donald Leslie, "Broadacres Geometry: 1934–35," *Journal of Architectural and Planning Research*, 5 (Summer 1988)

Johnson, Donald Leslie, *Frank Lloyd Wright versus America: The 1930s*, Cambridge, Massachusetts: MIT Press, 1990

Johnson, Donald Leslie, *The Progressives' City: Frank Lloyd Wright, Aesthetics and Rationalism 1893–1917*, 2000

Schapiro, Meyer, "Architect's Utopia," *Partisan Review*, 4 (March 1938)

Sergeant, John, *Frank Lloyd Wright's Usonian Houses: The Case for Organic Architecture*, New York: Whitney Library of Design, 1976

Wright, Frank Lloyd, "The City: Lecture 6," in *Modern Architecture: Being the Kahn Lectures for 1930*, Princeton, New Jersey: Princeton University Press, and Oxford: Oxford University Press, 1931; reprint, Carbondale: Southern Illinois University Press, 1987

Wright, Frank Lloyd, "Broadacre City: An Architect's Vision," *New York Times Magazine* (20 March 1932)

Wright, Frank Lloyd, "Today . . . Tomorrow," *American Architect*, 141 (May 1932)

Wright, Frank Lloyd, *The Disappearing City*, New York: Payson, 1932; 4th edition, as *The Industrial Revolution Runs Away*, New York: Horizon, 1969

Wright, Frank Lloyd, *An Autobiography*, New York: Longmans Green, 1932

Wright, Frank Lloyd, "Broadacre City: A New Community Plan," *Architectural Record*, 77 (April 1935)

Wright, Frank Lloyd, "Freedom Based on Form," *New Masses*, 16 (July 1935)

Wright, Frank Lloyd, *Frank Lloyd Wright: Collected Writings*, 5 vols., edited by Bruce Brooks Pfeiffer, New York: Rizzoli, and Scottsdale, Arizona: Frank Lloyd Wright Foundation, 1992; see especially vol. 2, *1930–1932*, 1992

Zellner, Peter, " 'The Big City Is No Longer Modern,' " *Daidalos*, (1998–99)

BRUSSELS, BELGIUM

Brussels, the capital of Belgium, played a vital role in the history of modern architecture at the turn of the century. Since 1890 a group of young architects such as Victor Horta (1861–1947), Paul Hankar (1861–1901), O. van Rijselberghe (1855–1929), and Henri van de Velde (1863–1957), to name just a few, were essential in creating a new art: the Art Nouveau. Versatile in many disciplines, their buildings would be designed into the finest detail encompassing building facades, interior spaces, decorative structures, furniture, wallpaper designs, doorknobs, and sometimes even the dress for the hostess. This aesthetic quest in search for perfect harmony would dominate the avant-garde architecture until the eve of World War I.

During the *Interbellum*, movements with more vigor and amplitude promoted a rationalization of the building process. In order to solve the problems of Brussels's overcrowded inner-city area, garden cities were developed in its suburbs. Notorious examples are the Cité Moderne (1923, St.-Agatha-Berchem) by Victor Bourgeois (1897–1962), the Kapelleveld (1926, St.-Lambrechts-Woluwe) by Huibrecht Hoste (1881–1957), and Le Logis (1927, Boisfort/Bosvoorde) by Jean-Jules Eggericx (1884–1963) and Louis van der Swaelmen (1883–1929).

Besides these collective habitations, these avant-garde architects also experimented with individual residences. Henri van de Velde's house in Tervuren (1928), Hoste's bourgeois house in Woluwe St. Pierre (1932) and by L.H. De Koninck's (1896–1984) Dotremont house in Uccle (1932) illustrate how, once liberated from traditional construction methods, their technical virtuosity reached a most refined plastic expression.

The designs for public buildings during that period were mainly experimentation grounds with the new material reinforced concrete and complex building programs. Horta's Palais des Beaux-Arts (1928) has both classical and Art Deco stylistic features and is built in reinforced concrete. The complicated plan reveals the architect's primary concern, namely, to accommodate a complex building program on an irregular sloping site. The Institut Bordet (1934) by Gaston Brunfaut (1899–) and Stanislas Jansinsky (1901–), with its white-colored balconies, form an objective expression of its hospital function. And the Sanatorium of Tombeek (1935) by Maxime Brunfaut (1909–) illustrates how by the end of the 1930s, architecture had become truly functional.

During the years following World War II, a succession of different architectural tendencies would leave their undeniable mark on the urban landscape. The North-South connection, a master plan developed back in the 19th century, took until 1945 to be completed. This urban intervention longitudinally dissected the city and left a whole area that needed to be redeveloped. A variety of public buildings in a number of styles were erected, such as the new colossal National Bank building (1945) by M. Van Goethem, the Kunstberg/Mont des Arts (1947) by J. Ghobert, the State Administrative Center (1955) by the group Alpha (H. Kuyck, M. Lambrichts, G. Riguier), and the Central Station (1952) designed by Horta and completed under M. Brunfaut.

Housing programs, both individual and collective ones, remained the most important architectural tasks during this postwar period. Villas, with facades in noble materials, such as natural French stone, adorned Brussels's most prominent boulevards leading to suburbs such as Tervueren and Uccle/Ukkel. Few of these buildings have a modern character. Exceptions are the residences in Uccle/Ukkel (1954) by L.J. Boucher (1929–), J.P. Blondel (1924–), and O. Filippone (1927–). Row houses, the most common type of townhouses in Brussels, formed continuous street elevations in new neighborhoods such as Evere, Koekelberg, and Woluwe. Awarded the Van de Ven Prize for architecture in 1954, E. Delatte's (1910–) design for his own house sets the standard: a garage and entry hall on the ground level, daytime spaces on the first floor, nighttime spaces on the second floor, and a brick facade. Apartment buildings were an attempt to change the monotony of this typology. Noteworthy examples are the apartment buildings (1949) by Josse Franssen in Schaarbeek, the duplex apartments in the high-rise tower (1954) by W. Van der Meeren in Evere, and the Model City on the Heysel/Heizel (1958) by R. Braem, Coolens, Panis, and Van Doosselaere and the firms L'Equerre and Structures. The latter created an entirely new, autonomous, harmonious, and lively neighborhood in close travel distance to downtown.

Whereas before World War II, modernism would be generated in Europe and emulated in the United States; after World War II, Europe borrowed ideas from America to further develop its cities. Public buildings such as the offices of the Prévoyance Sociale (PS), designed in 1957 by H. Van Kuyck (1902–), introduced the American technique of the curtain wall. The Corporate Headquarters Offices of the Bank Lambert (1965) were designed by Gordon Bunshaft (1909–90), a partner of Skidmore, Owings and Merrill. Although for the latter this project was merely an intermediate step in an evolving typology, for Brussels it represented a primer with its freestanding pillars that support the cross-shaped prefabricated concrete elements of the elevation. This procedure, which alleviated multiple shortcomings of the curtain wall, has been emulated in many projects. An example is the Glaverbel office building (1967, Watermael-Boisforts/Watermaal-Bosvoorde) by R. Braem, P. Gullisen, A. Jacqmain (1921–), and V. Mulpas, with its perfect circular plan and its elevation of discrete blue-stone slabs attached to consoles in reinforced concrete. By the end of the 1960s, Brussels, with its office towers, curtain walls, flat roofs, and freestanding columns, had developed after the American model.

During the 1970s and 1980s, Belgian architecture freed itself from the doctrines of the International Style and redirected its attention to its historical architectural and urban heritage. At first various retro styles, such as neoecclecticism, neo-Art Nouveau and neo-Art Deco, were rekindled; yet they did not, besides some ersatz products, make any valuable contributions. The Belgian capital in search for its own identity did not find a new architectural style. Noteworthy for the period are some remarkable architectural and urban rehabilitation projects. The beautiful Salon du Concert Noble designed by H. Beyaert in the 19thh century became an integral part of a new office building. And in 1983, it was decided that the new Museum of Modern Art (R. Bastin, L. Beeck) at the Place Royale/Koningsplein had to be built completely below ground around a central courtyard to minimally impact this historically significant urban context.

The last decade of the century is marked by a rekindled interest in qualitative architecture. Typical for the 1990s is the work of H. Daem and P. Robberecht (1950–) whose minimalist architecture are virtually invisible interventions in existing situations in order to celebrate a work of art or a significant restored building element. In the Hufkens gallery (1992), for example, the classical facade was carefully restored while the body of the house was remodeled into exhibit spaces. The back elevation, with its free-form composition contrasting open versus closed parts, is incontestably modern. It is furthermore continued in the roof where it provides idiosyncratic light wells that, in reference to V. Horta's nearby townhouses, help to illuminate the otherwise dark interior spaces.

Exemplary public buildings of the early 1990s are the projects by Ph. Samyn (1948–) and Partners. Their architecture may be characterized as contemporary high-tech executions of classical spatial compositions. His Brussimmo Office Building (1993), erected in the Leopold district where most of the European institutes have their headquarters, introduced the theme of the double skin. Consisting of two layers, it leaves a void for easy maintenance, to locate stairs, and to integrate the mechanical systems. By concentrating all secondary circulation and mechanical systems along the building's perimeter, a flexible plan is created.

Probably the most impressive building in the same area is the European Parliament (1998) by M. Bouquillon, J. van Pottelsberghe de La Potterie, and G. Maes. Whereas its spatial composition, with elliptic plan and central hall with vaulted ceiling, derives from classical sources, its materials and details are undeniably modern and executed with state-of-the-art technologies. Most important, it forms a new landmark for Brussels and symbolizes the city's new role as capital of the European community.

HENDRIKA BUELINCKX

See also **Art Nouveau (Jugendstil); Expo '58, Brussels; Bunshaft, Gordon (United States); Horta, Victor (Belgium); L'In-**

novation Department Store, Brussels; Palais Stoclet, Brussels; van de Velde, Henri (Belgium)

Further Reading

Bekaert, Geert, *Hedendaagse architectuur in België*, Tielt, Belgium: Lannoo, 1995; 2nd edition, as *Contemporary Architecture in Belgium*, translated by Ferdinand du Bois, 1995

Bontridder, Albert, *Dialoog tussen licht en stilte*, Antwerp, Belgium: Hélios, 1963

De Kooning, Mil (editor), *Horta and After: 25 Masters of Modern Architecture in Belgium*, Ghent, Belgium: Ghent University Press, 1999

Dubois, Marc, *Philippe Samyn: Architecture and Engineering, 1990–2000*, Basel, Switzerland, and Boston: Birkhauser, 1999

Jacobs, Steven, *Works in Architecture: Paul Robbrecht and Hilde Daem*, Ghent, Belgium: Ludion Press, 1998

Puttemans, Pierre, *Architecture moderne en Belgique*, Brussels: Vokaer, 1974

Strauven, Francis, *L'architecture en Belgique, 1970–80*, Louvain-la-Neuve, Belgium: CRA Unite Architecture, 1981

Van Bergeijk, Herman, and Otakar Mácel, *Birkhäuser Architekturführer: Belgien, Niederlande, Luxemburg: 20 Jahrhundert*, Basel, Switzerland, and Boston: Birkhauser, 1998; as *Birkhauser Architectural Guide: Belgium, the Netherlands, Luxembourg: 20th Century*, translated by Graham Broadribb

BRUTALISM

Brutalism (also called New Brutalism), narrowly defined, was the term used to describe the theory, ideas, and practice of a small number of young architects in Great Britain from 1950 to 1960. Broadly conceived, Brutalism came to describe an international approach to architecture that reflected social ideals, industrial and vernacular means, and humane goals.

Given the exigencies of building in Europe in the years immediately following World War II, namely, limited resources and unlimited demand, it was no surprise that the new generation of postwar architects saw before them not merely opportunity but the challenge to respond to circumstances that seemed unprecedented in European history. After World War I, architects seemed to approach the task of rebuilding in Europe with revolutionary idealism and an optimistic trust in mechanical technology. International Modernism seemed to represent not only all that was modern but also all that was valuable in a devalued and degraded world. The generation following World War II had less use for idealism, revolutionary or otherwise, and diminished trust in technology. It was in that context that the Brutalist apothegm "An ethic, not an aesthetic" acquired significance. The new generation embraced several precepts: first, that architecture absorbed existential weight; second, that building was the result not of reasoning but of ethical action; and finally, that International Style modernism was no more than shallow aestheticism. It was the radicalism of its approach rather than the persuasiveness of its early monuments that enabled Brutalism to force a transformation of the accepted conventions of modernism. Despite its short life as an identifiable movement, Brutalism came to occupy a central position in the redefinition of the history of 20th-century architecture.

The first built Brutalist work was the Secondary School at Hunstanton in Norfolk, England (Peter and Alison Smithson, 1954), which employed what seemed at first glance to be a Miesian aesthetic of pure structural clarity. For a building at that time in Britain to follow the example of Mies van der Rohe would have been provocative enough, but the Hunstanton School added another dimension to Miesian clarity: that of the mundane, the diurnal, the literal. Thereafter, the Smithsons turned their attention to larger questions, especially the need for a new approach to public housing in post–World War II Europe. Their new concerns resulted in no built works of their own, but their original ideas became profoundly influential. The next range of Brutalist buildings were to be the works of other young British architects; for example, the Terrace Housing (Howell, Howell, and Amis, Hampstead, 1956), Langham House Development (Stirling and Gowan, Ham Common, 1958), Architecture School Extension (Wilson and Hardy, Cambridge, 1959), Park Hill Development (Sheffield City Architect, Sheffield, 1961), and Engineering School Laboratories (Stirling and Gowan, Leicester, 1963), among others. All of those examples shared an unyielding emphasis on structural clarity, spatial simplicity, and material presence, and all contributed to the solidifying of the character of Brutalism in the general imagination.

The origin of the term Brutalism is not reliably attested, but the most plausible explanation comes from adaptation of the French phrase *beton brut* (rough concrete) to describe the material qualities of many buildings in Europe after World War II, qualities necessitated by a general lack of the time and resources necessary to obtain finer finishes. In particular, two works by the Swiss-French architect, Le Corbusier—the Unité d'Habitation (Marseilles, 1946–52) and the Maisons Jaoul (Neuilly, 1954)—played major parts in establishing the Brutalist model. In the first case, the Unité d'Habitation displayed unfinished, boldly concrete surfaces laid out in patterns directly descriptive of the processes of its fabrication. In Maisons Jaoul, Le Corbusier employed rough brickwork, tile-surfaced concrete vaults, and raw plywood, mimicking traditional vernacular building with industrial materials. To be sure, at least one Brutalist building had appeared in Britain by 1954, but that fact cannot obscure the role of Le Corbusier's works as precursors of the new wave. To the smooth white planes and elegantly balanced compositions of International Style (to whose definition Le Corbusier himself had made major contributions before 1939), Brutalism contrasted unfinished, natural-colored surfaces and seemingly awkward arrangements of parts, only too often revealing messy and formerly hidden mechanical functions. Indeed, even when smoothly finished, Brutalist buildings appeared crude and ordinary, with what some critics saw as willful perversity.

Again, although it was at first essentially a British phenomenon, Brutalism's reach soon included such European examples as the Architect's House (A. Wogenscky, Remy-les-Chevreuses, France, 1957), the Istituto Marchiondi (V. Vigano, Milan, Italy, 1959), and the Alder House (Rothrist, Switzerland, 1958) and a factory (Thun, Switzerland, 1960), both by Atelier 5. Furthermore, the catalytic role of Le Corbusier endured with his buildings for the Capitol Complex (Chandigarh, India, 1951–65), together with the monastery of La Tourette (Eveux-sur-l'Arbresle, France, 1955), all of which employed *beton brut* at heroic scale and with great expressiveness. In every case, the effect was of a kind of peasant or industrial vernacular, using the simplest materials in the simplest ways, applying them to modern programs at modern scale.

Nonetheless, despite its radical appearance, Brutalism could claim, if not legitimacy, at least ancestry in pre–World War II modernism. The early work of Hugo Haering (Farm Building, Garkau, Germany, 1925), and Antonio Sant'Elia (unbuilt Futurist projects, Italy, *c.*1911–14) were acknowledged sources. Before them, the German architects Peter Behrens, Bruno Taut, and Hans Poelzig could be included as forerunners. Equally, it would be wrong to ignore the role in the development of Brutalism and the spread of its ideas played by the contemporary architectural press. On the one hand, *Architectural Review*, the oldest continuing architectural periodical in Britain, gave much attention during the 1950s to vernacular tradition, early industrial monuments, and historic urban environments; on the other, *Architectural Design*, the newest, gave prominent place to the latest, the most provocative works. Between them, seen as they were across the world, they contrived both to inspire young British architects and to spread the message of the new British architecture.

Brutalism, or at least its influence, also traveled to the United States. In the Yale Art Gallery Extension (Louis Kahn, New Haven, 1949–53), which predated most British examples, surfaces were selectively coarse or smooth whereas composition was rigorously classical. A decade later, in the Yale Art and Architecture Building (Paul Rudolph, New Haven, 1961–63), which depended entirely on European models, surfaces were uniformly roughened, material choices were entirely aesthetic, and composition was wholly picturesque. In the Mummers' Theater (J. Johansen, Oklahoma City, 1970), surfaces were randomly rough, smooth, or colored; material choices were inconsistent; and composition was accidental.

Engineering Building, at Leicester University, England, designed by James Stirling (1959)
© Donald Corner and Jenny Young/GreatBuildings.com

Brutalism's historical origins shed light on the movement's profound worldwide influence, despite the fact that it was initiated by a small group of people in a relatively small place (or of limited geography). Before World War II, monuments of international modernism, based as it was on the industrialization of building, had been confined largely to the countries of its origin; namely, Germany, Austria, Czechoslovakia, France, and the Netherlands. Although spread had begun before 1939, the years of the war had interrupted that flow. After 1945 the triumph of international modernism seemed certain, and so it came to pass in the most highly industrialized country in the world, the United States, and in the work of architects trained in the 1930s. By contrast, the first post–World War II generation in Britain knew this history but rejected it. In that view, the war had shown that all those who had bought into the promise of an industrial utopia had been fatally compromised. What was needed was an architecture that was industrially based, but not ideological, and especially not political. Soviet Communism, Italian Fascism, and German National Socialism had each claimed leadership of the modern world and had employed architecture as demonstration of its claims. In the aftermath of the most destructive warfare in European, if not world, history, it seemed clear that architecture should assume a new role in society, a role dissociated from politics as such and focused on human needs in the simplest sense. It was in response to that perception that the first practitioners of Brutalism chose to employ exposed materials, rough textures, and seemingly awkward compositions, and it was those physical characteristics that came to typify the movement in the general understanding.

Despite the brevity of the list of genuinely Brutalist buildings, in Britain and elsewhere, the influence of Brutalism lay far less in the aesthetic concerns demonstrated in its built works than in the ethical concerns manifested in its challenge to accepted views. In that respect, Brutalism took its place beside other contemporary phenomena; namely, literature and film. The writings of Albert Camus and Jean-Paul Sartre and the films of Roberto Rossellini and Vittorio de Sica were only some of those manifestations of postwar despair, rejection, and existential rage. In Britain the works of writers such as John Osborne and John Braine, of painters such as Francis Bacon and John Bratby, and of sculptors such as Eduardo Paolozzi and Reg Butler displayed a rejection not just of the war and its seemingly pointless waste of lives and resources but also of the seemingly meaningless continuation of the attitudes and practices of the past.

At first, Brutalism seemed, even to its most ardent adherents, to be an idea isolated in time (the 1950s) and place (Britain). Its chronicler, Reyner Banham (*The New Brutalism*), had little confidence in Brutalism's future recognition as more than a minor episode in the history of 20th-century architecture. In both the senses, ethical and aesthetic, in which Brutalism came to be viewed, that estimate was too pessimistic. The ethical part of Brutalism survived because of its continuation of the principle established by A.W.N. Pugin and the Cambridge Camden Society as far back as 1840: The ultimate test of design is its social worth. The aesthetic aspect of Brutalism, assuming that the test of social worth has been met, follows directly from material character—itself, if truthful, socially worthy by definition. All over the built world today can be seen works that accept or challenge the issues that Brutalism brought to attention; namely, if building is for the people, should it not be of the people (vernacular forms)? If building is to invoke virtue, should it not itself be virtuous (truth in materials)? If building is to be meaningful, should it not embody meaning in itself (social worth)? The questions put by Brutalism have yet to be answered with finality, and that is its continuing legacy.

B. M. Boyle

See also **Banham, Reyner (United States); Concrete; Le Corbusier (Jeanneret, Charles-Édouard) (France); International Style; Kahn, Louis (United States); Parliament Building, Chandigarh; Rudolph, Paul (United States); Sant'Elia, Antonio (Italy); School; Smithson, Peter and Alison (Great Britain); Stirling, James (Great Britain); Unite d'Habitation, Marseilles Cité Radieuse**

Further Reading

The fundamental information on Brutalism appeared first in the pages of the British periodicals *Architectural Review* (1954–61) and *Architectural Design* (1954–57), which provided the only contemporaneous reporting on the movement and its works; most, but not all, of that record was resumed in Banham (1966, which also included much extraneous material). A useful summary is found in William Curtis (1983, chapter 24). The Smithsons' writings are the essential sources on Brutalism.

Banham, Reyner, *The New Brutalism. Ethic or Aesthetic?* London: The Architectural Press, 1966

Curtis, William, *Modern Architecture Since 1900*, Oxford: Phaidon Press, 1982; Englewood Cliffs: Prentice-Hall, 1983

Jencks, Charles, *Modern Movements in Architecture*, Garden City: Anchor Books, 1973 (see especially chapter 7)

Smithson, Alison, and Peter Smithson, "Louis Kahn," in *Architects' Yearbook 9*, edited by Trevor Dannatt, London: Paul Elek, 1960; New York: Chemical Publishing Co., 1960

Smithson, Alison, and Peter Smithson, *Without Rhetoric: An Architectural Aesthetic, 1955–1972*, London: Latimer New Dimensions, 1973

Webster, Helena (editor), *Modernism without Rhetoric: Essays on the Work of Alison and Peter Smithson*, London: Academy Editions, 1997

BUCHAREST, ROMANIA

As the capital of Romania, Bucharest can be also considered the primary source of the country's modern architecture, beginning in the second half of the 19th century and continuing throughout the 20th century. Like other major European capitals, the search to define an emblematic national character for Bucharest's architecture developed in relationship to historical precedents as well as the contemporary milieu.

The 19th century represented a period of major change for Bucharest in both political and cultural realms. The first half of the century encouraged Western European values of culture and civilization, thus announcing a massive import of several architectural currents—mainly neoclassicism and Romanticism—that progressively changed the Oriental aspect of the city. In 1859, as the principalities of Wallachia and Moldavia unified, Bucharest became the capital of the new state of Romania and, in 1878, after the country won its independence from the Ottoman Empire, the capital of the kingdom of Romania. This gain in political prestige was reflected in the architectural field by an important campaign of building monumental official institutions and luxury residencies, all inspired by the French eclecticism of the École des Beaux-Arts. French influence, dispersed through the work of French architects or Romanians trained at the École, became so considerable that the city was nicknamed "Little Paris." Urban planning followed the same way of modernization by assimilating the French model, as it happened for the creation of a series of boulevards inspired by Baron von Haussmann's Parisian model. Parallel to the spread of foreign currents, the first Romanian architects attempted to create a style based on a national expression in Bucharest, interpreting the rich heritage of historic and folk tradition.

As the majority of Romanian architects studied at the École des Beaux-Arts in Paris, even after the foundation of the School of Architecture in Bucharest in 1892, their production mirrored the French aesthetic (primarily the historical revivalism and academicism of Beaux-Arts or the neobaroque). Among the most important public buildings designed according to the French method were the Palace of the Chamber of Deputies (1907) and the Military Circle (1912), both by Dimitrie Maimarolu, and the Palace of the Bourse (1911) by Stefan Burcus. However, the magnificence of the French influence was reflected mostly in the sumptuous compositions of private dwellings, such as those designed by Ion D. Berindey (1871–1928) and Petre Antonescu (1873–1965).

In contrast, the development of a "national" style emerged as a reaction against the omnipresent foreign stylistic models. Its aesthetics exalted the local tradition, interpreting major examples from the Wallachian architecture of the 18th century (considered as the most representative) and assimilating the craftsmanship and ornamentation of the folk architecture. The first buildings to incorporate a Romanian-based style were private homes, designed in tribute to a historicist vision rather than the modern International Style. The General National Exposition in 1906, celebrating 40 years of the reign of King Carol I, brought the official consecration of what could be called an indigenous Romanian style of architecture. Its picturesque character made it increasingly popular for residential architecture, but it also developed a monumental dimension, suitable for the public programs, such as the Institute of Geology (1906) by Victor Stefanescu, the Ministry of Public Works (1910) and the Bank Marmorosch-Blank (1912), both by Petre Antonescu, the School of Architecture (1912–26) by Grigore Cerchez, and the Museum of National Art (1912–38) by Nicolae Ghika-Budesti.

The creation of greater Romania after World War I by the unification of the ancient kingdom with Transylvania, Bessarabia, and Bukovina initiated a flourishing period for the country that fully benefited its capital as well. Bucharest developed into the most vibrant economic and cultural center of Romania and doubled in population. The "national" style became the official architecture for all architectural programs, from administrative buildings to social housing designed by architects such as Antonescu, Paul Smarandescu, and Statie Ciortan.

Economic prosperity and a governmental legislation that encouraged construction transformed Bucharest into a huge building site. The penetration of new architectural ideas and modernist architecture was favored by several institutions and particularly among intellectual circles with shared progressive or avant-garde views. Modernist architecture never achieved an official status, but nevertheless it became the emblem of post–World War II dynamism. In fact, the first important modernist building, the ARO building (1929–31), was designed by Horia Creanga for such an institution: the insurance company Asigurarea Românească (ARO). Other important public buildings developed the potential of modernism, including those designed by Duliu Marcu, Rudolf Fraenkel, and Arghir Culina. On the other hand, the language of modern architecture—reductive geometries based on the grid, the elimination of ornamentation and historical references, the adaptation of technological materials such as steel and glass—was adopted largely in the housing programs by Horia Creanga, Ion Boceanu, Duliu Marcu, Tiberiu Niga, Octav Doicescu, and many others. Modernism was consecrated as a consumer architecture, and its various typologies of habitation, from the apartment buildings or villas to social housing, spread all over the city and to its suburbs. Several compact areas of the city were newly created during the 1930s, such as the central boulevards Take Ionescu and Bratianu and the marginal district Vatra Luminoasa, renovations that generated a completely new urban image. Among the industrial buildings, which were situated mainly at the periphery of the city, included the Malaxa Industries building (1930–40) by Creanga. Despite the austerity of the Creanga's modernist vocabulary, he reached a remarkable expressive force that remained unequaled in the production of the industrial architecture.

Modernist architecture also shaped the national style, the latter of which adopted the former's principles of formal simplicity and monumentality, developing a new expression and thus avoiding a certain regression induced by second-rate production. Modernism was embraced mainly by the young architects, such as Doicescu, Henriette Delavrancea-Gibory, and Constantin Iotzu.

By the end of the 1930s, the increased authoritarian politics of King Carol II, who declared his personal dictatorship in 1938, resulted in the promotion of a nostalgic classicism, common in the whole of Europe of the time. Frequently called "the style Carol II," this tendency became the symbol of the official architecture, and it found in Duiliu Marcu, architect of the Ministry of Foreign Affairs (1937–44), its most accomplished exponent.

The installation of the Communist regime brought, among other consequences, "The Socialist Reconstruction" of Bucharest, an ideological and architectural movement that conferred a "suitable" image upon the city as a new socialist capital; this period extended from 1952 to 1989. However, although they almost always ignored precedent, the interventions on the urban fabric did not radically modify the central area of the city until

The ARO (Asigurarea Românească) Building, Bucharest, Romania, designed by Horia Creanga (1931)
© Carmen Popescu

the last years of the Communist regime. The sole important intervention of the early years was that of the complex of buildings (1959–60), by Horia Maicu and collective, erected in the Palace Square, which also included the former royal palace, reconverted into the National Museum of Art. The 1950s were marked, more than anywhere else in the country, by the coexistence of Stalinist architecture with rationalism, actually a continuation of the interwar architecture. The classicist formalism of the Casa Scînteі (The House of the Spark, 1950–51, Horia Maicu, Ludovic Staadecker, M. Alifanti, and N. Badescu), of the Romanian Opera House (1952–53, Doicescu), and of the housing program (the districts of Vatra Luminoasa and Bucurestii Noi) was contemporaneous—and sometimes executed by the same architects—with works that displayed the strong and authentic rationalism of the 1930s to 1940s, such as the Baneasa Airport (1948; M. Alifanti, N. Badescu, A. Damina, and P. Macovei), the Pediatric Hospital "Emilia Irza" (1950; Gr. Ionescu), the Pavilion H of the Expositional Center (1953; A. Damian), and the Palace of the National Broadcasting (1960; T. Ricci, L. Garcia, and M. Ricci).

The 1960s and early 1970s brought an opening toward Western European culture, including architecture. At the same time, this period was one of intensive construction activity. Housing was built, mainly in the peripheral districts of Balta Alba, Drumul Taberei, and Berceni. However, the most interesting architecture of these years were the functionalist public buildings, such as the State Circus (1960; N. Porumbescu), the Dorobanti Hotel (1974; V. Nitulescu, P. Vraciu, and Al. Beldiman), and the campus of the Polytechnic Institute (1962–72; Doicescu and collective).

After a violent earthquake in the city in 1977, the idea of a socialist capital was invigorated with the building of the Civic Center, which was of national importance and was intended to solidify architecture's relationship to political totalitarianism and nationalism. This huge architectural complex, which was not yet completed in 1989, was situated at the limit of the historic center and was erected on a massively demolished area (about 500 hectares). During these years, the Bucharest architecture and particularly that of the Civic Center and the House of the Republic abandoned the previous principles of rationalism and functionalism in favor of a style that responded to the new ideological orientation.

The 1990s focused on the restoration of the area destroyed in the 1970s and 1980s and on the erection of the Civic Center. The international architectural contest "Bucharest 2000" (1995–96), organized by the Union of Romanian Architects, showed—particularly through the designers of the winning project (Meinhard von Gerkan and Joachim Zais, Germany)—viable solutions for articulating this area with the traditional urban fabric of the city and possibilities for synchronizing Bucharest architecture with contemporary European experiences.

CARMEN POPESCU AND NICOLAE LASCU

Further Reading

Bucharest in the 1920s–1940s: Between Avant-garde and Modernism, Bucuresti: Simetria, 1994

Centenar Horia Creanga 1892–1992, Bucuresti: Editura UAR, 1992

Constantin, Paul, *Arta 1900 in Romania*, Bucuresti: Meridiane, 1972

Echilibrul uitat. Timisoara 1991–1996, (Romanian catalog at the Venice Biennial), Bucuresti: Simetria, [1996]

Ionescu, Grigore, *Arhitectura pe teritoriul Romaniei de-a lungul veacurilor*, Bucuresti: Editura Academiei, 1982

Ionescu, Grigore, "Arhitectura romaneasca dupa al doilea razboi mondial," *Arhitectura*, no. 3–4 (1991)

Machedon, Luminita, and Ernie Schoffham, *Romanian Modernism: The Architecture of Bucharest 1920–1940*, Cambridge, Massachusetts, and London, England: MIT Press, 1999

BUDAPEST, HUNGARY

Budapest is the capital of Hungary, and is the industrial, commercial, and cultural center of the country. The city is situated on the Danube River, in the geographic center of the region. With the compromise between Hungary and Austria in 1867, a period of economic prosperity and a population growth of enormous speed began. In 1869 the three towns (Buda, Pest, and Óbuda) that were to be united four years later into Budapest had 280,349 inhabitants. At the turn of the century, Budapest already had a population of 733,350. In 1871 the first international competition in urban development was announced to restructure the capital. Its program underlined the importance of the Chain Bridge as the central connection between Buda and Pest. A system of boulevards and avenues was realized as the result of the competition and subsequent revisions, and the urban structure of Budapest today is determined by the large-scale realization of what was probably the most consistent attempt to create a bourgeois city in Europe.

The Danube is the determining element of the monumental cityscape, its sweep underlined by the closed building facades on the embankments. The architectural treatment of the riverfront and St. Marguerite Island, which became an urban park, was seen by many urban planners of the time as a major achievement. The problem of creating well-functioning connections between Pest and Buda was solved by a number of bridges. The Buda side is dominated by the Gellért Hill and the Castle Hill with the neobaroque Royal Castle (1880–91, Miklós Ybl and 1891–1905, Alajos Hauszmann) at its top. The business center is on the (flat) Pest side, whose riverfront is dominated by the colossal neo-Gothic Houses of Parliament (1904, Imre Steindl) and more recent hotels that replace those destroyed in World War II.

The basis of Budapest's prosperity was the grain-milling industry and the processing and sale of other agricultural goods in the Carpathian basin. Urban development was conducted by the Council of Public Works (1870–1949), a body related to the municipality as well as to the government. The downtown business and residential district was executed during the last three decades of the 19th century. The typical residential unit of Budapest was a block of rental apartments with an interior courtyard. Access to the individual flats was from open galleries in the courtyard. The quality of apartments and the social status of their inhabitants could differ within a one-block area. Upper-middle-class families built summer residences and villas on the green hills of Buda. Low-income families lived on the outskirts of the city, near industrial zones.

At the beginning of the 20th century, Budapest's architecture showed a pluralism of styles: beside the various neostyles (Stock

Exchange, 1905, Ignác Alpár), many variations of Art Nouveau emerged (Academy of Music, 1907, Korb and Giergl), indicating connections with Vienna and other European cities. Ödön Lechner, whose major work was the Postal Savings Bank (1901), and his followers tried to create a national style that aimed to express Hungarian identity, using ornaments of peasant embroideries and Oriental art. Early modern tendencies (Rózsavölgyi Building, 1912, Béla Lajta) and National Romanticism (Calvinist Church, 1912, Aladár Árkay) also emerged. Most of the architects graduated from the Technical University of Budapest, such as the group of National Romanticists known as the "Young Ones" (Károly Kós, Dénes Györgyi, Dezső Zrumeczky, Béla Jánszky, Valér Mende, and others). Their architecture was influenced by Scandinavian National Romanticism (Eliel Saarinen and Lars Sonck) as well as by the English Arts and Crafts movement.

The first social building program of Budapest was initiated by Mayor István Bárczy in 1908. As the result, between 1909 and 1913, Budapest built 25 blocks of flats and 19 colonies of small family houses for 6,000 families in three cycles (Wekerle housing estate, a garden city of Budapest, 1912–13, by Károly Kós and others) as well as 55 public schools. The apartment block on Visegrádi Street (1910, Béla Málnai and Gyula Haász) shows the emerging neoclassicism before World War I that put an end to the dynamic development. The multinational Austro-Hungarian monarchy lost the war and broke up into small national states in 1919. The economy recovered slowly during the 1920s. With most architects and artists of the avant-garde working abroad, the early 1920s was a period of a conservative neobaroque and other revivalist tendencies. A new, functionalist aesthetics could only break through from 1929 on. The Hungarian CIAM (Congrès Internationaux d'Architecture Moderne) group, with Farkas Molnár, József Fischer, Pál Ligeti, and György Masirevich as its most significant members, was radical and politically engaged but could realize only a few large-scale projects, such as the housing development (1934) on Köztársaság Square. However, the group built a number of villas for reform-minded individuals.

In the 1930s, Budapest's architecture started to show the impact of Italian rationalism, such as the Church in Városmajor (1936, Aladár and Bertalan Árkay). The real breakthrough occurred around 1935, when a "domesticated" modernism, stripped bare of its social aims, became accepted by a large part of the population. Many apartment and office buildings represent a very high aesthetic and technical quality, such as the Atrium cinema and apartments (1936, Lajos Kozma), the Dunapark apartment building (1937, Béla Hofstätter and Ferenc Domány), and the Financial Center (1939, László Lauber and István Nyíri). In the early 1940s, two large working-class housing estates of detached houses were built in Angyalföld and at Albertfalva, financed by the Social Security Fund.

World War II did not spare the city; the population, as well as housing, infrastructure, and economy, suffered enormous damages. Reconstruction work, which began immediately after the war, was a long process that included apartments being built on the lots of destroyed houses in Buda Castle by György Jánossy and by Zoltán Farkasdy (among others). In 1948 the Communist Party assumed power and introduced total state control over the production and distribution of goods, including housing. Now, urban and architectural planning took place exclusively in large, state-owned offices with hundreds of employees. During the 1950s, the development of large-scale industry was forced. The quality reached a higher level in works of the planning office IPARTERV, specialized for industrial buildings. An outstanding example of early postwar public building in the International Style was the Trade Union Headquarters (1949, Lajos Gádoros and others).

Between 1951 and 1953, the Communist Party forced the style of "socialist realism," following Soviet models (People's Stadium, 1953, Károly Dávid; Institute building "R" of the Technical University, 1955, Gyula Rimanóczy). In 1956 political oppression led to an uprising against Communism. The uprising was crushed by Soviet tanks, but the party was forced to begin a process of liberalization. Elements of a market economy were introduced in 1968. A large-scale building program to eliminate housing shortage had already been announced in 1960. Using traditional technology, housing estates of usually 2,000 flats were built in the inner residential zone. During the second half of the 1960s, four plants producing prefabricated building parts were set into operation, and housing estates of 10,000 flats were built in the transitory residential zone (Kispest, Budafok, Rákospalota, Békásmegyer, and Újpest). In the 1970s the peak decade of the housing production, the state built 105,907 flats, or 65.7 percent of the whole production. However, both the quantity and the quality of output were met with public dissatisfaction, giving rise to a search for an organic language of architecture as represented by the internationally publicized buildings of Imre Makovecz (funerary chapel, Farkasrét Cemetery, 1977). Efforts were made, by using standardized designs, to satisfy the needs for kindergartens, schools, stores, public health facilities, and other services. In 1970 the Master School of Architects, an important forum for the exchange of ideas that was closed in the 1950s, was reorganized. Buildings such as the CHEMOLIMPEX Office Building (1964, Zoltán Gulyás), the DOMUS Furniture Store (1974, Péter Reimholz and Antal Lázár), the MEDICOR Office Building (1975, Zoltán Gulyás and Péter Reimholz), and the RADELKIS Office Building (1978, Antal Csákváry) are in line with international tendencies of the time. Sports facilities with ingenious structures were built, such as Spartacus Swimming Pool (1983, Ádám Sylvester). Public transportation was strengthened by opening the east-west (1974) and north-south (1984) Metro lines.

The process of significant economic and political change had already begun before the fall of Communism in 1989. Most of the large state-owned planning offices collapsed or became privatized. Foreign capital and international businesses have been moving to Budapest. Transforming 19th-century apartment blocks, banks are settling in the downtown area (ING Bank, 1994, Erick van Egeraat and MECANOO Architects), and high-tech office buildings, such as the Siemens Headquarters (1999, Péter Reimholz and Antal Lázár), give the capital a late 20th-century skyline, at least in its details. New ensembles are developing, such as the Graphisoft plant (1998, Ferenc Cságoly and Ferenc Keller). Shopping malls are introducing American-style commercial architecture into the urban periphery. State-financed housing construction stopped, but private housing is on the rise. The reconstruction process of residential blocks of the inner city has started. Budapest has been developing from an industrial city into a tertiary economy city since the 1960s.

KATALIN MORAVÁNSZKY-GYÖNGY AND ÁKOS MORAVÁNSZKY

See also **Hungary**

Further Reading

Enyedi, György, and Viktória Szirmai, *Budapest: A Central European Capital*, translated by Vera Gáthy, London: Belhaven Press, and New York: Halsted Press, 1992

Lőrinczi, Zsuzsa, and Mihály Vargha (editors), *Építészeti kalauz: Budapest építészete a századfordulótól napjainkig* [Architectural Guide: Architecture in Budapest from the Turn of the Century to the Present], Budapest: 6 BT, 1997

BUENOS AIRES, ARGENTINA

Throughout the 20th century, several factors contributed to Buenos Aires's architectural significance. In the early decades of the century, when Buenos Aires was the capital of one of the wealthiest countries in the world, architects were commissioned to design luxurious residences and institutional buildings, many influenced by French and Italian styles. Later, different immigrant groups looking for status constructed important examples that followed European traits of Viennese secession, Italian liberty, and Catalan modernism. The rationalist architecture of the early 1930s and 1940s in Buenos Aires is one the most significant of the world. This era of architecture greatly influenced the present profile of the city. Also relevant are the examples of Brutalist architecture. The last decades of the century have been characterized by an interest in preserving this rich architectural heritage and by new architectural interventions related to the existing urban fabric.

Buenos Aires is situated by the estuary of the Rio de la Plata and the plains. The city became a federal district in 1880 and since then has gained more political, financial, and administrative power. In 1910 the mayor, Torcuato de Alvear, inspired by the Beaux-Arts influence and the Parisian example of Baron von Haussmann in the 1850s, provided the city with a framework of avenues, plazas, and parks.

In the early 20th century, the city consisted of a basic infrastructure of institutional buildings and magnificent private residences following Italian academic styles. Carlos Morra designed the former National Library (1901) and Victor Meano and Julio Dormal the Colon Theater (1908). Later, French influence dominated the city. Alexander Christophersen designed the Anchorena Palace (1909; today the Palace of Foreign Affairs). The Frenchman René Sergent designed three large residences, among them the Errazuriz Palace (1911). Utilitarian architecture followed English influence. Retiro (1914), the major train station, was designed by Conder, Conder, Farmer, and Follet, with the metallic structure produced by Morton and Co. in Liverpool. The opening of avenues such as May Avenue and North Diagonal completed a scheme that transformed Buenos Aires into the "Paris of South America."

In the 1920s, academic dominance was affected by two other tendencies, namely the importation of European-derived Art Nouveau and the reemergence of pride in the Spanish heritage and the Ibero-American roots of the city. Immigrants who found a taste of economic power sought expressions for their new status. Italians such as Mario Palenti, who designed Pasaje Barolo (1923), expressed this reaction against academic architecture; Joaquín García Núñez designed for the Spanish colony; and Martin Noel designed a residence that today houses the Museum Fernandez Blanco (1916), a neo-Colonial building with Spanish decoration and details. Also inspired by the Spanish High Renaissance is the Cervantes Theater (1921) by Aranda and Repetto. In the 1920s, Art Deco challenged the preference for traditional academic architecture. Deco details were linked to modern buildings: cinemas, parking garages, banks, and apartments. An important representative of this tendency is Alejandro Virasoro, who designed the House of Theater (1927), the Santander Bank (1926), and the Equitativa del Plata (1929).

Le Corbusier visited Buenos Aires in 1929 and gave a series of ten lectures, the most comprehensive of his career. Werner Hegemann followed him in 1931. Although both spoke of a harmonious synthesis, they offered different approaches to resolve the problems of the growing metropolis. Le Corbusier's influence was felt a decade later with the creation of the Austral Group and with the Plan for Buenos Aires (1938, in collaboration with Ferrari Hardoy and Kurchan). His enduring influence was felt also in many Brutalist projects in the following decades.

As a result of his visit, Le Corbusier was inspired by the gigantic landscape and wrote his book, *Precisions of the Present State of Architecture and City Planning* (1930). Similarly, Hegemann's ideas influenced the urbanist Carlos della Paolera and some projects by Jorge Kalnay.

Several factors, such as the academic influence, the Beaux-Arts model for the education of the architect, the German-language influence, and the Art Deco materials and detail, generated a series of buildings between the late 1930s and 1940s that has been characterized as part of the "School of Buenos Aires." At this time, major avenues helped define the city as a metropolis—Corrientes, Santa Fe, 9 de Julio, and General Paz—and the city acquired a more cosmopolitan atmosphere.

Alejandro Bustillo was the architect of the first modernist building of Buenos Aires, Maison Ocampo (1929). Yet, showing the eclectic nature of the time, he later developed a classical language, as in the headquarters of the Argentinean Central Bank (1939). Two important buildings are the COMEGA (1932) by Alfredo Joselevich and Enrique Douillet and the SAFICO (1934) by Walter Moll. By the early 1940s, modernism triumphed as the dominant style. The Kavanagh Apartment Building (1936) by Sánchez, Lagos and de la Torre, for example, evinces an extraordinary modernist silhouette within the urban landscape. This 30-story building won an Award of the American Society of Engineering (1994). Moreover, the Grand Rex Cinema (1937) by Alberto Prebish exhibits purist modern lines and architectural economy, and his Obelisk (1936), located at the intersection of three major avenues, remains a landmark and symbol of the city.

The apartments of Libertador and Lafinur (1937) by Sánchez, Lagos and de la Torre constituted a signpost of modern architecture in Argentina. The ateliers of Suipacha and Paraguay (1938) by Antonio Bonet, Vera Barros, and Lopez Chas suggest the flexibility, open plan, and experimentation with material but also mark one the first buildings to be distanced from orthodox rationalism in Buenos Aires.

Antonio Ubaldo Vilar produced works combining functionality and a pure formal language, namely the Central Headquarters (1943) of the Automobile Club of Argentina. With the arrival of Peron (1946–52 and 1952–55), industrialization and legislation to improve social conditions marked a new period in Buenos Aires. The city attracted immigrants from the interior

ATC (Argentina Televisora Color) Building, designed by Manteola, Sánchez Gómez, Santos, Solsona, Viñoly
© Jose Bernardi

of the country, requiring the populist regime to provide large housing complexes and infrastructure as well as buildings to meet needs for health care, education, and recreation.

At the middle of the century, Amancio Williams designed an unrealized proposal (1945) for an airport for the city designed to stand over the river on immense Le Corbusian *pilotis*. The study of the Regulatory Plan for the city (1947–49), done by Kurchan and Hardoy in collaboration with Le Corbusier, marks the Modern movement's maturity.

The most important work of the 1950s is the Theater General San Martin (1953–60) by Mario Roberto Alvarez and Macedonio Ruiz and, connected to it, the Cultural Center San Martin (1960–64) by Alvarez and Associates. Detailed with refinement and quality of materials, this building denotes the influences of the International Style.

In the 1960s, the work of Clorindo Testa, as in the Bank of London (1966), indicates a significant turning point in the city's architecture. Aesthetically derived from Le Corbusier's principles of reductivism and lack of ornamentation, the bank's exterior reflects the Brutalist use of concrete for rationalist ends. The Headquarters of the Bank of the City of Buenos Aires (1967) by Manteola, Sánchez Gómez, Santos, Solsona, and Viñoly is also significant: a box of glass bricks framed by a metallic structure, it was one of the first examples of recycled architecture in Buenos Aires.

A significant building of the 1970s is the ATC Argentina Televisora Color (1978) by Manteola, Sánchez Gómez, Santos, Solsona, and Viñoly, associated with Salaberry and Tarsitano, a landmark in the urban landscape. The National Library (contest won in 1962, construction began in 1972, and completed in 1992) by Testa, Bulrich, and Cazzaniga was remarkable for its underground storage of books and sculptured and elevated reading areas. Also characteristic of this period is the work of Jorge Roberto Alvarez and Associates, who produced works known for their durability, order, and asceticism. Among their buildings, SOMISA (1975) met a technological challenge to design all the building's parts within a tolerance of three millimeters.

In 1972 Catalinas Norte, in the Retiro area, began again to incorporate the river into the life of the city. The Conurban building (1973) by the Kocourek studio with Katzenstein and Llorens uses a curtain wall in the facade facing the river and brick in the facade looking to the city and is one of the best of the whole complex.

The Cultural Center (1980) in the Recoleta area by Bedel, Benedit, and Testa, a recycled Franciscan monastery, is today an active popular center of contemporary art, experimental art galleries, and shops. The complex was completed with the more whimsical Buenos Aires Design Center (1994) by Testa, Genoud, and Graci.

Since 1991 the Madero docks area (built in 1887–97) has been rehabilitated in one of the most successful urban interventions in the city's recent history. The utilitarian buildings of the dock have been recycled as apartments, restaurants, and shops as a natural extension of the center of the city. Several new towers have changed the profile of the city's skyline. The twin towers (1997) of High Palermo Plaza by Urgell, Fazio, and Penedo and the studio of Sanchez Gomez, Manteola, and Santos Solsona present an urban doorway to the Palermo area, enlivened by the Postmodernist and ornamental Alto Palermo Shopping (1990) by Juan Lopez.

Buenos Aires enters the 21st century immersed in the revolutionary changes in technology and the process of globalization. The city has successfully implemented new programs to recuperate areas of the city, open the city to its river, and rehabilitate buildings in Mayo, Rivadavia, and Corrientes Avenues. In addition, historical neighborhoods, such as San Telmo and Monserrat, have begun to be rebuilt. All these actions indicate that Buenos Aires is as interested in preserving its past as it is in constructing its future. The city, once called the "Paris of South America," is still recognized for its European heritage and remains one of the great metropolises of the world.

JOSE BERNARDI

See also **Alvarez, Mario Roberto (Argentina); Art Deco; Brutalism; Corbusier, Le (Jeanneret, Charles-Édouard) (France); Hegemann, Werner (Germany); Manteola, Sánchez Gómez, Santos, Solsona, Viñoly (Argentina); Rationalism; Testa, Clorindo (Argentina); Williams, Amancio (Argentina)**

Further Reading

Abitare, 342 (July/August 1995) (special issue devoted to Buenos Aires, with full text in English)

Le Corbusier, *Précisions sur un état présent de l'architecture et de l'urbanisme*, Paris: Crès, 1930; reprint, Paris: Altamira, 1994; as *Precisions on the Present State of Architecture and City Planning*, translated by Edith Schreiber Aujame, Cambridge, Massachusetts: MIT Press, 1991

Petrina, Alberto, and Liliana Aslan, *Buenos Aires, guía de arquitectura: Ocho recorridos por la ciudad*, Buenos Aires: Municipalidad de la Ciudad de Buenos Aires, 1994; 2nd edition, 1998

BUNGALOW

As the 19th century drew to a close and the 20th began, Victorian ideals and the domestic architecture that embodied them were coming under increased scrutiny. Beginning in the 1880s, the Arts and Crafts movement and its bungalows would transform the landscape of American domestic architecture and serve as a transitional housing form in the years prior to World War II. Between 1900 and 1930, the bungalow was the most widespread housing type in the country, from city to suburb.

Bungalows responded to a constellation of sociocultural forces and economic necessities, particularly to the Progressive Era philosophy of the Arts and Crafts movement. As the cost of previously unavailable household technologies such as indoor plumbing and electricity increased, the size of American homes was reduced to compensate for these expenses (which could add between 25 and 40 percent to a home's cost). At the same time, "simplicity" became a watchword of the Arts and Crafts movement, which was taking shape in the United States with the help of publications such as Gustav Stickley's *Craftsman* magazine. For Arts and Crafts proponents, the craftsman-inspired bungalow provided an economically advantageous, socially responsible, and artistic dwelling for members of the middle and working classes.

Bungalow scholar Clay Lancaster explains that "the word 'bungalow' originated in India, derived from the Bengali noun *bangla*, meaning a low house with galleries or porches all around" (see Lancaster, 1985). The first American bungalows appeared along the eastern seaboard as a type of resort architecture. Much grander in scale than the more modest bungalows that followed, these early bungalows nevertheless included the ample porches and exposed-framing construction that are typical of the form. Although not all scholars agree on this point, the architects who are usually credited with perfecting the bungalow style in the United States are Charles Sumner Greene and Henry Mather Greene. In addition to the Greenes, architect Frank Lloyd Wright's Prairie style of domestic architecture influenced midwestern bungalows. In California, where the bungalow was most popular, Arthur and Alfred Heineman were well known for pioneering the concept of the "bungalow court," featuring multiple bungalows around a central courtyard.

Beginning in the early 1900s, the Greene brothers designed a number of relatively inexpensive California homes as well as the "Ultimate Bungalows," for which they are best known (for example, the Blacker House [1907] and the Gamble House [1908]). The distinguishing features of the Greenes' style include (1) a heavy use of wood and natural materials, such as clinker brick and river stone; (2) exposed interior and exterior joinery; (3) the use of sleeping and living porches to enhance the occupants' contact with nature; (4) a concern for the "total design" of a home, including its textiles and furnishings; and (5) the use of relatively open floor plans. Many of these features are evident in simpler and smaller bungalows that feature natural building materials, wide porches with heavy (typically masonry) columns, and low-pitched roofs with exposed rafters and joinery. In addition to these features, many bungalows incorporate outdoor gardens with pergolas, porches specifically designed for sleeping, and prominent chimneys constructed of rustic materials.

Architectural historian Marcus Whiffen (1969) explains that "it was the bungalow as much as any other kind of house that led to the adoption of the 'living room' and the 'outdoor-indoor' living space—of craftsmanship, climatic adaptation, and harmony with the landscape."

The simple floor plans of most bungalows maximize the amount of interior space available by discarding the Victorian parlor in favor of a combined living and dining area, often separated by a colonnade or book arch. The typical bungalow plan provides a kitchen at the rear, a living-dining area with the living area at the front of the home, and two bedrooms with a bathroom between them. To maximize the bungalow's limited interior space, built-in furniture pieces, such as buffets, bookcases, and seating inglenooks, were integral features. Built-ins enhanced the beauty of a room with their natural woodwork while contributing to the reputation of the bungalow as an easily kept home.

Bungalows vary somewhat by region in terms of their exterior appearance, building materials, and interior plans. Bungalows in the eastern United States tend to exhibit an English influence, whereas west coast bungalows draw inspiration alternately from Japan and the Swiss chalet. Such observations are only guidelines, however, as the widespread diffusion of the bungalow through plan books and mail-order catalogs has functioned to minimize regional differences. The typically wooden exterior of the bungalow is also occasionally replaced or joined by stucco, brick, or stone. The most typical interior variation of the bungalow is the provision of an extra bedroom or breakfast area. In addition, many two-story homes can be characterized as bungalows despite the fact that the term usually denotes a one-story home. Two-story "bungaloid" homes (as Marcus Whiffen calls them) often feature dormer windows to maintain a relatively low profile appearance.

Potential home owners could build a bungalow from an architect's original plans, purchase bungalow plans from widely available catalogs such as *Radford's Artistic Bungalows*, or buy a prefabricated bungalow kit from companies such as Sears and Roebuck or Aladdin. Mail-order bungalows produced by Sears, Aladdin, and several smaller companies appeared in 1906 and reached their greatest popularity between 1910 and 1930. An estimated one-half million mail-order homes were produced between 1900 and the start of World War II in 1939. Today mail-order houses can be found throughout the country.

Beginning with the stock market crash of 1929 and continuing through the Great Depression, the popularity of the bungalow declined, as did interest in domestic building generally. The construction industry was dealt a sharp blow by the enduring economic crisis, with housing starts falling a precipitous 90 percent between 1925 and 1933. By the time the country emerged from World War II, the affordable mass-produced suburban house had eclipsed the picturesque bungalow. Nevertheless, the bungalow and its attendant philosophy of the simple life established attitudes about the home that persist today.

CYNTHIA DUQUETTE SMITH

See also **Arts and Crafts Movement; Greene, Henry M. and Charles S. (United States); Prairie School; Stickley, Gustav (United States); Wright, Frank Lloyd (United States)**

Further Reading

Architectural histories that focus on American domestic building are provided by Clark, Gowans, Whiffen, and Wright. Lancaster focuses on the bungalow form specifically. Additional sources below provide further information about the Arts and Crafts movement with respect to the bungalow and mail-order houses produced by Aladdin and Sears.

Aladdin Company, *Aladdin Homes: "Built in a Day" Catalog No. 29*, Bay City, Michigan: Aladdin, 1917; reprint, as *Aladdin "Built in a Day" House Catalog, 1917*, New York: Dover, and London: Constable, 1995

Clark, Clifford, Jr., *The American Family Home, 1800–1960*, Chapel Hill: University of North Carolina Press, 1986

Gowans, Alan, *The Comfortable House: North American Suburban Architecture, 1890–1930*, Cambridge, Massachusetts: MIT Press, 1986

King, Anthony D., *The Bungalow: The Production of a Global Culture*, Boston and London: Routledge and Kegan Paul, 1984; 2nd edition, New York: Oxford University Press, 1995

Lancaster, Clay, *The American Bungalow: 1880–1930*, New York: Abbeville Press, 1985

Rybczynski, Witold, *Looking Around: A Journey through Architecture*, New York: Viking, 1993

Schweitzer, Robert, and Michael W.R. Davis, *America's Favorite Homes: Mail-Order Catalogues as a Guide to Popular Early 20th-Century Houses*, Detroit, Michigan: Wayne State University Press, 1990

Sears, Roebuck and Company, *Honor Bilt Modern Homes*, Chicago: Sears, Roebuck, 1926; reprint, as *Small Houses of the Twenties: The Sears, Roebuck 1926 House Catalog*, Philadelphia, Pennsylvania: Athenaeum of Philadelphia, and New York: Dover, 1991

Stevenson, Katherine Cole, and H. Ward Jandl, *Houses by Mail: A Guide to Houses from Sears, Roebuck, and Company*, Washington, D.C.: Preservation Press, 1986

Trapp, Kenneth R., et al., *The Arts and Crafts Movement in California: Living the Good Life*, New York: Abbeville Press, and Oakland, California: Oakland Museum, 1993

Whiffen, Marcus, *American Architecture Since 1780: A Guide to the Styles*, Cambridge, Massachusetts: MIT Press, 1969; revised edition, 1992

Wright, Gwendolyn, *Building the Dream: A Social History of Housing in America*, New York: Pantheon, 1981

BUNSHAFT, GORDON 1909–90

Architect, United States

Gordon Bunshaft was a partner in the New York office of Skidmore, Owings and Merrill and was an adherent of European modernism as well as one of the leaders of a generation of architects who made buildings of glass, metal, reinforced concrete, and travertine familiar in North America. At his best, he created works of highly refined proportion, efficient function, imaginative construction, and adaptation to sites that were often difficult. His later works were often bulkier and simplified in geometric form; nevertheless they include imaginative solutions to complicated problems, humane consideration for those who work in them, and dramatic boldness. His work encompassed institutional buildings such as the Beinecke Library (1963) for rare books and manuscripts at Yale University (a building he thought might potentially be his most enduring work), the Hirshhorn Museum and Sculpture Garden (1974) on the Mall in Washington, D.C., and the presidential library for Lyndon Johnson in Austin, Texas (1971). Corporate headquarters built to his designs included Lever House (1952) in New York City, the Banque Lambert (1965) in Brussels, the American Can Company offices (1970) in Greenwich, Connecticut, and the National Commercial Bank (1983) in Jeddah, Saudi Arabia. Buildings for business constituted most of the works for which he became well known, although he also designed other types of structures. These included the Venezuelan Pavilion at the World's Fair of 1939 (held in New York City), the Istanbul Hilton Hotel (1955) in association with Sedad Eldem, a pristine cubic addition to the Albright-Knox Museum (1962) in Buffalo, New York, the Philip Morris Cigarette Manufacturing Plant (1974) in Richmond, Virginia (where garden courts alternate with work areas), the spectacular Haj Terminal at the Jeddah airport (in collaboration with the engineer, Fazlur Khan), and a one-story house for himself and his wife in Easthampton, New York.

Bunshaft was the son of immigrants from Russia and attended public schools in Buffalo, New York, before receiving his bachelor's and master's degrees in architecture from Massachusetts Institute of Technology (MIT). It was there that several of the younger instructors showed him the new forms, generated in Europe by Le Corbusier, Ludwig Mies van der Rohe, Walter Gropius, among others. Bunshaft found their work inspiring, but did not execute mere copies of their works; instead, he adapted European ideas to the specific circumstances of American commissions that differed in type, materials, location, and legal constraints. With the help of a Rotch Traveling Fellowship from MIT, Bunshaft visited Europe for several months in 1935–36, and then sought work in New York City. After working briefly for Edward Durell Stone, Raymond Loewy, and other practitioners, he secured a position in 1937 with the young firm of Skidmore, Owings and Merrill. Louis Skidmore's experience in exhibition design secured work for his firm at the World's Fair of 1939, and the firm expanded rapidly thereafter. Bunshaft returned to the office in New York, after serving in several branches of the military (1942–46), and became a partner in the firm in 1946.

Bunshaft's work on such varied projects as Manhattan House, a large apartment house in New York City, and the Fort Hamilton Veterans' Administration Hospital in Brooklyn, is characterized by a taste for geometric form, siting to enhance both efficiency and amenity, refined proportion, and attention to landscaping and ground-level amenity. These characteristics reappeared at Lever House (New York), a modestly sized corporate headquarters that was the first glass box, commercial office building in the city. During the next decade, Bunshaft designed other buildings that often appeared delicate despite their substantial size, including the glass-walled branch bank for the Manufacturers' Trust Company in Manhattan, the Connecticut General Life Insurance Company (1957) in Bloomfield, Connecticut, and the Reynolds Metals Company headquarters (1958) in Richmond, Virginia, where the company's aluminum formed a substantial part of the exterior surface.

During the 1960s, Bunshaft's style included attention to dramatic structure, with large boxlike buildings supported on small pin joints; the Beinecke Library is one example of the style, and another is the American Republic Life Insurance Company headquarters (1965) in Des Moines, Iowa. At this time, he used concrete more often than glass and metal, but continued his intense interest in designing the thinnest possible metal and glass curtain walls, as he used at 140 Broadway (1967) in New York City.

The taste for dramatic buildings continued into the 1970s, with sometimes-clumsy results, as in the Hirshhorn Museum. The museum is a doughnut-shaped building that attempted to mediate between the disparate shapes of neighboring museums. By contrast, praise abounded for his National Commercial Bank (Jeddah) where he ingeniously placed multistory openings on a prismatic, largely blank building, allowing partly cooled air to help ventilate the office tower in a hot, dry climate. The Teflon-covered tents at the terminal in Jeddah for the pilgrims to the annual Haj, earned universal admiration, providing as they do, an elegant, airy solution to climatic and social problems.

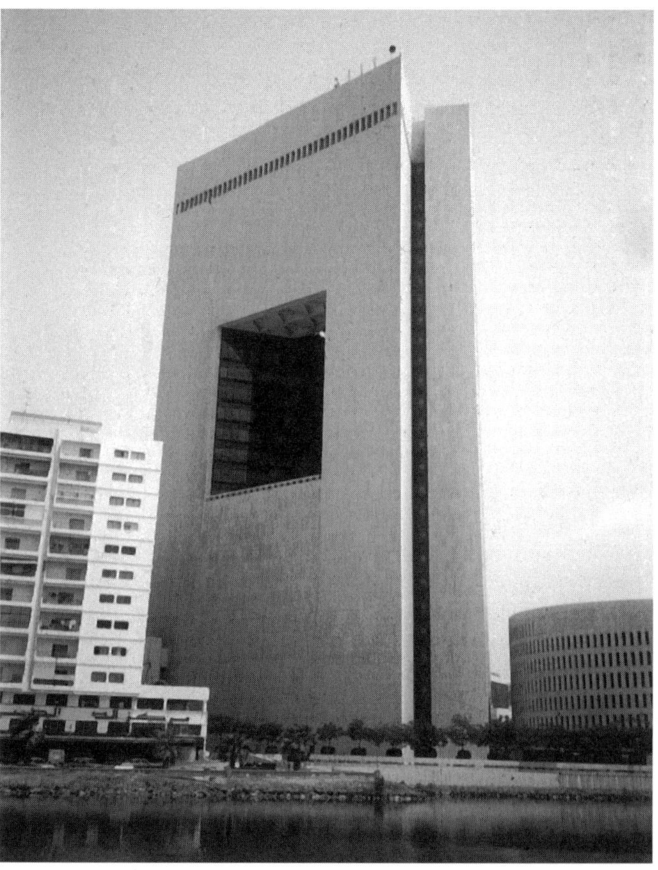

National Commercial Bank, Jeddah, Saudi Arabia, designed by Gordon Bunshaft (1983)
© Zouheir A. Hashem

These buildings are too intricate to have been designed by one person, and Bunshaft acknowledged his debts to his administrative partners as well as to his design assistants and engineers. His architectural colleagues included William S. Brown, J. Walter Severinghaus, Natalie de Blois, and Sherwood A. Smith. A practical person who was interested in specific situations rather than in theory, Bunshaft was a man of great energy, a decisive decision-maker with a habit of blunt speech, and a man of fundamental honesty.

His interests in landscaping and in the placement of works of modern art inside and outside the firm's buildings are lesser-known aspects of his work, but they were essential to his idea of good architecture. He favored the sculpture of Henry Moore, Joan Miró, Alberto Giacometti, and Isamu Noguchi, whose works were in the private collection that he and his wife willed to New York's Museum of Modern Art. His collection included paintings by Miró and Jean Dubuffet and modest examples of African sculpture.

His building designs earned him 12 First Honor awards from the American Institute of Architects, the Gold Medal of the American Academy and Institute of Arts and Letters, and the Pritzker Prize, which he shared with Oscar Niemeyer.

CAROL HERSELLE KRINSKY

See also **Gropius, Walter (Germany); Corbusier, Le (Jeanneret, Charles-Édouard) (France); Lever House, New York; Mies van der Rohe, Ludwig (Germany); Skidmore, Owings and Merrill (United States)**

Biography

Born in Buffalo, New York, 9 May 1909. Earned bachelor's degree, 1933; master's degree, 1935 in architecture, both at Massachusetts Institute of Technology; toured Europe and northern Africa on a Rotch Traveling Fellowship 1935–37. Married Nina Elizabeth Wayler 1943. Chief designer, New York office 1937–42 Skidmore and Owings, later Skidmore, Owings and Merrill; served in United States Army Corps of Engineers 1942–46; partner Skidmore, Owings and Merrill 1946–83; member, the President's Commission on the Fine Arts 1963–72. Visiting critic, Massachusetts Institute of Technology 1940–42; visiting critic, Harvard University, Cambridge, Massachusetts 1954–60; visiting critic, Yale University, New Haven, Connecticut 1959–62; trustee, Museum of Modern Art, New York from 1975; trustee, Carnegie-Mellon University, Pittsburgh, Pennsylvania from 1977. Fellow, American Institute of Architects; fellow, American Academy of Arts and Sciences; academician, National Academy of Design; honorary member, Buffalo Fine Arts Academy, New York 1962; honorary professor, Universidad Nacional Federico Villareal, Lima, Peru 1977; awarded Pritzker Prize (shared with Oscar Niemeyer) 1988. Died in New York, 6 August 1990.

Selected Works

Venezuelan Pavilion, World's Fair, New York, 1939
Lever House Corporate Headquarters, New York, 1952
Manufacturers Hannover Trust Bank Branch Headquarters, New York, 1954
Hilton Hotel (with Sedad Hakkí Eldem), Istanbul, 1955
Connecticut General Life Insurance Company Office Building, Bloomfield, 1957
Reynolds Metals Company Building, Richmond, Virginia, 1958
Chase Manhattan Bank, New York, 1961
Albright-Knox Art Gallery (addition), Buffalo, New York, 1962
Beinecke Library, Yale University, New Haven, Connecticut, 1963
Banque Lambert Building, Brussels, 1965
American Republic Insurance Company Building, Des Moines, Iowa, 1965
Marine Midland Building, 140 Broadway, New York, 1967
American Can Company Suburban Corporate Headquarters, Greenwich, Connecticut, 1970
Lyndon Johnson Presidential Library (with Brooks Barr Graeber and White), Austin, Texas, 1971
W.R. Grace Building, 1114 Avenue of the Americas, New York, 1973
Philip Morris Cigarette Manufacturing Plant, Richmond, Virginia, 1974
Hirshhorn Museum and Sculpture Garden, Washington, D.C., 1974
National Commercial Bank, Jeddah, 1983
Haj Terminal, Jeddah International Airport (with Fazlur Khan), Saudi Arabia, 1985

Selected Publication

"25-year Award Goes to Lever House," *AIA Journal* (March 1980)

Further Reading

Bush-Brown, Albert, *Skidmore, Owings and Merrill: Architecture and Urbanism, 1973–1983*, New York: Van Nostrand Reinhold, 1983
Danz, Ernst, *Architecture of Skidmore, Owings and Merrill, 1950–1962*, translated by Ernst van Haagen, New York: Praeger, and London: Architectural Press, 1962
Krinsky, Carol Herselle, *Gordon Bunshaft of Skidmore, Owings and Merrill*, New York: Architectural History Foundation, and Cambridge, Massachusetts: MIT Press, 1988
Menges, Axel, *Architecture of Skidmore, Owings and Merrill 1963–1973*, translated by E. Rockwell, New York: Architectural Book, and London: Architectural Press, 1974

BUREAUX D'ETUDES HENRI CHOMETTE

Architecture firm, France and West Africa

The Bureaux d'Etudes Henri Chomette were architectural firms created in 1949 by Henri Chomette, a French-born architect who established himself in Africa ten years before the independence achievements.

Active in Africa from 1949 until 1993 and concentrated in Francophone West Africa (Senegal, Ivory Coast, Burkina Faso, Benin, and Togo) and central Africa (Cameroon and Gabon), the Bureaux d'Etudes Henri Chomette in 50 years gained a sustained reputation based on the contribution of African architects, engineers, craftsmen, and artists in the building of modern African states.

Born in Saint-Etienne (a city near Lyon), Henri Chomette (1921–95) developed early a passion for architecture. A student of Tony Garnier in Lyon (1941–45), Othello Zavaronni, and Gustave Perret at the École des Beaux-Arts in Paris (1945–46), Chomette earned his degree in architecture in 1946. An admirer of Le Corbusier and intern in his atelier de la rue de Sèvres 35 in Paris, Chomette rapidly gained recognition as a major architect for the Reconstruction period after World War II throughout his practice in Paris, Le Havre, and Lille. In France, the difficult period of Reconstruction with "normalized architecture" and the takeover of geometers and engineers in the architectural project limited architects' initiative, creativity, and control over their projects for public buildings.

In 1948 Chomette won an international architectural competition for Haile Selassie's Imperial Palace in Ethiopia. The competition, organized by the International Association of Architects (UIA) in Paris, gave Chomette the opportunity to access another continent with major potentiality in terms of urban planning, architecture, and project management. Although never built, the Imperial Palace in Addis-Ababa nevertheless gave Chomette an official entrance to Ethiopia and to the African continent. In Ethiopia Chomette was commissioned for public buildings such as theaters, housing projects, the State Bank of Ethiopia (1949–53), and the Headquarters of the Organization of African Unity (1963). Appointed major urban planner, he also developed urban grids (1953) for the city of Addis-Ababa. He then moved to West Africa, where he established and managed architectural firms for more than 45 years.

As a liberal private-sector architect unlike his contemporaries (who were primarily salaried-employees paid by the French government and working temporarily in Africa), Chomette depended entirely on public and private commissions to manage his firms and pay his collaborators. Architectural firms connected to the private sector, the Bureaux d'Etudes Henri Chomette represented a body of professionals from architects to economists, from draftsmen to craftsmen, who autonomously managed the totality of the projects in any country in which they practiced.

Another fact differentiated architects working for the Bureaux d'Etudes Henri Chomette from their peers: their originality in reflecting and respecting African cultures, architectural patrimony, and environment in all steps of the projects, from beginning to finalization. In opposition to many practitioners of the time, who merely transplanted European architectural epitomes derived from the International Style and from all types of revivals (including classical, Normand, and Provençal), Chomette and his colleagues intensively produced both a local and a modern architecture considering cultures and their environment. In their quest for authenticity through simplicity, all partners of the Bureaux d'Etudes Henri Chomette clearly understood that modern architecture in Africa needed use technology in order to serve social values and to suit popular needs.

Romanticized imagery about giant thatch-roofed cabins in the middle of a modern city, as well as out-of-place urban-planning theories derived from "masters" such as Le Corbusier were not apropos in the architectural repertoire and agenda of Chomette's firms. The latter offered an African alternative based on society, economy, and technology during transitional periods preceding and following the independence processes.

Numerous projects in the heart of capitals such as Dakar, Abidjan, Niamey, Lome, and Cotonou, and in secondary cities are attributed to the Bureaux d'Etudes Henri Chomette. Their activity included urban planning, housing projects, public administrations, embassies, hospitals, schools, transportation, hotels, banks, private residences, and industrial buildings and structures.

The following buildings and structures cover only an infinitesimal portion of the substantial contributions of the Bureaux d'Etudes Henri Chomette in African architectural and urban landscapes: State Bank of Ethiopia (1953), City Hall of Abidjan (1956), National Palace of Benin (1963), Nour-Al-Hayat Mall (1965) in Abidjan, French Embassy (1966) in Ouagadougou,

SOS Children's Village International, Dakar, Senegal, designed by Henri Chomette in collaboration with Thierry Melot (1979)
Photo courtesy Bureaux d'Etudes Henri Chomette © Aga Khan Trust for Culture

National Saving Bank of Yaounde (1973), Charles de Gaulle Bridge (1967) in Abidjan, Department of Finances Building (1976) in Abidjan, Ivorian Society of Bank (SIB; 1976) in Abidjan, the Yopougon and Williamsville dwellings (1975) in Abidjan, and the School of Librarians (1980) in Dakar.

Similarities can be seen between the Bureaux d'Etudes Henri Chomette's early works in the 1950s and the later ones in the 1990s. Some of these concepts greatly influenced new generations of African architects, such as Abou Koffi, Andree Diop, and Habib Diene, who acknowledged the pioneering and quintessential work of the Bureaux d'Etudes Henri Chomette. Major innovations and concepts include the following:

1. Integration of cultural features and connections referring to the population concerned in the concept, design, spatial organization, and aesthetics of public and private buildings (the stairway of honor of the National Palace of Benin in Cotonou [1963] consisted of several royal insignias and seals of Abomey, former capital of the kingdom of Dahomey)
2. Use of local materials and modern techniques
3. Structural transformation of buildings (for the City Hall of Abidjan built in 1956, the facade was composed of revolving wooden panels for natural ventilation that later were turned into a revolving thermal double glazing in the 1970s)
4. Partnership with African craftsmen, artisans, and artists in all steps of the projects
5. Integration of Plastic Arts into the architectural project

One observes the longevity of the Bureaux d'Etudes Henri Chomette through a solid local structure and independent management, the knowledge and enforcement of all the rules connected with building markets throughout West Africa, and the quality of economically realistic and culturally oriented projects.

The quintessential partnership with local architects, engineers, craftsmen, and artists reinforced the cultural identity of the architectural work of the Bureaux d'Etudes Henri Chomette, whose existence and expression served primarily Africans by defining and designing a modern architecture completely African in its concept and its destination.

DIALA TOURE

See also **Corbusier, Le (Jeanneret, Charles-Édouard) (France)**

Biography

Born in Saint-Etienne, near Lyon in France, 1921; son of an established craftsman. Attended the École des Beaux-Arts, Lyon; studied under Tony Garnier, 1941–45. Moved to Paris in 1945 and studied under Othello Zavaronni and Gustave Perret at the École des Beaux-Arts, Paris, 1945–46. Major Architect for the Reconstruction, active in independent practice, Paris from 1947. Won international competition for Imperial Palace in Ethiopia 1948. Moved to Ethiopia 1949. Created and managed the Bureaux d'Etudes Henri Chomette 1949–93. Appointed major architect and urban planner for the city of Addis-Ababa 1953–59. Appointed architect and urban planner for the Upper-Volta government 1961–66. Gave numerous lectures in African Universities and Schools of Architecture. Published several influential works in *Africa*, 1964, *Architectures d'Outremer*, 1992, *Les 460 000 heures*, 1995. Exhibited at several national and international exhibitions including Expo '67, Montreal, 1967, Bouake, 1970. Died in Saint-Etienne, 1995.

Selected Works

Many of the buildings built by the Bureaux d'Etudes Henri Chomette are still in use today. Some that are well kept, such as the City Hall of Abidjan, Department of Finances Building in Abidjan, and National Palace of Benin, underwent major reconstruction over the years; others, such as the Ivorian Society of Bank, lost their original value after technical problems caused the deterioration of their main facades.

State Bank of Ethiopia, Addis-Ababa, 1953
City Hall of Abidjan, 1956
National Palace of Benin, Cotonou, 1963
Nour-Al-Hayat Mall, Abidjan, 1965
French Embassy in Ouagadougou, 1966
Charles de Gaulle Bridge, Abidjan, 1967
National Saving Bank of Yaounde, 1973
Yopougon and Williamsville dwellings, Abidjan, 1975
Department of Finances Building in Abidjan, 1976
Ivorian Society of Bank (SIB), Abidjan, 1976
School of Librarians, SOS Children's Village International (with Thierry Melot), Dakar, 1979

Selected Publications

Africa (November 1964) (special issue on modern architecture)
Architectures d'Outremer, edited by Institut Francais d'Architecture, 1992
Les 460,000 heures, 1995

Further Reading

The works of the Bureaux d'Etudes Henri Chomette were published in many international architecture magazines and in general publications about Architecture in Africa.

Bedarida, Marc, "L'influence française: Du rayonnement des Beaux-Arts au repli hexagonal," *Techniques et architecture*, 430 (1997)
Chapier, François, "Cotonou: Le Nouveau Centre et le Palais de la République," *Equipements et activités d'outremer*, 115 (1964)
Christin, Olivier, and Armelle Filliat, "Abidjan: Un urbanisme capital," in *Architectures françaises outre-mer*, edited by Maurice Culot and Jean-Marie Thiveaud, Liège: Mardaga, 1992
Depret, Roland, *Les Bureaux d'Études Henri Chomette: L'assimilation des pratiques traditionnelles dans l'architecture contemporaine*, Dakar: Aga Khan Program for Islamic Architecture, 1983
Dione, Mareme, "Dakar au fil des plans," in *Architectures françaises outre-mer*, edited by Maurice Culot and Jean-Marie Thiveaud, Liège: Mardaga, 1992
Kultermann, Udo, *Architecture nouvelle en Afrique*, Paris: Morancé, 1963
Rambert, Charles, "Tourisme et loisirs: Réalisations du Bureau d'Études Henri Chomette," *L'architecture d'aujourd'hui*, 70 (1957)

BURLE MARX, ROBERTO 1909–94

Landscape Architect, Brazil

Roberto Burle Marx was born in São Paulo, Brazil, on 9 August 1909. A painter, muralist, sculptor, designer, architect, botanist, and landscape architect, Burle Marx is said to be the greatest single influence on gardens since the development of the English tradition in the 18th century.

The son of a wealthy family of European descent (his father Wilhem was born in Trier, the same city as Karl Marx), Burle Marx moved with his family to Rio de Janeiro, where he was educated in music and the arts from an early age. Before entering the Brazilian School of Beaux Arts (ENBA) in 1930, Burle Marx spent two years in Europe, mainly in Germany. There, in an encounter that would influence his whole life, he fell in love with Brazilian native plants in a botanical museum. Not yet valued by the Brazilian elite, which at that time saw themselves as Europeans in the tropics, the Brazilian flora impressed the young Burle Marx. It is worth noting that in the 19th century, Brazilian cities imported plants and tree species for its gardens, following a tradition started by the Portuguese king João VI when he moved to Rio de Janeiro in 1808 and founded the *Jardim Botânico* (botanical garden) the following year. Burle Marx had traveled to dive into European culture, and instead he found his own. Returning to Brazil, he had as a mentor Henrique Melo Barreto, head of Rio's botanical garden.

At the ENBA, Burle Marx got in touch with a generation of extraordinary colleagues like Jorge Moreira, Carlos Leão, Luis Nunes, Affonso Reidy, and Oscar Niemeyer, under the advice of Lúcio Costa. Named director of the ENBA in 1930, Costa had changed the whole curriculum from one that was highly classical to one that introduced the methods and ideas of Le Corbusier and the Bauhaus. Despite its modernist inclinations, however, the ENBA did not reject its faith in drawing as an important part of the process, and Burle Marx would profit from both the rigor of academic sketching and the freedom of modernist composition.

After graduating in 1934, Marx moved to Recife, in the Brazilian northeast, with the task of supervising the renovation of the city's parks and public squares. A few works remain from this period, in which he mainly rebuilt gardens that already existed but, for the first time, introduced native plants into those compositions. In the northeast, he developed more and more his love for documenting, researching, and collecting native Brazilian plants—a task that he would continue through his whole life.

Returning to Rio in 1937, he was invited by Costa to collaborate on the gardens for the Ministry of Education (MES) building. A landmark of Brazilian modernism and one of the first high-rises to be built in accordance with Le Corbusier's "Five Points," the MES building had the French master himself as a consultant. After that, Burle Marx designed and executed a series of gardens that are landmarks of Brazilian modern architecture and almost always associated with a building by one of his colleagues. In Belo Horizonte, he designed the gardens around the Pampulha buildings (by Oscar Niemeyer) in 1942; in Rio, the garden in front of the *Santos Dumont* airport (by Roberto brothers) in 1952 and the gardens around the Modern Art Museum (by Affonso Reidy) and the whole *Flamengo* sea shore park in 1954–56.

Burle Marx used the topography as a field of work and integrated nature and building in a way that was unknown in Brazil, which was accustomed to the Iberian tradition of separation between city and nature. With an extensive knowledge of the plants' life cycles, especially those of the native flora, Burle Marx organized his gardens with natural elements the same way other artists worked on canvas with paint and brush. His creations were always multifaceted, and in his gardens he had a unique ability to anticipate the mature and organic three-dimensional composition from the plan only.

After designing exuberant gardens that represent the best of Brazilian architecture of the 1950s, Burle Marx also worked in Brasilia at the Foreign Affairs Ministry and the Army ministry (1965) and in Rio at the State Oil Company (1969) and the Xerox Building (1980). His most publicized landscape project might be the sidewalk and arborization of the Copacabana beach (1970). Many of his gardens in Brazil are now protected by federal and state conservation offices, and the firm Burle Marx and Cia continues his legacy. Burle Marx also worked outside the boundaries of Brazil and designed the sidewalks and gardens of Biscayne Boulevard in Miami, Florida, and the Ciudad del Este Park in Caracas, Venezuela. In close collaboration with other Brazilian outstanding modernist architects and in full compliance with Costa's intellectual idea of bridging the local and the universal, the modern and the antique, Burle Marx left an impressive body of work, unsurpassed by any other landscape designer of the 20th century.

FERNANDO LARA

See also **Bò Bardi, Lina (Brazil); Brasilia, Brazil; Costa, Lúcio (Brazil); Niemeyer, Oscar (Brazil); Pampulha Buildings, Belo Horizonte, Brazil; Rio de Janeiro, Brazil**

Further Reading

Adams, William, *Roberto Burle Marx: The Unnatural Art of the Garden* (exhib. cat.), New York: MoMA, 1991

Bruand, Yves, *Arquitetura Contemporânea no Brasil*, São Paulo: Perspectiva, 1981

Eliovson, Sima, *The Gardens of Roberto Burle Marx*, New York: Harry Abrams: Sagapress, 1991

Lemos, Carlos A.C., *Arquitetura Brasileira*, Sao Paulo: Melhoramentos, 1979

BURNHAM, DANIEL H. 1846–1912

Architect, United States

Daniel Hudson Burnham's directive to "make no small plans" remains a fitting summary for a man whose life and work was defined by the expansion, growth, and prosperity of well-to-do Americans in the decades that surround the turn of the 20th century. Not only did Burnham house businessmen and statesmen who drove the American commercial and political engine to its unmatched expansion, but he also defined and gave architectural expression to the building types and urban forms they brought to life.

Burnham was born into a family of modest means in rural New York. In 1855 his family moved to Chicago, drawn by the thriving new city's opportunities. At first, seeking his fortune elsewhere, Burnham made unsuccessful attempts to get an Ivy League education, mine for silver in the West, and run for public office in the late 1860s. Upon returning to Chicago, Burnham fell into architecture, rather than having been led by a muse to express himself in built form. From the start, Burnham saw architecture as a business opportunity. After working briefly for a series of architectural offices that included Loring and Jenney in 1872, Burnham settled in with Carter Drake and Wight, where he met John Wellborn Root. In the following year, the two men channeled their complementary interests and talents into opening their own firm. Root was more aesthetically inclined and detail oriented, and became the firm's primary designer, whereas Burnham's organizational and social skills were directed toward business matters and planning efforts.

Their first projects were residences for wealthy Chicagoans, and were characterized by an affinity for period styles and historical eclecticism. They included a house in 1874 for stockyard mogul John B. Sherman that was built on fashionable Prairie Avenue. This project was essential to Burnham's later development and professional life, and offered him access to the boardrooms of high-powered patrons; it became his social entrée to dinner parties following his marriage to Sherman's daughter. From this point, Burnham and Root were catapulted into the elite social and business circles in Chicago.

His patrons enhanced Burnham's natural inclination toward the entrepreneurial. Declaring that he was "not going to stay satisfied with houses," Burnham envisioned assembling a "big business to handle big things, deal with big businessman, and to build up a big organization, for you can't handle big things unless you have an organization" (Hines, 1974). His growing firm focused on office-building projects, for which Burnham laid out the plans, and they soon became the standard for this new building type; Root was responsible for the detailed designs. Burnham's functional, utilitarian designs were based largely on H, U, or square plans accommodating interior light wells, while exposing a maximum amount of the exterior walls to light and air. Their 11-story Rookery Building (1887) is a square plan with one double-loaded corridor wrapping a central light court; all of its offices opened onto either this court or the exterior. The efficient plan was matched by an innovative, iron-curtain, wall structure not evident under the building's brick and terra-cotta shell, articulated into five heavy layers, with a profusion of neo-Romanesque ornament. In contrast, the recently restored internal court—a delicate web of cast- and wrought-iron skylights and cantilevered stairways—is a dazzling display of late-19th-century building technology.

Whereas the Rookery showed indebtedness to 19th-century historicism, another office building constructed in the following decade pointed toward the future. The Reliance Building (1894) eschewed overt historical detail in favor of a more utilitarian, functional, structure-expressing language for which the Chicago School is well known. The 14-story steel frame was wrapped in fireproof terra-cotta and expressed clearly on the building facade through the slender, ribbonlike spandrels that wrap each story at floor level, leaving the greatest proportion of the facade open to glazing. Delicate foliate patterns in the terra-cotta and the building's original projecting cornice hearken to past traditions. However, the startling quantity of glass, the sparkling whiteness of the glazed spandrels with their pronounced horizontality, and the removal of vertical structural members from the facade foretold a new spirit in office-building design: a functional, honest expression of the structure that would reach fulfillment in the next century. Burnham's office buildings contributed to the development of the new building type, improving function and comfort. Whatever the outward expression of these buildings, their decorous designs made them impressive members of the urban landscape, suggestive of the growing wealth and prestige of their patrons, and the importance of the activities within their walls.

With Root's unexpected death in 1891, Burnham was forced to form other partnerships; the firm's name changed to D.H. Burnham and Co. and later to Graham Burnham and Company. Each firm built on the original Burnham and Root model, with Burnham overseeing every part of an increasingly hierarchical and specialized structure. Adopted from the world of business, this approach led architectural practice away from the atelier-based system, and toward the now common architectural practice. By 1910 Burnham's was the largest architectural firm in the world, with 180 employees, branch offices in New York and San Francisco, and buildings rising from Houston to London. Burnham was long an advocate for professionalism in architecture, and he lobbied for professional rights and served the American Institute of Architects (AIA) as president in the 1890s.

His growing fame and prominence in social and professional circles made Burnham an appropriate choice to direct the architectural planning of the World's Columbian Exposition of 1893 held in Chicago. It was not only a fair; the exposition was a city in miniature and inaugurated Burnham's practice as an urban planner. As director, Burnham took control of virtually every aspect including the hiring of workers, laborers, artists, and architects, and overseeing their work and the construction of all buildings. Burnham led the team of prominent architects in arranging a series of buildings around a centralized Court of Honor. To encourage harmony among the designs in response to the classical taste shared by many of the École-trained architects, the committee agreed to a uniform cornice height and a classical vocabulary for their individual buildings, which were to be grouped around the central Court of Honor. References to imperial and Renaissance Rome, Versailles, and post-Haussmann Paris were manifest in the fair's long axial boulevards, water elements, and monumental classical architecture. Although a variety of building styles were employed in the peripheral buildings, it was the images of the Court of Honor that made the fair famous, and influenced city planning afterward.

Aesthetics were not all that concerned Burnham in the planning of the Columbian Exposition. Although it was to be temporary, the grounds were needed to operate like a small-scale city: electrical, steam, gas, water supply, sewage, and transportation all had to be accommodated, which further prepared Burnham for the practical considerations of city planning. However, in this case, other urban challenges were conspicuously absent. For example, there were no slums, and no housing at all was designed or was to be included. Many questioned the appropriateness of this model for real, working cities, and it was deemed irrelevant by later historians and critics. However, the fair was enormously successful with the thousands of visitors who flocked to it, as well as the city officials across the country that were moved to inject some of the model into their own municipalities.

Following the success of the fair, Burnham's well-known administrative and planning skills were in great demand at the turn of the century. His most prominent commission was the Washington Plan of 1902. It was prompted by the capital city's centennial, renewed hope and prosperity following the depression of the mid-1890s, and the conclusion of the Spanish-American war. The plan began as a revival of Pierre Charles L'Enfant's 1793 scheme, from which departures had been made for time- and cost-saving reasons. The design team (Burnham and other alumni of the Columbian Exposition) studied such

Interior (waiting room), Union Station, Washington, D.C., designed by Daniel Burnham (1907)
© Historic American Buildings Survey/Library of Congress

precedents as Paris, Rome, and Versailles, focusing their attention on the Mall area. The main axes of the original plan had been abandoned with the placement of the Washington Monument. Burnham's reconfigured Mall disguised this imperfection by redrawing the axes to meet at the Monument. Burnham cleansed the Mall of its previous functions as pasture, lumberyard, and railroad center, making it a wide swath of elm-lined green space, bordered by cultural institutions. Office blocks and parks were planned for prime locations nearby. The next four administrations drew from Burnham's plan the groundwork for future development in Washington, and architects followed his precepts for layout and style. Significant additions to Washington that remained in keeping with the plan include Henry Bacon's Lincoln Memorial (1912), John Russell Pope's National Gallery of Art, and Burnham's Union Station (1907). Burnham's classicized plan for the capital—successor to and embodiment of the fulfillment of the westward march—suited the nation's cultural and political vision.

Burnham's plans for Cleveland (1903) and San Francisco (1905) proved, on smaller scale, the national influence of his city-planning ideals. His vision affected foreign countries as well; in 1904 Burnham designed the colonial Philippine cities of Manila and Baguio. These designs also paid homage to Beaux-Arts planning, with the city grid cut by diagonal boulevards and dotted with a citywide park system. However, within this imported framework, Burnham preserved local Spanish-Philippine building traditions. As such, his urban plans encourage comparison with other early-20th-century imperial capital planning, such as Sir Edwin Lutyens's design for the Viceroy's House (1913) in New Delhi, where Mogul and Buddhist features meld into an otherwise abstractly classical design.

No urban scheme of Burnham's was as sweeping as his Chicago Plan of 1909. Here, he accepted the challenge that included not only a city center or fairgrounds, but a complete city. Taking only the most general clues from the existing street grid and lakeshore, Burnham reorganized the city into a 20-mile-long recreational, lakefront park, backed by virtually endless commercial districts, with consistent cornice heights punctuated by interior parks. The existing grid of streets was improved functionally and aesthetically, railroad terminals were regrouped for better communication and reduced industrial sprawl, and the Chicago River was straightened for more effective water and riverside transportation. A great domed civic center dominated the skyline; from it, radial boulevards reached into the suburbs miles away.

While the Chicago Plan's aesthetics are often noted—particularly the seeming incongruence of Burnham's Beaux-Arts imposition on the existing industrial, commercial nature of the jagged city, a consistency remains with his earlier vision, to ennoble the businessman and his commercial empire. Burnham's Chicago was a commercial enterprise, aggrandized in a way that lent recognition to commercial activity as Chicago's primary cultural export. As early as the mid-1890s, Burnham had revealed the genesis of the plan as the city's moneymaking potential: an improved physical structure would increase productivity and wealth, and a fine-looking city would encourage the spending of travel dollars at home rather than abroad. Burnham's optimistic and, ultimately unrealistic vision, populated it with wealthy and successful business leaders with little room for anyone else. Even so, the grandeur of Burnham's vision directed much of Chicago's development in coming years: his double-decker boulevard was built as Wacker Drive, Michigan Avenue, was broadened in the 1920s, and various lakefront amenities were constructed in a landfill along the shore, now known as Grant Park.

Burnham's plans served the society that he knew best: the industrialists and politicians who endeavored to improve society through cultural gifts. With honorary degrees from Harvard, Yale, and Northwestern; membership in exclusive social and business clubs; extensive foreign travel; and a supporter of the arts, Burnham was among the elite of the architectural profession, who could afford to live as their clients did. Just as businessmen presented the city with museums and libraries, Burnham gave the gift of his talents to the people. Most of the city plans he completed were presented free of charge. Although some might judge this beneficence as misguided, Burnham was convinced of architecture's role in the improvement of society. In *Century Magazine*, he described the plan of Washington as complementary to the reformation called for among progressive politicians. He believed that aesthetic unity among buildings encouraged social harmony. He felt the ennobling forms of classical architecture were a language meant to uplift the populace, and express the strength and permanency of the political and social order. In his report for the Cleveland Plan, he wrote that the "jumble of buildings" present in most cities disturbed social peace. Architectural uniformity and harmony, as seen in ancient cities of the world, would encourage social harmony in modern America.

Attitudes about Burnham changed radically after his death in 1912. While once he was regarded as a powerful visionary, by the 1920s he was decried as a megalomaniac. During the 1930s, the threat of Fascism and its orderly, uniform architecture brought a chill to reviews of his grand designs. The aesthetic of classicism fell out of favor as modernism swept through the architectural academies and journals, and the few who discussed Burnham did so with derision, grieving his renunciation of the honest architecture of the Chicago School to follow classical, elitist, historicist, and irrelevant flights of fancy. Recent years have been kinder to Burnham, bringing an increased appreciation for the role of ornament in architecture after mid-century. It has lead to a reevaluation of Burnham's career. During the 1970s, the first serious biography of Burnham was written, as were a flurry of dissertations on his work and planning. His many contributions to architecture are appreciated today. Burnham's role in the development of the skyscraper, the planning of the modern office building, and city-planning concepts that were employed throughout the United States affects nearly every architectural office in operation today.

JHENNIFER A. AMUNDSON

See also **Chicago School; Flatiron Building, New York; Holabird, William, and John Wellborn Root (United States); Lutyens, Edwin (Great Britain); Plan of Chicago**

Biography

Born in Henderson, New York, 4 September 1846. Attended Chicago city schools; studied with a private tutor in Bridgewater, Massachusetts; apprentice in the office of Loring and Jenney, Chicago. Married Margaret Sherman: 5 children; sons Hubert and Daniel Jr. became architects and joined their father's firm. Entered large mercantile house, Chicago 1868; partnership with Laureau; draftsman, Carter Drake and Wight, Chicago 1872; partner in Burnham and Root with John Wellborn Root 1873–91; opened own office, Chicago 1891; directed the architectural planning of the World's Columbian Exposition, Chicago 1893; appointed chairman of the Commission of Fine Arts, Washington, D.C. 1910. Member, Chicago chapter, American Institute of Architects 1884; fellow, American Institute of Architects 1887; president, American Institute of Architects 1894. Died in Heidelberg, Germany, 1 June 1912.

Selected Works

All in Chicago unless otherwise noted

Burnham and Root:
Sherman House, 1874
Montauk Building, 1882
Rookery Building, 1887
Rand-McNally Building, 1890
Monadnock Building, 1890

D.H. Burnham and Company:
Reliance Building, 1894
Frick Building, Pittsburgh, 1901
Marshall Field Retail Store, 1902
First National Bank, 1903
Fuller (Flatiron) Building, New York, 1903
Railway Exchange Building, 1903
Union Station, Washington, D. C. 1907
Orchestra Hall, 1905
Wanamaker's Store, Philadelphia, 1909
Claridge Hotel, New York, 1910

Selected Publications

Burnham's papers are located in the Burnham and Ryerson Library, The Art Institute of Chicago.

The World's Columbian Exposition, the Book of the Builders, Being the Chronicle of the Origin and Plan of the World's Fair (with Francis Millet), 1894
"How to Set up an Architectural Office Composed of Specialists," *Inland Architect and News Report*, 35 (June 1900)
The Improvement of the Park System of the District of Columbia (with Charles Moore), 1902
"White City and Capital City," *Century Magazine*, 63 (February 1902)
Group Plan of the Public Buildings of Cleveland (with John M. Carrère and Arnold Brunner), 1903
Report on a Plan for San Francisco (with Edward F. O'Day), 1905
The Plan of Chicago (with Edward Benett and Charles Moore), 1909

Further Reading

Although somewhat dated, the best and most complete work on Burnham to date is Thomas S. Hines's *Burnham of Chicago*. Written by a close friend, Charles Moore's earlier account of Burnham's life and work benefits from intimacy of detail but suffers from a lack of scholarly discrimination. Jordy and Wiseman cover both Burnham's 19th- and 20th-century work.

Elliott, Thomas R., "Daniel Burnham: A Consistent Classicist," *Classical America*, 4 (1977)

Field, Cynthia R., "The City Planning of Daniel Hudson Burnham" (Ph.D. diss.) Columbia University, 1974

Hines, Thomas S., *Burnham of Chicago: Architect and Planner*, New York: Oxford University Press, 1974

Jordy, William H., *Progressive and Academic Ideals at the Turn of the Twentieth Century*, Garden City, New York: Doubleday, 1972

Moore, Charles, *Daniel H. Burnham: Architect, Planner of Cities*, New York: Houghton Mifflin, 1921

Wiseman, Carter, *Shaping a Nation: Twentieth-Century American Architecture and Its Makers*, New York: Norton, 1998

BUS TERMINAL

The coming of the automobile resulted in new building types that met the needs of motorized America, such as the filling station and motor lodge. In the early 20th century, the arrival of bus travel also initiated the construction of a new building type, the bus terminal. Although the architectural style of bus terminals has changed dramatically since their development in the early 1930s, their function and general program has remained relatively unaltered.

Early bus terminals typically included features found in rail stations, such as waiting areas and ticket offices; however, some architects viewed bus terminals as mysterious new building types that required analysis and evaluation. In the 1930s, seemingly rudimentary suggestions about bus terminal design were available from magazines such as *The Architectural Record* and *The Architectural Forum.*

Unlike rail stations, however, early bus terminals also required a loading balcony or platform to reach the rooftop luggage racks. By the late 1930s, buses had luggage compartments below the cabin floor, thus removing the need for loading balconies. Nonetheless, bus stations had to incorporate properly designed platforms that could accommodate several arriving and departing buses per day. As a result, the creation of a functional bus platform was a key concern for many architects. Contemporary professional magazines such as *The Architectural Forum* illustrated different types of bus platforms for uncertain architects. These early-20th-century platform designs, such as the island-

Greyhound bus station, in the streamlined art *moderne* style, Louisville, Kentucky (1938)

and-wheel types, continue to be used with contemporary bus terminals.

Architects of early-20th-century bus terminals employed a style that was consciously different from rail stations. During this period, some architects believed that bus travel could assert its viability through a standardized architectural presence with value as an advertising medium. The desire for stylistic uniformity resulted in the use of an art moderne or "streamlined" style, a manner influenced by contemporary industrial designs. From 1930 to 1950, most American bus stations employed the common elements of art moderne (or Deco), such as curved corners, semicircular window bays, and smooth surfaces. Like trains and automobiles, streamlined bus stations also used aerodynamic movement and efficient, modern services: a new dynamic building for a new dynamic form of travel. The New York Terminal for the Greyhound Lines (1935) is an excellent example of this newly developed building type and correlative imagery. Designed by Thomas W. Lamb, its curved walls, wraparound facade, rounded windows, and sleek materials epitomized bus terminal architecture in the early and mid-20th century.

Despite the bus terminal's clean, modern style, delays due to traffic and road conditions compromised its efficiency, and poor maintenance and clumsy designs undermined its appeal. Soon, bus stations were considered dark, dank, and inefficient shelters that catered to passengers "who are automatically marked down as second class citizens" (Dawson, 2000). In the second half of the 20th century, bus terminals lost their streamlined style but retained their dreary quality.

During the mid-20th century, attempts were made to transform the bus terminal's image from an uninviting and dangerous place to a modern and safe transit center. As a result, many bus terminals began incorporating expansive bus platform canopies that sheltered open, well-lit, and safe spaces. These elaborate canopies, which were normally supported by daring and intricate truss designs, achieved a sculptural quality and were sometimes the principal means of architectural expression. For example, New York City's George Washington Bridge Bus Terminal (1962), designed by Pier Luigi Nervi, was an early bus terminal to implement a dramatic and expressive trussed roof. Unfortunately, the waiting areas did not receive the same type of innovative architectural treatment.

Despite new canopy designs, bus terminals continued to be considered inhospitable and troublesome buildings. During the last two decades of the 20th century, however, several efforts were made to infuse a sense of safety and modernity to a formerly lackluster building type. Again, one of the hallmarks of contemporary bus terminals is a light and expressive canopy that is supported by an extravagant truss system. Nevertheless, current terminals are also characterized by waiting areas that are simpler and rely on an extensive use of glass. A recent example is the bus terminal for the North Greenwich Interchange (1997). Designed by Foster and Partners, the dominant feature is a sweeping birdlike canopy supported by a forest of metal, treelike members. The dramatic roof slopes to enclose a waiting area that the architects emphasized as an uncluttered and "safe, user-friendly environment" (Baillieu, 1998).

Terminals that need to fit within an existing urban fabric sometimes become part of mixed-use facility. These types of terminals typically resemble a commercial building more than a high-volume transit center. The Laredo Transit Center (1999) in Laredo, Texas, is a contemporary example of a mixed-use facility that had to conform to the city's urbanism and face a historic town square. Here, the Laredo Transit Center's unassuming facade hides a bus station (which serves local and long-distance passengers), a parking garage, and 16,000 square feet of rentable office space.

Mixed-use bus terminals have been built in urban centers around the world since the 1930s. Similarly, although the architectural style of bus terminals has changed since the early 20th century, the needs and functions have remained the same. Nonetheless, with a renewed dedication to constructing efficient and safe bus terminals, many cities will continue to witness this venerable building type.

MARC PERROTTA

See also **Art Deco; Nervi, Pier Luigi (Italy); Railroad Station; Transportation Planning**

Further Reading

Baillieu, Amanda, "Gimme Shelter," *RIBA Journal*, 105, no. 7 (1998)

"Bus Terminal: New York Terminal of Greyhound Lines, Thomas W. Lamb, Architect," *The Architectural Record*, 78 (September 1935)

Dawson, Layla, "Civilizing the Bus," *The Architectural Review*, 1240 (June 2000)

Fistere, John C., "Bus Terminal Construction," *The Architectural Forum*, 53 (December 1930)

Fistere, John C., "Bus Terminal Planning," *The Architectural Forum*, 53 (December 1930)

ITE Committee 5C-1, "The Location and Design of Bus Transfer Facilities," *ITE Journal*, 52, no. 1 (1982)

Moorhead, Gerald, "Plaza Transit," *Texas Architect*, 50, no. 2 (2000)

"National Trailways Bus Depot, Chicago, Illinois: Graham, Anderson, Probst, and White, Architects," *American Architect and Architecture*, 151 (July 1937)

Thomas Lamb, Inc., "The Bus Terminal," *The Architectural Record*, 81 (January 1937)

Melrose Community Center (2000), view from south garden, Bronx, New York
Designed by Diana Agrest and Mario Gandelsonas (United States)
© David Sunberg / ESTO. All rights reserved.

Alliance Franco-Sénégalaise (1994)
Kaolack, Senegal
Designed by Patrick Dujarric (France)
© Aga Khan Trust for Culture

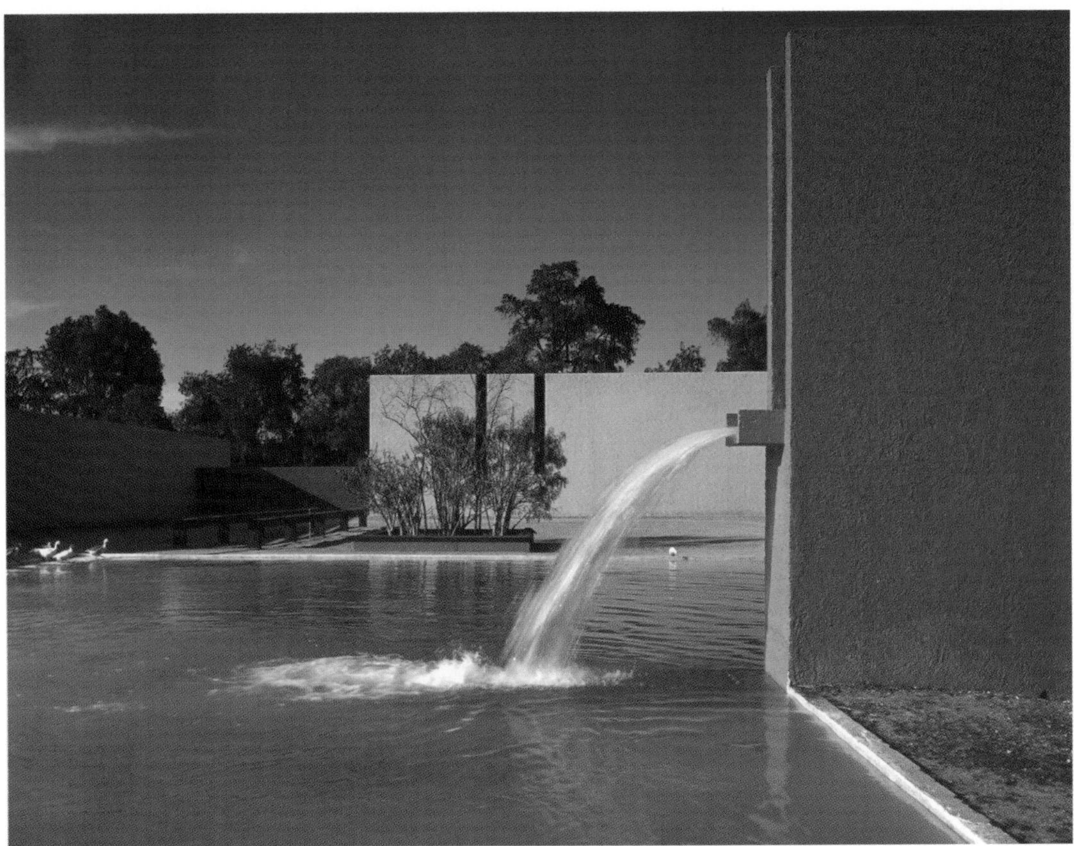

Cuadra San Cristóbal (1966–68), Mexico City, Mexico
Designed by Luis Barragán (Mexico) in collaboration with Andres Casillas de Alba
Photo by Armando Salas Portugal © Barragán Foundation, Switzerland / Artists Rights Society, New York

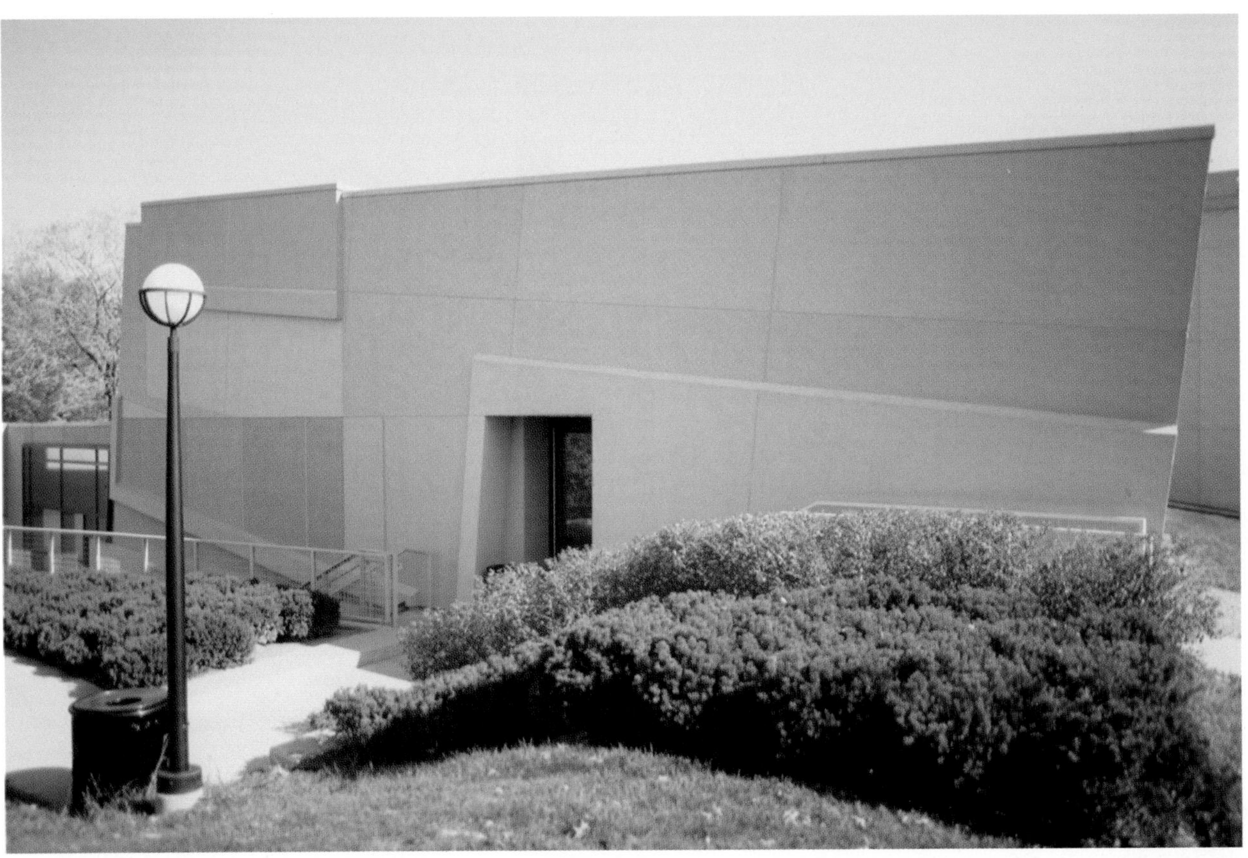

Arnoff Center for Design and Art (1996), University of Cincinnati, Ohio
Designed by Peter Eisenmann (United States)
© Mary Ann Sullivan

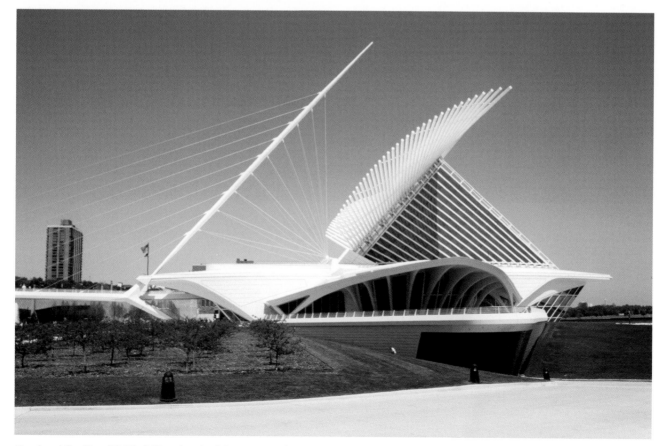

Groninger Museum (1993–95), Groningen, the Netherlands
Designed by Coop Himmelb(l)au (Austria)
© Margaritha Spiluttini. Photo courtesy Coop Himmelb(l)au

Quadracci Pavilion (2001), Milwaukee Art Museum, south terrace, view with wings open, Milwaukee, Wisconsin
Designed by Santiago Calatrava (Spain)
© Mary Ann Sullivan

Casa Malaparte (1938–40), Capri, Italy
Designed by Adalberto Libera (Italy)

Interior Designs of Hill House (ca. 1903), Helensburgh, Scotland
Designed by Charles Rennie Mackintosh (Scotland)
© Howard Davis / Greatbuildings.com

Casa Milá ("La Pedrera") (1905–10), Barcelona, Spain
Designed by Antonio Gaudí (Spain)
© Mary Ann Sullivan

Great Court Interior (1994–2000), The British Museum, London, England
Designed by Sir Norman Foster and Partners (Great Britain)
Photo by Nigel Young © Foster and Partners

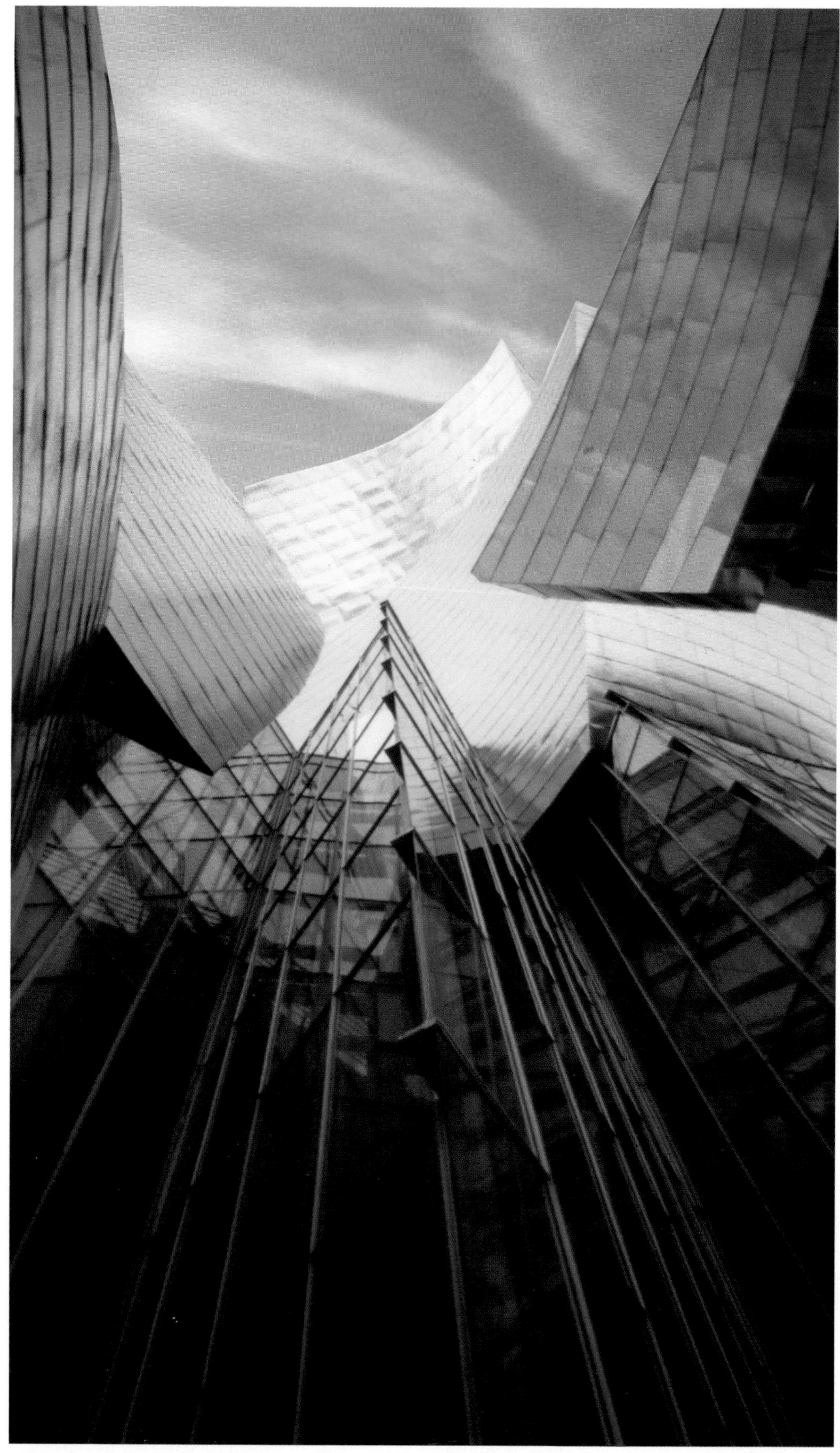

Sky court of the Guggenheim Museum (1991–97), Bilbao, Spain
Designed by Frank O. Gehry (United States)
© Dan Delgado *d2 Arch*

Eigen Haard Housing Estate (Building No. 3, corner) (1915–20)
Amsterdam, the Netherlands
Designed by Michel de Klerk (Netherlands)
© Elisabeth A. Bakker-Johnson

Color Construction. 1923. Project for a private house
Designed by Theo van Doesburg and Cornelius van Eesteren
Gouache and ink on paper, sheet, 22 1/2 x 22 1/2"
Edgar J. Kaufmann, Jr. Fund. (149.1947)
The Museum of Modern Art, New York
Digital image © The Museum of Modern Art, New York / Licensed by Scala / Art Resource, New York, and Artists Rights Society (ARS), New York

C

CAIRO, EGYPT

Though best known for its splendid World-Heritage-listed historic monuments, its inhabited Cities of the Dead (cemeteries), or its contemporary informal peripheries, Cairo is also a city that has experienced almost all international trends of modernism (in a broad sense) across the entire 20th century. The phenomenon can be traced back to the 1870s when an ambitious ruler, Khedive Ismâ'îl (r. 1863–79), known for his passion for architecture and his will to prove that his country was European rather than African, decided to transform the Egyptian capital according to the model of Paris.

Within less than a decade, new quarters (the actual city's center) were created at the edge of the historical core; streets were cut through the old fabric, and building types alien to the local context were introduced, starting with a Palace Hotel (1869) by Christopher G. Wray, an Opera (1869) inspired by La Scala in Milan, apartment buildings with commercial arcades, and town houses surrounded by gardens in the Second Empire's manner. Public parks and promenades, designed by landscape architects with Parisian experience, as well as a vast spa were built south of the city. The result was far from resembling Paris, but an enduring pattern was set among the local elite: the importing of the latest fashions from influential European capitals. Attracted by a growing market, architects, engineers, and contractors of European origin (mainly Italians, but also French, Germans, Austrians, and Armenians) began settling in Cairo, where they more or less reproduced the architecture of their native countries, occasionally using Moorish and later Mamluk motifs to add some sort of "local" touch to their constructions.

Both the eagerness of affluent patrons for innovations from abroad and the hegemony of French and Italian aesthetics continued all through the British occupation (from 1882 to 1922). Building in reinforced concrete started in 1894 and developed quickly. An early example is the Club des Princes (1899), a private theater designed by the prolific Antonio Lasciac, the favorite architect of the Khedivial family from 1895 to the late 1920s and author of a number of princely Italianate palaces still visible today—most of them now adapted to other uses, such as the administration offices of 'Ayn Shams University (1902, restored in 1997), featuring impressive metalwork and a large stained-glass opening in the Liberty style. Art Nouveau was actually short lived, as elsewhere, but flourished as well in its French and Belgian versions, while also producing some Secessionist buildings, among them the Shaarei Hashamaim Synagogue (1907) by Eduard Matasek. Paradoxically, the British influence appears to have been rather incidental. In residential architecture, it manifested mainly through some blocks of flats of red brick and Norman-inspired details, such as the St. David's building (1912), by Robert Williams, or the cottage architecture of the garden suburb of Ma'âdî (created in 1905).

Italianate villas and Parisian-styled apartment buildings constituted by far the dominant and lasting model. Department stores were of an unmistakable French inspiration, be it the luxuriant Orosdi-Back Store (1909) by Raoul Brandon, the Sednaoui Store (1913) by Georges Parcq (with fine iron skeleton), or the Tiring premises (1914) by Oskar Horowitz. The major public building of the period, and the first in Cairo for which an international competition was organized, the Museum of Antiquities (1902), typically featured a Beaux-Arts design by Marcel Dourgnon.

Yet the most spectacular development of the early decades of the 20th century was the building, starting in 1907, of the new town of Heliopolis in the eastern desert, 10 kilometers away from the city's center—and today included in Cairo's boundaries as one of its most fashionable residential districts. Initially a speculative development on a large scale imagined by the Belgian magnate Baron Edouard Empain, the enterprise turned to erecting a sustainable town, with its own facilities, transportation system, and services, generous public and open spaces, and varied types of housing intended to accommodate a large public, from working to upper-middle class. Due to the strict building regulations and standards of construction imposed by Empain and his architects (among them Ernest Jaspar and Alexandre Marcel), an architectural ensemble of remarkable homogeneity was achieved, although a variety of stylistic idioms were used: Moorish and Mamluk Revival, *Japonisme*, Indian style, French and Italian Renaissance, and Romanesque.

The prosperous 1920s and 1930s were dominated by an exuberant Art Deco manner, characterized by the extensive use of ornate stuccowork and elaborate metalwork. One of its best exponents was the firm constituted by Léon Azéma, Max Edrei,

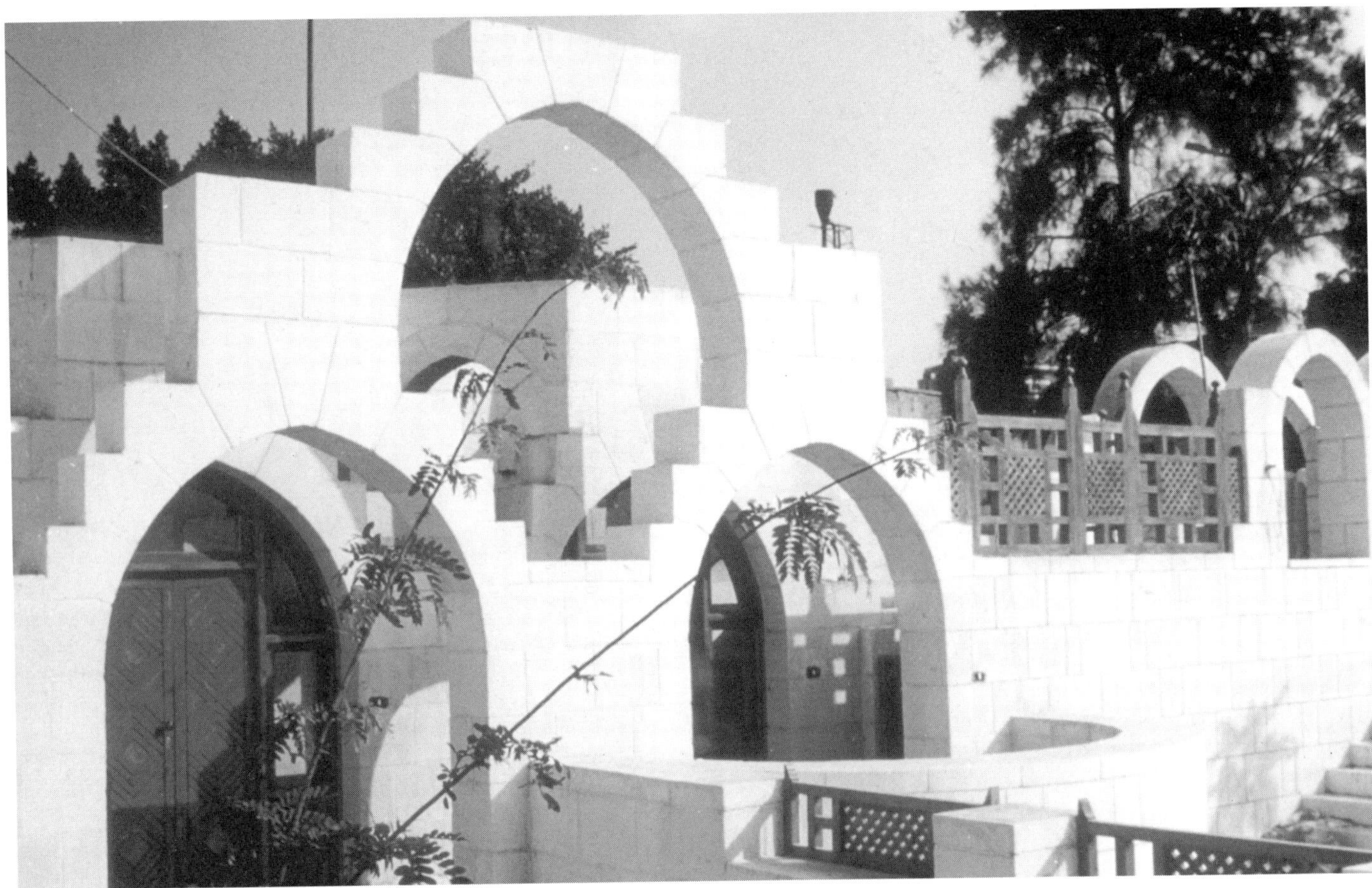

Cultural Park for Children (1992), Cairo, designed by Abdelhalim I. Abdelhalim
Photo by Barry Iverson

and Jacques Hardy. Founded in 1921 by classmates at the École des Beaux-Arts in Paris, the firm opened an office in Cairo after winning the competition for the Mixed Tribunals in 1924 and was extremely active until the completion of the project in 1929: Among the numerous villas and blocks of flats that it designed in Cairo, the Nahas villa (1927) and the highly decorated Rabbath Block (1927) deserve mention. Later examples of French modernism include the elegant work of Georges Parcq and Auguste Perret and, more largely, numerous apartment blocks by local architects educated in Paris and strongly influenced by Michel Roux-Spitz's or Pol Abraham's "modern classicism," such as Antoine Selim Nahas, Raymond Antonious, and Charles Ayrout. In contrast, grand public schemes, such as Cairo University's campus (1937) by Eric George Newmun and the Qasr al-'Aynî hospital (1937) by Charles Nicholas and John Edward Dixon-Spain, were more in line with the British academic classicism.

Another significant aspect of the interwar period was the emergence, due to the Egyptianization policies adopted after independence in 1922, of the first generation of indigenous professionals. Its initial major concern was the search for a genuine modern "national style," combining a contemporary language and references to the country's prestigious architectural heritage. Of note, in this respect, are Mustafa Fahmy's interesting attempts to synthesize the Pharaonic and Islamic legacies into modern designs, through using massive volumetry—the actual Museum of Modern Art (1936)—eventually mixed with Art Deco stylizations of the Mamluk repertoire—the Dâr al-Hikma (Doctors' Syndicate offices) (1941). In an expanding metropolis that had already reached 2 million inhabitants by 1937, the following generation, to which belonged Hasan Fathy as well as active and prominent figures such as Ali Labib Gabr and Mahmud Ryad, was more involved in planning and housing issues. Responsible for the layout of the new residential quarters created in 1948 on the left bank of the Nile (Muhandisin), Ryad also elaborated prototypes of low-density economic housing that were used in three major schemes of the postwar period: the garden suburbs of Madinat al-Tahrîr, Helmiyya al-Zaytûn, and Helwân, totaling 4,000 units completed in 1954. They were succeeded by radical advocates of the International Style. A leading figure was Sayyid Karim, author of several early high-rise buildings and, more important, the founder in 1939 of *al-'Imâra* (Architecture), the first architectural magazine in Arabic, which endeavored to disseminate the latest developments of the international scene into the Middle East. To the same generation belong Mustafa Shawqi and Salah Zeitun, both educated in the United States and claiming influence from Frank Lloyd Wright's organic architecture; Cairo International Airport (1961) is among the many projects they designed as partners. By the late 1950s, few European architects were still practicing in Cairo, and a major shift of the prevailing architectural references was occurring: Americanism was taking command.

Whereas Fathy's and his disciples' internationally-known researches based on vernacular models have left almost no mark on Cairo's landscape and physical environment, conventional international architecture of the 1960s, 1970s, and 1980s did have, in the form of taller and taller apartment towers and hotel blocks, unimaginative shopping malls, ugly multistoried parking buildings, and cheap public housing schemes. Quality design and fine execution, as found in the World Trade Center (1988) and Conrad International Cairo (1999) by Skidmore, Owings and Merrill's London office with Ali Nour El Din Nassar, remain rather exceptional. There are still very few redevelopment schemes dialoging with the surrounding fabric—as in the case of the Cultural Park for Children by Abdelhalim I. Abdelhalim (1992)—or seeking to integrate the preexisting architecture (e.g., the cultural ensemble formed by the new Opera designed by Nikken Sekkei Planners [1987] and reused former fair pavilions). With globalization entering the scene, approaches to architecture greatly diversified during the 1990s, ranging from the interpretation of tradition pursued by Abdelhalim Ibrahim Abdelhalim, to the deconstructionist collision of old and new praised by Ahmed Mito, author of the neo-Pharaonic new Supreme Court building (2000), whereas countless exclusive compounds, drawing on the American model of the service city and displaying "Spanish-style" villas with swimming pool and garden, are being built on the desertic outskirts of the congested metropolis at tremendous rate. Cairo is definitely entering the 21st century with a fast-changing morphology.

MERCEDES VOLAIT

See also **Aga Khan Award (1977–); Art Deco; Art Nouveau (Jugendstil); Egyptian Revival; Fathy, Hassan (Egypt); Gabr, A. Labib (Egypt)**

Further Reading

'Abd al-Jawad, Tawfiq Ahmad, *Misr al-'imarah fi al-qarn al-'ishrin* (Egyptian Architecture in the 20th Century), Cairo: Maktabat al-Anjilu al-Misriyah, 1989

Abdelhalim, Abdelhalim Ibrahim, "Egypt: Country Focus," *World Architecture*, 75 (April 1999)

Curtis, Eleanor, "Culture Clash: The Development of New Cairo," *Architectural Design*, 67: 11/12 (1997)

Myntti, Cynthia, *Paris Along the Nile: Architecture in Cairo from the Belle Epoque*, Cairo: The American University in Cairo Press, 1999

Volait, Mercedes, *L'Architecture moderne en Egypte et la Revue al-'Imara (1939–1959)*, Cairo: Centre d'Études et de Documentation Économiques, Juridiques et Sociales, 1988

Volait, Mercedes, "The Age of Transition: The Nineteenth and Twentieth Centuries," in *The Glory of Cairo: An Illustrated History*, edited by André Raymond, Cairo: The American University in Cairo Press, 2002

Volait, Mercedes, "Making Cairo Modern (1870–1950): Multiple Models for a 'European-style' Urbanism," in *Urbanism—Imported or Exported? Native Aspirations and Foreign Plans*, edited by Joe Nasr and Mercedes Volait, pp. 17–50, Chichester, U.K.: Wiley-Academy, 2003

CALATRAVA, SANTIAGO 1951–

Architect, Spain

Santiago Calatrava studied art and architecture in Valencia and pursued a degree in civil engineering at Zurich's Eidgenossische Technische Hochschule (ETH, or Federal Institute of Technology). After graduation, he worked at the ETH's Institute for Building Statics and Construction and Institute for Plane Statics and Light Construction. In professional practice for just 20 years, he currently has offices in Paris, Zurich, and Valencia, where he works on a number of large-scale architectural projects, on establishing his work as a standard by which later engineering design will be measured, and on winning countless awards including the 1992 Gold Medal of the Institute of Structural Engineers and the 1987 Auguste Perret UIA Prize.

Although Calatrava's work might be best characterized by the futuristic forms of his famous bridge designs, his oeuvre spreads far beyond the engineering wonders he has built. The architect has written that his motto is "Nature is both mother and teacher," and this philosophy is reflected clearly in the manipulation of seemingly unnatural materials like concrete that has dominated some of his stronger work. Nearly all of Calatrava's projects tackle complicated technical issues and are resolved in surprisingly elegant ways. Often inspired by nature, the organic forms that are his solutions leap to new technical heights in a synthesis of light, material, and form.

His most recognizable bridge design might be the Alamillo Bridge (1987–92) in Seville, Spain, spanning 820 feet (250 meters) over the Guadalquivir River. Originally proposed as a twin bridge with a connecting viaduct, the design would cross the river in two locations, approximately 1 mile (1.5 kilometers) apart. The twin bridges were designed so that their tall, inclined masts would reach toward each other, forming an implied triangle that had its apex far above the site. This scheme was ultimately abandoned and adjusted to a single bridge and viaduct, but the inclined mast was retained. The extraordinary weight of the mast (steel filled with concrete) angling back at 58 degrees was enough to support the roadbed without the need for counter-stay cables. This was a first in bridge design, and is a stunning sight. The 1640-foot (500 meter) viaduct served as an entrance gateway for Expo '92 in Seville, for which Calatrava also designed the Kuwait Pavilion. Typical of Calatrava's other works, this bridge was designed to seamlessly accommodate pedestrian traffic and connect with motor roads.

The Stadelhofen Station in Zurich presented Calatrava with a unique chance to make a mark on a city. The site the station was to occupy was challenging in that it varied greatly in elevation from end to end and was curved along its length. Other proposals for the station involved roofing over the area and hiding the bulk of the building underground. However, Calatrava saw this as an opportunity to show off the imperfections of the site. The station he designed is left open to reveal the entire workings of the structure to the viewer. Conceived as a collection of bridges, the project took full advantage of the dynamic qualities of the site.

Campo Volantin Footbridge (1990–98), Bilbao, Spain

Since the early years of the 21st century, Calatrava's work has become visible in the United States after years of almost exclusively European building. In 2002 his first American bridge was realized at the Turtle Bay Exploration Center in Redding, California, linking different sides of the park with the Sacramento River Trail System. The glass span and decking evoke weightlessness and contribute to a seamless integration into the site. The bridge's north-leaning mast doubles as a sundial.

The architect's largest United States commission to date will be the Oakland Cathedral (Oakland, California). Begun in November of 2000, Calatrava's design (not yet completed) will have movable glass-and-steel sections evocative of a pair of praying hands with the capability of opening skyward. Calatrava's other notable American commission—and the first to be completed in the States—was the Milwaukee Art Museum expansion (May 2001). The ingenious riverfront concrete and steel structure is topped with glass "fins" that open and close depending on exterior light; the architect has likened its movement to a bird in flight. A pedestrian bridge links the city to the museum and the landscaped shore of Lake Michigan. In the Milwaukee Museum building, Calatrava's affinity for Finnish-born Eero Saarinen's work (namely the curvilinear TWA [Trans World Airline] terminal at John F. Kennedy Airport) as an Expressionist modernist aesthetic is clear.

EUGENIA BELL

Selected Works

Schwarzhaupt Factory, Dielsdorf, Switzerland, 1982
Jakem Warehouse, Münchwilen, Switzerland, 1985
DOBI Office Building, Suhr, Switzerland, 1986
Wohlen High School, Wohlen, Switzerland, 1988
Lucerne Station Hall, Lucerne, Switzerland, 1989
Stadelhofen Station, Zurich, Switzerland, 1990
Alamillo Bridge, Seville, Spain, 1992
Montjuic Communications Tower, Barcelona, Spain, 1992
Kuwait Pavilion, for Expo 1992, Seville, Spain, 1992
Lyon Airport Station, Lyon, France, 1994
Buchen Housing Estate, Würenlingen, Switzerland, 1996
Alcoy Municipal Center, Alcoy, Spain, 1996
Orient Station, Lisbon World Exposition, Portugal, 1998
Campo Volantin Bridge, Bilbao, Spain, 1998
Sondika Airport, Bilbao, Spain, 1999
Oakland Cathedral, California, unfinished
Milwaukee Art Museum, Minnesota, 2001

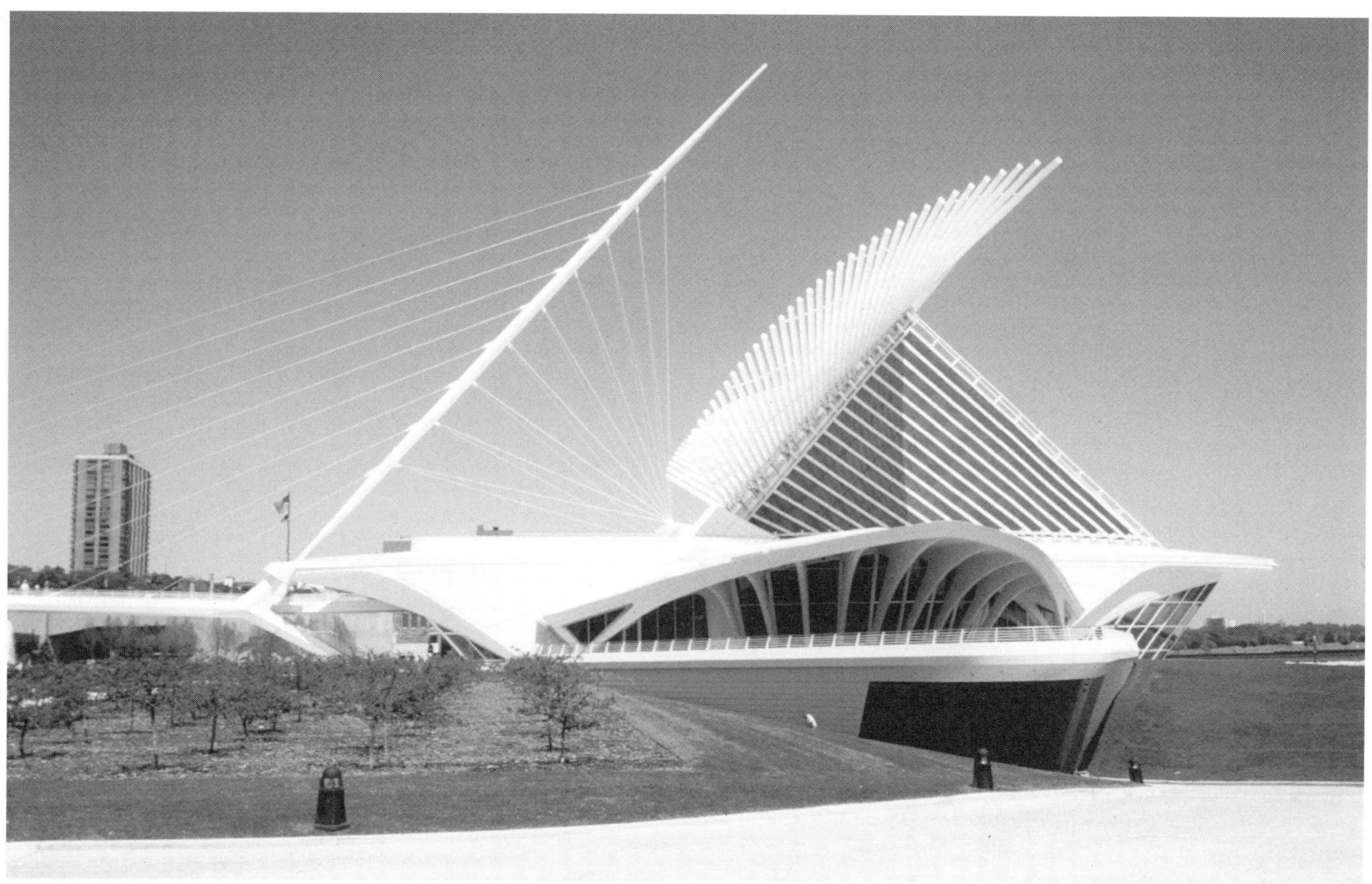

Quadracci Pavilion, Milwaukee Art Museum, South Terrace, view with wings open (2001)
Photo © Mary Ann Sullivan

Further Reading

Frampton, Kenneth, Anthony C. Webster, and Anthony Tischhauser, *Calatrava: Bridges*, Basel: Birkhäuser, 1996
Tischhauser, Anthony, and Stanislaus von Moos, *Calatrava: Public Buildings*, Basel: Birkhäuser, 1998

CAMPUS PLANNING

As the traditional college evolved into the modern university at the dawn of the 20th century, campus planning reached a new complexity. For more than 200 years, college campuses reflected the colonial models of Harvard College (1636), the College of William and Mary (1693), and Yale College (1717), the latter of which began as a few buildings with grass lawns. The evolution from simplicity to complexity saw varied interpretations of Gothic, medieval, and Georgian institutional architecture as the symbolism of higher learning grew more grandiose, corresponding with the growth and purpose of education in the nation.

A new awareness of the importance of scientific scholarship and rationalism changed the function and scope of education. Disregarding tradition, colleges became more specialized, emulating English and German models of the university that combined colleges. Johns Hopkins University (1867), for example, located its first campus in plain buildings on Baltimore's city streets, distinguishing itself from its predecessors by purposely ignoring the familiar picturesque settings that had guarded college learning. Like the political laboratories of German education, the university expressed a new scholarly purpose, one that was utilitarian and serious.

As complex universities replaced traditional colleges, they grew larger, replacing the memory of the village with the image of the city. Not incidentally, a new type of campus planning emerged that took its fundamental reference from urbanism. By 1900, campus planning fell under the thrall of the Beaux-Arts, which also had a great influence on urban planning as a result of the World's Columbian Exposition of 1893 in Chicago. With its ordered City Beautiful buildings and boulevards, the exposition emphasized stately systems of organization that implied not only virtue but order, characteristics eminently suited to the image of the university.

Educational institutions, faced with the need to integrate an increasingly complex array of facilities within a unified design, were easily drawn to the principles of the City Beautiful and its Beaux-Arts high-mindedness. After 1900, numerous articles appeared bemoaning the "un-unified character" of the campus. The main task facing the campus planner, noted A.A.D.F. Hamlin, the educator and architect, was to create a "unity of effect." Critical to this endeavor was the idea of the master plan. Campuses, like cities, took up the idea of planning in a swell of Progressive Era enthusiasm.

The influence of the Columbian Exposition was immediately evident in Henry Ives Cobb's 1893 plan for the University of Chicago. Stylistically linked to English Collegiate Gothic models, Cobb's plan lacked much of the elaborate Beaux-Arts detail evident in Charles McKim's 1894 (revised) plan for Columbia University, which was the first campus plan to really show the practicality of Beaux-Arts symmetry to meet the needs of the new multi-structure university. The designation "university" was part of the new plan, changed from Columbia College when Columbia moved from its small midtown location to its new site on upper Broadway, the former site of the Bloomingdale Asylum. McKim, who had studied at the École des Beaux-Arts and had designed a building for the Chicago exposition, produced a plan for Columbia that was eminently urban—absent dormitories, with buildings that abutted the street and an entrance on Broadway—while expressing an extremely formal presence that included a domed colonnaded main building hierarchically raised above the symmetrical campus. The Broadway entrance evoked a stately formalism, in tune with its Beaux-Arts influence, leading to a campus quadrangle, McKim's version of the Beaux-Arts *cour de honneur* (main courtyard).

Beaux-Arts campus planning soon became the rage. McKim, with his partners Mead and White, were hired to develop a new campus plan at Thomas Jefferson's University of Virginia, whereas Parker, Thomas and Rice designed a new Beaux-Arts campus for Johns Hopkins in 1904. Cass Gilbert produced an elaborate Beaux-Arts plan for the University of Minnesota in 1908. Olmsted's parklike plan for the University of California at Berkeley campus was put on the shelf, and a competition was held that awarded the commission for a new campus to a Frenchman, Emiule Bénard (almost all the entrants were Beaux-Arts trained), who created a grand and ornate campus plan. However, when Bénard, in a pique, refused to move to California to supervise its realization, John Galen Howard (who placed fourth in the competition) replaced him, substantially modifying Bénard's plan, softening it, and integrating other elements from the traditional American campus planning.

Beaux-Arts architecture fulfilled another need for the new university: it expressed a grand monumentality of permanence and importance that appealed to a new wealthy class of philanthropic benefactors who emerged in the early 20th century. Cloaking themselves in art and culture, these philanthropists set their sights on creating personal memorials. The philanthropic benefactor desired a worthy monument. With large sums of money being contributed to educational institutions, it became necessary to provide tangible evidence of the gifts beyond the expansion of research programs and academic pursuits. Gone was the notion of utilitarian educational structure, as evidenced in the new Parker, Thomas and Rice Beaux-Arts campus for Johns Hopkins in 1904. The campus of architectural grandeur had arrived.

John D. Rockefeller's endowment to the University of Chicago was bestowed without direct involvement in campus planning. However, Leland Stanford had no such hesitancy when he endowed Stanford University at the end of the 19th century, transforming Frederick Law Olmsted's plan for informal structures set carefully in the coastal foothills behind Palo Alto into a formal arrangement of buildings around a fully enclosed quadrangle. Anticipating Beaux-Arts formalism, the university was built on a flat site laid out with a formal axis. Stanford's ordered monumentality made a good fit with his desire for a proper personal monument. At the same time, it suited the emerging needs of the new expanding university.

So influential was the Beaux-Arts campus that it essentially defined campus planning in the first half of the 20th century. Even campuses that were developed in the 18th or 19th century rushed to modify their campus plans in the Beaux-Arts fashion in the early 1900s. The modifications to Olmsted's plans at the University of California at Berkeley and Stanford were emblematic of the changing tide. As Olmsted's firm was taken over by his two sons, it could not ignore the trend, and so it specialized in campus planning in the Beaux-Arts style, developing a plan for Harvard that emphasized strict symmetry and axiality.

Princeton University sometimes seemed to be at the whim of these changes, going from a symmetrical campus in the early 19th century to a more informal campus plan at the end of the century to a revised plan at the beginning of the 20th century by Ralph Adams Cram that emphasized a new axial order, even though Cram's plans, Gothic in style, also included many smaller spaces that ignored Beaux-Arts conventions. At the University of Wisconsin at Madison, the École-trained Paul Philippe Cret transformed the existing campus in 1908 with a new central axis, cross axes, and domed buildings laid out in a Beaux-Arts pattern. In 1910, Cass Gilbert redesigned the University of Texas at Austin with a new integrated pattern of formal quadrangles and a centralized tower monument.

With the expansion of higher education in the 20th century and the increasing presence of the large university, another trend developed that sought to reestablish the intimacy of the college campus. Although running not quite counter to Beaux-Arts principles, often embodying many of its formal characteristics, it nonetheless sought to bring about a more collegiate presence by looking back to the form of the English medieval college.

The principal physical expression of this nostalgia was the enclosed quadrangle, which evoked a kind of cloistered and secluded education that most 20th-century campus planning had moved beyond. If its principal metaphor was the monastery, it was nonetheless a very collegial monastery where intellectual life was hoped to thrive within a closed setting of fellowship.

The most popular advocate of this collegiate traditionalism was Cram, a political conservative who was opposed to the "Germanic secularism" of contemporary campus planning and sought to rectify it with romantic evocations of medieval architecture that relied on Gothic structures and closed quadrangles. Cram's Gothic campuses sprang up at West Point, Sweet Briar College, and Richmond College in Virginia as well as at Princeton.

As neo-Gothic enthusiasm spread, often in the form of a compromise between medievalism and classicism, new proponents took up the style. Around 1914, Charles Zeller Klauder designed Cram-influenced structures at Wellesley, Cornell, and Princeton. In 1925, he developed a campus plan for Concordia

Seminary in St. Louis that relied on Cram's formula of a cathedral tower and monastic buildings set around quadrangles. In Pittsburgh, Klauder was responsible for the towering 42-story Gothic Cathedral of Learning at the University of Pittsburgh, which dramatically expressed the underlying religious preoccupation of the neo-Gothicists. Built in 1926, the building seemed almost a moral corrective to the symbolic significance of the skyscraper. The university, Klauder seemed to be saying with his heaven-reaching edifice, relied on God, not Mammon.

Prior to World War II, campus planning stodgily resisted inroads by modern architecture. Although a few anomalies to the traditional campus were to be found, for the most part higher education regarded modern architecture with a frozen look of displeasure. By the 1940s, International Style structures began to reface American cities but exerted little influence on college campuses. Mies van der Rohe's 1938 plan for the Illinois Institute of Technology was a noted exception.

Also in 1938, Frank Lloyd Wright tried his hand at campus planning at Florida Southern College. The result was a geometrically fascinating arrangement of irregularly shaped buildings. However, like Wright's highly schematic urban plan, Broadacre City, it remained mostly a curiosity. Other notable experiments of the prewar era were Paul Rudolph's master plan for the Tuskegee Institute in Alabama and Walter Gropius and Marcel Breuer's plan for Black Mountain College. In New York City, Hunter College came forth with a brazen new International Style structure in 1942 but had few followers, even though the trend seemed serious in architectural magazines that debated the wisdom of "going modern" on the campus.

After World War II, society was recast socially, economically, and demographically. Huge increases in college enrollments forced the need for new campus planning. At the same time, however, college designers began to abandon the idea of the master plan in favor of growth contingencies that emphasized flexibility and adaptability.

The result was an abandonment of the fully integrated campus, as new, large unconventional structures began to be built to meet enrollment increases and fill in spaces on traditional campuses. Freed from the restraints of compatibility, university administrators concentrated on building programs that featured large, often out-of-scale improvements to dormitories, student unions, and laboratories.

An early example of the new attitude toward campus planning was Alvar Aalto's sprawling modern dormitory at the Massachusetts Institute of Technology in 1949, followed four years later by Eero Saarinen's three-pointed auditorium. At Yale University, a hodgepodge of new structures took defiant residence on the campus, including Louis Kahn's Art Gallery, Gordon Bunshaft's Rare Book Library, Paul Rudolph's Art and Architecture Building, and Philip Johnson's Science Center. When campus additions were conceived of as a group, as they were at the Harvard Graduate Center in 1949, they were often sited irregularly in unpredictable arrangements that defied the traditional norm of the college quadrangle.

The new campus planning was an aggressive repudiation of Beaux-Arts planning, with each new building conceived of as an individual unit, as dramatic and unpredictable as the times. When campus planners reached into the past, it was often no further than Paris in 1932, where Le Corbusier and Pierre Jeanneret established a vocabulary of forms at the Swiss Student Hostel that relied on masonry framing, minimal detailing, and the calibrated curtain wall.

When considerations were given to planning an entire campus, the presiding rationale was often based on organizing by function and accessibility. The new plan for the University of Illinois at Chicago Circle in 1965, for example, focused on developing specialized areas, instead of having separate buildings for each department, with circulation being the foremost priority.

The social upheavals of the 1960s challenged the traditions of formal education and brought about significant changes to education if not always campus planning. The University of California at Santa Cruz took a large step away from the traditional college campus with its 1963 master plan by John Carl Warnecke and Associates, which totally dispensed with the idea of formal symmetry and took the site's natural topography in the California coastal foothills as a basis for locating the campus' "cluster colleges."

The most innovative of the clusters was Moore and Turnbull's Kresge College, University of California, Santa Cruz, created like a rural compact village in sight of the ocean. At the same time the plan reached into the future, it evoked campus planning ideals from the past. Intact was the romantic notion of education isolated in nature. Recalling Jefferson's ideal of dialogue and proximity between students and faculty at the University of Virginia, the plan encouraged faculty to live on the campus in informal settings near where they teach. It also recalled Olmsted's original plan for the Berkeley campus by minimizing the proportion of land to buildings and keeping them informal—a university regulation prohibits any building taller than two-thirds the height of the coastal redwood trees that populate the area.

Another radical departure in campus planning came about after William Pereira's 1960 plan for the University of California at Irvine, planned around a series of concentric rings. Although Pereira's plan appeared to lack any overall design concept, it became a proving ground for the postmodern campus, especially after 1985, when Frank Gehry's three-pavilion structure for classrooms, engineering laboratories, and administrative facilities provided a new shock to the system for campus planning.

Along with structures by Robert Venturi, Eric Moss, and Charles Moore, Gehry's colorful collage of ramps, stairways, porches, and canopies created a furor at the time; it also might have served as an annunciation in campus planning, sweeping in an even freer, more unpredictable collection of ideas of what the campus should be.

RICK ADAMS

See also **Aalto, Alvar (Finland); Broadacre City (1934–35), Wright; Bunshaft, Gordon (United States); City Beautiful Movement; Corbusier, Le (Jeanneret, Charles-Édouard) (France); Cram, Ralph Adams (United States); Gehry, Frank (United States); Gilbert, Cass (United States); Kahn, Louis (United States); McKim, Mead and White (United States); Mies van der Rohe, Ludwig (Germany); Saarinen, Eero (Finland)**

Further Reading

Dober, Richard P., *Campus Design*, New York: Wiley, 1992
Dober, Richard P., *Campus Architecture: Building in the Groves of Academe*, New York: McGraw Hill, 1996

Gaines, Thomas A., *The Campus As a Work of Art*, New York: Praeger, 1991
Turner, Paul Venable, *Campus: An American Planning Tradition*, New York: Architectural History Foundation, and Cambridge, Massachusetts: MIT Press, 1984

CANADA

Canada's architecture has been intricately bound up with the nation's search for an identity distinct from European and American influences. At the dawn of the 20th century, the lingering effects of England's authority over Canadian political and economic affairs were still keenly felt, and Canadian architecture was held firmly in the thrall of Victorian trends. Although the major external influences on Canada's architecture originally came from France and Great Britain, movements popular in the United States began to attract notice as Canada directed more interest toward the nation with whom it shared a common geography and a history of recent settlement. Nonetheless, the new century also represented a coming of age for Canada's architects, as professional associations of architecture and engineering were established to ensure clients of minimum standards of practice and to enable Canadian architects to offer serious competition to British and American architects, who had been awarded many substantial contracts during the preceding years.

A significant factor affecting Canada's architectural evolution was the political autonomy that came with the costly sacrifices in World War I. This served as a national coming of age, and Canadians realized that they were now entitled to make their own decisions with regard to their country. The struggles during the Great Depression of the 1930s and the contributions to the World War II effort were followed by a high-spirited postwar era of booming population and extensive development. Canada's economy relies heavily on abundant natural resources, but technological innovation and development have diversified the country's research and manufacturing sectors. The perceived architectural colonialism of the early decades has evolved into an architectural vocabulary that reflects a maturing sense of independence and emerging national identity. There were several factors propelling this architectural evolution.

Immigration and Early External Influences

Canada had benefited greatly as a consequence of the global economic depression between 1873 and 1896. During the late 19th and early 20th centuries, publicity schemes and land grants attracted thousands of impoverished immigrants from the British Isles and Europe, in addition to young families who migrated from the eastern provinces to settle the western plains. In their new and harsh environment, the settlers experienced limited success at reproducing familiar architecture, and inevitably the use of locally available construction materials merged with cultural heritage, creating a distinctive Canadian "folk" architecture. Such original, vernacular design was particularly noticeable in regions settled by immigrants from Eastern Europe, the Ukraine, Russia, Scandinavia, Iceland, and China. The strict religious beliefs of some prairie settlers, such as the Doukhobors and the Hutterite Brethren, predetermined the form of their community-focused architecture.

With the massive immigration to the newly created prairie provinces of Manitoba, Saskatchewan, and Alberta, as well as British Columbia, governments embarked on an ambitious program to supply new settlements with essential services—legislative buildings, post offices, immigration and customs houses, policing, courthouses, and correctional facilities. The federal government architecture of the early 20th century closely adhered to precedents set by Thomas Fuller, chief architect of the Department of Public Works from 1881 until 1896. His carefully situated and finely detailed buildings with their rusticated masonry and textured surfaces contributed significantly to the High Victorian character still evident in many Canadian communities. However, Victorian eclecticism was gradually overtaken by more contemporary approaches to design, such as the Edwardian baroque, the Richardsonian Romanesque, the Château style derived from the Loire Valley of France, and the neoclassical Beaux-Arts tradition promoted at the 1893 World's Columbian Exposition in Chicago. The classical principles of rational clarity and ordered planning that were the hallmarks of the teachings of the École des Beaux-Arts influenced Canadian architectural education of this era. Whether the practitioners acquired their skills in Paris or from American architecture schools, many of Canada's early 20th-century architects converted to this multinational design philosophy.

As particular styles became associated with certain building types, Canadian architecture assumed a more consistent and less decorative character. Beaux-Arts classicism was expressed in the monumental legislatures designed and built in the prairie provinces between 1888 and World War I. These were highlighted by statuesque central domes and entrance porticoes with rhythmic arrays of double-height columns, strikingly similar to the Minnesota and Rhode Island state capitols. The sole exception was the Richardsonian Romanesque design of the Ontario Legislative Building (1892, Richard A. Waite) at Toronto's Queen's Park. Neoclassical vocabulary was further adapted to situations such as E.J. Lennox's Toronto Power Generating Station (1903–13) at Niagara Falls, where his client wished to create a majestic temple to new technology. This building is visually grounded by a large central block and pedimented entrance portico. The extremities of the side wings are anchored by smaller cubic blocks, and the entire facade is unified by the entablature and an imposing arrangement of Ionic columns—a grandiose shell for a utilitarian function.

Climate and the Natural Environment: Technological Innovation

As the first immigrants had discovered, the Canadian climate and physical geography ensured that, over a period of time, it proved expedient to adapt foreign styles and building technologies. Early in the 20th century, the National Research Council, a multidisciplinary institute of the federal government, saw the necessity for developing building materials and techniques to assist Canadians in their perpetual battle against the elements. The Institute for Research in Construction was established to develop materials, insulation, and construction standards suitable to every part of the country. This research led to specialized construction appropriate to Arctic conditions, such as cold temperatures, permafrost, low snow cover, and high winds. During the 1970s escalating energy costs fostered interest in solar design and collector panels, heat pumps, superinsulated windows, and low-emission glazing, culminating in the development of the R-2000 building system.

In addition, prefabrication and standardized housing designs have often been used to offset construction costs. During the World War II era, available housing was at a premium, forcing the federal government to establish Wartime Housing Limited to design and build thousands of small family homes. Many Canadian cities still retain neighborhoods of these "wartime" houses, originally considered to be an expedient yet temporary measure to alleviate the housing shortage. The lessons learned from such projects were adapted to other circumstances, where the lumbering, mining, pulp and paper milling, and hydroelectric power generation industries established company towns in remote parts of the country. On a site selected for an aluminum smelter because of its deep-water access to the Pacific, the hydroelectric power capacity of the Nechako River, and the broad alluvial plain on which a town could be built, the planned community of Kitimat, British Columbia, was created by Alcan Aluminum during the early 1950s. Referencing Ebenezer Howard's garden city concept, the model town included a greenbelt that encircled distinct residential and commercial districts.

Many of Canada's rapidly constructed northern and aboriginal communities are also distinguished by standardized and prefabricated buildings. Although the earliest of these quickly proved unsuited to the climatic extremes of the northern territories, recent buildings were more appropriately designed. They are now raised off the ground, with an insulating barrier under the main floor to prevent the building's heat from melting the permafrost; walls and roofs are totally insulated with no vented roof crawl spaces; and the windows are few and small in area. Even though these engineered structures are not necessarily architectural masterpieces, they are very characteristic of Canada's north. With continued improvements to materials and technology, northern communities now have many examples of a creatively designed yet pragmatic architecture. The Nunavut Legislative Assembly (1999), designed for the new northern territory by The Arcop Group and Full Circle Architecture, combines the latest in energy-conservation technology with a series of interior spaces and symbolic forms important to Inuit culture.

Geography and Transportation: Regionalism

For centuries, aboriginal communities existed along trade routes or wherever agriculture was viable, and with a growing European interest in Canada's natural resources, particularly furs and lumber, permanent settlements sprang up near trading posts and transshipment centers. In the late 19th century, completion of the first Canadian transcontinental railway (1886) expedited the shipment of goods and people and fostered the establishment of towns along its route. The western railway towns of wooden false-fronted buildings overlooking a broad Main Street greeted thousands of immigrants as they disembarked to begin their homesteading life. By contrast, government buildings, prosperous businesses, and financial institutions were usually constructed of brick or assembled from prefabricated components that had been shipped from the east. The thriving agricultural economy of the 20th century added another prominent feature to prairie towns: the grain storage elevator, or "prairie sentinel." These mammoth wooden structures, with steeply pitched roofs and the town's name boldly emblazoned on their sides, could be identified from a great distance. Industrial versions of these elevators can be found at the major Great Lakes and ocean ports, where a phalanx of massive concrete silos stretches along the waterfront, with the railway spur line on one side and the freighters tied up on the other. It was a complex such as this that attracted Le Corbusier's admiration for their honest industrial form.

The high costs of transporting goods, materials, and labor over immense distances and the climatic extremes in this, the world's second-largest country, continue to foster regionalism in Canadian architecture. Professional architects have incorporated local characteristics in their projects, as seen in Peter Rose's postmodern Bradley House (1979) in North Hatley, Québec. This country home evokes the spirit of a 16th-century Palladian villa, adopts Queen Anne Revival features prevalent in the community, and incorporates local building materials. One of the most outstanding examples of postmodern Canadian regionalism is the Mississauga City Hall and Civic Square (1986), designed by Edward Jones and Michael Kirkland to reflect both the maturity of this sprawling Toronto suburb and its roots as a rural farming community. A lofty clock tower presides over an intricate collage of massive agricultural forms, fronted by an open agora that is enclosed by modest colonnades. The dramatic interior spaces continue these historical references, and the intricate detailing and high-tech finishes imbue the building with a modern persona.

International Architecture and Canadian Identity

When Canada acquired dominion status with the 1867 confederation of four British provinces, Canadian sensibilities turned toward the picturesque neo-Gothic and its High Victorian interpretation. Used for religious buildings, educational institutions, and most outstanding, the Parliament Buildings in Ottawa (1865, Frederick Warburton Stent and Augustus Laver; 1866, Thomas Fuller and H. Chilion Jones), the neo-Gothic style defined Canada's affiliation with the British Empire. It was subsequently reproduced in the Centre Block (1927, John A. Pearson and J. Omar Marchand), which was redesigned and rebuilt following a disastrous fire in 1916. Even though the heavy masonry and mansard roofs of the Second Empire style had been popular for a brief period at the turn of the century, particularly in Québec, where it expressed the province's historic ties with France, Victorian neo-Gothicism remained the prevalent form of architectural expression in English-speaking Canada well into the 20th century. This style was evident not only in large public buildings but also in vernacular architecture, as manifested in the numerous white, clapboarded community churches and gable-fronted farmhouses of Ontario. Because it symbolized a valued affiliation with all things British, Victorian Gothic remained in vogue in the Canadian architectural landscape long after it fell from favor elsewhere.

Nonetheless, Canadians were becoming ever more preoccupied with defining their own distinctive and recognizable architectural style. The most successful of these efforts was achieved by a series of luxurious railway hotels, initiated at Québec City with the Canadian Pacific Railway's Château Frontenac (1892–93, Bruce Price). The last and undoubtedly most impressive of these, the Banff Springs Hotel, was constructed in two phases to enlarge the original wood-frame resort. Designed by the railway's own personnel, Walter S. Painter in 1911–14 and John Wilson Orrock in 1925–28, this building was characterized by steeply pitched roofs, multiple dormer windows, corner turrets, and solid massing. This unabashedly picturesque style has been termed either Northern French Gothic or Canadian Château. In acknowledging the effect of this Canadian architectural idiom, the federal government approved an urban plan for the national capital, Ottawa, which made particular reference to the appropriateness of the Château style. Consequently, several mansard-roofed government buildings were constructed in the vicinity of Parliament Hill during the Depression era. Even after World War II the federal government commissioned H.L. Allward and G.R. Gouinlock of Toronto to design the East (1949–56) and West (1954–58) Memorial buildings in this idiom. These interconnecting buildings successfully combined the Château style with the restrained and subtle detailing of the "stripped" classicism that had emerged during the 1930s.

Whereas the federal government was attempting to define a national style, John M. Lyle, a Toronto architect and teacher, encouraged his colleagues to study European modernism. Canadian architects and their clients were generally reluctant to wholeheartedly embrace new trends, and even John Lyle's own approach sought to combine traditional forms with a new language of ornament reflecting Canadian history and regional diversity. An example of his approach to modern classicism was the Bank of Nova Scotia (1930) in Calgary, which contained neoclassical elements compressed into the building's facade and highlighted by decorative imagery of western Canada, such as Mounties, aboriginal figures, horses, bison, wheat sheaves, and oil wells. Lyle's ideas were taken a step further by Ernest Cormier, who successfully combined attributes of the neoclassical, Art Deco, and moderne to create dramatic architectural statements. For his 1920s design of the Université de Montréal (1943), situated on the slopes of Mont Royal, Cormier arranged a brick and reinforced-concrete structural system in a symmetrical Beaux-Arts organizational plan, complemented by the precise, vertical piers that articulate the main elevation and delineate the tall, domed central tower.

It was not until after World War II, however, that most Canadian architects discarded historicism. With technological development instigated by wartime research and the booming population, architects largely ignored the International Style in its pure form and turned to the Modern movement. This trend first made inroads in Vancouver, nurtured by a vibrant community of young artists and designers led by Charles B.K. Van Norman, B.C. Binning, Frederic Lasserre, Robert A.D. Berwick, and Charles Edward Pratt, who were followed by Ron Thom and Arthur Erickson. The first Massey Gold Medal, jointly established by the Right Honorable Vincent Massey, governor-general of Canada, and the Royal Architectural Institute of Canada (RAIC), was awarded in 1952 to Semmens and Simpson for Vancouver's Marwell Place, one of Canada's earliest renditions of international modernism.

The 1950s and 1960s heralded an era of profound change and development that saw the destruction of many buildings, structures, and societal institutions. Glass-enclosed skyscrapers began to dominate the major Canadian cities, and Toronto in particular saw the emergence of the large, multidisciplined corporate design firm. One of most prolific of these was John B. Parkin Associates, renowned for its collection of rectilinear buildings designed in the international modern style. The characteristic traits of this design firm—formality, precision, and technology—are evident in the Ortho Pharmaceutical (1956) office's bold, white concrete frame; the dark recessed glazing with steel spandrel panels; and the adjacent manufacturing plant of white glazed brick and contrasting dark ribbon windows. The John B. Parkin firm, with Bregmann and Hamann, also worked with Mies van der Rohe on the Toronto-Dominion Centre (phase 1, 1969), a high-rise development in Toronto's financial district. The resulting pair of finely detailed black towers, with exposed I beams traveling the full height of the immense curtain walls, immediately became a city landmark.

Montréal experienced an exuberant proliferation of new architecture with its hosting of the world's fair, Expo 1967, during the centennial year of Canada's confederation. This celebration was an opportunity for the nation to showcase its achievements to the world, and the Expo pavilions were an eclectic sampling of architectural modernism. Two of the Government of Canada theme pavilions (1967) occupied a massive assembly of interconnected tetrahedrons constructed of exposed-steel space frames that were designed by the Montréal firm of Affleck, Desbarats, Dimakopulos, Lebensold, and Sise. Another remarkable Expo 1967 project was the experimental housing complex of prefabricated concrete block units, Habitat (1967). The original but unsuccessful intention of the young architect, Moshe Safdie, was to create a prototype for low-cost housing.

Although large urban centers benefited from these major design projects, smaller-scale regional architecture continued to flourish. Still a source of creative inspiration, the prairie provinces produced unique Expressionist projects by young architects. Their designs employed natural materials, sinuous lines, and organic forms to mold structures that successfully achieved the contradictory objectives of blending with the landscape and drawing the attention of the viewer. Partially set into a hillside, Clifford Wiens' St. Mark's Shop (1960) was an artisan's studio with a conical concrete roof, reminiscent of the tepees of the plains aboriginal cultures. In Manitoba, Étienne Gaboury's church for the Paroisse du Précieux Sang (1967) reflected recent changes to the Roman Catholic liturgy with a circular interior space, capped by a conical wooden roof that spiraled up to a strategically placed window at the apex. A third innovator was Douglas Cardinal, whose first major commission was St. Mary's Church (1968), constructed in Red Deer, Alberta. This structure of sinuously curving walls of red brick enclosing a semicircular nave displays what has become the architect's signature style. Above this looms a prestressed-concrete roof whose form resembles the experimental tensile fabric structures of the era.

The 1970s and 1980s saw the emergence of several architects, such as A.J. Diamond and Barton Myers, Raymond Moriyama (Moriyama and Teshima Architects), and Kuwabara Payne McKenna Blumberg Architects, who addressed the requirements of urban living. Given the sobriquet of late modernism, their design approach was typified by projects such as Edmonton's Citadel Theatre (1976) by Diamond and Myers, with Richard L. Wilkin. Occupying a busy corner site in the city center, the glass walls, awnings, and skylights of the reception area initiate a visual conversation between the people on the street and the theater's activities inside.

A growing concern over the destruction of the country's historic architectural fabric evolved into the heritage conservation movement. In addition to numerous local heritage initiatives, this received federal government support through the conservation programs of Parks Canada. Heritage conservation created a need for architects who were skilled at combining new technologies and public sensibilities with an appreciation for older structures and traditional building methods. One of the earliest projects was the midcentury reconstruction of the Fortress of Louisbourg, originally built by France on Île Royale during the early 18th century and subsequently destroyed by the British. The 1995 declaration of the British colonial port of Lunenburg, Nova Scotia (established 1753), as a World Heritage Site underlines the importance of Canada's architectural heritage.

Although modernism continued to dominate Canadian architecture during the last decades of the 20th century, a new technical style has evolved that merges urban modernism, industrially based design strategies, and the exuberant individuality of small innovative firms. This new style has been masterfully executed by several architects with roots, once again, in the western provinces. The design team of Patricia and John Patkau has been internationally recognized for their expressive geometric building forms that successfully reflect the inherent characteristics of the natural surroundings. The small scale of many of their projects has not precluded them from making bold and unapologetic architectural statements. In a similar vein IKOY Architects (formerly the IKOY Partnership), with principal architect Ron Keenberg, has become known for their High-Tech style, as evinced by the Conservation Laboratories (1996) for the National Archives of Canada in Gatineau, Québec. Glazed walls completely enclose the large, climate controlled archival storage vaults on top of which many conservation lab functions occur. The shallow arched roof is supported on intricately assembled columns, reminiscent of high-tension power transmission towers. As a major cultural institution, the National Archives has continued to reflect Canadian cultural identity via architectural expression.

Throughout the 20th century, Canadian architectural expression generally lagged a decade or so behind international tastes. Even when influenced by international trends, Canadian architecture has evinced a restrained and carefully considered personality, often because geography and climate have enforced a pragmatic respect for the economics of design and construction. In contrast the dramatic and varied natural Canadian landscape has inspired architects and encouraged a philosophy of limited interference with the environment.

For several decades Canada's major urban centers produced renowned architects of the Modern movement whose works speak the language common to the rest of the world. The search for a recognizable Canadian identity has colored efforts by regional architects to create a distinctive style rather than following the internationally approved but anonymous design trends. Unfortunately, their work has frequently gone unnoticed by the international architectural community, which fails to appreciate the environmental and cultural constraints under which Canadian architects work. As new technologies shrink the perceived disparities and distances between countries and settlement increases in the northern regions of the world, the 21st century may see a new appreciation for Canadian architecture and building technology.

RHODA BELLAMY

Further Reading

The growing recognition of the contribution of aboriginal cultures to Canadian society, combined with the effect of immigrants arriving from all corners of the globe, heralds an era of boundless architectural creativity in the 21st century. The following works enable the reader to explore Canadian architecture and acquire an understanding of its rich and diverse history. Alan Gowans's classic book, although somewhat dated, offers a perspective from the midcentury period. The most recent comprehensive survey of Canadian architecture is Harold Kalman's update to his previously published two-volume history. In Adele Freedman's collection of articles published in a major Canadian newspaper, she offers the reader some insight into the architectural issues that attracted public attention during the 1980s.

Bernstein, William, and Ruth Cawker, *Contemporary Canadian Architecture: The Mainstream and Beyond*, Toronto: Fitzhenry and Whiteside, 1982; revised edition, Markham, Ontario: Fitzhenry and Whiteside, 1988

Freedman, Adele, *Sight Lines: Looking at Architecture and Design in Canada*, Toronto, New York, and Oxford: Oxford University Press, 1990

Gowans, Alan, *Looking at Architecture in Canada*, Toronto and Oxford: Oxford University Press, 1958; revised and enlarged edition, as *Building Canada: An Architectural History of Canadian Life*, Toronto: Oxford University Press, 1966

Kalman, Harold, *A History of Canadian Architecture*, 2 vols., Toronto and New York: Oxford University Press, 1994; as *A Concise History of Canadian Architecture*, 1 vol., Toronto: Oxford University Press Canada, 2000

Maitland, Leslie, Jacqueline Hucker, and Shannon Ricketts, *A Guide to Canadian Architectural Styles*, Peterborough and Deddington: Broadview Press, 1992

Simmons, Geoffrey, *Bibliography of Canadian Architecture; Bibliographie d'architecture canadienne* (bilingual English–French edition), Ottawa: Society for the Study of Architecture in Canada, 1992

Wright, Janet, *Crown Assets: The Architecture of the Department of Public Works, 1867–1967*, Toronto; Buffalo, New York; and London: University of Toronto Press, 1997

CANBERRA, AUSTRALIA

Canberra (Australian Capital Territory) provides a showcase of Australian planning and architecture during the 20th century. The first parliament of the Commonwealth of Australia met in Melbourne in 1901. An international competition for the federal capital city of Canberra was conducted in 1911 and was won by Walter Burley Griffin and Marion Mahony Griffin of Chicago.

The so-called Departmental Board Plan was under way by 1913, designed by bureaucrats using features assembled from the competition entries. This procedure and its ugly product caused a public outrage, so Griffin visited Australia in late 1913, when he was appointed director of Federal Capital Works. The Griffins thus settled in Australia in May 1914, but their Canberra Plan was frustrated by wartime conditions, by quickly changing governments, and by hostile public servants—the authors of the discarded conglomerate plan. Griffin, having achieved very little, resigned in 1920 from any further involvement in Canberra. In 1921 Sir John Sulman headed the Federal Capital Advisory Committee, which was formed to procure the construction of the city and its suburbs. He fashioned a sparse garden suburbia and "introduced a modified mediterranean style of red tile roofs, white stucco walls, [and] simplified classical details."

The Griffins' Canberra Plan (1911, revised 1918) was consistent with the City Beautiful movement and with precedents by Daniel Burnham (e.g., the Chicago Plan, 1909). The basic geometry of the Griffins' Plan was put in place: the Land Axis, connecting Mount Ainslie, Capitol Hill, and a mountain peak beyond; the bisecting Water Axis; and the overlay of a triangle of broad avenues between Capitol Hill and the Civic and Municipal Centres via two bridges across the lake basin. These elements were fitted majestically into the terrain, but the building types that the Griffins had named for the key nodes were not adhered to. Their crystalline suburban road network was not established; of their building designs in Canberra, only a military general' gravestone survives intact.

Capitol Hill had been the site for the Griffins' major 1911 competition landmark, a national cultural archive building, a "ziggurat" that included imagery of Hellenic tombs and Oriental temples. The politicians in 1974 legislated that Capitol Hill instead become the site for a new parliament building. However, in 1914 Griffin had organized and then withdrawn a wartime international competition for a new parliament building on Camp Hill, a less elevated site on the Land Axis between Capitol Hill and the central lake basin. Louis Sullivan (Chicago), Otto Wagner (Vienna), John Burnet (London), and Victor Laloux (Paris) had been invited as judges. In 1927 John Smith Murdoch (chief architect, Commonwealth Works) completed a temporary Parliament House located below Camp Hill toward the lake. Consequently the politicians and government departments moved to Canberra from the interim capital, Melbourne.

Public servants have always been reluctant to relocate in Canberra. The city's development languished until Robert Gordon Menzies became prime minister in 1949. Menzies engaged the British town planner William Holford and the British landscape architect Sylvia Crowe to evaluate Canberra's prospects (Holford Report, 1957). Holford described Canberra as "a camel—a horse designed by a committee" and as "suburbs in search of a city," and recommended that the Griffins' denser city proposal be reinstated. Crowe nevertheless advocated the retention of Canberra as a garden city. The National Capital Development Commission (NCDC) was formed, directed by John Overall. The Molonglo River was dammed in 1963; at last the lake system was filled and was ironically named Lake Burley Griffin. The city has since been extended with distant suburban satellites on the postwar English model of new towns beyond a greenbelt, each with a civic center. Central Canberra became a park dotted with white modernist foci, but today it has improved in amenity and urban coherence as it has been gradually filled in with buildings.

A new Parliament House competition for Capitol Hill, conducted in 1980, was won by Romaldo Giurgola (Mitchell/Giurgola Thorp). The ziggurat-like configuration of the Griffins' projected capitol (1911) and its landscaped setting (1918) were the inspiration for Giurgola's scheme (1988)—the main central bulk of the reinforced-concrete building complex was contained within two curving retaining walls topped by a huge flagpole (Holford Report recommendation, 1957) supported by four stanchions ghosting the Griffins' originally proposed shape. The House of Representatives and the Senate were roofed with red tile, each house placed in a courtyard on either side of the curved walls. The public can still climb Capitol Hill and look down through the skylight on the Members' Hall. The Land Axis vista was architecturally emphasized: the colonnade of Giurgola's "Great Verandah" entrance appears integrated with the stripped classicism of Murdoch's temporary parliament building, today a national portrait gallery.

The NCDC (now disbanded) located a few monumental buildings off the Land Axis but within the Parliamentary Triangle between Capitol Hill and the lake's edge. Walter Bunning (Bunning and Madden and T.E. O'Mahoney) followed the lead of Walter Gropius and The Architects Collaborative (U.S. Embassy, Athens, 1956) with a classical peripteral colonnade (National Library of Australia, 1968). Colonel Madigan (Edwards Madigan Torzillo and Briggs) celebrated the architectural promenade: lofty cubic atrium and ramps (High Court of Australia Building, 1981) and diagonal and dogleg passageways through gallery spaces (Australian National Gallery, 1982). Concrete work by Louis Kahn, fractured forms by Richard Meier, and Paul Rudolph's design-by-section methods were the context for Madigan's idiosyncratic compositions. Lawrence Nield thematically referred to Palladio's Villa Rotonda, with compositional strategies and detailing informed by Le Corbusier (Science and Technology Center, 1988). The prime minister's department building (Edmund Barton Offices, 1974) by Harry Seidler was adjoined to the Triangle; scalloped, precast-concrete beams of great length were suspended between cylindrical service towers.

The Griffins intended for a community sports and recreation casino to terminate the Land Axis at the base of Mount Ainslie. Placed there instead was a sepulchral museum by Emil Sodersteen and John Crust (Australian War Memorial, 1941), twice sympathetically extended by Denton Corker Marshall (1988, 1999).

Where the Griffins envisaged a civic center—a town hall atop a knoll—nothing was ever built: this topographical prominence is a lawn that is densely surrounded by cypress trees. Sulman's shopping blocks, with pedestrian sidewalks enclosed by arcades and loggias, were built below it (Sydney and Melbourne Buildings, 1926). Roy Simpson (Yuncken Freeman Brothers Griffiths and Simpson) formed a distant plaza enclosed by offices (Civic Offices, 1961) and theaters (Canberra Theatre Center, 1965). Further around the knoll, Simpson alluded to the Greek temple in gray marble (ACT Law Courts, 1962).

Brian Lewis, Roy Simpson, and others were involved in the campus planning of the nearby Australian National University.

Professor Brian Lewis designed the residence (University House, 1952), and Simpson designed many student and academic department buildings (for example, University Union Plaza, 1975). Roy Grounds, initially desiring a shell structure, evolved a paraboloid reinforced-concrete dome in a ring-beam moat (Australian Academy of Science, 1958). Daryl Jackson and Evan Walker demonstrated an interest in muscular Brutalist forms in reinforced concrete (Canberra School of Music, 1976).

Markets, a railway station, and a city cathedral were never constructed at the Griffins' Municipal Centre, but a projected military function was. In their master plan (Russell, 1959) Skidmore, Owings and Merrill incorporated into the forecourt Richard Ure's aluminum obelisk (Australian-American Memorial, 1954); the buildings were by Buchan Laird and Buchan (Russell Defense Group Offices, 1966). The nearby carillon, a gift from the United Kingdom (Aspen Island, Central Basin, Lake Burley Griffin, 1970), was by Cameron Chisholm and Nicol.

Belconnen and Woden provide examples of civic center buildings in Canberra's satellite suburbs. John Andrews's works related to the Archigram projects of the 1960s (WodenTAFE College, 1981) and to International Brutalism (Cameron Offices, Belconnen, 1972). Concrete blocks and landscaped courtyards dominated the latter, connected by a "street in the air" to an extensive bus terminal. McConnel Smith and Johnson (Benjamin Offices, 1979), in similarly conceived public office blocks, color coded service towers to assist the users' identification and location of the parts. In startling contrast, Peter Corrigan (Edmond and Corrigan) referred to late 19th-century polychrome brick office–warehouses of Melbourne and Sydney (Belconnen Community Center, 1987). Daryl Jackson also made postmodern reference to traditional brickwork and school yards (Belconnen College, 1988).

Philip Cox, at another significant outlying site, the Australian Institute of Sport (Bruce, ACT), designed the dynamic (Bruce National Athletics Stadium, 1977) and the relatively inert (National Indoor Sports and Training Centre, 1981) in the spirit of 1950s tensile-steel structures in Melbourne. Daryl Jackson used expressive wave shapes and tight-skinned surfaces (Swimming Training Halls, 1983) and brightly colored bands (Basketball Indoor Courts, 1988). Allen Jack and Cottier arranged urban terraces to form wind-sheltered courts (AIS Halls of Residence, 1988).

The Griffins had proposed in their 1911 drawings to align public buildings along the lake's edges, and drew their reflections in the water. However, the Canberra Hospital (main ward block, Leighton Irwin, 1964, demolished) was, typically, placed in the middle of its peninsula site. Ashton Raggatt McDougall have recently placed here a series of building masses (National Museum, 1999) right at the water's edge, a tactic that will only enhance the Griffins' original vision for the city of Canberra.

Jeff Turnbull

See also **Brutalism; Burnham, Daniel H. (United States); City Beautiful Movement; Plan of Chicago; Seidler, Harry (Australia)**

Further Reading

Canberra: An Architectural Guide to Australia's Capital, Canberra: Royal Australian Institute of Architects, A.C.T. Chapter, 1982

Taylor, Jennifer, "The Special Case of Canberra," in *Australian Architecture since 1960*, by Taylor, Sydney: Law Book Company, 1986; 2nd edition, Melbourne: National Educational Division, Royal Australian Institute of Architects, 1990

CANDELA, FÉLIX 1910–97

Architect, Spain

Félix Candela's works in Mexico, the majority of which were executed between 1952 and 1968, provide some of the finest examples of functionality fused with plastic expression that exist in that nation to date. His forms are extremely reductive and simple, and his approach is clearly seen in works such as his ultrathin shells, particularly the hypar shell (1.5 centimeters) of the Cosmic Rays Pavilion (1952) at the new campus of the National Autonomous University in Mexico City and in the vaults of the Mexico City Stock Exchange (1955).

Candela's genius in devising new methods of calculating shell forms is illustrated by a variety of roof constructions, such as the simple umbrella, and short and long vaults. These structures attest to his technical expertise and his fluency in geometry as well as his sense of poetry, as seen in what are widely regarded as his free-edged masterpieces, Las Manantiales Restaurant (1958), where the structure, consisting of an octagonal groined vault composed of four intersecting hypars, appears, lotus-like, to float on the waters at Xochimilco, and La Jacaranda Night Club, designed in collaboration with Juan Sordo Madaleno (1957), an innovative shell derived from the intersection of three hypars, a form in complete harmony with the surrounding shoreline.

Candela arrived in Mexico City in 1939, part of the diaspora of Spanish intellectuals, architects, artists, and other professionals who were fleeing a country wracked by civil war. He encountered a vital nation emerging from a decade of revolution and another of reconstruction. Mexican architects and structural engineers were being called on to envision and construct innovative, multifunction structures on the city's unstable subsoil. Candela flourished in this environment; his work in the design and construction of prismatic slab shells of the Hidalgo, Convent, and Monte Alpas schools (1953) are examples of his concern for sound structural design and economy, as is his later work in designing the Zaragoza and Candelaria Metro Stations (1967). His work in residential construction is similarly marked by dedication to simplicity, whether in the execution of single-family homes (Romero residence, 1952) or apartment houses.

His construction firm, Cubiertas ALA, begun in 1950 in partnership with his brother Antonio and sister Julia, participated in Mexico's rapid industrialization in the postwar years, as it completed over 800 factories and warehouses in the 1950s and 1960s. Of particular significance among these works were those shells constructed for Bacardi and Company: the Bacardi Distillery (1955) and Bacardi Bottling Plant (1960), the former including a large, thin handkerchief dome over the fermenting tanks derived from a sphere of 24 m radius. These works, along with the Ciba Laboratories (1953), Aceros de Monterrey factory (1955), Lederle Laboratories (1955), and the High Life Textile Factory (1955), yield evidence of the considerable creative energies and resources dedicated to industrialization at that time, as well as attesting to Candela's growing fluency in the development of shell forms.

Throughout his career Candela stressed the limited nature of architecture. Unlike other architects and engineers practicing in postrevolutionary Mexico, such as Ricardo Legorreta, Alvaro Aburto, Enrique del Moral, and others, Candela did not believe that architecture could rectify complex social problems. As his works progressed from experimental funicular vaults to cylindrical shells and various umbrellas to the free-edge hypar, and in collaboration with prominent architects such as Enrique del Mora and Mario Pani, he continued to emphasize efficiency and economy. His final work in Mexico, the Palacio de Deportes for the 1968 Olympic Games, manifests his talents in structural mechanics and design.

Yet his work cannot be seen as strictly utilitarian. In his design of the Church of the Virgen de la Medalla Milagrosa (1953), he employed hyperbolic paraboloids to yield a concrete roof of only 4 centimeters' thickness, a sign of his technical genius. The resulting interior, however, indicates much more: the resulting internal space evokes the solemnity and mystery of Gothic architecture, a dramatic play of light and shadow that envelops and transports the worshiper to a different plane.

PATRICE OLSEN

See also **Legorreta, Ricardo (Mexico); del Moral, Enrique (Mexico)**

Biography

Born 27 January 1910, Madrid, Spain. Studied architecture at the Escuela Superior de Arquitectura in Madrid; graduated and began professional practice in 1935. Received a grant from the Academia de Bellas Artes de San Fernando (Spain) for study in Germany 1936; with the outbreak of civil war in Spain remained in Madrid, served the Republican cause in the Comandancia de Obras in Albacate, later promoted to Captain of the Engineers. Exiled to Mexico, chartered by the Society of Friends; arrived in Veracruz 1939. Worked in Chihuahua and Acapulco 1939–42. Formed partnership in Mexico City with another Spanish refugee, Jesús Martí 1942–46. Married Eladia Martín. Founded with his brother Antonio and sister Julia the construction firm Cubiertas ALA, specializing in design and construction of reinforced-concrete shell structures. Professor, Escuela Nacional de Arquitectura, UNAM 1953–70; University of Illinois-Chicago 1971–78. Received Gold Medal of the Institute of Structural Engineers 1961; Auguste Perret Prize of the UIA 1961; the Plomada de Oro from the Sociedad de Arquitectos Mexicanos 1963; the Grand Medaille d'Argent de la Recherche et de la Technique, Académie d'Architecture, Paris (1980); the Medalla de Oro of the Consejo Superior de Colegios de Arquitectos de España, Granada 1981; the Premio Antonio Camuñas, Madrid 1985. Named Charles Eliot Norton Professor of Poetry, Harvard University 1961–62; Jefferson Memorial Professor, University of Virginia 1966; Andrew D. White Professor-at-large, Cornell University 1969–74; honorary professor, Escuela Superior de Arquitectura de Madrid 1969; William H. Wood Chair of Architecture, University of Leeds 1974–75; honorary professor, Universidad Nacional Federico Villareal, Lima 1977. Emigrated to the United States 1971; became a naturalized citizen 1978. Died in 1997.

Selected Works

Fernández Factory, San Bartolo, México, 1950
Pisa Warehouse, San Bartolo, México, 1951
Cosmic Rays Pavilion (with Jorge González Reyna), UNAM, Ciudad Universitaria, Mexico City, 1952
Church of the Virgen de la Medalla Milagrosa, Mexico City, 1953
Hérdez Warehouse, San Bartolo Naucalpan, México, 1955
Lederle Laboratories, Coapa, México, 1955
Bacardi Distillery, La Galarza, Matamoros, Puebla, México, 1955
High Life Textile Factory, Coyoacán, México, 1955
Stock Exchange (with Enrique del Mora), México City, 1955
Coyoacán Market Hall, Mexico City, 1956
Music Pavilion (with Mario Pani), Unidad Santa Fe, México, 1956
Insignia, Tequesquitengo, Morelos, México, 1957
La Jacaranda Night Club (with Juan Sordo Madaleno), Hotel El Presidente, Acapulco, Guerrero, México, 1957
Las Manantiales Restaurant (with Joaquín Álvarez Ordóñez), Xochimilco, México, 1958
Chapel of San Vicente de Paul (with Enrique del Moral), Coyoacán, México, 1960
John Lewis Store (with Yorke, Rosenberg and Mardall), Stevenage, Herefordshire, England, 1963
Zaragoza Metro Station, Mexico City, 1967
Candelaria Metro Station, Mexico City, 1967
Palacio de Deportes for the Olympic Games (with Enrique Castañeda and Antoni Peyri), Magdalena Mixhuca, México, 1968
University of King Abdulaziz (as consultant of Project Planning Associates), Jidda, Saudi Arabia, 1975

Selected Publications

"Candela dice," *Calli* (México) 33 (May–June 1968)
"Cubierta prismática de hormigón en la ciudad de México," *Revista Nacional de Arquitectura* (México) (March 1950)
"Design and Construction in Mexico: Shell Construction," *Industrial Building* (September 1961)
"Divagaciones estructurales en torno al estilo," *Espacios* 15 (May 1953)
En defensa del formalismo y otros escritos, Bilbao: Xarait Ediciones, 1985
"Estereoestructuras," *Espacios* 17 (May 1953)
"Estructuras laminares parabólico-hiperbólicas," *Informes de la Construcción* (Madrid) (December 1955)
"Hacia una nueva filosofía de las estructuras," *Cuadernos de Arquitectura* (México) 2 (1961)
"The Shell as a Space Encloser," *Arts and Architecture* (January 1955)
"Shell Structure Development," *Canadian Architecture* (January 1967)
"Simple Concrete Shell Structures," *American Concrete Institute Journal* (December 1951)
"Toward a New Structure," *Architectural Forum* (January 1956)

Further Reading

Banham, Reyner, "Simplified Vaulting Practice," *Architectural Record* (September 1953)
Bowman, Waldo, "Umbrellas over Mexico City's New Buildings," *Engineering News Record* (May 1957)
Boyd, Robin, "Engineering of Excitement," *Architectural Review* (November 1958)
Buschiazzo, Félix E., *Félix Candela*, Buenos Aires: Instituto de Arte Americano e Investigaciones Estéticas, 1961
Campbell, Betty, "Félix Candela," *Concrete Quarterly* (July–September 1959)
"Candela: The Man Who Gave Concrete a Free Rein," *Concrete Quarterly* (Spring 1998)

Cervera, Jaime, et al., "Felix Candela, 'in memoriam,'" *Arquitectura Viva*, 58 (January–February 1998)
Cetto, Max L., *Moderne Architektur in Mexiko*, Stuttgart: Hatje, 1961; as *Modern Architecture in Mexico*, translated by D.Q. Stephenson, New York: Praeger, and London: Tiranti, 1961
Cueto Ruiz-Funes, Juan Ignacio del, "Félix Candela, el mago de los cascarones," *Arquine* (Winter 1997)
Faber, Colin, *Candela the Shell Builder*, New York: Reinhold, and London: Architectural Press, 1963
González Gortázar, Fernando (editor), *Arquitectura mexicana del siglo XX*, Mexico City: Consejo Nacional para la Cultura y las Artes, 1994
Holmes, Burton, and Thomas Creighton, "Recent Work of Mexico's Felix Candela: Can a Man Be Architect, Engineer, and Builder?" *Progressive Architecture* (February 1959)
McCoy, Esther, "Concrete Shell Forms—Félix Candela," *Arts and Architecture* (May 1957)
Mereles, Louise Noelle, "A Master Builder in Mexico," *World Architecture* 13 (1991)
Pinoncelly, Salvador, "La obra de Félix Candela," *Cuadernos de Arquitectura* 2 (July 1961)
Poniatowska, Elena, "Candela: El salto mortal de la arquitectura," *México en la Cultura* (May 1961)
Robina, Ricardo, "La iglesia," *Arquitectura* (December 1961)
Seguí Buenaventura, Miguel, *Félix Candela: Arquitecto* (exhib. cat.), Madrid: Instituto Juan de Herrera, 1994
Sharp, Dennis, "Sharp Angles: Umbrella Shells Mark a Watershed in Stevenage: Architects (1963): Felix Candela, with Yorke, Rosenberg, and Mardall," *Concrete Quarterly* (Winter 1995)
Smith, Clive Bamford, *Builders in the Sun: Five Mexican Architects*, New York: Architectural Books, 1967

CARACAS, VENEZUELA

In the early 20th century, Venezuela's economy changed from agriculture to oil production. For Caracas, its capital, this change implied growing in less than 100 years from just over 100,000 to more than four million people. With an area more than 300 times larger, the originally compact town between two creeks had expanded all over the valley.

Caracas's present appearance, and what is likely to prevail as its structure, is a product of the 20th century, expressing the paradigms of modernity with the shortcomings of historical disruptions and exaggerated optimism. Without a city project, unwilling to preserve a past it is eager to overcome, and open to foreign influences because of both intense and diverse immigration and its traditional inclusiveness, Caracas has myriad distinct and diffuse enclaves.

Founded in 1567, Caracas had, by the late 18th century, the size and structure that it would have at the start of the 20th century. After the death of dictator Juan Vicente Gómez (1935) and the return of government activities, this humble armature proved inappropriate for the capital emerging from those new conditions, and reflections flourished. In 1939, a team coordinated by French designer Maurice Rotival proposed to expand the city east and south with a system of diagonal avenues and gridded streets, stretching out the foundational grid with a pattern more able to interact with the valley's topography.

Although political turmoil prevented Rotival's plan from being pursued, the urban awareness that it awakened affected the city's form. Its building paradigms supported the first systematic urban codes (1942), applied on La Candelaria, the easternmost district of traditional downtown. Its fanlike plan modeled San Bernardino, a new section on the town's northeast edge. Further east, Roche's Altamira relied on monumental avenues and civic spaces for urbanizing a still-unconquered land. Although Avenida Bolívar, the plan's major urban space and its only initiated part, still awaits completion (even after Carlos Gómez's Parque Vargas project of the 1980s), it has become the city's most emblematic promenade.

Being French, Roche and Rotival's proposals evoked Parisian urban-planning paradigms. Dependencies from agricultural times had Venezuela looking to Europe for models; speaking French and following Paris's fashion was a symbol of architectural sophistication.

In fact, Venezuelan architects trained in France were to develop these urban transformations, displaying in the 1930s and 1940s a body of work still among the city's best. Among others, Carlos Raúl Villanueva's (1900–75) El Silencio (1942), a housing district on the western end of Avenida Bolívar; Luis Malaussena's (1900–62) Edificio París (1948), a skillfully articulated urban block; Carlos Guinand's (1889–1963) Casa Taurel (1941), an urban *palazzo* later to become a model in residential neighborhoods; and, very specially, Cipriano Domínguez's (1904–95) Centro Simón Bolívar (1949), an urban compound of government offices, retail spaces, squares, and parking facilities, introduced elements of modern architecture and a completely new urban monumentality. Architects coming from Europe would support and enrich these transformations. These architects include Manuel Mujica-Millán (Vitoria, 1897; Mérida, 1965), whose well-tempered eclecticism gained him the favor of both government and aristocracy, allowing him to build some of Caracas's first International Style buildings, and Arthur Kahn (Istanbul, 1910), whose Altamira building finely integrated urban grandeur and modern linearity in a piece that still commands this district's main space.

New economic conditions also brought new influences. With the increasing presence of American companies and the international scenario resulting from World War II, attention shifted from Europe to the United States. This shift correspondingly marked the replacement of urban design concerns by city-planning tools and of the influence of Beaux-Arts principles by those of International Style. Expressing this change are the Military Academy (1951) by Luis Malaussena and the Central University Campus (1945–65) by Carlos Raúl Villanueva. Whereas Academia Militar, ceremonially approached along Los Próceres promenade, elaborates on classical monumentality with somewhat abstract devices, Ciudad Universitaria's spatial interactions, playful corridors, and ever-changing territories of light and shadow introduce, with the rigor of its author's Beaux-Arts training, values of modernity that were to become quintessential to Caracas.

Architects now trained in the United States began to practice in an active situation that soon produced remarkable modern buildings. Simultaneously, under the guiding presence of Villanueva, these young architects participated in the founding of the School of Architecture (1955) at the Universidad Central de Venezuela. With Torre Polar (1957) by Vegas and Galia, Hotel Humboldt (1956) by Tomás José Sanabria, and even Ciudad Universitaria opening or just being built, the city adopted

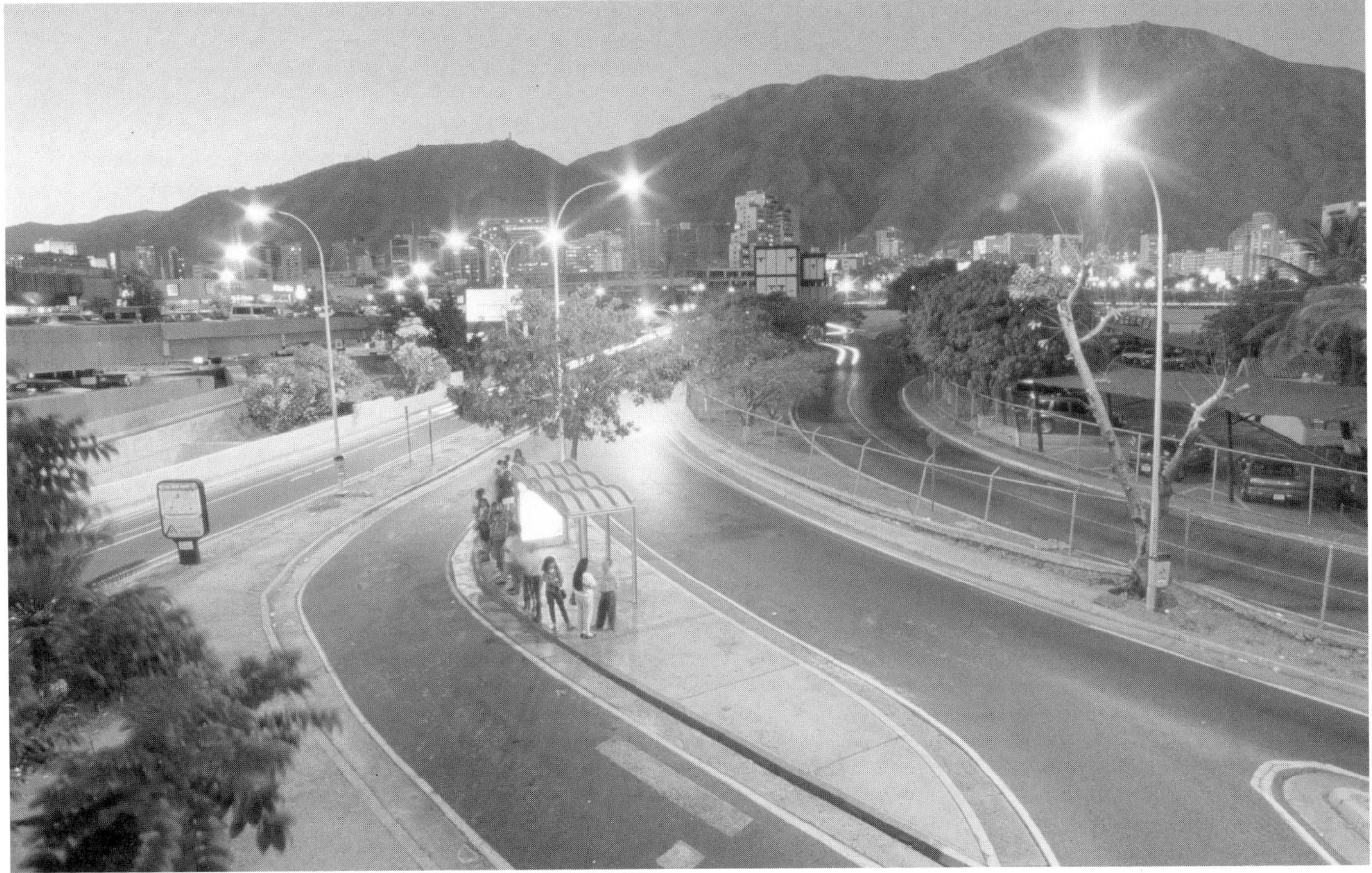

Overview of Section of Avenida Bolívar, Caracas, Venezuela (1996)
© Pablo Corral Vega/CORBIS

new architectural principles that guided the education of architects to come.

American planner Francis Violich's Plano Regulador de Caracas (1951) had no overall formal premise; instead, it evolved from land patterns of farms and villages along the main road built parallel to the river. Violich's plan turns that road into the main urban connector and turns existing farms into urban pockets to be developed as independent compounds. Loose as the plan proved to be, it established the urban system.

Under the excitement of new paradigms and prosperous circumstances, professional skills gained abroad and passed to new students resulted in some remarkable designs. Jorge Romero-Gutiérrez's Helicoide (1955), a strip of retail spaces wrapped around Roca Tarpeya hill; the lightness of Fruto Vivas' Club Táchira (1956) roof floating over the hill; and the folded structures of Alejandro Pietri's Estación de Teleférico (1956) formed an exciting inventory of buildings. Projects by foreign architects, such as Don Hatch's rationalist Edificio Mobil (1959), Emile Vestuti's urban articulations at Banco Unión (1955), and Angelo di Sapio's dynamic Edificio Atlantic (1956), brought Caracas local and international acclaim.

The coherent housing experiments developed at Taller de Arquitectura del Banco Obrero (TABO) permanently linked modern paradigms and hopes to Caracas's landscape. Under Villanueva's management, with the participation of young architects such as José Manuel Mijares and Carlos Celis-Cepero, TABO developed an ambitious public housing plan of high quality, modeled after Le Corbusian models. From Guido Bermúdez's Cerro Grande (1955) to "23 de enero" neighborhood (1955) or El Paraíso housing blocks (1957) and even beyond the now obvious mistakes of these urban strategies, TABO established modern convictions in the architectural context of Caracas.

In the early 1960s, affected by economic depression and a growing indifference from both government and public opinion, this promising environment seemed to fade into mediocre buildings. Public investment concentrated on infrastructure, making highway bridges and ramps the most significant constructions of the decade, their heroic scale both marking and disrupting the existing urban fabric.

This crisis extended itself well into the 1970s because of architectural education and standards. This situation sadly coincided with times of urban growth, which was encouraged by protective housing programs and laws. The heritage of modern architecture was enlivened by the mostly residential work of Jimmy Alcock (Caracas, 1932); the Louis Kahn-inspired work of Díquez, González, and Rivas; the few but remarkable buildings by Gorka

Dorronsoro (Caracas, 1939); and Jesús Tenreiro's (Valencia, 1936) early houses.

In the early 1970s, an underground transportation project was started; its first line opened in 1983. Directed by Max Pedemonte (Havana, 1936), the Metro project also clarified and qualified urban spaces along the lines. Despite the questionable quality of some actual interventions, the new public areas and pedestrian links allowed by them substantially transformed the way in which Caracas was used, connected, and understood.

Through emerging figures such as Carlos Gómez de Llarena (Zaragoza, 1939), Pablo Lasala (Zaragoza, 1940), Jorge Rigamonti (Milan, 1940), and Oscar Tenreiro (Caracas, 1939), the 1970s recuperated design interest and care. With Jesús Tenreiro, Gómez and Lasala founded in 1976 the Instituto de Arquitectura Urbana, an independent research organization that introduced issues of urban architecture and marked a new generation of architects, such as Joel Sanz (Higuerote, 1947) and Federico Vegas (Caracas, 1950), who, in competitions, exhibitions, and publications, promoted a more inclusive and complex understanding of the city.

Perhaps the most comprehensive planning effort of this kind was the new zoning code plan promoted by the city authority (1993–95). Acknowledging Caracas's fragmentary condition, different design groups were assigned different city sections to identify character, analyze problems, and promote potential solutions. Following a coding armature agreed on as an overall team, specific zoning regulations were designed for each area, realizing order not from borrowed paradigms but from the city's own form, history, and structure. Conducted by Francisco Sesto (Vigo, 1943), the project was developed, among others, by Enrique Larrañaga (Caracas, 1953) and Fernando Lugo (San Juan, 1953), who also proposed a new Building Codes Ordinance (1995) to coherently support the urban design strategy. Unfortunately, authorities resulting from the following election did not pursue the project.

Today, Caracas is still growing intensely and often puzzlingly. Unlike the town of the 1900s, this city is decidedly modern; like its earlier incarnation, however, it still lacks a plan.

ENRIQUE LARRAÑAGA

See also **Villanueva, Carlos Raúl (Venezuela)**

Further Reading

Gasparini, Graziano, and Juan Pedro Posani, *Caracas a través de su arquitectura*, Caracas: Fundación Fina Gómez, 1969

Moreno, Juan, *Monumentos históricos nacionales*, Caracas: Instituto del Patrimonio Cultural, 1998

Niño Araque, William, and Pedro Mendoza, *1950: El espíritu moderno*, Caracas: Fundación Corp Group, Centro Cultural, 1998

Valery S., Rafael, Marta Vallmitjana A., and Alberto Morales Tuker, *Estudio de Caracas: Evolución del patrón urbano desde la fundación de la ciudad hasta el período petrolero, 1567/1936*, Caracas: Instituto de Urbanismo, Facultad de Arquitectura y Urbanismo, Universidad Central de Venezuela, 1990

Vallmitjana A., Marta, et al., *El Plan Rotival: La Caracas que no fué: 1939–1989, un plan urbano para Caracas*, Caracas: Instituto de Urbanismo, Facultad de Arquitectura y Urbanismo, Universidad Central de Venezuela, 1991

CARRÈRE AND HASTINGS

Architecture firm, United States

Carrère and Hastings' designs of the early 20th century evoked the essence of the American Renaissance and Beaux-Arts classicism. Simple, understated forms as well as their coherent use of materials resulted in elegant compositions and French classical motifs.

John Mervin Carrère (1858–1911) left Rio de Janeiro, Brazil, to study architecture in Switzerland and eventually in Paris, at the École des Beaux-Arts, where he met his future partner. Hastings (1860–1929), a native New Yorker, joined the architectural division of the furniture-making and decorating firm Herter Brothers after study at Columbia University. He worked mainly under the guidance of Charles Atwood, who at that time was busy designing W.H. Vanderbilt's residence on Fifth Avenue. Both men settled in New York City in 1883, where they worked for the firm of McKim, Mead and White.

It was not until 1886—when Henry Flagler commissioned Carrère and Hastings (not McKim, Mead and White) to build a hotel in St. Augustine, Florida—that the new partnership officially opened offices. The success of the hotel's Spanish Renaissance design established the firm and brought other commissions from Flagler, who along with John D. Rockefeller had established the American institution of Standard Oil.

Carrère and Hastings would spend the next four years under Flagler's wing as they assisted in the creation of what the oil baron coined the "American Riviera." The Ponce de Leon (1888) was followed shortly thereafter by the Alcazar (1888), in which Spanish and Moorish motifs intermingled. The two architects not only looked to their past designs but also employed other influences that were appropriate to St. Augustine's Spanish past. The historical background of the city, as well as the designers' own interpretation of the Spanish style, formed the basis for the structures. In addition to the unique design, the construction was significant in that the architects used an innovative combination of concrete and coquina stone (a mixture of shell and coral). Flagler could not pay the architects in cash, and their fortune was secured when they were paid in Standard Oil stock.

Carrère and Hastings were responsible for designing some of the most luxurious country houses in the United States. Their work reached from Palm Beach, with Flagler's Whitehall mansion (1902), to Long Island, with the William K. Vanderbilt, Jr., residence (1903) in Long Neck, both sumptuous buildings whose elaborate landscaping and gardens existed as an extension of the house plans. The architecture was articulated by conforming to the layout of the grounds; as a result, the design of the house was initially conceived from within. The exterior elements, although important signifiers of style, became a secondary consideration.

Despite their important business and personal connections, it was Carrère and Hastings' ingenuity that ensured their professional success when they won the commission for the New York Public Library in 1897 over rivals McKim, Mead and White. The New York City Library was probably the most vital of Carrère and Hastings' creations as it marked the introduction of Beaux-Arts architecture into the realm of civic building. Unlike their hotels in St. Augustine, the library competition guidelines were strict and therefore required conservatism and political

New York Public Library, New York City, designed by John Carrère and Thomas Hastings (1897–1911)

savvy; the architects' solution was to embrace a French Renaissance Revivalism. The French Beaux-Arts style was easily adapted for such a project because of the general association with France and French culture, most notably Henri Labrouste's influential Bibliothèque Ste. Genevieve of 1851, a luxurious edifice that had established a standard for library buildings.

Carrère and Hastings' design was undoubtedly chosen because it best combined the necessary structural elements into one unified mass, achieved by using ornamental detail in a way that made the parts come together in a harmonious whole, an effect that is evident in the entranceway. The triple arcade within the central pavilion projects from the mass of the building and is flanked by decorative niches that house sculptural details. The large arched windows flanking each side of the entrance indicate the location of the large reading rooms within and are just one example of external design expressing internal function. However, it is in the rear of the building where this concept is most successful. The lower wall consists of divided windows housed in narrow slits that illuminate the book stacks, and the iron stacks are duplicated on the facade by stack-shaped windows. This modernist cue was used to soften the otherwise conservative design and symbolized Hastings' architectural doctrine "that direct and honest treatment of modern problems need not imply stark ugliness nor bizarre novelty of ornament."

The firm spent 14 years building the New York Public Library. It was this commission, along with Carrère's involvement in the Pan-American Exposition, that substantiated the firm and secured their national popularity. They subsequently secured other New York commissions including Richmond Borough Hall (1906), the New Theater (1909), and the design for the Manhattan Bridge (1911) as well as the House and Senate Office Buildings (1906) in Washington, D.C. In the end, the opening of the library in 1911 would have been a grand and auspicious occasion if not for the sudden death of Carrère, who had died unexpectedly two months earlier, after being fatally injured by a taxicab.

Jennifer Noelle Thompson

See also **Library; McKim, Mead and White (United States)**

Biography

John Mervin Carrère

Born in Rio de Janeiro, Brazil, 9 November 1858. Studied at the Institute Breitenstein, Switzerland; attended the École des Beaux-Arts, Paris, where he met Thomas Hastings; graduated

1882. Joined the firm of McKim, Mead and White, New York 1883. Opened office with Hastings, New York 1886; appointed chief architect for the Pan-American Exposition, Buffalo, New York 1891. Director and instructor, the American Academy at Rome. Fellow, American Institute of Architects 1891. Devoted end of his career to urban planning for Hartford, Connecticut, and Cleveland, Ohio. Died 1 March 1911.

Thomas Hastings

Born in New York City, 1 March 1860. Studied at Columbia University, New York; attended the École des Beaux-Arts, Paris, where he met John Mervin Carrère; graduated 1884. Joined the firm of McKim, Mead and White, New York 1884. Opened office with Carrère, New York 1886. Fellow, American Institute of Architects 1892. Maintained the office under the original tutelage after Carrère's death. Gold Medal, Royal Institute of British Architects 1922; Chevalier, Legion of Honor, France. Died in New York, 23 October 1929.

Firm of Carrère and Hastings

Founded in New York City 1886; lasted until Carrère's death in 1911; operated primarily in New York; famous works include the Ponce de Leon Hotel, St. Augustine, Florida 1888 and the New York Public Library 1911.

Selected Works

Ponce de Leon Hotel, St. Augustine, Florida, 1888
Alcazar Hotel, St. Augustine, Florida, 1888
Grace Methodist Episcopal Church, St. Augustine, Florida, 1888
Flagler Memorial Presbyterian Church, St. Augustine, Florida, 1890
Whitehall, Palm Beach, Florida, 1902
William K. Vanderbilt, Jr., Residence, Long Island, New York 1903
Senate Offices, Washington, D.C., 1905
House of Representatives Offices, Washington, D.C., 1906
Richmond Borough Hall, New York City, 1906
New Theater (Century Theater), New York City, 1909
New York Public Library (First prize, 1897 competition), New York City, 1911
Manhattan Bridge and Approaches, New York City, 1911
City Hall, Portland, Maine, 1911

Hastings Continuing in Firm's Name after Death of Carrère

Cunard Building, New York City (with Benjamin W. Morris), 1921
Macmillan Building, New York City, 1924
Standard Oil Building, New York City, 1926
Devonshire House, Piccadilly, London, 1926

Selected Publications

Preliminary Report for a City Plan for Grand Rapids (Carrère, with A.W. Brunner), 1909
"On the Evolution of Style" (Hastings), *American Architect* 97 (1910)

Further Reading

There is very little scholarship on the firm Carrère and Hastings. However, both principals wrote articles found in architectural journals of their day. In addition, they are always mentioned in texts about Beaux-Arts and the American Renaissance. See Blake's dissertation for the only scholarly text that spans the firm's entire career. See Doumato for complete bibliographies on Carrère and Hastings that include their own writings.

Blake, Curtis Channing, "The Architecture of Carrère and Hastings," Ph.D. diss., Columbia University, 1976
Desmond, Harry W., "The Complete Works of Messers Carrère and Hastings," *Architectural Record* (January 1912)
Doumato, Lamia, *John Mervin Carrère 1858–1911* (bibliography), Monticello, Illinois: Vance Bibliographies, 1985
Doumato, Lamia, *Thomas Hastings* (bibliography), Monticello, Illinois: Vance Bibliographies, 1988
Hastings, Thomas, *Thomas Hastings, Architect: Collected Writings*, edited by David Gray, Boston: Houghton Mifflin, 1933

CARSON PIRIE SCOTT STORE

Designed by Louis Sullivan, completed 1904
Chicago, Illinois

The Carson Pirie Scott (originally the Schlesinger and Mayer) Store in Chicago, designed and built in 1898–1904, was the last large commercial structure designed by Louis Sullivan. In later modernist historiography, this building was acclaimed for its forthright expression of steel-and-glass construction in its upper elevations. As such, Carson Pirie Scott was seen as a forerunner of the International Style in commercial architecture of the mid-20th century, epitomized by the later tall buildings of Ludwig Mies van der Rohe. Carson Pirie Scott was also pivotal in the international development of the department store as a building type in the late 19th and early 20th centuries. From a Postmodernist perspective of the 1980s, the building's outstanding feature is Sullivan's ornamental enrichment of the show-window frames along the two-story base that served to enhance the display of apparel to a largely female clientele.

Since 1881 the retail dry-goods firm of Leopold Schlesinger and David Mayer had occupied parts of a preexisting structure on the southeast corner of State and Madison Streets at the center of Chicago's retail shopping corridor along State Street. Over the years Schlesinger and Mayer had commissioned the firm of Adler and Sullivan (and afterward Louis Sullivan alone) to design remodelings and expansions of their quarters. The principal client was David Mayer, who commissioned Sullivan's design for the new Schlesinger and Mayer Store, first announced in May 1898. By this time, a group of new and projected buildings for retailing created by nearby competitors, as well as the high annual rental value of the corner property, had accentuated the need for a new building on the site. Sullivan's original design called for a uniformly 12-story steel-frame structure, including a rounded corner tower recalling that of the earlier building on the site. The original design also featured a cladding of white Georgia marble for the steel frame above the two-story base (the marble was changed to white enameled terra-cotta as built) and cast bronze for the ornamentally elaborate frames of the show windows on the lower two floors (the bronze became painted cast iron as built). The first three-bay section of the new Schlesinger and Mayer Store, built late in 1899, was only nine stories tall because of a height limit of 120 feet imposed on tall buildings by Chicago's city council. A relaxation of that limit to 240 feet in 1902 enabled construction of the corner and State Street sections of the building in 1903–04 to the originally designed height of 12 stories, extending seven bays down State Street south of the rounded corner.

The new building opened in October 1903 with additional interior work continuing into the spring of 1904. After the dissolution of the Schlesinger and Mayer firm, Carson Pirie Scott and Company acquired control of the building in August 1904.

In December, Carson's commissioned D.H. Burnham and Company to add five bays to Sullivan's 12-story structure, extending it 104 feet farther south on State Street. In 1948 the overhanging cornice and top-floor colonnade along the whole building were removed and replaced by a low parapet wall. In 1960–61 Holabird and Root designed an eight-story addition adjoining the Burnham bays to the south on State Street. In 1979 Carson Pirie Scott commissioned architect John Vinci to partially restore their landmark building, including cleaning the terra-cotta and replacing damaged pieces, repainting the cast-iron base to approximate Sullivan's original treatment, and restoring the main corner vestibule's interior. The structure has been in continuous use as a department store since it opened over a century ago.

When it was first completed, the Schlesinger and Mayer Store was considered a model for a modern department store and a major work in Sullivan's oeuvre. Sullivan's style of ornamental ironwork along the base was related to the processes of show-window display and newspaper advertising of women's apparel, whose seasonal variations and elaborate lacework corresponded to the ornament's foliate motifs and intricate design. Like other stores nearby, the first- and second-story plate-glass show windows also had upper lights filled with Luxfer prismatic glass to refract daylight into the depths of the sales floors. Originally, the store's architectural interiors included a third-floor ladies waiting and writing room and an eighth-floor restaurant featuring ornamentally elaborate sawed mahogany screens and columns with capitals of ornamental plasterwork, like the capitals visible atop the columns of the corner vestibule and the first, second, third, and fourth sales floors.

The need to maximize spatial openness and interior daylight for shopping (in an era when arc lamps were still the principal interior electrical fixtures for such buildings) led to Sullivan's design for the upper exterior elevations of Chicago windows (a wide, central, fixed glass pane flanked on either side by an operable sash window). Sullivan's upper fenestration is distinguished by its precise proportions (windows twice as wide as they are high, columns one-sixth the width of windows, and lintels between stories one-half the height of windows) and reveals of ornamental terra-cotta, a detail not reproduced in the Burnham bays down State Street. Overall, the Carson Pirie Scott Store exemplified Sullivan's often stated commitment to a modern American architecture wherein forms followed functions, in this case meaning the criteria of a department store as a novel building type then undergoing rapid development in metropolitan centers such as Chicago's State Street. Like Adler and Sullivan's and Sullivan's own earlier tall office buildings of the 1890s, as well as Sullivan's series of later bank buildings from 1906, Carson Pirie Scott exhibits the characteristics of Sullivan's architec-

Carson Pirie Scott Store, Chicago, designed by Louis Sullivan
© Greatbuildings.com

tural style: clear, simple massing; consistently precise proportions; forthright constructive expression; and botanically inspired ornament rendered in a variety of materials inside and out. This style embodied his broader aim of creating a modern architecture that eschewed dependence on historical styles and that would be culturally appropriate for the United States of the early 20th century.

JOSEPH M. SIRY

See also **Burnham, Daniel H. (United States); Holabird, William, and John Wellborn Root (United States); International Style; Mies van der Rohe, Ludwig (Germany); Sullivan, Louis Henry (United States)**

Further Reading

The comprehensive monograph on Carson Pirie Scott is by Siry. Other sources listed below include earlier detailed, or more recent, discussions of the building.

Bonta, Juan P., *Sistemas de significación en arquitectura y disziño*, Barcelona: Gili, 1977; as *Architecture and Its Interpretation: A Study of Expressive Systems in Architecture*, New York: Rizzoli, and London: Lund Humphries, 1979

Condit, Carl W., *The Chicago School of Architecture: A History of Commercial and Public Building in the Chicago Area, 1875–1925*, Chicago: University of Chicago Press, 1964

Frei, Hans, *Louis Henry Sullivan*, Zurich: Artemis, 1992

Giedion, Sigfried, *Space, Time and Architecture*, Cambridge, Massachusetts: Harvard University Press, and London: Oxford University Press, 1941; 5th edition, Cambridge, Massachusetts: Harvard University Press, 1967

Jordy, William H., *American Buildings and Their Architects*, Volume 3: *Progressive and Academic Ideals at the Turn of the Twentieth Century*, Garden City, New York: Doubleday, 1972; New York: Oxford University Press, 1986

Jordy, William H., "The Tall Buildings," in *Louis Sullivan: The Function of Ornament*, edited by Wim de Wit, New York: W.W. Norton, 1986

Manieri-Elia, Mario, *Louis Henry Sullivan 1856–1924*, Milan: Electa, 1995; as *Louis Henry Sullivan*, New York: Princeton Architectural Press, 1996; translated by Antony Shugaar with Caroline Green

Morrison, Hugh, *Louis Sullivan: Prophet of Modern Architecture*, New York: Museum of Modern Art and W.W. Norton, 1935; with introduction and revised list of buildings by Timothy J. Samuelson, New York: W.W. Norton, 1998

Siry, Joseph, *Carson Pirie Scott: Louis Sullivan and the Chicago Department Store*, Chicago: University of Chicago Press, 1988

Twombly, Robert, *Louis Sullivan: His Life and Work*, New York: Viking, 1986; Chicago: University of Chicago Press, 1987

CASA MALAPARTE

Designed by Adalberto Libera, completed 1963
Island of Capri

The Casa Malaparte is a villa on the island of Capri designed by the Italian rationalist architect Adalberto Libera (1903–63) for the writer and journalist Curzio Malaparte (1898–1957). The building's dominant position on its rocky outcrop reflect its expressive and outward-looking spirit. Its bold volumetric form and symmetrical planning reflects Libera's desire for "sincerity, order, logic and clarity above all" (Malaparte, 1989). All in all, it is a textbook example of modernist 20th-century architecture. At first glance, this might seem to be an accurate description of the Casa Malaparte. However, a closer examination reveals these seemingly uncontestable facts as increasingly problematic.

The Casa Malaparte is actually a curious and contradictory work that directly reflects the nature of its curious and contradictory client: Curzio Malaparte. Born Kurt Erich Suckert into a Protestant family, Malaparte denounced these roots when beginning his writing career by taking his mother's maiden name and then later, on his deathbed, converting to Catholicism. Malaparte is best known for his writings that glorified Mussolini and the Fascist Party, yet he was jailed by that same party between 1933 and 1935. While he subsequently tried to become a member of the Communist Party, Malaparte also served as a liaison officer for the U.S. Army after World War II. These examples are only the more concrete ones illustrating a soul who functioned in extremes and was always torn between opposites.

The architect Adalberto Libera, a member of the rationalist Gruppo 7, is best known for his works that helped advertise Fascist Italy: the staging of the Exhibition of the Tenth Anniversary of the Fascist Revolution (1932), and the Italian Pavilions at the World Expositions of Chicago (1933) and Brussels (1935). It is through these works that Malaparte most likely became familiar with Libera. Sometime in early 1938, Malaparte approached Libera to design a small villa on the island of Capri. The resulting design, which was submitted for approval to the Capri authorities in March 1938, was never built. For this reason, the attribution of the Casa Malaparte to Adalberto Libera can be questioned. However, Libera's initial design, although different from what was actually built, can be seen as the "foundation" of the eventual building.

Libera proposed a two-story, elongated rectangular building with rooms on one side and a corridor on the other. The linearity of the project took advantage of the linearity of its site: the Massullo promontory. The project stepped up in section toward the sea, using the lower portion's roof as a sheltered terrace. The external ground-floor walls of the project consisted of rough stone, presumably from the site, with the upper portion of the walls plastered smooth. These characteristics of the project can be seen in the building as built. However, this is where the similarity ends. Sometime during 1939, Libera and Malaparte lost touch concerning the villa. Without an architect, Malaparte, however, continued building, acting on advice from his builder, Adolfo Amitriano, and his circle of artist friends as well as on his own thoughts and inspirations.

The most significant change to Libera's initial project made by Malaparte is perhaps the defining element of the Casa Malaparte: the curious wedge-shaped staircase to the roof that extends for about one-third of the entire structure and gives the building its unique silhouette. This form has been attributed to Malaparte's memory of the Church of the Annunziata, experienced during his exile imposed by the Fascists on the island of Lipari. The staircase is a strange form, perhaps one that would never be designed by an architect, yet it solved several problems for Malaparte once he began to deviate from Libera's project. First, although oversized, the staircase provided access to the roof terrace, which Malaparte now placed on the very top of the building. Second, it unified the mass of the building into a single,

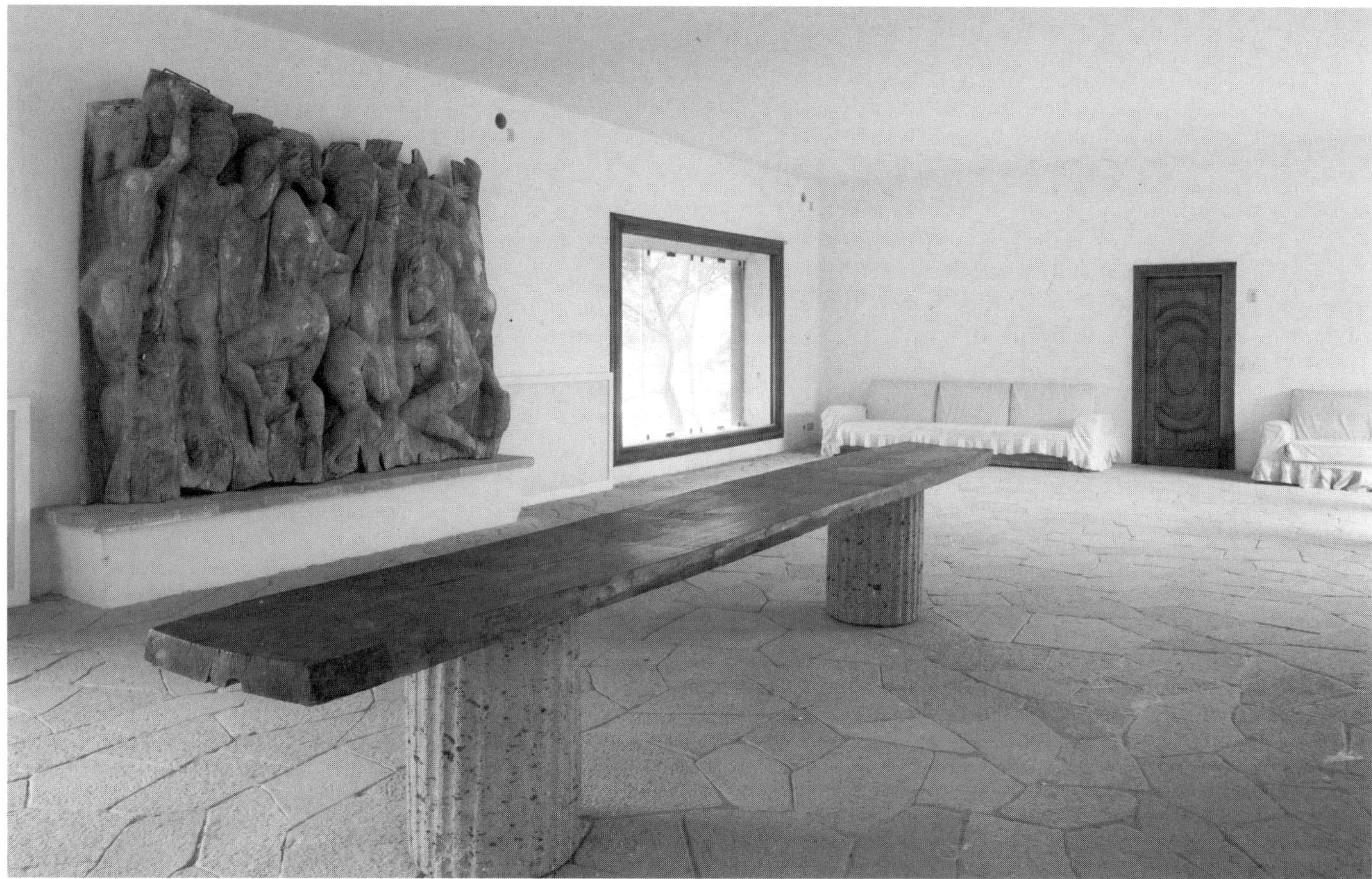

Casa Malaparte interior, Capri, by Adalberto Libera
© Roberto Schezen/Esto

streamlined whole instead of a series of awkward jumps, as Libera had proposed.

This unified mass, isolated on the rocky heights of a Mediterranean cliff, is what gives the building its heroic and romantic appeal. However, these same characteristics also strangely make the building belong to its natural surroundings: the building's linearity and the gradual slope of the staircase seem to echo the linearity of the site with its gradual ups and downs. In addition, the color of the building, often described as "Pompeian red," is also subject to this paradox: on the one hand, it is not the typical Mediterranean (and modernist) white, which would make it stand out from its natural surroundings of sea, rock, and low shrubs; on the other hand, the deep red is completely foreign to an island setting of natural blue, brown, and green tones.

Other changes that Malaparte made to Libera's original design were less noticeable than the staircase. Windows on the southwest facade were framed with a "braid of tufa stone," and iron security bars were installed on the ground floor. It is theorized that Malaparte did this to make the house seem more like a prison, again evoking memories of his exile. Yet, unlike a prison, the entire rooftop was to be used for sunbathing, with a sweeping modesty wall to protect Malaparte from prying eyes.

Libera's proposed interior configuration was completely changed by Malaparte from a single-loaded corridor to a symmetrical layout, with the principal room consisting of a large temple-like salon the entire width of the building. The building's entrance, however, was still located on the southwest elevation, and the resulting circulation pattern is clumsy: once one is inside the principal entrance, an awkward L-shaped stair leads upstairs to another awkward antechamber before the salon. In addition, to access the new basement accommodation below the external staircase, a secondary external entrance also exists on the southwest elevation. Although Malaparte masterfully reorganized the building into a symmetrical layout that more accurately reflects the linearity of the scheme, he was unable to follow this through to the circulation through the building.

In the end, the Casa Malaparte is an accurate reflection of the unusual "both/and" character of its client: it is a combined product of its architect, client, and builder; an example of both heroic modernism and humble vernacular traditions; an architectural work that both dominates and engages its natural surroundings; and a house that is both a prison and a temple. Indeed, Malaparte, on completion of the building, is known to have described his Capri villa as a "house like me" and "a self-portrait in stone."

Christopher Wilson

See also **Libera, Adalberto (Italy)**

Further Reading

Arets, Wiel, and Wim van den Bergh, "*Casa come me:* A Sublime Alienation," *AA Files* 18 (Autumn 1989)

Bostik, Joe, "The Surveyed House," *Lotus International* 60 (1989)

Hejduk, John, "Cable from Milan," *Domus* 605 (April 1980)

Malaparte, Curzio, "On the Island of Lipari," *AA Files* 18 (Autumn 1989)

McDonough, Michael, "Nature, Surrealism, and Folk Design Methodology in the Casa Malaparte," *A + U* 243, no. 12 (December 1990)

Safran, Yehuda, "On the Island of Capri," *AA Files* 18 (Autumn 1989)

Savi, Vittorio, "Orphic, Surrealistic: Casa Malaparte on Capri," *Lotus International* 60 (1989)

Talamona, Marida, "Adalberto Libera and Villa Malaparte," *AA Files* 18 (Autumn 1989)

Talamona, Marida, *Casa Malaparte*, New York: Princeton Architectural Press, 1992

CASA MILÁ

Designed by Antoni Gaudí, completed in 1910
Barcelona, Spain

Casa Milá, located at the corner of the Paseo de Gracia and the Calle Provenza in Barcelona, Spain, was designed and built between 1906 and 1910. It exemplifies the exuberant forms and distinctly personal architectural sensibility of Antoni Gaudí (1852–1926), whose work influenced the development of *Modernismo*, the Catalan adaptation of Art Nouveau. Popularly known as "La Pedrera" (The Quarry), the large apartment building, commissioned by wealthy businessman Pedro Milá i Camps and his wife, Rosario Segimón Artells, received widespread critical attention for its massive, undulating facade and innovative architectural and structural details. Although Casa Milá has been described as a precursor of the Einstein Tower (1921) in Potsdam, designed by Erich Mendelsohn (1887–1953), the explicitly organic references of Gaudí's structure exhibit closer stylistic affinities to Art Nouveau (Jugendstil) than to the German Expressionism of Mendelsohn's work.

Casa Milá is the last secular project undertaken by Gaudí before devoting his energies exclusively to the design and construction of the Sagrada Familia (1926), also in Barcelona. Gaudí began work on the Casa Milá during construction of another private residence he designed (1906) on the Paseo de Gracia, Casa Battlò. As with the earlier structure, the serpentine, organic appearance of Casa Milá results from the rhythmic alternation of concave and convex bays and balconies and is further heightened by the organic curves of the wrought-iron grillwork. Following a dispute with Milá over the inclusion of a religious sculpture on the facade of the building, Gaudí abandoned the project in 1909, leaving its completion to project contractor José Bayó Font. The building's interior and exterior decorative finishes were executed by Gaudí's assistant, José Jujol. The present appearance of the building reflects the conversion of the attic structure into apartments, executed by F.J. Barba Corsini in 1954.

The J-shaped plan of Casa Milá contains two internal courtyards whose rounded forms are consistent with the building's general lack of orthogonal planes and are echoed in the building's facade. One of the most significant aspects of Casa Milá is the open plan of each floor, achieved by Gaudí's use of columns rather than masonry bearing walls throughout the structure. This strategy, which anticipates the free plan advocated by modernists such as Le Corbusier, allowed architectural and structural autonomy for both the facade and the individual floors. Additional structural support was provided by an extensive framework of iron beams embedded in the floors, facade, and balconies, including an elaborate umbrella-shaped iron structure within the floor of the courtyard facing the Paseo de Gracia.

Among Gaudí's numerous innovative design elements was a spiral ramp intended to provide automobile access from the ground floor down to the basement garage and continuing up to the top floor of the building. Although the ramp was later deemed too large for the courtyard and never completed, the idea anticipates by almost 20 years the internal ramp designed by Le Corbusier for Villa Meyer (1925) in Paris.

Because of the influence of *novecentismo*, or 19th-century historical eclecticism, in Barcelona at the time Casa Milá was under construction, the building's unconventional facade met with a wide range of critical responses on completion. The visual plasticity, marine-inspired decorative elements, and grotto-like lobby spaces of Casa Milá were hailed by some contemporaries as the pure architectural expression of a Mediterranean sensibil-

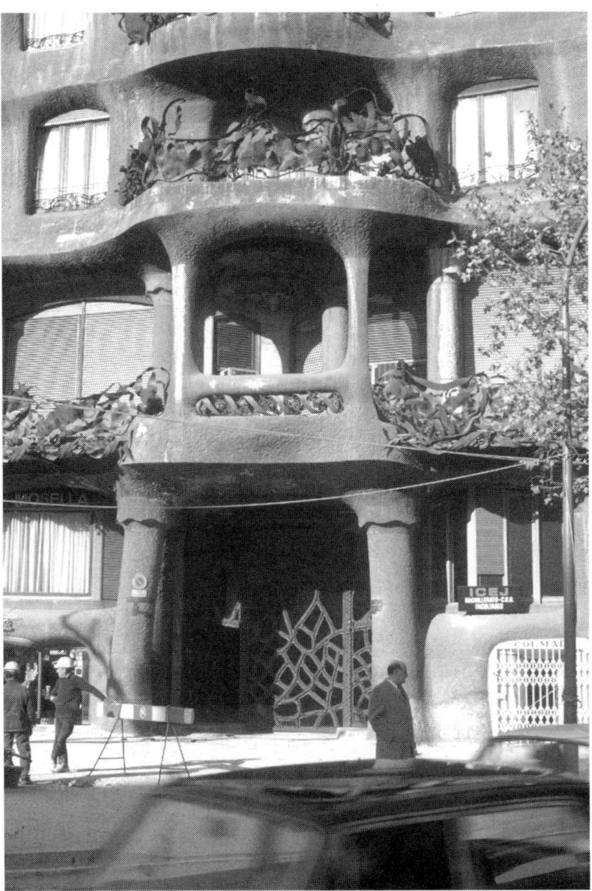

Casa Milá, close-up of entrance and balconies
© Howard Davis/GreatBuildings.com

Casa Milá (or La Pedrera), Barcelona (1905–10), Antoni Gaudí
Photo © Mary Ann Sullivan

ity, an interpretation strengthened by Gaudí's published comments praising Mediterranean light and shadow. It has also been suggested that the design of Casa Milá's facade was influenced by the massive, towered masonry structures of the Berber tribes in North Africa, a region visited by Gaudí in 1887.

The materials and decoration of the facade of Casa Milá, particularly the use of Catalonian limestone facing and ornate wrought-iron grillwork, reflect Gaudí's interest and background in local craft traditions. These choices also typify Gaudí's deep commitment to Catalan culture, which at the turn of the 20th century underwent a widespread social, political, and economic revival known as the *Renaixença*, or Catalan Renaissance.

Gaudí, a devout Catholic and follower of the cult of Mary, also intended Casa Milá to serve a symbolic religious function. The explicit Marian references embedded in the building's facade include an inscription of the prayer of the rosary along the cornice and a monumental sculpture group of the Virgin and two angels. The sculpture was intended for a niche in the facade above the corner of the Paseo de Gracia and the Calle de Provenza. However, a violent outbreak of anticlericalism in Barcelona in 1909 resulted in the owner's decision not to include the sculpture; Gaudí abandoned the project soon afterward.

The undulating attic and roof of Casa Milá serve as a base for the elaborate sculptural forms housing the building's ventilation shafts, chimneys, and access structures, which collectively produce Casa Milá's distinctive roofline. The roof is celebrated for its inventive use of Catalan vaults, which are composed of roof tiles laid end on end, supported by transverse ribs. This technique, which may be compared to concrete eggshell vaulting, permits great flexibility in the design of the vaults. In addition to the attic vaults at Casa Milá, which take the form of catenary arches, Gaudí used Catalan vaults at numerous other projects, including the roof of the school building of the nearby Sagrada Familia (1909). At Casa Milá, however, the attic arches stretch from the ground to the roof of the attic structure, recalling the arcaded corridors Gaudí designed for the Colegio de Santa Teresa de Jesús (1894) in Barcelona.

The decoration of the attic of Casa Milá represents a conflation of Gaudí's sculptural design aesthetic with local and regional artistic traditions. His use of *azulejos*, brightly colored ceramic tile fragments embedded in masonry, at Casa Milá, the Park Güell (1914), and other projects throughout his career contributed to the Catalan craft revival of the early 20th century. Although Casa Milá has received much critical attention as an Art Nouveau monument, its sculptural plasticity suggests a more three-dimensional—and more uniquely personal—design aesthetic than that of Art Nouveau.

KRISTIN A. TRIFF

See also **Art Nouveau (Jugendstil); Barcelona, Spain; Catalan (Guastavino) Vaults; Corbusier, Le (Jeanneret, Charles-Édouard) (France)**

Further Reading

Barba Corsini, F.J., "Edificio La Pedrera, Barcelona, España," *Habitat* (December 1955)

Collins, George Roseborough, *Antonio Gaudi*, New York: Braziller, and London: Mayflower, 1960

Nonell, Juan Bassegoda, *El gran Gaudi*, Sabadell, Spain: Ausa, 1989

Nonell, Juan Bassegoda, *Antonio Gaudi: Master Architect*, New York: Abbeville Press, 2000

Schoelkopf, R.J., "Antonio Gaudí: Architect, 1852–1926: Casa Milá," *Perspecta* 2 (1953)

Zerbst, Rainer, *Gaudi, 1852–1926: Antonio Gaudi i Cornet: A Life Devoted to Architecture*, Cologne: Taschen, 1985

CATALAN (GUASTAVINO) VAULTS

This historic vaulting technique, popular in Spain and the United States in the early 20th century, is also called "cohesive construction," "timbrel vault," "laminated vault," *voûte Roussilon* (in France), *bóveda tabicada* ("board vault," in Spain), and *volta a foglia* ("layered vault" in Italy). It uses thin, flat clay tiles (about 12 by 6 by 5/8 inches) in laminated shell structures, assembled with an extremely adhesive and fast-drying mortar into vaults, normally in three or more layers of overlapping tiles. The enormous stability stems from two major factors: the convergence of the tiles and mortar into a homogeneous, monolithic material that can absorb both compression and tension and the thin (single or double) curved surfaces that obtain additional strength by distributing them sideways as well as downward. Apart from being fireproof, the vault is lighter than any other masonry vault and produces only minimal lateral thrust at its springing points. As a result, it allows the placement of openings in the shell and the easy combination of several units and does not require outside buttressing or reinforcement beams. Skilled workers can erect even large vaults without scaffolding or formwork, as the lower rows of laminated clay tiles are usually strong enough when the mortar has dried to carry the workers placing subsequent layers.

The roots of this vaulting technique can be traced back to medieval and even Roman sources. The structure would typically be hidden from sight under plaster or suspended ceilings or used as permanent formwork. The late 19th century developed a new interest in the technique, which eventually flourished simultaneously in the first half of the 20th century both in Catalonia, Spain, and in the United States.

In the 1860s it was rediscovered in Catalonia as a cheap method of vaulting spaces for industrial buildings and warehouses. A prime example is the factory (1869–75; today called The Clock Building) for the Battlò brothers in Barcelona by Rafael Guastavino. Father and son Rafael Guastavino exhibited the method with great success at the Philadelphia World's Fair and subsequently proceeded to introduce the technique to the United States. The Guastavino Company (1885–1963) held 24 patents and was involved in the construction of more than 1,000 buildings all across the United States, Canada, and 11 other countries. During the 40 most active years of the company, the Guastavinos worked on some of the most spectacular public buildings of the day, including the Boston Public Library (McKim, Mead and White, 1898), Grand Central Terminal (Warren and Wetmore, 1913), and Pennsylvania Station (McKim, Mead and White, 1911) in New York, as well as private commissions, including the Biltmore Estate (Richard Morris Hunt, 1895) in Asheville, North Carolina. The widest span ever to be achieved with Guastavino tiles is the 66-foot-wide dome above the crossing of the cathedral of St. John the Divine (Cram and Ferguson, 1893 and later) in New York. Although American architects used Guastavino tiles mostly for conventional vaults and domes in historicist architecture, they frequently chose to expose the typical fish-grate pattern of the tiles on the underside of a vault or dome without any ornamental embellishment. These patterns can still be found in countless public structures.

Simultaneously, the method gained popularity among the architects of the Catalan *Modernismo* movement in northeastern Spain. (Although several medieval applications in Catalonia are known, there is no evidence that the method was exclusive to this region or had originated there.) Fired by a search for an independent Catalan architectural expression, several architects fully exploited the technique's structural and expressive potential for complex vaults, undulating walls, and rolling ceilings. Among the prime examples are Antoni Gaudí's small school building (1906) at the Sagrada Familia cathedral in Barcelona, which features both a curvilinear outside wall and a wavelike roof structure. Gaudí's contemporary, Lluis Domènech i Montaner, used the technique in the Palau de la Música Catalana (1905–08) and his Hospital de Sant Paul (1902–10), both in Barcelona. Cèsar Martinell built more than 30 agricultural cooperatives using the tiles in Catalonia between 1913 and 1919, and Lluís Muncunill i Parellada created perhaps the most radical application of the technique in his textile factory, Aymerich Amat i Jover (1907–09) in Terrassa, Catalonia, which features series of double-curved roof elements on cast-iron posts that both shelter the interior and provide northern skylights.

Eventually, the use of the technique succumbed to rising labor costs and new, cheaper building methods that began to dominate the building markets in the Western world after World War II. There were only occasional later applications, as in Luis Moya Blanco's St. Augustin church (1954) in Madrid or Le Corbusier's use of simple, flat Catalan vaults in his Maison Jaoul (1955) in Paris.

The two most spectacular applications since World War II have occurred outside the highly industrialized Western building markets. A Catalan mason brought the vaulting technique in the late 1950s to Cuba, where it was applied to the first major building project of Fidel Castro's government, a cluster of five art schools (Ricardo Porro, Vittorio Garatti, Roberto Gottardi, 1961–65, unfinished) featuring spectacular sequences of domes and barrel vaults.

The Uruguayan architect Eladio Dieste (b. 1917) has continuously applied the central principles of the Catalan vault since the late 1950s and improved it structurally by using steel reinforcement rods and tie bars in conjunction with double-curvature brick shells, thus increasing the span of each unit. Among Dieste's most stunning creations is a church (1958) in Atlantida, Uruguay, with undulating walls and ceiling based on a principle similar to that of Gaudí's school at the Sagrada Familia.

Palau de la Música Catalana, Barcelona (1908), designed by Lluis Domènech i Montaner
Photo © Mary Ann Sullivan

Equally important is a warehouse (1960) in Montevideo that is spanned by double-curved laminated shell structures similar to those in Lluis Muncunill's 1909 textile factory in Terrassa. The thin laminated masonry vaults have influenced the development of thin concrete shells (for example, in the work of Spanish architects Edoardo Torroja and Félix Candela) and Russian experiments with large vaults of prefabricated-concrete elements. A renewed interest in the technique has led to attempts at reviving the vaulting technique for the Western building market.

DIETRICH NEUMANN

See also **Barcelona, Spain; Casa Milá, Barcelona; Candela, Félix; Gaudí, Antoni (Spain); Grand Central Station, New York City; McKim, Mead and White (United States); Spain**

Further Reading

APT Bulletin: The Journal of Preservation Technology 30, no. 4 (1999) (special issue entitled "Preserving Historic Guastavino Tile Ceilings, Domes, and Vaults")

Araguas, Philippe, "L'Acte de naissance de la Boveda tabicada ou le certificat de naturalisation de la 'Voûte Catalane,' " *Bulletin Monumental* 156, no. 2 (1998)

Bannister, Turpin C., "The Roussillon Vault: The Apotheosis of a 'Folk' Construction," *Journal of the Society of Architectural Historians* 27 (October 1968)

Blanco, Luis Moya, *Bóvedas tabicadas*, Madrid: Ministerio de la Gobernación, Dirección General de Arquitectura, 1947; as *La arquitectura cortes y otros escritas*, 2 vols., Madrid: Colegio Oficial de Arquitectos de Madrid, 1993

Brunet, Cèsar Martinell, and Ignasi Solà-Morales Rubió, *Construcciones agrarias en Cataluña*, Barcelona: Colegio Oficial de Arquitectos de Cataluña y Baleares, 1975

Collins, George R., "The Transfer of Thin Masonry Vaulting from Spain to America," *Journal of the Society of Architectural Historians* 27 (October 1968)

Gulli, Riccardo, and Giovanni Mochi, *Bóvedas tabicadas: Architettura e costruzione*, Rome: CDP Editrice Edilstampa, 1995

Loomis, John A., *Revolution of Forms: Cuba's Forgotten Art Schools*, New York: Princeton Architectural Press, 1999

Parks, Janet, and Alan G. Neumann, *The Old World Builds the New: The Guastavino Company and the Technology of the Catalan Vault, 1885–1962*, New York: Avery Architectural and Fine Arts Library and the Miriam and Ira D. Wallach Art Gallery, Columbia University, 1996

CELEBRATION, FLORIDA

The town of Celebration, designed and built by the Disney Corporation near Orlando, Florida, is certainly the most prominent—and perhaps the most controversial—of the second generation of New Urbanism green-field projects. It followed the sole first-generation new town, Seaside, Florida, by about ten years.

Celebration is the New Urbanist stepchild of Walt Disney's original vision of EPCOT, the Experimental Prototype Community of Tomorrow. Presented in 1966, the drawings and the animated film showed a full-fledged city, organized as a radial system with business and commerce at the center, higher density apartments around a greenbelt, and an outer ring of clean factories and low-density neighborhoods. Shelved at Disney's death, the concept of the "Model City" was revived in the late 1980s under the direction chief operating officer Michael Eisner.

The design of what became Celebration was protracted over many years because it involved the careful testing of every facet of the project. Among the sources of inspiration were the reassessed tradition of the Anglo-American suburb, the new towns of John Nolen (1869–1937), Seaside, Florida, and other examples selected from Werner Hegemann and Elbert Peet's *The American Vitruvius* (1922). Following a series of competitions involving architects including Duany and Plater-Zyberk, Robert A.M. Stern, Gwathmey and Siegel, Helmut Jahn, and Charles Moore, the final master plan was the work of Stern, with Jaquelin Robertson and Associates. The town was officially launched on the 25th anniversary of Disney World in October 1996.

Buffered from the highway by golf courses and a 4,700-acre greenbelt of wetlands, the plan of Celebration remotely resembles EPCOT's original concept. The half-circular and radial plan of streets and neighborhoods, distorted by the environmental constraints, focuses on an artificial lake along which the mixed-use town center develops. A wide waterfront promenade, complete with a stepped embarcadero, parks, and fountains, harbors a series of restaurants and cafes stretching from the cinema complex (designed by Cesar Pelli) to the hotel. The one-block-long Main Street departs from the lake and terminates in a square, identified by the 52 columns of the town hall (designed by Philip Johnson), the circular post office (designed by Michael Graves), and the preview center (by Moore/Anderson Architects) with its Outlook Tower. The public school (by William Rawn), whose entrance faces a British-like crescent of town houses, is exceptionally neighborhood friendly.

Inspired by Frederick Law Olmsted's "Emerald Necklace" (Boston, 1878–95) and Martin Wagner's diagram for the greening of Berlin (1910), a system of "green fingers" penetrates into the town and articulates its neighborhoods. One finger prolongs the main street, which widens as a parkway on both sides of a canal and terminates at the golf course; another one bisects the school's property and embraces its playing fields. Smaller parks, creeks, and lakes remind of nearby Winter Park—another major inspiration for the design.

Celebration depends on connectivity and diversity: a system of navigable streets and a full range of housing types in addition to shops and office, school, and civic buildings. Most interesting are the Main Street apartments above shops (the open-air circulation is an innovative solution to the challenge of separate entrances) and the courtyard-type apartments along the canal. To avoid some of Seaside's problems, the mixed-use blocks of the center contain landscaped parking lots, and alleys give access to the private residential garages. Yet, diversity also meant some concession to more traditional zoning. The isolated office park or Celebration Place—two of the three buildings centered around an obelisk were designed by Aldo Rossi and completed in 1996—faces the regional highway; nearby and in visual contact with the town center is the community hospital. Residential-only satellite neighborhoods, organized around greens, are not quite in walking distance of the center.

The controversy swirling around Celebration, eliciting two books in 1999 as well as countless articles, is due less to its design than to its controlling concept. Its government is, in fact, a private association—not unlike the tens of thousands of homeowners' or property owners' associations, both common in the suburbs and increasingly in inner cities across the 50 states; yet, it was attacked as a first case of "private government by corporation." Most critics focused on the failure of the original public school's curriculum, conceived by Disney in collaboration with the Harvard School of Education. The experimental curriculum did not match the more conservative aspirations of the parents, and their civic dissatisfaction was presented as a failure in building a genuine community. Eventually, they succeeded in changing the course of the school.

Another controversial factor is the code or pattern book, written by Ray Gindroz of Urban Design Associates (Pittsburgh), that strictly defines the six permitted styles: Classical, Victorian, Colonial Revival, Coastal, Mediterranean, and French. The issue of individual freedom has been raised, as the precision and inflexibility of the code are unmatched in New Urbanism communities. However, the choice made in Celebration was to risk eliminating the exceptionally good design in order to avoid the kitsch and the very bad. As a mitigating factor, the civic structures and the mixed-use buildings along Main Street were not coded, but rather commissioned to first-rate architects who worked closely together.

Disney's decision to put the centrally managed main street and shops at the very center of the community and away from the main highway was well supported by the residents afraid of the impact of regional traffic on the community. Yet the development industry accused Disney of infringing one of the tenets of commercial practice, thus making the project unsustainable without subsidies—an allegation that Disney has strongly denied.

The most influential new town since Radburn, New Jersey (started in 1929), Celebration is being built out as planned—the alternative model to traditional suburban sprawl. However, its garden city-like density, its limited capacity for growth, and the absence of a structuring (local and regional) transportation system preclude its being the long-term solution to the challenge of smart growth in North America.

Jean-François Lejeune

See also **Disney Theme Parks; Duany and Plater-Zyberk (United States); New Urbanism; Seaside, Florida; Stern, Robert A.M. (United States)**

Further Reading

Dunlop, Beth, "From Fantasy to Traditional Planning," *Places* 12, no. 1 (Fall 1998)

Frantz, Douglas, and Catherine Collins, *Celebration, U.S.A.: Living in Disney's Brave New Town*, New York: Holt, 1999

Hegemann, Werner, and Elbert Peets, *The American Vitruvius: An Architect's Handbook of Civic Art*, New York: Architectural Book, 1922; reprint, edited and introduced by Alan J. Plattus, New York: Princeton Architectural Press, 1988

Kroloff, Reed, "Disney Builds a Town," *Architecture* 86 (August 1997)

Ross, Andrew, *The Celebration Chronicles: Life, Liberty, and the Pursuit of Property Values in Disney's New Town*, New York: Ballantine Books, 1999; London: Verso, 2000

Stein, Karen, "Place Making: Celebration Place, Celebration, Florida," *Architectural Record* 184, no. 1 (January 1996)

Stern, Robert A.M., and John Montague Massengale, "The Anglo-American Suburb," *Architectural Design* 51 (October 1981)

CENTER FOR INTEGRATED SYSTEMS, STANFORD UNIVERSITY

Designed by Antoine Predock, completed 1996
Palo Alto, California

The Center for Integrated Systems Extension Building (CISX, 1993–96) at Stanford University is an academic research and educational facility designed by Antoine Predock (1936–). The design is the result not only of a highly skilled architect's efforts but also of 50 years of successful educational initiatives and over a decade of thoughtful university planning.

Established in 1888, Stanford University undertook a Centennial Campaign funding drive during President Kennedy's term (1980–92) that resulted in raising $1.26 billion, at the time the largest amount in the history of American higher education.

This success was due in large part to the university's close ties with regional electronics and computer industries of Silicon Valley that sparked much of the economic growth of the last decade of the 20th century. Coinciding with this success was the development and adoption of *The Plan for the Second Century* in 1991, prepared by Hardy, Holzman, Pfieffer and the Office of the University Architect. This study examined the original intentions behind the Olmsted-Stanford Beaux-Arts campus plan, a century of sporadic growth, and the desire to promote natural landscaping. As a plan for revitalization, it presented a two-pronged approach to restore the original character of the institution and also to ensure that all future development would reinforce as well as extend characteristics of the original plan, a natural landscape, and the architectural environment in a cohesive manner. The most influential directives concerning new individual projects sought to harmonize building massing and material choices with the dominant Richardsonian Romanesque-Mission style of red clay roof tiles, arcades, and massive rough-faced sandstone walls of the Main Quad.

During the following term of President Casper (1992–2000), much of the plan was implemented. A good deal of Stanford's original infrastructure was restored or renovated, such as the Main Quad, dating from the original collaboration of 1887–1901 between U.S. Senator Leland Stanford, Frederick Law Olmsted, and Charles Coolidge, of Shepley, Rutan and Coolidge. Conformance with this plan was held to, as a bold initiative for growth was inaugurated that sought to ensure Stanford University's place at the forefront of academic/technological research as well as a place of significant architectural interest. In addition to the CISX building, other notable projects have included the William Gates Computer Sciences Building (1994–97) by Robert A.M. Stern and Partners and the Science and Engineering Quad (1995–99) by Pei, Cobb, Freed and Partners.

Stanford's Educational Initiative brought about a windfall of resources and ultimately the need for a campus revitalization strategy, all stemming from a partnership between academia and industrial entrepreneurs concerning electronic and computing systems that began in the early 1950s. The initiative was originally known as the Industrial Affiliates of Stanford in Solid-State Electronics and was developed in collaboration with a graduate program for members of the electronics industry known as the Honors Cooperative Plan. These programs bound together the educational training, research agenda, and pragmatic objectives of an emerging industry that contributed significantly to the development of the computer industry and Silicon Valley. The plan served as a model that ultimately led to a comprehensive program known as the Center for Integrated Systems (1983), which sought to coordinate scientific research and industrial development in related engineering disciplines at Stanford University. These developments culminated in the 1983 CISX building.

By the early 1990s, the need arose to expand the original 70,000-square-foot CISX building by Ehrlich-Rominger, Architects. A laboratory with additional support space of semi-industrial character was needed for a variety of experimental efforts. The location of the existing facility on campus was west of the Main Quad and presented an early opportunity to test the adopted revitalization plan. Because of the sensitive location and difficult technical requirements, a decision was made to host an invitation-only design competition. Predock's winning entry was distinct among the four competitors for achieving several desirable goals for coherent expansion.

Predock's solution comprised three parts: a new courtyard, the new addition, and a new hazardous materials/mechanical equipment area, for a total of 53,000 square feet. Rather than butting up against the existing building, Predock designed the addition as a discrete building that spatially defines the Main Quad, presenting a powerful logic for a building form that affords both an east entry visible from the Main Quad and a north entry for easy access. His plan strengthened the nodal entry to the new Science and Engineering Quad to the south and the Biological-Chemistry science area to the north, created a private interior courtyard for informal gatherings, and defined interior programmatic spaces.

The design suggests a traditional sense of solidity for which the Richardsonian Romanesque-Mission style is noted. A concrete plinth provides a visual base for the building, similar to the Main Quad. The building is faced with Indian (Delhi) fossilized sandstone veneer. The sense of weight is enhanced through contrast with a copper-clad concrete-vault form that floats within the CISX main entry arcade and that proportionally matches the Main Quad entry arches. Copper-sheet roof shingles are returned to cover the eave soffits, which, in conjunction with a continuous nine-inch strip window at the eave, also cause the upper roof mass to hover. Together the copper-sheathed roof and vault heighten the contrast and sense of gravity of the stone-faced building mass. The stonework and copper materials complement a sense of permanence in the unusual handling of mass and space that both delights and defies conventional sensibilities established by the original campus buildings. Overall, the design offers a 21st-century expression of a scientific endeavor that is genuine, rich, and appropriate in the context of the traditional architectural style of the original campus.

RANDY SWANSON

See also **Predock, Antoine (United States)**

Further Reading

"Antoine Predock's CIS Extension Is the Boldest New Building on Campus," *Stanford* (September–October 1996)

Baker, Geoffrey H., *Antoine Predock*, Chichester, West Sussex: Academy Editions, 1997

Chow, Phoebe, "Stanford Systems," *The Architectural Review* (November 1997)

Collins, Brad, and Juliette Robbins (compilers), *Antoine Predock Architect*, New York: Rizzoli, 1994

Collins, Brad, and Elizabeth Zimmermann (editors), *Antoine Predock Architect 2*, New York: Rizzoli, 1998

"Completed Competition Projects Tell the Story," *Competitions* 10, no. 1 (2000)

Hess, Alan, "Stanford Takes Welcome Turn toward the Abstract," *San Jose Mercury News* (3 May 1996)

Joncas, Richard, David J. Neuman, and Paul V. Turner, *Stanford University*, New York: Princeton Architectural Press, 1999

Neuman, David J., "New Time-Saving Standards at Stanford University," *Competitions* 4, no. 3 (1994)

Stephens, Suzanne, "The American Campus," *Architectural Record* 188, no. 2 (2000)

Stein, Karen, "Two California Campuses: Two Different Worlds: Antoine Predock Spans the Spectrum with a New Building for Each," *Architectural Record* 8, no. 97 (1997)

Turner, Paul Venable, *Campus: An American Planning Tradition*, New York: Architectural History Foundation, and Cambridge, Massachusetts: MIT Press, 1984

CENTURY OF PROGRESS EXPOSITION

Chicago, Illinois, 1933–34

The Century of Progress International Exposition, held in Chicago in 1933–34, played a pivotal yet often underrecognized role in the development and acceptance of modern architecture. The event was the largest architectural program realized in the United States during the depths of the Great Depression. It attracted the attention of influential architects and designers as well as building materials manufacturers and design critics. The innovative exhibition pavilions introduced more than 38 million fair visitors to then-current progressive ideas in modern architecture. Millions more became acquainted with the modern exposition designs through secondary sources, including a wide range of articles, newsreels, and souvenirs.

In 1928 a not-for-profit corporation was chartered to organize a world's fair to celebrate the centennial anniversary of the founding of Chicago. The fair organizers quickly realized that this theme was too narrow to attract enough international or even national interest to guarantee a successful event. Additionally, the recent financial fiasco of the Philadelphia Sesquicentennial International Exposition made it apparent that relying on a structure and character common to past expositions would result in a financial and cultural catastrophe. To ensure the success of the Chicago exposition, the organizers knew that they had to broaden the scope of the fair and present an event that would be perceived by critics and the public as appropriate to modern times. Consequently, the organizers adopted a more inclusive, forward-looking theme: the impact of scientific development on the betterment of humanity.

The members of the architectural commission for the exposition—Paul Philippe Cret, Raymond Hood, John Holabird, Edward Bennett, Hurbert Burnham, Arthur Brown, Harvey Wiley Corbett, and Ralph Walker—knew that their designs had to reflect the modern theme of the fair. The struggle of these notable, Beaux-Arts–trained architects to achieve this through coming to terms with recent developments in their field, as well as the changing conditions of modern life, is clearly evident in the preliminary schemes for the event. Early site plans consisted of neoclassical buildings laid out following a symmetrical *parti* that emphasized a strong sense of axiality. The long and narrow exposition site, financial limitations resulting from the Great Depression, the lack of a rigid building code, and the ephemeral nature of the event all served as sources of inspiration and limitation for the committee members in their efforts to create a modern world's fair. The final result was an asymmetrical layout of inexpensive yet innovative buildings of prefabricated materials.

The fairgrounds covered three and a half miles of new manmade land along the shore of Lake Michigan directly south of the Loop. Recently completed neoclassical buildings, including the Field Museum of Natural History, the Shedd Aquarium, and Soldier Field, framed the north end of the site. These historically derived buildings provided a monochromatic backdrop, reminiscent of Chicago's Columbian Exposition of 1893, which contrasted sharply with the colorful, modern exhibition pavilions that covered the fairgrounds.

Architects produced a wide range of building designs for the Century of Progress Exposition. These included large exhibition halls, futuristic model houses, progressive foreign pavilions, and historic and ethnic entertainment venues. Designs of the major pavilions ranged from the "ultramodern" yellow and blue Administration Building (Bennett, Burnham, and Holabird), with its silver, undulating entrance and factory fenestration, to the flat, windowless, streamlined Sears Roebuck Building (Nimmons, Carr, and Wright). Several of the main pavilions, including the Hall of Science (Cret), which served as the centerpiece of the fair, and the Electrical Building (Hood), were decorated with panels of bas-relief sculpture containing stylized, allegorical figures representing the sciences. Many other buildings, however, including most of the corporate pavilions, contained little or no applied ornament, except letters spelling out the company's name across their facades. Pavilions such as the Time and Fortune Building (Nicolai and Faro) and the Havoline Thermometer Tower (Alfonso Iannelli and Charles Pope) strove for more immediate corporate recognition by including giant reproductions of their products or related items as part of their building's design. Several other companies commissioned pavilions constructed out of their own new products. For example, the Owens-Illinois Glass Corporation Pavilion (Elroy Ruiz) consisted of a tower and two wings built out of glass bricks. A comprehensive color scheme, created by Joseph Urban, that articulated the individual exterior planes of the major buildings through the use of vivid hues, unified the diverse fair pavilions. At night, the use of dramatic lighting effects created a magnificent spectacle. The fair presented the largest quantity of electric lighting emitted at a single event up to that time and featured the first major application of neon in architectural lighting.

Millions of attendees stood in long lines to tour full-scale, modern houses on display in the Home and Industrial Arts Exhibit. For many visitors, the Chicago fair provided their first exposure to modern residential design. Most of the model houses were sponsored by building-material manufacturers. They promoted new construction materials, such as porcelain enamel panels or Rostone (a synthetic stone product), or demonstrated new uses for traditional building materials, such as "precast" brick walls. Other houses, including the Tropical House, focused less on materials and more on demonstrating new ideas in modern living. The House of Tomorrow, designed by George Frederick Keck, generated the greatest amount of attention. Keck designed his 12-sided glass residence to appear as futuristic as possible in hopes of making the aesthetics of modern architecture more familiar and thus more acceptable to the average American home buyer.

Because of poor economic conditions around the world, only a few nations constructed their own pavilions at the exposition. Most countries chose instead to promote themselves through national displays located in the general exhibition buildings. Notable exceptions included Sweden, Czechoslovakia, and Italy, which built large, modern pavilions. The Italian Pavilion (Mario De Renzi, Antonio Valent, and Adalberto Libera) consisted of an assemblage of dynamic forms that clearly expressed the major political goal of the displays inside: to increase support for Fascism among the American public. The basic composition of the building consisted of easily recognizable symbols of Italy's recent

Century of Progress Exposition, Chicago World's Fair (1933)

transportation achievements, including a thin, wing-shaped, horizontal canopy that hovered above the central entrance, and current political ideology, highlighted by an 80-foot-high steel-and-prismatic-glass tower in the shape of a *fascio littorio*.

Not all buildings were aesthetically modern. Event organizers wished to celebrate earlier cultural developments to provide a context from which visitors could measure current and future advances. Architecturally, the past was represented by re-creations of historic structures, such as Chicago's Fort Dearborn and the Maya Nunnery of Uxmal; ethnic settings for entertainment, such as the Belgium Village and the Streets of Paris; and a variety of other "midway" attractions. Although historical in formal characteristics, these buildings were constructed using modern materials.

The fair designers relied heavily on the use of new building materials to minimize construction costs. The exteriors of most of the pavilions consisted of wall panels produced from a variety of factory-made materials, including asbestos cement wallboard, precast gypsum board, plywood, metal siding, and laminated insulation board. In addition to aesthetics and cost, the factors involved in selecting a particular prefabricated material included strength and durability, weatherproofness, moisture resistance, relative resistance to combustion, lightness of weight, ease of securing to framework, and availability. A new type of Sheetrock, suitable for exterior use on temporary buildings, was the favored wall surface material for the large exhibition pavilions.

Factory-made panels were ideally suited to two major concepts in building construction gaining favor among progressive designers in the early 1930s: prefabrication and disposable architecture. Architects designing buildings for the exposition explored systematic construction techniques in their attempt to keep construction costs down to an affordable level despite sharp increases in labor and material costs and a significant decrease in available funds as a result of the poor economy. Workers assembled various types of standardized wall panels to steel framing in modern assembly-line fashion. Screwing or bolting the panels of the pavilions together provided for easy disassembly and salvaging of the building parts after the close of the exposition. This led proponents of "disposable architecture" to highlight the Chicago fair in American architectural journal discussions on the benefits of short-lived buildings.

The designers also looked toward new structural ideas for inspiration in the creation of modern yet novel-looking pavilions. Two forms of thin membrane roofing highlighted structural advances at the event. The first, used in the rotunda of the steel Travel and Transport Building (Bennett, Burnham, and Holabird), was the first major catenary roof constructed in the United States. The massive structure consisted of a drum with support cables traveling from the roof upward to the tops of 12 tall columns and then downward to anchors at the outer edge of a broader, lower level of the building. The Brook Hill Dairy (Richard Phillipp and Anton Tedesko), built for the second fair season in 1934, also demonstrated an advancement in roofing design. The building's five contiguous elliptical barrel vaults presented the first use of a multi-vaulted concrete-shell roof and probably the first applications of the Zeiss-Dywidag process for reinforced thin-shell vaulting in the United States. A third, less apparent structural development was an innovative system of low-cost pile footings. This proved more suitable than spread footings for the unstable conditions of the recently created land of the fairgrounds.

The exposition also provided an opportunity for designers to explore and promote innovative architectural ideas through unbuilt designs for the event. Frank Lloyd Wright, whose inability to work cooperatively with other architects kept him off the design commission, clearly realized the importance of the event in the development of American architecture. With encouragement from Lewis Mumford and other architectural critics, he presented three schemes for the fair at a meeting of the American Union of Decorative Artists and Craftsmen held in New York in February 1931. These conceptual designs explored housing the entire exposition in a skyscraper, under a massive tent structure, and on barges floating out on Lake Michigan. Industrial designer Norman Bel Geddes, who briefly served as a design consultant to the architectural commission, also promoted innovative ideas, including the concept of streamlining, through producing a series of unrealized, experimental theater and restaurant pavilions. Many of these designs, including a rotating aerial restaurant, were featured in his influential 1932 treatise *Horizons*.

In contrast to the first Chicago world's fair, which helped usher in a massive wave of neoclassical buildings throughout the United States, the Century of Progress Exposition played a less discernible role in the development of modern American architecture despite its tremendous public success. Although the exposition encouraged a greater acceptance of nonhistorical forms, few architects looked to the fair as a source of aesthetic inspiration for their modern building designs. Reasons for this ranged from the vast difference in functional needs between the temporary exposition halls and more permanent architecture to the drastic reduction in all construction starts in the 1930s. Also influential were the strong reactions of architectural critics to Wright's omission from the commission and, later, to the formal qualities of designs produced for the event. Although the direct aesthetic impact of the exposition on everyday architecture was limited, the designs did influence the formal qualities of buildings with similar functional needs, particularly the designs of later exposition pavilions. The Chicago fair's most significant contributions to the development of American architecture lay instead in the introduction and promotion of innovative building products and processes adaptable to both progressive and traditional designs.

LISA SCHRENK

See also **Cret, Paul Philippe (United States); Hood, Raymond (United States); Mumford, Lewis (United States); Wright, Frank Lloyd (United States)**

Further Reading

Few secondary sources exist on the 1933–34 Chicago Century of Progress Exposition. However, numerous articles were published on the architecture of the fair in contemporary architectural publications, including *Architectural Forum, Architect and Engineer, American Architect, Pencil Points, Engineering News-Record, Western Architect*, and *Architectural Record*. The exposition published several guidebooks and picture books, as well as *World's Fair Weekly*, a magazine for fair visitors. The most significant of several large archives on the exposition is the Century of Progress collection at the University of Illinois at Chicago, which contains over 1,000 linear feet of original records from the event. These include correspondence, plans, photographs, press releases, and published materials covering all aspects of the fair. The Lenox Lohr archive, also housed at the University of Illinois, contains additional materials from the exposition. Photographs, articles, pamphlets, and some drawings from the event can be found in various collections at the Chicago Historical Society. The University of Chicago owns the John Crerar Collection, a large pamphlet archive from the exposition. The Daniel Burnham, Jr., and Edward Bennett collections at the Ryerson and Burnham Libraries in the Art Institute of Chicago contain diaries, drawings, photographs, and other miscellaneous paper items relating to the architecture of the exposition.

Condit, Carl W., *Chicago, 1930–70: Building, Planning, and Urban Technology*, Chicago: University of Chicago Press, 1974

Doordan, Dennis P., "Exhibition Progress: Italy's Contribution to the Century of Progress Exposition," in *Chicago Architecture and Design, 1923–1993: Reconfiguration of an American Metropolis*, edited by John Zukowsky, Munich: Prestel, and Chicago: Art Institute of Chicago, 1993

Findling, John E., *Chicago's Great World's Fairs*, Manchester: Manchester University Press, 1994

Findling, John E., and Kimberly D. Pelle, editors, *Historical Dictionary of World's Fairs and Expositions, 1851–1988*, New York: Greenwood Press, 1990

Lohr, Lenox R., *Fair Management: The Story of a Century of Progress Exposition: A Guide for Future Fairs*, Chicago: Cuneo Press, 1952

Rydell, Robert W., *World of Fairs: The Century of Progress Expositions*, Chicago: University of Chicago Press, 1993

Schrenk, Lisa D., "The Role of the 1933–34 Century of Progress International Exposition in the Development and Promotion of Modern Architecture in the United States," Ph.D. diss., University of Texas at Austin, 1998

CHADIRJI, RIFAT 1926–

Architect, Iraq

The driving force behind Rifat Chadirji's work has been his attempt to reconcile contemporary social needs with new technology. His search for a regional modernism found expression in cement-concrete buildings and in his plans for Baghdad.

In the Iraq of the 1950s, a flowering of the arts included intensive discussions among architects, artists, writers, and intellectuals about the need for appropriate artistic expressions, influenced by both European ideas and local traditions. The architects Wilson and Mason, who practiced in Iraq in the 1940s and whose buildings interpreted local architecture employing indigenous master masons, also shaped Chadirji's ideas about regionalism. This approach stagnated somewhat after World War II, when new technologies that bypassed the contribution of the indigenous building industry were introduced. Architects such as Le Corbusier, Walter Gropius, and Frank Lloyd Wright visited Iraq in the 1960s, encouraging the local Iraqi architects to find their own expression of modern architecture. As a consequence, Chadirji sought to achieve a synthesis between traditional forms and materials and modern technology and building types. He studied local environmental features such as courtyards, screen walls, and natural ventilation. However, until the late 1960s his buildings were clearly functionalist and were determined by structural considerations and modern materials, as evidenced in his Monument to the Unknown Soldier (1959) and in his Tobacco Monopoly Offices and Warehouse (1969), both in Baghdad.

Chadirji articulated his ideas concerning a modernism informed by tradition in his written works, theories that can be seen in his villa for H.H. Hamood (1972), designed as a dramatic series of parallel vaults. As Chadirji noted, it was not until the early 1970s that he reached the view that the connection between form and structure was not inevitable. This realization led the architect to increased freedom of construction and the plastic possibilities of building form.

This sense of plasticity and a graphic approach to buildings characterize the facades of his buildings, as demonstrated in his published portfolio of etchings and drawings for the Federation of Industries and for the Ministry of Municipal and Rural Affairs. His buildings are characterized in plan by parallel walls and in elevation by facades of solid planes with indented openings, often with protruding tall, thin, arched windows and curving corners. The concrete buildings were usually designed to be faced in brick or, in other countries of the Middle East, in stone. Together with Mohamed Makiya, Chadirji's buildings influenced much of the architecture in the Arab Middle East in the 1970s and early 1980s.

In his analysis of built form, Chadirji led the way in the Middle East to reevaluate architecture's role in culture and politics. The effects of his contributions have been long lasting and include his vision of rapidly changing architectural forms as mediators between social needs and prevailing technology. The failure to come to terms with this, he postulated, partly explained the collapse of architecture seen in Iraq after 1945. Second, Chadirji saw the relationship between local traditional building and international modernism as one in which an "authentic regionalism" based on an abstraction of tradition and modernity could emerge. Third, in the 1960s, Chadirji was early to recognize the potential importance of the computer to design and urban planning such that computer technologies would enable the inhabitants of buildings and neighborhoods to participate in the design process.

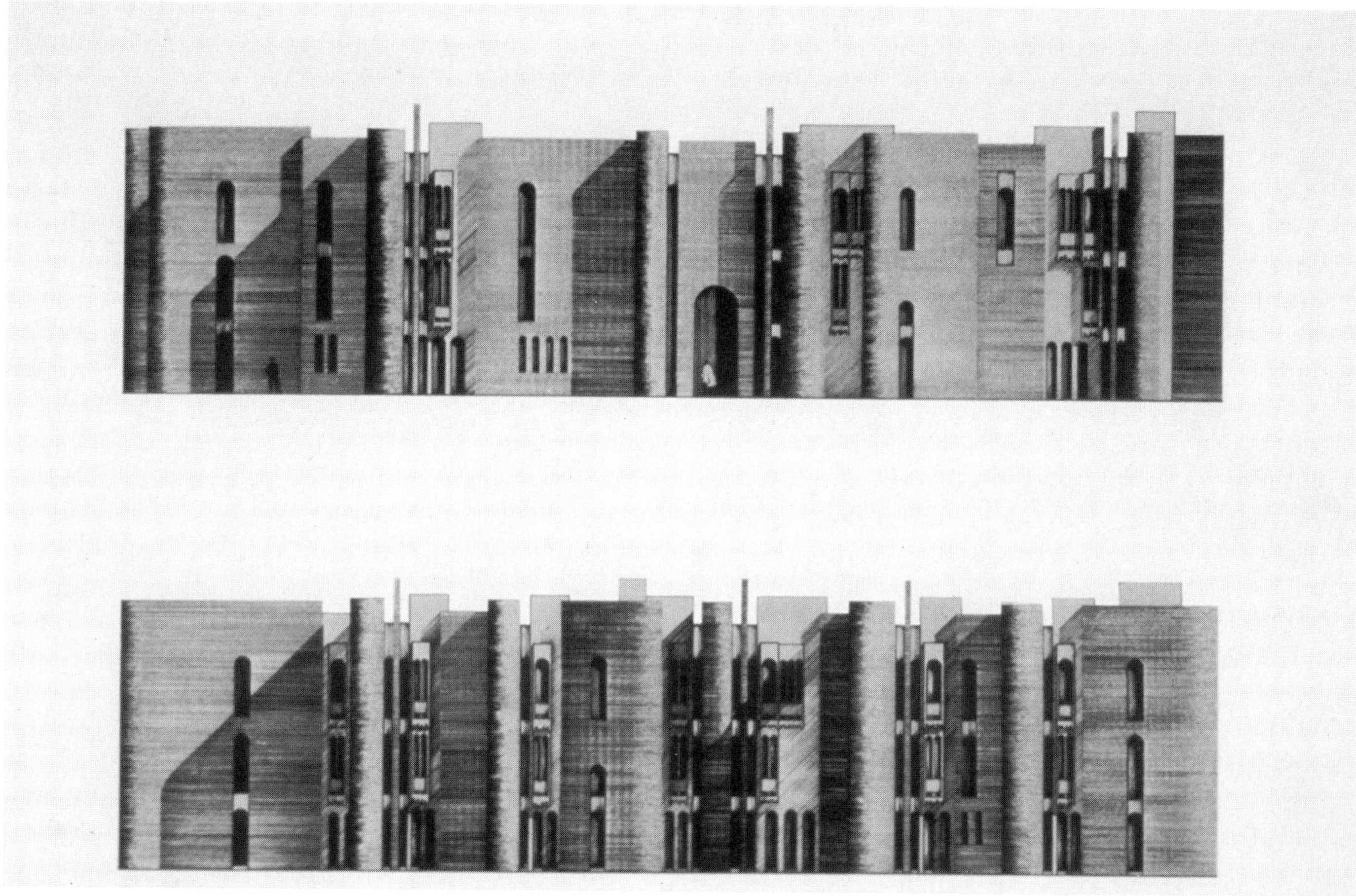

Black-and-white drawing, elevation study for Tobacco Monopoly Offices and Warehouse Complex (1969)
Photo by Rifat Chadirji © Aga Khan Trust for Culture

Chadirji's contribution to the urban built form of Baghdad has been remarkable, despite a turbulent political relationship with the authorities. In the late 1970s he was forced to abandon his practice when the Iraqi government imprisoned him. Surprisingly, in 1980 that same government appointed him counsellor to the mayor of Baghdad, with responsibility for an ambitious scheme for urban rehabilitation and development. This project was completed in 1983 for the international meeting of Non-Aligned Nations; it included a master plan, a citywide landscaping scheme, infrastructure development, urban conservation and urban design projects, housing, and commercial works. Proposals for building codes, conservation law, and economic development projects were all in his domain, and for two years he was one of the most powerful bureaucrats in the country.

Chadirji left Baghdad for the United States in late 1982 and subsequently completed his most significant book, *Concepts and Influences* (1986), and continued his research in the interrelationships among architectural theory and phenomena in physics and biology. The Chadirji Research Center in the United Kingdom is a major source of information about Iraq and includes an extensive archive of photographs from his father and his own detailed survey of Arab peoples and their physical world.

HASAN-UDDIN KHAN

Biography

Born in Baghdad, Iraq, in December 1926. Studied at the Hammersmith School of Arts and Crafts, London, 1946–52, earning a Diploma of Architecture. Founder and partner of Iraq Consult (1952–72). Married Balquis Sharara 1954. Worked for government organizations as director of buildings: Waqf (1954–57), Public Works, Department Health and Education (1957–58), Ministry of Planning (1958–59), and Ministry of Housing, Planning Department (1960–63). Returned to private practice from 1965 until 1980. Appointed counsellor to the mayor of Baghdad from 1980 to 1982. Arrived of the United States (Harvard University), where he was a Loeb Fellow (1983), Visiting Scholar at the Graduate School of Design (1984–86), Philosophy of Education Research Center (1985–92), and Graduate

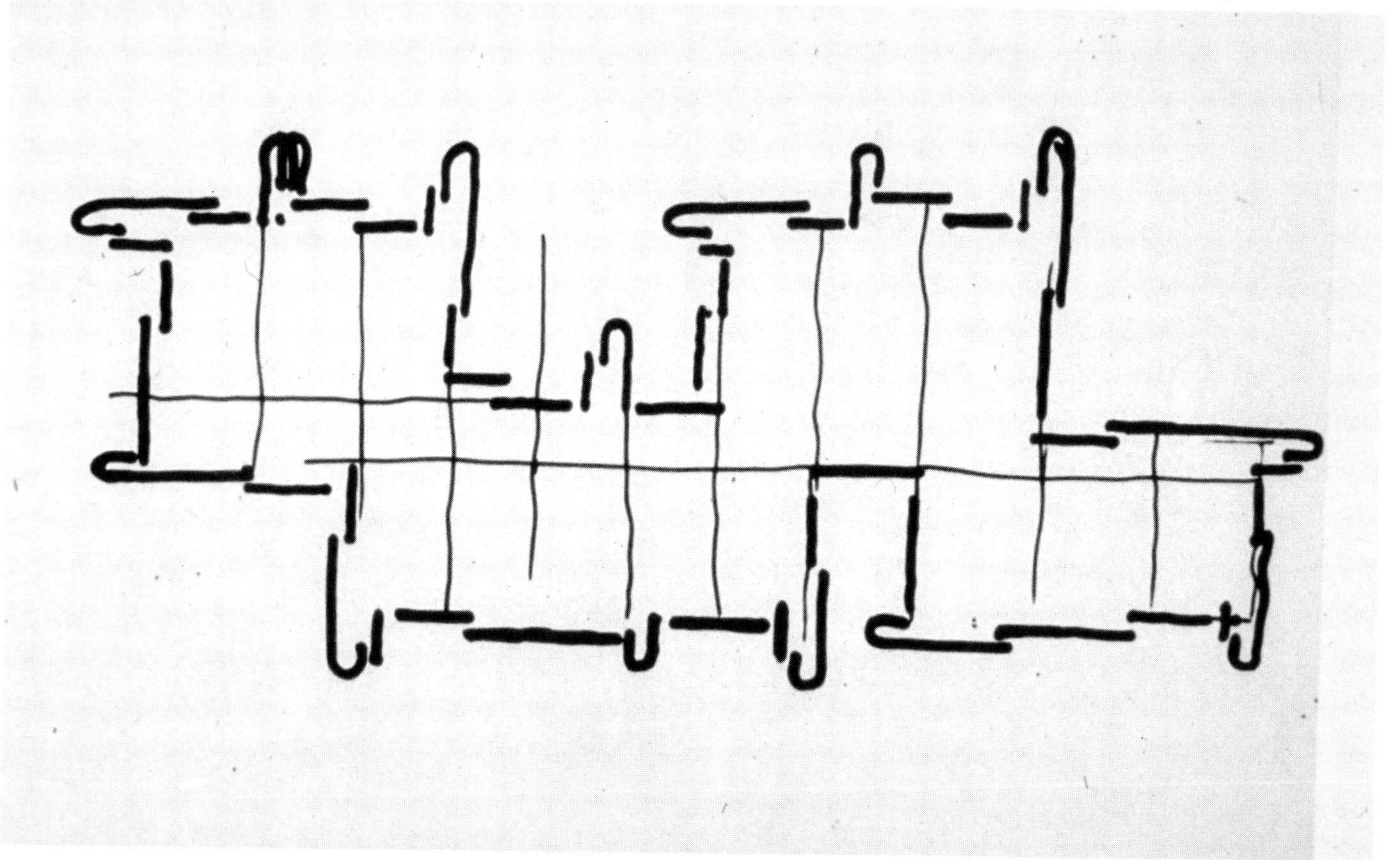

Black-and-white drawing, conceptual sketch for Tobacco Monopoly Offices and Warehouse Complex, 1969
Photo by Rifat Chadirji © Aga Khan Trust for Culture

School of Education (1987–92). Appointed a Visiting Scholar at the Aga Khan Program for Islamic Architecture at MIT (1986–92) and at the Bartlett School, University College London (1989–94). Established the Chadirji Research Center, Kingston-upon-Thames, in 1990. Recipient of the Bronze Medal, Barcelona International Furniture Design (1964), The Chairman's Award, Aga Khan Award for Architecture (1986), and Honorary Fellow of both the Royal Institute of British Architects (1982) and the American Institute of Architects (1987). Subject of over a dozen exhibitions in the Middle East and Africa between 1966 and 1975. "Modern Arab Architecture" exhibition at the Royal Institute of British Architects in London, 1978. Retired from practice, 1982; continues to live and work in England.

Selected Works

Works all in Baghdad, Iraq, unless otherwise noted
Wahab House, 1954
Munir Abbas Building, 1957
Monument to the Unknown Soldier, 1959
National Insurance Company Building, 1960
Waqf Office Building, North Gate, 1965
Iraqi Federation of Industries Administration Building, 1966
Iraqi Scientific Academy, 1968
Tobacco Monopoly Offices and Warehouse Complex, 1969
Kufa Cement Factory (with N. Fetto and P. Nay), 1969
Sheikh Khalefa Building, Bahrain, 1970
Qatar Cinema Complex, Doha, 1972
Villa Hamood, 1972
General Federation of Trade Unions Assembly Hall, 1973
Central Post Office, 1975
Cabinet Ministers' Building, United Arab Emirates (UAE), 1976
Al Ain Public Library, UAE, 1977
Rifat Chadirji House, 1979

Selected Publications

A Collection of Twelve Etchings, London: privately published, 1985
Portrait of a Father, London: privately published, 1985
Taha Street and Hammersmith, Beirut: privately published, 1985
Concepts and Influences: Towards a Regionalised International Architecture, London: KPI, 1986
The Ukhaidir and the Crystal Palace, Kingston-upon-Thames: CRC, 1991

Further Reading

"Architect of Baghdad: Rifat Chadirji" in *Middle East Construction*, Surrey, England: Sutton, 1984
Bofill, Ricardo, and Charles Knevit, "The Architecture of Rifat Chadirji: An Appraisal," *Process Architecture* (Tokyo) (May 1985)

Khan, Hasan-Uddin, "Regional Modernism: Rifat Chadirji's Portfolio of Etchings," *Mimar: Architecture in Development* (Singapore) 14 (October–December 1984)
Khan, Hasan-Uddin, *The Middle East*, Volume 5 of *World Architecture: A Critical Mosaic 1900–2000*, K. Frampton, Series Editor, Vienna: Springer, 2000
Kultermann, Udo, *Architekten der Dritten Welt*, Cologne: DuMont Buchverlag, 1980
Kultermann, Udo, "Contemporary Arab Architecture: The Architects of Iraq," *Mimar: Architecture in Development* (Singapore) 6 (July–September 1982)
Kultermann, Udo, *Contemporary Architecture in the Arab States*, New York: McGraw Hill, 1999
"Middle Eastern Realities at RIBA," in *Building Design* (London) 19 (January 1983)
Ali, M., "Rifat Chadirji," *Domus* (Milan) (December 1983)
Serageldin, Ismail (editor), "Chairman's Award: Rifat Chadirji," in *Space for Freedom*, London: Butterworth Architecture, 1989

CHANDIGARH, INDIA

Chandigarh is the modern, new state capital built by the government of India in the immediate aftermath of its independence from 200 years of colonial rule. On 15 August 1947, India's hard-won freedom was accompanied by a partition that established Pakistan as a separate country. As a result, the Indian state of Punjab lost its historic capital, Lahore, to Pakistan. Consequently, the search for a replacement capital for East Punjab was high on the agenda of the fledgling Indian nation-state.

A burgeoning sense of national pride focused attention on the search for this new capital, and the project took on great symbolic value as a demonstration of the new government's effectiveness, ideals, and abilities. Although the development of this new capital was ostensibly a state project, the central government took an active role in the endeavor, propelled by Prime Minister Jawaharlal Nehru's personal interest in it. Instead of choosing an existing city, Nehru advocated the making of a new capital that would express the ideals of the new nation-state, which was precipitously embracing modernism as a catalyst for change.

This kind of ideological momentum propelled the project quickly to a developmental stage. The new capital was intended to resettle not only the Punjabi government and university but also thousands of refugees displaced in the political upheaval. The new city was named Chandigarh after an existing village which had a temple dedicated to the Hindu goddess Chandi. A site for the project had been chosen by 1948, but in 1949 it was changed to its present location in an effort to reduce the number of people whom the project would displace. Even so, 24 villages and 9000 residents were forced to give up their land and relocate. They actively protested their displacement, but the project went forward, driven by the optimism and determination of the central government.

Although industrialization and modernization were key to Nehru's agenda, he did not actually prescribe a modernist architectural language for Chandigarh. The architectural vision for the city first took shape under A.L. Fletcher, the government of Punjab's "Officer on Special Duty" for the capital project. Of Indian descent, Fletcher was trained as a civil service officer under the colonial administration, which functioned through procedures sanctioned by the home government in London. In what could be considered a postcolonial reflex reaction, Fletcher turned to contemporary official town-planning practices of England to derive his vision for a modern Chandigarh.

In 1948, English town-planning practices were strongly influenced by the principles of the Garden City movement and Ebenezer Howard's 1898 book *To-Morrow: A Peaceful Path to Real Reform* (republished as *Garden Cities of To-Morrow* in 1902). Howard's fundamental goal was to invent new living environments that could coexist with industry without suffering from the congestion and squalor that resulted from industrial pollution and agglomeration of labor. By the 1930s, garden city principles had influenced the construction of several experimental new English towns, including Letchworth (1903) and Welwyn (1919), and Radburn, New Jersey (1929). Eventually, its principles were adapted to develop the greater London plan of 1944 and the New Towns Act of 1946, which was used to design a ring of new towns around London.

Fletcher recommended a vision for Chandigarh based on these ideas and proposed sending officials to England to recruit appropriate town planners and architects for Chandigarh. However, Nehru quickly vetoed this idea, saying, "There is too great a tendency for our people to rush up to England and America for advice. The average American or English town-planner will probably not know the social background of India. He will therefore be inclined to plan something which might suit England or America, but not so much India" (Kalia, 1987).

Instead, Nehru suggested Albert Mayer for the job. Mayer was an American town planner who had been strongly influenced by Lewis Mumford and Clarence Stein and who had been working on an innovative pilot project for rural development in the state of Uttar Pradesh and the urban development plan of greater Bombay. Although his ideas were quite close to those of the Garden City movement, he had made considerable effort to ensure that there was effective citizen participation in the design process based on the principle of what Mayer called "inner democratization." Nehru, attracted by Mayer's modern ideals and innovative practice, maintained friendly relations with him.

Mayer accepted the commission and began work on Chandigarh early in 1950, along with four (non-Indian) associates: Julian Whittlesey, Milton Glass, Clarence Stein, and Matthew Nowicki (a Siberian trained in Warsaw who joined the work on Stein's recommendation). The idea was that this team of architects would direct and supervise the work of a group of Indian architects who could continue the job after their departure. This apprenticeship model was carried through the remainder of the project.

Mayer's plan centered around the basic unit of a superblock that would serve the daily needs of a community with amenities such as markets and schools. A larger, three-block unit that he called the Urban Village was to house a theater, hospital, meeting hall, and additional shopping facilities. The Urban Villages were organized in a gridlike pattern, although the main streets in Mayer's plan were allowed to follow the natural topography and thus broke from the geometric rigidity of the grid.

With the institutional campuses of the government and Punjab University at the north, the city plan widened out in a triangular shape toward the south. A large business district was sited at the center of the city, and an industrial site was proposed at the southeast corner of the plan. Mayer's plan accounted for a future phase of southward expansion that could bring the town's projected population from 150,000 to 500,000. Architectural designs, including sketches and standards for the capitol complex, the commercial buildings (bazaars), and much of the housing, were taken on by Nowicki, who was largely responsible for envisioning the details that would determine the quality of life in Chandigarh. Nowicki's hand is also evident in a proposed continuous park system that linked the various parts of the city.

Following Nowicki's tragic and unexpected death in a plane crash on 31 August 1950, progress on the project was deterred by Mayer's increasing communication difficulties with the Indian bureaucracy. As a consequence, Punjabi state officials began a search for a new architect that resulted in the selection of the professional with whom the project is most often associated: Swiss-French modern architect Le Corbusier, who viewed Chandigarh as the superlative opportunity to model his theories on town planning in a manner more befitting his conception of the true potential and purpose of modern civilization. Modern Western civilization, according to Le Corbusier, had lost contact with the "essential joys" of life in its clamor for money. In India, with its rural and primitivistic way of life, Le Corbusier saw the potential of a civilization that was still in touch with these atavistic desires but had as yet to advance into modernity.

Le Corbusier's enchantment with this "humane and profound civilization" only served to reassure him of the veracity of his vision for a true modernism. There seemed to be a vindication at hand, and Le Corbusier set to work at the task of upgrading India to what he described "the second era of mechanization" (quoted in Sarin, 1982)

Le Corbusier redesigned the Mayer master plan; what had been named an Urban Village in Mayer's plan, Le Corbusier renamed a "sector." Each sector featured a green strip running north to south, bisected by a commercial road running east to west. Le Corbusier's plan comprised a smaller area than Mayer's (5380 acres versus 6908 acres) reorganized into a more rationalized, orthogonal order and rectangular shape. A light industrial zone was planned at the eastern limit of the city, with an educational zone on the western. Le Corbusier's strategy for organizing the city in the modular mode stemmed from his view of the city as a living organism. Well-defined cellular organization predicted orderly growth, with the unencumbered flow of traffic acting as vital circulation to link the city's head (the government complex) to its heart (the central commercial sector) and to its various extremities.

In the end, Le Corbusier was responsible only for the overall master plan of Chandigarh and almost nothing of the city itself. He prepared the guidelines for the commercial center, and in an adjoining sector he designed a museum and a school of art. The majority of the buildings within the city (other than those developed privately) were designed by Jeanneret, Fry, and Drew, with assistance from their Indian team. Housing designs for sectors 22 and 23 were the first to be developed. As most of Chandigarh's original housing was intended for government employees, it was decided that the housing costs would be determined by a set percentage of a government employee's income. Jeanneret, Fry, and Drew devised 13 (later 14) "types" of housing based on a spectrum of incomes from employees earning less than Rs. 50 per month to the chief minister. Each design was given a designation with a number (denoting the economic sector for which it was envisioned) paired with a letter (indicating the architect who designed it), type 13J or 14M, for example. All the designs were visibly "modern," exhibiting unornamented stark geometries broken only by sunscreening devices, such as deep overhangs and recesses, perforated screens, and open verandas. There was even a "frame-control" system devised to regulate all the construction that was privately developed.

Chandigarh's more adolescent years have been burdened by the onus of carrying out the idealistic and formalistic vision on which the city was founded while dealing with the massive housing and economic problems that are, in part, the legacy of this vision. It is one of the ironies of history that Chandigarh, born of a partition, once again found itself the center of a political divide. Punjab was further partitioned in 1965, creating the new state of Haryana. At that point, Chandigarh acquired the unique status of a centrally administered "Union Territory" while also functioning as the capital of both Punjab and Haryana. This was accompanied by the redrawing and reduction of the municipal boundary of the city and the location of Chandigarh right at the line of division.

This repartition resulted in the establishment and growth of "satellite" towns, bordering Chandigarh but legally in Punjab and Haryana. Now, "greater Chandigarh," originally designed for a population of 800,000, is approaching the one million mark. Although efforts are under way to increase the density of the city and to accommodate the changes, the most glaring omission of the city's "master plan" continues to be neglected by its new development plans. There is still no comprehensive plan to integrate the poorest dispossessed people, who form almost 20 percent of the city's population and cater to most of its service needs, into the urban fabric. They continue to live in illegal, substandard slums along the edges of the city.

In its ideological purity, Chandigarh belongs to the roster of cities such as Canberra, Brasilia, and Islamabad, pregnant with the brazen optimism of their time. Brought to life and now aging, it is one of the rare events of our modern era that, in its unadulterated realization, define a moment (in time, place, and theory) from which our distance offers a critical view.

VIKRAMADITYA PRAKASH WITH AMY POTTER

Further Reading

Constant, Caroline, "From the Virgilian Dream to Chandigarh," *The Architectural Review* (London), no. 1079 (1987)

Curtis, William J.R., *Le Corbusier: Ideas and Forms*, New York: Rizzoli, 1986

Curtis, William J.R., "L'Ancien dans le moderne," *Architecture en Inde*, Saint-Gobain, France: Electa Manteur, 1985

Correa, Charles, "Chandigarh: The View from Benares," in *Le Corbusier*, edited by H. Allen Brooks, Princeton, New Jersey: Princeton University Press, 1987

Doshi, Balkrishna V., *Le Corbusier and Louis I. Kahn: The Acrobat and the Yogi of Architecture*, Ahmedabad, India: Vastu Shilpa Foundation, 1993

Evenson, Norma, *Chandigarh*, Berkeley: University of California Press, 1966

Fry, Maxwell, "Le Corbusier at Chandigarh," in *The Open Hand: Essays on Le Corbusier*, edited by Russell Walden, Cambridge, Massachusetts: MIT Press, 1977

Gordon, Chris and Kilian Kist, Chandigarh Forty Years after Le Corbusier, *Architectura and Natura Quarterly: ANQ* (*c.*1990)

Kalia, Ravi, *Chandigarh: In Search of an Identity*, Carbondale: Southern Illinois University Press, 1987

Krustrup, Mogens, *Porte email: Le Corbusier, Palais de l'Assemblee de Chandigarh*, Copenhagen: Arkitektens Forlag, 1991

Le Corbusier, *Oeuvre complète 1946–1952*, edited by Willy Boesiger, translated by William B. Gleckman, Zurich: Éditions Girsberger, 1953

Le Corbusier, *Modulor 2, 1955: La Parole est aux usagers: Suite de "Le Modulor 1948,"* Boulogne: Éditions de l'Architecture D'aujourd'hui, 1955; as *Modulor 2, 1955: Let the User Speak Next: Continuation of The Modulor 1948*, translated by Peter de Francia and Anna Bostock, London: Faber and Faber, and Cambridge, Massachusetts: Harvard University Press, 1958

Le Corbusier, *Oeuvre complète 1952–1957*, edited by Willy Boesiger, translated by William B. Gleckman, New York: Wittenborn, 1957; 4th edition, Zurich: Les Éditions d'Architecture, 1966

Le Corbusier, "The Master Plan," *Marg (Pathway)*, 15 (December 1961)

Le Corbusier, *Oeuvre completè 1957–1965*, edited by Willy Boesiger, Zurich: Éditions de l'Architecture, 1965; 2nd edition, New York: Wittenborn, 1965

Le Corbusier, *Last Works*, edited by Willy Boesiger, translated by Henry A. Frey, New York: Praeger, 1970

Le Corbusier, *Le Corbusier Sketchbooks*, 4 vols., New York: Architectural History Foundation, Cambridge, Massachusetts: MIT Press, and London: Thames and Hudson 1981–82

Le Corbusier, *Cité Fruges and Other Buildings and Projects, 1923–1927*, New York and London: Garland, 1983

Moos, Stanislaus von, *Le Corbusier, Elemente einer Synthese*, Frauenfeld, Germany: Huber, 1968; as *Le Corbusier, Elements of a Synthesis*, Cambridge, Massachusetts: MIT Press, 1985

Nehru, Jawaharlal, "Mr. Nehru on Architecture," *Urban and Rural Planning Thought*, 2/2, (April 1959)

Nilsson, Sten Åke, *The New Capitals of India, Pakistan and Bangladesh*, translated by Elisabeth Ardréasson, Lund, Sweden: Studentlitteratur, 1973

Prakash, Aditya, *Chandigarh: A Presentation in Free Verse*, Chandigarh: Chandigarh Administration, 1980

Prakash, Vikramaditya, *Chandigarh's Le Corbusier: The Struggle for Modernity in Postcolonial India*, Seattle: University of Washington Press, 2002

Prasad, Susand, "Le Corbusier in India," *Architecture + Design*, 3/6 (September–October 1987)

Sarin, Madhu, *Urban Planning in the Third World: The Chandigarh Experience*, London: Mansell Publishing, 1982

Serenyi, Peter, "Timeless but of Its Time: Le Corbusier's Architecture in India," in *Le Corbusier*, edited by H. Allen Brooks, Princeton, New Jersey: Princeton University Press, 1987

CHANNEL 4 HEADQUARTERS

Designed by Richard Rogers Partnership, completed 1994
London, England

London's Channel 4 was founded in 1982 primarily to commission and air programs and films that had been created elsewhere by independent producers and to directly compete with large corporations, such as the BBC. By the late 1980s, the company employed more than 500 people whose offices were dispersed among several buildings in Bloomsbury. In 1990 the station decided to move to a single building that could handle the large number of employees as well as the channel's changing technological needs, brought about by its shift to digital broadcasting. Richard Rogers Partnership, a London firm, won the commission, and the resulting design, with its sense of openness and references to modern media technology, fit the image of a company known for its progressive, sometimes radical, programming.

The building is situated on a corner lot in Westminster, midway between the Houses of Parliament and Victoria Station. Targeted for housing, the site became available when the developer went bankrupt, and the borough of Westminster approved the use of the site by Channel 4 as long as the scheme included a certain number of residential flats. The competition brief also stipulated other requirements, such as 15,000 square meters of flexible office space, conference rooms, viewing and editing rooms, an underground parking garage, and a public garden.

The site plan consists of four rectangular blocks that surround a central landscaped garden. The southern and eastern wings—designed by Lyons Sleeman and Hoare, not Rogers—are the required residential blocks, consisting of 100 apartments. Rogers's input on the design of the flats was ignored after this portion of the site was sold to a separate developer to raise money for

Metal mesh screens cover the windows of the Channel Four Headquarters (1994), London, England, designed by Richard Rogers Partnership
© Gillian Darley; Edifice/CORBIS

Channel 4, which occupies the northern and western wings. The L-shaped layout of these two blocks, each four stories high and containing the offices, echoes the street-corner location of the building. They are joined by a soaring concave, glass-enclosed foyer containing the main entrance, accessible once one walks up a stepped ramp that leads from the street through a paved piazza. A lightweight glass bridge, covered by a steel-and-glass canopy, allows the visitor to peer down into the station's underground quarters. The basement space is a vestige of an earlier building whose construction had begun in the 1970s but had never been completed. The entrance facade is flanked by a tall vertical tower, topped by television antennae and containing the building's utilities as well as the elevators, whose movements are visible from the street.

On entering the curved reception area that links the two wings, one can see past it to a glass-walled public restaurant, several steps down from the entranceway. The open design—penetrated by red steel supports for the entrance canopy—allows the visitor immediately to see all the way through to the central garden area that lies behind the building. The steel cables and rods that support the curving glass entrance wall are slender yet clearly visible in the central atrium of the building. The upper floor of the concave portion of the building contains sliding-glass doors that lead from executive offices to a terrace that offers views to the garden below and overlooks the surrounding Westminster area.

Engineered by Ove Arup and Associates, the building is constructed on a concrete frame with gray aluminum cladding. The Arup firm developed an innovative technique to hang the curving glass wall from steel supports. The main structural elements are painted the same red as the supports for the entrance canopy, and the exterior walls of the office wings are almost fully glazed, serving two important purposes for the architect. First, it ensures that the horizontal traffic patterns of the people inside the building are visible, complementing the evident vertical movements of the lifts, both of which are meant to expose and highlight the constant activity and energy of the building's users. Second, Rogers's extensive use of glass walls in the Channel 4 Headquarters reveals his interest in transparency—the glazed entrance wall, for example, functions as a screen through which the visitor can see a series of windowed walls and glass blocks. The view is one of an overlapping sequence of metal and glass that continues until the eye is led through the final glazed wall of the ground-floor restaurant. Rogers intended the visitor to be drawn toward the building by noting the dynamism of its moving elements (such as the elevators) from afar and then visually to peel away each layer and each successive screen by moving through the building. The use of materials that appear light allows for complex, interpenetrating layers while still maximizing the views through and out of the building. The visual lightness was also meant to reduce the effect of a large office building's being placed in an already dense area of the city.

The obvious precedent, both aesthetically and conceptually, for the Channel 4 Headquarters is Rogers's formulation of a high-tech architecture as manifested in his Pompidou Center in Paris (1977, designed with Renzo Piano) and the Lloyd's Building (1987), his only other work in central London. Although smaller than these earlier works, the Channel 4 building reveals many of the same interests and concerns; the exposed steelwork in all three structures, the exterior lifts in the two London buildings and the Pompidou's external escalators, and the flexibility of the interior spaces call to mind the machine imagery and functionalist rhetoric of the early Modern movement. Rogers is part of a continuum that includes early 20th-century celebrations of the machine age as well as the futurist projects of the 1960s British collective, Archigram, whose interest in an adaptable architecture is paralleled in Rogers's work. The design for the Channel 4 Headquarters includes the possibility of reworking the interior space should the building someday serve a new tenant while still ensuring that the overall design housing the changeable aspects remains unchanged.

DEBORAH LEWITTES

See also **Piano, Renzo (Italy); Pompidou Center, Paris; Rogers, Richard (England)**

Further Reading

Burdett, Richard (editor), *Richard Rogers Partnership: Works and Projects*, New York: Monacelli Press, 1996

"Channel 4 Headquarters," *GA Document Extra* 02 (1995)

Davey, Peter, "Channel Vision," *Architectural Review*, 196/1174 (1994)

Davies, Colin, "Broadcast News: Channel 4 Headquarters," *Architecture*, 84/1 (1995)

Powell, Kenneth, *Lloyd's Building: Richard Rogers Partnership*, London: Phaidon, 1994

Powell, Kenneth, "A Building Tuned to Its Users," *Architects' Journal*, 201/14 (1995)

"Richard Rogers Channel 4 Television Headquarters," *A + U*, 10/301 (1995)

"Richard Rogers Partnership: Channel 4 Television Headquarters," *Architectural Design*, 65/9–10 (1995)

Sudjic, Deyan, *The Architecture of Richard Rogers*, London: Fourth Estate and Wordsearch, 1994; New York: Abrams, 1995

Sudjic, Deyan, *Channel 4 Headquarters, London: Architects, Richard Rogers Partnership*, London: Blueprint Media, 1996

CHAPEL OF NOTRE-DAME-DU-HAUT

Designed by Le Corbusier, completed 1956
Ronchamp, France

Le Corbusier's Chapel of Notre-Dame-du-Haut (1956) stands on a hill overlooking the village of Ronchamp, France, just miles from the Swiss border. A pilgrimage site since the 13th century, the building now receives as many students of architecture as worshipers of the Virgin Mary, to whom it is dedicated. Although it is now considered one of the masterpieces of modern architecture and a landmark work in Le Corbusier's formidable oeuvre, the building's peaceful hilltop setting belies a controversial history.

The courting of Le Corbusier (born Charles-Édouard Jeanneret in 1887) began in early 1950, when the task of rebuilding what remained of a war-wrecked chapel on Bourlémont hill was designated to La Société Immoblière (development corporation) de Notre-Dame-du-Haut. The corporation's original intention was to restore what remained of the existing chapel, which had been destroyed by German bombing in 1944. After reviewing the costs of restoration, however, it became clear to members of the corporation that complete reconstruction was a more sound decision. In need of an architect, the group turned to the Commission d'Art Sacré, the body of the French Church that made such recommendations, and specifically to two local members of the commission—Canon Ledeur of Besançon (the commission's secretary) and François Mathey—for suggestions on whom best to solicit for the new design. There was little doubt that they would nominate Le Corbusier.

Skeptical about a project for the Catholic Church, Le Corbusier, who was raised a Protestant, initially refused the offer to submit drawings for the chapel. Just a few months earlier, his design for a subterranean basilica at Sainte-Baume had been rejected, and it was no secret that the architect remained bitter about what he perceived as the Church's lack of vision. However, his interest was piqued on learning more about Ronchamp. The hilltop had been home to a third-century B.C. pagan temple and a number of different structures dating as far back as the 14th century A.D., when church records reveal worshipers first flocking to the site. Informed of the sanctity of the spot, Le Corbusier made his first visit to Ronchamp in June 1950. After many hours spent walking and sketching the hillside, the concept of building on the significant site became more appealing, and the architect began to reconsider.

It was undoubtedly the support and friendship of Ledeur, Mathey, and their colleague clergyman Pierre Marie Alain Couturier that led Le Corbusier to accept the commission and allowed him to carry out the controversial design. All three were leaders of a movement that aimed to revive the French Church through the application of contemporary art and architecture. Together, the trio offered Le Corbusier free rein, and, not surprisingly, Le Corbusier found it impossible to refuse.

The commission left him with a singular opportunity to manifest his belief in the integral relationship between architecture and nature and between nature and religious experience. His career and reputation established, the decision to accept the job was also in keeping with a resolution to take on only work with a personal resonance. The project at Ronchamp satisfied the architect on all counts.

The construction of Notre-Dame-du-Haut began in 1953, after the Besançon Commission d'Art Sacré approved a refined scheme for the building. The building was constructed of walls of sprayed untreated concrete (*béton brut* or *gunnite*) and whitewashed with a coat of plaster to leave a rough surface. In fact, the use of concrete was as much a pragmatic decision as an aesthetic one: Le Corbusier recognized the difficulty of transporting bulky materials up the hillside and the consequent fact that he would "have to put up with sand and cement."

The chapel's sweeping, earthen-colored roof—composed of a pair of parallel six-centimeter concrete shells—contrasts in both color and texture with the coarse, bright-white walls. Likened

Chapel of Notre-Dame-du-Haut (1956), Ronchamp, France, by Le Corbusier
© Dan Delgado *d2 Arch*

to everything from a nun's habit to a ship's prow, the form of the roof was consciously designed by the architect with a crab's shell in mind. The load is not carried by the walls themselves, as it appears to be, but by 16 pillars embedded in the north and south walls. The building's two principal facades orient toward the south and the east and are separated by a pinched wall that swiftly rises as it moves toward the corner. The south facade, with its gently sloping wall punctured by a series of openings for stained glass, holds the chapel's main entrance. Ranging in shape from small slots to deep recesses, the windows reflect the depth of the wall and create a mosaic of light on the interior. Le Corbusier's determination to employ this design element is apparent in his earliest conceptual sketches, but the final design became far more restrained. Adjacent to the wall, a two-ton enameled steel door bears the abstracted image of a giant open hand, a welcoming to those entering the chapel.

Although the architect claimed that the "requirements of religion have had little effect on the design," the eastern facade was specifically created to accommodate an outdoor chapel for 10,000 worshipers, the focal point of the annual pilgrimage masses at the hilltop.

The west facade, the only blind facade on the building, features a double-barrel gutter that runs rainwater into a receiving pool at ground level (rain collection was part of the program given to the architect by the parish). The rain pool contains three pyramids and a cylinder, all in *béton brut*—a sculptural composition vaguely reminiscent of Le Corbusier's roof garden for the Marseilles Unité d'Habitation (1947–53). These geometric elements provide textural and formal contrast to the gentle bulge of the outside wall of the chapel's confessional. The west facade curves around to the north, where a pair of towers are separated by the visitors' entrance.

On entering the chapel, light pierces through the south wall into the darkened space. Punched through the wall's thick membrane, clear windows offer a blurred view of the landscape beyond, painted panes pay tribute to the Virgin Mary, and colored glass filters light throughout the central space. Le Corbusier relieved the weight of the roof on the interior by separating the south and east walls from the ceiling with a narrow strip of light. The floor follows the natural slope of the hillside leading down toward the altar, which is situated beneath the highest point in the chapel. Three interior side chapels offer additional spaces for private services. All are placed in the bases of the chapel's periscope-like towers and benefit from the dramatically filtered light that pours down the towers' shafts.

Le Corbusier conceived of Ronchamp as a three-dimensional work of sculpture to be viewed from all sides and intended visitors to follow what he described as a "promenade architecturale" in order to capture a series of "événements plastiques" (plastic events) when approaching the building and entering its spaces. Le Corbusier's concept of architectural procession was clearly influenced by the architecture of the ancient Greeks and particularly by the staging of the Parthenon on the Athenian Acropolis—the prototypical sanctuary atop a hill and the architect's interpretive model for Ronchamp.

Even before it opened, the building and the architect were mercilessly attacked by critics, the Church, and the citizens of Ronchamp. The chapel was many things to its critics: a highly irrational building, a step backward for the Modern movement, and a nod to archaic technology dressed in modern appliqué. However, supporters saw it as an example of plastic poetry modified by the architect's rationalism, a logical progression in the development of the modernist idiom, and a place of intense beauty and feeling—a bold return to the architect's spiritual roots.

EUGENIA BELL

See also **Church; Corbusier, Le (Jeanneret, Charles-Édouard) (France); Unité d'Habitation, Marseilles**

Further Reading

Gans, Deborah, *The Le Corbusier Guide*, Princeton, New Jersey: Princeton Architectural Press, and London: Architectural Press, 1987; revised edition, New York: Princeton Architectural Press, 2000

Pauly, Daniele, *Le Corbusier: La Chapelle de Ronchamp; The Chapel at Ronchamp* (bilingual French-English edition), Basel and Boston: Birkhäuser, and Paris: Fondation le Le Corbusier, 1997

CHAREAU, PIERRE 1883–1950

Architect and designer, France

The work of Pierre Chareau is emblematic of the confluence of artistic and technological developments of high-modern architecture and design in Paris in the 1920s and 1930s. Endowed with talent, charisma, and good fortune, Chareau became an integral part of a group of progressive artists, designers, and their bourgeois patrons on the Left Bank. Although Chareau was an influential furniture designer, interior decorator, and architect of the period, his legacy hinges on his one architectural masterwork, the Maison de Verre (1932; House of Glass).

Pierre Paul Constant Chareau began his design career at age 16 as a tracing draftsman for the Parisian office of a British furniture and interior design firm, Waring and Gillow. During this professional apprenticeship, Chareau also attended the École des Beaux-Arts from 1900 to 1908. Although he never received a formal degree, he studied a wide variety of artistic disciplines, including painting, music, and architecture, before focusing on interior decoration. In 1904, Chareau married Dollie Dyte, a Londoner teaching English in Paris. This union proved critical to Chareau because it was one of Dollie's students, Annie Bernheim, who later became Chareau's most important patron.

At Waring and Gillow, Chareau rose to the rank of master draftsman before being conscripted into the French army in 1914. Once he was discharged in 1918, he established his own design firm in Paris. His first commission was to design the interiors and furniture for the apartment of Dr. Jean Dalsace and his new wife, Annie Bernheim-Dalsace, Dollie Chareau's former student. The Dalsaces also introduced Chareau to their circle of intellectual compatriots. As a result of his newfound connections, Chareau began to exhibit his furniture and continued to do so through the 1930s. This early furniture consisted of massive wood-framed pieces heavily influenced by the Art Deco style. By 1924 he started designing much lighter furniture using metal frames and surfaces. His work stood at the threshold between the tradition of craft and a modern industrial aesthetic.

By the mid-1920s, Chareau was well established within a group of designers referred to in Paris as *ensembliers*, or architect/decorators. This group consciously resisted the separate categorization of architect, decorator, and furniture designer. Chareau went beyond decorating surfaces by removing walls and traditional moldings of existing apartments to embody new modernist ideals of spatial fluidity and the elimination of ornament. Within the newly configured spaces, he would integrate fixed furniture pieces in conjunction with freestanding furniture arrangements. The results were Cubist-inspired assemblages of volume, surface, texture, and color. After a series of collaborative interior projects done with designer Robert Mallet-Stevens and others, he received his first architectural commission in 1926 for a clubhouse in Beauvallon, France, for Annie Dalsace's uncle.

It is at the Maison de Verre, however, that Chareau most clearly asserts his modernist vision. The Dalsaces commissioned Chareau in 1928 to design their home together with the offices of Dr. Dalsace's gynecological practice. Chareau embodied the avant-garde spirit by using industrial materials for residential construction such as exposed steel framing for the structure, translucent glass blocks for the enclosure, and Pirelli rubber tile on the floor. In addition, Chareau captured the dynamism of modern life by designing a kinetic architecture that could transform habitation of the space. For example, at the bottom of the main staircase, perforated metal screens either prevented the doctor's daytime clients from ascending the stairs or swung out of the way to invite the evening guests up to the great room on the second level. The large double-height space at the top of the stairs became a center of Parisian intellectual activity: it doubled as a theater for musical and literary performances while displaying the Dalsaces's acquired treasures of modern art.

In 1932 the Maison de Verre won Chareau wide recognition in the national and international press: it was clear that he had created a unique, forward-looking architecture. He was invited to join the editorial board of the new progressive architectural journal *L'Architecture d'aujourd'hui,* a position that he maintained throughout the 1930s. Chareau's production and development as an architect, however, were significantly limited by the worsening economic situation in Europe. To survive, he and his wife began to sell their painting collection of modern masters, including Georges Braque, Giorgio de Chirico, Paul Klee, Piet Mondrian, and Pablo Picasso. The only significant commissions that he received in the period leading up to World War II were the renovation of the LTT telephone company offices in 1932 and a weekend house outside Paris for his longtime friend, dancer Djémil Anik, in 1937.

In 1940, Chareau left France for New York to avoid the ravages of war. During the war, he kept busy by organizing exhibitions for the French Cultural Center. In 1947 his last significant commission was a weekend house and studio for the artist Robert Motherwell in East Hampton on Long Island. Here, Chareau adapted a military Quonset hut for the building's shell. A long bank of windows inserted along one edge of the large metal barrel vault and an exposed metal frame supporting the upper level in the interior were only a crude memory of the promise of an industrial aesthetic achieved in the Maison de Verre just 15 years prior.

After his death in New York in 1950, Chareau remained a relatively peripheral figure in 20th-century architecture because of his modest production of built works and the paucity of a written record or philosophy. However, a renewed interest in Chareau's work was evident in the second half of the 20th century, beginning with Kenneth Frampton's 1969 article on the Maison de Verre published in the journal *Perspecta.* Subsequently, Marc Vellay, the grandson of Jean and Annie Dalsace, collaborated with Frampton on the first comprehensive record of Chareau's output in 1984. Symptomatic of Chareau's marginal status, however, is that Frampton, who has been credited with resurrecting Chareau's reputation, did not mention him in his sweeping study of 20th-century architecture, *Modern Architecture: A Critical History,* published in 1980.

PETER H. WIEDERSPAHN

Biography

Born in Bordeaux, France, 3 August 1883; immigrated to the United States in October 1940. Married Dollie Dyte 1904. Studied painting, music, and architecture, École des Beaux-Arts, Paris 1900–08; apprentice in furniture design in the firm of Waring and Gillow, Paris 1908–14. Served in the French Army during World War I. Established private practice in Paris 1918; partners with Bernard Bijvoet 1925–35; a founder of the Union des Artistes Modernes; moved to New York 1940; organized shows for the French Cultural Center. Died in New York 1950.

Selected Works

Clubhouse (now altered), Beauvallon, 1928
Maison de Verre, Paris, 1932
LTT Telephone Company Renovation, Paris, 1932
Djémil Anik House, outside Paris, 1937
Robert Motherwell Studio (destroyed), East Hampton, New York, 1948

Selected Publication

"La Création artistique et l'imitation commerciale," *L'Architecture d'aujourd'hui* 11 (1935)

Further Reading

Baroni, Daniele, "Pierre Chareau, Protagonist of the Modern Movement," *Ottogano,* 21/81 (June 1986)

Blake, Peter, "Chateau Chareau," *Interior Design,* 65/6 (May 1994)

Chareau, Pierre, *La Maison de verre,* edited by Yukio Futagawa, Tokyo: A.D.A. Edita, 1988

Filler, Martin, and Marc Vellay, "House of Glass, Walls of Light: A Beacon of Modernism," *House and Garden,* 155/2 (February 1983)

Frampton, Kenneth, "Maison de verre," *Perspecta,* 12 (1969)

Futagawa, Yukio (editor), *La Maison de verre: Pierre Chareau,* Tokyo: A.D.A. Edita, 1988

Pierre Chareau: Architecte, un art intérieur (exhib. cat.), Paris: Centre Georges Pompidou, 1993

Taylor, Brian Brace, *Pierre Chareau, Designer and Architect,* Cologne: Taschen, 1992

Vellay, Marc, and Kenneth Frampton, *Pierre Chareau, Architect and Craftsman, 1883–1950,* New York: Rizzoli, 1984; London: Thames and Hudson, 1985

CHEN ZHI 1902–

Architect, China

Chinese architect Chen Zhi was born in Hangzhou, Zhejiang Province, in southeastern China. He had received a college education from Tsinghua School in Beijing before he was sent to the United States in 1923 to study architecture. He completed his Master of Architecture in 1928 at the University of Pennsylvania. During his student years, he won the Cope Prize Architectural Competition in 1926. In the summer of 1928, he went to New York to work for Ely J. Kahn for one year and then returned to China.

Chen joined the architecture faculty at Northeastern University in 1929. The school was founded by another University of Pennsylvania graduate, Liang Sicheng, with whom Chen also cooperated for design practice. Their projects included the campus buildings of Jilin University, Changchun City, China. However, Chen did not stay long; in late 1930 he departed for Shanghai.

In Shanghai, Chen established his lifelong career in architecture. In 1933 he was a partner of Huagai Architectural Office, a leading architectural firm in Shanghai for the following two decades. Among their major projects are the office building for the Ministry of Foreign Affairs in Nanjing, the Shanghai Grand Theater, and the Zhejiang Xinye Bank in Shanghai. These designs have reflected the influence of the American Beaux-Arts tradition that Chen and some of his partners studied and assimilated into their own work while in the United States.

In 1952 Chen left private practice to take positions in government-supported design institutions. He was one of the leading technical designers in Shanghai, where he was the chief architect for the East China Architectural Design Company and the president and chief architect of Shanghai Civil Building Design Institute.

Among the major projects that Chen designed or directed are the memorial tomb of Lu Xun, the Shanghai International Seamen's Club in Shanghai, and Friendship Hall in Sudan. Chen also participated in the design of the Memorial Building of Chairman Mao.

Chen's design philosophy emphasized nationalism in architecture. He believed that the new designs in China should reflect traditional and national architectural features and highlight the local characteristics in style. When he designed the Lu Xun Memorial Museum in Shanghai, he treated the gable walls with three steps—a typical feature from the vernacular architecture in Lu Xun's hometown, Shaoxing.

However, Chen does not favor an architectural conservatism. When he designed a commercial street in Minghang, he tried to express a new spirit with well-balanced volumes that, in the language of modernism, marry form with functionalism.

YUNSHENG HUANG

Biography

Born in Hangzhou, Zhejiang Province, China in 1902. Attended the Tsinghua School in Beijing, and the University of Pennsylvania, Philadelphia. Taught at Northeastern University and Zhijiang University in China. Chen's architectural teaching in Shanghai was affiliated with Zhijiang University, where he was department chairman, 1949–52.

Since 1952, Chen Zhi had been the chief architect at East China Architectural Design Company until his retirement.

CHICAGO, ILLINOIS

Although Chicago architecture has, within modernist architectural histories, been conflated with the "Chicago School," a term borrowed from literary criticism and applied to the distinctive residential work of Louis Sullivan, Frank Lloyd Wright, and their contemporaries, Chicago architecture is, in fact, more diverse and less insular than the modernist narrative suggested (Condit, Giedion, Hitchcock). Chicago School scholars' views were popularized in publications such as *Chicago's Famous Buildings* (1965), which asserted that "almost the whole history of what we call 'contemporary design' can be examined in Chicago. For Chicago is the birthplace of modern architecture" (see Siegel, 1993). More recently, however, some architectural historians have debunked the myth of the Chicago School and shown that other locales simultaneously witnessed similar design shifts.

Architectural historians have studied a range of types and styles, some typically American, some more innovative. Chicago designers, mostly recent migrants and immigrants, set many trends and standards in the 19th and 20th centuries. Several factors influenced the city's prominence on the national and international scene. Chicago, grid platted in 1830 and incorporated in 1837, grew rapidly into a great metropolis in large part because of its auspicious location. The city lies near the geographic center of the vast and fertile plains region, blessed also with abundant natural resources. Its location at the southwestern tip of the Great Lakes system and near the Mississippi River allowed Chicago to develop during the 19th century into a center of trade, finance, industry, and rail and water transport, second only to New York City. From the beginning this urban center attracted entrepreneurs. Their wealth and cultural aspirations supported skilled professionals and artists in many fields, including architecture. In many respects, the speculative fever of the 1830s persisted through the end of the millennium. Generous patronage for significant architectural works abounded, although only at the end of the century did preservationist ideals take root. Surviving works of special merit are embedded in the more common fabric of Chicago's built environment, which stretches from the downtown Loop, where the Chicago River meets Lake Michigan, across the flat prairie through an ever-expanding fan of suburbs.

In Chicago's Loop dozens of tall, speculative office buildings were constructed from 1880 through 1929 as investors sought to accommodate large and small businesses. The Marquette Building (1895), developed by the Brooks brothers and designed by Holabird and Roche, established a characteristic formula. This 16-story steel-framed structure has a U-shaped plan and cladding of dark brick and terra-cotta. The flat classicizing ornament is articulated into a base, shaft, and capital, thus giving the enormous block a sense of order within the gridded streetscape. The Conway Building (1915), by Graham, Anderson, Probst and White, is organized around a square light court, like many of Chicago's multitenant office buildings. Cream-colored terra-cotta ornament of classical character forms the tripartite schema of the exterior cladding. This structure, developed by the estate of merchant Marshall Field, became the model for premier commercial structures throughout the country during the 1920s. The fact that it resembles the earlier Marshall Field and Co. State Street Store (1902–14), by D.H. Burnham and Company, illustrates how these large Chicago design firms established the nation's business vernacular in the first decades of the 20th century. More distinctive are the pre–Depression-era corporate headquarters, such as the Wrigley Building (1924, Graham, Anderson, Probst and White) and the Gothic Revival Tribune Building (1925) by New Yorkers Howells and Hood. Another 1920s newspaper headquarters, the Chicago Daily News Building (1929, Holabird and Root), was more innovative as the first Chicago building to utilize air rights over railroad tracks. It was designed in the moderne-style stepped-back skyscraper type introduced in 1922 by Eliel Saarinen's second-place Tribune Tower scheme and replicated throughout the city and the nation.

Chicago's suburbs host significant structures from every decade of the century. Lake Forest, along the west shore of Lake Michigan, has possibly the nation's first automobile-oriented shopping center, Market Square (1917), designed by Howard Van Doren Shaw as a picturesque amalgam of European and American motifs. Oak Park, west of downtown, was home to Frank Lloyd Wright; he worked there and in Chicago from 1887 to 1910. Wright's suburban prairie house type, formulated around 1901, expressed a sense of shelter without emulating any historic model. His house (1903) for manufacturing company president Ward Willits in Highland Park extends in four directions on a cross-axial plan, anchored at the center by a fireplace core.

For those who wanted high-rise living without sacrificing domesticity or conventional imagery, Chicago architects designed many elegantly detailed apartment buildings. Some of Chicago's richest men commissioned their friend Andrew Rebori to design for them the 18-story luxury cooperative at 2430 North Lake Shore (1926), just one of many such structures overlooking lakefront parks on the north and south sides of the city.

These parks form part of an extensive public works program undertaken in Chicago following the World's Columbian Exposition of 1893. Civic designs were guided by the 1909 Plan of Chicago, sponsored by the Commercial Club. This ambitious document epitomized the City Beautiful movement in its depiction of an orderly and monumental urban region. Among the improvements that accorded with the plan were the south-side neighborhood parks and field houses (1903–11, Olmsted Bros. and Burnham and Co.); the bascule bridges across the Chicago River, notably Michigan Avenue Bridge (1920, Thomas G. Pihlfeldt, Hugh E. Young, and Edward H. Bennett); and several museums, including the Field Museum (1919) and Shedd Aquarium (1930), both by Graham, Anderson, Probst and White. All these structures are neoclassical in style. Private patronage also produced magnificent public buildings, for example, the Gothic Revival–style campus of the University of Chicago, which includes the Rockefeller Memorial Chapel (1928, Bertram Grosvenor Goodhue).

The Great Depression slowed Chicago building for over a decade. During 1932 the value of new construction shrank to 1 percent of the 1926 total. Nevertheless, some projects kept designers and builders at work. The 1933 Century of Progress Exposition was supported by magnates such as Julius Rosenwald of Sears, Roebuck and Company, Philip Wrigley, and Robert McCormick of the *Chicago Tribune*. It played a major part in the acceptance of modern architecture in Chicago during the next decades. Non-Chicagoans led the design team: Raymond Hood, Paul Philippe Cret, Ralph T. Walker, Harvey Wiley Corbett, and Arthur Brown, Jr. Chicago architects who participated were Edward H. Bennett, John A. Holabird, and Hubert Burnham. Louis Skidmore was selected to direct exhibition design, and he appointed his brother-in-law, Nathaniel Owings, to oversee concessions. They would later form Skidmore, Owings and Merrill (SOM), a design firm that profoundly shaped the Chicago skyline. The theme of the fair was "Science Finds—Industry Applies—Man Conforms." The official guidebook emphasized practicality, efficiency, and economy through the use of prefabricated and mass-produced materials. Its rhetoric resembled that in the 1932 New York Museum of Modern Art Modern International Style exhibition catalog. Less aesthetically precocious were the New Deal public works that saved Chicago's economy. Projects included the expansion of Lincoln Park, North Lake Shore Drive, public transit improvements, and large public housing projects: the Jane Addams Houses (1938), Trumbull Park Homes (1938), and Frances Cabrini Homes (1942 and later).

Rich and poor Chicagoans live in high-rise apartment buildings. Shortly after World War II several innovative large-scale projects were constructed on the "Gold Coast" north of downtown. Wealthy entrepreneurs, such as Herbert Greenwald and the McCormicks, financed these towers and commissioned modernist architect Ludwig Mies van der Rohe. His Promontory Point apartment complex (1949) used a reinforced-concrete frame. In collaboration with others, he designed two identical apartment towers (1949–52) at 860–880 North Lake Shore Drive. Mies employed a distinctive vocabulary of form: a clearly articulated structural grid based on an abstract mathematical order and filled by glass walls. Skidmore, Owings and Merrill's Miesian Lake Meadows Apartments (1950–60) makes up one of the city's largest postwar redevelopment projects. It was intended by the New York Life Insurance Company to provide racially integrated housing for middle- and upper-income families and included a shopping center, community club, and office building. The luxurious Lake Point Tower (1965–68), designed by George C. Schipporeit and John C. Heinrich (both Mies protégés), used an undulating three-lobed design inspired by a 1919 Mies project.

Mies' Modern style, the basis of the second Chicago School, was employed for many institutional and commercial projects. His structurally expressive Illinois Institute of Technology Campus (1939–58) was based on a 24-foot module: the bay span of steel and concrete frames. Mies designed Chicago's Federal Center (1964, 1975), a grouping of three buildings (a 30-story courthouse and office building, a 45-story office tower, and a single-story post office) oriented around a central plaza. In 1965 the combined firms of C.F. Murphy Associates; Loebl, Schlossman and Bennett; and Skidmore, Owings and Merrill employed a Miesian vocabulary for the Civic Center (now the Richard J. Daley Center). Skidmore, Owings and Merrill designed a host of office buildings in the Miesian spirit, including the Inland Steel Building (1955–57). Its stainless-steel utility tower contains service elements, allowing rental spaces in the adjoining blue-green glass tower to be free of structural obstructions. The 19-story building was one of the first tall buildings erected downtown after the Depression. This firm explored capabilities of materials and structural systems to the fullest extent in multiuse projects, such as the John Hancock Center (1965–70) and the Sears Tower (1974). The former building uses an exterior bracing system to attain a height of 1,107 feet, whereas the latter has a unique structural system of bundled tubes and rises to 1,454 feet. Its black aluminum–sheathed steel frame was the tallest building in the world at the time of construction.

Other architects of the postwar period employed more expressive or symbolic forms. The Crow Island School in suburban Winnetka, by Finnish immigrant architects Eliel and Eero Saarinen with Perkins, Wheeler and Will (1939–40), is a low, brick-clad structure. The picturesque massing resulted from the articulation of functional units. This was one of the first schools in the country to respond to the principles of progressive education. Bertrand Goldberg's Marina City (1963) was realized as two circular, 60-story concrete-frame towers. Loads are carried mainly by cylindrical cores. Forty floors of apartments rise above an 18-story parking garage and two-story utility space. Chicagoan Walter Netsch, a designer in the Skidmore, Owings and Merrill office, applied his "field theory" of design at the University of Illinois Chicago Circle Campus (1965–77). Netsch developed a generative principle of design based on rotated squares, resulting in elaborate and complex interpenetrations of space. Harry Weese's sculptural Seventeenth Church of Christ, Scientist (1968) was inspired by the designs of his friend Eero Saarinen. Its semicircular reinforced-concrete form is sheathed in travertine and capped with a lead-coated roof. Weese's Metropolitan Correctional Center (1975), a federal prison downtown, is an exposed reinforced-concrete building with a triangular footprint and abstractly ordered slit windows illuminating perimeter cells.

The firm of Naess and Murphy (later C.F. Murphy Associates and Murphy/Jahn) proposed a "new synthesis" of modern and historic elements. Their Prudential Building (1955) was inspired by architectural forms of the 1920s. At O'Hare International Airport, opened in 1963, their earliest Mies-inspired terminals were augmented in 1987 by Munich-born Helmut Jahn's United Airlines Terminal, whose forms recall railroad sheds. Among the firm's other projects are the Chicago Board of Trade addition (1981), complementing the original 1930 Art Deco design of Holabird and Root, and the controversial State of Illinois Center (1981–84), with its curvilinear glass exterior, terminating in a truncated ellipse, and a 17-story atrium. In the 1980s responses to specific sites and programs led to other signature designs in downtown Chicago. For example, New Yorkers Kohn Pedersen Fox designed the 333 West Wacker Building (1983) with a curved face, defining the bend of the Chicago River. Its green reflective glass facade rises 36 stories. The same firm designed the 311 South Wacker Building (1990), the world's tallest concrete-frame building. Hammond, Beeby and Babka employed a combination of forms drawn from Beaux-Arts classicism and 1880s commercial buildings in their 1988 competition entry for the Harold Washington Library Center, the country's largest public library building. It is located in the south Loop and was completed in 1991. In contrast, the firm of Tigerman, McCurry used a Gothic vocabulary to articulate the exterior of their Chicago Bar Association Building (1990).

Among historical restoration projects since the 1960s are some of Chicago's most beloved monuments: the Auditorium Building (1889, Adler and Sullivan, restored 1967 by Harry Weese), Orchestra Hall (1905, D.H. Burnham and Company, renovated 1967 by Harry Weese), the Art Institute (1893–1916, Shepley, Rutan and Coolidge, lobby restored 1987 by John Vinci), and Navy Pier (1916, Charles Sumner Frost, ballroom restored 1976 by city architect Jerome Butler). Since 1991 VOA Associates of Chicago have worked with public officials to turn Navy Pier into a multifunctional festival environment, containing diverse public, cultural, entertainment, and commercial facilities. Navy Pier differs significantly from earlier modernist single-purpose commercial projects, such as Old Orchard Shopping Center (1957, Loebl, Schlossman and Bennett) in Skokie. The Navy Pier project typifies Postmodern urbanism in the United States.

JOAN DRAPER AND ROBERT NAUMAN

See also **Burnham, Daniel H. (United States); Century of Progress Exposition, Chicago (1933); Chicago School; Giedion, Sigfried (Switzerland); Goodhue, Bertram Grosvenor (United States); Graham, Anderson, Probst and White (United States); Hitchcock, Henry-Russell (United States); Holabird, William, and John Wellborn Root (United States); Illinois Institute of Technology, Chicago; Jahn, Helmut (United States); Kohn Pederson Fox (United States); Mies van der Rohe, Ludwig (Germany); Office Building; Plan of Chicago; Sears Tower, Chicago; Skidmore, Owings and Merrill (United States); Skyscraper; Sullivan, Louis (United States); Tribune Tower International Competition (1922), Chicago; Wright, Frank Lloyd (United States)**

Further Reading

Bluestone, Daniel M., *Constructing Chicago*, New Haven, Connecticut: Yale University Press, 1991

Chicago Architects Design: A Century of Architectural Drawings from the Art Institute of Chicago, Chicago: Art Institute of Chicago, and New York: Rizzoli, 1982

Condit, Carl W., *Chicago, 1910–29: Building, Planning, and Urban Technology*, Chicago: University of Chicago Press, 1973

Condit, Carl W., *Chicago, 1930–70: Building, Planning, and Urban Technology*, Chicago: University of Chicago Press, 1974

Mayer, Harold M., and Richard C. Wade, *Chicago: Growth of a Metropolis*, Chicago: University of Chicago Press, 1969

Siegel, Arthur (editor), *Chicago's Famous Buildings: A Photographic Guide to the City's Architectural Landmarks and Other Notable Buildings*, Chicago: University of Chicago Press, 1965; 4th edition, revised and enlarged, edited by Franz Schulze and Kevin Harrington, 1993

Stamper, John W., *Chicago's North Michigan Avenue: Planning and Development, 1900–1930*, Chicago: University of Chicago Press, 1991

Willis, Carol, *Form Follows Finance: Skyscrapers and Skylines in New York and Chicago*, New York: Princeton Architectural Press, 1995

Zukowsky, John (editor), *Chicago Architecture, 1872–1922: Birth of a Metropolis* (exhib. cat.), Munich: Prestel Verlag, and Chicago: Art Institute of Chicago, 1987

Zukowsky, John (editor), *Chicago Architecture and Design, 1923–1993: Reconfiguration of an American Metropolis* (exhib. cat.), Munich: Prestel Verlag, and Chicago: Art Institute of Chicago, 1993

CHICAGO SCHOOL

Named for the city in which it materialized and flourished, the Chicago School of skyscraper design marked the emergence of the first truly American style of architecture. A concern for the economic use of materials in a speculative environment resulted in a radically new solution for the high-rise building, quite removed from the historicism and eclecticism of the past. Beginning in the mid-1870s and peaking in the early 1900s, the skyline of Chicago underwent an amazing transformation, evoking the "Brown City" designation made so famous in the critical work by Lewis Mumford. The so-called death of the Chicago School style in 1922 resulted in part from the ever-increasing popularity of the White City and coincided with the Chicago Tribune Tower Competition. Yet, with the 1938 arrival of Ludwig Mies van der Rohe at the Armour Institute of Technology (later renamed Illinois Institute of Technology), a so-called Second Chicago School of architecture emerged. This synthesis of late 19th-century structural efficiency and mid–20th-century materials demonstrated the long-ranging contributions of Chicago School architects, such as Louis Sullivan, on skyscraper design and modern architecture as a whole.

In 1871 the Great Fire decimated the central business district in Chicago, destroying 18,000 buildings and causing over $200 million in property damage. An area four miles long and nearly three-quarters of a mile wide was affected. Yet from this devastating loss, Chicago arose like a phoenix, reborn from the ashes, as speculators funded an enormous amount of commercial high-rise building. Their desire for economical and functional buildings contributed nearly as much to the aesthetic of the Chicago School as did the architects who flooded there seeking to define the skyscraper. The primary characteristics of the late 19th-century Chicago School included the economic use of and experimentation with modern materials, resulting in little applied ornamentation and a greater use of large glass windows.

As is the case in many urban centers, tremendous land costs made it desirable to build tall and to build in a very concentrated area. Architects responded to the challenges presented by speculators. In order to reap the greatest profit from their investment, investors required maximum profitability from the interior space, so high-rent offices with windows providing adequate natural lighting were preferred. The Chicago window was developed and was repeated across the wall surfaces: a large central pane flanked on either side by narrow, movable sash windows. In addition, as dictated by the building plots and in the desire for greater interior light, Chicago School skyscrapers tended to be either tall and narrow or to possess a U-shaped light court. Steel-cage construction provided far greater fire protection than wrought- or cast-iron framing, a concern in a city that had so recently suffered a catastrophic fire. The uniformity of the steel-frame grid improved construction time and aided in the ease of erection, yet the sodden soil demanded the use of caisson foundations and limited the heights to which architects could build. Masonry or terra-cotta encased the steel frame not only to express it clearly but also to provide fireproofing. With restrictive budgets, speculators, such as the Brooks brothers of Boston, also frowned on excessive and expensive ornamentation.

Most discussions of the Chicago School have emphasized the lack of exterior ornamentation and have focused on the aesthetics of form. This is not entirely the case, as recent scholars such as Bruegmann and Willis have argued. Speculators were willing to pay for some degree of ornamentation if it appealed to prospective renters. Thus, embellishments commonly appeared in lobbies or in courtyards, anywhere easily visible. However, the overt large-scale application of historicism did not seem appropriate, considering the use of modern technology. Thus, the bare-bones structural form of the steel-framed building became primarily its own ornament, along with its curtain walls filled with glass.

The most prominent Chicago School firms were Daniel Burnham and John Wellborn Root, William Holabird and Martin Roche, and Dankmar Adler and Louis Sullivan. These firms designed and built some of the best-known examples of Chicago School architecture, mostly in Chicago, although some of Sullivan's best work was in other cities. The influential figure that drew most of these men together was the structural pioneer William Le Baron Jenney, whose Home Insurance Building (1884–85) masterfully handled a steel rather than an iron frame for the first time. Burnham, Holabird, Roche, and Sullivan had worked in the office of Jenney during the 1870s. The important aesthetic influence on these men was Henry Hobson Richardson's tour de force, the Marshall Field Wholesale Store (1885–87) in Chicago. The strong simplicity and rationalization of form displayed by Richardson's structure galvanized similar approaches by Burnham and Root in their masonry-block Monadnock Building (1884–91, with its steel-cage addition, 1891–93), Holabird and Roche's Tacoma Building (1887–89), and Adler and Sullivan's Auditorium Building (1886–90).

Louis Sullivan in particular served as a strong proponent of the Chicago School style not only through his buildings but also through his theoretical writings. In his "The Tall Office Building Artistically Considered" (1896), Sullivan argued that the uniform solution for high-rise form lies in organicism, "that the life is recognizable in its expression, that form ever follows function." Thus, the natural verticality of the skyscraper, drawn by the steel-frame elements, should be articulated, and a clear distinction should be made between the base of the building, its honeycombed office middle, and its machinery top. In reality, Sullivan exploited mainly the vertical I beams, although the horizontal elements also maintained the grid, and at times he simply added decorative vertical elements that did not correspond to load-bearing members. He also continued to employ ornament on his facades, mostly terra-cotta Art Nouveau–like germinating seeds and leafy plants. Many European architects, such as the Adolf Loos, eschewed such details and rejected ornamentation as "degenerate," like the tattoos worn by criminals. However, his practical approach to handling the skyscraper also inspired European architects, such as the Dutchman Hendrick Petrus Berlage, who visited Chicago in 1911. In addition, Frank Lloyd Wright transmitted Louis Sullivan's ideas of organicism, not only in ornamentation but also in terms of form, to Europeans through his writings and work, as seen in his 1910 Wasmuth Portfolio. These important European connections, particularly through the Dutch rationalists and the German Werkbund, contributed to the spread of Chicago School ideals and helped facilitate the second Chicago School by expatriates displaced by World War II.

In the first decade of the 20th century, the Chicago School reached its zenith, especially in such works as Holabird and Roche and Louis Sullivan's Gage Group (1899–1900) and Sullivan's Carson Pirie Scott store (1898–99, 1902–04). The empha-

860–880 Lake Shore Drive Apartments (1948–51), designed by Ludwig Mies van der Rohe, Chicago
© Johnson Architectural Images/GreatBuildings.com

sis on modular design, with large amounts of glass surface and still somewhat historicist masonry, dominated the Chicago skyline and crept into other midwestern cities, such as St. Louis, Detroit, Cleveland, and Pittsburgh. Yet the aesthetic changed, as American architects just could not quite make a total commitment to modernism and reverted to a Beaux-Arts–inspired classicism that affected form, ornamentation, and materials. The event that spurred on this architectural reversal was the World's Columbian Exposition of 1893, coordinated by Daniel Burnham. Burnham's firm, D.H. Burnham and Company, and its successor firm, Graham, Anderson, Probst and White, came to dominate major high-rise design in the period leading up to the Great Depression in the style known as commercial, or Beaux-Arts, classicism. Replacing the characteristic flat roof was a more ornamental top, and the emphasis on heavy masonry over glass returned. New zoning laws in Chicago as well as other cities encouraged the setback style over the tall narrow or even U-shaped Chicago School type.

The 1922 Chicago Tribune Tower Competition substantiated the comeback of historicism in skyscraper design as Raymond Hood's winning Gothic-inspired creation beat out Eliel Saarinen's modernist design in the most important international architectural competition of the early 20th century. Instead of being a showcase for the Chicago School style, the competition ended up displaying the new conservatism of American design and hinting at the future ascendancy of European modernism. Interestingly, European entries, such as Walter Gropius and Adolf Meyer's, demonstrated a far greater appreciation for the Chicago School aesthetic than did those of native-born architects by referencing motifs such as the Chicago window. These Europeans had virtually no experience (except on paper) in designing commercial high-rise buildings, a primarily American phenomenon up until the post–World War II era. Thus, they were far more willing to embrace technological developments and imaginatively pursue new aesthetic solutions.

The German architect Ludwig Mies van der Rohe had demonstrated a substantial understanding of the Chicago School style in his Friedrichstrasse Office Building Project (1921) in Berlin with its honeycomb repetition of offices and lack of ornamentation. His early, unexecuted designs for office buildings possessed a rather organic sculptural quality, with undulating curves rather than straight lines, but he quickly moved away from this. By the time he arrived in Chicago to teach at the Armour Institute in 1938, he had begun to synthesize his ideas of material integrity and structural honesty with the tenets of the Chicago School. What he rejected was the use of heavy masonry or terra-cotta cladding over the steel cage. For him, the pure expression of materials meant exposing the frame and making it flush with the glass curtain wall, as visible in his Lake Shore Drive Apartments (1948–51) in Chicago. His masterpiece Seagram Building (1954–58) in New York, done with Philip Johnson, reveals the refinements that Mies made to the Chicago School style. He tempered the "proud, soaring" structure by emphasizing the monotonous horizontal banding of windows wrapping around the entire building. The steel grid dominates, creating a precise exercise in modulation heavily influenced by classical rhythms and order.

Coincidentally (or perhaps not), at the same time that Mies was reevaluating the Chicago School style, architectural historian Carl Condit published his landmark study *The Rise of the Skyscraper* (1952), which appraised the original Chicago School. With subsequent revisions and expansions by the author, now retitled *The Chicago School of Architecture*, Condit's remains the best work on this commercial style.

The so-called Second Chicago School, centered in Chicago and led by Mies until his death in 1969, emphasized bold structural form and expressive use of modern materials. The skeletal quality inherent in steel-cage construction was worshiped, not hidden behind masonry. Often International Style elements, such as *pilotis* or ribbon windows, merged with the Miesian glass block, creating a hybrid of modernism unique to American cities and American-based firms. The early work of Skidmore, Owings and Merrill adheres to these tenets, as visible in their early masterpieces the Lever House (1952) in New York and the Inland Steel Building (1954–58) in Chicago. Here, the glass box revealed the full maturation of the first Chicago School in the economic use of materials and modernist aesthetics that reject all historicism and ornamentation.

Skidmore, Owings and Merrill's John Hancock Tower (1970) in Chicago, with its exoskeletal cross bracing and clearly vertical articulation of structural members, signaled the ending of the Miesian manifestation of the Chicago School style. Postmodernism thus emerged, reconnecting with pre–Chicago School historicism. Yet, even in this form, a demonstration of the Chicago School heritage continued to manifest itself in either overt or subtle ways. Often these were found in Chicago-trained or Chicago-based architects, suggesting a form of architectural osmosis occurring. A prime example is Helmut Jahn, whose Xerox Center (1977–80) in Chicago appears very much like a stripped-down version of Sullivan's Carson Pirie Scott store. In a contextual way, Postmodern structures in Chicago and elsewhere have attempted to visually embrace the older Chicago School–style structures through the use of reflective plate glass and complementary height lines.

VALERIE S. GRASH

See also **Berlage, Hendrik Petrus (Netherlands); Burnham, Daniel H. (United States); Carson Pirie Scott Store, Chicago; Graham, Anderson, Probst and White (United States); Gropius, Walter (Germany); Holabird, William, and Martin Roche (United States); Hood, Raymond (United States); International Style; Lever House, New York; Loos, Adolf (Austria); Mies van der Rohe, Ludwig (Germany); Seagram Building, New York; Skidmore, Owings and Merrill (United States); Skyscraper; Sullivan, Louis (United States); Tribune Tower International Competition (1922), Chicago**

Further Reading

The best-known and most oft-quoted source on the Chicago School is Condit. For varying degrees of discussion on the manifestation of the Chicago School in the 20th century, see Bluestone, Goldberger, Huxtable, Pierson, Van Leewen, and Willis. The latter is particularly representative of current scholarship that reevaluates the skyscraper as economic indicator, not just aesthetic object. Andrew, Bruegmann, and Schulze handle individual Chicago School-inspired architects, while Berlage, Mumford, and Sullivan represent original sources.

Andrew, David S., *Louis Sullivan and the Polemics of Modern Architecture: The Present against the Past*, Urbana: University of Illinois Press, 1985

Berlage, Hendrik Petrus, *Hendrik Petrus Berlage: Thoughts on Style, 1886–1909*, translated by Iain Boyd Whyte and Wim de Wit, Santa Monica, California: Getty Center for the History of Art and the Humanities, 1996

Bluestone, Daniel M., *Constructing Chicago*, New Haven, Connecticut: Yale University Press, 1991

Bruegmann, Robert, *The Architects and the City: Holabird & Roche of Chicago, 1880–1918*, Chicago: University of Chicago Press, 1997

Condit, Carl W., *The Rise of the Skyscraper*, Chicago: University of Chicago Press, 1952; revised edition, as *The Chicago School of Architecture: A History of Commercial and Public Building in the Chicago Area, 1875–1925*, Chicago: University of Chicago Press, 1964

Goldberger, Paul, *The Skyscraper*, New York: Knopf, 1981

Huxtable, Ada Louise, *The Tall Building Artistically Reconsidered: The Search for a Skyscraper Style*, New York: Pantheon, 1984

Mumford, Lewis, *The Brown Decades: A Study of the Arts in America, 1865–1895*, New York: Harcourt Brace, 1931

Pierson, William Harvey, and William H. Jordy, *American Buildings and Their Architects*, 4 vols., Garden City, New York: Doubleday, 1970–78

Schulze, Franz, *Mies Van Der Rohe: A Critical Biography*, Chicago: University of Chicago Press, 1985

Sullivan, Louis, "The Tall Office Building Artistically Considered" (1896), in *America Builds: Source Documents in American Architecture and Planning*, edited by Leland M. Roth, New York: Harper and Row, 1983

Van Leeuwen, Thomas A.P., *The Skyward Trend of Thought: Five Essays on the Metaphysics of the American Skyscraper*, The Hague: AHA Books, 1986; as *The Skyward Trend of Thought: The Metaphysics of the American Skyscraper*, Cambridge, Massachusetts: MIT Press, 1988

Willis, Carol, *Form Follows Finance: Skyscrapers and Skylines in New York and Chicago*, New York: Princeton Architectural Press, 1995

CHILE

Chile is characterized by geographic isolation. Elongated and narrow, the country is confined by strong natural barriers: a bleak desert on the north, the freezing Antarctic area on the south, the towering Andes mountain chain on the east, and the Pacific Ocean on its entire western side. This separation, combined with the absence of a strong pre-Hispanic culture such as those that highly influenced other Latin American countries, greatly shaped the nation's architecture during the 20th century.

Because the population is mostly of European origin, there is a discontinuity between the cultural links with a different continent and the great distances from all the major centers of Western civilization. Architects and planners struggle to find Chile's own image, with very little historic precedent.

In the first two decades of the 20th century, Chilean architecture was dominated by a strong academic tradition. The influence of the École des Beaux-Arts produced important institutional and residential buildings. The Palace of Beaux-Arts (1910), by Emilio Jecquier, combined Bourbon language and diverse ornamental motifs. Jecquier also produced the buildings for the Catholic University in Santiago (1914), a complex of excellent harmony and urban significance. Any reaction to the academic style was slow and marked by discontinuity. Diverse movements were adopted according to the circumstances dictated by client needs or representational purposes, but the intense theoretical debate and the search for newness that characterized turn-of-the-century European architecture were absent in Chile.

The most important architects of the 1920s and early 1930s were Luciano Kulczewsky, Ricardo Larraín Bravo, Miguel Dávila, and Ricardo González Cortés, architects who exemplified a variety of current trends, including Art Nouveau, neo-Colonial expressions, and Art Deco tendencies.

The democratic government of Alessandri Palma in 1920 and later the dictatorship of Carlos Ibáñez began the process of modernization as well as the growth of administration and public services. In 1928 an earthquake hit the city of Talca. All these factors intensified Chile's modernization and brought rationalization in construction techniques.

A representative Art Nouveau building, presently used as the College of Architects of Santiago, was designed by Luciano Kulczewsky (1920). His own house (1920) was designed in the Gothic Revival style, another indication of Chile's conservative tastes. Looking to regional traditions, another prominent architect, Ricardo González Cortés, combined decoration inspired from aboriginal Mapuche forms and Art Deco. Two representative pieces of this tendency are the Caja de Crédito Hipotecario (1930) in Santiago and the Building of Public Services (1935) in Talca. This combination of regional forms and European styles indicated a desire to define a representative style.

Concurrently, the influence of the Chicago School manifested in the growing cities of Santiago and Valparaíso. The first skyscraper, the Ariztía (1921), was built in Santiago by Alberto Cruz Montt and Ricardo Larraín Bravo.

Rationalist architecture arrived in Chile when a new generation of architects returned from Europe after visiting important Modern monuments. Representative of this generation, Rodolfo Oyarzún, Roberto Dávila, Sergio Larraín, and Alfredo Johnson combined classical compositional devices with elements of modernism. Among the first modernist buildings, the Oberpaur (1930) in Santiago, by Sergio Larraín and Jorge Arteaga, incorporated elongated windows and a free plan. Similarly, the Hotel Burnier (1930) in Osorno was designed in a modernist language by Carlos Buchmann.

In his important and influential 1929 visit to Argentina, Le Corbusier met the Chilean diplomat Matias Errázuriz; the following year Le Corbusier designed a small vacation home for him, located in Zapallar. Together with the house for Madame Mandrot, near Toulon, the project for the Errázuriz house (unbuilt) was a radical departure from the white, purist architecture of the 1920s. Although the impact of this new style of house and the use of local materials did not immediately influence architecture in Chile, once regionalist styles were legitimated outside the country (in Finland and Mexico), they gained acceptance among Chilean professionals.

The assimilation of rationalist principles and a purist language characterized the 1930s. Rationalism dominated in the work of Sergio Larraín, Roberto Dávila, and Alfredo Johnson. These efforts were furthered when Dávila worked with Peter Behrens and Le Corbusier in 1932. The restaurant Cap Ducal (1936), by Roberto Dávila, is located in Viña del Mar, overlooking the Pacific Ocean, and exemplifies the modernist Chilean style. The Santa Lucia Building (1934) in Santiago, by Sergio Larraín and Jorge Arteaga, uses forms of refined modernism including circular windows. The Hogar Parque Cousiño (1939), by Aguirre and Rodríguez, isolated from any other urban reference, shows the assimilation of Bauhaus-designed elements—such as asymmetrical composition, *pilotis* (stilts), elongated windows, a terrace garden, and a free plan—combined with a rationalist formula.

In 1939 an earthquake in Chillán, the presidency of Aguirre Cerda, and the beginning of World War II created a new context for the development of a modern architecture in Chile. During the 1940s architects in Chile continued their experimentation with modernist forms. The Maritime Biology Laboratory in Montemar (1944), by Enrique Gebhard, shows the strong influence of Brazilian modernism. Also important were the Hogar Social Hipodromo Chile (1941), by Gebhard and Aguirre, which used modernist materials such as glass, brick, and concrete combined with a regional stone for its walls.

The publication of *Arquitectura y Construción* magazine, the incorporation of Chile in 1946 to CIAM (Congrès Internationaux d'Architecture Moderne), and Josef Albers's visit to the country in 1953 established modernist ideals in Chile. In the 1950s the proposals of CIAM influenced several habitation complexes, among them the Unidad Vecinal Portales (1957) by Carlos Bresciani, Fernando Castillo, Carlos Huidobro, and Hector Valdéz, a building that incorporated for the first time in Chile the separation of vehicular and pedestrian circulation.

After World War II the influence of American culture and the dominance of the International Style were evident. The new typology of a platform and tower appeared, as in the case of the Plaza de Armas building (1955), by Sergio Larraín, Emilio Duhart, Osvaldo Larraín, Sanfuentes, and Jaime Larraín. Another example is the Arturo Prat building (1956), by S. Larraín and Duhart. Parallel to the full incorporation of the International Style in the 1950s, some architects began to pay more attention to significant differences in architecture throughout the many regions of Chile. For example, the Hotel Antumalal (1952) in Pucón, by Jorge Elton, combines aboriginal craft, materials from the area, and landscape.

The 1960s were characterized by a new generation of architects and a diversity of tendencies. Emilio Duhart, who studied under Walter Gropius and later, in 1952, worked for six months with Le Corbusier in the project for Chandigarh, applied his experience to the building for the United Nations in Vitacura, near Santiago. Known as CEPAL (Comisión Económica para América Latina), it was designed in 1966 in collaboration with Christian de Groote. Duhart proposed a strong geometry with a simple square shape, an elongated body with a sculptural conic shape and expressive details. The building recalls the enclosed shape of Chandigarh's Palace of the Assembly. The strong plastic shapes contrast in their abstraction with the presence of the Andes in the background.

The lasting influence of Le Corbusier is seen in the Benedictine Monastery in Las Condes, Santiago de Chile. This monastery was built in a time spanning almost 30 years. The unity reached through diverse interventions is the most important lesson of the complex. The monastery was designed by Jaime Bellalta in 1954 and the cemetery by Brother Martin Correa in 1954. In 1964 P. Gros planned the hostel, and in 1965 Brothers Martin Correa and Gabriel Guardia designed the church. Jorge Swinburn planned the refectory (1974), while R. Irarrával designed both the access plaza (1975) and the library (1980). The complex is related to the topography of the hill and built with exposed concrete, white stucco on brick, and details in wood. The most prominent feature of the monastery is the church, consisting of two cubes slightly rotated that create a strong yet simple space for prayer and ritual. Light generates a serene atmosphere and provides the space with its spiritual character. This simple and austere church constituted a key piece in Latin American architecture, comparable to Cavari's Fátima church in Argentina, Oscar Niemeyer's church in Pampulha, and Eladio Dieste's church in Atlántida.

Process and collaboration throughout time characterize the Open City in northern Chile. In the 1960s a group of architects from the Catholic University of Valparaíso began to question both the principal tenets of the International Style and the relationship between client and architect. This challenge would culminate in the 1970s with the remarkable experience of the Open City. Located in the dunes of Ritoque, overlooking the Pacific Ocean, the buildings were erected without plans and based on a collaborative design inspired by the Maudés poets of France, a movement that proclaimed responsiveness to life and emancipation from rules.

Throughout the 1960s and part of the 1970s, Christian democratic and socialist governments emphasized the need for housing and other social programs. Among others it is important to mention the complex CORVI (1960), by Bruna Camus, Calvo Barros, Perelman, and Sepulveda, a project inspired by Le Corbusier's Unité d'Habitation at Marseilles.

Since the 1980s, the term *appropriate modernity*, coined by Cristian Fernandez Cox, has taken center stage in Latin American architectural debates. *Apropiada* denotes both the appropriations of modernity's values and ways to make it suitable to the Latin American context. A new sensibility characterized this architecture of the 1990s: a conscious effort to recover typologies rooted in the region, the search for cultural identity, the use of traditional technologies combined with modern devices, and the exploration of the unusual sculptural qualities of ordinary materials.

Edward Rojas's work exemplifies this approach. In his Modern Art Museum in Chiloé, outside the town of Castro, Rojas restored a warehouse built by Isaac Eskenazzi, who in the 1970s combined Modern aspects with regional typologies and materials. Rojas renovated the structure of the roof and floor and added a new building, a modest wooden shed. The combination of minimalist devices and regional types created a rich and simple museum adapted to the needs of the site and locale.

Mathias Klots's Hotel Terrantai in San Pedro is equally context driven. Located in Atacama, a dry, northern area of the country, the small hotel was structured around a communal space. The project incorporated an existing house and kept the low profile of the context, composed mostly of adobe constructions. Inside, the structure combines broad expanses of glass and bleached timber floorboards with Andean-style terracing and textured walls.

The Consorcio-Vida Building (1999) by Enrique Browne and Borja Huidobro, is located in an elegant area of Santiago. The western facade, elongated and rounded, has staggered steps and trellises that generate a vertical garden of 16 levels. Protected by trellises that add a second skin, plants reduce up to 60 percent of solar heat gain. The building represents an appropriate modernity, as it incorporates recent tendencies and languages with an attention to sustainable design, local influences, and the economic reality of the country. The El Cerro House (1994), by Cristián Undurraga and Ana Devés, exemplifies a subtle reference to several precedents and a respect for the site. Two elongated walls, submerged in the hill, contain all the functions of the home in several levels and a terrace. Because all access is lateral, the only portal in the facade opens to the garden. Refined and minimal, the project refers to multiple figurative types.

Enrique Browne speaks of the permeability of Chilean culture, also characterized by the lack of direct relationship between sociopolitical events and architectural production. At the beginning of the 20th century, the principles of rationalism were not fully understood. As in many other Latin American countries, Chilean architects were attracted to modernism by its technical appeal rather than the utopian and political origins that characterized contemporary changes in Europe.

Although 60 percent of the population is concentrated in the metropolitan area of Santiago, the country is geographically expansive. This situation has created a fertile ground for exploration of differences in materials and traditions as well as the regional adaptability to the rigors of extreme climatic conditions. An uncritical acceptance of modernist postulates has been transformed to a new respect for architectural heritage and the environment. One of the most important elements of 20th-century architecture in Chile is the tension and permanent dialectic between universal tendencies and the spirit of the place. Chile, with its economic prosperity and innovative spirit, is considered one of the most dynamic and active architectural cultures in Latin America.

JOSE BERNARDI

See also **Corbusier, Le (Jeanneret, Charles-Édouard) (France); Niemeyer, Oscar (Brazil); Parliament Building, Chandigarh; Santiago, Chile**

Further Reading

Boza Díaz, Cristián (editor), *Sergio Larraín G.M.*, Bogotá, Colombia: Escala, 1990

Klotz, Mathias, *Mathias Klotz*, Barcelona: Gustavo Gili, 1997

Pendleton-Jullian, Ann M., *The Road That Is Not a Road and the Open City, Ritoque, Chile*, Cambridge, Massachusetts: MIT Press and Chicago: Graham Foundation for Advanced Study in the Fine Arts, 1996

1er Premio Mies van der Rohe de Arquitectura Latinoamericana—1st Mies van der Rohe Award for Latin American Architecture, Barcelona: Fundació Mies van der Rohe, 1999

Riera Ojeda, Oscar (editor), *Ten Houses: Enrique Browne*, Gloucester, Massachusetts: Rockport, 1997

Riera Ojeda, Oscar (editor), *Ten Houses: Christian De Groote*, Gloucester, Massachusetts: Rockport, 1999

Roca, Miguel Angel (editor), *The Architecture of Latin America*, London: Academy Editions, 1995

2o Premio Mies van der Rohe de Arquitectura Latinoamericana—2nd Mies van der Rohe Award for Latin American Architecture, edited by Diane Gray, with Anna Bes, Ariadna Gilabert, Griselda Massó; translated by Richard Rees and Mireia Alegre, Barcelona: Fundació Mies van der Rohe, 2000

CHINA

The development of architecture in 20th-century China followed closely its political evolution. Starting out as an imperial regime nearly colonized by Western powers, China was declared a republic in 1911, only to fall into the chaos of the warlord period a year later. With the Japanese invasion of China in 1937, the country was engaged in eight years of warfare. When the Communists first took power in the country in 1949, after four years of civil war following the Japanese surrender, China enjoyed ten years of stability. A series of political campaigns took place between 1959 and 1976, disrupting the normal functioning of the country. In 1979 China adopted an economic open-door policy; foreign and multinational companies were invited to invest and trade in the country. This resulted in a booming economy and strong foreign trade in the last decades of the 20th century. Architectural style, spatial conception, architectural symbolism, the choice of architect, and construction technology were all directly influenced by the country's political, commercial, and cultural development.

Up until 1911, most buildings constructed in China were of the distinctive traditional style with a timber post-and-beam structure supporting a heavy and curved tile roof. In-filled wall between the timber frames was of timber, brick, or pounded earth construction. Buildings were normally of a single story; only an exceptional structure such as a pagoda or a town tower was of two- or multiple-storied construction. Several buildings were arranged around a courtyard, and a few courtyards lined up along a central axis or two or three axes made up a complex. Building types were extremely limited in traditional China, which included palaces, princes, and official residences, government offices, temples and altars, shops, academies, ancestral halls, houses, and gardens all sharing the same form, construction, and spatial layout. Western architecture appeared in China with the introduction of new building types from the West. These included churches, custom houses, railway stations, and commercial offices. Fine examples of churches include the neo-baroque Catholic South Church in Beijing of 1657 and the neo-Gothic Holy Trinity Cathedral in Shanghai, designed by Sir George Gilbert Scott and constructed in 1866. A small railway station was built outside the imperial gate of Beijing in 1900. The introduction of Western-styled buildings at the beginning of the 20th century set the scene for Chinese architecture and more dramatically, the International Style had by the end of the century completely obliterated the traditional architectural environment in the cities. The remaining Chinese characteristics are seen only in the buildings of nationalistic style. The architectural development can be divided into four periods: the introduction of Western-styled architecture (1900–28), the Modern movement or national style (1929–49), a period of pragmatism coupled with the search for a new national identity (1949–79), and a period of intense internationalization (1979–2000).

1900–28

With the signing of the Nanjing treaty with Great Britain in 1842, five port cities were designated for foreign trade where Western merchants could set up trading houses. In 1850 the British set up the first concession in Shanghai, and Western-style buildings and city planning began to appear in major cities of China. Most Western-style buildings in China in the 19th century were neo-Gothic and neoclassical churches, arcaded shop houses, embassy buildings, and industrial buildings. Many houses, shop buildings, and offices were also built in the Colonial style first seen in the British colonies of India and Southeast Asia. After the Boxer Rebellion of 1900, the influence of Western powers in urban China became more apparent, expressed visibly through the increased number of foreign concessions filled with Western-styled buildings. These buildings were designed by foreign architects and engineers following closely the stylistic development of European architecture. These foreign professionals brought with them the specialized discipline of architectural design, which hitherto had been carried out by master builders of the craft tradition.

Church buildings were designed according to denominational preference. The twin-tower Xujiahui Cathedral in Shanghai was completed in 1910, designed by British architect W.M. Dowdall in French Gothic for a Jesuit missionary. English red-brick Gothic Revival style can also be seen in many Protestant churches throughout the country. The Catholic church in the former French concession in Tianjin was built in the French Romanesque style and completed in 1916. These buildings with tall spires dominated the low skylines of traditional Chinese cities. In prosperous trading cities, however, more and more bank and commercial buildings reached greater and greater height. Many early bank buildings were in the neoclassical style, as in the West. The first bank building to be erected on the Bund in Shanghai was the St. Petersburg Russo-Asiatic Bank, completed in 1901 and designed by H. Becker. This was the first building in China to be constructed with reinforced-concrete, equipped with modern conveniences and an elevator. However, the most impressive of bank buildings in this age must have been the Hong Kong and Shanghai Bank building designed by British architects Palmer and Turner and completed in 1923. This seven-storied steel-framed building was decorated in the neoclassical style surmounted by an imposing dome.

Apart from these buildings that are shadows of their European prototypes, ecclectic-style buildings mixing traditional Chinese architecture with the Western style were also attempted. The earliest example in this style is the Peking Union Medical College in Beijing, designed by Harry Hussey between 1916 and 1918. The scale and proportion of these buildings are clearly Western classical in inspiration, whereas the details and the gigantic roof are Chinese. Many foreign architects adopted this style for residences, churches, and colleges, among whom the most accomplished was American architect Henry K. Murphy (1877–1954), who completed many university campus projects in what he called "Adaptive Chinese Renaissance" style (Cody, 1989).

1929–49

This period of modernist nationalism in architecture is significant in the development of 20th-century Chinese architecture in that many Chinese architects trained abroad returned to make important contributions to the architectural scene. Among these were Zhuang Jun, who returned from the University of Illinois, Urbana, in 1914; Liu Dunzhen returned from Japan in 1923; and Yang Tingbao, Tong Jun, and Liang Sicheng all graduated from the University of Pennsylvania and returned to China between 1927 and 1930. These architects either taught in the first architectural schools in China, worked for foreign architects in China, or formed partnerships in private practice. Their monumental designs with minimal decorations were a direct result from their monumental training in the Beaux-Arts tradition in the West. In this they followed the Hungarian architect L.E. Hudec, whose modernist architecture was first seen in a church completed in 1925 and some residences. The Chinese architects were increasingly given major commissions, such as government buildings, banks, hotels, commercial buildings, and academic buildings. Some high-rise buildings along the Shanghai Bund are also modernist in spirit. Chinese architects influenced by the Bauhaus also designed buildings with clean lines and devoid of decorations.

The other architectural style seen in this period was developed from the Chinese ecclectic style of the foreign architects working for foreign missions. With the Chinese style roof as the prominent feature of the style, it was considered as a national style promoted heavily by the newly formed national government at the end of the 1920s. Many government buildings were constructed in this style in the new capital, Nanjing (designated in 1927 and the planning of which was undertaken by Henry Murphy). In 1929 a competition for the mausoleum for Sun Yat-sen, the father of nationalistic China, was organized, and the brief clearly asked for a nationalistic style. The winning design submitted by Lu Yanzhi displays a symmetrical monumentality based on the Lincoln Memorial while incorporating distinctive Chinese elements, including the roof, bracket system, window surrounds, and decorative architrave. Just as the foreign architects saw in the style the representation of Chinese tradition, the government used the style for nation building. However, the style was increasingly criticized by the advocates of the Modern movement for being wasteful in material and for not representing the spirit of the modern society China was moving toward. Heated debates were fully argued in architectural journals for many years in the 1930s, only to be abruptly cut due to the Japanese occupation of eastern China between 1937 and 1945.

1949–79

After the setting up of the People's Republic of China, institutional buildings were designed following closely the Russian Monumental style. Between 1949 and 1957, Russian experts helped in building the new China by promoting the principle of neoclassicist monumentality with Chinese characteristics. Together with the first Five-year Plan, many new functionalistic buildings were constructed for the new social order. Invariably, these buildings are symmetrical both on the facade and in the internal layout. Over the central entrance is usually a high tower. This form had a long-lasting influence on the modern Chinese architectural style right through to the end of the century, due partly to the influence of the centralizing symmetry of traditional Chinese architecture. Two good examples are the Soviet-designed Beijing and Shanghai Exhibition Halls of 1954.

With the Communist rule also came the reform of architectural practice. Replacing the private architectural and engineering offices were many state-owned design institutes, which are comprehensive professional offices surviving to this day (Lin, 1988). At the end of the 1950s, Russian experts were expelled from China, and the leading design principle adopted was essentially nationalistic. However, unlike the earlier Chinese Renaissance style of foreign architects or the national style of the 1930s, the nationalistic style of this period was much restrained, using less of the massive tiled roof and relying more on minor traditional decorative elements. The ten major projects to celebrate the tenth anniversary of the founding of the People's Republic are important examples of this style. Completed in 1959, some of these buildings are located at the heart of Beijing, such as the Great Hall of the People (Zhao Dongri) and the Revolutionary and History Museum (Zhang Kaiji). And others served important political and infrastructure functions, such as the Cultural Palace of Nationalities (Zhang Bo) and the Beijing Railway Station (Chen Dengao). Other examples of this nationalistic style can be seen in other parts of the country, such as the Great Hall of the People in Chongqing (Zhang Jiade, 1954). Soon after the tenth anniversary, the country was thrown into turmoil again with many political movements culminating in the Cultural Revolution—all normal social activities stopped until 1976. However, there were also pragmatic functionalist buildings constructed even in this period, such as the extension to the Beijing Hotel (Dai Nianci, 1974).

1979–2000

With the liberalization of the Chinese economy in 1979, the nationalistic style continued to be adopted only for political purposes during this period of internationalization. This is particularly apparent in buildings along the main east-west boulevard of Beijing, Chang'an Jie, which are required by city officials to adopt national characteristics in their form. This is accomplished by adding small Chinese pavilions on otherwise multistoried modern buildings. However, there was also more genuine integration of the two forms, such as the Beijing Library (Yang Yun, 1987), the Beijing West Railway Station (Zhu Jialu, 1996), and the Peking University Library (Guan Shaoye, 1998). In these attempts large tiled roofs appeared again on top of tall buildings, much like the examples from the 1920s. The search for a new Chinese architecture had found a new interpretation in the Fragrant Hill Hotel completed in 1982. In it I.M. Pei used traditional elements from southern China, such as diagonal windows and whitewashed walls, integrated in modern and yet distinctive Chinese spaces. Similar examples designed by Chinese architects include the Queli Hotel in Qufu (Dai Nianci, 1984) and a housing design in Ju'er Hutong in Beijing (Wu Liangyong, 1990).

However, the most significant development of the period was the return of foreign architects to the Chinese architectural scene in the last two decades of the century. They were involved in joint ventures with local design institutes in the design of new hotels operated by major Western hotel chains, such as the Beijing Jianguo Hotel (1982), the Great Wall Sheraton of Beijing (1983), the Nanjing Jinling Hotel (1983), and the Crystal Palace Hotel (1987). These buildings served important purposes of introducing the International Style and modern construction technology to China, rapidly updating China from its 20-year isolation from the rest of the world. In the 1990s other commercial and cultural projects also benefited from international designers. These included the Beijing Chinese-Japanese Youth Center (Kisho Kurokawa, 1990), the Shanghai Center (John Portman and Associates, 1990), the Shanghai Grand Theater (Arte Jean Marie Charpentier and Associates, 1998), the Industrial and Commercial Bank of China Building, Beijing (Skidmore, Owings and Merrill, 1998), and the Bank of China, Beijing (I.M. Pei and Partners, 1999). Some of these were the first facilities built to international standards in China. The Shanghai Grand Theater has successfully utilized the curtain wall both as a symbol of modernization in the day and a bright jewel at night. The curved roof soaring into the sky is reminiscent of the traditional curved roof of south China and is a source of inspiration for many buildings in China. Although some architects were particularly sensitive to the local context, the majority designed massive curtain-wall buildings totally out of context with the surroundings. Sadly, these buildings became the icons of modernization and were copied all over China in a less-satisfactory manner.

With the development of Pudong district in Shanghai, imposing skyscrapers, unseen before in China, started to dominate the generally flat skyline. The two most notable examples from this district are the 421-meter-tall Jin Mao Building (Skidmore, Owings and Merrill, 1998) and the 460-meter World Financial Center (KPF Associates, 2000). These projects were mainly won in an international competition, which was becoming the norm for larger and joint-venture projects in the late 1990s. The foreign designers of these projects were clearly sensitive to the Chinese tradition within which the buildings are located. They often incorporated Chinese elements, motifs, or symbolism in their design. For example, the tallest building in China, the Jin Mau Building, was conceived as a Chinese pagoda with a shimmering curtain wall, whereas the Word Financial Center was designed to invoke the Chinese conception of the heaven as round and the earth as square.

Other than the nationalistic and International Styles, there are Chinese architects who boldly attempt architectural symbolism in building form. The Shanghai Museum is designed in the shape of an ancient bronze cauldron (Xing Tonghe, 1996), and the Memorial to the Victims of Japanese Massacre used a stark granite surface and dry landscape to evoke the extreme horror of the massacre (Qi Kang, 1985). However, the most controversial project that epitomizes the tension between internationalism and nationalism in architecture is the winning entry of the design competition for the National Grand Theater of China in Beijing. The design of Paul Andreu consists of a gigantic glass dome covering three separate theater structures. Located next to the Great Hall of the People, the heart of political China, this project has generated heated debates in the local architectural community and was put on hold in 2000. The stark contrast of the ultramodern structure with nationalistic architecture at such an important site and the cultural symbolism of the glass dome are two major objections to the scheme. On the other hand the supporters argue that China needs national icons of this sort to launch itself into the new millennium. This is perhaps a clear indication that Chinese architecture was standing at the crossroad at the end of the century. The desperate search for a Chinese identity has so far yielded no satisfactory answer. In the meantime, the pressure of commercial development has produced two extremes: well-conceived buildings designed by international offices and big design institutes in major cities, and mediocre buildings by the thousands all over the vast country.

PUAY-PENG HO

See also **Bank of China Tower, Hong Kong; Liang Sicheng (China); Lu Yanzhi (China); Wu Liangyong (China)**

Further Reading

Cody, Jeffrey, "Henry K. Murphy: An American Architect in China, 1914–1935," Ph.D. diss., Cornell University, 1989

Cole, Doris, "Building a New China," *Building in China*, 9 (1988)

Dai, Nianci, "On the Design of Queli Hotel," *Building in China*, 4 (1986)

Kurokawa, Kisho, *Kisho Kurokawa: From Metabolism to Symbiosis*, London: Academy Editions, and New York: St. Martin's Press, 1992

Lin, Chen, "The Beijing Building Design Institute," *Building in China*, 6 (1988)

Liu, Erming, and Yi Feng (editors), *Wai guo jian zhu shi Zhongguo zuo pin xuan* (International Architects in China: Selected Works since 1980), Beijing: Zhongguo ji hua chu ban she and Zhongguo da bai ke quan shu chu ban she, 1999

Liu, Erming, and Yi Feng (editors), *Zhongguo dang dai zhu ming jian zhu shi zuo pin xuan: Selected Works of Well-Known Chinese Architects* (bilingual Chinese–English edition), Beijing: Zhongguo ji hua chu ban she and Zhongguo da bai ke quan shu chu ban she, 1999

Portman, John C., "An Architecture for Contemporary China," *Building in China*, 12 (1990)

CHOISY, AUGUSTE 1841–1904

Architectural engineer and historian, France

François Auguste Choisy is in many ways the ideological link between significant individuals such as Eugène Viollet-le-Duc and Auguste Perret and Vitruvius and Le Corbusier; his influence on the beginnings of the Modern movement was fundamental. Born in 1841, Choisy was the son of an architect practicing in Vitry-le-François in northeastern France. His interests in mathematics and architecture quickly led him to the École Polytechnique under Léonce Reynaud, author of the influential *Traité d'architecture* (1860; Treaty on Architecture), and eventually to the prestigious École des Ponts et Chaussées. His professional career as civil engineer originated in 1865, while still within the junior ranks of the latter institution, when he was dispatched to the Rhone region; there, he began to investigate the significance of the surrounding Gallo-Roman monuments. During the same year he traveled to Greece, undertaking technical analyses of, among other monuments, the Parthenon; his work on stylobate and column curvature remains important within the study of classical architecture. Graduating second at the École des Ponts et Chaussées in 1866, he was awarded a travel bursary that he ultimately used to visit Italy.

In 1868 Choisy took on his official duties as engineer within the Département des Ponts et Chaussées at Rethel, France. In 1870 he met Viollet-le-Duc, who was already well known for his *Entretiens sur l'architecture* (1863–72; Commentaries on Architecture). Choisy remained with the government department for his entire career, moving up the ranks as chief engineer and eventually inspector general, all the while teaching architectural history at the École des Ponts et Chaussées, the École d'Horticulture de Versailles, and the École Polytechnique. His interests extended beyond historical studies, organizing the public works programs for the French installations at the universal expositions in Vienna (1873), Philadelphia (1876), Melbourne (1880), and Paris (1878, 1889, and 1900).

During his initial sojourn in Italy, Choisy began outlining his first substantial publication, *L'Art de bâtir chez les Romains* (1873; The Art of Roman Building). His interpretation of Roman building technique focused on brick masonry and vault construction; he emphasized that material and labor thriftiness was central to Roman construction, modeling his analyses in part on Robert Willis's work and ultimately comparing his own observations to the words in Vitruvius's *De architectura libri decem* (1st century B.C.; The Ten Books on Architecture). Choisy used a complex three-dimensional drawing technique, the plunging isometric, which allowed for the depiction of plan, elevation, section, and interior layout within single engravings. The work established him as an authority in classical architecture, and similar studies followed, including *L'Art de bâtir chez les Bizantines* (1883; The Art of Byzantine Building), *Études épigraphiques sur l'architecture greque* (1883; Epigraphic Studies on Greek Architecture), *L'Art de bâtir chez les Égyptiens* (1904; The Art of Egyptian Building), and his tour de force, *Histoire de l'architecture* (1899; The History of Architecture).

Comprehensive and systematic, Choisy's 1899 architectural history book was a textual and visual account of building methods in culture, time, and space; it included his own 1700 drawings, presenting the culmination of his lectures and studies, distilled within a comprehensive analysis of architecture from prehistory to the end of the 18th century. Each historical section was first contextualized within the broader work, with the technical aspects of building following immediately afterward. Choisy's thesis that form follows local environmental and cultural conditions was buttressed throughout the book, underscoring his view that architecture is generated by the collective and not the individual. To the historian, style and form derive from the creative use of materials, labor, and ideas; architecture is the result of the adaptations of historical precedents on the one hand and the solution to immediate problems on the other. The connection between form and technique was thus achieved, making the influence of Viollet-le-Duc abundantly clear. In his section on Gothic architecture, in fact, Choisy bases much of his discussion on the work of the latter as well as on Willis's, further elaborating their theories and subsequently contributing to the spread of their ideas.

As with his discussion of the Gothic, Choisy refined previous theories, particularly as they related to Greek architecture. He advanced the thesis that Greek builders did not rely solely on symmetry and axial alignment, as previous historians had often concluded; he noted that the ensemble of monuments interacted within more complex landscapes. He went back to his studies of the Parthenon—a model that Le Corbusier would echo just a few decades later. Coupled with Choisy's translation of Vitruvius's *Ten Books on Architecture* (published posthumously in 1909), the *Histoire de l'architecture* served as a base text for the theory expounded in Le Corbusier's *Vers Une Architecture* (1923; Toward a New Architecture). Le Corbusier turned to Choisy's history book for Parthenon and Acropolis details, pointing to symmetrical buildings arranged within asymmetrical site layouts and discussing the evolution of classical types. Central to Le Corbusier's thesis was that pure architecture works on an emotive level with the viewer. He termed *modénature*, the act of controlling emotion by visual stimulus; the term was translated in his *Vers Une Architecture* as "contour and profile." This, of course, was directly tied to Choisy's notion that the Greeks used contours and profiles to arrive at their optical corrections; Choisy borrowed from Vitruvius in his examination of moldings, adding his own ideas relating to the use of light in controlling the viewer's experience. Le Corbusier in turn followed Choisy and adapted ideas on light within his theoretical principles.

In 1903, just before his death, Choisy received the Royal Institute of British Architects' Gold Medal for his lifetime contribution to the study of architecture and, in significant ways, to the meaning of architectural history during the early 20th century.

DANIEL MILLETTE

See also **Corbusier, Le (Jeanneret, Charles-Édouard) (France)**

Selected Publications

L'Art de bâtir chez les Romains (The Art of Roman Building), 1873
L'Art de bâtir chez les Bizantines (The Art of Byzantine Building), 1883
Études épigraphiques sur l'architecture greque (Epigraphic Studies on Greek Architecture), 1883
Histoire de l'architecture (The History of Architecture), 1899
L'Art de bâtir chez les Égyptiens (The Art of Egyptian Building), 1904

Further Reading

Very little has been written on Choisy or his career. A brief synopsis by Annie Jacques is included within the 1991 edition of the *Histoire de l'architecture* (Paris; Inter-Livres). It includes quotes from Maurice d'Ocagne's (1930) short text on Choisy's writings; d'Ocagne was an engineer who replaced Choisy in one of his positions at the École des Ponts et Chaussées. More recently, Richard Etlin (1987) provides a careful study examining the links between Choisy and Le Corbusier, and Fernand Pouillon (1994) records an analytical commentary.

Etlin, Richard A., "Le Corbusier, Choisy and French Hellenism: The Search for a New Architecture," *Art Bulletin*, 69/2 (1987)
d'Ocagne, Maurice, *Auguste Choisy, et l'Art de bâtir chez les anciens*, Vannes: Lafolye et J. de Lamarzelle, 1930
Pouillon, Fernand, *Auguste Choisy*, Paris: Altimira, 1994

CHRYSLER BUILDING

Designed by William Van Alen, completed 1930
New York City

The Chrysler Building, designed by William Van Alen, stands 77 stories tall at Lexington Avenue between 42nd and 43rd

Streets in Manhattan, and is considered one of the most famous and admired skyscrapers in the world. The Chrysler Building owes this position primarily to its distinctive tower, which terminates in a series of curves that support a final pointed spire. At night, v-shaped light patterns mark the successive curves, keeping the structure conspicuous around the clock.

The building occupies an easily visible site, across the street from the Grand Central Terminal, where subway lines, commuter rail lines, and long-distance rail lines converge. Other buildings in the area attract less attention because their towers are rectilinear, and thus commonplace. Not only does the Chrysler spire draw attention at close range as well as from afar, but also the ground floor features tall, angular entrances, a lavishly decorated lobby, and beautifully inlaid elevator cabs. Several setbacks along the building's silhouette have easily visible decorations including metal eagles, winged radiator caps, and a brick frieze of Chrysler automobiles. The combination of stiff stylization and recognizable imagery marks a phase of the style known as Art Deco, an amalgam of French-inspired semi-abstraction and popular, easily intelligible subject matter. The decorative forms at the Chrysler Building are more energetic than the more classicizing ones used at the contemporary Waldorf-Astoria Hotel.

All this came about when Walter Chrysler, Jr., a free spirit in his family of automobile industrialists, obtained the building site and existing plans in 1928. Between 1925 and 1929, high-rise office construction in New York City expanded markedly, and a site convenient to public transportation was an ideal one for luring tenants in a highly competitive market. There are entrances to the subway and terminal system within the building, so that people could avoid walking outdoors to reach their workplaces.

To design the project, Chrysler employed William Van Alen, a socially well-connected architect trained in the neo-Renaissance tradition of the École des Beaux-Arts who accommodated his work to the stylistic preferences of his clients. For Chrysler he created a building that is seen as glamorous, amusing, and utilitarian all at once, although it is rarely considered to exemplify serious high art. Neither architect nor client was making a profound aesthetic or philosophical statement; the aim was pragmatic: to be distinctive, as a good advertisement is. Van Alen was probably prodded by Chrysler to design details in a more popular contemporary mode than was customary for this architect.

The owner hoped to capture additional publicity by building the world's tallest office building. The title was then held by 40 Wall Street, but Chrysler expected that his building in the newer office zone of midtown Manhattan would confirm a trend toward relocation of major firms to the Grand Central area. He did not achieve his goal because the owners of the nearby rival Empire State Building commissioned a last-minute change of design from their architects and erected a higher tower. Nevertheless, the Chrysler tower earns more aesthetic admiration.

The imaginations of architect and client were constrained by the zoning regulations of New York City, which decreed that buildings taller than specified limits had to be set back from the building line on several sides. The setback rules applied particularly to the silhouette above a legal multiple of the adjacent street width. Above that level, the building had to recede until it occupied only one-quarter of the site, at which point it could rise as a tower to any height that the owner desired; this accounts for the setbacks and tower of the Chrysler Building.

Chrysler Building, undated drawing (*c.*1928–30), designed by William Van Alen

Their imaginations were also constrained by the building code, which required provisions for safety and health, and also by the customs of the day. These determined that tenants would not rent office space that was more than 30 feet from perimeter windows, as deeper spaces were considered to lack sufficient light and air. Accordingly, owners and architects designed insets, courtyards, and other receding forms to produce maximal office space and minimal storage or service space, as the latter rented at lower rates per square foot.

No constraints seem to have operated when it came to decorating the Chrysler Building. At ground level, shops along the street and the entrances to the building were given angular decoration, much of it in metal that forecast vibrant embellishments inside. The lobby, entered from both Lexington Avenue and 42nd Street, appears triangular, thus unusual in a city where axial lobbies are the norm. The Chrysler's lobby is decorated in warm colors of inlaid wood, of metal, and of paint. Above the marble and granite walls, a ceiling mural by Edward Trumbull depicts the building, airplanes, the Chrysler automobile assembly line, and other emblems of modernity. The 30 elevator cabs are inlaid in wood veneer on steel, featuring simplified floral forms and geometric shapes, separated into panels.

The office floors have double-loaded corridors and office spaces that were standard at the period of their construction; several revisions have been made to parts of the interior since the building was completed in 1930. At the top of the tower is a tall space, furnished for dining and receptions. The exterior surface is made primarily of pale brick over a steel frame; stainless steel marks the entrances, decorative details, and the tower. Tower lighting, originally planned, was activated in 1981.

Minor alterations and restoration especially of the lobby, entrances, and ornamental features, followed several changes of ownership. In 1978 the New York City Landmarks Preservation Commission designated the Chrysler Building as a municipal landmark. This prevents the owners from changing the designated features unless severe economic hardship can be demonstrated. Aware of the building's prestige, owners have generally been willing to repair essential functional and ornamental features. The building is now admired as a delightful relic of an optimistic era in skyscraper building and an urban icon, although, having always functioned as an obvious self-advertisement, it has not been regarded as a seminal work of modern architecture.

CAROL HERSELLE KRINSKY

See also **Art Deco; Empire State Building, New York; Skyscraper**

Further Reading

Krinsky, Carol Herselle, "The Chrysler Preserved," *Art in America*, 67 (1979)

Robinson, Cervin, and Rosemarie Haag Bletter, *Skyscraper Style: Art Deco, New York*, New York: Oxford University Press, 1975

Stern, Robert A.M., Gregory Gilmartin, and Thomas Mellins, *New York 1930: Architecture and Urbanism between the Two World Wars*, New York: Rizzoli, 1987

Willis, Carol, *Form Follows Finance*, New York: Princeton Architectural Press, 1995

CHURCH

The term "church" refers both to the Christian congregational body and to the buildings in which public Christian worship takes place. Although churches share with secular sites functional attributes common to all types of built structures, they also are endowed with symbolic meanings consonant with their purpose as sites of sacred ritual. Because international modernism, which dominated the middle years of the 20th century, was self-referential, antiemblematic, and ahistorical in character, its practitioners sought new ways to express sacredness using space and light, with traditional forms reduced to subtle references. Since the 1960s, however, symbolism has been recognized as implicit in all architecture, countering the tendency Pier Luigi Nervi saw to "reduce the 'house of God's people' to a cold compound of human functions" (Bozzo, 1990).

Representations of sacredness respond to a number of different factors, including ritual practice and conventional signification. Many forms are ancient in origin, dating from the third century A.D., when public Christian observance first became legal under the Romans. Early Christians adopted the basilica from Greek and Roman courts of justice; the longitudinal interiors lit by a clerestory were ideal for congregational assembly. The introduction of transepts gave rise to the Latin-cross plan, seen as an emblem of that most fundamental of all Christian symbols. The Gothic rib vault, perfected in the Ile de France in the 12th century, then elevated the basilica to the status of quintessential Christian representation, because the Church of Rome was at the height of its influence across Europe. Not only did the basilican or processional plan continue to hold significance into the modern era, but also as recently as the early 20th century, Gothic churches still were being built in the traditional manner.

Centralized plans based on Roman tombs and Greek treasure houses were reserved for baptisteries and *martyria*. During the Renaissance, however, both centralized and Greek-cross plans enjoyed a wider use, because neo-Platonic aesthetics influenced architects to look on these forms as symbols of divine perfection. It was only in the wake of the Reformation that the Church of Rome decreed a return to more conventional sacred expression to articulate its opposition to dissent.

For Protestant sects such as the Huguenots in France, architecture became a channel through which to signify uniqueness. Classicist temples, on rectangular or octagonal plans with banked seating around a central pulpit, were well suited to the delivery of sermons, and they engendered a sense of communal worship. In many cases an ideologically determined simplicity, central to the practice of reformed worship, also was manifested not only in the temples of French Protestants but also in the early Puritan meetinghouses of New England. As for banked auditoriums, they were identified with Protestant observance, particularly after important German baroque examples such as the Frauenkirche in Dresden, and because burgeoning evangelical congregations in North America during the late 19th century were accommodated by necessity in church amphitheaters with adjoining Akron-plan Sunday schools. Catholic churches only adopted this type of iconography after the Second Vatican Council in the 1960s authorized increased congregational participation.

The significance of plan type and architectural vocabulary in representing sectarian allegiance also is indicated by a third important precedent from the 6th century, which holds particular meaning for Christians of the Eastern rite. The domed interior of the Hagia Sophia in Constantinople (now Istanbul), sustained on a square of four vast arches, mediates between longitudinal and centralized space with the inclusion of semi-domed apses on the east and west. So impressive was its interior that it became an equally potent symbol for the followers of Islam after the building's conversion to a mosque in 1453, when the Ottomans conquered the city.

In the opening years of the 20th century, the importance of tradition was affirmed through a renewed interest in Gothic architecture. The groundwork had been laid in the 1830s, when the Oxford Movement reintroduced Catholic principles into Protestant Episcopal practice and stimulated a move toward ecumenism. This in turn found architectural justification in the writings of 19th-century theorists such as A.W.N. Pugin, the ecclesiologists (formerly the Cambridge Camden Society), John Ruskin, and John Ninian Comper in Britain; and in Europe, through the writings of Eugene-Emanuel Viollet-le-Duc and Ro-

Crystal Cathedral, by Phillip Johnson and John Burgee, Garden Grove, California (1978–80) © G.E. Kidder Smith/CORBIS

mano Guardini, among others. Pugin, in particular, proposed that pointed or Christian architecture could edify society and at the same time exemplify rational design. By combining sacred tradition with the chief principle of modernism, Pugin earned a place among the pioneers of modern design and facilitated the survival of medieval forms into the 20th century. Liverpool's Anglican Cathedral by Gilbert Scott the younger, begun in 1904, affirmed the Gothic tradition in Britain, just as New York's Cathedral of St. John the Divine, begun by Heins and Lafarge in 1892 and continued by Cram and Ferguson, did in the United States.

With the development of modern materials such as steel and reinforced concrete, it was only a matter of time before convention gave way to new types of expression. French architects Anatole de Baudot and his student Auguste Perret drew on the writings of Viollet-le-Duc to translate traditional forms into modern materials. Baudot's St.-Jean-de-Montmartre (1904) was a groin-vaulted basilica executed in concrete, whereas Perret's Notre-Dame-Le-Raincy, featured a segmental, ferroconcrete shell vault extending the length of the nave. This approach also was explored by Karl Moser at St. Anthony in Basel, Switzerland (1927), and somewhat differently by Werner Moser in the Protestant church of Altstretten in Zurich, Switzerland (1941). Otto Bartning's Steel Church for the Press Exhibition at Cologne, Germany (1928), realized a similar project in steel and glass. In other instances, historical references were reduced to a minimum, as was the case with Corpus Christi Church in Aachen, Germany (1930), by Rudolf Schwarz and Hans Schippert, a simple concrete hall with clerestory windows with the merest trace of an ancient basilica.

Attempts also were made to translate Gothic vaulting into a contemporary idiom. For example, Antoni Gaudí conceived an extraordinary series of organic forms to complete the more conventional 1882 design his mentor Villar had proposed for Sagrada Familia in Barcelona. (More recently, Santiago Calatrava reinterpreted Gaudí's idiosyncratic vocabulary in his 1991 Tree of Life design for the nave and transepts of New York's St. John the Divine.) In a similar manner, the paraboloid concrete barrel vault with low transverse aisle vaults, which Domenikus Böhm adopted in the Catholic church of Christ the King at Bischofsheim (1926), invested the basilica with what Henry-Russell Hitchcock called "a strong emotional effect . . . both Gothic and Expressionist in tone." Two decades later, Oscar Niemeyer revisited the idea of the single bold paraboloid in his Church of St. Francis of Assisi, Pampulha, in Belo Horizonte, Brazil, and fashioned a transept from four undulating concrete shells. His approach found sympathetic affirmation in the work of Spanish-born Félix Candela, who also created a basilica of hyperbolic paraboloids for Santa María Miraculosa in Mexico City (1954).

Medievalism also pervades the regional expression of the Grundtvigs Church in Copenhagen, Denmark (1913 and 1921–40), by Vilhelm Jensen-Klint. Its massive, neotraditional brick facade harks back to Baltic vernacular, with an overscaled evocation of a pipe organ conjured from a cathedral portico.

By 1952 the boxy, steel-and-glass chapel Ludwig Mies van der Rohe designed as part of his campus plan for Chicago's Illinois Institute of Technology had formulated the fundamental problem of sacred architecture in the modern era—how to represent matters of the spirit in the stark, universal geometry of international modernism. A different approach was explored by Eero Saarinen and Associates in the interdenominational Kresge Chapel at the Massachusetts Institute of Technology (1955). Its simple cylindrical form, executed in red brick, was set on a moat of water that reflected dimly into the skylit interior, where a beam of light precipitated on an ethereal retable of suspended brass rectangles to invoke the divine as tangibly as any baroque *Gesamtkunstwerk* (total work of art). That same year Le Corbusier finished what has come to be recognized as the 20th century's most extraordinary example of sacred architecture, the Pilgrimage Chapel of Notre-Dame-du-Haut at Ronchamp, in the Vosges, France (1955). Sculptural and massive, the structure supported a soaring, sail-like roof on battened wedges of raw concrete, pierced only by deep window wells that send light refracting into the deeply protected refuge of the interior.

In the decades following these key syntheses, a variety of approaches were tested. Marcel Breuer, Hamilton Smith, and Pier Luigi Nervi designed a church of concrete, granite, and stained glass for St. John's University in Collegeville, Minnesota (1961), then announced its presence with a mammoth bell tower similar to the pylon of an ancient temple. Concrete was also Alvar Aalto's choice to create organic arcs of space in the Vuoksenniska Church (1958) in Imatra, Finland, and again for a church at Riola, Italy (1978). Less conventional still were the fortress-like blocks out of which Gottfried Böhm forged the Pilgrimage Church (1968) at Neviges, Germany, its plan lobed around a central pulpit. Equally powerful was the spectacular brick interior and fanned accordion roof that Paul Rudolph designed with Fry and Welch for the interdenominational Tuskegee Chapel (1969) at the Tuskegee Institute.

There were also consciously iconic approaches. Skidmore, Owings and Merrill opted for a symbolism of site with a series of geometric aluminum tetrahedrons, like the clustered wings of a plane, for the Air Force Academy Chapel (1963) at Colorado Springs, Colorado.

By contrast, St. Mary's Cathedral (1970) in San Francisco, by Pietro Belluschi, Pier Luigi Nervi, and others, took up a more ancient iconography. Their white sailing ship of poured concrete was a play on the concept of the nave or *navis*, the ship of souls, and the interior was conceived like a Gothic cathedral with stained-glass windows. Emblematic, too, of consumer culture and the role of the automobile in North American life was California's Garden Grove Community Church (1978) by Philip Johnson and John Burgee. Known as the Crystal Cathedral, its star-shaped hangar of steel and glass opened to accommodate drive-in participants in the service.

Another strategy stressed awareness of the natural environment. Frank Lloyd Wright's sensitivity for both materials and site extended in his religious works to a spiritual communion with nature. His First Unitarian Meetinghouse (1951) in Madison, Wisconsin, introduced a monumental window beneath a triangular copper gable, which opened up the sanctuary to its natural setting. His son, John Lloyd Wright, in turn took the approach a step further in the contemporaneous Wayfarer's Chapel at Palos Verdes, California, its glass enclosure, framed in redwood, sanctifying silent communion with the surrounding coastal scenery. Wright protégé E. Fay Jones refined the concept in the Thorncrown Wayfarer's Chapel (1981) for a hilltop site in the Ozark Mountains, near Eureka Springs, Arkansas, one of several similar structures the architect has since executed in other locations.

Some churches actually become one with the setting. Philip Johnson's Shrine at New Harmony, Indiana (1960), for example, consisted of a lobed, parabolic hood of timber, to focus upon the concept of the sacred without actually circumscribing the space. By contrast, in Sedona, Arizona, Ashen and Allen's Chapel of the Holy Cross (1965) was built into the red sandstone cliffs, while the domed Taivallahti Church (1969), in Helsinki, Finland, by Timo and Tuomo Suomalainen, was blasted into bedrock, the crater of which nested the footings of the interior. Stanley Tigerman's St. Benedict's Abbey (1978) at Benet Lake, Wisconsin, was buried in the ground to express humility. A similar integration executed in consciously vernacular terms by Auburn architecture professor Sambo Mockbee and his students, working collectively as the Rural Studio, was realized in the Yancey Chapel (1997) at Mason's Bend, Alabama. A lean-to dug into the earth and partly open to the sky, the chapel was built on a low budget for needy clients, without a specific plan and from scavenged materials, including old tires, rusted I beams, large trusses, pine from a century-house, tin from an old barn, and river slate.

Other architects have fused the geometry of international modernism with an appreciation for the natural setting. For example, in 1957 Finnish architects Heikki and Kaija Siren introduced a glass sanctuary wall into the linear geometry of their University Chapel in Otaniemi, Finland, locating the altar against a natural screen of fir trees. Similarly, contemporary Japanese architect Tadao Ando consciously combined the spirituality of East and West in his Church on the Water (1988) in Hokkaido. Its two-level structure, a roofless crown framed by four concrete crosses and a lower chapel with a glass wall overlooking a lake, aspired to "constructed nothingness" through a hybrid of geometry, nature, and materials that engaged the worshiper in a direct experience of nature.

More primal in their impact were the works of Hungarian architect Imre Makovecz, whose disturbingly anthropomorphic Mortuary Chapel (1977) in the Farkasret Cemetery, Budapest, is matched only by the ligamented viscera that frame his Roman Catholic Church (1990) in Paks, Poland. From cosmopolitanism to an experience of the sacred expressed in highly personal terms, religious architecture of the 20th century is a bricolage of tradition, ritual practice, formal expression, and an intangible articulation of spirituality.

ANGELA K. CARR

See also **Ando, Tadao (Japan); Calatrava, Santiago (Spain); Candela, Félix (Mexico); Corbusier, Le (Jeanneret, Charles-Édouard) (France); Chapel of Notre-Dame-du-Haut, Ronchamp, France; Gaudí, Antoni (Spain); Illinois Institute of Technology, Chicago; Mies van der Rohe, Ludwig (Germany); Nervi, Pier Luigi (Italy); Niemeyer, Oscar (Brazil); Notre Dame, Le Raincy; Saarinen, Eero (Finland)**

Further Reading

"Architectures Sacrées/Religious Architecture," *Techniques et architecture*, 405 (December 1992)

L'Art d'Eglise: Revue Trimestrielle, 45 (January–March 1977)

Bozzo, Gianni Baget, "Architettura e religione," *Domus*, 718 (July/August 1990)

Clausen, Meredith L., *Spiritual Space: The Religious Architecture of Pietro Belluschi*, Seattle: University of Washington Press, 1992

Cook, Peter, and Rosie Llewellyn-Jones, *New Spirit in Architecture*, New York: Rizzoli, 1991

Coppa and Avery Consultants, *Church Architecture: A Bibliographic Guide to Church Architecture in Selected Municipalities and Regions in the United States*, Monticello, Illinois: Vance Bibliographies, 1980

Davey, Peter (editor), "Theme Issue on Architecture and Religion," *The Architectural Review*, 190 (April 1992)

Eaton, Leonard K., *American Architecture Comes of Age: European Reaction to H.H. Richardson and Louis Sullivan*, Cambridge, Massachusetts: MIT Press, 1972

Frampton, Kenneth, and Yukio Futagawa, *Modern Architecture, 1851–1945*, 2 vols., New York: Rizzoli, 1983 (see especially volume 2: *Modern Architecture, 1920–1945*)

Gaskie, Margaret, "To Gather Together: Building Types Study 674, Religious Buildings," *Architectural Record*, 178 (January 1990)

Gieselmann, Reinhard, *New Churches*, New York: Architectural Book, 1972

Jodidio, Philip, *Contemporary American Architects*, Cologne: Taschen, 1993– (see especially volume 4, 1998)

Jodidio, Philip, *Álvaro Siza*, Cologne and New York: Taschen, 1999

Joedicke, Jürgen, *Geschichte der modernen Architektur*, Teufen, Switzerland: Niggli, 1958; as *A History of Modern Architecture*, translated by James C. Palmes, New York: Praeger, 1959; London: Architectural Press, 1961

Kennedy, Roger G., *American Churches*, New York: Stewart, Tambori and Chang, 1982

Kidder, G.E. Smith, *The New Churches of Europe*, New York: Holt, and London: Architectural Press, 1964

Klotz, Heinrich, *20th Century Architecture: Drawings, Models, Furniture from the Exhibition of the Deutschen Architekturmuseums, Frankfurt am Main*, New York: Rizzoli, and London: Academy Editions, 1989

LeBlanc, Sydney, *20th Century American Architecture: 200 Key Buildings*, New York: Whitney Library of Design, 1993; revised edition, as *20th-Century American Architecture: A Traveler's Guide to 220 Key Buildings*, 1996

Mannell, Steven, "Places of Worship I: In a Rational Light, Abbey Church St. Benoit-du-Lac, Quebec: Dan Hanganu, Architect," *The Canadian Architect*, 40 (October 1995)

Mazmanian, Arthur, *The Structure of Praise: A Design Study: Architecture for Religion in New England from the 17th Century to the Present*, Boston: Beacon, 1970

Mazria, Edward, "Edward Mazria: Sacred by Design," *Progressive Architecture*, 74–75 (March 1991)

Meyhöfer, Dirk, *Contemporary Japanese Architects*, Cologne: Taschen, 1994

Pehnt, Wolfgang (editor), *Encyclopedia of Modern Architecture*, London: Thames and Hudson, 1963; New York: Abrams, 1964

Placzek, Adolf K. (editor), *Macmillan Encyclopedia of Architects*, 4 vols., New York: Free Press, and London: Collier-Macmillan, 1982

Risebero, Bill, *Modern Architecture and Design: An Alternative History*, London: Herbert Press, 1982; Cambridge, Massachusetts: MIT Press, 1983

Sharp, Dennis, *A Visual History of Twentieth-Century Architecture*, London: Heinemann, Secker, and Warburg, and Greenwich, Connecticut: New York Graphic Society, 1972; revised and expanded edition, as *Twentieth-Century Architecture: A Visual History*, New York: Facts on File, and London: Lund Humphries, 1991

Shear, John Knox (editor), *Religious Buildings for Today*, New York: Dodge, 1957

Stern, Robert A.M., Gregory Gilmartin, and Thomas Mellins, *New York 1930: Architecture and Urbanism between the Two World Wars*, New York: Rizzoli, 1987

Stimpson, Miriam F., *A Field Guide to Landmarks of Modern Architecture in the United States*, Englewood Cliffs, New Jersey: Prentice-Hall, 1985

Wright, Lance (editor), "Manplan 5," *The Architectural Review*, 147 (March 1970)

CHURCH OF ST. FRANCIS OF ASSISI BELO HORIZONTE, BRAZIL

Designed by Oscar Niemeyer; completed 1943

In 1941 the mayor of Belo Horizonte, Juscelino Kubitschek, commissioned the architect Oscar Niemeyer to build a series of buildings around Pampulha lake. These included a yacht club, a dance hall, a casino, and a chapel, the latter of which is known as the Church of St. Francis of Assisi (1943). Under Kubitschek's influence Belo Horizonte, the capital of the state of Minas Gerais, aspired to compete with the two hitherto hegemonic metropolises, São Paulo and Rio de Janeiro. In 1938 the governor suggested the need for a tourist hotel in the colonial city of Ouro Preto, a project that would be also carried out by Niemeyer (1939). Kubitschek's desire to introduce modern elements in a city that still remained provincial and traditional motivated the urbanization of the lands edging the artificial lake in Pampulha, situated fifteen kilometers from the city center, and created for the recreation of Minas Gerais's new industrial bourgeoisie.

Niemeyer invited artists Alfredo Ceschiatti and Cándido Portinari and the landscape architect Roberto Burle Marx to collaborate on the Pampulha projects, including the Church of St. Francis of Assisi. In his designs Niemeyer abandoned the Cartesian system of composition in favor of freely curving forms in space.

The small church is shaped by three basic elements: the bell tower linked to the light access marquee, the nave covered by a freestanding vault, and the adjacent installations, covered by three smaller reinforced-concrete domes. The blind facade of the chapel, which faces the street, is embellished by a large mural by Cándido Portinari of Portuguese blue-and-white glazed tiles (*azulejos*) depicting scenes from the life of St. Francis of Assisi. The nave is designed in two parts: the area for the faithful worshipers, accessed through the horizontal slate of the choir, a low element that antecedes the surprise of the vault's parabolic expansion; and the altar space, lit from the ceiling's apex that establishes the difference in height between the two domes integrated in the central axis. From the darkness of the nave, the miracle of light illuminates the wall of the altar that is also covered with a painting by Portinari. From the exterior the chapel is apprehended through the continuous fluidity of the domes and the transparent bell tower that appears almost suspended in air by the light, curved, metallic supports.

Although these shapes were innovative for a religious building, Niemeyer was likely inspired by several precursors, including the parabolic hangars of the Orly Airport (1916–24, Eugéne Freyssinet) and the Orbetello Airport (1935–38, Pier Luigi Nervi), the curved ramps of the penguin pool at the London Zoo (1933–34, Berthold Lubetkin), and the Zementhalle in Zurich (1939, Robert Maillart). These lightweight shells foreshadowed the possibilities of reinforced concrete in the hands of talented structural engineers such as Félix Candela and Eladio Dieste in Latin America. Joaquim Cardozo, Niemeyer's engineer, participated in the creation of the church. The avant-gardism of Niemeyer's structure was widely rejected among the local clergy and the Minas Gerais bourgeoisie who did not accept such secular forms for a religious building; in fact, the church remained abandoned and converted to a radio station until 1959, when it became definitively a church.

The urbanization project of Belo Horizonte unfortunately did not prosper, and Pampulha began to decline, culminating in the contamination of the lake. Today, Niemeyer's buildings have been restored, and the area has been recuperated as a space for public leisure. Some European critics, in particular Bruno Zevi (1953) and Manfredo Tafuri (1979), argued that the chapel's freedom of design was overly formulist. The Italian critic Gillo Dorfles (1984) identified a nascent neobaroque modernism (or baroque rationalism) in Niemeyer's work. The French critic Jean Petit (1995) affirmed Niemeyer's autonomy from the prevailing European rationalism. According to Le Corbusier, an early mentor and collaborator, Niemeyer was able to marry the emotionalism of the baroque with the industrial and austere materials of reinforced concrete. Without question, Pampulha in the 1940s emerged as the forerunner of the expressive freedom of English and American Brutalism that emerged at the end of the Second World War.

ROBERTO SEGRE

See also **Burle Marx, Roberto (Brazil); Candela, Félix (Mexico); Church; Concrete Shell Structure; Corbusier, Le (Jeanneret, Charles-Édouard) (France); Costa, Lúcio (Brazil); Nervi, Pier Luigi (Italy); Niemeyer, Oscar (Brazil); Pampulha Buildings, Belo Horizonte, Brazil; Rationalism**

Further Reading

Botey, Josep Maria, *Oscar Niemeyer. Obras y proyectos*, Barcelona: G. Gili, 1996

Botey, Josep Maria, and Miquel Dalmau, *Oscar Niemeyer*, Barcelona: Caixa Barcelona, 1990

Bruand, Yves, *Arquitetura contemporâneo no Brasil*, São Paulo: Editora Perspectiva, 1981

Cavalcanti, Lauro, *As preocupações do Belo*, Rio de Janeiro: Taurus Editora, 1995

Dorfles, Gillo, *Architetture ambigue. Dal neobarocco al postmoderno*, Bari: Edizioni Dedalo, 1984

Niemeyer, Oscar, "De Pampulha ao Memorial da América Latina," *Módulo*, 100 (March 1989)

Papadaki, Stamo, *The Work of Oscar Niemeyer*, New York: Reinhold, 1950

Pereira, Miguel Alves, *Arquitetura, texto e contexto. O discurso de Oscar Niemeyer*, Brasília: Editora UnB, 1997

Petit, Jean, Lugano: Fidia Edizioni, *Niemeyer: Architetto e poeta*, 1995

Puppi, Lionello, *Guida a Niemeyer*, Milan: Arnoldo Mondadori, 1987

Sá Corrêa, Marcos, *Oscar Niemeyer*, Rio de Janeiro: Relume Dumará, 1996

Segawa, Hugo, *Arquiteturas no Brasil. 1900–1990*, São Paulo: Edusp, 1997

Tafuri, Manfredo, and Francesco dal Co, *Architettura Contemporanea*, Volume 2, Milan: Electa Editrice, 1979

Underwood, David, *Oscar Niemeyer and the Architecture of Brazil*, New York: Rizzoli, 1994

Zevi, Bruno, *Storia dell'architettura moderna*, Turin: Einaudi, 1953

CHURCH ON THE WATER

Designed by Tadao Ando; completed 1988
Hokkaido, Japan

Tadao Ando's Church on the Water (1988) signaled a critical shift in the designer's approach and for that reason was widely heralded in the international press. Ando's earlier residential works were structured private domains that were isolated from their surrounding urban contexts. The chapel, however, was a communal building designed for an idealized landscape, Ando's response to an earlier chapel on Mount Rokko (1986), rather than for a specific site or client. This is why published presentation drawings do not reflect the realities of the site, a point that would be otherwise odd, considering the importance of nature in the design. It is also the reason that such a long period passed between the building's design in 1985 and its construction in Hokkaido in 1988.

In the Church on the Water, nature becomes an active force. The sanctuary is essentially an open-ended shallow box, overwhelmed by a flat artificial pool. When the only separation between the two territories, a large glass wall, is rolled to the side, it erases any distinction between interior and exterior. Notably, this is also the only one of Ando's churches in which the altar area is depressed rather than raised, a gesture that increases the sense of spatial continuity and that is echoed in shallow terraces in the pond.

In the 1986 essay "Mutual Independence, Mutual Interpenetration," Ando wrote, "Within a site, architecture tries to dominate emptiness, but at the same time emptiness dominates the architecture. If a building is to be autonomous and have its own character, not only the building but the emptiness itself must have its own logic." There are clear parallels between Martin Heidegger and Eastern thought that make it difficult to determine the roots of Ando's phenomenology, but this character of nothingness, found in the blank pool, holds an important place in both philosophical systems. It is not God but, rather, man in nature that is the focus of this chapel. As Ando declared, "To experience God in this natural setting, perhaps, is to experience the encounter with one's own spirit" (Ando, 1989). Elsewhere, Ando goes further: "For me, the nature that a sacred space must relate to is man-made, or rather an architecturalized nature. I believe that when greenery, water, light or wind is abstracted from nature-as-is according to man's will, it approaches the sacred" (Ando, 1991).

The building was intended not as a religious structure but simply as a commercial chapel for wedding services. In a country where only an infinitesimal percentage of the population is Christian, the fashion of having "Christian" weddings is merely a reflection of Westernization. Thus, many of the conventional accoutrements of a church are unnecessary, in keeping with Ando's characteristic ascetic minimalism. With economic prosperity in the 1980s, young Japanese also embraced the larger Christian wedding ceremony as an opportunity for display. As a result, Ando's wedding chapels share with several other projects from the 1980s an irony: although he established a critical attitude in opposition to the comfort and decorative tendencies in architecture of the period, his works were embraced by the very consumer culture he denounced.

Some critics have implied that this was merely a "radical chic" gesture by fashionable Japanese, but it is worth noting that Ando's work was also compatible with a narcissism characteristic of the time. In 1986, Ando was developing a conception of space based on the physicality of the body and the use of the walls and floors as framing devices, articulated in his 1988 English-language piece "Shintai and Space." In Japanese, the word *shintai* has three meanings; the most common use of the word refers to religious icons and other objects intended for worship. In addition, the word indicates one's own body or a course of action. Had Ando used Japanese characters in writing his piece, he would have had to choose one of these meanings. In English, it was possible for him to fuse them; he explains that *shintai* refers not only to the body but also to "spirit and flesh" and declares that the *genus loci* of a site is grasped only through the *shintai*.

It is difficult not to measure the space with one's body. Small granite pavers in the sanctuary are only slightly more than shoulders' span in length. The markings of formwork on Ando's trademark concrete walls are the size of a single bed, and because the walls of this building are almost three feet thick, the imprints of form-tie separator cones are very close together. Risers are shallow and benches low, and the chairs for the nervous bride and groom are fragile perches. Thus, despite Ando's austere and even brutish use of unfinished concrete, the building has a delicacy and human scale.

Kenneth Frampton notes that the Church on the Water was "patently influenced" by Kaija and Heikki Siren's Otaniemi Chapel (1957) for the Helsinki Institute of Technology. The building is less often considered in literature today because the concepts that Ando initiated here are more skillfully carried out in subsequent works. The religious implications of architecture as a site for the body in nature are more convincingly executed in the later Water Temple (1992). The shallow proportions of the Church on the Water's sanctuary led to Ando's many outdoor amphitheaters, in which inconsequential stages and the lack of a backdrop make nature the real drama—including the first, the Theater on the Water (1987), planned for another site at the same Hokkaido resort. Even the avatar-like cross standing in the pool and the framework of crosses on the roof of the church later reemerged as freestanding colonnades forming spatial filters in Ando's works from the late 1980s.

Francesco Dal Co has written that Ando is "completing building after building with astonishing speed, but only able to do so by falling back on the design and conceptual procedures he had worked out in earlier researches." In this designer's work, it is often not the variations on concepts that are of interest but their genesis. More than 15 years after its completion, the Church on the Water remains a source of inspiration for the architect; it is clearly the model for Ando's Chapel of the Sea, completed at the end of 1999 as part of the Awaji Island Yume Butai.

DANA BUNTROCK

See also **Siren, Heikki and Kaija (Finland)**

Further Reading

Ando has written briefly on many of his works, both in English and in Japanese. The best of these are collected in the *Complete Works*, edited by Dal Co, which also includes a bibliography of primary and secondary sources. Images of the Church on the Water are most numerous in Drew and Frampton. The other books on this list offer a useful context, especially demonstrating the development of the ideas first explored in this chapel.

Ando, Tadao, *Tadao Ando: The Yale Studio and Current Works*, New York: Rizzoli, 1989

Ando, Tadao, *Tadao Ando*, Tokyo: Japan Architect, 1991

Ando, Tadao, *Tadao Ando, 1989–1992*, edited by Richard C. Levene and Fernando Márquez Cecilia, Madrid: El Croquis, 1993

Ando, Tadao, *Tadao Ando: Complete Works*, edited by Francesco Dal Co, London: Phaidon, 1995

Drew, Philip, *Church on the Water, Church of the Light: Tadao Ando*, London: Phaidon, 1996

Frampton, Kenneth, *Tadao Ando*, New York: Museum of Modern Art, 1991

Tadao Ando: Beyond Horizons in Architecture, Tokyo: Shinkenchiku-sha, 1992

CITÉ INDUSTRIELLE, UNE

Unbuilt project designed by Tony Garnier, completed 1917

Une Cité industrielle, Etude pour la construction des villes (An Industrial Town, Study for the Construction of Towns, 1901–04, 1917), Tony Garnier's vast and complex project consisting of 164 plates for an imaginary industrial town, incorporated classical, contemporary, and futuristic aspects. Modernist architects considered it a significant pioneering work in modernism, one that retained classical elements. Garnier himself, however, never participated in the Modern movement. He practiced architecture without being overly concerned with the conflicts between modernity and tradition. Later interpretations have compared the affinity of *Une Cité industrielle* with contemporary trends, such as the Garden City movement, debates on workers' housing, utopian literature, and the socialist tradition. *Une Cité industrielle* was foremost an innovation in regional and town planning.

Garnier won the Rome Prize in 1899 as a student at the École des Beaux-Arts in Paris and studied in Rome for four years. There he worked on *Une Cité industrielle* (which outraged the conservative Académie des Beaux-Arts) and a project for the restoration of the ancient city of Tusculum. Garnier exhibited drawings for *Une Cité industrielle* in 1904. The final, expanded 1917 version incorporated numerous projects that were realized in Lyons, Garnier's native city, to which he returned in 1905. The same year, Garnier met the 33-year-old radical-socialist mayor, Edouard Herriot. The two launched a program of construction that would last three decades.

Une Cité industrielle is an astoundingly thorough visualization, from its overall conception down to individual houses. Garnier emphasized zoning, circulation, hygiene, and industry, considering both communal and individual aspects of life in a town of 35,000 inhabitants. The general plan is based on the French academic tradition. However, the parklike setting and the emphasis on pedestrian routes are comparable to the English

Garden City movement led by Ebenezer Howard and to the ideas of Camillo Sitte. The site was to be near raw materials, sources of energy, and communication routes. The three main functions of the town—production, housing, and health facilities—are clearly distinguished. Residential and public areas are placed on a plateau, and the industrial complex is situated on the periphery by the river. At the center of the residential area is a cluster of public buildings, including an assembly hall, museums, libraries, theaters, and a sports center. Around the railroad station is a mixture of tall residential and commercial buildings, including an open market and a clock tower. Residential quarters are arranged on an urban grid divided into lots of 15 by 15 meters. Each building is linked to a pedestrian route so that people could cross the city in all directions independently of the roads. All houses are detached. Courtyards are eliminated, and every room is lit and ventilated directly from the outside. Each bedroom has at least one south-facing window that lets in plenty of sunlight. All the interior walls and floors are made of smooth material. Only half the residential area was to be built up, whereas the other half was to form a kind of a communal garden.

Garnier's emphasis on hygiene, space, and the separation of pedestrian and automobile traffic would resonate widely in the early 20th century. His conception of urban zoning would have a profound impact on 20th-century town planning. Le Corbusier, who met Garnier in 1907, was the first well-known architect to publicly acknowledge the influence of *Une Cité industrielle* in 1921. *Une Cité industrielle* relies on reinforced concrete for the buildings that gives them a bare and austere appearance. The houses are mostly free of ornamentation, with the exception of several classical sculptures. The simplicity of material and means of construction were to lead logically to great simplicity of expression in the structure, which then would support a variety of decorative arts. Such ideas reveal an affinity with traditional architectural theory, emphasizing preestablished harmonies. At the same time, Garnier's influence forced French architectural education to be more open to the concerns of New Urbanism.

Intellectual currents of the late 19th century provided inspiration for *Une Cité industrielle*. Many French intellectuals embraced ideals of social progress deriving from the socialist tradition of Charles Fourier, visions of a scientific and technological utopia espoused in both French and foreign novels, and renewed interest for antiquities. *Une Cité industrielle* resembles the ideal city in Emile Zola's *Travail* (1900–01); the assembly hall of *Une Cité industrielle* has inscriptions from *Travail*. The absence of a church, prison, court, police station, or military barracks fits with some of the contemporary utopian ideas, including the premise that society would provide medicine and basic foodstuffs. Garnier's premise rested on a systematic physical organization that would best sustain the needs of the individual in a regional setting. In Lyons, Garnier built a series of exemplary public buildings, such as a slaughterhouse-cattle market complex (1909–13), an Olympic stadium (1913) with Greco-Roman allusions, and the Grange-Blanche Hospital (1915), all of which were integrated into *Une Cité industrielle*. *Une Cité industrielle* enabled Garnier to integrate his conceptions into Lyons, an existing, complex city, and thereby contribute significantly to 20th-century architecture and urban planning.

HAZEL HAHN

See also **Garden City Movement; Garnier, Tony (France); New Urbanism; Urban Planning**

Further Reading

Guiheux, Alain, Olivier Cinqualbre, and Nicole Toutcheff (editors), *Tony Garnier: L'Oeuvre complète*, Paris: Centre Georges Pompidou, 1989

Jullian, René, *Tony Garnier, constructeur et utopiste*, Paris: Sers, 1989

Mariani, Riccardo (editor), *Tony Garnier: Une Cité industrielle*, New York: Rizzoli, 1990

Pawlowski, Krzysztof Kazimierz, *Tony Garnier et les débuts de l'urbanisme fonctionnel en France*, Paris: Centre de Recherche d'Urbanisme, 1967

Wiebenson, Dora, *Tony Garnier: The Cité Industrielle*, London: Studio Vista, and New York: Braziller, 1969

CITTÀ NUOVA (1914)

On 20 May 1914 Antonio Sant'Elia from Italy and Mario Chiattone from Switzerland, two young architects in the Italian avant-garde movement Il Nuovo Tendenze, exhibited drawings that illustrated fragments of a new urban metropolis. Chiattone's contribution, entitled "Structures of a Modern Metropolis," included several fine renditions of high-rise apartment buildings that presaged later developments in the 1920s and 1930s, but they were overshadowed by Sant'Elia's collection of drawings, entitled *La città nuova* (The New City), his vision of Milan in the year 2000. These drawings were accompanied in the exhibition catalog by a written text, a *messaggio* (or manifesto) on the problems of modern architecture, bearing Sant'Elia's name only. This polemical essay reappeared in a reworked form several weeks later, on 11 July 1914, as *L'architettura futurista* (Futurist Architecture), still authored by Sant'Elia, but bearing the unmistakable stamp of Filippo Tommaso Marinetti, the mouthpiece of Italian futurism.

Dispute still lingers over the precise relationship of Sant'Elia to Marinetti and to the futurist movement in general. Most critics agree that Sant'Elia was primarily a socialist who joined Marinetti's movement without much enthusiasm on account of its increasingly outspoken nationalist character, at odds with the more internationalist views of socialist thought at that time. But there is little doubt that Sant'Elia's vision of the new city, an urban environment infatuated with the awesome potential of mechanistic form, is futurist in concept, even if not specifically created under that banner.

Antonio Sant'Elia was born in Como, in northern Italy, in 1880. He studied architecture in Milan and later in Bologna, where he graduated at the age of 24. His studies were interrupted by a period of apprenticeship with the Villoressi Canal Company and some time spent in the works department of the commune of Milan. On his return to Milan from Bologna in 1912, Sant' Elia was in touch with the polemical futurist group under Marinetti's provocative leadership and clearly had sympathy with several of their aesthetic aims having to do with the dynamism and mechanized setting of futurist life in a truly modern metropolis.

The eleventh proposition of the original Futurist Manifesto, published by Marinetti in 1909, praises "the midnight fervor of arsenals and shipyards blazing with electric moons; insatiable stations swallowing the smoking serpents of their trains; factories hung from clouds by the twisted threads of their smoke; [and]

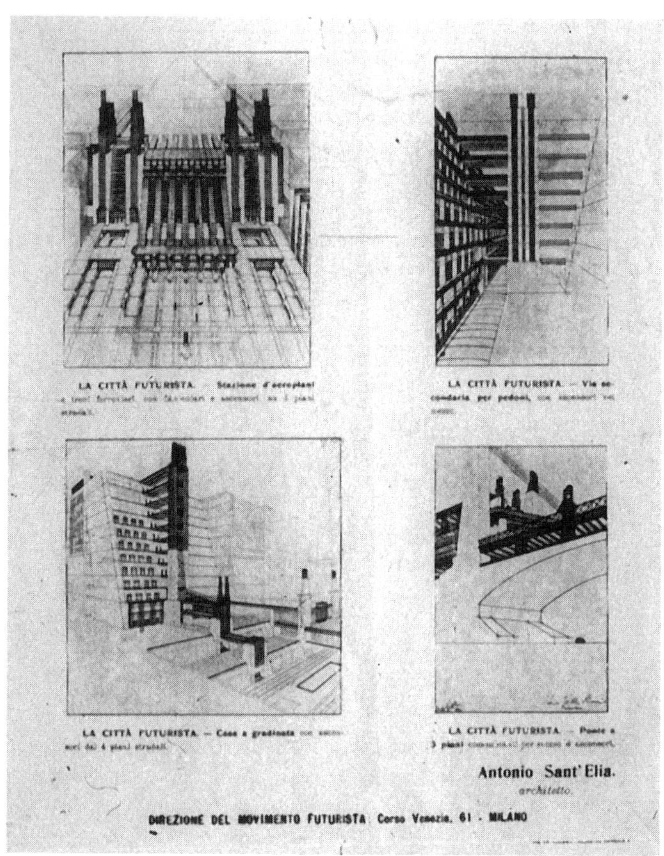

Antonio Sant'Elia, first page of the original pamphlet edition of the manifesto *L'architettura futurista* (Futurist Architecture)

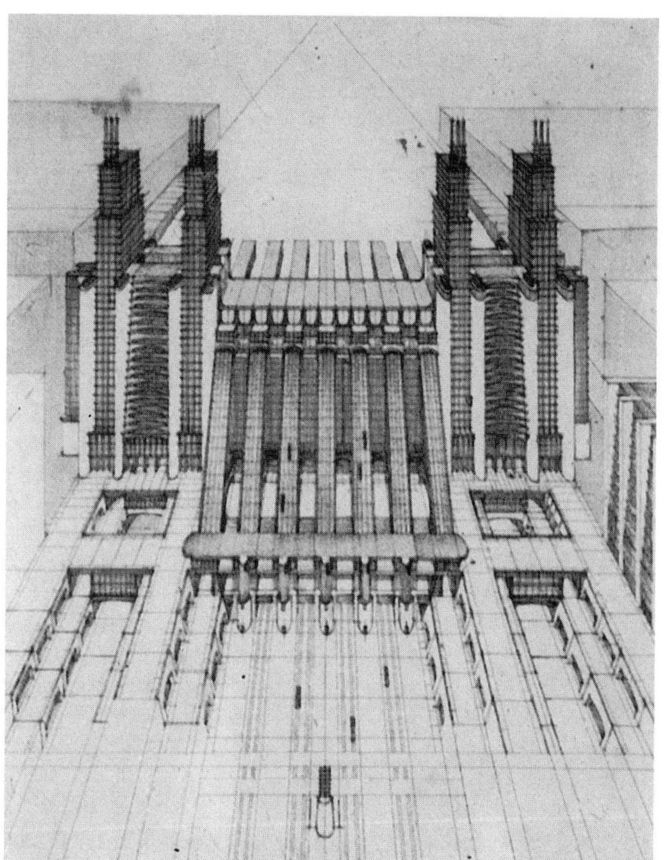

Antonio Sant'Elia, *La citta nuova*, plane and train station, with funiculars and elevators on three traffic levels; ink and pencil on tracing paper

bridges flashing like knives in the sun, giant gymnasts that leap over rivers."

This passage could serve as a preface for Sant'Elia's vision, and in a series (possibly hundreds) of provocative sketches made in 1912, 1913, and 1914, Sant'Elia sought to translate the spirit and content of mechanical innovations into architectural and urban form. Tall sculpted shapes define a city of rapid travel and technical purity, forms that owed much to the artifacts of the new industrial society such as power stations—an icon of Marinetti's futurist vocabulary—and engineering structures such as great dams. One of the most famous drawings, *Stazione aeroplani* (1914)—a study for the more finished version in *La città nuova* exhibition—illustrates a railway station shaped like a huge dam. Trains vanish beneath the great, sloping mass, raked by escalators and flanked by symmetrical towers, whereas to the rear an aircraft landing strip vanishes into the distance between clifflike slabs of buildings—a particularly dangerous transport interchange that reappeared in Le Corbusier's drawings a decade and more later.

Several lines in Sant'Elia's manifesto that accompanied his drawings at the 1914 exhibition echo the sentiments and wording of the Futurist Manifesto closely, but the text, put together by a colleague, Ugo Nebbia, from Sant'Elia's own words, indicates that the architect was quite capable of formulating futurist polemics and visions without any direct help (or interference) from Marinetti. Sant'Elia's words marry with his images to create a future world in which architects "must invent and rebuild *ex novo* our Modern city like an immense and tumultuous shipyard. . . . Elevators must no longer hide away like solitary worms in the stairwells . . . but must swarm up the facades like serpents of glass and iron."

In none of the drawings and sketches are conventional streets or buildings indicated. There is no indication of traditional urban structure. Instead, Sant'Elia depicts the city as a megastructure of connected building masses and multilevel movement systems, presaging the fascination with urban megastructures during the 1960s and 1970s. In this aspect his vision of the future city differs sharply from that of Tony Garnier, whose *Cité industrielle* of 1901–04, although relying on hydroelectric power and containing large industrial buildings and a modern train station, still contains residential areas comprising streets of neat homes surrounded by greenery. In Sant'Elia's vision, such residential quarters are superseded by stacked apartment houses, their stepped profiles lined with terraces and accessed by elevator towers and flying bridges.

It is not clear whether *Città nuova* was to replace the existing city fabric of Milan completely. However, in accordance with futurist principles that placed emphasis on the continual reinvention and rebuilding of the city, it is evident that by drawing a completely new urban world, Sant'Elia did want to inspire people to supplant existing cities. This cleared site approach was emphasized again in Le Corbusier's 1925 *Plan voisin* for central Paris and was to come true with many devastating consequences in American and European cities during the urban renewal period of the 1950s and 1960s.

With the wisdom of hindsight, it is easy to blame Sant'Elia's visions for some of the negative physical and social outcomes of this radical demolition approach that are evident to architects and planners at the end of the 20th century. But these visions were born of their time, and the world of fin-de-siècle Europe was vastly different; there was a growing sense, especially in Italy (only recently unified in 1861), that the old age was passing and a new one beginning, politically and in terms of technology.

For most of the 19th century, new technologies had little impact on the appearance of Italian cities, but the last quarter of the century saw massive changes, especially in the northern cities of Milan and Turin. These cities became major industrial centers in which new building types—train stations, large factories, and power stations—jostled side by side with older buildings. Electric lighting came to city buildings and streets, and these same thoroughfares became clogged with traffic and the new electric trams. This transformation of Milan—the home base of Marinetti and the futurists—from an Old World princely capital to an industrial metropolis galvanized futurist thought. Clearly the new world would not fit into the antiquated Renaissance palaces of Italian history; the young nation of Italy, with new technological power and potential, needed a correspondingly modern urban environment in which to flourish. But before this contemporary city could arise, Sant'Elia theorized, Italy had to be shaken from its architectural slumber and cast off the burden of its classical past and deadening architectural conventions.

This new urban world, created with an architecture of engineering directness and bold sculptural form, is illustrated precisely in Sant'Elia's drawings for *La citta nuova*. His forms, surfaces, and spaces destroyed the traditions and styles of classicism and historical eclecticism. Sant'Elia reworked several of his earlier sketches, transforming them from fluid Expressionist compositions to finely wrought illustrations, drafted with exquisite care and precision. Using black ink and black (occasionally blue-black) pencil on paper and tracing paper, Sant'Elia transmuted the flowing romantic images of his preparatory drawings into hard-edged perspectives that transcended other visualizations of the future metropolis. When compared with contemporary illustrations of future New York by R. Rummel (1911) and H. Wiley Corbett (1913), which comprise large, lumpen buildings and bridges clothed in standard historicist details, Sant' Elia presented an architecture of stark and flashing profile, developed with convincing engineering details that pushed new materials and technologies to their limits.

For the Nuovo Tendenze exhibition Sant'Elia selected 16 drawings comprising the Airplane and Train Station; the Casa Nuova apartment building and four other high-rise apartment buildings (referred to as "terraced houses") incorporating external elevators and sited adjacent to multilevel roadways; three power stations; a bridge; and six other detail or preparatory sketches. Taken together, these thoroughly worked out illustrations provided the most heroic and poetic conception of all the utopian visions of the 20th-century city. Compared to the polite, well-mannered comprehensiveness of Garnier's *Cité industrielle*, the rationalist bombast of Le Corbusier's *Plan voisin* (1925), or the idiosyncratic prairie aesthetic of Frank Lloyd Wright's Broadacre City (1934–35), Sant'Elia's imagination depicts, in a marvelous pictorial synthesis, a city infatuated with the majestic and liberating potential of the machine. Sant'Elia's tragic, if heroic, death at the battle of Monfalcone, on 10 October 1916, denied the world a more developed examination of this urban potential. The futurist architecture of *La città nuova* died with its precocious young author.

DAVID WALTERS

See also **Broadacre City (1934–35); Cité Industrielle, Une; Futurism; Sant'Elia, Antonio (Italy); Voisin Plan for Paris**

Further Reading

Banham, Reyner, *Theory and Design in the First Machine Age*, London: Architectural Press, and New York: Praeger, 1960

Caramel, Luciano, and Alberto Longatti, *Antonio Sant'Elia: L'opera completa*, Milan: Mondadori, 1987; as *Antonio Sant'Elia: The Complete Works*, New York: Rizzoli, 1988

Ulrich, Conrad (compiler), *Programme und Manifeste zur Architektur des 20. Jahrhunderts*, Gütersloh, Germany: Bertelsmann, 1964; as *Programs and Manifestoes on 20th-Century Architecture*, translated by Michael Bullock, Cambridge, Massachusetts: MIT Press, and London: Lund Humphries, 1970

CITY BEAUTIFUL MOVEMENT

Begun in the United States in the late 19th century, the City Beautiful movement enjoyed a relatively brief reign, fading into obscurity during the New Deal and the rise of modernism. City Beautiful architects and planners sought to bring elements of city planning, architecture, and landscape architecture into a harmonious unity. It aspired to many of the principles of baroque or neoclassical city design, which had transformed the medieval cores of European cities such as Rome from the reign of Pope Sixtus V in the late 16th century to Paris under the prefecture of Baron Georges Eugene Haussmann in the mid–19th century. Equally embedded in City Beautiful was a celebration of neoclassical architecture, transplanted to American soil by architects loyal to the aesthetic principles promoted by the École des Beaux-Arts in Paris.

Although its intellectual seeds were sown by a handful of 19th-century figures, such as landscape architect Frederick Law Olmsted and city planner Charles Mulford Robinson, the possibilities of the City Beautiful ideal were most dramatically portrayed at the World's Columbian Exposition, opening in Chicago in 1893. With Daniel H. Burnham in charge of the overall design and construction process, highly regarded architects such as Van Brunt and Howe; McKim, Mead and White; Peabody and Stearns; Adler and Sullivan; Burling and Whitehouse; Jenny and Mundie; and Henry Ives Cobb contributed designs for individual buildings and features. Rendered in a special type of plaster, their work resulted in magnificent exhibition halls designed in classical Greco-Roman and Renaissance architectural styles. Olmsted's landscaping talents infused the site plan of the fair and included a lagoon, canals, ceremonial plazas, promenades, gardens, fountains, and statuary. By the fair's end well over 20 million people had visited and returned to their home cities and countries around the world with an idealized vision of the future city. This idealized view characterized the City Beautiful movement wherever it was pursued, in small town and large city alike.

At its heart City Beautiful was less an aesthetic ideal and more fundamentally a concept that at that time was largely alien in North America, namely, that cities should result not from random and cumulative decisions by individual architects and builders but from a holistically conceived and visually coherent plan that prescribes siting, scale, and other design principles in a rational and balanced ensemble. A bold idea, to be sure, City Beautiful arose in the context of the reformist fervor that sought to transform politics, government, and social policy in the late 19th and early 20th centuries within an orderly and humanly scaled urban setting combining nature and planning.

Eight years after the exposition's close, the nation's capital became the first U.S. city to seriously pursue City Beautiful principles. As consultants to the McMillan Commission, Burnham, Olmsted, Charles F. McKim, and Augustus St. Gaudens sought to restore the essence of Washington's original 1792 plan as prepared by Pierre Charles L'Enfant and refined by Andrew Ellicott. The plan resulted in the removal of railroad tracks, a polluted creek, and several buildings from the Mall. The Mall was relandscaped in the tradition of French formalism. Building heights and massing were carefully limited, and structures were sited so as to enclose the Mall in a balanced and harmonious composition. Although many details have been altered, the 20th-century redevelopment of the Mall and environs in central Washington has more or less embraced the spirit of the McMillan Commission plan.

Several other communities followed suit. For example, Virgil G. Bogue's plan for Seattle (1911) and Edward H. Bennett's plans for Minneapolis (1917) and Denver (1917) also promoted City Beautiful ideals. However, for sheer aspirations and comprehensive vision of present and future conditions, the 1909 plan of Chicago knew no equal in terms of boldness and departure from the city's 19th-century status quo. Written by Burnham and Bennett, the plan prescribed a great civic center plaza in the downtown, framed by federal and state buildings and a new city hall; a lakefront park, its symmetrical jetties embracing a view corridor westward to the civic center; broad boulevards and diagonal avenues intersecting at magnificent circles and squares containing obelisks, columns, fountains, and decorative focal features; and carefully proportioned buildings built to uniform cornice heights. Today, in the city of skyscrapers and gridded streets, Grant Park, Wacker Drive, Michigan Avenue, and the city's associated cultural institutions and sprawling park system echo the grandiose utterances found in the plan.

Beyond Chicago, fragments of City Beautiful plans appeared in other cities. Burnham's modified plan for San Francisco resulted in construction of a civic center embraced by the domed neoclassical City Hall (1915), library (1916), courthouse (1926), and other civic and government edifices. Burnham, John M. Carrere, and Arnold W. Brunner prepared Cleveland's Group Plan (1903), which ultimately led to construction of that city's civic center, the Mall. Arrayed on its perimeter are a federal building (1910), courthouse (1911), city hall (1916), auditorium (1922), library (1925), Board of Education building (1930), and county building (1957). Civic center plazas or malls were added to Indianapolis, Denver, and St. Louis, all in the early 20th century.

Cleveland Group Plan (1903), designed by Daniel Burnham, John M. Carrère, and Arnold W. Brunner. View of central and north sections of the Mall.
© Dennis Gale

Other cities appropriated other City Beautiful conventions. Philadelphia's Benjamin Franklin Parkway (1919) is a grand avenue cutting diagonally through the city's grid system to visually link City Hall to the Philadelphia Museum of Art. Between them lie a grand circle and an oval providing open space for landscaping, statuary, and other decorative features. City Beautiful plans found reality in many state capitals, including Harrisburg, Pennsylvania; Austin, Texas; and Augusta, Maine. In these cities and others, carefully organized vistas, elevated public buildings, ceremonial boulevards, formalistic landscaping, and near uniform building heights bespeak the legacy of Burnham, Bennett, Olmsted, and others.

An irony of the City Beautiful movement was the fact that it emerged in opposition to the real American industrial city of the Gilded Age. Embedded in the times was a struggle among architects, landscape architects, engineers, artists, and civic leaders over the direction and meaning of the fledgling city-planning profession. Many sought to emphasize the functional elements of city planning, including efficiency, economy, safety, and reform of social conditions. Others insisted that the aesthetic and cultural attributes of European baroque ideals and neoclassical architecture would inspire civic pride, respect for democratic values, and cultural growth among citizens and visitors to American cities. With more than a century behind it, the City Beautiful legacy remains in American history a celebration of order, balance, symmetry, axiality, monumentality, and restraint.

DENNIS E. GALE

See also **Burnham, Daniel H. (United States); McKim, Mead and White (United States); Mumford, Lewis (United States); Parkways; Philadelphia (PA), United States; Plan of Chicago; Urban Planning**

Further Reading

One of the most authoritative texts is Wilson's *The City Beautiful Movement,* which examines the work of Burnham, Bennett, and others in several U.S. cities. A respected source on the World's Columbian Exposition is Burg's *Chicago's White City of 1893.* To place City Beautiful in the larger evolution of city planning history, Scott's *American City Planning since 1890* is an excellent departure point. For a less sympathetic treatment of the movement, Lewis Mumford's *Sticks and Stones* (chapter 6, "The Imperial Facade") will command the reader's attention.

Burg, David F., *Chicago's White City of 1893,* Lexington: University Press of Kentucky, 1976

Burnham, Daniel H., and Edward H. Bennett, *Plan of Chicago,* edited by Charles Moore, Chicago: The Commercial Club of Chicago, 1909; reprint, New York: Princeton Architectural Press, 1993

Gutheim, Frederick, and Wilcomb E. Washburn, *The Federal City: Plans and Realities: The History* (exhib. cat.), Washington, D.C.: Smithsonian Institution Press, 1976

Hines, Thomas S., *Burnham of Chicago: Architect and Planner,* New York: Oxford University Press, 1974

Issel, William, and Robert W. Cherny, *San Francisco, 1865–1932: Politics, Power, and Urban Development,* Berkeley: University of California Press, 1986

Kahn, Judd, *Imperial San Francisco: Politics and Planning in an American City, 1897–1906,* Lincoln: University of Nebraska Press, 1979

Mumford, Lewis, *Sticks and Stones: A Study of American Architecture and Civilization,* New York: Boni and Liveright, 1924; reprint, New York: Dover, 1955

Scott, Mel, *American City Planning since 1890,* Berkeley: University of California Press, 1969

Wilson, William H., *The City Beautiful Movement,* Baltimore, Maryland: Johns Hopkins University Press, 1989

CITY HALL

The city hall is an ancient building type, its origins found at least as far back as the classical Greek *bouleutrion,* the assembly chamber of the city-state. In medieval Europe the city hall took on a number of auxiliary spaces that complemented the council chamber, such as market halls, office spaces, and social rooms. Some, such as the Palazzo Pubblico in Siena or the Palazzo Vecchio in Florence, celebrated the corporate identity of the independent city with soaring towers and instructive works of art. As cities grew in size and administrative complexity, their city halls grew ever larger and assumed a prominence in the urban form of their cities that rivaled only the greatest sacred edifices. By the end of the 19th century, enormous piles, such as Alfred Waterhouse's Manchester Town Hall (1867–77) and John McArthur's Philadelphia City Hall (1871–1901), marked the seats of municipal authority with complex historical allusions and equally convoluted silhouettes.

At the beginning of the 20th century, it was unquestioned that a building typology as representational as a city hall would be expressed in a historical style. In northern Europe this historicism often meant an investigation of medieval forms, as the type was closely associated with its medieval antecedents and the National Romantic movement. Martin Nyrop's Copenhagen Town Hall (1892–1905) was the most significant example of the northern European city hall and a primary inspiration for Ragnar Östberg's Stockholm City Hall (1911–23), which fused medieval and Renaissance detailing with an extensive art program. In more southern nations, Renaissance and baroque models were often emulated. Contemporaneous city halls in the United Kingdom often interpreted the baroque. A. Brumwell Thomas appropriated Wren's vocabulary at St. Paul's to create his grand but rather literal Belfast City Hall (1897–1906), and John Belcher's Colchester City Hall (1897–1902) did much to establish the English "free baroque." Across the English Channel, the influential French architect and theorist Victor Laloux built several city halls modeled on those of the 17th century; his *hôtel de ville* (1898–1900) at Tours inspired several interpretations across the Atlantic.

In the United States many cities had built their city halls in the 1880s and 1890s, when the Richardsonian Romanesque style suited the desirable images of permanence and monumentality. Later, the civic improvement movement known as the City Beautiful encouraged many cities to build new city halls as the centerpiece of a multistructure civic center modeled on the "White City" of the World's Columbian Exposition of 1893 in Chicago. The most complete and successful of these efforts was built after the great earthquake and fire of San Francisco (1906); Bakewell and Brown's City Hall (1912–16) dominates the 15-block Civic Center with a 300-foot-high dome sometimes described as a Doric fusion of those of Hardouin-Mansart and Michelangelo. The skyscraper as city hall was first executed across the bay in Oakland, California, where Palmer and Hornbostel won a competition with a 14-story tower in 1911. The skyscraper idiom became more common in the 1920s and is best exemplified by Austin, Martin and Parkinson's Los Angeles City Hall, a severe classical tower, and G. Lloyd Preacher's Gothic skyscraper Atlanta City Hall (1928–30); Art Deco forms dominated the 1930s—Dietel and Wade and Sullivan Jones' Buffalo City Hall remains an important American example of this international movement. In some locales regionally important revival styles were employed to reinforce the city's past or to promote an idealized fictive past; Bakewell and Brown's Pasadena City Hall (1923–27) was an amalgamation of Mediterranean sources intended to evoke a Spanish heritage that the community did not actually possess.

The emergence of the Modern movement in Europe in the 1910s and 1920s was not often evidenced in city halls, largely because few new city hall projects were initiated between the wars and because the political nature of the type nearly precluded experimental form. Several notable exceptions were built. Willem Dudock's Town Hall (1924–30) for Hilversum, the Netherlands, is well known. Dudock contrasted several austere horizontal masses, including a primary volume containing the council chamber, with a soaring tower. Each mass interlocked with several others and yet remained distinctly legible, the assembly presenting a balanced composition in repose. Fritz Höger's Town Hall (1928–30) for Rüstringen, Germany, exemplified his interest in dramatic geometric form within the limitations of brick masonry; the ceremonial entry and council chamber are marked by an enormous 12-story tower, a pure solid broken only by a series of vertical fins and a clock tower on the primary elevation.

After World War II a large number of city centers in Europe required complete rebuilding. Naturally enough, in many places city halls were repaired or even reconstructed in order to preserve a continuity with prewar civic life. Some cities, particularly in Germany, adapted surviving structures to a new civic purpose, with the intention to build a representational structure at some time in the future. Most of the continent's new city halls were modern in orientation. Perhaps the most famous are those by Alvar Aalto, whose civic complexes for Säynätsalo (1950–52) and Seinajöki (1952–66) wove the town hall and auxiliary buildings into the landscape and demonstrated as much concern for the space between the buildings as for the buildings themselves. At Seinajöki the city hall is marked by its axial siting within the civic center and by a commanding monitor roof through which light pours into the council chamber.

American postwar city halls came in two forms: the unassuming suburban multipurpose civic building, which usually was designed on a decidedly domestic scale, and the overscaled, inner-city modernist monument, which usually served as the centerpiece of a large urban-renewal scheme. The former conception, city hall as ranch house or colonial farmstead, successfully served those residential communities that lacked a commercial center or a long civic tradition. The success of the second movement, the city hall as civic savior, has proven more troublesome, if only because so much more was at stake. Perhaps definitive of this latter form, Kallmann, McKinnell and Knowles' Boston City Hall (1963–69) commands its cleared plaza and the 18th- and early 19th-century harbor below it like a citadel. Although one can read the jumble of fenestration on the harbor elevation for a clue as to the location of the mayor's suite and the council chambers, much of the public's interaction with its municipal government is forced underground into several floors of bureaucratic offices below grade. This loss of dignified purpose continued into the late 20th century, in which many newer Sunbelt cities constructed city halls and civic campuses indistin-

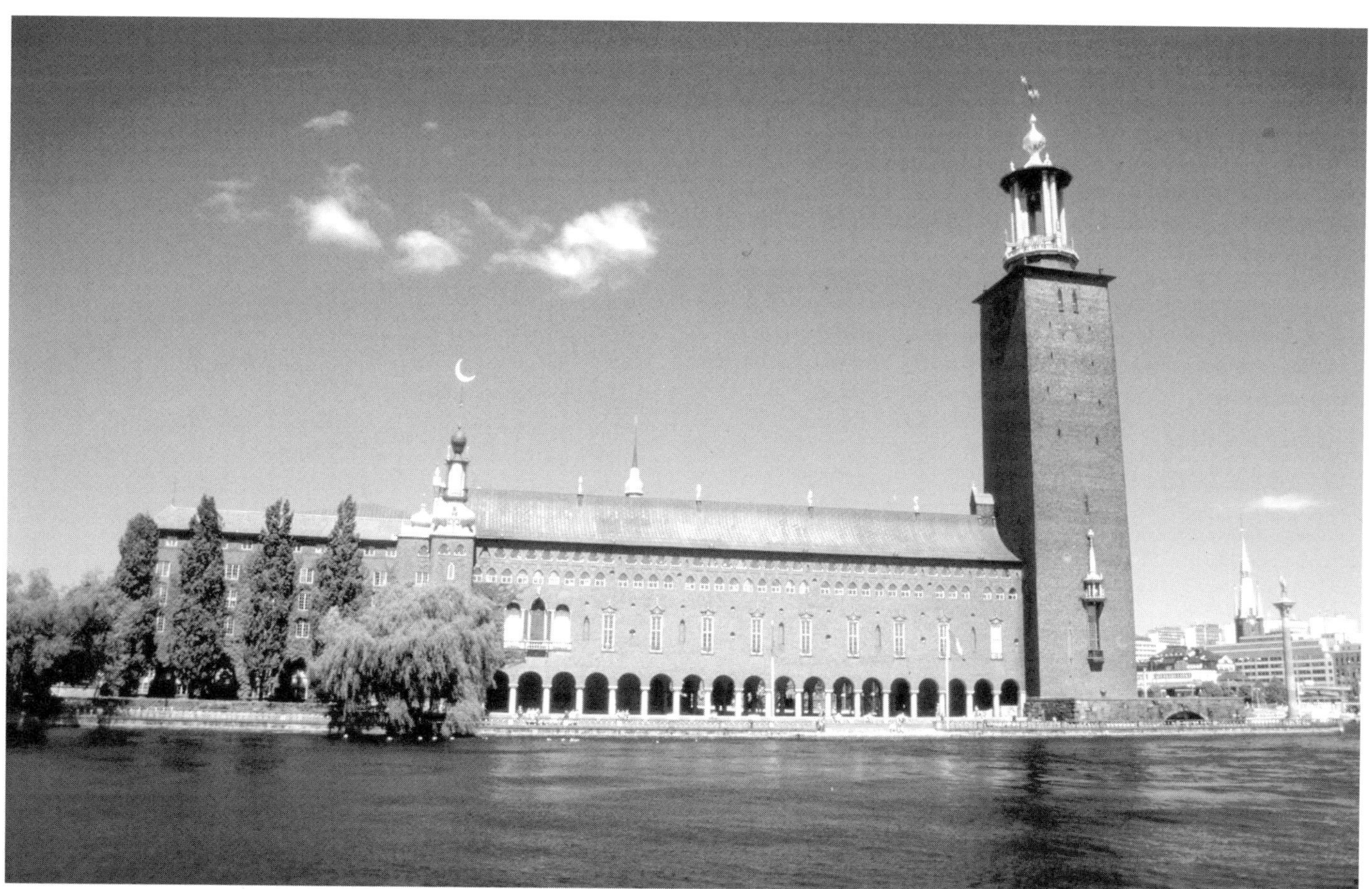

Stadshuset (Stockholm City Hall), designed by Ragnar Östberg (1911–23)
© Macduff Everton/CORBIS

guishable from the suburban business parks and hotel slabs that surround them.

At the end of the 20th century, the city hall regained its significance in architectural discourse, although not without some concern about the overwhelming scale that the modern city hall often possesses. Richard Meier's city halls restored the type to the center of urban life, but they did so without comment on the local architectural dialect. In The Hague (1987–95), Meier organized three colossal slabs of office space about an equally enormous atrium, creating within the city hall a public realm that functions independently of the often damp Dutch climate. One corner of the complex is punctuated by the cylindrical mass of the public library, a form that is repeated within the atrium at the council chamber; both are subordinated to the experience of the atrium, whose precise detail and sublime scale transport the viewer beyond the day-to-day life of the city.

Scale is again of paramount importance with Kenzo Tange's City Hall (1989–95) for Tokyo. This complex, spread over three blocks of the Shinjuku subcenter, is composed of two tower groups and an assembly building linked to the towers by skywalks. The axiality and geometric rigor of the plan recall the Beaux-Arts conceptions of the beginning of the century, even as the elevations refer to both traditional Japanese post-and-beam construction and modern integrated circuit boards. The orthogonal grids set up by the office tower blocks are complemented by the radial framework of the assembly building, whose sweeping hemicycle embraces a fan-shaped court reminiscent of the Piazza del Campo in Siena. The elliptical assembly hall is situated on axis to this court, elevated to the seventh floor, and in fact breaks the plane of the hemicycle to announce its presence. In his design Tange provides both a usable public space and an identifiable seat of authority (the council chamber) within a comprehensible assembly of office towers and stratified circulation. This synthesis of Western and native traditions represents a culmination of the typology in the 20th century and might serve as a worthy starting point for the city halls of the next.

JEFFREY THOMAS TILMAN

See also **Aalto, Alvar (Finland); City Beautiful Movement; Dudok, Willem Marinus (Netherlands); Meier, Richard (United States)**

Further Reading

Cornell, Elias, *Stockholm Town Hall*, Stockholm: Byggförlaget, 1992

Cramer, Max, Hans van Grieken, and Heleen Pronk, *W.M. Dudok: 1884–1974*, Amsterdam: Van Gennep, 1981

Draper, Joan Elaine, "The San Francisco Civic Center: Architecture, Planning, and Politics," Ph.D. diss., University of California at Berkeley, 1979

Feddes, Fred, et al., *The City Hall/Library Complex by Richard Meier in The Hague; Stadhuis/Bibliotheek*, Rotterdam: NAi, and The Hague: Gemeente, 1995

Gutheim, Frederick Albert, *Alvar Aalto*, New York: Braziller, and London: Mayflower, 1960

Hales, George P., *Los Angeles City Hall*, Los Angeles: Board of Public Works, 1928

"Koolhaas and OMA Win The Hague City Hall Competition," *Progressive Architecture* (April 1987)

Lebovich, William L., *America's City Halls*, Washington, D.C.: Preservation Press, 1984

"The New Tokyo City Hall Complex," *The Japan Architect* 3 (Summer 1991)

Östberg, Ragnar, *Stockholms Stadshus*, Stockholm: Norstedt, 1929; as *The Stockholm Town Hall*, Stockholm: Norstedt, 1929

"Richard Meier: City Hall and Central Library," *GA Document* 46 (1996)

Service, Alastair, *Edwardian Architecture: A Handbook to Building Design in Britain, 1890–1914*, New York and Toronto: Oxford University Press, and London: Thames and Hudson, 1977

Wilson, Richard Guy, "California Classicist," *Progressive Architecture* (December 1983)

CIUDAD UNIVERSITARIA CAMPUS AND STADIUM

Mexico City, Mexico

The Mexican National University, founded in 1553 by order of the Spanish emperor Charles V, is the oldest university on the American continent. Institutes and colleges of the National University were located in the historical center of Mexico City, but in the 1940s, the structural problems of organizing the increasing academic activities led Mexican politicians to commission plans for a new campus in the southern periphery of the city. Inspired by Madrid's university city of 1927 and by the tradition in the United States of suburban campus and university planning, the Mexican planners designated a seven-million-square-meter site of lava landscape at the Pedregal de San Angel for the university city. In 1953, four centuries after its foundation, the entire National University moved to Ciudad Universitaria.

The project of constructing a university city following contemporary urban planning and architecture standards had high symbolic importance for the Mexican government under President Miguel Alemán. Oil-exporting developing countries, such as Mexico, Venezuela, and Iraq, hoped to make their economic progress visible by building huge modern architectural projects for education. Although spatially different, the Mexican university city shared political and architectural aims with Carlos Raúl Villanueva's master plan of 1950 for the University City in Caracas and provided the model for Walter Gropius's and The Architects Collaborative's (TAC's) design for the New University of Baghdad, Iraq, in 1958.

The first urban plan for Ciudad Universitaria of 1946, by the architects Mario Pani and Enrique del Moral, characterized by axial Beaux-Arts structures, was soon revised because of the effect of the modern spatial concept of the UN headquarters in New York and also because of pressure from architecture students around Teodoro González de León. Together with José Luis Cuveas, a student of the former Bauhaus director and emigrant Hannes Meyer, Pani and del Moral in 1949 presented the definitive urban structure of Ciudad Universitaria. In a campus of 180 to 360 meters, the university buildings were placed like isolated monuments in open spaces. In the southern zone, the architects set sports and leisure installations, and west of the campus, separated by the north–south axis of the broad Insurgentes Avenue, the stadium. Curved internal roads, an idea of the Austrian-born architect Hermann Herrey, contrasted with the rectangular structures of campus buildings and opened magnificent views to the lava-stone landscape. Contemporary critics emphasized that this concept for the Ciudad Universitaria subtly interpreted the topographic conditions, such as various levels of lava stones and site-specific vegetation. The grand open campus space, marked by huge horizontal and vertical building volumes, reminded archaeologists of pre-Hispanic urban patterns.

Under the direction of the architect Carlos Lazo, a group of 150 Mexican architects, most of them alumni or students, elaborated the designs for the 30 university buildings. The outstanding buildings—Rectoría for the university's president and the central library—dominate the campus. Their cubic forms and vertical orientation contrast with the low-rise buildings for the faculties of philosophy and architecture. At the eastern edge of the central green campus, the tower of sciences marks the beginning of another subdivision, for the faculties of medicine, chemistry, and law. The smallest building on campus, the Pavilion of Cosmic Rays, was regarded as architecturally the most interesting. Here, in 1951, Félix Candela with Jorge González Reyna constructed his first shell building, which brought Mexico to the attention of international architecture magazines.

One of the principal intentions of modern Mexican architects at that time was to integrate artworks with the buildings to imbue International Style forms with national or local iconographic elements. Juan O'Gorman's Central Library shows all the contradictory aspects of this "integración plástica." The cubic high-rise is covered with a mosaic containing different worldviews and scientific concepts, graphically expressed in the manner of pre-Hispanic codices. The library's facades serve as huge canvases but do not integrate art and architecture. Other campus buildings show applied murals or ornaments, as in David Alfaro Siqueiros' relief mural at the Rectoría.

The most outstanding example of artistic intervention and structural integration into the landscape is the University Stadium, used for the 1968 Olympics. Its conical, oval form rises out of the surrounding lava rocks. Exterior walls are covered with rough, gray lava stones, yielding at the central entrance to an unfinished mural by Diego Rivera showing the development of sports from pre-Hispanic to modern times. For its combination of dynamic forms and archaic material, the University Stadium was admired worldwide as a model for site-specific entertainment architecture.

The Ciudad Universitaria and stadium complex forms claim a landmark of international standing. Together with the neighboring luxurious Pedregal housing development by Luis Barragán and Max Cetto, the Ciudad Universitaria adds ecological and topographical aspects to the modern urban concept of open spaces. The immense urban growth of Mexico City has, however, affected the Ciudad Universitaria. Originally planned for a community of 25,000 students and academics, the campus serves about 300,000, reflecting the increasing population of Mexico City (3.5 million in the 1950s, probably 20 million in 2000). New university satellites were planned in the 1970s and 1980s, among them the cultural center at the southern edge of Ciudad Universitaria. There, the National Library in raw concrete and the research institutes in modular functionalist forms are located between an open forum for contemporary sculpture and an ecological reserve. The circular Espacio Escultorio, which reveals the geologic origins of the site, was designed in 1978 by a group of Mexican artists under the direction of Mathias Goeritz.

Despite all intentions to decentralize higher education in Mexico, Ciudad Universitaria, with its dense concentration of science and culture, is still attractive and therefore exceeds its intended capacity. Uncontrolled urban growth endangers the generous open and green spaces of Ciudad Universitaria. The agenda for the 21st century will require protection of its urban, architectural, and artistic concept not only as a landmark but also as a lively space and as ecological compensation for the megalopolis.

PETER KRIEGER

See also **Barragán, Luis (Mexico); Candela, Félix (Mexico); Meyer, Hannes (Germany); Mexico City, Mexico; O'Gorman, Juan (Mexico); Villanueva, Carlos Raúl (Venezuela)**

Further Reading

Myers gives a contemporary perspective, as does Hitchcock. Detailed lists of architects and artists are in the architectural guide by Noelle and Tejeda. The official publication of the faculty of architecture (Sarukhan) contains a good collection of essays, photographs, and plans.

Burian, Edward R. (editor), *Modernity and the Architecture of Mexico*, Austin: University of Texas Press, 1997

Hitchcock, Henry-Russell, *Latin American Architecture since 1945*, New York: Museum of Modern Art, 1955

Myers, Irving Evan, *Mexico's Modern Architecture*, New York: Architectural Book, 1952

Noelle, Louise, and Carlos Tejeda, *Catálogo guía de arquitectura contemporánea: Ciudad de México*, Mexico City: Fomento Cultural Banamex, 1993

Sarukhán, José, et al., *La arquitectura de la Ciudad Universitaria*, Mexico City: Universidad Nacional Autónoma de México, 1994

CIUDAD UNIVERSITARIA

Designed by Carlos Raúl Villanueva, completed 1977
Caracas, Venezuela

The Ciudad Universitaria of Caracas (City University of Caracas, also known as the Universidad Central de Venezuela [UCV] or Central University of Venezuela), designed by the Venezuelan architect Carlos Raúl Villanueva, is regarded as the country's most important example of modernist architecture. Derived from Le Corbusier's works, the campus plan's Venezuelan-inflected organicism set a new standard for Venezuelan architects. The "synthesis of the arts" it proposed has never been surpassed. Despite the dilemma its association with the military government of General Marcos Pérez Jiménez (1948–58) presented for artists working on the project, its success with both Venezuelan elites and the international architectural community significantly influenced the course of Venezuelan architecture.

Villanueva's initial conception of the campus plan as well as early building designs make use of monumental axes and symmetrical disposition of masses—elements that betray his Beaux-Arts education. The University Hospital (1943), designed in the first phase of construction from 1944 to 1949, demonstrates this traditional approach. Villanueva modified the hospital's facade later in an attempt to integrate it with the rest of the campus; in subsequent stages of the design, both individual buildings and the overall plan become more flexible and organic. For example, in the second phase of construction (1950–52), Villanueva made the transition to a full-fledged modernism in the Olympic Stadium (1950). Recalling the Mexican architect Félix Candela's experiments in reinforced concrete, the oval grandstand of the stadium resembles the prow of a great ship; sustained by barely visible columns, its bulk seems to defy gravity. Strong contrasts of tropical light and shadow play important roles in this and later structures, and the architect's use of reinforced concrete to mold forms reappears as well.

The necessity for covered spaces and walkways because of the *caraqueño* tropical climate became a source of invention for Villanueva at the UCV. Citing the need to shelter students from the wind, rain, and sun, he covered the 1428-meter-long sidewalk that links various zones of the campus with a canopy of reinforced concrete, supported by columns, that appears to float above the ground. The covered sidewalk also acts as an orienting path through the free-form ground plan of the campus and terminates in the physical and spiritual center of the university, the Plaza Cubierta (Covered Plaza).

The Aula Magna (Amphitheater) and the Covered Plaza (third phase of construction, 1952–53) that surrounds it best embody the architect's principles of the synthesis of the arts, as well as his attempt to create an "outdoor museum" by integrating artworks and structures with the landscape. The Covered Plaza, an enormous roof of reinforced concrete, creates heavily shaded areas punctuated by light effects produced by *bris-soleil* walls cast in different patterns. Sculpture by Europeans Henri Laurens and Jean Arp, murals in materials as diverse as ceramic, mosaic, aluminum, stone, bronze, and glass by Fernand Léger, Antoine Pevsner, Victor Vasarely, and Venezuelans Mateo Manaure, Pascual Navarro, and Carlos González Bogen, among others, punctuate the space and are grouped so as to create smaller irregularly shaped areas under the canopy and just outside it. Many of these works make use of strong, saturated colors, which are set off by a backdrop of tropical foliage and bright sky.

Seen from above, the Aula Magna's cone-shaped auditorium is emphasized by repeating wing-shaped sections rising from the roofline in two tiers. The reference to flight on the exterior is manifested more explicitly in the interior, specifically in the acoustic panels designed by U.S. sculptor Alexander Calder, which he called Platillos Voladores or Nubes Acústicas (Flying Saucers or Acoustic Clouds, 1953). Huge, rounded shapes in various colors, attached to walls and ceilings, appear to float over the fixed auditorium seats. Critics cite the resulting marriage of form and function as the sole instance in which Villanueva achieved a synthesis of the arts at the university.

The School of Odontology (1957), from the fourth stage of construction (1954–58), demonstrates an important step in the evolution of Villanueva's designs for the campus. Citing the library at the Ciudad Universitaria in Mexico City as failing to integrate art and architecture because Mexican artist Juan O'Gorman's murals were figurative in style and, thus, mere decoration, Villanueva made use of polychromatic facades on the exterior of this building (Policromía, by Omar Carreño). He also commissioned Alejandro Otero and Oswaldo Vigas, among other artists, to design abstract murals in paint and mosaic for the exteriors of other buildings.

Constructed during the petroleum boom of the 1950s and supported by a military regime committed to renovating the capital city, the UCV played an important role in advertising the success of the dictatorship in achieving its goals of order and progress. Heralded in the Venezuelan press to this day as the jewel of Venezuelan architecture, through the years its significance as an architectural site has superseded its original political associations. Periodic calls are made in the press for its restoration, as its buildings and artworks have suffered significant deterioration and misuse. Built for four to five thousand students, the university today has an enrollment of over 50,000 and covers an area of 204 hectares, or 504 acres.

The UCV's influence on Venezuelan architecture, perhaps because of its audacity and scope, has been diffuse. Its celebration of the Venezuelan landscape through the lens of European modernism spawned no imitators, but it did legitimate modernism as a valid style for public architecture. In addition, a major consequence of Villanueva's synthesis of the arts has been the proliferation of public art projects throughout the city: large-scale art dominates the urban experience in Caracas. Freestanding sculptures and wall murals in subway stations, alongside highways, in plaza centers, and in buildings transform the city into a living exemplar of Villanueva's "outdoor museum."

International critics frequently compare Villanueva's UCV with Le Corbusier's designs for Chandigarh and Lucio Costa's for Brasília, because of these projects' similarities of scope and intention, but Villanueva's style is regarded as less fully realized. As one of the few extant examples of large-scale modernist experiments carried to fruition outside Europe, however, the UCV continues to be of interest to the international architectural community.

MARGUERITE K. MAYHALL

See also **Brasília, Brazil; Candela, Félix (Mexico); Chandigarh, India; Corbusier, Le (Jeanneret, Charles-Édouard) (France); Costa, Lúcio (Brazil); Villanueva, Carlos Raúl (Venezuela)**

Further Reading

No monographs have been published in the United States on the Ciudad Universitaria, and in Venezuela, the only recent book-length work deals with the works of art at the university. For these reasons, more general, and somewhat more dated, texts are in many cases the best available sources. The publications on Villanueva's career, or on Venezuelan architecture more generally, are the next best sources for information on and illustrations of the university, but readers should be aware that Villanueva's continuing status in the country as Venezuela's most revered architect precludes much critical analysis of his work within its sociopolitical context. Interested readers can also consult monographs on individual artists for more information.

Bullrich, Francisco, *New Directions in Latin American Architecture*, New York: Braziller, 1969

Damaz, Paul F., *Art in Latin American Architecture*, New York: Reinhold, 1963

Gasparini, Graziano, and Juan Pedro Posani, *Caracas a través de su arquitectura*, Caracas: Fundación Fina Gómez, 1969

Hitchcock, Henry-Russell, *Latin American Architecture since 1945*, New York: Museum of Modern Art, 1955

Moholy-Nagy, Sibyl, *Carlos Raúl Villanueva and the Architecture of Venezuela*, New York: Praeger, and London: Tiranti, 1964

Villanueva, el arquitecto (exhib. cat.), Caracas: Museo de Arte Contemporáneo de Caracas, 1988

Obras de arte de la Ciudad Universitaria de Caracas; Works of Art in the University City of Caracas (bilingual Spanish–English edition), Caracas: Universidad Central de Venezuela and Monte Avila Editores, 1991

Posani, Juan Pedro, *The Architectural Works of Villanueva*, Caracas: Lagoven, 1985

Spazio e società: Space and Society, Dossier Venezuela: Venezuela Dossier, 10 (1987)

CLASSICISM

In the 20th century architectural classicism continued in its centuries-old custom (traditional classicism) and also was appropriated by those who abstracted its principles in the modern effort for an ahistorical architecture (early modernism). Among those extending the classical tradition, the terms *classical* and *traditional* have been used as if interchangeable. However, most would use *traditional* as the more inclusive term referring to premodernist architectural habits in various cultures and societies around the world. Many would describe *classicism* as including a more specific species of traditional architecture drawing from the Western tradition of building.

The contrast in how traditional classicism was employed in the 20th century may be witnessed in the work of architects as apparently dissimilar as Walter Gropius and Paul Philippe Cret, both of whom utilized such fundamentals as bilateral symmetry, axes and cross axes as organizing plan elements, and proportional systems based on anthropomorphic sources. It would be of little consequence to identify as classical any building employing axes of symmetry in an organizational strategy, yet classical principles proved themselves useful throughout the century and to architects of every aesthetic preference. Buildings whose elevations and massing are as different as the Werkbund Pavilion (Cologne, 1914), First Church of Christ, Scientist (Berkeley, 1910), and Rockefeller Center (New York, from 1931) share fundamentally classical planning techniques of axes of symmetry disciplining complex building programs. After midcentury a notable exponent was Louis Kahn, trained in the University of Pennsylvania's Beaux-Arts program. Kahn employed the general geometries of classicism and axial organization, altering the classical ideals of ceremonial circulation laid out on primary axes separating the levels of important spaces into his theory of "servant" and "served" spaces, as seen in his 1963 Parliament Building at Dacca (in what is now Bangladesh).

Overt classical allusions were present in surprising places early in the 20th century, notably in the AEG Turbine Factory designed by Peter Behrens (Berlin, 1908), hailed for its sleek curtain wall and exposed structure. However, the impression of the classical temple is undeniable despite the obvious expression of the factory function, even if here the triangular pediment is replaced by the polygonal profile of the building's truss roof, and the colonnade is a series of steel columns. Through this metaphor Behrens could intentionally express that his era had elevated industrial tasks to the level of cultural endeavor; he could not have communicated such in a newly invented vocabulary. Here, classicism was essential for the meaning of this primary monument of the factory aesthetic. More ingenious with its use of the "elements" of classicism, Gunnar Asplund's Stockholm Public Library (1920–28) is massed with a simple cylinder rising from a low box, recalling at once the creative form play of neoclassical architect Ledoux and the elementary volumes into which the Pantheon might be broken down. Drawing from more specific classical lessons, Asplund applied ornament in its traditional civic role: Interior bas-reliefs illustrate scenes from Homer; the exterior frieze portrays elements of everyday life to enliven the building and to suggest the library's contents and function as well. As an important civic institution, the building's cylinder makes a typal reference to those buildings that have ranked high in the traditional hierarchy.

Critical attention has tended to favor modernist stylistic innovation over the application of classical principles. Even so, the recognizable signs of ancient building types and ornament—in particular the orders—were employed consistently by advocates of architecture's classical heritage through the 20th century. In the early part of the century, the design methods of American Renaissance architects proved helpful in lending an appropriately ceremonial appearance and organizational structure to complex buildings serving the modernity of 20th-century life. Notably, the Pennsylvania Station (McKim, Mead and White; New York, 1910) vividly recalled the Imperial Baths of Rome as it also utilized École des Beaux-Arts planning to skillfully organize the movements of travelers on foot, in taxis, and on trains. Such landmarks as the New York Public Library (Carrère and Hastings, 1911) and the Flatiron Building (Daniel Burnham, 1903) reveal classicism's value for expressive potential as well as its ability to organize large, complex buildings, whether they sprawl horizontally or soar vertically. Although these examples reveal a rigorous adherence to elements of Western classicism, the Viceroy's House in New Delhi (Edwin Lutyens, 1915–24) fused Western antique forms and proportional systems with Mogul emblems of authority to express the imperial station of the British Raj, revealing the conviction among colonial powers and their architects that the Western classical tradition could be adapted flexibly to other cultural contexts.

Following World War I, especially in the 1930s, the formal expression of classicism was changed, especially in the hands of architects and patrons who strove to articulate imperial ambitions architecturally, in a manner that some have described as "stripped." Their simplified but recognizable classicism embraced the monumental scale, sense of discipline, order, and bright whiteness associated with classical antiquity, but in a form void of the delicate ornament and visual refinements popular earlier in the century. This architecture has been roundly criticized for its appropriation by the Nazi party, specifically in Albert Speer's Zeppelinfeld (Nuremberg, 1936) and Gerdy Troost's House of German Art (Munich, 1934). Hitler's expression of nationalist sentiments through stripped classicism extended to his 1937 plan to reorder Berlin with long avenues, axes, and monumental classical buildings (including a triumphal arch dedicated to the Führer and a domed pantheon of Nazi heroes) drawing from the plans for Haussmann's Paris, imperial Rome, and L'Enfant's Washington. However, there is nothing inherently malevolent in the style itself, which appeared through the 20th century in buildings designed to represent the democratic capital of the United States, including the Pan-American Union (Cret, 1910) and the National World War II Memorial (Friedrich St. Florian, design competition 1998). The appeal of stripped classicism to a culturally diverse audience is apparent in such a case as the generation of architects from China who studied under Cret at the University of Pennsylvania and, on returning to their homeland, practiced an architecture that fused Western classicism with traditional Chinese methods. Thus several countries, from Italy and Germany to China and America, shared an affinity for this simplified classicism, drawing from it the expressive power and authority of ancient architecture, its usefulness to express values of civic decorum, and the forward-looking nature of its contemporary patrons.

The more visually obvious manifestations of classicism typified by McKim and Cret coincided with peaks in the publication of ancient and Renaissance treatises, whose appearance at the start and conclusion of the century reveals a significant readership of architects applying the lessons and details of these books in their buildings. Vitruvius's *De architectura* was continually published in the 20th century. Revealing its importance to architecture worldwide, the treatise was brought out in Spanish, French, Italian, German, and Latin; two notable English translations of Vitruvius mark either end of the century (1914 and 1999). Similarly, several versions of William Ware's *American Vignola* were published in the first decade of the century, and two more appeared in its final decades. These publication events correspond with the early flourishing of the classical tradition. Their interruption during the century's middle decades coincided with the apparent triumph of "orthodox," or high European, modernism, which by the 1960s was deemed by many as fundamental to the failure of urban renewal and slum clearance schemes, construction of disastrous CIAM-inspired public housing projects, and the demolition of historic structures (notably the 1963 destruction of the aforementioned Penn Station). As the architectural devastation visited on cities gave impetus to both a growing backlash against ahistorical modernist architecture and historic preservation initiatives, tradition and classicism emerged as viable correctives to the disasters of the Modern movement. Concurrently, several works of Renaissance theory appeared in the last four decades of the century: Alberti's *Ten Books on Architecture* was published in 1966 and translated in 1986; Palladio was retranslated in 1965 and again in 1997; and several of Serlio's books were reprinted in the 1970s, 1980s, and 1990s. In 1993 the Getty Center's Texts and Documents series added the 17th-century *Ordonnance for the Five Kinds of Columns after the Method of the Ancients* by Claude Perrault to its ambitious list of publications.

New theory drawing from the old also appeared in these later decades (notably Robert Venturi's *Complexity and Contradiction in Architecture*, 1966) and found a wide audience whose growing dissatisfaction with modernism stimulated the rise of Postmodernism. In its approach to infuse classical ornament with meaning relevant in an era of relativity, which has led to double-coding, Postmodernism at once acknowledges the importance and value of ornament and antique forms in architecture, at times with the intentional hazard of weakening the tradition by making such references ironic or comical. Postmodernism's contribution has been judged a mixed one. As early as 1979, Joseph Rykwert criticized it as an alternate modernist architecture.

Perhaps criticism of this sort drove some to find again what constitutes the tradition of classical architecture. The ever-increasing success of the New Urbanist founders, Andres Duany and Elizabeth Plater-Zyberk, to restore the traditional art of making cities has made evident that architectural historians, such as Yale University's former professor Vincent Scully, in professional schools where the curriculum is modernist, have had an important role. An event perhaps of more symbolic than substantive importance in the hoped-for ascendancy of classical architecture was HRH Prince Charles's criticism of the planned addition to Britain's National Gallery. In his now-famous speech presented on the 150th anniversary of the RIBA in 1984, he criticized the addition as a "monstrous carbuncle on the face of a much-loved and elegant friend" and advocated, as he continues to do, for a return to classical and traditional architecture. Remarkable are the number of academies such as the one in New York, organizing groups such as INTBAU in London, and university curriculums committed to classicism. Among the small group of such universities, the strongest, but unique in the United States, is the University of Notre Dame.

The most important polemicist for the architecture of traditional cities based on classical principles from the late 1960s continues to be Leon Krier, who in 2003 was the recipient of the first Driehaus Prize—the aim of which is to recognize annually the great contributors to the practice of classical architecture or traditional architecture and architectural preservation. Krier's language, illustrations, and civic designs have the force and clarity of a manifesto. He criticizes modernist architecture as a totalizing production which has substituted that which has been traditionally appreciated as truly engaging in buildings—including the accumulation of thousands of years of architectural accommodation to social, political, and environmental circumstances—which classical architecture is able to adapt. Presently, Poundbury, for which Krier has been the master planner and whose patron is Prince Charles, is being raised in Dorchester, England. In Krier's paper architecture, and now in this built architecture, he argues that the making of cities and the practice of classicism are disciplines best not separated. Many would say that the present interest in classical architecture is not a stylistic revival but a return to an important cultural habit of building.

JHENNIFER A. AMUNDSON AND CHRISTOPHER C. MILLER

See also **AEG Turbine Factory, Berlin; Asplund, Erik Gunnar (Sweden); Behrens, Peter (Germany); Burnham, Daniel H. (United States); Cret, Paul Philippe (United States); Flatiron Building, New York City; Gropius, Walter (Germany); Kahn, Louis (United States); Lutyens, Edwin (England); McKim, Mead and White (United States); Modernism; Pennsylvania Station, New York City; Postmodernism; Stockholm Public Library**

Further Reading

Curtis, William J.R., *Modern Architecture since 1900*, Oxford: Phaidon, 1987

Davis, Howard, *The Culture of Building*, New York: Oxford University Press, 1999

Economakis, Richard, "Will the *Real* Early Moderns Please Step Forward?" *Proceedings of the International Conference and Exhibition: The Other Modern: Building and Living, the Architecture of the City*, Bologna: A Vision of Europe, 2000

Krier, Leon, *Leon Krier: Architecture and Urban Design, 1967–1992*, edited by Richard Economakis, London: Academy Editions, 1992

Rykwert, Joseph, "Inheritance or Tradition," *Architectural Design* 49, 5/6 (1979)

Scott, Geoffrey, *The Architecture of Humanism: A Study in a History of Taste*, New York: Norton, 1999

Wiseman, Carter, *Shaping a Nation: Twentieth-Century American Architecture and Its Makers*, New York: Norton, 1998

CLIMATE

Climate is characterized by the global, regional, and local distribution of solar radiation, precipitation, temperature, wind, and humidity at the earth's surface. The earth–sun relationship that defines season combines with latitude, surface cover (land versus sea), the water cycle, and movement of air masses, to generate global weather patterns. As opposed to weather that takes place over a short time span, climate represents long-term trends that are averaged over a time scale of several decades. These trends are classified into climate types with names indicative of their dominant temperature and precipitation features. Knowledge of the macroclimate of a representative city or region, in combination with a qualitative understanding of local microclimate, allows architects, builders, city planners, and landscape architects to modify indoor and outdoor environments in ways that improve human comfort, reduce building energy consumption, and optimize site resource use.

Indigenous builders recognized the relationships between shelter and climate. James Marston Fitch, in his 1960 *Scientific American* article "Primitive Architecture and Climate," clarified the empirical and evolutionary wisdom of these builders to create efficient, comfortable, climate-responsive structures in all regions of the world. Fitch also challenged contemporary architects to demonstrate skill comparable to their "primitive" counterparts in designing energy- and resource-efficient structures that would satisfy their occupants' needs. This challenge became the focus of climate-responsive architecture for the 20th century: to combine the wisdom of indigenous builders with contemporary building science, technology, and design. The achievements of this era can be summarized in three main categories: refined regional guidelines for climate-responsive environmental design; new methods for assessing the relationship between climate, human comfort, and energy use in buildings; and an improved understanding of how urban environments influence climate.

Regional Climate Analyses and Design Guidelines

The most important contributions advancing architectural knowledge of climatic design in the 20th century occurred in the post–World War II era. In 1949 the American Institute of Architects' *House Beautiful* Climate Control Project was the first major contribution to the field, appearing both as a series of articles in the popular press and technical briefs in the *Bulletin of the A.I.A.* The principal author of these reports, climatologist Dr. Paul Siple, was hired by the American Society of Heating and Ventilating Engineers to create regional climate analyses and design data for a number of U.S. cities and their surrounding areas. The project—to analyze climatic data in terms of its implications for residential design—was the first major effort to summarize climate data for use by the architectural design community.

There have been subsequent publications of regional climatic design guidelines for buildings and their surrounding environments. The U.S. Department of Housing and Urban Development contracted with the American Institute of Architects' Research Corporation to publish *Regional Guidelines for Building Passive Energy Conserving Homes* (1980), which provides general climatic design recommendations for the continental United States and Hawaii. *Climatic Design* (Watson and Labs, 1993) and *Sun, Wind and Light* (Brown and Dekay, 2000) use design illustrations, monographs, rules of thumb, and case study examples to communicate architectural design strategies that respond to climate. Most works have been inspired by the ideas presented in the 1963 book *Design with Climate: Bioclimatic Approach to Architectural Regionalism* by Victor Olgyay, which has greatly influenced several generations of architects interested in climatic design.

Design Methods

The text *Design with Climate: Bioclimatic Approach to Architectural Regionalism* was a substantive addition to the architect's understanding of climate-responsive design beyond the provision of design guidelines. The author developed a quantitative method for assessing human comfort in relationship to exterior climate conditions. The "Bioclimatic Chart," as it is called, plots dry-bulb temperature against relative humidity and delineates a portion of the chart as the "comfort zone"; that is, the range of thermal conditions in which a sedentary young adult dressed in lightweight clothing would experience comfort in the shade. For climate conditions outside this zone, the chart indicates how modifications of sun, wind, and moisture can render comfort in spite of the naturally occurring conditions. The Bioclimatic Chart still enjoys a place in architectural design methods although it has evolved through the contributions of others. Givoni and Milne (1976) showed, in this case adopting the psychometric chart, how comfort can be achieved indoors through passive and low-energy design strategies. The relationship between human comfort, acclimatization, and appropriate building strategies is an emerging field of study as architects and engineers realize the need to optimize both energy consumption and environmental performance in buildings.

Computer software to analyze regional climate data and their design implications is another important development in design methods in the 20th century. The most notable software packages in this category are Climate Consultant from UCLA and METEONORM from Meteotest. Sources for U.S. climatological data used by these software packages and by other calculation methods include the National Oceanic and Atmospheric Administration (NOAA), the National Climatic Data Center (NCDC), and the National Renewable Energy Laboratory (NREL). When based on actual measurements, these data are compiled from a sparse observation network of weather stations on the ground or of sky-based instruments (such as satellites and weather balloons), typically recorded for agricultural or military purposes. When actual data are not available, they can be approximated using mathematical or statistical methods. Typical Meteorological Year (TMY2) data from NREL, for example, are based on actual measurements and mathematical models. Climate data are instrumental to climate analysis for building energy simulation software (e.g., Energy-10, Energy Scheming, Solar-5) that allows designers to estimate the effect of climate on indoor temperatures as well as building energy consumption. More research is needed for the application of these data to modeling of microclimates around buildings and open spaces at the city scale.

Climate Modification

Although the effects of urbanization on climate have been noted since Roman antiquity—from the writings of architect and engineer Marcus Vitruvius Pollio in the 1st century B.C. to the odes of Quintus Horatius Flaccus around 24 B.C.—measurement and modeling of these effects gained greater attention in the 20th century A.D. Motorized traverses of urban centers to measure air temperature gradients between cities and their surrounding rural countrysides began in 1917. The field of urban climatology, which examines the effect of cities on climate, has emerged as the principal discipline engaged in this study. Its purpose is to assess the effects of urban buildings, transportation systems, and industrial activities on the atmospheric and hydrologic cycles and their associated energy and water balances. Detailed studies of one climate phenomenon in particular, the urban heat island effect, preoccupied many scientists and researchers in the 20th century.

Urban heat islands are attributed to a combination of influences that cause air temperatures in cities to be higher than in surrounding suburban or rural areas. Cities exhibit increased thermal storage potential, for waste heat as well as incident solar radiation, by their massive construction materials commonly used in buildings and streetscapes (such as concrete and asphalt, respectively). The effect is more pronounced at night because cities have a slower rate of nocturnal radiant cooling than surrounding rural areas. Finally, cities experience less evaporative cooling because of increased runoff from paved surfaces and limited vegetation to retain moisture in urban environments. The urban heat island effect has been documented in cities throughout the world using satellite imagery and ground-based measurement. Because of the negative effect on cooling energy consumption in most cities (except in cold climates), design recommendations, such as white roofs and selective planting, are cited as mitigation measures for the urban heat island effect.

The question of climate change on a global scale fueled a central debate at the end of the 20th century. Large computer programs called GCMs (known as General Circulation or Global Climate Models) were being used by scientists to predict the magnitude of change in temperature and precipitation for changes in atmospheric concentrations of carbon dioxide. Evidence of climate change has also been detected in paleoclimatological records obtained from ice cores, for example. The Intergovernmental Panel on Climate Change (IPCC), formed in 1988 by the World Meteorological Organization and the United Nations Environmental Program, continues an internationally coordinated effort to investigate the hypothesis that surface temperatures worldwide have been increasing as a result of anthropogenic change and, to a lesser degree, natural climatic variability.

In the last two decades of the 20th century, world leaders and a wide array of international nongovernmental organizations (NGOs) convened to determine appropriate policy responses to global climate change. The most notable policy actions resulting from these landmark events were the 1987 Montreal Protocol to combat ozone depletion, the 1997 Kyoto Agreement for reducing greenhouse gases, and the 1992 Rio Summit "Agenda 21," a worldwide plan for global environmental action. The architectural and planning ramifications of climate change have yet to be translated into discernible actions, with a few exceptions such as the phasing out of chloro-fluorocarbons (CFCs) used in building materials and systems.

Environmental sustainability, as an approach to architectural design and urban planning, has renewed understanding of the importance of climate in the design of buildings, landscapes, and cities. As a result of developments in the 20th century, regional guidelines, design methods, and documentation of regional and global climate phenomena have advanced designers' abilities to predict environmental performance of buildings in their surroundings based on climate. From the bioclimatic skyscrapers of architect Kenneth Yeang to the solar planned subdivision of Village Homes in Davis, California, climate-adapted design has proven to be economically, aesthetically, and environmentally sound.

MARGOT MCDONALD

Further Reading

Historical perspective on climate-responsive architecture is described in Fitch and Bobenhausen (1999) and Fitch and Branch (1960). Design guidelines for climate-responsive architecture, rules of thumb, and case study examples can be found in the references (AIA Research Corporation 1980; Brown and Dekay 2000; Givoni 1998; Lechner 2000; Loftness 1981; Olgyay 1963; Siple 1949; Watson and Labs 1993). Site planning with microclimate and energy considerations can be found in Brown (1995) and Robinette (1983). Climate-related software is available through Milne (1991). Climate data are available through NCDC (1983) and NREL (1995). Additional reading on urban climatology is found in Givoni (1998), Landsberg (1981), Oke (1987), and Akbari et al. (1992). Global climate change is described in Houghton (1996).

AIA Research Corporation, *Regional Guidelines for Building Passive Energy Conserving Homes*, written for HUD, Office of Policy and Research, and the U.S. Dept. of Energy, Washington, D.C.: U.S. Government Printing Office, 1980

Akbari, Hashem, Susan Davis, Sofia Dorsano, et al., *Cooling Our Communities: A Guidebook on Tree Planting and Light-Colored Surfacing*, Washington, D.C.: U.S. EPA, DOE, and Lawrence Berkeley Laboratory, 1992

Brown, G.Z., and Mark Dekay, *Sun, Wind and Light: Architectural Design Strategies*, New York: Wiley, 1985; 2nd edition, 2000

Brown, Robert D., and Terry J. Gillespie, *Microclimatic Landscape Design*, New York: Wiley, 1995

Fitch, James Marston, and Bob Bobenhausen, *American Building: The Environmental Forces that Shape It*, New York: Oxford University Press, 1999

Fitch, James Marston, and Daniel Branch, "Primitive Architecture and Climate," *Scientific American*, 230 (December 1960)

Givoni, Baruch, *Climate Considerations in Building and Urban Design*, New York: Van Nostrand Reinhold, 1998

Houghton, J. (editor), *Climate Change 1995: The Science of Climate Change*, Cambridge: Cambridge University Press, 1996

Landsberg, Helmut E., *The Urban Climate*, San Francisco: Academic Press, 1981

Lechner, Norbert, *Heating, Cooling, Lighting: Design Methods for Architects*, New York: Wiley, 1992; 2nd edition, 2000

Loftness, Vivian, *Climate/Energy Graphics*, Washington, D.C.: Association of Collegiate Schools of Architecture, 1981

Milne, Murray, *Climate Consultant* and *Solar-5* software, UCLA Department of Architecture and Urban Design, http://www.aud.ucla.edu/energy-design-tools/, 1991

NCDC, *Climate Atlas of the United States*, Asheville, N.C.: U.S. Dept. of Commerce, Environmental Science Services Administration, Environmental Data Services, 1983

NREL, *TMY2s—Typical Meteorological Years Derived from the National Solar Radiation Data Base*, Golden, Colorado: National Renewable Energy Laboratory, 1995

Olgyay, Victor, *Design with Climate: Bioclimatic Approach to Architectural Regionalism*, Princeton, New Jersey: Princeton University Press, 1963
Oke, T.R., *Boundary Layer Climates*, New York: Routledge, 1978; 2nd edition, 1987
Robinette, Gary O., *Energy Efficient Site Design*, New York: Van Nostrand Reinhold, 1983
Siple, Paul A., "Regional Climate Analysis and Design Data," *Bulletin of the American Institute of Architects* (September 1949)
Watson, Donald, and Kenneth Labs, *Climatic Design*, New York: McGraw-Hill, 1983; 2nd edition, 1993

CODERCH Y DE SENTMENAT, JOSÉ ANTONIO 1913–84

Architect, Spain

José Antonio Coderch y de Sentmenat was a Catalan architect born in Barcelona. He completed his architectural education at the Escuela Técnica Superior de Arquitectura, Barcelona, in 1940, later teaching there as a professor between 1965 and1968. From 1936 to 1939, he fought in the Spanish civil war. Until he established his own private architectural practice in 1947, he gained architectural experience at the offices of the Director-General of Architecture in Madrid; the City Architect in Sitges, Spain; Obra Sindical del Hogar in Barcelona; and Barcelona's Naval Institute. He was an active participant in the architectural group Team X, which he joined in 1961. After an accomplished career in Spanish architecture, he died on 6 November 1984 in Barcelona.

Coderch was influenced by the work of Madrid architect Secundino Zuazu and greatly admired the work of Finnish architect Alvar Aalto. He admired popular Mediterranean architecture, adapting it with a contemporary modern idiom. This combination prompted Kenneth Frampton in *Modern Architecture: A Critical History* to refer to him as a "Catalan Regionalist." The first built example of this hybridization was Coderch's eight-story ISM apartment block (1951) in Barcelona.

Arguably one of Coderch's most significant contributions to 20th-century architectural thinking was his questioning of the importance of architectural geniuses. In his article "There Are No Geniuses That We Need Now," Coderch contests the need for great leaders with absolute doctrines and universal principles. Rather, he argues for a transfer of responsibility to individual architects, empowered by their devotion, goodwill, and honor, all guided by the architect's personal intuition. Similarly, he advocated for the return of an architectural "trade."

More recently, Coderch has been recognized for his contributions to post–World War II Spanish architecture. For example, Barcelona architect Ignacio de Solà-Morales has reappraised Coderch's work to demonstrate his lasting contributions. Although previously dismissed by some of his colleagues, Coderch has won new recognition among critics, leading to his receipt of the professional Merit Medal FAD, Barcelona, in 1977.

An important pursuit for Coderch was the deconstruction of pedagogical systems in architecture. His teaching and concern for the training of young Spanish architects were outlined most clearly in his "Letter to Young Architects" in *Quaderns d'Arquitectura i urbanisme* (174 [July–September 1987]). He contended that architectural students should engage with life rather than architectural history alone. His outspoken, aggressive, and reactionary position to architectural education is well known. His teaching has been characterized by his impatience with student laziness and ignorance. Despite this approach, he was forever hopeful of the impact of the independent architectural graduate.

Coderch's work has been described as inquisitive and transgressive. His interest lay in architectural form and its plasticity. One of his most renowned domestic projects, the Casa Ugalde (1951), exemplifies this interest. Influenced by its location in Cadeques, an isolated beach town near Barcelona, the Casa Ugalde translates the local vernacular into a piece of "modern" abstract architecture. Characterized by its framed views, the house exploits the landscape. In plan it has been described as both poetic and arabesque. An enormous shaded terrace moderates the effects of the Mediterranean sun. This interest in climatic control is reflected in a number of other important housing projects designed by Coderch. These include the single-family dwellings Casa Catasus (1956) in Sitges and Casa Uriach (1961) in L'Ametlla del Vallès. The experimentation in climatic control by Coderch continued in a number of multifamily-housing schemes, including the ISM apartments (1951) in Barcelona, the Il Girasol apartments (1966; inspired and translated as the sunflower) in Madrid, and the Las Cocheras apartment building (1968) in Barcelona. These projects used hinged panels, louvers, roll-down screens, balconies, and stepped facades to allow, black, or filter light into interior rooms.

Not all Coderch's work was residential. Two notable commercial projects that he designed are the Trade Office Building (1965) and Instituto Frances (1972) in Barcelona. Both projects exploit the glass facade made famous by German architect Ludwig Mies van der Rohe.

Exhibitions were another important activity in Coderch's career. His seven-by-eight-meter pavilion for the 1951 Ninth Trienniale in Milan sought to confirm the Spanish presence on the European architectural scene. A Spanish-made straw cloth sheet; a large, rotating natural finish timber shutter; and a table occupied the pavilion space and were decorated with sculptures, ceramics, and photographs of Spanish crafts. For this exhibition he was awarded a Gold Medal and a Grand Prize. He exhibited at the National Fine Art Exhibition in Madrid in 1960, received a Gold Medal for the Centre Pompidou in Paris in 1978, and exhibited at the Transformations in Modern Architecture Exhibition at the Museum of Modern Art in New York in 1979.

Coderch's early architectural career was relatively unrecognized. Exhibitions at the Centre Pompidou and the Museum of Modern Art toward the end of his career increased his profile, elevating acceptance of his work internationally and in his own country. The recently cited effect of his Casa Ugalde on the Cap Marinet House (1985–87) of Spanish architects Elias Torres and J.A. Martínez Lapeña in C.M. Arís's article in *El Croqius* reaffirms his contribution. His strong opposition to pedagogical systems in architecture and his poetic, climate-responsive designs contributed significantly to 20th-century architecture.

IGEA TROIANI

See also **Aalto, Alvar (Finland); Barcelona, Spain**

Biography

Born in Barcelona, 25 November 1913. Earned doctor of architecture degree at the Escuela Técnica Superior de Arquitectura,

Barcelona 1940. Served as a lieutenant in the Spanish civil war 1936–39. Married Ana Maria Giménez Ramos 1943; children: 4. Worked in the offices of the Director-General of Architecture, Madrid 1940–42, Offices of the City Architect, Sitges, Spain 1942–45, the Obra Sindical del Hogar, Barcelona 1944–52, and at the Naval Institute, Barcelona 1949–52; commenced a private architectural practice in Barcelona in partnership with J. Sanz Luengo 1947–67, after which he was in partnership with G. Coderch Giménez; joined Team X, 1961. Taught as a professor at the Escuela Técnica Superior de Arquitectura, Barcelona 1965–68. Died in Barcelona 6 November 1984.

Selected Works

Casa Ferrer Vidal, Cala d'Or, Majorca, 1946
Casa Garriga Nogués, Sitges, 1947
Casa Ugalde, Cadeques, 1951
Building, Barceloneta, or ISM Apartments, Barcelona, 1951
Pabellon de España, or Spanish Pavilion, Ninth Triennale, Milan, 1951
Casa Coderch, Cadeques, 1955
Casa Catasus, Sitges, 1956
Casa Senillosa, Gerona, 1956
Lamp Design, 1957
Casa Coderch Milá, Cadeques, 1958
Casa Tàpies, Barcelona, 1960
Casa Paricio, San Feliu de Codines, 1961
Casa Uriach, L'Ametlla del Vallès, 1961
Casa Rozès, Rosas, Gerona, 1962
Hotel de Mar, Palma, Majorca, 1962
Trade Office Building, Barcelona, 1965
Casa Gili, Sitges, 1965
Il Girasol Apartments, Madrid, 1966
Casa Entrecanales, Madrid, 1966
Las Cocheras Apartment Building, Sarria, Barcelona, 1968
Casa Raventós, Matadepera, 1970
Instituto Frances, Barcelona, 1972

Selected Publications

"There Are No Geniuses That We Need Now," *Domus* (1961)
"Letter to Young Architects," quoted in *Quaderns d'Arquitectura i Urbanisme*, 174 (July–September 1987)

Further Reading

Arís, Carlos Martí, "Other Versions of the Patio: On Two Houses by Torres Tur and Martínez Lapeña," *El Croquis*, 10/48 (April–May 1991)
Cabrero, Gabriel Ruiz, "A Long Converstion and a Gift," *Arquitectura* (Madrid), 73/294 (December 1992)
Frampton, Kenneth, *Modern Architecture: A Critical History*, London: Thames and Hudson, and New York: Oxford University Press, 1980; 3rd edition, Thames and Hudson, 1992
Leet, Stephen, "Mysterious Realities: The Genius of Jose Antonio Coderch," *Metropolis*, 11/10 (June 1992)
Sherwood, Roger, "Two Sunflowers," *Journal of Architectural Education*, 38/3 (Spring 1985)
Smithson, Alison (editor), *Team 10 Primer*, Cambridge, Massachusetts: MIT Press, 1962
Smithson, Peter (editor), "Team 10 at Royaumont," *Architectural Design*, 45 (November 1975)

COHEN, JEAN-LOUIS 1949–

Architectural historian, France

First trained as an architect, Jean-Louis Cohen subsequently earned a doctorate from the École des Hautes Études en Sciences Sociales. In 1994 New York University's Institute of Fine Arts awarded him the architectural history chair created for Henry-Russell Hitchcock and later occupied by Reyner Banham and Richard Pommer. Cohen stopped teaching between 1979 and 1983 to expand and manage France's government research funds for architectural history, theory, and technology.

An articulate writer, popular lecturer, commentator for the French media, and leader of research teams, Cohen has greatly contributed to expanding the knowledge and understanding of Western architecture and urbanism in the first half of the 20th century. His initial expertise on Soviet avant-garde architecture led him to study Le Corbusier's personal and theoretical effect in the Soviet Union as well as the career of French modernist and pro-Soviet architect André Lurçat.

Cohen's studies of cosmopolitan aspects of French architecture are also groundbreaking; with Hartmut Frank he directed a team that compared policies implemented by the Germans in Alsace-Lorraine in 1940–44 and by the French in the Baden and Saar regions in 1945–50. In addition he has analyzed the French infatuation with Italian architecture in the 1970s. The Centre Georges Pompidou entrusted him with the architecture section for its Paris-Moscow exhibit and named him scientific adviser for the mammoth 1987 retrospective "L'Aventure Le Corbusier." Although Cohen has organized shows on behalf of the Pavillon de l'Arsenal and Les Années 30 for the Musée des Monuments Français, his best-known curatorial endeavor remains "Scenes of the World to Come: European Architecture and the American Challenge, 1893–1960," a spectacular display of artifacts related to Europe's fascination with American architecture, organized by the Canadian Centre for Architecture in Montreal. The premise of the exhibition, as Cohen defined it, was that European architects and engineers were intrigued by the iron-and-steel structure that supported the classicizing facades of the World's Columbian Exposition of 1893 in Chicago. The following decades witnessed an ongoing interaction between European architectural practice and thinking and the contemporary American profession as the skyscraper and mass production reshaped urban environments.

Overall, Cohen's intent has been to explore how the complementary, and at times contradictory, social and aesthetic concepts of modernism, modernity, and modernization have affected the built environment on an international scale and to place these currents into a broader political and cultural context. Cohen has served on the editorial boards of *Architecture, Mouvement, Continuité, Casabella*, and *Design Book Review*. He sits on the boards of the Fondation Le Corbusier and the Canadian Centre for Architecture and is the only non-American member of the Council for Architecture and Design at New York's Museum of Modern Art. In 1998 his visibility, cosmopolitanism, sense of leadership, and organization, which are unparalleled among French architectural historians and critics, led to his nomination by the minister of culture as the head of the Institut Français d'Architecture and Musée des Monuments Français.

ISABELLE GOURNAY

See also **Corbusier, Le (Jeanneret, Charles-Édouard) (France); Paris, France**

Biography

Born 20 July 1949 in Paris; studied École Spéciale d'Architecture, Paris 1967–70; received diploma, Unité Pédagogique d'Architecture 6, Paris 1973; Researcher, Institut de l'Environment, Paris 1973–76; taught at the École Paris d'Architecture, Paris-Villemin 1975–96; Scientific Director, Secrétariat à la Recherche Architecturale, Ministère de l'Urbanisme et du Logement 1979–83; Associate Professor, École des Ponts et Chaussées 1980–89; received Ph.D. in art history, École des Hautes Études en Sciences Sociales 1985; Professor, Institut Français d'Urbanisme (Université Paris 8) 1996–98.

Selected Publications

(edited with Bruno Fortier) *Paris, la ville et ses projets* (*Paris, a City in the Making*), Paris: Editions Babylone, Pavillon de l'Arsenal, 1989

Le Corbusier and the Mystique of the USSR: Theories and Projects for Moscow, 1928–1936, Princeton, New Jersey: Princeton University Press, 1992 (first published in French in 1987)

(edited with André Lortie) *Des Fortifs au périf, Paris, les seuils de la ville*, Paris: Picard, Pavillon de l'Arsenal, 1992

"America: a Soviet Ideal," *AA Files*, 5 (January 1984)

Scenes of the World to Come: European Architecture and the American Challenge, 1893–1960, Paris: Flammarion, and Montreal: Canadian Centre for Architecture, 1995

André Lurçat (1904–1970), autocritique d'un moderne, Paris: Institut Français d'Architecture, and Liège, Pierre Mardaga, 1995

(Monique Eleb, co-author) *Casablanca, mythes et figures d'une aventure urbaine*, Paris: Hazan, 1999

"Modernism in Uniform: Occupation architecture in France and Germany (1940–1950)," in *Wars of Classification: Architecture and Modernity*, edited by Taisto H. Makela and Wallis Miller, New York: Princeton Architectural Press, 1991

Mies van der Rohe, London: E and FN Spon, 1995

(with Monique Eleb) "Paris, the 20th Century Architecture and Urbanism," *Architecture and Urbanism* (special issue) (1990)

COLLINS, PETER 1920–81

Architecture historian, England (became Canadian citizen 1962)

Peter Collins was one of the leading architectural historians of his generation and a doyen of the English-language historians and theorists of 20th-century architecture. Born in Leeds in Yorkshire in 1920, his architectural studies at Leeds College of Art began in 1936 (diploma in architecture in 1948) but were interrupted by seven years in the British army, serving in the Yorkshire Hussars; as an intelligence officer in the Middle East and Italy; and finally as captain, General Staff at the War Office, London. On graduation, he went to Switzerland and France to work on the design of reinforced-concrete structures, including working on Auguste Perret's reconstruction of Le Havre. In 1951 he returned to England to lecture in architecture at Manchester and, later, to begin graduate work there under Professor Cordingly. His Master of Arts thesis, "The Development of Architectural Theory in France in the Mid-Eighteenth Century," was completed in 1955. The year before that, he received a Silver Medal from the Royal Institute of British Architects for his essay "Jacques-François Blondel." In Paris in August 1953, he married Margaret Taylor of Ottawa, leading to his later relocation to Canada.

The year he completed his work at Manchester, Collins received a Fulbright Traveling Scholarship and an appointment to lecture in architectural history at Yale University. In 1956 he was appointed an associate professor at McGill University, and in 1962, he was appointed a full professor of architecture. He became responsible for reorganizing the undergraduate courses in the history and theory of architecture and completed a book that was inspired by his work with Perret, *Concrete: The Vision of a New Architecture*, earning him the Henry Florence Architectural Book Scholarship in 1960. In 1962 he became a Canadian citizen.

In 1965 Collins wrote his most successful book, *Changing Ideals in Modern Architecture*, which traces the intellectual development of modern architectural theories. It is the antithesis of a picture book. Buildings are shown as the result of thoughts based on the ideals of each age of Western culture. Collins recognized the importance of analogies and metaphors in architectural iconography. In this he followed in the footsteps of Geoffrey Scott's *The Architecture of Humanism* (1924).

That same year, during which he took a sabbatical leave from McGill, Collins returned to Yale as a research fellow to study at the University Law School, leading to a Master of Laws degree in 1971 from Queens College, Montreal, for his thesis "Amenity, a Study of Jurisprudential Concepts Which Affect the Legal Control of Urban Environments, and Their Relevance to Canadian Constitutional Law." Based on this, his last book, *Architectural Judgment* (1971), a comparative study in decision making in architecture and law, was published. In this seminal work, Collins explored the relevance of architectural journals and found them sadly wanting. Too often, they are seen to be editorial propaganda for favored architects and are filled with little effective criticism. In comparing them with law journals, Collins showed how the focus on a full understanding of precedent in the latter might well be an appropriate standard to which architectural journals might aspire, with the benefit of advancing standards of architecture. In this and his other writings, he constantly pointed to the social and cultural standards by which architecture should be judged.

An ideal teacher, always well prepared himself, Collins encouraged a rigorous attention to detail among his students. In addition about 100 essays and reviews have appeared with his name in most of the architectural periodicals in North America and England, and for a time he was architectural correspondent to the *Manchester Guardian*. He also wrote the article "Architectural Theory" for the *Encyclopaedia Britannica*. Early in his career, Collins developed a special love and knowledge of the architecture of France. This gave him standards by which to measure and allowed him to comment seriously on all kinds of architecture. An eye for humbug always aroused a quick response in him. In 1972 the American Institute of Architects' Architecture Critic's Citation recognized his eminent contribution to architectural thought.

W.P. THOMPSON

Biography

Born in Leeds, Yorkshire, 1920. Began architectural studies at Leeds College of Art 1936; received diploma in architecture 1948; studies were interrupted by seven years of service in the British army. Married Margaret Taylor of Ottawa 1953. Completed M.A. thesis, University of Manchester, 1955; received Fulbright Traveling Scholarship and an appointment to lecture in architectural history at Yale University 1955; appointed associate professor, McGill University 1956, and full professor of architecture 1962. Became a Canadian citizen 1962. Received Master of Laws degree, Queens College, Montreal 1971. Died 1981.

Selected Publications

Concrete: The Vision of a New Architecture: A Study of Auguste Perret and His Precursors, New York: Horizon, 1959
"In Search of a Flaw in Architectural Education," *Royal Architectural Institute of Canada Journal*, 36 (January 1959)
"Historicism," *Architectural Review*, 128/762 (August 1960)
"The Form-Givers," *Perspecta*, no. 7 (1961)
"Aspects of Ornament," *The Architectural Review*, 129/772 (June 1961)
"Furniture Givers as Form Givers: Is Design an All-Encompassing Skill?" *Progressive Architecture*, 44 (March 1963)
Changing Ideals in Modern Architecture, 1750–1950, 1965; 2nd edition, Montreal: McGill-Queens University Press, 1998
"The Philosophy of Architectural Criticism," *American Institute of Architects Journal*, 49/1 (January 1968)
Architectural Judgment, London: Faber; 1971
"Peter Collins: Selected Writings," *The Fifth Column*, 4/3–4 (Summer 1984)

Further Reading

Bland, John, and Derek Drummond, "Peter Collins (1920–1981)," *Society of Architectural Historians Newsletter*, 26/2 (April 1982)

COLOGNE, GERMANY

With the Rhine River winding slowly through the city and its towering cathedral spires, Cologne has long provided the German imagination with rich images of artistic and national Romanticism. Its idyllic landscape and key location on a major waterway have supported the city's evolution as an important commercial and industrial center. The history of Cologne's architectural developments in the 20th century clearly joins the two strands of artistic enchantment and dynamic economy.

The city's built landscape served a distinct defensive function at the close of the 19th century. Developments in military technology had brought about an increased target range of weapons, and Cologne's medieval city wall with its buffer zone leading up to fortification structures was insufficient to protect Cologne from enemy fire. In 1881 the Prussian government moved the inner medieval fortress ring outward, and the approximately one-square-mile, crescent-shaped area created by the relocation of the wall, Neustadt, was then quickly constructed. No longer cramped behind the 600-year-old city wall, Cologne's turn-of-the-century population of over 400,000 had room to continue its process of growth and urbanization. In 1907–14 the defensive structures underwent further alterations. The fortification numbered 182 units on the eve of World War I, and almost all these were subsequently torn down per the Treaty of Versailles, putting an end to Cologne's military and architectural status as a "fortress city." Konrad Adenauer, Cologne's lord mayor from 1917 to 1933, successfully convinced the Allies to allow a handful of the fortresses to remain as historical documents.

As modern military technology changed the location and layout of the city, suburbs dominated by factories began to crop up around the outskirts of the city. The population continued to grow, helped along by a pattern of incorporating communities, extending the geographic contours of the city eastward across the river. The industrialization and commercialization of Cologne brought about construction projects that facilitated the transportation of goods and people throughout the city. The construction of the Deutzer Bridge (1911–13) united both sides of the Rhine, and the widening and merger of existing alleys into the Gürzenichstrasse created a modern access road to the bridge on the east side of the river.

The construction of major department stores such as Kaufhaus Tietz (designed by Wilhelm Kreis, 1912–14) supported the trend toward urbanization. The Kaufhaus Tietz building, situated between Hohe Strasse and Gürzenichstrasse, represented a new architectural form with its symmetrical, imposing form and three glass-covered courtyards. In 1933 the Tietz firm was one of the first victims of the National Socialists' policy of "Aryanization." The Jewish family Tietz lost their position as head of the company, and the firm was renamed Westdeutsche Kaufhof AG. Allied bombing damaged the interior and the foundation of the building. In 1953 the firm was renamed once again, acquiring the simpler title Kaufhof Aktiengesellschaft, which it retains today.

Such monumental architecture reflected Rhineland architects' belief that they could affect the world with their constructions, and this conviction led to buildings that were assigned a pedagogical and therapeutic role by their designers. In 1914 Bruno Taut constructed one of the first Expressionist buildings with his polygonal Glaspalast (the glass palace) for the Werkbund Exhibition in Cologne, which took place on what are now the trade-show grounds. Under the pavilion's cupola, made up of diamond-shaped glass bricks, a band of six short rhymes by Paul Scheerbart celebrated the potential for architecture to improve society. Focusing primarily on glass and light, these included "*Das bunte Glas/zerstört den Hass*" (Colored glass/destroys hate) and "*Das Glas bringt uns die neue Zeit/Backsteinkultur tut uns nur leid*" (Glass brings the new era to us/Brick culture only pains us). The building, which has not survived, and the exhibition firmly established Cologne as a major figure on the international and national architecture stages.

Under Konrad Adenauer the city saw a number of new designs in the interwar period, from Rhine Romantic to international modern, but all with a decidedly German reference. Although the war had suffocated an explicitly Expressionist architectural movement, the prewar utopian vision of beauty, light, and glass continued to influence construction plans, particularly with reference to the emerging social interest in hygiene and sports and the growing population. Before the war Cologne's population numbered almost 600,000 inhabitants. By the mid-1920s this number rose to over 700,000. With the elimination of the fortress structures, city planners were free to push Cologne's

Maria Konigein, Cologne-Marienburg, Germany, designed by Dominikus Böhm (1954)

borders out further again, onto land that had once been reserved for defense purposes. The need for increased work and recreation spaces, combined with Expressionist influences and interwar local patriotism, brought about an explosion of new constructions in all sectors.

Inspired by the parks in the city of Düsseldorf, Adenauer created the greenbelts or rings encircling Cologne (1921–24). These areas consisted of a seven-kilometer-long inner ring and a 30-kilometer-long outer green ring that followed the fortification lines and incorporated the remaining forts in their landscape. Designed in part by the Hamburg architect and city planner Fritz Schumacher, the belts were part of the designs for Cologne that envisioned a unity of living, working, relaxation, and transportation. This connection between mind and body, accompanied an increased enthusiasm for sports as well, was symbolized by the stadium and swimming facility constructed by Adolf Abel in 1926, city planner from 1925 to 1930. Two monumental, matching buildings flanked the sport center's entrance, flat-roofed, with straight, imposing lines and massive brick pillars.

A further remnant of Fortress Cologne found a use for the construction of the Bastei restaurant (1923–24) by Wilhelm Riphahn, reconstructed by him in 1958 after it had been badly burned during World War II. Built on an abandoned structure of the fortress wall, the defensive tower houses three administrative and storage levels, and the kitchen is in a corner of the top floor, overlooking the street. The dining area projects over the river, a glass-paneled half circle like a Ferris wheel turned on its side and framed with steel struts, topped with a star-shaped flat roof and encircled by a terrace. The Expressionist reference to glass and jagged forms is unmistakable, but the Bastei also showed elements of an emerging functionalism, such as using glass to increase the view of the river. This peculiar interwar combination of Expressionism, functionalism, and local patriotism can also be seen in Riphahn and Caspar Maria Grod's Kölnsiche Zeitung, a newspaper building shaped like a ship's bow that alludes to the Rhine.

Ideas about light and green spaces extended to the new residential areas, and many of these constructions are exemplary of Cologne's Neues Bauen (New Building) movement. Riphahn and Grod's Blauer Hof estate (1926–28) in the Buchforst district, unusual for its block structure, provided residents with light, air, trees, and green courtyards. The architects designed the apartments of the neighboring estate, Weisse Stadt, at a slant to provide optimum lighting; its row-by-row layout of units became quite popular for housing. Their residential area Zollstock Siedling (1927–29) comprised apartments designed to reflect the shared economic and social status of the middle-class civil servants and private-sector residents. Each unit included a separate kitchenette instead of the combined kitchen and living area typical for the region, thereby demonstrating the residents' higher social status. The Melanchthon church (1929–30) there, designed by Theodor Merrill, intentionally provided Zollstock with a social center. The church sustained damage during the war and has been restored with some alterations.

Commercial buildings reemerged in the interwar period as important constructions. Jacob Koerfer's L-shaped Hansa-Hochhaus (1924–25), comprising a long, seven-story unit and a 17-story tower, presented a trend toward horizontal forms. Nevertheless, at more than 213 feet, it was briefly the tallest building in Europe. With its alternating rows of glass and limestone, the Dischhaus (1928–30), designed by Bruno Paul, represented a clearer modern emphasis on smooth, vertical, flowing lines. Destroyed in World War II, it has been rebuilt according to the original plans. The completion of the autobahn between Cologne and Bonn in 1932 offered infrastructural transportation support to these commercial projects.

The National Socialists' seizure of power in 1933 brought about a cleansing of the Martinsviertel quarter, a project actually developed under Adenauer to combat the poverty and crime rampant in that part of the city. The Nazis chased "undesirables" out of the area and expropriated great numbers of buildings from Jews. Architects fused old and new buildings together, creating a changed topography that evoked an idealistic image of a German medieval inner city. Nazi planners envisioned the inner city as a visual reference to the party's claims of a German heritage, whereas the surrounding modern city, with its monumental parade alleys, contributed to a sense of historical evolution.

World War II bombing almost entirely destroyed Cologne. The historic inner city lost 90 percent of its buildings, and urban areas saw irreparable damage to 70 percent of residences. The cathedral, although still standing, was badly damaged, as were many Romanesque churches. Only 40,000 people of the prewar 800,000 population continued to live in Cologne. The "Adolf Hitler Mountain," as locals referred to the overwhelming pile of rubble left by the destruction in the center of the city, disappeared only slowly over the years until 1955. Planners ripped down many 19th-century buildings in the postwar years, electing to reconstruct a number of the 1930s buildings in the massive neoclassical style of Nazism.

The postwar years focused on reclaiming Cologne's architectural past. In 1948 residents celebrated the 700th anniversary of the cathedral. In 1956 repairs to the building had been completed, allowing visitors once again full access to the city's icon. Dominikus Böhm and his son Gottfried continued the elder's interwar program of constructing new churches, using new materials such as concrete and circular styles that reflected changes in the function of the church as a center of community life. Dominikus Böhm had built the tower of his St. Engelbert Church (1930) standing apart from the main building, keeping the form of the main building as reflective of its purpose to unify the congregation. St. Maria Königin (1952–54), also designed by Dominikus Böhm, uses a south-facing picture window as the primary source of light, and its baptistery is entirely glass. Gottfried Böhm constructed the tower in 1960. The combination of round forms and straight lines in brick and concrete used in Dominikus Böhm's Christi Auferstehung Church (1968) provides an example of the plasticity typical of the Brutalism movement, evident as well in the architect Oswald Matthias Ungers's own private home and office (1958–59). The library annex in 1989 used almost exclusively cubes and squares and acquired an explicit humanistic, pedagogical function.

The architectural competition for the Wallraf-Richartz Museum in 1978 demonstrated the importance that discussions surrounding architectural projects have had in Cologne. Although neither James Stirling's Postmodern design for the museum nor Ungers's plan, which called for the museum building itself to open up new spaces in the city, was realized, both contributed to a new era of architecture in Cologne and Germany. The winning plan, by Peter Busman and Godfrid Haberer (1980–86), a reinforced-concrete structure with overhanging red brick walls, housed the Wallraf-Richartz, the Ludwig Museum, and the Philharmonic. Ungers later won a competition for the new Wallraf-Richartz Museum, which once again reflected his preference for cube forms. The museum opened for exhibits in January 2001 to critical acclaim for the architectural design as well as the display of the museum's holdings, successfully helping Cologne in its struggle to edge out Berlin as Germany's leading cultural city.

The end of the 20th century demonstrated the "cathedral city's" commitment to preserving its cultural heritage while looking forward architecturally. The ruins left by the war of the Church of St. Kolumba will be incorporated into a new building for the relocated diocesan museum of Cologne, a competition won by Peter Zumthor in 1997. The following year marked the 750th anniversary of the cathedral and a new series of reconstructions for that building. As restorers voice concern over the damage effected by pollution to the flying buttresses, the cathedral remains a looming reminder of the evolving role of the city's artistic and commercial past in the construction of its built landscape.

BENITA CAROL BLESSING

See also **Böhm, Gottfried (Germany); Taut, Bruno (Germany); Ungers, Oswald Mathias (Germany); Werkbund Exhibition, Cologne (1914); Zumthor, Peter (Switzerland)**

Further Reading

Architekten- und Ingenierverein Köln e.v., ed. *Köln—seine Bauten 1928–1988*, Cologne: J.P. Bachem, 1991

Hall, Heribert, *Köln, seine Bauten 2000*, Cologne: J.P. Bachem, 1999

Heinen, Werner, and Anne M. Pfeffer, *Köln. Siedlungen 1888–1938*, Cologne: J.P. Bachem, 1988

Kier, Hiltrud, *Kirchen in Köln*, Cologne: J.P. Bachem, 1999

Kierdorf, Alexander, *Köln. Ein Architektführer/An Architectural Guide*, Berlin: Reimer, 1999

Kierdorf, Alexander, Dieter Klein-Meynen, and Henriette Meynen, *Kölner Wirtschaftsarchitektur*, Cologne: Wienand, 1996

Koshar, Rudy, *Germany's Transient Pasts: Preservation and National Memory in Twentieth Century*, Chapel Hill: University of North Carolina Press, 1998

Wallraf-Richartz-Museum, *Köln*, Cologne: DuMont, 2001

COLOR

Color had always been fundamental to the visual and symbolic human experience of architecture until the advent of modernism, which largely dismissed its evocative effects as ornamental and unmodern. Subjugated for decades by the monochromatic architecture of the International Style, color reemerged in the latter half of the 20th century to again take its place as a significant design aspect of architectural form.

By the beginning of the 20th century, the scientific understanding of color through theories of physical light, pigments, and human perception was accepted within standard artistic methods and incorporated into art and design education. Following the color experiments of Cubism, the Dutch De Stijl movement conceptualized a spatial use of color to unify two- and three-dimensional forms. In *De Stijl Manifesto V* (1923), Cor van Eesteren, Theo van Doesburg, and Gerrit Rietveld argued, "We have given color its rightful place in architecture and we assert that painting separated from the architectonic construction (i.e. the picture) has no right to exist." This theory was followed rigorously in architectural examples, such as Gerrit Rietveld's Schröder-Schräder House, a design that dispersed painter Piet Mondrian's floating planes of color into three dimensions.

Design instruction at the Bauhaus carefully limited color application to abstract compositions and the intrinsic color of materials. Color theory and composition was one of the fundamental principles taught within the Preliminary ("Basic") Course, and color was considered to be instructional content of the same importance as building materials in later courses. Among the significant instructors at the Bauhaus who contributed to the evolution of color theory were Paul Klee, Johannes Itten, and Josef Albers.

Though methods of Bauhaus instruction became popular throughout architecture schools, color was largely dismissed as an aspect of architectural design because of the modernist dictum against ornamentation. White planar surfaces and structural elements became the formal language of modernism as it spread throughout the world as the International Style. Paradoxically, the work of a number of significant Modern architects still involved color theory and application. Bruno Taut combined practice as an artist with architectural design, as did Le Corbusier, who produced complex color schemes for particular elements within his buildings, sometimes examined through dozens of paint swatches and colored sketches (Unité d'Habitation, 1945–52). After being reconstructed in 1986, the richly colored stone surfaces of Mies van der Rohe's German Pavilion (1929)—known after its demolition only through black-and-white photographs—were recognized to be as intentionally spatial as the architectural forms themselves.

Among architects who designed through modernism's influence, Luis Barragán integrated color most fully into spatial effects. His Cuadra San Cristóbal in Mexico (1968) and the Francisco Gilardi House (1976), with its striking blue-walled dining room and floating red column over water, are among his most significant achievements.

By midcentury advances in engineering and psychology began to create new "functional" color sciences that ranged from thermal absorption of surfaces to human visual recognition. Schemes of colorization were classified for building safety and egress as well as for building components, such as wiring and mechanical systems. Renzo Piano and Richard Rogers used these as an aesthetic in the Pompidou Center (1977) by exposing major building systems on the exterior, painted in colors based on the appropriate standard. The building industry also began to institute color standards for the selection of building products and finishes.

The advent of Postmodernism in the 1960s returned the possibilities of color to architectural design. Robert Venturi argued against modernism through a reinvigorated interest in the complex, evocative, and ambiguous characteristics of architecture. His first significant built work, the Vanna Venturi House (1964), was painted a disturbing olive green, intentionally provoking arguments for and against the International Style's "white" architecture. Partnered with Denise Scott Brown and Steven Izenour, Venturi continued to incorporate bold color patterns and iconography in building design, echoing the graphic abstractions of pop art.

Other Postmodern architects began to use color profusely throughout their work, highlighting building surfaces and elements with sometimes raucous color combinations. Notable among these are Charles Moore (Piazza d'Italia, 1975–78), Aldo van Eyck (Mothers' House, 1973–78), Arquitectonica (Spear House, 1976–78), and Michael Graves, who abstracted the formal language of classical architecture and appropriated its muted "Italian" colors—yellows, ochers, and terra-cottas—in his Port-

Arnoff Center for Design and Art, University of Cincinnati, by Peter Eisenman (1996)
© Mary Ann Sullivan

land Public Services Building (1980). British architect James Stirling repeatedly used a signature yellow-green, which was applied to hand railings, window frames, and other details in a number of building designs (Neue Staatsgalerie, 1977–84). Following earlier work by Barragán, Ricardo Legorreta continued exploring abstractly modernist forms covered in vibrant, saturated colors typical of the vernacular traditions in his native Mexico (Solana, 1991).

As in the infrequent use of color in modernism, color in the Postmodern style was most often employed to give articulation to building elements. This application of color was more compositional than spatial because it tended to increase the contrast of elements to one another—making their tectonics and organization more evident—rather than manipulating space with the advancing and receding characteristics of colored surfaces.

Frank Gehry choose materials and finishes with consistent color, applying them individually to forms so that they could set off one another within a larger composition (Winton Guest House, 1982–87). Peter Eisenman often returned to a palette of pastel pinks, blues, and greens to distinguish various autonomous patterns in his deconstructed forms, but in a somewhat programmed manner that suggested an abdication of subjective color choice (Arnoff Center for Design and Art, 1988–96).

Though its scientific understanding grew enormously, color was rarely the subject of a cogent space-making design methodology. With the exceptions of De Stijl and a few singular buildings, this may remain the greatest unexplored possibility of 20th-century architecture.

CHRISTOPHER MONSON

See also **Arquitectonica (United States); Barragán, Luis (Mexico); Bauhaus; Corbusier, Le (Jeanneret, Charles-Édouard) (France); Cuadra San Cristóbal, Mexico; Cubism; De Stijl; Eisenman, Peter (United States); van Eyck, Aldo (Netherlands); Gehry, Frank (United States); German Pavilion, Barcelona (1929); Graves, Michael (United States); International Style; Legoretta, Ricardo (Mexico); Moore, Charles (United States); Neue Staatsgalerie, Stuttgart; Pompidou Center, Paris; Portland Public Services Building, Portland, Oregon; Postmodernism; Rietveld, Gerrit (Netherlands); Schröder-Schräder House (Utrecht); Scott Brown, Denise (United States); Stirling, James (England); Taut, Bruno (Germany); Unité d'Habitation (Marseilles); Vanna Venturi House, Philadelphia; Venturi, Robert (United States)**

Further Reading

Albers, Josef, *The Interaction of Color*, New Haven, Connecticut: Yale University Press, 1963

Chevreul, Michel-Eugene, *The Principles of Harmony and Contrast of Colors and Their Application to the Arts*, New York: Van Nostrand Reinhold, 1967

"Color Confessions by Contemporary Architects," *Daidalos*, 51 (1994)

Conrads, Ulrich (editor), "De Stijl Manifesto V" by Cor van Eesteren, Theo van Doesburg, and Gerrit Rietveld in *Programs and Manifestoes on 20th-century Architecture*, translated by Michael Bullock, Cambridge, Massachusetts: MIT Press, 1990

Heer, Jan de, *Kleur en Architectuur* (Color in Architecture), Rotterdam: Uitgevergij 010, 1986

Itten, Johannes, *The Art of Color: The Subjective Experience and Objective Rationale of Color*, New York: Van Nostrand Reinhold, 1969

Mahnke, Frank H., *Color and Light in Man-made Environments*, New York: Van Nostrand Reinhold, 1987

Mondrian, Piet, *Plastic Art and Pure Plastic Art*, New York: Documents of Modern Art, Wittenbon, 1947

Porter, Tom, *Architectural Color: A Design Guide to Using Color on Buildings*, New York: Whitney Library of Design, 1982

Riley, Charles A., *Color Codes: Modern Theories of Color in Philosophy, Painting and Architecture, Literature, Music, and Psychology*, Hanover, New Hampshire: University Press of New England, 1975

Rüegg, Arthur (editor), *Polychromie architecturale: Le Corbusiers Farbenklaviaturen von 1931 und 1959* (Le Corbusier's Color Keyboards from 1931 and 1959), Basell: Birkhäuser, 1997

Swirnoff, Lois, *Dimensional Color*, New York: Van Nostrand Reinhold, 1986

Venturi, Robert, *Complexity and Contradiction in Architecture*, 2nd edition, New York: Museum of Modern Art, 1977

COLQUHOUN, ALAN 1921–

Architect and historian, England

Determined to sustain the humane possibilities of architecture in a world without the master narratives of cultural authority and universal history, Alan Colquhoun has made rigorous contributions to the discipline as a theorist, writer, critic, and architect. Throughout the 1950s he was, according to Reyner Banham in *The New Brutalism*, "one of the guardians of the intellectual conscience of his generation of London architects" (1966). As an architect working in London, he was one of the earliest modernists to submit the clichés of modernism to functional and contextual critique in the hope of redefining architecture after the death of neoclassical repetition and the birth of ahistorical relativism.

Colquhoun's earliest connection was to the architects of a nascent movement called Brutalism (sometimes referred to as the New Brutalists) that was pioneered in England by Peter and Allison Smithson as an aesthetic response to the country's desire to rebuild after World War II using the heroic model of Mies van der Rohe's brand of modernism. Although the term "brutalism" suffers somewhat from negative associations with ugliness, severity, and a generally unpleasant form of modernism, the Smithsons' original aspirations for the style were rooted in a purist, truth-to-materials aesthetic. The Brutalists' rejection of provincial English architecture that Banham had criticized as "whimsical" would be measured by International Style standards, modernist forms, and classicism, as exemplified in their embrace of Mies, Le Corbusier, and Gerrit Rietveld. Colquhoun's early work and thought, however, have sometimes been referred to as a more refined Brutalism in that he allowed many demands of context to mitigate the starkness traditionally associated with brutalism. He could now be called a Postmodernist if one interpreted, in his words, "the postmodern to mean not only the revival of historical forms, but all those tendencies, apparently within modernism itself, that have modified its original content" (Colquhoun, 1989, ix). For Colquhoun there is no final or completed order to architecture, as any history leads to the object and activity of criticism. Colquhoun is committed to a critical and didactical engagement with architecture that fully incorporates the claim that no one, including himself, can offer a final argument from a final (universal) perspective.

Beginning in the middle of the 20th century, Colquhoun's writing explores the problems presented to architects by historical repetition and functional logic, problems that he has recently approached from an anthropological and philosophical turn to language. Colquhoun took pains to separate Modern architecture from the more purely visual or "picturesque" transformations of the 19th century by pointing out the distance from "Historicism," a distance increased by the didactic demands of Modern architecture. Early on, his critical interest was in the element of architecture that defined its connection to its age—that is, he wanted to know what it was that generated style in 20th-century architecture. Colquhoun explicitly linked this style to the function of the building such that "the visual hierarchy always reflects a functional hierarchy, an understanding of which intensifies the aesthetic pleasure derived from the forms." His later work expanded this notion with the assertion that there did not exist any singular style for any one context but there were "a multiplicity of 'language games' that may vary according to circumstance" (Colquhoun, 1988, 5). His work has been influenced to some extent by recent attention to language in social theory, particularly the works of the philosophers Walter Benjamin, Claude Lévi-Strauss, and Jean-François Lyotard. Colquhoun's discovery of a state of architectural affairs similar to the state of social science affairs offers him ways to examine the world without relying on universal commitments or teleological narratives.

Colquhoun's early theoretical and architectural work focused on the role of function in an attempt to conceptualize the building as a self-contained entity, the form of which was created out of the internal requirements of the building itself. On the other hand, his later work examines the question of the individual building as a part of larger spatial and historical contexts. The use of historical typology, however, is typically less important than concerns of logical function and abstraction.

Colquhoun's architectural work followed a trend coeval with his theoretical and critical work. He began his architectural career as a detail assistant to Tom Ellis and Lawrence Israel for the firm of Lyons, Israel and Ellis. There he worked on early Brutalist buildings, such as a workshop and scene-painting building for the Old Vic Theater in South London. In 1961 he formed a partnership with John Miller. In 1975 Richard Brearley became a partner, and Su Rogers became one in 1987, the year that the firm's name was changed from Colquhoun and Miller to the more descriptive Colquhoun, Miller and Partners. In the 1960s the firm's work focused on medium- to large-size public buildings, and by 1970 public housing comprised the largest part of their work. During the 1980s their work focused on museums, including their renovation work on Whitechapel Art Gallery in London that improved and reinterpreted the building's already diverse elements with a concern for the historical, social, and contextual fabric of the building's exterior and the functional utility of the building's interior.

CHAR MILLER

See also **Banham, Reyner (United States); Brutalism; Smithson, Peter and Alison (England)**

Selected Publications

Essays in Architectural Criticism: Modern Architecture and Historical Change, New York: Rizzoli, 1981

Colquhoun, Miller and Partners (with John Miller), Cambridge, Massachusetts: MIT Press, 1988

Modernity and the Classical Tradition: Architecture Essays, 1980–1987, Cambridge, Massachusetts: MIT Press, 1989

Further Reading

Banham, Reyner, *The New Brutalism: Ethic or Aesthetic?* London: The Architectural Press, 1966

COLUMBUS, INDIANA, UNITED STATES

In many respects, Columbus, Indiana, is a typical small town of the American Midwest with a population of only 32,000 and a single company dominating its economic and civic life. Its main street, laid out in 1821, retains much of its 19th-century character, as does its most visible public building, the Victorian Bartholomew County Courthouse (1874) on the town square. However, Columbus also possesses one of the densest concentrations of modern architecture in the United States, with more than 50 buildings designed by internationally known firms.

Columbus' involvement with modern architecture is due largely to the patronage of J. Irwin Miller, the (now retired) chairman of Cummins Engine Company. Miller was exposed to modernism as an undergraduate at Yale University, where he developed an enthusiast's interest in architecture and a belief in its potential to express the spirit of a community. In 1937, when his uncle and aunt donated land in downtown Columbus for their congregation's new church, Miller persuaded his relatives to give the commission to Eliel Saarinen, whose Cranbrook School of Art had deeply impressed him. Saarinen's First Christian Church (1942) is a restrained, boxlike structure of buff brick with a gridded limestone facade and a detached, shaftlike campanile. Furnishings for the church were designed by Saarinen's son Eero (Miller's classmate at Yale) and Charles Eames. The church's departure from its predecessor's Gothic Revival style caused local controversy on its completion, but eventually Columbus became receptive to modern architecture.

Miller continued to press the cause of modern architecture in the following decades, commissioning Eero Saarinen to design a series of buildings, including the North Christian Church and his own house. The church is a simple geometric composition of concrete and slate. Its hexagonal form, symbolizing unity, is articulated in steel by prominent roof ribs that rise to form a spire marking the centralized sanctuary within. The Miller house, one of Saarinen's few residential commissions, features a transformable open plan, a conversation pit, and plastic "scoop" dining chairs designed for the house. Saarinen also designed a new branch and central office for Miller's family's bank. The Irwin Union Bank and Trust (1954) was the first example of Miesian modernism in Columbus. Although its steel frame and transparent glass facade defied small-town expectations for a bank, its open plan and cageless teller stations were welcomed by patrons for their friendliness and informality. Subsequent Irwin Union branches and office additions were designed by Harry Weese (1958) and Roche Dinkeloo (1973).

Under Miller's aegis these firms also designed buildings for the Cummins Engine Company, including factories, offices, and research facilities. Roche Dinkeloo's Components Plant (1973) maximized manufacturing flexibility and productivity while enhancing the work environment for the plant's 2,000 employees.

Designing a 13-acre glass-and-steel shed set in a parklike campus, the architects utilized innovative air and noise pollution control systems and provided extensive views to the exterior. To avoid marring these views, the architects accommodated automobiles on the plant's roof. When the design was exhibited at the Museum of Modern Art in 1970, it was hailed as a prototype for the factory of the future. Roche Dinkeloo's corporate office complex (1984) for Cummins was as significant for its location as for its design. Determined to make downtown Columbus continually relevant to the life of the city, Miller chose to locate Cummins World Headquarters on three square blocks in the central business district rather than on the urban periphery. A long arc of a building with a sawtooth east facade embracing a public park, it is flanked by a covered public walkway that connects with nearby structures (post office, bank, and shopping mall) used by employees. The Roche Dinkeloo design also included the renovation of a brick building from 1881 that was part of the original garage and machine shop where the Cummins diesel engine was born.

The renovation of this building reflected architecture's burgeoning interest in adaptive reuse as well as Miller's own awareness of his company's local historical significance. As early as the 1960s, Miller hired Alexander Girard to renovate his family's 1881 Irwin Bank building to house his private offices. Although the interior was thoroughly modernized, the building's cast-iron-and-brick facade was restored to approximately its original appearance. This renovation was part of a master revitalization plan that Girard prepared for the Columbus Redevelopment Commission. Focusing on a ten-block area of downtown Columbus that had declined in the 1950s because of suburban retail competition, Girard preserved the Victorian character of the district while adapting it for contemporary use, introducing coherent signage and color coordination across the corridor's storefronts. This revitalization effort was given added impetus by the construction of the Courthouse Center and Commons (1973), a Miller-financed shopping and civic complex. Occupying a superblock site along Washington Street, the complex was designed by Cesar Pelli to minimize its obtrusive scale by respecting the cornice lines of nearby buildings. Its brown mirrored glass sheathing gives way on the Washington Street facade to clear glass, better connecting the enclosed commons with the life of the street. Inside is a Jean Tinguely sculpture fabricated of metal scraps collected from the Columbus area. This work is the focal point of the complex, serving as a popular public gathering place, thus satisfying Miller's desire that the Commons add vitality to downtown and become a contemporary equivalent to the town's original public plaza, namely, the courthouse square immediately to the south.

Miller's direct patronage brought a substantial amount of modern architecture to Columbus, but of even greater impact was the architectural program that he established through the Cummins Engine Foundation in 1954. Alarmed that post–World War II business and population expansion was negatively affecting Columbus' built environment and its quality of life, Miller proposed to improve both. His foundation would pay the architect's fees for any civic building in Columbus, provided that the designer be chosen from a list of six approved architects. That list, supplied by the foundation but compiled by an anonymous panel of national experts, is continually revised to include the names of architects appropriate for a specific project. There are no other restrictions, and the foundation distances itself from the selection and design process, declining to meet the chosen

Gateway Study for Columbus, Indiana (1991), designed by Venturi Scott Brown and Associates
© Venturi, Scott Brown and Associates

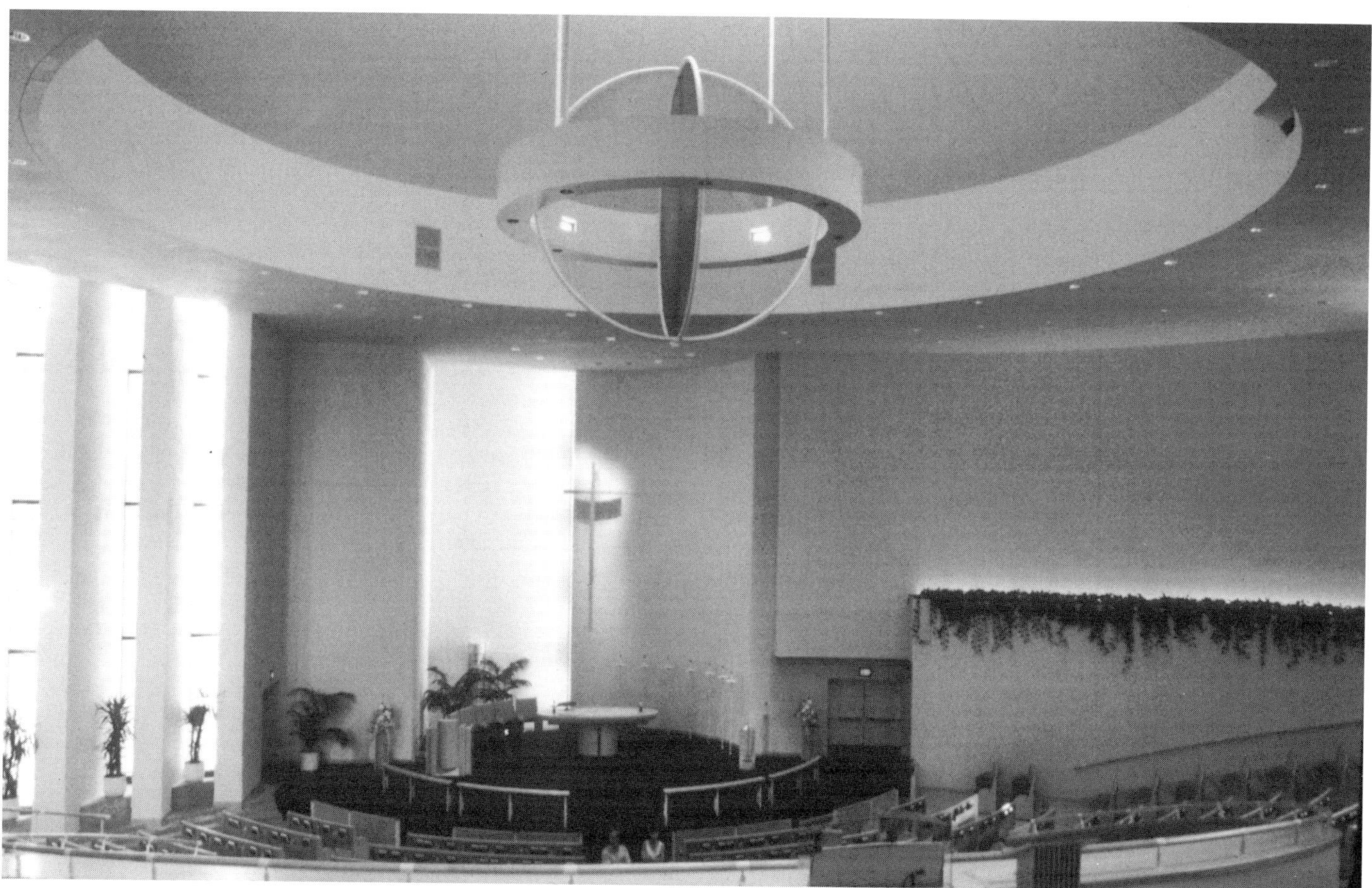

St. Peter's Lutheran Church, designed by Gunnar Birkerts, Columbus, Indiana (1988), interior
Photo © Mary Ann Sullivan

architect until his or her fee is paid. The Columbus School Board was the first local body to accept the foundation's offer, selecting Harry Weese to design the Lillian Schmitt Elementary School (1957). Subsequent schools were designed by Norman Fletcher and The Architects Collaborative (1962), Edward Larrabee Barnes (1965), Gunnar Birkerts (1967), John Johansen (1969), Eliot Noyes (1969), Mitchell-Giurgola (1972), Hardy, Holman, Pfieffer (1972), Caudill Rowlett Scott (1973), and Richard Meier (1982). Stylistically diverse—including concrete bunkers, megastructures, programmatic clusters, high-tech imagery, and neoindustrial forms—these buildings demonstrate a broad range of postwar modernism.

Other public buildings financed by the Cummins architectural program include Venturi and Rauch's Fire Station No. 4 (1967), which responds to the surrounding commercial vernacular through consciously banal design, signage, and materials; Roche Dinkeloo's Columbus Post Office (1972), the nation's first designed by privately paid architects and notable for its use of salt-glazed tiles (typical of midwestern grain silos) and Cor-ten steel; Skidmore, Owings and Merrill's City Hall (1981), with a concave glass facade set back from elongated brick cantilevers framing the entrance; and Don Hisaka's Law Enforcement Building (1991), designed in a neo-Victorian manner with brickwork and stone trim matching that of the adjacent courthouse.

Since the architecture program's inception, the Cummins Engine Foundation has spent nearly $15 million in design fees for more than 30 buildings. Although critics have complained that the program produces expensive buildings and favors high-style designers over local architects, it is generally regarded as a success. The program has been cited as a model of innovative public/private partnership, garnering praise from the National Building Museum, the American Institute of Architects, and the Pritzker Prize.

The impact of the Cummins architectural program has extended beyond the individual buildings that it has subsidized. It has contributed to an unprecedented level of architectural awareness and design excellence throughout Columbus, evident in the award-winning buildings erected without foundation support. These include I.M. Pei's Cleo Rogers Memorial Library (1969), which engages Saarinen's First Christian Church across a new public plaza; Gunnar Birkerts' St. Peter's Lutheran Church (1988), whose congregation selected Birkerts because they admired his Cummins-financed design for a nearby school; Skidmore, Owings and Merrill's plant for *The Republic* newspaper (1971), with its printing equipment dramatically revealed behind a transparent facade; and Caudill Rowlett Scott's switching center for Indiana Bell Telephone (1978), with its colorful street-level shafts. The latter two are fine examples of light industrial buildings sensitively designed as neighborhood enhancements.

Although many of Columbus' modern buildings are architectural landmarks, none exist as isolated monuments. Rather, housing the everyday institutions of the town, these buildings are an integral part of daily life. Taken together, they present a cohesive portrait of postwar architecture and planning, documenting changes in modernism and Postmodernism, urban renewal and historic preservation, and public policy and civic awareness and demonstrating the social benefits of good design.

GABRIELLE ESPERDY

See also **Barnes, Edward Larrabee (United States); Birkerts, Gunnar (United States); Pei, I.M. (United States); Roche, Kevin, and John Dinkeloo (United States); Saarinen, Eero (Finland); Saarinen, Eliel (Finland); Skidmore, Owings and Merrill (United States)**

Further Reading

The individual buildings of Columbus, Indiana, have been extensively written about in architectural journals. On the town of Columbus and its modern buildings as a group, the literature is substantial but introductory and popular, rather than analytic.

Antonelli, Paola, "An Architecture Collection," *Abitare* (March 1994)

Columbus, Indiana: A Look at Its Architecture, Columbus, Indiana: Visitors Center, 1974; 6th edition, 1991

Dana, Amy, "Revving Up to Quality," *Interiors* (May 1990)

Freeman, Allen, "Living in an Architectural Museum," *AIA Journal*, 69 (March 1980)

Glick, Jean Flora, "Camelot in the Cornfields," *Metropolis* (October 1988)

Goldberger, Paul, "Prairie Showplace," *New York Times Magazine* (4 April 1976)

Smith, G.E. Kidder, *The Architecture of the United States*, 3 vols., Garden City, New York: Anchor Press, 1981 (see especially volume 2, *The South and Midwest*)

Taylor, Robert M., Jr., *Indiana: A New Historical Guide*, Indianapolis: Indiana Historical Society, 1989

COMPETITIONS

Throughout the 20th century professional architectural competitions were a constant source of debate and controversy among those in the discipline. They were used as pedagogical tools, as means for determining excellence, as a method for awarding commissions, as battlegrounds of opposing ambitions, and as political tools. Competitions can discover new talent, challenge contemporary ideas about architecture, and involve the general public in a dialogue. As an institution within the practice of architecture, they are also capable of reflecting contemporary or predicting future trends.

The most common types of architectural design competitions are idea competitions and project competitions. Project competitions imply an intention and a commitment to build, whereas idea competitions are promoted as theoretical exercises in design intended primarily to promote discussion and attract awareness to a particular issue. An idea competition is most beneficial for dealing with problems with a broad social interest, exploring different ways of using a building material, bringing attention to the potentials of a site, or examining new approaches to a particular building form or type.

Competitions can also be open, limited, or invited and conducted in one or two stages. Open competitions are used for selecting an architect or firm for a real project. They can be done in one or two stages, and the client retains the right to modify the winning design. In the case of a two-stage competition, the purpose of the first stage is to narrow the field, and the winner is selected in the second stage. The benefit of a two-stage process is the opportunity for the architect to engage the client in a dialogue, an option not usually available in an open competition. Disadvantages of the open competition process include the risk of choosing an inexperienced architect, the possibility of receiving far too many submissions for the jury to evaluate adequately, the expense borne by the individual firms or architects who participate, and the selection of a project that is not economically viable to build.

In the case of an invited or limited competition, a few architects or firms are commissioned to submit designs and customarily are paid an honorarium for their participation. This type of competition is often used when it is important for the sponsor to obtain a limited number of solutions from qualified competitors.

Often, one of the first steps a sponsor takes in the competition process is the selection of a professional adviser to act as a competition consultant. The adviser, a qualified professional, is paid by the sponsor to advise on every aspect related to staging the competition. The professional adviser is expected to act as an impartial liaison between the client or sponsor and the competitors and to ensure that the competition is executed in a fair and equitable manner for both the client and the competitors. The adviser also assists the jury in their understanding of the competition program.

In an effort to ensure an open and fair competition process, many countries have adopted competition regulations and guidelines. The American Institute of Architects (AIA) issued its "Guidelines for Architectural Design Competitions" in 1976 (a revision of its 1972 code, which required AIA approval and participation in competitions). The AIA document is divided into the following seven parts: General Advantages and Disadvantages of Competitions, Definitions and Classifications, General Principles for the Conduct of Competitions, The Role of the Professional Adviser and Other Details for the Conduct of Competitions, The Jury and Judging Guidelines, Costs and Time, and Suggested Form of Architectural Design Competition Program.

For international competitions there is the "Regulations for International Competition in Architecture and Town Planning" of the Union Internationale des Architectes (UIA), published in 1974. The stated purpose of the UIA regulations is to outline the principles on which international competitions are based. The regulations are divided into two basic parts. The first consists of 51 articles divided into the following sections: General Provisions; Professional Adviser; Drawing Up the Conditions; UIA Approval; Registration of Competitors; Prizes, Honoraria, and Mentions; Insurance; Copyright and Right of Ownership; and Exhibition of Entries and Return of Designs. The second part includes instructions and recommendations to promoters.

Chicago Tribune Tower (1922)

One of the most significant 20th-century competitions was for the *Chicago Tribune*'s new office tower. An announcement for the open, international competition appeared in major American and European newspapers, in professional journals, and in the *Tribune*'s national and international editions in June 1922.

In a sense this was a two-stage competition, as in addition to the open entries, ten architects were invited to participate for a fee of $2000 each. The invited architects were to be judged with the ten best projects chosen from the more than 200 submissions received, the majority of which were from the United States. From this group of 20, three were to be awarded prize money of $50,000, $20,000, and $10,000. The composition of the jury (one architect, Alfred Granger, AIA, and four members of the Tribune Building Corporation) was a source of criticism by the AIA, which felt that the jury was heavily weighted on the side of the layperson.

From the outset the competition was highly publicized and extremely well documented. At the conclusion of the competition, the *Tribune* sponsored a touring exhibition of the perspective renderings to universities, public institutions, and office buildings. The publicity was intended to promote the *Tribune* as a newspaper committed to such lofty values as public education. In fact, during the period that the competitors were working on their submissions, the *Tribune* ran a series of weekly articles on the subject of historic and modern architecture that might have influenced some of the participants.

An important outcome of this competition was the exposure of a mass audience to modern architecture during the exhibition's 27-city tour of the United States and Canada. It was also a demonstration of the benefit of the competition process even to the so-called losers, as they profited from the exposure as well. In fact, it is often noted that Eliel Saarinen's second-place design (the last entry received) was regarded more highly than the more traditional, winning design of Howells and Hood.

League of Nations (1926)

The open, international competition of 1926 for the League of Nations Building in Geneva is generally regarded as a disaster in the history of 20th-century competitions. The building was intended to symbolize the effort to achieve greater international harmony and world peace, objectives that were to be reflected in the architecture. Politically charged from the outset, the initial jury of six men represented six different countries. Soon the jury grew to nine, with the result that three additional countries were represented (all Western European).

When the jury evaluated the 377 entries, they were unable to come to consensus on a winner. Most of the designs were deemed too expensive to build, and only Le Corbusier and Pierre Jeanneret had stayed within the budget. Problems with their drawings kept them from being named the winners. As a result each of the nine jury members chose a winner and two runners-up. None of the 27 architects nominated received more than one vote. Nine architects representing five different countries shared first prize. Immediately, Le Corbusier embarked on an unsuccessful campaign to convince the jury that his design should win.

The League of Nations intervened at this point, and a second round was scheduled with five jury members who did not represent any of the prize-winning countries. They too found the winners' design unsuitable. However, two voted for Le Corbusier and two for Vago. As a compromise four of the winners (all traditionalists) were commissioned to produce another new design.

In the meantime a sizable donation from the Rockefellers necessitated the search for a larger building site. When one was located, permission depended on the signature of Hélène de Madrot, the host of the 1928 meeting where the Congrès Internationaux d'Architecture Moderne (CIAM) was founded. She said that her permission was contingent on all the prize winners having the chance to submit new designs for the site. In addition, Le Corbusier would be allowed to clarify his design. Only Le Corbusier and Erich zu Putlitz took advantage of the opportunity, yet the jury decided to stand by their earlier decision. This competition is generally regarded as an example of the battle between the modernists and the traditionalists as well as a competition plagued by nationalistic allegiances.

Sydney Opera House (1956)

Despite such problems as drastically escalating construction costs, conflicting political ambitions, and the fact that the winning architect ultimately abandoned the project, the Sydney Opera House is today the much admired symbol of both Sydney and Australia. The competition was initiated by J.J. Cahill, prime minister of New South Wales, in an attempt to garner votes for the Labour Party.

In 1956 an open international competition was organized. Two hundred and thirty-three designs, all line drawings as required by the program, were submitted. The jury included Gobden Parkes, head of the Public Works Department, and three architects: J.L. Martin of Cambridge University, Henry Ingham Ashworth of Australia, and Eero Saarinen of the United States.

The winner, Jørn Utzon, had worked for and been influenced by both Alvar Aalto and Frank Lloyd Wright. Previous to the competition, his projects had consisted primarily of single-family residences. His inexperience became evident when he attempted to solve the problem of the construction of the roof shell structure. Eventually, under time constraints and political pressure, he resigned in 1966, relinquishing the project to Australians Peter Hall, David Littlemore, and Lionel Todd.

Boston City Hall (1962)

This open, two-stage competition for a new city hall and surrounding public open spaces was sponsored by the Government Center Commission of the City of Boston. The competition was announced in October 1961. Deadlines for the preliminary stage were 17 January 1962 and for the final stage 25 April 1962. The jury announced their decision on 4 May 1962. This competition is generally considered a successful example of an open competition because of its extraordinarily complete program and the establishment in 1958 of the Government Center Commission, which included representatives from the government, the business community, the architectural profession, and the building trades. This commission was charged with the task of developing the program for the competition.

Although the actual building itself has been a source of criticism by its users and others, the competition was exemplary for its fair and democratic urban practice for design. There was no evidence of political favoritism, and the competition provided the opportunity for a young, relatively unknown firm, Kallmann, McKinnell, and Knowles, to give the city an extraordinary design. More important, the Boston City Hall competition restored faith in the competition process in general.

Centre Nationale d'Art et de Culture Georges Pompidou (1971)

This competition is notable for its effect on architecture in general. With 681 proposals, at the time it was the most widely entered in the history of architectural design competitions. Officially commissioned by the Ministry of Cultural Affairs, the project was actually initiated by French President Georges Pompidou, who wanted to be remembered after the end of his seven-year term of office. The program was for a complex that could accommodate all forms of art and, perhaps more important, draw large numbers of visitors.

Among others the jury included architects Philip Johnson, Oscar Niemeyer, and Jørn Utzon. When it came time for the jury to assess the projects, Utzon was absent for health reasons. To maintain the international character of the jury, he was replaced by Herman Liebaers, Belgian director of the Royal Library in Brussels, and not by the original reserve jury member, French architect Henri-Pierre Maillard. In a nearly unanimous vote, the design of Renzo Piano and Richard Rogers was selected as the winner. The entry was cited for its use of only half the available site, the flexibility of the interior, and the transparency of the exterior.

Unfortunately, the enthusiasm of the jury was not shared by the public. Protests began as soon as the jury decision was announced and lasted for several years. A group of French architects even went so far as to attempt, through legal channels, to prevent the design from ever being built. That they were unsuccessful in these attempts is a tribute to President Pompidou, who himself was less than enamored of the project initially yet stood by the expertise of his jury. The jury was correct in noting that architecture was "entering a phase the effects of which will not be confined to France but which will make themselves felt throughout the world."

The competition was to have a lasting effect on architecture in Paris. Expanding on Pompidou's example, when François Mitterand became president of France in 1981, he initiated a series of competitions that resulted in the Grands Projets (Grand Projects).

Although architectural design competitions remain a source of controversy, they continue to be held because they provide many benefits despite drawbacks such as the cost of the competition to the client and to the profession, the possibility of selecting an inexperienced architect, and the absence of a dialogue between the client and the architect. They are an excellent source for discovering new talent and provide a venue for exploring new methods for conceiving architecture. They are usually able to maintain the focus on design rather than on other aspects of the architectural process. Competitions can also stimulate a public dialogue.

Although the major 20th-century architectural design competitions are too numerous to mention, many significant ones include Stockholm Town Hall (1902–05); Helsinki Railway Station (1903); Peace Palace, The Hague (1905); Nebraska State Capitol (1919); the Chicago Tribune Tower (1922); the Lincoln Memorial, Washington, D.C. (1922); League of Nations, Geneva (1926–27); Palace of the Soviets, Moscow (1931); Jefferson National Expansion Memorial, Washington, D.C. (1946); Termini Station, Rome (1947); Sydney Opera House (1956–57); Brasília Urbanization Plan (1956–57); Toronto City Hall (1958); FDR Memorial, Washington, D.C. (1960); Lawrence Hall of Science, University of California, Berkeley (1962); Congress Building, Kyoto (1962); University of California Arts Center, Berkeley (1965); NASA Kennedy Space Center, Cape Canaveral, Florida (1965); San Francisco Civic Center Plaza, California (1965); Amsterdam Town Hall (1967); Yale University Mathematics Building, New Haven, Connecticut (1970); American Pavilion, Osaka World's Fair (1970); Georges Pompidou National Center of Art and Culture (1971); High Court of Australia, Canberra (1972–73); Roosevelt Island Housing, New York (1975); Minnesota II (Capitol Building Annex, 1976–77); Park de la Villette, Paris (1976); Hong Kong and Shanghai Bank (1979); La Cité des Sciences et de l'Industrie, Paris (1980); Vietnam Veterans Memorial, Washington, D.C. (1980–81); Grande Arche de La Défense, Paris (1982); Opéra Bastille, Paris (1982); Ministry of Finance, Paris (1982); The Peak, Hong Kong (1982); Carré d'Art, Nimes (1984); New National Theater, Tokyo (1984); Shonandai Culture Center, Fujisawa (1985); Metropolitan Hall, Tokyo (1985); Brooklyn Museum of Art, New York (1986); City Hall, The Hague (1986); Tokyo Opera House (1986); Houston Museum of Fine Arts, Texas (1987); Media Park, Cologne (1987); Jewish Museum, Berlin (1988); Kansai Airport, Japan (1988); Center for Japanese Culture, Paris (1989); Chicago Public Library, Illinois (1991); the Reichstag, Berlin (1993); and the McCormick Tribune Campus Center at Illinois Institute of Technology (1998).

LINDA HART

See also **Boston City Hall; Grande Arche de La Défense, Paris; Jewish Museum, Berlin; Kansai International Airport Terminal, Osaka; Lincoln Memorial, Washington, D.C.; Pompidou Center, Paris; Reichstag, Berlin; Sydney Opera House; Tribune Tower International Competition (1922), Chicago**

Further Reading

Bergdoll, Barry, "Competing in the Academy and the Marketplace: European Architectural Competitions, 1401–1927," in *The Experimental Tradition*, edited by Hélène Lipstadt, New York: Princeton Architectural Press, 1989

Chicago Tribune Tower Competition, New York: Rizzoli, 1980

de Haan, Hilde, and Ids Haagsma, *Architects in Competition: International Architectural Competitions of the Last 200 Years*, with essays by Dennis Sharp and Kenneth Frampton, New York: Thames and Hudson, 1988

de Jong, Cees, and Erik Mattie, *Architectural Competitions 1792–1949*, Taschen, 1994

de Jong, Cees, and Erik Mattie, *Architectural Competitions 1950–Today*, Taschen, 1994

Lipstadt, Hélène, "Architectural Publications, Competitions and Exhibitions," in *Architecture and Its Image: Four Centuries of Architectural Representation: Works from the Collection of the Canadian Centre for Architecture*, edited by Eve Blau and Edward Kaufman, Cambridge, Massachussetts: MIT Press, 1989
Lipstadt, Hélène, "The Experimental Tradition," in *The Experimental Tradition*, edited by Hélène Lipstadt, New York: Princeton Architectural Press, 1989
Nasar, Jack L., *Design by Competition: Making Design Competition Work*. Cambridge: Cambridge University Press, 1999
Silver, Nathan, *The Making of Beaubourg: A Building Biography of the Centre Pompidou, Paris*, Cambridge, Massachusetts: MIT Press, 1994
Strong, Judith, *Winning by Design: Architectural Competitions*, London: Butterworth Architecture, 1996

COMPUTERS AND ARCHITECTURE

To realize an example of architecture, the object must be described. However, this in itself is insufficient—the process of realizing the object must itself be supported. It is in both these dimensions that computers have been of benefit in the practice of architecture in the 20th century. The use of computers in architectural design has been motivated by a number of factors and driven by others, and has come to reflect the evolution of practice through the last half of the 20th century.

The work of an architect started the century relying heavily on teams of colleagues, employees, consultants, and contractors; by the close of the century, although the practice of architecture was much the same, the picture had changed to include computing tools in almost every team and every practice, drawing the participants closer together through the whole sequence of events leading to the construction of a building. As this change took place, the challenge with the use of computing tools came to be recognized as the challenge of management, not technology.

Describing the Building

Buildings can be described in two ways. They can be described by performance (including quantities), or they can be drawn. Initially, computers were seen as manipulators of data in the simplest sense: calculators and organizers. Thus, when computers were first made accessible to designers, it was largely in the areas of planning and engineering that applications were first undertaken. In these fields, design could be seen to rely on the handling of large data sets as well as the manipulation of equations in the calculation of quantified results. More traditionally, a building is drawn: The geometries of the building are set forth by means of lines, straight or curved, or volumes. A second application of computers is in the creation and manipulation of graphics. Although computers could be applied to data manipulation and calculation with more simple interfaces of card readers and printers, architectural graphics required more sophisticated user interfaces such as display screens and input devices supporting pointing and drawing. Because the practice of architecture relies heavily on graphic communication, the development of computer graphic devices was highly influential on the spread of computer use in design. The evolution of computer graphics can therefore be considered discretely when reviewing the history of computer-aided architectural design.

Computer Graphics

The first implementation of such systems supporting what we might recognize as a computer graphics system can be found in 1950, when MIT's Whirlwind computer system was used to support a refreshed vector screen for display of graphics. This system can be considered a first-generation computer, running with vacuum tubes and consuming considerable space and power. Limitations in the interfaces as well as cost-effective access to computational systems meant that it was not until 1963 that Ivan E. Sutherland presented *Sketchpad*, the first full-fledged, operational computer-aided design system. This system ran on second-generation TX-2 computers, using transistors for computation, and refreshed vector displays and light pen for the user interface. Several other implementations of computer graphic systems were developed in academic settings during the early 1960s, leading to the conference "Architecture and the Computer" in 1964.

In late 1964 IBM demonstrated their DAC-1 system to support graphic interaction in automobile design. From the introduction of this system came increasing use of interactive computer-aided design systems by automobile and aerospace firms, so that by end of the 1960s, commercial use of computer graphics was proven, although only in applications that supported high-cost factors. The first computer graphic tool specifically for architectural application was ARK-2, introduced in the early 1970s.

General use of computers in architectural design had to wait until the early 1980s, when computer systems had reduced in cost by a factor yet again to make it feasible for large practices to purchase workstations. The final impetus for widespread use of computer graphics came when miniaturization of computer circuits was achieved and computing systems dropped by yet another factor. The personal computer was introduced (1982) and software developers provided tools that could be used in a normal office environment at a lower cost. As hardware became cheaper and hence more accessible, computers came to be widespread and were common tools in every design practice and activity.

Software developed initially to describe buildings as three-dimensional data models, but as workstations became more common, users demanded simpler two-dimensional descriptions for drawing, rather than digital modeling. As personal computers were adopted in practice, the most popular computer tools in practice were drafting systems. As the smaller workstations became more powerful, more complex software could be developed for use on these cheaper platforms, and rendering and presentation software became widely available. Initially capable of displaying only simple forms and colors, these software systems evolved to portray lighting, surface textures, and colors more accurately. By the 1990s such systems were being used in architectural practice to prepare animations of design ideas for presentation to clients, regulators, and potential users.

Traditionally, building designs are communicated visually by two-dimensional descriptions, such as in drawings, as well as by three-dimensional descriptions, such as models. From the start computer graphic systems supported three-dimensional descriptions, although it was not easy to convert these to paper-based drawings. Computer graphics thus came to be categorized into distinct tool sets: drawing tools in which two-dimensional descriptions are created and virtual reality systems in which the user interacts with three-dimensional representations. Some software avoids the problems of full three-dimensional representation with simulating three-dimensional forms by extruding two-dimensional shapes or assembling (as in a card model) two-dimensional drawings in a three-dimensional space. Virtual reality systems have proved to be cumbersome and overly complex for either designers or clients to use and, after 30 years of development, have not yet realized the benefits anticipated in architectural design.

As computers came to be used in design, it was found to be possible to describe forms digitally that may not be apparent or obtainable through manual methods of working. For example, parametric design came to be used—a method in which particular properties of a shape, dimensional or otherwise, could be adjusted as the design progressed. If the parameters were geometric, for example, the shape of a design might change according to other properties such as time or capacity. Using these computational attributes, designers have explored forms that are sufficiently complex to require computer-driven digital output devices such as robotic cutters or rapid prototyping machines. By use of these devices, a more sculptural architecture came to be explored by the end of the century (see, e.g., Gehry's works from the late 1990s). These sculptural forms also pushed the use of robotics in manufacturing of architectural components.

Nongraphic Descriptions

Graphic descriptions of a building are not sufficient to erect or maintain a building. Many aspects of design rely on quantitative analysis, such as the prediction of the energy consumption of a particular design. These quantitative design procedures typically lend themselves to automation and were the first type of design activity to which computers were applied. Numerous computer programs have been written to help designers estimate the cost of their design—its performance in various parameters such as energy, wind, noise, and structural behavior, among others. Later, these nongraphic analyses came to be integrated with graphics and the results of the calculations displayed on the digital model of the building proposed. Thus, the results of a structural analysis program can be shown with the building bending in digital wind.

The construction of a building is supported not only by drawings but also by textual descriptions, such as specifications of tabular quantifications of materials (e.g., bills of quantities). Computers are particularly useful in organizing and accessing large quantities of data; that is, as database management tools. In early software developments, applications were created that linked geometric descriptions to nongeometric descriptions, permitting the generation of text descriptions directly from graphical descriptions; for example, the automated printing of draft construction specifications.

With the recognition of the programmers that building design itself represents only a small portion of the life cycle of a building, computers have come to support facilities management through the remainder of the life cycle, tracking building use and maintenance. Computers now are extensively used in the management of buildings, both for monitoring and operating particular equipment within a building (which processes generate data that can be used in design analysis for subsequent designs) and for tracking usage and scheduling maintenance and replacement of elements.

Supporting the Process

The use of computer tools in architecture can be seen to track architectural theory in the 20th century, although perhaps time shifted by a few decades at the start. Initial applications of computers were quantitative and focused on calculating answers to specific questions arising in design. In the 1960s this application of computers fit well with the attitude that design was a problem-solving task in which specific design questions could be isolated and solved and the results integrated to produce a final answer. Design could be considered an optimization of solution searching in a well-defined problem space (see Simon 1981 for a particularly clear exposition of this perspective). In this approach to design, the architect can structure the problem space and inform the computer of the data to be considered, and the computer can search, through calculation and data manipulation, all possible permutations of solutions and identify the optimal answer. Computational tools were developed through the 1960s to solve particular problems, such as needs analysis and schedules of accommodation, minimization of energy consumption, optimization of space layouts, traffic flow analysis, and plan layouts based on synthesis of quantified factors. Applications were used in producing optimized standard plans for hospitals and schools, in designing industrialized construction methods, and in planning new urban centers and housing areas.

After a decade or more of such use, it became obvious that approaching design as segmented questions to be solved through individually optimized solutions did not adequately address the broader synthetic aspects of successful design. At the same time, computer tools had developed to the point that large databases could be stored for online access and querying. Research in artificial intelligence has led to successful rule-based computer programming tools to query databases and to simulate reasoning. This led to design applications being developed to support knowledge-based design processes. Drawing on successes in technical applications such as oil exploration, rule-based expert systems were developed for architectural design. In these, expert knowledge and reasoning processes were captured from successful designers and design domains to create knowledge bases in particular. The shift to knowledge-based design reflected a broader perception that architectural design needed to incorporate a wide range of issues, not merely those expressible in simple computational terms.

The third fundamental shift in computer-aided architectural design came about when the Internet provided widespread connectivity. Architectural design has always been practiced in teams, requiring that team members collaborate on the evolving description of a building and communicate these descriptions to one another to ensure that all team members work toward the same goal. By the mid-1990s such teams were commonly communicating by sending data between team members on disks or tapes, thereby bringing together the work of team members through the computer and facilitating the division of work to permit concurrent activities. On the advent of the Internet, communication moved away from physical media and toward purely digital forms, allowing projects to be built with the majority of communication in digital form. Thus, the computer and its connectivity came to support the collaborative production of buildings, bringing together not only architects but also consultants and contractors and enabling team members to proceed on their own tasks while maintaining close coordination of the parts.

Supporting the Business

The business of architecture has adapted to accommodate the use of computers. Tasks and duties in architecture extend beyond design and include project management, research, and construction administration. In these functions as well as design, computers have come to be essential tools. For example, in construction administration Internet-based communication enables the construction administrators to observe construction progress using Web-cam video images transmitted from the site back to the office. Robotics is being applied to particular construction projects to execute procedures not easily carried out by hand, to speed up construction times, or to reduce the dangers to which people are exposed on-site. Workers in remote site offices can access online drawings and documentation as easily as their colleagues in the main office. Project managers can access online current financial information and use this to complete projects on budget and schedule. Using digital technologies, team members, including clients, have been drawn together and coordination has been improved through better communication. By the end of the century, several e-commerce web sites were actively supporting design communication, component sourcing, and construction processes.

THOMAS KVAN

Further Reading

Mitchell, William J., *Computer-Aided Architectural Design*, New York: Van Nostrand Reinhold, 1977

Simon, Herbert, *Science of the Artificial*, 2nd edition, Cambridge, Massachusetts: MIT Press, 1981

Zampi, Giuliano, and Conway Lloyd Morgan, *Virtual Architecture*, New York: McGraw-Hill, 1995

CONCERT HALL, HÄLSINGBORG, SWEDEN

Designed by Sven Markelius, completed 1932

The Hälsingborg Concert Hall was built in 1932 on Drottninggatan opposite St. Jörgen's Square. Hailed as a pioneering work of functionalism, it is also the first monumental exponent of the modern style in Sweden. The long and complicated history reflects changes that occurred in the first decades of the 20th century, not only architecturally but also socially.

In 1911 a permanent orchestra was established in Hälsingborg with its spa. In 1915 it was suggested that the local authorities should erect a society house (Borgarnas Hus) with a concert space. Because public funding was not forthcoming, the industrialist Henry Dunker suggested in 1916 a corporate venture; Dunker managed to secure a majority of shares and became, in practice, the builder. Later, it gave him the possibility to offer unflagging support for the radical new ideas of the architect.

From the outset two lines were represented in the building committee: the idea of a multipurpose society house and the idea of a single-purpose concert hall. Initially, the first idea came to influence the various projects proposed, whereas the latter idea won out in the end. In 1918, on their own initiative, two young architects, Sven Markelius and Olof Lundgren, submitted drawings for a hotel, including a concert space and assembly rooms, that was never realized. They had already won an architectural competition for a local residential area that only Markelius was commissioned to execute as his first independent project.

In 1925 an architectural competition was announced for a society house containing a concert hall, spa, assembly rooms, lecture halls, banqueting halls, and a movie theater. Among the invited architects, Markelius appeared once more and was subsequently awarded the commission.

Architecturally, the 1920s in Sweden are famed for their classicism, internationally dubbed "Swedish Grace." Following the lead of his former employer, Ivar Tengbom, whose famous Stockholm Concert Hall was conceived in 1920 and inaugurated in 1926, Markelius originally turned his eye to classical architecture to find his inspiration. The main facade of his final winning contribution offered an austere prostyle Roman temple front with columns of giant order based on the temple of Hadrian, thereby strongly resembling its Stockholm forerunner. Even the rectangular ground plan for the concert hall was based on classical precepts.

Meanwhile, social and cultural conditions changed. In response to this, Markelius made new drawings in 1929–30. Jadelius has shown that he then felt that contemporary needs were better served with a more anonymous, democratic architecture that did not demand a classical humanistic education from its audience. Thus, when the project was finalized, all traces of classicism had been stripped from the proposed building. Professional critics were thrilled at the result, but locally there arose a furor, as the architect had not bothered to inform the authorities of the change in formal character. In the end the architect was sued but won in court because he had followed all legal stipulations as to security and hygienic issues.

In keeping with the tenets of functionalism, the exterior form now emanated from the bold plan, which was based on strict rationality and separation of functions. The building was given an L shape, but with semicircles bulging out from each side of the entrance wing. The latter part of the building contained three floors and was considerably lower than the major wing, where the concert space and the movie theater below were housed.

The members of the audience were expected to arrive by car and enter the concert hall under a cantilevered roof carried by straight pillars that was supposed to protect from inclement weather. Tickets could be purchased in a specially designed space on the first floor. The visitor would then proceed to the cloakrooms placed inside the semicircles, whose very shape and organization were designed to facilitate an efficient decloaking and a smooth flow toward the main vestibule preceding the concert hall. Originally, both a restaurant and an outdoor cafe were intended for the audience, the former placed below the cloakrooms and the latter on top of them on the roof. Eva Rudberg has pointed out similarities between the larger auditorium and Alvar Aalto's Finnish Theater (inaugurated in 1928) in Åbo.

Because music consumption had become the main purpose, the acoustics became of paramount importance. Although in 1929 Markelius visited the paradigmatic Salle Pleyel, built in 1927 to house the Paris orchestra, he chose to retain the rectangular form of the concert hall rather than copying Lyon's irregular plan based on bisecting parabolas. Still, Lyon was contracted to aid him in improving the acoustics in Hälsingborg. Even though the acoustics turned out to be excellent, the rectangular plan was later criticized, as it was regarded an unfortunate remnant of classical form. Therefore, the Hälsingborg Concert Hall did not gain followers in its interior arrangements, and the concert hall that was erected in Gothenburg had other inspirational sources.

The exterior was highly acclaimed by the critics, with its stark, white concrete walls enlivened by huge areas of glazing and the side buttressing necessary to support the roof over the concert hall. In particular, the glazing of the entrance facade is a major feature, intended to entice passersby into the building. From the outside one may follow the flow of the entering well-dressed audience until people vanish inside the concert space. This spectacle was meant by the architect to create a living decorative effect, making any other ornament superfluous. In other spaces, the glazing served the people inside the building, as in the restaurant, where the opening of the wall offered a spectacular view over the sea. Unfortunately, the dining room was felt to be discouragingly naked and simple and never became a success. After only two years, this space was given over to the city library. Despite this and other minor changes, the Hälsingborg Concert Hall has not seen much alteration and is still considered a masterpiece of the functionalist era.

BRITT-INGER JOHANSSON

See also **Aalto, Alvar (Finland); Sweden**

Further Reading

Jadelius, Lars, "Folk, form och funktionalism: Om allmänt och gemensamt i offentlighetens arkitektur—Med utgångspunkt från Hälsingborgs Konserthus," Ph.D. diss., Chalmers Tekniska Högskola, 1987

Rudberg, Eva, *Sven Markelius: Arkitekt*, Stockholm: Arkitktur Förlag, 1989; as *Sven Markelius: Architect*, edited by Olof Hultin, translated by Roger Tanner, Stockholm: Arkitektur Förlag, 1989

CONCRETE

It is difficult if not impossible to imagine the 20th century without concrete. Surely the landscape of modernity and modernization would be unrecognizable without it. By 1900 concrete may indeed have been considered modern, but as pointed out by technical manuals throughout the century, it was by no means a new material. Ancient builders put it to use, most notably the Romans, who built walls (faced with brick) and arcuated spans (the 145-foot span of the Pantheon's dome the most famous and well-preserved example). This classical pedigree appealed to many architects of the early 20th century, although modern concrete practice had more recent origins. Europeans experimented with it in the 18th century, when the English engineer John Smeaton used a form of hydraulic cement (a cement that hardens underwater) to rebuild the wall and lighthouse at Eddystone off the Cornwall coast in 1756. The French began their own experiments some 30 years later, using a combination of clay and cement from limestone. Louis Vicat perfected hydraulic cement around 1800, and by 1850 Joseph Monier was producing concrete flowerpots and sewer pipes using wire mesh and timber molds. In 1824 the English bricklayer John Aspdin invented a type of cement dubbed "Portland," after the stone it resembled. This high-strength variety proved crucial, for it became, and remains, the standard binding agent in the concrete used today. Portland cement was exported to the United States at the end of the American Civil War, and as in much of Europe, concrete frame structures were constructed for a variety of industrial uses. Particularly valuable for fireproof attributes, concrete effectively insulated the iron or steel embedded within. In some places, such as the American northeast, they were a relatively common sight by the start of the 20th century. By 1887 the French engineer and building entrepreneur François Hennebique patented a host of techniques for embedding steel bars in concrete.

How best to utilize concrete and how to appreciate and interpret its cultural meaning remained one of the more interesting and politically volatile architectural debates of the century. This ongoing state of flux involved more than technical development. By the end of World War II engineers, architects, builders, and others helped develop concrete as a common building material across the globe. From great hope to corporate or state-induced eyesore, perhaps no other material would be perceived in so many contrasting ways during the 20th century. One of several materials embraced by avant-garde architects for its revolutionary prospects, critics would come to vilify the material, associating it with the oppressive characteristics of modern power structures. Through it all the material maintained a pragmatic usefulness.

Technical Aspects

Concrete is a composite material produced by mixing a paste of cement and water with inert materials called aggregates. Because concrete is mixed and poured, it is well suited for molds and can be molded around reinforcing steel, a practice so common that by 1900 nearly all concrete structures were reinforced in some way by steel hidden from view. The first ingredient, cement paste, is the binding agent, and a number of different types were developed throughout the century. Consisting of Portland cement and water, this paste hardens via a curing process called hydration. The second ingredient, aggregates, varies considerably in size from sand particles to 3-inch rocks mixed with the paste. Lightweight varieties of concrete substitute these aggregates for expanded shale, slate, or slag to reduce the finished product's weight. Because concrete's usefulness is complicated by its own dead load, a variety of engineers and builders have sought inventive alternatives. One of the more unusual experiments was conducted by the American architect Bernard Maybeck (1923), who sought a low-cost remedy for the housing shortage after a fire devastated a portion of Berkeley, California. In a clothes-washing drum he combined cement paste, water, and sand; added some chemicals; and after mixing the concoction he dipped burlap sacks into the tank and pasted them onto wooden wall studs to form a concrete cladding. Calling this technique Bubble Stone for its unique appearance, Maybeck boasted that home owners could use it themselves because an average man could lift a hay-bale-sized chunk of this "stone" above his head.

Well-made concrete enjoys significant resistance to compression, but unlike steel it has little strength against tensile stress. The compressive strength of concrete is primarily based on the ratio of water to cement. Experiments both in the field and in laboratories led engineers in an ongoing effort to increase the material's strength and decrease curing time. Generally speaking, the smaller the ratio of water to cement paste (i.e., the less water compared to cement paste), the stronger the concrete.

Once mixed, concrete is poured into molds called formwork, which may vary from a hole dug out of the earth for a foundation, to wood boards bolted together, to fiberglass panels. In some cases an entire substructure of forms must be constructed, itself a self-supporting structure requiring careful design and inspection by engineers and contractors. In order to ensure a more controlled mixing process, concrete elements are often poured in a factory or in a semiremote location on the building site set aside for the purpose. The pour is crucial because laborers must work the paste and aggregates evenly throughout the formwork so that they do not shift prelaid rebar out of its intended positions. Pipes and conduits that must pass through the finished concrete must be set into position prior to the pour as well and remain undisturbed by laborers' efforts to fill the forms. As the mix is spread within the formwork, laborers must ensure that all voids are filled and that the aggregate is evenly distributed. The more fluid the mix, that is, the greater the ratio of water to cement paste, the more workable the pour. Increasing the water makes for easier construction, but weakens compressive strength. In colder climates air-entraining agents are often added to increase workability and resistance to the heaving resulting from water turning to ice.

Concrete must be mixed for a sustained period of time, so that the finished product exhibits the properties of strength and durability designed by engineers. The development and widespread marketing of gasoline-powered automobiles and trucks have had an influence in the mixing process, especially in the United States. The truck was both a prerequisite and a consequence of the parallel development of concrete construction. Improvements in road construction, a development that was facilitated by the concrete industry, in turn facilitated the widespread acceptance of the automobile. Likewise, the cement-mixing gasoline-powered truck is ideally suited to concrete construction because while en route from the factory the truck mixes the cement paste, water, and aggregates in a revolving drum. Once poured and left to remain still, concrete sets in up to three days, then cures for usually one month, depending on the type of ingredients in the mixture and the climatic conditions at the site or factory. After engineers determine the concrete is strong enough to support its own weight, laborers remove the formwork for reuse at the next pour. In cold conditions curing concrete must be covered to ensure the temperature necessary for developing a designed compressive strength. Curing is a chemical process (not a process of desiccation) in which water reacts with the cement paste and generates heat. Although hydration can occur even when concrete is underwater, even well-made concrete is not completely watertight. Over time exposed surfaces tend to absorb water that can pass into interior space. Other liabilities were discovered throughout the century, such as the material's poor insulating properties and the particularly dangerous problem called creep. Horizontal concrete structural members (slabs and beams) develop the tendency to gradually deflect over long periods of time, and this can become so severe as to make buildings uninhabitable. Structural engineers devised prestressing strategies to counter this creeping deflection.

Properties of strength and workability have not monopolized experimentation. Designers and builders have devised myriad ways of altering the construction process to obtain specific aesthetic effects. Various admixtures, especially those added at the end of a pour, have been used to alter the color of the finished material. Paolo Soleri experimented with using mounds of sand as a formwork in building concrete shells and half domes in the Arizona desert, even using the red and yellow color of the local sand and clay as part of the cement paste and aggregate mixture (Arcosanti, *c.*1970). These colors were transferred to the finished product. The subtractive volume of the formwork, and even the texture of its interior surfaces, has absorbed the attention of architects interested in manipulating the texture and the quality of concrete's finished surface. Ornamental aggregates have been left exposed to give concrete a more rustic appearance, and a variety of surface treatments have been developed to alter the appearance of the finished concrete. The 1960s and 1970s in particular was a period in which concrete surfaces were used as a finish on a massive and widespread basis. Paul Rudolph's Art and Architecture Building at Yale University (1964) was a grand experiment in finish treatment, where the architect and contractor devised a method of using grooved forms that left corresponding vertical fins that ran the full seven-story height of the building's towers. Workmen removed the forms and then with hammer and chisel knocked away a portion of the fins to create a rusticated and jagged finish. The resulting grooves channeled rainwater down the facade in a controlled manner, which in turn limited the effect of stains on the finished surface, and at a distance the rough texture of the towers blended into the neo-Gothic architectural context of the neighborhood.

Stylistic Issues

By 1920 concrete helped inspire architects to visualize massively scaled cities, and for the next 40 years they sought to refashion the urban landscape in a wholly new and modern reconfiguration of the 19th-century city. With the turning over of the colonial order following World War II, much of the world embraced concrete and its promise, but by the last quarter of the century, the material's own success wrought a searing critique against its aesthetic properties and monolithic application. Finally, in the hands of a few architects across the globe, concrete once again continued as a material with striking aesthetic possibilities at the close of the century.

The fact that steel-reinforced concrete structures were already fairly common by the start of the 20th century, at least in parts of Western Europe and North America, is attested to by the number of notable works designed and constructed between 1900 and 1910. Thomas Edison was already promoting his "monolithic houses" by that time, Frank Lloyd Wright had designed Unity Temple (Oak Park, 1906), Antoni Gaudí had begun construction on his Casa Milá apartment block (Barcelona, 1905), and Auguste Perret had completed the apartment house at 25 bis, rue Franklin (Paris, 1903), followed by a concrete-frame garage (Paris, 1905). Although concrete had already been employed for some 30 years as an industrial building material, by the turn of the century it was still too new to be associated with industrialism. That distinction belonged to iron and steel, the constituent elements of a landscape troubled by smokestacks and locomotives. Many architects and engineers also looked to concrete as an alternative to stone, perhaps because of the many similarities between the two materials. The weight of stone tended to be a prime factor as a building material, requiring extensive formwork during construction. Concrete was perceived as the thinking man's building material, requiring a scientific mind to fully exploit its properties, which helped rehabilitate its status as a rough and crude version of stone. Mixtures and ratios, after all, required experimentation and theorizing by engineers who took out patents on their ideas. The possibility of creating a monolithic structure excited architects who understood that with concrete each element (walls, columns, floor, and roof) would resist loads as one integrated structure. This was an important and tantalizing potential, because for many architects in the early 20th century, the key problem of the day was finding a way to bring pragmatic considerations of the engineer together with the architect's taste for beauty and formal unity.

The French architect Perret is generally looked to as the first 20th-century architect to fuse the new medium of concrete with existing attempts to find a modern and modernized expression of architecture. Greatly influenced by the ideas of Viollet-le-Duc, Abbé Laugier, and especially his mentor Julien Guadet, he sought to extend and embrace classical ideas about proportions and order to the technology of the 20th century. He saw concrete as an ideal medium for creating frame structures, articulating columns in a clear and rational expression of their structural use, rather than clothing and thus obscuring them in cladding. To emphasize the trabeated character of the structural frame at the apartment building at 25 bis, rue Franklin, Perret designed the street-facing fenestration as large as local ordinances allowed. The structure was not clearly articulated; however, Perret used a subtle technique of varying color and texture to distinguish what was load bearing from what was not. By varying the color and texture of the facade panels and by recessing windows and cantilevering the second floor beyond the ground floor ever so slightly, Perret deemphasized the mass-wall characteristics of the concrete. The effort to read the facade like a frame-and-panel assemblage, a more truthful reading of the structure, was Perret's way of maintaining continuity with the neorational ideas of the past.

The engineer, builder, and pioneer in concrete construction, François Hennebique, acted as consultant on Perret's project. Hennebique had several patents for concrete members already, and unlike the architect who strove for a homogeneous and uniform structural expression, Hennebique articulated the joints between column and beam by thickening the columns and extending the beams in a cantilevered bracket (Hennebique House, Paris, 1904). Engineers such as Robert Maillart and Eugene Freyssinet, however, were the first to appreciate concrete's nonrectilinear potential. Maillart designed arcuated bridges whereas Freyssinet built factories with curvilinear concrete-shell roofs, and perhaps their lack of concern over spatial enclosure allowed them the freedom to experiment more easily with form and thus more fully capitalize on the unique prospects of the material. Late 19th-century experiments with concrete reinforced by wire mesh produced curvilinear ship hulls that prefigured this later engineering development. Perret by necessity had to think in terms of both space and structure, and influenced by the architectural concerns of his day, he was less willing to depart from the rectilinear norm that marked architectural design at the turn of the century. Although concrete may have seemed an alternative to the industrial steel aesthetic, ironically architects increasingly saw in the material an opportunity to use it as a medium for expressing the machine age.

For many repetition of the rectilinear module was the key. Le Corbusier's influential post–World War I solution to the housing shortage in Flanders was the Domino housing project. Six concrete columns, three horizontal slabs, foundation blocks, and switchback stairs comprised the fundamental elements of this kit of parts, and the articulation between column and slab was without beams, the trabeation fully embedded and embodied in the clean and ornament-free lines of the steel-reinforced concrete. Le Corbusier asserted this system was an economical solution that could be mass-produced, with wall elements added to complete this housing scheme. Although this model had little practical application during and immediately after the war, it was nonetheless a powerful inspiration among architectural thinkers who sought a fit between modern materials and modern architectural aesthetics. As an idealized shelter, stripped of non-load-bearing elements and reduced to the purity of column and horizontal planar members, it was hailed as a bold gesture toward a new symbolic architectural representation free of historical iconography.

Thirty years later Le Corbusier was busy designing an entire city (Chandigarh, India) out of concrete and masonry, but in 1946 he remarked on an important transformation of thought that had taken place. From a "machine infatuation" to a more "spiritual" pursuit of the material's potential, he claimed that architects now sought to tease out less sterile formal aspects of concrete. The small music pavilion for the Phillips Company at the 1958 World Exposition in Brussels reveals how concrete could be thought of as more than a respite from historical reference. As a technologically sophisticated building material ripe with technical problems, it was deemed ideal for creating a space that celebrated a marriage between multiple and technologically sophisticated art forms. The project architect, Iannis Xenakis, designed the general layout, leaving Le Corbusier to concentrate on finding formal expression to match the "electronic poem" composed by Edgard Varèse, the multimedia piece that combined visual projection with electronic sound. The architects devised a hyperbolic paraboloid shell to enclose the exhibition space, believing that using concrete here would be economical because this complex form could be created with straight lines and repetitive rectilinear sections. The shells of the paraboloid needed to be thin—too thin, in fact, to cast in place—so the architects sought the expertise of engineers in devising a system of prestressed panels formed on sand in a nearby warehouse, then bolted together and stiffened by longitudinal precast ribs.

The Phillips Pavilion, however, was an exception. For the most part, concrete had supplanted stone as the building material of weight and dignity. Although engineers occasionally utilized its fluid-form properties to advantage (see especially the most famous case, the Chapel Notre-Dame-du-Haut by Le Corbusier), architects typically bowed to the thrift of rectilinearity. Concrete remained a conservative but increasingly popular building material. Louis Kahn's Salk Institute (1959–65) is perhaps the best example illustrating how an architect could use the modernist idiom to create dignified space. The blank gray laboratory facades alternating with fenestration and the mass of concrete stair towers created a serene yet monumental outdoor court. Kahn christened this space "sublime," a term repeated by critics at a loss to surpass the analysis of the designer. The spiritual quality of this central but little-used space was the result of the architect's effort to bring together in an artistic treatment two disciplines that seemed to be yawning further apart in the 20th century. Again, architecture was to marry the rationalism of science to the romanticism of art, a marriage many architectural thinkers believed was more important than ever after World War II and the advent of what many thought was the ultimate work of science, the atomic bomb. It was, in fact, the technical demands of materials like concrete that led architects like Pier Luigi Nervi, a pioneer in the use of concrete himself, to insist that "architecture is and must be a synthesis of technology and art," rather than "separate aspects" of a building process. The architect's role was changing—no longer an agent of technological change, but a mediator of technology. Nervi gave a series of lectures at Harvard University in the early 1960s urging students and practitioners to embrace a disciplinary unity, a sentiment that belied anxieties over the architect's weakening influence. The technical demands of concrete forced engineers to specialize in its design and maintenance, a task few architects were capable of handling competently.

Although a naïve booster of a synthesized design process, Nervi was at least prescient about one aspect of concrete's future. In those same lectures he predicted that concrete would be utilized as the principal building material in ever-larger public and commercial projects. Across the globe governments and government agencies, as well as wealthy groups of profit-interested private companies, had already been forcing dramatic interventions in the landscape. Urban renewal and new towns, often composed of large-scale multiblock buildings, housing blocks, hotels, convention centers, and government administration centers, came to dominate wherever they were built. Modernist vocabulary did not change by this embrace of the large and the hard as much as it grew in scale. The Brutalism movement grew out of this application of concrete and masonry, and the multilane freeway elevated on giant-sized piers designed entirely by civil and structural engineers came to mark the American urban landscape in particular. Even before Nervi finished his lectures, a skepticism of this progressive gigantism gained momentum, particularly with such books as Jane Jacobs's *The Death and Life of the Great American City* (1964). She fronted a chorus questioning the inhumane character that resulted in part from gross-scaled concrete construction. Although but one of many building materials put to use in this boom, concrete had finally supplanted steel as the epitome of modernity's failings. Architects who achieved fame via an expertise in the design of the monolithic concrete environment watched as their careers withered into obscurity (see especially Paul Rudolph).

The rise of critical regionalism as a critique of modernism, and especially the development of Postmodern architecture, has meant a shift away from the monolithic at many scales. The large-scale concrete block has given way in architectural importance to smaller works that have been built in a whole range of locales across the world. Even large-scale building complexes have been commissioned in smaller pieces to a handful of architects. By the end of the 20th century, however, concrete continued to offer a small number of architects the possibilities of abstract design in a medium affording a range of formal possibilities limited not so much by physics as by budgets.

Although concrete remained a vital structural material, as an aesthetic medium it was perceived as a stylistically austere means of creating minimalist space but only at great expense. Architects such as Enrique Norton of Mexico City and Tadao Ando of Osaka relied on many techniques from the modernist boom, using concrete as a decorative as well as spatial and structural medium. They went to the trouble of designing the formwork themselves to create a grid of indentations punctuated by bolt holes left over from the forms during curing. In House Le by Norton (Mexico City, 1995), the three-story concrete facade was articulated with this pattern in a way that softened the otherwise massive plane while maintaining an expression of urban privacy that embodies the heart of this compact courtyard house. Ando's austere but elegant Church of the Light (Osaka, 1989) used a similar texture derived from impressions left by the formwork. In this case the partitioning of the concrete walls by the grid of form lines gave the finished surface a taut effect, one that makes the mass wall seem more like a tensile surface. The small size of the church, coupled with the application of simple but stark openings articulating one space from the next, meant that as the principal finish material, the concrete was not overwhelming or oppressive.

Political and Economic Influences

Concrete persistently teased architects with the allure of its fluid form and sculptural potential. Steel-reinforced concrete has indeed been designed and constructed as curvilinear elements, but such practice proved expensive because forms typically had to be customized and could not be used repetitively. Using concrete as a finish material meant ensuring a smooth and visually clean and stainless appearance. This required increased care, skill, and on-site inspection, which translated into higher budgets. It is perhaps ironic that at the end of the century, when curvilinear forms had become an obsession for many architects in a wide variety of materials, concrete had become associated with a rectilinearity that Perret would have appreciated 100 years earlier. The Stone Cloud House by Kyu Sung Woo (Seoul, 1996) reveals the pragmatic uses concrete was often put to at the end of the century. The villa encloses a courtyard that spatially unites the extended family, each unit of the family dwelling in spaces enclosed by cast-in-place concrete bearing walls, but finished with stone from a local quarry. The stone is arranged in a pattern of square-panel courses that echo the stone flooring as well as the rectilinearity of the various spatial units that enclose the courtyard. The pattern is also vaguely reflective of the concrete it hides and adorns.

The success of concrete as a building material early in the century stemmed in large part from the argument by builders, engineers, and architects that concrete was cheaper than timber and stone. This was true only because the majority of labor required in creating concrete structures demanded less skill and training than stonemasonry. Concrete construction demanded a shift in thinking, a shift that had profound consequences in the construction industry at large. At the turn of the century those few architects, engineers, and contractors who insisted on the application of steel-reinforced concrete strove to bring science into a practice dominated by a craft tradition. In their view the demands of concrete construction meant that technical innovation would prevail over what was perceived as the monopoly of an artisan class.

Unlike stone construction, a monumental material that concrete ultimately came to supplant in many respects, concrete requires a small group of highly skilled technicians to ensure a proper and safe construction process. This stratification of labor between the skilled engineers and foremen, and the unskilled and in some cases untrained laborers, proved to be an important and distinctive aspect of the modernization of the building industry as a whole and became typical of virtually every modernizing industry. Demanding empirical testing both in the laboratory and in the field, as well as inspections that only well-educated and trained engineers were capable of, this new organization effectively diminished the power of older family and regional-based trade networks. These older craft unions, as historian Amy Slaton has argued, the bricklayers and the stonecutters in particular, "had little influence in the concrete industry, and technological advance helped render their diminished role both possible and permanent" (2000).

The success of this managerial transformation has been amply demonstrated by the widespread synthesis of the concrete construction industry across the globe, particularly in the post–World War II period, and its effect on other construction trades. Steel-reinforced concrete structures, many resembling in skeletal form Le Corbusier's Dom-ino house, have appeared in regions where unskilled labor is plentiful. The limiting factor in such construction tended to be set by the cost of reinforcing steel rather than the technical expertise of the engineering profession in the newly liberated nations, many of which realized an acute need for large-scale buildings to house new political, financial, and domestic populations. Many governments, particularly in the Soviet Union, as well as myriad newly independent nations after the war, built large-scale projects in concrete to house the populace. Urban renewal in the United States and postwar reconstruction largely funded by the Marshall Plan vaulted concrete into a position as the preeminent building material during the 1950s and 1960s and even later. In some regard the modernist effort to make architecture relevant to social and economic problems, an effort epitomized by massively scaled visions of new cities such as Le Corbusier's plans to remake Paris, came as near realization during this period as it ever would. Although concrete was by no means the only material put to use in these grand visions, by the 1970s it was a material that not only seemed to epitomize modernity and modernization both materially and politically, it had become inextricably associated with the problems of excess and scale in both socialist and capitalist planning.

JERRY WHITE

See also **Ando, Tadao (Japan); Brutalism; Le Corbusier, Le (Jeanneret, Charles-Édouard) (France); Chapel of Notre-Dame-du-Haut, Ronchamp, France; Dom-ino Houses (1914–15); Gaudí, Antoni (Spain); Maillart, Robert (Switzerland); Nervi, Pier Luigi (Italy); Norten, Enrique (Mexico); Perret, Auguste (France); Precast Concrete; Reinforced Concrete; Salk Institute, La Jolla, California**

Further Reading

For technical information the best sources in the United States can be had from the American Concrete Institute and the many publications and manuals published by that organization. General works of architectural history are useful for the story of concrete over the 20th century and its early period in the 19th century. Peters's *Building the Nineteenth Century* is an especially good investigation of how technology influenced the practice of building, whereas Frampton's *Studies in Tectonic Culture* provides an interesting study of materials and architectural thought. For the economic transformation as played out in the concrete industry, Slaton's *Reinforced Concrete and the Modernization of American Building* is excellent.

Billington, David P., *Robert Maillart: Builder, Designer, and Artist*, Cambridge and New York: Cambridge University Press, 1997

Monk, Tony, *The Art and Architecture of Paul Rudolph*, Chichester, West Sussex: Wiley-Academy, 1999

Nervi, Pier Luigi, *Aesthetics and Technology in Building*, translated by Robert Einaudi, Cambridge, Massachusetts: Harvard University Press, 1965

Parker, Harry, *Simplified Design of Reinforced Concrete*, New York: Wiley, and London: Chapman and Hall, 1943; 7th edition, by Parker and James E. Ambrose, New York and Chichester, West Sussex: Wiley, 1997

Peters, Tom F., *Building the Nineteenth Century*, Cambridge, Massachusetts: MIT Press, 1996

Slaton, Amy E., *Reinforced Concrete and the Modernization of American Building, 1900–1930*, Baltimore, Maryland: Johns Hopkins University Press, 2001

Slessor, Catharine, *Concrete Regionalism*, London and New York: Thames and Hudson, 2000

Stoller, Ezra, and Daniel S. Friedman, *The Salk Institute*, New York: Princeton Architectural Press, 1999

Treib, Marc, *Space Calculated in Seconds*, Princeton, New Jersey: Princeton University Press, 1996

CONCRETE-SHELL STRUCTURE

Concrete-shell structures consist of a thin membrane of concrete in compression. The earliest practical applications of concrete shells in architecture took place in Germany during the early 1920s. The basic mathematical formulas for shell designs were developed by Franz Dischinger and Ulrich Finsterwalder, employees of the Dyckerhoff-Widmann engineering firm. Dischinger, along with Walther Bauersfeld of the Carl Zeiss Optical Company, designed the first major concrete-shell roof for the Jena Planetarium in 1924. To create the 82-foot hemispherical dome, a thin layer of concrete was sprayed over a skeletal frame of reinforcement bars. This technique became known as the Zeiss-Dywidag, or "Z-D," process. By the 1930s employees at Dyckerhoff-Widmann, along with engineers in Spain, France, and Italy, began designing other forms of concrete-shell roofs,

Kresge Auditorium Massachusetts Institute of Technology, shown from the rear, roof being replaced, designed by Eero Saarinen (1955)

including barrel vaults, octagonal domes, and hyperbolic paraboloids.

The introduction and early promotion of concrete shells in the United States stemmed primarily from the efforts of one man: Anton Tedesko. By 1932 Tedesko, an employee of Dyckerhoff-Widmann, had moved to the United States and persuaded the Chicago engineering firm of Roberts and Schaefer to acquire the American rights to the Zeiss-Dywidag process. The first building in the United States to take advantage of this technique was the Brook Hill Farm Dairy Pavilion, built in 1934 for the Century of Progress International Exposition in Chicago. The multi-barrel-vaulted building was designed by Richard Philipp. Roberts and Schaefer served as design consultants. Within months the engineering firm was also involved in the design of a concrete-shell dome for the Hayden Planetarium at the American Museum of Natural History in New York City.

Articles on these buildings, appearing in both engineering and architectural journals, promoted concrete shells as an ideal solution for roofing large, unobstructed spaces, as they eliminated the need of rafters, purlins, or heavy trusses and were considered fireproof. The development of reusable formwork in the construction of concrete barrel vaults made shell roofs economically competitive with steel-truss designs.

Roberts and Schaefer dominated the American concrete-shell market prior to World War II. By 1941 the firm had built concrete shells covering almost ten million square feet of area. Most of their commissions during these years consisted of barrel-vaulted airplane hangars and sports halls. Included was the Hershey Sports Arena in Hershey, Pennsylvania, which, when completed in 1936, was roofed by the largest concrete shell in the world. During World War II concrete shells provided an ideal alternative to steel trusses for roofing large structures, including the many warehouses, factories, and hangars built to meet war-related needs. Benefits of concrete shells recognized by the military included speed of construction, ability to withstand intense heat, and, if the structure became damaged, ability to change distribution of stress.

After the war other American architects and engineers became involved in the creation of concrete shells. Most notable was the New York engineering firm of Ammann and Whitney. The company developed its own barrel-vaulted shell design, which it then used in the construction of a series of wide-span airplane hangars, including a double hangar for American Airlines (1948) at Midway Airport in Chicago. In the mid-1950s the firm worked with Eero Saarinen on several of the architect's innovative shell designs, including the curved, equilateral triangular-shaped roof of Kresge Auditorium at the Massachusetts Institute of Technology and the fluid, bird-shaped Trans World Airline Terminal in New York.

The organic shape of Saarinen's TWA Terminal reflected a desire among architects around the world in the 1950s to take advantage of the ability of shell structures to be molded into a wide range of artistic forms. The Spanish engineer Félix Candela explored a variety of hyerbolic paraboloidal forms in his designs for thin-shell buildings in Mexico, such as the dramatically cantilevered entrance canopy of the Ciba Plant (1955) in Churubusco. In Italy, Pier Luigi Nervi explored the use of concrete ribs in aesthetically pleasing designs to strengthen large concrete roofs, including the shallow dome of the Palazzetto dello Sport (1957) in Rome. Le Corbusier's hyperbolic paraboloidal shell design for the Phillips Pavilion (1958) at the Brussels International Exposition was just one of several exhibition halls at the event to include a concrete-shell roof. Roberts and Schaefer also experimented with new shell forms in the late 1950s, as illustrated in their involvement with I.M. Pei on the roof design for his May D and F Department Store (1958) in Denver, Colorado, which consists of four large back-to-back gables.

At the First Congress of the International Association for Shell Structures, held in Madrid in 1959, the Swiss engineer Heinz Isler presented a paper in which he illustrated new techniques for creating nongeometric shell forms. This led to further explorations into the expressive potential of concrete shells. Isler's own design for the Sicli Company Building (1969) in Geneva includes a flowing roof form supported at seven points. A massive concrete shell in the shape of a Paleozoic trilobite roofed the Velodrome at the 1976 Olympics in Montreal. Although a major advantage of thin-shell concrete is its usual low economic cost, the use of shells was a principal factor in the exorbitant cost of the Sydney Opera House (1957–73) by Jørn Utzon. The complexity of the billowing, sail-like forms that compose its roof resulted in an engineering nightmare. It took approximately 380,000 man-hours and 2,000 computer hours to complete the design.

During the last two decades of the 20th century, creative development in the design of thin shells significantly waned. The few concrete shells that were constructed consist primarily of simple cylinders and hemispheres on industrial buildings, such as bulk-storage facilities. Milo Ketchum, a major designer of thin shells, suggested several factors for the decline in an unpublished essay titled "What Happened to Shells?" His reasons included the fact that the cost of concrete shells is usually more difficult to calculate than the cost of precast, prestressed concrete slabs or steel roof systems, two building forms that received extensive publicity in these years. Thin shells, in contrast, no longer had a charismatic promoter, such as Tedesko or Candela, touting the benefits of their use. As a result most engineers and architects were not fully aware of the aesthetic and structural possibilities of concrete shells. Ketchum predicted, however, that sometime in the future the relative cost of structural steel would rise to a point where once again designers would be drawn to the aesthetic, structural, and economic benefits of concrete shells.

LISA D. SCHRENK

See also **Precast Concrete**

Further Reading

Billington, David P., *Thin Shell Concrete Structures*, New York: McGraw-Hill, 1965; 2nd edition, New York and London: McGraw-Hill, 1982

Condit, Carl W., *American Building Art*, 2 vols., New York: Oxford University Press, 1960

Condit, Carl W., *American Building: Materials and Techniques from the First Colonial Settlements to the Present*, Chicago: University of Chicago Press, 1968; 2nd edition, 1982

Cowan, Henry J., *Science and Building: Structural and Environmental Design in the Nineteenth and Twentieth Centuries*, New York: Wiley, 1978; London: Wiley, 1979

Elliott, Cecil D., *Technics and Architecture: The Development of Materials and Systems for Buildings*, Cambridge, Massachusetts, and London: MIT Press, 1992

Joedicke, Jürgen, *Schalenbau: Konstruktion und Gestaltung*, Stuttgart, Germany: Krämer, 1962; as *Shell Architecture*, New York: Reinhold, and London: Tiranti, 1963

Mainstone, Rowland J., *Developments in Structural Form*, Cambridge, Massachusetts: MIT Press, and London: Allen Lane, 1975; 2nd edition, Oxford and Boston: Architectural Press, 1998

Melaragno, Michele G., *An Introduction to Shell Structures: The Art and Science of Vaulting*, New York: Van Nostrand Reinhold, 1991

Milo Ketchum archive <www.ketchum.org/milo/> (includes a great deal of information on concrete shells)

CONGRÈS INTERNATIONAUX D'ARCHITECTURE MODERNE (CIAM 1928–)

The Congrès Internationaux d'Architecture Moderne, founded in Switzerland in 1928, was related to earlier European avant-garde efforts, such as the German Werkbund's 1927 Weissenhofsiedlung in Stuttgart, and to journals such as the Swiss *ABC: Beiträge zum Bauen*. Some of its initial impetus also came from Le Corbusier's attempts to overturn the 1927 rejection of his entry in the League of Nations competition in favor of a Beaux-Arts design. The first CIAM meeting, sponsored by the French-Swiss noblewoman Hélène de Mandrot, resulted in the issuing of the La Sarraz Declaration, signed by 24 European architects, which demanded that architecture should be taken away from the classically oriented Beaux-Arts schools of architecture and linked to the general economic system. It invoked Taylorist ideas about the need to design for minimum working effort through the rationalization and standardization of building components and emphasized that architects should seek to influence public opinion in favor of the new architectural approaches. By its second congress, held in Frankfurt in 1929, CIAM began to be the most important international organization of the Modern movement in architecture, with delegates on its governing council, the CIRPAC (Comité International pour la Réalisation des Problèmes d'Architecture Contemporaine) from Belgium (Victor Bourgeois), Denmark (Ed Heiberg), Germany (Ernst May), England (C.J. Robertson, later replaced by Wells Coates), Finland (Alvar Aalto), France (Le Corbusier), Hungary (Farkas Molnár), Italy (Alberto Sartoris), the Netherlands (Mart Stam), Norway (Lars Backer), Poland (Szymon Syrkus), Sweden (Sven

Markelius), Switzerland (Hans Schmidt), Spain (Fernando Garcia Mercadal, later replaced by Josep Lluis Sert), the United States (Richard Neutra), and the Soviet Union (Moisei Ginzburg), along with its Swiss president, Karl Moser, and secretary-general, Sigfried Giedion, a Zurich art historian and critic. Its membership shifted many times over the rest of its history, although Le Corbusier and especially Giedion remained central throughout, until the decision in 1959 by a group of former CIAM "youth members" led by Alison and Peter Smithson and Aldo van Eyck to cease using the name.

The published results of the second and third congresses included plans from the associated exhibitions that traveled across Europe, the first on housing for the lowest-income wage earners and the second on the rational site organization of housing districts. The approach taken reflected the ideas of the architectural avant-garde at the time: the importance of efficiently designed, sanitary, and well-lit minimum apartment housing and the related need to site the buildings for repetitive low-cost construction and maximum solar exposure for every unit. By 1931 a self-selected core group within the congress, which included Le Corbusier, Giedion, and the new president, the Dutch town planner Cornelis van Eesteren, determined that the next congress, to be held in Moscow in 1932, should be devoted to the theme of the "Functional City." In contrast to what he called the "cardboard architecture" of classical urbanism, van Eesteren and other CIAM members advocated an approach to city planning based on the most rational siting of "functional elements," such as workplaces and transportation centers. This idea was linked to the belief that city planning should be based on the creation of separate zones for each of the CIAM "four functions" of dwelling, work, recreation, and transportation, an idea already stated in part in the La Sarraz Declaration. Changes in Soviet architectural policies led to repeated postponements of the fourth congress, and it was eventually held on a cruise ship traveling from Marseilles to Athens and back in July–August 1933. CIAM members from Austria, Belgium, Britain, Canada, Czechoslovakia, Denmark, Finland, France, Hungary, Germany, Greece, Italy, the Netherlands, Norway, Poland, Spain, Switzerland, and Yugoslavia analyzed the same-scale plans of 33 modern cities prepared by CIAM groups from most of these countries, along with additional plans from Dalat, Vietnam; Bandung, Netherlands Indies (now Indonesia); and Baltimore, Detroit, and Los Angeles. The disputed results of this congress were eventually published in Greece in late 1933 and formed the basis of what Le Corbusier would later style *La Charte d'Athènes* (*The Athens Charter*).

After 1933 CIAM was greatly affected both by the Soviet shift toward what came to be known as socialist realism, which often resulted in an overscaled neoclassicism, and by the Nazi proscription of the Modern movement in Germany. CIAM activities were ended in the Soviet Union, and German CIAM members such as Walter Gropius and Mies van der Rohe eventually relocated to Harvard University (1937) and the Illinois Institute of Technology (1938) in the United States, respectively. After several years of delegate meetings, the fifth CIAM congress was held in Paris in 1937 on the theme of "Housing and Recreation." Associated with this congress was Le Corbusier's "Pavillon des Temps Nouveaux" at the 1937 Paris Exposition, which included large murals illustrating the CIAM four functions and a display of the CIAM 4 "doctrine of urbanism," which he termed *La Charte d'Athènes.* Following this, Giedion, who gave the Charles Eliot Norton lectures at Harvard in 1938–39, advocated that the next CIAM congress be held in the United States, but no CIAM congresses occurred again until 1947. In the interim Giedion and Sert set up a New York CIAM chapter in 1944, and Le Corbusier went from attempting to influence the occupation Vichy government to successfully allying himself with the Allied victors. CIAM and *La Charte d'Athènes*, finally published in Paris in 1943, became immensely influential in the postwar years, particularly in Latin America and eventually in the decolonizing nations of the former European empires. This was due both to Le Corbusier's own efforts, such as his working with Brazilian architects in Rio de Janeiro in 1936 and with Argentine architects on several occasions, and to the efforts of Sert, who developed urban master plans with Paul Lester Wiener in Brazil, Peru, Colombia, Venezuela, and Cuba. Sert became president of CIAM in 1947, but the first two postwar congresses, CIAM 6, held in Bridgwater, England (1947), and CIAM 7, held in Bergamo, Italy (1949), were unable to develop any clear new approaches. CIAM 8, "The Heart of the City," held near London in 1951, was more successful in this regard and was one of the earliest efforts to discuss the issue of urban public space in the transformed postwar circumstances of modern architecture. Its combining of the Italian and Polish CIAM groups' concerns about historic centers with Le Corbusier, Sert, and Wiener's fascination with the design of new monumental cores suggested a different basis for modern architecture beyond the design of social housing, one that looked both backward to the classical tradition and forward to a later generation's interest in reconstituting urbanity in late 20th-century cities.

In 1952 the CIAM Council decided to begin efforts to hand over CIAM to the "youth members," and the first step in this direction was to increase their participation at CIAM 9, which was held in Aix-en-Provence, France, in 1953. In the confused developments that followed, a youth group charged with organizing the tenth congress and eventually known as Team X (Ten) emerged, with Alison and Peter Smithson of England, Aldo van Eyck and Jacob Bakema of the Netherlands, and Georges Candilis as important voices. CIAM 10, held in Dubrovnik, Yugoslavia (now Croatia), in 1956 was the last regular CIAM congress, and there the decision was made to dissolve all existing CIAM groups. A selected group of 30 members, including members of Team X, were to plan the next congress. This was eventually held at Otterlo, the Netherlands, in 1959 and was published as *CIAM '59 in Otterlo.* At this congress it was decided to discontinue the use of the name CIAM.

CIAM's influence on architecture and architectural education has been extensive, ranging from the plans of the new capitals of Chandigarh, India (Le Corbusier, Jeanneret, Fry, and Drew, 1950), and Brasília, Brazil (Costa and Niemeyer, 1955), to efforts such as the Harvard Urban Design program, established by Sert in 1960. Although the name CIAM was no longer used, in many ways Team X, which lasted until 1981, was a continuation of some aspects of CIAM, including the latter's emphasis on the importance of a small avant-garde of like-minded architects meeting to develop urbanistic doctrines and the use of architectural magazines and visiting design teaching positions to disseminate ideas. Much of the criticism of CIAM since its demise has concerned its specific formal strategies of urban reorganization, which were deliberately intended to break with all previous patterns of urban development to help bring into being a more rational and collectivist society. By the 1950s CIAM members were themselves questioning specific aspects of these "functional city" strategies, although they did not challenge the basic premises of CIAM activities. Since 1960 CIAM has been extensively criticized and is usually understood as an extension of the work of Le Corbusier; in part this is true, but it oversimplifies the organization's complex history.

Eric Mumford

See also **Athens Charter; Brasília, Brazil; Chandigarh, India; Corbusier, Le (Jeanneret, Charles-Édouard) (France); Sert, Josep Lluís (United States); Smithson, Peter and Alison (England); van Eyck, Aldo (Netherlands); Weissenhofsiedlung, Deutscher Werkbund (Stuttgart, 1927)**

Further Reading

CIAM, "Constatations du IVe Congrès," *TECHNIKA CHRONIKA—Les Annales Techniques*, 44–46 (November 1933); as "Statements of the Athens Congress, 1933," in *Het nieuwe bouwen Internationaal/International: CIAM, Volkshuisvesting, Stedebouw; Het nieuwe bouwen Internationaal: CIAM, Housing, Town Planning*, by Auke van der Woud, Delft, Netherlands: Delft University Press, 1983

CIAM, "La Sarraz Declaration," in *Programme und Manifeste zur Architektur des 20. Jahrhunderts*, edited by Ulrich Conrads, Berlin: Ullstein, and Gütersloh, Germany: Bertelsmann, 1964; as *Programs and Manifestoes on 20th-Century Architecture*, translated by Michael Bullock, Cambridge, Massachusetts: MIT Press, 1970

CIAM-France, *La Charte d'Athènes*, Paris: Plon, 1943; as *The Athens Charter*, by Le Corbusier, translated by Anthony Eardley, New York: Grossman, 1973

Giedion, Sigfried, *A Decade of New Architecture*, New York: Wittenborn, 1951

International Congress for Modern Architecture 1930, Brussels, Belgium, *Rationelle Bebauungsweisen*, Frankfurt: Englert und Schlosser, 1931

International Conference for Modern Architecture 1937, Paris, France, *Logis et loisirs*, Boulogne-sur-Seine: Editions de l'Architecture d'Aujourd'hui, 1937

International Congress for Modern Architecture, *CIAM 8: The Heart of the City*, edited by J. Tyrwhitt, José Luis Sert, and E.N. Rogers, New York: Pellegrini and Cudahy, and London: Lund Humphries, 1952

International Congress for New Building, Zurich, Switzerland, *Die Wohnung für das Existenzminimum*, Frankfurt: Englert und Schlosser, 1930

Mumford, Eric, *The CIAM Discourse on Urbanism, 1928–1960*, Cambridge, Massachusetts: MIT Press, 2000

Newman, Oscar, *CIAM '59 in Otterlo*, New York: Universe Books, London: Tiranti, and Stuttgart, Germany: Kramer, 1961

Sert, José Luis, *Can Our Cities Survive? An ABC of Urban Problems, Their Analyses, Their Solutions, Based on the Proposals Formulated by the CIAM*, Cambridge, Massachusetts: Harvard University Press, and London: Milford and Oxford University Press, 1942

CONNELL, WARD AND LUCAS

Architecture firm, England

The London-based architectural firm Connell, Ward, and Lucas was founded in 1933 by two architects from New Zealand—Amyas Connell (1901–80) and Basil Ward (1902–76)—and one from England—Colin Lucas (1906–84). Connell and Ward arrived in England in the 1920s and studied at the Bartlett School of Architecture, University of London; in 1926 both won prizes to study architecture in Rome. Lucas studied at the University of Cambridge and in 1928 formed a building company whose main goal was to experiment with concrete construction. Although the partnership lasted only six years and was disbanded in 1939, it was nonetheless one of the leading modernist firms active in Britain during the 1930s, and the architects were important, vocal proponents of modern architecture.

Before forming the partnership, the three were already known in architectural circles for innovative projects. Connell designed High and Over (1928–31), a home for the art historian and archaeologist Bernard Ashmole, who later became the director of the British Museum in London. Located on a 12-acre site in Buckinghamshire, High and Over is often considered the first significant modern house built in England. Local residents protested that its white-walled exterior, ribbon windows, and Y plan were incongruous in the rural setting. In 1930 Lucas designed the first reinforced-concrete house in England, Bourne End in Buckinghamshire. Bourne End's extensive glazing, unornamented surfaces, and flat roof show a strong identification with the modernist language of the International Style. With Connell in 1932, Ward designed New Farm in Surrey, a home with an open, spacious plan whose structural system was modeled on Le Corbusier's Dom-ino Houses.

In 1933 Connell, Ward, and Lucas not only officially established their partnership but each became a founding member of the MARS (Modern Architectural Research) Group, the British branch of CIAM (Congrès Internationaux d'Architecture Moderne). The firm's involvement with MARS is indicative of the architects' support for the Modern movement in general, as well as their interest in architectural developments on an international scale, innovations in technology and construction, and solutions for mass housing. Despite opposition from the British building industry, the architects consistently developed new building techniques to make the walls of their reinforced-concrete structures progressively thinner, and they rightly looked at their own work as experimental.

The firm's commitment to the new architecture, as International Style and modernist works were often described, was immortalized in a 1934 BBC radio debate titled "For and Against Modern Architecture," when Connell agreed to be challenged on the air by architect Reginald Blomfield. Connell, who had been unknown to the public before the debate, responded boldly to Blomfield's fierce attacks on the International Style for its foreignness, its overemphasis on function, its lack of an artistic vocabulary, and its break with venerated traditions. Blomfield criticized the use of the flat roof in a thinly veiled attack on French and German modernism derived from Le Corbusier and Walter Gropius's Bauhaus aesthetics, respectively. A transcript of the debate was made public, Connell emerged as a public figure, and the firm began to receive more commissions.

One of the partnership's most well known works is a house at 66 Frognal Way (1938) in Hampstead, London. Built for a lawyer and his family in a neighborhood of neo-Georgian villas—one of which was owned by Blomfield—the house celebrated the elements Blomfield despised: unornamented, white exterior walls; ribbon windows; a free plan; and a free facade.

Once again basing the structural system on Dom-ino Houses, Connell, Ward, and Lucas used their ample experience with reinforced concrete to puncture the house with gardens, concrete patio slabs on all three levels, a sun deck, and an observation point. A colorful, lush interior, most of whose furnishings the architects designed, is masked by the unadorned street facade. The design of the house, first made public in 1936, resulted in a series of lawsuits precipitated by Blomfield, accusing the architects of destroying the character of the neighborhood. The comparatively unquestioned presence of E. Maxwell Fry's modernist Sun House (1936) around the corner is most likely testament to Blomfield's personal hatred of Connell.

Although Connell, Ward, and Lucas is most famous for designing private homes, in 1935 it participated with other MARS members in a competition for public housing. The firm's entry—reinforced-concrete flats (apartments)—did not win, but in that same year the firm built other blocks of low-cost flats; the first, Kent House, is in the Chalk Farm neighborhood in London, and the second, in Surrey, was designed as an extension of a Regency-style house. The blunt modernist style of this addition was criticized for clashing with the existing, more traditional building.

Despite the firm's defense of modernism and its controversial works, a 1936 design for the Newport Civic Building, with its overt references to Ragnar Östberg's Stockholm Town Hall (1909–23), seemed to Connell, Ward, and Lucas's peers to have betrayed the modernist cause. Several MARS Group members objected to the design's particular use of brick, its classical symmetry, and its symbolism of function, and the firm was forced to explain and defend the work in front of a MARS meeting. An attempt to officially censure Connell, Ward, and Lucas was abandoned, but from that point on, the three had little interaction with the group, despite remaining members for several more years.

With few commissions at the beginning of World War II, Connell, Ward, and Lucas closed in 1939 and did not reopen after the war. Each of the three architects continued to practice on his own. Connell went to Nairobi, Kenya, and established a new firm, TRIAD. His works include the Aga Khan Platinum Jubilee Hospital (1959) and the Parliament Buildings (1963); he returned to England in 1977. Ward set up a new firm as well, became the Lethaby Professor of Architecture at the Royal College of Art in London, and then led the School of Architecture at the Manchester College of Art. Ward's firm designed the microbiology building (1960) at Oxford University as well as a store and office block (1967) at the Glasgow Airport. Lucas joined the Housing Division of the London County Council (LCC); under his supervision the LCC designed the important Alton West Estate (1955–59) at Roehampton, a housing scheme inspired by Le Corbusier's Unité d'Habitation in Marseilles (1946–52).

The work of Connell, Ward, and Lucas is marked by a consistent willingness to experiment with modern materials and forms. Its use of concrete, steel, and glass and its identification with the pared-down elements of modernist works was unusual for the rather conservative architectural climate of England in the 1930s, but it shows the architects to have been imbued with the same spirit as that of first-generation modern architects in continental Europe.

DEBORAH LEWITTES

See also **Congrès Internationaux d'Architecture Moderne (CIAM, 1928–); Corbusier, Le (Jeanneret, Charles-Édouard) (France); Dom-ino Houses (1914–15); International Style; London, England; Unité d'Habitation Marseilles**

Selected Works

High and Over, Amersham, Buckinghamshire, 1928–31
Bourne End, Buckinghamshire, 1930
New Farm, Surrey, 1932
Kent House, Chalk Farm, London, 1935
Project for reinforced working-class flats 1935
Film Studios for Sound Cit Ltd., Shepperton, Middlesex, 1936
House for Philip Proudman, 26 Bessborough Road, Roehampton, London, 1938
66 Frognal Way, Hampstead, London, 1938

Further Reading

The special issue of *Architectural Association Journal* contains essays by Henry-Russell Hitchcock and others. The two subsequent issues of the journal (December 1956 and January 1957) contain short letters by Peter Smithson and Colin Rowe, commenting on the importance of Connell, Ward, and Lucas. The book by William Curtis contains a section on Connell, Ward, and Lucas.

"Connell, Ward and Lucas," *Architectural Association Journal*, 72 (November 1956)
Curtis William, *English Architecture 1930s: The Modern Movement in England 1930–9; Thoughts on the Political Content and Associations of the International Style*, Milton Keynes, England: The Open University Press, 1975
Modern Architecture in England, New York: The Museum of Modern Art, 1937.
Sharp, Dennis, "British Modern Architecture of the 30s. The Work of Connell, Ward and Lucas," *A+U*, 240 (September 1990)
Sharp, Dennis (editor), *Connell, Ward and Lucas: Modern Movement Architects in England, 1929–1935*, London: Book Art, 1994
Thistlewood, David, and Edward Heeley, "Connell, Ward and Lucas: Towards a Complex Critique," *Journal of Architecture*, 2/1 (1997)

CONSTRUCTION MANAGEMENT

Construction management refers to those management services performed by an architect, engineer, or contractor under separate or special agreement with the owner of a construction project. Traditionally, these services are not a part of the architect's or engineer's basic services, but additional services.

Often these services are included in a comprehensive service or construction management contract. The construction management contract formalizes the arrangement wherein responsibilities for coordination and accomplishment of project planning, design, and construction are given to a single construction firm.

Construction management services include nine primary activities: developing and operating the overall management system, estimating the project cost, project planning, project scheduling, reduction of project time duration, resource management, project time control, the project cost system, and contract administration.

Developing and operating the overall management system provides for the general management of the project from its conception through any warranty period. It is the oversight mechanism that ties all phases of a project together.

Estimating the project cost affords the owner and potential construction contractor a measure of the complexity of a project as well as a way of seeing whether finances are adequate. Project cost estimating is an iterative process that starts often at the time of project conception and continues until the project completes its warranty period.

Project planning is a general planning process that details the steps by which a project can be accomplished. Project planning often continues throughout the entire project implementation period.

Project scheduling is tied to project planning and attempts to attach work or time periods to each of the project implementation steps. Often the project scheduling process is undertaken within the framework of a formal scheduling process, often incorporating the critical path method (CPM).

Reduction of project time duration is the iterative process whereby the project schedule is adjusted to reflect time constraints imposed either by the project owner or the contractor and subcontractors.

Resource management looks at the availability of labor, equipment, and material resources during the course of the project. Often resource management is a subfunction of the project scheduling function and is accomplished during the scheduling function.

Project time control is a general management function that provides an accounting of labor and equipment expenditures in terms of time and money on various project activities. Often performed on-site by the clerk of the works, project time control is often incorporated along with the resource management and project scheduling activities to provide the owner and contractor with an overall project status report.

Project cost system is the activity that provides the project owner and contractor with detailed information regarding the status of project expenditures. In addition to the management of payments, the project cost system provides management of change orders and other construction contract modifications.

Contract administration is a general function that provides for a review of construction contract provisions to ensure that both the owner and contractor comply with the provisions of the contract between them.

According to the Construction Management Association of America, modern construction management takes several forms, the most common being Traditional Design Build, Construction Management at Risk, Multiple-Prime Contracting, and Agency Construction Management Services.

Traditional Design Build remains the most common form. Here the owner engages an architect or engineer who prepares the design of the complete facility, including construction drawings, specifications, and contract packages. Once completed, the design package is offered to interested general contractors who prepare bids for the work and execute contracts with subcontractors to construct various specialty items. Usually, but not always, the contractor submitting the lowest bid that meets all of the project specifications is selected to perform the construction. This contractor is then responsible for constructing the facility in accordance with the design. The architect–engineer may also assist the owner in administering the construction contract, including determination of project progress, for interim payments made to the contractor. Some disadvantages of the Design Build Process are that the process is time-consuming, as all design work must be completed before solicitation of the construction contract; the owner generally faces exposure to contractor claims over design and construction issues because the owner accepts liability for design in its contract with the contractor; the contractor pursues a least-cost approach to completing the project, requiring increased oversight and quality review by the owner; and the absence of a contractor's input into the project design may limit the effectiveness and constructibility of the design. Important design decisions affecting both the types of materials specified and the means of construction may be made without full consideration of a construction perspective.

Construction Management at Risk is a system adopted and promoted by many large general contracting firms. It is similar to the Traditional Design Build approach in that the construction manager acts as a general contractor during construction. Yet, although the construction manager holds the risk of subletting the construction work to trade subcontractors and guaranteeing completion of the project for a fixed, negotiated price following completion of the design, in this approach the construction manager also provides advisory professional management assistance to the owner before construction, offering schedule, budget, and constructibility advice during the project-planning phase. Thus, rather than dealing with a traditional general contractor, the owner deals with a hybrid construction manager/general contractor. Besides providing the owner with the benefit of preconstruction services, which may result in advantageous changes to the project, the Construction Management at Risk form offers the opportunity to begin construction before completion of the design. The primary disadvantages cited in the Construction Management at Risk form involve the contractual relationship among the architect, engineer, general contractor, and owner once construction begins. Once construction is under way, the construction manager converts from a professional advisory to the contractual role of the general contractor. Often, tensions over construction quality, the completeness of the design, and effects on the schedule and budget can arise because of this change. Interests and stakeholding can also become similar to the Traditional Design Build system, and adversarial relationships may result.

Multiple-Prime Contracting is a system in which the owner holds separate contracts with contractors of various disciplines, such as general construction, structural, mechanical, and electrical. In this system the owner, or its construction manager, manages the overall schedule and budget during the entire construction phase. Work in each construction discipline is bid separately, allowing the flexibility of awarding construction contracts on the first portions of the project as soon as the respective aspect of design is completed. Furthermore, the system allows the owner to have more control over the project schedule, as the owner sets the schedule for bidding individual portions of the work. For example, if an initial phase of construction is delayed, the owner may reduce liability for delays by postponing the bidding of follow-on work. The problems primarily arise from lack of coordination and contractor delay issues. Although the general construction prime contractor is often given contractual responsibility to coordinate the work among trades, including schedule, this contractor lacks the contractual authority to dictate the schedule of another contractor.

Agency Construction Management Services, or construction management-for-fee, encompasses a range of services provided by a construction manager on behalf of an owner. It is a common misconception that Agency Construction Management Services represents a distinct project delivery system. In fact it consists of a distinct set of services that are applicable to any project delivery system. These services can be used by the owner as necessary to extend or supplement the owner's own expertise and that of its own staff and to manage the construction process to help address some of the shortfalls of the project delivery system chosen. A construction manager working as an agent of the owner primarily provides the benefit of independent, professional services provided on the owner's behalf throughout the project. In contrast to some other project participants, the Agency Construction Management Services manager has no stake in the project—in either its design or construction—and maintains a fiduciary duty to act on the owner's behalf and to provide impartial advice concerning the construction project. The Agency Construction Management Services form may include predesign and design services such as selection of a design team, budget and cost estimating, constructibility review (a review of design plans and specifications will help the owner verify that the design as presented is clear to the contractor, poses no construction conflicts, and is economically feasible to build), value engineering, and contract bidding. Construction services include construction inspection and surveillance, project controls, and change order review.

When considering whether to use Construction Management Services, an owner may wish to consider the following items to determine the proper delivery method: type of project, size of project, owner capabilities, time considerations, and likelihood of changes.

DENNIS RANDOLPH

CONSTRUCTIVISM

For the 15 or so years of its existence, from the first years of Soviet power to the early 1930s, Constructivism endeavored to alter conceptions of architectural space, to create an environment that would inculcate new social values, and at the same time to use advanced structural and technological principles. Paradoxically, the poverty and social chaos of the early revolutionary years propelled architects toward radical ideas of design, many of which were related to an already thriving modernist movement in the visual arts. For example, El Lissitzky's concepts of space and form, along with those of Kazimir Malevich (1878–1935) and Vladimir Tatlin (1885–1953), played a major part in the development of an architecture expressed in "stereometric forms," purified of the decorative elements of the eclectic past. The experiments of Lissitzky, Vasily Kandinsky, and Malevich in painting and of Tatlin and Alexander Rodchenko (1891–1956) in sculpture had created the possibility of a new architectural movement, defined by Lissitzky as a synthesis with painting and sculpture.

In its initial phase, Constructivism was closely associated with radical design studios. The preeminent institution was named VKhUTEMAS (the Russian acronym for "Higher Artistic and Technical Workshops"), following a reorganization of the Free Workshops in 1920. In 1925 it was reorganized yet again, subsequently to be called the Higher Artistic and Technical Institute (VKhUTEIN). VKhUTEMAS–VKhUTEIN was by no means the only Moscow institution concerned with the teaching and practice of architecture in the 1920s, but it was unique in the scope of its concerns (which included the visual and the applied arts) as well as in the variety of programs and viewpoints that existed there before its closing in 1930.

Theoretical direction for VKhUTEMAS was provided by the Institute of Artistic Culture (INKhUK, also founded in 1920), which attempted to establish a science "examining analytically and synthetically the basic elements both for the separate arts and for art as a whole." Its first program curriculum, developed by Kandinsky, was found too abstract by many at INKhUK, and Kandinsky soon left for Germany and the Bauhaus. However, the concern with abstract, theoretical principles did not abate with Kandinsky's departure.

Indeed, the issue of theory versus construction became a major source of factional dispute in Russian modernism. The crux of the debate between the rationalists, or formalists, and the Constructivists lay in the relative importance assigned to aesthetic theory as opposed to a functionalism derived from technology and materials. Constructivist ideologues maintained that the work of the architect must not be separated from the utilitarian demands of technology. The Constructivist theoretician Moisei Ginzburg (1892–1946) accused the rationalists of ignoring this principle.

ASNOVA, the main rationalist group that included Nikolai Ladovsky (1881–1941), Vladimir Krinsky (1890–1971), Nikolai Dokuchaev (1899–1941), and for a time Lissitzky, countered by accusing the Constructivists of "technological fetishism." Yet both groups shared a concern for the relation between architecture and social planning, and both insisted on a clearly defined structural mass based on uncluttered geometric forms and drew inspiration from modernism in painting and sculpture.

The importance of "pure" artistic experiments in spatial constructions to the evolution of the principles of Constructivism is demonstrated in the work of Alexander Rodchenko, who in 1921 defined construction as the contemporary demand for organization and the utilitarian application of materials. Equally influential was the work of Lissitzky and Malevich, whose abstract architectonic models (Lissitzky's "Prouns," and Malevich's *planity* or *arkhitektony*) represented the ultimate refinement in "pure" spatial forms. For Malevich, architectonic forms were a logical extension of his "Suprematism." Even as art (and sculpture) continued to exert a profound influence on the development of modern architectural design, so architecture came to be seen as the dominant, unifying element in a synthesis of art forms.

The most dramatic expression of artistic form as a function of material revealed in space was Tatlin's utopian project for a monument to the Third International (1919–20), intended to be 400 meters in height, with a spiral steel frame containing a rotating series of geometric forms. The monument was dismissed as technologically infeasible when the large model constructed by Tatlin was brought to Moscow for exhibition and discussion. Yet the designs of Tatlin, Lissitzky, and other architects and students at the VKhUTEIN workshops gave notice of a new movement that glorified the rigorous logic of undecorated form as an extension of material and that intended to participate fully in the shaping of Soviet society.

Commissariat of Agriculture (1929–33) by Aleksei Shchusev, Moscow

In the early 1920s, the evolution of Constructivist ideas at INKhUK passed through a number of polemical phases (the term *konstruktivizm* was still broadly interpreted and had not yet acquired the "functionalist" architectural emphasis of the mid-1920s). The pure-art faction, influenced by Kandinsky, was opposed by the "productionists" (associated with the Left Front of the Arts), who anticipated an age of engineers supervising the mass production of useful, nonartistic objects. A reaction to both sides, particularly the former, led in 1921 to the formation of a group of artists–constructivists: Alexander Vesnin, architect; Aleksei Gan, art critic and propagandist; Rodchenko, sculptor and photographer; Vladimir and Georgii Sternberg, poster designers; and Varvara Stepanova (1894–1958), artist and set designer.

Until 1925 the Constructivists had little more to show in actual construction than their more theoretically minded colleagues, the rationalists. The exigencies of social and economic reconstruction drastically limited the resources available, particularly for structures requiring a relatively intensive use of modern technology. In fact, the most advanced of Constructivist works in the early 1920s were wooden set designs by Alexander Vesnin, Varvara Stepanova, and Liubov Popova.

By 1924 Constructivist architects, whatever their tangible achievements, had acquired vigorous leadership in the persons of Alexander Vesnin and Moisei Ginzburg. In 1924 Ginzburg's book *Style and Epoch* appeared in print and established the theoretical and historical base for a new architecture in a new age, devoid above all of the eclecticism and aestheticism of capitalist architecture at the turn of the century. The following year the Constructivists founded the Union of Contemporary Architects (OSA), and in 1926 the Union began publishing the journal *Contemporary Architecture*, edited by Ginzburg and Vesnin.

Perhaps the most accomplished example of the functional aesthetic is Ginzburg's own creation, the apartment house for the People's Commissariat of Finance (1928–30) at Narkomfin, designed in collaboration with Ivan Milinis. The smaller scale of the Narkomfin building (intended for 200 residents) contributed only marginally to a solution for resolving the urban housing crisis, but it illustrates Ginzburg's statements on the necessary interdependence of aesthetics and functional design, from the interior to the exterior. Built to contain apartments, as well as dormitory rooms arranged in a communal living system, the interior was meticulously designed, like that of many Constructivist buildings. The main structure, adjoined at one end by a large block for communal services, rested on *pilotis* (now enclosed), and the structure culminated in an open-frame solarium. The front, or east, facade of the building is defined by the sweeping horizontal lines of window strips and, on the lower floors, of connecting balconies.

Ginzburg's concept of functionalism for the Narkomfin project shows similarities to the work of Gropius and De Stijl. The closest affinity, however, is with Le Corbusier's notion of the Unité d'Habitation. (Le Corbusier and Ginzburg were personally acquainted, and in 1927 the French architect was included on the board of *Contemporary Architecture.*) Larger communal apartment buildings of the period were necessarily less refined in detail, yet a few examples, such as Ivan Nikolaev's massive eight-story dormitory (1000 rooms, each six square meters, for 2000 students) built in 1929–30 on Donskoi Lane in south Moscow, were strikingly futuristic in the streamlined contours of their machine-age design.

Other notable examples of Constructivist architecture in Moscow include the Izvestiia Building (1927) by Grigory Barkhin (1880–1969), the Zuev Workers' Club (1927–29) by Ilya Golosov (1883–1945), the State Trade Agency (1925–27) in Gostorg by Boris Velikovsky (1878–1937), and the Commissariat of Agriculture (1929–33) by Aleksei Shchusev (1873–1949).

The most productive proponents of Constructivism were the Vesnin brothers: Leonid, Viktor, and Alexander. Among their most significant works are the Mostorg Department Store (1927–29), the club for the Society of Tsarist Political Prisoners (1931–34), and a large complex of three buildings (1932–37) to serve as a workers' club and House of Culture for the Proletarian District, a factory and district in southeast Moscow.

Constructivism was by no means confined to Moscow. Many other Soviet cities, such as Leningrad, Nizhnii Novgorod (or Gorky), Sverdlovsk, Novosibirsk, Kazan, and Kharkov, saw the implementation of major projects that illustrated the extent to which ideas developed by the Constructivists had been assimilated into architectural practice. In Kharkov a massive complex of several buildings known as the State Industry Building (Gosprom, 1926–28) was designed by an architectural team headed by Sergei Serafimov (1878–39). In Sverdlovsk, whose entire city center was redesigned with the participation of architects such as Moisei Ginzburg, a large housing and office development known as Chekists' Village (1929–38) was designed by I. Antonov, V. Sokolov, and A. Tumbasov.

In Leningrad, which under the direction of Sergei Kirov had begun to recover from its precipitous economic and political decline following the revolution, Constructivist architecture was particularly noticeable in the design of administrative and cultural centers for the city's largest outer districts, where workers' housing was under construction. (The historic central districts of the city remained largely intact by virtue of a comprehensive preservation policy and the limited resources of an abandoned capital.)

One of the earliest examples of Constructivism in Leningrad was the Moscow-Narva District House of Culture (1925–27; later renamed the Gorky Palace of Culture) by Alexander Gegello (1891–1965) and David Krichevsky. Essentially a symmetrical structure designed around a wedge-shaped amphitheater of 1900 seats, the compact building demonstrated the beginnings of a functional monumentality dictated by actual circumstances—ignored in the earlier Workers' Palace and Palace of Labor competitions.

The construction of a number of model projects occurred in the same district, including workers' housing (1925–27) by Gegello and others on Tractor Street, and a department store and "factory-kitchen" (1920–30; to eliminate the need for cooking at home) in a streamlined early Bauhaus style by Armen Barutchev (1904–76) and others, and the Tenth Anniversary of October School (1925–27) designed by Alexander Nikolsky on Strike Prospekt. The centerpiece of the district (subsequently renamed Kirov) was the House of Soviets (1930–34) designed by Noi Trotsky (1895–1940). Its long, four-story office block, defined by horizontal window strips, ends on one side in a perpendicular wing with a rounded facade and on the other in a severely angular ten-story tower with corner balconies.

A similarly austere, unadorned style emphasizing the basic geometry of forms was adopted by Igor Ivanovich Fomin (1903–) and A. Daugul (1900–41) for the Moscow District House of Soviets (1931–35) on Moscow Prospekt. Yet the facade, composed of segmented windows of identical size, signifies the repetition of an incipient bureaucratic style rather than the streamlined dynamic of earlier Constructivist work.

Despite the appearance of late examples of Constructivist architecture, such as the Pravda Building (1931–35) by Panteleimon Golosov (1882–1945), Soviet architectural design during the 1930s increasingly adopted historicist approaches to the articulation of structure, whether derived from variants of neoclassicism or skyscraper Gothic. Only in the 1960s did critical interest in Constructivist concepts and innovations begin to revive.

Although the Constructivist legacy was long ignored in the Soviet Union, it must be emphasized that Constructivism and the related art of the avant-garde experienced considerable success in Europe. Lissitzky, who spent 1922–25 in Germany, served admirably as a propagandist for the movement, and ties between INKhUK and the Bauhaus were close. During the 1920s many Russian artists active at VKhUTEMAS and INKhUK visited the West (Kandinsky, Malevich, Gabo, and Pevsner), while Western architects visited, and in many cases worked in, the Soviet Union (Bruno Taut, Ernst May, Erich Mendelsohn, and Le Corbusier). Exhibitions of modernist Soviet art were held in various European cities as well as in New York, and Western journals, such as *L'Esprit Nouveau* and *De Stijl*, wrote of Constructivism and of the latest developments in Russian architecture. Western interest in the legacy of Constructivism continues to this day in the form of numerous publications and major museum exhibitions devoted to the work of the Constructivists.

William C. Brumfield

See also **Ginzburg, Moisei (Russia); Mendelsohn, Erich (Germany, United States); Russia/Soviet Union; Taut, Bruno (Germany); Vesnin, Alexander, Leonid, and Viktor (Russia)**

Further Reading

Constructivism is likely the most extensively studied topic within Russian architectural history. Western scholars, as well as Russian specialists such as Khan-Magomedov, have written prolifically on the movement as a whole and on specific architects and artists associated with it.

Barkhin, M.G., et al. (editors), *Mastera sovetskoi arkhitektury ob arkhitekture* (Masters of Soviet Architecture on Architecture), 2 vols., Moscow: Iskusstvo, 1975

Bliznakov, Milka, "The Realization of Utopia: Western Technology and Soviet Avant-Garde Architecture," in *Reshaping Russian Architecture*, edited by William Brumfield, New York: Cambridge University Press, 1991
Borisova, Elena A., and Tatiana P. Kazhdan, *Russkaia arkhitketura kontsa XIX–nachala XX veka* (Russian Architecture of the End of the 19th Century and the Beginning of the 20th), Moscow: Izd-vo "Nauka," 1971
Brumfield, William Craft, *A History of Russian Architecture*, Cambridge and New York: Cambridge University Press, 1993
Brumfield, William Craft, and Blair A. Ruble, *Russian Housing in the Modern Age: Design and Social History*, Washington, D.C.: Woodrow Wilson Center Press, and Cambridge and New York: Cambridge University Press, 1993
Cohen, Jean Louis, *Le Corbusier et la mystique de l'URSS: Théories pour Moscou, 1928–1936*, Brussels: Mardaga, 1987; as *Le Corbusier and the Mystique of the USSR: Theories and Projects for Moscow, 1928–1936*, translated by Kenneth Hylton, Princeton, New Jersey: Princeton University Press, 1991
Cooke, Catherine, *Russian Avant-Garde Theories of Art, Architecture, and the City*, London: Academy Editions, 1995
Ginzburg, Moisei Iakovlevich, *Stil i epokha*, Moscow: Gosudarstvennoe Izdatelstvo, 1924; as *Style and Epoch*, translated by Anatole Senkevitch, Cambridge, Massachusetts: MIT Press, 1982
Khan-Magomedov, Selim O., *Alexandr Vesnin and Russian Constructivism*, New York: Rizzoli, 1986
Khan-Magomedov, Selim O., *Pioneers of Soviet Architecture: The Search for New Solutions in the 1920s and 1930s*, translated by Alexander Lieven, edited by Catherine Cooke, New York: Rizzoli, and London: Thames and Hudson, 1987
Khazanova, V.E., *Sovetskaia arkhitektura pervykh let Oktiabria, 1917–1925 gg.* (Soviet Architecture of the First Years of October, 1917–1925), Moscow: Nauka, 1970
Kopp, Anatole, *Constructivist Architecture in the USSR*, London: Academy Editions, and New York: St. Martin's Press, 1985
Lissitzky, El, *Russland: Die Rekonstruktion der Architectur in der Sowjetunion*, Vienna: Schroll, 1930; as *Russia: An Architecture for World Revolution*, translated by Eric Dluhosch, Cambridge, Massachusetts, and London: MIT Press, 1970
Lodder, Christina, *Russian Constructivism*, New Haven, Connecticut: Yale University Press, 1983
Paperny, Vladimir, *Kultura "Dva": Sovetskoya arkhitekura, 1932–1954*, Ann Arbor, Michigan: Ardis, 1984
Riabushin, A.V., and N.I. Smolina, *Landmarks of Soviet Architecture, 1917–1991*, New York: Rizzoli, 1992
Senkevitch, Anatole, *Soviet Architecture 1917–1962: A Bibliographical Guide to Source Material*, Charlottesville: University Press of Virginia, 1974
Tupitsyn, Margarita, *El Lissitzky: Beyond the Abstract Cabinet*, New Haven, Connecticut: Yale University Press, 1999

CONTEMPORARY CITY FOR THREE MILLION INHABITANTS

Urban design by Le Corbusier, 1922

Exhibited in 1922 at the Salon d'Automne in Paris, the Contemporary City for Three Million Inhabitants was Le Corbusier's first comprehensive urban-planning project. Accompanied by a 100-square-meter diorama, it consisted of a rigidly geometric, centralized orthogonal plan with monumental axes, uniform modern buildings, vast expanses of open space covering 85 to 95 percent of the surface, and a system of highways. The project was seen simultaneously as a breathtaking modern vision and as the destruction of the familiar urban setting. Influence on the project ranged from American gridded cities, Peter Behrens' work, and Tony Garnier's *Une Cité industrielle* (1901–04, 1917; An Industrial Town) to Bruno Taut's utopian *Die Stadtkrone* (1919; The City Crown). By 1922 Le Corbusier was one of the major figures of the Modern movement, and the Contemporary City marked a high point in a period of extraordinary activity. It incorporated two ideas that he had been developing since 1915. One was the *ville pilotis*, a city built on stilts, which had independent skeletons rather than supporting walls and was inspired by Eugène Hénard's *Rue future* (1910; Street of the Future). The other was the Dom-ino House, which would be the basis of most of his houses up to 1935. While developing a standardized, universal house form, he also sought to develop the urban context of his architecture. The Contemporary City was aimed at achieving fundamental, standardized principles of town planning.

Four times the size of Manhattan, the City consisted of a series of concentric, rectangular belts. At the center was the administrative and business section of 24 cruciform 60-floor towers that were spaced far apart. Their plan profile recalled Khmer or Indian temple forms and symbolized the centrality of the secular power of control. The towers had evolved from the ideas that Le Corbusier had published in *L'Esprit Nouveau* in 1921, following the suggestions of Auguste Perret. The cruciform tower was opposed to the American skyscraper, which in 1920 appeared as a viable urban form. What was new was not the cruciform shape but the rigid geometry that was part of the purist machine aesthetic.

The next two rings contained residential blocks of *immeuble-villas*, six stacked-up duplexes with garden terraces that were either grouped around vast interior courtyards or arranged in a linear pattern of "setback," or *redent*, formation. Each represented a different conception of the city. In the former the cellular perimeter blocks formed streets, with the vertical plane forming both a barrier and a linking screen. The *redent* blocks, taken from Hénard, represented the wall-less, "antistreet" idea. They were to allow for a maximum of open view, lighting, variation, and rhythm. This open-city idea would culminate in the Ville Radieuse (Radiant City), an elevated city with a continuous park at the ground level. Surrounding the residential area of the Contemporary City was a wide greenbelt, beyond which lay garden cities for workers and industrial districts, a port, or a sports complex.

The *immeuble-villa*, an adaptation of the Citrohan House, is the most enduring contribution of the Contemporary City. The *immeuble-villa* was worked out in detail and exhibited as the Pavilion of L'Esprit Nouveau in 1925. It contributed to the formation of the five essential elements that Le Corbusier published in 1926 as *Les 5 Points d'une architecture nouvelle* (Five Points for New Architecture): the *pilotis*; free plan; free facade; long, horizontal sliding windows; and roof garden. Both the cruciform towers and the apartment blocks posed a possible rational solution to the urban problems of overcrowding and traffic congestion. Although Le Corbusier's emphasis on air, light, and greenery recalled the garden city, his solution was radically different in its emphasis on centralization and increased densities. Another major aim of the project was facilitating traffic. Fast automobile traffic was completely separated from the pedestrian traffic. Elevated highways intersected the city and were joined to a peripheral highway system. Pedestrian traffic was to take place amid parks and gardens. Despite the abstract and general character of the Contemporary City, its program addressed the postwar situation of Paris. Next to the Contemporary City, Le Corbusier exhibited a small sketch proposing an adaptation of the plan to the situation of Paris. In 1925 the reorganization of Paris was the theme of the Voisin Plan for Paris.

The influence of the Contemporary City was immense. As Le Corbusier remained an outsider of the planning establishment and received few design commissions, his influence was largely indirect. Yet the Contemporary City formed the basis of one of the most pervasive urban images of the 20th century, a conception of environment that underlay every radical major city plan discussed through the 1960s. The project synthesized many prevalent concepts of urban design, including the idea that the modern city represented a problem to be solved and the idea of the separation of the road, pedestrian route, and buildings.

Although much more developed than most precedents, the Contemporary City contained utopian and dystopian characteristics. Many streets would, in reality, be practically empty of pedestrians. Related is the preoccupation with nature. Derived partly from the tradition of Parisian urban planning incorporating public gardens, the idea of bringing nature into the city was more philosophical than practical and reflected Le Corbusier's deep belief in nature and an interest in broad vistas. In practice, from the office high-rises one would lose any contact with nature. Amid the lower, residential blocks, the parks had a more useful function. Whereas Le Corbusier continuously evolved any given type, unfortunately the midcentury American urban-renewal projects ignored Le Corbusier's *immeubles-villas* and only replicated the towers, which now served as the model for social housing.

The undifferentiated open space also posed difficulty in developing varied types and sizes of open space for a range of uses. Moreover, one of the most decisive consequences of the cutting off of the building from the land was the separation of architecture and landscape design, which in practice made the total environment suffer. Not only shortfalls but the apparent success of large-scale planning has also generated concern. The philosophy underlying the Contemporary City was inspired by regional syndicalism emphasizing the idea of participation and the Fourierist notion of harmony and collaboration. Ideologically, the Contemporary City was a middle-class utopia of social order based on management and technology that prefigured the cities of the industrialized world in the post–World War II era.

HAZEL HAHN

See also **Apartment Building; Behrens, Peter (Germany); Cité Industrielle, Une (1901–04); Corbusier, Le (Jeanneret, Charles-Édouard) (France); Dom-ino Houses (1914–15); Garnier, Tony (France); Taut, Bruno (Germany); Ville Radieuse (*c.*1930)**

Further Reading

Benton, Tim, *The Villas of Le Corbusier, 1920–1930*, New Haven, Connecticut: Yale University Press, 1987

Blake, Peter, *The Master Builders*, New York: Knopf, 1960

Curtis, William J.R., *Le Corbusier: Ideas and Forms*, Oxford: Phaidon, and New York: Rizzoli, 1986

Etlin, Richard A., *Frank Lloyd Wright and Le Corbusier: The Romantic Legacy*, Manchester and New York: Manchester University Press, 1994

Frampton, Kenneth, *Le Corbusier*, New York: Thames and Hudson, 2001

Le Corbusier, *The Ideas of Le Corbusier on Architecture and Urban Planning*, edited by Jacques Guiton, translated by Margaret Guiton, New York: Braziller, 1981

Lucan, Jacques, editor, *Le Corbusier, une encyclopédie*, Paris: Centre Georges Pompidou, 1987

Moos, Stanislaus von, *Le Corbusier: Elemente einer Synthese*, Frauenfeld, Switzerland: Huber, 1968; as *Le Corbusier: Elements of a Synthesis*, Cambridge, Massachusetts and London: MIT Press, 1979

Moos, Stanislaus von, editor, *L'Esprit nouveau: Le Corbusier et l'industrie, 1920–1925*, Berlin: Ernst, 1987

Passanti, Francesco, "The Skyscrapers of the Ville Contemporaine," *Assemblage*, 4 (1987)

Raeburn, Michael, and Victoria Wilson, editors, *Le Corbusier: Architect of the Century*, London: Arts Council of Great Britain, 1987

Serenyi, Peter, editor, *Le Corbusier in Perspective*, Englewood Cliffs, New Jersey, and London: Prentice Hall, 1975

Turner, Paul Venable, *The Education of Le Corbusier*, New York: Garland, 1977

CONTEXTUALISM

For many centuries architectural theory and practice have regarded the contextual compromise of architecture with its urban, regional, and sociocultural setting as a basic demand. Alberti's definition of the logical and necessary connection between urban and architectural design was long a guideline for integral city planning. Nevertheless, extreme urban growth and concentration of rural masses in late 19th-century cities challenged traditional models of urban contextuality, producing vast standardized speculative housing units and industrial facilities. Defining new architectural and urban concepts to guarantee identification of the city's inhabitants became a central topic of 20th-century architectural debates. Against the strict geometric patterns of new urban agglomerations, Camillo Sitte in 1889 proposed a structural revitalization of traditional, picturesque cityscapes. His proposal influenced the planning of new urban quarters in the early 20th century as well as Postmodern debates of the 1980s. Avant-garde planners of the 1920s, especially Le Corbusier and Ludwig Hilberseimer, rejected Sitte's ideas and instead proposed a radical new paradigm composed of semi-industrial, standardized architectural elements in functionally separated and geometrically ordered spaces that dismissed all relation to the city's history. Only after the destruction of European cities during World War II could these modernist planners realize their ideas on a scale beyond that of a few prewar suburban housing developments *(Siedlungen)*. Modernist postwar reconstruction in West Germany, urban renewal in the United States, crude modernization programs in Latin America (including Mexico, Venezuela, and Brazil), and Soviet functionalism during the Khrushchev administration in the 1960s fostered supposedly rational standards in urbanism and architecture. Their prefabricated boxlike buildings in open, linear, and one-dimensional spaces virtually required the destruction of the city's existing, contradictory, but memorable structural contexts. Historical monuments and traditional city cores lost their function as cultural orientation points and sites of social identification.

Nevertheless, with few exceptions (such as the ideal modernist city of Brasília, Brazil), urban reality confirmed the city's capacity to adapt even contrasting urban patterns. When modern urban elements were implanted in historic settings, the result was a kind of collage with both isolated elements and other features that were integrated into a new concept of spatial references. Colin Rowe and Fred Koetter's *Collage City* emphasized several contemporary revisions of modern architecture and urbanism. These included late modernist dissidents of Team X centered around Aldo van Eyck, Aldo Rossi's treatise *The Architecture of the City* (1966), and later Robert Venturi's *Complexity and Contradiction in Architecture* (1966). These theoretical approaches recognized the city's multidimensionality and rejected dogmatic and exclusive modernist concepts. Contextualism as a method of architectural planning tended to respect the architectural heritage and interpret its complex relation within the urbanistic frame. In *Collage City* aesthetic fractures and structural conflicts were rehabilitated as creative forces in the contemporary design process. Even the monuments of modern architecture and commercial vernacular buildings formed part of a new, intricate, and vivid urban network that was meant to inspire various processes of identification. Based on empirical and psychological studies of the city form—elaborated mainly by Kevin Lynch and supported by Michel Foucault's philosophical idea of the "heterotopia"—contextualism since the 1960s became an important paradigm in urban and architectural thinking.

The two most influential architectural tendencies of the last three decades of the 20th century were Postmodernism and deconstructivism. Both used and transformed the idea of contextualism. Postmodern architectural thought and ideology reduced the complexity of the concept to a mere retrospective view of historically isolated forms and images of the preindustrial city. Prince Charles's *Vision of Britain*, with its anti-Modern tone, tried to revitalize neoclassical harmony of architecture and the urban setting. The long-term effect of Postmodern contextualism can be seen in the "New Urbanism" of the 1990s, which attempted to replicate and codify urban patterns of the 19th and early 20th centuries, as in Celebration (Florida), built by the Disney Corporation.

By contrast, deconstructivist architectural thought interpreted contextualism within less-obvious references and relations of the urban texture. Peter Eisenman's designs—such as the City of Culture of Galicia in Santiago de Compostela, Spain (2000–present)—demonstrate that deconstructivist contextualism tends to be self-referential, nonintegrative, or even superficial.

At the end of the 20th century, fragmentation and dissolution of urban contexts were caused mainly by megaprojects, such as shopping malls or spectacular museum buildings sited in degenerated urban landscapes (such as the Bilbao port area in Spain that was radically altered by Frank Gehry's 1997 Guggenheim Museum). These globalized megaprojects often ignore the historical complexity and structural diversity of the site-specific contextualism and question subtle balances of the collage city.

Despite European trends of the 1990s—as in Berlin after the German reunification or in the Olympic city of Barcelona—to reanimate the characteristic metropolitan urbanism of 1900, fragmentation became the dominant mode of architectural theory and practice. Contextualism at the beginning of the 21st century still bears symbolic importance for the social constitution of city culture and, moreover, became a matter of urban ecology. Faced with potential global hyperurbanization, ecology as a universal discipline continues to stimulate reflection on contextualism.

PETER KRIEGER

See also **Brasília, Brazil; Celebration, Florida; Corbusier, Le (Jeanneret, Charles-Édouard) (France); Deconstructivism; Eisenman, Peter (United States); van Eyck, Aldo (Netherlands); New Urbanism; Postmodernism; Regionalism; Rossi, Aldo (Italy); Rowe, Colin (United States); Team X (Netherlands); Venturi, Robert (United States)**

Further Reading

Corbusier, Le, *The City of To-morrow and Its Planning*, New York: Payson and Clarke, 1929

Cullen, Gordon, *The Concise Townscape*, London, 1961

HRH The Prince of Wales, *A Vision of Britain. A Personal View of Architecture*, London, New York, Toronto, Sydney, Auckland, 1989

Koolhaas, Rem, and Bruce Mau, *S, M, L, XL: Office for Metropolitan Architecture*, edited by Jennifer Sigler, New York: Monacelli Press, 1995

Lynch, Kevin, *The Image of the City*, Cambridge, Massachusetts: MIT Press, 1960

Rowe, Colin, and Fred Koetter, *Collage City*, Cambridge, Massachusetts: MIT Press, 1978

Rossi, Aldo, *L'architettura della città*. Padua: Marsilio, 1966

Valena, Tomás, *Beziehungen. Über den Ortsbezug in der Architektur*, Berlin: Ernst und Sohn, 1994

Venturi, Robert, *Complexity and Contradiction in Architecture*, New York: Museum of Modern Art, 1966

COOK, PETER (1936–) AND CHRISTINE HAWLEY

Architects, Great Britain

Peter Cook is best known as a member of the infamous (but famously talented and far-reaching) collaborative, Archigram. After studying architecture at the Bournemouth College of Art and the Architectural Association in London under Peter Smithson, Cook worked at the office of James Cubitt and Partners in London.

In the early 1960s Cook, along with Ron Herron and Michael Webb, self-published the journal *Archigram*. More than a critical review of architecture, the magazine served as a vehicle to exhibit their own futuristic house and urban plans through their beautiful, colorful, collaged drawing styles. The group was formalized as Archigram Architects in 1968—a partnership that lasted through 1976. The power of the Archigram group, as Cook has said, was "its creative creation of the antidote to boredom."

In 1976 Cook opened a practice with his former student Christine Hawley. Though many of their collaborative efforts remain strictly in the "project" category, Cook's own work is still geared toward the city and echoes Archigram's experimental city studies. "At various times I have delighted in the idea of the anti-city," he says. "Plugged-In," "Instant," and "Layered" are just a few of Cook and Hawley's joint, unbuilt projects.

Cook has had several teaching appointments at the Architectural Association in London, where he still works as a consulting critic. He is presently professor of architecture and head of the department of architecture at both the Bartlett School of Architecture of the University College in London and at the Staedelschule in Frankfurt. Christine Hawley is professor of architectural studies and dean at Bartlett School of Architecture, where they both encourage experimental student work. The few built projects the two have embarked on exhibit a broader design than their imaginary cities, in spite of the built work's logistical constrictions.

EUGENIA BELL

See also **Archigram**

Further Reading

Cook, Peter, *Experimental Architecture*, London: Studio Vista/St. Martin's Press, 1975

Cook, Peter, *Six Conversations*, London: Architectural Monographs Academy Editions, 1993

Cook, Peter (editor), *Archigram*, New York: Princeton Architectural Press, 1999

Cook, Peter, and Rosie Llewellyn-Jones, *New Spirit in Architecture*, New York: Rizzoli, 1991

Peter Cook, Tokyo: A + U, 1989

COOP HIMMELB(L)AU

Architecture firm Austria

The Viennese architecture and design firm Coop Himmelb(l)au was founded in 1968 by Wolf D. Prix and Helmut Swiczinsky. The name Coop Himmelb(l)au (Heavenly Blue Cooperative or Heavenly Building Cooperative) is a play on words that reflects the linguistic and philosophical nature of their work best expressed through the postwar international deconstructivist movement.

The roots of Coop Himmelb(l)au's work are markedly futuristic and organic. Well-known early projects include the Reiss Bar (1977) and the club café Roter Engel (1981), with its fractured and fissured facade in the First District of Vienna, as well as the inventive Humanic shoe store branches (1979–81) in Vienna and in Mistelbach. The Kon'yo Arts and Crafts Shop in Tokyo (1986) and the two Funderwerk factory-glazed-entry additions in St. Veit/Glan (1988) are also significant statements of their design thinking.

The Falkestrasse rooftop addition of 1988 in Vienna, with its winglike winter garden roof and aquiline attitude, created an international sensation, raising the international community's awareness of Coop Himmelb(l)au as an established design entity.

Coop Himmelb(l)au's 1987 competition-winning entry for the new town of Melun-Senart, located on the southern periphery of Paris, is an urban-planning scheme to connect three small settlements. The three-phase proposal defined a triangular region composed of a dense settlement node completed by radial "force lines" created by the TGV railway lines and the N6 emanating from this center. A "web" of streets of small houses would be built, and two dense "beams" of loft apartments would be interlaced with the scheme, activating the urban environment. Finally, the long housing blocks would also be vertically separated and horizontally interconnected to allow for enhanced public circulation.

In 1987 Coop Himmelb(l)au developed a challenging scheme for the renovation of the classical Viennese theater, the Ronacher. A modern and flexible theater facility was to be located in a strictly historically protected 19th-century theater facade. Coop Himmelb(l)au created the perfect inwardly turned "black box" environment—high-tech and accessible for both the public and its personnel. The opening of a multilevel interior volume and utilization of a flexible assembly system for the stages ensured that spaces of differing sizes could be custom configured. Additionally, two restaurants and bars were planned to alleviate high-traffic conditions. The tension and the counterbalancing forms to ease this transition are clearly evident in the execution of the added facade elements that function as vertical circulation to the roof terrace with its open-air stage, videothek, and café/bar. The rooftop theater, with new stage house below, cantilevers and pivots over the classic Ronacher's roof, sheltering the terrace and adding to the drama of the interplay of old and new.

The Groniger Museum's East Pavilion (1993–94) was Coop Himmelb(l)au's contribution to a tripartite museum scheme with overall design by Studio Mendini, Milan, Italy. In the museum the need for spatial exhibition volumes using natural light and artificial lighting was combined with the primary intention of providing multiple viewpoints from which to experience the art. The flexible exhibition system that comprises the "interior skin," as well as the varying levels of the interior circulation, allows the possibility of several viewing platforms from which a given work of art can be experienced. The museum was prefabricated and was assembled economically, using computer-directed shipbuilding methods. The original architectural sketch was greatly enlarged to create the evocative signature graphic on the exterior.

The commanding UFA Cinema Center (1998) in Dresden, Germany, sited on an unusual polygonal area, directly addresses with its crystalline lobby void the solid drum-shaped kinetoscope of the former UFA Palace. The building, which houses eight cinemas in its solid mass, acts as a foil to the glazed atrium volume of the lobby with its circulation canyon of staircases and lift shafts. The café spaces located on the ground floor, combined with the hourglass-shaped suspended bar composed of tension cables and rings, provide quiet zones in the public interior, allowing the lobby to be reacted to in an urban manner as one would a "passage." The constant movement of movie patrons and casual visitors electrifies the space, as persons are in perpetual movement through the lobby as if in a clockwork.

Located in the southern Simmering district, the Gasometers (the original natural gas depot for Vienna) now stand void of their equipment. In 1999 one of four aligned cylindrical brick masonry buildings with spacious interior atrium volumes was developed for adaptive reuse. Coop Himmelb(l)au's proposal includes commercial space and maintains cultural activities in areas that attend the new residential spaces. The multipurpose utilization, combined with spatial density, creates a complex urban node on the periphery that is strengthened by its prominent historical reference. Buried in the body of the Gasometer volume is an encapsulated theater rising in height to the equiva-

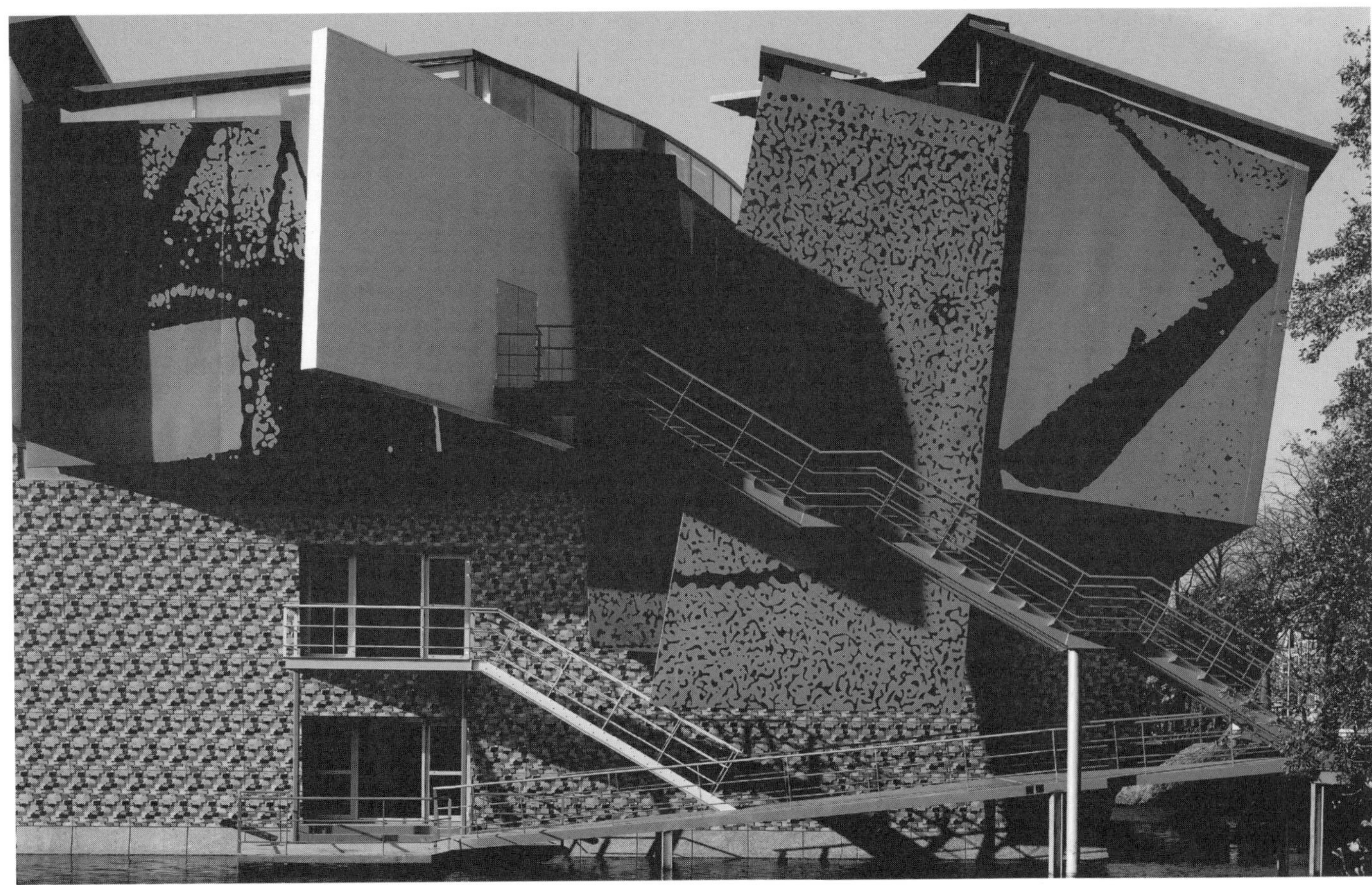

Groninger Museum, the Netherlands (1993–94)
© Margaritha Spiluttini. Photo courtesy Coop Himmelb(l)au

lent of three adjacent levels. Adjoining the theater is commercial and entertainment space that includes a café with an underground garage directly below. From this base the 15-story apartment tower grows. The semicircular plan is concealed behind a clamshell-shaped curtain wall that allows light penetration whereas atrium views allow sunlight to penetrate through the dome of the Gasometer.

Showcased under a great arcing roof floating above the spacious plaza level, Coop Himmelb(l)au's Entertainment and Shopping Complex is one of nine buildings being developed by a team of prominent international architects for the JVC Center in Guadalajara, Mexico (in planning). Sixteen cinemas, along with diverse restaurants and clubs, exist as independent solid elements punctuating the volume between the ground plane and the protective sun-filtering roof. Vertical circulation in the solids is clustered with restaurants and clubs, and a series of connecting cross-decks unites the multiple solids on a variety of different levels. One of the most prominent of the structures, a structurally complex twisting "beak," dramatically cantilevers over a serenely expansive reflecting pool, mirroring its arc in reverse and providing a respite from the center's activities. In addition to architecture and design, Coop Himmelb(l)au has developed a portfolio of household products and furnishings, thus completing a diverse and comprehensive architectural practice.

Celeste M. Williams and Dietmar E. Froehlich

See also **Deconstructivism**

Biographies

Wolf D. Prix

Born in Vienna, 13 December 1942. Attended the Technische Universität, Vienna. Founding partner of Coop Himmelb(l)au 1968. Professor of a master class of architecture, Hochschule für Angewandte Kunst, Vienna 1990; visiting professor, Southern California Institute of Architecture, Los Angeles; visiting professor, Architectural Association, London; visiting professor, Harvard University, Cambridge, Massachusetts.

Helmut Swiczinsky

Born in Poznan, Poland, 13 January 1944. Attended the Technische Universität, Vienna. Founding member, Coop Himmelb(l)au 1968. Visiting professor, Architectural Association, London.

Frank Stepper

Born in Stuttgart, Germany, 1955. Attended the Technische Universität, Stuttgart. Partner, Coop Himmelb(l)au from 1989. Studio instructor, Southern California Institute of Architecture, Los Angeles.

Coop Himmelb(l)au

Established in Vienna in May 1968 by Wolf D. Prix, Helmut Swiczinsky, and Rainer Michael Holzer; Holzer resigned in 1971; Frank Stepper joined the firm in 1989. An office in Los Angeles was opened in 1987; honorary member, Ehrenmitgliedschaft bei dem Deutscher Bund 1989; exhibited in London 1988, Museum of Modern Art, New York 1989, Osaka 1990, Paris 1993.

Selected Works

CM Pavilion for Cincinnati Milacron, Düsseldorf, Birmingham, 1974, 1977, 1979
Reiss Bar, Vienna, 1977
Humanic-Filiale, Mistelbach, Austria, 1979
Humanic-Filiale, Vienna, 1981
Roter Engel, Vienna, 1981
Atelier E. Baumann, Vienna, 1985
Loft Zugmann, Vienna, 1985
Passage Wahliss, Vienna, 1986
Kon'yo Shen'the, Tokyo, 1986
Direktionsetage ISO-Holding AG, Vienna, 1986
Dachausbau Falkestrasse, Vienna, 1988
Groninger Museum, East Pavilion, Groningen, The Netherlands, 1994
Büro- und Forschungszentrum Seibersdorf, Seibersdorf, Austria, 1995
Biennale Pavilion, Venice, 1995
SEG Wohnturm, Vienna, 1997
UFA Palast Dresden, Dresden, 1998

Selected Publications

GA Document, 45 (December 1995)
"Coop Himmelb(l)au: Gasometer B2, Simmering, Vienna, Austria," *GA Houses*, 48 (March 1996)
"Coop Himmelb(l)au: Groninger Museum, Groningen, Netherlands 1993–1994," *A+U*, 310/7 (July 1996)
Coop Himmelb(l)au: Offene Architektur Ent würfe 1980–1984, Berlin: Aedes Galerie für Architektur und Raum, 1984
Coop Himmelb(l)au. Sie Leben in Wien, Eine Ausstellung und ein Buch, Vienna: Galerie im Taxispalais, 1975
Coop Himmelb(l)au: Architecture Is Now: Projects, (un)Buildings, Actions, Statements, Sketches, Commentaries: 1968–1983, translated by Jo Steinbauer and Roswitha Prix, New York: Rizzoli, 1983
Blaubox/Blue Box, 1988
Coop Himmelb(l)au: 6 Projects for 4 Cities, 1990
Die Faszination der Stadt, 2nd edition, edited by Oliver Gruenberg, Robert Hahn, and Doris Knecht, 1992
Coop Himmelb(l)au Austria—From Cloud to Cloud. Biennale di Venezia, 1996

Further Reading

Architektur muß brennen, Technische Universität Graz, Graz, Austria: Galerie H, 1980
Construire le Ciel, Paris: Centre Georges Pompidou, 1992
De Sessa, Cesare, *Coop Himmelb(l)au: Spazi atonali e ibridazione linguistica*, Turin, Italy: Testo e Immagine, 1998
Ent-würfe 1980–1984, Hamburg, Germany: Galerie Kunst + Architektur, 1985
Feuerstein, Günther, and Christiane Feuerstein, *Visionary Architecture in Austria in the Sixties and Seventies: Inspirations, Influences, Parallels; L'Architettura visionaria nell'Austria degli anni sessanta e settanta: Ispirazioni, influssi, paralleli; Visionäre Architektur im Österreich der sechziger und siebziger Jahre: Inspirationen, Einflüsse, Parallelen* (trilingual English-Italian-German edition), Klagenfurt, Austria: Ritter Verlag, 1996
Freireiss, Kristin, and Hans Jürgen Comerell (editors), *Die Wiener Trilogie + Ein Kino. Drei Wohnbauten in Wien und ein Kino in Dresden*, Berlin: Galerie Aedes East, 1998
Frischzellen für die Stadt. Konzept für Erholungs- und Freizeitanlagen in Wien und München. Eine Studie im Auftrag der MA19, Vienna: 1973
Giovannini, Joseph, "Art with Attitude: Groninger Museum, Groningen, Netherlands," *Architecture* (September 1995)
Noever, Peter (editor), *Architecture in Transition: Between Deconstruction and New Modernism*, Munich: Prestel, 1991
Noever, Peter (editor), *The Havana Project: Architecture Again*, Munich and New York: Prestel, 1996
Papadakis, Andreas, Catherine Cooke, and Andrew Benjamin (editors), *Deconstruction: Omnibus Volume*, New York: Rizzoli, and London: Academy Editions, 1989
Pearson, Clifford, "Ten Top Firms Shape a Brand New Town at the Edge of Guadalajara," *Architectural Record* (June 1999)
Skyline: Projekt für das Hamburger Bauforum 1985, Berlin: Aedes Galerie für Architektur und Raum, 1985
"Wie es Euch gefaellt: Theaterprojekt Ronacher, Vienna," *Deutsche Bauzeitung*, 125/6 (June 1991)

LE CORBUSIER (JEANNERET, CHARLES-ÉDOUARD) (FRANCE) 1887–1965

Architect, France (born in Switzerland)

Le Corbusier (né Charles-Édouard Jeanneret) was born in Switzerland, although he studied and worked primarily in France. In 1905, when still in his teens, Le Corbusier was commissioned by one of the trustees at the school where he studied—La Chaux-de-Fonds—to design the Villa Fallet. Charles l'Eplattenier, a painter and mentor to the young Le Corbusier, arranged for him to be helped by a local architect, René Chappalaz. The house was constructed of freestone, rendered and decorated with stylized fir-cone patterns, with the steep roofs and all-round balcony traditional in the region.

In 1907 the fee for this commission enabled Jeanneret, in the company of fellow student Léon Perrin, to travel to Italy, where they visited 16 major northern Italian cities, including Siena, Florence, and Venice. In Tuscany, Jeanneret visited the Carthusian monastery of Ema, an experience that had a profound effect on him. In late 1907, still in the company of Perrin, he visited Budapest and then Vienna, where he met Josef Hoffmann and other members of the Wiener Werkstätte. Two more houses for La Chaux-de-Fonds were commissioned: the Jaquemet and Stotzer houses. He worked on their design during a stay in Vienna of four and a half months in 1908, again receiving help from Chappalaz. Both these houses are of wood and stone, in the regional style.

Later in that year Jeanneret went to Paris, where he approached Franz Jourdain, Henri Sauvage, Eugène Grasset, and finally Auguste Perret, for whom he worked for 16 months. Another formative influence was that of Tony Garnier, whom he met in Lyons.

Jeanneret returned to La Chaux-de-Fonds in 1909 and joined a group of his former associates who styled themselves Ateliers d'Art Réunis. The following year he was given a grant from the School of Art, on the initiative of L'Eplattenier, to study and to report on the decorative-arts movement in Germany. He attended the Deutsche Werkbund Congress in Berlin and acquired a new perspective on the relationship between art and modern industrial production, which took him even further from his earlier Arts and Crafts years. Deeply impressed by Peter Behrens's AEG Turbine Factory, he worked for five months in his studio, alongside Walter Gropius and Mies van der Rohe, although he does not appear to have formed close friendships and eventually fell out with Behrens.

In the spring of 1911, Jeanneret left Germany and set off on another major formative journey that lasted six months: the "voyage d'orient." Traveling with his friend Auguste Klipstein, he visited Czechoslovakia, Serbia, Bulgaria, Romania, Turkey, Greece, and Italy, which this time included Pompeii and Rome. He returned to La Chaux-de-Fonds in November to teach and to help form a new design section at the Art School.

The next commission was for a house for his parents in 1912, a medium-size villa close to the Maisons Fallet, Stotzer, and Jacquemet, with a studio and a music room. Essentially classical in form, with white cubic and cylindrical forms under a pyramidal roof, it has strong echoes of the houses by Behrens at Hohenhagen that Jeanneret had visited, in particular the Haus Schroeder. The Villa Favre-Jacot at Le Locle (1912) also resembles Behrens's Hohenhagen houses, and the Jura regionalism of the earlier houses has been wholly abandoned. Aligned along a terrace on a steep hillside and approached from the side, the striking feature of the composition of this house is the circular court greeting the visitor, the diameter of which was the turning circle of M. Favre-Jacot's car. This courtyard is embraced by concave single-story wings from the body of the house and counterpointed by the convex entrance porch, which leads inside to a cylindrical two-story vestibule with a double staircase wrapped around it. The sequence of movement outside and inside the house is an early expression of one of the most characteristic elements of the architect's future buildings: an architectural processional way.

In 1914 Jeanneret visited the Deutsche Werkbund Exhibition in Cologne, the buildings of which vividly demonstrated the properties of industrial materials such as concrete, glass, brick, and steel.

At the outbreak of war, which he did not expect to last long, Jeanneret thought that the first priority would be for rapidly constructed houses in the devastated areas. With the help of an engineer, Max du Bois, who ran a reinforced-concrete building firm, he planned the Dom-ino housing type. Based on a standardized concrete skeleton unit consisting of three rectangular horizontal slabs supported on six slender stanchions placed well back from their edges, there were no capitals or beams or transitional brackets between the vertical pillars and the horizontal planes; the slabs were quite flat underneath. The three slabs were to be of pot tiles with steel reinforcement and connected by two dogleg staircases cast as part of the whole. The exterior skin of windows and walls could be of any configuration, and the interior partitions might be placed in an infinite variety of ways. This design formed the nucleus of his later architectural language.

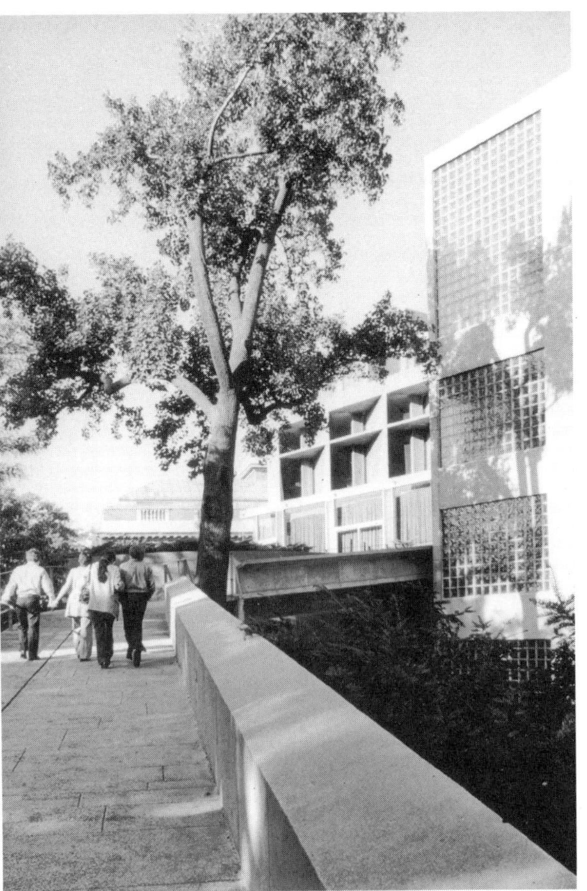

Carpenter Center for the Visual Arts, Harvard University, Cambridge, Massachusetts (with Josep Lluís Sert), 1963
© G.E. Kidder-Smith, Courtesty of Kidder-Smith Collection, Rotch Visual Collections, M.I.T.

The Villa Schwob (1916), however, in the rue de Doubs, was a major turning point, the first building that the architect (the later Le Corbusier) considered to be representative of his oeuvre. From the beginning he conceived the building in terms of a reinforced-concrete frame with brick in-filling walls. The site slopes steeply away to the south. Aligned alongside the road, the facade rises straight from the sidewalk. It is a three-story house flanked by a high wall extending along the street on either side of the entrance; the single-story kitchen wing, attached to the house, is hidden behind this wall. Behind the rectangular volume containing the hall and staircase, on the north (or road) side, the basic form of the house is roughly a cube, but with the addition of two apsidal-ended projections to the east and west. Inside, the plan is splendidly open, with a two-story-high central living room, from which the dining room and drawing room open on either side, terminating in bay windows, and another window, the full height of this space, opens onto the garden and extended views over the landscape. To the left and right of this window, the space is open on one side into the library and on the other to a study. The style is fundamentally one of unadorned classicism, but the house is so subtle and complex that references in its design have been convincingly identified with buildings as diverse as Hagia Sophia in Istanbul, Michelangelo's St. Peter's, and villas by Palladio as well as contemporary works by Hoffmann and Frank Lloyd Wright. It was the first house in La Chaux-de-Fonds to have a flat roof.

In the winter of 1916–17, Jeanneret moved to Paris. Max du Bois helped him to find work as a consultant to the Société d'Applications du Béton Armé. Soon he met the painter Amédée Ozenfant. Jeanneret began painting seriously in 1918 and, with Ozenfant, held an exhibition at the Galerie Thomas. They called themselves "purists" and published their manifesto *Après le Cubisme* in the catalog.

Active in a number of unsuccessful business enterprises associated with building construction, in 1920 Jeanneret, Ozenfant, and Paul Dermée launched the magazine *L'Esprit Nouveau*, which ran for 28 issues until 1925. He began at this time to use the name Le Corbusier. In 1922 his first Paris house, the Villa Besnus, was begun, and he set up a studio in partnership with his cousin Pierre Jeanneret. This was the year he met Yvonne Gallis, a fashion model, later to be his wife.

The Villa Besnus at Vaucresson was a flat-roofed oblong house with white-painted smooth cement wall surfaces; the facade was asymmetrical, with horizontal and vertical strips of windows; a porch with a balcony above and an oriel window project from the flat rectangular plane. There are no moldings or classical details, and the formal language is derived from Cubism.

Le Corbusier's second Paris commission was a studio house for Amédée Ozenfant, completed in 1924. This cubic building—smooth, white, and with huge metal-framed windows—had sawtooth factory-style windows as part of its roof, and throughout, the aesthetic is one of modern industrial engineering. In brilliant counterpoint to the rectangular forms is the white-walled exterior spiral staircase leading to the entrance.

In 1923 Le Corbusier published *Vers Une Architecture*, based on the articles he had published in *L'Esprit Nouveau*. It rapidly became one of the most influential and widely read architectural writings of the 20th century, with its resonant aphorisms and persuasive rhetoric supported by powerfully evocative photographs and drawings.

In 1924 the industrialist Henri Frugès, after reading Le Corbusier's book, commissioned an estate of houses at Pessac near Bordeaux. It was intended to provide affordable housing for the Frugès employees and others, as a new garden suburb, but of the 150 or so dwellings planned, only 51 were built. They were of four types: a row of houses linked by arcades, detached houses, "gratte-ciel" double houses, and houses grouped in blocks of six. All were constructed of reinforced-concrete frames with non-load-bearing walls, continuous ribbon windows, roof gardens, and terraces. The houses were painted green, red, blue, yellow, and maroon on different sides when finished in 1926. The provision of light and ventilation, terrace space and kitchen, and bathroom and storage facilities was ahead of its time, but difficulties of construction created severe financial problems, and the houses were very much modified by later owners. Today they are being restored.

At the 1925 Exposition des Arts Décoratifs in Paris, Le Corbusier exhibited the Pavillon de l'Esprit Nouveau, a freestanding villa. The double-height living room had a gallery at the back, providing kitchen, bathroom, and bedrooms half the height in the divided space. A prototype from the Immeubles-Villas project of 1922, this interior arrangement was to remain a favorite theme of the architect. A covered double-height terrace was to one side, a young tree on the site penetrating through a circular opening in its roof. Adjacent curved dioramas exhibited the model of the Ville Contemporaine (1922) and the Plan Voisin. The Plan Voisin was a project to apply the Ville Contemporaine to the center of Paris and to flatten a vast area just north of the Ile de la Cité. Eighteen glass skyscrapers and lower housing complexes would be laid out in a gridiron plan. This scheme provoked much hostility at the time and has always been difficult to evaluate by later critics.

A twin house, La Roche/Jeanneret (1923–25), was for the Swiss art collector Raoul La Roche, a bachelor who invested in *L'Esprit Nouveau*, and for Le Corbusier's newly married brother Albert. The two white-painted dwellings blend together as a single composition from the outside. At right angles to them, across the end of the Square du Docteur Blanche (a narrow cul-de-sac in the 16th district), La Roche's studio gallery is a raised, curved, second-floor form, apparently supported on a single slender pillar. The interior of this house is celebrated for the complexity and drama of its shapes and spaces, with its three-story-high entrance hall and the long, curving ramp in the gallery. At the back the reinforced-concrete construction demonstrates its versatility by allowing for an old tree growing at an angle from a neighboring garden to be accommodated by modeling a concave inverted funnel shape into the composition of the building.

Another house in Paris was the Maison Cook (1925–27) at Boulogne-sur-Seine, a cubic building sandwiched between other houses. It unequivocally expressed Le Corbusier's "Five Points of a New Architecture": the *pilotis*, which lifted the building into space; the *plan libre*, whereby interior walls could be arranged at will; the *façade libre*, an exterior cladding free from load-bearing constraints; the *fenêtre en longueur*, or horizontal band of windows; and the *toit-jardin*, the flat roof that could be used as a terrace garden. The Maison Planeix (1924–28) has, by contrast, a formal and symmetrical facade, as does the Villa Church (1928) at Ville d'Avray. Two houses for the Weissenhofsiedlung in Stuttgart (1926–27), built at the invitation of Mies van der Rohe and sponsored by the Werkbund, also demonstrate the Five Points.

The double house Villa Stein/de Monzie (1926–28) at Garches, Les Terrasses, was Le Corbusier's most ambitious work yet and was soon recognized as one of his masterpieces. This palatial and luxurious villa is very complex spatially, inside and out, with the spectacular orchestration of solid and void climaxing in a series of terraces descending to the garden in an elegant *promenade architecturale*. Le Corbusier once mentioned his desire to re-create "the spirit of Palladio," and it has been shown that the plan, despite its astounding fluidity, very precisely follows the grid of Palladio's Villa Malcontenta (1550–60).

The villa Les Terrasses was followed by another, if anything more remarkable for its beauty and originality: the Villa Savoie (1928–30) at Poissy.

A bitter disappointment for Le Corbusier was his entry for the competition launched in 1926 for the League of Nations Headquarters in Geneva. Although it excited much favorable interest, his entry was disqualified and finally excluded. He was successful, however, with his submission to the Soviet Central Union of Consumer Cooperatives (Centrosoyuz) of designs for their Moscow headquarters, having been invited in 1928 to participate in a limited competition. Some aspects of this project, a gigantic office building to accommodate some 3500 employees, echo the League of Nations design. It was not completed until 1936.

Le Corbusier was a founder/member of Congrès Internationaux d'Architecture Moderne (CIAM) in 1928 and collaborated with Charlotte Perriand on the design of a range of tubular steel furniture that continues in to be in production today. The first volume of his *Oeuvre complète* was published in 1929 by Boesiger; Le Corbusier married Yvonne Gallis and took French nationality the following year.

Between 1929 and 1933, Le Corbusier designed and realized the Cité de Refuge in Paris for the Salvation Army. This building suffered from grave defects of ventilation, and Le Corbusier was made to insert opening windows in 1935; he restored the bomb-damaged facade in 1948–52, adding a concrete *brise-soleil.* A design for the Palace of the Soviets (1931–32) was rejected in favor of a Russian competition entry in the Renaissance style.

Over the same period, Le Corbusier was much more successful with the Swiss Pavilion at the Cité Universitaire (1931–33), a building that had widespread influence internationally, with its clear separation of parts. A single-story foyer and communal area of irregular plan (one wall of which is constructed of rough stone) passes underneath the long rectangular block of dormitories for 51 students, raised on thick *pilotis,* which show the marks of the wooden shuttering into which the concrete was poured. To one side the curved staircase tower is again a separate entity. The whole building unites and contrasts curved and straight forms, materials, and surfaces.

In 1936 Le Corbusier worked with Oscar Niemeyer and Lúcio Costa on the Ministry of Education and Public Health building in Rio de Janeiro. His major preoccupation with urban planning during the period 1931–42 was with plans for the city of Algiers, which finally came to nothing.

During World War II, under the Vichy government of France, Le Corbusier at first sought to work for the authorities but was eventually obliged to retreat to Ozon in the Pyrenees, devoting 1942–44 to painting and writing and beginning to devise the system of proportion he called "The Modulor." His cousin Jean, who joined the Resistance, would not work with him for a number of years after the war because of his attempts to collaborate.

Soon after the liberation, he was asked by Raoul Dautry, minister of reconstruction, to design prototypes for mass housing. The result was the Unité d'Habitation at Marseilles (1947–52), another key building of its time. *Béton brut*—rough, board-marked concrete—was used for an 18-story block of flats incorporating many services. The concept was inspired by the ideal of the oceangoing liner and the Phalanstery schemes for communal living advocated by Charles Fourier in the 19th century. Other versions of the Unité were built at Nantes-Rezé (1952–53), Briey-en-Forêt (1957–61), Firminy-Vert (1965–68), and Berlin (1957–58).

In 1950 the English architects Edwin Maxwell Fry and Jane Drew proposed to the Indian authorities that Le Corbusier be invited to work on Chandigarh, a new capital city for the Punjab. Together with Pierre Jeanneret, he collaborated with these architects to design this vast project, concentrating mainly on the huge and spectacular official buildings of the Capitol complex. Other major commissions in India followed throughout the 1950s, notably in Ahmedabad. At the same period, two religious buildings of his in France, the Chapel of Notre-Dame-du-Haut (1950–55) at Ronchamp and the monastery of Sainte-Marie de la Tourette (1953–59), were immediately acclaimed.

This fertile period also included the Maisons Jaoul (1956) in Paris, the Brazilian Pavilion (1959) with Lúcio Costa to house Brazilian students at the Cité Universitaire in Paris, and Le Corbusier's only American building, the Carpenter Center for the Visual Arts (Cambridge, Massachusetts, 1961–63) with Josep Lluís Sert.

Le Corbusier received the Gold Medal of the Royal Institute of British Architects in 1953 and that of the American Institute of Architects in 1961. Throughout his life he was inspired by the polarities of the architecture of Mediterranean civilization stretching back to antiquity and the potential of the most modern technology of his day.

ALAN WINDSOR

See also **AEG Turbine Factory, Berlin; Arts and Crafts Movement; Chapel of Notre-Dame-du-Haut, Ronchamp, France; Congrès Internationaux d'Architecture Moderne (CIAM); Contemporary City for Three Million Inhabitants; Costa, Lúcio (Brazil); International Style; Paris, France; Parliament Building, Chandigarh; Perriand, Charlotte (France); Sert, Josep Lluís (United States); Unité d'Habitation, Marseilles; Villa Savoye, Poissy, France; Ville Radieuse (*c.*1930); Voisin Plan for Paris; Weissenhofsiedlung, Deutscher Werkbund, Stuttgart (1927)**

Biography

Born Charles-Édouard Jeanneret, 6 October 1887 in La Chaux-de-Fonds, Switzerland; father was a watch and clock dial painter; mother, née Perret, was a musician. Left elementary school in 1901 for the School of Art (La Chaux-de-Fonds) to become an apprentice engraver. Mentored by painter Charles L'Eplattenier. Died 27 August 1965 while swimming at Cap Martin, leaving many unfinished projects.

Selected Works

Villa Faure-Jacot, Le Locle, 1912
Villa Jeanneret, La Chaux-de-Fonds, 1912
Villa Schwob, La Chaux-de-Fonds, 1916
Villa Besnus, Vaucresson, 1922
Ozenfant House and Studio, Paris, 1924
Villas La Roche/Jeanneret, Paris, 1925
Quartiers Modernes Frugès, Pessac, 1926
Houses for the Weissenhofsiedlung, Stuttgart, 1927
Maison Cook, Paris, 1927
Maison Planeix, Paris, 1928
Villa Church, Ville d'Avray, 1928 (destroyed)
Villa Stein/de Monzie, Les Terrasses, Garches, 1928
Villa Savoye, Poissy, 1930
Moscow Headquarters for Centrosoyuz, Moscow, 1936
Cité de Refuge, Paris, 1933
Swiss Pavilion, Cité Universitaire, Paris, 1933
Ministry of Education and Public Health Building, Rio de Janeiro (with Oscar Niemeyer and Lúcio Costa), 1936

Unité d'Habitation, Marseilles, 1952; other versions built at Nantes-Rezé, 1953; Briey-en-Forêt, 1961; Firminy-Vert, 1968; and Berlin, 1958
Chapel of Notre-Dame-du-Haut, Ronchamp, 1955
Maisons Jaoul, Paris, 1956
Brazilian Pavilion, Cité Universitaire, Paris (with Lúcio Costa), 1959
Monastery of Sainte-Marie de la Tourette, Eveux, 1959
Parliament Building, Chandigarh, 1960
Carpenter Center for the Visual Arts, Harvard University, Cambridge, Massachusetts (with Josep Lluís Sert), 1963

Further Reading

Benton, Tim, *Les Villas de Le Corbusier et Pierre Jeanneret, 1920–1930*, Paris: P. Sers, 1984; translated into English as *The Villas of Le Corbusier 1920–30*, New Haven, Connecticut: Yale University Press, 1987
Boudon, P., *Lived-in Architecture: Le Corbusier's Pessac Revisited*, London: Lund Humphries, 1972
Cohen, Jean-Louis, *Le Corbusier and the Mystique of the USSR, 1928–1936*, Princeton, New Jersey: Princeton University Press, 1992
Curtis, William J.R., *Le Corbusier, Ideas and Form*, London: Phaidon, 1986
Evenson, Norma, *Chandigarh*, Berkeley: University of California Press, 1966
Guiton, Jacques, *The Ideas of Le Corbusier on Architecture and Urban Planning*, translated by Margaret Guiton, New York: Braziller, 1981
Moos, S. von, *Le Corbusier, Elements of a Synthesis*, Cambridge, Massachusetts: MIT Press, 1979
Rowe, Colin, *The Mathematics of the Ideal Villa and Other Essays*, Cambridge, Massachusetts: MIT Press, 1976
Sbriglio, Jacques, *Le Corbusier, L'Unité d'Habitation de Marseille*, Marseilles: Editions Parenthèses, 1992
Serenyi, Peter, *Le Corbusier in Perspective*, Englewood Cliffs, New Jersey: Prentice-Hall, 1975
Steinmann, Martin, and I. Noseda (editors), *La Chaux-de-Fonds et Jeanneret (Avant Le Corbusier)* (exhib. cat.), Niederteufen: Arthur Nigli, 1983
Taylor, Brian Brace, *Le Corbusier at Pessac*, Cambridge, Massachusetts: Carpenter Center, Harvard University, 1972
Taylor, Brian Brace, *Le Corbusier, La Cité de Refuge, Paris 1929/33*, Paris: Equerre, 1980; as *Le Corbusier, The City of Refuge, Paris 1929/33*, Chicago: University of Chicago Press, 1987
Turner, P.V., *The Education of Le Corbusier, a Study of the Development of Le Corbusier's Thought, 1900–1920*. New York: Garland, 1977
Walden, R. (editor), *The Open Hand: Essays on Le Corbusier*, Cambridge, Massachusetts: MIT Press, 1977
Le Corbusier, Architect of the Century (exhib. cat.), London: Arts Council of Great Britain, 1987
Le Corbusier, Le Passé à réaction poétique (exhib. cat.), Paris: Caisse Nationale des Monuments Historiques et des Sites, 1988
Le Cobusier, *Vers Une Architecture*, Paris: Vincent, Fréal, 1923; as *Towards a New Architecture*, translated by Frederick Etchells, London: John Rodker, 1927; frequently reprinted in many languages
Le Corbusier, *Précisions sur un état présent de l'architecture et de l'urbanisme*, Paris: Vincent, Fréal, 1930
Le Corbusier, *Modulor*, Paris: Editions de l'Architecture, 1948; as *The Modulor*, translated by Peter de Francia and Anna Bostock, London: Faber and Faber, 1954
Le Corbusier, *Les Carnets de la recherche patiente; Ronchamp*, Paris: 1957; reprinted with a translation by Jacqueline Cullen, Verlag Gerd Hatje, 1991
Le Corbusier et Pierre Jeanneret Oeuvre Complète, 8 vols., edited by Willi Boesiger, Zurich: Girsberger, 1930 onward: Vol. 1 1910–29, Vol. II 1929–34, Vol. III (edited by Max Bill) 1934–38, Vol. IV 1938–46, Vol. V 1946–52, Vol. VI 1952–57, Vol. VII 1957–65, Vol. VIII 1965–69
The Le Corbusier Archive, 32 vols., edited by H.A. Brooks, New York: Garland Paris: Foundation Le Corbusier, 1982–84

CORPORATE OFFICE PARK, ESTATE, AND CAMPUS

Associated largely with the post–World War II era of economic expansion and the monumental growth in power and size of American business organizations, the architecture of corporate office parks has its antecedents in designs as different as Rockefeller Center (1927–45), by Reinhard and Hoffmeister, with H. W. Corbett and Raymond Hood, in New York City, and Walter Gropius's Werkbund Factory and Administration Building (1914) in Stuttgart, Germany. Although corporate office parks are often reviled today by "signature architects" in favor of other, more prestigious commissions, many of the early examples of this form of architecture were designed by such well-known masters as Frank Lloyd Wright and Eero Saarinen.

The history of U.S. corporate office park architecture is tilted toward the second half of the 20th century. Before 1945 large-scale construction in the United States was slowed because of the Great Depression, the materials shortages spawned by World Wars I and II, and the fledgling (relative to the post–World War II era) nature of the corporate, Fordist regime of capital accumulation that would come to define the American economy until the 1970s. The development and rise of the corporate office park was spurred, first and foremost, by the growth, in both size and wealth, of U.S. corporations. Along with such growth, corporations saw a need for centralized headquarters that accommodated the increasing division of labor that such growth necessitated, that provided working spaces to enforce such hierarchical divisions, and that offered corporations the opportunity to develop a positive—and marketable—public image through the design of their offices. The low-rise and open-plan corporate campus is today a nearly ubiquitous presence in suburbs of most U.S. cities.

Aside from the previously mentioned efforts, perhaps the most famous corporate office park built before World War II was Frank Lloyd Wright's Johnson Wax Administration Building (1936–39) for S.C. Johnson and Son in Racine, Wisconsin. Modestly described by Wright as "one of the world's remarkably successful structures," the curvilinear building is perhaps best known for the columns that support it. Resembling concrete mushrooms, the columns were thought insufficiently strong by city engineers, and Wright had to build a test column to prove that his design was capable of handling many times the load necessary. The test was, as we all know, a great success for both Wright and S.C. Johnson and Son. The publicity surrounding the opening of the building (the image of which was used in advertising for the company), in the estimates of Johnson Wax's own publicity department, was worth around $2 million. The

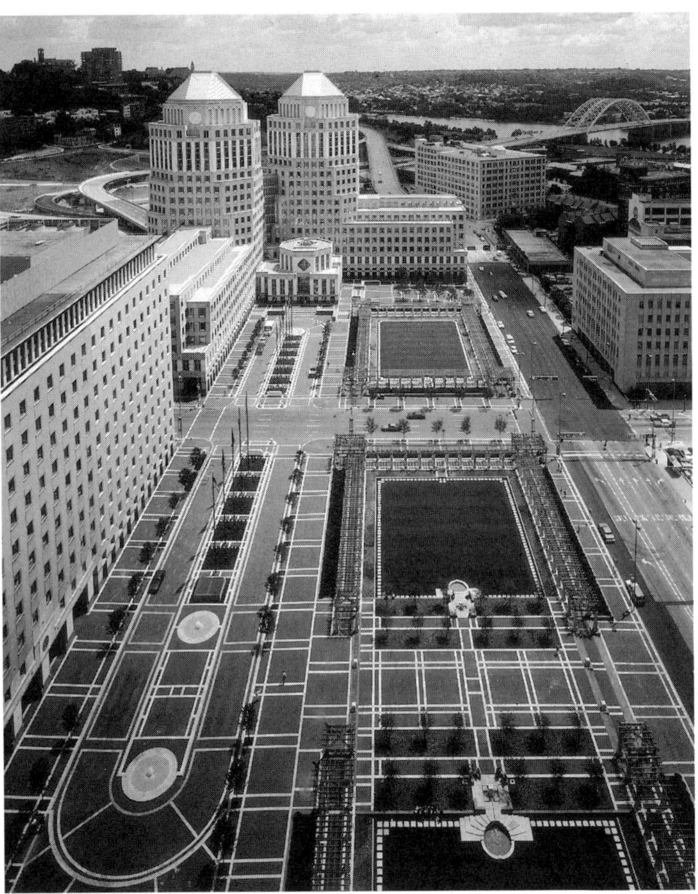

Procter and Gamble Headquarters, Cincinnati, Ohio, designed by Kohn, Pedersen and Fox, 1982–85
© Timothy Hursley

fame that it garnered Wright also played a significant role in advancing his career.

By the late 1940s and early 1950s, a number of American corporations were in the process of building new headquarters. Unlike their urban predecessors, Rockefeller Center and the Johnson Wax Administration Building, the majority of these corporate office parks, exploiting the development of the interstate highway system, were built in suburban settings. As such, suburban developments, such as the General Motors Technical Center (1948–56) in Warren, Michigan, materialized a host of complex social dynamics, including the increasing wealth and prestige of the American corporation, the appropriation by popular culture of the aesthetic impulses of modernism (the GM Technical Center was designed by Eliel and Eero Saarinen, whose use of glass and steel in forms both clean and regular set the standard for many postwar corporate office parks), the technological advancements made in air conditioning and fluorescent lighting, the waning political power of urban centers in the postwar economic boom, and the racially exclusive nature of American society (e.g., by 1960 the GM Technical Center employed 4153 employees; only six were African American). One of the lasting achievements of Saarinen's design for General Motors was his ability to create a composition that suggested the corporation possessed both economic and cultural authority. Eero Saarinen would employ the same modernist idioms in his designs for other suburban corporate office parks, including the John Deere and Company Headquarters (1957–63) in Moline, Illinois, and the IBM Watson Research Center (1957–61) in Yorktown Heights, New York.

Until the 1970s modernism was the style of choice for the majority of corporate office parks. As the rest of the architectural world went, however, so too did corporations, and throughout the 1970s and 1980s a number of office parks were built that are nearly or wholly Postmodern. These include the Procter and Gamble World Headquarters (1982–85), designed by Kohn, Pedersen Fox Associates, in Cincinnati, Ohio, and the College Life Insurance Building (1967–71), by Roche and Dinkeloo, in Indianapolis, Indiana. The explosive growth of the computer industry in California in the last 30 years spawned a number of significant office parks in Silicon Valley and surrounding areas. Among the more famous examples are the IBM Santa Theresa Programming Center (1976) by McCue Boone Tomsick; the Oracle campus (1989–98) by Gensler Associates, in Redwood Shores; Electronic Arts (1998) by Skidmore, Owings and Merrill, in Redwood Shores; and Silicon Graphics International (1996) by Studios Architects, in Mountain View.

BENJY FLOWERS

Further Reading

Book-length studies of corporate office park/estate/campus architecture and history are still relatively rare. Articles on various aspects of this form, however, are plentiful and address a variety of technocratic, theoretical, and stylistic issues and concerns.

"Arquitectura dey hoy: Edificios para oficinas," *Escala*, 27/165 (1994)

Cohn, David, et al., "Corporate Ego: A Thing of the Past?" *World Architecture*, 64 (March 1998)

Harwood, Elain, " 'Prestige Pancakes': The Influence of American Planning in British Industry since the War," *Twentieth Century Architecture*, 1 (Summer 1994) (special issue)

MacCormac, Richard, "The Dignity of Office," *Architectural Review*, 190/1143 (May 1992)

Schwarzer, Mitchell, "Beyond the Valley of Silicon Architecture: On Architecture and the Embodiment of Value," *Harvard Design Magazine* (Winter/Spring 1999)

Walton, Thomas, *Architecture and the Corporation: The Creative Intersection*, New York: Macmillan, and London: Collier-Macmillan, 1988

CORREA, CHARLES MARK 1930–

Architect, India

In 1958 Charles Mark Correa was awarded two commissions that would showcase his approach to architecture: the Pavilion for the All India Handloom Board in New Delhi (1958) and the Gandhi Smarak Sangrahalaya, a museum and archive at Mahatma Gandhi's ashram on the banks of the Sabarmati River in Ahmedabad (1963). Designed and built in six months, the temporary Handloom Pavilion consisted of a series of stepped earth-filled platforms contained within a square enclosure of sun-dried bricks and shaded by freestanding wood and handloom-fabric parasols. The exhibition unfolded as the visitors in the first sequence ascended the platforms and then, in the second sequence, descended in a spiral manner. The subtle interplay of enclosed and semienclosed spaces brought about by a shifting axis, later to become a leitmotif of Correa's work, also formed the central device in the Gandhi Sangrahalaya.

The existing buildings in Gandhi's ashram were whitewashed one-story masonry structures with tiled roofs, some of which had a linear arrangement, while others, such as Gandhi's own residence, were wrapped around a small courtyard. Correa's addition addressed this typology in an assemblage of pavilions arranged around a central water court, only four of which, containing archival material, were enclosed. The tiled-roof structures were supported on a modular system of masonry columns and reinforced-concrete beams that also served as rainwater conduits. The result was a serene atmosphere: alternating open and covered spaces, the dapple of light and shade, a few carefully chosen trees in the courtyards, the reflection of the water, and the breeze from the river. The profoundly antimonumental gesture of the Gandhi Sangrahalaya, in fact, monumentalized the "village" idea central to Gandhi's philosophy. It augmented a decisive departure in 20th-century architecture from accepted canons of monumentality and the memorialization of national heroes. These two early projects also challenged the heroic modernism then unfolding in Chandigarh and Ahmedabad in the works of Le Corbusier.

In over 140 projects that have followed, Correa has used a minimal set of formal devices—the stepped platform reminiscent of wells and river ghats, the open-to-sky space in the form of terraces and courts, the freestanding parasol roof, the split-level space to minimize full-height walls, the shifting axis of pedestrian movement, the square module, and the framed view—to create a complex spatial repertoire. Although the importance of open-to-sky space takes the form of generous terrace gardens and courts sculpted from the sloping site and enhanced by judicious framing of the lake view at Bharat Bhavan in Bhopal (1981), the same principle is used to carve out double-height garden terraces and provide an environmental buffer of verandas and service spaces in the high-rise Kanchenjungha Apartments in Bombay (1983). In both cases it is the subtle manipulation of the building section belying the apparently simple plan arrangements that enabled him to attenuate the microclimate and at the same time make sculptural statements. In the Permanent Mission of India to the United Nations in New York City (1992) and the Alameda Park Project in Mexico City (1994–), these spatial voids/framed views became giant "urban windows"—his signature—that address the urban scale while offering the

Spiral staircase, Inter-University Center for Astronomy and Astrophysics
Photo by Charles Correa © Aga Khan Award for Architecture

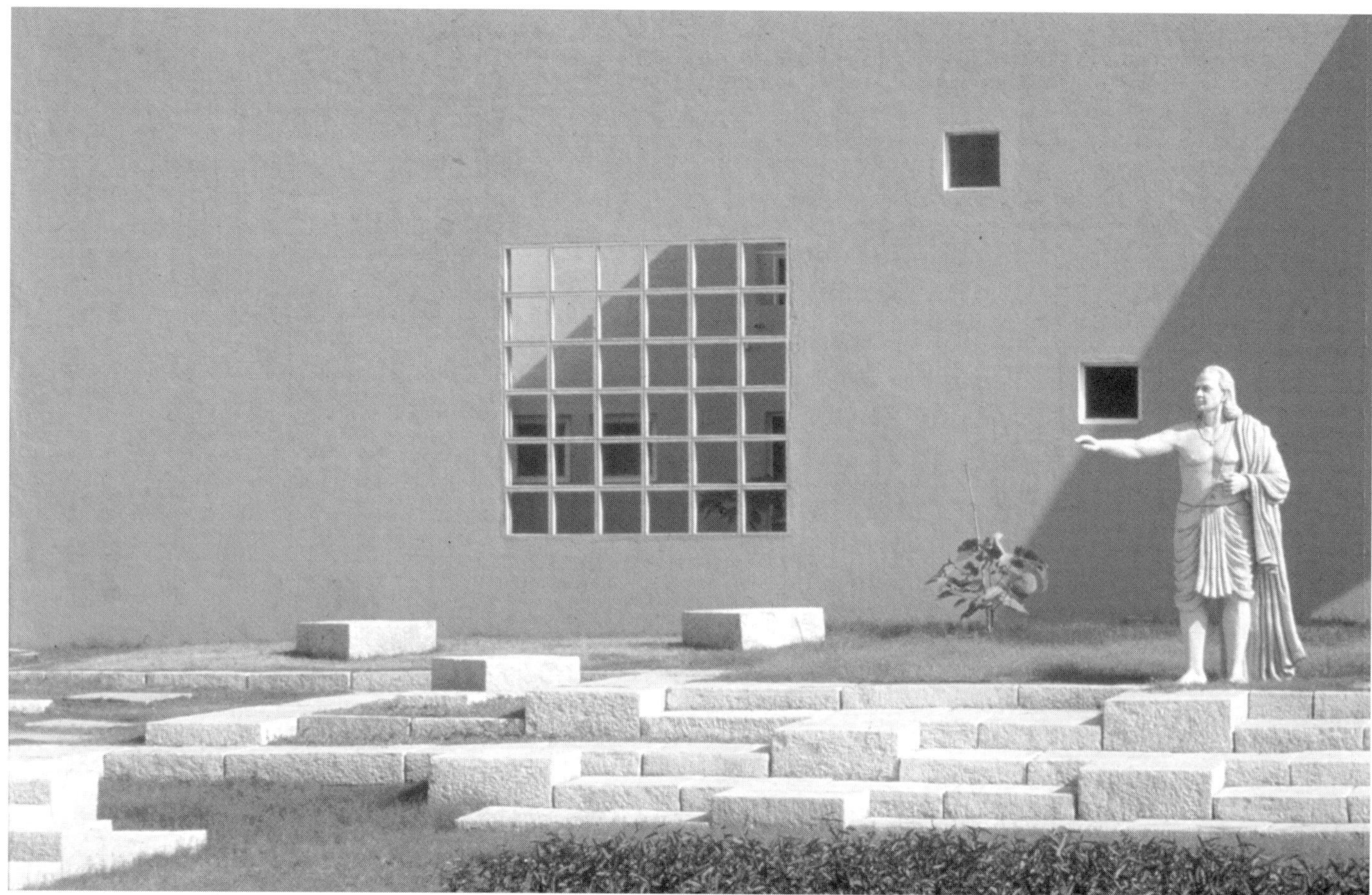

Inter-University Center for Astronomy and Astrophysics, Pune, view of courtyard facade (1992)
Photo by Charles Correa © Aga Khan Award for Architecture

outsider a hint of the layered spaces inside. His formal principles apply as well for a luxury condominium as they do for low-cost housing. As he noted in a postcolonial manifesto—*The New Landscape* (1985)—both rich and poor, grand monuments and vernacular buildings, share the same landscape.

His writings presented alternate possibilities for building practice and urban planning. In an unusual move for an architect, he argued that the solution to the problem of so-called Third World housing resided not in more innovative technology or new materials or even better architectural design, but in sociospatial equity and a great deal of common sense. He himself, however, designed several low-cost housing schemes (e.g., Belapur, 1986) in response to what he labeled the "belligerently anti-visual" approach to low-cost housing among architects. His "housing bill of rights" included concepts such as incrementality, pluralism, identity, income generation, disaggregation, and the "equity plot"—in urban areas each family should be allotted a plot between 50 and 75 square meters. Many of his ideas seemed to ignore the complexity of urban problems, and yet he was fully cognizant of the deep sociopolitical implication of his suggestions. In urging an integral look at the landscape that would overcome barriers between different institutions and experts, Correa was essentially questioning the fundamentals of economic and physical planning theory and the design process that had failed to answer housing needs around the world—whether in India, the United States, or the former Soviet Union. Many of his concepts have been successfully used at an architectural scale, but implementation at an urban level remains unfulfilled. His writing displays a rare clairvoyance and profound belief in the possibilities of a socialist democracy and the "third option"—the term "Third World," he reminded his readers, was coined not to facilitate an ordinal ranking of nations but to generate the possibility of an alternative, "one different from Joseph Stalin's USSR and John Foster Dulles' USA."

Since the 1970s, like many architects around the world, Correa has included more features of popular culture, color, and allusion to enrich his primary architectural vocabulary, which had already been formulated by the first decade of his practice. The brilliant color scheme of the tourist resort of Cidade de Goa in Dona Paula (1982) that exceeded the modernist primary palette was accentuated with trompe l'oeil to create a "city" that was part imagined, part illusory, and part real. He has successfully used paintings and sculptures (often in collaboration with well-known artists) to enhance the spatial architectonics (for example, in the Kala Academy in Panaji, Goa, 1984; the British Council in New Delhi, 1992; and the Inter-University Center of Astronomy and Astrophysics in Pune, 1992), and in doing so has been instrumental in resituating painting as a legitimate accompaniment to contemporary architecture. This interest in popular sources has also been increasingly accompanied by a vocabulary that attempts to root his architecture not just in the vernacular but in what he calls the mythic values of Indian tradition. Not surprisingly, some of this early experimentation in vocabulary (the *kudil*, "individual suite"; *otla*, "raised platform"; and *chattai*, "rush mats") took place in resort hotels that paid homage to ethnic chic and government patronage of India's craft tradition. The now ubiquitous *kunds* (rectangular pools) and mandalas (cosmic diagrams) appearing in Correa's recent projects were most flamboyantly used in the Jawahar Kala Kendra Museum in Jaipur (1992) with its nine-square mandala plan, stone inlaid symbols of planets, and brilliantly painted, overscaled murals. When read against the architect's explanatory texts, they indicate a complex negotiation between the ascribed position of a Third World architect, who is expected to express his regional identity (as opposed to a "Western" architect, who is not), and the desire to supersede such binding propositions.

By aligning the aesthetic inspiration from a local tradition with a universal language of science and metaphysics, he attempts to reverse the route and the terms through which universal principles were supposed to enter the world of modern architecture. In a practice that has spanned four continents and a vast range of government institutions, corporate offices, museums, hotels, and residential designs, Correa has employed an architectural syntax that fluidly travels between contexts and serves as one of the most convincing critiques of the principles of a universalized modernism and its Euro-American bias.

Apart from his own ruminations on architecture, there are three monographs on Correa and scores of articles that comment on individual projects, a complete list of which is available in the 1996 monograph.

SWATI CHATTOPADHYAY

Biography

Born in Hyderabad, India, 1 September 1930. Attended St. Xavier's College, Bombay 1946–48; studied at the University of Michigan, Ann Arbor, under Buckminster Fuller and Walter Sanders 1949–53; received a bachelor's degree in architecture 1953; studied at the Massachusetts Institute of Technology, Cambridge, Massachusetts, under Buckminster Fuller and Lawrence Anderson 1953–55; received a master's degree in architecture 1955. Married Monika Sequeira Kamat 1961: 2 children. Partner, G. M. Bhuta and Associates, Bombay 1956–58. Private practice, Bombay from 1958; chief architect, City and Industrial Development Corporation, Government of Maharashtra 1971–74. Albert Bemis Professor, Massachusetts Institute of Technology 1962; visiting critic, Graduate School of Design, Harvard University, Cambridge, Massachusetts 1974; Bannister Fletcher Professor, University College, London 1974; visiting critic, University of Bombay 1976 and 1977; Arthur Davis Visiting Professor, Tulane University, New Orleans, Louisiana 1979; visiting critic, Massachusetts Institute of Technology 1981; visiting critic, University of Pennsylvania, Philadelphia 1982; consultant to UN University, Tokyo 1982–83; visiting critic, Columbia University, New York 1984. Fellow, Indian Institute of Architects 1964; member, council, Indian Institute of Architects from 1964; member, Western Board, Reserve Bank of India from 1973; member, Steering Committee, Aga Khan Awards, Paris from 1977; honorary fellow, American Institute of Architects 1979; chairman, National Commission on Urbanization 1985–88; fellow, Royal Institute of British Architects 1993. Gold Medal, Royal Institute of British Architects 1984; Gold Medal, International Union of Architects 1990; Aga Khan Award for Architecture 1998.

Selected Works

Handloom Pavilion, Industrial Fair, Delhi, 1958
Gujarat Low-Cost Housing (first prize, competition), Ahmedabad, 1962
Gandhi Smarak Sangrahalaya (museum and archive addition), Ahmedabad, 1963
ECIL Offices, Hyderabad, 1967
Bharat Bhavan, Bhopal, 1981
Cidade de Goa, Dona Paula, 1982
Kanchenjungha Apartments, Bombay, 1983
Kala Academy, Goa, 1984
Low-Income Housing, Belapur, 1986
British Council, New Delhi, 1992
Inter-University Center for Astronomy and Astrophysics, Pune, 1992
Jawahar Kala Kendra Museum, Jaipur, 1992
Indian Mission to the United Nations, New York, 1992
Almeda Park Project, Mexico City, still under construction as of 2001

Selected Publications

Charles Correa, 1984; revised edition, edited by Hasan-Uddin Khan, 1987

Further Reading

Ashraf, Kazi Khaleed, and James Belluardo (editors), *An Architecture of Independence: The Making of Modern South Asia*, New York: Architectural League of New York, 1998
Bhatt, Vikram, and Peter Scriver, *After the Masters*, Ahmedabad: Mapin, 1990
Khan, Hasan-Uddin (editor), *Charles Correa*, revised edition, New York: Aperture, and Singapore: Concept Media, 1987
Prakash, Vikramaditya, "Identity Production in a Post-Colonial Indian Architecture: Re-covering What We Never Had," in *Post-Colonial Space(s)*, edited by Gülsüm Baydar Nalbantoglu and Chong Thai Wong, New York: Princeton Architectural Press, 1997

COSTA, LÚCIO 1902–1988

Architect, Brazil

Lúcio Costa (b. Toulon, France 1902, d. Rio de Janeiro Brazil 1988) played a seminal role in introducing modern architecture and urbanism to Brazil. A dedicated teacher, he often included talented younger designers in important projects. Costa tempered modern European methods with local materials, building techniques, and vernacular design traditions, thus contributing significantly to the development of a modern Brazilian expression. During his lifetime he fostered appreciation for Brazil's unique architectural heritage and was active in the historic preservation movement, particularly in his later years.

As a 1924 graduate of the Escola Nacional de Belas Artes in Rio de Janeiro, he participated in the neo-Colonial movement. His promise as an articulate designer in that style helped secure his position as the director of the Escola in 1930 at age 28. Yet Costa's interests in such European modernists as Walter Gropius, Mies van der Rohe, and Le Corbusier were further galvanized by the latter's brief visit to Rio in 1929. Costa soon became a major force for the dissemination of the ideas of Le Corbusier and CIAM (Congrès Internationaux d'Architecture Moderne) in Latin America. His reforms at the Escola included appointments of progressive architects to the faculty to teach modern design. Costa hired São Paulo–based modernist Gregori Warchavchik to teach architectural composition, and the two established a local practice from 1931 to 1933. Although popular with students, the new appointments soon aroused the enmity of the traditional faculty. By year's end they forced Costa's resignation. A six-month student strike ensued, resulting in the retention of many reforms. With Warchavchik, Costa's work demonstrates a decidedly International Style flavor. Their innovative Vila Operária apartments (1933) in Rio's Gamboa district with its flat roofs, terraces, and facade of angled volumes is equal to the best European work of the period.

Despite his commitment to progressive social and architectural ideologies, Costa steadfastly held that contemporary architects had much to learn from Brazil's colonial heritage. Rather than simply copy the past, he sought a modern expression for Brazil's architecture, one taking into account the country's climate, landscape, and unique mélange of indigenous, European, and African cultures. Costa's neo-Colonial designs attested to his beliefs. His residence (1942) for Argemiro Hungria Machado in Rio, although in a traditional style, evinced rational planning and clarity in massing. The house surrounded a patio and garden, with internal spaces opening freely onto sheltered external ones. Costa's residential architecture best characterizes the continuing dialogue in his thought between modernist theory and local building techniques and traditions.

Costa's first major commission to draw international attention was his collaborative design for the headquarters (1936–43) for the Ministry of Education and Public Health. Disregarding the results of a competition dominated by traditional architects, Minister Gustavo Capanema requested Costa to create a design expressing the progressive agenda of his new ministry. Costa formed a team of local architects, many his former students, and later secured Le Corbusier's participation as a consultant. Le Corbusier's three-week visit produced two projects, including one for an alternative site. The Brazilian team (Oscar Niemeyer, Carlos Leão, Jorge Moreira, Affonso Eduardo Reidy, and Ernani Vasconcelos) developed one of these projects for the original site, with significant changes by Niemeyer. Ricardo Burle-Marx designed the gardens with indigenous plants, and Cândido Portinari ornamented the exterior with traditional-style tiles. The Ministry constituted one of Brazil's earliest and most important modern public buildings. Its native translation of the Le Corbusian idiom drew widespread attention from the international architectural press and was much imitated after World War II. Costa again collaborated with Niemeyer on the Brazilian Pavilion at the New York World's Fair in 1939, thus continuing the synthesis of Brazilian and modernist forms encapsulated in the Ministry building.

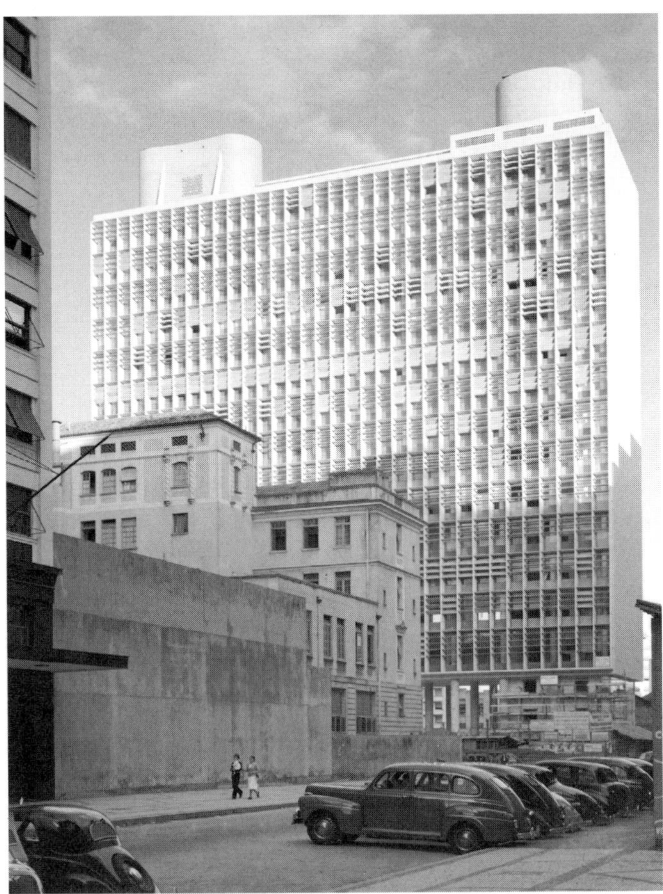

Ministry of Education and Public Health, Rio de Janeiro, Brazil, designed by Lúcio Costa and Oscar Niemeyer

Costa's designs for multiple dwellings demonstrated his concern for more comprehensive planning. His Parque Guinle complex (1948–54) included three of six projected apartment blocks in a verdant setting, closely following ideas suggested by CIAM in the Athens Charter. The horizontal slab apartments, ranging from seven to eight stories, included single- and double-level units, open communal areas on the interiors, and parking at ground level. As usual the architect incorporated indigenous building materials and forms, including wooden louvers and ceramic tiles. Costa's design won the award for multifamily habitations at the First Biennial Exposition in São Paulo in 1953.

The architect's winning design in the 1956 international competition for the Pilot Plan of Brazil's new capital secured his fame as an architect and planner. The cross-shaped organization of Brasília carefully divided major functions into two main zones, one official and the other mainly residential. The plan, often likened to the shape of an airplane, both recalls and far exceeds the scale of Washington, D.C., because of its monumental axis. This axis terminates in the Plaza of Three Powers, encapsulating the three branches of government. At the opposite end, government is countered by the mass media in Costa's television tower. The "wings" contain apartment blocks interspersed with small shops, restaurants, and churches. A theater, bus station, shopping malls, and hotel and banking sectors stand at the intersection of the two axes. Although much criticized, this city of two million inhabitants presently enjoys lower crime and many amenities lacking in Brazil's other crowded urban centers. Costa's unrealized design (1968) for the Barra de Tijuca, a suburban beach resort in Rio, offered a comprehensive development interspersing park spaces and conservation areas with private residences on a regional scale.

Costa's lifelong involvement with Le Corbusier has sometimes obscured his central role in Brazilian modernism in the international arena. Although frustrated by Le Corbusier's efforts to take credit for ideas developed by Brazil's young designers, Costa remained loyal, collaborating with Le Corbusier in the design of the Brazilian Pavilion (1956) at the Cité Universitaire in Paris and as an architectural consultant from 1950 to 1953 for the team overseeing the UNESCO seat in Paris. The lack of any major study in English to date has impeded a broader appreciation and understanding of Costa's important contributions as architect, writer, and teacher in the development of modernism in the mid-20th century.

LINDA S. PHIPPS

See also **Brasília, Brazil; Brazil; Le Corbusier (Jeanneret, Charles-Édouard) (France); Niemeyer, Oscar (Brazil); Rio de Janeiro, Brazil; São Paulo, Brazil**

Selected Works

Vila Operária apartments (with Gregori Warchavchik), Rio de Janeiro, 1933
Argemiro Hungria Machado Residence, Rio de Janeiro, 1942
Ministry of Education and Public Health Headquarters, Rio de Janeiro, 1943
Brazilian Pavilion, New York World's Fair (with Oscar Niemeyer), 1939
Parque Guinle Complex, Rio de Janeiro, 1954
Pilot Plan (project) for Brasília, Brazil, 1956
Barra de Tijuca beach resort (unexecuted), Rio de Janeiro, 1968

Selected Publications

Sobre arquitetura, Pôrto Alegre, Brazil: Centro dos Estudantes Universitários de Arquitetura, 1962
Registro de uma vivência, São Paulo: Empresa das Artes, 1995
"In Search of a New Monumentality," participant in print symposium, *Architectural Review* (London), 104 (September 1948)
"Razões da nova arquitetura," "Uma escola viva de belas-artes," "Depoimento de um arquiteto carioca," "Autobiografia," in *Arquitetura moderna brasileira: Depoimento de uma geração*, Alberto Xavier, editor, São Paulo: Associação Brasileira de Ensino de Arquitetura, 1987
"Memoria del plano piloto de Brasilia," in *Lucío Costa* edited by Jorge O. Gazaneo, Buenos Aires: Instituto de Arte Americano e Investigaciones Estéticas, 1959
"Comments on Brasilia," in *Doorway to Brasilia*, edited by Aloisio Magalhaes, Philadelphia: Falcon Press, 1959

Further Reading

Bruand, Yves, *Arquitetura contemporânea no Brasil*, translated from the French by Ana M. Goldberger, São Paulo: Editora Perspectiva, 1981
Bullrich, Francisco, *New Directions in Latin American Architecture*, New York: Reinhold, 1969
Evenson, Norma, *Two Brazilian Capitals; Architecture and Urbanism in Rio de Janeiro and Brasilia*, New Haven, Connecticut: Yale University Press, 1973
Ferraz, Geraldo, "Warchavchik & Lúcio Costa," in *Warchavchik e a introdução da nova arquitetura no Brasil: 1925 a 1940*, São Paulo: Museu de Arte de São Paulo, 1965
Guimoraens, Ceca, de, *Lúcio Costa: Um certo arquiteto em incerto e segular roteiro*, Rio de Janeiro: Relume Dumara, Prefeitura Rio Arte, 1996
Harris, Elizabeth Davis, "Le Corbusier and the Headquarters of the Brazilian Ministry of Education and Health, 1936–45," Ph.D. diss., University of Chicago, 1984.
Hitchcock, Henry-Russell, *Latin American Architecture since 1945*, New York: Museum of Modern Art, 1955
Mindlin, Henrique, *Modern Architecture in Brazil*, New York: Reinhold, 1956
Santos, Cecília Rodrigues dos, et al., *Le Corbusier e o Brasil*, São Paulo: Tessela, Projecto Editora, 1987

COUNTRY CLUB

From its origins at the end of the 19th century as a converted farmhouse to its maturity as a fully developed building type, the country club has been most popular in British and North American locations suitable to the wealthy classes and to the requirements of outdoor sport. Farmhouses originally met these requirements and were less expensive to convert and augment than building new structures. At the same time, some members undoubtedly preferred the ambience of a farmhouse over a new building. While the farmhouse has continued to serve as a model for clubhouse design, club leaders have increasingly opted to construct new buildings rather than convert old ones.

When converting a farmhouse into a clubhouse, designers were forced to develop a site plan that centered on the farmhouse's location. However, on an undeveloped site the clubhouse location was determined not only by its proximity to a road but also by how to develop the best golf course. Using the high ground was a key criterion for engineering a club's grounds. The clubhouse had to be on high ground to accommodate sewer and water needs. The high ground also had to be sufficiently large in area to handle tennis courts, parking, and auxiliary buildings kept near the clubhouse. Once basic service needs were met, aesthetics dominated the choice of clubhouse location. The architect located the clubhouse and designed a landscape to create aesthetic vistas—from the building to the golf course and vice versa. Because members often wanted the clubhouse to be the focal point atop a hill, problems of shading and wind were handled through landscaping. Whereas physical constraints played a role in clubhouse location, aesthetics was the primary means to convey a prestigious setting.

Although golf was the major outdoor sport at a time when equestrian sports were in decline, the popularity of tennis led to the building of new and additional tennis courts that were typically near the clubhouse. In moderate climates a totally new addition was the swimming pool. The Wichita, Kansas (1913), Peninsula, California (1914), and San Antonio, Texas (1917), country clubs provided swimming pools with their new clubhouses. Some clubs, such as Wichita and Ridgewood, New Jersey, provided dance pavilions for outdoor dances, but most clubs held dances indoors and used verandas and porticoes as an outer room for fresh air. Although architects introduced some new design features, automobile sheds, parking lots, and tennis courts were the primary additions that changed the clubhouse's outdoor setting.

In the period 1900–20, architectural styling became more important and reflected the values and lifestyles of the club's members. Progressing increasingly from remodeled farmhouses to architect-designed clubhouses, the country club changed in its scale, setting, and appearance. Some of the oldest institutions, such as the Country Club in Brookline, remained in converted farmhouses. The prestigious Piping Rock Country Club of St. Louis, Missouri, built a new two-story clubhouse that was visually modest with wood-slat siding. In contrast the Bellereive Country Club of St. Louis built a three-story Georgian brick structure with a clerestory and dome on its roof as well as a large two-story portico. Clubs with wealthy members could afford grand clubhouses built with expensive materials and in a style that conveyed a stately appearance.

Architectural styling for country clubs during the early 20th century was diverse. The Brae Burn and Vesper country clubs in Massachusetts, the Country Club of Virginia in Richmond, and the Chevy Chase in Washington, D.C., were all designed in a tradition characteristic of the region. In the Midwest country clubs were designed in a variety of styles, including Classical Revival, Colonial, Tudor, and Shingle. Midwestern architects trained in the East undoubtedly imported traditional designs from the East Coast. Some country clubs in the Southwest and California decided to build clubhouses in the Mission style, which was indigenous to the region. The San Antonio (1917) and the Santa Barbara (1918) country clubs both adopted the style, which recognized the region's ethnic heritage.

Although the country club was a new American building type, many clubhouse functions duplicated what earlier city clubs provided. Beyond the obvious needs, such as a kitchen, plans for many country clubs included a ballroom and stage, bedrooms for members, and game rooms. Bedrooms continued to be important because of transportation limitations. At the Houston Country Club, bachelors rented upstairs bedrooms, as they had done historically in men's city clubs. Elites still preferred to have the clubhouse as a place for guests to spend the night. Although the club setting had changed, many habits of club life remained the same.

In the 1920s there was an increasing demand for architects who were knowledgeable about clubhouse design. In this prosperous decade, most new clubs could afford a new clubhouse, especially when club organizers and a real estate developer worked together to relate the country club's development to an adjoining elite housing subdivision. Early country clubs benefited from the initial economy of converting a farmhouse into a clubhouse. However, with a growing, active membership, a club had to either renovate the clubhouse or build a new one.

Architects increasingly suggested that the clubhouse's best location was just below a hilltop, a location that allowed for air ventilation without the building experiencing extreme wind velocities. Moreover, locating a clubhouse below the hilltop offered the possibility of some shading and a scenic backdrop to golfers approaching the clubhouse. Minimizing the clubhouse's distance from a main road reduced on-site road construction, and locating the entrance road on the high ground reduced grading costs and erosion problems. For the golf course, designers reiterated the need for the nine-hole loop plan, the 1st and 10th tees as well as the 9th and 18th greens being near the clubhouse. However, they acknowledged the difficulties of maintaining this principle when a club decided on developing a 36-hole course and wanted other sports activities around the clubhouse. Designers needed to avoid steep grades, especially at the end of a round, to prevent golfers from becoming overfatigued. Providing or keeping trees allowed for windbreaks along fairways, scenic backdrops for greens, visual barriers between parallel holes, and visual walls to hide ugly surroundings. Landscape design was critical for creating a sense of entrance to the club's grounds and to integrate the clubhouse with surrounding sports facilities and the golf course. The general goal was to blend efficiency with the picturesque.

Architects developed basic clubhouse plan types. First, the most illustrated type was the finger plan. Basic functions, such as the lounge and dining rooms, were in a central building, and building wings typically housed locker rooms, guest bedrooms, and sometimes an indoor swimming pool. This plan type worked best for large clubs that had multiple functions. With a large building complex, the building wings enabled the architect to orient the floor plan to existing land contours and provide a V or U stage set that looked on the golf course. Second, the corridor plan type connected the major club functions along a single corridor. This type was most adaptable in small country clubs, where an architect could easily organize a small number of functions along a corridor spine that was not excessively long. Another alternative for the small country club was the great hall plan. The club's main dining room or lounge served as a central space with the club's other functions surrounding it. In a large country club, an architect had difficulty placing all the club's functions around the great hall. Finally, there was the courtyard plan. The courtyard served as a pivotal open space around which architects organized a club's functions, but, as in the great hall plan, all a club's activities could not always be efficiently arranged around a central space. However, these four plan alternatives were ideal types, and architects with commissions for large country clubs designed a variety of hybrids, enabling them to incorporate some types best suited for small country clubs.

Architects emphasized interior design and decor more than they had in the past by focusing on the need for the clubhouse's interior to convey a feeling of family, dignity, and comfort. They paid special attention to the fireplace's design and placement in the main room because it was the symbolic center of club social life. The recommended dining room, lounge, and great hall height was at least a story and a half to give dignity and importance to the club's main social spaces. The staircase design was important not only as a social place centrally located to club activities but also as an integral feature for particular traditional building styles that conveyed the visual dignity that club members wanted.

In the 1920s perhaps the main design anomaly in relation to the country club ideal was the men's grillroom. Although the country club was promoted as a family club, men dominated its membership rosters and club definitions of social terrain. Men particularly enjoyed the grill as a place to eat and drink after a round of golf, where their dress and language could be informal. The grillroom had its historic roots in city social clubs that were exclusively for men, and it was continuing that traditional exclusivity in the country club.

In the United States architectural styling in country clubs continued to repeat past practices and regional styles, with some minor variations. The clubs in Florida and California almost universally adopted Spanish or Italian styles of architecture, whereas those in New England were influenced by American Colonial, English, Georgian, and French farmhouse design. Spanish Colonial became a popular style in Florida during its real estate boom in the 1920s. In the Southwest architects used the Pueblo style, as seen at the Trinidad Country Club of Trinidad, Colorado. Modernism, however, was largely missing. In 1924 Frank Lloyd Wright produced schematic drawings for the Nakoma Country Club of Madison, Wisconsin, but a new, conservative board of governors rejected his innovative design proposal. Thus, by the 1920s architects had incorporated all the major styles used for other building types in the United States into clubhouse design.

In the early postwar era, modernism became the dominant style. By the 1950s progressive architects had rejected the classical styles for modernism, and this shift is seen in country club designs of the time. Glass, steel, and concrete were the basic materials used to express this modernist style. In the 1940s Chicago's Tam O'Shanter Club and the Des Moines, Iowa, Golf and Country Club built two of the first clubhouses that exemplified the International Style. Organic architecture reflected the influence of Wright, who designed buildings to fit into the site rather than to dominate it. His architecture emphasized indigenous building materials, and in the 1950s some architects were highly influenced by his buildings that used asymmetrical plans and triangular forms. Completed in 1958, the Paradise Valley Country Club of Scottsdale, Arizona, exemplified the Wrightian influence. There were clubhouse designs that mixed these two modernist variations by using the rectilinear formalism and flat roofs of the International Style while using indigenous materials that gave the appearance of organic architecture. Regardless of the particular purity or mix of modernist options, newly organized country clubs chose modernism as it increasingly became the most popular architectural style in the nation.

Some country clubs that built a modernist style clubhouse later replaced it with a traditional design. Modernist architecture removed the traditional building cues that conveyed an elite lifestyle. Club members soon longed for a return to heavy timber and stone in clubhouse construction. By the 1980s architects returned to using historic styles, although some clubs in western states still preferred the modernist style. Members of the Sedgefield Country Club of Greensboro, North Carolina, so adamantly preferred their Tudor-style clubhouse that they restored it. Some architectural firms revived some of modernism's early beginnings. In 1994 Klages, Carter, Vail and Partners designed the Coto de Caza Country Club of California in a manner that reflected the Arts and Crafts style of Bernard Maybeck and the Greene brothers. Architects began taking a personal approach to choosing an architectural style for the country club and its clubhouse. They visited club members' homes to determine what style they would find most comfortable in their club life. Thus, modernism's popularity fell as country club members sought building styles that better reflected their tastes and values.

Some changes in plan layouts in the postwar era were directed largely by the introduction of air conditioning. In the past verandas were often part of a clubhouse plan, but air conditioning now made these porches obsolete. Attempts to create cross ventilation or to have high ceilings for better air circulation were no longer needed as long as an air-conditioning system was installed. By the 1950s automobile ownership was common, and most roads were paved; there was no longer a need for club members to remain overnight at the clubhouse. Women were increasingly provided equal treatment with men and women jointly used the same rooms for socializing. The men's grillroom often became simply the grillroom in new country clubs. Women were also taking a more active role in sports, and larger women's locker rooms reflected this involvement. Thus, the country club's floor plan reflected both technical and social changes throughout the 20th century.

JAMES MAYO

See also **Greene, Henry M. and Charles S. (United States); Maybeck, Bernard R. (United States)**

Further Reading

Gordon, John S., "The American Country Club," *American Heritage*, 41 (September 1990)

Mayo, James M., *The American Country Club: Its Origins and Development*, New Brunswick, New Jersey: Rutgers University Press, 1998

CRAFTSMAN STYLE

Reaching the height of its popularity in the first decades of the 20th century, the Craftsman style in America was informed by both European and Japanese architectural design. The Craftsman style and the Arts and Crafts movement, of which Craftsman was a part, hearkened back to medieval times, when the creative labor of human beings rather than the constant hum of machinery was the driving force behind the built environment and craft objects. The Craftsman movement would reinvigorate handicraft, return the skilled artisan to a position of respect, and serve as a reminder that honest labor could be joyful rather than dehumanizing. In England the Arts and Crafts movement originated with such thinkers and architects as John Ruskin, William Morris, C.R. Ashbee, and M.H. Baillie-Scott. On the Continent, Craftsman buildings tended to use more masonry than wood, to incorporate tiled roofs, and to use half-timbered exterior ornamentation with Tudor overtones. The American Arts and Crafts movement drew on these influences while adapting itself to liberal capitalism and the varying climates and landscapes of the United States. The movement and its design principles were popularized through such publications as Gustav Stickley's magazine *The Craftsman*. In contrast to the Victorian buildings that preceded them, Craftsman structures eschewed applied ornamentation in favor of the natural beauty of construction materials and a simplicity of line. Perhaps the greatest irony of this preference for simplicity and honesty of materials was the reality that much Craftsman joinery, in both architecture and furniture, was extremely elaborate and difficult to execute.

The Craftsman style reached its fullest expression mainly in domestic rather than public buildings. The style was characterized by the use of natural building materials, such as brick, stone, and regionally available woods. A hallmark of Craftsman design was the use of exposed joinery on both the exterior and the interior of buildings, an art arguably brought to its most dramatic realization in the Blacker House (1907) and Gamble House (1908), designed by Charles Sumner Greene and Henry Mather Greene in Pasadena, California. It is in the work of the Greenes that the Japanese influence on the Craftsman style is most apparent, particularly in the roof supports, lanterns, and reflecting pool on the rear terrace. In addition to natural building materials and exposed joinery, Craftsman domestic structures generally featured low-pitched roofs that served to anchor the buildings to their surrounding landscape. Even the three-story Gamble House appears relatively low to the ground. In addition the tasteful use of stained and art glass as well as prominent fireplaces (often incorporating handmade tiles as a decorative element) surrounded by inglenooks or seating areas were components of the style. The homes typically (although not universally) worked toward an open plan, minimizing obstacles between rooms. Craftsman style was also characterized by a belief in comprehensive design where it was possible. In homes designed for wealthy clients by Frank Lloyd Wright and the Greene brothers, for example, furniture, lighting fixtures, textiles, and accessories were all designed as integral parts of the domestic space rather than as afterthoughts.

In the United States the work of the Greene brothers is perhaps most frequently associated with the Craftsman style at its best. Indeed, David P. Handlin (1979) has argued that California was the most active region of the country for Arts and Crafts design. The Greenes' "Ultimate Bungalows" in Pasadena and additional projects throughout the state, such as the Thorsen House (1908) in Berkeley, provide the best-preserved and most fully articulated examples of the style. Peter Davey describes the Greenes' style as one "in which complexity was built up from elements of great simplicity, an architecture of timber in which beam was piled upon beam, rafter upon rafter to form ordered nests of smooth sticks with great overhanging eaves and projecting balconies to provide shade from the sun. Every member and every joint is made explicit" (1980, 212). Craftsman-style buildings on the West Coast tended to draw on the work of the Greenes and on Stickley's *Craftsman* designs, incorporating more wood than stone, including shingles, and ample porches enhanced with rough stones or masonry.

In addition to the Greenes, Frank Lloyd Wright's Prairie style is recognized as a part of the Arts and Crafts movement despite the visible differences between Wright's designs and those of other Craftsman architects. While the Greenes were busy on the West Coast, Wright was changing domestic architecture in the Midwest. His own home and studio (1889) in Oak Park, Illinois, exhibit many of the features described previously, such as the tasteful use of art glass, prominence of natural woods, and fireplace inglenook. Further, Wright's Robie House (1906–09) in Chicago demonstrates the clean horizontal lines, spectacular woodwork, free-flowing space, and dramatic central fireplace which were key elements of Wright's Prairie style. An excellent example of the Craftsman style applied to a public building is Bernard Maybeck's First Church of Christ Scientist (1909–11) in Berkeley. The exposed brackets supporting the low-pitched roof and dramatic windows exemplify the Craftsman style on a large scale.

With the onset of World War I, the Arts and Crafts movement in America began to decline in popularity. The ideals that gave rise to the movement were losing their appeal for many, and the allure of mass-produced housing components made possible in part through the advances of wartime construction became increasingly hard to resist. The simplicity of the Arts and Crafts movement was gradually replaced by the even more simplified International Style, with its clean lines and blank facades. Even so, in almost any town in the country, one can still feel the influence of the Craftsman style and its domestic architectural ideals.

CYNTHIA DUQUETTE SMITH

See also **Arts and Crafts Movement; Ashbee, C.R. (England); Bungalow; Greene, Henry M. and Charles S. (United States); House; Mackintosh, Charles Rennie (Scotland); Maybeck, Bernard R. (United States); Stickley, Gustav (United States); Wright, Frank Lloyd (United States)**

Further Reading

Davey, Peter, *Arts and Crafts Architecture: The Search for Earthly Paradise*, London: The Architectural Press, 1980

Handlin, David P. *The American Home: Architecture and Society 1815–1915*, Boston: Little, Brown, 1979

Kardon, Janet (editor), *The Ideal Home 1900–1920: The History of Twentieth Century American Craft*, New York: Abrams, 1993

Lancaster, Clay, *The American Bungalow*, New York: Abbeville, 1985

Makinson, Randall L., *Greene & Greene: Architecture as a Fine Art*, Salt Lake City, Utah: Peregrine Smith, 1977

McCoy, Esther, *Five California Architects*, New York: Praeger, 1975

Stickley, Gustav, *Craftsman Homes: Architecture and Furnishings of the American Arts and Crafts Movement*, New York: Dover, 1979

Trapp, Kenneth R., Leslie Green Bowman, et al., *The Arts and Crafts Movement in California: Living the Good Life*, New York: Abbeville, 1993

CRAM, RALPH ADAMS 1863–1942

Architect, United States

Ralph Adams Cram was without question the foremost practitioner of the Gothic style of architecture of his day in the United States, but he was a writer and advocate of no less energy and stature. The author of 24 books and scores of magazine and journal articles, Cram was a member of the faculty of the Massachusetts Institute of Technology from 1914 to 1922, and he toiled ceaselessly to advance his reasons for the continuation of an architectural tradition stretching back to medieval times.

Born in Hampton Falls, New Hampshire, Cram lacked the money to attend college and instead became an apprentice in the Boston architectural firm of Rotch and Tilden. Through his expanding circle of acquaintances in the Boston artistic world, Cram fell under the influence of the work of the English designer-writers John Ruskin and William Morris and came to admire the work of Henry Vaughan, an English Gothicist (and follower of George F. Bodley) who would go on to design the National Cathedral in Washington, D.C.

Cram was a devotee of high-church Anglicanism, a belief that made his enthusiasm for the Gothic more than merely stylistic. Indeed, art and religion to Cram were virtually inseparable. In his view the Gothic was not a style of the past but rather one that was capable of continuing evolution and that embodied the highest spiritual aspirations. "My idea," he wrote in his 1936 autobiography, "was that we should set ourselves to pick up the threads of the broken tradition and stand strongly for Gothic as a style for church building that was not dead but only moribund and perfectly susceptible of an awakening to life again."

So vigorously did Cram pursue the Gothic that he has come to be thought of almost exclusively as a Gothic architect, but he was also highly skilled in the classical, Byzantine, Georgian, and Lombard styles.

Over his long career, Cram worked with numerous collaborators, but his most fruitful association was with Bertram Grosvenor Goodhue, who joined him in 1891 and soon became a partner in the firm. Cram's greatest strength was in the development of the plan and the overall composition of a building, whereas Goodhue proved a master at detail. Among the many brilliant ecclesiastical buildings that they designed together, the finest example of their combined talents is St. Thomas Episcopal Church on New York City's Fifth Avenue, completed in 1914. A serenely confident sense of mass and space is enlivened with striking ornamentation, especially in the enormous reredos, or sculptural screen, behind the altar. Designed by Goodhue and executed by the sculptor Lee Lawrie, it creates an almost theatrical focus for the earnest overall composition.

Despite the unabashed historicism of St. Thomas, Montgomery Schuyler, the distinguished architecture critic, saw the beginnings of a new architectural direction lurking beneath its details. "In the block," Schuyler wrote, "without a single toolmark of ornament, the new St. Thomas's would already be a noble building. The highest praise the decoration of such a building can deserve is that it heightens and develops the inherent expression of the structure."

Cram's far grander but less elegant design for the completion of the Cathedral of St. John the Divine (begun by the firm of Heins and La Farge), also in New York, marks the high point of the Gothic revival in the United States.

Much of Cram's finest work was done at private boarding schools, such as Phillips Exeter Academy, and on college and university campuses. He was a consulting architect to Bryn Mawr, Mount Holyoke, and Wellesley and did work at Rice, Sweetbriar, and Williams, but he is best known in this area as the supervising architect of the Princeton University campus, where his most powerful buildings include the chapel and the graduate school (1911–29). In explaining his dedication to the Gothic as the most appropriate style for educational institutions, Cram wrote that the late Gothic of the colleges at Oxford and Cambridge was "the only style that absolutely expresses [the] ideals of an education that makes for culture and . . . character."

With his partners Bertram Goodhue and Frank Ferguson (who was responsible primarily for engineering), Cram also oversaw the design of several major buildings at the U.S. Military Academy at West Point, most notably the Cadet Chapel (1903–

Phillips Exeter Academy, Exeter, New Hampshire (1932)
© Arne Hodalic/CORBIS

14). The architects exploited the dramatic site above the Hudson River to the full. The concept of a Gothic fortress rising from the heights commanding a great river seemed both programmatically and symbolically correct. No better icon of Cram's integration of his spiritual and architectural muscularity exists than that above the main door, which is embellished with a cross in the form of a sword hilt.

The image of the sword was one that Cram used later in life, as the influence of Le Corbusier and the other leading European modernists began to be felt in the United States, much to Cram's dismay. "These things," he wrote, referring to the stripped elements of the new aesthetic, "seem to me to be a betrayal of trust, a vicious though unintentional assault on the basic principles of a sane and wholesome society." The modernist idea, he went on, "has its own place and it may and should go to it. Its boundaries are definite and fixed, and beyond them it cannot go, for the Angel of Decency, Propriety, and Reason stands there with a flaming sword."

CARTER WISEMAN

Biography

Born in Hampton Falls, New Hampshire, 16 December 1863. Apprenticed to the architectural firm of Rotch and Tilden, Boston. Opened office with Charles Wentworth, Boston 1887; partner, Cram Wentworth and Goodhue, Boston 1897–99; partner, Cram Goodhue and Ferguson, Boston 1899–1910; partner, Cram and Ferguson, Boston from 1911. Faculty member, Massachusetts Institute of Technology, 1914–22. Fellow, American Institute of Architects. Died in Boston, 22 September 1942.

Selected Works

Richmond Court, Brookline, Massachusetts, 1899
Cadet Chapel, United States Military Academy, West Point, New York, 1914
St. Thomas's Church, New York City, 1914
Chapel and Graduate College, Princeton University, Princeton, New Jersey, 1929
Federal Building, Boston, 1930
Sweet Briar College, Sweet Briar, Virginia, 1932
Phillips Exeter Academy, Exeter, New Hampshire; library, dormitories, gymnasium, inn, and administration building, 1932
Wheaton College Chapel, Norton, Massachusetts, 1934
Rice Institute Campus, Houston, 1941
Cathedral of St. John the Divine, New York City, 1941

Selected Publications

Church Building, 1901
Impressions of Japanese Architecture, 1905
Ministry of Art, 1914
The Substance of Gothic, 1917
The Catholic Church and Art, 1930
My Life in Architecture, 1936

Further Reading

Horowitz, Helen Lefkowitz, *Alma Mater: Design and Experience in the Women's Colleges from Their Nineteenth-Century Beginnings to the 1930s*, New York: Knopf, 1984; 2nd edition, Amherst: University of Massachusetts Press, 1993
Kidney, Walter C., *The Architecture of Choice: Eclecticism in America 1830–1930*, New York: Braziller, 1974
Shand-Tucci, Douglass, *Ralph Adams Cram, American Medievalist*, Boston: Boston Public Library, 1975
Turner, Paul Venable, *Campus: An American Planning Tradition*, New York: The Architectural History Foundation, and Cambridge, Massachusetts: MIT Press, 1984
Whiffen, Marcus, and Frederick Koeper, *American Architecture 1607–1976*, Cambridge, Massachusetts: MIT Press, 1981
Wiseman, Carter, *Shaping a Nation: Twentieth-Century American Architecture and Its Makers*, New York: Norton, 1998

CRANBROOK, MICHIGAN

Twenty miles northwest of Detroit in Bloomfield Hills, Michigan, Cranbrook is an educational complex comprising a house and garden, a church, three schools, an art academy, and a science institute. It was developed by George Gough Booth (1864–1949), publisher of the *Detroit News* and a chain of smaller papers, and his wife, Ellen Warren Scripps Booth (1863–1948), daughter of newspaper magnate James Edmund Scripps.

In 1904 the Booths purchased a large farm in Bloomfield Township and named it for the ancestral home of Booth's father in Cranbrook, County of Kent, England. Aided by Booth's sketches, Albert Kahn (1869–1942) prepared plans for their English Arts and Crafts country house (1908) overlooking the estate. The Booths commissioned American and European artisans and craftsmen to create tapestries, wood carvings, furniture, metalwork, glasswork, fine bookbindings, and other decorative pieces in an arts-and-crafts aesthetic for the house. The Booths subsequently began transforming their estate into an educational complex distinguished for its architecture, gardens, fountains, pools, and sculpture.

Booth articulated the vision for Cranbrook, assembled advisers, collaborated with architects, artists, and craftsmen to form and furnish it, and, together with his wife, provided the financial means to execute it. Finnish-American architect Eliel Saarinen (1873–1950) designed many of the campus's plans and buildings between 1925 and 1942.

The first community gathering place, the Meeting House (1918), was built to the English cottage designs of Booth and his son, Henry Scripps Booth, then a student of architecture at the University of Michigan. Its rambling additions and tower adapted the glacial fieldstone, brick, and half-timber building for use as the Brookside School for Young Children (1922–1930s).

The Booths commissioned Oscar H. Murray (1883–1957) of Bertram Grosvenor Goodhue and Associates to design the late Gothic Revival Christ Church (1929) as the spiritual cornerstone for Cranbrook and the Bloomfield Hills community. Leading contemporary Arts and Crafts artisans and craftsmen created superb ornamental detail and furnishings for the stone church.

In 1925 Saarinen, a visiting professor of architecture at the University of Michigan in Ann Arbor, accepted Booth's invitation to develop a visionary plan for an art academy at Cranbrook. Having won second prize in the Chicago Tribune Tower competition of 1922, Saarinen had come to Chicago with his family to see the American Midwest.

Saarinen's first completed work in America was the Cranbrook School for Boys (1929). His plans, based on the sketches of Henry Scripps Booth and his university classmate, J. Robert

F. Swanson, after George Gough Booth's preliminary designs, presented a campus of remodeled farm buildings (1911). Remodeling proved too costly, so Saarinen revised the plan, retaining much of the arrangement of the farm buildings. The exquisitely crafted brick buildings topped with red tile–clad gabled roofs are grouped around a quadrangle, courts, and terraces in the manner of English collegiate quadrangles. For the school Saarinen won the Gold Medal Award of the Architectural League of New York for 1934.

Booth attributed the origins of Cranbrook Academy of Art, a working place for creative art expressive of the time, to his visit to the American Academy in Rome in 1922. Utilitarian brick buildings with studios and living quarters (1928–1930s) flank Academy Way with courts and plazas facing gardens to the east. The propylaeum of the modern monumental art museum and library (1942) forms the focus for the formal gardens, pools, fountains, and sculpture. The precursor to the art academy was the group of European artists and craftsmen—including Swedish sculptor Carl Milles, Finnish ceramicist Maija Grottel, and others—who assembled at Cranbrook to enhance the buildings and grounds of the institutions.

The Kingswood School for Girls (1931) comprises two connected rectangular wings that form quadrangles with a succession of long, low projecting wings. The low-pitched, copper-clad hipped roof with broad overhanging eaves; the horizontal bands of windows; the spreading out of the brick building toward the periphery of the dramatic site on Kingswood Lake from the higher condensed center; and the open interior spaces are reminiscent of the Prairie architecture of Frank Lloyd Wright. The Saarinen family collaborated in unifying the buildings, interiors, and furnishings. Loja Saarinen created curtains, upholstery, and rugs; Eero Saarinen designed furniture and lead-glass windows; and Eva Lisa (Pipsan) Saarinen Swanson did the interior decoration for the dining room, auditorium, and other spaces.

At the Cranbrook Institute of Science, Saarinen expanded the temporary cinder-block building with an observatory (1931) designed by George Gough Booth with a simplified modern flat-roofed brick structure (1938) that was reflected in a pool animated with sculptures by Milles.

The Booths established the Cranbrook Foundation in 1927 to endow and support the institutional development of Cranbrook. In 1973 the Cranbrook Foundation and five of the original six Cranbrook institutions reorganized as the Cranbrook Educational Community. The sale of Cranbrook's ownership in Booth Newspapers in the 1970s and in the Evening News Association in 1986 and other financial strategies realized funds needed to support massive restoration and construction work to mark its centennial in 2004. This master plan is setting the course for the future, enabling the community to meet the changing needs of education, a diverse student body, and a more public role.

The result is a northern access to the campus off Woodward Avenue, the main thoroughfare from Detroit to northern communities; four extraordinary new buildings and additions to existing buildings that are compatible with the Saarinen and Booth campus; and the restoration of the historic buildings, art, and landscaping. The new wing of early childhood, science, and music rooms at the Brookside School (1997) by Peter Rose responds to the small size and scale, irregularity, and childlike qualities of the historic buildings. The natatorium (1999) at the Cranbrook School by Tod Williams and Billie Tsien opens to nature by means of retractable oculi and hydraulically powered louvered wall panels. The spacious studio addition to the museum (2001) by Rafael Moneo has gallery, studio, and fabrication spaces that permit the creation of large artworks. The new wing to the science institute (1998) by Steven Holl, entered through a spectacular light laboratory, straddles the wings of Saarinen's older building to connect with and form an interior courtyard with the older building. Thus, Cranbrook continues stewardship of its National Historic Landmark campus while making concrete its visionary role.

KATHRYN BISHOP ECKERT

See also **Arts and Crafts Movement; Campus Planning; Goodhue, Bertram Grosvenor (United States); Moneo, Rafael (Spain); Saarinen, Eero (Finland); Saarinen, Eliel (Finland); School; Williams, Tod, and Billie Tsien (United States); Wright, Frank Lloyd (United States)**

Further Reading

Balmori, Diane, "Cranbrook: The Invisible Landscape," *Journal of the Society of Architectural Historians*, 53/1 (March 1994)

Benson, Robert, "The Cranbrook Community Examines Its Future," *Inland Architect*, 5 (September/October 1987)

Christ-Janer, Albert, *Eliel Saarinen*, Chicago: University of Chicago Press, 1948; revised edition, 1979

Clark, Robert Judson, et al., *Design in America: The Cranbrook Vision, 1925–1950*, New York: Abrams, 1983

Eckert, Kathryn Bishop, *Cranbrook*, New York: Princeton Architectural Press, 2001

McMechan, Jervis Bell, *Christ Church Cranbrook: A History of the Parish to Commemorate the 50th Anniversary of the Consecration of the Church, 1928–1978*, Bloomfield Hills, Michigan: Christ Church Cranbrook, 1979

Pound, Arthur, *The Only Thing Worth Finding: The Life and Legacies of George Gough Booth*, Detroit, Michigan: Wayne State University Press, 1964

White, Lee A., et al., *Cranbrook Institute of Science: A History of Its Founding and First Twenty-five Years*, Bloomfield Hills, Michigan: Cranbrook Institute of Science, 1959

Wittkopp, Gregory (editor), *Saarinen House and Garden: A Total Work of Art*, New York: Abrams, 1995

CRET, PAUL PHILIPPE 1876–1945

Architect, United States

Paul Cret can be seen as one of the leading examples of the architectural generation that formed the bridge between neoclassicism and modernism.

Whereas many American architects, starting with Richard Morris Hunt, traveled to France to study at the Ecole des Beaux-Arts, Cret was a native. Born in Lyons in 1876, he studied at the École from 1897 to 1903, absorbing its principles of rationality and symmetry and its devotion to the sources of classicism. Although he distinguished himself in his studies and might have flourished professionally in France, in 1903 Cret accepted a position on the faculty of the University of Pennsylvania in Philadelphia. While there, he helped establish the university's school of architecture as one of the most influential in the United States, counting among his students Louis I. Kahn, who would go on to prominence in later life.

In his own practice, Cret concentrated heavily on civic buildings, to which he brought a steadily more refined style of Beaux-Arts classicism. Describing his professional goals in the early 1930s, he wrote, "The characteristic of this practice is the planning of important city improvements, the planning of government . . . buildings and important memorial buildings." However, the aim of his aesthetic was to convey, as Elizabeth Grossman has written in her 1996 monograph, *The Civic Architecture of Paul Cret*, an "intimate monumentality."

Cret eagerly adopted new construction techniques, particularly in the use of steel framing, but he remained committed to the essentially Beaux-Arts idea that the architecture of a building should flow from an analysis of its program. He was averse to the idea that a building should make a personal statement about its creator.

Cret's earliest major commission was won in a competition he entered in association with Albert Kelsey for the International Bureau of American Republics, later called the Pan American Union, in Washington, D.C., completed in 1910. The building was richly ornamented, but beneath the trim lay a rigorous organization of masses and spaces that gave it a fundamental sculptural power.

Cret interrupted his career to return to his homeland and serve with the French army during World War I. (He was first an infantryman and later an interpreter on the staff of American General John Pershing, commander of the American Expeditionary Force; the frontline experience left him partially deaf.) On his return to the United States, Cret embarked on a gradual simplification of the ornamental palette that he had employed on the Pan American Union building, reducing columns to flat piers, stripping them of capitals and bases, and eliminating moldings.

This austere aesthetic, powerfully exemplified by the Hartford County Building (1930) in Connecticut and the Folger Shakespeare Library (1932) in Washington, D.C., proved especially effective for the many memorials that Cret designed for the dead of World War I both in France and in such American cities as Providence, Rhode Island. However, his reach extended well beyond these high-minded structures to include such mundane projects as the Central Heating Plant for Washington, D.C.

Although some have argued that Cret's "stripped classicism"—which he preferred to call "new classicism"—reflected a return to conservative sources in reaction to the upheavals of World War I, a more convincing argument can be made that Cret was seeking a version of a style in whose fundamental principles he still believed but whose embellishment had become overly familiar and socially suspect. He suffered among other critics for the superficial similarities of his work to that of contemporary architects in Italy and Germany, whose less sensitive

Folger Shakespeare Library, East Capitol Street facade
Photo © Mary Ann Sullivan

Folger Shakespeare Library, Art Deco detail
Photo © Mary Ann Sullivan

forms and spaces created in the service of authoritarian regimes were given a political overtone of racial "purity."

Cret retired from the University of Pennsylvania faculty in 1937 and a year later was awarded the Gold Medal by the American Institute of Architects. In his acceptance speech, Cret said, "In the art of Architecture, collective effort counts more than individual industry in giving form to the ideals of a period."

Cret died on 8 September 1945 during an inspection tour of a building site in North Carolina. His vision of a "new classicism" had long since been overtaken by modernism, but with the discrediting of that movement later in the century, Cret's evolved investigations of traditional forms began to take on renewed stature, especially as durable architectural citizens of the American urban fabric.

CARTER WISEMAN

Biography

Born in Lyons, France, 21 October 1876; immigrated to the United States 1903; naturalized 1927. Studied at the École des Beaux-Arts, Lyons; attended the École des Beaux-Arts, Paris 1897–1903. Private practice 1907; collaborated with the firm of Zantzinger, Borie, and Medary. Served in World War I. Member, planning commission, Chicago's Century of Progress Exposition of 1933 1928. Professor of design, University of Pennsylvania, Philadelphia 1903–37; pupils included Louis I. Kahn. Critic, Philadelphia T-Square Club; critic, Pennsylvania Academy of Fine Arts. Gold Medal, American Institute of Architects 1938. Died 8 September 1945.

Selected Works

International Bureau of the American Republics (now Organization of American States; with Albert Kelsey), Washington, D.C., 1910
Indianapolis Public Library (with Zantzinger, Borie, and Medary), 1927
Detroit Institute of Arts (with Zantzinger, Borie, and Medary), 1927
Providence War Memorial, Rhode Island, 1929
Hartford County Building (with Smith and Bassette), Connecticut, 1930
Folger Shakespeare Library, Washington, D.C., 1932
Aisne-Marne Memorial, near Chateau-Thierry, France, 1933
Flanders Field Chapel, Wareghem, Belgium, 1933
Federal Reserve Bank, Philadelphia, 1934
Federal Reserve Board Building, Washington, D.C., 1937
Naval Memorial, Gibraltar, Spain, 1937

Selected Publications

"The École des Beaux-Arts: What Its Architectural Teaching Means," *Architectural Record*, 23 (1908)
"Modern Architecture," in *The Significance of Fine Arts*, 1923

Further Reading

Burchard, John, and Albert Bush-Brown, *The Architecture of America*, Boston: Little, Brown, 1961; revised edition, 1966
Grossman, Elizabeth Greenwell, *The Civic Architecture of Paul Cret*, Cambridge and New York: Cambridge University Press, 1996
Handlin, David P., *American Architecture*, London: Thames and Hudson, 1985
Kidney, Walter C., *The Architecture of Choice: Eclecticism in America 1880–1930*, New York: Braziller, 1974
Whiffen, Marcus, and Frederick Koeper, *American Architecture 1607–1976*, Cambridge, Massachusetts: MIT Press, 1981
White, Theophilus B., *Paul Philippe Cret: Architect and Teacher*, Philadelphia, Pennsylvania: Art Alliance Press, 1973
Wiseman, Carter, *Shaping a Nation: Twentieth-Century American Architecture and Its Makers*, New York: Norton, 1998

CUADRA SAN CRISTÓBAL

Designed by Luis Barragán, completed 1968
Mexico City, Mexico

The Mexican Pritzker laureate Luis Barragán (1902–88) designed Cuadra San Cristóbal in collaboration with his protégé Andrés Casillas in 1967–68. The Cuadra San Cristóbal, along with the design of his own house and the Chapel of Capuchinas Sacramentarias, are premier examples of Mexican contemporary architecture. His house, built in 1947, undoubtedly demonstrates a period of maturity in Barragán's career, and the Chapel of Capuchinas Sacramentarias (1952–55) is a masterpiece in its exploration of light, demonstrating great refinement and sophistication. These three works together represent the pinnacle of "emotional architecture," conveying nostalgia and spirituality as defined by Barragán's Creole heritage.

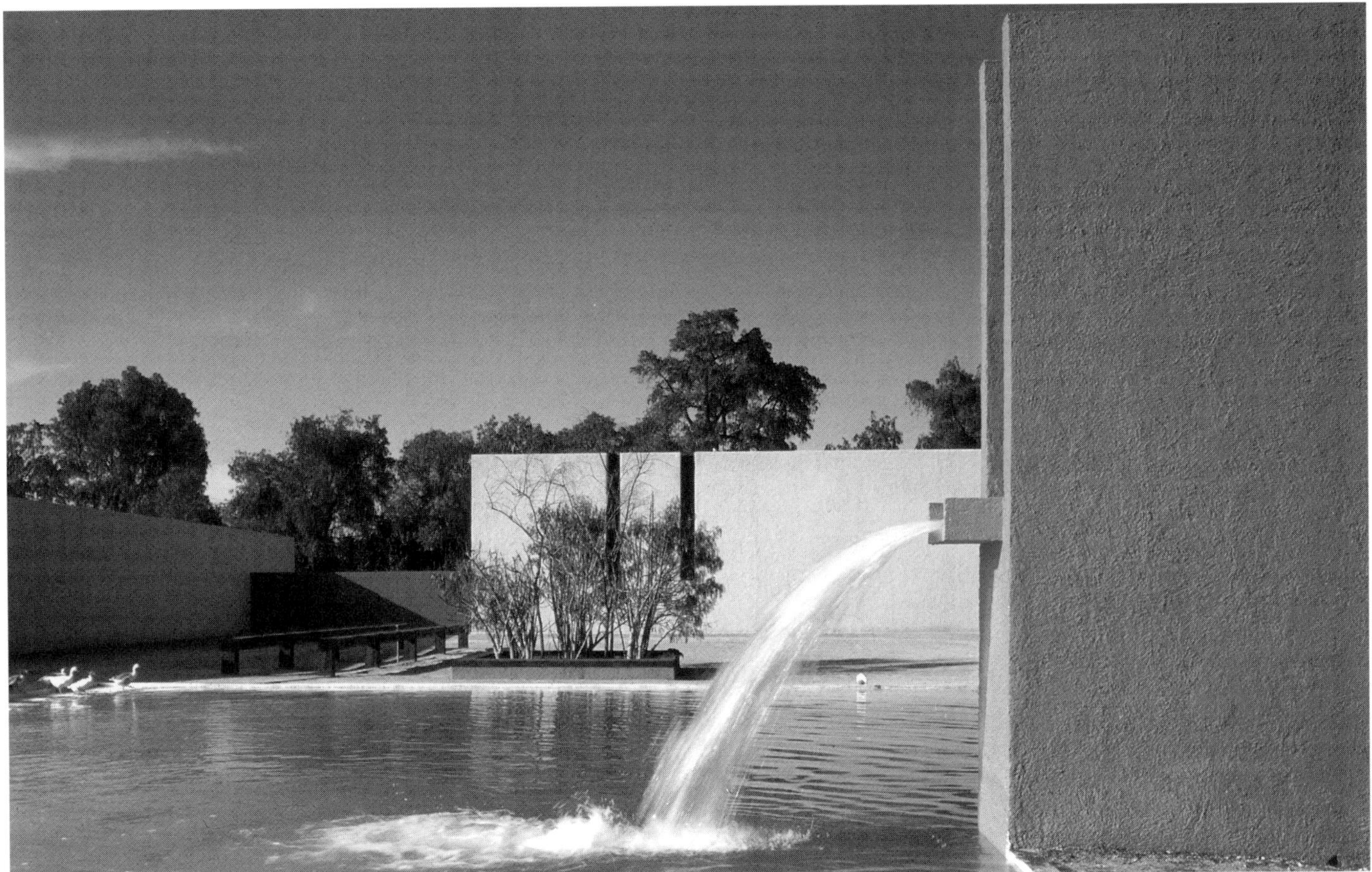

Luis Barragán (in collaboration with Andrés Casillas de Alba), Cuadra San Cristóbal, Los Clubes, Mexico City, 1966–68
Photo Armando Salas Portugal © Barragán Foundation, Switzerland/Artists Rights Society, New York

Born in Guadalajara, Mexico, Barragán spent his childhood in the now nonextant family hacienda of Los Corrales in La Sierra del Tigre. He acquired a taste for the vernacular in the small towns of Jalisco and developed his innate sensibility of light, color, texture, and to a greater extent, myth, silence, solitude, and serenity.

Cuadra San Cristóbal was one of Barragán's most comprehensive and complex mature works. His designs were heavily influenced by conversations with his friends (the humanist Ignacio Díaz Morales and the artist Jesús Reyes Ferreira) and the written works (poetry and essays) of Marcel Proust, Charles Baudelaire, and Valle Inclán.

Barragán sought out metaphysics, surrealism, ethics, and psychology rather than the conventional texts of his discipline for inspiration. *Les Jardins enchantés* (The Enchanted Gardens) and *Les Colombiers* (The Dovecotes), written and illustrated by the French landscape architect Ferdinand Bac (1859–1952), as well as Cyril Connolly's *The Unquiet Grave*, influenced Barragán's first houses. J.M. Buendía explains how *Boris Godounov* (published in 1925), with colorful illustrations by Choukhaeff, influenced Barragán to use color combinations from this book in some of his works.

As a concluding phase of the Cuadra San Cristóbal project, Barragán developed the public park Las Arboledas in 1958. He designed a comprehensive program of entrances, plazas, the great red wall, and the fountains El Bebedero and El Campanario (The Spout and The Belfry, 1959). Barragán intended Las Arboledas to become a horse lovers' paradise. However, the development became a popular destination for middle-class suburbanites. In 1963 Barragán, himself an accomplished equestrian, purchased a series of plots within Las Arboledas that he called Los Clubes. He planned this development as an exclusive and private equestrian experience, catering specifically to the elite. The Fuente de los Amantes (The Lovers' Fountain, 1964), Cuadra San Cristóbal, and the home of the Egestrome family reflect a powerful refinement of Barragán's phenomenological explorations of exterior space. The sounds of water emerging from scuppers and horses' hooves in contact with the stone paving evoke sounds of the streets of Mazamitla, demonstrating a physical and psychological connection to memory. The fragmentation of space through the use of enormous walls that are often punctured and juxtaposed to visually frame the landscape and the reflective surfaces of pools of water enrich what is a surrealist space with metaphysical contradictions. Barragán's architecture relies less on theoretical principles and rational formulas than on emotional and subjective experiences.

Barragán presented the design for Cuadra San Cristóbal as a gift to the Egestrome family under the condition that a large plot of land would be purchased for the project. Andrés Casillas explains that before the design, he and Barragán visited several small towns and haciendas in the state of Mexico. These visits evoked images of the project that were then developed through models and perspective sketches. The first model of the complex was exactly what was to be constructed later, excluding the enormous pink wall with two slotlike cuts for vertical ventilation that required approximately 70 sketches before the final proposal. According to Casillas, Barragán designed by dividing the project into isolated moments, individually created and later integrated into the whole. For Barragán there was no bad proposal: all proposals had considerable potential. He would often make changes in a project during its construction. In San Cristóbal he would tie lengths of cloth to wooden poles to mock up the position of a wall, as was the case with the with wall that defines the entrance to the complex. Barragán would also mount colored paper over the unfinished white walls to see whether the deep pinks, maroons, and purples would blend with the light and mood of the environment. Almost always immersed in a creative act of emotion and intuition, his process was devoid of rational thinking.

JAVIER GÓMEZ ALVAREZ-TOSTADO

See also **Barragán, Luis (Mexico); Mexico; Mexico City, Mexico; University Library, UNAM, Mexico City**

Further Reading

Ambasz, Emílio, *The Architecture of Luis Barragán*, New York: Museum of Modern Art, 1976

Artes de México, 23 (1994) (special edition entitled "In the World of Luis Barragán")

Burian, Edward R. (editor), *Modernity and the Architecture of Mexico*, Austin: University of Texas Press, 1997

Buendía Júlbez, José María, Juan Palomar, and Guillermo Eguiarte, *Luis Barragán*, Mexico City: Reverte Ediciones, 1996; as *The Life and Work of Luis Barragán*, translated by Margaret E. Brooks, New York: Rizzoli, 1997

Riggen Martínez, Antonio, *Luis Barragán, 1902–1988*, Milan: Electa, 1996; as *Luis Barragán: Mexico's Modern Master, 1902–1988*, translated by Christina Bennett, New York: Monacelli Press, 1996

San Martín, Ignacio (editor), *Luis Barragán: The Phoenix Papers*, Tempe: Arizona State University Center for Latin American Studies Press, 1997

CUBA

Even for the most jaded architect, Cuba represents one of the most fascinating and beautiful places in the world. Today Cuba has become a "must see" destination for architects. Although some American architects have been granted permission to visit the country by the U.S. government, most have traveled illegally, risking large fines and possible prison sentences to visit what some call the "Paris of the West." Cuba has one of the largest intact collections of historic buildings of any country in the world (going as far back as 500 years), including one of the largest intact collections of Spanish colonial architecture and the largest collection of Soviet-era prefabricated buildings.

Cuba's architectural prominence dates back to the origin of the New World. Comparisons and contrasts between the historical architectural brilliance and its current state of decay offer captivating images and insights into Cuban history, development, and design.

Cuba provides a wide range of architectural styles, which some call the most beautiful in the world—pre-Columbian, Spanish colonial, Art Deco, International, Soviet, Postmodern, and Retro-Cubano. UNESCO has declared Trinidad and Old Havana world heritage sites. Moreover, the National Arts School and Las Terrazas have also been declared architectural masterpieces by UNESCO and others.

Located only 90 miles from the United States, Cuba is one of the few truly socialist countries left in the world. Socialist Cuba has created a radically different economic, social, and cultural life for its citizens. Architecture is intended to serve the masses' needs of efficient and affordable housing, schools, hospitals, offices, and industrial production space. Ornamentation, excess, and waste are all frowned upon. The irony of Castro's socialist revolution was that the imperialist architecture of Spanish colonialism was replaced with imperialist Soviet International Style. Efforts to create a unique and original Cubano style free from other styles have largely been a failure.

One of the great myths and disappointments is that Havana has a large collection of Art Deco and Art Nouveau buildings. Some exist, but only a few are notable and deserving of attention, such as the 1930 Bacardi building designed by Esteban Rodríguez Castells, Rafael Fernández Ruenes, and José Menéndez and the López Serrano apartment building built in 1932 by Ricardo Mira and Miguel Rosich. The 1947 Collegio de Arquitectos by Fernando de Zarraga and Mario Esquiroz is another example.

Spanish colonial revival style has a major presence in Cuba. Coming from this tradition is the widely praised Hotel Nacional, which was completed in 1930 by the highly respected New York architectural firm of McKim, Mead and White. Another successful building is the Havana train station by architect Kenneth H. Murchison.

Modern architecture before the revolution produced the widely praised Solymar apartments built in 1944 in Central Havana by Manuel Copado. These apartments celebrate the sea with wide circular balconies that represent ocean waves. This building, and the Tropicana Cabaret designed in 1951–56 by Max Borges Recio, are representative of the sensual and curvy Modern architecture. Borges also designed the Nautical Club in 1953 in the Playa area of Havana. This building celebrated the sea and shipping industry by tying together two distinct structures. One symbolizes a large container ship sailing in the other, the Nautical Club, representing the curvy ocean waves. Another spectacular presocialist building with nautical leanings is the house of Maria Melero (built between 1940 and 1942 by architect Herminio Laduerman) in the Playa area of Havana. The building has portholes for windows and features the command bridge of a ship. Many believe this distinctive architecture reflects Cuban culture and its relationship to the sea, sensuality, sun, and salsa.

Before and after Cuba's socialist revolution there was a burst of Modern and monumental architecture. The Modern architec-

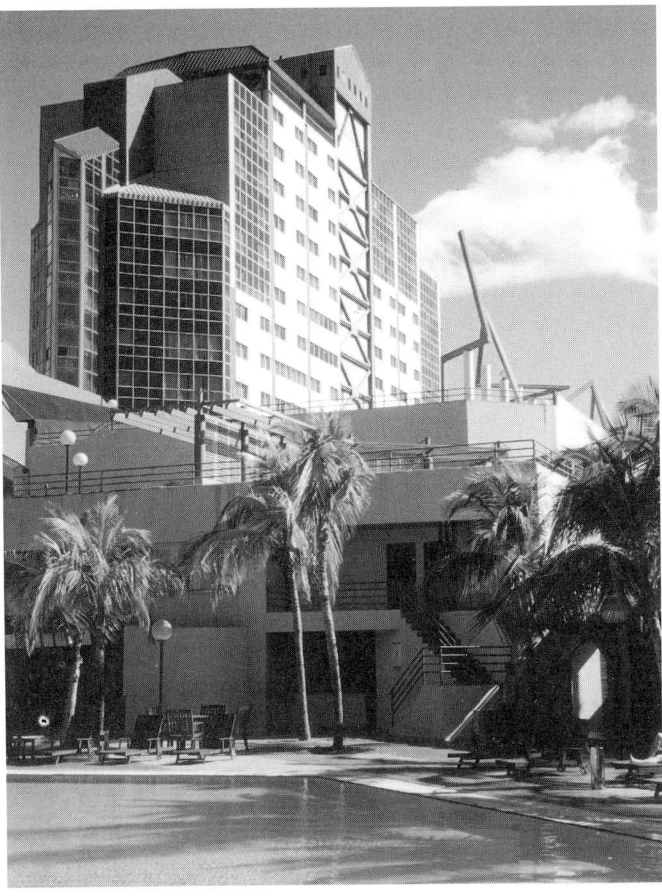

Santiago Hotel, José Antonio Choy (1991)
© Roberto Segre

ture movement was controversial because these buildings were not adapted to Havana's patterns of extreme hot weather—rooms became hotter because the ceilings were lower, windows were fewer, and heat could not escape to higher floors. Moreover, the individualism of the Spanish colonial or even Art Deco was lost to a repetitive sharp angular design. Architect Richard Neutra was a major influence on this movement. Few are aware that Neutra helped design two buildings in Cuba, one of which (house of Alfred de Schultess, 1956) won the National College of Architects' Gold Medal Prize and has been called the most beautiful house designed by a non-Cuban architectural firm. The best representation of this Modern architecture was captured by the architect Miguel Gaston's house, built in 1952. This house is spectacular because the pool gives the illusion of floating into Havana Bay and becoming one with it. Nearby, the Riviera Hotel by Polevitzky, Johnson and Associates, built in 1957, is notable for providing balconies for every room. The building curves nicely, like a wave, in a seaside teal color. It is very sleek and sensual; this building also tips its hat to the influence of Morris Lapidus's Fontainebleau Hotel in Miami Beach.

Cultural and political ideology is difficult to separate from Cuban architecture. Shortly after Wallace K. Harrison and Max Abramovitz designed the United Nations Building in New York, they designed the United States Embassy in 1953, which fits awkwardly among the historic buildings of Havana's Malecón. This building was widely criticized by Cuban architects because of its excessive glass and windows that did not open, creating a cooling problem. Unlike the grace and substance of the United Nations Building, this building looks like a typical suburban American office center building, whose dark frame, glass walls, and 20-foot-high metal fences become the embodiment of how the socialist government wants its citizens to see America: big, dominating, impersonal, ugly, and uncaring. This building has become a frequent site of anti-American demonstrations.

Cuba also uses its large public squares for public rallies. José Martí is honored in Havana's Plaza de la Revolución, a collective effort built between 1938 and 1952. In Santa Clara a stark square honors Che Guevara, and in Santiago another commemorates revolutionary leader Antonio Maceo. If the goal of monumentalism is to make the person feel small and powerless against the state, these squares and others like it seem to be effective in achieving this goal.

Churches are largely Spanish colonial in design with the exception of the modernist Jewish temples. Interestingly, the most striking church in Cuba, built in 1927, is a Spanish revival called El Cobre near Santiago. Of particular significance is the church's spectacular placement, rising out of the trees at the bottom of a mountain range.

Perhaps the most important 20th-century watershed architectural event was the building of the National Art Schools (begun in 1961; never completed). The lead architect was Ricardo Porro, who sought to celebrate Cuba's African roots in a conglomeration of buildings with separate schools for visual arts, music, and dramatic arts. Construction was stopped and abandoned because of ideology. Critics argued that it was wasteful and inefficient to spend many hours training brick craftsmen to build highly sophisticated Catalonian vaults instead of using reinforced-steel concrete. The Soviet-aligned architects not only defeated the National Arts School, but they also were able to get Castro to pass a law requiring that all new building projects use mass industrial production techniques similar to those employed in the Soviet Union. This was the demise of architecture in socialist Cuba. Architectural styles, historically imported from Spain and Italy and later France, England, and America, found a new exporter of architecture in the Soviet Union, which produced faceless, cold, mass-production concrete housing free of individualization. Housing became a symbol of the state and no longer a symbol of the self. The vast majority of architects and planners, attacked as part of the bourgeois class, left Cuba after the revolution because they felt that they had lost a great deal of professional and personal freedom. Cuba now allows families who receive dollars from the tourist industry or from relatives overseas to build prefab, low-rise single-family concrete housing units and allows builders to personalize them with stone, seashells, wood, and different color paints. The best example of what is called "micro brigade housing" was built in the early 1990s near the Santiago Bay luxury boat harbor.

Housing and places of work were designed to maximize production of space. Playful, individualistic, and human-scale housing production became almost nonexistent during the socialist era. In the conference on Fifty Years of Cuban Architecture, architects passed resolutions and demanded greater influence in how buildings are to be designed, ideally to reflect Cuban culture. The National Union of Architects and Engineers has also denounced the hotel and shopping mall designs of European and Canadian corporations, the designs of which represent a "cookie-cutter" approach, failing to integrate Cuban cultural amenities and aesthetics—balconies, more rounded buildings, stained glass, tile floors instead of carpeting, louvered doors, fanlights above doorways, and louvered window shutters that open. Most of these new hotels seem like second-rate versions of Hyatt hotels in third-rate cities.

When the Soviet International school defeated the Cubano National Arts School, Cuba decreed that all future architecture must follow the Soviet model of rational, scientific, and efficient design. The Soviet school was greatly influenced by the work of Le Corbusier. All schools, residences, hospitals, and offices were to be built using laborsaving devices based on the factory model—no more inefficient design. It is difficult to quantify a reliable number of how many prefabricated housing units were built in Cuba, but the estimate is approximately one million. The Cubans insist that everyone is guaranteed a house, food, education, and transportation, yet many dislike the houses for their lack of character and personality. The Cuban lament is that you need a house number to find your own place. Over 100,000 units were lost due to lack of upkeep during the socialist period. Many blame this on Cuban housing law, which did not factor in maintenance and repair of roofing, walls, and plumbing. The average Cuban pays about $2 per month for an apartment.

One development that Castro boasted would be a model socialist city and the envy of the world is Alamar. More than 100,000 units were constructed there. Today, this formalistic, factory-built concrete design is roundly considered a major architecture and planning failure. Even Cuban architects call it a dormitory devoid of services, shops, style, and exuberance. Much of it stands abandoned and incomplete. Instead of building in the cities, Castro wanted new housing developments to be outside the city. For Alamar residents the average commute time is three hours per day back and forth to available work in Havana. It is a good example of "socialist sprawl." These buildings do demonstrate Cuban ingenuity for using unorthodox materials such as wall partitions made out of processed sugarcane waste. Perhaps the most successful building design is CUJAE, which is the flagship Cuban university for planning, architecture, and engineering. CUJAE was a collective effort built in the early 1970s by untrained builders. This building is located near Havana International Airport about 30 minutes from downtown Havana. A more interesting and successful result is achieved when old and new are fused together. Las Ruinas Restaurant in Lenin Park, also near the airport, was built atop the ruins of a stone church by architect Joaquín Galván in 1971. Here he recaptures the Cuban Spanish colonial style of blurring what is inside and outside.

Near Alamar is the Pan-American Village, which makes the best use of prefabricated materials by putting Cuban accents on the design: more curves, a main promenade like Havana's famous Paseo del Prado, shops on the ground floor, homes on the second to fifth floors, design that incorporates brick, and an individualistic style and a skyline that is not uniform. The design team was headed by Roberto Caballero and building was completed in 1991. The Pan-American complex is somewhat successful because it adapts Soviet prefab buildings into a modern version of Spanish colonial design. The only problem is that this should have been built in Havana, close to jobs.

Postmodern Architecture

In 1991 José Antonio Choy was the lead architect who put together two of Cuba's most important pieces of Postmodern architecture: the Santiago train station and Santiago Hotel. Choy does not get much credit in Cuban architecture books because few architects make the 14-hour drive from Havana to eastern Cuba. Choy's work is similar in many ways to Frank Gehry's in its use of unusual building materials, sharp and bold angles, and nonfunctional, playful, and provocative spaces. Corrugated metal is prominent. For Cuba these buildings represent a bold departure from the highly rationalized Soviet style of modular design that is faceless, cold, predictable, uninspiring, and demoralizing. Yet Cuban citizens see this building as extravagant, inefficient, and wasteful. Both these buildings are far more political and powerful because of their symbolism. Hotel Santiago salutes the mighty sugar mills of the past with a Postmodern design. It is important because it stands against the faceless rationalization of communism by saying the world is illogical, confusing, and confounding. It says that beauty cannot be found in a simple straight line but in a curved line that sometimes goes nowhere. The Santiago train station is even more radical and utilizes stairs climbing up three flights to nowhere, a bridge that is without function, large pillars that support nothing, and large square blocks tossed randomly on the front entrance. The Gehry corrugated metal and storm fences are here, too. More interesting is that this building was built at a time when Russians were cutting financial support for Cuba. The train building is a powerful commentary on socialist Cuba—broken, unfinished, and illogical.

The biosphere of Las Terrazas is a one-hour drive west of Havana in Pinar del Río. Las Terrazas has undergone a significant reforestation program that utilizes community gardens, recycling, papermaking, and trees that grow through the buildings. UNESCO has declared this a world biosphere. Castro has declared that the future is in ecotourism. The Hotel Moka was designed by Mario Girona in the early 1990s as a green building in which trees are allowed to grow through rooms, hallways, and decks. The red tile used here is another salute to the Spanish colonial era.

Prado Neptuno is representative of the movement for Retro-Cubano, which was built in 1999 by Roberto Gottardi, one of the architects who helped design the National Arts School. It is a Cuban salute to Frank Lloyd Wright, combining mosaic tiles, architectural lighting effects, and an emphasis on local materials. This building has been widely praised as a new chapter in Cuban architecture.

Callejón de Hamel, located in Central Havana, is an inspiring example of how to revitalize an inner-city neighborhood through art that reflects the history, hopes, and desires of its people.

The movement is led by a painter known as Salvador, who was untrained and has taught other nonpainters to create murals that celebrate African-based religion, urban life, love, and sex. The murals that cover six-story housing blocks are incredible in their ability to turn a bleak neighborhood into one that is colorful, exciting, and inspiring for both residents and tourists. This is one of the few places where large murals are allowed to exist free of the usual prosocialist political propaganda.

Socialism meant the end of architecture in Cuba. Very little has been written on Cuban architecture under socialism. Only a handful of reliable and useful books exist on the topic in English or Spanish. Two of the best books were written by Americans: *Cuba: 400 years of Architectural Heritage* by Rachel Carley and *Revolution of Forms: Cuba's Forgotten Art Schools* by John A. Loomis. The very best Cuban writer on architecture is Eduardo Luis Rodríguez, whose chief role is to document significant pieces of architecture for restoration and preservation. Although highly regarded internationally, Rodríguez has been reluctant to write critical articles on architecture under socialism. Interestingly, his most recent book on Modern architecture in Havana, published by Princeton University Press, stops in 1965—skipping 36 years of socialist architecture, which is probably of greater interest than many of the derivative buildings he reviews. Until recently, foreign travel to Cuba, especially outside Havana, has been difficult. If foreigners do publish articles critical of Cuban socialist architecture, they face a possible ban on future travel to Cuba. More scholarship is needed that documents, analyzes, reviews, and evaluates Cuban architecture, especially during the socialist period.

JOHN I. GILDERBLOOM

Further Reading

Carley, Rachel, *Cuba: 400 Years of Architectural Heritage*, New York: Whitney Library of Design, 1997

Codrescu, Andrei, *Ay, Cuba! A Socio-Erotic Journey*, New York: St. Martin's Press, 1999

Ellena, María, Martín Zequieira, and Eduardo Luis Rodríguez Fernández, *Guia de arquitectura: La Habana colonial, 1519–1898*, Havana: Agencia Española de Cooperación Internacional, and Seville, Spain: Junta de Andalucía, Consejería de Obras Públicas y Transportes, 1993

The Journal of Decorative and Propaganda Arts, 22 (2002) (special issue on Cuba)

Loomis, John A., *Revolution of Forms: Cuba's Forgotten Art Schools*, New York: Princeton Architectural Press, 1999

Miller, John, and Susannah Clark (editors), *Havana*, San Francisco: Chronicle Books, 1996

Rodríguez, Eduardo Luis, *The Havana Guide: Modern Architecture, 1925–1965*, translated by Lorna Scott Fox, New York: Princeton Architectural Press, 2000

Segre, Roberto, Mario Coyula, and Joseph L. Scarpaci, *Havana: Two Faces of the Antillean Metropolis*, New York and Chichester, West Sussex: Wiley, 1997

Stanley, David, *Cuba: A Lonely Planet Travel Survival Kit*, Hawthorne, Victoria, and Oakland, California: Lonely Planet, 1996

CUBISM

The aesthetic movements of the early 20th century were frequently and closely connected with new ideas in architecture. Futurism, the Dutch group De Stijl, the purist manifesto of Le Corbusier and Ozenfant, Suprematism and Constructivism in Russia, and Expressionist German painting resonated with the development of modernist ideas and forms in architecture. However, the question of the relationship of Cubist painting and sculpture to architecture is not straightforward. Rather, Cubism was a point of departure, contributing to the development of new concepts in Modern art.

In 1907 and 1908, Pablo Picasso and Georges Braque, inspired by the aperspectival, cubic treatment of space in the paintings of Paul Cézanne and by primitive African art, developed a radically new approach to the object in their paintings. When they showed their new paintings at the Salon des Indépendants in 1909, the critic Louis Vauxcelles referred to Braque's landscapes as "bizarreries cubiques." Vauxcelles' remark was immediately adopted in Parisian art circles, giving a name to the new approach: Cubism. Cubism represented a break with the painterly tradition since the Renaissance. The object was not represented in the central perspective but rather was deconstructed into prismatic surfaces, simultaneously representing different perspectives on the canvas. This formal analysis reduced what was depicted to geometric elements, similar to the relationship between words and syntax.

The new approach of Braque and Picasso quickly became a movement, as other artists, each with his own interpretation of Cubist principles, joined in the experiment. Albert Gleizes, Jean Metzinger, Robert Delaunay, the brothers Duchamp, Fernand Léger, Juan Gris, and many others went through a shorter or longer Cubist period in their work. Cubism also quickly spread beyond France, influencing art in many countries for some time. The break with classical perspective and the composition of the image independent of observation of nature opened up possibilities for abstract art, futurism, and other movements. These developments took place very quickly between 1909 and 1915 and were accompanied by changes in other art forms, including architecture and its theory, in the years ahead. The new poetics expressed in Guillaume Apollinaire's poem "Zone" of 1912 and the first atonal composition by Arnold Schoenberg of 1909 serve as examples for poetry and music.

Architecture, however, remained relatively untouched by Cubist painting and sculpture during this time with only two exceptions, and these were incidents rather than profound stimulation for new architectural developments: the *Maison Cubiste* project of Raymond Duchamp-Villon (1912) and the work of the group *Skupina Výtvarných* (Group of the Visual Artists) in Prague.

Duchamp-Villon (1876–1918) was a sculptor who belonged to a group of Cubist artists in Puteaux, outside Paris. For the exhibition of the group's work at the Salon d'Automne in 1912, Duchamp-Villon and others presented the *Maison Cubiste* project, a kind of *Gesamtkunstwerk* (total work of art) complete with furniture and articles of use. For lack of space and organizational problems, only the first story of the model was built in the Grand Palais. This work is known only from pictures of the plaster model and charcoal drawings.

The two-story facade has a traditional, symmetrical arrangement. Cubist principles are visible only in the details; traditional cornice and pillars, as well as the door and window frames, were replaced by broken surfaces and prismatic shapes. These plastic forms are abstract, and the overlap between them is the architectural equivalent of the painterly principle of superimposed planes.

The *Maison Cubiste* was the attempt of a sculptor to apply the principles of contemporary painting to architecture. By contrast the acceptance of Cubism by the *Skupina Výtvarných* group in Prague in 1911 was more systematic. Besides several painters and the sculptor Otto Guttfreund (1889–1927), the architects Josef Chochol (1880–1957), Josef Gocár (1880–1945), and

Pavel Janák (1882–1956) were cofounders of the group. They were active in architecture, interior design, arts and crafts, and set design and expressed themselves at the level of theory.

The interest of these architects in the latest developments in painting represented a reaction against the Wagner school's dominant rationalism and leaning to social engineering. Cubism seemed to offer an opening to a more artistic approach to architecture. In 1910 Janák—himself one of Otto Wagner's students—published an article in the journal *Styl* titled "From Modern Architecture to Architecture," noting that Modern architecture had an exclusively practical orientation and had no interest in questions of space, material, and form.

However, the transposition of the principles of Cubist painting to architecture turned out to be a formidable task because of fundamental differences in the two art forms. In fact the Prague architects only adopted the principle of decomposition, that is, the fragmented representation of the image, and applied it to the design of the facade. The plane of the facade was undermined by slanting, prismatic forms that replaced the traditional, orthogonal composition of the facade. The result was comparable to the detail in the *Maison Cubiste.* This approach had very little spatial significance, except in a few architectural sketches and installations for exhibitions and in the Kurhaus at Bohdanec (health administration building) (1911–12) by Gocár and the apartment building (1912) on Neklan Street in Prague by Josef Chochol, which demonstrate a spatial application of these principles. However, most of the architects concentrated on facades while their plans remained conventional.

The underlying theory of the Prague group was different from Cubist painting. The main objective was to achieve a plastic unity in the design of the facade through dynamism and movement. They were concerned with movement in an abstract sense, as an expression of the will to form, which subdues matter. These Czech architects saw the Wagner school's visible honesty in construction and use of material as imposed by matter, materialist, and devoid of spiritual content. Historian Alois Riegl's formulation of *Kunstwollen* (the will to art), in contradiction to the function, material, and technique of the artwork, and the theories of Theodor Lipps and Wilhelm Worringer, which were based on the subjective nature of observation and intuition, positioned themselves against the rationalism and materialism of contemporary art theory in the same spirit.

Prague's architectural Cubism, which became increasingly more formal and decorative after 1914, and even became a sort of national style of the Czechoslovak Republic between 1918 and 1925, in actuality brought forth an Expressionist architecture—at least within the framework of architectural history, in which the notion of Cubist architecture simply does not exist. From the point of view of aesthetic conception and analysis of style, the Prague designs are related to the Amsterdam School and to German Expressionism, with which it is sometimes possible to identify direct, formal similarities. There are also formal similarities with the work of the Moscow group Zhivskulptarch, which attempted the integration of painting, sculpture, and architecture between 1918 and 1920 under the leadership of the Cubist sculptor Boris D. Korolyov. The work of the architects Nikolai A. Ladovsky and Nikolai I. Istselenov from this short period is distinctively Expressionist.

The significance of Cubism in painting to Expressionist architecture amounts to the most definite, direct relationship between the two art forms. The causal connection rests formally in the decomposed fragments and prismatic forms of Cubist painting, which led to comparable three-dimensional forms in architecture. A deeper connection may reside in the anticlassical aspect of Cubism, particularly the break with classical perspective since the Renaissance. An anticlassical stance was also characteristic of Expressionism.

With respect to the relationship between modernist architecture and Cubism, it is interesting that the protagonists of renewal in the 1920s sometimes took positions against Cubism, or at least referred to it with considerable reserve, without identifying with it. The purism of Amédée Ozenfant and Le Corbusier may have been a further development following in the wake of Cubism, but their 1918 manifesto "Après le Cubisme" does not evince much appreciation for the movement. The manifesto rejected Cubist principles and called Cubism as a whole an esoteric game of ornamental forms. Instead, there is an emphasis on rational arrangement in the construction of an image, on a sort of standardization of the depicted object, and on the plastic values of the image. The purist manifesto represented a return to the classical tradition; elements of purist painting are significant for the architectural work of Le Corbusier, including the aesthetic concept of a standard and the emphasis on plastic values.

The direct influence of Cubism on modernist architecture is more difficult to identify. Although some authors, such as Sigfried Giedion, Reyner Banham, and Colin Rowe, see Cubist painting as an important impulse for the work of Le Corbusier and Walter Gropius, that remains a matter of interpretation. Without a doubt the pathbreaking role of Cubist painting in general led to an analogy with the pathbreaking role of modernist architecture, but this would appear to be more a matter of legitimation than a causal connection. Some aspects, such as the reduction of the object to geometric forms, spatial penetration, and transparency, bear a programmatic relationship to the conception of architecture of the pioneers of architectural modernism, but it is not clear whether these derive from Cubism or whether they were discovered because of Cubism.

Historically speaking, these aspects of architecture cannot be traced back exclusively to Cubism. The reduction of building volumes to geometric forms may as well be connected to Roman church architecture or the work of Enlightenment architects Claude Ledoux and Etienne Boullée. It was no accident that the work of Ledoux and Boullée received attention in 1933, precisely in relation to Le Corbusier. Transparency in architecture had earlier been applied in the iron-and-glass buildings of the engineers of the 19th century, whereas in Cubist painting transparency is more conceptual than visually present. Moreover, penetration and simultaneity in Cubist painting are closer to deconstructivist architecture than to Gropius's Bauhaus aesthetic. It is also possible to doubt the exemplary nature of the supposed rational construction of the image of analytical Cubism, already seen as not rational enough immediately after World War I.

Another problem that complicates the reception of Cubism in architecture is the confusion between "Cubist" and "cubic." As early as the 1920s, the word "cubist" was applied by some writers to the new, unornamented architecture that relied on the arrangement of stereometric volumes. The work of Adolf

Loos, J.J.P. Oud, Willem M. Dudok, and others has been called Cubist in this fashion, and as such the descriptor seems to be a global designation of form rather than a connection to be French avant-gardism in painting.

That contradictory pronouncements have been made about Cubism and architecture may be related to the fact that the artistic revolution of Cubism was a symptom, not the cause, of a new experience and interpretation of a changing world. A similar phenomenon took place in other movements, and architecture was one of them.

OTAKAR MÁCEL

See also **Amsterdam School; Corbusier, Le (Jeanneret, Charles-Édouard) (France); De Stijl; Deconstructivism; Loos, Adolf (Austria); Wagner, Otto (Austria)**

Further Reading

Banham, Reyner, *Theory and Design in the First Machine Age*, London: Architectural Press, and New York: Praeger, 1960; see especially chapter "Architecture and the Cubist Tradition"

Barr, Alfred Hamilton, *Cubism and Abstract Art*, New York: Museum of Modern Art, 1936

Blau, Eve, and Nancy C. Troy (editors), *Architecture and Cubism*, Montreal, Quebec: Canadian Centre for Architecture, and Cambridge, Massachusetts: MIT Press, 1997

Burkhardt, François, "Notes on Cubism in Czech Architecture," *Lotus International*, 20 (1978)

Golding, John, *Cubism: A History and an Analysis, 1907–1914*, London: Faber, and New York: Wittenborn, 1959; 3rd edition, Cambridge, Massachusetts: Harvard University Press, and London: Faber, 1988

Hamilton, George Heard, and William C. Agee, *Raymond Duchamp-Villon: 1876–1918*, New York: Walker, 1967

Lamarová, Milena, "Cubism and Expressionism in Architecture and Design: The Prague Cubist Group," *Lotus International*, 20 (1978)

Margolius, Ivan, *Cubism in Architecture and the Applied Arts: Bohemia and France, 1910–1914*, Newton Abbot, Devon, and North Pomfret, Vermont: David and Charles, 1979

Ragghianti, Carlo L., "Architettura moderna e cubismo," *Zodiac*, 9 (1962)

Švestka, Jiri (editor), *1909–1925: Kubismus in Prag. Malerei, Skulptur, Kunstgewerbe, Architektur*, Stuttgart, Germany: Hatje, and Düsseldorf, Germany: Kunstverein, 1991

Vegesack, Alexander von (editor), *Tschechischer Kubismus, Architektur und Design: 1910–1925*, Weil am Rhein, Germany: Vitra Design Museum, 1991; as *Czech Cubism: Architecture, Furniture, and Decorative Arts, 1910–1925*, New York: Princeton Architectural Press, 1992

CULTURAL CENTRE JEAN-MARIE TJIBAOU, NOUMÉA, NEW CALEDONIA

Designed by Renzo Piano; completed 1998

Since the mid-19th century, the Melanesian island community of New Caledonia in the South Pacific Ocean has been a French territory. Prized for its valuable nickel deposits, sections of New Caledonia have been extensively mined by the French, leaving the countryside a disturbing mélange of natural landforms and man-made quarries. The desire for cultural recognition became the catalyst for a strong Kanak nationalist movement, which formed in the 1980s. However, despite growing French recognition of the plight of the Kanak people, by 1988 the movement had been largely unsuccessful political extremists assassinated. In the following year, civil unrest grew in New Caledonia, among the Kanak leader, Jean-Marie Tjibaou, and several of his followers. Tjibaou's death, and the rift it symbolized between the French government and the native Kanak people, led French President Mitterand to support the construction of a cultural center in New Caledonia as the first step in a process of political and cultural reconciliation. A limited international architectural competition for the Tjibaou Cultural Centre was held in 1991, and a design from architect Renzo Piano and his Building Workshop was awarded first prize.

The site for the building is a spectacular promontory on the Tina Peninsula at the eastern edge of New Caledonia's capital city, Nouméa. The promontory, a densely vegetated strip of land, lies between a small lagoon and the Bay of Magenta. It is sufficiently close to the city that it fulfills Tjibaou's aims for such a center to be accessible to urban Kanaks, yet it is also within the natural landscape. Piano's winning scheme features a picturesque, and perhaps romanticized, cluster of structures that closely resemble overscaled traditional huts. In this preliminary scheme, these huts, or "cases," as they are known in French, are distributed around a narrow spine that runs along the ridge of the promontory. Despite being criticized for its complex technical detailing and its heavy-handed formal references to regional culture, Piano's preliminary design was strongly supported by the Kanak people, and work was begun on the project in 1992.

In its final form, as completed in 1998, the Tjibaou Cultural Centre consists of a central open spine with three clusters of cases, ten in total, all to the southeastern side of the spine. To the opposite side is a series of lower, rectilinear volumes, which are recessed up to three stories deep into the site. The largest of these volumes, a 400-seat theater, is also extended into the landscape to create an outdoor performance space. A public car park is at one end of the promontory, and visitors approach the building obliquely, first seeing the distinctive roof silhouette of the cases before rising up from the lower, lagoon side to the main entry. The spine is entered, as is appropriate for a visitor to a Kanak building, at right angles approximately one-third of the way along its length. An underground tunnel, roughly parallel to the spine, provides for servicing to all areas of the development.

Each of the ten cases is circular in plan and is clad, for three-quarters of its circumference, in a double layer of vertical timber ribs that support a system of in-fill panels comprising horizontal timber slats and glass and timber louvers. The inner wall of timber ribs is vertical, whereas the outer wall bows out from the base of the circle and is tied back at its apex like a billowing timber sail. Both inner and outer ribs are cut away at the rear, or lower, side adjacent to the circulation spine, and a steeply inclined circular metal roof is supported on the inner wall. At their peaks the tallest of the timber ribs reach a height of approximately 90 feet (28 meters) and are clearly visible from the distance. All of the joints are steel, and the ribs are constructed of iroko wood, which is naturally termite resistant and is able to be laminated. The gap between the inner and outer rib walls is carefully controlled to capture light winds to cool the structure while allowing the interior to be sealed in the event of cyclones.

Cultural Centre Jean Marie Tjibaro, Nouméa, New Caledonia, by Renzo Piano

Internally, the cases house gallery spaces, a multimedia library, and several small lecture theaters. The three clusters, although not as obvious as they are in the original scheme, still divide the cases into different functional zones, with the public galleries toward the northeast and the more private, or controlled, galleries to the southwest.

The cases, which come in three sizes, are the most visible and iconic elements of the design. They recall the structure, texture, and spatial distribution of the traditional Kanak village. They also have a natural tactility and level of detail that are similar to the complexity of the surrounding vegetation (particularly the tall Norfolk Island pines). The cases successfully evoke a regional cultural form, the Kanak village, without resorting to kitsch representation and without demeaning local tradition. This is arguably the buildings' greatest success—they are both stridently modern in technology and detailing yet able to capture some sense of the spirit of the land and its people. For this reason the buildings are often identified with critical regionalist practices that reject overt mimicry of traditional forms in favor of designs that capture some aspect of regional tectonics, light quality, or spatial practices.

MICHAEL J. OSTWALD

See also **Piano, Renzo (Italy)**

Further Reading

Buchanan, Peter, *Renzo Piano Building Workshop: Complete Works*, Volume 2, London: Phaidon, 1995

Buchanan, Peter, *Renzo Piano Building Workshop: Complete Works* Volume 4, London: Phaidon, 2000

Piano, Renzo, *Renzo Piano: Sustainable Architectures*, Barcelona: G. Gili, 1998

CURTAIN-WALL SYSTEM

The curtain wall, one of architecture's most provocative metaphors, is surprisingly difficult to pin down with a precise definition. Because it can be examined from multiple perspectives—in terms of functional relationships, as an aesthetic object, or as a mass-produced system available within the construction marketplace—some ambiguity is both inevitable and provocative.

In the first case, the curtain wall is defined in terms of its functional relationship to the building's structure. It then refers to the cladding, or enclosure, of a building as something both separate from and attached to the building's skeletal framework. Where load-bearing walls provide both structure and enclosure, there can be no curtain wall. However, difficulties emerge within this first definition when the question of "in-fill" is considered: are conventional windows (or other in-fill material), when fixed inside the boundaries of a structural frame, considered to represent curtain-wall construction? Such construction is certainly "attached" to the structural frame but not exactly "hanging" from it. When is a window just a window within a frame, and when does it transform into a curtain wall? The answer might have more to do with one's aesthetic bias than with the actual functional relationship between cladding and structure.

From a functional perspective, curtain walls necessarily appeared precisely at the same time as skeletal frameworks—toward the end of the 19th century. Yet the first such walls were often strikingly similar to the thick masonry walls that they might have been expected to supersede. Although no longer load-bearing structures, relatively thick masonry curtain walls continued to be used in steel-and concrete-framed buildings for other reasons. First, thinner masonry walls—before the development of internal cavities to block the migration of moisture through the wall—tended to have problems with water penetration. Second, lighter facades consisting of metal or glass panels were often considered aesthetically unsuitable for serious works of architecture because of a legacy and tradition that linked monumental architecture to masonry construction. Third, the use of more modern cladding alternatives required breakthroughs in environmental control technologies—air conditioning and insulation being the most important—before they could be deployed over large surface areas enclosing habitable spaces. Finally, building code officials, increasingly sensitive to the real danger of urban conflagrations, prevented the use of new, lightweight materials in exterior walls—even after other technical and environmental issues had been addressed—if they were unable to match the proven fire resistance of masonry.

Although defined initially in terms of its functional relationship to structure, toward the middle of the 20th century the curtain wall began to be alternatively defined by its function as an environmental filter—as a membrane mediating between desired interior conditions and variable exterior circumstances. Sunscreens (*brises-soleil*), double glazing, and pressure-equalized rain screens were among the functional responses to this concern, culminating in the late 20th century's technologically sophisticated "bioclimatic" designs. In these "green" buildings, an array of computer- and user-controlled devices may be embedded within the curtain wall to encourage the use of fresh air and natural daylighting while at the same time aiming to improve user comfort, reduce energy consumption, and promote a "sustainable" lifestyle.

Curtain walls can also be defined as the embodiment of an aesthetic intention—the second of the three perspectives mentioned previously. Numerous such curtain-wall themes can be identified in 20th-century architecture. They coalesce, in general, around the revolutionary "new" materials of metal and glass: metal (as industrialized, mass-produced, streamlined panel), glass (as transparent or reflective surface, crystalline solid, or harbinger of an enlightened culture), or metal and glass com-

Willis Faber and Dumas Building (1975), designed by Sir Norman Foster and Michael Hopkins, Ipswich, England
© Ken Kirkwood

bined (as woven "fabric" or abstract grid). Still, other more traditional materials and systems, including stucco, concrete, brick, and stone veneer, have also played a role in validating the curtain wall within various aesthetic domains and not merely as the by-product of functional considerations. The ideal of an all-glass skin perhaps was the most persistent curtain-wall theme of the 20th century. Starting with metal window systems containing relatively small glass panes and moving toward larger glass sizes with smaller mullion profiles, the most technically advanced glass walls of the late 20th century managed to eliminate mullions entirely, whether by using the glass itself as a structural material, relying on structural sealant joints, or by pinning the glass to elegantly detailed lightweight steel substructures.

Ironically, the initial aesthetic formulation of the modern metal-and-glass curtain wall preceded the invention of multistory skeletal frameworks. Greenhouses were being built in Europe, even in the mid-17th century, with large areas of glass divided by wooden, and later iron, mullions. By the mid-19th century, skins of metal and glass were commonly used for the roofs of markets, gallerias, and train stations. London's Crystal Palace of 1851 was extremely influential not only in validating the architectural use of iron and glass but also in foreshadowing its rationalization as an industrialized system.

It is as a system—the third perspective mentioned previously—that the curtain wall became widely available within the building construction marketplace. Early 20th-century curtain walls tended to be unique and custom made, fabricated individually from the cast iron, rolled steel, and plate glass that were just beginning to appear as industrialized commodities. However, by the mid-1930s the emerging sheet-metal technologies (and aesthetics) associated with the mass production of airplanes and automobiles began to be seriously adapted to building construction, especially the development of metal curtain-wall panels. Starting at the end of World War II, the 20th century's ubiquitous metal-and-glass curtain-wall systems—repetitive grids of extruded aluminum mullions and horizontal rails fastened to a building's structural skeleton and supporting panels of glass or metal—increasingly began to appear on commercial and institutional buildings. The newly invented float process made large areas of glass even more feasible beginning in the 1950s.

Other panelized curtain-wall systems also appeared as cladding options: these included composite metal panels containing lightweight cores of honeycombed material or foam plastic insulation sandwiched between two layers of thin sheet metal (aluminum or steel); precast concrete panels, custom designed for each job but still manufactured within a rationalized, systematic production setting; and thin stone veneer panels, factory cut to a thickness as little as one inch, then attached to the building's structure using proprietary metal clips and anchors. Even traditional brick and stucco became integrated into manufactured curtain-wall systems: brick as part of layered cavity wall systems and stucco, most commonly in the form of EIFS (exterior insulation and finish systems), consisting of thin polymer-based plaster laminae applied with fiberglass reinforcing mesh to a surface of rigid foam insulation. Among the numerous architects or designers associated with the development of curtain-wall technology or its aesthetic refinement, a partial list would include Nicholas Grimshaw, Norman Foster, Walter Gropius, Le Corbusier, Richard Meier, Jean Nouvel, I.M. Pei, Cesar Pelli, Jean Prouvé, Peter Rice, Kevin Roche, Ludwig Mies van der Rohe, Eero Saarinen, Ken Yeang, and the firm of Skidmore, Owings and Merrill.

JONATHAN OCHSHORN

Further Reading

The history of curtain walls in 20th-century architecture may be pieced together from readings in architectural histories and from monographs describing the work of individual architects or designers. For the development of early 20th-century curtain walls in Chicago, see Condit. A discussion of the rival cast-iron tradition may be found in Gayle. For a general text examining modern curtain-wall systems, see Sands. An overview of curtain-wall systems may be found in Allen. Discussion and details of early "modernist" 20th-century curtain walls are in Ford. For examples of state-of-the-art "glass walls," see Bramante as well as Rice and Dutton. For details of a more recent oeuvre incorporating metal curtain-wall panels, see Flagge and Hamm. For examples of "green" curtain-wall designs, see Yeang and Davies and Lambot.

Allen, Edward, *Fundamentals of Building Construction: Materials and Methods*, New York: Wiley, 1985; 3rd edition, 1999

Bramante, Gabriele, *Willis Faber and Dumas Building: Foster Associates*, London: Phaidon, 1993

Condit, Carl W., *The Rise of the Skyscraper*, Chicago: University of Chicago Press, 1952; revised edition, as *The Chicago School of Architecture: A History of Commercial and Public Building in the Chicago Area, 1875–1925*, Chicago: University of Chicago Press, 1964

Davies, Colin, and Ian Lambot, *Commerzbank Frankfurt: Prototype for an Ecological High Rise*, Boston: Birkhäuser, 1997

Flagge, Ingeborg, and Oliver Hamm (editors), *Richard Meier in Europe*, Berlin: Ernst und Sohn, 1997

Ford, Edward R., *The Details of Modern Architecture*, 2 vols., Cambridge, Massachusetts: MIT Press, 1990

Gayle, Margot, and Carol Gayle, *Cast Iron Architecture in America: The Significance of James Bogardus*, New York: Norton, 1998

Huber, Benedikt, and Jean-Claude Steinegger (editors), *Jean Prouvé: Prefabrication: Structures and Elements*, London: Pall Mall Press, and New York: Praeger, 1971

Rice, Peter, and Hugh Dutton, *Le Verre structurel*, Paris: Éditions du Moniteur, 1990; 2nd edition, 1995; as *Structural Glass*, London: Spon, 1995

Sands, Herman, *Wall Systems: Analysis by Detail*, New York: McGraw-Hill, 1986

Yeang, Ken, *Bioclimatic Skyscrapers*, London: Artemis, 1994

CZECH, HERMANN 1936–

Architect, Austria

Early on, Hermann Czech studied architecture, philosophy, and film while working as a theorist and publicist of architecture. The Viennese architects Adolf Loos and Josef Frank left a lasting impression on his theory and, subsequently, on his work. Czech's development as an architect was further influenced by the architectural work of Arbeitsgruppe 4 and the theoretical positions of Konrad Wachsmann.

According to Kenneth Frampton, Czech's work reflects a subtle mixture of a postulation of oblique ironies and a directly reflected modest reality. His field of intervention is the interior of the building that, after completion, looks like nothing has happened. However, at the same time, these spaces display residual qualities available for the distraction of the inattentive mind. In 1980 Czech wrote, "Architecture is not life. Architecture is

Kleines Café I (Little Cafe I), Vienna (1970)
© Hermann Czech, Vienna. Photo Celeste M. Williams and Dietmar E. Froehlich

background. Everything else is not architecture" (Czech, in Frampton, 1980).

In his Kleines Café/Little Café (1970, 1973–74; Vienna), Czech realizes the concept of a *Stehcafe* (a mixed function of café and bar), which he inserted in an existing building in downtown Vienna and successively expanded and restructured until 1985. The multiangled, mazelike wall structure and the tiny floor space necessitated interventions to visually expand the space, thus engaging in a playful use of architectural vocabulary. The design of the stairs and the doors recalls Loos's *Raumplan* tradition.

Other restaurants with "new urban" interiors are the Wunder-Bar (1976; Vienna), Restaurant Salzamt (1981–83; Vienna), and the restaurant in the Kurhaus Baden-Baden (1988), which show his concept of "many-layered-ness," where he is trying to find a link with history by means of the introduction of elements that in their turn speak of this history. His method of irony suggests a sophisticated relationship through the appropriate architectural means.

Czech's universal outlook rejects a falsely exceptional architecture. Instead, frugality, discretion, and community-mindedness are the main characteristics of his position, as exemplified in the restaurant in the Schwarzenberg Palace (1982–84; Vienna). Here he converted the lower ground floor of the palace, solving the problems regarding kitchen, servicing, and banqueting previously prevalent in all the floors. The plan's organization, the vaults, and the relationships of all the levels yielded an exemplary architectural and preservational achievement referencing not the ideal baroque palace but the historical reality of constant change over time.

Similar are his intentions in the MAK Café (1991–93) in the Museum of Applied Arts in Vienna, where, inside an old space of the museum, the café corrects the lack of connection with the street by having all the new elements point to the immediate surroundings or to the city. The space itself remains almost untouched except for the two new bar stands pointing toward the new exit to the museum garden. Fixed and mobile partitions separate the café from the restaurant. Here again, Loos's ambiguous and erratic statements are placed into a new field of reference through Czech's ironic quotations.

Perception is forced to acknowledge more than the image of an object in his Dicopa Offices (1974–75) in Vienna, a complex restructuring and remodeling of offices with support spaces, all set in a tiny space of a historic building. The "not true to scale," almost urbanistic spaces are justified by their "service" value.

Czech's buildings want to appear as a spontaneous reaction to different needs: the idea of Josef Frank's "accidentism" (adaptation to circumstances) in the formation of the environment forms the central issue in Czech's architecture. The design becomes a "nonevent" seeking to blend into its surroundings. This position rejects types and systems, replacing them with the concern for the real, which can be seen early on in his House M. (1977–81) in Schwechat, where he again interprets Loos's *Raumplan* and Frank's "accidentism." The interwoven sequence of interior spaces flows around a skeletal system with four columns reaching through the whole house. The stairs also wind around the verticality of the columns, constantly changing the spatial quality and meaning of the stairs.

Czech's architecture sometimes is called a silent architecture, an architecture at second sight, or a veiled architecture that does not reveal itself immediately, where one is encouraged to look behind the veil to uncover the world. Czech's own approach to architecture could be compared with his assessment of Frank's dialectic position that architecture is anchored in the ideal and in the real, in the personal as well as in the general.

In his Apartment Building Petrusgasse (1985–89) in Vienna, Czech shows that subsidized housing should behave neutrally toward later modifications. The units can be joined vertically and horizontally. Functions do not primarily guide the layout of rooms and relationships. According to Czech, such a building can become the expression of its contents in time only through adaptation or interpretation—it has to remain silent at first. The expression of an apartment building, for example, can come only through the users.

Czech is trying to retrieve and recompose fragments to constitute an architecture better attuned to the existing, a kind of "self-developing and regenerating" architecture. Despite his position of "spontaneity," Czech is manipulating the fragments skillfully and with artifice to create architecture that is superimposing cultured tradition on the everyday.

Czech has been called a determined and complicated architect, designing between the discreet and the formally excessive. He seems to work independent of trends, continuing to develop his own architectural language as he goes forward. The meaning of his elements is ever changing because of unusual syntactic relationships.

The design concept for the Rosa-Jochmann-School (1991–94) in Vienna reveals itself in the interior rather than on the surface. Functional considerations were behind this merging of the corridor and the hall school type; the tracts of this elementary school form two interior courtyards, with the classrooms being organized in small groups. Access to the school is via the first floor, using a bridge coming from the upper ground level. An-

Residential and office development (enclosing a subway terminal track for turnback operation), Vienna (1997) © Harald Schoenfellinger, Vienna. Photo Celeste M. Williams and Dietmar E. Froehlich

other sensitive and multilayered approach to the task at hand can be revisited in his Bank Austria Client Service Center renovation (1992–97) in Vienna. The building was finished in 1915, becoming one of the first reinforced-concrete-skeleton buildings with a classicist facade in Vienna. Having been damaged during World War II, it was undergoing its first major renovation in the 1970s. In 1991 the building became the headquarters of the bank, the entry was moved, and a new staircase accessed the new teller lobby. The traditional entry and the three naves of the teller lobby remained in their entirety, whereas the former offices were integrated into the main space, where a new mezzanine level transforms the space into an office landscape.

Czech, who also designs exhibits and furniture, is working with the self-evident and the accidental in his writings as well as in his buildings. Nevertheless, his architecture is always "guided" by spatial thinking that takes into account the overall urban and architectural context.

DIETMAR E. FROEHLICH AND CELESTE M. WILLIAMS

Biography

Born in Vienna, 10 November 1936. Studied architecture at the Technical University and the Akademie der Bildenden Künste, Vienna; studied film at the Hochschule für Musik und Darstellende Kunst, Vienna 1954–56; studied philosophy, University of Vienna 1957–60. Architecture critic, *Die Furche*, Vienna 1963–67; correspondent, *A + U*, Tokyo 1963–67. Assistant professor, Kunstgewerbeschule, Vienna 1974. Visiting professor at numerous universities.

Selected Works

Restaurant Ballhaus, Vienna, 1962
Subway network design for Vienna (with Arbeitsgruppe 4), 1967
Kleines Café, Vienna, 1970, 1974
Apartment Klemmer, Vienna, 1972
Antiquariat Loecker und Woegenstein, Vienna, 1973, 1979
Office renovation Dicopa, Vienna, 1975
Wunder-Bar, Vienna, 1976
Addition to Villa Pflaum, Altenberg, 1979
Interior for M. and H. Poeschl, Vienna, 1980
Art Dealership/Gallery Hummel, Vienna, 1980
House M., Schwechat, 1981
Restaurant Salzamt, Vienna, 1982
House S., Vienna, 1983
Underground renovation (restaurant, bar, lobby, kitchen, staff rooms, banquet halls), Schwarzenberg Palace, Vienna, 1984
City Park Bridge, Vienna, 1987
General planning of U3-West (subway), Vienna, 1988
Kurhaus, Baden-Baden, Germany, 1988
Store Arcadia in Vienna State Opera, 1988
Apartment Building Petrusgasse, Vienna, 1989
Housing Wien Ottakring, 1990
Café in Museum for Applied Arts (MAK-Café), Vienna, 1993
Glazing ("greenhouse") of loggia of Vienna State Opera, 1994
Housing Brunnergasse, Perchtoldsdorf/Vienna, 1994
Rosa-Jochmann-School (elementary school), Vienna, 1994
Renovation Bank Austria, 1997

Selected Publications

"Das Wiener U-Bahn-Netz als Entwurfsproblem," *Bauforum* (January–February 1968)
"Christopher Alexander und die Wiener Moderne," *A + U* (March 1984)
"The Diction of Otto Wagner," *A + U* (July 1977)
"The Loos Idea," *A + U* (May 1978)
"On Rigour," *9H*, 8 (1989)
"A Mode for the Current Interpretation of Josef Frank," *A + U* (November 1991)
"Selbstkritik der Moderne," in *Österreichische Architektur im 20. Jahrhundert*, catalogue (1995)
"Zur Abwechslung," *Selected Writings on Architecture*, Vienna: Löcker Verlag, 1996

Further Reading

Achleitner, Friedrick, "Franks weiter wirken in der neueren Wiener Architekur," *Umbau* (August 1986)
Almaas, Ingerid Helsing, *Vienna: A Guide to Recent Architecture*, London: Ellipsis, 1995
Almaas, Ingerid Helsing, *Vienna: Objects and Rituals*, London: Ellipsis, 1997
Frampton, Kenneth (editor), *A New Wave of Austrian Architecture*, New York: Institute for Architecture and Urban Studies, 1980
Gijsberts, Pietar Jan, "Architecktuur als Achtergrond. Theorie en Werk van Hermann Czech," *De Architect* (November 1990)
Hermann Czech, Options in Architecture (exhib. cat.), London: 9H Gallery, 1987
"Hermann Czech—The Architectonic Object: A Monograph of His Works," *Werk, Bauen + Wohnen*, 6 (1996) (special issue)
Mostaedi, Arian, *Bars and Restaurants*, Barcelona: Carlos Bcoto and Josep M. Minguet, 1999
Ohta, Yasuhito, " 'Museums of the World' Series: The Ultimate in Networking 2: From Museums for Objects to Museums for Space," *Space Design*, 395/8 (August 1997)
Steiner, Dietmar, "An Amalgam of Adaptation and Rejection: On the Continuity of Viennese Architecture," *9H*, 5 (1983)
Steiner, Dietmar, "Beyond Vienna," in *Emerging European Architects*, edited by Wilfried Wang, New York: Rizzoli, and Cambridge, Massachusetts: Harvard University Press, 1988
"Vienna and 'Vienna,' " *Lotus International*, 29 (1981) (special issue)

CZECH REPUBLIC AND CZECHOSLOVAKIA

The Slavic people, from whom the Czechs and Slovaks originated, have inhabited the territory of 20th-century Czechoslovakia since the 5th century. The Tatar and Turkish invasions and occupations over previous countries did not kill the spirit of the Czech and Slovak people, who, divided for 11 centuries, were unified in the 20th century. Despite centuries of ethnic oppression, and Germanization and Hungarization by foreign rulers, the language, culture, and national identity of the Czechs and Slovaks have survived.

The new republic of Czechoslovakia arose from the ruins of the Austro-Hungarian Empire in 1918 after World War I. The accord between the Czechs and the Slovaks was ratified in the Cleveland and the Pittsburgh declarations. The founders of the republic were its first president, Tomas Masaryk, and Garrigue Milan Rastislav Stefanik. The foundation of democratic principles gave the intellectuals of the young republic a new platform of liberal ideology. Influential in the cultural sphere was the Devetsil (the Nine Powers), an avant-garde group of artists, writers, architects, musicians, and actors, started in 1920 in Prague and in 1923 in Brno. Architect Josef Havlicek was one of the founding members, and the activist writer and graphic designer Karel Tiege was the leader of the group. They published a journal and organized lectures and exhibitions. The ARDEV (the Architects of Devetsil) members maintained contact with a number of representatives of the international avant-garde and invited them to visit and lecture in Czechoslovakia. Among them were Theo van Doesburg, Laszlo Moholy-Nagy, Jacobus Johannes Pieter Oud, Walter Gropius, Le Corbusier, Amédée Ozenfant, and Adolf Loos. The visits of Loos, a native of Brno, were particularly influential. The ARDEV members, concerned with the situation of social housing, produced studies of communal housing. These ideas came from the socialist ideals of Soviet Constructivism. In 1932 Karel Tiege, who was also an art critic and a theorist of architecture, summarized the housing studies in his book *Nejmensi byt* (The Smallest Flat).

At the turn of the 20th century, Czech, Moravian, and Slovak architects contributed to Art Nouveau. Czech Art Nouveau architecture was not based merely on an endeavor to dispense with historicism and to create original and independent principles of form and decorative elements of new style. A pupil of the Viennese modernist architect Otto Wagner, Prague architect Jan Kotera (1871–1923), preferred a functional layout and volume to counter the aesthetics of eclecticism. Simultaneously, Kotera emphasized truthfulness in architecture to counter a slavish imitation of historical motifs. He required a creative search for the new. Finally, Kotera's design principles emphasized a building's purpose and the clear expression of its structural elements. In 1910 Kotera was appointed professor of architecture at the Academy of Fine Arts in Prague. His teaching was very influential on the new generation of architects in Bohemia (Czechia).

In the midst of Art Nouveau, the evolution of modern Czech architecture was characterized by a rather homogeneous design philosophy noted for its rationalism. Apart from the work of Kotera, this rationalism is seen in the designs of the rest of the pioneers of Czech modern architecture (Otakar Novotny, Josef Gocár, and Pavel Janák), Slovak modern architecture (Dusan Jurkovic, Michal Harminc, and Emil Bellus), and Moravian modern architecture (Arnost Wiesner, Jan Visek, Jiri Kroha, and Bohuslav Fuchs). Their familiarity with the progressive ideas of Otto Wagner, Adolf Loos, P.H. Berlage, Henry van de Velde, Tony Garnier, Auguste Perret, and Peter Behrens fueled the process. Kotera consistently enhanced serviceability and simplicity of form, using traditional building materials. His first significant Art Nouveau building, the Peterka House (1899–1900) on Wenceslas Square in Prague, is a mixed-use row building. Other notable Art Noveau projects include the National House in Prostejov, the Chamber of Commerce Pavilion (1908) at the exhibition in Prague, and the Municipal Museum (1906–12) in Hradec Kralove.

Kotera's significant residential architecture also includes the Laichter Apartment House (1908–09) and his own villa (1908–09), both in Prague, noteworthy for their careful fenestration and brick and stucco finishes. Similarly, in the Laichter Apartment House, the materials for the five-story structure are brick and stucco. Devoid of any embellishment, the asymmetrical composition of the building's plan and corresponding facade features an offset cantilevered mass. The restraining simplicity and the lack of decor distinguish these designs.

The Mozarteum (Urbanek Department Store, 1912–13) in Prague is a symmetrical composition separated from its neighbors by a rectangular concrete frame topped by a triangular gable. The building's dynamic facade is a precedent to Kotera's Cubist period. His 1913 entry in the competition for the monument to Zizka on Vitkov Hill in Prague represents an articulate application of the Cubist language widely accepted among Czech modernists.

The search for a new architecture preoccupied many early 20th-century architects. Social and political changes were accompanied by a search for national identity. Architects returned to their ancestral origins for elements specific to the people and their region. Architect Dusan Jurkovic (1868–1947) relied on traditional peasant wooden architecture. He was interested in the indigenous architecture of villages and in the Arts and Crafts movement. After studies in Vienna, Jurkovic's first built works were the mountain resort buildings located in Radhost and Rezek. In his Luhacovice Spa (1902–03), the half-timber construction buildings for lodging, dining, and services were designed in the Art Nouveau style. During World War I, in 1916–18, Jurkovic designed for the military command in Krakow a series of soldier cemeteries, monuments, and grave markers located in southeastern Poland. Here, inspired by the indigenous architecture, he used carved wood. A singularly important work of Jurkovic's is the Memorial to General Stefanik (1925–28) at Bradlo. Working conscientiously with the landscape, Jurkovic designed stations (1936–38) for the cable car to the Lomnicky *stit* (peak) in the High Tatras. A leader in modern architecture in Slovakia, Jurkovic designed the four stations by combining the natural features of each site with the demands of technical operations and human habitation.

Architect Vladimir Karfik (1901–96) apprenticed with both Le Corbusier (1924–25) and Frank Lloyd Wright (1927–29). From 1930 to 1946, he was the chief architect of the Bata Company, where he developed "Zlin Architecture," based on an efficient and economic construction system of a distinctive industrial image applied to a variety of building types. The Zlin Architecture construction system was used for a number of one-factory towns in Czechoslovakia and abroad. After World War II, Karfik was appointed to the new school of architecture at the Slovak Technical University in Bratislava, where he was one of the most influential professors.

The history of Czechoslovakia has been tumultuous. In 1938 Nazi Germany forced the European powers to agree to divide the country into a Czech protectorate and the Slovak Republic. After World War II, Czechoslovakia reunited, but soon the population faced another catastrophe with the communist political takeover in February 1948, when the Soviet government took over Czechoslovakia. Architects had to give up private offices to become employees in large state-controlled design institutes. Functionalism was condemned as an expression of a bourgeois cosmopolitanism.

Despite the oppressive conditions, extraordinary buildings were designed under the totalitarian regime. The 1969 International Union of Architects (UIA) Perret Award was given to the Television Tower (1963–71) on Jested Hill near Liberec, designed by Karel Hubacek. Hubacek started a groundbreaking architectural office in Liberec, Atelier SIAL, which now runs an architecture school. From this office came the project of the Department Store Maj (1973–75) in Prague, designed by Miroslav Masak (b. 1932), Martin Rajnis (b. 1944), and Johnny Eisler (b. 1946). The husband-and-wife team of Jan Sramek (1924–78) and Alena Sramkova (b. 1929) designed the Main Train Station (1972–79) and the CKD Building (1976–83), both in Prague.

The carefully sited crematorium (1967) in Bratislava by Ferdinand Milucky broke out of socialist realism. For his work Milucky was awarded the prestigious Herder Prize in 1999. A prolific designer, Jan Bahna made a number of proposals for revitalization of Bratislava, among them the Department Store Dunaj (1990–92), designed with Fedor Minarik, Lubomir Zavodny, and Martin Fabry. The young Prague architects known as the Golden Eagles, the D.A. Studio, and the Brno group of the Municipal House have also been rediscovering the heritage of Czechoslovak functionalism of the interwar period. This can be seen in the Fitness Center (1991) in Ceske Budejovice by Jiri Stritecky and Martin Krupauer, the Riviera Swimming Pool (1986–92) in Brno by Petr Hrusa, and the Rowing Race Course (1989) at Racice by Zbysek Styblo, Tomas Kulik, and Jan Louda.

Czechoslovakia had contributed significantly to the international fairs, including the all-glass pavilion built for the 1937 Paris Exhibition by Jaromir Krejcar (1895–1949). At the 1958 World Expo in Brussels, the pavilion designed by Frantisek Cubr (1911–76), Josef Hruby (1906–88), and Zdenek Pokorny (1909–84) won the award for the most visited exhibition.

Several architects have contributed to 20th-century architecture in Czechoslovakia. These include the Villa Mueller (1928–30) in Prague by Adolf Loos, the Villa Tugendhat (1928–30) in Brno by Ludwig Mies van der Rohe, the synagogue (1928–31) in Zilina by Peter Behrens, the Villa Palicka (1932) in Prague by Mart Stam, and the National Netherlands Building (1992–95), known as the Fred and Ginger, in Prague by Frank Gehry and Vladimir Milunic.

Peter Lizon

See also **Art Nouveau (Jugendstil); Loos, Adolf (Austria); Prague, Czech Republic; Tugendhat House, Brno, Czech Republic**

D

DARMSTADT, GERMANY

The Darmstadt artists' colony was founded in West Germany in 1899 by Grand Duke Ernst Ludwig von Hessen of Darmstadt, grandson of Queen Victoria and the last ruler of the formerly independent state, which became part of the German Empire in 1871. Ernst Ludwig was one of the most influential of the new patrons of contemporary architecture and design movements in the early 20th century. He was familiar with the English Arts and Crafts movement because of his frequent trips to England and his having already commissioned Baillie Scott in 1897 to design furniture and interior decorations for the dining and drawing rooms of his palace at Darmstadt. C.R. Ashbee was invited to design the light fittings, and his Guild and School of Handicraft in London was asked to make both furniture and fittings. The colony was a response to a memorandum prepared for the parliament and important local people by Alexander Kock, proprietor of a local wallpaper factory. He and others acknowledged the important role that the applied arts might play in future economic development. Aware of English developments, the memorandum included ideas for the development of homes for artists and ateliers for applied art. Seven artists were invited to form the colony on the Matildehöhe, and they were to design and direct the production of goods by other craftspeople and workshops. The outcomes were published and promoted by Kock through his journals, *Zeitschrift für Innendekoration* and *Deutsche Kunst und Dekoration*, the latter a German imitation of the English *The Studio*. Twenty-three artists worked there at various times from 1899 to 1914, when the venture ceased.

Parklike grounds (already containing a reservoir), the Russian Chapel, and a number of villas were offered by Ernst Ludwig. The colony was to be a "living and working world" and to form a public exhibition, *Ein Dokument Deutscher Kunst* (A Document of German Art), to be held in 1901. The intention was to show the public a model style of home decoration in individually designed artists' houses. The artists—Hans Christiansen, Paul Bürck, Patriz Huber, Josef Olbrich, Peter Behrens, Ludwig Habich, and Rudolf Bosselt—were given a three-year contract and a housing subsidy, although they had to pay construction costs themselves. Work started immediately, and the resulting villa suburb formed the main part of the exhibition, creating an event in the field of architecture and interior decoration that bore witness both to the individuality of the members and to the collective strength of the colony. Olbrich organized the layout of the exhibition in 1901, designing most of the buildings himself. Architecture included not only Olbrich's Ernst-Ludwig-Haus, the artistic center, and a theater but also various temporary structures and the artists' houses themselves. Writings of the artists reveal that they were concerned with aesthetic rather than functional considerations. No reference is made to machinery, mass production, or cost-effectiveness in projects undertaken by the colony. In one of three articles on the Darmstadt colony by W. Fred in *The Studio*, Behrens gave a cogent analysis of the aims of the Arts and Crafts in Germany: "Architecture is the art of building, and comprises in its name two ideas: the mastery of the practical and the art of the beautiful. There is always something exhilarating in being able to combine in one word the two ideas—that of practical utility and that of abstract beauty—which unfortunately have too often been opposed to each other." The architecture and design at the colony showed progressive unification of the practical and the beautiful, going beyond the possibilities of artistic hand production to the wider field of industry.

Built on a gradient, the two-story Ernst-Ludwig-Haus, a long, low, shedlike design with unbroken walls, dominates the other buildings. Its principal feature is the omega-shaped central doorway, with richly painted and gilded stucco decoration, flanked by Ludwig Habich's colossal statues of Adam and Eve. The two bronze figures in the door niches, goddesses of victory by Bosselt, harmonize well with Olbrich's gold decoration behind them. Internally, the upper story contained a central hall, intended for small exhibitions. To the right and left, several colonists had two rooms each, placed one behind the other, to provide useful, well-lit spaces. The lower story contained living rooms for the bachelors along with the general fencing, gymnastic, and recreational rooms.

Grouped around the atelier were the private houses, which adhere to two basic types: (1) a narrow design with large, pitched roofs and irregularly placed windows with small panes, derived largely from English Domestic Revival work, and (2) those with flat, veranda-like roofs, developed by Wagner and Hoffmann, that echo the simplicity of the Italian villa. The Villa Habich is reminiscent of Hoffmann's Villa Henneberg (1900) near Vienna, with its emphasis on the square block of the house with larger windows, sudden projection, and a flat roof extending far out over the walls. The Glückert II house is a compromise between the two types.

The exterior and interior decoration witness the diversity and richness of Olbrich's vocabulary, in which he repeats linear border patterns and mold forms derived from nature into stucco and plaster. All his designs provide interesting color harmonies and demonstrate a simplification of form, tending toward geometry, but all bear the hallmark of quality, craftsmanship, and respect for materials. The first story of Olbrich's own house had glazed tiles on the facade.

Behrens designed his own small villa, employing a compact plan. The exterior shows the free interpretation of vernacular forms combined with an attempt at structural rationalism that contrasts with the picturesqueness of Olbrich. He employed brick and green terra-cotta tiles to invoke the vernacular of the Baltics, which he admired. Internally, curvilinear echoes of Art Nouveau are outweighed by simplified forms that are more in accordance with contemporary Viennese trends. The pavement running between the artists' houses is designed in a black-and-white linear geometric pattern, formed out of small flat cobbles and serving to unite the individually designed villas.

The exhibition of 1901 was a financial failure, and the critical reception was mixed, although it was recognized as an important point in the development of German design. A less ambitious exhibition followed in 1904, responding to the criticism that objects were too expensive and sometimes "eccentric." Olbrich created a "group of three houses" representing average homes. Here, modest shapes, simple motifs, and plainer materials recalled vernacular work.

The colony was represented at the Paris Exhibition of 1900, at Turin in 1902, and at St. Louis in 1904. In 1907, Olbrich designed the Hochzeitsturm (Wedding Tower) and the Municipal Exhibition Halls as the crowning feature of the Mathildenhöhe site. The motif of a five-fingered hand raised in benediction, with its asymmetrically placed banded windows running around the corners, is thought to have influenced Gropius' design for the Chicago Tribune Tower competition entry of 1922. Architects such as Behrens demonstrated their talents in designing architecture, furniture, silver, jewelry, glass, and porcelain. Behrens left the colony in 1903 and, as was the case of many others who had begun their careers at Darmstadt, enjoyed national and international acclaim.

A final exhibition was organized at Darmstadt in 1914. Albin Müller, who took over the artistic management after Olbrich's death, designed new buildings and facilities specifically for this purpose. These were destroyed in 1944.

HILARY J. GRAINGER

Further Reading

Bott, Gerhard, Ingrid Dennerlein, and Carl Benno Heller, *Kunsthandwerk um 1900: Jugendstil; Art Nouveau; Modern Style; Nieuwe Kunst*, Darmstadt, Germany: Roether, 1965; 2nd edition, revised by Carl Benno Heller, 1976

Ein Dokument deutscher Kunst: Darmstadt 1901–1976, 6 vols., Darmstadt, Germany: Roether, 1977–79

DE CARLO, GIANCARLO 1919–

Architect, planner, and writer, Italy

Architect and planner, educator and editor, writer and speaker, thinker and innovator, Giancarlo De Carlo is well known in his native Italy and abroad as a founder of Team X and as a pioneer in participatory architecture. Born in Genoa, the son of a naval engineer, he studied structural engineering at Milan Polytechnic from 1939 to 1943. On graduation, he was called for naval service to Greece. In Milan from 1943 to 1945, De Carlo was active in the Resistance movement and in anti-Fascist circles together with Giuseppi Pagano, Franco Albini, and other members of the Movimento di Unità Proletaria. At the same time, his interest in architecture was stimulated by Le Corbusier's *Oeuvre complete* and Alfred Roth's *Die Neue Architektur*. Following the end of World War II, De Carlo published critical works on Le Corbusier and William Morris. From 1948 to 1949, De Carlo studied at the Venice School of Architecture and collaborated with Albini on the development plan for Reggio Emilia.

De Carlo's career in both architecture and city planning was launched in the 1950s, together with his expanding intellectual circles, the latter including Carlo Doglio, Delfino Insolera, and Italo Calvino. In addition, he was briefly a member of the editorial board of *Casabella*. A participant in CIAM (Congrès Internationaux d'Architecture Moderne), De Carlo became known as a modernist who honored the heritage of the past.

Few architects who emerged in the generation following World War II have been as prescient in perceiving the problems and possible solutions in contemporary architecture and urbanism. Both part of and counter to the mainstream, De Carlo has succeeded because of his deeply embedded historical consciousness and his total immersion in the problems of contemporary society. A master craftsman, De Carlo harbors enormous respect for technological inventions and the design principles of modernism, including its utopian goals. Nonetheless, he has protested against the rigidity of the Modern movement and the International Style. In his multifaceted career, however, his name will inevitably be linked with Urbino, the hill town in the Marches, where Renaissance architecture reached its summit in Federigo da Montefelto's Ducal Palace. His work in Urbino is ongoing, beginning with his master plan and now clearly visible in his buildings for the University of Urbino.

When international modernism was at its zenith, De Carlo condemned the preoccupation with style divorced from the social realities of the day. While remaining open to the enriched possibilities of Postmodernism, he decried its superficiality, even frivolity. In fact, he believed that architecture was too important to be limited to the narrow domain of architects. Rather, it is the architect's "responsibility" to humanity that constitutes the basis of their life and work. Evidence of this creed is found in De Carlo's housing complexes, where he encourages participation between architect and users, a type of collaborative planning fully cognizant of the needs of inhabitants. Mindful of the inhumanity—and severe lack—of postwar housing, with its disregard for scale, social realities, and historical circumstances, he challenged the idea of "minimum living standard" as set forth at the CIAM conference in Frankfort (1929). Instead, De Carlo advocated an architecture based on current problems, one that considered the urban context as the primary force.

Still, a paradigm for architect/client collaboration is the Village Matteotti (1969–74) in the industrial town of Terni, 60 miles northeast of Rome. Meetings with the steelworkers and their families led to a continuous partnership in planning with the architect, who assumed the role of educator as well as designer and builder. Here, every phase of the project was considered in conjunction with the users, who were directly involved in all phases of construction. When completed, the Village Matteotti raised the standard for workers' housing. Unlike Terni, the housing at Mazzorbo, begun in 1950 on an island in the Venetian lagoon, focused primarily on morphological considerations. Because of the distinct identity of Mazzorbo's residents, De Carlo emphasized the unique setting and a strong vernacular tradition in his effort to design new forms that evoke the past by articulating it and enriching it with the use of local color and variety in building types and plans.

Beginning with his town plan (1958–64), De Carlo's work in Urbino continues to this day. It was the Collegio del Colle, the dormitories for the University of Urbino (1962–66), that initiated the dialogue between the old city and its surroundings. Additions to the college from 1973 created patterns that conform to the topography of the landscape, always simulating the memory of earlier times and fostering a greater sense of community among the students.

Many of De Carlo's proposals have since come to fruition: restoring the Mercatale, reviving the old approach from Rome, and providing access to students and tourists along Francesco di Giorgio's 15th-century ramp (discovered while restoring the 19th-century theater) leading to the Ducal Palace. Abandoned buildings have been rehabilitated and converted to modern facilities. Brilliant insertions in the town fabric are demonstrated by the glass-enclosed hemicycle of the School of Education, which seems to be carved from the surrounding walls, and the courtyard of the Law School, its domes illuminating the spaces below. Contradictions between inside and outside contribute to the continuity between old and new.

Aside from appointments as visiting professor at Yale University, the Massachusetts Institute of Technology, Cornell University, and the University of California at Berkeley, De Carlo was professor in the schools of architecture at the Universities of Venice and Genoa. In 1976 he founded the ILAUD (International Laboratory for Architecture and Urban Design). This forum of international students meets annually in an Italian city, such as Urbino or Siena, to develop projects for the adaptive reuse of old buildings, such as the Hospital of Santa Maria della Scala in Siena, the renewal of industrial areas in Genoa, or new interventions in the Arsenal in Venice. In addition to these pursuits, De Carlo, always a prolific writer, founded *Space and Society*, an Italian/English quarterly journal that addresses global architectural topics.

Since 1995 De Carlo has entered competitions for the School of Architecture in Venice and for the redesign of three piazzas in Trieste. Recent projects include university facilities, civic works, and conversions in Pavia, Siena, Catania, the Republic of San Marino, Lastre a Signe, Pistoia, Venice Lido, and Urbino. The latter includes the "Data of Francesco di Giorgio," and the restoration and transformation of a city observatory into a multimedia center. It is little wonder that De Carlo has been made an honorary citizen of Urbino and that, on the occasion of his 80th birthday in 1999, he was given the key to the city of Venice.

A CIAM delegate from 1952 to 1959, a member of Team X, and an honorary member of the American Institute of Architects from 1975, the American Academy for Arts and Sciences from 1978, and the Royal Institute of British Architects from 1981, De Carlo has been the recipient of prestigious awards, including the Patrick Abercrombie Prize (1963), the Wolf Prize (1988), the Gold Medal of the City of Milan (1995), and the Grand Prix "A/mbiente" in Buenos Aires (1999). In addition, De Carlo has been awarded the *doctor honoris causa* from the Oslo School of Architecture, the Heriot-Watt University in Edinburgh, the Université Catholique-Louvain, the Université de Genève, the Buenos Aires School of Architecture, and the Faculty of Humanities in Catania. On the occasion of receiving the Royal Gold Medal of the RIBA (1993), De Carlo spoke of "promising signs . . . emerging from our present state of confusion." Proving to be both realist and idealist, he hopes that "perhaps organizing and giving form to the three-dimensional physical space will become architecture's raison d'être once more."

NAOMI MILLER

Biography

Born in Genoa, Italy, 12 December 1919. Studied structural engineering, Milan Polytechnic; degree in engineering 1943; attended the Institute of Architecture, Venice 1948–49; degree in architecture 1949. Private practice, Milan from 1950; member, Team X 1952–59; member, Italian Group of CIAM 1952–59; assistant editor, *Casabella* magazine 1954–56; founder, ILAUD (International Laboratory of Architecture and Urban Design) 1975; director, *Spazio e Società*, Milan; director, ILAUD. Professor of urban design, Institute of Architecture, Venice from 1955; professor of architectural composition, University of Genoa from 1983; and visiting professor, Yale University, Massachusetts Institute of Technology, Cornell University, and the University of California from 1966 to mid-1970s. Fellow, Royal Institute of British Architects from 1981; honorary member, American Academy of Arts and Sciences from 1978; honorary member from 1975, American Institute of Architects; member, National Academy of San Luca, Rome. Royal Gold Medal, Royal Institute of British Architects 1993.

Selected Works

Master Plan, Reggio Emilia (with Franco Albini), 1948
Spontaneous Architecture Display, Triennale, Milan, 1950
INA-Casa Apartment Buildings, Arona, Baveno, Stresa, 1951
Master Plan, Urbino, 1964
University of Dublin (competition project; incomplete; with Armando Barp), 1964
Collegio del Colle, Free University, Urbino, 1962–66; addition, 1981
Matteotti Quarter (reconstruction; incomplete), Terni, 1974
Development Plan, University of Pavia, 1975
Faculties of Jurisprudence and Education, Free University, Urbino, 1976
Development Plan, Mazzorbo, Venice, 1979
Teatro Sanzio (reconstruction), Urbino, 1979
Development Plan for the San Miniato District, Siena, 1979
Istituto Statale d'Arte, Urbino, 1982
Development Plan for the Breda District, Pistoia, 1985

Selected Publications

Questioni di architettura e urbanistica, 1965
Urbino: la storia di una città e il piano della sua evoluzione urbanistica, 1966; as *Urbino: The History of a City and Plans for Its Development*, translated by Loretta Schaeffer Guarda, 1970
An Architecture of Participation, 1972
Gli spiriti dell' architettura, 1992; 2nd edition, 1999
Nelle città del mondo, 2nd edition, 1998
Io e la Sicilia, 1999

Further Reading

De Carlo is a prolific writer, and important accounts of his work appear in books that he authored or edited. Numerous articles are found in architectural periodicals from 1977 on and in annual ILAUD (International Laboratory for Architecture and Urban Design) reports. The only monograph in English is that by Benedict Zucchi.

Brunetti, Fabrizio, and Fabrizio Gesi, *Giancarlo De Carlo*, Florence: Alinea, 1981
De Carlo, Giancarlo, "Legitimizing Architecture: The Revolt and Frustration of the School of Architecture," *Forum* 23, no. 1 (1972)
Mioni, Angela, and Etra Connie Occhialini (editors), *Giancarlo De Carlo: immagini e frammenti*, Milan: Electa, 1995
Rossi, Lamberto, *Giancarlo De Carlo: architetture*, Milan: Mondadori, 1988
Zucchi, Benedict, *Giancarlo De Carlo*, Oxford and Boston: Butterworth Architecture, 1992

DE KLERK, MICHEL 1884–1923

Architect, the Netherlands

Michel de Klerk, in collaboration with his colleagues and in his own brief, but prolific, practice, was the creative inspiration for the Amsterdam School, a name first given to a group of young architects advocating an Expressive modernism in the years around 1915. Unlike other early Modern movements, the Amsterdam School was not an organized movement. It had no manifesto, journal, or official spokesperson. Although de Klerk wrote almost nothing, he was widely recognized as the leader of the movement through the aesthetic and visionary examples of his competition entries, built projects, graphic design, and furniture design.

During a brief period, corresponding to the years of his independent practice from 1911 until his death in 1923, the Amsterdam School radically changed the city's urban landscape. These architects, including de Klerk, J.M. van der May, Piet Kramer, and others, contributed an architecture that expressed the personal aesthetic visions of the architects, advanced the conditions of modernity, and contributed to an extension of Amsterdam's urban, architectural, and construction traditions.

Working-class housing in Amsterdam became de Klerk's most well known and projects. Especially important are his three housing blocks (1913–15, 1915–16, and 1917–20) in the Spaarndammerburt, a west Amsterdam working-class district, built for the Eigen Haard (Our Hearth) housing association. The third block, *Het Ship* (The Ship), is the most widely recognized and has become the iconic project of the Amsterdam School. The working-class housing for the De Daggerad (The Dawn) Association in Amsterdam South (1919–22) in collaboration with Piet Kramer is also widely recognized.

Born in Amsterdam's Jewish district to a family of 21 children, de Klerk grew up in poverty after his father died in 1886. Apparently more interested in drawing than in school, his work was accidentally discovered by the architect Eduard Cuypers, nephew of Petrus J.H. Cuypers (1827–1921), the famous neo-Gothic architect of Amsterdam's two monumental 19th-century buildings, the Rijksmuseum (1876–85) and Amsterdam Central Railway Station (1882–89). At age 14, de Klerk entered Cuypers's office as an apprentice in 1898 and remained until 1910 with interruptions for travel to England, Germany, and Scandinavia after 1906. While in Cuypers's employment, he also attended evening school in the Architecture Department of the Industrial School of the Society for the Working Class. Although there is little evidence recording de Klerk's influence in Cuypers's office, he gained increasing responsibility, supervising the building of major projects and preparing designs for publication in Cuypers's journal, *Het Huis—Oud en Nieuw* (The House—Old and New). He began his independent practice in 1911, soon after his marriage to Lea Jessurun, an administrative assistant in Cuypers's office. Several of de Klerk's initial projects—the second prize entry to the Water Tower Competition (1912), his collaborative work with the Kramer and the architect Van der May on the Scheepvaarthuis (1912–16) and the first housing block in Spaarndammerburt (1913–14)—became lasting inspirations for the later work of the architects of the Amsterdam School.

De Klerk's architectural projects occurred in two very different settings: urban and suburban. His suburban work, influenced by a variety of vernacular and folk sources—Dutch farmhouses, Scandinavian wood buildings, and German half-timber houses—were joined with his inventive combination of building plan, facade and detail into designs for picturesque cottages and villas. Few, however, were built. Exceptions are the Bileken House (1914) in Hilversum and the Barendsen House (1923) in Aalsmeer. These are far less fantastical, however, than the villas designed by other architects associated with the Amsterdam School. Just as his suburban work revealed inventive combinations of sources, his urban projects, especially his working-class housing, flowed from equally diverse sources but were formed within the context both of Amsterdam's urban traditions and of the emergence of the modern city.

The clients for de Klerk's most important urban housing were the housing associations Eigen Haard and De Daggerad. Formed after the adoption of the Dutch Housing Act of 1901 and Amsterdam's adoption of the first municipal building code in 1905, these associations not only sponsored the construction of working-class housing but also encouraged participation by architects to contribute to the aesthetic qualities of Amsterdam and the living conditions of the working class. With his projects in the Spaarndammerburt and in Amsterdam South, de Klerk provided a counterpoint to the emerging dogma of modern housing and modern urbanism, which culminated in the Congrès Internationaux d'Architecture Moderne's Athens Charter of 1932, advocating the functional city. Like his suburban cot-

Freedom Lane Housing (Vrijheidslaan Housing, 1921), Amsterdam, by Michel de Klerk

tages and villas, his stylistic sources for urban housing were far-reaching, including the English Arts and Crafts, exotic motifs from the then Dutch Indonesian colonies, and other folk traditions. However, these are extracted from their rural sources and compressed into the traditional urban block structure of Amsterdam's expansion plans. In contrast to emerging conventions of modern housing and modern urbanism, he submerged repetitive individual housing units into larger compositions of formal parts derived from his personal interpretations of local context. Finally, he applied Amsterdam's bricklaying traditions to the elaborate detailing of the street wall. Rooflines, roof drains, doorways, windows, mailboxes, and stairwells became sculptural celebrations of everyday urban life of the street and formed the visual symbols of collective residences of the working class. None of de Klerk's housing projects referred even indirectly to Amsterdam's mannerist architectural traditions. Instead, he, along with his colleagues in the Amsterdam School, expanded the 17th-century rings of canals and elegant merchants' houses by building equivalent modern symbols of working-class urban identity.

The expressionist and anticlassical stance of de Klerk's projects explains his disappearance from modern architectural history. Modernism found its lineage from Karl Friedrich Shinkel's Berlin, composed of the classical layered orders of column and beam, to Hendrik P. Berlage's masonry arcade and rationalistic pure skeleton building, expressed potently in the Amsterdam Stock Exchange. De Klerk's alternative Modern expressionism, like Bruno Taut in Berlin, became only a footnote in the treatises of modernism. Only since the 1980's have de Klerk's projects been reexamined to find the evidence of not only a parallel stream of anticlassical Modern architecture but also a vital modern urbanism that favored local conditions, context, and expressive urban form.

RICHARD DAGENHART

See also **Amsterdam, Netherlands; Amsterdam School; Arts and Crafts Movement; Berlage, Hendrik Petrus (the Netherlands); Taut, Bruno (Germany)**

Biography

Born in Amsterdam, the Netherlands, 24 November 1884. Apprenticed in the office of Eduard Cuypers 1898–1910. Attended evening school in architecture at the Industrial School for the Society for the Working Class during the period 1898–1906. Traveled to England, Scandinavia, and Germany 1906–10. Married Lea Jessurun 1910. Independent practice in architecture, graphic design, furniture design, and portraiture 1911–23. Died 24 November 1923.

Selected Works

Scheepvaarthuis, Amsterdam, 1916
Spaarndammerburt Housing for the Eigen Haard Association, Amsterdam 1920
Bileken House, Hilversum (severely altered), 1914
Rijksacademie (State Academy of Fine Arts), Competition Entry, 1918
De Daggerad Association Housing, Amsterdam, 1922
Facades for Amsellaan Housing, Amsterdam, 1923
De Hoop, Royal Rowing and Sailing Club, Amsterdam (constructed 1923–24 posthumously)
Barendsen House, Aalsmeer (constructed 1923–25 posthumously)

Further Reading

Bock, Manfred, Sigrid Johannisse, and Vladimir Stissi, *Michel de Klerk: Bouwmeester en tekenaar van de amsterdamse school, 1884–1923*, Rotterdam: NAI, 1997; as *Michel de Klerk: Architect and Artist of the Amsterdam School, 1884–1923*, 1997
Casciato, Maristella (editor), *The Amsterdam School*, Rotterdam: 010 Publishers, 1996
Stieber, Nancy, *Housing Design and Society in Amsterdam: Reconfiguring Urban Order and Identity, 1900–1920*, Chicago: University of Chicago Press, 1998

DE STIJL

De Stijl architecture offers dynamic conceptions of spatial relationships in reaction to conventionally static, grounded architecture from the beginning of the 20th century. Spatial innovation, based on principles developed by the De Stijl painter and writer Piet Mondrian from the philosophical-mathematical writings of M.H. Schoenmaekers, is clearly evident in three iconic De Stijl projects from the mid–1920s: Theo van Doesburg and Cornelis van Eesteren's *Maison d'Artiste* and *Maison Particulière* and Gerrit Rietveld's Schröder House in Utrecht, the Netherlands. These modernist touchstones represent the synthesis of ideal universal projections of space and everyday manipulations of life embedded within art. Architecture proved to be the ideal art form to represent De Stijl through its ability to transform space, surface, universal ideas, particular situations, exterior, and interior.

De Stijl as a collective modernist movement remains difficult to codify. Begun as a virtual assemblage of avant-garde artists based in the Netherlands, it was founded and controlled by the painter, writer, and architect Theo van Doesburg (1883–1931). To characterize De Stijl as a truly united group or school of artists and architects is to misrepresent the vicissitudes of a movement whose members were never in the same place at the same time. Van Doesburg, the proselytizer for De Stijl, presented it to the world as a close-knit, avant-garde collaborative unit of like-minded individuals with common goals.

The work of De Stijl was disseminated primarily through its periodical, *De Stijl*, published irregularly from 1917 to 1929 and in 1932 as a memorial issue for van Doesburg. Van Doesburg, as its editor, published art, architecture, graphic design, essays, and manifestos for an increasingly international audience. *De Stijl* as a collection of diverse projects coalesced under van Doesburg in a desire to achieve international unity through "the sign of art."

The clearest way to distill De Stijl is to examine its ideas made evident in painting, sculpture, graphic design, and, most significantly, architecture. Mondrian and van Doesburg strove to achieve an ideal unity through projecting the tension of opposites—a dialectical formation on its way to achieving synthesis through articulating and then annulling issues of the individual versus the universal, nature versus spirit, particular versus general. This was to be achieved through reform of past cultural conditions via *Nieuwe Beelding*, or new forming (Neoplasticism). Van Doesburg attempted radical change through De Stijl, derived from the international conflicts of World War I. He strove for universal synthesis rather than Dutch nationalism, as evidenced in "Manifesto 1 of 'De Stijl,' 1918," published in Dutch, French, German, and English as "De Stijl," "Le Styl," "Der Stil," and "The Style" De Stijl set out to negate the concept of style in a universal language through communicative art and architecture, and the concise format of the manifesto was its primary textual vehicle. Van Doesburg contended that art (including architecture) embodies the spiritual force of life. He scrutinized the historical development of art as culminating "inevitably" in De Stijl as "The Style," to synthesize all previous styles into a homogeneous purity. His ideological construct, looking simultaneously back into history and forward to a new art, codified polar opposites to create beauty in tension and synthesis. His manner of carrying out this process demanded collective work in all the arts, an ultimately unfulfilled desire.

The painter Piet Mondrian (1872–1944) was De Stijl's spiritual leader, providing its philosophical foundation (Neoplasticism) and language for representing pure relations of contrasts via horizontal-vertical oppositions and utilizing the primary colors red, blue, and yellow with the noncolors black, white, and gray. Beyond his neoplastic painting, Mondrian projected spatial architectural compositions and created rigorous interior designs for his own studio spaces in Paris and New York. Mondrian championed the development of De Stijl architecture, typically praising most built and unbuilt projects.

An early, perhaps the first, De Stijl work of architecture, appearing in its magazine in 1919, was the Villa Henny in Huis ter Heide, the Netherlands, by Robert van't Hoff (1887–1979), designed in 1915. This often published reinforced-concrete house was inspired by the residential architecture of Frank Lloyd Wright, whom van't Hoff visited in the United States in 1914. The rectilinear, flat-roofed house features white planar surfaces with gray bands of trim, standing aloof from its natural setting. Interior rooms project symmetrically off a central space, a theme later transformed by van Doesburg. Other early De Stijl projects typically involved interior alterations of existing rooms, such as a children's bedroom by Vilmos Huszár from 1920 and a doctor's clinic by Gerrit Rietveld from 1922, demonstrating a process of re-forming the past on the way to ideal De Stijl architecture.

The formal debut of De Stijl architecture took place in 1923 under van Doesburg at Léonce Rosenberg's *Galerie L'Effort Moderne* in Paris. This exhibition, *Les Architectes du Groupe "de Styl,"* displayed drawings, photographs, and models by van Doesburg, Cornelis van Eesteren, Vilmos Huszár, Willem van Leusden, J.J.P. Oud, Gerrit Rietveld, Jan Wils, and (surprisingly) Ludwig Mies van der Rohe, who contributed a photograph of his 1922 Glass Skyscraper model. This grouping of De Stijl architects (which at this time also included the Russian artist-architect El Lissitzky) indicates the expansive assembly of international members for the movement. Two projects attracting great attention from critics and later widely disseminated through publications and other exhibitions were the *Maison d'Artiste* (Artist's House) and the *Maison Particulière* (Private House). Both were developed by van Doesburg in collaboration with van Eesteren (1897–1988) specifically for the Paris exhibition. The *Maison d'Artiste* and the *Maison Particulière*, to be built of "iron and glass" and "concrete and glass," respectively, provided literal and figurative models for future construction. As siteless, dynamic, spatial objects, each contains asymmetrical volumes rotated about central voids, projecting primary-colored planes as floors, walls, and ceilings into surrounding space. Van Doesburg constructed a model of the *Maison d'Artiste* and photographed it from below as an object suspended in space to display its ability to confront space and time and to expose its "sixth facade." Van Doesburg prepared axonometric "counter-construction" drawings for the *Maison Particulière*. These drawings emphasize the oblique relationships between pure planes and convey the abstract qualities of infinite extension without grounding them to a fixed vanishing point as in perspective. These axonometric constructions sought to liberate space and surface from earthly associations, or, as van Doesburg wrote in point 10 of his manifesto "Towards Plastic Architecture," "This aspect, so to speak, challenges the force of gravity in nature."

The furniture maker and architect Gerrit Rietveld (1888–1964), an early De Stijl participant who contributed a jewelry store design and assisted as a model builder for the Paris exhibition, produced the most significant work of De Stijl architecture, the Schröder House in Utrecht, completed in 1924. Rietveld's *Red Blue Chair*, initially produced without color in 1918, successfully mediated the transfer of De Stijl principles from painting to architecture. This seemingly simple wood chair, painted in the primary colors plus black in 1922 or 1923, is simultaneously articulated and synthetic and allows space to flow through it uninterrupted. It, as well as the 1923 Maison Projects, inspired the De Stijl principles demonstrated in the Schröder House. This tiny two-story structure provides rich flexibility in its contrasting relations of elements and sliding partitions, allowing for closed or open living arrangements. As a house of options, or a cabinet to live in, it functions pragmatically and abstractly, attached to a series of row houses and opened wide to the surrounding environment. Although constructed primarily with traditional timber frame and brick in-fill, it appears as an a-material, innovative, anti-box in its exterior photographed images and its projecting pinwheel plan. Its innovatively detailed connections and built-in furnishings emphasized the house as a total work of art. Rietveld drifted away from his associations with van Doesburg and De Stijl after the Schröder House but continued a long career building throughout the Netherlands by developing architectural relationships from De Stijl.

J.J.P. Oud (1890–1963), an urban architect practicing in Rotterdam, published essays and projects in the periodical *De Stijl* but held a tenuous relationship to De Stijl and van Doesburg after 1921. Van Doesburg collaborated with Oud on several residential projects, adding stained glass and painted color patterns to Oud's architecture. Oud was simultaneously a pragmatist and an experimenter, as evident in his Wright-inspired Purmerend Factory project from 1919, a large industrial concrete volume nestled into an office area with a complex shallow-space facade. As a socially minded architect for the city of Rotterdam, he designed several expedient public housing projects there. His Spangen Housing (1919–21) and Tusschendijken Housing (1921–24), both displayed in the 1923 De Stijl exhibition, achieved efficiency and economy through standardization and use of brick as an everyday exterior material while including horizontal-vertical articulations of corner elements related to spatial De Stijl ideas. His Kiefhoek Housing (1925–29) contained a-material primary-color elements as a type of De Stijl village. His temporary Superintendent's Office (1923) for Oud-Mathenesse Housing was a De Stijl folly in primary colors and cubic forms, derived from the paintings of Mondrian and van Doesburg. Oud's Cafe de Unie, built in Rotterdam in 1925, was bombed during World War II and reproduced at another location in the city in 1986, signifying its architectural stature conveyed through publications. Its facade, a billboard manifesto advertising De Stijl, displays a low-relief composition of primary colors with integrated signage.

After 1924, van Doesburg and Mondrian clashed over appropriation of the diagonal into the rectilinear compositions characteristic of De Stijl painting. Mondrian developed his diamond compositions, rotating the frames of his paintings 45 degrees while retaining the horizontal-vertical relationships of the rectilinear elements themselves to emphasize extension of the boundaries of the artwork beyond the inconsequential oblique frame. Van Doesburg, on the other hand, began at this time to invert Mondrian's strategy, employing diagonal relationships of lines and planes within an orthogonal frame. Influenced by these interrelated yet oppositional developments, van Doesburg reified their spatial implications in two rooms of the Cafe Aubette (dawn), constructed within an 18th-century building in Strassbourg, France, between 1926 and 1928. The complex commission was carried out in conjunction with Hans Arp and Sophie Täuber Arp, who designed other rooms. This ultimate fusion of art and life using De Stijl ideas in combination with off-the-shelf materials, furniture, and lighting fixtures resulted in an ideal De Stijl forum. By re-forming the spaces of this nightclub with striking manifestations of line and color in relation to the bodily activity of dancing and the projection of cinema, van Doesburg temporarily accomplished De Stijl synthesis through unity from the tension of opposites. The Small Dance Hall's primary-color panels on the walls and ceiling align orthographically with the rectilinear room, resulting in a clear fusion of surface and space. Enacting van Doesburg's transition into "elementarism" and influenced by the oblique "counter-construction" drawings from the *Maison Particulière*, his Cinema-Dance Hall features diagonal color patterns extending through the room's corners to dismantle the confines of the space. In the Cafe Aubette, reconstructed in 1995, the projection of cinema and the gestures of bodies in motion establish a kinetic dialogue between art and life. Synthesizing architecture, painting, sculpture, and applied arts as *Gesamtkunstwerk*, or total work of art, van Doesburg created the ultimate De Stijl space and representation of modernism: a dialectically constructed avant-garde cafe-salon interiorized as spatial art rather than occupying rooms with art hung on the walls.

Van Doesburg built a simple house for himself and his wife, Nelly, in Meudon-Val-Fleury, outside of Paris, between 1927 and 1930. Succumbing to tuberculosis, he died in a sanatorium in Davos, Switzerland, in 1931. De Stijl as an avant-garde movement unfortunately expired with van Doesburg. Subsequent developments of modernist and contemporary architecture have been crucially reliant on the spatial conceptions of the De Stijl architects, from the works of Le Corbusier and Marcel Breuer to Peter Eisenman, John Hejduk, and MVRDV. De Stijl architecture engaged space and surface in a simultaneously elemental and universal manner, proposing meaning and spirituality within abstraction and "pure" relations of forms.

MARK STANKARD

See also **Color; Glass Skyscraper (1920–21); Lissitzky, El (Russia); Mies van der Rohe, Ludwig (Germany); Oud, J.J.P. (Netherlands); Rietveld, Gerrit (Netherlands); Schröder-Schräder House, Utrecht, Netherlands; van Doesburg, Theo (Netherlands)**

Further Reading

Writings on De Stijl seldom focus specifically on architecture, typically integrating multiple aspects of De Stijl. Many more books and articles on De Stijl, Piet Mondrian, Theo van Doesburg, Gerrit Rietveld, J. J. P. Oud, Vilmos Huszar, and other De Stijl participants, from the time period itself to the present, are available in several languages.

Barr, Alfred H., Jr., *De Stijl 1917–1928*, New York: Museum of Modern Art, 1952

Blotkamp, Carel, et al., editors, *De Stijl, the Formative Years*, translated by Charlotte I. Loeb and Arthur L. Loeb, Cambridge, Massachusetts: MIT Press, 1986

Boekraad, Cees, Flip Bool, and Herbert Henkels, editors, *De Nieuwe beelding in de architectuur; Neo Plasticism in Architecture: De Stijl*, Delft: Delft University Press, and Den Haag: Haags Gemeentemuseum, 1983

Bois, Yve-Alain, "The De Stijl Idea," *Art in America* 70, no. 10 (November 1992)

De Stijl 1 and *De Stijl 2* (Amsterdam: Athenaeum, 1968). Reprint of the periodical *De Stijl*, edited by Van Doesburg, from 1917–1929, and 1932.

Friedman, Mildred, editor, *De Stijl 1917–1931: Visions of Utopia*, Minneapolis, Minnesota: Walker Art Center, and New York: Abbeville Press, 1982

Jaffé, Hans Ludwig C., *De Stijl, 1917–1931; the Dutch Contribution to Modern Art*, Amsterdam: Meulenhoff, and London: Tiranti, 1956

Michelson, Annette, "De Stijl, Its Other Face: Abstraction and Cacaphony, or What Was the Matter with Hegel?" *October* 22 (Autumn 1982)

Mondrian, Piet, *The New Art—The New Life: The Collected Writings of Piet Mondrian*, edited and translated by Harry Holtzman and Martin S. James, Boston: G.K. Hall, 1986

Troy, Nancy J., *The De Stijl Environment*, Cambridge, Massachusetts: MIT Press, 1983

DECONSTRUCTIVISM

Deconstructivism is a theoretical term that emerged within art, architecture, and the philosophical literature of the late 1980s and early 1990s. The movement refers mainly to an architectural language of displaced, distorted, angular forms, often set within conflicting geometries. With origins in the ideas of French philosopher Jacques Derrida (*b.* 1930), deconstructivism generated an iconoclastic style of the avant-garde whose principle architectural exponents included Coop Himmelb(l)au, Zaha Hadid, Behnisch and Partners, Bernard Tschumi, Peter Eisenman, Morphosis, Rem Koolhaas, Daniel Libeskind, and Frank Gehry, among others. Curiously, while these and other architects have continued to practice in a related formal language, the terms once used to describe their work have long since dropped out of usage.

Deconstruction in the field of architecture owes its origins to two parallel events that took place in 1988. One was an exhibition titled "Deconstructivist Architecture" held at the Museum of Modern Art in New York City; the second was a conference titled "Deconstruction in Art and Architecture" held at the Tate Gallery in London. The different terms employed by the organizers to describe their respective events highlighted their differing trajectories. The exhibition in New York—originally to be called "Neo-Constructivist Architecture" with reference to a revival of the Russian stylistic movement from the early part of the 20th century—highlighted the formal language emerging in the work of a group of avant-garde architects, including several of those aforementioned. The event in London, meanwhile, stressed the connection to Derridian philosophy.

Deconstruction emerged out of the poststructuralist tradition of literary theory, which, in opposition to structuralism, stressed the slippage and fluctuation of meaning that is always at work in the process of linguistic and cultural signification. Derrida first used the term to refer to a mode of inquiry that sought to expose the paradoxes and value-laden hierarchies that exist within the discourse of Western metaphysics. Although deconstruction dismantles or analyses such concepts, it was never meant to be nihilistic, according to Derrida. Rather, it serves as an epistemological method of engagement with the world. Although Derrida once described the philosopher as a "would-be architect," always searching for secure foundations on which to construct an argument, the links between the philosophical term and architecture are clearly metaphorical. Derrida's sense of the word is a method and not a style.

The connection between Deconstruction and architecture stemmed largely from Bernard Tschumi's use of Derrida's ideas in his competition-winning 1983 design for the Parc de la Vilette in Paris. Tschumi proposed a nonhierarchical grid of dispersed pavilions instead of a more traditional building, echoing deconstruction's own challenging of linguistic arrangements. Later, Derrida himself collaborated with Peter Eisenman in the design of a small section of the landscaping of the park, and he subsequently wrote a commentary on Tschumi's project, reading the random play of forms as metaphors for the aleatory or contingent play of meaning in language. Derrida significantly referred in this piece to the "architecture of architecture." In other words, if thinking about architecture is itself already a social construct, one might conclude that what needs to be deconstructed are not the architectural forms themselves but rather the theoretical assumptions that lie behind the design of those forms.

In effect, there were two competing events claiming Deconstructivism as their own; it either referred to a purely stylistic phenomenon, or it referred to a broad intellectual shift that encompassed not only philosophy but all the visual arts. As Bernard Tschumi noted, "The multiple interpretations that multiple architects [have given] to deconstruction [have become] more multiple than deconstruction's theory of multiple readings could ever have hoped."

UFA Palast: Dresden, Germany (1998), designed by Coop Himmelb(l)au of Austria
© Gerald Zugmann. Photo courtesy of Coop Himmelb(l)au

The Museum of Modern Art's exhibition might have more suitably retained the term "Neo-Constructivism," even if the architecture that had inspired the movement also included the work of Suprematist architects, such as Kazimir Malevich. There is clear evidence of a revival of interest in these forms—stripped of their social and political connotations—within the formal experimentations during the 1980s at the Architectural Association in London by architects such as Zaha Hadid of Iraq. Certainly, as far as many architects were concerned, the connections with philosophy remained a side issue in what was essentially a stylistic movement that did much to break the stranglehold of the harsh rectilinearity of modernist architecture (derived from International Style, a movement incidentally also spurred by the Museum of Modern Art, New York, earlier in the century) but that nonetheless remained within the trajectory of modernism. As such, the deconstructivist style in architecture relates to what art historian and critic Hal Foster has termed a postmodernism of resistance, or a rupture of formal invention or a moment of recuperation within a cyclical, historical process that leads to ever-new emergent expressions of modernisms.

Derrida himself consistently refused to articulate what, if any, connection there was between his work and the architecture of the same name. Meanwhile, Tschumi conceded that although certain philosophical ideas that dismantled concepts had become remarkable conceptual tools, they "could not address the one thing that makes the work of architects ultimately different from the work of philosophers: materiality." As a result, the terms "deconstruction" and "deconstructivism" soon fell out of favor within the architectural literature. Yet, paradoxically, at almost the same moment the architectural language to which they referred began to enjoy popular support. With the construction, in particular, of Gehry's Guggenheim Museum in Bilbao, this once shockingly radical and irreverant approach to architecture emerged out of the shadows of the avant-garde to become a mainstream architectural movement sanctioned by the public.

NEIL LEACH

See also **Coop Himmelb(l)au (Austria); Eisenman, Peter (United States); Gehry, Frank (United States); Guggenheim Museum, Bilbao, Spain; Hadid, Zaha (Iraq); Koolhaas, Rem (Netherlands); Libeskind, Daniel (United States); Morphosis (United States); Museum of Modern Art, New York City, United States; Nouvel, Jean (France); Postmodernism; Post-structuralism; Tschumi, Bernard (France)**

Further Reading

Derrida, Jacques, "Letter to Peter Eisenman," *Assemblage*, 12 (August 1990)

Derrida, Jacques, "Point de folie—Maintenant l'architecture," in *Rethinking Architecture: A Reader in Cultural Theory*, edited by Neil Leach, London and New York: Routledge, 1997
Derrida, Jacques, "Why Peter Eisenman Writes Such Good Books," in *Rethinking Architecture: A Reader in Cultural Theory*, edited by Neil Leach, London and New York: Routledge, 1997
Johnson, Philip, and Mark Wigley, *Deconstructivist Architecture: The Museum of Modern Art, New York*, Boston: Little Brown, 1988
Papadakis, Andreas, Catherine Cooke, and Andrew E. Benjamin (editors), *Deconstruction: Omnibus Volume*, New York: Rizzoli, and London: Academy Editions, 1989
Wigley, Mark, *The Architecture of Deconstruction: Derrida's Haunt*, Cambridge, Massachusetts: MIT Press, 1993

DEMOLITION

Traditionally, the conclusion of building projects has drawn people together to celebrate cultural progress. Thousands toured the Crystal Palace during and after its construction in mid-19th-century London; in 1937, 200,000 pedestrians each paid a nickel to cross the newly opened Golden Gate Bridge in San Francisco; in 1974 the topping-out of the Sears Tower with a special white beam signed by 12,000 workers was covered by a throng of press.

Just as historically, and also in the name of progress, building demolition has emphasized the symbolic role of buildings by calling attention to changes in cultural values and temporal powers as the old is swept away in favor of the new. The destruction of Persepolis in 331 B.C. by Alexander the Great indicated the triumph of Hellenistic culture over the Mesopotamians; the order by Pope Julius II to condemn Constantine's basilica and thereby make way for a new St. Peter's epitomized the papal desire to link itself with an interpretation of Roman antiquity specific to Renaissance values. In both cases, an idea of advancement lay behind the destruction. In the former, an enemy was specifically and violently obliterated to establish the superiority of the victor; in the latter, progress was manifest through a new architectural expression replacing one considered outmoded. Rarely is building demolition a purely pragmatic act; at its theoretical base, demolition is the antithesis of memorial building.

The notion of progress has taken many forms across the 20th century alone. Often associated with the midcentury idea of clearing historic downtowns to make way for modernist projects, such architectural improvements have also worn the dress of classicism. Decades before the first Congrès Internationaux d'Architecture Moderne (CIAM)-inspired demolitions, dozens of buildings were scrubbed from Philadelphia's 17th-century grid to make room for the diagonal sweep of the Benjamin Franklin Parkway (1909–19). The City Beautiful boulevard and its associated Beaux-Arts buildings suggested a new decorum and civility for the modern city. Such classically draped progress was usually carried out in small parcels compared with the urban renewal of midcentury, when acres of urban fabric were razed.

A particularly focused and infamous example, the 1974 Urban and Rural Systemization Law enacted under the Ceausescu regime inaugurated a period of mass demolition in Romania. With the ultimate goal of consolidating 7,000 towns and villages (over half of those extant in the countryside) with 500 agro-industrial centers, building demolition became a tool in the formation of a more perfect Communist state by leveling the differences among ethnic identities and variations between standards of living in town and country along with the country's architectural heritage. At least 29 towns had been almost totally razed by the end of 1989, when the destruction came to an end with the overthrow of Ceausescu.

Most mid-century demolition carried out under the banner of urban renewal was a combination of social engineering and also a principle that older buildings, representing an outmoded way of life, were simply obsolete. Displaced by the construction of malls and the rising use of online shopping, the Sears Mail Order Center in Kansas City (1925) was demolished in 1997, and in the following year the 23-story Hudson Department Store (1911), the tallest department store in the country, was felled in Detroit. By indicating an adjustment in cultural relevance, the planned demolition of these buildings illustrates the concerns of the 1990s just as their construction revealed the values of a century ago.

More infamously, the destruction of hundreds of housing projects, starting in the 1970s, sounded the coda for one of the Modern movement's greatest efforts, the provision of efficient, low-cost public housing. Iconic photographs from 1972 of Pruitt-Igoe (St. Louis, 1952–55) crumbling in a cloud of smoke are as potent symbolically of the demise of modernism as well-known detail images of the Gallerie des Machines are of its rise. The news coverage of such demolitions and reconstruction of mixed-income, 19th-century-style town homes on many of their sites (most ironically exemplified in Baltimore, where new row houses replace the towers, which themselves replaced 19th-century townhouses) illustrate the cycle of urban housing planning values in America.

The loss of particular monuments has often been a catalyst to energize groups, which have lobbied for the protection of whole neighborhoods and districts in addition to single buildings. Ironically, the preservationists have also been to blame for the destruction of scores of historic industrial and vernacular buildings in their efforts to present a tidy historical vignette. Scores of dependency buildings that sheltered the lives of slaves were demolished at Colonial Williamsburg in the 1920s; 30 years later the creation of Independence National Historical Park in Philadelphia demanded the demolition of significant mid-19th-century buildings; both projects used demolition to clear distasteful mistakes of history for a sanitized image of Colonial life.

Across the 20th century, methods of demolition have differed from project to project, depending on the particular building's structural material, scale, environment, and accessibility to the site. Techniques range from the simplest procedure of pulling down by hand or with wire rope, to the use of demolition balls and pusher arm machinery, to the planning for explosives and the use of "bursters," steel cylinders inserted into predrilled holes that "burst" concrete by means of either hydraulic power or gas expansion.

As methods changed in precision and predictability they transformed the nature of demolition from the brute, droning labor of the wrecking ball to a quick and dramatic event that is often enhanced with the marching bands and fireworks displays once reserved for ribbon-cutting ceremonies. Especially in the last decades of the 20th century, as the work of demolition began to resemble entertainment, demonstrators against the destruction of particular buildings were joined at the contested sites by growing audiences seeking entertainment. Most famously, Controlled Demolition Incorporated (CDI) has raised the destruction of buildings to spectator sport. Between 1950 and 2000 the firm was responsible for the destruction of some 7,000 structures worldwide, often employing the technique of implosion. This high-tech method has been coupled with pyrotechnics and new communications technologies to draw worldwide audiences numbering in the millions of spectators via satellite.

The captivating nature of this entertainment is shown by the inclusion of CDI's 1994 demolition of Las Vegas' Landmark Hotel in a movie, while still shots of other imploded buildings were collected for calendars. For all their 20th-century popularity, these theatrics may not find such widespread draw in the 21st. Perhaps indicating a new mood, on the heels of the September 11 terror attacks, the implosion of the Desert Inn (Las Vegas, October 2001) was a low-key event, carried out in the middle of the night and without fanfare. The collapse of the World Trade Center towers, captured on film and replayed innumerable times, has likely squelched the enthusiasm once held for this kind of destructive entertainment.

JHENNIFER A. AMUNDSON

See also **Athens Charter (1943); City Beautiful Movement; Congrès Internationaux d'Architecture Moderne (CIAM, 1927-); Historic Preservation; Pruitt-Igoe Housing, St. Louis, Missouri**

Further Reading

Giurescu, Dinu C., *The Razing of Romania's Past*, New York: World Monuments Fund, 1989

Huxtable, Ada Louise, *Goodbye History, Hello Hamburger*, Washington, D.C.: The Preservation Press, 1986

Nye, David E., *American Technological Sublime*, Cambridge, Massachusetts: The MIT Press, 1994

Pledger, David M., *A Complete Guide to Demolition*, Lancaster: The Construction Press Ltd., 1977

www.controlled-demolition.com

DENMARK

A diversity of styles was represented in Denmark at the turn of the century, from the Art Nouveau commercial building (1907) designed by Anton Rosen for one of Copenhagen's main shopping streets to the Dutch Renaissance–inspired Student Union Building (1910) by Ulrik Plesner and Aage Langeland-Matthiessen. In response to the lack of a defining style, many architects began to search for a "national architecture" that would be based on Danish traditions rather than on movements originating in other parts of Europe. The first step in this direction resulted in the Abel Cathrine's Foundation Building (1885–86) by H.B. Storck; however, the most instrumental figure in the search for a national architecture was Martin Nyrop. Commissioned to design the Copenhagen Town Hall during the final decade of the 19th century, Nyrop sought to create a building that reacted to reliance on applied Renaissance-inspired ornament that characterized many buildings at the time and that responded to Danish material traditions and Nordic mythology via well-integrated details. The attention to material and detail is also evident in Nyrop's Bispebjerg Hospital (1907–13) and in the addition to Vallekilde High School (1907–08). Nyrop's wish for a national architecture was shared by P.V. Jensen Klint, who was responsible for the design of Grundtvig's Church (1913–40), which was clearly inspired by Danish brick traditions and the architecture of parish churches.

The debate concerning an appropriate style intensified during the first decade of the 20th century and culminated in a decisive event in 1910 precipitated by suggested alterations to Vor Frue Church, originally designed by C.F. Hansen and constructed between 1811 and 1829. The brewery owner Carl Jacobsen offered to donate a spire for the church, and although many of the older generation of architects were in agreement, Carl Petersen and a number of younger architects argued that it would destroy the church and greatly compromise the building; ultimately, the church was fitted with a Doric tower that was in keeping with the original neoclassical building. Carl Petersen's allegiance to Neoclassicism is evident in the Faaborg Museum (1912–15), which clearly acknowledged the work of Hansen. The culmination and the demise of neoclassicism are represented in Hack Kampmann's Copenhagen Police Headquarters (1925). Like the police station, Kampmann's other work was characterized by a theatrical formalism, as evidenced in the Århus Theatre (1898–1900), the Customs House (1895–97) in Århus Harbor, and the National Library (1898–1902) in Århus.

The transition from Neoclassicism to the Nordic adaptation of the Modern movement, commonly referred to as functionalism, is most clearly seen in the area of housing, as living standards and housing shortages were of political and social importance in Denmark following World War I. One of the leaders in improving housing was Copenhagen's Public Housing Association (KAB), which oversaw the construction of the Studiebyen demonstration project (1920–24) to examine alternatives for single-family houses, duplexes, and row houses. Among the architects participating were Thorkild Henningsen and Ivar Bentsen, Anton Rosen, and the influential teacher and architect Kay Fisker. During the same period, Henningsen and Bentsen were also commissioned by the KAB to build a series of row houses around Copenhagen that provided small back and front gardens while maintaining the street wall that was characteristic of traditional housing in provincial Danish towns. Large-scale housing projects undertaken at this time were five- or six-story blocks organized around an open interior court, as seen in Povl Baumann's municipal housing (1919–20) at the corner of Hans Tavsensgade and Struensgade in Copenhagen and Kay Fisker's Hornbækhus (1922–23). The transformation from closed housing blocks to freestanding parallel rows of flats can be traced through Ved Classens Have (1924) by Carl Petersen, Povl Baumann, Ole Falkentorp, and Peter Neilsen; Solgården (1929) by Peter Hansen; and finally the freestanding parallel blocks of housing at the Blidah Park housing estate designed by a group of architects that included Edvard Heiberg, Karl Larsen, and Ivar Bentsen. The complete transition to functionalism is evident in Vordroffsvej 2 (1929) and in the Vestersøhus housing complexes by Kay Fisker and C.F. Møller.

During the 1930s, two new tendencies developed, the first characterized by the adherence to the ideals of the Modern movement with the acceptance of Danish building traditions and form language and another that favored the aesthetic criteria of modernism. The former tendency can be seen in the buildings at Århus University, which were initiated in 1931 by Fisker,

Møller, and Paul Stegmann. Those architects who adhered to the stylistic tendencies of the Modern movement included Vilhelm Lauritzen, whose restrained formalism and elegant detailing are illustrated in the Radio Building (1937–47), Gladsaxe Town Hall (1937), and Kastrup Airport Terminal (1939). At the end of the 1930s, Mogens Lassen, who was influenced by the ideas of Le Corbusier, constructed a series of houses that successfully reconciled ideas imported from France and Germany and the attention to material and detail that characterized Danish architecture.

Arne Jacobsen revealed his affinity for the aesthetic sensibilities of the Modern movement in the Bellavista housing complex from 1934, which employs a flat roof and brick walls rendered smooth and painted white. Like the previous generation of architects, Jacobsen's work was characterized by a formal simplicity and attention to detail. These tendencies are revealed in the town halls in Århus (1937–42), Søllerød (1940–42, designed in association with Flemming Lassen), and Rødovre (1955). In 1960, Jacobsen completed the tallest building in Denmark up to that time, the SAS Hotel, which was based on Skidmore, Owings and Merrill's Lever House in New York. One year later, the commission for the new headquarters of the National Bank of Denmark (1965–78) was awarded to Jacobsen and completed after his death by his successor firm Dissing & Weitling.

Whereas some architects continued to work within the dictates of international modernism during the 1940s and 1950s, others looked to the American West Coast and Japanese architecture for inspiration. Houses by Jørn Utzon, Erik Christian Sørensen, and Vilhelm Wohlert revealed a concern for the relationship between interior and exterior, clearly expressed structure, and spatial variety using a series of standard elements. The most notable examples of these ideas are Utzon's Kingo Houses (1958–60) and Fredensborg Terraces (1962–63) and Jørgen Bo and Vilhelm Wohlert's Louisiana Museum, a complex that has continually grown by accretion from its inception in 1958.

A number of influences are visible in Danish architecture of the 1960s, including that of the work of Utzon, as seen in the dense, low-rise housing projects Ved Stampedammen (1965), Carlsmindepark (1965), Åtoften (1966), and Nivåvænge (1966). Another influence that was evident at the time was the work of the Finnish architect Alvar Aalto, who together with Jean-Jacques Baruël had won a competition for the North Jutland Art Museum in 1958. Aalto's influence is evident in Paul Niepoort's Sønderborg Church (1961) and Børglum Kollegium (1967); Jørgen Bo, Karen Clemmensen, and Ebbe Clemmensen's Blaagaard State Teachers College and Enghavegård School complex (1962–66); and Baruël's Sønderborg Business College (1964–74). Erik Christian Sørensen continued to emphasize the importance of structural clarity and material honesty in the First Church of Christ Scientist (1967), which revealed an affinity for the work of the Swedish architect Sigurd Lewerentz. The work of Lewerentz and the American architect Louis Kahn influenced the work of Inger and Johannes Exner, especially Nørrland Church (1966–70) and Islev Church (1967–70). The Exners

Århus University Main Building, Copenhagen, Denmark, designed by C.F. Moller, Kay Fisker, and Povl Stegmann (1942–46)
© Kevin Mitchell

went on to develop a greater personal expression in the Church of the Resurrection (1984), Lyng Church (1994), Skæring Church (1994), and an extensive restoration of Koldinghus Castle between 1972 and 1974.

At the end of the 1960s, a number of monolithic buildings inspired by the affiliation of architects known as Team X and their concern for adaptable structures and rough materials appeared in Denmark, including Gehrdt Bornebusch, Max Brüel, and Jørgen Selchau's Holbæk Teachers College (1967) and Esbjerg Teachers College (1967–73) and Friis and Moltke's Risskov County High School (1968–69), Danish Contractors Association School (1967–68), and Scanticon Training Center (1967–69). The most refined building constructed in this idiom was Erik Christian Sørenson's Viking Ship Museum (1967–68), which is supported by an elegantly proportioned, roughly formed concrete structure.

In the 1970s, a series of notable churches were constructed in Denmark, including Friis and Moltke's Ellevang Church (1973–74), C.F. Møller's Ravnsbjerg Church (1975–76), and Johan Otto von Spreckelsen's churches at Vangede (1974) and Stavsholt (1979–81), both of which reveal the influence of Louis Kahn. One of the most significant religious buildings to appear during this period was Jørn Utzon's Bagsværd Church (1974–76), which reflects his preoccupation with prefabricated building components and the relationship between free expression and clear structural logic.

A number of dense, low-rise housing developments were constructed during the 1970s. One of the most notable was Fællestegnestuen's Flexibo housing development, which incorporated a system of structure and light partitions that allowed residents to adapt the location of the walls to their particular way of living. In 1978, Tegnestuen Vandkunsten completed Tingården 1 and 2, which was the first public housing development in which future users were consulted during the planning stage. Along with Fællestegnestuen, Tegnestuen Vandkunsten has been influential in housing in Denmark with projects such as Jystrup Savværk (1983–84), Garvergården (1986–88), and Diana's Have (1991–92).

The concern for housing extended into the 1980s and 1990s, resulting in many large-scale developments, including the Sandbakken housing development (1988–80) by C.F. Møllers Tegnestue and the Dalgas Have development (1989–91) by Henning Larsens Tegnestue. Larsen has made significant contributions to Danish architecture in the latter half of the 20th century, beginning with the Glostrup Chapel and Crematorium (1960) and the Vangebo and Saint Jørgens elementary schools (1960), designed in association with Gehrdt Bornebusch, Max Brüel, and Jørgen Selchau. Like many other Danish architects during this period, including Nielsen, Nielsen, and Nielsen (Holstebro Congress and Cultural Center, 1990–91; Vingsted Center, 1993), Larsen's work is characterized by experimentation in a range of styles and the search for an appropriate expression, from the postmodern buildings at Dalgas Have to the neomodernist BT Building (1993–94) in Copenhagen.

The search for an appropriate expression and a defining style is evident in the new urban quarters that have been constructed to provide housing and services. The new neighborhood surrounding the Høje Taastrup station (1985–present) takes inspiration from the work of Leon Kreir and employs traditional town-planning principles in an attempt to provide an overall framework for development. Two major housing exhibitions that resulted in new suburban centers, Blangstedgård (1987–88) and Egebjerggård (1985–96), resulted in a range of individual structures that vary in quality and bear little relation to each other or to the overall development plans.

Buildings that resulted from competitions during the late 1980s and early 1990s also reveal the lack of a defining style that is characteristic of recent Danish architecture. In 1988, a competition was held for a new Museum of Modern Art to be built south of Copenhagen. Completed in 1996 by Søren Robert Lund, this building is one of the few in Denmark that appears to have been influenced by the briefly fashionable deconstructivism. Two recent additions to major buildings in Copenhagen have resulted from competitions in the 1990s: the Royal Library (1993–99) by Schmidt, Hammer, and Lassen and the National Gallery (1998) by C.F. Møllers Tegnestue. Both of these additions illustrate a current tendency to create buildings appearing as freestanding objects that bear little relation to the immediate context.

Whereas some architects have aggressively experimented with a range of styles imported from abroad, others have quietly worked to develop an architecture devoid of superficial effects. Of particular note are the summer cottage (1985–87) on the island of Læsø, the Holstebro Art Museum (1981, addition 1991) by Hanne Kjærholm, and the work of the firm Fogh and Følner, including the Bornholm Art Museum (1993), Egedal Church (1990), and Tornbjerg Church (1994). Perhaps the most significant contributions to the development of an architecture sympathetic to material and context have come from Gerhdt Bornebusch, as evident in the Danish School of Forestry (1981–92) in Nødebo, the extension and renovation of the National Museum (1990–92), and the Danish Forest and Landscape Institute (1995).

Although 20th-century Danish architecture has been subject to influences from a variety of countries, very few foreign architects have built in Denmark. It is interesting to note that two major exceptions were both from Finnish architects: Alvar Aalto's North Jutland Art Museum and Heikkinen and Komonen's European Film College (1992–93). However, Danish architects established an impressive record of obtaining significant commissions abroad during the latter half of the century, including Utzon's Sydney Opera House (1956–73) and National Assembly Building (1971–83) in Kuwait, Arne Jacobsen's St. Catherine's College (1962) at Oxford, Henning Larsen's Ministry of Foreign Affairs (1980–84) in Riyadh, and Johan Otto von Spreckelsen's Le Grande Arch (1982–90) in Paris.

KEVIN MITCHELL

Further Reading

A comprehensive account of 20th-century architecture in Denmark has yet to be published in English; the most up-to-date works remains Faber (1963) and Faber (1968). For information on individual architects, see Drew, Faber (1964), Faber (1991), Jørgensen, and Solaguren-Beascoa de Corral.

Drew, Philip (editor), *Sydney Opera House: Jørn Utzon*, London: Phaidon Press, 1995

Faber, Tobias, *Dansk arkitektur*, Copenhagen: Det Danske Selskab, 1963; as *A History of Danish Architecture*, translated by Frederic R. Stevenson, Copenhagen: Det Danske Selskab, 1978

Faber, Tobias, *Arne Jacobsen*, Stuttgart, Germany: Verlag Gerd Hatje, London: Tiranti, and New York: Praeger, 1964
Faber, Tobias, *New Danish Architecture*, New York: Praeger, and London: Architectural Press, 1968
Faber, Tobias, *Jørn Utzon, Houses in Fredensborg*, Berlin: Ernst and Sohn, 1991
Fisker, Kay, and Francis R. Yerbury (editors), *Modern Danish Architecture*, London: Benn, and New York: Scribner, 1927
Jørgensen, Lisbet Balslev, Jørgen Sestoft, and Morten Lund, *Vilhelm Lauritzen: en moderne arkitekt*, s.l.: Bergiafonden and Aristo, 1994; as *Vilhelm Lauritzen: A Modern Architect*, translated by Martha Gaber Abrahamsen, s.l.: Bergiafonden and Aristo, 1994
Lind, Olaf, *Copenhagen Architecture Guide*, Copenhagen: Arkitektens Forlag, 1996
Møller, Erik, Jens Lindhe, and Kjeld Vindum, *Aarhus City Hall*, Copenhagen: Danish Architectural Press, 1991
Norberg-Schulz, Christian, and Tobias Faber (editors), *Utzon: Mallorca*, Copenhagen: Arkitektens Forlag, 1996
Skriver, Poul Erik (editor), *Moderne dansk arkitektur*, Copenhagen: Dansk-Norsk Foundation, 1966; as *Guide to Modern Danish Architecture*, translated by David Hohnen, Copenhagen: Arkitektens Forlag, 1969
Solaguren-Beascoa de Corral, Félix, *Arne Jacobsen*, Barcelona: Gili, 1989
Utzon, Jørn, *Sydney Opera House: Sydney, Australia, 1957–73*, edited by Yukio Futagawa, Tokyo: A.D.A. Edita, 1980
Utzon, Jørn, *Church at Bagsvaerd, near Copenhagen, Denmark, 1973–76*, edited by Yukio Futagawa, Tokyo: A.D.A. Edita, 1981
Woodward, Christopher, *Copenhagen*, Manchester: Manchester University Press, 1998

DEPARTMENT STORE

The department store is so named for its administrative organization, which combines centralized marketing, customer service, deliveries, and accounting with separately managed departments for each type of stock, staffed by specialized buyers and sales personnel responsible for the unit's profitability (Clausen, 1985). An index of emerging monopoly capitalism in the second half of the 19th century, these large-scale retail enterprises initially grew because of innovative sales practices, such as fixed pricing, free access to goods, low markups, and liberal rights of return and exchange. Higher sales, in turn, yielded volume discounts and prompted increased diversification. Urbanization and population mobility, facilitated by public transportation, were instrumental in their growth from a single storefront into vast premises occupying an entire city block. So significant was their effect on the urban fabric that the construction of a new department store might signal both the demise of smaller establishments and the relocation of entire shopping districts.

Often opulent in their appointments, these emporia democratized luxury and opened new avenues of consumption for an upwardly mobile middle class seeking the status of high fashion at bargain-basement prices. In particular, large stores offered a protected setting for women shoppers, whose circumscribed lives nevertheless included the management of household accounts. Attending them were women assistants, whose consciousness of their requirements and lower wages than their male counterparts spelled increased profit margins for the retailer. In effect, the department store was one stage on which some of the major societal changes of the period were enacted (Benson, 1986).

Its built forms typically consist of large, open floors sustained on metal framing: in Europe, design is based on the tradition of the shopping arcade, in North America, on that of the wholesale warehouse. Large areas of plate glass, together with skylights, brought natural light into the interior to facilitate inspection of goods. Display windows lined the sidewalks, and commodious entrance portals ushered in the passersby. So successful were these stores at promoting consumption that writers of the day described them as "cathedrals of commerce" or "museums of merchandise." The professional expertise formerly lavished only on important public monuments now forged these tangible symbols of Gilded Age secularization (Clausen, 1987).

Elite architectural designs were emblems of corporate identity for retailers competing in an international market. The range of goods was comparable to that of any world's fair exhibition hall. Aristide Boucicaut's palatial Bon Marche of 1869–87 was the first Parisian precedent, its conventional exterior concealing an iron frame that carried massive floor loads. Ecole-trained Jean-Alexandre Laplanche ornamented the iron technology of Louis Auguste Boileau, a pairing duplicated in the second phase by the design of Boileau's son Louis Charles and the framing of engineer Gustave Eiffel. Among the stores that followed were the chic Au Printemps of 1881 by Paul Sedille and the more populist Grands Magasins de la Samaritaine of 1905 by Frantz Jourdain, a colorful Art Nouveau confection of frankly revealed steel and glass (Clausen, 1987).

In North America, A.T. Stewart's Marble Palace of 1848 in New York and its cast-iron successor of 1859–62 designed by John Kellum established the Renaissance *palazzo* as the vocabulary of choice well into the 20th century for such legendary retail giants as Macy's, Gimbels, and Marshall Field's of Chicago. Refined by James MacLaughlin in the John Shillito store of 1877–78 in Cincinnati and by William Le Baron Jenney, whose designs for Chicago's first and second Leiter stores of 1878–79 and 1889, respectively, marked the emergence of the curtain wall, the retail *palazzo* reached its finest culmination in the grid of horizontals and verticals that Louis Sullivan conceived for the Schlesinger-Mayer store (later the Carson Pirie Scott store) of 1899–1904, also in Chicago (Harris, 1987).

Twentieth-century examples were equally varied. Alfred Messel concealed the metal frame of Berlin's Wertheim department store of 1896–1904 beneath historicizing facades, notwithstanding an 1820s proposal by his countryman Karl Frederick Schinkel for shop fronts with large panes of glass between masonry piers. Similarly, Gordon Selfridge's London department store of 1910, on which Graham, Burnham, and Company of Chicago served as consultants, led the British vogue for Beaux-Arts design, a precedent also adopted by the Hudson's Bay Company for its flagship stores in western Canada. By contrast, Victor Horta's now demolished Grands Magasins a l'Innovation of 1901 in Brussels frankly expressed a metal-and-glass facade beneath an arc of granite. In the Far East, meanwhile, the Renaissance *palazzo* was the choice for China's Sincere, Wing On, and Wangfujing department stores and for Japan's Mitsukoshi (MacPherson, 1998).

The 1920s brought a revolution in department store design, as Erich Mendelsohn of Germany and William Marius Dudok of the Netherlands adopted the steel and glass of International modernism. Mendelsohn's Stuttgart (1926–28) and Chemnitz (1928–30) Schocken stores and his 1927 Petersdorff store in

Breslau, as well as Dudok's now demolished Bijenkorf store of 1929–30 in Rotterdam, defined a new aesthetic that fused Bauhaus purity with curvilinear expressionism. A similar idiom was introduced in 1938 in London with the Peter Jones department store by William Crabtree, Slater and Moberley, and C.H. Reilly.

Within a decade, the private car had transformed the North American city. In Los Angeles, Bullocks Wilshire of 1929 by John and Donald Parkman acknowledged this reality with an innovative Art Deco design in a suburban location fronting on a parking lot. Ten years later, a streamlined fortress of reinforced concrete and glass block was adopted by its competitor, Coulter's-Wilshire, heralding the advent of the blank facade adopted at the same period by the chain of Sears and Roebuck and later to become the norm for all suburban department stores from the 1960s on. From individual branch stores in the suburbs, the department stores became chains that anchored regional shopping centers, such as Seattle's Northgate of 1950 (Clausen, 1984). Downtown stores in the United States declined until the renaissance of the 1970s reintroduced them into multiuse complexes, such as the Broadway Plaza of 1974 in Los Angeles. Other solutions included the Toronto Eaton Centre of 1974–77 by Zeidler Roberts Partnership, a private galleria of smaller specialty shops built for a major retailer, to draw pedestrian traffic from adjoining city streets. Likewise, in the mid-1980s, Nichii Obahiro of Japan proposed a vast climate-controlled garden to attract customers confined by the rigors of a harsh winter. As the department store became but another contour of the shopping mall, its most distinctive contemporary residue was found in the prophetically ruinous facades that SITE conceived in the 1970s for the now vacant catalog showrooms of Best Products.

Angela K. Carr

Further Reading

Benson, Susan Porter, *Counter Cultures: Saleswomen, Managers, and Customers in American Department Stores, 1890–1940*, Urbana: University of Illinois Press, 1986

Clausen, Meredith L., "Northgate Regional Shopping Center—Paradigm from the Provinces," *Journal of the Society of Architectural Historians*, 43 (May 1984)

Clausen, Meredith L., "The Department Store—Development of the Type," *Journal of Architectural Education*, 39/1 (1985)

Clausen, Meredith L., *Frantz Jourdain and the Samaritaine: Art Nouveau Theory and Criticism*, Leiden: E.J. Brill, 1987

Clausen, Meredith L., "Department Stores," and "Shopping Centers," in *Encyclopedia of Architecture: Design, Engineering, and Construction*, 4 vols., edited by Joseph Wilkes, New York: Wiley, 1989

Harris, Neil, "Shopping—Chicago Style," in *Chicago Architecture, 1872–1922: Birth of a Metropolis*, edited by John Zukowsky, Munich: Prestel, and Chicago: Art Institute of Chicago, 1987

Harris, Neil, "The City That Shops: Chicago's Retailing Landscape," in *Chicago Architecture and Design, 1923–1993: Reconfiguration of an American Metropolis*, edited by John Zukowsky, Munich: Prestel, and Chicago: Art Institute of Chicago, 1993

Lancaster, William, *The Department Store: A Social History*, London: Leicester University Press, 1995

Leach, William, *Land of Desire: Merchants, Power, and the Rise of a New American Culture*, New York: Pantheon Books, 1993

MacPherson, Kerrie L. (editor), *Asian Department Stores*, Richmond, Surrey: Curzon, and Honolulu: University of Hawaii Press, 1998

Pevsner, Nikolaus, *A History of Building Types*, Princeton, New Jersey: Princeton University Press, 1976

DEUTSCHER WERKBUND

Recognized as a distinct group on the occasion of the Third German Exhibition of Applied Art in Dresden in 1906, the Deutscher Werkbund (German Arts and Crafts Society) was an association of artists, architects, industrialists, and merchants contending with the revolutionary changes in the economic, social, and cultural fabric of 19th-century Europe and America. Founders of the Werkbund included Berlin architect Hermann Muthesius; Friedrich Naumann, author and *Arbeitskommissar* (Director of Work) for the Berlin "industrial combine" Allgemeine Elektricitäts Gesellschaft (AEG); and Karl Schmidt, director of the Dresdner Werkstätten für Handwerkskunst (Dresden Workshop for Manual Art). Muthesius and Naumann authored two books that provided much of the Werkbund's platform: Muthesius's *Das Englische Haus* (1904; The English House), a critical overview of what he perceived as an ideal model for a native craft culture, and Naumann's *Die Kunst im Maschinenzeitalter* (1906; Art in the Epoch of the Machine), a treatise on the role of craft and industrial production. Initial membership of the Werkbund included 12 architects and 12 industrial firms. Architects included such important figures as Peter Behrens, Theodor Fischer, Josef Hoffmann, J.M. Olbrich, Bruno Paul, and Paul Schultze-Naumburg; associated firms included both associations and traditional firms, such as Peter Bruckmann and Söhne, Kunstdruckerei Kunstlerbund Karlsruhe, and the Wiener Werkstätte. Yet the Deutscher Werkbund was not only a recognized organization but also a coalescence of myriad points of view into a movement—a movement that continues to resonate across the full array of contemporary design disciplines.

With the industrial revolution, the traditional roles of art and architecture—modes of cultural production that had been heretofore understood as institutionalized extensions of state and economic power—were increasingly called into question. Gottfried Semper, a 19th-century Dresden architect, teacher, and political exile, wrote two books on the influence of sociopolitical conditions on style that were to become seminal works for members of the Deutscher Werkbund: *Wissenschaft, Industrie und Kunst* (1852; Science, Industry and Art), a treatise examining industrial production and mass consumption on the entire field of applied art and architecture, and *Der Stil in den technischen und tektonischen Künsten oder praktische Ästhetik* (1860–63; Style in Industrial and Structural Arts or Practical Aesthetics). Coupled with contemporary scientific, economic, and industrial developments, Semper's writings—publications that were themselves influenced by anthropology and the natural sciences—provided much of the impetus for a rethinking the role of art and architecture in modern German society during the 19th and 20th centuries. Accordingly, members of the Deutscher Werkbund recognized that the shifting attitudes toward the arts and crafts were not merely based on stylistic motivations but were the result of a more generalized critique of cultural production and its place within society. Thus, individuals associated with the Werkbund recognized the social responsibility of the artist and architect. This led to the Werkbund's acknowledgment (in the footsteps of 19th-century English theorists Augustus Welby

Pugin, William Morris, and John Ruskin) of the significance, indeed power, of a coherent, exemplary range of industrial and consumer products on the world stage.

Germany (a loose federation of duchies and nation-states until 1866) had long suffered from the perception that its art and architecture exposed a general ignorance of tasteful "culture." Although Germany was traditionally recognized for the manufacture of efficient, practical, and cost-effective goods and products (most notably its instruments of war), these products were usually criticized—often rightfully—as being of inferior design quality. The Werkbund sought to correct this perception, if not reality, by seeking to broadly inculcate a seamless marriage between economy, form, and artistic taste. This new vision—as a practice and an idea—was referred to by the term *Zweckkunst*, a word that translates literally as "functional art." As a new approach to design, the application of principles derived from *Zweckkunst* would better not only consumer products for use by the Germans themselves but also competitive products for export purposes. In promoting the nation's manufactured goods, the Werkbund also sought to articulate a fundamental revision of the nation's *Kultur* (culture). Germany was to be perceived no longer as a militarist—if efficient—nation devoid of the cultural élan of the rest of Europe but as a participating, sophisticated equal on the world stage. Thus, the strength, wealth, and spirit (in accordance with Semper, among others) was implicitly, if not explicitly, rendered by the products that it produced. (It should be noted that this faith in domestic products was not specific to Germany but exemplified a more general trend throughout Europe and the Americas whereby capitalist economic models for industrial production and economic development were increasingly seen as extensions of national culture.)

In the 1910s, Walter Gropius, who, with fellow German architect Adolf Meyer, advanced some of the newer techniques and materials in their architectural work of the period, expressed the need for Germany's advance of the arts and architecture as key to its general economic development. In so doing, Gropius also extended the Werkbund's vision of a vernacular aesthetic bearing the true spirit of German *Kultur*: "Compared to other European countries, Germany has a clear lead in the aesthetics of factory building." Stating that America was the "motherland of industry," Gropius pointed to the industrial architecture of the Americas, "whose majesty outdoes even the best German work of this order. The grain silos of Canada and South America, the coal bunkers of the leading railroads and the newest work halls of the North American industrial trusts, can bear comparison, in their overwhelming monumental power, with the buildings of ancient Egypt." These "humane and aesthetic sensibilities" (Banham, 1980, 80) were not completely in line with all members of the Werkbund, in particular Hermann Muthesius, the architect who would become the de facto spokesman of the Deutscher Werkbund for a period of time, setting the stage for the Werkbund's internal divisions.

Documents and activities of the Werkbund serve to chronicle the emergence and subsequent development of the organization's approach to the allied arts and architecture, including the inherent conflicts of the Werkbund's position. In 1907, Muthesius published his "Aims of the Werkbund" on behalf of the society. His earlier reports on British domestic architecture (1904–07), showcasing the advances of the English Arts and Crafts movement for his German audience, along with his advocacy of engineering and standardization in projects such as the Eiffel Tower, station halls, and bicycle wheels, had already lent Muthesius notoriety, if not credibility, among his peers. In "Aims of the Werkbund," Muthesius proposes what may be regarded as a "call to arms" for artists, architects, and their associates, an argument that he supports with the suggestion that cultural production has not enjoined the revolutionary changes of the day and that it is not only the social but also the spiritual responsibility of his compatriots to embrace change. Indeed, Muthesius not only emphasized the material and technical problems confronted by his contemporaries but also heralded a "spiritual purpose" for the arts and architecture, a purpose that extended to the economy as a whole—what Frederic Schwarz (1996) refers to as the pursuit of a "spiritualized economy" (75). Accordingly, architectural culture "remains the true index of a nation's culture as a whole . . . without a total respect for form, culture is unthinkable, and formlessness is synonymous with lack of culture. Form is a higher spiritual need" (Conrads, 27). In addition, Muthesius saw his project for the arts and architecture as a logical expression of Germany's vocation, a nation that enjoyed, according to Muthesius, its "reputation for the most strict and exact organisation in her businesses, heavy industry, and state institutions of any country in the world." For Muthesius, the will to "pure Form" (elaborated as *Zweckkunst*, the synthesis of form and function) was an extension of the nation's "military discipline" and, consequently, a manifestation of its *innerste Wesen* (inner being).

Seeking to counter Muthesius' arguments in "Aims of the Werkbund," the Belgian architect Henry van de Velde joined Muthesius in propounding what became the internally contradictory document "Werkbund Theses and Antitheses"—irreconcilable differences that both architects expressed publicly during the proceedings of the Werkbund Congress of 1914. Whereas Muthesius proclaimed "concentration and standardization as the aims of Werkbund design" (a statement implicitly supporting the collective project of the design arts, including architecture), his colleague, van de Velde, defined the essential nature of the argument as a struggle between two opposing ideals: "Type *(Typsierung)* versus Individuality." Although it is true that van de Velde was espousing what was already a rear-guard position by suggesting that artists are first and foremost "creative individualists," the argument did not end with the imminent success of a standardized economy. Dispensing with any attempt at dialectical fusion, both architects wrote several axioms supporting their stances regarding standardization and creative freedom. Presented on the occasion of the first great exhibition of the Deutscher Werkbund in Cologne in July 1914, the document, coupled with the ideologically diverse designs for the exhibition (as in Peter Behrens's Neoclassicism versus Gropius and Meyer's model office building and factory, Faguswerk), continued to affect discussions surrounding cultural production and arts and design education well into the future. It should be noted, however, that both Muthesius and van de Velde maintained a belief in the spiritual nature of cultural production, but Muthesius sought a universal set of values, reflected by a dominance of "good taste." It is also significant that Gropius, founder of the Staatliches Bauhaus Weimar in 1919—a program that, not incidentally, was housed in the building where van de Velde had directed his own state-funded School of Arts and Crafts—partook in the discussions surrounding the aims and directions of the Werkbund. These same ideological differences would have a bearing on the formulation and development of Gropius's Bauhaus pedagogical programs as well.

The Deutscher Werkbund Austellung (Exhibition) of 1927 in Stuttgart, also referred to as the Weissenhofsiedlung Stuttgart, exhibited built prototypes of experimental housing. The exhibit, including houses and apartments designed by an international array of architects (Le Corbusier, Mart Stam, J.J.P. Oud, Mies van der Rohe, Hans Scharoun, and Gropius, among others), represented the maturity of the Werkbund's vision. The 1927 exhibition underlined the transition of the Deutscher Werkbund from an organization to a movement, a movement no longer confined to Germany but international in scope.

ELIZABETH GAMARD

See also **AEG Turbine Factory, Berlin; Arts and Crafts Movement; Bauhaus; Bauhaus, Dessau; Behrens, Peter (Germany); Fagus Werk, Alfeld, Germany; Gropius, Walter (Germany); Muthesius, Hermann (Germany); van de Velde, Henri (Belgium); Weissenhofsiedlung, Deutscher Werkbund, Stuttgart (1927)**

Further Reading

Banham, Reyner, "Germany: Industry and the Werkbund," and "The Factory Aesthetic" in *Theory and Design in the First Machine Age*, by Banham, London: Architectural Press, and New York: Praeger, 1960; 2nd edition, Cambridge, Massachusetts: MIT Press, 1980

Burckhardt, Lucius (editor), *The Werkbund: History and Ideology, 1907–1933*, translated by Pearl Sanders, Woodbury, New York: Barron's, 1980; as *The Werkbund: Studies in the History and Ideology of the Deutscher Werkbund, 1907–1933*, translated by Pearl Sanders, London: The Design Council, 1980

Frampton, Kenneth, "The Deutsche Werkbund: 1898–1927" in *Modern Architecture: A Critical History*, by Frampton, London: Thames and Hudson, and New York: Oxford University Press, 1980; 3rd edition, London: Thames and Hudson, 1997

Hermann Muthesius, 1861–1927 (exhib. cat.), Berlin: Akademie der Kunste, 1977

Kirsch, Karin and Gerhard Kirsch, *Die Weissenhofsiedlung: Werkbund Ausstellung "Die Wohnung," Stuttgart, 1927*, Stuttgart, Germany: Deutsche Verlags-Anstalt, 1987; as *The Weissenhofsiedlungen: Experimental Housing Built for the Deutscher Werkbund, Stuttgart, 1927*, translated by Michael Knight, New York: Rizzoli, 1994

Lane, Barbara Miller, *Architecture and Politics in Germany, 1918–1945*, Cambridge, Massachusetts: Harvard University Press, 1968

DHAKA, BANGLADESH

Dhaka (spelled as Dacca until 1983), the capital of Bangladesh, with a 1999 population of 9.3 million in an area of 1,528 square kilometers, is one of the densest cities of the world. Situated in the deltaic plain of Bengal, in the midst of a maze of rivers and canals, it is the last big urban stop on the great Gangetic stream as it cascades into the sea. The name Dhaka has often been used synonymously, and rather incorrectly, with Louis Kahn's Capital Complex project that forms only a precinct—a significant one—in this burgeoning metropolis.

The literal meaning of the name Dhaka is "concealed." The enigmatic name might have originated from the "dhak" trees that are presumed to have been common in the area or the renowned 16th-century Dhakeswari Temple. Dhaka went through waves of decay and growth, from sporadic settlements datable to 10th century AD to a Mughal provincial capital in the 17th century and a deteriorated condition in the 18th c. until its consolidation as a thriving city in late 19th century The strategic location of Dhaka in the fertile and riverine land-mass of Bengal, once known for the fabled fabric muslin, and later for the world's largest jute production, made it the prime city in the region. As the capital city of Bangladesh, Dhaka is now an administrative, educational, commercial, and industrial center that includes the highest concentration of export-oriented garment industries.

Like similar cities undergoing rapid transformations, Dhaka is also a city of social, economic, and developmental contrasts. Despite bearing the typical afflictions of so-called developing cities (overpopulation, pollution, traffic problems, housing crisis, etc.), Dhaka is the center of an exuberant Bengali culture expressed in its literary and artistic life and various urban rituals and festivities.

Once located on the northern banks of the river Buriganga, Dhaka has grown largely toward the north, being delimited on all other sides by rivers and mostly fertile agricultural land subject to heavy flood. The extent of greater Dhaka now comprises the river port of Naryanganj in the south and the industrial town of Tongi and Gazipur on the north. Although most of Dhaka city is still on a higher level, population increase in recent times has driven people to build on the low-lying flood-prone areas.

The city is now constituted of roughly five distinct urban morphologies: (1) the so-called old city, the original settlement that grew along the river Buriganga and later developed into a thriving Mughal city, with its jostling mixed-use buildings, narrow, winding streets, and legendary neighborhood *(moholla)* traditions; (2) the so-called colonial part, the site of new governmental, cultural, institutional, and residential buildings, especially around the Ramna area in a bungalow and garden typology; (3) post-1947 developments of a mixture of regulated and planned residential areas, and sporadic commercial and institutional pockets; and (4) vast amorphous areas of semi- and unplanned growth, often with inadequate infrastructure, symptomatic of planning incapacity in addressing demographic and economic pressures. The fifth morphology is that of the exclusive National Capital Complex, better known as Sherebanglanagar that represents Kahn's vision of a government and civic complex.

The unassuming status of Dhaka belies its substantial role in the history of the Indian subcontinent. Historically, Dhaka has experienced paradoxical political orientation: On the one hand, it was the base of a Muslim ideology that led to the formation of Pakistan, and on the other hand, it was home to a Bengali nationalism that eventually led to the breakup of Pakistan and the formation of Bangladesh.

A strong Muslim culture was established with the consolidation of Mughal rule over Bengal in 1596, making it the eastern edge of a vast empire ruled from Delhi and Agra. For the nearly 150 years that Bengal was a Mughal province, the capital vacillated between Dhaka, Rajmahal, and Murshidabad, and with that fluctuated the economic and cultural spirit of the city. Dhaka went into a slow decline when it finally lost its capital status in 1704, as the Mughal administration left town with all its pomp and resources. The slump was deepened when the

Bangladesh College of Arts and Crafts (1956), designed by Muzharul Islam
© Aga Khan Trust for Culture

English wrested control of Bengal (1757) and established Calcutta as the base of their trading outfit. The economy of Dhaka was particularly hurt when its legendary *muslin* production was literally destroyed by English trade and tax machinations. Population would decrease drastically (from 450,000 in 1765 to 69,000 in 1838), and buildings would be overrun by vegetation. Dhaka would not gain a new momentum until the beginning of the 20th century under different English policies.

Since the 19th century Dhaka and Calcutta have played out a sort of tale of two cities in the history and psyche of modern Bengal. As Dhaka came to be seen, and in some ways projected itself, as the bearer of a Muslim culture, Calcutta became, despite or because of a stronger English presence, a Hindu-dominant city. The partition of Bengal into two provinces in 1905 that established Dhaka as the capital of East Bengal, again annulled in 1911, triggered a nationalist uprising that was to be a basis of the Indian independence movement. It was in Dhaka that the Muslim League took root as a political party in 1906 whose leadership was eventually to go to the Bombay-based M.A. Jinnah in the articulation of a separate state for Muslims. That political program was realized in the partitioning of India and the formation of Pakistan in 1947. Pakistan was to be constituted of two provinces, separated physically by India, where Dhaka became the capital of the eastern province. The argument for a Capital Complex in Dhaka came up as a result of this improbable condition when the government decided to transfer the parliamentary business between the central capital in Islamabad in West Pakistan (designed as a brand-new city by Doxiadis) and Dhaka (where a "Second Capital" was to be built). The defeat of the Pakistan Army in Dhaka during the Bangladesh Liberation War in 1971 represented the ascendance of a Bengali nationalist ideology and the establishment of the city as the capital of an independent country.

Dhaka has been described variously as "the city of mosques," with every conceivable neighborhood hosting a structure or two, and the city with "ba-anno bazaar, tepanno goli" (52 bazaars and 53 alleys), referring to the intricate network of winding streets forming the fabric of the old city. Although the profusion of mosques bespeak of a predominant Muslim culture since the Mughal era, there are 8th-century Buddhist ruins in the Savar area and various Hindu structures, including the well-known 16th-century Dhakeswari Temple.

Although Mughal building activity focused primarily on forts, *katras* (special dwellings), and mosques, residential neighborhoods of that time established morphology of dense, cellular buildings and courtyards along commercially active streets, traces of which can still be seen in parts of the old city (such as Shakhari Bazar, Islampur). Buildings of the colonial era were devoted mostly to administrative and institutional types that shifted stylistically between European neoclassical and quasi-Mughal modes. The typology of the bungalow in a garden setting became established at that time as a mode of urban dwelling that is followed even today in planning strategies despite the densification of the city.

Modern architecture was introduced in the city by two buildings that received immediate iconic status when they were built in 1954–56: The Bangladesh College of Arts and Crafts and the Public Library (presently Dhaka University Library), both designed by Muzharul Islam. These and other distinctive buildings, including the Science Laboratories (1959), N.I.P.A. Building (1969), buildings for Jahangirnagar University (1969), the National Archives (1979), and dozens of residences, established an international reputation of Muzharul Islam as a committed architect attempting to reconcile modernity with place and climate. A few foreign architects also contributed toward the process of establishing a modern architectural paradigm for Dhaka in such projects as the Kamlapur Railway Station by the American architect Robert Bouighy (1961), the Teachers-Students Center at Dhaka University by the Greek architect-planner Constantin Doxiadis (1963), and of course, the Parliament complex by Louis Kahn (1963–84). Architects of later generations have pursued diverse interests, exemplified in such notable projects as the Savar Monument by Mainul Hossain (1976), S.O.S. Youth Village by Raziul Ahsan (1984), housing complexes by Bashirul Haq and by Uttam Saha, and the Liberation Monument by Urbana Architects (2000). Although thoughtful and creative architectural work prevails in Dhaka, the city has seen very few compelling models of large-scale urban development.

The monumental and epochal architecture of Kahn's Capital Complex that put Dhaka on the international architectural map is a 1,000-acre site devoted to the parliament complex, government offices and residences, and a host of institutional buildings. The Parliament Building, the crown of the Complex, along with adjoining brick buildings presented a stunningly new and yet mythopoeic vocabulary for the city and the region. At the same time, the buildings in an environment of lakes, parks, gardens, and orchards offered a vision of a deltaic urban composition. It is perhaps poignant that when the city has moved away, both physically and strategically, from its deltaic roots the Capital Complex curiously evokes that condition.

KAZI K. ASHRAF

See also **Islam, Muzharul (Bangladesh); Kahn, Louis (United States); Mosque; National Assembly Building, Sher-e-Bangla Nagar, Dhaka**

Further Reading

Ahmed, Sharif Uddin, *Dacca: A Study in Urban History and Development*, London: Curzon Press, and Riverdale, Maryland: Riverdale, 1986

Ahmed, Sharif Uddin (editor), *Dhaka: Past, Present, Future*, Dhaka: Asiatic Society of Bangladesh, 1991

Bradley-Birt, F.B., *The Romance of an Eastern Capital*, London: Smith Elder, 1906; reprint, Delhi: Metropolitan Book, 1975

Islam, Nazrul, *Dhaka: From City to Megacity: Perspectives on People, Places, Planning, and Development Issues*, Dhaka, Bangladesh: University of Dhaka Press, 1996

Siddiqui, Kamal, et al., *Social Formation in Dhaka City: A Study in Third World Urban Sociology*, Dhaka, Bangladesh: University of Dhaka Press, 1990

DIENER AND DIENER

Architecture firm, Switzerland

The practice of Diener and Diener was formed as it exists now in 1975, when the son, Roger Diener (1950–), joined his father, Marcus Diener, in the elder's 30-year-old practice in Basel, Switzerland. From 1978 until 1984, the younger Diener collaborated primarily with Wolfgang Schett and Dieter Righetti, who already worked in Marcus's practice. Other key members of the Diener and Diener design team included Jens Erb and Andreas Ruedi; both joined the firm in 1983 and have remained perhaps the most influential members of the group. Roger Diener has taught at the ETH (Eidenössiche Technische Hochschule Zurich) Lausanne and at Harvard University's Graduate School of Design.

Diener and Diener are best known for their large residential complexes and housing plans, which are most recognizable by their simple features and severe facades. The firm has also won a number of town-planning commissions. Their designs are sophisticated and functionalist, adhering to the most positive traits of the modern philosophy while using the most unpretentious methods and materials possible.

When Diener and Diener first began designing large-scale apartment complexes in the late 1970s, postmodernism was at its height in Europe. The team wisely steered clear of these stylistic leanings and made their own mark with simplicity as their goal. The team's modern vocabulary, attention to function, and commitment to a variety of materials and construction methods set the firm apart. Their trademark materials have remained stone and colored concrete. The firm interprets the culture and history of Basel through many of their buildings, either via the facade and its conscious relationship to the urban design and street or in their pedestrian choices of materials. Diener and Diener employ design methods such as gridded mullions and lourves, and that often reappear throughout a range of different types of buildings, from office buildings to apartments.

The Hammerstrasse Apartment Complex (1981) in Basel exemplifies the firm's design preferences. Diener and Diener's challenge was to sensitively link the 19th-century urban plan to the new housing complex. The firm's design is an analogous display of a traditional peripheral apartment block of the late 19th century, where residences face the street, and communal space and walkways abound behind a row of studios. Apartments open up to the rear courtyard through large windows. Smaller apartments of different designs are intended for singles and the elderly, and larger units are intended for small families or communal living situations. Floor plans are of the utmost importance. The appeal to external variety is answered in the many different facings, ranging from corrugated aluminum to green glass and painted concrete. In many of the firm's residential buildings, windows will span nearly the entire wall to allow for light and a sense of space without encroaching on the proportions of the room.

Because most of their commissions are communal in nature—offices or housing estates—Diener and Diener developed early on a sensitivity to the role of the individual within the society. Naturally, they questioned the differences between the individual and the collective and how to express this in built form. They developed interrelationships between the city center and residential neighborhoods, neighborhood streets and courtyards of houses, and this space and the apartment with the apartment's relationship to everything around it. Within this scheme, it is the spaces where all these relationships intersect that define Diener and Diener's approach to space. Each project is unique, even when details are repeated from previous commissions, and reflects the urban environment around it. The firm has been key to the unique development of buildings in Switzerland. This is particularly true in the Basel area, where the government obliges architects to consider the urban pattern, the region's culture, and its inhabitants when planning a minor housing estate or a full city plan. A discipline to use minimal means and available materials and a consideration of the purpose of the task at hand are paramount. Diener and Diener feel a responsibility to both the inhabitant and the existing environment and display not only a fresh approach to functionalism but also an ethical humanism not seen in contemporary architecture.

EUGENIA BELL

Biography

The firm began as the private practice of Marcus Diener, Basel, Switzerland, in 1945; he was later joined by Wolfgang Schett and Dieter Righetti; his son, Roger Diener, became a member of the firm in 1975 and the name was changed to Diener and Diener; Jens Erb and Andreas Rudi joined the firm in 1983.

Selected Work

Hammerstrasse Apartment Complex, Basel, Switzerland, 1981

Selected Publication

Das Haus und die Stadt (Roger Diener), 1995

Further Reading

Bideau, André, "You See What You See: Gedanken zu einer Ausstellung über neuere Arbeiten von Diener Diener," *Werk, Bauen + Wohnen*, no. 7–8 (July–August 1998)

Diener and Diener, *Architecture d'aujourd'hui*, 299 (June 1995)

Diener and Diener, *Arkitektur*, 97/5 (August 1997)

Jehle-Schulte Strathaus, Ulrike, and Martin Steinmann (editors), *Diener und Diener*, Basel, Switzerland: Wiese, 1991; as *Diener and Diener*, translated by Claire Bonney, New York: Rizzoli, 1991

"Latterday Modernists," *Architectural Review*, 189/1127 (January 1991)

"Potsdamet Platz, Kothener Strasse," *Lotus International*, 80 (1994)

"Transparency in Architecture and the City: Swiss German Architecture," *Space Design*, 2/401 (February 1998)

DIESTE, ELADIO 1917–2000

Architect and engineer, Uruguay

Eladio Dieste was born in Artigas, Uruguay, in 1917. He received his engineering degree in 1943 from the University of the Republic in Montevideo, where he taught structures from 1943 until 1973. In 1953 Dieste begin his association with the engineer Eugenio Montañez. For almost half a century, Dieste conducted research and worked with reinforced brick. He developed structural masonry techniques using brick for water tanks, factories, horizontal silos, churches, towers, and bus stations.

Dieste recognized that the conditions that generated modern architecture in Europe and North America were distinct from those in Latin America. He reasoned that the design opportunities presented in Latin American countries did not demand that solutions resemble those produced in developed nations. He therefore understood that each culture could integrate technological change in its own manner, according to its own reality.

Dieste relied on the rational economic use of construction materials and methods, a respect for natural resources, and a knowledge of materials' properties. Convinced that development results from using regional techniques and technologies, he proposed construction methods and materials that considered the social and economic conditions of his country and the regions where he worked. Because Dieste used brick, one of the oldest and most humble construction materials, his work proved that it is possible to combine austerity and beauty and to understand local conditions while experimenting rigorously.

Dieste employed the principles of simple and double curvature in concrete and transferred it to brick and reinforced ceramic. This structural innovation allowed him to benefit from the characteristics of the new material. His use of brick, as opposed to concrete, offered lightness, responded to deformations, sustained the test of time, and minimized maintenance. Because ceramic brick is more resistant to temperature changes than concrete, it offers excellent thermal insulation. It is also inexpensive, acoustically resilient, and easy to repair or modify.

Dieste experimented with two principal structural types: the Gaussa vault and the self-supporting vault. The Gaussa vault contains a double curvature that combines brick, iron, and mortar. The word *Gaussa*, coined by Dieste, refers to vaults that he employed to cover large spaces using a minimal amount of reinforcement. The second type of vault that he often employed was designed to be completely self-supporting. In both cases, he relied on skills of regional workmen and used machinery that he designed and assembled.

One of the best examples of Dieste's work can be seen in the celebrated Atlántida church (1960, formerly a rectilinear warehouse. Dieste conceived a series of linear brick walls that are straight at the base and begin to undulate in the middle as they approach a double-curvature, continuous membrane roof. The conoidal-shaped walls and the Gaussian vaults create a monolithic and powerful form. The spatial light recalls Le Corbusier's Notre-Dame-du-Haut, Ronchamp, yet its conceptual distinction is seen in the changing brick textures and sculptural lightness. The bell tower is constructed with reinforced brick.

Dieste's search for structural expression and formal richness is also achieved in the Church in San Pedro, Durazno (1971). This church was built over the ruins of a parish church that had been destroyed by fire. The old parish followed the traditional layout of a central nave and two aisles separated by columns. The new structure consists of three folded slabs, two walls slanting toward the interior, and the roof, all of which are constructed of reinforced-brick membranes. The church follows the plan of the former parish but eliminates the columns between the nave and the side aisles, achieving a unified space. The interior is sober, enriched only by an altar and a rosette that is made up of a five-centimeter-thick hexagonal screen that is unified by iron spokes. The brick bell tower can be climbed to admire the landscape.

In the late 1960s, Dieste collaborated with the Brazilian government to build a series of markets, the most significant of which is the enormous structure for the market at Porto Alegre. Its central pavilion spans 47 meters and contains double-curved vaults and skylights. Dieste designed other areas of the complex with self-supporting vaults.

While exploring structural innovations with the Gaussa vault, Dieste began to experiment in the early 1960s with self-supporting vaults. He first used these light, supporting structures in his home (1962). Later, in Salto, Uruguay, he designed several buildings: the Municipal Bus Terminal (1974), the factory for the soft drinks "Refrescos del Norte" (1978), and the Turlit Terminal (1980) for a private bus company. He continued to develop these vaults at the Production Halls of Massaro Industries (1978) in Joanicó, Uruguay, where he constructed prestressed vaults for the roof structure that spanned 35 meters between pillars. One of these self-supporting vaults, only 10 centimeters thick, cantilevered 16 meters out from the entrance of the building. His explorations culminated with works at "Lanas Trinidad" (1979–91) in Alta, where he constructed vaults spanning up to 40 meters. In the Shopping Center of Montevideo (1985), his explorations resulted in the reinterpretation of the thematic ideas vested in the Atlántida church. An undulating line in the middle of the wall mediates the wall's form, which this time is straight at the base and the top. The undulating characteristic in the wall expresses structural pressure exerted by the set of two self-supporting ceramic vaults of the roof. This characteristic further absorbs lateral thrust and wind pressure. The floor slab is part of the entire structural system. It illustrates Dieste's ability to integrate his formal sensitivity and material knowledge with structural demands.

Since the 1960s, Dieste's work has been seriously studied in Latin America. His ideas inspired those interested in the development of an architecture that responds to a Latin American context. Outside Latin America, both his structural innovations and his poetic approach to construction received only peripheral attention. He remains lesser known than other Hispenic structural innovators, such as Felix Candela or Eduardo Torroja.

A refined and subtle beauty characterizes Dieste's work. It embodies sophisticated yet simple structures that combine varying brick-changing tonalities and patterns with technical rigor. His projects reflect three major considerations: an expressive force of local tradition, an integration of artistic and moral issues, and a knowledge of material property and capabilities.

JOSE BERNARDI

Biography

Born in Artigas, Uruguay, 10 December 1917. Received a degree in engineering from the University of the Republic, Montevideo, 1943. Married Elizabeth Friedham Utke, 1944: 11 children. Engineer in the Ministry of Public Works, Montevideo, 1943–45; engineer at the Represa Rincón del Bonete, Montevideo, 1945–46; chief engineer, Head Architectural Technical Office, Ministry of Public Works, Montevideo, 1946–48; chief engineer, Viermond SA, Montevideo, 1948–55. Founder and chief engineer, with Eugenio R. Montañez, of the firm Dieste and Montañez, from 1955. Consultant engineer, Salto Grande and Palmer Dams, Uruguay, from 1973. Professor of engineering, University of the Republic, Montevideo, 1943–45; visiting professor and lecturer, University of Buenos Aires, from 1959. Member, National Academy of Engineering, Uruguay, 1966. Died in Montevideo, Uruguay 19 July 2000.

Selected Works

Atlántida Church, Canelones, Uruguay, 1960
Eladio Dieste House, Montevideo, Uruguay, 1962
San Pedro Church (restoration), Durazno, Uruguay, 1971
Central Market, Porto Alegre, Brazil 1971
Municipal Bus Terminal, Salto, Uruguay, 1974
Refrescos del Norte Factory, Coca-Cola Exporter, Salto, Uruguay, 1978
Production Halls, Massaro Industries, Joanicó, Uruguay, 1978
Turlit Terminal, Salto, Uruguay, 1980
Shopping Center, Montevideo, Uruguay, 1985
Lanas Trinidad, Alta, Uruguay, 1991

Selected Publications

Problems of the Foundations of Turbo-Alternators, 1969
Buckling of Double Curvature Shells, 1970
The Action of Wind Over Long-Span Industrial Buildings, 1972
Reinforced Ceramic Hollow Towers, 1972

Further Reading

Anderson, Stanford, *Elado Dieste: Innovation in Structural Art*, by Princeton Architectural Press, 2003
Dieste, Eladio, *Eladio Dieste: la estructura cerámica*, Bogotá, Colombia: Escala, 1987
Eladio Dieste: 1943–1996 (exhib. cat.), 2 vols., Seville: Consejería de Obras Públicas y Transportes, 1997
Escolano, Victor Pérez, "Rigore e autenticita nell'opera di Eladio Dieste," *Lotus International* 98 (1998)
Waisman, Marina, and César Naselli, "Eladio Dieste," in *10 arquitectos latinoamericanos*, by Waisman and Naselli, Seville: Consejería de Obras Públicas y Transportes, Dirección General de Arquitectura y Vivienda, 1989

DISNEY THEME PARKS

Walt Disney's theme parks personify many of the trends that appeared in the media-saturated culture of postwar America, concentrated as entertainment centers for the leisure society. At Disneyland in California and its younger and larger sibling, Walt Disney World in Florida, Disney's genius for authoring modern, cinematic fables was brought to life in an amalgamation of high-tech paraphernalia and scenographic artistry. Visitors to the parks are able to live for a time in something like a movie set or, better yet, a compact sequence of numerous movie fantasies. The principle behind Disney's success was an uncanny ability to re-create the concept of place in Postmodern terms, as realms of inhabitable simulations and imagery that resonated well with a public raised on nostalgia and the vicarious thrills of the movies and who yearned for a more benign form of urbanism than the one confronting them daily. Combining aspects of amusement parks and world fairs, they purified America's public life in a new form of recreational spaces whose spectacular popularity made them an architectural metaphor for America's consumer culture.

Disney had set out his intentions in a plaque located at the entrance to Disneyland when it opened in 1955 on a site in Anaheim, California, a suburb of Los Angeles: "Here you leave today and enter the world of yesterday, tomorrow and fantasy." Disneyland's popularity was instantaneous. Designed largely by the in-house "Imagineers," a talented group of artists, artisans, and technicians who became the anonymous midwives of Walt Disney's vision, the park was shaped around explicit narrative concepts in which buildings played the roles of symbolic characters in a landscape of picturesque settings and sequenced storybook relationships. The plan for Disneyland was based on a simple, almost classical diagram of axially joined thematic precincts: Main Street, a stage-set reconstruction of a small 19th-century American town, began at the entrance and terminated in a central hub in front of the towering fantasy figure of Sleeping Beauty's Castle. From there paths led off like the spokes of a wheel to Frontierland, Adventureland, Fantasyland, and Tomorrowland.

The structure of the plan was filled out with lavish figural architectural settings that replicated images drawn largely from popular culture, many of them planted by Disney's own animated films. The Disney strategy was to invert the form-follows-function formula of modern architecture: by wrapping the attractions and their elaborate supporting technology in scenographic costumes, the park was constructed like a stage set. Most of the elaborate machinery that made the park work and the vast network of underground tunnels and utilities that served and serviced the surface imagery were made invisible to create the illusion that the purified simulations were operating independently, effortlessly, and without distractions.

Disney's vision of delight was filled with unabashed sentimentality and nostalgia; Disneyland took the form of a small town of the kind that was rapidly disappearing from the American scene. However, the town that was being portrayed was a denatured one, a deliberate contrivance built of images that were idealized and mythical. The architecture at Disneyland was designed to look right in ensembles of well-proportioned spaces, formal relationships, and illusionary scale that were achieved, for example, by reducing the buildings on Main Street to five-eighths scale to make them appear more toylike and friendly. However, the park was also technically sophisticated and well planned and engineered: As noted by many observers, Disney had produced something that had eluded real cities, a truly integrated system of multilevel mass-movement systems that included people movers, nonpolluting vehicles, monorails, pedestrian concourses, and vast urban infrastructure.

Disneyland was hemmed in by uncontrolled peripheral growth that limited its size and left it marooned in Los Angeles's sprawl. When Disney began scouting sites for a second park, his plans were far more expansive and ambitious. He had begun to think in utopian terms, imagining a vast urban plan that included not simply a single park but a series of them as well as an industrial park and residential community. Where Disneyland is a day trip, Walt Disney World becomes a weeklong expedition consisting of the Magic Kingdom as well as EPCOT, Disney MGM Studios, Pleasure Island, several water parks, two shopping centers, and dozens of hotels, all organized into an interconnected unit more than 180 times larger than Disneyland.

Disney's principle interests focused on EPCOT, an acronym for "Experimental Prototype Community of Tomorrow." He envisioned an idealized city based on modern planning principles that, in one of its iterations, was contained under a vast glass bubble to ensure a perfect climate. The plan reflected some of the ideas of the 19th-century English planner Ebenezer Howard's radial garden cities, rendered here in sleek, futuristic architecture. Commerce was located in a dense cluster of modern towers at the center surrounded by a series of expanding rings containing apartments, a green belt, and finally low-density, suburban-style neighborhoods. Reflecting Disney's interest in transportation technology, the city was to be linked by a monorail and a network of people movers. Disney imagined the city as a demonstration of the potentials for a modern city built along scientific principles as an alternative to the degradation he saw in the environments of America's cities. He described EPCOT as "a planned, controlled community, a showcase for American industry and research, schools, cultural and educational opportunities. In EPCOT there will be no slum areas because we won't let them develop."

However, the EPCOT that was built in 1982 after Walt Disney's death resembled nothing so much as a world's fair. The World Showcase, a collection of nationality pavilions designed to show typical architecture or familiar landmarks of the represented countries, was arranged in a loop around a man-made lagoon. Future World, the other part of the park, featured giant corporate-sponsored pavilions, including General Motors ("motion"), Exxon ("energy"), and Kodak ("imagination"). The two parts of the park are separate realms, each with different architectural treatments. Where the Future World pavilions are huge, nondescript sheds with little exterior detail or figuration beyond their lumpy shapes, the buildings in World Showcase are elaborately crafted inside and out, many of them using traditional crafts of the represented countries. The central figure is a huge, silver geodesic dome symbolizing "Spaceship Earth," reminiscent of the United States Pavilion at Expo '67 in Montreal.

Scholar Alfred Heller summed up the disappointment of many who had expected a more ambitious agenda for EPCOT. Writing in *World's Fair Quarterly*, he said, "It's not an experimental community or a prototype community or an experimental prototype of a community. It's not a community at all. It may be a prototype adult amusement park for the world of tomorrow." Disney's dream of creating a real residential community would have to wait until Celebration Florida was constructed in the early 1990s. By then, however, the vision had changed to the terms of the new urbanism. Celebration looked more like Main Street in the Magic Kingdom than the futurist city Disney originally imagined for EPCOT.

Michael Eisner, Walt Disney's successor as head of the Disney enterprises, developed an enthusiasm for architecture that led to the commissioning of buildings by some of the most distinguished architects of the day. Eisner provided a fertile ground for Postmodern architects to push the limits of convention in a succession of flamboyant buildings that were clearly influenced by Disney's philosophy of playfulness, irony, and wit. Michael Graves's designs for the Swan and Dolphin hotels (1989 and 1990, respectively) at Walt Disney World in Florida, the first of these large commissions, were startlingly colorful buildings, decorated inside and out with grotesque, overscaled details and sculptures, the most outrageous of which were the pairs of enormous swans and dolphins perched on their roofs. The hotels seemed to push the Postmodernist tendencies then on the rise into the realm of self-parody by subverting the well-composed facades with Disney-style kitsch.

Confidence in the success of the theme park formula led to the packaging of plans and technology for Tokyo Disney, which opened in 1983. However, Disney officials had set their eyes on Europe and a site in Marne-la-Vallee, a short distance outside Paris. Euro Disney (now Disneyland Paris) presented the designers with a number of new problems, among them the cultural question of how to make the essentially American imagery compelling in a country that had its own traditions and its own real castles. They decided to intensify the American theme rather than attempting to replicate local traditions. Convinced of the importance of creating a destination resort rather than simply a freestanding park, Disney officials embarked on an ambitious plan that included not only the park itself, which was in many respects simply a more refined copy of Walt Disney World in Florida, but a surrounding village of six hotels as well. Like the international buildings in the World Showcase, each hotel at Euro Disney was designed to evoke scenes of America, including Michael Graves's Art Deco urban landscape; Robert Stern's Newport Bay Club, modeled after a New England yacht club and the Cheyenne, a back-lot, western movie set; Antoine Grumbach's romantic Sequoia Lodge, resembling the rustic wood and stone hotels in America's national parks; and Anton Predock's haunting, minimalist Hotel Santa Fe, which on one side evoked the vernacular architecture of the American Southwest and on the other a drive-in movie theater complete with a billboard "screen" picturing Clint Eastwood. A sixth and the largest of the hotels, a High Victorian confection designed by the Disney Imagineers, served as an entrance into the park. Frank Gehry was given the assignment of designing a shopping and dining concourse called Festival Disney linking the hotels with the theme park that he made into a strip-center version of main street with a promenade of abstract, metal-skinned building forms punctuated by aluminum-clad pylons, all heavily garnished with neon and diner-style kitsch.

All Disney's built projects have been the subject of considerable critical attention. From their inception, the theme parks in particular were easy targets for social critics, who made them into sacrificial symbols of American consumer culture. To many architects and critics, the term "Disney" became synonymous with fakery and disingenuousness. However, the ambience of Disney was the art of the simulation—"masterpieces of falsification," as semiologist Umberto Eco wrote; and as long as they remained corralled within the precincts of the theme parks, they were the circumscribed experiences of entertainment.

However, architecture itself was shifting away from modernist ideals and into a romance with the ingratiating image. The proliferation of the synthetic over the natural had invaded the whole culture; as cultural geographer Edward Soja put it, a new wave had "carried hyperreality out of the localized enclosures and tightly bound rationality of the old theme parks and into the geographies and biographies of everyday life, into the fabric and fabrication of exopolis." With certain reservations, urbanists often marveled at the consummate skill with which the parks were put together and managed. Architectural historian Reyner Banham praised Disneyland as "an almost faultless organization for delivering, against cash, almost any type at all of environmental experience that human fancy, however inflamed could ever devise" (1971). Architect Charles Moore described the park as "the most important single piece of construction in the West in the past several decades" (1965).

Disney was an analogical thinker; his particular kind of inventiveness was to see the new possibilities available by investing in things already at hand or in memory. It was a combination of nostalgia and pragmatism: building the new out of reinterpretations and recombinations of what had become before. This also became one of the principles of the New Urbanism, a movement that rejected the urban experiments of modernism and sought instead to create urban models patterned on the things that worked in the past. In a somewhat curious involution, the art and science of Disneyland were being imitated in real-life places—in the malls, in resorts, and in the redevelopment of towns and townscapes. The theme park and the realities of living communities were beginning to join seamlessly together. However, to do so, as Disney demonstrated, required a purification of the sources and a simplification of the problem and a strong measure of central control.

BRUCE C. WEBB

See also **Amusement Park; Art Deco; Banham, Reyner (United States); Gehry, Frank (United States); Graves, Michael (United States); Moore, Charles (United States); Postmodernism; Shopping Center; Stern, Robert A.M. (United States)**

Further Reading

Banham, Reyner, *Los Angeles: The Architecture of Four Ecologies*, New York: Harper and Row, and London: Allen Lane, 1971

Dunlop, Beth, *Building a Dream: The Art of Disney Architecture*, New York: Abrams, 1996

Eco, Umberto, *Faith in Fakes*, translated by William Weaver, London: Secker and Warburg, 1986; as *Travels in Hyperreality*, translated by William Weaver, San Diego, California: Harcourt Brace Jovanovich, 1986

Fjellman, Stephen M., *Vinyl Leaves: Walt Disney World and America*, Boulder, Colorado, and Oxford: Westview Press, 1992

Marling, Karal Ann (editor), *Designing Disney's Theme Parks: The Architecture of Reassurance*, Montreal, Quebec: Canadian Centre for Architecture, and Paris and New York: Flammarion, 1997

Moore, Charles W., "You Have to Pay for the Public Life," *Perspecta: The Yale Architectural Journal* 9–10 (1965)

Sorkin, Michael, "See You in Disneyland" in *Variations on a Theme Park: The New American City and the End of Public Space*, edited by Sorkin, New York: Hill and Wang, 1992

DOM-INO HOUSES

Housing design by Le Corbusier, 1914–15 and later

Between 1914 and 1915, Le Corbusier, partly encouraged by his friend Max du Bois, conceived of a standardized system of construction using reinforced concrete, which was to provide the structural basis of most of his houses through the mid-1930s. These were the Dom-ino prefabricated houses with independent skeletons. The frame was to be completely independent of the floor plans of the houses. Derived from the Hennebique frame, it consisted of six thin concrete columns that simply carried two horizontal slabs as the floors. The columns and slabs were connected by staircases. Apart from this structural core of the houses, nothing else was fixed, thus permitting a great flexibility to suit demands on the basis of aesthetics, climate, composition, or view. The floor plan was also extremely flexible, as interior partitions were independent of the grid. This utterly simple and clear "open plan" method did away with load-carrying walls. Supporting beams for the ceiling slabs were eliminated. The vertical supports, recessed with respect to the exterior walls, allowed the facade to be freestanding, allowing windows to go easily around corners. The houses were to be built of standardized elements to be attached to one another in a wide variety of combinations, allowing for a great range in the grouping of the houses. This was not only a highly innovative idea from the technical standpoint but also an entirely new method of construction that promised rapid, economical mass housing.

At this time, reinforced concrete was still a relatively unused material for construction. After Tony Garnier and Auguste Perret, Le Corbusier was one of the first to advocate its use. For Dom-ino houses, there was to be a special on-site arrangement for pouring concrete to produce completely smooth and even floor slabs. A contractor would provide the frames. Other, specialized contractors would furnish different, mass-produced building material on the order of the architect-planner or the client. After windows and doors had been attached, the exterior walls would be built.

The system was conceived as a solution for the post–World War I rebuilding problem. At the time, reports of war devastation in Flanders were the major news. Dom-ino houses demonstrate Le Corbusier's awareness of housing not only as an important social and architectural problem but also an industrial process. Construction would be transformed into a scientifically run, large-scale activity. The Dom-ino house marked a significant step in Le Corbusier's quest for developing a standardized, rational solution to the problem of housing.

The name "Dom-ino" invites several levels of interpretation. "Dom-ino" invoked *domus*, Latin for "house." As a patent industrial label, it was also a play on the word *domino*, appropriate for a standardized house. In plan, the six-point supports resemble a rectangular domino chip. The physical form of the houses could also be interpreted in terms of dominoes, with the columns as domino dots and the zigzag pattern of a group of these houses as formations of dominoes. Le Corbusier also saw Dom-ino as a product (the architectural equivalent), in both form and mode of assembly, of a perfectible industrial object. Experiments with the Dom-ino prototype and the Citrohan House of 1920–22 were based on his belief that a perfectible housing type could be formulated. He expressed this belief in the famous phrase "a house is a machine for living" in *L'Esprit nouveau* in 1921. Widely misinterpreted as a functionalist statement, this meant that a house could be just as rationally produced as any object-type. In *Vers une architecture* (Toward a New Architecture), Le Corbusier wrote, "if we erase all rigid notions of the house from our hearts and minds and look at the question from a critical and objective point of view, we will inevitably arrive at the 'house-tool,' the mass-production house within everyone's reach, incomparably healthier than the old (even morally) and imbued with the beauty of the working tools of our daily lives." The universal house-machine was to provide aesthetic pleasure as well as functional efficiency and healthy surroundings.

Dom-ino houses were not built in Flanders during the war; its principles as economical housing only began to be applied in 1928 in France with the passing of the Loucheur Law, which was aimed at building 200,000 low-income housing units. In the meantime, the principles of the Dom-ino house were applied to the elegant Villa Schwob in La Chaux-de-Fonds, Switzerland (1916), which successfully synthesized the potential of the Hennebique frame and stylistic elements drawn from elsewhere. It is one of the first concrete-frame villas in Europe. The Dom-ino house was further evolved into the Citrohan House, which was exhibited at the Salon d'Automne of 1922. Much more sophisticated than the Dom-ino house, the Citrohan House represented for the first time a duplex design with a double-height living space, a mezzanine, and children's bedrooms on the roof. This marked the initial development of one of Le Corbusier's characteristic spatial treatments: interlocking spaces of different, proportional heights. These superimposed duplexes with two-to-one interior space, spiral staircases, and garden roofs would be a major recurrent theme and also figure as the villa blocks of the Contemporary City for Three Million Inhabitants (1922). This type was derived from the 19th-century artist's atelier and the *mégaron* of Mediterranean architecture.

Le Corbusier's houses up to 1935 evolved from the structures of the Dom-ino house and the Citrohan House and consisted of freestanding columns and cantilevered floor slabs. The almost cubelike Cook House (1962) in Boulogne, one of the high points of this period, incorporated mechanistic analogies and the aesthetics of purist painting. The Villa Stein/de Monzie (1927) in Garches, with a unique outdoor room that is half inside and half outside, demonstrated the potential of the Dom-ino skeleton to become a superimposed or overlapping set of layers. The Orbus Plan (1932) included small Dom-ino house cells for the working class. Le Corbusier considered his formulation of the elemental form of pure column and pure slab as central to his lifelong oeuvre.

HAZEL HAHN

See also **Corbusier, Le (Jeanneret, Charles-Edouard) France; Garnier, Tony; Perret, Auguste; Functionalism; Contemporary City for Three Million Inhabitants**

Further Reading

Boesiger, Willy, and Hans Girsberger (editors), *Le Corbusier, 1910–65* (trilingual German–French–English edition), Zurich: Éditions d'Architecture, New York: Praeger, and London: Thames and Hudson, 1967; 3rd edition, Zurich: Verlag für Architektur, 1991

Corbusier, Le, *The Ideas of Le Corbusier on Architecture and Urban Planning*, edited by Jacques Guiton, translated by Margaret Guiton, New York: Braziller, 1981

Curtis, William J.R., *Le Corbusier: Ideas and Forms*, Oxford: Phaidon, and New York: Rizzoli, 1986

Frampton, Kenneth, *Modern Architecture: A Critical History*, London: Thames and Hudson, and New York: Oxford University Press, 1980; 3rd edition, London: Thames and Hudson, 1992

Frampton, Kenneth, *Le Corbusier*, translated by Frank Straschitz, Paris: Hazan, 1997; English edition, New York: Thames and Hudson, 2001

Frampton, Kenneth, and Roberto Schezen, Le Corbusier: Architect of the Twentieth Century, New York: Abrams, 2002

Lucan, Jacques (editor), *Le Corbusier, une encyclopédie*, Paris: Centre Georges Pompidou, 1987
Raeburn, Michael, and Victoria Wilson (editors), *Le Corbusier: Architect of the Century*, London: Arts Council of Great Britain, 1987
Serenyi, Peter (editor), *Le Corbusier in Perspective*, Englewood Cliffs, New Jersey, and London: Prentice Hall, 1975

DOSHI, BALKRISHNA V. 1927–

Architect, India

Balkrishna V. Doshi belongs to the generation of architects that commenced working soon after India's independence in 1947. Influenced by the thinkers of the independence movement, Doshi's career is devoted to establishing an identity for the contemporary Indian architecture, and he has accomplished this by rooting his work in the regional context, marrying his designs with the local environment, and building on India's rich architectural and building traditions.

Born in 1927 in Poona (Pune), a city near Bombay (Mumbai), Doshi was raised in a religious family that was engaged in the traditional carpentry business. Observing his drawing skills, his art teacher encouraged him to pursue architectural education. In 1947, Doshi joined the J.J. School of Art in Bombay; unhappy with the course of studies, he quit the program in 1950 and decided to go to London, where he met Le Corbusier at CIAM (Congrès Internationaux d'Architecture Moderne). Following that meeting, Doshi moved to Paris to work with Le Corbusier, who at that time was designing the city of Chandigarh and other large Indian commissions as well as his influential European projects, such as La Tourette and Jaoul House. Profoundly influenced by Le Corbusier's work, Doshi returned to India in 1955 to look after the master's projects in Chandigarh and in Ahmedabad, where he also chose to settle.

The first decade of Doshi's work was strongly influenced by the work of Le Corbusier, including key projects from this era, such as the low-cost housing for the workers of the Ahmedabad Textile Industry Research Association (ATIRA) and the Physical Research Laboratory (PRL; 1957) in Ahmedabad and the Institute of Indology (1957), also in Ahmedabad. The Institute of Indology is an exposed-concrete structure with sun breakers and large overhangs or "parasols," devices used by Le Corbusier in his Indian buildings. However, in this project Doshi also managed to make a regional architectural statement. The building is subdivided into small units and looks like it could have been built using wooden post-and-beam elements. Large verandas and natural cooling and ventilation also remind us of the traditional wooden *havalies*, half-timber courtyard dwellings of Guajart. Moreover, the refined proportions, fine workmanship, and elegant finishes of the Indology Institute make it more delicate compared to Le Corbusier's *béton brut* style of Indian projects.

The second phase of Doshi's practice was tempered by the work of the great American architect Louis I. Kahn. Doshi invited Kahn to design the facilities for the Indian Institute of Management (IIM) complex in Ahmedabad. From the beginning of 1960s until the sudden death of Kahn in 1974, Doshi and he remained close friends and associates. This relationship touched Doshi's work in several ways: his use and choice of materials became refined, the play of geometry in his buildings got richer, and buildings started to demonstrate great depth and concern for light and shade and spirituality, all hallmarks of Kahn's work. Some key buildings from this phase of Doshi's work include the Township (1964) for Gujarat State Fertilizers in Baroda (Vadodra), the School of Architecture (1966, first phase) in Ahmedabad, the Township (1968) for the Electronics Corporation of India in Hyderabad, and the Parikh Residence (1974) in Ahmedabad. Kahn's design influence is evident in two township projects in which Doshi employed simple but efficient load-bearing wall structures and clean geometry to organize unit plans and to control the entry of light into each dwelling. Doshi's School of Architecture building, with its heavy load-bearing brick walls and industrial north lighting, also closely resembles Kahn's IIM complex, its dormitory and classroom areas in particular.

Doshi's active involvement in education coincides with his second phase of practice. In 1962, he and several colleagues established the Ahmedabad School of Architecture, which has become the Center of Environmental Planning and Technology, comprised of schools of planning, interior design, and building construction and a visual arts center. Doshi is also the founder and director of the Vastu-Shilpa Foundation, a nonprofit group for studies and research in environmental design. Doshi has regularly served as a visiting professor at most leading American and European universities, inspiring a new generation of designers and planners.

The last 25 years of Doshi's architectural work has been the most exuberant, and no doubt the richest, phase of his work. This architecture owes little to his mentors and more to the cultural and building traditions of India. Projects from this time blend beautifully with their surroundings and, more important, convey a sense that they are somehow Indian. Important projects from this phase are the Indian Institute of Management (1977) in Bangalore; the Administrative Complex (1979) for the Madhya Pradesh Electricity Board in Jabalpur; Sangath (1979), the architect's own office, in Ahmedabad; the Gandhi Labor Institute (1980) in Ahmedabad; Aranya low-cost housing (1983) in Indore; and the Diamond Bourse (1994) in Bombay (Mumbai).

Aranya is truly a model housing project for a developing nation such as India. A 6500-plot development, 65 percent of which is reserved for very poor clients, Aranya is inspired by the traditional lifestyle and patterns of living observed in low-income neighborhoods. To maintain marketability of high-income plots and to avoid segregation, each income groups' plots are configured around a sophisticated arrangement of plots and public open spaces in concentric rings in six distinct sectors. Large open spaces are avoided, but that space is evenly distributed in small parcels to accommodate various cottage industries and the spillover of home-based income generation. The principles of Doshi's recent architectural projects are also uniquely inspiring. Architecture is not entirely form related but is ordered by simple principles, such as the systemic collection and shedding of rainwater in the design of Sangath and the Gandhi Labor Institute and the apparently irregular fanning of the towers to maximize natural lighting in the offices of the Diamond Bourse. The use of simple design *parti* allows Doshi to compose his buildings as a loose approximation of traditional places and to build them in harmony with the climate, culture, and construction practices of India, making his projects captivating and memorable.

Vikram Bhatt

Sangath, (1979) view of the vaulted and flatroof buildings around the terraced court, Ahmedabad, India
Photo by Joseph N. St. Anne

Biography

Born in Poona, India, 26 August 1927. Attended Fergusson College, Poona 1946; studied at the J.J. School of Art, Bombay 1946–50. Married Kamala Parikh 1955: 3 children. Senior designer with Le Corbusier, Paris, for major buildings in Chandigarh and Ahmedabad, India 1951–57; represented Le Corbusier and supervised his projects in Ahmedabad 1954–57. Private practice, Ahmedabad from 1956; practiced under the firm name of Vastu-Shilpa 1956–77; member, Advisory Board, *Architecture + Urbanism*, Tokyo from 1971; senior partner, Stein, Doshi, and Bhalla, Ahmedabad and New Delhi from 1977. Visiting professor, Washington University, St. Louis, Missouri 1958, 1960, 1964, 1967, 1977, 1980; visiting professor, University of Pennsylvania, Philadelphia 1964, 1967, 1968, 1977, 1982, 1984; visiting professor, University of Illinois, Urbana-Champaign 1977; visiting professor, Rice University, Houston, Texas 1977; Paul Philippe Cret Professor of Architecture, University of Pennsylvania, Philadelphia 1984; distinguished professor, School of Architecture and School of Planning, Ahmedabad 1987; visiting professor, Berlage Institute, Amsterdam, the Netherlands 1991. Founder and honorary director, School of Architecture, Centre for Environmental Planning and Technology, Ahmedabad 1962–72; founder and honorary director, honorary dean, School of Planning, Centre for Environmental Planning and Technology, Ahmedabad 1972–78; founder and director, Vastu-Shilpa Foundation for Studies and Research in-Environmental Design from 1978; dean emeritus, Centre for Environmental Planning and Technology, Ahmedabad from 1981; founder and honorary director, Kanoria Centre for the Arts, Ahmedabad from 1984. Member, Team X 1967–71; fellow, Indian Institute of Architects 1971; fellow, Royal Institute of British Architects 1971; honorary fellow, American Institute of Architects 1971; member, Building International, London 1972–76; vice president, Council of Architecture, Government of India 1973–74; member, Scientific and Technical Advisory Council, Kent State University, Ohio from 1975; member, steering committee, 1998 Aga Khan Awards for Architecture. Aga Khan Award for Architecture 1995.

Selected Works

Low-cost housing for workers of the Ahmedabad Textile Industry Research Association (ATIRA), Ahmedabad, 1957
Physical Research Laboratory (PRL housing), Ahmedabad, 1957
Institute of Indology, Ahmedabad, 1957
Science Faculty Buildings for Gujarat University, Ahmedabad, 1959
Township for Gujarat State Fertilizers, Baroda (Vadodra), 1964
School of Architecture, Ahmedabad, 1966

Township for the Electronics Corporation of India, Hyderabad, 1968
Premabhai Hall, Ahmedabad, 1972
Parikh Residence, Ahmedabad, 1974
Indian Institute of Management, Bangalore, 1977
Administrative, Laboratory, Dormitory and ancillary facilities for the International Crop Research Institute for Semi-Arid Tropics, Hyderabad, 1977
Administrative Complex for the Madhya Pradesh Electricity Board, Jabalpur, 1979
Sangath, architect's own office, Ahmedabad, 1979
Gandhi Labor Institute, Ahmedabad, 1980
Aranya low-cost housing, Indore, 1983
Maharashtra Institute of Development Administration, Poona (Pune), 1987
National Institute of Fashion Technology, New Delhi, 1990
Diamond Bourse, Bombay (Mumbai), 1994

Selected Publications

Between Notion and Reality, 1986
"Planning for a Community—Vidyadhar Nagar," *International Social Science Journal* (August 1990)

Further Reading

Belluardo, James, and Kazi Khaleed Ashraf (editors), *An Architecture of Independence: The Making of Modern South Asia: Charles Correa, Balkrishna Doshi, Muzharul Islam, Achyut Kanvinde*, New York: Architectural League of New York, 1998
Bhatt, Vikram, "Architecture for a Developing India," *Harvard Design Magazine* (Summer 1999)
Bhatt, Vikram, and Peter Scriver, *After the Masters: Contemporary Indian Architecture*, Ahmedabad: Mapin, 1990
Curtis, William J.R., *Balkrishna Doshi: An Architecture for India*, New York: Rizzoli, 1988
Lang, Jon T., Madhavi Desai, and Miki Desai, *Architecture and Independence: The Search for Identity—India, 1880 to 1980*, Delhi and New York: Oxford University Press, 1997
Steele, James, *Rethinking Modernism for the Developing World: The Complete Architecture of Balkrishna Doshi*, New York: Whitney Library of Design, and London: Thames and Hudson, 1998

DUANY AND PLATER-ZYBERK

Architecture and town planning firm, United States

The firm of Duany and Plater-Zyberk and Company (DPZ) was formed in 1980. They have designed a number of award-winning, internationally published buildings that explore the transformation of local building tradition through classical systems of order. Their early Key Biscayne houses—Hibiscus (1981), De la Cruz (1983), Vilanova (1985)—and commercial buildings, such as Galen Medical (1983), in Boca Raton, reflect the grounding of abstract principles of architectural ordering borrowed from Le Corbusier's evolutionary theories of modernism as derived from classicism.

As architecture students at Yale University in the early 1970s, Andrés Duany and Elizabeth Plater-Zyberk absorbed the university's eclectic approach to the study of architecture with a growing emphasis on the craft-based tradition of building exemplified in early America's vernacular architecture. The theories of Vincent Scully, who decried the fierce effects of urban redevelopment schemes and proposed a view of architecture that included reconsideration of the traditional language of construction, laid the groundwork for what would become the DPZ practice.

Duany and Plater-Zyberk joined the architecture faculty of the University of Miami in 1974 and 1979, respectively. Their dual commitment to architecture education and practice established their methods of working. Léon and Rob Krier, along with Colin Rowe, were among the leading theorists who inspired the firm's expansion of an architectural method to the design of neighborhoods and the development of plans for towns and cities and laid the foundation for an approach to town planning that is architecturally conceived. The first town design (Seaside, 1979, on Florida's panhandle) was an experiment in establishing specifically designed spaces that ensure urbanity through ordinance. DPZ's subsequent Traditional Neighborhood Development Ordinance further codified the process of translating physical design to legal prescriptions for land use, allocation, and regulation. The textual and graphic codes of the ordinance establish the regulating plan; urban, architectural, and landscape regulations; and street type. Beginning in Seaside, DPZ generally exempts public buildings from such regulations to distinguish civic monument from domestic and commercial fabric. DPZ moved from new-town design to improvements in existing communities with an emphasis on reinforcing neighborhood identity and ensuring physical predictability through ordinance.

In 1988, Duany and Plater-Zyberk founded what is now the Town Design program at the University of Miami to actively engage and train graduate students in the process of designing and building towns and communities. Duany and Plater-Zyberk, with faculty and practitioners from across the nation, cofounded the Congress for the New Urbanism (CNU), which expands the pioneering work of the founders from an initial academic inquiry into a national movement for urban reform. The CNU advocates the development and redevelopment of towns and cities through a cohesive effort marked by a coordination of architecture and infrastructure with environmental, social, and economic initiatives.

Moreover, the architects have focused on buildings that enhance community. DPZ has engaged inner-city building with Florida projects such as the Mission San Juan Bautista (1996), a small mission church in Wynwood; La Estancia (1997), a migrant workers' housing complex in Tampa; and the DPZ office (1990) near Miami's Calle Ocho. Public projects such as the Florida City Civic Complex (1996), done with Lidia Abello and Derrick Smith, directly address issues of urbanism and use formal properties of space and light to demonstrate civic principles, as in the linkage of the main hall's skylight illumination of the interior with the action of a government in the "sunshine," Florida's law that mandates that all discussions of public officials on public issues be held with appropriate notice and in a public forum.

Concepts of urbanism rooted in local tradition are at the foundation of DPZ's urban design projects around the world, including the development of Kemer Village (1992) in Istanbul, Turkey, and Dos Rios (Manila, 1999) in the Philippines. Consistency of materials, structure, organizing devices, and use of local traditions gives DPZ's architecture a close and specific association with the conditions of the site, first as a historic, cultural entity, then as an environmental and social ecology, and then as an architectural continuum. The buildings and urban projects

Aerial view, Kentlands, Maryland, 1991 project designed by Duany and Plater-Zyberk
© Duany and Plater-Zyberk

Master Plan, Kentlands, Maryland (1991)
© Duany and Plater-Zyberk

demonstrate DPZ's central philosophy, which values architecture as the agent of community and as essential to a civil society.

JOANNA LOMBARD

See also **Arquitectonica (United States); New Urbanism; Suburban Planning; Urban Planning**

Biography

Andrés Duany

Born in New York, 7 September 1949; son of Andrés J. Duany, real estate developer and builder. Studied architecture at Princeton University, Princeton, New Jersey 1971. Received a graduate degree in architecture from Yale University, New Haven, Connecticut 1974; studied at the École des Beaux Arts, Paris. Worked in the offices of Ricardo Bofill and Robert A.M. Stern. Founded Arquitectonica with Bernardo Fort-Brescia, Hervin Romney, Laurinda Spear, and Elizabeth Plater-Zyberk; partner, Andrés Duany and Elizabeth Plater-Zyberk, Architects and Town Planners from 1980. Professor, University of Miami from 1974; cofounder, Town Design Program, University of Miami 1988; cofounder, Congress for New Urbanism.

Elizabeth Plater-Zyberk

Born in Bryn Mawr, Pennsylvania, 10 December 1950; daughter of Josaphat Plater-Zyberk, architect, and Maria Plater-Zyberk, gardener. Studied architecture at Princeton University, Princeton, New Jersey 1972; graduate degree from Yale University, New Haven, Connecticut 1974; teaching assistant to Vincent Scully at Yale. Architectural intern with Venturi Rauch and Scott-Brown. Founded Arquitectonica with Bernardo Fort-Brescia, Hervin Romney, Laurinda Spear, and Andrés Duany; partner, Andrés Duany and Elizabeth Plater-Zyberk, Architects and Town Planners from 1980. Professor, University of Miami from 1979; cofounder, Town Design Program, University of Miami 1988; cofounder, Congress for New Urbanism.

Selected Works

The Town of Seaside, Florida, 1979
Hibiscus House, Coconut Grove, Florida, 1981
Galen Medical Building, Boca Raton, 1983
De la Cruz House, Key Biscayne, 1983
Vilanova House, Key Biscayne, 1985
Blount Springs, Alabama, 1988
Downtown Plan, Mashpee Commons, Massachusetts, 1988
Windsor, Florida, 1989
Avalon Park, Florida, 1989
Duany Plater-Zyberk Office, Miami, 1990
Kentlands, Maryland, 1991
Kemer Village, Istanbul, 1992
Cleveland Central Commons Neighborhood, 1993
Mission San Juan Bautista, Wynwood, Florida, 1996
Florida City Civic Complex (with A + S Architects), 1996
La Estancia, Tampa, 1997
Dos Rios, Manila, 1999

Selected Publications

Andrés Duany

"Principles in the Architecture of Alvar Aalto," *Harvard Architecture Review*, 5 (1986)
"En Loge," in *Zero Hour*, edited by Charlotte Milholland, 1987
"The Future of La Habana," in *One World: Shared Cultural Influences in the Architecture of the Americas*, 1997

Elizabeth Plater-Zyberk

"The Three Traditions of Miami," in *Miami: Architecture of the Tropics*, edited by Maurice Culot and Jean François Lejeune, 1992
"It Takes a Village to Raise a Child," in *Suburbs and Cities: Changing Patterns in Metropolitan Living*, 1994
"The Wrecker's House," in *Black and White: A Journal of Architecture and Ideas*, 3 (1997)

Andrés Duany and Elizabeth Plater Zyberk

"The Town of Seaside," *The Princeton Journal: Thematic Studies in Architecture*, 2 (1985)
"Andrés Duany, Elizabeth Plater-Zyberk," *Metamorfosi*, 6–7 (September 1988)
"The Neighborhood, the District, and the Corridor," in *The New Urbanism*, edited by Peter Katz, 1994
"The Second Coming of the American Small Town," *The Wilson Quarterly* (Winter 1992)
"Site Planning," in *Architectural Graphic Standards*, 1994
Suburban Nation: The Rise of Sprawl and the Decline of the American Dream (with Jeff Speck), 2000

Further Reading

Both Krier and Scully locate the intellectual center of the work of DPZ. Krieger and Lennertz organized an exhibition at Harvard's Graduate School of Design, and the subsequent book—which features essays by Vincent Scully, Patrick Pinnell, and Leon Krier—remains the most comprehensive collection of DPZ's urban work. Mohney and Easterling curated an exhibition on Seaside at the Architectural League of New York, and the subsequent book continues to be the most complete representation of the planning, design, and construction of Seaside. Duany and Plater-Zyberk's own book with Jeff Speck, *Suburban Nation*, offers a complete summary of the values and process of the urban projects.

Duany, Andrés, Elizabeth Plater-Zyberk, and Jeff Speck, *Suburban Nation: The Rise of Sprawl and the Decline of the American Dream*, New York: North Point Press, 2000
Krieger, Alex, and William Lennertz (editors), *Andrés Duany and Elizabeth Plater-Zyberk: Towns and Town-Making Principles*, New York: Rizzoli, 1991
Krier, Leon, "The Reconstruction of Vernacular Buildings and Classical Architecture," *The Architects' Journal*, 12 (12 September 1984)
Mohney, David, and Keller Easterling, *Seaside: Making a Town in America*, New York: Princeton Architectural Press, and London: Phaidon, 1991
Scully, Vincent, *American Architecture and Urbanism*, New York: Holt Reinhart and Winston, and London: Thames and Hudson, 1969; revised edition, New York: Holt, 1988

DUDOK, WILLEM MARINUS 1884–1974

Architect, the Netherlands

Willem Marinus Dudok, a city architect for Hilversum, the Netherlands, a small town southeast of Amsterdam, is well known for his distinctive contribution to the modernism of the early 20th century. His architecture provided a compositional strength and visual richness that transformed the otherwise traditional and conservative community of Hilversum into the modern age.

Born in 1884 in Amsterdam to musician parents, Johannes Cornelis and Cornelia Bertha (née Holst), Dudok claimed that his architectural design was influenced more by the great composers than by the great architects. Much to the disappointment of his parents, though, rather than pursue music, Dudok chose a career in the army. He attended Alkmaar Cadet School and later Breda Military Academy, where he was trained in military engineering, with a focus on fortification planning. Over time, he taught himself architecture, and when he was promoted to lieutenant-engineer in the Royal Engineering Corps, he joined a team that planned and built fortifications that were to surround Amsterdam, possibly his first experience with building. In 1913, he left the army and began work as the deputy director of Public Works for the town of Leiden, moving to Hilversum two years later to become the Director of Public Works. He later became the city architect in 1928, a position he held until his retirement in 1954.

Throughout Dudok's long career in Hilversum, he is credited with building almost all its public buildings and is thought to have been instrumental in producing a town development plan that was based on the English Garden City movement promoted by Briton Ebenezer Howard (1850–1928). Of Dudok's 150 realized projects over his 50-year career, 80 percent were within Hilversum's local government area, and only four were outside the Netherlands. Dudok was at his zenith between 1916 and 1930, when he designed 13 public housing estates, some of which contained up to 180 buildings. In addition, he designed 11 schools and extended two others. Other more utilitarian projects included a sports park, an abattoir, pumping stations, and public utilities. The building that became an icon and career acme, however, was the Hilversum Town Hall. Although his design influence pervades the town, no other structure is as much of a masterpiece. The Marriage between art and geometry succeeded with the culmination of his modernist philosophy into a premier object d'art.

Dudok claimed to have acquired his ideas of architectural truth from Karel P.C. de Bazel (1869–1923) and Hendrik Petrus Berlage (1854–1934). De Bazel was a Theosophist whose mysticism and architectural theory permeated the planimetric and volumetric geometry of his designs. Berlage was also widely published; his works included a collection of six essays titled *Thoughts on Architecture and Its Development* (1911), thought to be one of his more important anthologies. It was Berlage, considered the "Father of modern architecture," who first introduced the work of Frank Lloyd Wright (1867–1959) to European architects. His interest and great admiration caused him

Community Bath (1926) Hilversum, Netherlands, by Willem M. Dudok

to pronounce that Wright was a master, "whose equal is yet to be found in Europe." The Wrightian philosophy of form and space definition was particularly espoused by the De Stijl and the Amsterdam School movements.

Dudok also recognized Wright's innovative design: "I saw his work for the first time . . . and immediately recognized his greatness." He was impressed by the "poetic spirit" and "harmonious construction" of his spaces. As a result, Wright then heavily influenced Dudok's subsequent work, but Dudok was also thought to have been affected by Amsterdam School Expressionism, De Stijl functionalism, Delft School traditionalism, Cubism, and Dutch vernacular. Dudok's eclectic style was sometimes mistakenly referred to as a "hybrid" of some or all of these elements. Dudok's independent approach to modernism made him one of the most influential architects working in the Netherlands between the two world wars. This nonconformist unique style is also sometimes attributed to his informal architectural training.

Dudok's lifelong passion for music was reflected in the rhythm, mood, and character of the proportions of his architecture, unifying it and enhancing its sculptural expression. This response to modernism was restrained by the soft craftsmanship of the built form. Dudok managed to express the ideals of modern architecture while still retaining the traditional values of composition, craftsmanship, and materials but most importantly, monumentality. Dudok emphasized that "monumentality is the most pure expression of the human sense of harmony and order." The monumental building stressed not only the essential material elements but also its spirituality. Its value transcended the human experience and entered the spiritual realm. This architectural theology in the form of built reality formed a model for many later architects throughout Europe and the United States. Unfortunately, as his "style" was repeatedly duplicated, his individuality and stylistic superiority diminished. By the 1950s, his architecture no longer contained the artistic and spiritual qualities that were inherent in the earlier works.

Dudok was celebrated in worldwide publications of his work. By 1924 international books and journals showcased his projects, giving great attention to the town in which he did most of his work. Hilversum briefly became an architectural mecca, attracting admirers to study and perhaps worship Dudok's work.

Dudok's architecture earned several awards, including the gold medals of the Royal Institute of British Architects (RIBA) in 1935, the American Institute of Architects (AIA) in 1955, and the French Academy of Architecture in 1966. In his own country, he received several other awards, including knighthood.

Dudok's other notable projects include the Municipal Baths (1921) in Hilversum, the columbarium of the creamery (1926) in Westerveld, The Netherlands students' house of the Cité Universitaire (1927) in Paris, "De Bijenkorf" (1929) in Rotterdam, the Monument on the Zuyderzee Dyke (1933), and the H.A.V. Bank (1934–35) in Schiedam. Dudok's independent style produced a range of modernist buildings, making him a defining force in the Modern movement and a premier architect of his time.

Elisabeth A. Bakker-Johnson

See also **Amsterdam School; Berlage, Hendrik Petrus (The Netherlands); Cubism; De Stijl; Garden City Movement; Hilversum Town Hall; Wright, Frank Lloyd (United States)**

Further Reading

An exhaustive list of available material can be found in Langmead 1996.

Groenendijk, Paul, and Piet Vollaard, *Gids voor moderne architectuur in Nederland* (Guide to Architecture in the Netherlands), Rotterdam, The Netherlands: Uitgeverij 010 Publishers, 1987

Holzbauer, Wilhelm, "Willem Marinus Dudok. Town Hall, Hilversum, The Netherlands, 1928–31," *Global Architecture: An Encyclopedia of Modern Architecture* 58 (1981)

Langmead, Donald, *Willem Marinus Dudok, A Dutch Modernist: A Bio-Bibliography*, Westport, Connecticut: Greenwood Press, 1996

Magnee, Robert M.H. (editor), *Willem M. Dudok*, Amsterdam: G. van Saane "Lectura Architectonica," 1954

Whittick, Arnold, *European Architecture in the Twentieth Century*, New York: Abelard-Schuman, 1974

Wit, Wim de (editor), *The Amsterdam School: Dutch Expressionist Architecture, 1915–1930*, New York: Cooper-Hewitt Museum, The Smithsonian Institution's National Museum of Design; London and Cambridge, Massachusetts: MIT Press, 1983

DUIKER, JOHANNES 1890–1935

Architect, the Netherlands

Although relatively unknown outside his native land during his brief life span, today Johannes Duiker is recognized as among the foremost representatives of the *Nieuwe Bouwen*, the Dutch version of functionalism, or *neue Sachlichkeit* (New Objectivity). The buildings of his maturity, composed of crystalline volumes of great purity, executed without superfluous details, rationally fulfill function while expressing modernity in all its spare beauty. The exciting possibilities of 20th-century technique are transformed into radiant forms that engage the mind and lift the spirit.

Duiker's work cannot be discussed without citing two other Dutchmen, Bernard Bijvoet (1889–1980) and the civil engineer Jan Gerko Wiebenga (1886–1974), with whom Duiker frequently collaborated, thus honoring one of the ideals of the modern movement: its stated emphasis on architecture as a cooperative profession. Although Duiker's lyrical architectural vision dominates, realization of the oeuvre is a result of teamwork.

Like so many of their peers, Duiker and Bijvoet would achieve recognition through competitions. Already in 1913 they won first prize for a church, never built, but their entry of 1916 for the Karenhuizen, an elders' hostel in Alkmaar, became their first executed work (1918). They next triumphed in the most prestigious contest of the day, that for the Academy of Fine Arts in Amsterdam in 1917 (Michel de Klerk, the leader of the Amsterdam School, came in second); although their striking design, heavily influenced by Frank Lloyd Wright, would never be erected, the prize money allowed them to establish a partnership that would continue even after Bijvoet moved to Paris in 1925 to work for Pierre Chareau.

Duiker's production can be divided into three phases. In the first, from 1913 to 1923, he employed the traditional Dutch vocabulary of brick with stone trim, wooden sash, and tile roofs and followed the lead of H.P. Berlage, the doyen of Dutch architecture. The majority of commissions from this period are domestic, whether for groups of urban townhouses or clusters of villas at Kijkduin (1919–23), all in The Hague. The next, transitional period is foreshadowed in the entry to the Chicago Tribune Competition (1922), which is indebted to De Stijl, a movement that Duiker would later criticize for its aestheticism. However, it was in 1924, when Duiker discovered skeletal structures, that the major shift toward a personal language appeared. This occurred at Stommeerkade 64 (1924) in Aalsmeer, a country house supported by a wooden frame and based on novel motifs: shed (monopitch) roofs, window bands that turn the corner, a projecting circular stair, and horizontal wooden siding. The interior spaces are clearly articulated in the exterior massing. It is but a short step to the reinforced-concrete-and-steel skeletons and glazed curtain walls of Duiker's mature phase, which commenced with the Laundry in Diemen (1924; extension 1925), built for the Koperen Stelenfonds (KSF, Copper Wire Fund) of the ANDB (Netherlands Diamond Workers Union), which raised money by retrieving and selling copper wire used in the diamond polishing process.

The encounter with this new client might have occurred as early as 1919 and was brought about through Berlage's recommendation. It equals in importance Duiker's introduction to skeletal construction, for several major projects were commissioned by this socially conscious body dedicated to the well-being of employees of one of the main industries in Amsterdam, namely, the preparation of diamonds for the international market. The most extensive was for the sanatorium Zonnestraal (Sunshine) in Hilversum, which received its definitive formulation in 1925 and was completed in 1928 to great acclaim. The program was perfectly suited to Duiker's growing concern with health, and he utilized his new mastery of concrete construction to fashion a luminous series of buildings intended to speed recovery from tuberculosis, an occupational hazard of the diamond workers.

Duiker's concurrent preoccupation with mass production and the tall building resulted in a book, *Hoogbouw* (1930), and a block of flats in The Hague, Nirwana (1927–30), both done in collaboration with Wiebenga. American skyscrapers had captured the European imagination and led to many fantastic projects, above all in Germany and the Netherlands, but the modestly scaled Nirwana, comprising six stories of apartments set between a ground story and a penthouse, seemed eminently feasible. It was intended as a prototype, but despite structural innovations, the envisaged economies did not come about, and the handsome building with its ingeniously designed corner windows remains a unique example.

In 1928, Duiker joined the polemical Amsterdam group De 8, founded in 1927, and was elected president in 1932. That same year he became the first editor of *De 8 en Opbouw*, the periodical published jointly with the similarly functionalist *Opbow* (Construct), established in 1920 in Rotterdam. From 1932 to 1935, Duiker filled its pages with thoughtful commentary on the nature of the new architecture and, by extension, the new society, shaped by scientific progress and mechanization, that it was to serve. When the *Nieuwe Bouwen* was criticized for its utilitarianism, Duiker responded that it was spiritual rather than monetary economy he sought, utilizing new materials to dematerialize architecture and embody the quickened tempo of modern life.

The four-story Fresh [Open-Air] School for the Healthy Child, (Amsterdam, 1929–30) complements Duiker's interest in hygiene, manifested at Zonnestraal, and maintains the vocabulary of exposed reinforced-concrete frame and window walls. Set behind an entry building that dramatically spans the existing dwellings on the Cliostraat in Amsterdam, the school demonstrates how Duiker achieved magic with the simplest and most direct means.

One year before his death, Duiker received commissions for three significant buildings, including the newsreel cinema Cineac (Amsterdam, 1934), ingeniously fitted onto a miniscule plot and identified by a striking neon sign set high above the street, and the department store Winter (Amsterdam, 1934), its transparent curtain wall stretching the length of the facade to facilitate tempting views of the merchandise. He also began work on the Grand Hotel and Theater Gooiland (1934–36) in Hilversum; after his death, Bijvoet came from Paris to see to its execution, apparently adding a few touches of his own.

Although Duiker rarely left the Netherlands, he was conversant with international architectural events. With Wiebenga he submitted an entry to the League of Nations competition, and although he was not present at the founding meeting of the Congrès Internationaux d'Architecture Moderne (CIAM) in 1928, he participated in its third conference on Rationelle Bebauungsweisen (1930) by sending a project for exhibition. Throughout his professional career, Duiker followed advances in the natural sciences and mathematics, believing that they pointed the way to an architecture that would free rather than constrain its occupants and encourage them to pursue a wholesome lifestyle invigorated by physical health and spiritual enlightenment.

HELEN SEARING

See also **Amsterdam, the Netherlands; Berlage, Hendrik Petrus (the Netherlands); De Stijl; the Netherlands; Open-Air School, Amsterdam; Zonnestraal Sanatorium, Hilversum, the Netherlands**

Biography

Born 1 March 1890 in The Hague, son of a school principal and a teacher. Enrolled in the Technische Hogeschool, Delft 1907; studied under Henri Evers and J.F. Klinkhamer; graduated with degree of *bouwkundig ingenieur* 1913. Married 1) Hermina Valken, 1919 (divorced 1925), two children. Lived with and later married 2) Lucy Kupper (1925), who managed his office. Worked for Henri Evers, Rotterdam, 1913–16, established partnership with Bernard Bijvoet 1917–25, located first in The Hague, then in nearby Zandvoort; independent practice in Amsterdam 1925, but continued collaborations, first with Bijvoet and then with Wiebenga; joined De 8, 1928, elected president 1932. Editor, *De 8 en Opbouw*, 1932–35; with Wiebenga conducted studies about the technical aspects of tall buildings and of prefabrication; died in Amsterdam 23 February 1935.

Selected Works

With Bijvoet

Karenhuizen home for the elderly, Krelagestraat, Alkmaar (modernized), 1918

Residential village Kijkduin (14 villas, some semidetached), Scheveningselaan, The Hague, 1923

House for A. Suermondt, Stommeerkade 64, Aalsmeer, 1924
Laundry for the KSF, Diemen, 1924; extended 1925 (demolished)
Country house "Doelzicht," Hilversum (demolished), 1925
Open-Air School, Amsterdam, 1930
Building for service personnel, Zonnestraal, Hilversum, 1931
Grand Hotel and Theater "Gooiland," Hilversum, 1936

With Bijvoet and Wiebenga

Zonnestraal Sanatorium, Henri ter Meulen and Dresselhuys pavilions, ateliers, Loosdrechtse Bos 7, Hilversum (restored), 1928

With Wiebenga:

"Nirwana" flats, Willem Witsenplein, The Hague, 1930

Duiker alone

Third Trade School (first commissioned with Bijvoet, 1921), Zwaardstraat 6, Scheveningen, 1931
Cineac, Amsterdam (altered), 1934
Winter Department Store, Amsterdam (altered), 1934

Selected Publications

Hoogbouw, 1930; reprinted as *Hoogbouw (1930) met een nawoor van Manfred Bock*, 1930

Further Reading

For a catalogue raisonné of Duiker's works, see *J. Duiker bouwkundig ingenieur* (1982).

Boga, Thomas (editor), *B. Bijvoet en J. Duiker (1890–1935)* (exhib. cat.), Zurich: Eidgenossischen Technischen Hochschule, 1975. Essay in English by Robert Vickery

Buch, Joseph, *Een eeuw Nederlandse architectuur, 1880–1990; A Century of Architecture in the Netherlands, 1880–1890* [bilingual Dutch-English edition], Rotterdam: NAi publishers, 1993

Casciato, Maristella, *Johannes Duiker 1890–1935: Le Scuole*, Rome: CLEAR (Cooperativa Libraria Editrice Architettura), 1982

Derwig, Jan and Erik Mattie, *Functionalisme in Nederland; Functionalism in The Netherlands* [bilingual Dutch-English edition], Amsterdam: Architectura et Natura, 1995

Duiker, Johannes, *Jan Duiker*, Barcelona: Gustavo Gili, 1989

Duikergroep Delft, *J. duiker bouwkundig ingenieur: constructeur in stuc en staal*, Rotterdam: Stichting Bouw, 1982

Fanelli, Giovanni, *Architettura moderna in Olanda*, Florence: Firenze, Marchi and Bertolli, 1968; as *Moderne architectuur in Nederland, 1900–1940* [bilingual Dutch-English edition], translated by Wim de Wit, Gravenhage: Staatsuitgeverij, 1978

Idsinga, Ton, *Zonnestraal: Een nieuwe tijd lag in het verschiet*, Amsterdam: Arbeiderspers, 1986

Loghem, Johannes Bernandres van, *Bouwen-Bauen-Bâtir-Building, Holland*, Amsterdam: Kosmos, 1932

Milelli, Gabriele, *Zonnestraal, il sanatorio di Hilversum*, Bari: Dedalo Libri, 1978

Molema, Jan, *The New Movement in the Netherlands, 1924–1936*, Rotterdam: 010, 1996

Rebel, Ben, *Het Nieuwe Bouwen: het functionalism in Nederland, 1918–1945*, Assen: Van Gorcum, 1983

Zoetbrood, Ronald, *Jan Duiker en het sanatorium Zonnestraal*, Amsterdam: Van Gennep, 1985

DULLES INTERNATIONAL AIRPORT

Designed by Eero Saarinen and Associates, completed 1962
Chantilly, Virginia

This airport, located 28 miles southwest of Washington, D.C., was conceived as the international gateway to the nation's capital. President Eisenhower made the final site selection in 1958, and the Civil Aviation Authority (CAA) commissioned Eero Saarinen and Associates to build the first American airport designed specifically to handle jet airplanes. In a quirk of timing, this symbol of international welcome was named for Eisenhower's secretary of state, John Foster Dulles, the bellicose point man for America's Cold War policies before his death in 1959. The airport design was innovative on several counts, including its automobile traffic pattern (with separate levels for arrivals, departures, and parking) and its controversial "mobile lounges," which detach from the main terminal building to ferry passengers out to airplanes parked next to the runways. In 1962 these odd-looking vehicles were considered a breakthrough in airport efficiency and passenger comfort. The model was never copied at any other airport, although the mobile lounges do remain in use at Dulles Airport, supplemented by a few fixed gates added to the airport in the mid-1990s. Modifications to the airport were far more visible in 1997, as work commenced to extend the main terminal building 300 feet at either end, doubling its original length. Undisturbed by these alterations, the pagoda-inspired air traffic control tower (initially planned to include an observation deck) continues to oversee the airport, providing a strong vertical accent to balance the emphatic horizontality of the site and the enlarged terminal building.

Saarinen had anticipated the need for expansion, designing the pavilion-like terminal as a set of 15 modular bays that were easily replicated by the builders of the additions. The bays, each 40 feet wide, are framed by rows of concrete piers standing a monumentalizing 65 feet tall along the main facade and then dipping to 40 feet in height on the air side of the pavilion as a sheltering gesture for passengers arriving aboard the mobile lounges. As at the TWA Airport Terminal (1962), also designed by Eero Saarinen and Associates and located at New York's John F. Kennedy Airport, custom-styled concrete supports were required to make possible the unique roof form at Dulles, justly celebrated for its bold upward sweep from back to front. Saarinen described the roof as "like a huge continuous hammock suspended between concrete trees [and] made of light suspension-bridge cables between which the concrete panels of the roof deck fit." The piers of the opposing colonnades slant away from each other to counteract the load of the poured-in-place slabs carried by the cables. However, as the architect acknowledged, "we exaggerated and dramatized this outward slope [of the piers] to give the colonnade a dynamic and soaring look as well as a stately and dignified one." The desired effect was to maintain some connection with Federal traditions of static, neoclassical architecture while still pulling off the kind of grand expressive gesture that Saarinen saw as essential, given the use of the building.

Saarinen did not live to see the airport completed, as he died during surgery for a brain tumor in 1961. Two of his associates, Kevin Roche and John Dinkeloo, inherited the firm and supervised the construction of Dulles Airport together with the engineering firm of Ammann and Whitney and airport consultant Charles Landrum. Roche recalls the early stages of the work, when all discussion of the appearance and structure of the airport were held in abeyance for 14 months after the commission was received while the functional scheme for the passenger concourse was worked out. Any Saarinen staffer traveling by plane was under strict orders to note the time taken to check-in, to walk

Dulles Airport, by Eero Saarinen, at Chantilly, Virginia (1958–1962)
© Donald Corner and Jenny Young/GreatBuildings.com

to the departure gate, and to receive baggage at every airport they visited. According to Roche, Saarinen always traveled with a stopwatch, methodically recording such details and, invariably, reaching his gate at the last possible moment, "just to drive me crazy."

Having boiled down the passenger data to produce an ideal plan, comprising the concourse and mobile lounges, Saarinen brought in friends Charles and Ray Eames to produce a documentary that was intended to help sell the airlines on the scheme. Airline officials were not fully convinced by the ten-minute cartoon short, "The Expanding Airport." However, the CAA came down firmly on Saarinen's side, alerted by the film to the fact that the proposed 1000-foot-long pavilion concourse would have to stretch to 8000 feet if they opted for a conventional "finger-terminal" airport of equal capacity.

Their plan for the new airport approved, Saarinen and his design team embarked on the search for a suitable form for its main pavilion. Dozens of sketches, now in the archives at Yale University, show what a remarkable variety of shapes were considered—rows of barrel vaults and of ziggurats as well as jagged roof forms, as if drawn by Picasso. Ultimately, Saarinen looked back to his own work, on the cable-strung roof of the Ingalls Hockey Rink (1959), built by the firm on the Yale campus in New Haven, Connecticut. The hammock form that evolved for the airport pavilion has since been celebrated to the point where the U.S. Postal Service printed a 20-cent stamp to honor the building as part of a series in the 1980s dedicated to American architecture. Suitably, a jet airplane is seen on the stamp, climbing into the sky (but in a direction perpendicular to the runways, as if it somehow took off from the concourse roof).

Heralded as "The Temple of Travel," the central pavilion itself appears to hover above the flat plains of the airport runways. Approached by car, Dulles Airport can be seen as a "Jet-Age Parthenon," resting on an "Acropolis" created by the tiers of roadways stacked up at its front. In its thrusting expressionistic posture, the pavilion is also reminiscent of designs by Erich Mendelsohn, particularly that portrayed by his 1914 sketch, "Architectural Fantasy." In turn, Saarinen's airport buildings (if not his mobile lounges) have inspired imitation, as in Renzo Piano's Kansai Airport (1994) at Osaka, Japan, and in an airport design by Santiago Calatrava for Bilbao, Spain. That Saarinen knew that he and his firm had created something special at Dulles is evident from comments made just two months before his death: "I think this airport is the best thing I have done. . . . Maybe it will even explain what I believe about architecture." At the very least, he matched the feat performed by his father, architect Eliel Saarinen, at the Helsinki Train Terminal (1914) in Finland by likewise providing his country with a transportation gateway that is a masterpiece of its genre.

DAVID NAYLOR

See also **Airport and Aviation Building; Helsinki Railway Station, Finland; Saarinen, Eero (Finland); Saarinen, Eliel (Finland)**

Further Reading

Dulles International Airport was spotlighted as being among the last works fully attributable to Eero Saarinen in the monograph by Allan Temko and in the compilation of Saarinen's remarks as edited by his widow, Aline Saarinen. Aline Saarinen also participated, with Edgar J. Kaufmann, Jr., in a documentary film, "Eero Saarinen Architect (1910–1961)," filmed largely inside the main concourse at Dulles and distributed in 1967 by Columbia University Press. Since the 1960s, only infrequent attention has been paid to the airport, despite its reputation worldwide.

Brodherson, David, " 'An Airport in Every City': The History of American Airport Design," in *Building for Air Travel*, edited by John Zukowsky, Chicago: The Art Institute of Chicago, 1996

Kaufmann, Edgar J., Jr., "Our Largest Airports: Dulles International Airport, O'Hare International Airport," *Progressive Architecture*, 44 (August 1963)

McQuade, Walter, "A New Airport for Jets," *Architectural Record*, 127 (March 1960)

Nakamura, Toshio (editor), *Eero Saarinen*, Tokyo: A + U Publishing, 1984

Saarinen, Aline B. (editor), *Eero Saarinen on His Work*, New Haven, Connecticut: Yale University Press, 1962; revised edition, 1968

Temko, Allan, *Eero Saarinen*, New York: Braziller, 1962

Tzonis, Alexander, Liane Lefaivre, and Richard Diamond, *Architecture in North America since 1960*, Boston: Bulfinch Press, and London: Thames and Hudson, 1995

DÜSSELDORF, GERMANY

As a German industrial and commercial center in the Prussian Rhine province, Düsseldorf expanded rapidly in the last quarter of the 19th century, serving as the banking and trading center for the heavily industrialized *Ruhrgebiet* (Ruhr Valley) to the east. Industrialization and continuous development as a trade-fair center shaped the city and its architecture along the Rhine River. Noteworthy commercial and administrative structures were built in the first half of the 20th century, but during World War II much of the city was destroyed by Allied bombing raids. Although some prewar buildings were undamaged or restored, a great deal of construction in the 1950s and 1960s transformed the cityscape, with many notable achievements. In 1946, the Allied occupation designated Düsseldorf the capital of the new state of Northrhine-Westphalia, and, as a result, prominent new structures associated with state capital status have enhanced the city's architectural character.

Düsseldorf has long been a center for art and architectural study. Under the German Empire, the city had two art institutions: an Academy of Art (Kunstakademie) and a School for Arts and Crafts (Kunstgewerbeschule). Both offered courses in architecture and design. The Kunstakademie continues to be a leading center for study. However, the Kunstgewerbeschule closed in 1918, torn between the reformist and conservative tendencies of the 20th century. The Kunstgewerbeschule was an important center for aesthetic reform under Peter Behrens' directorship (1903–07). A number of innovative designers were attracted to the school, including Rudolf Bosselt, Fritz Helmuth Ehmcke, and J.L.M. Lauweriks. Behrens was followed by Wilhelm Kreis, an architect with much more conservative views. Kreis purged the school of Behrens' appointees and ultimately presided over the institution's dissolution in 1918, an approach to the rivalry between art academies and schools of applied arts mockingly referred to as the "Düsseldorf solution." Kreis continued to teach architecture at the Kunstakademie, where he had held a joint appointment since 1913. Relatively unknown today, Kreis enjoyed fame and success in a career spanning four German regimes: the Second Empire, the Weimar Republic, the Third Reich, and West Germany. Through his teaching and commissions, Kreis strongly affected Düsseldorf's architectural heritage.

Düsseldorf has a wealth of innovative buildings. German architecture between 1900 and 1914 was typified by bourgeois monumentalism, a stylized architecture that melded Jugendstil (Art Nouveau) with historicism, serving as a bridge between 19th-century historicism and the 20th-century search for new forms and ideas. One of the most important Wilhelmine buildings is the Tietz Department Store (now Kaufhof), built in 1907–09 to designs by J.M. Olbrich on a given floor plan. Together with Alfred Messel and Wilhelm Kreis, Olbrich was one of the most influential architects of German department stores. Olbrich used the colonnade and shop window front made famous by Messel's Wertheim store but added new sculptural interest to the roofline. Buttresses and columns covering the steel frame served to unify the monumental exterior. Olbrich's four-part windows, running the height of the building, became a basic motif of German department stores. The interiors and light courts were not restored after World War II destruction.

Despite teaching for years in Düsseldorf, Peter Behrens designed only one building there, the Mannesmann Building; it was built in 1911–12 after he left the city. Here, Behrens sought to combine his interest in innovative design with the need for display inherent in a corporate headquarters. Behrens' building was inspired by Italian *palazzi*. On a steel frame, he used rusticated stone for the foundation, dressed stone for the upper levels, and a steeply pitched roof. The fenestration, geometric harmony, and horizontal emphasis are typical of Behrens' classical tendencies and were widely imitated. The interior incorporated innovative engineering based on a system of pillars using a normal module that allowed organizational flexibility. The module was a "normal office": a six-person desk with heater and office furniture. Even in the executive offices, all office walls were movable partitions. The free treatment of the interior and the exterior emphasis on blocky, objective forms were design landmarks in German corporate architecture.

Poured-concrete construction and innovative brick Expressionist architecture dominated the interwar period. Düsseldorf also became home to Germany's first skyscraper, the Wilhelm Marx House (1922–24) by Kreis. The building included a stock exchange, shops, and administrative offices. Concrete and elaborate brick designs alternate on the exterior, culminating in geometric brick tracery crowning the tower and lending a distinctive silhouette to the building. Another brick Expressionist building, the Stumm Concern Headquarters (1922–24), was the work of Paul Bonatz, the architect of Stuttgart's Central Train Station.

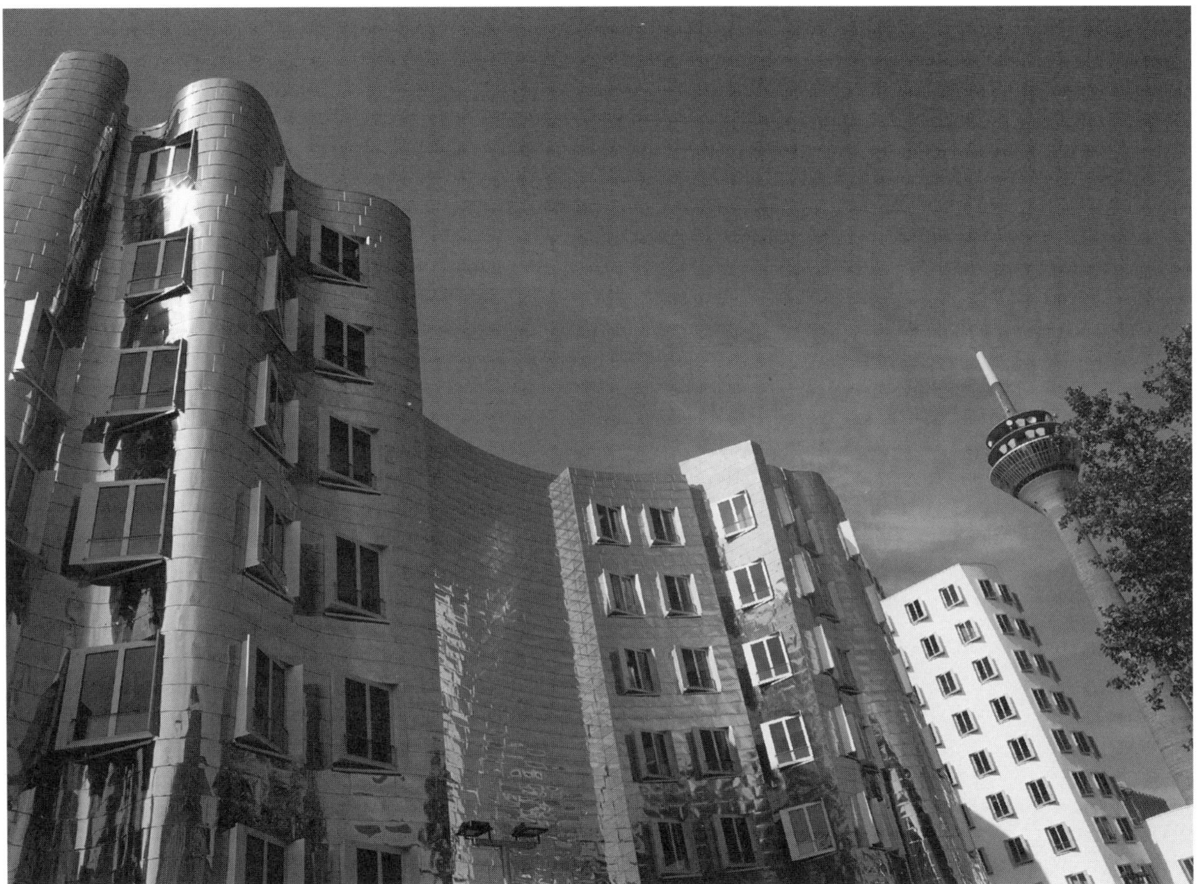

Der Neue Zollhof (1999), designed by Frank O. Gehry

The Stumm building drew on American examples to create a concrete frame decoratively clad in bricks.

The most important interwar project was the Ehrenhof (1925–26), a group of buildings designed by Wilhelm Kreis as part of the "GESOLEI" (*Gesundheitspflege, soziale Fürsorge und Leibesübungen*) exposition, an event combining elements of design show, amusement park, trade fair, and education fair. The Ehrenhof itself was a group of four stylistically unified permanent buildings arranged around a plaza: Planetarium (a multipurpose meeting hall), Economics Museum, Art Museum, and Rhine Restaurant. The complex was intended to combine contemporary architecture, sculpture, and landscaping ideas in an urban plaza that would serve as a cultural center for social interaction and give closure and balance to the Rhinefront as part of the city plan. On the whole, the Ehrenhof exemplifies Weimar design at its best but also presages the monumental classicism of the 1930s (particularly during the Third Reich) at which Kreis excelled. Flat roofs and horizontal lines dominate the museum buildings, where stone foundations contrast with decorative use of brick and sculpture. The Planetarium is a striking, circular building with brick arcades and a low dome reminiscent of Near Eastern forms. Gutted by fire in World War II, the Planetarium was restored in the 1970s as a concert hall.

Postwar Düsseldorf became a center for innovative architecture, and recent developments sealed Düsseldorf's reputation as an architectural mecca. In 1960, Düsseldorf received a new symbol in the Thyssen Tower, popularly known as the "Dreischeibenhaus" (Three-Slab House), built in 1957–60 to designs by the firm Helmuth Hentrich and Hubert Petschnigg. The nickname refers to its geometric conception as three tall, narrow slabs. At a height of 95 meters with 25 floors, its steel-frame and glass/aluminum-curtain-wall construction was a milestone for German corporate architecture. Although its height and starkness were controversial, the tower was celebrated as an emblem of German economic recovery.

Another subject of debate as a symbol was the State Parliament (*Landtag*), completed in 1988 following a 1979 competition won by the firm of Eller, Maier, Moser, Walter and Partner. The parliament features a circular plenary hall surrounded by two multilevel wings and an interplay of convex and concave rounded forms intended to symbolize the complex but open nature of democracy. Nonetheless, the building's monumentality has been criticized for embodying a sort of economic hubris. Although a state parliament, the building is larger and more imposing than the Federal Parliament built in Bonn in the same era.

Düsseldorf continues to be a center for arts innovation. Museum Insel Hombroich is an art environment, an innovative approach to museum conception located on an island 15 kilometers south of Düsseldorf in Neuss. The complex was begun in 1982 by Karl-Heinrich Müller, a real estate tycoon, and has been open to the public since 1986. There is no single museum building. Instead, the island is conceived as a space for art in a landscape shaped by Bernhard Korte. An art collection is housed in pavilions, or "walk-in sculptures," designed by Erwin Heerich. By 1997, there were 11 pavilions in a large park. The concept behind the complex was to blend art and nature and to juxtapose ancient Chinese, Persian, and Khmer art with contemporary works, allowing their merits to speak to the viewer directly, without any signs or labels to identify the artworks. Heerich's pavilions also include ateliers and studios for artists in residence. The collection includes work ranging from Rembrandt through Matisse to Alexander Calder.

The redevelopment of Düsseldorf's Rhinefront in the 1990s has also recently attracted critical attention. Between 1993 and 1995, a major thoroughfare along the Rhine River was rerouted into a tunnel. The goal was to reincorporate the river into the life of the city by making space for terraces, parks, and cafes above the tunnel. The resulting Rhine Promenade has been critically admired and popularly successful. The Promenade combines paths with seating spaces and pools running roughly north to south from the State Parliament to the Ehrenhof.

In a second project, the Rhine Harbor is being redeveloped to transform most of the harbor area into office spaces, especially for multimedia firms. The "Media Harbor," or "Creative Mile," combines retention of the 1896 harbor as a technological landmark with experimental architecture by international leading architects, including Frank O. Gehry, Steven Holl, David Chipperfield, and many others. It is frequently described as a permanent architecture exhibit. In particular, Gehry's Neue Zollhof office tower complex (1999) broke new ground by making deconstructionist architecture potentially economical. Gehry's free-form shapes were adapted to mass-production methods via computer simulation and poured forms in order to meet the builder's engineering demands. The harbor project promises to attract attention for several years to come.

TIMOTHY PURSELL

See also **Behrens, Peter (Germany); Expressionism; Gehry, Frank (United States); Germany; Olbrich, Josef Maria (Austria)**

Further Reading

Gehry, Frank O., *Der neue Zollhof Düsseldorf*, Essen: Verlag Peter Pomp, 1999

Heerich, Erwin, *Museum Insel Hombroich*, Stuttgart, Germany: Hatje, 1996

Mai, Ekkehard, "GESOLEI und PRESSA: zu Programm und Architektur rheinischen Ausstellungswesens in den zwanziger Jahren," in *Rheinland-Westfalen im Industriezeitalter*, edited by Kurt Düwell and Wolfgang Köllmann, volume 4, Wuppertal, Germany: Peter Hammer, 1984

Moeller, Gisela, *Peter Behrens in Düsseldorf: die Jahre von 1903 bis 1907*, Weinheim, Germany: VCH, 1991

Nerdinger, Winfried, and Ekkehard Mai, editors, *Wilhelm Kreis: Architekt zwischen Kaiserreich und Demokratie, 1873–1955*, Munich: Klinkhardt und Biermann, 1994

Schepers, Wolfgang, and Stephan von Wiese, editors, *Der Westdeutsche Impuls, 1900–1914: Kunst und Umweltgestaltung im Industriegebiet: Düsseldorf, eine Grossstadt auf dem Weg in die Moderne* (exhib. cat.), Düsseldorf: Kunstmuseum Düsseldorf, 1984

E

EAMES, CHARLES ORMAND 1907–78 AND RAY KAISER EAMES 1912–88

Architects and designers, United States

Charles and Ray Eames believed that good design was a means to better living. With their architecture, furniture design, films, and exhibitions, the Eameses sought to change the way people thought about everyday objects and daily life. Using new, low-cost, pre-fabricated construction materials, they set out to make good design inexpensive and accessible.

Charles and Ray formed their professional partnership in 1941, the year they married and moved to Los Angeles. However, all the work was submitted solely under Charles's name until 1947, at which time the design firm became known as the Eames Office. In recent studies, feminist historians have attempted to assert Ray's importance in the partnership, claiming for her some of the recognition she did not receive during her lifetime. Ray, who studied under Hans Hofmann and at the Cranbrook Academy of Art in Michigan, contributed an abstract sculptural sense, an aesthetic refinement, and an eye for detail to their design work. With two years of architectural training at Washington University in St. Louis, several years in architectural firms, and some experience with mechanics and manufacturing, Charles brought technical knowledge and engineering skills to the professional partnership. The Arts and Crafts ideals of Cranbrook had a lasting effect on the Eameses' holistic approach to design.

The Eameses' best-known and most influential architectural work is the house they designed for themselves: Case Study #8 (1949). The Case Study House Program, sponsored by the journal *Arts and Architecture* under John Entenza, was initiated in 1945 as a venue for architects to produce innovative prototypes for postwar American living. Designed for specific clients who were mainly professionals or the artistic elite, the Case Study Houses focused on aesthetic and technological innovation. Charles collaborated with Eero Saarinen on the initial plan for Case Study #8 in 1945; however, the design was substantially revised by the Eameses before construction. Interested in the work of European modernists Ludwig Mies van der Rohe, Walter Gropius, Marcel Breuer, and others, the Eameses adapted the spare, functional machine aesthetic to their interest in individual expression. The Eames House was the first Case Study House to use a steel frame, and the innovative adaptation of prefabricated construction and industrial material to residential architecture proved very influential. To the Eameses, a house was an exhibition space for the occupants. Because the designs were published in *Arts and Architecture* and the finished buildings were open to the public for six to eight weeks *before* their occupation by the clients, this architectural program was accessible to an extensive audience. Charles also collaborated with Saarinen on a house for John Entenza, Case Study #9 (1949), which was built on a lot neighboring the Eames House at Pacific Palisades. The Case Study Houses came to define a new kind of Californian style, and the Eames House in particular captured public attention and helped define the image of what was modern and American in the postwar period, both within the United States and internationally.

Other notable architectural works include the showroom for the Herman Miller Furniture Company (1949) in Los Angeles, designed shortly after the company began manufacturing the Eameses's furniture. Using steel-frame construction and a glass facade of windows and opaque panels, the exterior of the showroom, as well as the concept of a flexible interior space, was similar to the Eames House. Two unrealized competition entries for public projects in the 1940s, City Hall (1943) designed with John Entenza, and a proposal for the Jefferson National Expansion Memorial (1997), attempted to create a spatial arrangement of elements that opened the channels of communication between government and citizens. Projects from the 1950s include the Max De Pree House (1954) in Zeeland, Michigan, designed for the son of the president of the Herman Miller Furniture Company, and the Griffith Park Railroad (1957), which was a miniature railroad station in a Los Angeles park. There were a number of other unrealized buildings, including a house for Billy Wilder (1950), a project for low-cost mass housing commissioned by the Kwikset Lock Company of Anaheim (1957), and a Birthday House for Hallmark Cards (1959). They did not take on any architectural projects in the 1960s or 1970s.

After 1949, the Eameses began to concentrate more on furniture design, toys and decorative objects, films, and later exhibi-

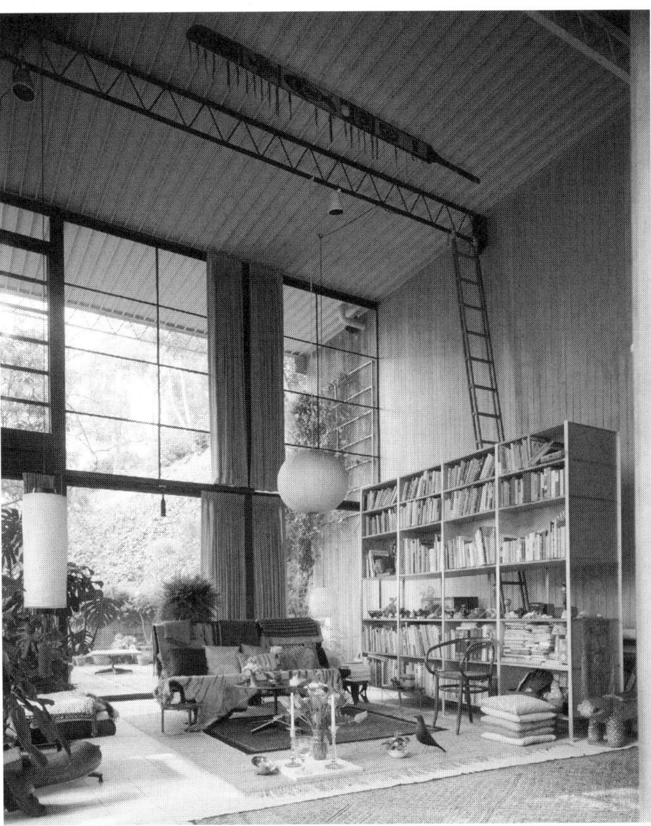

Eames House, Santa Monica, California (1949), designed by Charles and Ray Eames

tions. Between 1945 and 1978, more than 40 furniture projects designed by the Eames Office were commercially produced. The Herman Miller Furniture Company began to manufacture, market, and distribute furniture from the Eames Office in 1946, and the designs soon gained international recognition. As in their architectural projects, they adapted wartime techniques and materials, such as plywood, metal, and plastic (resin and fiberglass), to new purposes. Responding to functional and technical challenges rather than market demand, the domestic, corporate, and institutional furniture ranged from inexpensive and mass-produced styles to high-priced models.

Film, multimedia, and exhibition design appealed to the Eameses's desire to communicate ideas. Educational presentations were their specialty, and they delighted in producing everything from independent films to further the public understanding of science to films for corporate clients who eagerly embraced the medium as a training and marketing tool in the 1950s and 1960s. *Glimpses of the U.S.A.* (1959), a multiscreen film presentation about everyday life in America, was commissioned by the U.S. Department of State as part of a cultural exchange for the American National Exhibition in Moscow. With this project, Charles and Ray helped define the image of America to an international audience during the Cold War.

For the Eameses, solving design problems was a way of making the world a better place. While their architecture made an important contribution to the development of Californian modernism, the functionalist philosophy that informed it contributed to all of their design work. The Eameses wanted people to see beauty in the everyday, and in all its forms, their design is a celebration of life.

SARAH BASSNETT

See also **Saarinen, Eero (Finland); Smithson, Peter and Alison (England); Steel Frame Construction**

Biography

Charles Eames was born in St. Louis in 1907. He spent two years in the architecture program at Washington University, and during this time, he began working for a large architectural firm, Trueblood and Graf. In 1930, he and Charles Gray started their own office in St. Louis, and then in 1933, Eames left for an eight-month trip to Mexico. After a brief period with the Historic American Buildings Survey, his next venture was another architectural firm, Eames and Walsh. In 1938, he went to the Cranbrook Academy of Art to pursue a fellowship, and he stayed on to set up a design department. Here, he met his life-long friends, Eliel and Eero Saarinen and Ray Kaiser. In 1941, Charles and his first wife, Catherine Woermann, were divorced, and he married Ray. The same year, Charles and Ray moved to Los Angeles to work on their own design projects, although in the first few years, Charles also worked in the art department at MGM. In 1943, the Eameses opened their office in 901 West Washington Boulevard. This is where the Eames Office remained until after both Charles and Ray had died. The Eameses began designing furniture in 1944, and in the 1950s and 1960s, they also produced a wide range of films and exhibitions. Charles received many awards, including the AIA Gold Medal Award in 1957. He lectured at the California Institute of Technology from 1953 to 1956 and at Harvard University from 1970 to 1971. He was also granted numerous honorary doctorate degrees.

Ray Kaiser was born in Sacramento in 1912. From 1933 to 1940, she studied with Hans Hofmann, first in New York, and later at the Cranbrook Academy of Art. During this time, she was involved with the group, American Abstract Artists. Ray and Charles met at the Cranbrook Academy of Art in 1940, and they married and moved to Los Angeles in 1941. Between 1942 and 1947, Ray designed covers for *California Arts & Architecture*, and she began to collaborate with Charles on a wide range of design projects. Together they produced a vast body of work. Their partnership lasted until Charles died in 1978. For the last ten years of her life, Ray continued her work at the Eames Office, she gave public presentations of film and multi-media projects, and she worked on a two books. Over the years, Charles's and Ray's work has been the subject of numerous exhibitions, including a retrospective at the Museum of Modern Art in New York in 1973.

Selected Works

Eames and Gray, Sweetser House, St. Louis, Missouri (1931)
Eames and Walsh, St. Mary's Church, Helena, Arkansas (1935–1936)
Eames and Walsh, Dean House, Webster Groves, Missouri (1936)
Eames and Walsh, Dinsmoor House, Webster Groves, Missouri (1936)

Eames and Walsh, Meyer House, Huntleigh Village, Missouri (1936–1938)
Charles and Ray Eames, Case Study House #8, Santa Monica (Pacific Palisades), California (1949)
Charles Eames and Eero Saarinen. Case Study House #9, Santa Monica (Pacific Palisades), California (1949)
Charles and Ray Eames, Herman Miller Furniture Company, Los Angeles, California (1949)
Charles and Ray Eames, Max De Pree House, Zeeland, Michigan (1954)
Charles and Ray Eames, Griffith Park Railroad, Los Angeles, California (1957)

Selected Publications

Eames, Charles, "City Hall," *Architectural Forum* (May 1943)
———, "City Hall," *Arts & Architecture* (June 1943)
———, "Design, Designer and Industry," *Magazine of Art* (December 1951)
———, "Design Today," *California Arts & Architecture* (September 1941)
———, "The Exploring Eye: Sun Mill," *Architectural Review* (February 1959)
———, "Language of Vision: The Nuts and Bolts," *Bulletin of the American Academy of Arts and Sciences* (October 1974)
———, "Organic Design," *California Arts & Architecture* (December 1941)
———, "A Prediction: Less Self-Expression for the Designer." *Print* (January–February 1960)
———, "What is a House?" *Arts & Architecture* (July 1944)
Eames, Charles, and Ray Eames, *Eames Report*, Los Angeles: Eames Office, 1958
Eames, Charles, and John Entenza, "Case Study Houses 8 and 9 by Charles Eames and Eero Saarinen, Architects," *Arts & Architecture* (December 1945)
Eames, Ray, and Philip and Phylis Morrison, *Powers of Ten*, Redding, Connecticut: Scientific American Library and W.H. Freeman, 1982
Eames, Ray, John Neuhart, and Marilyn Neuhart, *Eames Design: The Work of the Office of Charles and Ray Eames*, New York: Harry Abrams, 1989

Further Reading

Albrecht, Donald (editor), *The Work of Charles and Ray Eames: A Legacy of Invention*, New York: Harry Abrams in association with the Library of Congress and the Vitra Design Museum, 1997
Banham, Reyner, "Architecture IV: The Style That Nearly . . . ," *Los Angeles: The Architecture of Four Ecologies*, London: Penguin Press, 1971
Demetrios, Eames, An Eames Primer, New York-Universe Publishing, 2001
Kirkham, Pat, *Charles and Ray Eames: Designers of the Twentieth Century*, Cambridge, Massachusetts and London: MIT Press, 1995
McCoy, Esther, *Modern California Houses*, New York: Reinhold, 1962; 2nd edition, *Case Study Houses 1945–1962*, Los Angeles: Hennessey and Ingalls, 1977
Neuhart, John, Marilyn Neuhart, and Ray Eames, *Eames Design: The Work of the Office of Charles and Ray Eames*, New York: Harry Abrams, 1989
Smith, Elizabeth A.T. (editor), *Blueprints for Modern Living: History and Legacy of the Case Study Houses*, Cambridge, Massachusetts: MIT Press, 1990
Smithson, Alison, and Peter Smithson, *Architectural Design*, "Eames Celebration," special issue (September 1966)
Smithson, Alison, and Peter Smithson, *Changing the Art of Inhabitation*, London: Artemis London, 1994
Steele, James, *Eames House: Charles and Ray Eames*, London: Phaidon, 1994

EARTHEN BUILDING

Building in earth is one of the world's oldest technologies, and traces of buildings constructed in earth 4000 years ago still survive in the arid regions of the Middle East and China. Its versatility (earth can be formed into building materials in at least half a dozen different ways), its durability, and its economy have ensured its survival as a vernacular building system in many parts of the world. The same qualities led to its revival in the 20th century in those parts of the world where the availability of suitable soils, the prevalence of arid-zone climatic conditions, the high cost of industrialized building materials or components, or the survival of a culture of building in earth have favored the introduction of earth-based building materials and systems.

Of the several different ways of building in earth, monolithic earth construction, where hand-formed balls of wet clay, with or without natural additives, are built up in courses and left to dry and set, is probably the oldest and the most widely dispersed throughout the world. Buildings in cob (Southwest England), in mud (Central Europe), and in swish (West Africa) are a few of the many local vernacular manifestations of this method of construction. Almost as old, and confined to the more arid regions of the globe is adobe: sun-dried brick formed out of the local soil mixed with water, with or without natural additives, and either hand-molded or cast in timber molds. In more humid regions of the world, where timber is, or was, more readily available for building, wet clay was commonly daubed onto an interwoven vegetal armature on a timber framework in *wattle and daub* construction. (Although the term "daub" derives from the same Arab root as "adobe," this system is not indigenous in the arid-zone Arab homelands of the Middle East but was prevalent throughout much of northwest Europe, and still is in many parts of sub-Saharan Africa.)

A more complex technology is required to build in *pisé* (rammed earth), where sieved earth, dampened and with or without natural additives, is rammed into timber formwork (normally made of timber planks), with the walls being built up in courses, and left to dry. Of considerable antiquity, this method was common in the lands surrounding the Mediterranean in the ancient Roman period (3rd century B.C. through the 4th century A.D), and has survived in many of those lands to the present day. Equally ancient examples have been found in Central Asia and China, where its use has also survived.

A more recent development is the manufacture of earth blocks in metal molds, compressed under either manual lever arm or hydraulic pressure, and the similar stabilized earth blocks, where a binding agent—cement, lime, or bitumen—is added in small quantities to the sieved earth to give greater compressive strength and water-resistance to walls built in these materials.

Although the use of these technologies is usually restricted to wall construction, adobe and *pisé* and monolithic earth are used in the construction of roofs, whether flat, vaulted, or domed, and of upper floors. All these materials and compressed or stabilized earth blocks are used in staircases and paving.

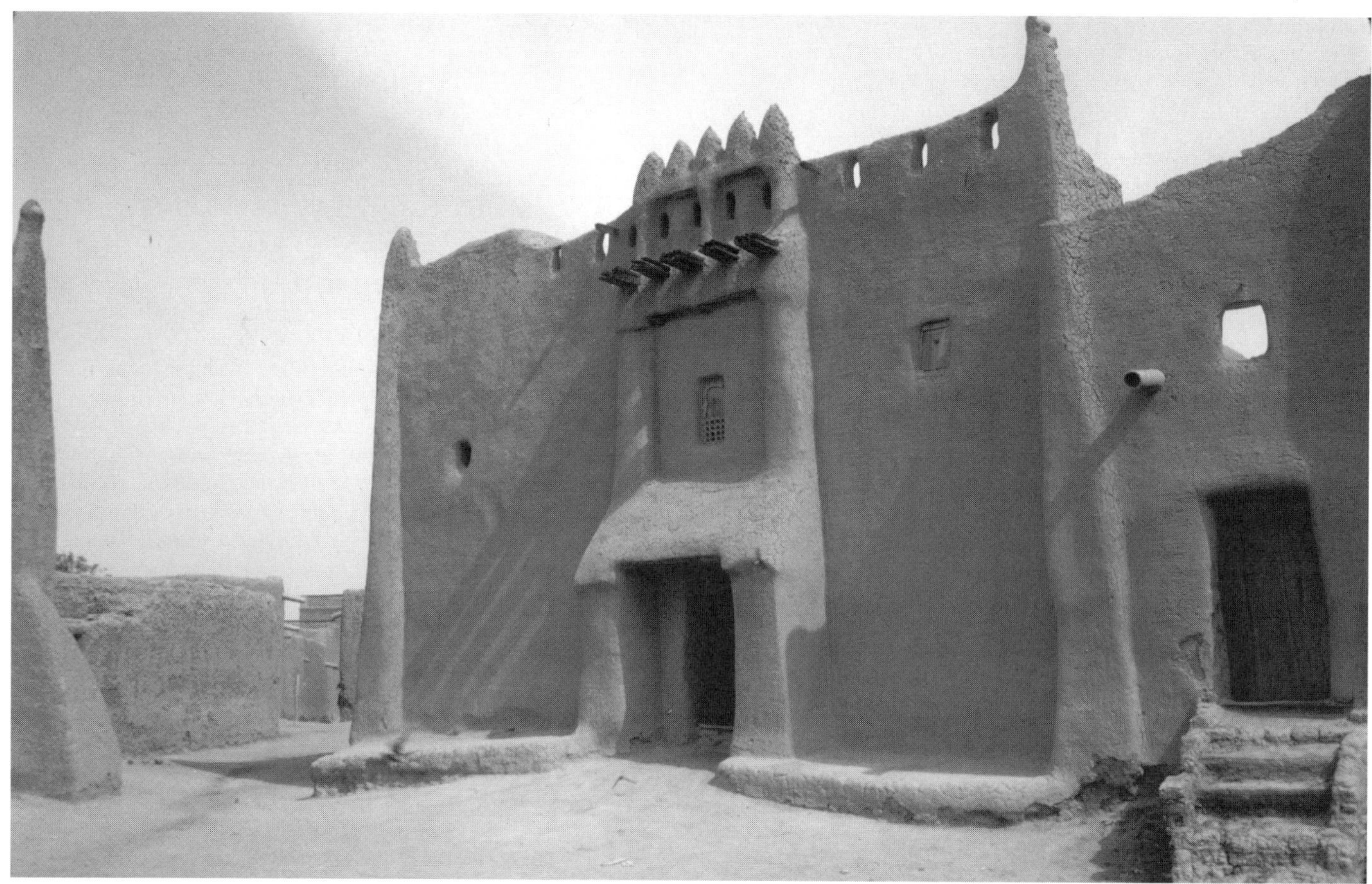

Newly rendered private dwelling, Djenne conservation project, begun in 1996 by the Dutch Government and Mission Culturelle. The city is built entirely in earth.
© Aga Khan Trust for Culture

Closely related to the above technologies are construction in sod or peat cut from the ground—found in Ireland, Scandinavia, and North America—and blocks cut or molded from gypsum—found in parts of North Africa and Arabia.

Inevitably, with increasing industrialization and urbanization and the commercialization of building construction skills, by 1900 these traditional technologies had fallen into disuse in the more developed countries of the world and were already going down-market in the less developed countries (colonies of European metropolitan nations and independent African, Asian, and Latin American nations). More damagingly, traditional maintenance skills and practices were being neglected, and many traditional vernacular buildings were falling into decay through neglect, with the result that earthen buildings were acquiring a reputation for nondurability.

Several factors, however, led to a revival of interest in earthen building around the turn of the century. First, among architects, the Arts and Crafts Movement in the United Kingdom and National Romanticism and Regionalism in Northern and Central Europe had popularized traditional building materials and construction systems: thatch and shingles for roofs, for example, and earthen materials for walls. In the decade after 1900, Edwin Lutyens and Charles F. A. Voysey in England explored the potential of cob, clay lump, and clunch in country houses, and in Hungary, Karoly Kos exploited the plasticity of monolithic earth construction in country houses, most notably in the Artists' Colony, Godollo.

Across the Mediterranean, in Africa, the high noon of European colonial imperialism was opening up the cultural heritage of the continent to European observers; not only in sculpture, jewelry and textiles, but in vernacular building also. The vigor, spontaneity, and decorative quality of African arts and crafts, increasingly extensively collected (or pillaged) and brought to Europe by colonial officials and adventurers, led to a revolution in the fine arts in the decade before World War I (1914–18): Cubism and Fauvism owe much of their appeal and their power to their African sources of inspiration. The effect on architectural formal and stylistic development was less early and less obvious. To French colonial administrators and missionaries attempting to lay down the infrastructure of colonial government and Christian evangelism in North and West Africa, the venerable monuments of Africa's precolonial past, almost all of which had been built of earthen materials, provided obvious prototypes for their own rudimentary building projects. A particularly notable example is the R. C. Cathedral of the Seven Dolours of Mary in Navrongo, Ghana (1907–10), built by the White Fathers throughout, as are most of the older surrounding mission buildings, in *pisé*. Navrongo Cathedral is now a designated National Monument in Ghana. British colonial administrators and missionaries were generally not so venturesome, but a successful example of British colonial building in adobe is the Kano Museum, in Kano, Northern Nigeria. The Anglican Namirembe Cathedral (1913–19), designed by English architect Temple Moore, in Kampala, Uganda, also contains much adobe brickwork in its interior walls.

The splendors of the monumental earthen architecture of Algeria, Morocco, and the French Sudan were widely publicized in Europe, however, and the restoration in 1905 of the ancient Great Mosque of Djenne, Mali, originally built in the 15th century of adobe and monolithic earth, became a cause célèbre among avant-garde architects in France. A generation later, Le Corbusier paid tribute to the architectural and environmental quality of the adobe and *pisé* buildings of the ancient towns of the M'zab, in Algeria, in his *African Notebooks*, and subsequently, in the dynamic, organic form of his pilgrimage chapel at Ronchamp, France, for which the towns were a primary source of inspiration. In the outbacks of Australia and South Africa, as the arid zones there were being opened up for colonial settlement, earthen buildings were often the only materials available to the early settlers. In both territories, sun-dried earth bricks were frequently manufactured out of termite molds.

In the Americas, adobe was still a living tradition, and architects in the arid zones of the United States were exploiting its plastic qualities in major buildings. The Fine Arts Museum, Santa Fe, New Mexico (1917) by Rapp and Rapp, in a pastiche of vernacular styles, was less innovative than the later house projects by Frank Lloyd Wright and Rudolph Schindler in New Mexico and Arizona.

The collapse of the building industry in much of Europe in the aftermath of World War I gave an added boost to earthen building. British Architect Clough Williams-Ellis, in addition to designing and building in earthen materials on his own estates in North Wales—most notably at Portmeirion—was largely instrumental in popularizing earthen building through his book *Building in Cob, Pisé and Stabilised Earth*, first published in 1919. In it, he convincingly advocated the use of *pisé* for utilitarian housing and industrial and agricultural buildings. A second, amplified and updated edition, edited by J. C. Eastwick-Field, was published in 1947 in the aftermath of World War II, when similar economic conditions prevailed and a severe shortage of conventional building materials led to a revival of the techniques advocated by Williams-Ellis a generation earlier. By this time, however, national and local governments had become major providers of housing—for the poor, the homeless, war veterans, and refugees—and many examples of low-cost housing, in *pisé*, adobe, and later in compressed or stabilized earth blocks, survive in all continents. An example of such housing is the Queen's Park Estate, in Bulawayo, Zimbabwe, built between 1948 and 1953 by then-colonial government of Southern Rhodesia for returning war veterans and immigrants.

Contemporary with this development was the pioneer village of New Gourna, near Luxor, in Upper Egypt, designed by Egyptian architect Hassan Fathy to be built throughout in adobe. At the time, this project was regarded as a failure because most of the villagers from whom it was designed refused to move into the new village. New Gourna itself, and Fathy's advocacy of earthen building, was not widely appreciated until some decades later, following the publication of his seminal work *Housing for the Poor*, in 1973. Fathy, however, was not alone in Egypt, a country in which there were many surviving examples of adobe building, both from remote antiquity and in the present—for the Nubian builders of Upper Egypt had retained the traditional skills and knowledge of their ancient forebears—in advocating building in adobe. His enthusiasm and commitment was shared by his contemporary, Wissa Wassef, who in the 1950s began building his magnum opus in adobe, the group of buildings that eventually became the Ramses Wissa Wassef Arts Centre, Harrania near Giza (1951–70).

The development of the CINVA Ram and other types of simple block-making machines was a parallel response to the severe shortage of building materials after World War II, the repercussions of which were as severe in the British Commonwealth and European colonial countries and in Asia and Latin America as they were in Europe. The pioneer work of developing the machine was carried out in Colombia, South America, in the early 1950s, with the aim of producing a machine that was inexpensive to produce, simple to operate, and easy to transport to the peri-urban areas of South America's rapidly expanding cities. Subsequently, the principles of design and production of manually operated block-making presses was taken up by governmental and intergovernmental agencies and nongovernmental organizations as a major tool in the task of providing shelter for the homeless in all continents.

Meanwhile, in the arid-zone "sunshine states" of the United States, adobe had been widely promoted as a popular and environmentally appropriate building material, especially for housing and tourist facilities. In the earlier, midcentury phase of this development, architects and builders sought to create buildings in a pastiche Indian pueblo or Spanish colonial style, inspired by the surviving examples of the genuine article in early mission compounds and Native American settlements. This adobe revival had been gathering momentum for most of the century and had remained as much real estate developer driven as architect driven. Fathy's advocacy of the material since the 1970s has given all earthen materials a higher profile and a greater sense of authenticity and architectural quality. This factor, together with the influential exhibition on "Des Architectures de Terre" (Architectures in Earth) at the Center Pompidou in Paris, France, in 1982, and the accompanying book on the same subject by Jean Dethier, has resulted in a veritable avalanche of adobe and *pisé* building throughout the warmer arid-zones of the globe and in the construction of many examples of earthen architecture of high quality that look well in the landscape and that provide an interior climate that is thermally comfortable—comparatively cool summer and warm in winter—and economical to maintain.

More innovative projects in the United States paid particular attention to the energy conservation and thermal comfort potential of adobe buildings. More significant developments included LaLuz Residential Estate, Albuquerque, New Mexico (1975), designed by Antoine Predock. Both he and William Lumpkin, architect of several houses in New Mexico such as the Balcomb Residence Santa Fe (1978), are architects who have revitalized and energized the adobe tradition in the United States. Given the increasingly high cost of energy, earthen building materials, which require little energy to produce, and earthen buildings, which require comparatively little energy to maintain at a comfortable temperature, are likely to retain their popularity and their prestige in the 21st century.

ANTHONY D. C. HYLAND

See also **Fathy, Hassan (Egypt); Great Mosque of Niono, Mali; Ramses Wissa Wassef Arts Centre, Giza, Egypt; Wassef, Wissa (Egpyt)**

Further Reading

Bourgeois, J.L., *Spectacular Vernacular—The Adobe Tradition*, New York: Aperture Foundation, 1996

Dethier, Jean, *Des Architectures de Terre*, Paris: Centre Georges Pompidou, 1982

Dethier, Jean, *Down to Earth*, New York: Facts on File, 1983

Fathy, Hassan, *Architecture for the Poor*, Chicago The University of Chicago Press, 1973

Keable, Julian, *Rammed Earth Structures—A Code of Practice*, London: Intermediate Technology Publications, 1996

Linstrum, Derek, "The Architecture of the Twentieth Century: Africa," in Sir Banister Fletcher's *A History of Architecture*, 20th edition, Oxford: Architectural Press, 1996

Williams-Ellis, Clough, *Building in Cob, Pisé and Stabilized Earth*, London: Country Life, 1919; revised and expanded edition, Shaftersbury: Donhead Publishing, 1999

EDGE CITY

"Edge city" is one of many terms used to describe the large, sprawling conglomerations of commercial, retail, and residential development that proliferated along the beltways of United States metropolitan peripheries in the 1980s. Coincident with the advances in telecommunications, economic restructuring, and deregulation that began in the 1970s, edge cities exemplify the privatization, decentralization, and dispersion of development that is characteristic of digital media and the global economy. Joel Garreau defined five criteria that characterize a full-blown edge city: "five million square feet of leasable office space or more; six hundred thousand square feet of retail space or more; a population that increases at 9 AM on workdays—marking the location as primarily a work center, not a residential suburb; a local perception as a single end destination for mixed use—jobs, shopping, and entertainment; and a history in which, thirty years ago, the site was by no means urban; it was overwhelmingly residential or rural in character" (1991, 425). As of 1991, Garreau found 119 mature and 74 emerging edge cities in the United States.

Largely low-rise, low-density landscapes, edge cities typically evolve around suburban spoke-and-hub highway intersections. The automobile access provided by these intersections encourages the nearby development of office parks, regional shopping malls, retail strips, franchises, and apartment complexes. Each use is visually and functionally isolated from its neighbors by parking lots, united only by the heavily trafficked arterial roads connecting them. Sylvan corporate campuses and gated residential communities also follow this pattern, typically locating on cul-de-sacs off the main arterials.

Suburbs initially used zoning to exclude industrial uses. New economies however, replaced traditional manufacturing jobs with clerical jobs that posed less threat to health and property values. Electronic media, meanwhile, reduced the need for face-to-face communication. The information basis of much of the service economy, the expanding suburban middle class, and the rise in automobile ownership further allowed many operations to be moved to cheaper land on the urban periphery. Corporate headquarters also often moved out of the cities to lush suburban estates to be closer to the executives' homes and country clubs. These moves were aided by the interstate beltway system. Initially constructed to allow through traffic to bypass major cities, beltways also provided easy access to cheap, minimally administered land and proximity to the many non–unionized and educated suburban women entering the labor force. In addition, market deregulation, federal insurance, and the demand for greater financial returns in the 1980s encouraged lenders to speculate in real estate investment, much of it in the booming edge cities.

The growth of edge cities reflects the general growth of U.S. suburbs. Between 1970 and 2000, suburbs experienced growth rates double and triple that of cities, accounting for 60 to 85 percent of new construction, new investment, and new jobs. Suburban office stock, for example, increased 300 percent during the 1980s, and by 1993 the suburbs had half again as much office stock as that in cities. Similarly, declining urban populations in the 1970s prompted large-scale retail stores to move to the booming suburbs. Although population grew 10 percent in the 1980s, retail floor space grew 80 percent, mostly because of the feverish construction of suburban shopping malls in edge cities. Residential development has also migrated, as the declining real wages of the middle class have encouraged the search for ever-cheaper housing at the periphery. In pursuit of cheaper land, less-congested highways, and new markets, new edge city growth has manifested itself in urban-sprawl patterns of ever-lower overall densities and ever-escalating automobile use. In the 1990s, this prompted new urbanist efforts to reconfigure edge cities into more compact, transit-oriented development as well as the Environmental Protection Agency's Smart Growth policies.

Other names for edge cities emphasize their various characteristics. "Exurbs" or "urban sprawl" are popular and also emphasize distance from the city center. Richard Louv's (1983) early writing on the subject and his use of the term *anticity* emphasized not simply the physical distance from the city but also the deliberate way in which new master-planned communities at Irvine, California, or outside Houston and Phoenix have turned their backs on the city. By the late 1980s, the agglomeration of such developments led to the coining of more terms. *Cyburbia* and Robert Fishman's *technoburb*, for example, emphasize these regions' participation in the digital economy, exemplified by California's Silicon Valley and Boston's high-tech corridor along Route 128. The U.S. Congress's Office of Technological Assessment reinforces this role by its use of the term *postindustrial metropolitan development*. Jonathan Barnett has focused on the unplanned and haphazard process of their maturation; he cites Tysons Corner, Virginia, as a prime example. A sleepy crossroads in the 1960s, by the 1990s Tysons Corner had two very large malls and as much office space as downtown Washington, D.C., but no sidewalks and notorious traffic jams.

Edge city remains the most commonly used term, both for its simplicity and because of the wealth of description and study given to it in Garreau's definitive book as well as in critical discussion that followed. However, Garreau's unwavering enthusiasm for the developers of edge cities as cowboy pioneers and innovative entrepreneurs responding to new needs and desires has not been shared by many other authors on the subject. The critics of edge cities find them banal, highly privatized, fragmented, and destructive to both environmental and communal sustainability. Garreau dismisses such critics as elite, moralizing snobs and raises the question whether the market responds to and promotes individual freedoms better than planners and designers. The discourse on edge cities is continuing to grapple with this and related questions.

ELLEN DUNHAM-JONES

See also **New Urbanism; Suburban Planning; Urban Planning**

Further Reading

Augé, Marc, *Non-lieux: Introduction à une anthropologie de la Surmodernité*, Paris: Seuil, 1992; as *Non-Places: Introduction to an Anthropology of Supermodernity*, translated by John Howe, London and New York: Verso, 1995

Barnett, Jonathan, *The Fractured Metropolis: Improving the New City, Restoring the Old City, Reshaping the Region*, New York: HarperCollins, 1995

Beauregard, Robert A., "Edge Cities: Peripheralizing the Center," *Urban Geography* 16, no. 8 (1995)

Downs, Anthony, *New Visions for Metropolitan America*, Cambridge: Massachusetts: Lincoln Institute, and Washington, D.C.: Brookings Institution, 1994

Dunham-Jones, Ellen, "Temporary Contracts: The Economy of the Post-Industrial Landscape," *Harvard Design Magazine* (Fall 1997)

Fishman, Robert, *Bourgeois Utopias: The Rise and Fall of Suburbia*, New York: Basic Books, 1987

Garreau, Joel, *Edge City: Life on the New Frontier*, New York: Doubleday, 1991

Koolhaas, Rem, "What Ever Happened to Urbanism?" and "Bigness" in *Small, Medium, Large, Extra Large: Office for Metropolitan Architecture*, Rem Koolhaas, and Bruce Mau, edited by Jennifer Sigler, New York: Monacelli Press, 1995; 2nd edition, 1998

Leinberger, Christopher B., "Metropolitan Development Trends of the Late 1990s: Social and Environmental Implications" in *Land Use in America*, edited by Henry L. Diamond and Patrick F. Noonan, Washington, D.C.: Island Press, 1996

Leinberger, Christopher B. and Charles Lockwood, "How Business Is Reshaping America," *Atlantic* (October 1986)

Louv, Richard, *America II*, Los Angeles: Tarcher, 1983

Scheer, Brenda Case and Mintcho Petkov, "Edge City Morphology: A Comparison of Commercial Centers," *Journal of the American Planning Association* 64, no. 3 (Summer 1998)

Sorkin, Michael (editor), *Variations on a Theme Park: The New American City and the End of Public Space*, New York: Hill and Wang, 1992

U.S. Congress, Office of Technology Assessment, *The Technological Reshaping of Metropolitan America*, Washington, D.C.: U.S. Government Printing Office, 1995

EDUCATION AND SCHOOLS

Licensure of architects began around the turn of the 20th century as a means of enforcing higher professional standards. At the turn of the century, architects could prepare for the licensing exam by a variety of different educational and training experiences; a few schools existed for students with the financial means necessary to pursue a full-time education. Students lacking this economic freedom could learn by working in architecture firms, perhaps supplementing office training with evening studies. The traditional system of apprenticeship decreased as formal education became recognized as an important characteristic of the profession, and by the end of the 20th century, the educational requirement for licensure has become nearly universal.

Professional regulation varies from country to country and, within the United States, from state to state. Elements of preparation for practice presently include education, internship, demonstration of competence by examination, and continuing education. In the United States, an accredited professional degree, along with internship and examination, is the gateway to both the title architect and the practice of architecture in nearly all states.

There are some important differences in the various approaches to architectural education around the world. An important issue for the architectural profession at the beginning of the 21st century is the impact of globalization on preparation for architectural practice. The countries of the European Community have recently completed a survey of the national systems of higher architectural education in Europe. The ability to practice throughout the European Community will require some greater agreement on educational qualifications for architectural practice. The issue of reciprocity between the United States and Canada is also under discussion. Within the United States, the ability to gain reciprocal registration for practice in multiple states is facilitated by a national system of accreditation for schools of architecture. A professional body, the National Architectural Accrediting Board (NAAB), sets criteria for education leading to a professional degree. The NAAB recognizes the variety of models that exist for architectural education. Rather than regulating the type of school or dictating curricula, the NAAB criteria establish areas and levels of learning for students of accredited programs. In Canada, the Canadian Architectural Certification Board (CACB) accredits schools of architecture.

According to data published by the Association of Collegiate Schools of Architecture in 1994, there are 118 schools offering professional degree programs in architecture in North America, with 108 of these schools in the United States and ten in Canada. There are 199 schools in Central and South American countries, 63 architecture schools in Africa and the Middle East, and 425 schools spread throughout Europe. There are 315 schools in Asia, mainly concentrated in Japan, the People's Republic of China, South Korea, the Philippines, and India. Australia has 19 schools of architecture and New Zealand has two.

Institutional settings for architectural education vary. Within the university, architecture may exist as its own school or may be a department of a comprehensive college. Architecture departments may be organized under the umbrella of the arts, or may exist within colleges of engineering, as in many Asian universities.

Architecture may also be taught within its own school independent of a university, for example the Architectural Association School of Architecture in England or the Frank Lloyd Wright School of Architecture in the United States. Architecture may be taught as a discipline within an art school or may exist as a department of a technical school, such as the Eidgenossische

Technische Hochschule of Zurich (ETHZ) in Switzerland or the Illinois Institute of Technology in Chicago in the United States.

The variety of settings for architectural education stems from the historic development of the profession in Europe ranging from the first guild-based school for architecture in Prague (established in 1353 for the court architect's apprentices) to the Royal Academy of Architecture founded in Paris in 1671, where a rational approach based upon the study of classical architecture challenged the medieval traditions of the craft guilds. While formal education for architects was developing in France, the office apprenticeship remained the traditional English system for educating architects. In the early eighteenth century, apprenticeship was replaced by the pupilage system in which students paid fees for office instruction. Another type of architecture school, the Ecole Polytechnique, was founded in Paris in 1795. The technical school became a model for architectural education in German cities and in Prague, Vienna, and Zurich.

While the Polytechnic, where architecture was taught in a scientific context, became the dominant model in the Germanic countries, French architectural education came to be dominated by the École des Beaux-Arts, which grew out of the French Academy, where architecture was taught in the context of the arts. There were two parts to the École education, lectures on history and technical subjects at the school and design studies in the *atelier* or studio where a practicing architect served as patron to a group of students working on design projects.

In the United States, the earliest forms of architectural education were borrowed from British apprenticeship and French academic systems. The Beaux-Arts Society of Architects, later the Society of Beaux-Arts Architects (SBAA), was founded in 1894 to promote education. The SBAA issued programs for atelier students working under the direction of patrons (practicing architects). The SBAA also provided the mechanism for exhibition, judging, and publication of student work. In 1904, the SBAA established the prestigious Paris Prize, modeled on the French Prix de Rome (Rome Prize).

American universities began to offer architectural education in the latter half of the 19th century; the first was the Massachusetts Institute of Technology (MIT) in Cambridge in 1865. By the turn of the century, architectural education was offered in 13 American universities including Columbia University, New York, Cornell University, Ithaca, University of Pennsylvania, Philadelphia, George Washington University, Washington, D.C., and elsewhere. In Canada, the University of Toronto was the first, in 1890, to offer architectural education, followed by McGill University in Montreal.

The Beaux-Arts Institute of Design (BAID) was established in 1916 and incorporated under the Regents of the State of New York to take over the educational functions of the SBAA. The programs of the BAID were followed in schools as well as in the independent studios. Atelier activity peaked around 1929. As the number of students who worked by day and studied in the ateliers by night waned, the schools came to dominate architectural education by the middle of the century.

New developments in Europe were transforming architectural education as well. The state Bauhaus was founded in 1919 in Weimar, Germany; its program (developed primarily by German architect Walter Gropius) applied modern or new materials and industrial techniques to the problems of design, bringing together all of the arts and crafts. The avant-gardism of the Bauhaus, its ideology and teachers, came under attack by the Nazis; the faculty fled for France, the Netherlands, the United States and elsewhere, eventually bringing Bauhaus modernism to American schools of architecture. In 1936 Gropius became chair of the department of architecture at Harvard University and his colleague Marcel Breuer joined the faculty. In 1938, Ludwig Mies van der Rohe assumed the directorship of the Illinois Institute of Technology; Laszlo Moholy-Nagy went to teach at the Institute of Design in Chicago in 1937 and Josef Albers to Black Mountain College, North Carolina in 1940. This influx of European architects came to dominate the Beaux-Arts historicism of the American schools of architecture. The Beaux-Arts ateliers withered as the university became recognized as the locus for the modern architectural education. Following World War II, the G.I. Bill helped to make a university education affordable for many Americans.

The entry of women into architectural education began with Julia Morgan, the first American woman to attend the École des Beaux-Arts in Paris. The first American school to teach architecture to women, The Cambridge School, was begun by Henry Atherton Frost in 1915 to tutor women denied admission to the male bastion of Harvard University. Although many American universities became co-educational, relatively few women studied architecture until the 1970s. Women remain a minority in a number of schools and women are under-represented on architecture faculties. Moreover, architecture programs developed in several historically black colleges and universities in America. Hampton University, then known as Hampton Institute, first offered course work in architecture in 1889; Tuskegee University, then known as the Tuskegee Normal and Industrial Institute, began offering Certificates in Architecture in 1893; architecture degree studies began at Howard University in 1911. Today, there are seven historically black colleges and universities with accredited architecture programs. People of color continue to be under-represented among students and faculty in most American schools of architecture.

A system of educational degrees developed within the university system. In the United States, these include the *pre-professional architecture degree* (a bachelors degree awarded for an unaccredited education focused on the study of architecture); and the *professional architecture degree* (an accredited undergraduate Bachelor of Architecture [B. Arch.] or an accredited graduate Master of Architecture degree [M. Arch.]). Degree nomenclature and programs of study vary somewhat around the world. A third type of degree is a *post-professional architecture degree*, offered to students who already hold a professional degree in architecture. Post-professional education gives students the opportunity for specialization and in-depth study in design, history and theory, technology, environment and behavior, computer visualization, historic preservation, tropical architecture, or other fields of interest. The post-professional degree may be a Master's degree, a doctorate, or a Ph.D.

There are three possible courses of study leading to a professional degree in architecture. 1) The student may complete a B. Arch program, generally in five years. 2) The student may obtain a pre-professional undergraduate degree, then complete a two-year professional M. Arch. program. This option is generally known as the four-plus-two program. 3) The student may obtain an undergraduate degree in any field, then complete a professional M. Arch. program of three to four years duration.

The five-year Bachelor of Architecture degree was introduced at Cornell University in 1922. The four plus two program was introduced in the 1960s along with the possibility of studying architecture exclusively at the graduate level. The diversity of paths to a professional degree offers a variety of advantages. General studies help architecture students develop into well-educated professionals capable of understanding the needs of clients and the society. The B. Arch. program necessarily limits liberal arts courses because of the many required professional courses. The four-plus-two program gives students an additional year of study, freeing more time for liberal studies. The graduate professional program gives students an opportunity to major in another subject in college, then concentrate architectural studies into three to four years of graduate education.

Art courses, particularly focusing on drawing, are excellent preparation for architectural education, which places a premium on visual communication. The ability to draw expressively is considered to be more important to a beginning architecture student than the mechanical skills taught in high school drafting courses. High school courses in mathematics, at least including trigonometry, and in the physical sciences, are important preparations for technical coursework in architecture. Writing and speaking skills are also crucial for success in architecture school. A broad academic preparation is important for the architecture student because the study of architecture draws heavily upon a variety of disciplines. The basic components of the architecture curriculum are design, history and theory, technology, practice, and general education. The various programs have developed their own approaches, emphases, and strengths. Design studio integrates material learned in the other courses.

The studio design education is an experience common to most architecture schools and sets architectural education apart from other degree programs in the university. Studio designates both a physical setting and a course of study. The studio is a second home to the architecture student, who claims territory with a drafting table and often personalizes the space with computers, partitions, cabinets, and domestic effects such as sofas, refrigerators, and stereo equipment. Studio is generally conducted three afternoons a week. Students are expected to work independently in studio for many additional hours.

Studio education follows the project method developed in France. The instructor assigns a design project by means of a project statement outlining the parameters of the project, carefully circumscribed to focus the students' efforts on a particular set of learning objectives. The project schedule helps students learn to manage their time to complete work by the assigned deadline.

During a typical studio afternoon, students work independently, sketching, drafting with manual equipment or on the computer, and building study models. The instructor circulates around the studio giving individual criticism, often sketching on tracing paper to explain ideas and suggest new directions for development of each student's project. As the deadline nears, students work around the clock to resolve designs, construct models, and draft presentation drawings. This intense final effort is called the *charrette*, named after the carts that were drawn through the streets of Paris carrying student projects to the École des Beaux-Arts.

The project culminates in a final review. Students present their projects individually to a jury of faculty, sometimes augmented by visiting faculty from other schools, practicing architects, and sometimes clients. The jury critiques the project for the benefit of the assembled students. In the best of circumstances, the review is an important educational experience, helping to prepare students for presentations to clients and review boards in professional life.

History and theory are taught in lectures and seminars. A survey of architectural history is common to architectural programs. Seminars tend to reflect the interests of faculty, and theory courses may draw upon art history, environmental psychology, phenomenology, sociology, and other disciplines.

Architectural technology includes structures, environmental controls, construction materials and methods, and construction documentation. The emphasis on technology and the extent to which technology is integrated into the design studio varies by program.

A course in professional practice generally occurs in the final year of study. Students are introduced to the privileges and responsibilities of professionals, the legal and ethical environment of practice, the myriad issues of managing practices, and project processes.

Architecture schools may offer opportunities to learn by working in architectural offices. A few schools, such as Kansas State University, offer an internship program in the fourth year of study. The University of Cincinnati, the Boston Architectural Center, and Drexel University offer opportunities to pursue six years of concurrent academic and work credits.

Architecture schools are staffed by full-time faculty who may concurrently practice architecture and by adjunct faculty who teach part-time and maintain full-time practices. Full-time architecture faculty generally have at minimum a Master of Architecture degree, which may be a first professional degree or a post-professional degree. Some subjects, for example history of architecture, tend to be taught by faculty with Ph.D. degrees. Full-time faculty are subject to assessment by the same standards as other university faculty, that is, evaluation based upon teaching, scholarly work, and service. There is a continuing need for architecture faculty is to press universities to recognize creative and professional work as credentials for promotion and tenure.

In the United States and Canada, architecture faculty are represented by the Association of Collegiate Schools of Architecture (ACSA). ACSA sponsors conferences at the national and regional levels, providing venues for faculty to present scholarly and creative work. ACSA publishes a quarterly journal, the *Journal of Architectural Education*, as well as a monthly news magazine. European faculty are represented by the European Association of Architectural Education (EAAE). EAAE holds annual meetings, publishes a journal, *Stoa*, and a newsletter.

In the United States, mandatory continuing education was pioneered by the American Institute of Architects (AIA) as a means to distinguish AIA members from other architects. The AIA requires thirty-six learning units of continuing education per year for maintenance of membership. Learning units may be earned by attending educational programs and conferences or by self-reporting a variety of educational experiences in a broad spectrum of subjects. The state boards soon began to take up the idea of mandatory continuing education as a requirement for renewal of licensure. The thrust of continuing education for the states is keeping abreast of new knowledge in the area of health, safety, and welfare.

MADLEN SIMON

See also **Bauhaus; Bauhaus, Dessau; Institute for Architecture and Urban Studies**

Further Reading

Detailed information on North American schools of architecture and contact information for schools of architecture around the world may be found in the *Guide to Architecture Schools*. The *Architect's Handbook of Professional Practice* details professional requirements. The Bannister, Bosworth, and Boyer studies examine the status of architectural education at three points in the 20th century. Anthony and Cuff describe the studio education and jury system.

American Institute of Architects, *Handbook of Architectural Practice*, Washington, D.C.: Press for the American Institute of Architects, 1920; 12th edition, as *The Architect's Handbook of Professional Practice*, edited by David S. Haviland, 1994

Anthony, Kathryn H., *Design Juries on Trial: The Renaissance of the Design Studio*, New York: Van Nostrand Reinhold, 1991

Bannister, Turpin C., and Francis Rufus Bellamy, editors, *The Architect at Mid-Century*, 2 vols., New York: Reinhold, 1954; see especially vol. 1, *Evolution and Achievement*

Bosworth, Francke Huntington, Jr., and Jones, Roy Childs, editors, *A Study of Architectural Schools*, New York: Scribners, 1932

Boyer, Ernest L., and Lee D. Mitgang, *Building Community: A New Future for Architecture Education and Practice*, Princeton, New Jersey: Carnegie Foundation for the Advancement of Teaching, 1996

Cuff, Dana, *Architecture: The Story of Practice*, Cambridge, Massachusetts: MIT Press, 1991

Drexler, Arthur, editor, *The Architecture of the École des Beaux-Arts*, New York: Museum of Modern Art, and London: Secker and Warburg, 1977

Hegener, Karen Collier, and David Clarke, editors, *Architecture Schools in North America*, Princeton, New Jersey: Peterson Guides, 1976; 4th edition, as *Guide to Architecture Schools in North America*, Washington, D.C.: Association of Collegiate Schools of Architecture Press, 1989; 5th edition, as *Guide to Architecture Schools*, edited by Richard E. McCommons and Karen L. Eldridge, 1994

Mabardi, Jean François, and Renato Girelli, editors, *The National Systems of Higher Architectural Education in Europe*, Milan: Unicopli, 1997

EGYPTIAN REVIVAL

This architectural and decorative arts style is among the most easily identifiable of all revivalist styles. Early Egyptian architecture has been studied, admired, and emulated throughout time. The arch was used in ancient Egypt for what is believed to be the first time, and the ancient Greeks considered Egypt the source of all civilizations. During the Renaissance, Egyptian motifs were incorporated into the decorative arts, and many architectural and decorative traditions to follow were influenced by Egyptian ornament.

For centuries, Egypt was inaccessible to foreigners because of its relative isolation and strict religious and political restrictions. Early examples of the style were fanciful and highly interpretive, with no effort made for accuracy until the 19th century, when archaeological discoveries in Egypt captured the popular imagination. In 1798, Napoleon initiated a military campaign into Egypt and sent numerous scholars and researchers to excavate archaeological sites, resulting in a 22-volume treatise, *Description de l'Egypte* (1829), a text that would later become a major source of inspiration for designers. In addition, in 1799, the Rosetta Stone, a basalt slab covered in hieroglyphics, was discovered by Napoleon's troops. Rubbings of the stone were made and sent to several European scholars, foremost of whom was Jean Francois Champollion, who deciphered the hieroglyphics and identified the Greek and demotic scripts inscribed on the stone. These events fueled a further fascination with the Egyptian style, but a pervasive romantic interpretation of these findings diluted its historically accurate application.

The Egyptian Revival style is expressed primarily in two ways—as a specific massing with corresponding structural elements that evoke the architecture of ancient Egypt and as decorative ornament that is applied to a conventional building. In the case of architectural massing, each example of Egyptian Revival is configured with distinctive, exotic features. Frequently, buildings in this style suggest the architecture of dynastic Egypt in multiple ways—with battered (slanted) walls; columns that resemble bundles of bound stalks with lotus, papyrus bud, or flowering blossom capitals; tall window frames that mimic the battered walls and; an overall massing effect with heavy, thick walls and strong, simple geometric volumes. In addition, an Egyptian Revival structure may include an Egyptian gorge or cavetto cornice—a partially rounded, outwardly concave molding at the roofline. Another common device is a pylon, a pair of towers with battered walls that flank an entrance and is reminiscent of the monumental gateway into an ancient temple. In terms of applied ornament, the Egyptian designs are incised or affixed, usually to the surface of a fairly conventional building. The affixed elements are often in the medium of terra-cotta. One of the most commonly used symbols is the winged sun disk flanked by serpents, which represents the sun goddess joining the sun god Ra in his journey across the sky. The disk symbolizes eternity, the wings serve as the spirit, and the serpents represent wisdom. Another popular icon is the scarab beetle, which represents the sun god and symbolizes life eternal.

There are limited examples of the Egyptian Revival style in Europe, but it is a phenomenon found primarily in the United States, in cities both large and small. The style became popular during the 1830s, the 1850s, the end of the 19th century, and the 1930s, during the Art Deco era. During the 19th century, architects in the United States, most of whom had received classical training in Europe, were attempting to assimilate the conventional and classically academic architecture of Europe to the different geography and available building materials of the country. It was a time of great experimentation in the design and adaptation of popular Greek Revival, neoclassical, and Renaissance styles. However, because Egyptian architecture was not completely embraced by the traditional vocabulary of academic and Beaux Arts architects, it remained a stylistic experiment that was not popularized by a definitive school of American architects. Nonetheless, architectural structures including jails, monuments, cemetery structures, theaters, churches, and Masonic lodges were built in this style, including Robert Mills's Washington Monument (Washington, D.C., 1833); Thomas U. Walter's Debtors' Apartments (built 1835, demolished 1968) at Moyamensing Prison in Philadelphia; H. H. Richardson's Ames Monument (1882), located near Laramie, Wyoming; and Thomas

Paul Gerhardt's Marmon Hupmobile Auto showroom, Chicago (1910)
© Rima Krutulis

B. Stewart's Medical College of Virginia (Richmond, 1845). Daniel Burnham and John Root's Monadnock Building (1891) in Chicago is a remarkable 16-story office structure built of traditional brick and mortar that evokes ancient Egyptian architectural forms in its severe simplicity. It is a tall, narrow tower, devoid of all traditional ornament, that an architectural critic once likened to a chimney.

American Masonic lodges, in particular, have had an interesting relationship with the Egyptian Revival style, and many well-known architects were Masons. The Egyptian Hall of the Masonic Temple (1873) in Philadelphia by architect James Windrim, a heavily embellished, large, high-ceilinged room, and the Masonic Temple (1912) in Charlotte, North Carolina, by architects Hooks and Rogers, are two examples. The theatrical aspects of this style provided a backdrop for the secret rites and clandestine activities for which the Masons are known.

In the 20th century, the Egyptian Revival style reached its zenith in the Art Deco era of the 1930s. The development of polychromatic terra-cotta as a decorative architectural medium and Art Deco's abstract geometric design often manifested in quasi-Egyptian ornament. The style was popular in the design of theaters and commercial buildings. The best-known example of this type is the fully restored Egyptian (Ada) Theater (1927) in Boise, Idaho, by architects Tourtelotte and Hummel. A good example of a commercial application is the Reebie Storage and Moving Company headquarters (1923) in Chicago by architect George Kingsley—an otherwise conventional building profusely ornamented both inside and out with Egyptian design. Another example is Paul Gerhardt's Marmon Hupmobile Auto showroom (1910) in Chicago, an unexpectedly pleasing storefront with a heavily embellished temple facade. A submission to the Tribune Tower Competition of 1923 by Alfred Fellheimer and Stewart Wagner, architects from New York, is a large obelisk with clear Egyptoid references. Also noteworthy is the use of the lotus blossom in a stylized Art Deco pattern incised above some of the Chrysler Building's elevator cab doors.

After the 1930s, very few structures were built in the Egyptian Revival style until the 1970s, when it resurfaced in the redesign of the entrance to the Louvre (Paris, 1970–77) by I. M. Pei, in which a prominent feature is a pyramid structure. Also notable is the design of the Luxor Casino and Hotel (1993) in Las Vegas by architect Vernon Simpson. This massive casino/recreation complex incorporates a pyramid, a sphinx, and Egyptian interior decor, bridging the distinction between revivalism and theme-based novelty that has often typified this stylistic form.

RIMA KRUTULIS

See also **Art Deco; Historicism**

Further Reading

Carrott, Richard G., *The Egyptian Revival, Its Sources, Monuments and Meaning, 1808–1858*, Los Angeles: University of California Press, 1978

City of Chicago Department of Planning and Development, Reebie Storage Warehouse, Landmark Designation Report, September 1, 1999

Clichy, Bodo, *Architecture of the Ancient Civilizations in Color*, New York: Viking Press, 1966

Curl, James Stevens, *The Egyptian Revival: A Recurring Theme in the History of Taste*, Manchester: Manchester University Press, 1994

EIGEN HAARD HOUSING ESTATE

Designed by Michel de Klerk, completed 1920
Amsterdam, the Netherlands

The Eigen Haard Housing Estate in Amsterdam, the Netherlands, consists of three blocks of housing in the *Spaarndammerbuurt*, a residential district for workers that occupies approximately 54 acres in the northwest part of Amsterdam. Designed by Michel de Klerk (1884–1923) between 1914 and 1920, this complex has been recognized as his finest achievement in the field of housing, depicting his Expressionist style and ultimately becoming one of the symbolic structures of the Amsterdam School.

Inspired by contemporary ideas that can be traced to the teachings of H.P. Berlage (1856–1934), de Klerk was committed to the basic Berlage credo of "truth in architecture" as expressed through the unity of spatial organization and material use. In opposition to the abstract Cubism of the De Stijl movement, Berlage emphasized experimentation with the artistic potential of practical solutions and the role of rhythmic architectural forms in the evocation of moods, thus preparing the way for the Expressionism of the Amsterdam School.

After the passing of the *Woningwet* (Netherlands Housing Act of 1901), which encouraged the sponsorship of low-cost housing, and the National Housing Council, founded in 1913, which unified the large number of Dutch housing societies, the Amsterdam architectural milieu between 1915 and 1930 involved extensive public housing. Although initially built as low-rise, one- or two-family houses, Amsterdam saw a rising popularity in three- and four-story apartment buildings that were built around communal courts. These *tuindorpen* (garden villages) were based on the English Garden City movement and the principles of Briton Ebenezer Howard (1850–1928).

Because the post–World War I building commissions were almost solely public housing and because of the presumption that good housing was a means of elevating the working class to a higher social level, architects of the Amsterdam School instinctively became involved with the public housing projects. The first block of the *Spaarndammerbuurt* complex was commissioned by contractors Hille and Kamphuys, not by the Eigen Haard (One's Own Health) housing association, which commissioned the second and third building units. A misprint in the Amsterdam School publication *Wendingen* (Trends) in 1924 erroneously attributed all three structures to Eigen Haard, and it has been thus reported ever since.

The four- and five-story first and second blocks, constructed in 1914 and 1915, respectively, flank the *spaarndammerplantsoen*, the small communal park. The third building, designed in 1917, with its intimate *pleintje* (small public square) and characteristic spire, forms a triangular block perpendicular to the earlier two buildings and across *Oostzaanstraat* (East Zaan Street) and is similar in concept to the first two but different enough to gain additional attention from his many critics. The urban fabric is defined by the "urban block" consisting of the three-unit cluster and their accompanying community square. The three blocks are articulated differently, each with structural and decorative qualities that establish a specific character that is enhanced by bold contrasts in shape, texture, and color. Examples of this sculptural aesthetic can be seen through de Klerk's eloquent use of brick and by the apparent rigidity of the strong axial composition that is counterpoised by seemingly arbitrary apertures, cylinders, cones, cantilevered balconies, textured planes, curved wall masses, multi-paneled windows, and multi-angled roofs. The extraordinary range of formal design variations elevated the buildings from simply housing construction to works of art.

Detailing, technique, and massing distinguished de Klerk's work from that of his contemporaries. His creative and picturesque use of brick combinations, such as clinkers, corrugated bricks, and regular bricks laid in a double-stretcher Flemish bond pattern, may have reflected Berlage's distaste for smooth-faced brick and stucco but not his belief of honesty in materials. De Klerk did not feel that the simulated was deceptive but instead believed that traditional effects of materials had a more enduring value and therefore sometimes produced a hand-sculpted look with machine-made masonry units. Also, by adroitly molding a diverse yet unified assemblage of housing units into these large-scale blocks, de Klerk was able to further contrast with the lack of rhythm and the monotony of the existing housing stock.

Following Berlage's philosophy of architectural truth in the definition and enrichment of the exterior spaces, de Klerk applied geometric emphasis on major spatial divisions. Parabolic, curvilinear, and hemicylindrical forms define entrances, stairs, and window separations, respectively, and decorative hoists indicate attic storage areas.

De Klerk's lack of pretension in his artistic treatment of all building types, regardless of their intended function or end users, gained him due respect by some of his colleagues but especially with the residents of the Eigen Haard housing units. This nondiscriminatory approach to design allowed those in the working class to also experience the sculptural qualities of subsistence by enriching their perceptual experiences.

Others felt, however, that this method of design was indeed pretentious. The curvilinear forms were deemed illogical, the ornamentation embellishments were criticized as structurally dishonest, and the overall design was thought to have no connection to traditional architecture. Critics complained that his projects were too opulent and wasteful, whereas others defended that the dignified dwellings were the work of an "extraordinary artist" and showed a high degree of sophistication and therefore had cultural significance and value.

Eliciting feelings from euphoria to nausea, the *Spaarndammerbuurt* complex became such a subject of criticism that one critic went so far as to accuse de Klerk of creating details that were "not only doubtful, but contrived, bizarre and unsound." It was also said that the "total design leans toward the ridiculous or the overrefined, and then towards decadent" (see Gratama,

Eigen Haard Housing Estate, Amsterdam
Eigen Haard Housing complex, designed by Michel de Klerk, Building #1, front facade
© Elisabeth A. Bakker-Johnson

1915). Perhaps because of the publication of these comments in the widely circulated *Bouwkundig Weekblad*, the words "bizarre," "individual," and "decadent" became inextricably linked to de Klerk and ultimately to the Amsterdam School as a whole.

De Klerk's engagingly provocative design of the Eigen Haard Housing Estate reflected his desire to solve each building problem independently with an unpredictable artistic composition. Although once thought to have little in common with the major monuments of the 20th century, this complex now stands as a monument itself for the masterful artistry and audacious individualism of its architect who, because of an untimely death, was not able to further develop these skills.

ELISABETH BAKKER-JOHNSON

See also **Amsterdam School; Apartment Building; Berlage, Hendrik Petrus (Netherlands); De Klerk, Michel (Netherlands); De Stijl; Expressionism**

Further Reading

Curtis, William J.R., editor, *Modern Architecture since 1900*, Oxford: Phaidon, 1982; Englewood Cliffs, New Jersey: Prentice-Hall, 1983; 3rd edition, Oxford: Phaidon, and Upper Saddle River, New Jersey: Prentice Hall, 1996

Frank, Suzanne S., *Michel de Klerk (1884–1923): An Architect of the Amsterdam School*, Ann Arbor, Michigan: UMI Research Press, 1984

Futagawa, Yukio, and Wilhelm Holzbauer, editors, *Eigen Haard Housing, Amsterdam, 1913–1919; Apartment Blocks, Henriette Ronnerplein Amsterdam, 1920–1921*, Tokyo: A.D.A. Edita, 1980

Gratama, Jan, "Kroniek LXX," *Bouwkundig Weekblad* 36, no. 33 (1915)

Whittick, Arnold, *European Architecture in the Twentieth Century*, 2 vols., London: Crosby Lockwood, and New York: Philosophical Library, 1950

Wit, Wim de, "De architectuur der Amsterdamse School," in *Nederlandse architectuur, 1910–1930: Amsterdamse School*, edited by Wim Crouwel, Amsterdam: Stedelijk Museum, 1975

Wit, Wim de, *The Amsterdam School: Dutch Expressionist Architecture, 1915–1930*, New York: Cooper-Hewitt Museum, and Cambridge, Massachusetts: MIT Press, 1983

EINSTEIN TOWER, POTSDAM, GERMANY

Designed by Erich Mendelsohn, completed 1921

True to modernism's precepts, the Einstein Tower in Potsdam, Germany, designed and built by Erich Mendelsohn from 1919 to 1921, is one of the most unique expressions of avant-garde architecture of the early 20th century.

Born in 1887, Mendelsohn was drawn to architecture at a young age. Like so many artists and architects at the fin-de-siècle, he believed that a new era was dawning, and that new forms of architecture were necessary for the modern epoch. In 1913 Mendelsohn met the astrophysicist Erwin Finlay Freundlich; the two men discovered shared interests and developed an enduring friendship. Freundlich introduced Mendelsohn to the then-unpublished radical theory of relativity by Albert Einstein, ideas that would profoundly influence European intellectual thought, as well as the visual arts, for years to come. Freundlich; was interested in making observations that would confirm Einstein's new theory, and Mendelsohn sought to adapt Einsteinian principals to built forms endowed with expressive plasticity. Unfortunately, both mens' plans were interrupted by the outbreak of World War I. In 1917, Mendelsohn was sent to the Western front.

During the war, Mendelsohn sketched continuously. These small sketches, in ink, of factories and observatories are remarkable for their abstract forms and stark play of light and dark. Mendelsohn began creating images of an architecture without reference to history or style. He indicated in his letters to his wife that these images came to him as fleeting visions that he labored to jot down before they vanished.

In 1918, Freundlich decided to build his own observatory in Potsdam where he could explore and apply Einsteinian principles. He immediately sent detailed information to Mendelsohn on the front. Early studies for the observatory for Freundlich are among Mendelsohn's sketches.

Mendelsohn began serious work on the Einstein Tower in May 1920. Construction began in the summer of 1920; the exterior was completed by October 1921, and the project was generally finished by 1924. The plan, in keeping with modernist reductivism, was relatively simple; a vertical shaft was required down which light was reflected into a horizontal underground observation chamber. The finished building consisted primarily of a three-story tower supporting an observatory cupola, a ground-floor workroom, a second-floor room, and the underground observation area.

However, the appearance of the structure is less like a device for scientific experiment than like a ship, airplane, or vehicle of transport already in motion across the landscape. The conceptual program was perhaps more complex than the functional one: Mendelsohn consciously strove to make a design devoid of right angles, that was molded rather than built, and that architecturally expressed the dynamic interchange of mass and energy inherent in Einstein's theory of relativity. For this reason, he emphasized the interplay of mass and light, drawing on his impressionistic wartime sketches. The observatory was to be constructed of poured-in-place concrete, the only material Mendelsohn thought capable of expressing the dynamic possibilities of the new age. In the end, because of cost considerations and material wartime shortages, the underground portion was built in concrete, but the shaft of the tower was constructed of brick with a plaster finish.

The windswept form of the building reflects the conglomeration of a number of ideas and influences. In part, Mendelsohn's thinking had been influenced by the German Expressionist writers and painters, such as Wassily Kandinsky, whose meetings he attended. Kandinsky's metaphysical exploration of a new German Zeitgeist shaped by spiritual rather than rational forces proved particularly influential for Mendelsohn's architecture.

The organic vitality of Jugendstil interior design and architecture was equally influential. Jugendstil (or German Art Nouveau) derived its sinuous and curvilinear motifs from nature, particularly from vines and trailing plants, which suggested fecundity and irrationality in their sensuous curving stems. The first-floor plans of the Einstein Tower seem to be derived from Jugendstil organicism, as seen in the ovoid entry porch, chrysalis-like stair chamber, and the curvaceous walls of the workroom, all of which evince references to germination and plantlike growth.

Finally, Mendelsohn's concern for energy, dynamism, and vitalism led him to the ideas of the Italian Futurists and their manifestos, particularly to the work of artist Umberto Boccioni. For example, Boccioni's sculpture, *Unique Forms of Continuity in Space*, of 1913—a virtual icon of Futurist ideals of power, movement, and violence—would seem to echo in the sense of undulating movement that is evoked by the curving walls of Mendelsohn's Einstein Tower. In particular, the swept forms of the legs in Boccioni's soldierlike sculpture find their way into the surrounds of the Tower's first-floor windows, suggesting a kind of protective cowling against movement through some medium, as if the building were really a vehicle designed for travel.

The Einstein Tower became the most famous, albeit often misunderstood and esoteric, German building after World War I. Despite the fact that Einstein himself referred to the building in a private aside to Mendelsohn as organic, the architect's intentions that the building formally embody the physicist's theories was not generally perceived. In his later work, Mendelsohn continued to explore formal dynamism, but the work was much more linear and rational, using steel and glass, brick, and concrete slab. He never built anything like the Einstein Tower again.

The building functioned successfully as an observatory, yet its formal influence on other architects seems to have been minimal. In this regard, it is a victim of its own originality and uniqueness. It was a vision, but perhaps not visionary.

LAURENCE KEITH LOFTIN III

See also **Art Nouveau (Jugendstil); Expressionism; Germany; Mendelsohn, Erich (Germany, United States)**

Further Reading

Beyer, Oskar (editor), *Briefe eines Architekten*, Munich: Prestel-Verlag, 1961; as *Eric Mendelsohn: Letters of an Architect*, translated by Geoffrey Strachan, London and New York: Abelard-Schuman, 1967

James, Kathleen, *Erich Mendelsohn and the Architecture of German Modernism*, Cambridge and New York: Cambridge University Press, 1997

Stephan, Regina, *Erich Mendelsohn: Architekt, 1887–1953*, Ostfildern-Ruit, Germany: Hatje, 1998; as *Eric Mendelsohn: Architect, 1887–1953*, translated by Melissa Thorson Hause, New York: Monacelli Press, 1999

Whittick, Arnold, *Eric Mendelsohn*, London: Faber and Faber, 1940; 2nd edition, London: Hill, 1956

EISENMAN, PETER D. 1932–

Architect and theorist, United States

As an architect, writer, educator, and theorist, Peter Eisenman has consistently striven to reveal the critical function of architecture. His commitment to maintaining architecture as a critical practice has led him to adopt the role of architectural impresario, inciting, supporting, and publishing the research and production of subsequent generations of architects. Eisenman's writings, most notably "Notes on Conceptual Architecture: Towards a Definition" (1971), "The Futility of Objects" (1984), and "The End of the Classical, the End of the Beginning, the End of the End" (1984), have become seminal texts within architectural theory.

Eisenman was the founder and director of the architectural think tank the Institute for Architecture and Urban Studies (IAUS; 1967–82). At the IAUS, Eisenman was also one of the founders and editors of *Oppositions*, a seminal and influential journal of architectural criticism. It was during this period as well that a 1969 CASE meeting and exhibition at the Museum of Modern Art, New York, cited Eisenman, Michael Graves, Charles Gwathmey, John Hedjuk, and Richard Meier as "The New York Five." The Five, also known as "the Whites" (because of their penchant for using pure white forms) shared an interest in formal abstraction.

Studying under Colin Rowe at Cambridge University, Eisenman wrote a doctoral dissertation ("The Formal Basis of Modern Architecture," 1963) that reflects Rowe's influence; it also reveals how early it was that Eisenman expanded formal analysis beyond the purely compositional to explore the structural possibility of architecture. He contributed to the broadening of the discipline of architecture by turning to linguistics, philosophy, and art theory; namely, Structuralism, Poststructuralism, Deconstructivism, and other approaches including the writings of French philosophers Jacques Derrida, Gilles Deleuze, and Félix Guattari.

Eisenman, Peter (United States)
Wexner Center for the Visual Arts (1983–89), Ohio State University

Between 1967 and 1980, Eisenman designed a series of houses that focused on revealing the process of performing architectural abstraction. These houses, numbered rather than named and documented with scientifically precise serial axonometrics, represented research into the generation, transformation, and decomposition of architectural form. The first four houses—House I (1967–68) in Princeton, New Jersey; House II (1969–70) in Hardwick, Vermont; House III (1969–71) in Lakeville, Connecticut; and House IV (1971, unbuilt)—examined within architecture what Noam Chomsky called "deep structure": a self-referential language devoid of semantic content. Beginning with House VI (1975) in Cornwall, Connecticut, Eisenman moved away from the compositional, transformative formalism of the early houses in favor of what he called a "decompositional" approach, a strategy that focused more on relations and process than on the formal qualities of the final object.

On founding his practice in 1980, Eisenman turned from the domestic to the urban scale. The interest in the structure of the grid that had marked his houses was translated into a horizontal-generating device in the Cannaregio Town Square housing competition entry (1978) in Venice and the acclaimed Berlin Housing project (1982–86) in Berlin. Eisenman's first significant public building in the United States was the Wexner Center for the Visual Arts (1983–89) at Ohio State University, which was the first project to actively engage the ground plane. The Wexner can be understood as a constructed fiction: a fragmented and reordered reconstruction of an armory tells one version of the story, whereas another version is revealed by the gridded spine, which registers the discrepancy between the campus and urban grids. The University Art Museum (1986, unbuilt) for Long Beach, California, and the Choral Works/Parc de la Villette project (1986) in Paris, designed with French philosopher Jacques Derrida, all illustrate an archaeological approach by which historic or existing forms were taken from a site and then scaled according to a fictive scenario.

If the transition from the houses to the artificial excavation projects can be understood as a move from object to site, Eisenman's subsequent career shift represented a turn from Cartesian geometries to supple geometries. This transition, facilitated by computer-aided design, was initiated with a series of projects that engaged the Deleuzian concept of folding. In these works, most notably the Rebstock Park Master Plan (1991) in Frankfurt, Germany, attention is still paid to the site, but the design solution is one of folding the ground plane rather than extruding it. Here, the architecture and the site fold into each other, creating a continuous sequence across the site, which throws into question distinctions between horizontal and vertical. This manipulation of the existing site grew even more complex with subsequent projects, such as the Arnoff Center for Design and Art (1988–96) at the University of Cincinnati, which employed a dynamic, nonlinear mathematical operation to produce a sinuous, torqued curve that, when juxtaposed with the repeated Cartesian geometry of the existing building, creates what theorist Sanford Kwinter has referred to as a "Piranesi-effect of unforeseeable complexity" (p. 13).

Recent projects, most notably the Staten Island Institute of Arts and Sciences (1997–present) in New York City and the Galicia City of Culture (2000–present) in Santiago de Compostela, Spain, continue this Piranesian propensity. Derived from complex computer technologies, the generated geometries are fluid and smooth, creating extremely graceful, innovative forms. Although the computer has been instrumental in aiding Eisenman's generation of complex forms, it is even more significant for its role in shifting his intellectual focus. If the early houses sought the critical within the performance of the process, this highly complex current work cites the critical within possibilities of performance; that is, within any aspect of the work, any possibility inherent to the work. As he describes the Galicia City of Culture design, "[It] produces a new kind of center, one in which the coding of Santiago's medieval past appears not as a form of representational nostalgia but as an active present found in a tactile, pulsating new form—a fluid shell."

Eisenman's work continues to challenge the limits of architectural form and the boundaries of architecture, landscape, and urbanism; meanwhile, Eisenman the impresario continues to further the intellectual project of architecture through his writings, lectures, and provocations.

SARAH WHITING

See also **Color; Computers and Architecture; Deconstructivism; Institute for Architecture and Urban Studies; Museum; Rowe, Colin (United States); Poststructuralism; Structuralism**

Biography

Born 12 August 1932 in Newark, New Jersey; received Bachelor's degree, Cornell University, Ithaca, New York 1955; Master's degree in architecture, Columbia University, New York 1960; M.A. and Ph.D. from Cambridge University, Cambridge, England 1963. Irwin S. Chanin Distinguished Professorship, Cooper Union for the Advancement of Science and Art, New York City 1967; taught at Cambridge University, England 1960–1963; Princeton University, Princeton, New Jersey 1963–67, Established Eisenman/Robertson Architects with Jaquelin Robertson 1980.

Selected Works

House I, Princeton, New Jersey, 1968
House II, Hardwick, Vermont, 1970
House III, Lakeville, Connecticut, 1971
House VI, Cornwall, Connecticut, 1975
Cannaregio Town Square (competition entry), Venice, Italy, 1978
Berlin Housing project, Germany, 1986
Wexner Center for the Visual Arts, Ohio State University, 1989
Rebstock Park Master Plan, Frankfurt, Germany, 1991
Arnoff Center for Design and Art, University of Cincinnati, Ohio, 1996
Staten Island Institute of Arts and Sciences, New York City, (1997–present)
Galicia City of Culture, Santiago de Compostela, Spain (2000–present)

Selected Publications

Houses of Cards, New York: Oxford, 1987
"Extra Edition: Peter Eisenman," *A + U* (1988)
Unfolding Frankfurt, Berlin: Ernst & Sohn Verlag, 1991
Re:working Eisenman, London: Academy Editions, 1993
Eisenman Architects, Mulgrave, Australia: The Images Publishing Group, 1995
Diagram Diaries, London: Thames and Hudson, 1999

Further Reading

Bédard, Jean-François, *Cities of Artificial Excavation: The Work of Peter Eisenman, 1978–1988*, Montreal: Centre Canadien d'Architecture and New York: Rizzoli, 1994
Kwinter, Stanford, The Eisenman Wave, in *Eisenman Architects Selected and Current Works*. Mulgrave, Australia: Images Publishing Group, 1995
Krauss, Rosalind, "Death of a Hermeneutic Phantom: Materialisation of the Sign in the Work of Peter Eisenman," *A*+U (January 1980)

ELDEM, SEDAD HAKKÍ 1908–1988

Architect, Turkey

Sedad Hakkí Eldem was the leading proponent of a regionalist and tradition-conscious modernism in 20th-century Turkish architecture. Born in Istanbul as the descendent of an elite Ottoman family, Eldem spent his childhood in Geneva, Zurich, and Munich, where his father served as an Ottoman diplomat. He studied architecture in the Imperial School of Fine Arts in Istanbul (1924–28; the school was established in 1882 by his great-uncle Osman Hamdi Bey), which was based on the École des Beaux-Arts. After graduation, he spent two formative years in Europe (1928–30), visiting the offices of Le Corbusier and August Perret in Paris and working with Hans Poelzig in Berlin. His beautifully rendered sketches, titled "Anatolian Houses," dating from this period also reflect his fascination with Frank Lloyd Wright's prairie houses, which were inspirational for his own vision of the modern Turkish house. In 1931, he returned to Istanbul to start his own practice and joined the faculty at the Academy, where he taught continuously for 48 years.

Eldem's architectural training at the Academy coincided with the end of the Ottoman revivalist (or national style) in Turkey. By 1930, that style was replaced by the International Style–influenced German and Austrian modernism of Ankara, the symbol of the new Kemalist Republic. Critical of the academicism of the former and the formal sterility of the latter, Eldem posited the traditional Turkish residential vernacular as the only viable source of a modern and national architecture. He devoted a lifetime to the theorization, codification, and promotion of the "Turkish house" as a distinct cultural and plastic type spread throughout the vast territories of the Ottoman Empire, especially in Istanbul, the Balkans, and northern Anatolia. In 1934, he established the National Architecture Seminar at the Academy to study and document hundreds of such traditional houses, which, he argued, already embodied modernist qualities in the rationality of their floor plans and the constructional logic of the timber frame clearly manifest in their facades. Although much of this material perished in the Academy fire of 1948, it constitutes the core of his *Türk Evi Plan Tipleri* (1954; Plan Types of Turkish Houses) and his monumental *Türk Evi* (1984; Turkish House), conceived in five volumes. In addition to these seminal works, Eldem published numerous monographs on individual pavilions, kiosks, and houses of Istanbul as well as a two-volume documentary of the city's engravings and old photographs.

Eldem's early built works were largely private houses in Istanbul based on traditional Turkish plans and displaying the characteristic tile roofs, wide overhanging eaves, and modular repetition of projecting windows above the ground floor. These features became his distinct personal style, which he elaborated in numerous private villas for wealthy clients, mostly along the banks of the Bosphorous, well into the 1980s. In most examples, the modular grid that acted as the generator of the plan, and the facade versus the in-fill panels within the grid were distinctly articulated in different materials and colors. His masterpiece, the paradigmatic Taslík Coffee House in Istanbul (1950; demolished in 1988 and rebuilt on an adjacent site), is a reinforced concrete replica of a 17th-century shore mansion on the Bosphorous.

The larger and more monumental public buildings of Eldem's early career were also informed by his quest for a rationalist conception of modern Turkish architecture. Working in partnership with Emin Onat and in close association with Paul Bonatz, Eldem became the leading proponent of what was termed "National Architecture Movement" in the 1940s, epitomized by the Faculties of Sciences and Letters of the University of Istanbul (1942–44). This building is organized around a series of open courtyards and displays the classicizing tendencies of the period in its use of monumental tall colonnades and stone facing. The main facade is an elongated version of Eldem's Turkish house idea, blown up in scale and lifted above a monumental colonnade on the ground level with clear allusions to Paul Bonatz's Stuttgart Railway Station (1912–28). In the courtyards, Eldem adopted the Ottoman walling technique of alternating brick and stone layers, also used by Bruno Taut in the Faculty of Humanities Building in Ankara (1937–38).

The most acclaimed scheme of Eldem's long career, however, was the Social Security Administration Complex in Zeyrek, Istanbul (1962–64), which won an Aga Khan Award in 1986. The program is skillfully scaled down and fragmented into smaller blocks, and the scheme conforms to the topography of the triangular site sloping toward the old neighborhoods of Zeyrek, with its narrow streets and wooden houses. In its sensitivity to the scale and architectural character of one of the few remaining traditional neighborhoods in Istanbul, the design marks the shift in Eldem's attitude from the more monumental nationalist classicism of the 1940s to a more contextualized modernism of the 1960s.

SIBEL BOZDOGAN

See also **Istanbul, Turkey; Social Security Complex, Istanbul; Turkey; Vernacular Architecture**

Biography

Born Ömer Sedad in Istanbul, 18 August 1908; adopted family name of Eldem 1934. Studied architecture, Academy of Fine Arts, Istanbul, 1924–28; traveled and studied, Paris, Berlin, England, 1928–30. Married Fahire Hanim, 1941. Worked in the office of Hans Poelzig, Berlin, 1929–30. Private practice, Istanbul from 1931; member, and for several years chairman, Central Committee of Antiquities, Istanbul, 1931–41; member, Central Committee for the Protection of Cultural Properties, Istanbul, 1941–45; member, Council of the Monuments and Sites, Istanbul, 1962–78; member, Turkish Foundation for Environmental and Historical Protection, Istanbul, 1978–88; member, Faculty of Architecture, Academy of Fine Arts, Istanbul, 1930; created National Architecture Seminar, Academy of Fine Arts, Istanbul, 1934; head of department, Faculty of Architecture, Academy of Fine Arts, Istanbul, 1941–46; head, Design Bureau for Major Projects, Ministry of National Education, Istanbul, 1944. Member, Union of Fine Arts, Istanbul, 1932; member, Turkish Architects' Union, Istanbul, 1934–54; honorary fellow, Royal Institute of British Architects, 1946; member, Turkish Chamber of Engineers and Architects, Istanbul, 1954. Aga Khan Award for Architecture 1986. Died in Istanbul, Turkey, 7 September 1988.

Selected Works

State Monopolies General Directorate (First prize, 1934 competition), Ankara, 1937
Faculty of Sciences, University of Ankara (partially built; with Paul Bonatz), 1943
Faculties of Sciences and Letters, University of Istanbul (with Emiun Onat), 1944
Taslík Coffee House, Istanbul, 1950; dismantled 1988 and rebuilt on adjacent site
Social Security Agency Complex, Zeyrek, Istanbul, 1964
Indian Embassy Residence, Ankara, 1968
Dutch Embassy Residence, Ankara, 1977
Palace of Justice, Sultanahmet, Istanbul (with Emiun Onat), 1978
Rahmi Koç House, Tarabya, Istanbul, 1980
Hilton Hotel, Istanbul (with Skidmore, Owings and Merrill), 1984

Selected Publications

Bursa Evleri, 1948
Türk Evi Plan Tibleri, 1954
Yapi: Geleneksel Yapi Metodlari, 1967
Rölöve I (with F. Akozan and K. Anadol), 1968
Köskler ve Kasirlar, 1969
Anadoluhisari'nda Amucazade Hüseyin Pasa Yalisi, 1970
Köskler ve Kasirlar II, 1974
Türk Mimari Eserleri, 1975
Türk Bahçeleri, 1976
Rölöve II (with F. Akozan and K. Anadol), 1977
Köçeoglu Yalisi, 1977
Sa'dabad, 1977
Istanbul Anilari, 1979
Bogaziçi Anilari, 1979
Topkapi Sayayi: Bir Mimari Arastirma (with F. Akozan), 1982
Sedad Hakki Eldem: 50 Yillik Meslek Jubilesi, 1983
Türk Evi I: Osmanli Dönemi, 1984

Further Reading

Bozdogan, Sibel, "Profile: Sedad Hakkí Eldem," *Mimar*, 24 (1987)
Bozdogan, Sibel, "The Legacy of An Istanbul Architect: Type, Context and Urban Identity in Sedad Eldem's Work," in *Die*

Architektur, Die Tradition und Der Ort, edited by Vittorio M. Lampugnani, Ludwigsburg: Wustenrot Stiftung, 1999

Bozdogan, Sibel, Suha Özkan, and Engin Yeral, *Sedad Eldem: Architect in Turkey*, Singapore: Concept Media, and New York: Aperture, 1987

Eldem, Sedad Hakkí (editor), *Sedad Hakkí Eldem: 50 Yíllík Meslek Jubilesi* (Sedad Hakkí Eldem: 50 Years in the Profession), Istanbul: Mimar Sinan Üniversitesi, 1983

Gercek, Cemil, and Leyla Baydar (editors), *Sedad Hakkí Eldem: Büyük Konutlar* (Sedad Hakkí Eldem: Large Residences), Ankara: Yaprak Kitabevi, 1982

ELEVATOR

The invention of a safety device for the elevator made possible the construction of high-rise buildings, thus enabling the traditionally horizontal city to turn to the vertical. In the mid-nineteenth century hotels and commercial stores were among the first building types to deploy elevators; with improvements in elevator technology, office buildings and apartment buildings adopted them. As structural advances made possible taller buildings new elevator technologies made possible easy and safe access to those floors.

Hoisting and lifting devices were long a common feature in mines, on building sites, and for the loading of ships. Rarely more complicated than a pulley with a winch turned by hand or animal, or later powered by steam, the particular danger of these early forms of hoist was the absence of a safety device. Stretched or frayed ropes or cables might break causing the platform to hurtle to the ground. The key invention that made the hoist or lift safe for humans was a safety device that prevented free-fall disaster and its inventor was Elisha Graves Otis (1811–1861).

Born in Halifax, Vt., the son of a farmer and part-time inventor, Otis left high school and moved to Troy, New York in 1829 where he opened a sawmill and manufactured carriages and wagons. In 1851 he moved to Yonkers, New York where he worked for a bedstead manufacturer and while installing machinery in a new factory he developed a hoist that incorporated a number of new features, including an automatic ratchet device to hold the platform in place should the hoist rope break. He received a number of orders for the device and to publicize it, held a demonstration at the American Institute Fair at P.T. Barnum's Crystal Palace in New York in 1854. While standing on a platform that was raised to a height of thirty or forty feet above the ground he cut the supporting rope. As viewers gasped the platform remained in place and Otis announced to the assembled crowd, "All safe, gentlemen, all safe." Though a relatively crude device—lugs were driven into the platform when tension from the hoisting rope was broken—and the stop abrupt, the device was effective.

The first orders received by the company were for freight elevators which were able to exploit the steam power present elsewhere in the building to raise and lower the platform, but on 23 March 1857 Otis installed an elevator in the new five-story china and glassware shop of E.V. Haughwout and Company at 488 Broadway in New York. In addition to the safety device demonstrated at the Crystal Palace, Otis installed a freestanding two-cylinder belt-driven steam engine that enabled elevators to be built in buildings without their own extensive special power sources thus enabling elevators to be installed in buildings other than factories. (The Otis Company remains one of the largest manufacturers of elevators today.) The first steam-driven elevator in Chicago was installed in 1864 in the Charles B. Farwell Store at 171 North Wabash Avenue.

With the construction of tall buildings, notably in New York and Chicago, the need for efficient elevators necessarily increased and engineers experimented with different types. In 1859, a Boston engineer Otis Tufts built a screw-type elevator was built in the Fifth Avenue Hotel in New York City. Tufts called his device a "vertical screw railway," effectively a large central screw, ninety feet long and 12 inches in diameter, which raised and lowered the platform. Slow and relatively expensive, the screw-type of elevator also had an unnervingly jerky movement. Another elevator type was developed by Cyrus W. Baldwin for the Hale Elevator Company in Chicago. It employed a hydraulic system that acted under water pressure and was first installed in the warehouse of Burley and Company on West Lake Street in Chicago in 1870. The hydraulic elevator was particularly effective in the highest of the new skyscrapers and was demonstrated at the Eiffel Tower in Paris (1889).

Conversion to electric operation begun in the 1880s brought distinct advantages and enabled the diffusion of the elevator to private apartment houses and smaller office buildings. Traditionally elevators required a special operator, skilled at meeting the floor levels, and opening and closing the gates. "Watch your step," was the traditional elevator operator's call to passengers when he (or she) failed to meet the floor level exactly. But electric operation, using push-button controls introduced first in the 1890s meant that apartment dwellers themselves could operate the elevators. Electric elevators had the advantage of clearing the basements of complex and noisy machinery. In New York, as Cromley has pointed out, the electric elevator also helped introduce a new double-lot sized flat building, typically of seven stories. Because of the elevator it was possible to charge rents equably from floor to roof which not only compensated for the cost of the elevator but made residents feel more secure: all fellow residents were of the same income bracket.

Elevators were not only expensive to build but as building heights increased it became necessary to add more of them to expeditiously transport people to the upper floors. More elevators, however, consumed more of the floor plate, cutting down on rental income. In order to reduce this theft of space, experiments were also tried with double-height elevators stopping at even and odd floors. Staggered tubes with elevators running express to a point one-third or one half of the way up the building, and with passengers required to change elevators for local service for the remainder of the journey are commonplace today.

In addition to its practical virtues, the elevator has also been a potent design symbol for 20th century architects. Among Antonio Sant'Elia's drawings for his *Città Nuova* (1914), for example, was one project for an apartment house with the elevator projecting from the slanted exterior of the building. This elevator served as a potent symbol of modernity. In William van Alen's Chrysler Building, in New York City (1930) the elevator doors were decorated with hardwood veneers forming stylized flower patterns and the interiors of the elevator cars were decorated with elaborate marquetry. The effect of the lobby and its decoration was like a lush underwater world from which the elevators would speed one to the light. Louis A. Kahn exposed the elevator shafts and covered them with brick, giving them the character of medieval towers on the Richards Medical Research Laboratories, Philadelphia, Pa (1957–64). In the 1960s exposed elevators on the interior of the building became part of the kinetic pleasures of the atria built by John Portman in hotels such as the Hyatt Regency in Atlanta (1967) and elsewhere. This form of exposed elevator has been imitated, generally with rather baleful results, in shopping malls throughout the world.

NICHOLAS ADAMS

See also **Chrysler Building, New York City; Città Nuova (1914); Grain Elevator; Kahn, Louis (United States); Portman, John C. (United States)**

Further Reading

Cromley, Elizabeth Collins, *Alone Together: A History of New York's Early Apartments*, Ithaca, New York: Cornell University Press, 1990

Elliott, Cecil D., *Technics and Architecture: The Development of Materials and Systems for Buildings*, Cambridge, Massachusetts: MIT Press, 1992

Landau, Sarah Bradford, and Carl W. Condit, *Rise of the New York Skyscraper, 1865–1913*, New Haven, Connecticut: Yale University Press, 1996

ELLWOOD, CRAIG 1922–1992

Industrial Designer, United States

Craig Ellwood is credited with designing some of the most elegant modern houses built in California in the 1950s and 1960s, but he was not educated as an architect. Born Jon Nelson Burke, in Clarendon, Texas, Burke established in 1946 a small construction company to take advantage of the house-building opportunities offered by the G.I. Bill. To avoid any recriminations should the business fail, the company operated under the fabricated name of "Craig Ellwood Inc." The company did fail, although Burke retained the name Craig Ellwood for professional reasons, adopting it legally in 1951.

Ellwood then worked as a cost estimator for a firm of modern-house builders in Los Angeles, Lamport, Cofer, Salzman, while operating from the same address as "Craig Ellwood, Industrial Designer." While there, Jack Cofer asked him to design his first house, for Milton Lappin, in 1948. Although somewhat awkwardly planned and derivative of Frank Lloyd Wright's Sturges House in Brentwood (1939), it was nevertheless published in the *Los Angeles Times Home Magazine* in 1950 and brought in further commissions which encouraged him to set up, illegally, as "Craig Ellwood, Architect."

In October 1949 the first house credited to Ellwood—the Broughton House—appeared in *Arts & Architecture* followed by the Hale House (Beverly Hills, 1949). That year Ellwood also priced the Eames House (Case Study House 8) for Lamport, Cofer, Salzman. The speculative house he later built for Henry Salzman was published in *Arts & Architecture* as Case Study House 16 in April 1952, and with this building Ellwood's reputation was ensured.

The qualitative difference between the Lappin House and the Salzman House is noticeable. Ellwood had clearly learned something from Cofer, and probably something too from Robert Peters, who drew crisp, modernist perspectives for him as early as 1950.

Ellwood's houses were greatly influenced by the reductivism of Mies van der Rohe as well as Charles Eames and Richard Neutra. Characterized by the use of exposed, lightweight steel or timber framing, and by floating wall planes separated by a shadow-line or "flash-gap" detail, they were spare, modernist, and invariably elegant. Recognition came with Case Study House 16 and international success with the Maypole Apartments (1953) which won the Collective Dwelling Category of the 1953–54 São Paolo Biennale. Often formal in arrangement, sometimes symmetrical in plan, and frequently launching into the landscape, Ellwood houses populated the more exclusive Los Angeles suburbs and included the Zack House, Crestwood Hills (1952); the Anderson House, Pacific Palisades, (1954); the Pierson House (1954) and the Hunt House (1957), Malibu; the Smith House, Crestwood Hills (1958); the Korsen House, Beverly Hills (1959); the Rosen House, Brentwood (1962), and the Kubly House, Pasadena (1965). Overseas, readers of *Arts & Architecture* saw Ellwood's homes as the epitome of Californian chic. It was in England and Australia however that Ellwood's influence was most keenly felt, his aesthetic providing one basis for Hi-Tech architecture. What Mies van der Rohe had established as purely aesthetic functionalism with the Farnsworth House (Plano, Illinois, 1950), Ellwood had adapted into an accessible and fashionable vernacular architecture.

The Ellwood style translated less well in larger commercial buildings. Although the South Bay Bank (Los Angeles, 1958) and the Westchester Post Office (1959) are undeniably elegant, the Carson/Roberts Building (Los Angeles,1960) misrepresents its steel frame as an ill-conceived concrete structure. But at the Scientific Data Systems site in El Segundo (1968), where the administration and manufacturing buildings are pavilions in an open landscape, a successful industrial expression is found. Landscape and architecture came together most dramatically in Ellwood's last building, the Art Center College of Design in Pasadena, California (1977), which was conceived as a huge truss spanning a canyon, a final realization of a theme often repeated in earlier schemes and buildings.

NEIL JACKSON

See also **Eames, Charles and Ray (United States); Los Angeles (CA), United States**

Biography

Born Jon Nelson Burke, in Clarendon, Texas, 22 April 1922; raised in southern California; drafted into the US Army Air Force in 1942; established small construction company (1946) under the fabricated name of "Craig Ellwood Inc.," the name Burke adopted legally in 1951. Established his own office in Los Angeles 1948. Worked as a cost estimator for a firm of modern-house builders, Lamport, Cofer, Salzman (Los Angeles); shared an office with architect Emiel Becsky (1951–53); took graduate classes in Engineering at the University of California, Los Angeles (1949–53). Employed architects in his firm: Ernie Jacks (1953), Jerrold Lomax (1953–62), Philo Jacobsen (1961–63), Gerald Horn (1962–65), James Tyler (1966–77), some of whom became Associates but not Partners. In 1977 Ellwood

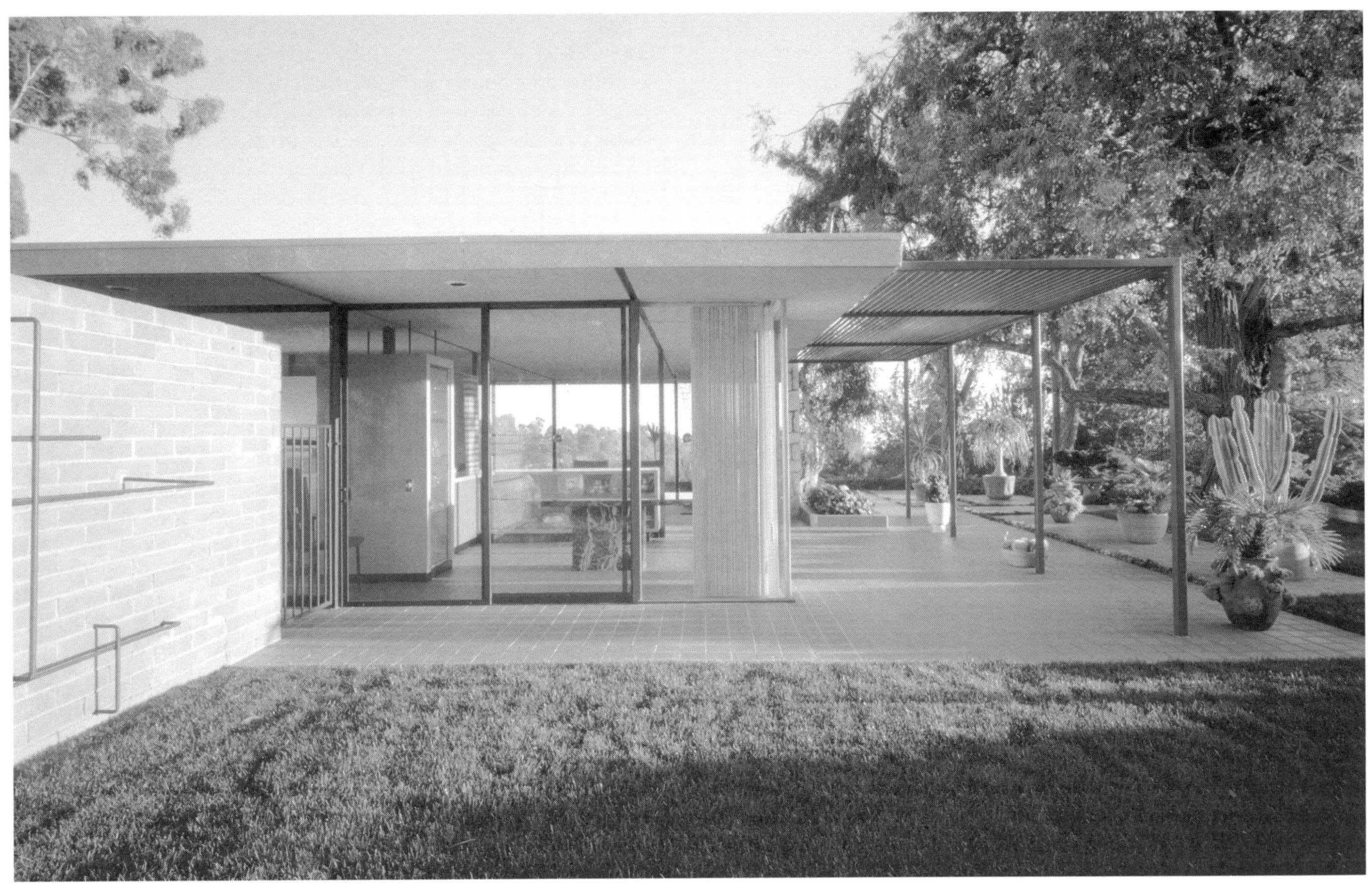

Craig Ellwood House and patio Bel Air, California

closed his architectural practice, moved to Arezzo, Italy, where he died, 29 May 1992, of an aneurism.

Selected Works

Lappin House, Los Angeles, 1948
Zack House, Crestwood Hills, 1952
Anderson House, Pacific Palisades, 1954
Pierson House, Malibu, 1954
Case Study House #16, Los Angeles, 1954
Case Study House #17, Los Angeles, 1955
Smith House, Los Angeles, 1955
Hunt House, Malibu, California, 1955
South Bay Bank, Los Angeles, 1958
Hale House, Beverly Hills, 1959
Korsen House, Beverly Hills, 1959
Rosen House, Brentwood, 1962
Kubly House, Pasadena, 1965
Art Center College of Design in Pasadena, California, 1977

Further Reading

There are no publications that cover the whole extent of Ellwood's oeuvre. The other sources shown here discuss Ellwood's work in broader contexts and thus are more general.

Banham, Reyner, *Los Angeles, The Architecture of Four Ecologies*, London: Allen Lane, and New York: Harper and Row, 1971

Clausen, Meredith, "The Pasadena Art Center and the Curious Case of 'Craig Ellwood'," *Casabella* 664 (1999)

Jackson, Lesley (editor), *Contemporary: Architecture and Interiors of the 1950s*, London: Phaidon, 1994

Jackson, Neil, *The Modern Steel House*, London: Spon, and New York: Van Nostrand Reinhold, 1996

McCoy, Esther, *Modern California Houses: Case Study Houses, 1945–1962*, New York: Reinhold, 1962; 2nd edition as *Case Study Houses 1945–1962*, Los Angeles: Hennessey and Ingalls, 1977

McCoy, Esther, *Craig Ellwood: Architecture*, Venice: Alfieri, 1968; Santa Monica, California: Hennessey and Ingalls, 1997

Pérez-Méndez, Alfonso (editor), "Craig Ellwood, 15 Houses," *2G International Architecture Review* 12 (1999)

Slert, Charles, *12 Los Angeles Architects*, Pomona, California: Cal Poly, 1978

Smith, Elizabeth A.T. (editor), *Blueprints for Modern Living: History and Legacy of the Case Study Houses*, Cambridge: MIT Press, 1989

EMBASSY

Few buildings are more symbolically charged than an embassy, the tangible emblem of a nation's foreign presence. With complex programs, embassy office buildings, or chanceries (not to be confused with ambassadorial residences), house diplomatic and consular offices, some of which are open to the public and some not. They also host numerous government agencies, including trade, agriculture, public health, law enforcement, and defense. Thus, they serve many clients with varied agendas.

Historically speaking, no country has more expansively explored this building type as a tool of cultural diplomacy than the United States, which, however, did not create its own diplomatic architecture until the third decade of the 20th century. Embarrassing comparisons between U.S. facilities and those of Germany, England, France, and Japan and a feeling that independent wealth should not be a prerequisite for diplomatic service prompted Congress to pass legislation authorizing construction of the first foreign buildings in 1926. Until then, American diplomats lived abroad at their own expense, and diplomatic properties were either leased or acquired by gift. Impressive embassies in Tokyo (1931, Raymond and Magonigle) and Paris (1932, Delano and Aldrich) quickly followed. Another, in Helsinki (1938, Harrie T. Lindeberg), was modeled after "Westover," an 18th-century plantation house in Virginia.

Following World War II, America's need for overseas office space soared, and the State Department's Office of Foreign Buildings Operations (FBO) embarked on a vastly expanded building program financed initially by foreign credits. [In 2001, FBO was reorganized and renamed the Bureau of Overseas Buildings Operations (OBO).] What made the postwar embassies so striking was FBO's daring decision to retain modernists for high-profile projects in capitals such as Rio de Janeiro (1952, Harrison and Abramovitz) and Stockholm (1954, Rapson and van der Meulen).

Critics in Congress reacted to the modern architecture and its International Style association with dismay and called for a return to classical tradition. However, with the Soviet Union building its own classically detailed embassies, FBO defended modern architecture as an expression of American ideals. To promote its program, it created an architectural advisory panel of experts in 1954. Spokesman for the panel, Massachusetts Institute of Technology Dean Pietro Belluschi, called for designs that were both "friendly" and "distinctly American," urging respect for local history, climate, and context. Thus, embassies challenged architects to combine newness with perceived tradition and to reconcile modernism with the uniqueness of place. Architects coveted FBO commissions as opportunities to try out new ideas, sample exotic themes, and create recognized monuments.

The period from 1954 through 1960 was the heyday of the American foreign building program in terms of scope and the quantity of new work on the boards. FBO retained promising young architects for projects in, for example, Kobe (1958, Minoru Yamasaki), Accra (1959, Harry Weese), and Tangier (1959, Hugh Stubbins) and also turned to well-known leaders of the profession for jobs in Athens (1959, Walter Gropius), Karachi (1959, Richard Neutra and Robert Alexander), and The Hague (1959, Marcel Breuer). Billboards for America and its foreign-policy aspirations, these prominent landmarks welcomed the public with their libraries, exhibition halls, and other cultural attractions.

Edward Durell Stone's design (1959) for the New Delhi embassy was among the most memorable. Stone made a conscious effort to link his design metaphorically to Indian tradition with a scheme that featured a pierced sunscreen and a temple-like plan. A diplomatic success, the embassy was hailed as a symbol of American commitment to India when it opened in 1959. Critical debate over the London building (1960, Eero Saarinen) and congressional deadlock over the Dublin embassy (1964, John Johansen) demonstrated clearly that embassy architecture was part of a larger political process.

As American facilities became targets of protest in the 1960s, security grew as a concern. State Department officials considered the need first for perimeter fences and then for walls. They barred architects from using devices such as sunscreens, limited the use of glass, banned *pilotis*, and eventually closed or relocated embassies, such as Accra, that could not be secured.

Suicide bombings in Beirut in 1983 prompted a major security overhaul. In 1985, Admiral Bobby R. Inman chaired a review panel that called for strict new construction standards. Projects designed to meet the so-called Inman standards included chancery compounds in Amman (1992, Perry Dean Rogers), Nicosia (1993, Kohn Pedersen Fox), Santiago (1994, Leonard Parker Associates), Lima (1996, Arquitectonica), and Bangkok (1996, Kallmann, McKinnell, and Wood). Some resembled prisons, whereas others were slightly more welcoming, but the openness once associated with these unique public buildings was lost amid escalating fears.

Bombings of U.S. embassies in Nairobi and Dar-es-Salaam in 1998 reinforced opinion that such facilities should not be sited in densely built downtown areas and that they needed better protection. In 1999, FBO hired Hellmuth, Obata, and Kassabaum to design replacement embassies for the two East African capitals. Both are landscaped walled compounds away from traffic and away from other buildings, with structures designed to look open but engineered to withstand a bomb blast.

The State Department finds itself caught in the same dilemma facing other government agencies; namely, how to use design to represent democracy in a high-risk world. This situation is particularly apparent in Berlin, where the State Department has planned an embassy of great symbolic significance. The site faces the Pariser Platz and is also bordered by busy streets, and it is almost adjacent to the city's foremost monument, the Brandenburg Gate. The site belonged to the United States before World War II and thus holds special meaning today. As an indication of the project's importance, FBO held a competition (only the second in its history) and selected a winning scheme by Moore Ruble Yudell, and Gruen Associates in 1997. The design accents America's democratic heritage through carved inscriptions from the Declaration of Independence and artwork inspired by the American flag, but given security concerns, its interiors will be seen by few. Moreover, lacking a security setback, the project has been delayed as diplomats, politicians, and security experts agree on how to proceed.

Less targeted by terrorists, other nations face fewer design constraints. Canada's new chancery (2001) in Berlin, for example, boasts a prime location, and the building itself is designed to be inviting and accessible. It houses embassy offices in a nine-story mixed-use structure that also features a pedestrian arcade, shops, and rental apartments. With walls of Douglas fir from British Columbia and floors of Quebec maple, and with a design that conveys quiet strength, the embassy is an expression of Canadian national identity, according to its Toronto architects, Kuwabara Payne McKenna Blumberg.

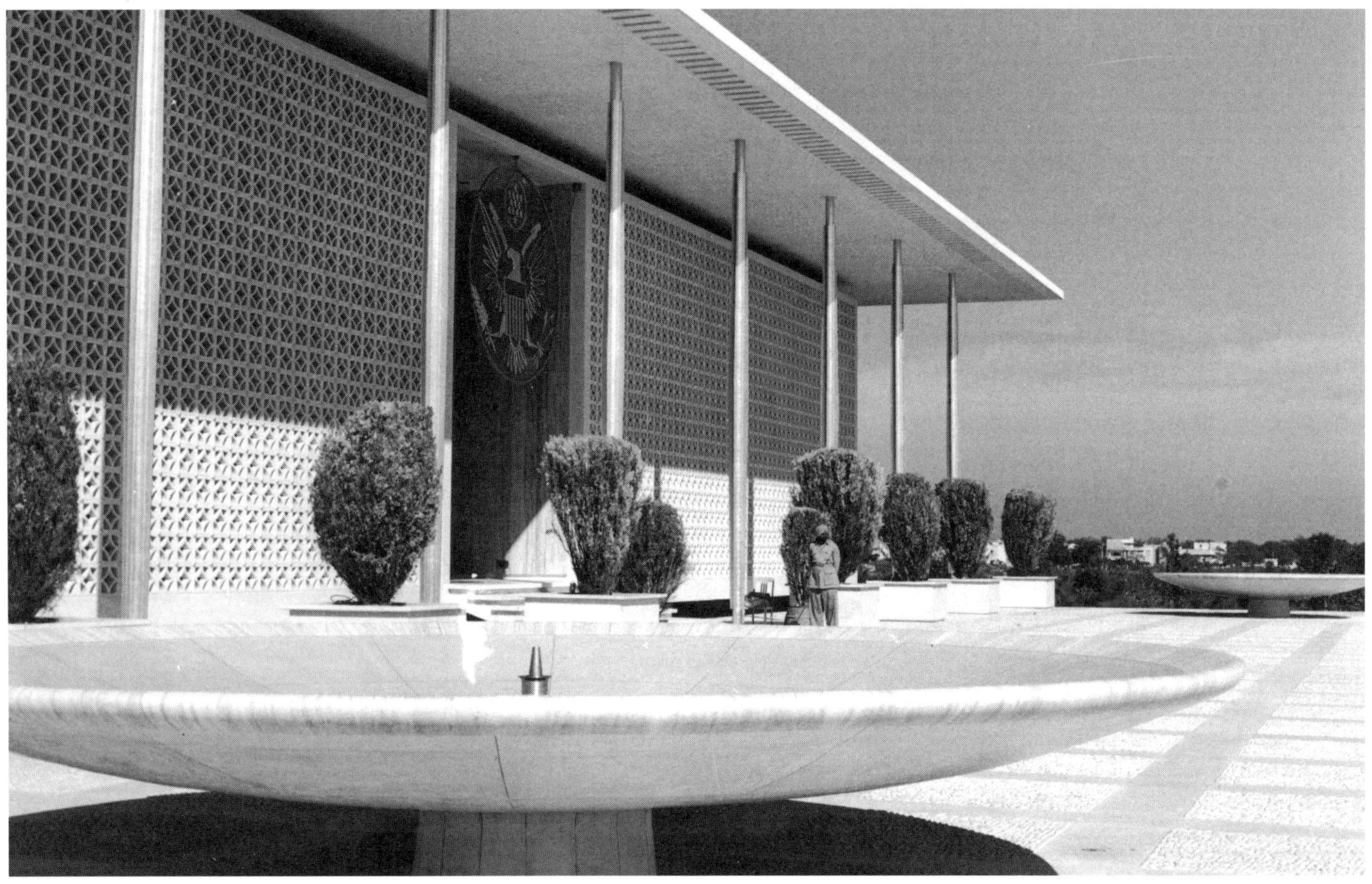

U.S. Embassy, New Delhi, designed by Edward Durell Stone (1959)
© Edward Durell Stone Papers (MC 340), box 119, photograph number USE 94. Special Collections, University of Arkansas Libraries, Fayetteville.

Another of Berlin's many new architectural attractions is the Nordic Embassy complex, for which Vienna-based Berger and Parkkinen Architekten prepared the master plan (1999). An unusual (and diplomatic) departure from tradition, the complex includes chanceries of Denmark (Nielsen Nielsen and Nielsen), Finland (Viiva Arkkitehtuura), Iceland (Palmer Kristmundsson), Norway (Snøhetta), and Sweden (Wingårdh Arkitektkontor), all designed together on a single site.

Like the United States, Great Britain oversees a worldwide building program. London architects Allies and Morrison garnered critical acclaim for the new British embassy (1995) in Dublin, as did Jestico and Whiles for the British embassy (1997), a restored historic villa, in Riga.

The extent to which security shapes embassy design varies, depending on who is building, and where. In the United States, for example, where the host government can provide dependable protection, foreign missions can build embassies that they could not build where such protection is lacking. On Washington's Embassy Row, Finnish architects Mikko Heikkinen and Markku Komonen designed Finland's chancery (1994) as a glass-walled showplace for Finnish design and craftsmanship. If security concerns the Finns, it does not show in their architecture.

Nearby, at the entrance to Washington's Rock Creek Park, Italian architects Piero Sartogo, Nathalie Grenon, and Susanna Nobili, in association with Leo A. Daly of Washington, have designed an Italian embassy (2000) that combines the grandeur of the past with modern sensibility. An homage to the Italian *palazzo*, it is a major cultural statement of Italy's presence in the United States and features a spectacular glass-topped atrium, brightly colored interiors, exterior walls of perfectly matched blocks of pink Italian marble, and a display of Italian-made furnishings. Security is a priority, but the architects have made a clear effort to downplay its impact.

No nation has a more prominent site in Washington than Canada, whose embassy sits at the foot of Capitol Hill, directly across from the National Gallery of Art on Pennsylvania Avenue. Canadian Arthur Erickson designed it in 1989 as a complement to existing buildings in Washington's Federal Triangle. Its formality and location underscore the importance of U.S.–Canadian relations. The U.S. embassy (1999) in Ottawa stands directly across from the Canadian houses of Parliament, making the same point. Skidmore, Owings and Merrill designed the building to be "virtually accessible," if not actually so.

In Washington, numerous other nations have built smaller but no less distinctive chanceries as part of the 28-acre International Center, an enclave of diplomatic buildings northwest of downtown. The State Department helped these countries build modern buildings by offering low-cost, long-term leases. Israel,

Jordan, Ghana, Bahrain, Egypt, Kuwait, Singapore, Austria, and Ethiopia are among those with embassies there, each supposedly representing its own design theme. Ethiopia, for example, hired RTKL to design an embassy (2000) that emphasizes the country's history and hospitality and makes use of its best-known building material: stone. Eventually, 19 chanceries will be located at the center.

Through their foreign buildings, nations large and small, rich and poor, support building programs that reveal their political, economic, and cultural ambitions. With nations more globally interconnected, embassy buildings will remain singularly important on the international landscape. Moreover, the threat of transnational terrorism makes outstanding architecture evermore precious, as evidence of a commitment to a shared future.

JANE C. LOEFFLER

See also **Breuer, Marcel (United States); Gropius, Walter (Germany); Harrison, Wallace K., and Max Abramovitz (United States); Kohn Pederson Fox (United States); Neutra, Richard (Austria); Stone, Edward Durell (United States); Washington, D.C., United States; Yamasaki, Minoru (United States)**

Further Reading

Few secondary sources deal with this building type. Loeffler's *The Architecture of Diplomacy: Building America's Embassies* provides a thorough overview of the American experience and includes a selected bibliography. A far more extensive bibliography exists in her doctoral dissertation (George Washington University, 1996).

Huxtable, Ada Louise, "Sharp Debate: What Should an Embassy Be?" *New York Times Magazine* (18 September 1960)

Loeffler, Jane C., "The Architecture of Diplomacy: Heyday of the United States Embassy Building Program, 1954–1960," *Journal of the Society of Architectural Historians*, 49/3 (September 1990)

Loeffler, Jane C., *The Architecture of Diplomacy: Building America's Embassies*, New York: Princeton Architectural Press, 1998

Sullivan, Joseph G. (editor), *Embassies under Siege: Personal Accounts by Diplomats on the Front Line*, Washington, D.C.: Brassey, 1995

Therrien, Marie-Josée, "Au-delà des frontières, l'architecture des chancelleries canadiennes, 1930–1992" (Ph.D. dissertation), Laval University, 1999

Tuch, Hans N., *Communicating with the World: U.S. Public Diplomacy Overseas*, New York: St. Martin's Press, 1990

United States Advisory Panel on Overseas Security, *Report of the Secretary of State's Advisory Panel on Overseas Security*, Washington, D.C.: United States Department of State, 1985

United States Department of State, *Report of the Accountability Review Boards on the Embassy Bombings in Nairobi and Dar es Salaam*, Washington, D.C.: United States Department of State, 1999

Vale, Lawrence J., *Architecture, Power, and National Identity*, New Haven, Connecticut: Yale University Press, 1992

EMPIRE STATE BUILDING

Designed by Shreve, Lamb and Harmon; completed 1931
New York City, New York

The Empire State Building is arguably the world's most famous skyscraper, and has been since its completion in 1931. Although it relinquished the title of world's tallest building in the early 1970s, the Empire State Building epitomizes the commercial skyscraper, a late 19th-century American invention that captured public attention and imagination around the world as a symbol of America's rise to global economic preeminence.

The Empire State Building was the brainchild of two men: John Jacob Raskob, former chief financial officer of General Motors, and Alfred Smith, former governor of New York. In the late 1920s, Raskob and Smith decided to build the world's tallest building as a way to attract tenants to a midtown Manhattan site on Fifth Avenue that had been owned by the Astor family. They began to raise money for their building in 1929. Raskob and Pierre du Pont, the latter of the famous chemical family, were the main investors. The project was entirely speculative, proceeding without a guaranteed "anchor tenant," unlike the Chrysler or Woolworth buildings. Raskob and Smith's gamble was seriously threatened in October 1929 when "Black Thursday" struck, inaugurating the Great Depression just two months after the first public announcement of the Empire State Building project. Construction continued in the hope that an economic turnaround was near, but even after its completion in 1931, the building faced adversity. The Empire State Building was only half full when it opened, and throughout the 1930s the occupancy rate never exceeded 25 percent. Critics coined the nickname "The Empty State Building" to describe the spectacular but barely used Goliath. The fact that the building was able to survive these lean years adds to the Empire State Building's fame, just as its continued construction during the Depression made it a public symbol of hope for better times ahead.

In 1929, Raskob and Smith enlisted the New York architectural firm of Shreve and Lamb to design a 65-story building for the site. William F. Lamb, chief designer for the project, created a building in the popular "setback style" to comply with the prevailing New York zoning laws. These laws required a building to become thinner as it rose higher; theoretically, a skyscraper could reach any height as long as it covered less than one-quarter of its site. Lamb responded to the restrictions by creating a simple, elegant building that gradually stepped skyward to a flat top. However, Raskob not only wanted a towering skyscraper, he also wanted to trump corporate foe Walter Chrysler, who was building a headquarters just blocks from the Empire State Company's Manhattan site. In August 1929, as the Chrysler Building was rising, Raskob's dream of a 1000-foot, 80-story tower had been announced to the public. Chrysler kept his architectural plans secret, depriving Raskob and others of knowing just how tall his new building would be. As it neared completion, Chrysler decided to add a needlelike spire to the top to bring the height to 1048 feet. Raskob retaliated by ordering his architects (now Shreve, Lamb and Harmon) to add six stories to the Empire design, making the building 1050 feet and topping Chrysler by less than a yard. By December 1929, Raskob was insecure about this slim margin of victory; the architects and engineers appeased him by proposing a 200-foot dirigible mooring mast to crown the building. As constructed, the Empire State Building's 102 stories soared to a height of 1250 feet, just over 200 feet taller than the Chrysler Building. Raskob had won the battle.

The Empire State Building was designed to satisfy the setback requirements by rising in a series of ever-narrowing blocks. The exterior was sheathed in Indiana limestone with a minimum of decoration. Geometric designs in the aluminum spandrels and fluted stone corners are the only ornamentation. The darkened spandrels are contrasted with light, continuous mullions to em-

Empire State Building, designed by Shreve, Lamb and Harmon (1931)
© Museum of the City of New York Print Archives

phasize verticality. Although the Empire State Building's attractive setback style and amazing height draw the most attention, its interiors were equally impressive. The building contained an incredible 2.1 million square feet of rentable space—almost twice the amount of Manhattan's second-largest building. The opulent lobby was a shining example of Art Deco design, with marble walls; aluminum, platinum, and chromium finish; reflected light; and a stainless-steel relief of the building against the outline of New York State.

In addition to being aesthetically pleasing, the Empire State Building was a marvel of construction. Its steel skeleton was state of the art for the period. More spectacular was the speed with which the building was constructed—only 18 months passed from the first sketches to the opening ceremonies. Actual construction was accomplished in an almost unbelievable 11 months. The structural frame took only 25 weeks. Much of the praise for this rapid erection goes to the organizational scheme developed by the general contractors, Starrett Brothers and Eken.

On 1 May 1931, President Herbert Hoover pressed a button in Washington, D.C., and the lights went on in the Empire State Building, officially opening the world's tallest building. During an opening ceremony at the building, attended by New York Governor Franklin Delano Roosevelt and Mayor Jimmy Walker, Al Smith aptly described the new architectural wonder as "a monument for generations to come." It stood tall and unchallenged over midtown Manhattan, proudly proclaiming the triumph of American corporate capitalism even on the verge of its darkest hours.

Despite the lack of tenants in its early days, the Empire State Building has been a critical and popular success from the very beginning. During the lean years, income from the popular 86th- and 102nd-floor observation decks helped keep the building open. Beyond its place in the climax of the movie *King Kong*, it has remained a tremendous tourist attraction for over half a century. The building became a cultural icon, symbolizing New York and American prosperity and ingenuity. The Empire State Building lost the title of world's tallest building after a 41-year reign when the New York's World Trade Center opened in 1972, but it has never lost its mystique. The Empire State Building is the archetypal skyscraper; although subsequent buildings have been built higher, none have equaled it in grace and beauty or approached it in the public's imagination.

DALE ALLEN GYURE

Further Reading

Bailey, Vernon H., *Empire State: A Pictorial Record of Its Construction*, New York: Rudge, 1931

Douglas, George H., *Skyscrapers: A Social History of the Very Tall Building in America*, Jefferson, North Carolina, and London: McFarland, 1996

"The Empire State Building: New York City," *Architecture and Building*, 54 (1931)

Goldman, Jonathan, *The Empire State Building Book*, New York: St. Martin's Press, 1980

Hine, Lewis W., *Lewis Hine: The Empire State Building*, Munich and New York: Prestel, 1998

James, Theodore, Jr., *The Empire State Building*, New York: Harper and Row, 1975

Lamb, William F., "The Empire State Building: VII. The General Design," *Architectural Forum*, 54/1 (1931)

Stern, Robert A.M., Gregory Gilmartin, and Thomas Mellins, *New York, 1930: Architecture and Urbanism Between the Two World Wars*, New York: Rizzoli, 1987

Tauranac, John, *The Empire State Building: The Making of a Landmark*, New York: Scribner, 1995

Willis, Carol (editor), *Building the Empire State*, New York: Norton, 1998

ENERGY-EFFICIENT DESIGN

In the popular imagination, energy-efficient design has been understood to be a by-product of the oil embargo initiated by the Organization of Petroleum Exporting Countries (OPEC) on 19 October 1973. On that date, Western consumers of fossil fuels became painfully aware of the energy-intensive nature of their built environment and their fragile dependence on foreign energy sources. The practice of energy-efficient design gained public recognition only after the related conditions of overconsumption and scarcity became so dramatically apparent. The political drama of the mid-1970s, however, only documents the prior suppression of long-emergent scientific doctrines.

The German physical chemist Rudolf Clausius (1822–88) was one of the first to articulate the second law of thermodynamics, which he expressed in 1865 as the concept of *entropy*. On the basis of his observation of thermal transfer, Clausius argued that one could not finish any real physical process with the same amount of energy as that with which one started. Once energy is expended, changing it from a usable form to an unusable one, it cannot be replaced. In any closed system—such as our solar system—entropy measures the amount of energy not available to do work. By the 1920s, this modern understanding of basic physics prompted natural scientists to develop the doctrines of *energy economics*. These doctrines express various ethical and economic imperatives to expend energy as efficiently as possible, thus delaying the inevitable chaos associated with advanced states of entropy.

Despite the proliferation of neo-Malthusian predictions in the scientific community, energy economics found little support among architects or in the realm of public policy until the effects of World War II were realized by energy-poor nations such as Germany. In the postwar era, concerns for the national security of energy-importing nations stimulated numerous government-sponsored research programs intent on rationalizing energy production and consumption. These pragmatic proposals for rationalization were bolstered by the ideological proposals of the political Left. Marxists in general sought to transform architectural production into a science capable of completing the modern project.

In the United States during the 1950s, Victor (1910–) and Aladar (1910–) Olgyay published research that reintroduced the concerns of biology, meteorology, and engineering into architecture. This research culminated in the appearance in 1963 of the influential *Design with Climate: A Bioclimatic Approach to Architectural Regionalism*. In 1968, the founding of EDRA (the Environmental Design Research Association) documented the academic acceptance of the Olgyays's scientific approach to architectural design. This approach is clearly expressed by Buckminster Fuller's (1895–) Dymaxion Principle, which promotes maximum gain for minimum energy input. In minds less energetic than Fuller's, however, the principles of energy-efficient design produced many projects distinguished only by low rates of energy consumption. The relentlessly quantitative nature of the scientific approach to architecture eventually came into conflict not only with traditional formalists but also with those intent on conserving nature in other than instrumental terms.

The term *ecology* was first used by the German zoologist Ernst Haekel (1834–1919) in his *Generelle Morphologie* of 1866. Although Haekel did not fully develop the scientific concept as it is understood today, he did help popularize the notion that biological entities cannot be understood outside their natural environment. He argued from a philosophically monist position that is opposed to the Cartesian dualist assumptions of Western science. It is not surprising, then, that the latter-day supporters of ecology, awakened by the 1962 publication of Rachel Carson's *Silent Spring*, would reject a purely quantitative approach to the conservation of nature. In their holistic view, the reductive assumptions of modern science are understood to be the source of resource depletion and environmental degradation—not their cure.

Many historians argue that *ecologism* emerged as a somewhat romantic idea at the beginning of the 20th century in Germany, England, and North America. Ecologism, however, did not mature as a political idea until it merged with the concept of energy economics in the era of the OPEC-induced energy crisis and the Vietnam War (1961–75). In that politically divisive climate, the proponents of ecologism and those of economic development clashed with increasing intensity. A significant contribution to the tentative resolution of that conflict has been the concept of *sustainability*, first used in "World Conservation Strategy," a 1980 publication by the International Union for the Conservation of Nature and Natural Resources (IUCN). In that document, the seeming opposition of nature conservation and economic development is subsumed in the synthesis of *sustainable development*, meaning "those paths of social, economic, and political progress that meet the needs of the present without compromising the ability of future generations to meet their own needs." More developed definitions, such as that proposed by the planner Scott Campbell in 1996, understand the concept of sustainability to be a set of related but competing discourses in which the economic interests evident in the socially constructed concept of energy efficiency are balanced with the interests of environmental protection and social equity.

In Europe, the scientific—as opposed to the romantic—interpretation of sustainability has been appropriated by the practitioners of the high-tech aesthetic, such as Sir Norman Foster (1935–), Nicholas Grimshaw (1939–), Thomas Herzog (1941–), Renzo Piano (1937–), and the engineering firm of Ove Arup. In the 1970s, these designers were concerned principally with the expressive potential of structure. At the end of the century, however, their interests turned equally to the energy engineering problems inherent in the environmental control of large buildings. Foster's Commerzbank project (1994) in Frankfurt, Grimshaw's British Pavilion (1992) at the Seville World Fair, Thomas Herzog's exhibition hall (1995) for the Deutsche Messe in Hanover, and Piano's office building (1998) for Daimler-Benz at Potsdammerplatz in Berlin are significant works that demonstrate the formal incorporation of energy engineering into architecture.

In North America, the concepts of energy efficiency and sustainability have been associated more with the environmental impact of material selection and the reduction of embodied energy in buildings than with expressive technology. The Croxton Collaborative's design for adaptive reuse of the National Audubon Society office building (1992) in New York; the Advanced Green Builder Home (1997) by the Center for Maximum Potential Building Systems of Austin, Texas; and William McDonough's proposal for the Environmental Studies Center (1999) at Oberlin College are equally significant examples of how the concept of energy efficiency has evolved into a more complex approach to the conservation of both natural and social systems.

In its most rigid form, energy-efficient design has been characterized as an attempt to reconstitute the practice of architecture as a purely instrumental applied science. In its most expansive form, however, energy-efficient design challenges society to understand buildings not as static objects of aesthetic value but rather as dynamic entities that participate in a complex system of natural energy flows and political consequences.

STEVEN A. MOORE

Further Reading

The literature that investigates this topic is spread between the disciplines of architecture, engineering, economics, climatology, environmental studies, and physics. The titles listed here are those related to architecture.

Bramwell, Anna, *Ecology in the Twentieth Century: A History*, New Haven, Connecticut: Yale University Press, 1996

Campbell, Scott, "Green Cities, Growing Cities, Just Cities: Urban Planning and the Contradiction of Sustainable Development," *APA Journal*, 62/3 (Summer 1996)

Carson, Rachel, *Silent Spring*, Boston: Houghton Mifflin, 1962; London: Hamilton, 1963

Daniels, Klaus, *Technologie des ökologischen Bauens*, Basel and Boston: Birkhäuser, 1995; as *The Technology of Ecological Building*, translated by Elizabeth Schwaiger, Basel and Boston: Birkhäuser, 1997

Givoni, Baruch, *Man, Climate, and Architecture*, Amsterdam and New York: Elsevier, 1968; 2nd edition, London: Applied Science, 1976

International Union for Conservation of Nature and Natural Resources, *World Conservation Strategy: Living Resource Conservation for Sustainable Development*, Gland, Switzerland: IUCN, 1980

Meadows, Donella H., Dennis L. Meadows, and Jorgen Randers, *The Limits to Growth*, New York: Universe Books, 1972

Olgyay, Victor, *Design with Climate: Bioclimatic Approach to Architectural Regionalism*, Princeton, New Jersey: Princeton University Press, 1963

Watson, Donald, and Kenneth Labs, *Climatic Design: Energy-Efficient Building Principles and Practices*, New York: McGraw-Hill, 1983

ENGINEERED LUMBER

The most influential engineered wood products of the 20th century may be classified quite simply as wood composites—recombinations of wood and wood fibers that overcome many of wood's natural limitations and extend its usefulness. Surprisingly, however, in this century of rapid scientific progress, most of the notable new lumber products have been rather modest steps forward—chemical improvements on essentially mechanical 19th-century inventions.

Plywood, the trade name adopted by the Veneers Manufacturers Association in 1919, is a perfect example of a product that became truly viable only in the 20th century. The industrial process of cutting thin layers of wood veneer by either peeling logs or slicing them, along with the concept of adhering layers of veneer together, was first introduced in France around 1830. Furniture makers such as Thomas Sheraton and the Steinway company began using laminated wood veneers in the mid–19th century, and in 1884 a factory in Reval, Estonia, began manufacturing three-ply birch seats for bentwood chairs. By 1870, a practical version of the rotary veneer lathe had been developed in the United States. However, the development of a structural wood veneer panel that could be used in everything from airplane fuselages to wall sheathing depended on the discovery of reliable, waterproof adhesives. That did not take place until after 1933, when German companies began manufacturing a new type of synthetic, heat-activated resin glue. Previous to the 1930s, plywood had been manufactured with a variety of other types of adhesives, such as blood albumin glue, casein glue (made from milk curd), and soybean glue, but its application was rather limited by its adhesives' vulnerability to moisture and light. Once these limitations were removed, plywood quickly replaced dimensional lumber as the most efficient material for flooring, wall sheathing, roofing, and concrete forms.

Like plywood, the origins of glue-laminated timber lie in the 19th century. First used in 1893 in Basel, Switzerland, glu-lam timbers are composed of many small, dry boards, laminated together with glue and/or metal fasteners, to form extremely deep, long, stable timbers. At first, glu-lam timbers could be used only indoors, where they would not be exposed to harmful moisture or radiation. After the 1930s, however, new adhesives made it possible to use glu-lam timbers practically anywhere. Glu-lam timbers have several advantages over long single timbers cut from old-growth logs. First, they can be made from much smaller logs grown in rotation. Second, because they are made from smaller selected planks, their composition is highly predictable. Third, they can be manufactured to practically any size or shape. Glu-lam timbers have many architectural applications, but their one weakness is their reliance on the strength and longevity of the adhesive.

Numerous new products have been developed on the plywood and glu-lam themes since the 1970s. One is a composite wood joist manufactured in an I-beam cross section. The webbing is usually made from long sheets of plywood or oriented strand board, and the flanges are made either from a parallel-laminated plywood product called micro-lam or from a material called Para-lam. The joists are much stronger and more stable than traditional wood joists and are perfectly uniform. Naturally, they rely completely on the strength of their glue bonds. Para-lam is a type of glu-lam timber, but rather than being made up of 2-by lumber, it is made of thousands of long, thin strips of wood approximately one-eighth by one-half inch in cross section and up to a few feet in length. In the manufacture of a Para-lam timber, a long bundle of spaghetti-like strands is coated in glue, compressed as it is squeezed through gigantic rollers, dried by microwave, and chopped off to convenient lengths. It can be manufactured to virtually any length or cross section. In the United States, Para-lam is superseding traditional glu-lam beams in many applications.

Not all engineered lumber requires chemical adhesives for its manufacture. One product in particular, which was an essential part of America's war arsenal during World War II, was a compressed particle or fiber panel, often called Masonite or Hardbord. It was manufactured throughout the 20th century out of many types of agricultural and lumber waste and by many different processes. Ordinarily, sawdust or wood chips were finely ground, boiled into a slurry, and then strained, pressed, and dried into hard sheets. Fiberboard relied on the natural bonds between the wood fibers themselves for its strength. Because it could be manufactured in practically limitless quantities out of extremely low cost materials, it became popular for housing projects of all types both before and after World War II. Partly for this reason, fiberboard has come to be synonymous with temporary, cheap construction. Its extremely limited insulating properties have also been far exceeded by fiberglass and rigid-foam insulation, and as an interior finish it has been superseded in both cost and simplicity by gypsum wallboard.

Oriented strand board (OSB) is a recent variation on the fiberboard-panel theme and has been on the market since the 1980s. In OSB, small, flat chips of softwood approximately one to four inches in size are gouged out of waste scraps from sawmills and low-quality logs. The chips are mixed into a gooey resin and then are laid and pressed flat in a hard matrix of resin and wood chips. Sheets of OSB are ordinarily cut to four- by eight-foot panels and come in a variety of thicknesses. Particleboard is manufactured in a very similar way out of sawdust. Both of these products are finding wider use. Oriented strand board is an extremely inexpensive sheathing material, although it is weaker and more moisture sensitive than plywood, and painted particleboard takes an extremely hard, smooth finish for interior detailing and exterior siding.

The engineered lumber products described here have been designed to decrease the cost of housing and the use of scarce timber resources while increasing the reliability of structural designs and the palette of architectural options. Unfortunately, many "innovative" products, such as finger-jointed studs, cobble together pieces of poor-quality lumber to create flimsy replacements for an already cheap existing product. Many engineered wood products also require careful handling and can maximize their strength and efficiency only if they are installed perfectly. Because the engineered timbers of the 20th century are composites designed to combine small, cheap, plentiful strips, scraps, and planks into larger units, nearly all of them also rely on chemical adhesives, which can release toxic gases and deteriorate under certain conditions. Despite these drawbacks, there is no doubt that engineered lumber is the rational, ingenious, and optimal solution to many of the environmental, economic, and political dilemmas that Western nations faced throughout the 20th century and will certainly face in the 21st.

A. Gordon MacKay

Further Reading

Elliot, Cecil D., *Technics and Architecture: The Development of Materials and Systems for Buildings*, Cambridge, Massachusetts: MIT Press, 1992

Haygreen, John G., *Forest Products and Wood Science: An Introduction*, Ames: Iowa State University Press, 1982; 3rd edition, 1996

Jester, Thomas C., editor, *Twentieth-Century Building Materials: History and Conservation*, New York: McGraw-Hill, 1995

Schniewind, Arno P., *Concise Encyclopedia of Wood and Wood-Based Materials*, Cambridge, Massachusetts: MIT Press, and Oxford: Pergamon, 1989

Wilson, Forrest, "Wood: Holding Its Place through Decades of Change," *Architecture: The AIA Journal* 87, no. 2 (February 1988)

ENTREPRENEURSHIP DEVELOPMENT INSTITUTE OF INDIA

Designed by Bimal Patel; completed 1987
Near Ahmedabad, India

Commended by the Aga Khan Award for Architecture (1992) for the "confident use of formal elements growing out of the Indo-Islamic architectural heritage," the Entrepreneurship Development Institute of India, designed by Bimal Patel, can be conceived as a series of open courtyards and transitional arcade spaces that provide a primary organizational framework for various scattered buildings. Situated on the outskirts of Ahmedabad near the Bhat village, this institute is the outcome of an enterprising collaboration between its director, Dr. V.G. Patel, and the architect.

The institute is formally organized as fragmented buildings that are laid out in an L shape and unified by a system of corridors. It is entered through a plaza that is shaded with trees. The entrance kiosk, with its green pyramidal roof, is the pivot from which two axes extend. The first axis has the administrative offices and training and research centers and ends in the library. The second axis has two sets of residential quarters, a kitchen, and a dining hall and ends at the water tower.

The first axis proceeds straight ahead as one enters the kiosk. It has a reception area off to one side and shows glimpses of the major courtyard, which sets off an austere yet monumental looking residential building that has a gateway flanked by squat circular towers at a distance. One is drawn through this axis that has alternating courtyards extending from it on one side; these courtyards house the administrative part of the complex, with research and training areas on the opposite side. It ends with a poetic view of a plain exposed-brick wall that has a window set in it, framing the trees outside. The library sits adjacent to this space. Staircases off this axis lead to the upper level, which has a low corridor that follows the lower one on one side and is connected across to offer views of the lower corridor and courtyards. The second axis, which leads to the residential quarters, is interspersed with circular areas that look like squat towers from the exterior and that are used for various activities, including indoor games such as table tennis, and as sitting areas.

The buildings are constructed of exposed load-bearing brick and have reinforced-concrete lintels and frames, with flat concrete and corrugated galvanized-steel roofs—all materials that are associated with low-cost building. These materials have been meticulously detailed with great refinement. The buildings are low, two-story structures that are connected through corridors and walkways, which also surround the various courtyards. The smaller courtyards are paved and have water bodies and trees that help create shade and enhance the natural ventilation system, and the large courtyard between buildings is landscaped with grass and has trees surrounding it. This project has been extolled for its low maintenance, easy replicability, and concern for saving energy through the use of courtyards for natural ventilation.

Although formally there is an aspect of monumentality that is emphasized by the circular tower-like forms, by the framed views, and by the uniformity of courtyards (as well as the materials used), this aspect is reversed in terms of the scale, as the buildings are quite low in comparison with the scale of the courtyards they surround. In addition, stepping-down devices on the roof accentuate the low scale. The formal alignment and deflections that frame particular vistas are geared toward underscoring special areas of the institute. The corridors that unify the institute contribute to the visual delight by alternating between light and shade, with courtyards opening on the sides. In addition to these corridors are alternate views of flat and arched lintels spanning adjoining courts, staircases leading up to the walkways at the upper level, a variety of framed views at both the upper and the lower level, and a rhythm in the arcades.

The project is greatly indebted to the vocabulary used by Louis Kahn in the Indian Institute of Management in Ahmedabad and can ultimately be summarized as encompassing a

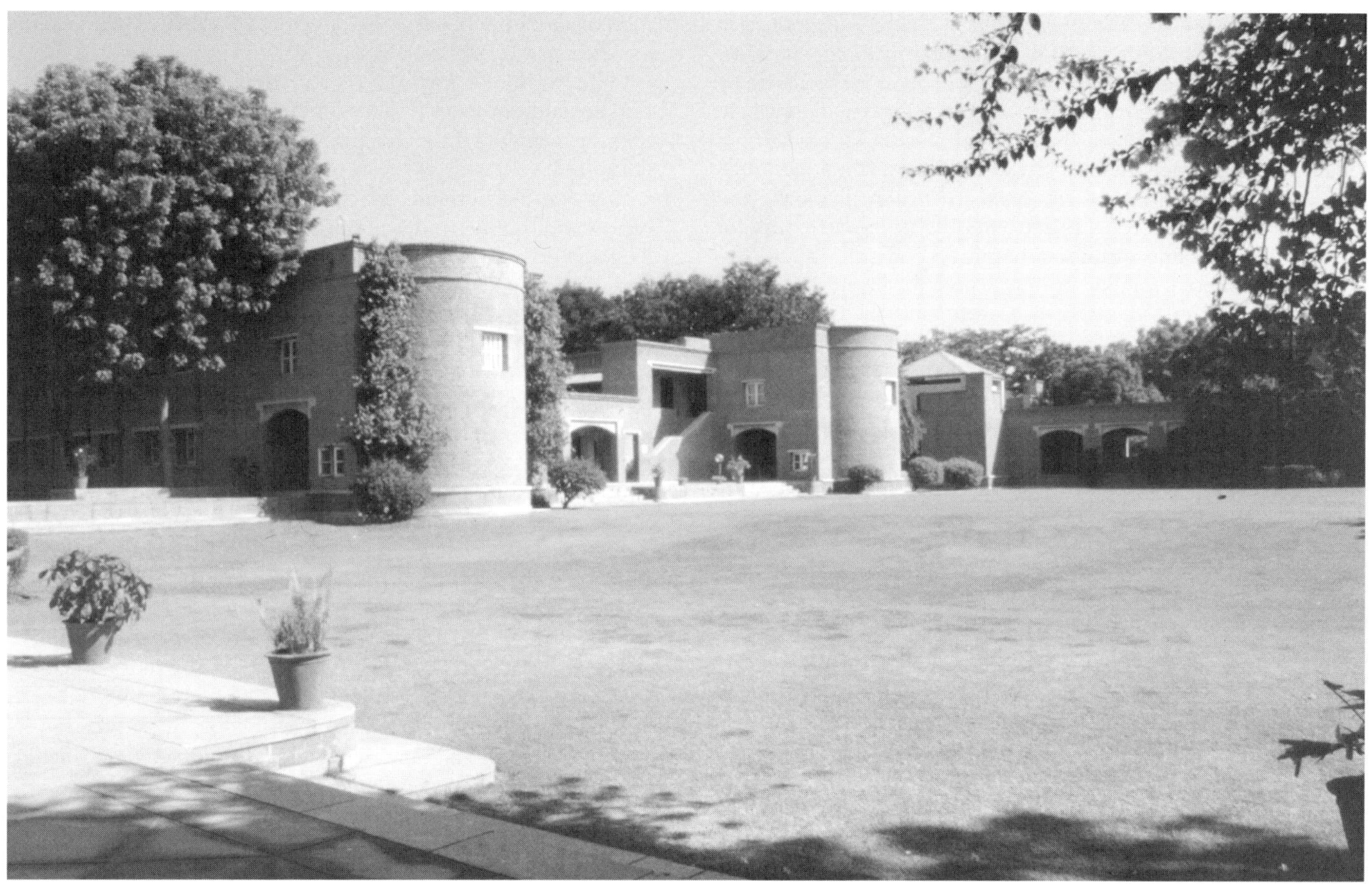

Entrepreneurship Development Institute of India, Ahmedabad
© Aarati Kanekar

restrained and refined monumentality. It is noteworthy that this was the architect's first major commission.

AARATI KANEKAR

See also **India; Indian Institute of Management, Ahmedabad**

Further Reading

Bhatia, Gautam, "Indian Archetypes," *The Architectural Review*, 197/1179 (May 1995)

Chauhan, M., "Spatial Experiences: Entrepreneurship Development Institute, Ahmedabad," *Architecture + Design*, 5/5 (July–August 1989)

Sabiki, Ranjit, "India: Significant for Its Vernacular Sensitivity and Its Simplicity," *Architecture: The AIA Journal*, 78/9 (September 1989)

ENVIRONMENTAL ISSUES

Environmental degradation became an issue in those locales where citizens suffered the unintended consequences of modern industrial development. In England, workers first experienced the grim conditions associated with the Dickensian city in the mid-18th century. In the rest of Europe and North America, the degraded industrial landscape emerged by the mid-19th century, and globally such conditions emerged in the 20th century. By the end of that century, the condition of the environment had become an issue not only for the world's industrial workers but also for an increasingly diverse population who could no longer isolate themselves from the fouled water, polluted air, and multiple health hazards that derive from industrial capitalism.

Historians and philosophers attribute the emergence of a degraded natural environment to various sources. The historian Lynn White, Jr. (1907–), for example, argued that the anthropocentric assumptions of mainstream Christianity are largely responsible for the instrumental view of nature held in those Western societies where industrial capitalism first developed. It is that instrumental logic, according to White, that has made nature appear to humans as available for exploitation and consumption. Postmodern philosophers of nature, such as Arne Naess (1912–), construct a slightly different narrative. Naess and the deep ecologists who followed him have tended to see the origins of the degraded natural world in the foundational assumptions of such early moderns as the French philosopher René Descartes (1596–1650) and the English natural philosopher Francis Bacon (1561–1626). Most historians agree that the Cartesian and Baconian creeds became popularly accepted in Western society by about 1850. Although this modern reconceptualization of nature became dominant by the mid-19th century, it did not extinguish contrary views. The idealization of nature by the French philosopher Jean Jacques Rousseau (1712–78) and the counter-modernism of the German philosopher Friedrich Nietzsche (1844–1900) set the stage for the 20th-century reassessment of our relationship to the natural world.

In the view of the German philosopher Martin Heidegger (1889–1976), the sum of mainstream Christian and philosophically modern doctrines has been to institutionalize what he describes as "modern technological thinking"—a form of consciousness in which nature is understood as a static human resource or reserve. Heidegger's influential criticism of modern science and technology would resonate throughout the 20th century.

The reaction against modern environmental degradation predictably emerged in those locales that were most affected by industrial excess—England, Germany, and North America. In England, the Arts and Crafts movement, through the writings of John Ruskin (1819–1900) and the socialist utopian projects of William Morris (1834–96), articulated a particularly nostalgic critique of industrialization. Those who followed Ruskin and Morris—principally the architect Raymond Unwin (1863–1940) and the planner Ebenezar Howard (1850–1928)—constructed progressive visions of urban life that attempted to both rationalize and beautify industrialization in the form of the garden city. In this tradition, English environmentalism has generally been associated with progressive politics. However, architects such as C.F.A. Voysey (1857–1941) and Baillie Scott (1865–1945), who enabled the retreat of industrialists to stylish houses in the as-yet-unpolluted countryside, can be associated with conservative politics.

As with the English Arts and Crafts movement, the German and Austrian architects saw a return to craft as the best defense against industrialization and environmental degradation. The German Romantic attitude is exemplified by the self-consciously picturesque Darmstadt artists' colony designed principally by Joseph Maria Olbrich (1867–1908). That village-like refuge from industrialization embodies the emergent romantic environmentalism that became a powerful conservative force in the Weimar era of Germany. Although there were Bauhaus- or Deutsche Werkbund–influenced environmentalists, such as the landscape architect Leberecht Migge (1881–1935), who affiliated themselves with progressive political causes, environmentalism in Germany between the world wars was more commonly associated with the blood-and-soil rhetoric of anti-modern nationalists and National Socialists. Architects of the Bauhaus, Hannes Meyer (1889–1954) chief among them, did articulate various progressive positions advocating the production of a hygienic environment for industrial workers.

In North America, those agrarian pastoralists who descended from Thomas Jefferson (1743–1826) and Henry David Thoreau (1817–62) developed a two-sided critique of industrialization: those who favored environmental preservation and those who favored environmental conservation. On the side of preservation were those romantics, such as John Muir (1838–1914), who advocated creating nature preserves that would remain forever untouched by development. On the side of conservation were those pragmatists, such as Gifford Pinchot (1865–1946), who advocated environmentally responsible development. As these two camps matured under the New Deal administration (1933–45) of President Franklin D. Roosevelt (1882–1945), social elites and technocrats came to dominate both. The principal environmental concern of social elites was aesthetic, while the principal environmental concern of technocrats was natural resource sufficiency and balancing the accounts of energy economics.

Frank Lloyd Wright's (1867–1959) organic approach to architecture emerged within these debates. In projects such as Fallingwater—the Edgar J. Kaufmann house (1936) at Bear Run, Pennsylvania—Wright's careful attention to the integration of the building with the natural conditions of the site, as well as his attention to solar orientation and to the use of local materials, supports those who argue that Wright's architecture is environmentally inspired. Other historians, however, argue that Wright's architecture responded to the environmental consequences of industrialization in only a metaphoric, not a material, sense. For example, Wright's proposal for Broadacre City (1935) exemplifies rather than critiques the American suburban attitude toward nature. It is the consumptive quality of suburban American land use practices that has produced the related environmental conditions of urban sprawl, universal dependence on the automobile, carbonization of the earth's atmosphere, and global warming—a cause-and-effect relation that gained increasing credibility among scientists at the century's end.

Following in the tradition of Wright, the organic architecture of Bruce Goff (1904–82), Paolo Soleri (1919–), Herb Green (1929–), and Bart Prince (1947–) can be characterized as profoundly anti-urban. Supporters of organic architecture argue that it is, at the very least, a proto-environmentalist position. Detractors, however, argue that organic architecture has achieved only the aestheticization of suburban life, thus masking the environmental consequences of the American automobile culture. The growing suburban population has tended to ignore the progressive environmental degradation in North America until the mid-1960s. In the absence of public consciousness, environmental issues were the concern of the poor who lived in the shadow of industrial production, the technocrats who wished to manage it from above, and the social elites who found it aesthetically unpleasant.

In the 1960s, however, several conditions conspired to change the political complexion of environmentalism. First, the sanctity of science as an objective body of knowledge came into question by such critical theorists as Herbert Marcuse (1898–1979). If science could be understood as ideological and itself a source of environmental degradation, Marxists found it increasingly difficult to distinguish between science and the capitalist economy that commissioned it. Second, white middle-class citizens, especially the so-called Woodstock generation, increasingly criticized the technocratic capitalist economy because, like the poor, they too had begun to experience serious environmental degradation. Following the 1962 publication of *Silent Spring* by Rachel Carson (1907–64) and the political confrontation of the Vietnam War (1961–75), environmentalists of the Left, such as Barry Commoner (1917–), inspired a new generation who embraced architecture as a medium of environmental and political action.

The critique of modern architecture that emerged in the late 1960s can be characterized as having two fronts, one aesthetic and one environmental. On the aesthetic front were those populists, such as Robert Venturi (1925–), who argued for a linguistic approach to architecture. Those who followed Venturi's aesthetic critique, Robert A.M. Stern (1939–) and Michael Graves (1934–) among them, became associated with a popular historicism that was much appreciated by corporate clients such as Walt Disney and the suburban developers of shopping malls. On the second front of the critique of modern architecture were those lesser-known environmentalists, such as Steve Baer (1938), who dropped out of conventional society to form alternative cooperatives, such as *Zomeworks* in northern New Mexico. For example, Baer's Davis house (1976–77) at Corrales, New Mexico, employed a variety of passive solar techniques that enabled his client to live independent of commercial power sources. Most of those activists who followed Baer's environmental critique of modern architecture rejoined conventional practice in the 1980s and produced a body of architecture distinguished mostly by its energy efficiency. The counterculture environmental architecture of the 1960s and 1970s was deeply influenced by the "dymaxion" principles and geodesic constructions of R. Buckminster Fuller (1895–) expressed through utopian interpretations of both the future and the past.

In the 1970s and 1980s, postmodern environmentalists in Europe and North America routinely characterized modern architecture as both inhumane and inherently anti-nature. In this reactionary view, modern architecture, like the modern science and technology that enabled it, was understood to be the principal source of environmental degradation, not its cure. Under scrutiny, however, such claims appear to be ideological and reflect the romantic assumptions of environmentalists in that era. More careful analysis suggests that within modern architecture there is a continuous, if not constant, tradition of concern for environmental issues, even among those major figures most often accused of abusing natural processes. The California projects of Richard Neutra (1892–1970), the works of Alvar Aalto (1898–1976), and even the later works of Le Corbusier (1887–1965) can be understood as thoughtful attempts to design human environments in sympathy with the natural energy flows of a particular site. Neutra's Kaufmann Desert House (1946–47) at Palm Springs and Le Corbusier's experiments with natural ventilation at La Tourette (1957–65) are particularly good examples that document the skill of modern architects in addressing environmental issues.

It is such site-sensitive modern architecture that the historian Kenneth Frampton (1930–) has described as "Critical Regionalism." Frampton described a set of related design attitudes that might provide resistance to both the globalizing tendencies of modern technology and the repressive social codes associated with local building traditions. To illustrate his hypothesis, Frampton pointed to the works of Mexican architect Luis Barragán (1902–), the early projects of Swiss architect Mario Botta (1943–), the houses of Australian architect Glenn Murcutt (1936–), as examples of sensitivity to site and context. Frampton's writings have generated a powerful proto-environmentalist discourse that paved the way for the ecologically inspired architecture that appeared at the end of the century.

Although the ecologically inspired architecture of the 1970s lost momentum when the energy crisis of 1973 waned, it enjoyed a significant resurgence at the end of the century. Under the rubric of green architecture and/or sustainable development, European and North American architects produced a wide variety of projects that responded to the ever-expanding list of environmental concerns. The term "sustainability" was first used in a 1980 publication by the International Union for the Conservation of Nature (IUCN), "World Conservation Strategy." Although the definition of sustainable development is widely contested, the concept attracted a broad following in both developed and developing nations by the early 1990s. In a 1987 publication by the UN World Commission on Environment and Development, *Our Common Future*—also known as *The Brundtland Report*—the concept was defined as "development that does not destroy or undermine the ecological, economic or social basis on which continued development depends." Subsequent international summit meetings on the environment—the first at Serrado Mar near Rio de Janiero, Brazil (1992), and the second at Kyoto, Japan (1997)—vigorously debated the political implications of sustainable development as a concept. The charged nature of the international debate reflected the environmental and social effects of economic globalization at the end of the century.

Although sustainable architecture had gained considerable visibility and support at the century's end, it would be a mistake to characterize it as a single, coherent ideology much less a style. Rather, selected environmental issues confronting the late century gained resonance with a number of competing and frequently opposed traditions within architecture. Two British scholars, Simon Guy (1963–) and Graham Farmer (1965–), identified six distinct factors that characterize the concept of sustainability in terms that are alternately progressive and conservative, high tech and low tech, romantic and pragmatic. Guy's and Farmer's six categories (or "logics") are particularly helpful in relating particular environmental issues to distinct constituencies and include the eco-technic, eco-centric, eco-aesthetic, eco-cultural, eco-medical and eco-social.

"Eco-technic" logic uses technologies to treat environmental problems. The term defines projects of those architects and engineers who work at a global scale, relying on the language of technology and scientific research. This type of architecture often appears modern, commercial, and future-oriented; the architects employ "hi-tech," and energy-efficient construction methods, such as the photovoltaic production of electrical energy. Projects by Norman Foster and Partners (Commerzbank Frankfurt, 1997), the Renzo Piano Workshop (*Cite Internationale*, Lyon, 1995), or by the engineering firm Ove Arup exemplify an eco-technic logic in architecture.

"Eco-centric" logic in architecture is focused on reconstructing a spiritual relation between humans and nature. These architects envision the world as fragile and therefore rely on systemic ecology and other holistic approaches as a source of environmental knowledge. Eco-centric buildings are understood to be consumptive, but can be redeemed through employing such renewable technologies as straw-bale construction. The natural harmony envisioned by those who support eco-centric architecture is exemplified by the projects of Brenda (1949–) and Robert Vale (1948–) in the United Kingdom (the Autonomous House, 1975) and by the "Earthships" (1983–90) of Mike Reynolds (1945–) in New Mexico.

"Eco-aesthetic" logic in architecture is less concerned with energy efficiency and the sanctity of nature than with metaphor and meaning. This group of architects prizes iconicity, organics, and a non-linear approach to design. In this characterization of sustainable architecture, human consciousness of nature is transformed as much by organic expressionism as by new ecological knowledge. Eco-aesthetic architecture is exemplified by the dramatic concrete constructions of Santiago Calatrava (1951–), the fusion of landscape and architecture found in the works of SITE, and the complex organic forms of Frank Gehry (1929–).

"Eco-cultural" logic involves the local cultural consequences of global technological change. Space, in this tradition, is understood as phenomenological and bioregionally unique. Typologically appropriate constructions are generally realized through "passive," "low-tech," or "vernacular" technologies, such as adobe construction, that focus cultural practices. Exemplars of eco-cultural logic, however, include the technologically inventive houses of Glenn Murcutt (1936–) in Australia, the works of Charles Correa (1930–) in India, and the midcentury works of Egyptian architect Hassan Fathy (1900–89).

"Eco-medical" logic is concerned principally with medical and health issues. According to the eco-medical, the modern built environment is characterized as polluted and even hazardous—the consequence of "sick building syndrome" that results from the use of volatile chemical compounds in tightly constructed buildings coupled with inadequate natural ventilation. The technologies employed by the practitioners of eco-medical logic are "passive, nontoxic, natural, or tactile," and are deployed to ensure individual health and well-being. The *Baubiologie* (building biology) movement in Germany and the Gaia group in Norway are practitioners of eco-medical logic.

The final environmental logic identified by Guy and Farmer is the "eco-social," which concerns itself with social participation in reproducing those natural processes that enhance all life. In this tradition, ecological space can be interpreted only in the social context of power relations. One cannot consider the health of the forest, for example, without also considering the health of forest workers. Eco-social design, then, relies on sociology and social ecology in architecture construction that is democratic, participatory, and locally managed. In the United Kingdom, Ralph Erskine (1914–) has employed eco-social logic in most of his projects, as have Lucien Kroll (1927–) in Belgium and Peter Hubner (1939–) in Germany.

Each of the environmental logics identified by Guy and Farmer concern themselves with a different set of environmental issues and attract citizens with differing political and economic interests. There is, of course, considerable fluidity in the ideological boundaries described in these various logics, but it is less the exclusive quality of the categories that is important than the diversity of those citizens who are attracted to them. Indeed, by the year 2000, the degraded condition of the environment had become a significant issue not only to exploited workers but also to average citizens in every country. On this account, a new breed of environmental activists exemplified by the industrialist Paul Hawken (1946–) and the co-directors of the Rocky Mountain Institute, Amory (1947–) and Hunter Lovins (1950–), predict that environmentally inspired technology will come to dominate architectural production in the 21st century.

STEVEN A. MOORE

See also **Barragán, Luis (Mexico); Foster, Norman (England); Fuller, Richard Buckminster (United States); Goff, Bruce (United States); Neutra, Richard (Austria); Stern, Robert A.M. (United States); Sustainability and Sustainable Architecture; Venturi, Robert (United States)**

Further Reading

The literature articulating the environmental issues of the twentieth century, as well as that proposing courses of action, is located within the disciplines of architecture, planning, environmental engineering, environmental studies, environmental history, ecology, social ecology, public policy, philosophy, science and technology studies, and other related disciplines. The texts cited below are a small, representative sample.

Advancing Sustainable Development: The World Bank and Agenda 21, Washington, D.C: World Bank, 1997

Carson, Rachel, *Silent Spring*, Boston: Houghton Mifflin, and Cambridge, Massachusetts: Riverside Press, 1962; London: Hamish Hamilton, 1963

Frampton, Kenneth, "Toward a Critical Regionalism: Six Points for an Architecture of Resistance" in *The Anti-Aesthetic: Essays on Postmodern Culture*, edited by Hal Foster, Port Townsend, Washington: Bay Press, 1983; as *Postmodern Culture*, London: Pluto Press, 1985

Guy, Simon, and Graham Farmer, "Re-Interpreting Sustainable Architecture: The Place of Technology," *The Journal of Architectural Education* 54, no. 3 (February 2001)

Heidegger, Martin, *The Question Concerning Technology and Other Essays*, translated by William Lovitt, New York and London: Harper and Row, 1977

International Union for Conservation of Nature and Natural Resources, *World Conservation Strategy: Living Resource Conservation for Sustainable Development*, Gland, Switzerland: International Union for Conservation of Nature and Natural Resources, 1980

Jones, David Lloyd, *Architecture and the Environment: Bioclimatic Building Design*, Woodstock, New York: Overlook Press, and London: King, 1998

Lyle, John Tillman, *Regenerative Design for Sustainable Development*, New York and Chichester, West Sussex: Wiley, 1994

Næss, Arne, *Ecology, Community, and Lifestyle: Outline of an Ecosophy*, translated and revised by David Rothenberg, New York and Cambridge: Cambridge University Press, 1989

Olgyay, Victor, and Aladar Olgyay, *Design with Climate: A Bioclimatic Approach to Architectural Regionalism*, Princeton, New Jersey: Princeton University Press, 1963

Vale, Brenda, and Robert Vale, *Green Architecture: Design for an Energy-Conscious Future*, London: Thames and Hudson, and Boston: Little Brown, 1991

White, Lynn, Jr., "The Historical Roots of Our Ecological Crisis," *Science* 155, no. 3767 (March 1967)

World Commission on Environment and Development, *Our Common Future*, Oxford and New York: Oxford University Press, 1987

ERSKINE, RALPH 1914–

Architect, England

Although English by birth and training, Ralph Erskine has spent the majority of his working life in Sweden. Born in North London, Erskine was sent to the coeducational Friends' School at Saffron Walden near Cambridge (1925–31), where many of his political and ethical values were formed. In 1932, he entered the Regent Street Polytechnic, at first to study surveying, and then architecture. Among his fellow students was Gordon Cullen, the illustrator, whose townscape drawings were to have an important influence on the representation of the postwar New

Towns in Britain. Following qualification, Erskine sought work with the new modernist firms in London but ended up working for planner and architect Louis de Soissons, then active in the design of Welwyn Garden City, the first of Ebeneezer Howard's garden cities.

Attracted by the humane modernism of the International Exhibition in Stockholm (1930) and the work of architects such as Erik Gunnar Asplund, Uno Ahrén, and Sigurd Lewerentz, Erskine left England for the summer in May 1939. He found work with the firm of Weijke and Ödéen in Stockholm. With the outbreak of war in September 1939, Erskine lost his job but, on being turned down for the Quaker Ambulance Corps, decided to stay in Sweden. In 1944–45, he studied architecture at the Royal Academy of Art in Stockholm. During the war, he was able to build very little: a house (known as The Box) for himself and his wife at Lissma near Djupdalen in 1941–42 made with materials scavenged on site (reconstructed 1989–93), a modernized log cabin country house (*stuga*) for the inventor Baltzar von Platen at Djupdalen, and a rustic ski lodge and summer holiday center at Lida Friluftsgård. At war's end, Erskine opened a practice in Drottningholm on the outskirts of Stockholm.

Much of Erskine's practice has been in housing, and he has specialized in involving the community in the process of design. An early housing project at Gyttorp (1945–55), for example, used bright colors for the concrete houses to provide a lively effect. Housing at Gästrike-Hammarby (1948) involved extensive community consultation and careful attention to the formation of public spaces based on principles he had learned while working with Louis de Soissons. At Landskrona (1968–71), there was a special effort to adapt the housing design to the local environment, and at Nya Bruket (1973–78) in Sandviken, where Erskine was responsible for the shopping street and surrounding housing, special community centers were included along with satellite parking to ensure a peaceful residential area.

Architecture for colder climates has also directed Erskine's practice. At Luleå in northern Sweden, he built a community center and interior shopping mall (1954–56) following new American models. In 1959, he presented his ideas on Arctic housing to the Otterlo meeting of CIAM (Congrès Internationaux d'Architecture Moderne) and laid out the town plan for Svappavaara (1963–64) in Lapland. A long, wall-like building was designed to shield the community from the Arctic winds, leaving the south side open to the sun. Erskine later also planned the community at Resolute Bay (1973–77) in the Nunavut Territories, Canada, a difficult undertaking not only because of the extreme climate (it is close to magnetic north) but also for the complex mixture of Inuit inhabitants and North American scientists that reside in the community. Neither Svappavaara nor Resolute Bay was completed to plan.

Erskine returned to England in 1962 to participate in a project for replanning the center of Cambridge. In 1968–69, he received the commission for a postgraduate residential hall at Clare College, Cambridge. His aim was to create "an open ended and attractive environment which was free from memories of medieval and Renaissance monumentality or opulence, [and] to ally ourselves with new society builders rather than the establishment." The effect of the two-story brick apartments and study halls is modest, with narrow walkways overhung by wooden balconies.

The best known of Erskine's works is known as Byker Wall (1969–81) at Newcastle-upon-Tyne. The traditional home of Newcastle's shipyard craft workers, the area was overcrowded and run down by the mid-1960s, a possible target for demolition and redevelopment. Instead, the District Council Housing Committee decided to improve the quality of the existing housing and reinforce the character of the community. A long perimeter-wall apartment block snaking around the crest of the hill and enclosing low-rise terraced housing was built, and transportation links to the surrounding communities to foster economic development were planned. Like Erskine's social housing in Sweden, cars were excluded from the residential area. Extensive consultation with the local community led to the preservation of the density of the old neighborhood, and the striped brick exterior cliff wall (facing the new roadway) evoked a medieval defensive system, providing visual identity for the development. On the interior of the wall, wood balconies faced the landscaped interior, creating a village-like intimacy.

The Byker Development was much praised in Sweden, and thereafter Erskine was hired to help with planning of the new site for Stockholm University at Frescati in 1971. The library and student center (Allhuset) recalls Erskine's links to Team X, although the overall effect of the central hall today, with its exposed structural members and glass roof, tends to remind visitors, regrettably, of a shopping mall or an airport.

In the 1980s and 1990s, Erskine's work has taken on new scale. In 1981, the Drottningholm office staff was cut drastically to allow him to refocus on design. A new cooperative office was opened in Stockholm, Arken-Erskinearkitekterna AB, with which Erskine could collaborate but that he did not run. Products of this new freedom include two office towers (The Ark, London, and Lilla Bommen, Göteborg), the vast bus center and office complex (Vasaterminalen) in Stockholm, and the Aula Magna at Stockholm University.

Lilla Bommen, headquarters for Skanska, a development and construction firm, is located at the entry to the Göta Canal, and the building recalls a giant navigational aid (buoy or lighthouse) with brown, cream, and red stripes and a periscope-like public atrium-observation tower. Unlike the typical vertical rental tower, the Ark was conceived of as being funnel shaped, the edges prowlike. The exterior is a reddish-brown copper color, and the overall effect is nautical. On the inside are a series of interior terraces suspended over an open atrium. Above is a glass wall that allows the interior to fill with natural light, and there is a wood ceiling. The interior, with its white walls and blond wood, provides its Scandinavian character.

The Aula Magna, near the entrance to the Frescati campus, is attached to Erskine's earlier Student House (Allhuset). Holding 1200 people in a main auditorium, the central gathering space is surrounded by smaller classrooms and open communal study facilities. The site was located on a south-facing incline with a height differential of ten meters, and the building flows across the slope in a series of terraces and around a group of a venerable oak trees. The central auditorium has been designed for effective acoustics both from the stage to the auditorium and for more democratic exchange among members of audiences, and the circulation spaces, which double as study alcoves and terraces, provide an appealing topography to what might have been dead space.

It is sometimes difficult to define the qualities of a building by Erskine. Working process is generally dominant: local materi-

Byker Redevelopment project, Newcastle-upon-Tyne (1981), designed by Ralph Erskine
© Howard Davis/GreatBuildings.com

als and community needs take precedence. The forms recall a variety of Scandinavian and modern northern European architects: Reima Pietilä, Alvar Aalto, and even Hans Scharoun come to mind. The jutting balconies and unpainted wood surfaces often seem handmade. The character of his environmental planning reminds one that his Regent Street Polytechnic classmate was Gordon Cullen: whose drawings often show hot-air balloons floating above traffic-free urban walkways. There is also, quite frequently, a high-tech quality to Erskine's work, sometimes reminiscent of Buckminster Fuller but also expressed in raw concrete or corrugated sheet steel, exposed structural supports, and playful adaptations to climatic factors: raised roofs to provide insulation, suspended balconies for sun without trapping cold air, waterwheels at the ends of gushing downspouts to provide colorful motion, and sunlight deflectors leading to skylights to open the dark center of a room to light.

Nicholas Adams

Biography

Born in Mill Hill, north London, 24 February 1914; settled in Sweden 1939. Studied, Regent Street Polytechnic, London 1932–37; degree in architecture 1939; attended the Royal Academy of Arts, Stockholm 1944–45. Married Ruth Monica Francis 1939 (died 1988): 3 children. Private practice, Drottningholm, Sweden from 1946; partners with Aage Rosenvold; branch office, Byker Estate, Newcastle, England 1968. Guest professor, Eidgenösische Technische Hochschule, Zurich 1964–65; guest professor, McGill University, Montreal 1967–68. Associate, Royal Institute of British Architects 1937; member, Royal Town Planning Institute 1938; member, Team X from 1959; member, Swedish Arkitekts' Riksförbund 1965; honorary fellow, American Institute of Architects 1966; foreign member, Swedish Royal Academy of Arts 1972; fellow, Royal Society, London 1984; honorary member, Royal Society of Arts, London 1985. Commander, Order of the British Empire 1978; Officier, Ordre des Arts et des Lettres, France 1986; Gold Medal, Royal Institute of British Architects 1987.

Selected Works

The Box, Lissma, near Djupdalen, for the Erskines (reconstructed 1989–93, near Drottningholm), 1942
Housing, Gyttorp, 1944–55
Housing, Gästrike-Hammarby, 1948
Ski Hotel, Borgafjäll, Lapland, 1950
Housing, Avesta, 1953
Shopping center, Luleå, 1956

Villa Nordmark, Södertälje, 1962
Erskine house, Drottningholm, 1963
Housing, community plan, Svappavaara, 1964
Housing, offices, shops, church, Kiruna, 1966
Clare Hall, Clare College, Cambridge, England, 1969
Housing, Landskrona, 1971
Housing, offices, shops, Barberaren, Sandviken, 1972
Housing, Eaglestone, Milton Keynes, 1973
Housing and township plan, Resolute Bay, Nunavut Territories, Canada, 1977
Housing, Nya Bruket, Sandviken, 1978
Housing, Byker Development Project, Newcastle-upon-Tyne, 1981
University Library; Student Center, Frescati, Stockholm, 1982
City Terminal and World Trade Center (Vasaterminalen), Stockholm (in collaboration with Arken-Erskinearkitekterna AB, Tengbom Arkitektkontor), 1989
Juristernas Hus, Stockholm, 1990
Lilla Bommen, Göteborg (in collaboration with White Arkitektur), 1990
Town Center and housing, Tappström and Gustavalund, Ekerö, 1991
The Ark, Hammersmith, London (in collaboration with Rock Townsend; Lennart Bergström Architects), 1992

Aula Magna, Frescati, Stockholm, 1998
Erskine's drawing archive is located at the Swedish Architecture Museum, Stockholm. Materials related to the Byker Development Project are located at the Royal Institute for British Architects Library, London.

Selected Publications

"Building in the Arctic," *Building Design* (May 1960)
"Primer for Subarctic Communities," *Perspective* (1963)
"Construire dans le Nord," *L'architecture d'aujourd'hui*, 38sh134 (1967)
"Indigenous Architecture: Architecture in the Subarctic Region," *Perspecta*, 8 (1963)
"Architecture and Town Planning in the North," *Polar Record*, 89 (1968)
"Democratic Architecture, the Universal and Useful Art: Projects and Reflections," *Royal Society of Arts*, 130sh5314 (1982)

Further Reading

Caldenby, Claes, Jöran Lindvall, and Wilfried Wang (editors), *20th-Century Architecture, Sweden*, Munich: Prestel, 1998
Collymore, Peter, *The Architecture of Ralph Erskine*, London and New York: Granada, 1982; revised edition, London: Academy Editions, 1994
Egelius, Mats, *Ralph Erskine: The Humane Architect*, London: Architectural Design, 1977
Egelius, Mats, *Ralph Erskine, Arkitekt*, Stockholm: Byggförlaget, 1988; as *Ralph Erskine, Architect*, Stockholm: Byggförlaget, 1990
Hall, Thomas (editor), *Frescati: Huvudstadsuniversitet och arkitekturpark*, Stockholm: Stockholm University Informationsenheten, 1998
Pearman, Hugh, *The Ark, London: Architect Ralph Erskine*, London: Wordsearch, 1993

ESCALATOR

The term "escalator" was developed by the Otis Elevator Company to describe the moving stairway systems they began producing at the turn of the twentieth century. Otis Elevator maintained exclusive use of the term until the 1930's when "escalator" was declared to be in the public domain.

Elevators provide quick and easy access over long vertical distances and thus were necessities in the high-rise building type that began to evolve at the end of the nineteenth century. The escalator provides both vertical and horizontal displacement, usually in an open environment, making it more appropriate in buildings where only a few floors need to be connected. The funicular, or inclined elevator, was the predecessor of both the vertical elevator and the escalator. It evolved into use where the vertical distances were great and intermediate landings were usually not required such as a ski lifts. Pittsburgh, PA once boasted fourteen funiculars to move people around the hilly city and they remain an integral part of the transportation system in Naples, Italy and other parts of Europe.

The predecessor to the modern escalator was the flat stepped "Seeberger" escalator introduced to the public at the Paris Exposition in 1900. The design necessitated passengers step off or on the upper landing at an angle to the direction of travel creating a safety hazard. The "Reno" type, patented about the same time as an "endless conveyor or elevator," consisted of a series of slightly inclined flat platforms on a conveyor. A Reno type escalator installed in the 59th Street Station of the New York subway system at the turn of the century remained in use until 1955. Both the "Reno" and "Seeberger" escalators included continuous rotating handrails and were manufactured by the Otis Elevator Company.

A much earlier moving stairway system, patented in 1859, was the Ames revolving stair. Its demise was the equilateral treads that forced passengers to awkwardly jump off and on at right angles to the direction of travel as the tread rotated around the gear.

Other early 20th century improvements to the design of escalators included flat steps with cleats or combs, and boarding areas parallel to the direction of travel. Developments during the mid-century include metal treads (instead of wood), glass balustrades, sleeker lines, and safety enhancements. A late 20th century innovation was the development of the radial configuration.

Related to escalators are moving walks, both horizontal and inclined designed to speed the movement of passengers over long distances. Early types, such as the one introduced at the 1893 Chicago World's Columbian Exposition, were refined conveyor belts. Modern moving walkways, incorporating much of the technology used in escalator design, are familiar sights in airport terminals. Inclined moving walkways are often found in retail establishments to enable shoppers to move shopping carts from level to level. Elevators were a key design feature in department stores, museums, concert halls, and other early 20th century building types built to satiate the need of the burgeoning middle classes to spend and to be seen. Escalators continue to be used to create opportunities for enticing shoppers in department stores and shopping malls to view enticing merchandise displays.

The construction of extensive underground and elevated commuter rail systems in British, European and American cites contributed to the need for experimentation in the development of machines to facilitate the transport of large groups of people over relatively short distances. Escalators enable the management of people in transportation centers by dispersing surges of users into a uniform flow and quantity. Moscow boasts the fastest speeds, about 200 feet per minute for escalators traveling into the deepest subway tunnels. Speed is limited to 100 feet per minute in most other countries for safety reasons.

During the first half of the 20th century, banking halls were often located on the second floor in new high-rise buildings. Escalators provided easy access to the banking hall from the street allowing patrons to observe who was going in and out, whom they were with, and, what they were wearing. Today lobbies of grand hotels and convention centers perform the same function; they allow guests to see and be seen during their leisurely ascents or descents while adorned in their finest garments and jewelry. The escalators in the lobby of the PSFS (Philadelphia Saving Fund Society) Building (Philadelphia, PA) originally transported patrons to a banking hall that was recently converted to the ballroom of a luxury hotel.

Escalators also provide excellent opportunities for viewing monumental architectural spaces such as those in the East Wing of the National Gallery of Art (Washington, D.C.) or panoramic views of the natural environment. Architects often use escalators as design features within large open spaces. They can be arranged in crisscross or parallel configurations creating bold aesthetic statements.

The process of designing spaces for escalators includes extensive analysis of a building's function, the number of occupants, peak periods of use, and knowledge of how people traverse through space as individuals and in groups. Adequate queuing distances must be provided at both the top and bottom of landings to allow for large numbers of people to embark and disembark in an orderly fashion. This is particularly important in rail facilities when the platform edges may be located near the escalators. Subway stations feel grossly oversized during much of the day, except at rush hour when they seem barely adequate to safely contain the passengers in the space.

Escalator configurations (tread width, angle of travel, speed, and design features) are standardized by code to ensure passerby safety and to make the process of incorporating escalators into a design less difficult for architects and engineers. Safety requirements minimize opportunities for innovative aesthetic modifications to escalator systems. Balustrades, the most prominent feature, may have tempered glass (clear or tinted), bronze, or, stainless steel safety panels. Panels may be etched with designs to enhance their appearance or to tie the escalator to the building's design theme. Handrails may be colored or lights may be mounted under them to emphasize this feature. Trusses (the structural support) may be exposed such as at the Zurich Trade Fair in Switzerland or clad in mirrors, ornamental metals or decorative stone.

KATHRYN PRIGMORE

See also **Elevator**

Further Reading

Strakosch, George R. (editor), *The Vertical Transportation Handbook*, 3rd ed., New York: John Wiley and Sons, 1998

EXHIBITION BUILDING

The development of exhibition buildings is inseparable from international world expositions. Historian Nikolaus Pevsner demonstrated that the 20th-century exhibition building has 19th-century origins, with stylistic and programmatic links to the conservatory and market hall.

Expositions are brief events usually lasting only one season, although they may consume up to ten years of planning effort. The buildings serve to display the innovative technological, industrial, economic, scientific, and cultural ideas of the participating nations. The Bureau International des Expositions (BIE), which administers these events, selects a timely theme that serves as a catalyst for each event. Themes provide an informational and organizing principle that guides much of what is designed and constructed. Themes have been celebratory, such as "The Age of Discovery" for Expo '92 in Seville, marked by the 500-year anniversary of the sailing of Columbus to the New World, or more frequently address a global concern, such as "Progress and Harmony for Mankind" at Expo '70 in Osaka. Although most buildings must be erected in a short period of time and are subsequently destroyed, those that come to symbolize the event are often saved and serve as powerful symbols for the city and issues they commemorate. The great exposition of London in 1851 had the Crystal Palace by George Paxton and that of Paris in 1889 the 300-meter-high Eiffel Tower by Gustave Eiffel, and in Chicago in 1893 the collective works surrounding the grand canal came to be known as "The White City." These landmark exhibitions and their symbolic buildings remain extraordinarily potent and have influenced most exposition efforts throughout the 20th century.

The first period of 20th-century exhibition buildings occurred through the late 1920s. These buildings are generally characterized as being retrospective both stylistically and historically, in correspondence with the imperialistic tendencies of the dominant Western nations. Although innovative structural and material applications led to the increasing scale of construction, these armatures were often surrounded in wooden lath and plaster known as "staff," molded into classical elements. The formal results were often awkward, as the proportion of classical encasements conflicted with large-scale steel structures. Despite some occasional structural inventions, most exhibition buildings served as stylistic props, with much attention given to their exterior facades. Highly acclaimed for resolving these formal problems, the Petite Palais by G. Girault and the Grand Palais by H. Deglave appeared at the Paris Exposition of 1900, which initiated the theme "A Century in Retrospect." In 1914, when the Deutscher Werkbund's exhibition was held in Cologne, Walter Gropius's model factory and Bruno Taut's Glashaus became icons of 20th-century architecture and modernism. Another popular building in this era was the Palace of Fine Arts by Bernard Maybeck for the Panama-Pacific International Exposition of 1915 in San Francisco. Sited on the bank of a lagoon, the overscaled classical Roman features contributed to a contemplative and melancholy setting that captured the spirit of the time, as the destruction and waste of World War I was occurring.

An exception to this era's general tendency occurred in 1929 at the Barcelona Exposition, where Ludwig Mies van der Rohe was responsible for the design of the German Pavilion. This was an elegant single-story building that relied on simplicity, scale, proportion, and quality materials for its sense of ornament. The design and its furnishings became the most celebrated pavilion at the exposition and a model for modern architecture. After

Court of the Universe, by McKim, Mead and White, from the Panama—Pacific International Exposition, San Francisco (1915)
© Museum of the City of New York, from the Monograph of the Work of McKim, Mead and White, Vol. IV, plate 386

the event, it was dismantled but lost. It was reconstructed in 1979 using the original plans.

The second period of exposition development was initiated by the global economic depression of the 1930s. Futuristically oriented and intentionally utopian, these expositions promoted an optimistic vision of a better life for all. The vision was to be fueled by scientific innovations, tempered by government guidance, and fulfilled by new methods of industrial mass production. Throughout this decade, the large-scale steel structures of exhibition buildings were mainly cubic volumes with flat roofs. The styles employed were a streamlined art moderne, a futuristic European modernism, a stripped-down classicism that tended toward the monumental, or a new simple functionalism. Breaking free from classical iconic constraints, many buildings successfully promoted a refreshed aesthetic sensibility. Starting with the theme "A Century of Progress" for the Chicago Exposition of 1933–34, representative examples include the Hall of Sciences by Paul Cret; the Crystal House by George Fred Keck, which also housed the Dymaxion automobile (1934) of Buckminster Fuller; and the Hall of Transportation by Holabird, Burnham, and Bennett. Following in this venue was the Paris Exposition of 1937, where nationalistic pride was baldly displayed at all pavilions, but the most memorable overscaled and forceful pavilions were for the Soviet Union by Boris Iofan and for Germany by Albert Speer. At the New York Exposition of 1939, "Building the World of Tomorrow" came to be symbolized by the sculptural composition of the Trylon and Perisphere (Wallace Harrison and Andre Foulinhoux), a 213-meter-high triangular spire and a 60-meter-diameter sphere.

Expositions after World War II maintained the futuristic tendency begun in the 1930s but sought a greater application of science and technology for peaceful purposes. Memorable exhibition buildings were the result of greater formal and structural experimentation. Continuing the exhibition hall's legacy of vast enclosed space, Pier Luigi Nervi designed his famous halls for the Turin Expositions of 1948, 1950, and 1961, notable for their inventive use of concrete. At the Brussels Exposition of 1958, the theme "Scientific Civilization and Humanism" was symbolized by the Atomium (Andre Waterkeyn), a geometric form of an iron molecule 102 meters in height and made up of nine spheres. They were finished in high-gloss aluminum alloy and housed a restaurant, viewing platform, and displays devoted to the peaceful use of atomic power. The nationally competitive nature of the expositions continued with the United States Pavilion by Edward D. Stone, a 104-meter-diameter rotunda with a free-span roof structure of concentric cables. Juxtaposed with this was the Soviet Pavilion by Abramov, Boretsky and Poliansky using a symmetrical tensioning system and steel mast supports to carry an aluminum skylight system that achieved a clear span of 48 meters. What was achieved was a symbolic expression of technical and scientific prowess that was to be pursued through the 1970s. Following on these efforts were the Seattle Space Needle of Exposition '62, Frei Otto's tensile fabric construction for the pavilion of the Federal Republic of Germany, Buckminster Fuller's welded spherical space frame for the United States Pavilion, and the concrete cantilevered high-density housing complex of Moshe Safdie (known as Habitat), all at Expo '67 in Montreal.

Since 1970, exhibition buildings have generally continued to be designed along a similar trajectory in attempting to symbolize technical and scientific progress. Technical and scientific endeavors have shifted. The development of expositions has also suffered with the growing ease of global transportation. The attention of society has moved away from the heroic expectations and awe that had been imparted by this building type as similar applications of innovative structural/spatial systems became common for regional sports, transportation, and institutional facilities. By maintaining the exposition formula, advanced building techniques have only served to heighten the sense of spectacle at subsequent exhibitions. However, an exception should be noted that might signal the introduction of a third period of exposition building development. At Expo '92 in Seville, the British Pavilion, by Nicholas Grimshaw and Partners, blended both high- and low-technical methods to produce a building that offered insightful and globally relevant approaches to achieving comfortable but dramatic environments without the customary demands on environmental resources. The appearance of this building underscores the unique venue that expositions can serve as a platform to explore and present a conscious range of building options for the future of mankind.

R. Swanson

See also **Century of Progress Exposition, Chicago (1933); Exhibition Hall, Turin, Italy; Expo 1958, Brussels; Expo 1967, Montreal; Expo 1992, Seville; Exposition Universelle, Paris (1900); Fuller, Richard Buckminster (United States); German Pavilion, Barcelona (1929); Grimshaw, Nicholas, and Partners (Great Britain); Lisbon World Exposition (1998); Maybeck, Bernard (United States); Mies van der Rohe, Ludwig (Germany); Nervi, Pier Luigi (Italy); Otto, Frei (Germany); Panama Pacific Exposition, San Francisco (1915); Safdie, Moshe (Canada, Israel)**

Further Reading

Expo '85 Architecture; "Kagaku banpaku Tsuba '85" kenchiku no kiroku (bilingual English-Japanese edition), Tokyo: Architectural Institute of Japan, 1985

Friebe, Wolfgang, *Architektur der Weltausstellungen: 1851 bis 1970*, Stuttgart, Germany: Kohlhammer, 1983; as *Buildings of the World Exhibitions*, translated by Jenny Vowles and Paul Roper, Leipzig: Edition Leipzig, 1985

Gelernter, David Hillel, *1939: The Lost World of the Fair*, New York: Free Press, 1995

Greenhalgh, Paul, *Ephemeral Vistas: The Expositions Universelles, Great Exhibitions, and World's Fairs, 1851–1939*, Manchester: Manchester University Press, 1988

Heller, Alfred, *World's Fairs and the End of Progress: An Insider's View*, Corte Madera, California: World's Fair, 1999

Mattie, Erik, *World's Fairs*, New York: Princeton Architectural Press, 1998

Pevsner, Nikolaus, *A History of Building Types*, Princeton, New Jersey: Princeton University Press, and London: Thames and Hudson, 1976

Rydell, Robert W., *World of Fairs: The Century-of-Progress Expositions*, Chicago: University of Chicago Press, 1993

EXHIBITION HALL, TURIN

Designed by Pier Luigi Nervi; completed 1950

The Exhibition Hall of Turin (1949–50) represents a significant achievement in the building arts of the 20th century. Built in the city of Turin among the vestiges of war-torn Italy, it was designed, engineered, and built by Italian engineer Pier Luigi Nervi. Widely known for its innovative adoption of new building materials and construction techniques, the Exhibition Hall is an eloquent example of the use of reinforced concrete and ferro-cement. The large, unobstructed spans of the main hall and the exuberant elegance of its articulated roof structure were made possible by the pioneering efforts and structural ingenuity of its builder. A building commissioned to showcase the promise of Italy's postwar industrial production called for display areas of vast dimensions, and the undulating concrete canopy of the Turin Exhibition Hall achieved just this.

Its construction epitomized modern architecture's postwar fascination with structural engineering. The building's appearance was derived from its structural logic and process of assembly. The elasticity and plasticity of poured-in-place concrete, the flexibility of prefabricated ferro-cement shells, and the ability to calculate and thus control the building's static forces were significant factors in determining its final shape. In building the Exhibition Hall, no boundary separated the architectural search for form from the engineering imperative to quantify structure.

Programmatically, the Exhibition Hall was a quintessentially modern building. Along with factories, warehouses, bridges, and power plants, exhibition halls were utilitarian structures born of the industrial revolution. From turbine engines to plumbing fixtures, exhibition halls collected and displayed the products of mechanization. A progenitor of the Turin Hall was the Crystal Palace, designed by Sir Joseph Paxton for London's Great Exhibition of 1851; like the later Exhibition Hall, it too was built of prefabricated components. However, unlike the Turin Hall, the Crystal Palace was built of iron and glass and achieved interior spans of only 100 feet. Only 100 years later, the use of reinforced concrete and ferro-cement would result in clear spans of nearly 300 feet.

An invited competition was launched for the construction of a new Exhibition Hall to be located on the site of the former Palace of Fashion. A general urgency to rebuild existed throughout Europe, and as the Exhibition Hall was essential in helping to generate future economic growth for Italy, its building schedule was but a mere eight months. The lack of building materials, particularly wood for the erection of formwork, further exacerbated the difficult conditions under which the participants were asked to devise an architectural solution. The existing palace, destroyed during World War II, was rebuilt by engineer Biscaretti di Ruffia. The design commission and building tender for the new Exhibition Hall, however, was entrusted to the engineer-

Exhibition Hall, Turin, Italy, interior longitudinal view, designed by Pier Luigi Nervi (1949)
© Donald Corner and Jenny Young/GreatBuildings.com

ing team of Nervi and Bartoli. The economical nature of their proposal, with its inexpensive use of materials, managed use of labor, speed of erection, and avoidance of wooden formwork, made it the favored solution. The mastery that Nervi and Bartoli had previously achieved in the construction of large-span structures, such as the Florence Stadium (1929–32) and the airplane hangers of Orvieto and Orbetello (1937–43), bore confidently on the future success of their daring proposal.

The complex was built in two stages, the first structure being completed in 1949 and the second a year later. The initial building, Salone B (Agnelli), was spatially, materially, and structurally the more extravagant of the two. It comprised two interconnected spaces, the main hall a rectangular barrel-vaulted enclosure measuring 328 by 262 feet and the smaller hall an apsidal room, with a half-dome 130 feet in diameter attached to one end of the main hall. With respect to the cross section, the height at the center of the main hall rose to over 60 feet, and 25-foot-wide mezzanines were built at the base of the two rows of supporting piers. The second building, Salon C, measured 213 by 230 feet and was also roofed with a concrete vault of both precast and poured-in-place elements.

The project's success can be attributed to its inventive construction process. To build during the harsh winter months and reduce the total time required for construction, Nervi devised a three-part process wherein the first two parts proceeded simultaneously. On site, the main structural supports of Salone B were built using poured-in-place reinforced concrete, whereas off-site, the prefabricated sections of the vaulted roof were cast independently using ferro-cement. Once the main structural piers and floors were in place, the installation of the roofing members proceeded without the need for additional formwork. The individual roof sections, measuring 8 by 13 feet and folded in the profile of a sinusoidal wave, were aligned and arched into the desired profile of the vault and bound to each other using poured-in-place concrete, the whole made possible by the use of movable metal scaffolding. The final phase of construction required bonding the roof shells to the poured-in-place piers. This was achieved via the on-site pouring of reinforced-concrete rib beams. They spanned from pier to pier and were poured within the upper and lower extremities of the roof section. It was this system of in situ concrete beams that ensured that the prefabricated roof shells and the structural piers worked together monolithically.

Still, the most significant characteristic of the Exhibition Hall was its extensive use of precast ferro-cement. This new material was used here for the first time in the construction of a large-span building, and the best person disposed to do so was its inventor, Nervi. In 1943, Nervi registered two patents for ferro-cement and built four boats using the material. Its ability to be light in weight, thin in section, and difficult to pierce, yet structurally sound, made it a viable alternative to wood for the construction of navigational vessels. Ferro-cement represented an entirely new way of conceiving roof structures and exterior building skins. It inverted the traditional manner in which concrete and steel were combined. Whereas reinforced concrete involved the insertion of steel rods within the body of concrete, ferro-cement involved a concrete coating over a body of steel. Layers of small-diameter steel mesh were intertwined and coated with a mixture of cement mortar (cement and sand) and folded into a range of contours intrinsic to its process of construction. The ability to bend the mesh into various shapes rendered possible the construction of very thin yet structurally sound slabs. The roof section of the Exhibition Hall was of an undulating corrugated profile whose strength was contained in only an inch and a half of ferro-cement.

The Exhibition Hall is an architectural and structural marvel of the postwar era. Its means of construction bear witness to the power of invention in the act of building and to the hidden potential in uniting the search for form with the measure of materials.

FRANCA TRUBIANO

See also **Concrete; Concrete Shell Structure; Exhibition Building; Nervi, Pier Luigi (Italy); Pre-cast Concrete**

Further Reading

Claudio, Greco, "Pier Luigi Nervi and 'ferro-cemento'," *Domus* 766 (December 1994)

Huxtable, Ada Louise, *Pier Luigi Nervi*, New York: George Braziller, Inc., 1960

Mateovics, Ernst, "Nervi and the art of 'correct construction'," *Architect's Journal* (June 1996)

Nervi, Pier Luigi, *Developments in Structural Technique, The Architect's Journal* (October 1955)

Nervi, Pier Luigi, *The Place of Structure in Architecture*, Architectural Record (July 1956)

Nervi, Pier Luigi, *Aesthetics and Technology in Building*, Cambridge, Massachusetts: Harvard University Press, 1965

Nervi, Pier Luigi, *Structures*, New York: F.W. Dodge Corporation, 1956

The Works of Pier Luigi Nervi, New York: Frederick A. Praeger, 1957

"Exhibition Hall," *Architectural Forum* 95 (July 1951)

EXPO 1958, BRUSSELS

Expo 1958 opened as the first major international exhibition since the end of World War II. As a world's fair, the exhibition in Brussels continued the century-old tradition of economic and technological competition among participating nations. Although technology and commerce were important aspects of the fair, its organizers cast the event as a cultural exchange, a celebration of the art and culture of the atomic age. To this end, the various pavilions (representing 43 nations and a variety of corporations) celebrated the broad spectrum of contemporary architecture, from the glass-and-steel modernism of Vjenceslaw Richter's Yugoslavian Pavilion to the hyperbolic paraboloid of Guilliame Gillet's French Pavilion. Amid the spectacular variety of architecture present at the fair loomed the specter of the Cold War (the American press referred to the event as a cultural Cold War). The United States and the Soviet Union faced off, the Soviets displaying their technological prowess with a model of the *Sputnik* satellite and the Americans emphasizing a rhetoric of democracy, prosperity, and freedom. Against this backdrop, the fair's towering theme building, the Atomium (modeled on a steel molecule), called attention to the benefits of atomic energy in an era when nuclear war seemed ever more likely.

No single architectural style governed the fair, and this allowed each participant to explore a variety of forms, materials, and technologies. A number of buildings celebrated structure and engineering, drawing on recent developments in precast concrete, tensile structures, and modern materials, such as plastic. Overall, the fair was characterized by the swooping, projecting, and dynamic geometric forms so popular in the structural exhibitionism of the 1950s. Amid the profusion of parabolas, cantilevers, concrete, and glass, two pavilions stood out: the American Pavilion, for its imperialistic and political overtones, and the Philips Pavilion, for its innovative combination of space, light, and sound.

The American Pavilion epitomized the economic and cultural competition that pervaded the fair. Located on a choice location next to the rectangular glass-and-steel Soviet Pavilion (dubbed "the refrigerator" by American commentators), Edward Durell Stone's circular pavilion housed a series of exhibits intended to showcase the cultural and technological achievements of the United States. The U.S. government viewed the fair as a chance to elevate American prestige in Europe, to counter Soviet propaganda, and to divert attention away from its crushing defeat in the space race (the Soviets had been the first to successfully launch an earth-orbiting satellite, *Sputnik*, in 1957). To this end, the Department of State and the American Institute of Architects chose Edward Durell Stone, the architect of the United States Embassy (1954–58) in New Delhi, as the architect for the pavilion. Stone designed a circular building with no internal supports and an elaborate roof structure comprised of tension cables and concrete compression rings (resembling a bicycle wheel laid on its side) supporting translucent plastic panels. Stone wrapped the exterior of the building with a slender colonnade and a plastic grillwork, combining classical forms and motifs with strikingly modern materials (a recurring theme in Stone's architecture).

The pavilion designed for the Philips Corporation remains one of the most interesting of the exhibition. Philips Electronics (a major international producer of items ranging from lightbulbs to loudspeakers and tape recorders) decided to commission a unique multimedia work of art for the exhibition instead of the typical trade show display of products. Philips commissioned Le Corbusier to design a pavilion to house a unique multimedia exhibit that combined a musical composition by the modern composer Edgard Varèse titled *Poèm Èlectronique* with a collage and film by Philippe Agostini. Le Corbusier created a striking design for the pavilion, combining a hyperbolic paraboloid and a conic section. The building consisted of a thin shell of concrete sprayed on a tensile structure of steel cables, surrounding an open plan on the interior (the expressive nature of Le Corbusier's design recalls his Chapel [1955] at Ronchamp). Varèse's eight-minute composition filled the unique acoustics of the structure, and the projected imagery covered the abstract geometries of

The Atomium (Molecule Building) from the World Exposition in Brussels (1958) was composed of nine aluminum spheres 55 feet in diameter connected by aluminum tubes. Inside the spheres are a restaurant (top sphere), bar, atomic exhibit, and other attractions. The spheres are linked by elevators and escalators running inside the tubes.

the interior of the building. This overwhelming sensory and intellectual experience left many visitors confused; nonetheless, Varèse's work stands as a significant example of spatial composition in 20th-century music.

Although the fair and its architecture received little scholarly attention following its close, there was a resurgence of interest in the fair in the 1990s. As part of the ongoing reappraisal of modernism in architecture, the fair epitomizes the variety of modernist idioms available to architects and clients in the late 1950s. In addition to Le Corbusier's Philips Pavilion, there has been a rediscovery of Norwegian architect Sverre Fehn's own version of modernism (Fehn's Norwegian Pavilion combined pinewood, plastic, and bush-hammered concrete in a more humanizing and organic version of Miesian modernism). Other scholars have focused on the role of the fair in the complex relationship between the United States and the Soviet Union during the height of the Cold War.

Regardless of the political overtones of the Brussels World Exhibition, the public saw the fair as a stunning success, both for its optimistic view of technology and for the sheer exuberance of much of the fair's modern architecture. At a time when the public was tiring of modernism (particularly the corporate idiom of rectilinear glass-and-steel architecture), the celebration of structure and dynamic architectural forms seen at the Brussels World Exhibition reinvigorated interest in the possibilities of modern architecture. Although experiments into the expressive and sculptural possibilities of concrete in architecture had been under way for nearly a decade (particularly in the work of Matthew Nowicki, Félix Candela, and Pier Luigi Nervi), the fair called attention to and promoted some of the more innovative possibilities of modern architecture, setting the stage for the overwhelming public acceptance of works from Jørn Utzon's Sydney Opera House (1973) to Eero Saarinen's TWA Terminal (1962) at John F. Kennedy Airport in New York.

MATTHEW S. ROBINSON

See also **Chapel of Notre-Dame-du-Haut, Ronchamp, France; Corbusier, Le (Jeanneret, Charles-Édouard) (France); Fehn, Sverre (Norway); Saarinen, Eero (Finland); Stone, Edward Durell (United States); Sydney Opera House; TWA Airport Terminal, New York; Utzon, Jørn (Denmark)**

Further Reading

Although there are no comprehensive works dealing solely with the Brussels World Exhibition, several recent works address the broader cultural and architectural significance of world's fairs. Both Robert Haddow and Robert Rydell have explored the political circumstances behind the United States presence at the Brussels fair, placing the U.S. pavilion in the broader cultural and political context of the Cold War. Erik Mattie's *World's Fairs* provides an overview of the architecture of most of the major exhibitions since 1851. Marc Treib's creative and exhaustive treatment of Le Corbusier's Philips Pavilion provides insight into the more innovative aspects of the Brussels fair's architecture. Finally, the critic Howard Taubman presents an interesting contemporary viewpoint of the fair in the context of cultural competition.

"Architecture at Brussels: Festival of Structure," *Architectural Record* 123 (June 1958)

Haddow, Robert H., *Pavilions of Plenty: Exhibiting American Culture Abroad in the 1950s*, Washington, D.C.: Smithsonian Institution Press, 1997

Mattie, Erik, *World's Fairs*, New York: Princeton Architectural Press, 1998

Rydell, Robert W., *World of Fairs: The Century-of-Progress Expositions*, Chicago: University of Chicago Press, 1993

"Sverre Fehn, Norwegian Pavilion, World Exhibition Brussels, Belgium, 1956–1958," *A + U* 340 (January 1999)

Taubman, Howard, "Cold War on the Cultural Front," *New York Times Magazine* (13 April 1958)

Treib, Marc, *Space Calculated in Seconds: The Philips Pavilion, Le Corbusier, Edgard Varèse*, Princeton, New Jersey: Princeton University Press, 1996

EXPO 1967, MONTREAL

Planned and constructed in just four years, the 1967 Universal and International Exhibition (Expo '67), held in Montreal, Canada, was an extraordinary achievement for the quality of its urban planning, integrated transportation systems, and space frame architecture.

After visiting the 1958 World's Fair in Brussels, Canadian senator Mark Drouin, together with Montreal mayor Sarto Fournier, petitioned the federal government to apply for a world exhibition to celebrate Canada's forthcoming centennial in

1967. The request, submitted to the Bureau International des Expositions (BIE) in Paris, fell short, however, as the 1967 exposition was awarded instead to the Soviet Union to celebrate the 50th anniversary of the revolution. When the Soviet Union bowed out on 1 April 1962 because of the exposition's tremendous estimated cost, Canada immediately reapplied. In November 1962, the BIE granted Canada permission to stage a "first category" exhibition, which stipulated in part international participation, a contemporary theme, and minimal commercial content.

The Canadian Corporation for the 1967 World Exhibition (CCWE) was to manage the fair in Montreal. Its theme, "Man and His World," was inspired by French author and aviator Antoine de Saint-Exupéry's book *Terre des Hommes*. Four subthemes were additionally chosen—"Man the Explorer," "Man the Creator," "Man the Producer," and "Man in the Community"—with separate pavilions devoted to each.

In January 1963, architects Bedard, Charbonneau, and Langlois agreed upon a site, using the city waterfront and a man-made island offshore in the St. Lawrence River connected to existing Ile Sainte-Hélène, an early 19th-century military installation turned into a park. Preparation of the site began in August 1963, and construction was completed ten months later. Fifteen million tons of landfill, dredged from the river and excavated from Montreal's accelerated subway construction in preparation for Expo, was used to double the size of Ile Sainte-Hélène (with the original island left as a public park) and to create the new Île Notre-Dame. Under the management of Commissioner General Pierre Dupuy, Colonel Edward Churchill was placed in charge of the Installations Department. In the project's early stages, Van Ginkel & Associates, a local urban-planning office, was charged with developing the site design, but for the final site plan the BIE commissioned Montreal architects André Blouin, Fred Lebensold, and Guy Desbarats. In December 1963, the master plan for Expo '67 was submitted to the Canadian Parliament for approval, and the completed site was turned over to the CCWE the following July for the infrastructure and pavilions.

The principal architects and planners of Expo '67 included Edouard Fiset as chief architect, Adele Naudé (from Harvard) as site plan designer, and architect-urbanist Steven Staples (from the Massachusetts Institute of Technology) as head of the planning team. The site design borrowed from various influences, including the 1964–65 New York World's Fair, modernist urban-planning and North American suburban shopping center layouts, and the ideas of MIT planning professor Kevin Lynch.

Expo's 285-hectare site was divided into four main activity poles: (1) the entrance and administration buildings, which were constructed as permanent structures, at Cité-du-Havre in Pointe-Saint-Charles and on Mackay Pier in the port; (2) the extended southwestern end of Ile Sainte-Hélène with pavilions, Place-des-Nations public square, and connected to the Cité-du-Havre by the new Concordia Bridge (Beaulieu, Trudeau & Associates, engineers; Claude Beaulieu, consulting architect); (3) the Île Notre-Dame, where most of the pavilions were located; and (4) the La Ronde amusement area on the northern end of Ile Sainte-Hélène. Because the St. Lawrence River surrounded the site, water was a major motif expressed by the lagoons and canals on Ile Notre Dame, two small lakes on Ile Sainte-Hélène, and the placement of the most preferred pavilion sites on the water's edge.

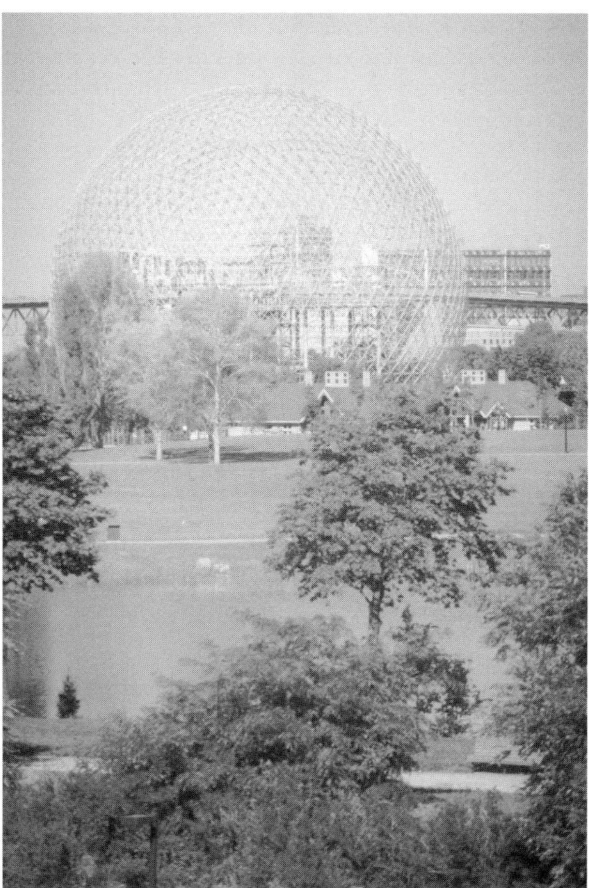

U.S. Pavilion at Expo 1967, by Buckminster Fuller and Shoji Sadao, at Montreal, Canada (1967)

To unify the site, the largest national pavilions were grouped as poles of attraction with theme pavilions and train stops nearby. These anchor poles were placed at the extreme ends and around the periphery of the activity areas to create striking perspectives and vistas and a flow of people by the smaller pavilions, shops, sculptures and fountains, entertainment stages, and kiosks in between. Scenic perspectives were created by specific alignments and orientations, and, except for the more important pavilions, the size of the architecture was restricted to a human scale.

Transportation to and around the Expo site was remarkably well integrated, and aimed to make the fair easily navigable. From large parking lots at Cité du Havre and at Longueuil on the river's south shore, the primary conveyor was the Expo Express rapid-speed train operating on elevated tracks. The main secondary system was a slower, elevated monorail train bought from the 1964 national exposition at Lausanne, Switzerland. Other means of moving about the site included boats and ferries in the canals and lagoons, cable cars over La Ronde, and trailer trains driving on roads separated from the pedestrian paths. Motor vehicles were banned from the site except for service vehicles on periphery routes. Apart from the Expo Express train, the island site could be accessed from the city by subway to Ile Ste-Hélène, hovercraft, and ferry or from one of several bridges.

Fifty-three private pavilions and 60 others representing 120 countries were erected for Expo '67. For the most part, the buildings were experimental, contemporary in design, and expressively modernist. One of many guidelines imposed for the pavilions stipulated a light and temporary rather than a massive and permanent appearance. As a result, the most significant structural forms were built of prefabricated, modular elements assembled in striking sculptural forms, such as the covering of the West German Pavilion, made of a suspended cable mesh system designed by architect Frei Otto. However, the most significant system by far was space frame construction utilizing aluminum tube components, most impressively in Buckminster Fuller's geodesic dome for the United States Pavilion and the flexible assembly of Walter Eykelenboom's Netherlands Pavilion.

Experiments in prefabricated, low-cost housing were also of architectural note at Expo '67, particularly the Cuban Pavilion (Baroni, Garatti, Da Costa, architects) and Habitat '67 (Moshe Safdie, architect, with David, Barott, Boulva, associated architects). Whereas the former featured a bolted steel frame and brightly painted aluminum panel walls, the latter was constructed of factory-produced concrete units assembled as a large prototype community housing project.

The creation of the Expo '67 site and its superb urban design ultimately have had a longer-lasting impact than any of the fair's architecture, as only space frame systems have found substantial applications in today's buildings. At present, half a dozen of the original pavilions remain, including the French and Quebec Pavilions, which have been modified and merged to form the Montreal Casino, and the United States Pavilion, recycled into an environmental information center. The islands are now known as Jean Drapeau Park, Montreal's largest green space.

MICHÈLE PICARD

See also **Exhibition Building; Fuller, Richard Buckminster (United States); Otto, Frei (Germany); Safdie, Moshe (Canada, Israel)**

Further Reading

Dupuy, Pierre, *Expo 67: Ou la découverte de la fierté*, Ottawa, Ontario: Les Éditions de la Presse, 1972

Expo 67: Official Guide Officiel (bilingual English-French edition), Toronto, Ontario: Maclean-Hunter, 1967

Fiset, Edouard, "Expo 67: Introduction of an Urban Concept in the Planning of the Exposition," *Royal Architectural Institute of Canada Journal* 42, no. 5 (1965)

Fulford, Robert, *This Was Expo*, Toronto, Ontario: McClelland and Stewart, 1968

Images de villes idéales—Les expositions universelles; Civic Visions, World's Fairs (bilingual English-French edition), Montreal: Canadian Centre for Architecture, 1993

Les objectifs du plan directeur; Master Plan Design Intent (bilingual English-French edition), Montreal: Canadian Corporation for the 1967 World Exhibition, 1963

Rowan, Jan, editor, " 'Editorial' and 'Commentary and Analysis': The Architect's Expo," *Progressive Architecture* 48, no. 6 (1967)

Staples, Steven, "Planning for Success: Reflections on Expo 67," *World's Fair* 12, no. 4 (1992)

EXPO 1992, SEVILLE

The international exposition at Seville, Spain in 1992 attracted over 36 million visitors, making it one the most successful exhibitions of its kind in the world. At least eight billion dollars was spent on 111 pavilions, buildings and landscape architecture, infrastructure and other services. There were 108 participating countries, 17 independent communities, 23 international organizations and 7 companies with their own buildings, all included on a list that went far beyond the expected number of participants. The purpose of Expo 1992 was to celebrate the 500-year anniversary of the arrival of Christopher Columbus to America. The project was managed by two general commissioners, Manuél Olivencia Ruíz and Emilio Casinello Aubán. Two proposals for master plans were accepted—one by Emilio Ambasz, the other by the firm Fernández Ordoñez, Junquera and Pérez Pita—and the latter was chosen.

An entirely new infrastructure was created for the Spanish exposition, including highways, bridges, a new opera house (designed by L. Marín, A del Pozo and E Yanez), an international airport (by R. Moneo), a bus station (J.Cuenca), and a railway station (A. Cruz, A.Ortíz), for the first high speed train that runs from the capital city of Madrid to Seville in two hours and thirty minutes. Expo 1992 was officially inaugurated by H.M. Juan Carlos I, king of Spain, on April 20, 1992.

The site was divided into three well defined sections: the international participants were located at the north in straddle theme avenues, Spain and the provincial pavilions were placed around an artificial lake along the east side of the complex, and environmental theme pavilions, gardens and the introductory halls were built near the monastery of *Santa María de las Cuevas* south and southeast of *Cartuja* Island.

Sustainable architecture included water mist sprays as cooling devices and natural and artificial shades everywhere to protect visitors from the extreme summer temperatures. An open theater, *El Palenque* (designed by J.M. de la Prada), was built for concerts, pageants, and additional cooling shade.

The eight bridges that connect the Old City with *Cartuja* Island were internationally acclaimed and deserve a particular notice. Designed by Santiago Calatrava and resembling a gigantic harp, the 142-meter *El Alamillo* Bridge was suspended by cables with extraordinary sophistication. The *Barqueta* Bridge (by Arenas and Pantaleón) is an equally extraordinary structure.

The pavilions could be divided in different types including vernacular buildings, high-tech buildings, historic or folkloric structures, and massive structures. Vernacular buildings were in large part constructed of wood, such as the Hungarian Pavilion (by I. Makovecz) constructed of a massive oak tree with its roots visible under a glass floor, representing the wisdom of past ages. The Japanese Pavilion, designed by Tadao Ando, was an allegory to traditional wood-crafting techniques, with a structure built with an intricate system of joinery avoiding the use of nails. The Finnish Pavilion, designed by Sanaksenaho, Rouniainen, Jaaskelainen, Tirkkonnen and Kaakko, was an unusual example of simplicity and cultural representation. It comprised two parallel blocks, the first known as the keel, representing the tradition of boat making. The other built with steel as characteristic of the industrial culture as counterpart, represented the machine.

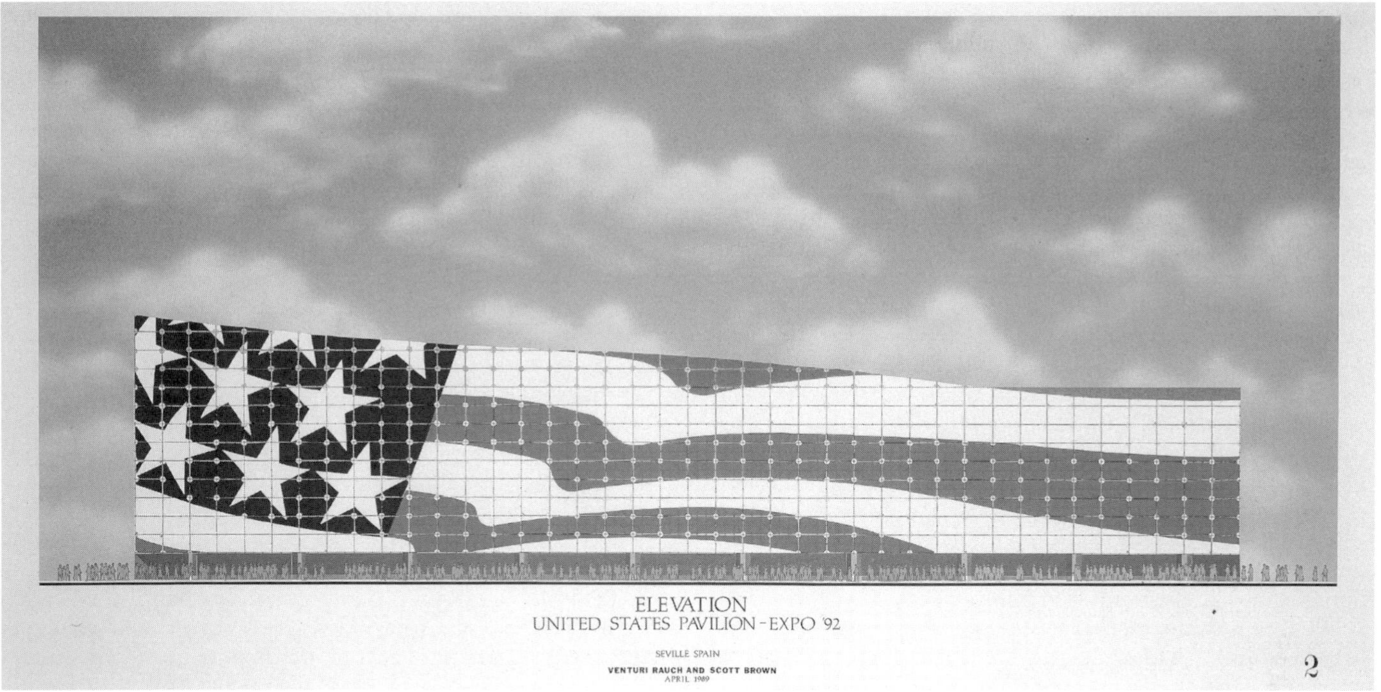

Design competition for U.S. Pavilion (1989), Expo 1992 by Venturi Rauch amd Scott Brown

The narrow gap between the two structures was named the "hell throat," and referenced the rugged Finnish landscape.

Among the high-tech buildings, those from the United Kingdom stood out, in particular, the British Pavilion, designed by Nicholas Grimshaw. This environmentally sensitive structure comprised a glass box with solar panels roof slabs, and curtains of mist and water falling over a glass wall to cool the building and generate electricity at the same time. The German Pavilion (by H. Muhlberger and G. Lippsmeier), inspired by dirigibles and flying machines, included an elliptical roof suspended by cables from an inclined post that supported it, and a building constructed with polycarbonate shields.

Among the historic and folkloric representation included pavilions from Morocco, India, Malaysia, Saudi Arabia, Thailand, Mauritania, Philippines and Indonesia. The Moroccan Pavilion, in particular, blended fountains, tiles and Moorish ornamentation.

JAVIER GOMEZ ALVAREZ-TOSTADO

See also **Calatrava, Santiago (Spain); Exhibition Building**

Further Reading

Rispa, Raúl, Cesar Alonso de los Ríos, and María José Aguzaga, (editors). *Expo 1992: Seville. Architecture and Design* (exhib. cat.), Italy: Electa 1992.
Fernández Galiano, Luis, "Sevilla Silicio y Silicona" *Arquitectura* # 6. Mexico (Summer 1992)
Russell J.S., Cohn D., "Spain's Year: Barcelona and Seville," *Architectural Record 8*. U.S. 1992.

EXPOSITION UNIVERSELLE, PARIS (1900)

The Paris Exposition Universelle of 1900 was meant by its sponsors to be both a retrospective summation of the material progress of the 19th century and a hopeful harbinger for the 20th. The 1900 event was the fifth Paris Exposition of the 19th century. Paris had hosted ever-larger events every 11 years since 1856, and expectations ran high for the greatest exposition ever in 1900. The 1889 Exposition Universelle, which had celebrated the centennial of the French Revolution, was France's first truly international fair and had been an unqualified success, both intellectually and economically, despite a shaky start. The 1900 Fair also had its share of initial uncertainties. The Dreyfus Affair threatened the Exposition with an international boycott, and the bitter of the winter of 1889–1900 and heavy spring rains further complicated the project, so although the Exposition officially opened with great ceremony on 14 April, paying customers were not admitted to the grounds for several more weeks.

The Exposition was laid out on several large precincts within Paris and in the Bois de Vincennes east of the city (the latter being the site of the Games of the Second Olympiad). Despite the fact that the Commissioner General of the Exposition, Alfred Picard, had graduated from the École des Ponts et Chaussées in the 1860, the 1900 Exposition did not have the large, showstopping engineering feats of 1889; French engineers concentrated their efforts in the construction of the Métro, notable for architect Hector Guimard's Art Nouveau stations and Victor

Laloux's Gare d'Orsay, which carried fair visitors from the provinces to the Exposition gates. The buildings and landscape features of the Exposition were awarded to architects and engineers within the closed circle of the French academies in the hope that the aesthetic presentation of the Fair would be in uniform good taste. The result was less than hoped for. Although there was no single spectacular building, and there were several important permanent constructions that were very well received, the grounds were more noteworthy for the wide assortment of temporary constructions that were aesthetically adventurous and even controversial.

The permanent monuments for the capital city were the Pont Alexandre III, which leapt across the Seine in one graceful arch, and the Grand and Petit Palais. The bridge continued the line of the newly established Esplanade des Invalides across the river past the two Palais to the Champs Elysées to the north. The Grand Palais, home to the contemporary art exhibitions (whose content was completely controlled by the Academie des Beaux-Arts), was designed by the team of Henri Deglane, Albert Louvet, and A.E.T. Thomas. The building hid behind Deglane's imposing Neoclassical central pavilion and sweeping colonnades an enormous steel-and-glass atrium, which spanned the length of the building. Charles Girault's Petit Palais, perhaps the architectural success of the Exposition, housed a retrospective fine art exhibit. Girault skillfully handled the difficult transitions at the odd corners necessitated by the building's trapezoidal plan and yet reveled in the free-Baroque classicism then fashionable among the faculty at the École des Beaux-Arts. The building's primary motif, a high arched entry that cut into a low steel dome, was adopted by French-trained architects around the globe in the years after the Exposition.

The temporary structures of the Exposition did not feature the restraint found in those structures that were intended to be permanent. Although some of them were interesting in their adoption of past architectures to modern purposes, others were simply novel. The Palace of Electricity, the home of the Exposition's dynamos and generators, terminated the Champs-de-Mars to the south and presented the viewer with a riot of baroque architectural elements, none of which were particularly related to one another. The whole was crowned by an allegorical extravaganza that set Electra in ecstasy atop a chariot, behind which rose a spiky steel-and-glass sunburst that if scaled down would be at home in any early-1960s rumpus room. The whole Palace, however, was nothing but a backdrop to the real feature of the site, the Chateau d'Eau, an immense waterfall 100 feet wide that gushed water over its terraces at the rate of 1.5 million gallons an hour. The whole was lit at night with colored light, the fountains bubbling and water jets dancing in a spectacle that was said to rival the fountains at Versailles.

The most controversial structure at the Exposition was probably René Binet's Porte de Concorde. This strange, oversized gateway sheltered the ticket booths and check stations under a steel dome, which was supported by three yawning arches encrusted with floral ornament. Two soaring minarets flanked the structure to further punctuate the work. The whole was studded with electric lights, so that the building shimmered with colored light at night. Although the architecture was not lauded for its novelty, true vitriol was reserved for crowning sculptural ornament, a 20-foot high statue of "The City of Paris," represented by a woman in revealing evening dress. Many Parisians were scandalized by the statue's lifelike flesh tones and immodest vestments and claimed that the statue more truly represented the city's prostitutes than the genteel women of Paris. Whatever the claims of her sartorial miscalculation, "La Parisienne" was a functional success—her ample gates welcomed as many as 60,000 guests an hour on the high fête days.

The 1900 Fair is perhaps most important architecturally for its national pavilions and cultural presentations. Nations of the first rank were given large lots on the Quai des Nations, where an impressive, if riotous, mélange of national styles were presented. Twenty-three nations constructed their own edifices, and all but one of these were evocations of particular nation's architecture. Britain, for example, constructed a Tudor-style house, whereas Germany built a very large baroque city hall, and Italy fused the Duomo at Siena with St. Mark's at Venice to create a rather unnatural hybrid palazzo. The one pavilion that did not denote its nation's architectural traditions was that of the United States, where American architects designed a Beaux-Arts pavilion. Boasting a triumphal arch entry-porch and a high steel-and-copper-clad dome, the building resembled a diluted version of Richard Morris Hunt's Administration Building at the World's Columbian Exposition of 1893. Of all the national pavilions, perhaps that with the most lasting importance to the history of architecture was Gesellius, Lindgren and Saarinen's Finnish Pavilion. This work, located in the second rank of national pavilions behind the Quai des Nations, juxtaposed the fortresslike character of its exterior stone walls and high tower with the softer, more introspective feel of its great hall, which was trimmed and roofed in native Finnish woods and ornamented with representations of the country's native flowers and woodland creatures. A landmark in the National Romantic style, the pavilion cemented Eliel Saarinen's international reputation as an architect capable of powerful yet sensitive work.

The colonial exhibitions at the grounds of the Palais du Trocadero were less culturally sensitive. Building on the ethnographic displays of the 1889 Exposition, the European powers were encouraged to celebrate their colonial holdings with simulations of these exotic locales. Natives of each land were brought to Paris to demonstrate folkways and perform religious and dance ceremonies for the public within well-crafted evocations of their homes in what can only be described as a human zoo. Across the river, the grounds in and around the Champs de Mars again hosted scientific and industrial exhibits. The Palais des Machines was again pressed into service for the Exhibition, but it was hardly noticed among the sea of similar iron-and-glass structures in the precinct. The decorative arts and light manufactures were displayed in pavilions along the Esplanade des Invalides. This implied a clear separation from the fine arts, located across the Pont Alexandre III, and the crafts. As a result, the works of masters such as Emile Gallé, Louis Comfort Tiffany, and René Lalique were not viewed either in the Grand Palais or in the national pavilions, but in their own small storefronts. In fact, despite the fact that the Fair would later be remembered as the event that popularized the Art Nouveau, only the Austrians and Germans exhibited the new forms in their national presentations.

The twin objectives of the Exposition—the reflection on the past and the foreshadowing of the future—were fulfilled admirably. The environmental design and art designed and collected for the event summed up decades of 19th-century academic eclecticism as practiced in official French art institutions. At the same time, the industrial and scientific exhibits showcased the industrial design, electrical technology, and military equipment that would lead to much of the material culture and political crises of the new twentieth century. Like any world's fair, the Universal Exposition of 1900 asked its participants to leave behind the social, economic, and political strife of the outside world once they crossed into the Exposition grounds. For a few days the visitor was asked to believe that the ideals of universal brotherhood and economic prosperity were not only possible, but also imminent. In hindsight, of course, the Exposition proved to be a brief respite from the *realpolitik* that would lead Europe into the chaos of the First World War. Within a few years, the political and social optimism espoused by the Exposition's promoters soon proved as illusory as the Potemkin village that was the fairgrounds itself.

Jeffrey Thomas Tilman

See also **Exhibition Building; Metro Station, Paris; Paris, France; Saarinen, Eliel (Finland)**

Further Reading

Drexler, Arthur (editor), *The Architecture of the École des Beaux-Arts*, New York: Museum of Modern Art, and London: Secker and Warburg, 1977

Evenson, Norma, *Paris: A Century of Change, 1878–1978*, New Haven, Connecticut: Yale University Press, 1979

Luckhurst, Kenneth W., *The Story of Exhibitions*, London and New York: Studio, 1951

Mandell, Richard D., *Paris 1900: The Great World's Fair*, Toronto: University of Toronto Press, 1967

The Parisian Dream City: A Portfolio of Photographic Views of the World's Exposition at Paris, St. Louis, Missouri: Thompson, 1900

Tuchman, Barbara Wertheim, *The Proud Tower: A Portrait of the World before the War, 1890–1914*, New York: Macmillan, and London: Hamilton, 1966

EXPRESSIONISM

The postimpressionist revolution in late 19th-century painting eventually brought the opposite of figurative representation, namely, Expressionism. If representation was no longer the main goal of art, the expression of one's inner spiritual self offered itself as an alternative. In the first decade of the 20th century, this direction was taken primarily by German artists, most successfully by the two movements Der Blaue Reiter and Die Brücke. Painters such as Wassily Kandinsky and Ernst Ludwig Kirchner used art to express the soul and their emotional reactions to the modern era. Their paintings introduced a cryptic, abbreviated style to art. The origin of a design in the creator's self and a drawing technique that was not concerned with exact figural representation were among the main impulses for Expressionist architecture.

Centered primarily in Germany and the Netherlands, Expressionist architects, just like their mainstream International Style colleagues, tried above all to cope with the industrial age. However, like their namesakes in painting, they attempted to express this age instead of representing it. Apart from this artistic goal, Expressionist architecture also dealt with communal concepts. Immediately after World War I, the massive physical and human destruction that had been caused by the first large-scale mechanical warfare engendered an anti-industrial feeling. Industry had excelled in manufacturing death machines that resulted in utter destruction. Such a common enemy brought forth thoughts about fraternization, community, and democracy. Especially in Germany, the postwar reality was difficult to bear. The shock of having lost the war brought with it the feeling that an era had passed and that it was time to orchestrate the rebirth of communal life and the arts. With its propagation of exactly such goals, Expressionism offered a feasible way to cope with the problems of the early 1920s in Europe. Expressionism rejected the machine age as the foundation of artistic creation. In architecture, this came out as the opposition to design as conditioned only by utility, materials, construction, and economics. Instead, Expressionism advocated that political and artistic revolution were the same by transposing the social uprising into artistic activity.

Apart from the origin in painting, immediate stylistic sources of Expressionism in architecture are found in Art Nouveau and other late 19th-century attempts at renewal, especially in the work of Hendrik Petrus Berlage, Frank Lloyd Wright, and Otto Wagner. Art Nouveau (Jugendstil) was particularly favored because it had rejected industrial construction methods and displayed a rather romantic longing in its naturalistic decorative structures. However, Expressionist architects had quite an open attitude toward the past. The styles in which all the arts had combined to produce decorated forms were preferred sources for inspiration. From Egypt came the concepts of cave and tower. Gothic architecture provided examples for the social and communal purposes of architecture and showed the triumph of expression over function. Far Eastern architecture was an important source because it combined architectural and sculptural forms and because of the mystical doctrines that informed this architecture.

The particular mind-set of Expressionist architects was also influenced by literary and philosophical sources, found primarily in Nietzsche and Kierkegaard. From Nietzsche came the admonition to let primitive instincts, not conscious self-control, determine artistic creations, whereas Kierkegaard emphasized the psychological background for this style in the spiritual searching and feeling of despair that were produced through the material instability.

The most significant heritage of Expressionism is that it attempted to solve the problems of the world through mainly symbolic architecture. Architects felt that they had to act on behalf of society and believed that they had to force people to realize their happiness through building. In those years, the spiritual realm was very far removed from reality. Expressionist architecture had a strong utopian urge. It was the search for a new reality, a new sense of life, and a new ethics of humanity. Many of the projects are indeed on a cosmic scale. This stemmed primarily from architects aiming to create their designs directly from their own visions. They let their hands draw the designs automatically and tried to exclude the mind from participating in the sketching. Their designs came out of an uncontrollable inner necessity and an inner spiritual life. The architects felt themselves to be the instruments of an absolute, metaphysical will and saw their task as transforming this spirit into reality. They wanted to achieve the direct transformation of consciousness into pure activity and did not pay much consideration to the objects that resulted from this. Theirs was an architecture that appealed to the intellect through feeling. With such practices, Expressionist architects found their modernity independently, unlike the International Style, which found its modernity through representation. Like the International Style, Expressionism avoided the literal imitation of traditional styles, but it also focused on expressing ideas. The Expressionist conception of the building was that of a total work of art that would present an aesthetic unity and thus become communal art. In this sense, architecture was spiritual.

In terms of form, Expressionist architects had a preference for cavelike interiors and towerlike exteriors. Inside their buildings, one felt enveloped not by walls and ceiling but by an encompassing membrane. Interiors felt physically oppressing on the inhabitant, who had to use sight, touch, and other synesthetic senses to understand his or her whereabouts. The theme of the cave was articulated in the exterior through a tectonic treatment of the building surfaces. The tower shape was articulated mostly by fashioning buildings as crowns, be they in the city or on the top of mountains.

In Germany, Paul Scheerbart instigated the preference for glass and crystals among Expressionist architects. Scheerbart can best be described as one of the fathers of science fiction in Germany. Apart from providing technical information in his book *Glasarchitektur* (1914), Scheerbart also promoted glass building for its generation of a new morality. Glass stood for brighter awareness, clearer determination, and utter gentleness. It represented the search for light and higher truth—the clarification of the soul—and can generally serve as a social catalyst. Glass buildings can function as shelter as well as extend garden architecture. This transparent material forces the users to continually relate to their environment, both the natural and the cosmic one. Glass buildings resemble states of emotion and suggest infinite space. In its mineral form, as crystal, glass became a symbol for the new life. Thus, glass and crystal forms presented the milieu that would give birth to the new culture.

Many Expressionist architects gave glass a special role in their designs. Bruno Taut, the organizer and indefatigable theoretician of Expressionism, was particularly taken with Scheerbart's ideas. He accepted the purifying potential of glass and crystal in his designs. These were especially notable in the Glass Pavilion he designed in 1914 for the glass industry at the Cologne Werkbund exhibition. There, Taut added a cosmological component. Glass was used as the material that enabled the reconciliation of mind and matter. The Glass Pavilion created primarily an experience for the user in the form of a purification ritual. It was intended to introduce a lighter building method and highlight the effects of glass to architecture. It is assembled from a centralized building with an addition at the back. The pavilion consists of a geodesic dome on a concrete base. Prism glass in reinforced-concrete frames was used for both the walls and the stair treads leading up to the glass hall. This is covered by a crystal-shaped dome assembled from reinforced-concrete ribs and colored-glass panels resting on prism glass. Visitors took a predetermined path that ultimately led them to the cascade room on the lower level. Water flowed down glass steps and terminated in a recess in which pictures from a kaleidoscope were projected. The procession through this pavilion was characterized by seductive anticipation and an increasingly intense experience of space. In Taut's later *Alpine Architecture* (1919), glass was used on an increased scale by designing glass pavilions on mountaintops.

As such endeavors suggest, Expressionism was a romantic movement. It can rightfully be criticized for not having been able to resist the seduction from formal aspects of architecture at the expense of all other concerns. Many Expressionist designs look like they are ready to depart. This notion of mobile architecture was aimed to symbolize metamorphosis and transcendence. Taut's early apartment buildings of the 1910s exemplify these goals. In these large structures, he attempted to engender a communal impression through color and facade articulation. Similarly, Erich Mendelsohn's early sketches express a dynamic feeling. These designs show forms that are derived from structure and the expression of the purpose of the building. They are rather abstract renderings of these intentions. The essence of the projects is artistic, not architectural, as they are not primarily meant to be realized. Mendelsohn wanted to formulate a new style based on industrial forms and materials. The gesture of drawing coincides with aerodynamic lines, producing a formal expression of "industrial" energy. Following the contour of a form with one's eyes is the only thing needed to understand the design. In his Einstein Tower (1924) in Potsdam, Germany he attempted to represent energy through mass. The form of the tower wants to show the movement that is immanent in the building mass. Thus, there is a melding of technical function and monumentality. The building implies the potential to leap forward, as if it contained energy.

Concerns with materials and meaning produced other variations. Fritz Höger's Chile House (1923) in Hamburg, for example, was a speculative office building in the tradition of the Hamburg Kontorhaus (commercial office building). The structure is a frame built entirely of brick. Thus, it became a counterpart to the other Expressionist material: glass. Brick alluded to a craft tradition and was better suited to Hamburg's damp climate. The bricks were vitrified. In its form, the Chile House evokes the image of a ship. Its sharp corners parallel the crystalline forms of other Expressionist architects. In general, the form alludes to many images, such as a fish or a flag.

A group of younger architects formed the Crystal Chain under Taut's leadership. This was mostly a group of solitary criers in the wilderness of the industrial world who formed a magic circle of mystery among themselves. Most of the members shared the wish for large-scale buildings that would bring all the arts together. The letters they wrote to one another document their attempts to go back to the roots, the origins, of creative architectural activity. Among the most charismatic members was Hermann Finsterlin, who had studied natural sciences and considered himself to be the Darwin of architecture. His conception of architecture was almost biological, dealing primarily with form and showing an evolution that dealt with biological urges and species, not with style. Similarly, he considered his visionary designs to be natural living organisms assembled from basic shapes. His sketches show strong anthropomorphic similarities.

In Dutch Expressionism, designing was seen primarily as an individual struggle of the architect's vision against materials and the construction reality. Unlike the ideological emphasis of German Expressionism, the Dutch School's buildings are characterized by a tendency toward composition and construction. Their architecture is distinguished by an emphasis on the plastic force of the building form. Buildings were designed and constructed according to the principles of organic growth found in nature. This was an architecture that looked like sculpture, in which materials were molded to enclose space. The architects used hand-formed bricks and tiles in various colors and shaped chimneys, balconies, towers, and ornamentation as sculptural additions to the building form. In this manner, purely functional parts were transfigured into symbolic aspects expressing the joy of everyday life. This merger between architecture and sculpture successfully expressed the inner aspirations of the architect and his clients. Building outlines are simple and firm and articulated in sinuous rhythms. This allowed architects to display emotion in their designs by endowing the building materials with their spirit and gave their buildings a unique character that allowed the inhabitants to identify with their homes. Architecture as art could be created only through an inward struggle. Through all of this, the architects expressed the essential character of society as a communal whole. In their buildings, architects tried to anticipate a better future, which also reflected a nostalgic longing for the social fabric symbolized in medieval architecture.

Consequently, most Dutch Expressionist work is found in the area of communal, low-income workers' housing. Michel de Klerk and Piet Kramer attempted to renew the existing Dutch communal housing traditions rather than inventing something completely novel. They generally used traditional materials and construction systems rather than the new industrial materials and structures. De Klerk's buildings excel at making conventional forms more piquant, primarily by presenting truncated shapes. He linked the individual elements and units of his forms in a dynamic manner. Masses rise and fall rhythmically, and large wall expanses are broken by terraces. His Eigen Haard Housing Estate (1913–21) in Amsterdam is a masterpiece in sculptural modeling. De Klerk wanted to make people happy through forms. Here, he created a fantastic environment. The overall forms follow closely the requirements of urban architecture—namely, those of articulating the traffic flow of the street—whereas individual details and facade articulations are Expressionist. There are many references to the sea and the nautical world in the forms and facades. Tile work and polychromatic brickwork are used to provide these impressions. Cylindrical forms further emphasize the corners of the buildings and are used to articulate communal entrances. Tower forms are also meant to express the village nature of this estate. The entire building complex and its details allude hypothetically to remnants from past, medieval cultures.

Rudolf Steiner represents the theosophical wing of Expressionism. His work may also serve as an example for the innovative use of new materials of this movement. In his Goetheanum (1927) in Dornach, he exploited reinforced concrete to achieve an imaginative shape. This produced a unique design that has no sources or progeny. Its form and details repeat a basic motif that Steiner had determined at the outset of the design. Nothing in the building exists in isolation: every part and detail strives toward the next one. Steiner's purpose was simply to find the way to the spirit through architecture. In this, he also showcases the mood of ideological and religious awakening of Expressionism. He was above all interested in alluding to the spiritual states that loom behind physical reality. For him, architecture was the medium that stimulates forms of thought that lead to spiritual rejuvenation.

With the German economic recovery of 1923, Expressionism ceded to a more sober, pragmatic approach to architecture. Constructing cheaply and abundantly became more pressing needs than spiritual rejuvenation. In Amsterdam, for example, architects were forced to use prefabricated building elements to reduce construction costs. A craft-oriented look was replaced by industrial forms, and individualistic designs lost out against the representation of a sober objectivity. Ultimately, the International Style mainstream prevailed. Expressionist architecture was given a bad reputation as the scapegoat for the adverse political reality in Germany after 1933. Siegfried Giedion denigrated its designs as "Faustian outbursts against an inimical world," "fairy castles to stand on the peak of Monte Rosa," or "concrete towers as flaccid as jellyfish." The early chroniclers of the International Style accused it of having reversed the push for a new architecture that the signs of the year 1914 announced. These evaluations continued the denunciation of Expressionism at the 1937 "Degenerate Art" exhibition in Munich, organized by the National Socialists. It was this event that prompted Marxist critics to proclaim that the same forces that had led to Expressionism also had led to Fascism. Expressionism was not even accepted as a style; it was accorded value only as the manifestation of the revolutionary fervor that existed in Germany after World War I. Although the movement was credited with tearing down the cultural heritage of the 19th century, it was accepted only as a synonym for opposition and lost out against the International Style.

The view of Expressionism as simply a revolt has in the meantime ceded to one that appreciates it as a style favoring personal creative liberty over the scientific rationality of the International Style. Beginning in the 1950s with the Englishman Reyner Banham, architectural critics began to reevaluate functionalism. Ultimately, this development resulted in the postmodern dismissal of the International Style. It was also felt that Expressionism could not satisfactorily be dealt with from only a purely formal, stylistic perspective. Expressionism is instead seen as a broad cultural phenomenon that encompassed a variety of artistic methods. Concurrent with this scholarly reevaluation came a resurgence of typically Expressionist forms in architecture. Acclaimed modernists, such as Le Corbusier and Alvar Aalto, created designs in which human activity and existence were seen as the central architectural metaphors. Architects such as Eero Saarinen and Jørn Utzon spearheaded the neo-Expressionist movement. The material innovations that were produced in the American war industry finally allowed architects to build expressive formal fantasies. Eero Saarinen's TWA Terminal (1962) at Kennedy Airport in New York and Utzon's Opera House (1973) in Sydney testify to this situation. Original Expressionists, such as Hans Scharoun and Mendelsohn, realized their earlier visions in such designs as the Philharmonic Hall (1963) in Berlin and Park Synagogue (1953) in Cleveland. Another significant part of neo-Expressionism is centered around the Waldorf Schools, which had been founded by Rudolf Steiner and which continue to imbue its school buildings, especially in England, with values identical to those that informed Steiner's Goetheanum.

HANS MORGENTHALER

See also **Berlin Philharmonic Hall; De Klerk, Michel (Netherlands); Eigen Haard Housing Estate, Amsterdam; Einstein Tower, Potsdam, Germany; Gaudí, Antoni (Spain); Giedion,**

Sigfried (Switzerland); Glass; International Style; Mendelsohn, Erich (Germany, United States); Saarinen, Eero (Finland); Scharoun, Hans (Germany); Steiner House, Vienna; Sydney Opera House; Taut, Bruno (Germany); TWA Airport Terminal, New York; Utzon, Jørn (Denmark); Wagner, Otto (Germany); Werkbund Exhibition, Cologne (1914); Wright, Frank Lloyd (United States)

Further Reading

Benson, Timothy O., editor, *Expressionist Utopias: Paradise, Metropolis, Architectural Fantasy*, Los Angeles: Los Angeles County Museum of Art, 1993

Borsi, Franco, and Giovanni Klaus Koenig, *Architettura dell'Espressionismo*, Genoa: Vitali e Ghianda, and Paris: Fréal, 1967 (contains summaries in French, German, and English)

Casciato, Maristella, editor, *La Scuola di Amsterdam*, Bologna: Zanichelli, 1987; as *The Amsterdam School*, Rotterdam: 010 Publishers, 1996

Conrads, Ulrich, and Hans G. Sperlich, *Phantastische Architektur*, Teufen, Switzerland: Niggli, 1960; as *The Architecture of Fantasy: Utopian Building and Planning in Modern Times*, translated, edited, and expanded by Christiane Craseman Collins and George R. Collins, New York: Praeger, 1960; as *Fantastic Architecture*, London: Architectural Press, 1963

Franciscono, Marcel, *Walter Gropius and the Creation of the Bauhaus in Weimar: The Ideals and Artistic Theories of Its Founding Years*, Urbana: University of Illinois Press, 1971

Pehnt, Wolfgang, *Die Architektur des Expressionismus*, Stuttgart, Germany: Hatje, 1973; 3rd edition, Ostfildern-Ruit, Germany: Hatje, 1998; as *Expressionist Architecture*, translated by J.A. Underwood and Edith Küstner, New York; Praeger, and London: Thames and Hudson, 1973

Pehnt, Wolfgang, *Architekturzeichnungen des Expressionismus*, Stuttgart, Germany: Hatje, 1985; as *Expressionist Architecture in Drawings*, translated by John Gabriel, New York: Van Nostrand Reinhold, and London: Thames and Hudson, 1985

Sharp, Dennis, *Modern Architecture and Expressionism*, New York: Braziller, and London: Longmans, 1966

Whyte, Iain Boyd, *The Crystal Chain Letters: Architectural Fantasies by Bruno Taut and His Circle*, Cambridge, Massachusetts: MIT Press, 1985

VAN EYCK, ALDO 1918–

Architect, the Netherlands

Advocating a new set of architectural concerns for postwar society, Aldo van Eyck belonged to the long tradition of Northern European experimentalism characterized by an attention to detail and craftsmanship coupled with a profound social commitment. His oeuvre comprises a vast array of tectonic ideas worked out within the programs of socially relevant structures, contributing greatly to modern architectures moral core.

Van Eyck was born in Driebergen, the Netherlands, on 16 March 1918; spent his primary and secondary school years in England; and took his architectural training at the Eidgenössische Technische Hochschule in Zürich. After a stint in the Dutch army, he returned to the Netherlands and found employment in the Public Works Office (then under the direction of Cornelius van Eesteren), charged with the task of refabricating the war-ravaged city of Amsterdam. In 1952, he began private practice in The Hague and Amsterdam, in partnership first with Theo Bosch and later with his wife, Hannie van Eyck-van Roojen.

Aldo van Eyck's introduction to the architectural community at large came during the eighth meeting of CIAM (Congrès Internationaux d'Architecture Moderne) at Hoddeston, England, where his playground projects in Amsterdam caught the attention of Siegfried Giedion, the organization's secretary-general and one of its founding fathers. Giedion reacted enthusiastically, writing, "These simple elements are grouped so subtly—with a background of the De Stijl movement and modern art which injects some kind of vitamin into the whole thing . . . (they also) fulfill another function. A formerly useless piece of waste ground has been transformed by an extremely careful layout into an active urban element. One need only provide the opportunity and we—the public, who are also maybe children of a kind—will know how to use it" (see Giedion 1952).

Giedion's comments confirmed the duality of van Eyck's architectural paradigm; namely, the coalescence of avant-garde form and a humanistic concern for the ethos of environment, a combination that van Eyck called "labyrinthine clarity." Not incidentally, van Eyck's interest in the fine arts was cultivated throughout a long friendship with Giedion's wife, Carola Giedion-Welcker, a prominent art historian and a champion of Klee, Miro, Mondrian, and others. Through her tutelage, van Eyck maintained a lifelong attachment to aesthetic ideals that would continue to inform his work. His Sonsbeek Pavilion (1966–) in Arnhem, a temporary space for an exhibition of modern sculpture, was a successful use of orthogonal and curved planes used to create a small city within which to literally traverse the presented artistic landscape. Putting architecture in the service of art, van Eyck drew attention to the interrelatedness of the two practices, using contextuality and contiguity to point to the potential enrichment of life through aesthetic means.

The years immediately following World War II saw a radical shift in the direction charted for contemporary architecture. Taking action against the devastation and destruction delivered on European nations necessitated a move away from utopian functionalism and toward a revitalization of associative perspective and a sense of belonging, and a younger generation of architects, known as Team X, were charged with reorienting CIAM toward these goals. However, whereas key members such as Alison and Peter Smithson maintained strong ties to the formalism of Le Corbusier and Mies van der Rohe, van Eyck advocated an approach to architecture that sought to underscore the eternal and immutable realities of humanity's relationship to built form. By reconciling "twin phenomena," such as inside and outside, that denied the possibility of easy dialectics, van Eyck sought to identify an "in-between" realm that would, in the architect's own words, "reconcile conflicting polarities."

The property of "in-between" was best exemplified by his most celebrated building, the Children's Home (1957–60) in Amsterdam: what van Eyck called "a home for children in the context of architecture." Playing with the notion of the module, the orphanage dispenses with traditional organization of space by creating a set of pavilions pinwheeling around a central axis; the resulting plan borrows heavily from De Stijl's modularity while providing strong diagonals that challenge orthogonal ordering. Surprising occurrences of semiprivate spaces within the confines of the building bring a sense of the outside indoors,

van Eyck, Aldo (Netherlands)
Hubertus House, Amsterdam (ca. 1959), designed by Aldo van Eyck
GreatBuildings.com

and the privacy of living quarters is ensured by their location at the periphery of the building, away from heavily trafficked areas. The result is a series of intimate spaces that adhere through a nonhierarchical yet clearly articulated modular program.

Although the school of Dutch structuralism, to which van Eyck's name is often attached, never really resolved its relationship to the larger conditions of structuralism as obtained in literary criticism and anthropology, van Eyck's own career drew from both of these disciplines in a more coherent fashion. Throughout his life, he maintained a vital attention to writing (especially during his stint as editor of the Dutch journal *Forum* from 1959 to 1963), his ideas developing within the fundamental framework of his notion of "relativity," or the belief that human history unfolds in a way not subordinated to preordained principles but rather through the multivalency of reciprocal relations among people, things, and ideas. In 1959, van Eyck and his wife traveled to Sudan to study the habitats of the Dogon, having already visited the Sahara earlier in the decade. It was there that his notions of the perpetuity of humanity's customs of existence found their inspiration and justification. Many of the themes arising from his ethnographic research recurred in later projects, such as the Hubertus House (1975–79) in Amsterdam, a home for single mothers and their children that underscores van Eyck's responsiveness to social needs. A functionalist glass-and-steel recessed entryway ties the new polychromatic structure to an adjacent older building, maintaining the sense of historical order while insisting on the need for growth. Within the structure, lodgings presented as a set of scaled-down row houses provide a sense of familiarity as well as reinforcing the architect's conviction that functionalism is not the enemy of history but rather has the capacity to expand and enrich one's understanding of time and place.

In 1990, van Eyck was awarded the Gold Medal of the Royal Institute of British Architects, an award fitting his significant contributions to 20th-century architecture.

Noah Chasin

Biography

Born in Driebergen, Netherlands, 16 March 1918. Attended the Building School, The Hague 1938; studied at the Eidgenössische Technische Hochschule, Zurich 1939–43. Married Hannie van Roojen 1943: 2 children. Architect for the Public Works Department, Amsterdam 1946–50. In private practice, The Hague and Amsterdam from 1952; partnership with Theo Bosch 1971–

82; partnership with Hannie van Eyck-van Roojen from 1982; editor, *Forum*, Amsterdam 1959–63, 1967. Lecturer in art history, Enschede Art School, Netherlands 1951–55; tutor at an art school, Amsterdam 1951–66; tutor, Academy of Architecture, Amsterdam 1956–61; visiting critic and lecturer: University of Pennsylvania, Philadelphia, Washington University, St. Louis, Missouri, Harvard University, Cambridge, Massachusetts, Tulane University, New Orleans, Louisiana, School of Architecture, Singapore, University of Trondheim, Norway 1961–68; professor, Institute of Technology, Delft since 1968; guest professor, Eidgenössische Technische Hochschule, Zurich 1977–78; Paul Philippe Cret Professor of Architecture, University of Pennsylvania 1978–83. Member, De 8 en Openbouw, Amsterdam from 1946; Dutch delegate to CIAM since 1947; member, COBRA (Copenhagen, Brussels, and Amsterdam) 1948–51; member, Team X from 1953; honorary member, Staatliche Kunstakademie, Düsseldorf 1979; member, Royal Academy of Arts and Sciences, Belgium 1981; honorary fellow, American Institute of Architects 1981; honorary member, Bund Deutscher Architekten, Germany 1983. Royal Gold Medal, Royal Institute of British Architects 1990.

Selected Works

Tower Room (conversion), Zurich, 1946
Approximately 650 children's playgrounds, Amsterdam, with the Public Works Department, 1948–79
Van Eyck Apartment (conversion), Amsterdam, 1949
Children's Home, Amsterdam, 1960
Sculpture Pavilion, Arnhem, Netherlands, 1966
Hubertus House, Amsterdam (with Hannie van Eyck), 1979
ESTEC/ESA New Conference Center and Restaurant, Noordwyk, Netherlands (with Hannie van Eyck), 1986

Selected Publications

"CIAM 6, Bridgewater: Statement Against Rationalism" (1947), in *A Decade of Modern Architecture*, by Sigfried Giedion, 1954
"Dogen," *Forum* 7 (1949); reprinted as "The Interior of Time: A Miracle of Moderation," in *The Meaning of Architecture*, edited by Charles Jencks and George Baird, 1969
"Wij Ontdekken Stijl," *Forum* 4 (1949)
"Het Verhaal an een Andere Gedachte," *Forum* 7 (1959)
"What Is and Isn't Architecture," *Lotus International* 28 (1980)
"Aldo van Eyck: Annual RIBA Discourse," *Royal Institute of British Architects Journal* (April 1981)
"By Definition," *Dutch Forum* (June 1982)

Further Reading

Aldo v. Eyck: projekten, 1962–1976, Groningen, Netherlands: Van de Beek, 1981
Bohigas, Oriol, "Aldo van Eyck, or, A New Amsterdam School," *Oppositions* 9 (1977)
Hertzberger, Herman, Addie van Roijen-Wortmann, and Francis Strauven, *Aldo van Eyck: Hubertus House; Hubertushuis* (bilingual English–Dutch edition), Amsterdam: Stichting Wonen/Van Loghum Slaterus, 1982
Lefaivre, Liane, and Alexander Tzonis, "Aldo and Hannie van Eyck: ESTEC," *A + U* 4, no. 247 (1991)
Giedion, Siegfried, "Historical Background to the Core," in *The Heart of the City: Towards the Humanization of Urban Life*, edited by J. Tyrwhitt, J.L. Sert, and E.N. Rogers, New York: Pellegoini and Cudahy, 1952
Nicolin, Pierluigi, "The Web and the Labyrinth," *Lotus International* 11 (1976)
Strauven, Francis, *Het Burgerweeshuis van Aldo van Eyck: een modern monument*, Amsterdam: Stichting Uitgeverij, 1987; as *Aldo van Eyck's Orphanage: A Modern Monument*, Rotterdam: NAi, 1996
Strauven, Francis, "The Dutch Contribution: Bakema and van Eyck," *Rassegna* 52, no. 4 (1992)
Strauven, Francis, *Aldo van Eyck: relativiteit en verbeelding*, Amsterdam: Meulenhoff, 1994; as *Aldo van Eyck: The Shape of Relativity*, Amsterdam: Architectura en Natura, 1998
Zevi, Bruno, "Children's Home in Amsterdam," *Architettura* 6 (1961)

EYRE, WILSON, JR. 1858–1944

Architect, United States

In 1901, Wilson Eyre's interest in domestic architecture and interior furnishings led him to help found the magazine *House and Garden*, a journal that was the mouthpiece for the Arts and Crafts movement in Philadelphia. Espousing the beauty of well-integrated gardens and homes, the magazine was coedited and illustrated by Eyre until the magazine changed hands in 1905. By then, Eyre was a noted specialist in the design of country houses in Pennsylvania, and his commissions took him as far afield as New Hampshire, Louisiana, Delaware, and Michigan, leading him to establish a second office in New York City.

In 1912 he joined the firm of Gilbert McIlvaine (1880–1939) as a principal designer. However, his architectural practice waned during the 1920s and 1930s, ultimately collapsing with McIlvaine's death in 1939. By the time of Eyre's own death five years later, he had designed nearly 350 buildings, most of them domestic and suburban in nature but also including a pair of hospitals, a museum, several churches and college buildings, one office building, and a miscellany of lesser-scaled commercial and retail establishments.

Although Eyre's work primarily reflected his English-inspired eclectic taste, he mastered an architectural expression that would be eclipsed by modernism, which might explain his relative obscurity at the end of the century. In retrospect, his unwillingness to embrace the latest modern style is not surprising, as its proponents made problematic just the sort of vague historicity that typified Eyre's architectural vocabulary.

Eyre sought to forge a truly American or, in many of his Philadelphia projects, a truly Pennsylvanian architectural expression out of an architectural tradition dominated by Europe and England. In this regard, he can be compared with contemporary California architects, such as Bernard Maybeck (1862–1957), Irving Gill (1870–1936), and Charles (1868–1957) and Henry (1870–1954) Greene, who sought regional styles of building. Eyre's country houses often featured asymmetrical massing in picturesque arrangements with a blend of traditional and original forms and details. Large buildings allowed Eyre to fully exercise his architectural eye, although he decried the excessive use of ornament as well as the slavish copying of period styles. In rural or suburban settings, Eyre strove to recall a rusticated proto-English aesthetic without resorting to re-creating outright Tudor, Jacobean, or Elizabethan houses.

Eyre's typically designed his houses based on a system of zones: one that comprised of dining room, parlor(s), bedrooms of the homeowners, and a servants' zone consisting of kitchen, pantry, servants' quarters, and other functions of utility. Eyre often manipulated form to visually distinguish one function from the other, pushing out or pulling in walls in an effort to articulate zones as wings or multistory masses. Consistent window head and/or sill heights, as well as a continuous eave height, were elements used to horizontally wrap both zones together in an integrated composition. This approach to design was more evident in his suburban commissions than in his urban houses, as the former afforded the opportunity to conceive buildings as freestanding objects surrounded by and shaping an equally malleable garden space.

The Charles Lang Freer House (Detroit, 1890), a major commission, comprised a three-story mass capped by a dominating hip roof with gables and two prominent ashlar chimneys protruding above. This overall form abutted a two-story wing of spaces that included the kitchen, servants' dining room, shed, and stable, a lesser form also punctuated by gables, chimneys, and the rounded masonry arch of the shed. The "served" wing was organized in plan around a stand-alone fireplace located within the central stairway hall, a space at the culmination of a carefully designed arrival sequence. The fireplace with its wood-carved mantle was situated as a freestanding object in the center of the great hall (an unusual design move for Eyre, who usually articulated such elements as part of the wall plane), partly obscuring the stairway wrapping around the hall. Eyre was a careful designer of furnishings as well as of the larger planning and articulation of building forms, and his clients looked to their architect for exquisite detailing and a commitment to high-quality materials and craftsmanship.

In the Conklin House (Huntington, Long Island, 1905–10) the three-story central mass was flanked symmetrically by two lesser wings, one containing servant spaces and the other a study and a music room; the upper floors were dedicated to bedroom spaces and a playroom. The central space is a double-height living room with a stair gallery, with quartered white oak–paneled walls and ceiling stained a dark greenish brown. Five carefully placed paintings taken from a European monastery were intended by architect and owner to accompany the heavy timber aesthetic of the box beams overhead and their accompanying knee braces. However, the focal point of this central space was a pipe-organ panel arranged in a triptych-like composition at the far end of the space. The intended effect was to impart a refined sense of the antique.

Eyre's attempts to create fine details within nostalgic and tastefully proportioned masses has placed him in the company of other contemporary Philadelphia architects, such as Walter Cope (1860–1902), John Stewardson (1858–96), and Frank Miles Day (1861–1918). High standards of construction remained a hallmark of Eyre's work, and this extended well beyond his own drawing board and onto those of the artists and artisans whom he enlisted in many of his commissions. He associated closely with a number of American artists, including Maxfield Parrish (1870–1966) and Alexander S. Calder (1898–1976), and he took great effort to meld an artist's work or a collected art object into his own so that the overall aesthetic effect was perceived harmoniously.

JERRY WHITE

See also **Gill, Irving (United States); Greene, Henry M. and Charles S. (United States); Maybeck, Bernard R. (United States); Regionalism**

Biography

Born to American parents in Florence, 31 October 1858; arrived in the United States 1869. Received no formal architectural training outside one year at Massachusetts Institute of Technology; apprenticed to James Peacock Sims, architect, Philadelphia (1882); Sims died that year; Eyre took over the practice at the age of 24. Lecturer, University of Pennsylvania 1890–92; in 1912 became principal designer in a new partnership with Gilbert McIlvaine; awarded the 1917 Pennsylvania American Institute of Architects' Gold Medal. Published in *Architectural Record* (1903–20); awarded an honorary degree from the University of Pennsylvania (1926). Died in Philadelphia, 21 October 1944.

Selected Works

Charles Lang Freer House, Detroit, 1890
Neill House, Philadelphia, 1891
Mauran House, Philadelphia, 1891
Mask and Wig Club, Philadelphia, 1893
Conklin House, Huntington, New York, 1910
W.T. Jeffords House, Glen Riddle, Pennsylvania, 1917

Further Reading

No book-length treatment of Eyre's architectural practice has been published. To appreciate Eyre's success and acclaim in his own day, however, one need only thumb through period journals such as *Inland Architect and Builder, American Buildings, American Architect and Building News,* and *Architectural Record* to note the frequency with which his work was published and praised as both tasteful and modern.

"Graced Places: The Architecture of Wilson Eyre" www.upenn.edu/GSFA/Eyre/Eyreintro.html

Brunk, Thomas, "The House That Freer Built," *Dichotomy* 3, no. 4 (1981)

Fahlman, Betsy, "Wilson Eyre in Detroit: The Charles Lang Freer House," *Winterthur Portfolio* 15, no. 3 (1980)

The Old House Journal 26, no. 5 (1998) (special issue devoted to Eyre)

Teitelman, Edward, "Wilson Eyre in Camden: The Henry Genet Taylor House and Office," *Winterthur Portfolio* 15, no. 3 (1980)

F

FACTORY

The history of the factory as a building type in the 20th century parallels that of architecture in general. However, as a new typology, it has had a fluctuating status in the profession between that of "building" and that of "architecture." For early modern architects, the factory became the epitome of modernism both as a building type that signified the modern era and in the technological innovations that were necessary to create these buildings for the production of goods. This was the building type in which form truly necessitated following function because the buildings are directed by the manufacturing processes inside, from automobiles to wartime machinery and computers. The increasing dominance and changes in methodologies for mass production influenced the spatial and structural needs of the factories. These developments were translated into innovations in building technologies with new uses for reinforced concrete, steel, large glass and metal curtain walls, open floor space, lightweight suspension systems, tent structures, and prefabricated kits of parts.

In terms of form, early 20th-century factories sustained the look of the previous century's multistory buildings as a result of the high cost of land that was often near the water's edge for easy shipping of products. In addition, before the advent of the conveyor belt, moving goods vertically by cranes and gravity was still easier than pulling them horizontally. This is seen in the multistory factory that Albert Kahn designed for Henry Ford in Highland Park near Detroit in 1909, a factory that then influenced Giaccomo Matte-Trucco's design of the Lingotto Fiat Factory in Turin, Italy, in 1913.

Advances in the strength of concrete influenced factory design, such as in the Larkin Plant (1907) in Buffalo, New York, built over 10 years by R.J. Reidpath & Son. This factory could withstand larger window spans to increase natural light in the building compared with 19th-century brick-pier construction with small windows. Concrete improved fireproofing and allowed for faster construction, especially when it could be prefabricated in pieces. Engineers played extremely important roles in the development of new building systems for factories, such as Ernest Ransome's reinforced-concrete system, the Ransome Bar. Ransome simplified the systems of the French engineer Francois Hennebique so that the floor slab continued to the face of the building and became a stringcourse, with vertical pieces forming lintels and sills. Precast structural wall units could be set in place and then cast as the floor in an early prefabricated system with in-fill in brick. Later, prefabricated systems were developed in concrete, metals, and glass curtain wall systems, emphasizing the use of the factory building as a testing ground for new technologies.

In Berlin Peter Behrens designed the AEG Turbine Factory (1908–09) with Mies van der Rohe and developed a new curtain wall system of glass and steel that allowed light into the vast open space. Unusual at the time, the steel pier is exposed and the skeleton revealed, creating a monumentality and a heroic metaphor for industry. The recessed glass facade influenced the later curtain wall systems.

Factories were experimental not only in terms of structure and form but also in terms of the management of the workers inside. Ford, who adopted the ideas of Frederick Taylor on employee performance, believed that by providing a decent workplace, workers would be more productive. Paternalistic in his attitude, Ford desired light and air in the factories, encouraging Albert Kahn to use skylight monitors for daylighting. Throughout the Great Depression, Ford influenced other factory owners to consider the well-being of the workers because it affected their morale. Ford eventually paid workers well enough for them to be able to afford his own product, which gave rise to a working class with expendable income.

These American industrial buildings and the work of Behrens influenced the designs of numerous European modern architects of the early 1920s and 1930s, such as Le Corbusier, Gropius, and Mendelsohn. Walter Gropius, with Hannes Meyer, designed a new building in 1913 for the Fagus Shoe Last company in Alfeld an-der-Liene, Germany. The primary feature, the glazed workshop block, was a departure from the heavier, piered structures and was based on the Bauhaus ideology in its lightness and transparency.

During World War II, Kahn and others designed primarily factories with one story, which had many advantages. They were faster to build, distributed power horizontally, and allowed more light into the building. The one-story shed-type building allowed for larger machines and more flexible and open floor plans for the new horizontal assembly-line production, which could then be shifted easily to the truck- and train-based transportation systems, with train lines running close to or even through a manufacturing plant.

The placement of the administration buildings was also a focus in the layout of a factory complex. Early in the century, the administration buildings were usually in a separate head house away from the plant. Alvar Aalto designed two paper mills in Finland; one, the Toppila Pulp Mill (1930–33) in Oulu, was a design primarily for the director's buildings and outbuildings, whereas the Sunila Pulp Mill (1936–38) at Lotka also included housing. Aalto also influenced the placement of the mill on the existing bedrock and incorporated the forms of technology in his design.

In the 1950s postwar era, steel was still in high demand, so factories had to be built in concrete. One of these was the Brynmawr Rubber Ltd. South Wales, Architects' Co-Partnership, which achieved the largest shell dome structure at its time in order to have huge open floor. The increasing automation and mass production dictated open floors, wide bays, and daylighting to reach the inner factory. The single story continued to solve this problem best. Both Richard Rogers' factory for Inmos in England and Nicholas Grimshaw's factory for Igus in Germany exemplify the high-tech prefabricated kit of parts and repetitive modules that became widely used in the 1980s. The Financial Times Printing Plant in London, designed by Grimshaw, with large windows into the processing area, brought printing into the public view.

In the 1950s workers' satisfaction and their motivation became a focus of corporate executives, so that architects improved the quality of places for socialization, such as workers' lounges, cafeterias, and athletic facilities, and the Japanese influenced the concept of teamwork, leading to different spatial arrangements. The head offices became a part of the main building structure, so that the entire factory was under one roof for easy communication between research teams and the production-line workers. With the advent of computer-directed manufacturing, the need for flexible, adaptable, and expandable spaces became increasingly dominant. Factory buildings throughout the 20th century have become an innovative system in which architects to explore new aesthetic issues, combined with practical building function, technological systems, and rapid construction, that are profitable for the client while attending to the worker.

NINA RAPPAPORT

Further Reading

Banham, Reyner, *A Concrete Atlantis: U.S. Industrial Building and European Modern Architecture, 1900–1925*, Cambridge, Massachusetts: MIT Press, 1986

Bucci, Federico, *Albert Kahn: Architect of Ford*, New York: Princeton Architectural Press, 1993

Hildebrand, Grant, *Designing for Industry: The Architecture of Albert Kahn*, Cambridge, Massachusetts: MIT Press, 1974

Jaeggi, Annemarie, *Fagus: Industriekultur zwischen Werkbund und Bauhaus*, Berlin: Jovis, 1998; as *Fagus: Industrial Culture from Werkbund to Bauhaus*, New York: Princeton Architectural Press, 2000

Powell, Kenneth, *Richard Rogers: Complete Works*, London: Phaidon, 1999

Reed, Peter, *Alvar Aalto: Between Humanism and Materialism*, New York: Museum of Modern Art, 1998

FACTORY AND INDUSTRIAL TOWN PLANNING

The 20th century witnessed the sublevation of industrial town planning, the culmination of nearly 200 years of experimentation by employers in mining, lumber milling, and manufacture. Examples of purpose-built settlements can be found in antiquity, but it was the industrial revolution that propelled modern planning and development, creating a distinctive and easily recognized type. Where a single enterprise owned the site and employed an architect or landscape architect to design the factories and housing, there was real opportunity to advance the science of planning and reduce environmental despoliation.

Before Parker and Unwin planned the garden city of Letchworth, England, for Ebenezer Howard and his benefactors, they planned the factory town of New Earswick (1902) for Benjamin Rowntree. Rowntree was a manufacturer who developed New Earswick as a single-enterprise town, following Lever and Cadbury, who earlier had founded Port Sunlight (1887) and Bourneville (1895), model industrial villages. The use of contour planning and the generous allotment of parkland in the design of industrial villages was well known in the 19th century and would be employed in the first garden cities. The principal difference between the two is that the industrial village or factory town owed its existence to the business enterprise, whether extractive or manufacturing, and was subordinate to the mine, mill, or factory, which could occupy a prominent site—sometimes the center of town. The garden city, on the other hand, put community first and then hoped to attract industry, and that industry was usually relegated to a peripheral site. True garden cities were tenant associations of joint stockholders who were prohibited from engaging in property speculation. In the factory town, the business enterprise was the landlord, and where housing was sold it usually was financed by the enterprise or one of its subsidiaries. In most instances, however, the housing was maintained by the company and available only to employees and their families through rental agreements.

The better factory towns of the 20th century offered a variety of houses in construction, size, and style and made them available for purchase through a company-backed building-and-loan association. Two- and four-family houses, as well as terraces or row houses, eventually gave place to single-family residences in North America. The use of contour planning as opposed to orthogonal blocks not only produced more interesting and less repetitive layouts but also reduced street paving and utility lines. Public space in the form of parks was sometimes incorporated into the plan. Schools and community facilities symbolized the employer's commitment to the community, and the architecture could be exceptional. Unity in plan with variety in architecture could be obtained through the selection employment of recognized design firms, such as McKim, Mead, and White (Roanoke Rapids, North Carolina, 1900) or George B. Post and Sons (Eclipse Park, Wisconsin, 1915). In Europe and North America, many of the more prominent architects and landscape architects received commissions to design industrial housing estates and factory towns.

Stand-alone single-enterprise developments included Neponsit Garden Village (1907) and Indian Hill (1912), Massachusetts; Kistler (1918) and Kohler (1915), Wisconsin; Kincaid

(1914), Illinois; Goodyear Heights (1913) and Firestone Park (1916), Ohio; Alcoa (1919), Erwin (1914), and Kingsport (1915), Tennessee; Corey (Fairfield, 1909) and Kaulton (1912), Alabama; and Torrance (1912), California, in the United States and Temiscaming (1917) and Arvida (1926) in Canada. In later years, several were incorporated into larger, neighboring communities. This early group favored the planning principles employed in the garden cities, although in the case of landscape architects such as Warren Henry Manning, John Nolen, Ossian C. Simonds, and Earle Draper, their indebtedness was to the Olmsted firm far more than to Parker and Unwin.

In the interwar and post–World War II period, it is not North America but rather Scandinavia and Europe that offer the better examples of industrial town planning.

The work of Alvar Aalto in Finland, especially at Sunila (1937–39), the lumber town, combines creative planning and contemporary housing in a majestic setting. Aalto, always the independent, managed to separate the mill from the housing and communal buildings through careful site analysis. The architectural forms are contrasted in a most interesting way with the natural setting. In Germany and Hungary, following the reconstruction, there were several important new industrial towns. Sennestadt and Wulfen, two German new towns of the 1960s, associated with extractive industries, experimented with mid- and high-rise housing in the *Zeilenbau*, or parallel row, arrangement celebrated by the Congrès Internationaux d'Architecture Moderne (CIAM). Dunaujvaros, Kazincbarcika, Tiszaszederkeny, and Komlo, Hungary, built in the 1960s and 1970s, are mining and chemical towns that, like the German towns, combine contemporary architecture in carefully zoned land uses that separate the industrial activities from the residential and recreational areas.

Most new towns are mixed economy, and the single-enterprise industrial town is no longer a sought-after or viable type in North America and Western Europe. However, second- and third-tier countries, whose economies are based on extracting and processing raw materials for export, will continue to build industrial towns in locations where existing towns and lack of transportation are inadequate to meet demands for industrial growth. These new communities will benefit from the example of the previously mentioned towns.

John S. Garner

See also **Aalto, Alvar (Finland); Congrès Internationaux d'Architecture Moderne (CIAM, 1927-); Factory; Garden City Movement; Urban Planning**

Further Reading

There is no shortage of contemporary accounts of individual industrial towns in architectural and planning journals. In the decade 1910 to 1920, there are dozens of essays in such serials as *The American City* and *Architectural Record.* Secondary sources, especially the more inclusive, are difficult to find. The following, however, should be of some assistance.

Crawford, Margaret, *Building the Workingman's Paradise: The Design of American Company Towns*, London and New York: Verso, 1995

Garner, John S. (editor), *The Company Town: Architecture and Society in the Early Industrial Age*, New York: Oxford University Press, 1992

Golany, Gideon (editor), *International Urban Growth Policies: New Town Contributions*, New York: Wiley, 1978

Gregotti, Vittorio (editor), *Company Towns, Rassegna 70*, Bologna: Editrice Compositori and CIPIA, 1997

Taylor, Graham Romeyn, *Satellite Cities: A Study of Industrial Suburbs*, New York: Appleton, 1915

FAGUS WERK

Designed by Walter Gropius and Adolf Meyer; completed 1911, with subsequent expansions
Alfeld-an-der-Leine, Germany

In 1910 spurred on by a dare from his former employer, Behrens Hannoverian Carl Benscheidt had visions of opening a competing shoe factory. After he secured a site just across the road from his former workplace in Alfeld, Germany (but with better rail access and three hectares to build on), Benscheidt founded Fagus GmbH in March 1911 and approached the Hannover architect Eduard Werner (1847–1923) to design his new factory. Not only had Werner designed the plans for the Behrens factory in 1897 (which was three times larger than Fagus would be), but he had the invaluable experience of knowing the calculations and work involved in building a shoe last factory. In Werner's plan, the Fagus complex would amount to a row of brick buildings (or half timbered in the case of the warehouses), all with different functions along the production line. With the exception of the administrative rooms, the production houses were fairly utilitarian in nature. Benscheidt had already expressed his dissatisfaction with this aspect of Werner's slightly Gothic design, and in 1911, he commissioned Walter Gropius (1883–1969) and Adolf Meyer (1881–1929) to redesign the facades of the entire complex. Gropius had done some exemplary work for the AEG Motor Company years before in Berlin while under the tutelage of architect Peter Behrens, and the buildings there had not only set new standards in factory design—practically making them works of art—but, in keeping with the time, had also created architecture as advertisement. It was decided that Werner would remain in charge of the project as a whole and in charge of the interior spaces and "outfitting of the buildings." However, it is the influence of Gropius and Meyer that gives meaning to a contemporary understanding of the Fagus Werk. Gropius viewed this opportunity in Alfeld as the perfect collaboration between industry and the arts—the primary aim of the Deutscher Werkbund—and it would turn into a long-term project that would occupy Gropius and Meyer until the end of their partnership in 1925. Because of Gropius's media presence during the building of Fagus, his adopted leadership of the building program, and his frequent writings within the Werkbund on the Fagus Werk, he is often credited solely with the design of the factory; indeed, it has been difficult to trace exactly what Meyer's contributions were. However, Meyer considered the conceptualization of the factory a truly collaborative effort and kept a personal archive of drawings throughout the life of the project.

In the spring of 1911, Gropius and Meyer submitted their plans for the complex; these deviated from Werner's in the positioning of the different buildings, creating courtyard space rather than the static row of structures proposed in the Werner plan.

Their plan gave the building a much broader exposure toward Hannover and, thus, to the trains that frequently passed the factory's property. Benscheidt never agreed to this plan, and the building was executed with its facade in a competitive stance toward Behrens's, as originally conceived. The pair ended up making few changes to the original Werner plan and retained the overall layout of the factory complex.

However, they succeeded in carrying out a more unified scheme through their use of materials and color. All Fagus buildings, for example, have a 40-centimeter-high purple-black brick base that projects from the facade by four centimeters and seems to allow the yellow-bricked rising walls of the building to float; windows in all the buildings appear to be cutouts from the cubical structures that contain them, although the window shapes and sizes differ from building to building. Perhaps the most daring design feature of the Fagus Werk—and the one that makes the building so significant and recognizable—is the vertical bands of windows that wrap around the main building, creating the illusion of a floating curtain wall. It was presumed that to accomplish this, the architects would have to employ some new construction technology, when in fact the frame construction was based entirely on Werner's original projections of a brickwork building with an iron ceiling beam. A staircase on the clear-span side of the building acts like a stabilizing column to the glass-clad structure. Buildings in the Fagus complex—other than the famous, often photographed main office building—included the production hall, sawmill, warehouse, and punch-knife department. All these buildings were visually unified with their yellow brick, terra-cotta roof tiles, gray-slate roofs and glazing, and black bases. The interiors of the public spaces of the office structure and the production hall were planned by Gropius and Meyer down to the smallest details. The waiting room exuded order, lightness, and success; glass panes offered views of the main offices from the waiting rooms, which were friendly and informal. The architects designed dust-free work conditions and placed the machines in sequence with the production process in a light-filled work environment. The design offered employees a commissary, washrooms, lockers, and later, housing.

An expansion to the Fagus Werk, led by Gropius and Meyer, began in 1913. Additions were attached to existing structures, and the main building and production hall were enlarged, the latter to three times its original size. Although hardly a challenging job for the architects, the expansion allowed them to suggest the application of a glazed facade to the production hall and the punch-knife department. This permitted them to provide a unified appearance to the entire complex. During World War I, the work progressed slowly as Gropius enlisted and Meyer took a job with a steel company. However, Benscheidt continued to make plans for the expansion, and drawings continued to be made. In 1915 some construction was allowed to commence, and the dominant characteristic of all Fagus buildings emerged: the floor-to-ceiling glazed and enclosed building corner.

EUGENIA BELL

See also **Curtain Wall; Factory; Glass; Gropius, Walter (Germany)**

Further Reading

Banham, Reyner, *Theory and Design in the First Machine Age*, London: Architectural Press, and New York: Praeger, 1960; 2nd edition, 1967

Jaeggi, Annemarie, *Fagus: Industriekultur zwischen Werkbund und Bauhaus*, Berlin: Jovis, 1998; as *Fagus: Industrial Culture from Werkbund to Bauhaus*, translated by Elizabeth M. Schwaiger, New York: Princeton Architectural Press, 2000

Gordon, B.F., "The Fagus Factory," *Architectural Record*, 169/7 (1981)

Scheffauer, Herman George, "The Work of Walter Gropius," *Architectural Review*, 56 (1924)

FALLINGWATER

Designed by Frank Lloyd Wright; completed 1937
Bear Run, Pennsylvania

Fallingwater, as the architect Frank Lloyd Wright named the house that he designed for Edgar and Lillian Kaufmann, was commissioned shortly after the Kaufmanns' son, Edgar, Jr., joined Wright's newly formed Taliesin Fellowship in Spring Green, Wisconsin. Founded following the Great Depression, the Taliesin Fellowship was instrumental in Wright's emergence at the age of 70 from 15 years of obscurity, signaled by the construction of the Johnson Wax Building (1939, Racine, Wisconsin), Taliesin West (1940, Scottsdale, Arizona), the first "Usonian House" for Herbert Jacobs (1937, Madison, Wiscon-

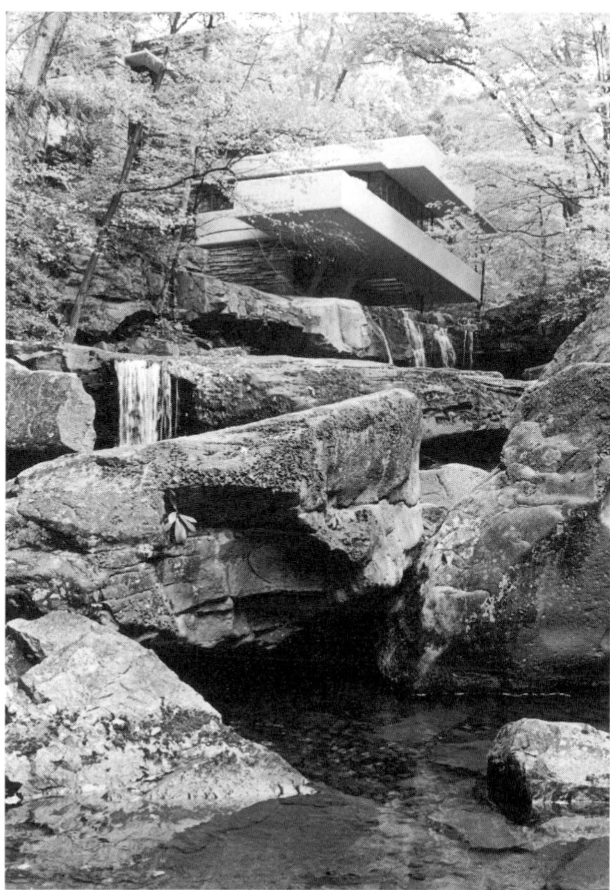

Fallingwater, Bear Run, Pennsylvania (1937)

Interior (living room), Fallingwater, Bear Run, Pennsylvania
© James Reber. Photo courtesy The Frank Lloyd Wright Archives

sin), and Fallingwater. After visiting the site for the Kaufmann house in 1934, a full nine months passed without any drawings or other evidence that Wright was working on the design of the house. In a famous story told by his Fellowship apprentices, Wright drew up the design in the two hours that it took Kaufmann to drive from Milwaukee to Spring Green on a Sunday morning in September 1935.

Wright's design is first and foremost a brilliant piece of site planning. Kaufmann had expected the house to be built to the south of the stream, looking north to the waterfall. However, Wright sited the house to the north of the stream, above the waterfall, so that the house opens to the south sun. As a result, it is the sound of the waterfall, not the view of it, that permeates the experience of Fallingwater. Fallingwater is also the greatest example of Wright's capacity to draw the spaces and forms of his architecture out of the very ground on which it is built. The house is anchored to the earth by vertical piers of sandstone quarried 500 feet from the waterfall, the stones set to resemble the natural strata of the rock exposed along the streambed. The floors of the house are constructed of broad horizontal cantilevered reinforced concrete slabs that appear to float effortlessly over the stream, for the structural beams are hidden between the flagstone floors and plastered ceilings. As a result of these two complementary systems of construction, Fallingwater is anchored to the ground by the stone piers even as its spaces float along with the motion of the stream.

The spaces within Fallingwater are at once surprisingly small, with only 2,885 square feet of enclosed space, and incredibly generous, opening in three directions to the east, south, and west onto large exterior terraces that almost double the floor area of the house. Glazing, set in red-painted steel frames, runs in continuous bands around three sides of the main living and dining room, opening at the corners in celebration of the spatial freedom given by the cantilevered structure. Wright detailed the house so as to reinforce the integration of interior and exterior space, creating delightful moments such as the glass that runs right into the stone wall without any vertical framing at the kitchen and small bedrooms and the flagstones that are set into the floor of the living room so that they appear to continue unbroken beneath the glass doors and out onto the terrace overlooking the waterfall.

Perhaps the most poetic moment in this most natural house is the "hatch" that Wright designed at the east side of the living room, whose glass doors may be opened to give access to a suspended concrete stair leading down to the stream below. Descending these stairs, we pass through the stone floor to find light stairs floating over water, in which is reflected the sky, the roar of the waterfall behind us reverberating off the enormous concrete slab overhead. In the living room, the dark gray color of the bedrock ledge under the shallow water and the way in which the light is reflected from the rippling surface of the stream are matched exactly by the waxed gray flagstone floor on which we stand. The fireplace in the opposite corner, a half-cylinder stone cavity running from floor to ceiling, built directly into the sandstone wall, has as its hearth the original boulder of the site, on which the Kaufmann family formerly took picnic meals. This boulder, left unwaxed, rises above the waxed flagstone floor like the dry top of a stone emerging above the water of the stream.

In Fallingwater, Wright captured the perfect essence of our desire to commune with nature, to dwell in a forested place, and to be at home in the natural world. Fallingwater is often considered Wright's greatest work, for he was first and foremost an architect of the American house. In its startling integration of ancient stone walls anchored to the bedrock and modern reinforced concrete terraces hovering among the leaves of the trees, Fallingwater is both an organic, site-specific critique of the placeless products of the International style and one of the greatest masterpieces of the modern movement. At the time of its construction, Fallingwater was an instant success, the famous perspective view from below the waterfall serving as the background when Wright's photograph appeared on the cover of the 17 January 1938 issue of *Time* magazine, in which he was profiled and the house introduced to the world. More than any other single work, Fallingwater signaled Wright's return to preeminence in American architecture and initiated his final two decades of incredibly prolific practice.

In its 60 years of existence, Fallingwater has proven to be one of the most influential designs of 20th-century architecture, inspiring architects both near and far. This last is exemplified by Alvar Aalto, whose Villa Mairea (1939, Noormarkku, Finland) is indebted to Wright's design both in its overall form and in its numerous natural details. Fallingwater is also, and perhaps more important, ever more popular with the general public, as demonstrated by the fact that nearly 150,000 people visit the house every year, this despite its remote site. In recognition of the unique and unmatched importance of this design, Fallingwater was named the best American building of the last 125 years by the American Institute of Architects. Fallingwater is today, without question, the most famous modern house in the world, reflecting its inspired embodiment of humanity's fundamental and timeless desire to be at home in nature.

ROBERT MCCARTER

See also **Villa Mairea, Noormarkku, Finland; Wright, Frank Lloyd (United States)**

Further Reading

Two very different but highly complementary accounts of Fallingwater are found in Hoffmann's comprehensive architectural history and in the inhabitant and client's view given by the son who apprenticed for Wright, Kaufmann, Jr. Insight into Wright's design process from the point of view of one of the apprentices for Fallingwater can be found in Tafel. A superb photographic survey is contained in Futagawa.

Futagawa, Yokio, *Frank Lloyd Wright, Selected Houses*, volume 4: *Fallingwater*, Tokyo: A.D.A. Edita, 1990

Hoffmann, Donald, *Frank Lloyd Wright's Fallingwater: The House and Its History*, New York: Dover, 1978; 2nd edition, 1993

Kaufmann, Edgar, Jr., *Fallingwater: A Frank Lloyd Wright Country House*, New York: Abbeville Press, 1986

Levine, Neil, *The Architecture of Frank Lloyd Wright*, Princeton, New Jersey: Princeton University Press, 1996

McCarter, Robert, *Fallingwater, Frank Lloyd Wright*, London: Phaidon Press, 1994

McCarter, Robert, *Frank Lloyd Wright*, London: Phaidon Press, 1997

Tafel, Edgar, *Apprentice to Genius: Years with Frank Lloyd Wright*, New York: McGraw-Hill, 1979

FALLOUT SHELTER

The fallout shelter was a highly specialized building type developed in the 1950s in response to the escalating Cold War tensions between the United States and the Soviet Union. Faced with the realization that conventional structures would provide little or no protection from an atomic blast, civil defense officials in the United States undertook a concerted campaign to convince the American public of the necessity of building fallout shelters in their houses and backyards. In addition to these personal shelters constructed of brick, concrete block, or corrugated metal, efforts were undertaken to identify sufficiently reinforced and structurally sound areas of existing buildings to designate as larger-scale public fallout shelters. Construction of personal fallout shelters peaked between 1958 and 1962, when a series of international crises pushed the world ever closer to the brink of nuclear annihilation. During this period the fallout shelter became an integral part of U.S. nuclear policy and was extensively promoted in the popular media as a viable solution to surviving and even winning a nuclear war. Although relatively few people actually built the structure, the fallout shelter was emblematic of the way Americans chose to confront the atomic bomb and nuclear policy.

The first attempts to develop reinforced structures to protect inhabitants from an atomic blast grew out of air raid shelter design from the World War II era. Although these shelters offered a degree of security against conventional weaponry, the atomic detonations over Hiroshima and Nagasaki underscored their futility in an age of atomic weaponry. In the early 1950s, the knowledge that the USSR possessed atomic weapons, combined with the American intervention in Korea, led many architects, engineers, and civil defense officials to contemplate the design of atomic bomb-resistant structures. These early studies concentrated primarily on the obvious physical effects of an atomic explosion, which could extend several miles from ground zero, and underscored the expense of designing sufficiently reinforced structures. However, it was the discovery of radioactive fallout in the mid–1950s that provided the impetus for effective shelter design. Far more lethal than the physical destruction accompanying a blast, fallout consisted of irradiated particles of dust and debris carried aloft by the explosion and dispersed hundreds and even thousands of miles downwind. With the realization that vast areas of the country could be covered under a blanket of radioactive particles, civil defense officials acknowledged that although those nearest a blast would be vaporized, sufficiently prepared citizens could safely wait out the decay of fallout in cozy backyard shelters.

As early as 1955 at least one company marketed a prefabricated shelter, the imaginatively named Kiddie Kakoon, which consisted of a large metal storage tank retrofitted with shelves

U.S. Naval Base, Pearl Harbor, fallout shelter, (date unknown) Honolulu County, Hawaii
© Historic American Buildings Survey/Library of Congress

and bunk beds. Although these early attempts met with limited sales, following the USSR's launch of *Sputnik* in 1957 Americans were increasingly ready to accept the idea of a fallout shelter. Throughout the 1950s and early 1960s, a number of companies offered a variety of prefabricated shelter designs. With the publication of *The Family Fallout Shelter* by the Office of Civil Defense and Mobilization (OCDM) in 1959, the U.S. government articulated a comprehensive plan for civil defense based on the construction of small-scale single-family fallout shelters. The plans presented in the brochure were frequently republished in the popular media, outlining the essential components of a successful shelter design while providing relatively inexpensive plans for shelter construction.

The fallout shelter plans provided by the OCDM fell into two main categories: those that could be constructed within an existing basement and those separate from the main house. Suitable shelter materials ranged from brick and concrete block to large sections of corrugated metal buried under several feet of earth. Regardless of its intended location, a shelter had to be designed to fulfill the following three criteria: it had to be constructed of dense enough materials or buried deep enough to block out as much radiation as possible; it had to provide some means of filtered ventilation to avoid the intake of radioactive particles; and it had to be comfortable and well stocked enough for a family to remain inside for several days or weeks. Architecturally, these criteria were met by solid materials, airtight construction, a baffle entrance with a tight-sealing door, and multiuse interior space that was comfortable enough for a family to eat, sleep, and entertain one another.

Beyond the accommodation of these basic concerns, the actual design of fallout shelters was relatively unremarkable. Besides the telltale hump in the otherwise flat Bermuda grass of suburbia, most shelters did not have a distinct exterior presence. The interior of the shelter focused on fulfilling its unique functional considerations as efficiently as possible. Several popular magazines did present images of shelters converted into clubhouses and playrooms or painted with imaginative scenes in an attempt to make the idea of building a shelter more palatable to the general public.

Although the single-family fallout shelter remained the most visible part of the civil defense initiatives of the 1950s and 1960s, some policymakers argued unsuccessfully for the construction of massive community-based shelters. However, more successful was the program initiated in the early 1960s that was designed to identify and designate sufficiently protected spaces as public fallout shelters. Despite persistent attempts by civil defense officials to convince large segments of the population to construct their own fallout shelters, scarcely 200,000 shelters were built or purchased by 1963. Even as the interest in shelter building peaked during the Cuban Missile Crisis of 1962, a public debate began to rage over the efficacy and moral implications of shelter building. New discoveries suggested that people would have to remain in shelters for years before radioactivity would drop to safe levels, and many debated the morality of what they saw as the vigilante mentality of shelter builders. The final blow to fallout shelter design came with the Nuclear Test Ban Treaty of 1963, which effectively pushed nuclear testing underground and out of sight.

Although most family fallout shelters now lie neglected in suburban backyards, others have found life as storm shelters, storage rooms, and even wine cellars. The late 1990s saw a limited resurgence of interest in fallout shelter design as some attempted to prepare for the possibility of civil unrest accompanying the year–2000 computer bug.

MATTHEW S. ROBINSON

Further Reading

Walter Karp's article provides the best overview of the fallout shelter craze of the early 1960s, with particular attention to the accompanying moral debate. For an overview of the American reaction to the atomic age see the lucid and insightful account by Paul Boyer. Margot Henriksen probes the deeper significance of the bomb and the role of fallout shelters in helping to foster the American culture of dissent in the 1960s. Edward Teague's lengthy bibliography surveys government publications as well as architectural journals at the expense of several significant articles in the popular media. For actual examples of shelter designs the most representative sources are those published by the OCDM, particularly the frequently duplicated *The Family Fallout Shelter*. The early approaches to the design of atomic bomb shelters is documented in the *Architectural Record* article "Buildings Can Be Built to Resist A-Bombs." "Fallout Shelters" presents the architectural requirements for effective fallout protection, while the *Life* magazine special issue "How You Can Survive Fallout" presents several home-built and prefabricated shelter designs.

Boyer, Paul, *By the Bomb's Early Light: American Thought and Culture at the Dawn of the Atomic Age*, New York: Pantheon, 1985

"Buildings Can Be Built to Resist A-Bombs," *Architectural Record* 112 (August 1952)

"Fallout Shelters," *Architectural Forum* 108 (April 1958)

Henriksen, Margot A., *Dr. Strangelove's America: Society and Culture in the Atomic Age*, Berkeley: University of California Press, 1997

Karp, Walter, "When Bunkers Last in the Backyard Bloom'd," *American Heritage* 31 (February/March 1980)

Life 51 (15 September 1961) (special issue entitled "How You Can Survive Fallout")

Office of Civil and Defense Mobilization, *The Family Fallout Shelter*, Washington, D.C.: U.S. Government Printing Office, 1959

Teague, Edward H., *Fallout Shelter Architecture: A Bibliography*, Monticello, Illinois: Vance Bibliographies, 1985

FARNSWORTH HOUSE

Designed by Ludwig Mies van der Rohe, completed 1951
Plano, Illinois

Commissioned in 1945 and finished in 1951, the Farnsworth House is generally regarded as one of Ludwig Mies van der Rohe's most elegantly conceived and precisely constructed buildings, easily the finest residence he put up in his later, American career. Among his completed house designs, only the Tugendhat House (1930) in Brno, which dates from his years in Germany, is considered comparable in quality.

The most striking feature of the Farnsworth House is its outer aspect. The walls consist of floor-to-ceiling glass mounted behind a simple frame made up of eight steel wide-flange piers, four to a side, that support a roof slab and a floor slab, the latter raised some five feet above the ground. The plan is rectangular, with the axis running east and west and the interior giving on to a deck on the west. Symmetry is qualified by a terrace located next to the main structure along the western edge of the south, or front, elevation. The house surveys a lawn that extends 50 yards to the north bank of the Fox River. A short flight of cantilevered steps provides access from the ground to the terrace, whereon a second flight, parallel to the first, rises to the deck. At that point, the visitor turns right to enter the double-door portal. All steel components of the house have been sandblasted and painted white.

Much of this description seems a reasonable confirmation of Mies' reputation as a classicist, although his inclination to deviate from that classification is apparent in the asymmetrical position of the terrace and in the subtlety—which has escaped the attention of many—of locating the portal closer to the south wall than to the north.

Mies' reason for the latter device stems from his layout of the unpartitioned interior. The single volumetric element is a core that contains two bathrooms, the kitchen facilities, and a tightly packed space through which all utilities descend via a cylindrical tube to the ground. Since the core has been deflected slightly to the northeast, the surrounding space is implicitly divided by varying sizes: the largest, a parlorlike area, with a fireplace, to the south (overlooking the river); a smaller, dining area to the west; a long, narrow kitchen to the north; and a sleeping area to the east. By placing the portal slightly closer to the south, the visitor on entry is likely to concentrate his attention on the living area, while the dining area appears to gain more space for itself. The principal articles of furniture now in place were designed by Mies, although with the exception of a large teak storage cabinet done specifically for the house, they are reproductions dating from his German years. The floor is heated by radiation facilitated by a small forced-air furnace in the utility space. The house is now air conditioned, although originally the only ventilation was provided by opening the entry door and/or a pair of hopper windows on the opposite, or east, elevation.

Such a summary should suffice to suggest the reductivist simplicity of the design. Words, however, do not convey the certainty of the proportions and the excellence of the materials, most notably the travertine floors and the prima-vera wood cladding the core. One of Mies' most impressive effects is gained by his decision to raise the structure above the ground. While the functional purpose of that move was to protect the house from the floods that occur regularly along the river, the elevated height simultaneously and indivisibly accomplishes an aesthetic end, leaving the house—especially in view of the transparency of its window walls and the whiteness of its framing members—in a seeming state of levitation.

The house exerted an impact on Mies' later work and on the larger, American architectural scene as well. It was one of the

Farnsworth House, north elevation

first examples of a building type, the clear-span pavilion, that, perhaps more than any other, preoccupied Mies throughout his post–World War II career. In addition, it attracted a huge amount of attention from critics and designers alike, some of it negative—especially from observers who found the very idea of a steel-framed glass house a grievous departure from traditional concepts of domesticity—but most of it enthusiastically affirmative. Philip Johnson, long an admirer of Mies, offered up the ultimate compliment by fashioning his own house in a manner perceptibly indebted to the Farnsworth House. The Johnson design diverged from Mies' in several respects: it was built on a symmetrical plan, with neither a terrace nor a deck nor even a substantial core, but its very form (not to mention its excellence) rested in large part on Johnson's imitation of the Farnsworth model.

The Farnsworth House cannot be fairly discussed without some consideration given its client and its subsequent owner. In requesting Mies to design the house in 1945, Dr. Edith Farnsworth, a distinguished Chicago nephrologist with a substantial knowledge of the arts, knew full well the merits of the architect whom she had chosen to produce a weekend retreat for herself just south of the town of Plano, about 60 miles from Chicago. Mies in turn appreciated the fact that Farnsworth, as a single woman using the house only intermittently, would impose relatively few complicated domestic requirements on him. Client and designer worked easily and cordially together in the early stages of the project. It was Farnsworth, in fact, who voted to employ travertine, one of Mies' favorite stones, for the floor surfaces, and the quality of the house profited further from her willingness to increase the budget, thus enabling Mies to use not only finer materials but also more expensive construction devices than had been anticipated in his first sketches (piers welded rather than bolted to the floor and roof slabs, among other things).

Nonetheless, a relationship that began on a warm footing grew chilly as the 1940s wore on, and eventually a degree of hostility was reached that ended in a legal battle. The reasons have never been made completely clear, but to all appearances Farnsworth at one point decided that Mies not only had gone too far in overspending the means she provided him with but, in her view, also had disregarded some of her more pressing requests in the process. Mies had his own opinion about both charges, and when he sued her for underpayment, she countersued him for professional incompetence, and the matter ended only when the court ruled in his favor.

Despite the rupture of their friendship, Farnsworth kept the house until 1968, when she sold it to a man who turned out to be its ideal owner. Lord Peter Palumbo, a wealthy British real

Farnsworth House, south elevation, detail of porch seen from southwest

estate developer, had known and admired the house and its architect since his schoolboy years. In 1968, having commissioned Mies to design an office building on a site he owned in London, Palumbo learned that Farnsworth had put her Fox River house up for sale. He approached her directly, and by 1972 he had taken full command of the property. He made all the changes necessary to put the house in premium condition and to keep it that way. It was he who elected to outfit it with Mies' furniture, to install air conditioning, and to hire the landscape architect Lanning Roper to improve the grounds. Hardly least, Palumbo bore the enormous cost of repairing the house following a disastrous flood in 1996 that rose unexpectedly well above the five-foot level, ruining all the prima-vera wood of the core, breaking two of the window walls, and destroying all the furniture.

After a half century of existence, the Farnsworth House has assured itself a lofty place in the annals of modern architecture, testimony both to the gifts of Mies van der Rohe and to his ultimate good fortune in having had a client as knowing (notwithstanding her eventual displeasure) as Edith Farnsworth and as sensitive, conscientious, and generous as Peter Palumbo.

FRANZ SCHULZE

See also **Johnson, Philip (United States); Mies van der Rohe, Ludwig (Germany); Tugendhat House, Brno, Czech Republic**

Further Reading

Schulze, Franz, *The Farnsworth House*, Chicago: Lohan Associates, 1997

Tegethoff, Wolf, *Mies van der Rohe: Die Villen und Landhousprojekte*, Essen, Germany: Bacht, 1981; as *Mies van der Rohe: The Villas and Country Houses*, translated by Russell M. Stockman, edited by William Dyckes, New York: Museum of Modern Art, 1985

FASCIST ARCHITECTURE

Fascist architecture denotes the spectrum of architectural projects that were built, theorized, ritualized, and polemically debated by Fascist political regimes of World War II. Extreme right-wing totalitarian dictatorships were forcibly installed in Italy (1922–43), Germany (1933–45), and Spain (1939–75). The Italian Fascist Party under the leadership of Benito Mussolini, the National Socialism Party headed by Adolf Hitler, and the Falange Espanola Party led by General Francisco Franco formed coercive governments whose absolute power abolished all forms of political opposition. Public utilities, commercial exchanges, processes of industrialization, as well as the production of art and architecture were controlled and regulated by the state; and it was in Italy and Germany that architecture played a seminal role in the advancement of Fascist ideologies.

The very term *Fascism* (or *fascismo* in Italian) was derived from the Latin word *fasces*, denoting an ornamental object of political and military authority carried by ancient Roman lictors during public ceremonies. As early as 1919, Mussolini adopted the fasces as the emblem of the Fascist Party, intent as he was on associating the glories of ancient Rome with the future triumphs of his Fascist state.

Throughout the Fascist era in Italy architecture was used as a rhetorical device; it became the preferred vehicle for launching Fascist propaganda. It most forcefully portrayed, in the solidity of its materials and the vastness of its measures, the sublimity of imperial power. Buildings, piazzas, and ruins were privileged backdrops for public demonstrations, ritual reenactments, and oratorical theatrics; spectacles aimed at cultivating a Fascist body politic. Italian architects Giuseppe Terragni, Marcello Piacentini, Adalberto Libera, Giovanni Michelucci, and Giuseppe Pagano participated in the design of new building types, the inauguration of new colonies, the restoration of ancient monuments, the staging of political rallies, the mounting of exhibits, and the publication of polemical journals; activities that contributed to the construction of the new Roman Empire.

From the outset, Mussolini launched a massive building campaign. The modernization and nationalization of transportation and communication networks necessitated the design and construction of building types new to Italian soil. Modern and efficient railway stations and post offices were built throughout Italy. Florence's Santa Maria Novella train station (1932–34), designed by Gruppo Toscano (a six-member group of Florentine rationalists), and Rome's Palace of Postal and Telegraphic Services, designed by BBPR (Banfi, Belgiojoso, Peresutti, and Rogers), were only two of the many building projects sponsored by the state. It was the invention of the Casa del Fascio (House of the Fascist Party), however, that most captivated the Italian imagination. Used primarily as the local headquarters of the Fascist Party, versions of this new building type were erected throughout the Italian peninsula. Typically sited in the center of town, the structure rivaled the church's dominance and evidenced the ceaseless presence of Il Duce. The most celebrated Casa del Fascio was built in Como (1932–36) and designed by Giuseppe Terragni. Its monumental austerity, abstract formalism, and frontal transparency made it the building most representative of both Italian Fascism and modernism.

Mussolini also commissioned the construction of entirely new towns in the southern regions of the Roman Campania, in Sardinia, in the Greek Dodecanese, and in the colonies of northern Africa. The towns of Littoria, Carbonia, and Guidonia were built on reclaimed swampland, whereas the occupied cities of Tripoli, Bengazi, Kos, and Rhodes were resettled with Italian farmers. Predappio (1925), Mussolini's hometown, was the first to be built with wide avenues, monumental civic buildings, and a vast civic piazza. Littoria (1932), named after the lictor who had carried the ceremonial fasces during antiquity, was built with the knowledge of ancient Roman foundation rites.

Antiquity was equally of issue in the Fascist policy of "isolamento": the valorization and preservation of rhetorically significant buildings. In an attempt to make visible select architectural masterpieces from imperial Rome, monuments from the first century BC were liberated from thousands of years of historical and material growth. With the demolition of entire city blocks, the Mausoleum of Caesar Augustus (63–14 BC) became one such site. Symbolic of the burial ground of Rome's founding emperor, the unearthing of its sublime circular structure was completed in 1937, the 2,000th anniversary of his birth. With a similar intent, Mussolini effected vast transformations to the via dell'Impero (present-day via dei Fori Imperiali) by physically connecting the ruins of the Colosseum with the administrative center of Fascist Rome—Piazza Venezia. In an effort to valorize the Roman Forum and the Forum of Augustus, the via dell' Impero was designed as a monumental avenue for ceremonial and military parades.

Alongside the building of large-scale architectural interventions, architects also participated in the design and construction of exhibits. Throughout the Fascist era, the mounting of state-sponsored public exhibitions was a significant vehicle for the promotion of both architectural ideas and Fascist polemics. In March 1931, the International Movement for Rational Architecture (MIAR) opened its second exhibition with a critique of contemporary Italian architecture. The likes of Pietro Maria Bardi, Edoardo Persico, and Alberto Sartoris called for the radical alliance of Fascist doctrine with modern architecture, for only in this way could a true renewal of the country take place. In 1932, to mark the tenth anniversary of the Fascist takeover of power, the *Mostra della Rivoluzione Fascista* (Exhibit of the Fascist Revolution) featured the work of architects Libera, Mario Renzi, and Terragni, its pavilions manifesting the allegiance of modernism to Fascist doctrine. However, it was the Universal Exposition of 1942 (EUR'42) that placed the Italian Fascist state on display through its vast complex of monumental pavilions, designed under the leadership of Piacentini. Although the events of the war halted its completion, the polemics surrounding the construction of EUR'42 forcefully pitted the modern rationalists against the more conservative neoclassicists.

Journals, periodicals, and newspapers were also significant venues for the dissemination of both architectural theory and Fascist propaganda. The printed word and image had become highly effective means of communication, and as a former journalist Mussolini was well aware of this truth. Marcello Piacentini served as editor for *Architettura*, and *Quadrante* was edited by Pietro Maria Bardi. *Casabella* was founded in 1928, and in 1933 Giuseppe Pagano had become its editor. Along with *Quadrante, Casabella* had been a vocal supporter of the Italian rationalists, and in the final years of the Fascist regime, with increasing criticism levied against the state, the magazine was ordered to cease production. As a result, architects Pagano and Banfi were deported to German death camps.

In Germany, the totalitarian regime of National Socialism, led by the Fuhrer Adolf Hitler, also privileged architecture in the communication of its ideologically charged political agenda. In Nazi Germany architecture, of all the visual arts, was materially, spatially and structurally most representative of the dictatorial power of the III Reich, a state intent on the political and military conquest of the Western world.

In this venture was implicated architect Albert Speer, who in 1937 was named by Hitler Inspector General of Buildings (GBI, Generalbauinspektor). The title attributed to Speer expansive decision-making powers and the mandate to make of Berlin a capital embodying the tenets of National Socialism. Guided by Hitler's own artistic imagination, Speer embarked on the conceptualization and design of the largest building project initiated by any totalitarian regime, the construction of a new urban plan for the city of Berlin. The enormous project envisioned the rezoning of a vast territory of the city through which the destruction of tens of thousands of homes would have been assured.

If actualized, the plan would have forcibly introduced a monumental north/south axis five kilometers long, originating at the southern limit of the Tempelhof and Schoeneberg districts and terminating at the city's northern limit, the Spree. Lined with granite-clad buildings, the axis would have housed the most politically significant buildings representative of the III Reich's major ministries and centers of power. At its northern end, the axis was designed to incorporate the colossal Pantheonlike shaped building called the Great Hall, conceived to gather nearly 200,000 spectators in mass celebrations of National Socialism. But steps from the Brandenburg gate, the Great Square immediately to the south of the Great Hall would have been surrounded by Hitler's Palace, the High Command of the Armed Forces, the New Chancellery, and the Old Reichstag. And although the New Chancellery was inaugurated in January 1937, Speer would have designed all of the square's new buildings.

Completed as planned, the monumental scale of the north/south axis would have engendered a sense of domination never before achieved by human artifice. And notwithstanding Hitler's defeat that ensured the demise of the Berlin project, Speer incorporated many of its architectural strategies in earlier projects for another German city, Nuremberg. In 1936, Speer completed the redesign and extension of its Zeppelin Field, a parade ground for the mass gathering of 100,000 citizens. In the austerity of its neoclassical colonnade and in the massive extension of its 1,000-foot reviewing stand was achieved a rhetorical and ideological backdrop for the orchestration of party rallies and for gatherings of the Hitler Youth movement.

Thus, in both Fascist Italy and Nazi Germany, architecture was used as a highly articulated tool of political propaganda. That architects were directly involved in the production and communication of such beliefs should not be overlooked but rather the source of continued study.

FRANCA TRUBIANO

See also **Italy; Libera, Adalberto (Italy); Terragni, Giuseppe (Italy)**

Further Reading

Albert Speer, Architecture 1932–1942, Bruxelles: Aux Archives d'architecture Moderne, 1985

Ades, Dawn, et al. (compilers), *Art and Power: Europe under the Dictators, 1930–1945* (exhib. cat.), London: Hayward Gallery, 1995

Andreotti, Libero, "The Aesthetics of War: The Exhibition of the Fascist Revolution," *Journal of Architectural Education* 45 (February 1992)

Doordan, Dennis P., *Building Modern Italy: Italian Architecture, 1914–1936*, New York: Princeton Architectural Press, 1988

Ghirardo, Diane Yvonne, *Building New Communities: New Deal America and Fascist Italy*, Princeton, New Jersey: Princeton University Press, 1989

Ghirardo, Diane Yvonne, "Architecture and Culture in Fascist Italy," *Journal of Architectural Education* 45 (February 1992)

Jaskot, Paul, *The Architecture of Oppression*, London: Routledge, 2000

Kostof, Spiro, *The Third Rome, 1870–1950: Traffic and Glory*, Berkeley, California: University Art Museum, 1973

Miller Lane, Barbara, *Architecture and Politics in Germany 1918-1945*, Cambridge, Massachusetts: Harvard University Press, 1968.

Millon, Henry, "Some New Towns in Italy in the 1930s" in *Art and Architecture in the Service of Politics*, edited by Millon and Linda Nochlin, Cambridge, Massachusetts: MIT Press, 1978

Schumacher, Thomas L., *Il Danteum di Terragni, 1938*, Rome: Officina Edizioni, 1980; enlarged and revised edition, as *The Danteum: A Study in the Architecture of Literature*, Princeton, New Jersey: Princeton Architectural Press, 1985

FATHY, HASSAN 1900–1989

Architect and teacher, Egypt

More than any other 20th-century architect, Hassan Fathy raised the status of earth building among architects worldwide. Building in earth—adobe or *pisé*—has a long and honorable history, and in those parts of the world where stone and timber are scarce and expensive, earth has remained the most economical and widely used building material. This is certainly true in Egypt and most Arab countries. But even there, as in most of Europe, earth, at the turn of the 20th century, had come to be identified with poverty and backwardness, and earthen building materials were increasingly perceived by architects and the professional middle classes in general to be old fashioned and impermanent. A handful of architectural devotees of earth building advocated and promoted its use, but by and large, commercial vested interests in the brick, cement, steel, and asbestos industries almost completely sidelined earthen building materials.

Fathy, in common with many Egyptian architects of his generation, studied in France, at the Ecolé dex Beaux Arts in Paris, and like them he acquired a love for the historic architecture of his homeland, and for the Mameluke and Ottoman architecture of his native city, Cairo, in particular. But unlike most of them, he acquired also a love for the traditional vernacular architecture of the Egyptian countryside, and chiefly for the Nubian architecture of Upper Egypt. Soon after his return from Egypt to France, he was appointed to the staff of the Department of Architecture at the School of Fine Arts in Cairo, of which he became Head in 1938. Under his direction, annual field study visits to the various regions of Egypt were introduced into the curriculum.

Fathy's growing reputation in this field brought him the commission, in 1946 from the Egyptian government, to design and build a new village, on flat fertile land closer to the Nile, for the inhabitants of Old Gourna, an ancient village close to the Valley of the Kings at Thebes, who had made a living for generations by robbing historic artifacts from the Pharaonic tombs and selling them to tourists and dealers. Before this commission, his architectural practice had consisted, in the main, of private houses for affluent middle-class clients: the New Gourna commission transformed his practice and almost broke him, financially and psychologically. His plan for the new settlement, his designs for each one of the buildings in it, housing and public buildings, incorporating as far as possible the architectural traditions of the Upper Nile valley and the building skills of the Nubians, and his direction of the building process, were based on long and close observation of, and consultation with, the community for which he designing. Unfortunately, on completion of the main phase of building in 1953, the people of Old Gourna refused to move form their old homes and to forfeit their traditional illegal source of income. The buildings of New Gourna were not occupied, and they remained empty for decades.

However, Fathy persevered—he remained faithful to his vision of an architecture deriving from and drawing its inspiration from the building traditions of the Egyptian people. His own architectural practice continued, in its modest way, until the publication in 1969 of his account of the genesis of the New Gourna project by the Egyptian Ministry of Culture became a turning point in his career. The Archaeology Department of the University of Chicago had been actively engaged in the exploration, interpretation, and conservation of the Pharaonic remains in Thebes for decades and had come to rely on, and admire, Fathy's profound knowledge of the building traditions of the area. Therefore, the department sponsored the re-publication of his account of New Gourna under a new title, *Architecture for the Poor: An Experiment in Rural Egypt*, in 1973.

The reissue of the New Gourna story coincided with the worldwide fuel crisis, following the Arab–Israeli war of 1973, and in the use of locally available building materials and building craft skills and the application of traditional principles of climatic comfort was seen the recipe for the affordable and locally sustainable rural development of which the developing countries of the world, in all continents, were in desperate need. Architects and architectural students from all continents in increasing numbers made the pilgrimage to New Gourna, or to Fathy's home in Cairo, on the top floor of the ancient house in Dar Al-Gabbani at the foot of the Citadel, where Fathy was to spend the last years of his life.

This historic house, acquired by the Aga Khan and over a period of years restored under Fathy's direction, came to serve as a demonstration of the design principles that Fathy advocated. Here he established the International Institute of Appropriate Technology, of which he served as director for several years.

In the final decade of his life, Fathy undertook a vast range of commissions including Dar Al-Islam, the Moslem arts and crafts community in New Mexico, and the Desert Research Centre for the American University of Cairo, at Sadat City, the vast new city in the desert overlooking the oasis of Wadi Natrun. The execution of these latter projects would have been impossible without the support and assistance of the young architects, Egyptians and others, who were attracted by his philosophy and personality, and whose assistance he so generously acknowledged. Notable among these architects was Abdel Wahid El-Wakil.

Anthony D. C. Hyland

See also **Africa: Northern Africa; Aga Khan Award (1977–); Cairo, Egypt; Earthen Building**

Biography

Born 23 March 1900 in Alexandria, Egypt; educated at Ecole des Beaux Arts in Paris; graduated from High School of Engineering, Architectural Section, University of King Fuad I (now University of Cairo), Cairo 1926. Appointed to the Faculty of Fine Arts School, Cairo 1930; chaired the Architecture Department there 1938–48. Designed and exhibited first mud brick projects—country houses for Lower Egypt 1937; Constructed first mud brick structures incorporating the inclined vault—experimental housing in Bahtim, Egypt, commissioned by the Royal Society of Agriculture 1941; delegated to the Antiquities Department to design and supervise the project of New Gourna Village at Luxor, to displace the inhabitants of the Old Gourna from the Antiquities Zone 1946–53. Appointed Director of the School Building Department, Ministry of Education 1949–52. Delegated Consultant to the United Nations Refugee World Assistance 1950; joined Doxiades Associates in Athens as consultant. Lecturer on Climate and Architecture at the Athens Technical Institute. Member of the Research Project for the City of the Future 1957–62. Director of Pilot Projects for Housing, Ministry of Scientific Research, Cairo; designed High Institute of Social Anthropology and Folk Art for the Ministry of Culture, Cairo; worked as Consultant to the Minister of Tourism, Cairo; delegated by the United Nations Organization for Rural Development Project in Saudi Arabia 1963–65. Lectured on philosophy and aesthetics in Town Planning and Architecture Department at al-Azhar University 1966. In 1980, awarded the first Chairman's Award by the Steering Committee of the Aga Khan Award for Architecture; in 1985, awarded the first Gold Medal of the International Union of Architects; in 1987, short-listed for the RIBA Gold Medal. He died 30 Novermber 1989.

Selected Works

Mohammed Fathy Villa, Giza, 1938
Said al-Bakri Villa, Cairo, 1942
Stopplaere House, Luxor, 1950
Zaki Willa, Cairo, 1951
New Gourna, Luxor, 1948–53
Arab Refugee Housing, Gaza, Palestine, 1957
New Bariz, Kharga Oasis, Egypt, 1967
Nassif House, Jeddah, Saudi Arabia, 1973
Wedha Mosque and Islamic Centre, Cairo, 1974
Holiday Village, island of Tahr al Bahr, Luxor, 1977
Akil Sami House, Dahshur, Egypt, 1978
Dar Al-Islam, Abiquiu, New Mexico, United States, 1980
Desert Research Centre, Sadat City, 1982
Talhouni Residence, Shuna, Jordon,1988

Selected Publications

Gourna: A Tale of Two Villages, Cairo: Ministry of Culture, 1969
The Arab House in the Urban Setting: Past Present and Future, London: Longman, 1972
Architecture for the Poor: An Experiment in Rural Egypt, Chicago: University of Chicago Press, 1973 (first published in 1969 under the title *Gourna, A Tale of Two Villages* Cairo: Ministry of Culture)

Hassan, Fathy, et al., Hassan Fathy, *Architecture d'Aujourd'hui* (1978)
Natural Energy and Vernacular Architecture: Principles and Examples with Reference to Hot Arid Climates, edited by W. Shearer, United Nations University, 1986

Further Reading

Durkee, Abdullah N., "Hassan Fathy in New Mexico," *Via* (1984)
Khan, Hasan-Uddin, "Poete de l'architecture: Hassan Fathy," *Connaissance des arts* (1990)
Kultermann, U., "Contemporary Arab Architecture: The Architects of Egypt," *Mimar* (1982)
Petruccioli, Altilio, et al., "Hassan Fathy," *Casabella* (1998)
Richards, J.M., Ismail Serageldin, and Darl Rastorfer, *Hassan Fathy*. Singapore: Concept Media and London: Architectural Press, 1985
Steele, James, "Hassan Fathy," *Architectural Monographs* (1988)
Steele, James, *An Architecture for People: The Complete Works of Hassan Fathy*, London: Thames and Hudson, 1997

FAVELA

Favela, the term that identifies shantytowns in Brazil, originates from poverty settlements in Rio de Janeiro and is derived from a type of bush that is abundant in the semiarid Canudos area in the northern state of Bahia. Rio's favelas coincide with the occupation of the Santo Antônio and Providência hills (*morros*) in the city center. In 1897, soldiers who returned from the Canudos War—a military campaign in the northeastern region of Brazil—received permission to temporarily settle on these sites, where they built shacks of cardboard and wood. Morro da Providência received the name Morro da Favela (favela hill) in reference to the previously mentioned bush. In 1904, 100 houses existed, and by 1933 the number had grown to 1500.

By the 1920s, favelas had spread to other hills of the city: Morro dos Telégrafos, Mangueira; Morro de São Carlos, Vila Rica (Copacabana area); Pasmado (Botafogo); and Babilônia (Leme). This expansion even reached the city suburbs. The growth of favelas was driven by the lack of a government policy to address the housing problems of the poorest members of society. In 1888, Brazil proclaimed a law of freedom for slaves; it was the last country to do so in Latin America. The urban reforms of the early part of the 20th century almost eliminated tenement houses (*cortiços*) in the city center; such houses sheltered approximately 100,000 people in 1890.

The peasants' migration from the northeastern rural areas to the capital intensified the settlement in the hills wherever vacant land was available near workplaces. The same development took place in areas near primary transportation lines that connected the city center to the northern zone of the city where industries were located: railroads and, later, wide avenues. By the 1920s, one of the main suburban favelas had emerged near the Madureira railroad station, right in front of the Imperial Palace (Quinta da Boa Vista).

The favela, throughout its history in Rio de Janeiro, was considered mainly an undesired component of the urban structure. This vision was present at the beginning of the 20th century in the programs of Mayor Pereira Passos (1903–06) and with the Agache Plan in the 1930s.

The importance of the favela and its presence in the city context were recognized and taken into consideration only to control public hygiene and epidemics. From the 1940s to the 1960s, the slums were considered to be an urban-order disruption, and their population was seen as alien to the urban society, so the government policy for favelas was simply to remove them from areas near the "formal" city. The Alliance Progress, a U.S. government aid program, was created to resettle the *favelados*, who rejected the program, which foresaw single apartment blocks located far in the periphery. At the same time, religious organizations, municipal initiatives, and sensitive architects (such as Carlos Nelson Ferreira dos Santos) helped several communities transform precarious shacks into houses of bricks and concrete and to furnish technical infrastructures, such as stairs, electricity, water supply, sewage, and garbage systems. Most of the favelas are still concentrated along the railroad system in the northern area of Rio; others are old, traditional settlements near the "noble" southern neighborhoods, such as Botafogo, Copacabana, Ipanema, Leblon, and São Conrado, with a privileged view over the marvelous natural environment. Rocinha, one of the largest and steadiest favelas of the city, has almost 100,000 inhabitants; Vidigal has 10,000, and Santa Marta 5000. The latest report shows that in 1999, one million people were living in 600 favelas in Rio de Janeiro.

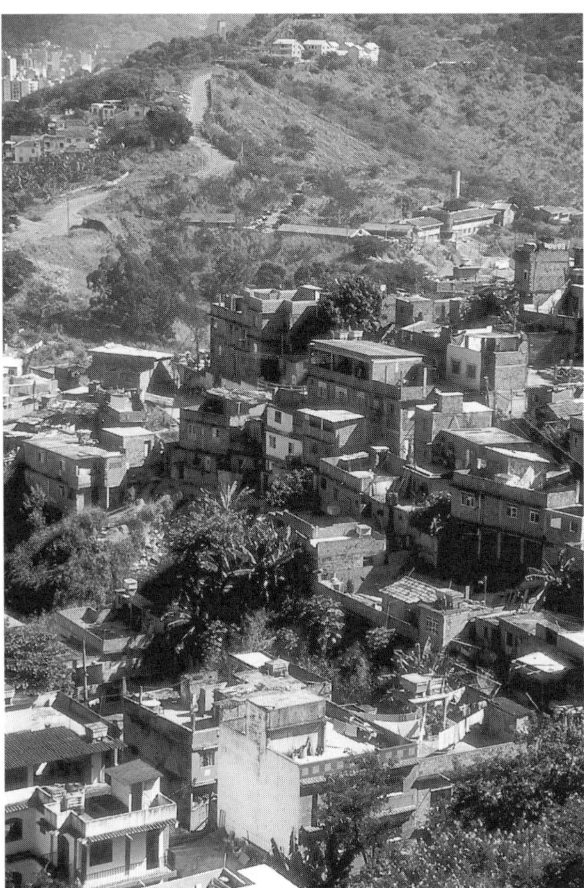

Favela in Vidigal section of Rio de Janeiro
© R. Segre

One could define as romantic the claim that there are some positive social, cultural, and urban components in those settlements, denying the negative opposition between "formal" and "informal" city. The free articulation of volumes and colors of housing units along the hills was admired by Le Corbusier during his visit to Rio in 1929. Bernard Rudofsky, who lived for several years in Brazil, recognized the spatial and formal quality of irregular urban structures and its vernacular huts before writing his book *Architecture without Architects*. The relationship between medieval cities and modern metropolises as defined by the French historian Jacques Le Goff is present in the favelas' urban structure. However, this free composition is related to individual and social appropriation of space that creates for inhabitants a sense of community and solidarity. This is reaffirmed by religious activities that make up the syncretism of Afro-Brazilian rituals and by the meaning of popular music (samba) and carnival shows, icons of *carioca* culture around the world. Some of the most important and oldest *escolas de samba* of Rio's carnival belong to traditional favelas: Salgueiro, Mangueira (Estação Primeira de Mangueira); Serrinha (Império Serrano); Formiga; and Borel (Unidos da Tijuca). Writers, poets, singers, and film directors used favelas as the main subject of their creative work. In Brazil, several films assumed this popular environment: in the 1950s, Frenchman Marcel Camus directed the film *Orfeo Negro*, which diffused the life and music of Rio's favelas, as did *Favela dos meus amores* (Humberto Mauro, 1935), *Rio 40 graus* (Nelson Pereira dos Santos, 1955), *Como nascem os anjos* (Murilo Salles, 1990), and *Orfeu* (Caca Diegues, 1998). However, there is a dark side of favelas: In the last two decades, lottery managers and drug dealers have taken over control of the population.

In the 1990s, the municipal government of Rio de Janeiro, with the initiative of the former secretary of urbanism, architect Luiz Paulo Conde (city mayor in 1997), and the secretary of housing, architect Sérgio Magalhães, decided to develop a long-term plan to integrate the "informal" city (favelas) into the "formal" urban structure. The key change in the municipal government's programs is the replacement of the idea of dealing only with the deficit of adequate housing for a policy that focuses on "producing the city" through readdressing the urban deficit.

The new program, Favela-Bairro, started serving 90 favelas with a population of 300,000 inhabitants and counted on an investment of U.S. $300 million, of which 40 percent came from the City of Rio and 60 percent from the Inter-American Development Bank (BID). To integrate the favela into the urban fabric of the formal city, the program includes the following key actions: (1) completing or constructing main urban infrastructures; (2) providing environmental changes that ensure that favelas look like standard neighborhoods; (3) introducing visual symbols of the formal city as a way to identify favelas as neighborhoods (paved streets, parks, urban furnishings, and public services); (4) consolidating and inserting favelas into the planning process of the city; (5) implementing social types of activities, such as setting up day care centers for children, income generation processes, training programs, and sporting, cultural, and leisure activities; and (6) promoting the legalization of land subdivision and providing individual land titles.

In 1994, the housing secretariat organized, in cooperation with the Brazilian Institute of Architects (IAB, Instituto de Arquitetos do Brasil), a competition for designing a methodology to develop improvements, beginning with 18 medium-size favelas (between 500 and 2500 dwellings). An important innovation was the organization of 15 teams, led by architects who participated in the competition that presented new ideas and methodological approaches. The competition included firms of young architects, such as Planejamento and Arquitetura, Fábrica Arquitetura, Arquitraço Cooperativa, and Archi 5 studios, as well as those of older, prestigious works, such as Paulo Casé, Luis Acciolli, and Maurício Roberto, who for the first time would undertake design for the poorest members of Rio's population. This initiative promoted a new relationship between technical expertise and the degraded areas of Rio de Janeiro to attempt to improve the quality of life of people living in favelas.

ROBERTO SEGRE

See also **Brazil**

Further Reading

Abreu, Maurício de A., *Evolução urbana do Rio de Janeiro*, Rio de Janeiro: IPLANRIO, 1988

Amaral de Sampaio, Maria Ruth (editor), *Habitação e cidade*, São Paulo: FAU-USP, FAPESP, 1998

Bonduki, Nabil, *Origens da habitação social no Brasil: arquitetura moderna, lei do inquilinato e difusão da casa própria*, São Paulo: Estação Liberdade, 1998

Casé, Paulo, *Favela: uma exegese a partir de Mangueira*, Rio de Janeiro: Relume Dumará, 1996

Cidade inteira: a política habitacional da cidade do Rio de Janeiro, Rio de Janeiro: Prefeitura da Cidade do Rio de Janeiro, Secretaria Municipal de Habitação, 1999

Duarte, Cristiane Rose, Osvaldo Luiz Silva, and Alice Brasileiro (editors), *Favela, um bairro: propostas metodológicas para intervenção pública em favelas do Rio de Janeiro*, São Paulo: Pro-Editores, 1996

Fessler Vaz, Lilian, and Mauricio Abreu, "Sobre as origens da Favela," in *Anais do IV Encontro Nacional da ANPUR*, 1 (1991)

Magalhães, Sergio F., "L'esperienza di Rio de Janeiro: Favela-Bairro," *Abitare*, 374 (1998)

Morro da Providência: memórias da "Favella," Rio de Janeiro: Prefeitura da Cidade do Rio de Janeiro, 1992

Ribbeck, Eckhart, "Favelas, Drogen und Folklore," *Stadt Bauwelt*, 134 (1997)

Segre, Roberto, *Las estructuras ambientales de América Latina*, Mexico City: Siglo Veintiuno Editores, 1977

Valladares, Licia do Prado, *Passa-se uma casa*, Rio de Janeiro: Zahar Editores, 1978

Zaluar, Alba, and Marcos Alvito, *Um século de favela*, Rio de Janeiro: Fundação Getulio Vargas Editora, 1998

Zuenir Ventura, *Cidade partida*, São Paulo: Companhia Das Letras, 1994

FEDERAL CAPITAL COMPLEX, BRASÍLIA

Designed by Oscar Niemeyer, completed 1960
Brazil

The free and vigorous forms of Oscar Niemeyer's works, such as Pampulha (1943) and Canoas House (1954), were already internationally recognized when he visited Europe in 1954. Niemeyer was impressed by classical buildings he saw there—their monumentality and their sense of permanence. This led him to introduce new concepts in his architecture. Niemeyer started to emphasize pure and concise forms as well as single volumes dictated by structure in order to achieve monumentality. The opportunity for Niemeyer to concretize this new vision came when he was commissioned to design the buildings of Brasília, the new planned capital of Brazil, built between 1957 and 1960.

Adopting the main principles of modern urbanism, Lucio Costa's plan for Brasília achieved an appropriate expression of a capital with two axes crossing each other in right angles. The composition, resembling a plane, is very simple, unified, clear, and elegant. In the curved wings of the north-south axis (road axis), Costa placed the residential areas. The east-west axis (monumental axis) is a sort of dorsal spine that organizes the entire plan. At the east end of the monumental axis, Costa located the governmental center, Three Powers Square, as a focus of the composition.

The Three Powers Square is a great esplanade for public ceremonies and provides an aesthetic and symbolic space for all the city houses. Following Costa's triangular scheme, Niemeyer placed in each vertex a building representing the three main powers: Planalto Palace (executive), National Congress (legislative), and Supreme Court (judiciary). Niemeyer concentrated his major efforts on the creation of this ensemble.

Niemeyer conceived these palaces as an entity, conferring formal unity and a general classical monumentality on them. He created three poles of visual attraction with many perspectives. The buildings are self-contained objects in the vast landscape, separated by large surfaces of stone paving that provides a free space to admire them and creates a scenic civic place. The ensemble of the Three Powers is a unique architectural complex in which classicism is joined with lightness.

From far away, the powerful National Congress (1958–60) appears, announcing the termination of the axis. Niemeyer placed two domes on a vast platform that emphasizes the horizontality of the complex. Based on a play of volumes, the complex was intended to express formally the duality of the two assemblies. According to Bruand, the inverted dome, the Chamber of Deputies, symbolizes the more democratic facet of this assembly, whereas the smaller dome, the Senate, appears to be more reclusive (see Bruand, 1971). Between the domes, two high thin slabs are placed, housing the secretariat. The balance of the final composition is also achieved by contrasts between vertical and horizontal lines, between curves and straight lines, and between the pure forms of platform, twin towers, and

National Congress Complex, Brasilia, Brazil (1958–1960)
© Bettmann/CORBIS

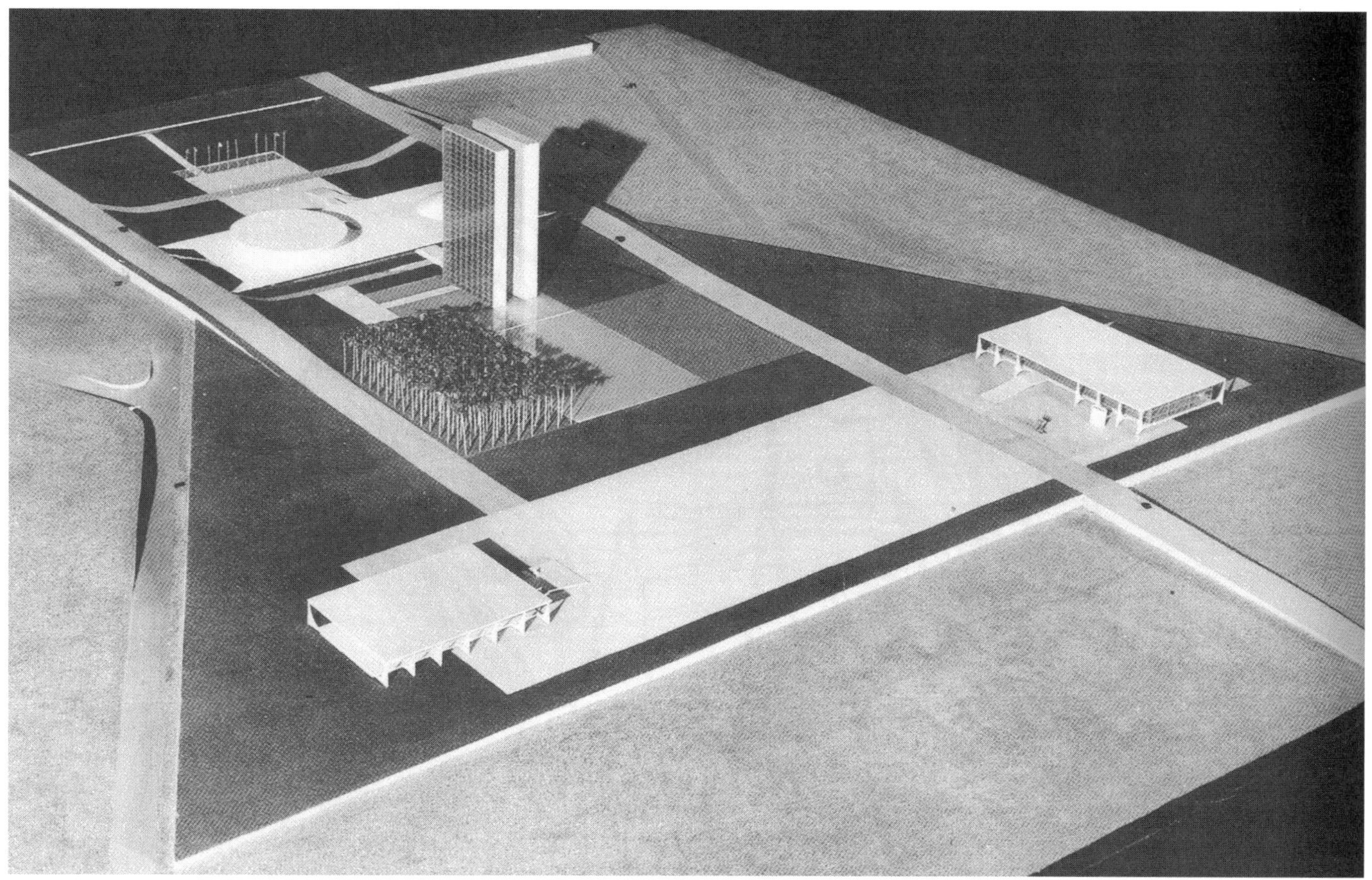

Oscar Niemeyer, model, National Congress Complex
(1958–60), Brasilia, Brazil
(published in: Damaz, Paul, Art in Latin American Architecture, New York: Reinhold, 1963, p.120)

domes. It was designed in order to preserve the openness of the mall while maintaining its symbolical importance.

In the other vertices of the triangle are the Planalto Palace and the Supreme Court (1960). Both buildings are rectangular glass boxes encased in a peristyle with magnificent colonnades. Niemeyer, in order to enhance the whole, reduced the number of formal elements and emphasized the single motif of the curving colonnade as the strongest facet of the composition. The delicate and curving colonnades, barely touching the ground, endow the buildings with lightness and grace. The widely projecting roof slabs supported by thin columns create many opportunities to frame the vast landscape. As they are inscribed in a larger composition, they have similar features, differentiated by disposition and size that confer unity upon the esplanade as imagined by Costa. Whereas the Planalto Palace is taller and more delicate, the Supreme Court is closer to the ground, communicating stolidity and stability. Whereas Planalto's long side is facing the square, the Court has its narrow side facing it. This arrangement creates different perspectives but maintains axiality and unity, which provide the classical character required by institutions.

The innovative motif of colonnades is a variation of that of Alvorada Palace (1958), the official residency of the president, located near the ensemble although not part of it. One of his most acclaimed works, Alvorada Palace had its image widely diffused and became a symbol of the country. The curving and slender columns, delicately touching the ground, graciously support the shaded veranda. As David Underwood noted, the airy structure "synthesizes Brazilian charm with European decorum, classical nobility with baroque plasticity." Niemeyer's ethereal and fluid suspended palaces are meaningful freestanding objects in the vastness of the square.

The mall also includes two rows of ministry buildings. These discrete and anonymous blocks are aligned consecutively in order to create a sort of scenic and ceremonial space, directing the attention to the Three Powers Square. Closer to this square are the Ministries of Justice (1960) and Foreign Affairs (1965–67), designed differently from the others. In these buildings, Niemeyer adopted a Brutalist aesthetic; at same time, however, they are refined and sophisticated. Instead of delicate colonnades, Niemeyer opted for heavy concrete porticoes as expressive elements. At the end of the mall is located the Metropolitan Cathedral (1958–70), one of Niemeyer's masterpieces. The volume is formed by a structure of 16 boomerang-like ribs, expressing the essence of the cathedral. The entrance through an underground passage leads the spectator to experience a dramatic contrast from the shadows to an intensely illuminated and mystical space. The most recent contribution by Niemeyer is the Pantheon of Democracy (1985), a poetic, fluid, and dynamic structure that closes the open side of the Three Powers Square.

As soon as Brasília was completed, it was both praised and criticized. In the architectural field, it was celebrated by many critics. However, others pointed out the failure of the climatic adaptation of the buildings and its rupture with traditional Brazilian living. Siegfried Giedion criticized the lack of coherence of the monumental axis, as it fails to reproduce a theatrical perspective. Although the capital was conceived as a coherent whole, it is not felt by the pedestrian, who feels powerless in such a vastness. Sybil Mohóly-Nagy pointed out the autoritarianism and the monumentalism of the new city. James Holston shows how Brasília failed regarding its social purposes (Holston, 1989). In a moment in which the principles of modern urbanism were under fire, Brasília seems to have been born already old.

Nevertheless, the attacks on modern urbanism and the fact that Brasília was a social failure eclipsed some positive aspects of its architecture. First was Brasília's role in the discussion of modern architecture and monumentality. Niemeyer's delicate and lighter classicism proved that modern architecture could also be monumental and symbolic without regressing to the massive authoritarianess of 1930s government buildings. Second was Brasília's unique image. Niemeyer sucessfully created an image for the city based on a repetition of some patterns, fostering formal unity although admitting variations in textures and materials that contributed to the city's inclusion in the World Heritage List of UNESCO. Third was Brasília's role as a symbol for the country. Brasília was planned to foster a new Brazilian man, a proof of the capacity of a country to build its future. Much more than housing institutions, the main achievement of Niemeyer was the creation of a cultural image for a modern state, providing poetic and symbolic forms.

FERNANDO DINIZ MOREIRA

See also **Brazil; Brasília, Brazil; Brutalism; Costa, Lúcio (Brazil); Niemeyer, Oscar (Brazil)**

Further Reading

Association Internationale des Critiques d'Art (AICA), La Cite Nouvelle, *Architecture, Formes + Fonctions*, 7 (1960–1961)

Bruand, Yves, *L'Architecture Contemporaire au Brésil*, Paris: Université de Paris, 1971 Evenson, Norma, *Two Brazilian Capitals: Architecture and Urbanism in Rio de Janeiro and Brasília*, New Haven, Connecticut: Yale University Press, 1973

Gorovitz, Matheus, *Brasília: Uma questão de escala*, São Paulo: Projeto, 1985

Haskell, Douglas, "Brasília: A New Type of National City," *Architectural Forum* 113 (November 1960)

Holston, James, *The Modernist City: An Anthropological Critique of Brasília*, Chicago: University of Chicago Press, 1989

Mohóly-Nagy, Sybil, "Brasília: majestic concept or autocratic," *Progressive Architecture* (October 1959)

Niemeyer, Oscar, "Depoimento/Testimonianza," *Zodiac* 6 (1960)

Niemeyer, Oscar, *Minha experiência em Brasília*, Rio de Janeiro: Vitória, 1961

Niemeyer, Oscar, *Meu sósia e eu*, Rio de Janeiro: Revan, 1992

Niemeyer, Oscar, J.O. Penna Meira, Carlos Alves Souza, et. al., "Brésil, actualités: Brasília," *L'architecture d'aujourd'hui* 31 (June–July 1960)

Petit, Jean, *Niemeyer, poéte d'architecture*, Paris: Bibliothèque des Arts, and Lugano, Italy: Fidia Edizioni d'Arte, 1995

Puppi, Lionello, *Guida a Niemeyer*, Milan: Mondadori, 1987

Underwood, David Kendrick, *Oscar Niemeyer and the Architecture of Brazil*, New York: Rizzoli, 1994

Underwood, David Kendrick, *Oscar Niemeyer and the Brazilian Free-Form Modernism*, New York: Braziller, 1994

FEHN, SVERRE 1924–

Architect, Norway

Sverre Fehn began his career after graduating from the Oslo School of Architecture in 1949. He is one of a number of post–World War II Norwegian architects who believed in bestowing universal modernism with both regional and site-specific values, espousing an architecture that, while always rational, recognized local crafts and culture, mythology, and folklore. His concerns with the topography of the site, climate, local identity, and tectonics are central to issues of both regionalism and phenomenology in architecture.

In 1950, Fehn joined the Progressive Architect's Group of Oslo, Norway (PAGON), a division of the Congrès Internationaux d'Architecture Moderne (CIAM), along with his former teacher Arne Korsmo, architectural theorist Christian Norberg-Schulz, and design collaborators Grung and Ostbye, among others. CIAM was a network concerned with how ideas of modern architecture and town planning were communicated internationally. Although CIAM had no direct influence on his own work, he would have been acquainted with many leading contemporary architects and artists through his association with the Congress.

Between 1952 and 1953, on the advice of Jørn Utzon, Fehn made a journey to study the so-called primitive architecture of Morocco. This journey was seminal to his recognition of eternal themes in architecture, values that existed long before being embraced by the functionalist doctrine of modernist theory. Fehn remarked on the mutual harmony between the structure of natural and man-made place and the relationship between the ground and constructed form, as well as the clarity, simplicity, and common sense of regional architecture regarding systems of environmental control, planning, and construction and how these systems characterized rituals of habitation. It was a journey of recognition rather than discovery that helped Fehn see clearly the character of his native Norway as well as the qualities in the works of earlier modernist masters, such as Le Corbusier, Louis Kahn, Ludwig Mies van der Rohe, and Frank Lloyd Wright.

The poetic modernism of Fehn's architecture derives from a unified and formal relationship between the site and the physical and psychological dimensions of the program and of the people who inhabit his buildings—reduced to a conceptual clarity and expressed through material construction. He describes architecture as a necessary interference with nature, in opposition to it yet also revealing the character of the landscape. His buildings articulate a relationship between earth, sky, and horizon, a recurring theme that is developed through his writings and drawings.

Fehn's buildings are generally constructed of concrete or brick and wood used in a modern rather than traditional way: mass construction to anchor the building to the ground and timber construction to articulate openings in walls or the connection between roof and wall. His timber detailing is reminiscent of the traditions of Nordic boat building and of Japanese architecture. Modular repetition and geometric configuration of structure give spatial definition to both interior volume and exterior surface. The ground plane of his interiors often relates to the natural topography of the site and to external views.

The works of Fehn date back to 1949, when he, with G. Grung, won an international competition for the design of the Craft Museum at Lillehammer. The winning project was never built. Subsequent works and projects typically have been for houses and museums but also include designs for religious, community, education, and recreational buildings.

During the late 1950s and early 1960s Fehn's designs for the Norwegian Pavilion at the Universal Exposition in Brussels (1958), now demolished, and his Pavilion of the Nordic Nations in the Gardens of the Biennale (1962) in Venice, Italy, garnered recognition. Both buildings employed Miesian qualities of a regular grid with a free plan and featured roofs that masterfully controlled the natural light within the exhibition spaces. The Schreiner House (1963) in Oslo, named "Hommage au Japon" by Fehn for its references to spatial relationships and construction in Japanese architecture, consisted of a structural timber fame around a brick central service core—a device developed from his time in the 1950s with Jean Prouvé, an architect noted for his industrialized fabrication and servicing systems. Planning and volumetric geometry developed with the designs of the houses for Arne Bodtker (1965) and his brother Carl (1967, extension 1985).

The masterpiece of his work in the late 1960s and 1970s, however, is the Archbishopric Museum (1979) in Hamar. The site is a ruined medieval fort over which a 19th-century U-shaped barn was built. Space, light, time, and the programmatic requirements of the museum are brought together by a series of concrete ramps and walkways that pass through the barn structure, hover over the medieval excavations, and lead into the courtyard. Parallels with this project can be made to the Castelvecchio Museum by Carlo Scarpa, whom Fehn met while working on the Pavilion of the Nordic Nations in Venice. Fehn's

Archbishopric Museum, Hamar, Norway (1979)
© Richard Dargavel

Archbishopric Museum, Hamar, Norway (1979), interior

ability to develop a clear dialogue among client, site, structure, and form is further exemplified by the Villa Busk (1990) in Bamble. A rocky outcrop chosen by Fehn dictates the physical dimensions and orientation of the house, the linear form of which is broken by a cross axis from the entrance of the main house to a timber tower that in turn provides visual and physical links to the fjord. As with the Hamar museum, a modulated timber structure distinguishes between roof and wall and allows for views out and light in. Fehn's approach set out in Villa Busk is continued in different contexts with the Glacier Museum (1991) in Fjærland and the Aukrust Museum (1996) in Alvdal.

Much of Fehn's work has been in suburban or rural locations, some inaccessible for long periods because of the harsh winter climate. Certain competition projects, notably his design for the Royal Theatre of Copenhagen in Denmark, confirm his capability for both large and urban projects.

RICHARD G. DARGAVEL

See also **Denmark; Expo 1958, Brussels; Glacier Museum, Fjaerland Fjord, Norway; Mies van der Rohe, Ludwig (Germany); Norberg-Schulz, Christian (Norway); Norway; Scarpa, Carlo (Italy); Utzon, Jørn (Denmark)**

Biography

Born in Kongsberg, Norway, 14 August 1924. Studied at the Oslo School of Architecture; degree in architecture 1949. Married Ingrid Løuberg Pettersen 1952: 1 child. Private practice, Oslo from 1949. Received scholarship from the French government to work in Paris for the office of Jean Prouvé 1953–1954. While in Paris befriended Le Corbusier. Professor, Oslo School of Architecture 1971; Carnegie Distinguished Professor, Cooper Union, New York 1980. Designed the Exhibition of Medieval Art (1972) and the Exhibition of Chinese Warriors (1984–85) at the Art Museum, Hovikodden. Lecturer, Architectural Association, London 1981–89; Saarinen Professor, Yale University, New Haven, Connecticut 1986. Founder, Norwegian division of CIAM; member, Order of Leopold, Belgium. Awards include the Grand Gold Medal from the Académie de l'Architecture of Paris 1993; the Henry Tessenow Prize 1997; and the Pritzker Prize for Architecture 1997.

Selected Works

Retirement Home, Okern, Oslo (with G. Grung), 1955
Norwegian Pavilion at the Universal Exposition in Brussels, Belgium, 1958
Pavilion of the Nordic Nations in the Gardens of the Biennale, Venice, Italy, 1962
Schreiner House, Oslo, 1963
A. Bodtker House, Oslo, 1965
Community Centre, Boler, Oslo, 1972
Villa, Norrköping, Sweden, 1964
C. Bodtker Houses 1 and 2, Oslo, 1967; extension, 1985
Sparre House, Skedsmo, 1967
Archbishopric Museum of Hamar, 1979
School for Deaf Children, Skadalen, Oslo, 1977
Atelier Holme, Holmsbu, 1997
Brick House, Bærum, 1987
Villa Busk, Bamble, 1990
Glacier Museum, Fjærland, 1991
Prototype Ecological House, Norrköping, Sweden, 1992
Aukrust Museum, Alvdal, 1996

Selected Publications

Norberg-Schulz, Christian, and Gennaro Postiglione, with an introduction by Francesco Dal Co, *Sverre Fehn: Works, Projects, Writings, 1949–1996*, New York: Monacelli Press, 1997
Nobuyuki Yoshida (editor), *Sverre Fehn Above and Below the Horizon,* A + U, 340/1 (1999)

Further Reading

Fjeld, Per Olaf, *Sverre Fehn: The Thought of Construction*, New York: Rizzoli, 1983
Giardiello, Paulo, *"Sverre Fehn, tra natura e artificio," Casabella*, 60 (June 1996) [Aukrust Museum]
Gronwold, Ulf, "Archaic Modernism: Two Houses, Oslo," *Architectural Review*, 179 (February 1986) [Bodtker House 1 and 2]
Lavalou, Armelle, "Sverre Fehn: Un Moderne en Norvège, avec l'esprit du lieu," L'architecture d'aujourd'hui, 287 (June 1993)
Miles, Henry, "Horizon, Artefact, Nature," *Architectural Review*, 200 (August 1996) [Villa Busk]
Norri, Marja-Riitta, and Marja Kärkkäinen (editors), *The Poetry of the Straight Line: Five Masters of the North*, Helsinki: Museum of Finnish Architecture, 1992

FEMINIST THEORY

Feminist theory in 20th-century architecture encompasses identification of gendered power relations in architectural and urban form and discourse, critique of masculine dominance in the design professions, and creation of "feminist" and "feminine" architectural practices. Influenced by feminism in philosophy, literature, cultural studies, and the social sciences, feminist architectural theory has embraced histories of women in architecture, new types of architectural practice, and the reconceptualization of the "feminine" itself. In architecture, feminist theory has three main tendencies, all of which address gendered power relations and the injustice of masculine domination in architecture. Some theorists celebrate the differences between men and women and take an overtly feminist approach to the critique and reconstruction of architectural practice and history. Others emphasize the struggle for equal access to training and jobs in architecture and for recognition of women's competence in the profession. Another group focuses on theories of gender difference and representation in the built environment, architectural discourse, and cultural value systems.

Feminist architectural theory has its sources in 19th-century feminist thought and the revival of feminism in the 1960s. Betty Friedan's book *The Feminine Mystique* (1963) marked the emergence of a second wave feminism in the United States and, later, around the world. This feminism emerged from the civil rights and anti–Vietnam War movements of the 1950s and 1960s, just as 19th-century feminism developed from abolitionism. "Women's liberation" focused on the pursuit of civil rights and equality. During the 1960s and 1970s, this strategy evolved into the analysis and challenge of gendered power relations. Feminists recognized that while the struggle for equality is ongoing, it left intact the epistemological and representational sources of inequality. They turned their critique to language, social relations, spatial hierarchies, education, history, art, and other means for preserving gender-based relations of power.

In light of the new emphasis on representation and language among feminists, the work of Simone de Beauvoir became central to feminist theory; her book *The Second Sex* is considered one of the greatest works of 20th-century feminist theory (published in France in 1949, translated into English in 1952). Its importance lies in the clarity with which Beauvoir summarized women's condition; in *The Second Sex*, she traced the history of women's reduction to objects for men, their status as man's Other without control over their actions or subjectivity. Beauvoir demonstrated that this assumption dominates social, political, and cultural life. Further, she noted that women internalize this objectified vision as normal and enact their prescribed roles within patriarchy.

Feminist theorists and architects have created alternative practices and histories of architecture. In liberal feminism, there has been a conscious continuity between feminist history, theory, and practice, on the premise that changes to representation of the past contribute to the struggles of living producers. Doris Cole, Dolores Hayden, and Susanna Torre, for example, produced explicitly feminist histories of women in architecture and design. Others, such as Doreen Massey and Leslie Kanes Weisman, authored critiques of the sexism and discrimination against women embedded in and enforced by the built environment. Prominent women practitioners, such as Denise Scott Brown and Patricia Conway, have been advocates for women in professional institutions and critics of masculinism in architecture culture.

Gender theories have been produced by specialists in many disciplines as well as architecture, such as philosophy, anthropology, geography, film studies, and cultural studies, the result of increased interest in theory among architects and in architecture among theorists of other discourses. French philosophy and psychoanalytic theorists, including Hélène Cixous, Jacques Derrida, Luce Irigaray, Julia Kristeva, and Jacques Lacan, have had a particularly strong impact on feminist theory in architecture. The range of gender theory in architecture encompasses textual analysis and philosophical inquiry (Bergren, Grosz, and Ingraham); architectural history read through feminist, postcolonial, psychoanalytic, and poststructural theory (Çelik, Colomina, and Friedman); critical interpretations of gender and identity in architecture culture and the built environment (McLeod and Sanders); and complex work that interrogates gender construction and blurs the boundaries between theory and practice (Bloomer and Diller). This work can be created by men and women since women's equality is not the central, political aim of gender theory; it analyzes and ultimately rejects the dichotomy between masculinity and femininity.

According to early feminist theorists, the sexual binary male/female constructs a series of negative values that define the female as passivity, powerlessness, death, the natural, irrationality, and the Other, whereas the male connotes activity, power, life, the cultural, rationality, and the Self. This hierarchical value system is imbedded with oppositions relating to sexual difference. It generates meaning by placing terms such as "nature" and "culture" in opposition; meaning is acquired only by acknowledging the other term. A crude model for understanding sex and architecture might define the masculine as the alienating, technological outsides of buildings and the feminine as their nurturing, comfortable insides. In this formula, the phallus/exterior stands alone, projects, occupies space as an object, and is coupled with technology and logic. The womb/interior, in this account, protects, creates space, shelters humans, and is affiliated with sensuality and materialism. The problem with such a theory is that it reduces architecture to a series of biologically-based metaphors without interrogating the social and cultural constitution of the linked terms. That is, it attributes fundamentally "feminine" or "masculine," universal essences to female and male biology (their sex), which are represented in cultural and social phenomena such as buildings.

In the 1970s, feminists made a crucial distinction between biological *sex* (their sexual organs and their biological functions as women) and *gender* (their social identity and the cultural associations of the feminine). The term "sex" seemed, to many feminists, to consign men and women to fixed roles, and they seized on "gender" as a more fluid, socially constituted category. Beauvoir's famous assertion "One is not born a woman, but, rather, becomes one" summarizes the split between sex and gender. Sex implied that being a woman was an innate, biological state, whereas gender connoted the process by which female humans became "women." Beauvoir noted that "the individuals that compose society are never abandoned to the dictates of their nature; they are subject rather to that second nature which is custom. . . . It is not merely as a body, but rather as a body subject to taboos, to laws, that the subject is conscious of himself." Gender is, therefore, a culturally and socially constructed category of difference, not fixed or stable; according to feminist theorists, it has no "natural" basis.

The idea that there is an "essential" women's nature or experience was further challenged during the 1980s; feminist theorists rejected "essentialism" because it reduced women to a homogeneous image based on their bodies (their biology) and a universal "woman's experience" that was the same for all women regardless of their age, race, or class. Women of color criticized white feminists for creating an exclusively white, middle-class image of women. Informed by critiques of essentialism, feminists have scrutinized dominant, stereotypical images of women and assumptions about gender roles, often through a parody of the pervasive mechanisms of the media. Writers and critics such as bell hooks and Adrian Piper have investigated the ways racial difference is interconnected with sexual difference in dominant regimes of power.

Recent feminist theory has challenged the sex/gender dichotomy itself as an ideological construct. Judith Butler has defined gender as more than the imposition of meaning on "sex"; gender is the very cultural and discursive processes by which the sexes are established, according to Butler. Lesbian critics, such as Monique Wittig, have challenged the heterosexual bias of straight feminism and the inadequacy of the male/female binary, positing a transgressive character of lesbian identity, neither stereotypically "feminine" nor "masculine." The essays collected by Joel Sanders in *Stud* explore such reconceptualizations of gender, sexuality, and identity in architectural discourse and design.

Feminist theorists in architecture have turned to a critique of the masculinist underpinnings of architectural discourse, both written and formal. A central concern of feminist theory has been the definition of the architect as a masterful, socially isolated individual whose genius and vision are imprinted on his designs. The conflation of the male body, illustrated by Vitruvius's famous diagram of a male circumscribed by a circle and a square, exemplifies the dominance of a masculine norm in architecture. It is precisely this model that feminist theorists reject, seeking new models of identity and practice. The interrogation of the architect's position in society informs feminist practices such as Matrix and Liquid Incorporated founded on collaboration rather than individual, competitive action. Diana Agrest has critiqued the history the Vitruvian model and provided an alternative based on the theory of *écriture féminine* (feminine writing). According to Agrest, women can place themselves outside the system of architecture by reconfiguring their marginal position and creating an architecture of the repressed, denied, excluded, and hidden.

More recently, feminist theory in architecture has returned to the themes of the body and the everyday experience of women. Feminists have used fashion, the home, and domesticity as a central theme in their work and have produced commentaries, parodies, historical critiques, performances, and alternative practices to critique architecture culture. Jennifer Bloomer's work, for example, plays with language to create new forms of thought and expression in both writing and design. Her essay and project "Abodes of Theory and Flesh: Tabbles of Bower" reads the foundational texts of architecture, from the Renaissance to the present in order to analyze the relationships between the feminine and ornamentation, the masculine and structure. In a series of important essays (see the works by Agrest, Coleman, and Fausch), Mary McLeod has dissected gender, fashion, modernity, "otherness," and the everyday in relation to the feminine in architecture culture.

The simultaneous appearance in 1996 of three major anthologies of feminist writing on architecture signaled the significance of feminist architectural theory. These collections joined a growing body of work (see, for instance the works by Bergren, Colomina, and Fausch) that interrogates the social construction of sexual difference in architectural history, theory, and practice. In their introduction to *The Sex of Architecture*, Diana Agrest, Patricia Conway, and Leslie Kanes Weisman claim that "women writing on architecture today are exploring history, the uses of public space, consumerism, and the role of domesticity in search of 'ways into' architecture, often through alternative forms of practice and education." Francesca Hughes, in *The Architect: Reconstructing Her Practice*, contends that "the absence of women from the profession of architecture remains, despite the various theories, very difficult to explain and very slow to change. . . . One simple and obvious reason for [the lack of feminist criticism in architecture] is the very small number of architects who might choose to apply feminist criticism to architecture: a constituency most easily identifiable as women architects." By contrast, Debra Coleman, Elizabeth Danze, and Carol Henderson, editors of *Architecture and Feminism*, propose a strategic relationship between architecture and feminism that would be forged "out of the desire to produce intertextual work that contests an unjust social order."

PATRICIA MORTON

See also **Agrest, Diana, and Mario Gandelsonas (United States); Postmodernism; Poststructuralism; Scott Brown, Denise (United States)**

Further Reading

Agrest, Diana, *Architecture from Without: Theoretical Framings for a Critical Practice*, Cambridge, Massachusetts: MIT Press, 1991

Agrest, Diana, Patricia Conway, and Leslie Kanes Weisman (editors), *The Sex of Architecture*, New York: Abrams, 1996

Beauvoir, Simone de, *Le deuxième sexe*, 2 vols., Paris: Gallimard, 1949; as *The Second Sex*, translated by H.M. Parshley, New York: Knopf, 1952; London: JonathanCape, 1953

Bergren, Ann, "Architecture, Gender, Philosophy," in *Strategies in Architectural Thinking*, edited by John Whiteman, Jeffrey Kipnis, and Richard Burdett, Chicago: Institute for Architecture and Urbanism, 1992

Berkeley, Ellen Perry, and Matilda McQuaid (editors), *Architecture: A Place for Women*, London and Washington, D.C.: Smithsonian Institution Press, 1989

Bloomer, Jennifer, "Abodes of Theory and Flesh: Tabbles of Bower," *Assemblage* 17 (April 1992)

Brown, Denise Scott, "Room at the Top? Sexism and the Star System in Architecture," in *Architecture: A Place for Women*, edited by Ellen Perry Berkeley and Matilda McQuaid, London and Washington, D.C.: Smithsonian Institution Press, 1989

Butler, Judith P., *Gender Trouble: Feminism and the Subversion of Identity*, New York: Routledge, 1990

Çelik, Zeynep, "Le Corbusier, Orientalism, Colonialism," *Assemblage* 17 (1992)

Cole, Doris, *From Tipi to Skyscraper: A History of Women in Architecture*, Boston: i press, 1973

Coleman, Debra, Elizabeth Danze, and Carol Henderson (editors), *Architecture and Feminism*, New York: Princeton Architectural Press, 1996

Colomina, Beatriz (editor), *Sexuality and Space*, New York: Princeton Architectural Press, 1992
Fausch, Deborah, et al. (editors), *Architecture: In Fashion*, New York: Princeton Architectural Press, 1994
Friedan, Betty, *The Feminine Mystique*, New York: Norton, and London: Gollancz, 1963
Friedman, Alice T., *Women and the Making of the Modern House: A Social and Architectural History*, New York: Abrams, 1998
Grosz, Elizabeth A., *Space, Time, and Perversion: Essays on the Politics of Bodies*, New York and London: Routledge, 1995
Hayden, Dolores, *The Grand Domestic Revolution: A History of Feminist Designs for American Homes, Neighborhoods, and Cities*, Cambridge, Massachusetts: MIT Press, 1981
Hughes, Francesca (editor), *The Architect: Reconstructing Her Practice*, Cambridge, Massachusetts: MIT Press, 1996
Ingraham, Catherine, *Architecture and the Burdens of Linearity*, New Haven, Connecticut: Yale University Press, 1998
Massey, Doreen, *Space, Place, and Gender*, Cambridge: Polity, and Minneapolis: University of Minnesota Press, 1994
Matrix, *Making Space: Women and the Man-Made Environment*, London: Pluto Press, 1984
Millett, Kate, *Sexual Politics*, Garden City, New York: Doubleday, and London: Virago, 1970
Moi, Toril, *Sexual/Textual Politics: Feminist Literary Theory*, London and New York: Methuen, 1985
Morton, Patricia, "The Social and the Poetic: Feminist Practices in Architecture, 1970–1999," *Magasin för aodern arkitektur* 26 (2000)
Pollock, Griselda, *Vision and Difference: Femininity, Feminism, and Histories of Art*, London and New York: Routledge, 1988
Rendell, Jane, Barbara Penner, and Iain Borden (editors), *Gender Space Architecture: An Interdisciplinary Introduction*, London and New York: Routledge, 2000
Sanders, Joel (editor), *Stud: Architectures of Masculinity*, New York: Princeton Architectural Press, 1996
Torre, Susana (editor), *Women in American Architecture: A Historic and Contemporary Perspective*, New York: Whitney Library of Design, 1977
Weisman, Leslie Kanes, *Discrimination by Design: A Feminist Critique of the Man-Made Environment*, Urbana: University of Illinois Press, 1992

FENG SHUI

Feng Shui dates from before the earliest dynasty in China, when its principles were first used to locate family graves to ensure good luck for all future descendants. Loosely translated as "wind and water," the term *Feng Shui* refers to the practice of discerning the harmonic arrangements of natural elements so as to enhance the flow of the life force, or Chi; for Western audiences, the term is most directly defined as "geomancy" or "divination." In the context of design, Feng Shui encourages a healthy and ecological approach to the built environment, such that humans and nature live together in the best possible relationship. In creating a sensitive environment, Feng Shui not only balances the natural forces of the universe but also cares for the psychic well-being of humankind. Feng Shui does not deny the cyclical forces of nature, which ultimately ensure that good and bad luck ebb and flow at different times; rather, its primary goal is to achieve the optimum balance between contrasting opposites to the benefit of human existence.

Feng Shui's principles center on the idea that the Chi must flow freely in and around the human environment. A positive flow of Chi will have a positive influence on humankind, allowing one's labors to reach their highest level of success. According to Feng Shui masters, the Chi can radiate with lesser and greater force up from the earth. The strength of the Chi can be read from the natural elements and the physical appearance of a location. For example, mountains and volcanoes show where the Chi has risen above the earth, whereas arid deserts demonstrate a lack of Chi. Feng Shui masters can measure the quantity of Chi present in an area by observing the soil and vegetation and noting the position of natural elements, such as mountains and waterways, relative to a particular site. Humankind is also an element in determining the relationship between the earth and the Chi, and the human body can, like the earth, demonstrate a good or bad flow of Chi. Healthy bodies are seen as a reflection of a good and positive flow of Chi, whereas sickness indicates an unhealthy element. Because there is no end and no beginning to Chi, humans can be both the cause and the solution to the negative flow, such that the person influences the flow of the Chi in the environment or the environment affects the level of Chi in the person. In either case, the problem can usually be corrected by following the guidance of a Feng Shui master.

In observing the flow of the Chi, Feng Shui requires that the contrasting forces of nature be balanced in harmonic arrangements. This principle is explained through the concepts of Yin and Yang, which are identified by a half-white, half-black circle. Yin and Yang represent dualities, or opposites, within the Chi, such that together they balance into a whole. For example, Yin is dark, passive, and female, whereas Yang is light, active, and male. Generally, these primordial forces are seen as complementary, and they symbolize the harmony of the universe, for without the one, there cannot be the other. Feng Shui seeks to balance the two by matching the Yin elements with the Yang. In terms of landscape, an area that is rich in Yin might lack Yang and thus will not bring good fortune to the owner. In many cases, however, a deficiency of either Yin or Yang can be corrected by the placement of certain objects—mirrors, fishbowls, or plants—to reflect and enhance the flow of the missing element.

Feng Shui masters can further discern the flow of Chi through the use of trigrams. Like coins, trigrams have two outcomes, whole or broken, which are represented by one long straight line or two short ones, respectively. Trigrams usually come in sets of three, thus making eight individual arrangements of long and short lines. Each of these patterns represents a quality (nature, heaven, earth, thunder, mountain, fire, wind, lake, and water), and they may also represent family relationships, directions, time, and change. When properly aligned with a compass, trigrams can ensure that the proper placement of furniture, doorways, windows, and rooms occurs under the most favorable conditions. Trigrams can been seen as types of omens, but they also ensure that the cycles of humans and nature are respected and remind humanity that the universe is never static.

The principles of Feng Shui encourage buildings to be placed, designed, and arranged with reference to particularly lucky attributes within the landscape. Feng Shui masters recommend that houses and offices be sheltered on their north side by a mountain or hill and that a source of water be placed to the south. Houses should always face south to appreciate the sun and the fresh winds from that direction, and they should be set up on the land rather than down in a hollow. In plan, houses should not have windows or doors opposite each other and should not have sharp angles or tight proportions. Particular rooms should be located farther from others; for example, the kitchen should not open directly onto the living room, and the stove should be in the southeast corner. For interior decor, beds should be elevated from the ground and should not face the west, unless the resident's astrology says otherwise. Beds should also not be positioned opposite open doors or too near the windows, as this will affect sleeping patterns. Other furniture may be placed according to a Feng Shui compass that directs which sections of the room will be lucky, thus encouraging the prosperity of the family.

Feng Shui is still practiced today not only the East but in the West as well. In China, Feng Shui masters are routinely consulted for readings on projects that range from houses to skyscrapers. Most recently, I.M. Pei's Hong Kong Bank was positioned according to Feng Shui principles, with a hill behind it and a gentle slope leading to the harbor in front. Once completed, the Hong Kong Bank was regarded as having favorably respected the principles of Feng Shui, unlike its neighbor, the Bank of China, whose sharp corners, domineering scale, and shiny facade negatively affected the surrounding neighborhood. Residents complained that the Bank of China's mirrorlike facade reflected bad elements back to the neighborhood and that the sharp angles cut into the local businesses like knives. Since its completion, the Bank of China has not been well regarded by the population and has had some trouble finding tenants. In the West, Feng Shui has become popular among designers who respect the principles of harmony and balance with nature, and Feng Shui experts are routinely consulted for interior decorating and even for architectural design. Despite their age, the principles of Feng Shui resonate with a modern society that still strives for a healthy, balanced lifestyle.

CATHERINE W. ZIPF

See also **Bank of China Tower, Hong Kong; Pei, I.M. (United States)**

Further Reading

Many useful books that explain the principles of Feng Shui are readily available in any local bookstore. Most of these books address the application of Feng Shui to the home; see O'Brien for an example. A good history of Feng Shui can be found in Rossbach (1998). For information on Feng Shui in the garden, see Keswick.

Brown, Simon, *Feng Shui*, San Francisco: Thorsons, 1996

Hyder, Carole J., *Wind and Water: Your Personal Feng Shui Journey*, Minneapolis, Minnesota: Hyden Enterprises, 1998

Keswick, Maggie, *The Chinese Garden: History, Art, and Architecture*, New York: Rizzoli, 1978

Knapp, Ronald G., *China's Living Houses: Folk Beliefs, Symbols, and Household Ornamentation*, Honolulu: University of Hawaii Press, 1999

O'Brien, Joanne, and Kwok Man Ho, *The Elements of Feng Shui*, Shaftesbury, Dorset, and Rockport, Maine: Element Books, 1991

Rossbach, Sarah, *Feng Shui: The Chinese Art of Placement*, New York: Penguin, 1991

Rossbach, Sarah, *Feng Shui Design: From History and Landscape to Modern Gardens and Interiors*, New York: Viking Press, and London: Sidgwick and Jackson, 1998

Simons, T. Raphael, *Feng Shui Step by Step*, New York: Crown, 1996

Skinner, Stephen, *The Living Earth Manual of Feng Shui: Chinese Geomancy*, Boston and London: Routledge and K. Paul, 1982

Wydra, Nancilee, *Feng Shui: The Book of Cures*, Chicago: Contemporary Books, 1996

FERRISS, HUGH 1889–1962

Urban designer, United States

Best known for his dramatic depictions of the monumental architecture of a futuristic, urban utopia, Hugh Ferriss contributed significantly in the 1920s and 1930s to an appreciation for urban design within academic and professional circles, but more so among a lay audience. Although he was a licensed architect, he chose not to build. He dedicated his career to drawing, writing, and urban planning, becoming the preferred renderer and consultant to some of the most notable practitioners of his day. Although Ferriss shared with his modernist peers a belief in architecture's agency in improving urban society, he rejected the industrial references assumed in many of their proposals. He sought to invest his designs with a spirituality that he felt absent both in international style modernism and in an America dominated by corporate activity; the skyscraper—the new icon of that activity—became his fundamental subject. His writings remained less polemical and ultimately less influential than those of his modernist contemporaries, whereas his widely circulated images became more influential. Although the last decades of Ferriss's career paled in comparison to his earlier notoriety, in the 1940s he could still be lauded by such populist magazines as *Time* as "U.S. architecture's most grandiose seer."

Ferriss's fame as an urban-design visionary proceeded from a pragmatic issue. After New York City passed its zoning ordinance in 1916, which was intended to improve the access of light and air into cavernous streets, new buildings were required to reduce their massing as they rose in height. Ferriss's "four stages" zoning envelope studies, published in 1922 in collaboration with the architect Harvey Wiley Corbett, show the gradual erosion of a tall block into a series of variously sized, adjacent, parallel slabs and were the first studies to make architectural sense of this zoning legislation. He championed his zoning solution, stating that the "efficiency and health of city life must be accepted as mandatory requirements," and he reinforced his brand of modernistic architectural moralism and determinism, saying, "We are not contemplating the new architecture of a city . . . we are contemplating the new architecture of a civilization." In 1930, the historian and critic Sheldon Cheney wrote, "More than any other architect . . . Ferriss influenced the imagination of designers, students, and public. Many a building of 1928–29 looks like a fulfillment of a Ferriss idealistic sketch of four or five years earlier." Indeed, his zoning study became a model for tall structures throughout the United States.

Most of Ferriss's renderings stemmed from commercial commissions for clients who wished to join, for their benefit, 1920s economic optimism with the progressive spirit that his drawings invoked. He also collaborated frequently with architects of the caliber of Raymond Hood and Wallace Harrison and became the public-image-giver to projects such as Rockefeller Center, the United Nations, Lincoln Center, and the New York World's Fair. Despite the fact that Ferriss had an aesthetic penchant for the architecture of modern capitalism, he recognized the skyscraper as "a symbol of an age in which there is no spirituality." Yet he believed that capitalism's power might be used to reform the city. His commercial work became intellectual and formal fodder for his theoretical explorations, which strove to reinvest architecture with humanistic dimension. Unlike most of his modernist peers, who may also be called "visionary," Ferriss maintained that modern technology was stifling the human spirit and chose to regard the city as an extension of nature rather than the machine. He emphasized organic, geological, and metaphysical analogies in reference to the "crystalline" properties of his architecture. Ultimately, Ferriss's intentions rarely transcended symbolic gesture.

Ferriss's best-known publication, *The Metropolis of Tomorrow* (1929), was a testament to his rendering talents, his idealism, and his commitment to fashioning structures whose effect would restore architecture's lost emotional content. The book was divided into three parts. The first part, "The City of Today," features many of the tower renderings that established his career. The second part, "Projected Trends," depicts work ranging from his realistic zoning studies to such fantastic proposals as multitiered streets clinging to the 20th story of a building facade. Ferriss recognized the far-fetched nature of his proposals, yet he surmised that they were nonetheless inevitable. The final part of the book, "An Imaginary Metropolis," summarizes his design theories for a utopian city. In his Metropolis, vast boulevards slide through a midrise urban fabric and link mile-high towers with gardens arranged on the ledges of their stepped-back massings. For all its visionary appearance, it was formally little more than a City Beautiful scheme; with no provision for industrial sectors or housing, it addressed only a bourgeois citizenry. The city's core, comprised of a triangulated business, art, and science zone punctuated by a soaring "tower of philosophy," underscored Ferriss's desires for a humanistic city yet proffered no plausible social, political, or economic theory by which to implement the new society. Ironically, the publication of his urban scheme coincided exactly with the financial collapse of 1929, sobering his faith in architecture's reach.

Ferriss's second book, *Power in Buildings: An Artist's View of Contemporary Architecture* (1953), was far less ambitious in scope. Produced following a journey across the country, the book portrays what he considered to be America's most inspirational structures, ranging from recently completed hydroelectric dams to pre-Columbian pyramids. Almost embarrassed by his earlier naïveté, he began to dedicate his drawing skills to built and pending designs rather than imaginary architecture; his rejection of capitalism's ability to work for social change is signaled by the book's near absence of high-rise towers.

Although Ferriss was alternately considered an architectural theorist and a delineator of remarkable talent, history has established him only as the latter. Ferriss rejected the Beaux-Arts representational tenets that he was taught at Washington University in St. Louis; he felt that emphasis on two-dimensional drawing—plans, sections, and elevation—was foreign to human experience. Likewise, he rejected the isometric representations used by his staunchly modernist peers, stating that such techniques yielded passionless images and, by extension, passionless architecture. Ferriss conveyed his ideas nearly exclusively through perspective. The drawings for which he ultimately became renowned were noteworthy not for their accuracy (he took technical liberties in order to show multiple vantage points in one view) but for their emotive capacity. Ferriss-conceived architecture revealed through a subtractive process, leaving ultimately finely chiseled masses where historical ornament was subjugated to smoothly massed surfaces. After building up layers of carbon, he would begin to reveal the form of his subject through erasure, yielding scenes whereby his architecture would appear as a brilliant beacon. If the purpose of the setback ordinance was to suffuse the city of darkness with light, then his system of erasure and the dark-to-light techniques of his drawings were an appropriate parallel to this transformation. Although Ferriss's work continued to be well received by the general public, professional and academic communities tended to be less generous. In 1954, six years before Ferriss's death in New York City, the architectural historian Vincent Scully dismissed Ferriss as "the last in a line of romantic-classic architectural artists which began with Piranesi and Boullee."

PAUL DUBELLET KARIOUK

See also **Hood, Raymond (United States); Harrison, Wallace K., and Max Abramovitz (United States); Rockefeller Center, New York City; United Nations Headquarters, New York City**

Biography

Born in St. Louis, Missouri, 12 July 1889. Attended the School of Engineering and Architecture at Washington University in St. Louis from 1906–11; moved to New York City in 1913; between 1913 and 1915, employed by Cass Gilbert during the final stages of the Woolworth Building. Married Dorothy Lapham, an art editor and illustrator for *Vanity Fair*, in 1914. In 1915 opened his own freelance rendering office, which he maintained until his death; included renderings in the 1925 "Titan City Exhibition" in New York City—the most significant exploration to that date of the future city; invited to hang his first solo show, "Drawings of the Future City," at New York's Anderson Galleries 1925; his publication in 1929 of *The Metropolis of Tomorrow* coincided with the start of the Great Depression; renderer and consultant to the New York World's Fair ("Building the World of Tomorrow") 1936–39; awarded an "Arnold W. Brunner" grant from the Architectural League of New York in 1940 and began journey across the United States, collecting material for *Power in Buildings* (1953); solo show at the Whitney Museum of American Art, New York 1942; renderer and consultant to the United Nations design project 1946–49. President of the New York chapters of the Architectural League and American Institute of Architects. Died in New York City, 29 January 1962.

Selected Works

Zoning Envelope Studies (with Harvey Wiley Corbett), New York City, 29 January 1922

World's Fair (delineator and design consultant), New York City, 1939

Rockefeller Center (delineator and design consultant), New York City, 1940

United Nations Headquarters (delineator and design consultant), New York City, 1949

Selected Publications

"Truth in Architectural Rendering," *Journal of the American Institute of Architects*, 13 (March 1925)
The Metropolis of Tomorrow, 1929; reprinted, 1986
"Rendering, Architectural," in *The Encyclopaedia Britannica*, 14th edition, 1929–61; revised 1961–73 and retitled "Architectural Rendering"
"How Hugh Ferriss Draws," *American Architect*, 140 (July 1931)
Power in Buildings: An Artist's View of Contemporary Architecture, 1953

Further Reading

Although Ferriss's name was a common fixture in the daily press of his time (owing both to the number of his writings and the frequency with which his work was reviewed in the press), very few in-depth studies of his work have been undertaken. The larger portion of Ferriss's archive resides in the Avery Architectural Library, Columbia University.

Huxtable, Ada Louise, "Looking Back at the World of Tomorrow," *New York Times Magazine* (January 1975)
Leich, Jean Ferriss, *Architectural Visions: The Drawings of Hugh Ferriss*, New York: Whitney Library of Design, 1980
Santuccio, Salvatore, "L'architettura 'Dark' nei disegni del Giovane Ferriss," *Parametro*, 168 (September–October 1988)
Willis, Carol, "The Early Works of Hugh Ferriss" (Master's thesis), Columbia University, 1976
Willis, Carol, "Drawing towards Metropolis," in reprint edition of *The Metropolis of Tomorrow*, by Hugh Ferriss, Princeton, New Jersey: Princeton Architectural Press, 1986
Willis, Carol, "Unparalleled Perspectives: The Drawings of Hugh Ferriss," *Daidalos*, 25 (September 1987)

FIAT WORKS (LINGOTTO), TURIN, ITALY

Designed by Giacomo Matté Trucco completed 1916–1926

In 1916 the Italian automobile company Fiat, with Giovanni Agnelli at its helm, began the construction of a modern factory that would take ten years to build and that epitomized the American multistory concrete factory as established by architect Albert Kahn for Henry Ford in the Highland Park Plant outside of Detroit in 1912, but with its own innovations. Fiat's earlier factories, typical of the time, were traditional multistoried brick structures in the center of cities. With Lingotto Fiat Works, Fiat moved out of Turin, south of the center, to the west of the Po River on the via Nizza. There they could improve their production methods and built a production space at an unprecedented scale for European industries.

In 1912, Agnelli, Fiat's founder, impressed with Ford's automobile plants which he had seen in Detroit, returned to Italy with the desire to build a factory similar both in construction and production techniques. By hiring an engineer, Giacomo Matté Trucco, to head the development, Agnelli immediately signaled the direction of the project. Construction began in 1916 as a way to promote work and labor instead of war. It also established his dynasty and the company's growth; similar to the patriarchal attitude of Ford, he wanted to help the working class.

Matté Trucco, trained at the Politecnico (Polytechnic Institute) of Turin as an industrial engineer, spearheaded the production engineering and building planning. Based on Taylor's scientific theory of efficency for productive work and constant mechanization of labor force, the production line was a continuous flow from the entering of the raw materials to the assembly of the parts, and to the completion of a car and was exemplary in factory design at the time.

The factory complex consisted of a main production building with smaller buildings for preassembly work, and a separate office building, called the Palazzina (little palace), completed in 1921. The design of the management offices was more traditional than the plant itself, with a doric portico at its entrance. The main production building was often compared to a skyscraper lying on its side and was without cellars or basements. It comprises two long workshops that run parallel for a third of a mile and connected at the ends, creating an elongated ring. At regular intervals, the long sides are linked by towers—two inside and one at each end—to create the four interior courtyards. At the south end is a square press-shop; on the north, a five-story building is part of the assembly workshop.

The building composition exemplified efficient auto production of the time: Assembly was begun on the ground floor, then cars were then taken up spiral ramps to consecutive upper floors for further assembly and, finally, to the roof for a test drive on the track. This was actually opposite to the Ford system, where the auto parts were taken up to the top floor and then the car was assembled as it descended to lower floors and finally out to the street. However, by the time Fiat Works was built, it was out-of-date, as Ford had begun his single-volume one-story factories.

Fiat Works is significant as one of the first modular concrete buildings in Europe. Matté Trucco was influenced by the work of the French engineer François Hennébique, whose structures Matté Trucco had seen with his engineer father. Matté Trucco repeated a square reinforced concrete module, 19 feet 8 inches by 19 feet 8 inches by 16 feet 5 inches high, to construct a 1664-foot-long (1/3 mile) by 264-foot-wide and 88-foot-high building with four interior courtyards.

Within the modular concrete grid there are over 2000 steel sash–awning multiple-paned windows that admit plenty of daylight to the interior spaces. Square concrete columns with chamfered edges that, architectural critic and historian Reyner Banham noted, were like those in the factories in the United States, are spaced six meters apart to create as open an interior as possible. More innovative were the perforated horizontal beams with regular rectangular holes for pipes and conduits.

The two major engineering accomplishments include the one-kilometer-long rooftop test track and the two poured-in-place spiral ramps at the north and south ends of the factory. The truck-size ramps are outstanding sculptural constructions that move cars to the roof track for testing without eliminating valued manufacturing space. The ramps were also used for hand trucks and for pulling car parts floor to floor. The ovular rooftop test track with banked curves at each end allowed cars to be tested at speeds up to 60 miles an hour, exceeding normal highway speeds at the time.

Renowned architects praised Fiat Works when it was completed. Le Corbusier described the factory after his visit there in the 1920s as where "the windows in a grille-like pattern are

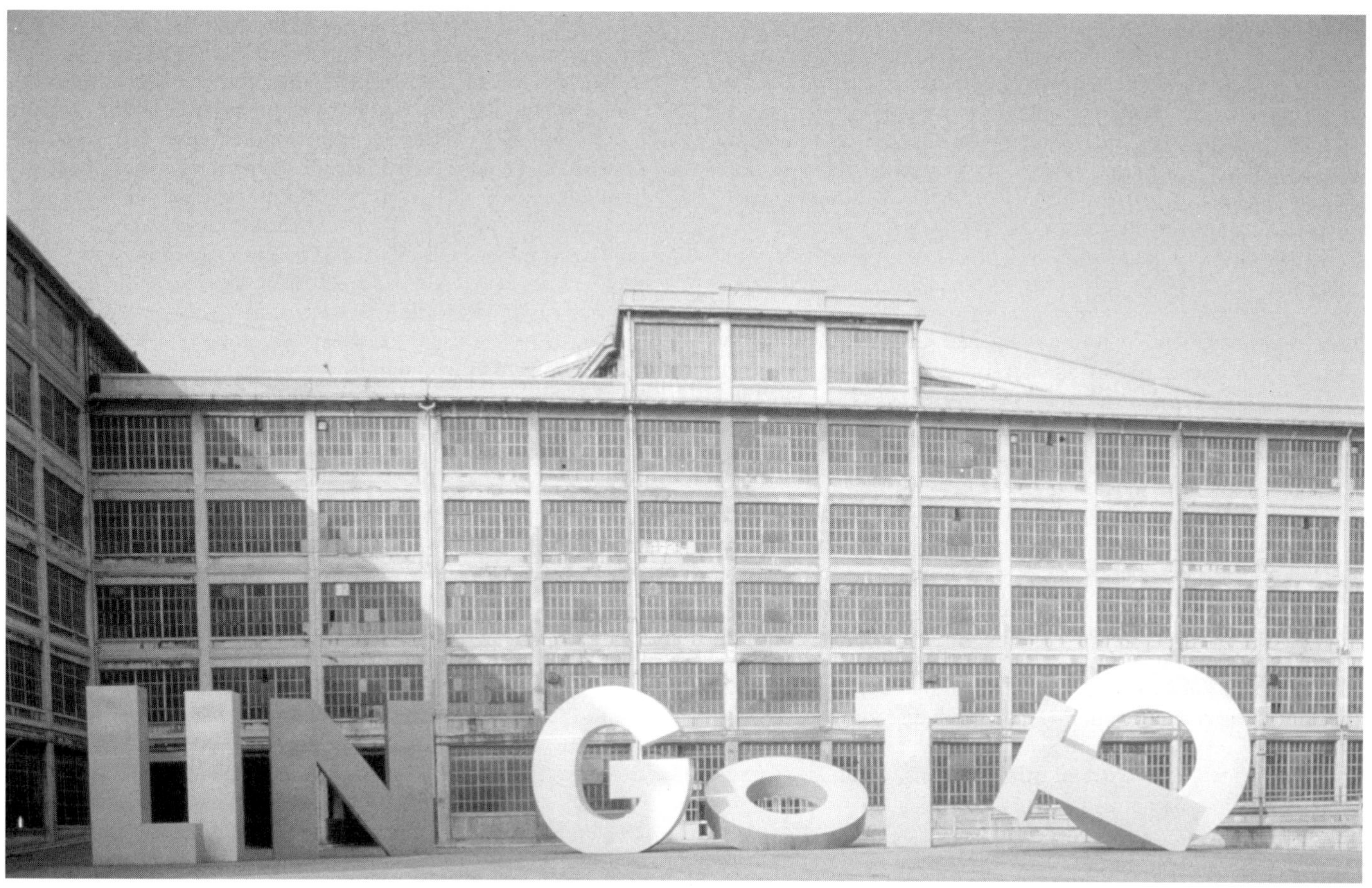

Lingotto Fiat Works, Turin, Italy (1926)
© Francesco Venturi/CORBIS

too numerous to count. The top is like that of a taffrail of a ship, with decks, chimneys, courtyard and catwalks. Surely one of industry's most impressive sights. . . . It is the Esprit Nouveau factory, useful in its precision and with the greatest clarity, elegance and economy" (Banham, 1986).

Edoardo Persico wrote of it in 1927 as the "ultimate metaphysic of form" and said of the track, "so here the car and its speed are celebrated in a form that presides over the work of the factory below, not only in terms of unity but also following a secret standard that governs the ends of things."

The building is significant not only in architectural history but in social history as well. After it was built, it had to be part of emergency plans for post–World War I assistance. During the Depression, the company had the normal internal troubles. In 1943, it was bombed, but the structure resisted destruction as Turin workers faced Mussolini. Then in the 1980s, when the plant closed, demolition was considered. Instead, Fiat held an ideas competition for reuse, which architect Renzo Piano won, and subsequently transformed the building complex into a conference center that opened in 1995.

NINA RAPPAPORT

See also **Banham, Reyner (United States); Concrete: Factory; Kahn, Albert (United States); Píano, Renzo (Italy)**

Further Reading

Banham, Reyner, *A Concrete Atlantis: U.S. Industrial Building and European Modern Architecture*, Cambridge, Massachusetts: MIT Press, 1986

Persico, Edoardo, *Tutte le Opere, 1923–1935*, edited by Giulia Veronesi, 1964, Milan: Edizioni di Comunita, as quoted in Reyner Banhan, *A Concrete Atlantis*, Cambridge, Massachusetts: MIT Press, 1986

Rappaport, Nina, "Linking Lingotto to the City and the Future," *Historic Preservation News* (October/November 1993)

FINLAND

Twentieth-century Finnish architecture, with few exceptions, has moved within the flow of contemporaneous international developments. Within this larger construct, Finnish architects have simultaneously developed qualities that are particular to the cultural and natural condition of the country. Over the past half-century, the Finns have not forsaken modernism but have continued to examine and inspect its potential, creating a legacy of superb works in architecture and planning.

Toward the end of the 19th century, a growth in national self-awareness occurred in Finland as well as in other European countries. Although this nationalism was partially based on an interest in seeking national cultural origins, it was also fostered by the establishment and growth of democratic institutions that accompanied industrial development. In response to the repression of the regime of Czar Nicholas II during the 1890s, Finland sought political independence through national self-assertion. Within the Finnish arts, the search for a national cultural identity resulted in a movement known as National Romanticism.

With the 1849 edition of the *Kalevala*, the Finnish national folk epic, the arts were provided with powerful poetic imagery that led to the development of a national form of artistic expression that moved from painting to music and eventually to architecture. The music of Jan Sibelius and the paintings of Akseli Gallén-Kallela express this urge toward national identity. For architects, the question of the period was, What qualities were required for a national architecture? The Finnish Pavilion for the 1900 Paris World's Fair, by the firm Gesellius Lindgren and Saarinen, was the first occasion for a public expression of National Romanticism. The work contained many of the formal features that would characterize National Romantic architecture: picturesque compositions with irregular asymmetrical plans and masses employing tactile and rough materials. Ragged and irregular building volumes and profiles are complemented through the use of heavily rusticated masonry surfaces, protruding log ends, and numerous textural variations in materials. Often, the ornamentation featured motifs derived from Finnish nature and folklore: bears, squirrels, and other animals, along with pinecones, tree boughs, and the occasional character from folklore were sculpted decorative motifs.

The work of Gesellius, Lindgren and Saarinen and of individuals such as Lars Sonck, Selim Lindqvist, Usko Nyström, and the architect Vivi Lönn exemplified the very best of Finnish National Romanticism. Hvitträsk (1902), the home and studio of Gesellius, Lindgren, and Saarinen, combines the organizational pattern of a Finnish vernacular farm complex with massing elements from medieval stone churches. The interiors continue these direct references and include an interlocking log living space and a sitting room decorated like medieval church vaults. The Pohja Insurance Building (1901) and several apartment complexes in Helsinki are of rough masonry construction that references the work of American architect Henry Hobson Richardson. Among the most powerful works of the period was the firm's National Museum (designed 1901, completed 1915), which incorporates direct references to Finnish medieval churches and fortresses. Lars Sonck's best work of the period includes the Eira Hospital (1905), a bank interior (1904), and the Richardson-influenced Telephone Building (1905), all located in Helsinki. However, his Tampere Cathedral (1907) is a true masterpiece: it is a fully integrated work of art and architecture, assimilating a variety of references into a bold, assertive building. Other important works of the period include Usko Nyström's evocative Valtion Hotel in Imatra (1903) and Onni Tarjanne's National Theater (1902). Many of the works of this period were important cultural buildings symbolizing Finland as an emerging nation with a sophisticated population.

Finland had several women architects practicing during this period, all of whom attended the Polytechnic Institute in Helsinki. Although Signe Hornborg and Signe Lagerborg-Stenius engaged in major commissions during the National Romantic period, it was Vivi Lönn who was a major force during the first two decades of the 20th century. Her best National Romantic work, all located in Tampere, included the Finnish Girl's School (1902), the Alexander School (1904), and the Central Fire Station (1908), along with other educational and domestic projects.

Two buildings, although appearing National Romantic, signal the movement toward a more classical approach to design among Finland's architectural leaders: Eliel Saarinen's (the partnership was dissolved by 1907) Helsinki Railroad Station (1914) and Lars Sonck's Helsinki Stock Exchange (1911). Both works have a classical restraint and control and eschew the compositional excesses of National Romanticism. Although National Romanticism had provided Finland with an international reputation, the style seemed regressive and heavy. The younger architects desired to generate a purer and more rational form of expression. The exaggerations of National Romanticism gave way to a classicizing tendency emergent throughout Scandinavia before World War I.

Finnish classicism of the 1920s is exemplified by the use of simply proportioned geometric volumes with sparsely decorated stucco surfaces. The flat, stuccoed surfaces with crisply modeled classical appointments recall the neoclassicism of early 18th-century Finnish architects Carl Ludwig Engel and Carlo Bassi and the simple classically inspired architecture found in the towns and villages throughout Italy. Despite their classical uniforms, the buildings of the 1920s contain a number of nonclassical characteristics. The plan orders are often distorted, making use of asymmetrical compositions rather than axial or symmetrical ones. A freer disposition of plan elements occurs to accommodate both functional necessities and the exigencies of context. The work of Hilding Ekelund, J.S. Siren, Erik Bryggman, Sigurd Frosterus, and Alvar and Aino Aalto embrace this direction.

Two major works, J.S. Siren's Finnish Parliament House (1931) and Sigurd Frosterus's Stockmann's department store (1930), both in Helsinki, are serious realizations of Nordic classicism. The Parliament House, with its columned front surmounting a monumental flight of stairs, is an essay in restraint and repose. The interiors are well resolved and expertly detailed, creating an integrated work of form, space, and decoration. The Stockmann's department store is more muscular in bearing because of its use of masonry. The massive vertical brick facade, clear profiles, and culminating copper roof are balanced by the large, skylit interior central space.

Four women architects made major contributions during this period: Eva Kuhlefet-Ekelund, Kerttu Rytkönen, Elsa Arokallio, and Elsi Borg. Kuhlefelt-Ekelund designed one of the exceptional buildings of the era, the Private Swedish Girl's School (1929) in Töölö. Rytkönen executed the exciting, more idiosyncratic Salus hospital (1929) in Helsinki. Arokallio's work for the Ministry of Defense as well as in private practice and her Kauhava barracks (1928) are marked by a strict and elegant classicism. A crowning work is Elsi Borg's Jyväskylä Rural Parish Church (1928), with its clear geometric shapes, arresting details, and expressive use of color.

Commercial buildings in addition to housing complexes were executed in this form of classicism. This was a period of growth and urban expansion in Finland's major cities—Turku, Helsinki, Tampere, and Jyväskylä—and the simplicity of the forms and their responsiveness as urban design elements made classicism a suitable style for these developments. Buildings in the 1920s by Alvar and Aino Aalto in Jyväskylä and Turku and by

Jyväskylä Worker's Club, designed by Alvar Aalto (1925)
Photo © Päijäne 1924/Alvar Aalto Archives

Erik Bryggman in Turku exemplify these characteristics, especially the Aaltos's Defense Corps building (1926) in Jyväskylä and Southwestern Agricultural Cooperative (1929) in Turk and Bryggman's two blocks of flats (mid-1920s) in Turku.

Hilding Ekelund's "Art Hall" (1929) and Töölö Church (1930), both in Helsinki, and the Aaltos's Worker's Club (1925) in Jyväskylä represent, in contrast, the free play of expression found in this form of classicism. These works, while using elements of the classical language, often exhibit exaggerated, even mannered, qualities in the overall composition or the detailing.

Many of Helsinki's suburban developments date from this period and are composed of apartment blocks executed in this form of classicism to achieve a harmonious cityscape. The streetscapes along Mäkelänkatu and Museokatu in Helsinki are examples of this unified intention. Martti Välikangas's Käpylä Garden Suburb (1925) in Helsinki combines classical motifs and decoration with a simple vernacular-inspired building while demonstrating an understanding of the most up-to-date town-planning principles.

Finnish Functionalism

Finnish awareness of the new ideas emerging from continental Europe began in the 1920s, as Scandinavian journals began publishing the work of the French, German, Dutch, and Russian avant-garde. At this time, Finnish architects were especially open to currents from the outside and willing to participate in theoretical and polemical discussions. Architects such as Alvar and Aalto and Erik Bryggman, among others, traveled throughout Europe to visit the seminal works of the new architecture and to attend meetings of CIAM (Congrès Internationaux d'Architecture Moderne). In particular, Aalto's firsthand knowledge of avant-garde developments not only was instrumental in the promulgation of Finnish functionalism but quickly established him as among its leaders.

Accepting both the formal canons and the social programs of modernism, Finnish functionalism was characterized by use of the "free" plan; the separation of structure from building envelope, with the structure (usually of concrete) being detached from the "free" facade; and a machine imagery created by taut-skinned, white cubic volumes with minimalistic industrial detailing. The architects further accepted the modern bias for buildings sited in open, park-like settings. In built works as well as in proposals, portions of extant urban fabric were opened to automobile access and the perceived health-giving qualities of sun, air, and greenery.

Although a number of Finns directly experienced the major new works on the Continent—which led to extremely sophisticated buildings being executed in this small country—Aalto's knowledge of his peers' work and his quick assimilation of modernism's industrial detailing techniques were wryly commented on by Hilding Ekelund in 1930: "With the same enthusiasm as the academics of the 1880s drew Roman baroque portals, Gothic pinnacles, etc. in their sketchbooks for use in their architectural practice, Alvar Aalto noses out new, rational-technical details from all over Europe which he then makes use of and transforms with considerable skill" (Mikkola 1980, 75).

The Aaltos's *Turun Sanomat* Newspaper Building (1929) in Turku and Tuberculosis Sanatorium (1933) in Paimio are seminal pieces of Finnish functionalism, as they have fully incorporated Le Corbusier's "Five Points of a New Architecture." However, Aalto was by no means the lone practitioner, and by the early 1930s, a number of especially fine examples of modernism existed throughout Finland. Exemplary works, embracing both modernism's formal canons and social programs, were also produced by Erik Bryggman, Viljo Revell, Erkki Huttunen, Oiva Kallio, and P.E. Blomstedt.

P.E. Blomstedt, who worked with his architect wife Märta, completed two small but excellent works: the Kannonkoski Church (1933) and the Kotka Savings Bank (1935). After his death in 1935, Märta Blomstedt, with Matti Lampén, completed the Pohjanhovi Hotel (1936) in Rovaniemi, one of the most important works of the period. The "Glass Palace" (1935) in Helsinki by Viljo Revell embraces modernism through expression of its program of restaurants, shops, and a cinema, all part of the central bus station, as well as for its machine aesthetics. Bryggman's library tower (1935) for the Åbo Akademi in Turku, the exceptional Helsinki Olympic Stadium (1940) by Yrjö Lindegren, and a series of works by Erkki Huttunen—the Cooperative Shop (1933) in Sauvo, the Kotka Town Hall (1934), and the SOK warehouse and office building (1938) in Oulu—are all examples of the acceptance of functionalism in Finland.

Although many architects continued to actively embrace functionalism, criticism of its propositions began to emerge during the mid- to late 1930s. This criticism initially concerned tectonics and materiality. As modernist works appeared in Finland and the forces of nature and the effect of climate began to act on them, architects questioned the advisability of using Mediterranean-inspired building forms in the harsh northern environment. To modify functionalism's astringent forms and material palette, Finnish architects incorporated traditional pitched-roof forms; brick, tile, and stone cladding; and punched window openings. Traditional norms modified functionalist "ethics," providing more corporeal substance and regional character to the work.

In the Aaltos's work, this change can be seen initially in the evolution of the design for the Viipuri Library (1935) and their residence (1936) in Munkkiniemi. However, the Finnish Pavilion at the 1936 Paris World's Fair and the Villa Mairea (1939) are the pivotal works that reveal and codify the directions that Aalto took over the next three decades of his production (Aino Aalto died of cancer in 1949). Erik Bryggman's elegant Resurrection Chapel (1940) in Turku is another example of this movement toward a more experiential and tactile architecture. In both the Villa Mairea and the Resurrection Chapel, the interplay between nature and the architecture is an essential characteristic of the design. A number of housing complexes and service facilities for factory complexes by Aalto, Aarne Ervi, and Viljo Revell exploit this play between built form and the natural setting.

Postwar Developments

At one level, Aalto's work dominated Finnish developments in the post-World War II era. The Säynätsalo Town Hall (1952), Rautatalo office building (1955), National Pensions Institute (1956), House of Culture (1958), and Vouksenniska Church (1959) all reinforced his international standing and independent direction. However, Finland during the 1950s and 1960s was more than Aalto.

Whereas Aalto went his own way, the majority of Finnish architects continued to practice an evolved form of modernism influenced by Mies van der Rohe and others. Their buildings are characterized by their direct approach in the use of reinforced concrete and steel along with brick and wood, coupled with rational planning and organizational techniques. Examples include Viljo Revell's Palace Hotel (1952, with Keijo Petäjä) in Helsinki and Vatiala Cemetery Chapel (1962); the numerous housing complexes by Arne Ervi; Yrjö Lindegren's Serpent house (1951), Kaija and Heikki Siren's National Theater addition (1954) and Otaniemi Chapel (1957); and Aarno Ruusuvuori's Hyvinkää Church (1961) and Huutoniemi Church (1964). Less Romantic in conception than Aalto's contemporaneous works, these buildings expanded the rationalist aspect of modernism while incorporating more expressive spatial exploration with a richer material vocabulary.

Often, this period in Finnish architectural development is viewed as the quiet, golden age of the century, a result of Aalto's code of not discussing his architecture, coupled with the general preference of a material palette relying on brick and wood. However, this was not necessarily the norm, and in fact much influence should be accorded the work and theoretical writings of Aulis Blomstedt. Blomstedt aimed to develop an objective theory of architecture that was verified through practice, with simplicity, austerity, and abstraction becoming essentials in his designs. His terrace housing complex (1954) in Tapiola and Worker's Institute (1959) in Helsinki are essays in his rigorous process of thinking and doing, as are a series of abstract graphic and installation pieces that he did to study proportion. In addition to practicing, Blomstedt was a professor at the Helsinki University of Technology, and his influence is seen in the works of his students—Kristian Gullichsen, Juhani Pallasmaa, Erkki Kairamo, and Kirmo Mikkola, among others—executed during the 1970s and 1980s.

New towns were also a feature of Finnish postwar development, especially around Helsinki. Because of the city's growth in the 1950s, a series of planned garden suburban developments was created. The most famous was Tapiola Garden City, begun in 1952, which embraced the Finn's particular enthusiasm for living close to nature. The plan for Tapiola comprised three neighborhoods grouped around a city center and separated by green zones. The shopping and administrative center (1961) was designed by Aarne Ervi. The housing complexes were done by the best of Finland's architects: Aulis Blomstedt designed flats (1961), terrace houses (1964), and studio housing (1965); Viljo Revell executed flats (1958) and a complex of tower blocks (1960); Aarno Ruusuvuori designed the Weilin and Göös printing works (1964) and the parish church (1965); and H. and K. Siren contributed a complex of terrace houses (1959).

By the late 1960s, Finnish architects were either exploring a more expressive modernist language or working toward a more rationalist, abstract form of expression. The first can be seen in the Helsinki City Theater (1967) by Tima Penttilä; the Taivallahti Church, or famous "church in the rock" (1969), by Timo and Tuomo Suomalainen; the Sibelius Museum in Turku (1968) by Woldemar Baeckman; and the Kouvola City Hall (1969) by Saarnio and Leiviskä. The second, influenced by Blomstedt, can be seen in the more purist architecture of the Villa Relander in Muurame (1966) by Kirmo Mikkola and Juhani Pallasmaa, the Moduli 225 system of construction (1970) by Kristian Gullichsen and Pallasmaa, and the Liinasaarentie multifamily housing (1971) and semidetached housing (1980), both in Espoo, by Erikki Kairamo. Aarno Ruusuvuori's sauna (1968), designed for industrial manufacture and commissioned by Marimekko, is a true essay of architectural purity achieved with the most minimal gestures.

While a duality was established between Aalto and Blomstedt, another design force emerged in Finland during the late 1950s that appeared to bridge the two: Reima Pietilä and his architect wife Raili Paatelainen. Their early work—beginning with the Finnish Pavilion at the 1958 Brussels World's Fair and including the Kaleva Church (1960) in Tampere, the "Dipoli" student union (1964) at Otaniemi, and the Suvikumpu housing (1969) in Tapiola—is both distinctive and Expressionistic yet rational. Although their work often seems to emerge from the site, somewhat akin to Aalto's, there is still a controlled abstract quality to their architectural conceptions, as Pietilä learned much from Blomstedt and was influenced by his writings and thinking. After the critical success of these projects, Pietilä had a decade-long hiatus in his work and did not receive a significant building project in Finland until the commission for the Hervanta Community Complex in suburban Tampere in 1975. Although Hervanta was not of the quality of their earlier work, the Pietilä's last works—the Lieksa Church (1982), the Tampere City Library (1983), and most especially the Finnish President's Official Residence (1993)—regain an intense and expressive architectural power.

The Past Quarter-Century

Contemporary Finnish architects carry forward both the rational and the expressive threads present in the past half-century of architectural production. The best work combines both threads into a rich experiential architecture that also builds on a deep understanding of program and site. Architects such as Ruusuvuori, Pallasmaa, Gullichsen, and Kairamo are joined by Käpy and Simo Paavilainen; Juha Leiviskä; Pekka Helin and Tuomo Siitonen; Mikko Heikkinen and Markku Komonen; the threesome of Matti Nurmela, Kari Raimoranta, and Jyrki Tasa; and the group MONARK, among others, in creating some of the very best work recently done in Finland.

The Olari Church and Parish Center (1981) in Espoo, the new Parish Center (1989) in Paimio by Käpy and Simo Paavilainen, and the numerous churches by Juha Leiviskä—the Church of St. Thomas (1975) in Oulu, the Myyrmäki Church and Parrish Center (1984) in Vantaa, the Kirkkonummi Parish Center (1984), and the Männistö Church (1992)—are true instruments for manipulating natural light. Leiviskä in particular, whose churches are organized as series of parallel white planes, creates through a combination of baroque exuberance and Nordic coolness wonderfully engaging settings for light to play in. In his other works, as exemplified by the German Embassy (1992) in Helsinki and the art museum (1988) in Kajanni, Leiviskä demonstrates his mastery of the use of the wall as the primary organizing element in his architecture.

Juhani Pallasmaa took a breather from architecture for about a decade. He was director of the Museum of Finnish Architecture for five years and spent much time writing on the theory and philosophy of architecture and doing graphic design and artistic projects. When he returned to architecture, his work, as best witnessed in his Rovaniemi Art Museum (1986) and Finnish Institute (1991) in Paris, extends his earlier rationalism toward a more considered, thoughtful experiential expressiveness. Like many of his colleagues, Pallasmaa designs furniture and art objects and does graphic design: however, more in keeping with Aalto, these endeavors seem to more directly influence his architecture.

The work of Arkkitehdit Ky runs a range of expressive techniques, depending on which of the design principals—Kristian Gullichsen, Erikki Kairamo, or Timo Vormala—is in charge of the project. Gullichsen's work, best seen in his Parish Center (1983) in Kauniainen and Pieksämäki Cultural Center (1989), is a demonstration of the concept of "building as wall," which structures the entire site and overall spatial order. Kairamo's work is more "Constructivist" in expression, as demonstrated in his semidetached houses (1990) in Espoo and the much celebrated Itäkeskus Tower and Commercial Center (1987) in Helsinki. Vormala's architecture is more vernacular and traditional in expression, yet it is grounded in modernism, as seen in the apartment complex (1980) in Varisto, Ventaa, and the block of flats (1984) in the Näkinpuisto section of Helsinki. The firm also produced the highly visible and significant extension to the Stockmann's department store (1989) in central Helsinki.

The range and scope of work executed by Pekka Helin and Tuomo Siitonen is impressive for its conceptual strength as well as detail execution. Their UKK Institute for the Study of Health and Fitness (1983) in Tampere; the Swimming Hall and Multipurpose Hall (1986) in Hollola; the UNIC Ltd. headquarters (1991) in Helsinki; their exquisite Sibelius Quarters housing complex (1993) in Borås, Sweden; and the North Karelian Provincial Library (1992) in Joensuu, among other works, demonstrate the diversity of their projects.

A series of very interesting building complexes have been executed by Matti Nurmela, Kari Raimoranta, and Jyrki Tasa. These include the Lippajärvi Daycare Center (1983), the Post Office (1984) in Malmi, the Library (1984) in Kuhmo, and the Commercial Center (1989) in Pori. The Cultural Center (1989) for Tapiola by Arto Sipinen and the unique Finnish Pavilion for the 1992 Seville World's Fair by MONARK are additional examples of the range of architectural thinking occurring in Finland today. And then there is the expressive and excellently executed work of Mikko Heikkinen and Markku Komonen: Their Finnish Science Center "Heureka" (1988) in Helsinki, the Rovaniemi Airport (1992), and the Finnish Chancery (1993) in Washington, D.C., all bespeak an elegant clarity in organization as well as detail quality.

Over the course of the 20th century, Finnish architects have desired to create an architecture of both place and time. In doing so, they have created a tradition of executing strong architectural ideas and conceptions and developing them toward a rich and expressive result. The architecture of 20th-century Finland is not one of overly complex ideas executed in a simple-minded fashion but, rather, that of substantive concepts that are worked and elaborated into a palpable, meaningful, and fully experiential architecture.

WILLIAM C. MILLER

See also **Aalto, Alvar (Finland); Helsinki, Finland; Helsinki Railway Station, Finland; Paimio Sanatorium, near Turku, Finland; Pietilä, Reima, and Raili (Finland); Saarinen, Eero (Finland); Saarinen, Eliel (Finland)**

Further Reading

A number of works on modern Finnish architecture exist, as do several general surveys on the overall architectural history of the country. Most of the works lack true comprehensiveness, and often the sections on Functionalism and postwar architecture devote too much discussion to Alvar Aalto at the expense of other significant architects. Aalto's work notwithstanding, there is a much more rich and varied body of work representing those periods. The importance of Aulis Blomstedt to postwar Finnish developments and the critical reaction many young architects of the 1960s and 1970s had to the dominance of Aalto (versus how he was viewed internationally) do not often receive the attention they should. A comprehensive and detailed assessment of 20th-century Finnish architecture is still needed. The Museum of Finnish Architecture continues to be an excellent source for exhibitions and publications on both historical and contemporary developments in the architecture of Finland.

Helander, Vilhelm, and Simo Rista, *Suomalainen Rakennustraide; Modern Architecture in Finland* (bilingual Finnish-English edition), Helsinki: Kirjayhtyma, 1987

Mikkola, Kirmo, "Finland: På spaning efter en nutid" ["Finland: Looking for the Present Times"]. In *Nordisk Funktionalism* [*Nordic Functionalism*], edited by Gunilla Lundahl, Stockholm: Arkitektur Förlag, 1980

Nerdinger, Winfried (editor), *Alvar Aalto: Toward a Human Modernism*, Munich and London: Prestel, 1999

Nikula, Riitta, and Kristiina Paatero (editors), *Sankaruus ja Arki: Suomen 50-luvun miljöö; Heroism and the Everyday: Building Finland in the 1950s* (bilingual Finnish-English edition), Helsinki: Museum of Finnish Architecture, 1994

Poole, Scott, *The New Finnish Architecture*, New York: Rizzoli, 1992

Quantrill, Malcolm, *Finnish Architecture and the Modernist Tradition*, New York and London: Spon, 1995

Richards, J.M., *800 Years of Finnish Architecture*, North Pomfret, Vermont, and Newton Abbot, Devon: David and Charles, 1978

Salokorpi, Asko, *Modern Architecture in Finland*, New York: Praeger, 1970

Suhonen, Pekka, *Neue Architektur in Finnland*, Helsinki: Tammi, 1967

Suomen Rakennustaiteen Museo, *Profiles: Pioneering Women Architects from Finland*, Helsinki: Museum of Finnish Architecture, 1983

Tempel, Egon, *New Finnish Architecture*, New York: Praeger, 1968

Wickberg, Nils Erik, *Byggnadskonst i Finland*, Stockholm: Lindqvist, 1959; as *Finnish Architecture*, Helsinki: Otava, 1959

FISKER, KAY 1893–1965

Architect, Denmark

Kay Fisker was one of the early proponents of functionalism in Danish architecture. Taking his point of departure from the early 20th-century Danish Neoclassicism so prevalent in the 1910s and 1920s, he developed a type of functional building design specific to the Danish language of materials. In this way, Fisker took his inspiration first from functional theorist and practitioner Louis Sullivan and only later from his contemporaries among the European architects, such as Mies van der Rohe, Walter Gropius, and Le Corbusier. Fisker's successful bridging of these two styles in his practice (with partner C.F. Møller from 1930 to 1941), along with his steadfast promotion of functionalist ideals in his teaching at the Academy of Fine Arts in Copenhagen and abroad and as a writer for architectural publications (including the Danish journal *Arkitekten*), proves his place as one of the most influential figures in modern architecture in Denmark is justified.

Fisker first melded regional expression with functionalist principles in a student project, with Aage Rafn, for a small railroad station (1915) on the island of Bornholm. A study in form, the end-gabled station, with little architectural detail other than patterning of the brick exterior, set the stage for Fisker's drawing on traditional Danish building types for his simplified structures. Fisker was able to expand on his application of functionalist principles to large-scale architecture beginning in the 1920s, specifically, on new forms of housing called for after the world wars. It is for his work in this area that Fisker is best known today.

The housing shortage in Denmark, particularly in Copenhagen, after World War I led to substantial government funds allotted to large-scale housing projects. Fisker's early housing block Hornbækhus (1922) helped define a new type of structure meeting the needs of modern Danes. The architect conceived of this rectangular apartment block, which enclosed a large central garden, as a series of identical apartment modules, both modern ideas at the time. This early solution, however, expressed functionalism through the lingering vocabulary of Neoclassicism. The symmetrical brick exterior is broken only by marching rows of uniform windows running across the entire facade of the building. Fisker's early publication with F.R. Yerbury, *Modern Danish Architecture* (1927), championed the neoclassical as the most appropriate style of the day. It is this sense of regularity, of preoccupation with massing and form, that remained the hallmark of Fisker's architecture even after he abandoned the neoclassical style in the 1930s.

The introduction of international functionalism, introduced through exhibitions in Berlin and Stockholm in 1930, provided Denmark with a break from Neoclassicism. This new practical vocabulary had a decisive effect on the direction of Fisker's later apartment houses and other structures. After some experimentation, Fisker applied a more attractive and humanistic solution to the blocks of flats while still retaining their regional qualities. His Vestersøhus housing project (1935, 1938) features brick facades broken up with rectangular projecting balconies paired with windows, giving the structure a pleasing proportion and appearance. This was no mean task with such an inherently long and monotonous building type, although by this time the enclosed street block, seen in Hornbækhus, had been abandoned. Fisker, in his 1948 article "The History of Domestic Architecture in Denmark," described this new functional aspect of balconies as helping to "accentuate facades in the rhythm of the new architectural style, facades which . . . were to give honest expression to the plan behind them" (Fisker, 1948). This break from classicism also led to siting becoming a more important aspect of Danish modern architecture, especially on the newly developed outskirts of Copenhagen. Vestersøhus, by example, is picturesquely placed with its main facade facing a Copenhagen lake. In addition, the state's involvement with these residential estates meant that it exercised aesthetic control, employing the same architects for later additions to ensure visual unity.

In the period following World War II, Fisker made significant contributions to the new trend of terraced apartment houses of smaller separate units set about in a parklike area. The grouping of several smaller housing blocks together throughout such massive estates became a typical way of breaking up the monotony of large-scale residential projects while providing more light and a neighborhood feel. Buildings in these complex developments related to the natural site and to one another in a way that the long housing blocks could not. Fisker's Voldparken estate (Husum, 1949–51) is a celebrated example of this type of housing block evolution in which the previously mentioned solutions are applied. Fisker again concentrated on overall form and massing, keeping in mind native qualities. Each house, for example, is constructed of warm indigenous brick with a hip roof. The long facades are again relieved through Fisker's use of balconies that ingeniously project from the building at an angle. Fisker also designed a school (1951–57) at Voldparken.

Many of the qualities of Fisker's large-scale housing projects were appropriate for his most well known project. In 1931, Fisker, along with partner C.F. Møller and Povl Stegmann, won the competition for the new Århus University campus (1932–68) in Århus, Denmark. It was only the country's second university, and the state broke with the classical, formal situation of an urban campus in favor of a modern one. The setting was undeveloped land marked by rolling hills, existing groves of trees, and glacial streams that were dammed to create two small lakes. The university buildings were to be informally nestled into this park setting while respecting the natural terrain. The architects strove for uniformity in the architectural vocabulary of the structures, and this program was adhered to in later additions (Stegmann left the project in 1937 and Fisker in 1945, after which C.F. Møller was the sole architect). Fisker's university buildings again recall traditional Danish structures, with their cubist forms, pitched roofs of yellow tiles, and unbroken yellow-brick exteriors, but on a much larger scale. Therefore, the buildings, beginning with the strong, unornamented Institute for Chemistry, Physics, and Anatomy (1932–33), although clearly expressing the new functionalism, still project the monumental qualities typical of Fisker's work.

The transition between Neoclassicism and Danish functionalism in Fisker's architecture can also be traced in his silver designs for A. Michelsen in the 1920s, whereas his domestic and ship interiors display a more modern progressivism. This influence can be seen in the work of his students, such as Jørn Utzon, who went on to international fame.

JENNIFER KOMAR OLIVAREZ

See also **Copenhagen, Denmark; Denmark; Utzon, Jørn (Denmark)**

Biography

Born in Copenhagen, Denmark, 14 February 1893. Attended Gustav Vermehren's School of Architecture, Copenhagen 1909; studied at the Academy of Fine Arts, School of Architecture, Copenhagen 1909–20; studied English housing legislation, London 1919; traveled and studied, Italy, France, India, China, Japan 1920–22. Editor, *Arkitekten* 1919; assistant to Edvard Thomsen, Academy of Fine Arts, Copenhagen 1919–20. Private practice, Copenhagen from 1920; partner with C.F. Møller, Copenhagen 1930–41. Visiting lecturer, Technical School, Helsinki 1928; professor of architecture, Academy of Fine Arts, Copenhagen from 1936; dean, Architectural School, Academy of Fine Arts, Copenhagen from 1941; visiting professor, Graduate School of Design, Harvard University, Cambridge, Massachusetts 1952; visiting professor, Massachusetts Institute of Technology, Cambridge 1952 and 1957; visiting lecturer, Tulane University, New Orleans, Louisiana 1952; visiting lecturer, Georgia Institute of Technology, Atlanta 1952; visiting lecturer, Royal Technical School, Stockholm 1954. Member, Royal Academy for the Liberal Arts, Stockholm 1936; chairman, Academic Architects Society, Copenhagen 1940; member of the council, State Building Research Institute, Copenhagen 1946; honorary corresponding member, Royal Institute of British Architects 1946; member, Society for Architectural History 1947; member, Royal Society of Arts 1948; extraordinary member, Heinrich Tessenow Gesellschaft 1948; member, Danish Architects National Association 1952; honorary member, Architectural League of New York 1952; honorary fellow, American Institute of Architects 1955; vice president, academic council, Copenhagen 1959; extraordinary member, Society of Architectural Historians, Philadelphia 1960; extraordinary member, Akademie der Künste 1960. Died in Copenhagen, 21 June 1965.

Selected Works

Hornbækhaus Cooperative Society Housing, Borups Allé and Stefansgade, Copenhagen, 1922
Vestersøhus I Housing, Vester Søgade, Copenhagen, 1935
Vestersøhus II Housing, Vester Søgade, Copenhagen, 1938
University (first prize, 1931 competition; with Povl Stegmann until 1937; with C.F. Møller until 1945), Aarhus, 1945
Voldparken Housing, Husum, Denmark, 1951
National Council for Unmarried Mothers Administration Building and Home, Copenhagen, 1955
Voldparken School, Husum, Denmark, 1957
Interbau Housing, West Berlin, 1957

Selected Publications

Modern Danish Architecture (with F.R. Yerbury), 1927
Kobenhavnske boligtyper (with others), 1936
Trends in Danish Architecture 1850–1950 (with Knud Millech), 1951
Danish Architectural Drawings 1660–1920 (coeditor with Christian Elling), 1961

Further Reading

These selections represent most of the writings on Kay Fisker in English, with the addition of the most recent Danish biography by Tobias Faber

(1995). Surveys of Danish architecture by Tobias Faber (1963, 1968) and Esbjørn Hiort (1954, 1959) are the most helpful English sources on Fisker's work.

Anderson, Stanford, "The 'New Empiricism—Bay Region Axis': Kay Fisker and Postwar Debates on Functionalism, Regionalism, and Monumentality" (translation of essay in Faber 1995), *Journal of Architectural Education*, 50/3 (February 1997)
Faber, Tobias, *A History of Danish Architecture*, Denmark: Det Danske Selskab, 1963
Faber, Tobias, *New Danish Architecture*, translated by E. Rockwell, New York, Praeger, 1968
Faber, Tobias (editor), *Kay Fisker* (in Danish), Copenhagen: Arkitektens Forlag, 1995
Fisker, Kay, "The History of Domestic Architecture in Denmark," *Architectural Review*, 104/623 (November 1948)
Fisker, Kay, "The Moral of Functionalism," *Magazine of Art*, 43 (February 1950)
Hiort, Esbjørn, *Nyere Dansk Bygningskunst*, Copenhagen: Gjellerups, 1949; as *Contemporary Danish Art*, translated by Eve M. Wendt, Copenhagen: Arkitektens Forlag, 1958
Hiort, Esbjørn, *Modern Danish Silver*, Copenhagen: Gjellerups, and New York: Museum Books, 1954
Langkilde, Hans Erling, *Arkitekten Kay Fisker* (with English summary), Copenhagen: Arkitektens Forlag, 1960
"M/S Kronprins Frederik/Kay Fisker: Architect," *Architectural Review*, 101/602 (February 1947)

FLATIRON BUILDING

Designed by D.H. Burnham and Company; completed 1903
New York, New York

With its striking shape, prominent location, and exceptional height, the Flatiron Building was one of New York's most discussed and distinctive skyscrapers at the beginning of the 20th century. It was originally named the Fuller Building after the George A. Fuller Company, which had served as the building's developer and builder and was one of its original occupants until moving to a new building in 1929. From its lofty quarters, the New York office of the Fuller Company oversaw as general contractors the construction of several of the city's most prominent buildings. However, few called this skyscraper the Fuller Building; the triangular lot from which this tower rises quickly led to the building's popular moniker, the Flatiron.

The architect of the building was D.H. Burnham and Company of Chicago. Daniel H. Burnham (1846–1912) had established himself as one of America's most prominent architects and planners. By the time the Flatiron was being designed and built (1901–03), Burnham was devoting much of his time to big plans. Among other things, he played an important role in the development of the Senate Park Commission Plan (1901–02) for Washington, D.C. Concurrently, his large architectural office was designing numerous buildings across the country. Burnham oversaw the operation but left much of the creative work to several talented designers in the firm, including Frederick P. Dinkelberg, who appears to have had an important hand in the architectural design of the Flatiron.

At 21 stories or 307 feet tall, the Flatiron Building was one of the taller skyscrapers in New York when it was built. The building's structural steel frame, with extensive wind bracing, reflected the recent acceptance of the all-steel skeleton for skyscrapers in New York, after the pioneering efforts of the Chicago School (in which Burnham and his former partner John W. Root had played a key role). The limestone and terra cotta that cover the building are of the same light monochrome. The rustication and heavily ornamented patterns of these walls, as well as the conservatively sized windows, give the façades a heavy appearance, even though these are not load-bearing walls. The multistory oriels in the midsection, which are prominent in many of Burnham's Chicago buildings, are just barely perceptible on the busy, more enclosed skin of the Flatiron. This greater visual weight becomes especially evident in comparison with Burnham's earlier and even his contemporary work in Chicago. It is as if this Midwest-bred approach to skyscraper design became more formal when it came east to New York.

Stylistically, the design of the Flatiron draws from the classical tradition, with French Renaissance motifs. Ever since Burnham played a pivotal role in the staging of the 1893 World's Columbian Exposition in Chicago, he became increasingly enamored with Beaux-Arts classicism, an attraction that found its broadest expression in his involvement in the City Beautiful movement. The Flatiron is a vertical extension of a Renaissance palazzo: the tripartition of the overall design into a distinct base, a repetitive midsection, and a crowning cornice is now extended over 20 stories, making the whole appear column-like. If the Flatiron had been a building of a more traditional height, it could have fit comfortably in a contemporary City Beautiful plan with radial avenues carving triangular lots in a Parisian manner. But the Flatiron is not of a traditional scale. Its enormous height stretches its classical garb uneasily. It is not a part of a larger choreographed urban ensemble; in fact, it stands isolated as a freestanding tower on its own small urban island bound by 22nd Street, Broadway, and Fifth Avenue. The diagonal slice that Broadway makes through Manhattan's grid as it skirts past Madison Square creates the site's right triangle. The long, thin triangular footprint of the Flatiron extrudes up through all its stories. With all three façades facing streets, this tall, thin building was designed to always have very well-lit office spaces.

The most acute angle of the Flatiron points north. Early 20th-century commentators often likened this sharply curved corner of the building to a ship's prow. When seen at an angle from Madison Square, the building can appear to have little depth, like a wall leaned precariously against the sky. The gravity-defying illusion of the building is further enhanced by the enormous cornice projecting aggressively from the top of the building, giving the whole affair a top-heavy appearance. Although the building is in the flat-topped tradition of the Chicago School, its arrow-like north angle can make the Flatiron appear as if its horizontal cornice is pointing skyward in photographs. The striking visual presence of this uncommon vertical mass is what made the building instantly famous both with tourists and those in the arts grappling with the nature of New York's modernity. Did D.H. Burnham and Company intend all of this drama in the Flatiron? Perhaps not; the elements of the design fit in comfortably with the general development of the firm. It was the unconventional triangular lot, coupled with exceptional height, that transformed architectural conventions into something unique.

In the first years after completion, the Flatiron Building received considerable attention from various sources. In 1903 the

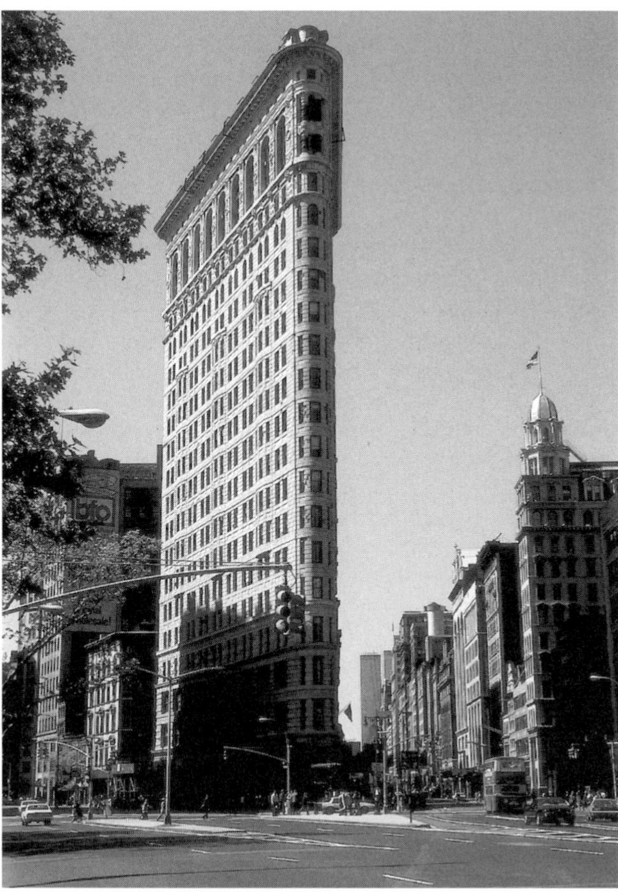

D.H. Burnham and Company, Flatiron Building, 1900–03, New York
© Craig Zabel

New York Herald reported that strong, swirling winds were congregating at the building's base and playing havoc with pedestrians. One writer for *Munsey's Magazine* in 1905 contemplated the ironies of contemporary civilization in New York from a godlike vantage point high up in the Flatiron. A 1903 essay in *Camera Work* discussed whether the Flatiron would lead to a rethinking of aesthetics. Photographers responded most profoundly to the visual challenge of the Flatiron. Photographs by Alfred Stieglitz and Edward Steichen taken soon after the building's completion established the Flatiron's iconic presence upon the modern imagination. However, these early photographs typically veil the Flatiron in the atmospheric effects of nature; the building's stylistic pretensions erode as the sublime vertical mass becomes dominant.

In 1903 the Flatiron stood in relative isolation near Madison Square, since the city's other early skyscrapers were clustered further south on Manhattan. However, ever-taller skyscrapers soon dwarfed the Flatiron: the 700-foot Metropolitan Life Tower (1909) arose on the other side of Madison Square, and the Empire State Building (1931) was built several blocks to the north on Fifth Avenue. From the tops of both of these buildings one had new yet belittling views of the Flatiron. Today, the Flatiron is one of New York's oldest extant skyscrapers and retains its theatrical and unsettling presence amid the ever-growing concentration of Manhattan's skyscrapers.

CRAIG ZABEL

See also **Burnham, Daniel H. (United States); Chicago School; City Beautiful Movement; Empire State Building, New York; Skyscraper**

Further Reading

For further detailed discussion of the Flatiron Building, see especially Landau and Condit, and Zukowsky and Saliga. Hines develops the context of the architect, while Starrett develops the context of the builder. Kreitler and Schleier examine the artistic response to the Flatiron.

Allan, Sidney (Sadakichi Hartmann), "The 'Flat-Iron' Building—An Esthetical Dissertation," *Camera Work* 4 (1903)

"The 'Flatiron' or Fuller Building," *Architectural Record* 12, no. 5 (1902)

Goldberger, Paul, *The Skyscraper*, New York: Knopf, 1981

Hines, Thomas S., "No Little Plans: The Achievement of Daniel Burnham," *The Art Institute of Chicago Museum Studies* 13, no. 2 (1988)

Kreitler, Peter Gwillim, *Flatiron: A Photographic History of the World's First Steel Frame Skyscraper*, Washington, D.C.: American Institute of Architects Press, 1990

Landau, Sarah Bradford, and Carl W. Condit, *Rise of the New York Skyscraper, 1865–1913*, New Haven, Connecticut: Yale University Press, 1996

Nash, Eric P., *Manhattan Skyscrapers*, New York: Princeton Architectural Press, 1999

Saltus, Edgar, "New York from the Flatiron," *Munsey's Magazine* 33, no. 4 (1905)

Schleier, Merrill, *The Skyscraper in American Art, 1890–1931*, 2 vols., Ann Arbor, Michigan: UMI Research Press, 1986

Starrett, Paul, *Changing the Skyline: An Autobiography*, New York and London: Whittlesey House, 1938

"Whirling Winds Play Havoc with Women at Flatiron," *New York Herald* (31 January 1903)

Zukowsky, John, and Pauline Saliga, "Late Works by Burnham and Sullivan," *The Art Institute of Chicago Museum Studies* 11, no. 1 (1984)

FOSTER, NORMAN 1935–

Architect, England

Together with architects Richard Rogers, Nicholas Grimshaw, and Michael Hopkins, Norman Foster is credited with pioneering the design style known as High-Tech in Britain in the early 1970s. Although in the United States the term refers principally to an architectural style, in Britain High-Tech points to a more rigorous approach in which advanced technology is acknowledged as representing the "spirit of the age." The aesthetics of industrial production and machine technology are celebrated and embodied in the methodology of design production. Industry is a source for both technology and imagery.

After working in the city treasurer's office in Manchester Town Hall and serving for two years in the Royal Air Force, Foster studied at the University of Manchester (1956–61) and at Yale University (1961–62). In 1963, he formed Team 4 in London, collaborating with his wife, Wendy, and Su and Rich-

Great Court at The British Museum (extension), London, 1994–2000
Photo by Nigel Young © Foster and Partners

ard Rogers, whom he had met at Yale. An early commission was for a house in Cornwall for Richard Rogers's parents-in-law, the Brumwells, and their art collection. Marcus Brumwell had been a founder of Misha Black's design consultancy, DRU, and this connection was to lead to further commissions. The house is half buried in the contours of the site and takes full advantage of the dramatic coastal position; the bridge spanning the steep gully between road and turfed roof presages some of Foster and Roger's later preoccupations. Another significant early work was the controversial Reliance Controls Factory (1967) at Swindon. Here, Foster's interest in tense metal skins for buildings and Roger's predilection for expressing structural bracing externally are anticipated. There was also a concern for civilizing working conditions, which was to become a hallmark of Foster's commercial buildings.

Foster Associates was founded in London in 1967 and includes eight partners in addition to Norman and Wendy Foster (Loren Butt, Chubby S. Chhabra, Spencer de Gray, Roy Fleetwood, Birkin Haward, James Meller, Graham Phillips, and Mark Robertson). It has become an immensely successful practice with an international profile. Their first significant commission was the Olsen line passenger terminal and administration building (1971) in London's Dockland. Here, Foster declared his concern of breaking down the "distinction between us and them, posh and scruffy, front office and workers' entrance." Throughout the early 1970s, Foster brought his commitment to a patrician elegance to a whole range of modestly scaled buildings, offices, schools, shops, and some factories.

The celebrated headquarters of the Willis Faber Dumas offices (1975) in Ipswich boasts a curved glass facade that reinforces the street boundaries and harmonizes with the urban environment. Two floors of office accommodation for 1300 people are elevated and placed between amenity and support areas above and below, including a swimming pool and gymnasium on the ground floor and a restaurant pavilion set in the landscaped garden roof. The Sainsbury Centre for the Visual Arts (1978), built to house the Sir Robert and Lady Sainsbury Collection, comprises an ingeniously adaptable structure that allows any part of the external walls and roof to be changed quickly to provide different combinations of glazed, solid, or grilled aluminum panels. A single, large, span roof covers two exhibition galleries, the School of Fine Arts, a large reception area, the university faculty club, a public restaurant, and storage facilities. The latter requiring more space, Foster designed the fan-shaped Crescent Wing, completed in 1991. This addition is introduced discretely into the landscape and does not destroy the integrity of the main building. The Renault Distribution Centre (1983) at Swindon is based on a structural module—a masted, lightweight suspended roof that repeats itself. Stansted Airport Terminal (1991) followed, with its dramatic roof structure surmounting the vast open space of the main building. Such great "neutral space envelopes," capable of accommodating differentiated functions, are a feature of Foster's work. While being committed to the High-Tech movement, which celebrates the aesthetic of industrial production, Foster is also concerned with what he describes as design "development," evinced in the Hong Kong and Shanghai Banking Corporation Headquarters (1985), described as the most expensive office building ever constructed. Here, all the main elements of the building, often prefabricated off-site, result from the close collaboration of architect and manufacturers, ensuring high levels of craftsmanship and quality of detail. Stansted witnesses a similar concern for detail, with the architect designing carpets, seating, checkout desks, and retail outlets. More recent works include a contribution to Stockley Park (1984), Heathrow, Middlesex, a business park attracting international companies; the ITN Headquarters (1991); Riverside Offices and Apartments (1990), including Foster's own apartment, both in London; and the Library (1992) at Cranfield Institute of Technology, Bedfordshire, England.

Hilary J. Grainger

See also **Airport and Aviation Building; Hongkong and Shanghai Bank, Shanghai; Renault Distribution Center, Swindon, England; Rogers, Richard (England); Sainsbury Wing, National Gallery, London**

Biography

Born in Manchester, England, 1 June 1935. Attended the University of Manchester School of Architecture and Department of Town and Country Planning 1956–61; studied, Yale University

Great Court at The British Museum (extension), London, 1994–2000

School of Architecture 1961–62; master's degree in architecture 1962. Married 1) architect Wendy Cheeseman 1964 (died 1989): 4 children; married 2) Begum Sabiha Rumani Malik 1991. Served in the Royal Air Force 1953–55. Partner, with Wendy Foster and Richard Rogers, Team 4, London 1963–67; partner, with Wendy Foster, Foster Associates, London from 1967; now Sir Norman Foster and Partners. Member, Board of Education and Visiting Examiner, Royal Institute of British Architects 1971–73; vice president, Architectural Association, London 1974; council member, Royal College of Art, London from 1981; member, Royal Institute of British Architects; member, Royal Academy of Arts; member, Ordre des Architetes Français; member, International Academy of Architects, Sofia; associate, Académie Royal de Belgique; honorary fellow, American Institute of Architects; fellow, Society of Industrial Architects and Chartered Society of Designers; honorary member, Bund Deutscher Architekten. Royal Gold Medal, Royal Institute of British Architects 1983; knighted 1980.

Selected Works

Reliance Controls Factory, Swindon, Wiltshire, 1967
Fred Olsen Passenger Terminal and Operations Centre, Millwall, London, 1971
Willis Faber Dumas Country Head Office, Ipswich, Suffolk, 1975
Sainsbury Centre for the Visual Arts, University of East Anglia, Norwich, 1978
Norman and Wendy Foster House, Cannon Place, Hampstead, London, 1979
Renault Distribution Centre, Swindon, Wiltshire, 1983
Stockley Park, Heathrow, Middlesex, 1984
Hong Kong and Shanghai Banking Corporation Headquarters, Hong Kong, 1985
Riverside Offices and Apartments, London, 1990
ITN New Headquarters, London, 1991
Stansted Airport Terminal, Essex, England 1991
Crescent Wing (addition), Sainsbury Centre for the Visual Arts, University of East Anglia, Norwich, 1991
Cranfield Institute of Technology Library (First prize, 1989 competition), Bedfordshire, 1992
Commerzbank Headquarters, Frankfurt, Germany, 1997
Hong Kong International Airport, Chek Lap Kok, 1998
Chek Lap Kok, Hong Kong China, 1998
Great Court at the British Museum, London, England, 2000

Selected Publications

Foster, Norman, "Exploring the Client's Range of Options," *Royal Institute of British Architects* (June 1970)

Foster, Norman, "Recent Work," *Architectural Design* (November 1972)
Foster Associates, *Architectural Design*, 47/9–10 (1977)

Further Reading

In the catalog that accompanied the Royal Academy of Arts Exhibition in London in 1986, Sudjic provides one of the most useful contextualizations of Foster's work. The catalog also includes a list of works and biographical details to date.

Banham, Reyner, *Foster Associates*, London: RIBA, 1979
Norman Foster, Architect: Selected Works 1962/84, Manchester: Whitworth Art Gallery, 1984
"Recent Works of Foster Associates," *A + U* (February 1981)
Sudjic, Deyan, *New Architecture: Foster, Rogers, Stirling*, London: Royal Academy of Arts, 1986

FRAMPTON, KENNETH 1930–

Architect, historian and critic, United States

Kenneth Frampton is an architect, historian, and theorist based in New York. As an architect with Douglas Stephen and Partners from 1961 to 1966, when he designed an eight-story (48-unit) apartment block, Craven Hill Gardens (1964), in Bayswater, London. It received a Ministry of Housing award and is now a Grade Four historic monument.

In 1962, Frampton also became a technical editor for *Architectural Design* and improved the depth and quality of the magazine's coverage of new work, such as the Smithsons' Economist Building in London. In 1965, he accepted a teaching position at Princeton University through the efforts of Peter Eisenman, then a young professor there who had studied at Cambridge University with Colin Rowe. While at Princeton, he became a member of the Institute for Architecture and Advanced Studies (IAUS) in New York and eventually one of the editors of its influential historical and theoretical journal, *Oppositions* (1972–82). While a professor at Columbia University (1972–73), with Theodore Liebman and others, he was involved in the design of an innovative low-rise, high-density, low-income housing project, Marcus Garvey Village, in Brownsville, Brooklyn, for the New York State Urban Development Corporation.

Frampton is perhaps best known for the concept of "critical regionalism," which he first advanced in two articles in 1983. Influenced by the writings of the philosopher Martin Heidegger, Frampton argued that local building culture and climactic influences could provide a form of resistance to what he saw as the homogenizing and environmentally destructive forces of worldwide capitalist development. A vehement critic of the ironic manipulation of formal imagery characteristic of Postmodernism, since the 1980s he has asserted the importance of the tectonics of building, a position reflected in his *Studies in Tectonic Culture* (1995). In addition to his position at Columbia, he has taught in recent years at the University of Virginia, the Berlage Institute in Amsterdam, the ETH (Swiss Federal Institute of Technology) in Zurich, the EPFL (Swiss Federal Institute of Technology) in Lausanne, and the Accademia di architettura in Mendrisio, Switzerland.

Frampton's international advocacy for an environmentally and culturally appropriate modern architecture has gained him considerable respect around the world, although in the 1990s some have charged him with being too naively idealistic about the role of architecture in contemporary society in light of the immense changes being wrought by computing and the spread of a global consumer economy. His response is that our mode of building has an important role to play in addressing issues of sustainability and global warming, and he continues to insist that the "architectural profession has an ethical responsibility for projecting works which have a critically creative character."

ERIC MUMFORD

See also **Eisenman, Peter (United States); Museum of Modern Art, New York City; Postmodernism**

Biography

Born in Woking, England, 1930; attended the Architectural Association in London, architectural degree, 1957. Worked as architect for Karmi, Melzer, Karmi and Yashar/Eytan in Israel, 1958–59; returned to London (1960) to work for Douglas Stephen and Partners, 1961–66; received Ministry of Housing award for Craven Hill Gardens (1964). Became a technical editor for *Architectural Design* (1962); began teaching at Princeton University (1965); while there became a member of the Institute for Architecture and Advanced Studies (IAUS), New York, and eventually one of the editors of its journal, *Oppositions* (1972–82). Professor at the Columbia University School of Architecture (1972–73); taught at the Royal College of Art in London (1974–77); then returned to Columbia where he is today the Ware Professor of Architecture. Chairman of the Columbia Division of Architecture (1986–89), director of Columbia Ph.D. program (1993–). Recipient of numerous awards and honorary degrees, including American Institute of Architects' National Honors Award (1985), ACSA Topaz Medallion (1990), and has served on many design juries, including the Aga Khan Awards (1999).

Selected Publications

"Maison de Verre," *Architectural Design* 81 (April 1966)
"America 1960–1970: Notes on Urban Images and Theory," *Casabella* 35 (December 1971)
"Twin Parks As Typology," *Architectural Forum* 138 (June 1973)
"On Reading Heidegger," *Oppositions* 4 (1975)
"Two or Three Things I Know about Them: A Note on Manhattanism," *Architectural Design* 47, no. 5 (1977)
Modern Architecture: A Critical History, New York: Oxford University Press, 1980; 3rd edition, London: Thames and Hudson, 1992
Idea As Model (with Sylvia Kolbowski), New York: Institute for Architecture and Urban Studies, Rizzoli International, 1981
Modern Architecture and the Critical Present, London: Architectural Design, 1982
"Towards a Critical Regionalism: Six Points for an Architecture of Resistance," in *The Anti-Aesthetic*, Hal Foster (editor), Port Townsend, Washington: Bay Press, 1983
"Prospects for a Critical Regionalism," *Perspecta* 20 (1983)
"Homage to Iberia: An Assessment," in *Building in a New Spain: Contemporary Spanish Architecture*, edited by Pauline Saliga and Martha Thorne, 1992
"An Anthropology of Building," in *Companion to Contemporary Architectural Thought*, edited by Ben Farmer and Hentie Louw, London and New York: Routledge, 1993

"Modernization and Mediation: Frank Lloyd Wright and the Impact of Technology," in *Frank Lloyd Wright, Architect*, edited by Terence Riley, New York: Museum of Modern Art, 1994

Studies in Tectonic Culture, Cambridge, Massachusetts: MIT Press, 1995

"Typology, Cosmology, and Construction Methods," in *Japanese Building Practice:* Frampton, Kenneth, Kudo, Kunio, Vincent, Keith (editors) *From Ancient Times to the Meiji Period*, New York: Van Nostrand Reinhold, 1997

Frampton, Kenneth, Spector, Arthur, Reed, Lynne (editors), *Technology, Place, and Architecture: The Jerusalem Seminar, 1996* (editors) New York: Rizzoli, 1998

"The Legacy of Alvar Aalto: Evolution and Influence," in *Alvar Aalto: Between Humanism and Materialism*, edited by Peter Reed, New York: Museum of Modern Art, 1998

"The Mutual Limits of Architecture and Science," in *The Architecture of Science*, edited by Peter Galison and Emily Thompson, Cambridge Massachusetts: MIT Press, 1999

"Seven Points for the Millenium: An Untimely Manifesto," *Architectural Review* 206 (November 1999)

Frampton, Kenneth (editor), *World Architecture, 1900–2000: A Critical Mosaic*, Wein: Springer, 1999

Further Reading

Jameson, Frederic, *The Seeds of Time*, New York: Columbia University Press, 1994

Koolhaas, Rem, "Doubletake: Review Reviewed," *AV Monographs* 73 (September/October 1998)

Powell, Kenneth, "Pragmatic Idealist," *Architects' Journal* (7 March 1996)

Scott-Brown, Denise, "Reply to Frampton," *Casabella* 35, nos. 359–360 (December 1971)

FRANK, JOSEF 1885–1967

Architect, Austria

Josef Frank was among the leading Austrian representatives of the Modern movement. He was a founding member of the Congrès Internationaux d'Architecture Moderne (CIAM), and, as vice president of the Austrian Werkbund, he oversaw the planning and construction of the 1932 Vienna Werkbundsiedlung. In the early 1930s, however, Frank emerged as one of the most important and vocal critics of what he saw as the totalitarian orthodoxy within the various strands of modernism. For the remainder of his life, until he stopped practicing in the early 1960s, he sought alternatives to what he perceived as the banality and uniformity of much of the building of his time.

Frank studied architecture with Carl König, Max Fabiani, and others at the Vienna Technische Hochschule, graduating in 1910 with a dissertation on the churches of Leon Battista Alberti. While still a student, he flirted briefly with the Art Nouveau (Jugendstil), but he soon abandoned the style in favor of the renewed historical eclecticism that dominated much of Central European design in the period after 1905. Around 1909 Frank formed a partnership with two of his former classmates from the Technische Hochschule, Oskar Strnad and Oskar Wlach. Together, the three young architects specialized in houses and interiors for the city's *haute bourgeoisie*. In the period just prior to 1914, Frank realized several houses, mostly notably the Scholl House (1913–14), which, despite its lingering neoclassicism, showed marked parallels with Adolf Loos's stark prewar villas. Frank, however, was much more radical in the composition of his facades and furnishings, which often relied on complex and asymmetrical arrangements.

After World War I, Frank devoted himself to finding solutions to Vienna's severe housing shortage. In the early 1920s he designed a series of housing projects in and around Vienna that were based on the ideas of reduction and repetition. Frank's early postwar works continued to draw on historical precedents, but by 1921 he began to develop a simplified form language, one that reflected the growing development of *sachlich* (objective) architecture throughout Central Europe. This was especially evident in Frank's designs for several apartment buildings for the Vienna municipality, including the Wiedenhofer-Hof (1924–25) and the Winarsky-Hof (1924–26). The housing blocks, which were published in many of the leading international architectural journals of the time, brought Frank increasing notoriety and led to an invitation from Ludwig Mies van der Rohe to participate in the 1927 Weissenhofsiedlung in Stuttgart.

Frank's contribution to the Weissenhof exhibition, a double house, was widely lauded for its straightforward appearance and innovative constructional ideas. Frank's colorful and florid interiors, however, which included furnishings and textiles from his shop Haus and Garten (House and Garden; founded in 1925 with Wlach), drew strong criticism from many of the other participants and observers who condemned them for being "conservative," "feminine," "obtrusive," and "middle class." Frank responded to the charges in an article titled "Der Gschnas fürs G'mut und der Gschnas als Problem" ("Frippery for the Soul and Frippery as a Problem"), in which he argued that the stripped-down, functionalist style of the radical modernists simply did not respond to most people's psychological needs. He repeated these criticisms in his book *Architektur als Symbol: Elemente deutschen Neuen Bauens* (1931; [Architecture as Symbol: Elements of German Modern Architecture]). Many of Frank's subsequent designs similarly constituted immanent responses to the modernist vanguard.

Because of the poor state of the Austrian economy in the postwar period, Frank was able to realize only a handful of residences for private clients, the most import of which was the Villa Beer (1928–30) in Vienna. Like Loos's famed *Raumplan* (space plan) houses of the 1920s and early 1930s, the three-and-a half-story residence consisted of intricate arrangement of interlocking volumes on different levels, and it stands, along with Loos's Müller House and Mies' Tugendhat House, as one of the most significant modernist explorations of the possibilities of a new spatial ordering.

In 1933, in response to the Nazi seizure of power in Germany and the growth of anti-Semitism in Austria, Frank immigrated to Sweden and settled in Stockholm, where he became the chief designer for the interior design firm Svenskt Tenn. He continued to produce designs for houses into the early 1960s, but increasingly after 1937 he devoted himself to furniture design, churning out hundreds of ideas for chairs, tables, and cabinets as well as textiles, rugs, and other objects for the home. The softened, cozy eclecticism that Frank developed in his designs for Svenskt Tenn was widely admired and imitated throughout Scandinavia and contributed to the rise of what later became known as Swedish or Scandinavian modern design.

From 1941 to 1946, Frank lived in New York City, but he was unable to establish himself in the United States, and he returned to Sweden and resumed his work for Svenskt Tenn. Frank continued to reflect on the problems of modern architecture, however, and in the late 1940s and early 1950s he produced a series of designs for houses based on the principles of non-orthogonal geometry and chance ordering. He spelled out these ideas in a manifesto titled "Accidentism," which was published in the Swedish design review *Form* in 1958. By that time, Frank was largely a forgotten figure, and his bold proposals attracted little attention. Many of his ideas for an architecture of complexity and contradiction, however, presaged the rise of Postmodernism in the 1960s.

CHRISTOPHER LONG

See also **Congrès Internationaux d'Architecture Moderne (CIAM, 1927-); Loos, Adolf (Austria); Mies van der Rohe, Ludwig (Germany); Tugendhat House, Brno, Czech Republic; Weissenhofsiedlung, Deutscher Werkbund (Stuttgart, 1927)**

Biography

Born in Baden, Austria, 15 July 1885. Studied architecture, Technische Hochschule, Vienna 1903–10. Worked with Bruno Möhring for a year in Berlin 1908–09. Private practice, Vienna from 1910; founder, Haus and Garten, Vienna 1925; supervisor, Österreichischer Werkbund Exhibition, Vienna 1929. Settled in Sweden 1933; worked as interior designer, Svenskt Tenn. Professor, the Kunstgewebeschule, Vienna 1919–25; professor, New School for Social Research, New York 1942–43. Contributor, Weissenhofsiedlung, Stuttgart 1927; representative, CIAM 1928; member, Deutscher Werkbund; member, vice president, Österreichischer Werkbund. Died in Stockholm, Sweden, 8 January 1967.

Selected Works

Scholl House, Vienna, 1914
Wiedenhofer-Hof (apartment building), Vienna, 1925
Winarsky-Hof (apartment building), Vienna, 1926
Villa Beer, Vienna, 1930
Bunzl House, Ortmann, Austria, 1914
Nursery School (Kinderheim), Ortmann, Austria, 1921
Hoffingergasse Housing Project, Vienna, 1925
Claëson House, Falsterbo, Sweden, 1927
House, Weissenhofsiedlung, Stuttgart, 1927
House, Vienna Werkbundsiedlung, 1932
Sebastian-Kelch-Gasse Apartment House, Vienna, 1928
Leopoldine-Glöckel-Hof (apartment building), Vienna, 1932
Bunzl House, Vienna, 1936
Wehtje House, Falsterbo, Sweden, 1936

Selected Publication

Architektur als Symbol: Elemente deutschen neuen Bauens, 1931

Further Reading

A detailed, scholarly catalog of Frank's designs appears in Stritzler-Levine. A complete catalog of Frank's textile designs is included in Wängberg-Eriksson (1999). For a catalog raisonné of Frank's architectural works, see Long and Welzig.

Long, Christopher, *Josef Frank*, Chicago: University of Chicago Press, 2002

Spalt, Johannes (editor), *Josef Frank, 1885–1967: Möbel und Geräte und Theoretisches*, Vienna: Hochschule für Angewandte Kunst, 1981

Spalt, Johannes, and Hermann Czech (editors), *Josef Frank, 1885–1967* (exhib. cat.), Vienna: Hochschule für Angewandte Kunst, 1981

Spalt, Johannes (editor), *Josef Frank zum 100. Geburtstag am 15. Juli 1985* (exhib. cat.), Vienna: Hochschule für Angewandte Kunst, 1985

Spalt, Johannes (editor), *Josef Frank, 1885–1967: Stoffe, Tapeten, Teppiche* (exhib. cat.), Vienna: Hochschule für Angewandte Kunst, 1986

Stritzler-Levine, Nina (editor), *Josef Frank, Architect and Designer: An Alternative Vision of the Modern Home*, New Haven, Connecticut: Yale University Press, 1996

Wängberg-Eriksson, Kristina, *Svenskt Tenn: Josef Frank och Estrid Ericson: En konsthistorisk studie*, Stockholm: Stockholms Universitet, 1985

Wängberg-Eriksson, Kristina, *Josef Frank—Livsträd i krigens skugga*, Lund: Signum, 1994

Wängberg-Eriksson, Kristina, *Josef Frank: Textiles Designs*, Lund: Signum, 1999

Welzig, Maria, *Josef Frank (1885–1967): Das architektonische Werk*, Vienna: Böhlau Verlag, 1998

FRANKFURT, GERMANY

Frankfurt am Main was, next to Berlin, perhaps Germany's most important center of 20th-century architectural developments. Its attempts to initiate an era of "New Building" with innovative social housing programs and extensive public works construction in the 1920s and its impressive post–World War II rebuilding program that culminated with the creation of a publicly funded "Museum Mile" in the 1980s have given Frankfurt an architectural prominence that far outweighs its modest size. The building of dozens of Europe's tallest skyscrapers has made Frankfurt's skyline similarly distinctive.

Located on the Main River at the edge of western Germany's densely populated Rhein-Main industrial area, Frankfurt is the capital of the German state of Hesse and one of Europe's most important banking, commercial, industrial, and transportation centers. It began the 20th century as a province of Prussia under the guidance of Mayor Franz Adickes (1846–1915), who initiated a series of reform-minded urban-planning policies. Before World War I, visitors and professionals from the nascent field of urban planning flocked to admire Frankfurt's new streets, boulevards, parks, housing projects, public transit system, sanitation, and land development schemes. The unique brand of municipal socialism created by Adickes gave the city government broad powers to create a beautiful and well-ordered city that planning officials throughout Germany, England, and the United States envied and sought to copy.

Despite these reforms, Frankfurt, like most other German (indeed European) cities, suffered a tremendous housing shortage at the end of World War I in 1918. Although some remedial reforms were implemented immediately after the war, major improvements did not come until the enactment of the Dawes Plan and the infusion of American money and loans in 1923 and the election of Social Democrat Ludwig Landmann as mayor in 1924. Landmann further reorganized the city government and the tax laws to allow for more efficient planning and construction of housing and public works and hired the young architect Ernst May from Breslau in Silesia to take control of all building and construction departments in the city. Although May did not solve the housing crisis he inherited, he initiated an unprecedented program of innovative research, planning, and construction that once again drew the attention and participation of many of the Europe's leading architects and planners.

May's program called for the greater part of the population to live in a series of new decentralized satellite cities clustered around the old city core, to which they would be connected with high-speed roads and public transit. Based on older ideas of the Garden City movement that May had learned as a student of Raymond Unwin in England, the new housing estates provided high-density low-rise housing for middle-income workers both in large blocks and in long row houses. Whereas early satellites developments such as Bruchfeldstrasse (1926–27, E. May), Römerstadt (1927–28, E. May), and Praunheim (1927–29, E. May) were often laid out with more traditional curved streets and courtyards, the latter ones, such as Westhausen (1929–30, E. May), Hellerhof (1929, M. Stam), and Am Lindenbaum (1930, W. Gropius), were laid out in rigid, uniform rows oriented north to south to maximize the solar orientation of each apartment and allow for greater standardization of building components.

To realize his ambitious plans, May reorganized the municipal construction industry, making the process faster, cheaper, and better. Through the help of some national building research grants (RFG), he rationalized the municipal production of materials and standardized building components, including the lightweight, prefabricated-concrete panels that were assembled into cubic, flat-roofed housing. May and his team, including Grete Schütte-Lihotsky, Martin Elsässer, Adolf Meyer, Emil Kaufmann, and Ferdinand Kramer, worked hard to define an "existence minimum"—the optimal and most efficient apartment layout for a given family size. The floor plans, the furnishings, and especially the "Frankfurt Kitchens" were completely redesigned and mass produced according to the latest American efficiency theories of C. Frederick, Frederick Taylor, and Henry Ford in order to minimize costs and work for the housewife. The resulting "New Building" was, like engineering, striving to be completely objective, rational, and efficient not only in its construction system but also in its aesthetic and social organization.

The housing program was complemented by an ambitious school-building program, new libraries, parks and recreation areas, new wholesale markets and electrical substations, and the implementation of a whole series of social and cultural reforms to help transform Frankfurt into a more modern home of the proverbial "New Man." May publicized Frankfurt's reforms in the avant-garde magazine *Das neue Frankfurt* (The New Frankfurt), which circulated the innovative ideas to Europe, the United States, Japan, and the rest of the world. Frankfurt's successes led the Congrès Internationaux d'Architecture Moderne (CIAM) holding its second congress in Frankfurt to inspect, admire, and share May's achievement of building over 10,000 new apartments in five years. Le Corbusier, Mies van der Rohe, Walter Gropius, and many other avant-garde architects of the Modern movement marveled at the new housing, infrastructure, advertising graphics, and schools in the "New Frankfurt" and modeled many new standards on the Frankfurt prototypes.

Deutsche Bank, by ABB Architects (1984), Frankfurt

In 1930, May and his team of architects left Frankfurt because of increasing pressure from Germany's radical right, who labeled May's modern brand of architecture "Bolshevik" and un-German. They went to the Soviet Union, where they had even greater experimental planning projects. Construction on the "New Frankfurt" continued until 1933, when Hitler's Nazi regime took over political power of Germany and championed a more traditional, handcrafted, pitched-roof architecture. Although architectural development slowed, Frankfurt's banking, transport, and industrial base made it an important center for Nazi wartime production. Two of the world's largest chemical companies, Hoechst and the former I.G. Farben, makers of the gas used in Nazi concentration camps, had their headquarters in new buildings in Frankfurt, the former in a brick Expressionist building by Peter Behrens (1924), the latter in a monumental, stone-clad, 10-story curved building by Hans Poelzig (1931). After World War II, Poelzig's office building was used as headquarters for the U.S. Army, and after 1995, it was slowly converted into university facilities.

From the fall of 1943 to September 1944 and especially on the night of 22 March 1944, the historic center of Frankfurt was almost completely destroyed by Allied bombings: of 47,500 buildings, fewer than 8000 survived at least in part. After the war, expecting to become the headquarters of Allied occupation forces, Frankfurt's planners elected to reconstruct their city based primarily on considerations of efficient traffic arteries and large building lots rather than restoring the original medieval city fabric. After rubble removal in the late 1940s, rebuilding started in the 1950s alongside West Germany's economic recovery. The modern, International Style buildings designed by May's colleague Ferdinand Kramer as well as well-known younger architects, such as Egon Eiermann, Sep Ruf, and Gottfried Böhm, still dominate downtown Frankfurt. With the relocation of the West German Central Bank to Frankfurt in 1957, the city grew rapidly into the largest banking and stock exchange center of Germany, the home of one of Europe's largest and architecturally significant convention centers, with exhibit halls by F.V. Thiersch (1907), O.M. Ungers (1984), and Helmut Jahn (1989), and home to Europe's largest and busiest train station, one of the busiest airports in the world, and some of Germany's busiest Autobahn crossings.

In the late 1970s, citizens began to demand more spending on cultural affairs and the creation of a more humane cityscape. They voted to restore and reconstruct their war-torn central Römer Square with its surrounding 16th-century merchants' houses, using traditional half-timber framing techniques. The city also began the creation and construction of a series of world-class museums, most of which were located on a short stretch of riverbank across from the downtown in the more traditional Sachsenhausen neighborhood. Unger's German Architecture Museum (1984) and Richard Meier's Museum of Applied Arts (1985) added on to early 20th-century villas, whereas the German Postal Museum (1990, G. Behnisch), the Museum of Modern Art (1991, H. Hollein), and the Schirn Kunsthalle (1985, D. Bangert, B. Jansen, S. Scholz, and A. Schultes) are completely new structures.

Although the tall banking towers had already earned the city the nicknames "Bankfurt," "Mainhattan," and "Chicago on the Main," during the final decade of the century Frankfurt added a whole series of Europe's tallest and most innovative new skyscrapers. The trend started with Ungers' Torhaus (1984) and Jahn's Messeturm (1991) at the convention center. On the skyline, the blue-glass twin towers of the Deutsche Bank (1984) downtown were soon joined by the DG Bank "Crown" tower (1993) by Kohn Pederson Fox and the Commerzbank Tower (1997) by Sir Norman Foster, which contains large multistory atriums every eight floors with trees to help condition the building's air. Frankfurt's recent designation as the home of the European Union's new central bank has only fueled the construction boom—the Landesbank Hessen is planning a tower by Peter Schweiger, and German Telekom is planning a skyscraper by Richard Rogers. The second "New Frankfurt," created alongside the new museums and banks, has once again become a fertile ground for architectural innovation and admiration.

KAI K. GUTSCHOW

Further Reading

Kalusche is the best and most up-to-date guidebook to individual buildings. Many studies exist of the "New Building" in Frankfurt in the 1920s, of which Mohr is the most authoritative, and Bullock perhaps the best English summary. Hirdina's anthology of articles from *Das neue Frankfurt* provides invaluable contemporary source material. The recent museums and skyscrapers are reviewed in countless architecture periodicals.

Bullock, Nicholas, "Housing in Frankfurt 1925–1931 and the New Wohnkultur," *Architectural Review*, 163 (1978)

Fehl, Gerhard, "The Niddatal Project: The Unfinished Satellite Town on the Outskirts of Frankfurt," *Built Environment*, 9 (1983)

Henderson, Susan Rose, "A Setting for Mass Culture: Life and Leisure in the Nidda Valley," *Planning Perspectives*, 10 (1995)

Hirdina, Heinz (editor), *Neues Bauen, neues Gestalten: Das Neue Frankfurt, die neue Stadt, eine Zeitschrift zwischen 1926 und 1933*, Berlin: Elefanten, 1984

Jonak, Ulf, *Die Frankfurter Skyline: Eine Stadt gerät aus den Fugen und gewinnt an Gestalt*, Frankfurt and New York: Campus, 1997

Kalusche, Bernd, and Wolf-Christian Setzepfandt, *Architekturführer, Frankfurt am Main; Architectural Guide, Frankfurt am Main* (bilingual German-English edition), Berlin: Reimer, 1992; 2nd edition, 1997

Ladd, Brian, *Urban Planning and Civic Order in Germany, 1860–1914*, Cambridge, Massachusetts: Harvard University Press, 1990

Lane, Barbara Miller, *Architecture and Politics in Germany, 1918–1945*, Cambridge, Massachusetts: Harvard University Press, 1968

Mohr, Christoph, and Michael Müller, *Funktionalität und Moderne: Das neue Frankfurt und seine Bauten, 1925–1933*, Frankfurt: Fricke, 1984

Prigge, Walter, and Hans-Peter Schwarz (editors), *Das Neue Frankfurt: Städtebau und Architektur im Modernisierungsprozess, 1925–1988*, Frankfurt: Vervuert, 1988

FREY, ALBERT 1903–1998

Architect, United States

Albert Frey holds a unique place in the history of 20th century Californian architecture as an uncompromising modernist of the European school, a pupil of Le Corbusier, and an exponent of high-tech and rationalist architecture who lived out his long life in the hills above Palm Springs, California.

Frey spent the early part of his career working for Belgian modernist architects Jules Eggericx and Raphael Verwilghen in Brussels, where he was involved with rebuilding housing following the Great War. He returned to Switzerland in 1927 to work for the firm of Leuenberger, Fluckiger before moving to Paris in 1928 to work for Le Corbusier and Pierre Jeanneret for nine months. In Le Corbusier's atelier he sat between Charlotte Perriand and Jose Louis Sert, working on the Centrosoyus Administration Building in Moscow (1933) and the Villa Savoye (1931) at Poissy. Here he was introduced to *Sweet's Catalogue* and, like Richard Neutra before him, found himself drawn to the American dream of a technological future.

Upon his arrival in New York in September of 1930, Frey began working with A. Lawrence Kocher, architect and editor of *Architectural Record*, in a partnership that would last until 1935. The most significant building of Frey's early career was the exhibition house designed for the 1931 Allied Arts and Building Products exhibition at the Grand Central Palace in New York. Called the "Aluminaire House" because of its ribbed aluminum cladding and its qualities of lightness and airiness, it was strongly influenced by Le Corbusier's Maison Citrohan (1920) projects and Maison Cook at Boulonge-sur-Seine (1926–27), as well as Frey's own investigations of mass housing, as evidenced in schemes published in *Architectural Record* in April 1931. The aluminum- and steel-framed house, with its innovative floor and wall construction, was subsidized by subscriptions Frey raised from manufacturers and erected in ten days. Following the exhibition it was bought by the architect Wallace Harrison, disassembled in six hours and moved to his estate on Long Island. It has now been rebuilt at the New York Institute of Technology, at Islip, Long Island.

In 1934 Frey traveled to Palm Springs, California, to supervise the building of the Kocher-Samson office building for Kocher's brother, a medical doctor. While there he met John Porter Clark and, terminating his partnership with Kocher, began working with Clark in a partnership that continued almost uninterrupted until 1957. A brief interlude in New York in 1938–39, where he worked on the Museum of Modern Art for Philip L Goodwin, and on a design for the Swiss Pavilion for the World's Fair with Kocher that is reproduced most memorably in his book, *In Search of a Living Architecture.*

Frey's philosophy was evinced in the first house he built for himself in 1940. Assembled out of industrial-type materials, Frey House 1 (Palm Springs, 1940) was a simple cubic cabin with extending wall planes and an over-reaching, flat roof probing the landscaped desert around it. These ideas were further explored in the Hatton House and Guest House (1945) and the Loewy House (1947), all in Palm Springs. The extension of Frey House 1 in 1947 and again in 1953, with the introduction of bright, electric colors and profiled metal and ribbed fiberglass cladding, gave it a noticeably futuristic quality while at the same time incorporating it within the planting and water pools of its natural site. Although an experimental house, its idiosyncrasies were a direct responses to the particularities of its desert condition.

With Clark he built a number of crisp, more conventionally modernist buildings, including elementary and secondary schools in Palm Springs and Needles, and hospitals at Banning and Palm Springs. These long, low, planar buildings spread out against the desert landscape, external circulation, play or convalescing areas taking advantage of the climate. Joined in partnership in 1952 by Robson Chambers, Clark and Frey built the Palm Springs City Hall (1957) using a palette of traditional and industrial materials. The design was sensitive to both function and climate, the administrative offices forming a low, steel-screened T-shaped building with the council chamber expressed as a jagged, masonry block at one end. Concrete and steel *portes cochère*, one circular and the other square, marked the respective entrances to the council chamber and the city hall, the circular form of the former corresponding to the void within the latter.

Frey House 2 (1965) was built on a mountainside on axis with and overlooking the centre of Palm Springs, the City Hall visible in the distance. Raised on a concrete-block podium which incorporated the car port below and the swimming pool above, the house appeared to be no more than a glass and steel lean-to cabin, carelessly decaying in the desert landscape. The architecture is literally subsumed in Nature as a giant rock pushes through a glass wall, separating the sleeping from the living area and providing, by way of its mass, a thermal regulator.

NEIL JACKSON

See also **Aluminum; Aluminaire House, Long Island, New York**

Biography

Born in Zürich, Switzerland, 18 October 1903; studied architecture at the Institute of Technology in Winterthur, training in traditional building construction; worked in 1925 for architects Jean-Jules Eggericx and Raphael Verwilghen in Brussels, Belgium, where he was involved with rebuilding housing following the Great War; returned to Switzerland (1927) where he worked for Leuenberger, Fluckiger before moving to Paris (1928) to work for Le Corbusier and Pierre Jeanneret for nine months. Arrived in New York, 5 September 1930; worked with Philip L. Goodwin (1938–39) on the design of New York's Museum of Modern Art. Established partnership with John Porter Clark, Palm Springs, 1934–57; Died 14 November 1998 in Palm Springs.

Selected Publications

In Search of a New Architecture, New York: Architectural Book Publishing, 1939, and Santa Monica: Hennessey + Ingalls, 1999

Further Reading

Golub, Jennifer, *Albert Frey: Houses 1 and 2*, New York: Princeton Architectural Press, 1999

Jackson, Neil, *The Modern Steel House*, London and New York: Spon, 1996

Jackson, Neil, "Aluminaire House, USA (Kocher and Frey)," in *Modern Movement Heritage*, edited by Allen Cunningham, London: Spon, 1998

Jackson, Neil, "Desert Pioneer," *The Architectural Review* 1147, no. 9 (1992)

Rosa, Joseph, *Albert Frey, Architect*, New York: Rizzoli International, 1990

FULLER, RICHARD BUCKMINSTER 1895–1983

Architect and philosopher, United States

The American Richard Buckminster Fuller has been variously labeled architect, engineer, author, designer–inventor, educator, poet, cartographer, ecologist, philosopher, teacher, and mathematician throughout his career. Although not trained professionally as an architect, Fuller has been accepted within the architectural profession, receiving numerous awards and honorary degrees. He thought of himself as a comprehensive human in the universe, implementing research for the good of humanity. Born in Milton, Massachusetts, on 12 July 1895, he was the son of Richard Buckminster Fuller, Sr., and Caroline Wolcott (Andrews) Fuller. His father, who worked as a leather and tea merchant with offices in Boston, died when Fuller was 15 years of age. Fuller's first design revelation came to him when, in kindergarten in 1899, he built his first flat-space frame, an octet truss constructed of dried peas and toothpicks. As a boy, vacationing at his family's summerhouse on Bear Island, Maine, he became an adequate seaman and developed an appreciation of nature's provision of principles of efficient design. He followed the philosophy of Pythagoras and Newton, that the universe comprises signs, or patterns of energy relationships, that have an order to them. Fuller used the term "valving" for the transformation of these patterns into usable forms. According to Fuller, these patterns in nature were comprehensive and universal. "Synergy" was the name that Fuller gave to the integrated behavior patterns discovered in nature.

Fuller attended the Milton Academy (1904–06) and Harvard University (1913–15) and was expelled twice while at Harvard. He worked in a few industries and then enlisted for two years of service in the U.S. Navy (1917–19). This experience in industry and with the Navy helped him gain knowledge of technical engineering processes, materials, and methods of manufacturing, which he would apply this knowledge to future inventions. When one of his two daughters, Alexandra, died of influenza at age four (1922), Fuller became obsessed with her death. Five years later, on the brink of suicide, he decided instead to devote the rest of his life to helping humanity by converting ideas and technology designed for weaponry into ideas for "livingry." At the age of 32, he started an experiment, Guinea Pig B (the "B" stood for "Bucky," his nickname), to discover how an individual with a moral commitment and limited financial means could apply his knowledge to improve humanity's living conditions by technological determinism. This experiment continued until his death at age 88. Thus, his technological and economical resources belonged to society. He believed in the same moralistic drive to develop better housing for the masses through mass production that many of the European modernists did, but Fuller's forms and design principles were quite different.

Among the proliferation of books that Fuller published during his life, the first, *4D Time Lock* (1928), propagated his lifetime philosophy. The term "4D" meant "fourth-dimensional" thinking, adding time to the dimensions of space to ensure gains for humanity instead of personal gains only. The first patent of the 4D designs was a mass-production house, first known as 4D and later as the Dymaxion House (1927 model; 1928 patent). A hexagonal structure supported on a mast, the house was to be air deliverable and based on his strategy of "design science," which sought to obtain maximum human advantage from minimum use of energy and materials. Using the analogy of airplane technology, he chose materials such as steel-alloy cables and the Duralumin mast. After developing the Dymaxion House, Fuller was to engage in developing prototypes of the Dymaxion Vehicles (1937) and the Dymaxion Bathroom (1940). Later he developed the Dymaxion Deployment Unit (1944), a lightweight corrugated-steel shelter made from modified grain bins. Thousands of these units were bought by the U.S. Army Air Corps for use as flight crew quarters. The Dymaxion Deployment Unit became the basis for Fuller's Wichita House (1946). These

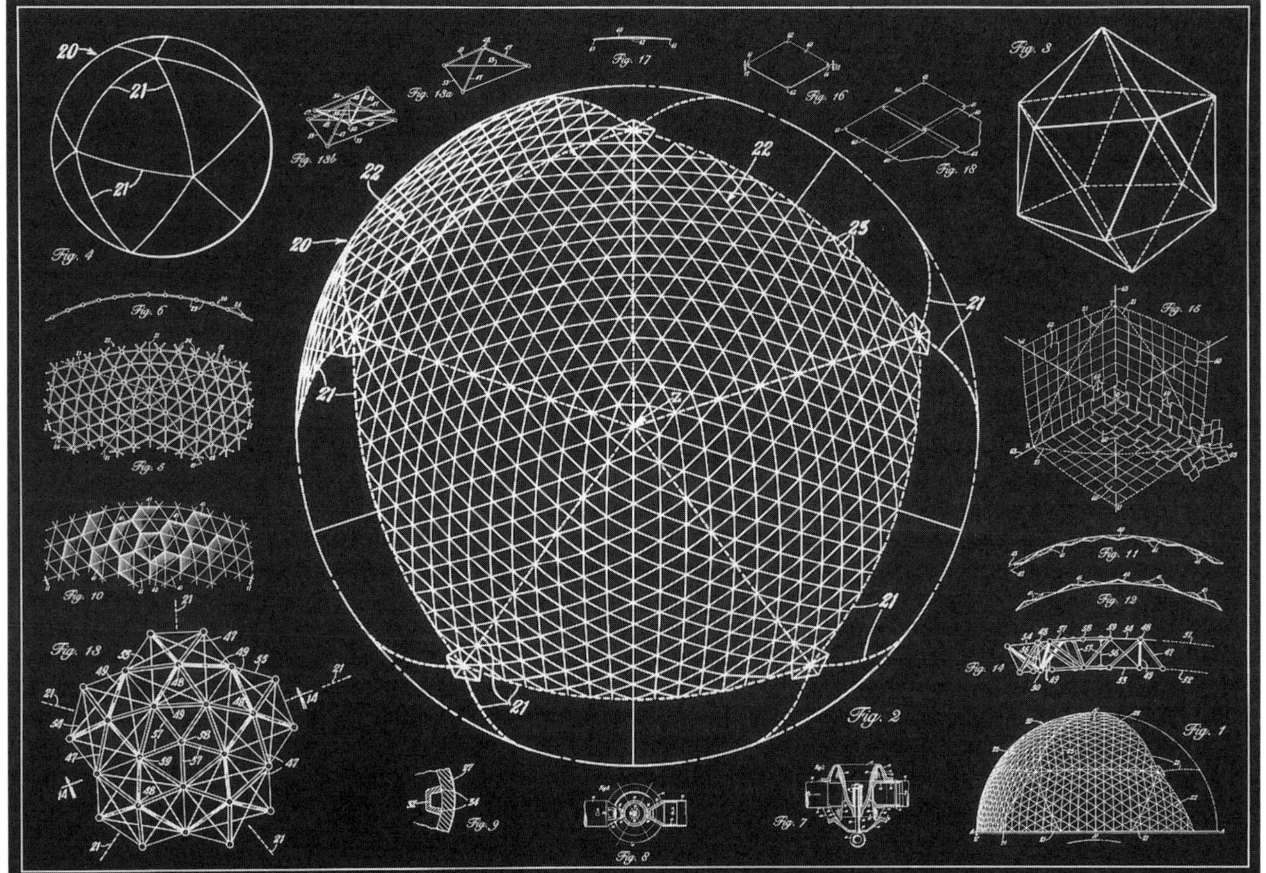

Construction plan of the geodesic dome, designed by R. Buckminster Fuller

houses were built to be used as full-size family dwellings, weighing four tons each, and were to be assembled on aircraft production lines built during the war. Another of Fuller's Dymaxion inventions was the Dymaxion Airocean World Map (1946). This map transferred the spherical data of a globe onto a two-dimensional surface.

Fuller, however, is best known for inventing the geodesic dome (1954), a triangulated space-enclosing technology. According to Fuller, this type of structure encloses the maximum internal volume with the least surface area. Designs such as the domes were based on synergy and its connection with mathematics, using such forms as the tetrahedron, octahedron, and icosahedron. Fuller brought into the dome structure ideas concerning the dome's tensile ability by introducing a new structural geometry and advancing mechanics into the dome form. He tried to emulate in this structure the atom's form, including the compound curvature trussing of its dynamic structure. Although this domical design was not new in its elementary form, it was new in its manner of employing these principles in a human-made structure. Numerous domes have appeared all over the world for domestic as well as large-scale industrial use, including the Union Tank Car Company (1958), Baton Rouge, Louisiana; the Climatron Botanical Garden (1961), St. Louis, Missouri; the U.S. Pavilion (1967) at Expo '67, the World's Fair, Montreal, Canada; and the Spruce Goose Hangar (1982), Long Beach, California.

As noted by architectural historian Kenneth Frampton in his book, *Modern Architecture: A Critical History* (1980), Fuller has influenced future generations of architects, most notably the Japanese group the Metabolists, the British group Archigram, Moshe Safdie, Alfred Neuman, Cedric Price, and Norman Foster. A few semiotician scholars liken him to Joyce, but whereas Joyce sought to obscure language intentionally, Fuller sought to emphasize a precise meaning. Often he would invent words for this purpose, as displayed in his numerous writings and lectures. Later in life, he entered into partnership with Shoji Sadao in New York and Sadao and Zung Architects in Cleveland, Ohio (1979–83). Fuller died on 1 July 1983 in Los Angeles, California, from a massive heart attack; his wife died three days later.

REBECCA DALVESCO

Biography

Born in Milton, Massachusetts, 12 July 1895. Studied, Milton Academy, Milton, Massachusetts 1914–1906; Harvard University, Cambridge, Massachusetts 1913–15; attended, United States Naval Academy, Annapolis, Maryland 1917. Married Anne Hewlett, daughter of architect James Monroe Hewlett 1917: 2 children. Served, United States Navy 1917–19. Assistant export manager, Armour and Company, New York 1919–21; National Accounts Sales Manager, Kelly-Springfield Truck Company 1922; president, Stockdale Building System, Chicago 1922–27. Founder and president, 4D Company, Chicago 1927–32; editor and publisher, *Shelter*, Philadelphia 1930–32; founder, director, chief engineer, Dymaxion Corporation, Bridgeport, Connecticut 1932–36; assistant to the director of Research and Development, Phelps Dodge Corporation, New York 1936–38; technical consultant, *Fortune*, New York 1938–40; vice president, chief engineer, Dymaxion Company, Delaware 1940–50; chief mechanical engineer, United States Board of Economic Warfare, Washington, D.C. 1942–44; special assistant to the Deputy Director of the United States Foreign Economic Administration, Washington, D.C. 1944; chairman, chief engineer, Dymaxion Dwelling Machine Corporation, Wichita, Kansas 1944–46; chairman, Fuller Research Foundation, Wichita 1946–54; president, Geodesics Incorporated, Forest Hills, New York from 1949; president, Synergetics Incorporated, Raleigh, North Carolina 1954–59; president, Plydomes Incorporated, Des Moines, Iowa from 1957; chairman, Tetrahelix Corporation, Hamilton, Ohio from 1959; editor-at-large, *World Magazine*, New York 1972–75; senior partner, Fuller and Sadao, Long Island from 1979; chairman of the board, R. Buckminster Fuller, Sadao and Zung Architects, Cleveland, Ohio from 1979; senior partner, Buckminster Fuller Associates, London from 1979. Research professor 1959–68, university professor 1968–75, distinguished university professor 1972–75, professor emeritus from 1975, Southern Illinois University, Carbondale; Charles Eliot Norton Professor of Poetry, Harvard University 1962–63; Harvey Cushing Orator, American Association of Neuro-Surgeons 1967; Nehru Lecturer, New Delhi 1969; Hoyt Fellow, Yale University, New Haven, Connecticut 1969; fellow, St. Peter's College, Oxford 1970; World Fellow in Residence, consortium of the University of Pennsylvania, Haverford College, Swarthmore College, Bryn Mawr College, and University City Science Center, Philadelphia, and consultant to the Design Science Institute, Philadelphia 1972–83; tutor in design science, International Community College, Los Angeles 1975. President, Triton Foundation, Cambridge, Massachusetts 1967; consultant to architects, Team 3, Penang, Malaysia from 1974; international president, MENSA, Paris 1975; international president, World Society for Ekistics, Athens 1975; member, National Academy of Design; fellow, American Institute of Architects; fellow, Building Research Institute of the National Academy of Sciences; life fellow, American Association for the Advancement of Science; member, National Institute of Arts and Letters; fellow, American Academy of Arts and Sciences; member, Mexican Institute of Architects; honorary member, Society of Venezuelan Architects; honorary member, Israel Institute of Engineers and Architects; honorary member, Zenralvereiningung der Architekten Österreichs; honorary member, Royal Society of Siamese Architects; honorary member, Royal Architectural Institute of Canada; Ben Franklin Fellow, Royal Society of Arts; honorary fellow, Royal Institute of British Architects; honorary fellow, Royal Academy of Fine Art, the Netherlands. Royal Gold Medal, Royal Institute of British Architects 1968; Gold Medal, American Institute of Architects 1970; R. Buckminster Fuller Chair of Architecture established at the University of Detroit 1970. Died in Los Angeles, 1 July 1983.

Selected Works

Dymaxion House (design), 1927 model/1928 patent
Dymaxion Car (prototype; patented), 1937
Dymaxion Bathroom (prototype; patented), 1940
Dymaxion Deployment Unit (prototype; patented), 1944
Dymaxion Airocean World Map, 1946
Wichita House, Kansas, 1946
Geodesic Dome (patented), 1954
United States Air Force Early Warning Systems Domes, Arctic Circle, 1954
Union Tank Car Company Quarter Sphere, Baton Rouge, Louisiana; Los Angeles; and Wood River, Illinois, 1958
Climatron Botanical Garden, St. Louis, Missouri, 1961

United States Pavilion (destroyed), Expo 1967, Montreal, 1967
Spruce Goose Airplane Hangar, Long Beach, California, 1982

Selected Publications

4D Timelock, 1928
The Dymaxion World of Buckminster Fuller (with Robert W. Marks), 1960
Ideas and Integrities, 1963
Nine Chains to the Moon, 1963
Operating Manual for Spaceship Earth, 1968
Synergetic Explorations in the Geometry of Thinking (with E.J. Applewhite), 1975
Synergetics 2: Further Explorations in the Geometry of Thinking (with E.J. Applewhite), 1979
Buckminster Fuller Sketchbook, 1980
Inventions: The Patented Works of Richard Buckminster Fuller, 1983

Further Reading

Applewhite, E.J., *Cosmic Fishing: An Account of Writing Synergetics with Buckminster Fuller*, New York: Macmillan, 1977
Baldwin, Jay, *BuckyWorks: Buckminster Fuller's Ideas for Today*, New York: Wiley, 1996
Edmondson, Amy C., *A Fuller Explanation: The Synergetic Geometry of R. Buckminster Fuller*, Boston: Birkhäuser, 1987
Fuller, R. Buckminster, *Synergetics Dictionary: The Mind of Buckminster Fuller*, 4 vols., edited by E.J. Applewhite, New York: Garland, 1986
Hatch, Alden, *Buckminster Fuller: At Home in the Universe*, New York: Crown, 1974
Kenner, Hugh, *Bucky: A Guided Tour of Buckminster Fuller*, New York: Morrow, 1973
Marks, Robert, *The Dymaxion World of Buckminster Fuller*, New York: Reinhold, 1960
McHale, John, *R. Buckminster Fuller*, New York: Braziller, 1962
Meller, James (editor), *The Buckminster Fuller Reader*, London: Cape, 1970
Pawley, Martin, *R. Buckminster Fuller*, New York: Taplinger, and London: Trefoil, 1990
Robertson, Donald W., *Mind's Eye of Richard Buckminster Fuller*, New York: Vantage Press, 1974
Sieden, Lloyd Steven, *Buckminster Fuller's Universe: An Appreciation*, New York: Plenum Press, 1989
Ward, James (editor), *The Artifacts of R. Buckminster Fuller: A Comprehensive Collection of His Designs and Drawings*, 4 vols., New York: Garland, 1984

FUTURISM

Italian in origin and concept, futurism was first theorized by Filippo Tomaso Marinetti in a manifesto published on 20 February 1909 in the French daily *Le Figaro*. Futurism soon became a movement central to the process of radical artistic renovation carried out by the European avant-garde. It dealt both with cultural debates specific to Italian art of the first two decades of the 20th century and with crucial discourses of the European artistic revival in general. While affecting primarily the arts in the more restrictive sense of the term—under the influence of Umberto Boccioni, Carlo Carrà, Gino Severini, and Mario Chiattone—its most notable representatives in Italian architecture were Giacomo Balla and Antonio Sant'Elia but also, in various degrees, such architects as Adalberto Libera and Angiolo Mazzoni, among others. The close collaboration between futurist artists and architects is evidenced by the fact that the first and only exhibition of futurist architecture held in Italy of the period was curated by a painter, Fillia, who also edited journals on topics such as "The Futurist City" and in 1932 wrote a book, *La Nuova Architettura*, in which he gave a comprehensive view of the significance of the movement.

Most sensitive to the challenges of the new "machinist society" (Le Corbusier) among the avant-garde artists and architects, the promoters of futurism were concerned primarily with expressing movement and mechanical speed, which they saw as essential determinants of modernity. The futurists extended their artistic vision to the study of the latest conquest of modern science with an undivided enthusiasm for all of what they perceived to be radical facts of the contemporary civilization. They rejected emphatically the old canons of static prespectival representation and invoked instead the redemptive force of the universal dynamism brought about by the machine, itself central to the new forms of visualization.

Such a proposition was translated in architecture first through visionary representations of cities shaped by speedy automotive vehicles and later through the redefinition of the Modern movement's functionalist themes in terms of extreme flexibility and mobility (Libera's imaginary villas, Mazzoni's control tower for the Florentine train station, and Le Corbusier's inhabited highways).

The best-known early projects of futurist architecture are Sant'Elia's and Mario Chiatone's urban experiments exhibited in Milan in 1914. The spatial relationships of the city fabric were determined in the first place by an elaborate system of monumental arteries distributed hierarchically through and underneath huge "streamlined" skyscrapers, anticipating the post–Art Deco aesthetics of the 1930s, including Libera's entrance to the commemorative *Mostra della Rivoluzione Fascista* (1932) or his analogous Italian Pavilion of the 1933 Century of Progress Exposition, Chicago. Sant'Elia's pre–World War I "città nuova" projects informed significantly Marinetti himself, who published *Manifest of Futurist Architecture*, commonly regarded as one of the most important documents of modern Italian architecture.

The thrust that futurism put on solving problems of motorized transportation and its diversification according to speed and purpose—including strict segregation of pedestrian circulation—had a significant influence on Le Corbusier's 1922 speculative Contemporary City for Three Million Inhabitants, the touchstone of pre-Chandigarh Le Corbusian urbanism. This influence can be seen as well in the Amsterdam Rokin project by Mart Stam and that of other European architects, Le Corbusier's Plan Obus in particular. Whereas at the eve of World War II the early Russian artistic and literary avant-garde evolved a genre with a similar name—the Cubo-Futurism of Kasimir Malevich, Khruchenikh, and Khlebnikov—with little significant connection with the Italian movement proper, the postrevolutionary Soviet Constructivism (Chernikhov's mechanical architecture, Melnikov's dynamic garages and exploded theaters, Mayakovsky's "urban poetry," or Dziga Vertov's cinematic constructions) played a significant role in the development of futurism in Italy (Libera's and Giuseppe Terragni's rooms at the 1932 *Mostra*).

After Düsseldorf, where he designed the interior of the Lowenstein house, Balla conceived the interior of the via Milano Bal-Tic-Tac ballroom (1921) in Rome, often seen as the first experiment in avant-garde architectural aesthetic in Rome. Vittorio Marchi, who wrote two books on futurist architecture in 1924 and 1928, designed the Pirandello Theater in Rome.

In Italy, where modern and experimental architecture was never banished under Fascism—and indeed was favored by Mussolini—the futurists emphatically tied their fate to the new regime and imploded with it in time. Still, the extraordinary mass development of automobile circulation after the country recovered from the disasters of both war and Fascism and the increased need, under the circumstances, for pedestrian segregation along with the desire to emphasize the particular urban character of mechanized transportation have led urban planners since the early 1960s in Italy to search back for the still-valid aspects of the futurist credo.

DANILO UDOVICKI-SELB

See also **Città Nuova (1914); Constructivism; Contemporary City for Three Million Inhabitants; Corbusier, Le (Jeanneret, Charles-Édouard) (France); Libera, Adalberto (Italy); Russia and Soviet Union; Sant'Elia, Antonio (Italy); Terragni, Giuseppe (Italy)**

Further Reading

Apollonio, Umbro, *Futurismo*, Milan: Mazzotta, 1970; as *Futurist Manifestos*, New York: Viking, and London: Thames and Hudson, 1973

Balla, Giacomo, *Ricostruzione futurista dell'universo*, Milan: Direzione del Movimento Futurista, 1915; reprint, in *Balla, Depero: Ricostruzione futurista dell'universo*, Modena, Italy: Fonte d'Abisso, 1989

Boccioni, Umberto, *Manifesto tecnico della scultura futurista*, Milan: Direzione del Movimento Futurista, 1912

Calvesi, Maurizio, *Le due avanguardie: Dal futurismo alla pop art*, Milan: Lerici, 1966

Clough, Rosa Trillo, *Futurism: The Story of a Modern Art Movement*, New York: Philosophical Library, 1961

Doordan, Dennis P., *Building Modern Italy: Italian Archictecture, 1914–1936*, New York: Princeton Architectural Press, 1988

Drudi Gambillo, Maria, and Teresa Fiori, editors, *Archivi del Futurismo*, 2 vols., Rome: De Luca, 1958–62

Humphreys, Richard, *Futurism*, Cambridge and New York: Cambridge University Press, 1999

Marchi, Vittorio, *Architettura futurista*, Foligno: Campitelli, 1924

Marinetti, Filippo Tommaso, *Le futurisme*, Paris: Sansot, 1911; reprint, Lausanne: L'Age d'Homme, 1980

Nash, John Malcolm, *Cubism, Futurism, and Constructivism*, London: Thames and Hudson, 1974; Woodbury, New York: Barron's, 1978

Portoghesi, Paolo, *L'eclettismo a Roma, 1870–1922*, Rome: De Luca, 1968

Rye, Jane, *Futurism*, London: Studio Vista, and New York: Dutton, 1972

Scrivo, Luigi, *Sintesi del futurismo: Storia e documenti*, Rome: Bulzoni, 1968

Taylor, Joshua Charles, *Futurism*, New York: Museum of Modern Art, 1961